INVESTIGATIVE CRIMINAL PROCEDURE

INSIDE THIS CENTURY'S MOST (IN)FAMOUS CASES

Second Edition

■ ■ ■

Brian R. Gallini

Dean & Professor of Law
Willamette University College of Law

AMERICAN CASEBOOK SERIES®

WEST
ACADEMIC
PUBLISHING

American Casebook Series is a trademark registered in the U.S. Patent and Trademark Office.

© 2019 LEG, Inc. d/b/a West Academic
© 2023 LEG, Inc. d/b/a West Academic
    860 Blue Gentian Road, Suite 350
    Eagan, MN 55121
    1-877-888-1330

West, West Academic Publishing, and West Academic are trademarks of West Publishing Corporation, used under license.

Printed in the United States of America

ISBN: 978-1-68561-157-6

This book is dedicated to three people:
my wife, Beth; and my boys, Braxton and Caden.
Beth—I remain grateful for your unwavering support
and for traveling along this journey with me.

PREFACE

I was dismissive when first approached about writing this casebook. "Just what the world needs, another casebook," I thought. But then I paused and reflected on what I might contribute. No, the world does not need another casebook in general, but maybe students need this one. So many casebooks out there include the same basic make up: long excerpts from the scholarly literature, excerpts from Supreme Court cases, and a series of notes and questions following the chosen excerpted cases. I doubt that approach continues to suit the modern law student.

Meanwhile, the investigative criminal procedure course is just different. The subject matter touches everyone, lawyers and nonlawyers alike. After all, what police can and cannot do impacts us all. And, whether students want to or not, they are going to take the investigative criminal procedure course in law school. Rarely is it a tough sell though. After all, more than 300 million people have downloaded the first season of hit podcast *Serial*, and 19.3 million people watched Netflix's documentary series, *Making a Murderer*, within 30 days of its launch. Those numbers reflect the reality that criminal procedure is an intriguing and constantly evolving area of the law that seemingly captures the public interest unlike other law school courses.

Collectively, I came to believe that the time has come to provide a criminal procedure casebook that brings law students into the courtroom. Today's students, after all, expect more from their upper-level courses and, in particular, a different experience from that provided by a traditional "cases and notes" casebook. They want courses that teach them substantive law in a way that captures their attention *and* hones their practical skills.

That, in short, is what this book tries to do. It relies heavily on practical materials to guide students through the substantive law. In an effort to engage students and present "the big picture," each chapter focuses on a specific "real-world" defendant, such as O.J. Simpson (former NFL running back), Richard Kuklinski (mafia's most prolific hitman), and John Wayne Gacy (one of this country's most prolific serial killers)—among numerous other (in)famous defendants.

Organizationally, each chapter begins with an introductory description highlighting the relevant legal aspects from the particular defendant's case. Each chapter also tries to lay out the law in an easy to digest format. Core cases are then presented in a logical and easy to follow order. There is no hiding the ball in this book.

To further explore the topics presented by each defendant's case, the book provides professor and students access to an online case file repository. The repository includes the actual litigation documents from each case, such as complaints, search warrants, transcripts, and other resources like interrogation videos. One chapter's effort to introduce students to a particular defendant takes them inside the Supreme Court, including access to private, white-glove Supreme Court filings associated with that defendant's case. All of these documents apply to the concepts found in the corresponding chapter through a series of "Questions, Comments, Concerns?" often listed at the end of the core cases.

By including case files for every selected defendant, professors who adopt the casebook may customize their criminal procedure course by selecting only the files that meet the specific needs of their students. To my mind, this feature is critical. After teaching investigative criminal procedure myself for several years, I have learned first-hand that the ability to tailor the course drastically improves student participation and success.

By focusing so heavily on defendants—rather than rely more traditionally on core cases and scholarship alone—my hope is to offer a fresh approach to teaching the investigative criminal procedure course. I admit, however, that this is lofty goal: to dramatically change the way law schools teach investigative criminal procedure. And I won't achieve it alone. So, if you enjoy using this book or otherwise have feedback (positive or negative), I hope to hear from you. Your feedback will be critical to improving the text for future editions.

A few housekeeping notes before we begin. You should know that I have edited nearly all of the cases included in this book. You'll know I have removed text when you see: * * *. You should also know that I have removed numerous footnotes from the cases as well. The footnotes that are included retain their original numerical designation.

On a personal note, I am lucky to have so many people to thank for their help in assisting with the completion of this project. So many in fact that I'm scared to list them lest I leave someone out. But here goes.

For their incredible research assistance, let me thank (in alphabetical order) the following amazing people who I've been lucky enough to call my students:

Alex Carroll

Gene Allen Franco

Beth Kanopsic

Krystin Kennedy

Erin Nelson

Spencer Sims-Bowling

Shannon Stroud

Within that exceptionally talented group, I would specifically recognize contributions to the first edition from Spencer Sims-Bowling and Gene Allen Franco, and to the second edition from Alex Carroll. In the lead-up to preparing this second edition, Alex dedicated extraordinary time and effort to this project. This edition is better because of him.

Closer to home, thanks are owed to my family for their support. I would like specifically to recognize my parents, Marc and Linda Gallini, and my father and mother-in-law, Chris and Camille Forrest. Thank you to my brother, Dan, and his wife, Karen. Thank you also to my brothers-in-law Matt and Brady, and to their wives, Chrysten and Firen. Last but hardly least, I owe special thanks to my wife, Beth, who somehow did not run out of patience with me while I worked long hours on this project.

A final thanks to Tessa Boury who, while working for West many years ago, somehow talked me into this project. It turns out you were right after all. I did have something to contribute.

BRIAN GALLINI

October 2022

ABOUT THE AUTHOR

Brian Gallini is Dean and Professor of Law at the Willamette University College of Law. Since he joined the College in March of 2020, the law school has recruited the largest and most academically well-credentialed 1L class in more than a decade, secured the second-largest gift in the College of Law's history, posted the highest ten-month gold standard employment numbers on the West Coast, and has committed itself to critically evaluating its approach to diversity, equity, and inclusion. Through Gallini's service on Oregon's Alternatives to Bar Exam Task Force, he has also facilitated national conversations about reform to attorney licensure.

These shared accomplishments have taken place against the backdrop of the pandemic, wildfires, a historic ice storm, and the College of Law's important presence at the epicenter of protests for racial justice and equity. No matter the circumstance, Gallini has prioritized an inclusive governance approach with active participation from faculty, students, and staff.

His scholarship, which focuses primarily on law enforcement discretion in the context of interrogation methods, consent searches, and profiling, has been published in some of the nation's top law journals. Gallini teaches a variety of doctrinal criminal courses. He has developed seminars and taught overseas. He is interviewed regularly by local, state, national, and international media outlets to provide legal perspective on current events.

Gallini regularly presents papers at a variety of conferences, roundtables and colloquia. He has twice won the Southeastern Association of American Law Schools Call for Papers competition, and he was named the 2017 SEC Faculty Achievement Award Winner. His work has been published in the *Washington Law Review, Hastings Law Journal, George Mason Law Review*, and *Tennessee Law Review*—among others. His expert commentary has been featured in global media outlets, including *The Wall Street Journal, L.A. Times, Chicago Tribune, Christian Science Monitor*, and *Arkansas Democrat-Gazette*, and distributed through the *Associate Press*.

In the classroom, Gallini teaches Criminal Law, Criminal Procedure I & II, and Federal Criminal Law. He also teaches several seminars he has developed, including Problems in Police Discretion, Crime & the Supreme Court, and Lawyers & Leadership. Gallini has taught criminal courses internationally in St. Petersburg, Russia, and in Lodz, Poland. For his teaching, he has received the University of Arkansas School of Law award for outstanding teaching and the graduation award for hooding.

Gallini received a Bachelor of Arts in Russian studies from the College of the Holy Cross in Worcester, Massachusetts. He earned a Juris Doctor form the University of Michigan Law School where he served as the articles editor on the *Michigan Journal of International Law.* He earned a Master of Laws from Temple University Beasley School of Law in Philadelphia.

Following graduation, Gallini served as a judicial clerk to the Honorable Robert W. Clifford on the Maine Supreme Judicial Court. He then practiced white-collar criminal defense at the Washington, D.C., office of Duane Morris LLP, before leaving private practice to clerk for the Honorable Richard Allen Griffin on the U.S. Court of Appeals for the Sixth Circuit. After his clerkship, Gallini entered academia. He taught for two years at the Temple University Beasley School of Law in Philadelphia and taught for twelve years at the University of Arkansas School of Law.

Outside of academia, Gallini coached ice hockey for more than a decade. Before coming to Arkansas, he served as the head coach for the University of Pennsylvania men's Ice Hockey Team and coached the University of Arkansas men's Ice Hockey Team from 2009–18. While coaching at Arkansas, he amassed five conference titles, three appearances at the Division III National Tournament, and was voted the 2013–14 SECHC Coach of the Year.

Gallini is an avid runner and enjoys spending time exploring the Pacific Northwest with his family. He lives in Salem with his wife Beth, their two sons, Braxton and Caden, and Atlas, their anxious Weimaraner who often disrupts Zoom calls.

SELECTED FEDERAL
CONSTITUTIONAL PROVISIONS
(QUICK REFERENCE)

Amendment IV. Search & Seizure

The right of the people to be secure in their persons, houses, papers, and effects, against unreasonable searches and seizures, shall not be violated, and no Warrants shall issue, but upon probable cause, supported by Oath or affirmation, and particularly describing the place to be searched, and the persons or things to be seized.

Amendment V. Grand Jury Indictment for Capital Crimes; Double Jeopardy; Self-incrimination; Due Process of Law; Just Compensation for Property

No person shall be held to answer for a capital, or otherwise infamous crime, unless on a presentment or indictment of a Grand Jury, except in cases arising in the land or naval forces, or in the Militia, when in actual service in time of War or public danger; nor shall any person be subject for the same offence to be twice put in jeopardy of life or limb; nor shall be compelled in any criminal case to be a witness against himself, nor be *Miranda* deprived of life, liberty, or property, without due process of law; nor shall private property be taken for public use, without just compensation.

Amendment VI. Jury Trials for Crimes & Procedural Rights

In all criminal prosecutions, the accused shall enjoy the right to a speedy and public trial, by an impartial jury of the State and district wherein the crime shall have been committed, which district shall have been previously ascertained by law, and to be informed of the nature and cause of the accusation; to be confronted with the witnesses against him; to have compulsory process for obtaining witnesses in his favor, and to have the Assistance of Counsel for his defence.

Amendment XIV. Citizenship; Privileges & Immunities; Due Process; Equal Protection

Section 1. All persons born or naturalized in the United States, and subject to the jurisdiction thereof, are citizens of the United States and of the State wherein they reside. No State shall make or enforce any law which shall abridge the privileges or immunities of citizens of the United States; nor shall any State deprive any person of life, liberty, or property, without due process of law; nor deny to any person within its jurisdiction the equal protection of the laws.

SUMMARY OF CONTENTS

TABLE OF CONTENTS

TABLE OF CASES

The principal cases are in bold type.

INVESTIGATIVE CRIMINAL PROCEDURE

INSIDE THIS CENTURY'S MOST (IN)FAMOUS CASES

Second Edition

CHAPTER 1

COURSE PLACEMENT & THE IMPORTANCE OF LAWYERING

■ ■ ■

I. WHERE INVESTIGATORY CRIMINAL PROCEDURE FITS

Law schools typically offer two different criminal procedure courses, leading students to wonder how the courses interrelate, if at all. At the risk of generalizing, one course focuses on police investigation while the other course focuses on prosecution. Together, the courses cover the legal rules and procedures for determining whether a person is guilty of a substantive criminal offense (think for example: the Model Penal Code).

This book, as the title suggests, focuses on investigations. As the semester proceeds, we will learn about the techniques government actors can constitutionally employ to investigate crime. Generally speaking, the law governing post-conviction appeals alongside death penalty procedures falls outside the purview of this course's coverage.

This first chapter covers where investigative criminal procedure fits within the criminal justice system before briefly examining the importance of lawyering. In the first section of this chapter, we consider the makeup of a typical state (not federal) defendant and evaluate the ordinary procedural stages (from initial investigation through post-conviction remedies) of the criminal justice system. We then briefly consider the incorporation doctrine and its application to the investigative criminal procedure course.

In the second section, we diverge from other criminal procedure texts and cover what qualifies as constitutionally "effective" defense counsel. We begin with *Strickland v. Washington*, the Supreme Court's seminal effective defense decision. Other than *Miranda v. Arizona*, there is arguably no case more famous than *Strickland*. But *Strickland* is also one of the saddest and most disappointing cases in the Court's history. As you will see, the Supreme Court's rulings on effective assistance of counsel fall short of the ethical standard that we should hold ourselves to as lawyers. Accordingly, effective assistance of counsel is the most important topic we will cover in this book—no other topic in this book matters unless you commit to being a good lawyer. It really is that simple.

One more introductory note is appropriate before we begin. This book comes with an online repository of "Casefiles." The Casefiles contain litigation filings from some of the most notorious criminals in recent history, including James Holmes, O.J. Simpson, Dzokhar Tsarnaev, and John Wayne Gacy, among many others. Those defendants and the filings in their respective cases play a critical role in our journey together. Each topic in this book is joined by an accompanying famous defendant and the real filings on the particular issue from their case. Accordingly, it is critical that you keep access to your online casefile repository close by as we make our way through the semester.

A. AN OVERVIEW OF THE CRIMINAL PROCESS

Pinpointing the "typical" state court criminal procedural process is an impossible task. This is because there is no single American criminal justice process; the steps in the process vary from jurisdiction to jurisdiction and may vary even within a single jurisdiction. But there is often commonality in the terminology and general structure governing the prosecution of state criminal cases. What's written below is an organizational starting point for our course. It is hardly an exhaustive treatment of the myriad of issues raised by each procedural step in our justice system.

Regardless of the precise verbiage, however, it's critical that we are constantly mindful of the role of discretion at all steps, beginning with the specific police officer and extending to the defendant, prosecutor, and judicial official (e.g., suppression or trial judge). These actors, in other words, may or may not elect to invoke or utilize many of the procedures described below. Let's consider each step briefly. You will find a quick reference chart following the description of each procedural step.

The investigation. Processing a person through the criminal justice system begins with the police investigating an incident—reported or otherwise—and identifying a "suspect." Investigations typically break into three separate categories: reactive, proactive, and prosecutorial.

Reactive investigations, as they sound, react to something, such as police observations, a 911 call, or an informant's tip. During a reactive investigation, law enforcement may rely on witness interviews, suspect interviews, and a variety of other investigative methods. Much of our course focuses on evaluating the constitutionality of police behavior during reactive investigations.

Proactive investigations are those initiated by the police in an effort to prevent or detect crime. Perhaps the most obvious example is the so-called "sting operation," where officers try to catch a perpetrator committing a crime. An officer, for example, could pose as a child in a chat room to catch a child molester. Alternatively, a member of law enforcement may pose as a hitman to catch a person planning a murder-for-hire. Regardless of scenario, officers in a proactive investigation rely on investigative methods like using informants, undercover officers, and/or electronic monitoring.

Last is the prosecutorial investigation. Perhaps the best example of a prosecutorial investigation is the "grand jury investigation." During a grand jury investigation, a prosecutor uses his or her subpoena power to direct a witness to appear before the grand jury to testify or present specific physical evidence. Grand jury investigations often occur in larger scale investigations into white-collar crimes. For reasons not relevant here, prosecutorial investigations are more relevant to adjudicatory criminal procedural than investigatory criminal procedure.

Arrest. At this stage, our "suspect" becomes an "arrestee." Two primary issues often arise in arrest litigation. First, was there sufficient probable cause to support the arrest? Second, did the arrest take place with or without a warrant? We'll discuss each issue in more detail later. But for now, it suffices to say that, once investigating officers believe a crime has occurred, the next step is to arrest the suspected perpetrator.

Booking. During the booking process, our arrestee is taken to a police station, jail, or some other holding facility. The arrestee then undergoes a booking process where he and his belongings are inventoried, and his mug shot is taken. He may also undergo a warrant and background check, health screenings, and even give a DNA sample. These booking procedures, however, are clerical. Importantly, at this stage, the arrestee has not yet been charged with a crime.

Post-arrest investigation. After the arrestee is booked, officers may elect to undertake a post-arrest investigation, which may include placing the arrestee in a lineup or showing other prospective witnesses the arrestee's picture in a photographic lineup. Law enforcement might also collect a handwriting or hair sample from the arrestee to compare with other evidence collected as part of the pre-arrest investigation.

Charging decision. Once the investigation is complete, police prepare and send an arrest report to the prosecutor for review. The prosecutor then determines whether to charge the arrestee or dismiss the case. The arresting officer may make recommendations about what crimes should be charged, but the prosecutor retains the sole discretion to make the charging decision.

Complaint filed. Assuming the prosecution elects to proceed, the prosecutor files a "complaint" signaling the formal commencement of criminal proceedings. At this point, the arrestee becomes a "defendant." In felony cases (our focus), the complaint is a straightforward document that identifies the defendant, the charged offenses, and a factual summary supporting the defendant's involvement in the offenses.

Judicial review. Assuming the arrest occurred without a warrant and the defendant remains in custody, he must receive judicial review of his case in accordance with *Gerstein v. Pugh*, 420 U.S. 103 (1975). This from of review (known as *Gerstein* review) requires an independent magistrate to determine *ex parte* whether probable cause supports the charged offense and whether the defendant should remain detained pending trial. Importantly, *Gerstein* review must occur within forty-eight hours of arrest, and the defendant must be released if the magistrate determines that probable cause does not support the charged offenses. That circumstance, however, is a rarity; as Steve Bogaria describes in his book, *Courtroom 302: A Year Behind the Scenes in an American Criminal Courthouse* 16 (2005), "[u]sually the defendant has barely reached the bench before [the magistrate] has made his detached judgment that there is 'probable cause to detain.'"

Before proceeding further, it is worth noting that *Gerstein* review need not occur when the defendant is arrested pursuant to an arrest warrant. After all, in those cases, a neutral and detached magistrate has already determined that probable cause supports the charged offenses. Likewise, no judicial review is necessary when the defendant is indicted because, in those case, a grand jury has already made the independent probable cause determination.

First appearance. Once the complaint is filed, our defendant must appear before a magistrate. If the complaint was filed immediately upon arrest and the defendant remains in custody, then many jurisdictions will fold *Gerstein* review into the first appearance. During the first appearance, the magistrate: (1) informs the defendant of the charges against him and of his rights (e.g., to silence, to counsel), (2) describes the next step in the criminal process, and (3) sets the defendant's bail. As part of setting bail, the magistrate can generally choose from a range of options in roughly two categories: non-financial release or financial release.

Notably, a majority of states permit a magistrate to deny bail entirely in the interest of community safety. Often called "preventative detention," pretrial detention was once considered inconsistent with the presumption of innocence. Over time, that concern has largely faded as preventative detention has grown increasingly common.

The split between information and indictment jurisdictions. In some state jurisdictions, criminal charges proceed by information, and in other jurisdictions charges proceed by indictment.

In an "information jurisdiction," formal charges are filed via an "information." That document is a formal charging instrument authored by the prosecutor. A preliminary hearing is typically held to determine whether sufficient evidence exists to bind the defendant over for trial. At the hearing, the prosecution must prove that probable cause exists to believe that the defendant committed the crime. Although a probable cause determination occurred earlier as part of the *Gerstein* hearing, the preliminary hearing is an adversarial proceeding where the defendant is represented by counsel. The purpose of the hearing is to determine whether sufficient evidence exists to require the defendant to stand trial. If the magistrate elects to bind the defendant over for trial, then the information replaces the complaint as the controlling charging document.

Other jurisdictions permit, and some even require, the prosecution to obtain a grand jury indictment for a felony prosecution. In "indictment jurisdictions," the indictment serves as the formal charging instrument. An indictment, which is signed by the prosecutor, serves to inform the defendant of the charges against him, though it is not evidence of his guilt. A prosecutor can obtain an indictment only by presenting their case to a grand jury. That presentation is what we mean by grand jury review. A screening grand jury might sit for between one and several months, hearing cases in a closed session led by the prosecution. During these presentations, the grand jury members hear only from the prosecution; the defendant has no right to offer his own evidence, be present, or have counsel present on his behalf.

If the grand jury issues a "true bill"—a written decision signed by the foreperson of the grand jury indicating that probable cause exists to believe that the defendant committed the charged offense—then the indictment replaces the complaint as the accusatory instrument. Finally, it is worth noting that Grand juries rarely decline to indict. As former Chief Judge of the New York Court of Appeals Sol Wachtler famously commented, a prosecutor can persuade a grand jury to "indict a ham sandwich."[1]

Arraignment. After the indictment or information is filed, the defendant is arraigned. Arraignment serves a variety of functions. For example, the court informs the defendant about the charges against him and determines whether the defendant has counsel, would like counsel appointed for them (if indigent), or whether the defendant wishes to represent themselves pro se. But perhaps most importantly, the defendant at arraignment is for the first time asked to enter a plea. If the defendant enters a plea of not guilty, then the judge sets a date for trial. Trials, however, are uncommon; approximately ninety-four percent of state cases are resolved through plea negotiations,[2] a process described below.

Motion practice. At or after arraignment, the parties are free to file pretrial motions. Those motions can cover a variety of topics, but common motions seek to (1) sever charges or defendants, (2) request discovery, (3)

---

[1]   Editorial, *Do We Need Grand Juries?*, N.Y. Times (Feb. 18, 1985), http://www.nytimes.com/1985/02/18/opinion/do-we-need-grand-juries.html.

[2]   Erica Goode, *Stronger Hand for Judges in the 'Bazaar' of Plea Deals*, N.Y. Times (Mar. 22, 2012), http://www.nytimes.com/2012/03/23/us/stronger-hand-for-judges-after-rulings-on-plea-deals.html.

suppress evidence, (4) change venue, (5) allege a defect in the charging instrument, and (6) assert a speedy trial violation. Because an overwhelming majority of state cases are resolved via guilty plea, competent defense attorneys are wise to litigate all viable pretrial issues (while reviewing all available discovery—discussed below) *before* finalizing a plea.

Discovery. Between the arraignment and trial, the prosecution (and sometimes the defendant) must turn over information about the case. This process, called discovery, is rooted simultaneously in a jurisdiction's rules of criminal procedure alongside the due process clauses of both the state and federal constitutions. From a strictly rules-based standpoint, discovery commonly takes one of two forms: "closed" and "open" discovery. Closed file discovery means that the state need not turn over its entire file. Rather, the state must only turn over what's required by the governing rule of criminal procedure. Open file discovery, on the other hand, means that the state's entire file is open to the defense for review and analysis. From the defense perspective, it's hard to overstate the importance of meticulous discovery collection and review before finalizing a guilty plea.

Plea negotiations. Plea negotiations typically commence after the filing of formal charges. In its strictest definitional form, a plea bargain is the product of an agreement between the prosecution and defense, where the prosecution makes certain concessions in exchange for the defendant's guilty plea. An important question in this context is whether any perceived prosecutorial concession is actually the result of overcharging.

Regardless of the bargain's merits, the trial court must evaluate whether to accept the defendant's guilty plea by ensuring that the plea is voluntary, and knowingly and intelligently made. A trial court must be satisfied that: (1) the defendant is aware of the direct consequences of the plea; (2) no threats or misrepresentations were made to the defendant to obtain the plea; (3) the defendant was represented by competent counsel; (4) the defendant is competent; (5) the defendant knows the constitutional protections being forfeited; (6) the defendant understands the crimes to which he is pleading guilty; and (7) a "factual basis" exists to support the plea.

Trial. In the rare case where no guilty plea occurs, the defendant proceeds to trial. Criminal trials are similar to their civil counterparts with four major exceptions. First, the prosecution must prove the defendant's guilt beyond a reasonable doubt. Second, the defendant retains a presumption of innocence throughout the totality of the trial. Third, the defendant has the right not to testify (and the prosecution may not ask the jurors to draw any inference from the defendant's decision not to testify). Finally, evidence obtained by the state in an unconstitutional manner may not be introduced.

At the conclusion of the trial, the case is submitted either to the jury or, in the case of a bench trial, to the trial court judge where the judge acts as the finder of fact. Assuming submission to a jury, the jury, which can range in size between six to twelve members, must then deliberate, and it must usually (though not always) be unanimous in reaching a verdict of guilty or not guilty in state felony cases.

Sentencing. Following a guilty verdict, the defendant is sentenced. Most commonly, the jury's work is done and the judge will now determine the defendant's sentence. As part of doing so, the judge sets a date for sentencing and orders the preparation of a presentencing report. The presentencing report typically includes details about the offender's background, the crime itself, and a recommended sentence. A sentence commonly takes one or a combination of the following forms: (1) imprisonment, (2) fines or other financial sanctions, and (3) community release—most commonly in the form of probation.

Appeals. Following a conviction or guilty plea, the defendant may directly appeal his case to the state intermediate appellate court as a matter of statutory (not constitutional) right. Some states, however, do not have intermediate appellate courts (e.g., Maine). In those jurisdictions, the courts of last resort will hear the defendant's appeal.

Collateral remedies. Following exhaustion of state appellate court remedies, the defendant can file for habeas relief in federal court. The particulars of habeas law are best reserved for an entirely separate course, but it is worth pausing to mention that commonality exists in every federal habeas filing. In each case, the defendant must argue that his state trial violated one or more of his federal constitutional rights.

Overview Quick Reference Chart

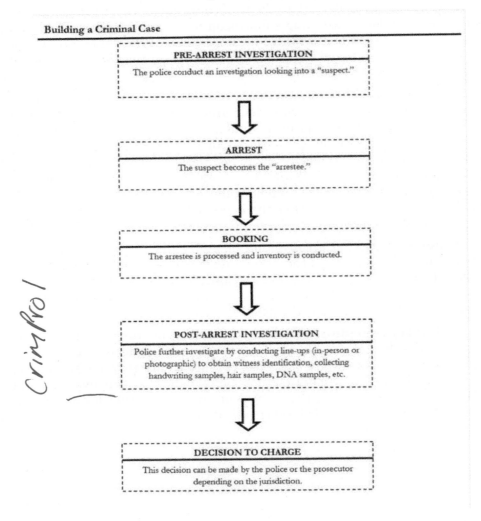

Formal Court Proceedings

FILING THE COMPLAINT

Arrestee becomes a "defendant"
This is usually where the police officer will hand off the case to the
prosecuting attorney and the formal court proceedings commence.

MAGISTRATE REVIEW

This is an ex parte review to determine if probable cause exists.
This takes place if and only if the defendant remained in custody
following a warrantless arrest.

FIRST APPEARANCE

Defendant is brought before a Magistrate Judge and bail is set

INFORMATION JURISDICTION

A preliminary hearing is held to
determine whether or not probable cause
exists. Once probable cause is established
the prosecutor files an information that
replaces the complaint.

INDICTMENT JURISDICTION

This requires a grand jury to review the
evidence and determine whether or not
probable cause exists as to whether or
not the defendant committed the crime.
Once the grand jury determines that
probable cause exists the prosecutor files
an indictment that replaces the
complaint.

ARRAIGNMENT

This is where the defendant is informed of the charges against him
and enters a plea of guilty, not guilty, or nolo contendere.

PRE-TRIAL MOTIONS

Certain motions should be made leading up to trial. These motions
include motions to suppress, change of venue, challenging the
charging document, etc.

TRIAL

When a defendant opts to go to trial he is presumed innocent until
proven guilty beyond a reasonable doubt. The defendant has the
right to not take the stand and illegally obtained evidence must be
excluded.

SENTENCING

A sentence can take on many different forms including financial
sanctions, community release, or incarceration.

APPEAL

The defendant has first appeal as of right.

COLLATERAL REMEDIES

Following exhaustion of remedies in state court, the defendant may
challenge his conviction in federal court.

B. UNDERSTANDING INCORPORATION

The topic of incorporation relates to whether the Bill of Rights, initially designed to limit the federal government, also imposes limitations on state governments. The reach of the Bill of Rights into state affairs matters is particularly relevant to the criminal procedure context because, as we've discussed already, the vast majority of the cases we address in this class arise at the state level. Accordingly, we briefly cover the topic here.

To start, the Bill of Rights consists of the first ten amendments to the Constitution. These amendments were ratified in 1971 to serve as limitations on the federal government. Nearly a century later, the Fourteenth Amendment was ratified. Section 1 of the Fourteenth Amendment limits state action through three clauses: the Privileges and Immunities Clause, the Due Process Clause, and the Equal Protection Clause. The question therefore became what relationship exists, if any, between the Fourteenth Amendment and the Bill of Rights.

How we resolve this question matters a great deal. Consider, for example, a scenario where the Bill of Rights does not apply to state governments at all. In that scenario, the Fourth Amendment would prohibit only federal actors from engaging in unreasonable searches and seizures; the Amendment would pose to restriction on state actors. Hypothetically, then, state actors could seize evidence in violation of the Fourth Amendment and simply turn it over to federal prosecutors. That certainly feels uncomfortable. But consider another scenario: what if every single provision of the Bill of Rights applied to the states? In that scenario, criminal procedure, as a topic, would hardly align with the concept of federalism.

Following the Fourteenth Amendment's ratification, several incorporation theories emerged. Three are worth briefly summarizing: (1) fundamental rights, (2) total incorporation, and (3) selective incorporation.

- **Fundamental rights:** The fundamental rights theory, championed by Justice Felix Frankfurter, asserts that there is no relationship between the Fourteenth Amendment and the Bill of Rights. Rather, "[t]he Fourteenth requires only that states honor basic principles of fundamental fairness and ordered liberty—principles that might indeed happen to overlap wholly or in part with some of the rules of the Bill of Rights, but that bear no logical relationship to those rules." Akhil Reed Amar, *The Bill of Rights and the Fourteenth Amendment*, 101 YALE L.J. 1193, 1196 (1992).

- **Total incorporation:** The theory of total incorporation, promoted by Justice Hugo Black, asserts that the Fourteenth Amendment "made applicable against the states each and every provision of the Bill, lock, stock, and barrel—at least if we define the Bill to include only the first eight amendments." *Id.*

- **Selective incorporation:** Finally, the selective incorporation theory, from Justice William J. Brennan, asserts that the analysis should "proceed clause by clause, fully incorporating every provision of the Bill deemed 'fundamental' without deciding in advance whether each and every clause would necessarily pass the test."

Ultimately, Justice Frankfurter's fundamental rights approach won the day. That said, given the Court's direction these last several decades, it feels as though Justice Black's total incorporation approach emerged victorious. The Court over time has, in piecemeal fashion, gradually incorporated specific rights—holding them applicable to the states. In the realm of criminal procedure, all but one provision of the Bill of Rights applies to the states (the Grand Jury Clause of the Fifth Amendment does not apply to the states).

Bottom line for purposes of this course: think of the Fourteenth Amendment as a bridge over which the Fourth, Fifth, and Sixth Amendments travel from the Bill of Rights to act as limiters on state action. Thus, when we discuss the Fourth, Fifth, and/or Sixth Amendments in this course, what we are really saying is the Fourth/Fourteenth Amendment, Fifth/Fourteenth Amendment, and Sixth/Fourteenth Amendment.

In our one incorporation case, *Malloy v. Hogan*, the Court wrestles with whether the Fifth Amendment's self-incrimination clause applies to the states. Can you identify which incorporation theory the Court relies on in *Malloy*?

Before reading the case, you might notice the date of its publication— 1964. That year was the middle of a period during which the Supreme Court, led by Chief Justice Earl Warren, was expanding individual rights. Although Earl Warren served as Chief Justice from 1953 until 1969, commentators often refer to the "Warren Court" to mean the time spanning from 1961, when Justice Arthur Goldberg replaced Justice Felix Frankfurter, to 1969, when Chief Justice Warren retired. During that timeframe, the Court published several controversial opinions relating to indigent criminal defense in trial and appellate representation, marital privacy, and state voting rights. Those cases, alongside so many others from the Warren Court, sparked national public outcry. "Impeach Earl Warren" signs littered the countryside, and the Court faced criticism from critics like the American Bar Association and the National Association of Attorneys General—among others. Congress even sought to refuse authorization of a pay increase for the Justices. Suffice it to say that the Court was not particularly popular with the public at the time of *Malloy*.

MALLOY V. HOGAN

378 U.S. 1
Supreme Court of the United States
March 5, 1964, Argued; June 15, 1964, Decided
No. 110

MR. JUSTICE BRENNAN delivered the opinion of the Court.

In this case we are asked to reconsider prior decisions holding that the privilege against self-incrimination is not safeguarded against state action by the Fourteenth Amendment.

The petitioner was arrested during a gambling raid in 1959 by Hartford, Connecticut police. He pleaded guilty to the crime of pool selling, a misdemeanor, and was sentenced to one year in jail and fined $500. The sentence was ordered to be suspended after ninety days, at which time he was to be placed on probation for two years. About sixteen months after his guilty plea, petitioner was ordered to testify before a referee appointed by the Superior Court of Hartford County to conduct an inquiry into alleged gambling and other criminal activities in the county. The petitioner was asked a number of questions related to events surrounding his arrest and conviction. He refused to answer any question "on the grounds it may tend to incriminate me." The Superior Court adjudged him in contempt and committed him to prison until he was willing to answer the questions. Petitioner's application for a writ of habeas corpus was denied by the Superior Court, and the Connecticut Supreme Court of Errors affirmed. The latter court held that the Fifth Amendment's privilege against self-incrimination was not available to a witness in a state proceeding, that the Fourteenth Amendment extended no privilege to him, and that the petitioner had not properly invoked the privilege available under the Connecticut Constitution. We granted certiorari. We reverse. We hold that the Fourteenth Amendment guaranteed the petitioner the protection of the Fifth Amendment's privilege against self-incrimination, and that under the applicable federal standard, the Connecticut Supreme Court of Errors erred in holding that the privilege was not properly invoked.

The extent to which the Fourteenth Amendment prevents state invasion of rights enumerated in the first eight Amendments has been considered in numerous cases in this Court since the Amendment's adoption in 1868. Although many Justices have deemed the Amendment to incorporate all eight of the amendments, the view which has thus far prevailed dates from the decision in 1897 in *Chicago, B. & Q. R. Co. v. Chicago*, 166 U.S. 226, which held that the Due Process Clause requires the States to pay just compensation for private property taken for public use. It was on the authority of that decision that the Court said in 1908 in *Twining v. New Jersey*, [211 U.S. 78] that "it is possible that some of the personal rights safeguarded by the first eight Amendments against

National action may also be safeguarded against state action, because a denial of them would be a denial of due process of law."

The Court has not hesitated to re-examine past decisions according the Fourteenth Amendment a less central role in the preservation of basic liberties than that which was contemplated by its Framers when they added the Amendment to our constitutional scheme. Thus, although the Court as late as 1922 said that "neither the Fourteenth Amendment nor any other provision of the Constitution of the United States imposes upon the States any restrictions about 'freedom of speech' . . . ," *Prudential Ins. Co. v. Cheek*, 259 U.S. 530, 543, three years later *Gitlow v. New York*, 268 U.S. 652, initiated a series of decisions which today hold immune from state invasion every First Amendment protection for the cherished rights of mind and spirit—the freedoms of speech, press, religion, assembly, association, and petition for redress of grievances.

Similarly, *Palko v. Connecticut*, 302 U.S. 319, decided in 1937, suggested that the rights secured by the Fourth Amendment were not protected against state action, citing, 302 U.S., at 324, the statement of the Court in 1914 in *Weeks v. United States*, 232 U.S. 383, 398, that "the Fourth Amendment is not directed to individual misconduct of [state] officials." In 1961, however, the Court held that in the light of later decisions, it was taken as settled that ". . . the Fourth Amendment's right of privacy has been declared enforceable against the States through the Due Process Clause of the Fourteenth . . . ." *Mapp v. Ohio*, 367 U.S. 643, 655. Again, although the Court held in 1942 that in a state prosecution for a noncapital offense, "appointment of counsel is not a fundamental right," *Betts v. Brady*, 316 U.S. 455, 471; *cf. Powell v. Alabama*, 287 U.S. 45, only last Term this decision was re-examined and it was held that provision of counsel in all criminal cases was "a fundamental right, essential to a fair trial," and thus was made obligatory on the States by the Fourteenth Amendment. *Gideon v. Wainwright*, 372 U.S. 335, 343–344.

We hold today that the Fifth Amendment's exception from compulsory self-incrimination is also protected by the Fourteenth Amendment against abridgment by the States. Decisions of the Court since *Twining* and *Adamson* have departed from the contrary view expressed in those cases. We discuss first the decisions which forbid the use of coerced confessions in state criminal prosecutions.

Brown v. Mississippi, 297 U.S. 278, was the first case in which the Court held that the Due Process Clause prohibited the States from using the accused's coerced confessions against him. The Court in *Brown* felt impelled, in light of *Twining*, to say that its conclusion did not involve the privilege against self-incrimination. "Compulsion by torture to extort a confession is a different matter." But this distinction was soon abandoned, and today the admissibility of a confession in a state criminal prosecution is tested by the same standard applied in federal prosecutions since 1897, when, in *Bram v. United States*, 168 U.S. 532, the Court held that "in criminal trials, in the courts of the United States, wherever a question arises whether a confession is incompetent because not voluntary, the issue is controlled by that portion of the Fifth Amendment to the Constitution of the United States, commanding that no person 'shall be compelled in any criminal case to be a witness against himself.'" Under this test, the constitutional inquiry is not whether the conduct of state officers in obtaining the confession was shocking, but whether the confession was "free and voluntary: that is, [it] must not be extracted by any sort of threats or violence, nor obtained by any direct or implied promises, however slight, nor by the exertion of any improper influence. . . ." In other words, the person must not have been compelled to incriminate himself. We have held inadmissible even a confession secured by so mild a whip as the refusal, under certain circumstances, to allow a suspect to call his wife until he confessed.

The marked shift to the federal standard in state cases began with *Lisenba v. California*, 314 U.S. 219, where the Court spoke of the accused's "free choice to admit, to deny, or to refuse to answer." The shift reflects recognition that the American system of criminal prosecution is accusatorial, not inquisitorial, and that the Fifth Amendment privilege is its essential mainstay. Governments, state and federal, are thus constitutionally compelled to establish guilt by evidence independently and freely secured, and may not by coercion prove a charge against an accused out of his own mouth. Since the Fourteenth Amendment prohibits the States from inducing a person to confess through "sympathy falsely aroused," *Spano v. New York*, [360 U.S. 315, 323], or other like inducement far short of "compulsion by torture," *Haynes v. Washington*, [373 U.S. 503], it follows *a fortiori* that it also forbids the States to resort to imprisonment, as here, to compel him to answer questions that might incriminate him. The Fourteenth Amendment secures against state invasion the same privilege that the Fifth Amendment guarantees against federal infringement—the right of a person to remain silent unless he chooses to speak in the unfettered exercise of his own will, and to suffer no penalty, as held in Twining, for such silence.

This conclusion is fortified by our recent decision in *Mapp v. Ohio*, 367 U.S. 643, overruling *Wolf v. Colorado*, 338 U.S. 25, which had held "that in a prosecution in a State court for a State crime the Fourteenth Amendment does not forbid the admission of evidence obtained by an unreasonable search and seizure[.]" *Mapp* held that the Fifth Amendment privilege against self-incrimination implemented the Fourth Amendment in such cases, and that the two guarantees of personal security conjoined in the Fourteenth Amendment to make the exclusionary rule obligatory upon the States. * * * We said in *Mapp*:

We find that, as to the Federal Government, the Fourth and Fifth Amendments and, as to the States, the freedom from unconscionable invasions of privacy and the freedom from convictions based upon coerced confessions do enjoy an "intimate relation" in their perpetuation of "principles of humanity and civil liberty [secured] . . . only after years of struggle," *Bram v. United States*, 168 U.S. 532, 543–544 . . . . The philosophy of each Amendment and of each freedom is complementary to, although not dependent upon, that of the other in its sphere of influence— the very least that together they assure in either sphere is that no man is to be convicted on unconstitutional evidence.

* * * *Mapp* necessarily repudiated the *Twining* concept of the privilege as a mere rule of evidence "best defended not as an unchangeable principle of universal justice but as a law proved by experience to be expedient." 211 U.S., at 113.

* * * The State urges, however, that the availability of the federal privilege to a witness in a state inquiry is to be determined according to a less stringent standard than is applicable in a federal proceeding. We disagree. We have held that the guarantees of the First Amendment, the prohibition of unreasonable searches and seizures of the Fourth Amendment, and the right to counsel guaranteed by the Sixth Amendment, are all to be enforced against the States under the Fourteenth Amendment according to the same standards that protect those personal rights against federal encroachment. In the coerced confession cases, involving the policies of the privilege itself, there has been no suggestion that a confession might be considered coerced if used in a federal but not a state tribunal. The Court thus has rejected the notion that the Fourteenth Amendment applies to the States only a "watered-down, subjective version of the individual guarantees of the Bill of Rights," *Ohio ex rel. Eaton v. Price*, 364 U.S. 263, 275 (dissenting opinion). * * * What is accorded is a privilege of refusing to incriminate one's self, and the feared prosecution may be by either federal or state authorities. It would be incongruous to have different standards determine the validity of a claim of privilege based on the same feared prosecution, depending on whether the claim was asserted in a state or federal court. Therefore, the same standards must determine whether an accused's silence in either a federal or state proceeding is justified. * * *

Reversed.

While MR. JUSTICE DOUGLAS joins the opinion of the Court, he also adheres to his concurrence in *Gideon v. Wainwright*, 372 U.S. 335, 345.

MR. JUSTICE HARLAN, whom MR. JUSTICE CLARK joins, dissenting.

[Omitted.]

MR. JUSTICE WHITE, with whom MR. JUSTICE STEWART joins, dissenting. [Omitted.]

II. THE IMPORTANCE OF LAWYERING

Nothing that you learn in this course will matter unless you have a deep appreciation for the impact of your decisions as a lawyer in the outcome of the case. Indeed, quality of lawyering matters arguably more than anything else—on both the prosecutorial and defense sides. On the defense side, the Supreme Court's treatment of the constitutional standard governing the minimal competency is, in a word, disappointing. But it nonetheless provides a sobering reminder that we, as lawyers, must own our actions because the Supreme Court's Sixth Amendment standard will permit almost anything to pass as constitutionally acceptable representation.

To that end, we begin our first substantive topic and meet Adnan Syed, best known for his role in NPR's first *Serial* podcast. In doing so, we evaluate the actions of Syed's trial lawyer, M. Cristina Gutierrez, before and during her representation of Syed at his trial for the murder of Hae Min Lee. We'll consider in some depth one of the Supreme Court's most disappointing cases, *Strickland v. Washington*, alongside an illustrative state decision demonstrating what defense behavior the *Strickland* standard arguably permits. Along the way, we'll consider alternative methods of evaluating a so-called *Strickland* claim while learning some of the history surrounding *Strickland* and why that history might provide a basis for overruling the decision.

A. MEET ADNAN SYED

On February 25, 2000, Adnan Syed was convicted of murdering his former girlfriend and classmate, Hae Min Lee. Lee, a gifted and talented student at Woodlawn High School in Baltimore, Maryland, who vanished after school on January 13, 1999.

Adnan Syed   Hae Min Lee

Investigators initially treated Lee's disappearance as a runaway or missing person case until her body was discovered buried in a shallow grave nearly a month later. Soon thereafter, an anonymous phone call implicating Syed, coupled with the testimony of a former Woodlawn High student, Jay Wilds, led to Syed's arrest for first-degree murder.

Cristina Gutierrez

As prosecutors and police built their case against seventeen-year-old Syed, Syed's family hired M. Cristina Gutierrez to represent him at trial. Gutierrez was a well-known criminal defense attorney who had been involved in a number of high profile cases during the 1990s.[3] But in 1999,

---

[3]   Gus Sentementes, *Maria C. Gutierrez, 52, criminal defense lawyer*, BALTIMORE SUN, January 31, 2004.

Gutierrez began suffering from the effects of multiple sclerosis, which reportedly included loss of vision and memory.[4]

In December 1999, Syed's first trial resulted in a mistrial. His second trial ended on February 25, 2000, with a conviction of first-degree murder, kidnapping, robbery, and false imprisonment. Syed was sentenced to life in prison.

After unsuccessful direct appeals, Syed hired C. Justin Brown to represent him in post-conviction proceedings. Syed filed a Petition for Post-Conviction Relief on May 28, 2010, alleging ineffective assistance of trial counsel, among other claims. The Baltimore City Circuit Court held a hearing in October 2012. The court denied Syed's petition. [See Casefile Document 1.]

On June 30, 2015, Syed filed a Motion to Re-Open Post-Conviction Proceedings in the Circuit Court, followed by a Supplement to the motion on August 24, 2015. [See Casefile Documents 2 & 3.] The Circuit Court granted Syed's motion on November 6, 2015, for the limited consideration of two of Syed's claims: (1) Gutierrez's failure to contact a potential alibi witness and (2) the reliability of the cell phone/cell tower evidence used by the State to corroborate Jay Wilds's testimony. [See Casefile Document 4.]

Specifically, the court first considered whether Gutierrez rendered ineffective assistance when she failed to contact Asia McClain, another Woodlawn High School student, and to investigate her as a possible alibi witness. McClain and Syed were high school acquaintances. Shortly after Syed's arrest, McClain contacted him via multiple letters to tell him that she remembered seeing him in the library after school the day that Lee was murdered. Syed repeatedly relayed this information and gave McClain's letters to Gutierrez, as evidenced by her case notes, but she never contacted or considered McClain as a potential alibi.

Syed argued that Gutierrez's failure to contact McClain constituted deficient representation because McClain's testimony provided Syed with an alibi for the precise time Lee was murdered. To present their theory, the State developed a timeline of events based on Wilds's testimony and Syed's cell phone records. According to their timeline, Syed strangled Lee after school in the Best Buy parking lot at 2:36 p.m. However, according to McClain's recollection of that day, Syed was in the library visiting with her from 2:30 p.m. to 2:40 p.m.

Although Gutierrez had notice of McClain's recollection, neither she nor her staff ever contacted McClain. After the first trial in 2000, McClain wrote and signed two separate affidavits affirming that she saw Syed in

---

[4]   As a result of her illnesses, the Maryland Court of Appeals would ultimately announce on May 24, 2001 that Gutierrez had consented to her own disbarment. Gutierrez passed away on January 30, 2004.

the library around 2:30 p.m. on January 13, 1999, and that no one from the defense team ever contacted her.

In considering "the alibi" claim, the Circuit Court applied the two-prong inquiry articulated in *Strickland v. Washington*, 466 U.S. 668 (1984), to evaluate whether Gutierrez's representation deprived Syed of his Sixth Amendment right to effective assistance of counsel. Regarding the first prong, identification of the acts or omissions that were deficient, the court found that Gutierrez's "failure to investigate McClain as a potential alibi witness fell below the standard of reasonable professional judgment."

Nevertheless, the court denied relief on "the alibi" claim under *Strickland*'s second "prejudice" prong. That prong requires a petitioner to show a reasonable probability that, but for trial counsel's deficient performance, the trial would have resulted in a different outcome. The court found that Gutierrez's failure to investigate McClain was not prejudicial because her testimony "would not have undermined the crux of the State's case: that [Syed] buried the victim's body in Leakin Park at approximately 7:00 p.m. on January 13, 1999." Thus, the "alibi claim" did not meet *Strickland*'s standard for ineffective assistance of counsel.

The court also denied relief on Syed's second claim—the "*Brady*" claim. In support of that claim, Syed argued that the State failed to disclose potentially exculpatory evidence (a fax cover sheet disclaiming the reliability of the cell phone records used against Syed) and, as such, violated *Brady v. Maryland*, 373 U.S. 83 (1963). However, the court found that Syed waived this claim because by not raising it in a prior proceeding.[5]

Finally, the court considered Syed's third claim for post-conviction relief: that Gutierrez rendered ineffective assistance when she failed to cross-examine the State's cell tower expert about the disclaimer contained in the fax cover sheet. At trial, the State relied on two incoming calls to corroborate Wilds's testimony that Syed buried Lee's body in Leakin Park at approximately 7:00 p.m.—the "crux" of the State's case. The State presented a cell tower expert to explain this evidence. Gutierrez failed to cross-examine the expert about the disclaimer included in the cell phone records cover sheet.

According to the court, the disclaimer raised the possibility that the State's evidence linking Syed's phone records to Leakin Park at the time of the burial "may not reliably have reflected the corresponding cell site of an incoming call." Thus, "a reasonable attorney would have exposed the misleading nature of the State's theory by cross-examining [the State's expert about the disclaimer]." The court found that Gutierrez's "deficient performance in failing to confront the State's cell tower expert regarding

---

[5]   The court proceeded to evaluate the merits of the *Brady* claim despite Syed's waiver, eventually concluding that the State did not violate *Brady* by failing to turn over the fax cover sheet disclaimer.

the disclaimer created a substantial probability that the result of the trial was fundamentally unreliable."

Consequently, on June 30, 2016, the court granted post-conviction relief with respect to this third claim, vacated Syed's convictions, and granted Syed's request for a new trial. [See Casefile Documents 5 & 6.] The State appealed the Circuit Court's order but, on March 29, 2018, the Maryland Court of Special Appeals affirmed the Circuit Court's order. [See Casefile Document 7.]

B. WHAT IS "EFFECTIVE ASSISTANCE" OF COUNSEL?

The right to counsel arises from the Sixth Amendment, which provides, "In all criminal prosecutions, the accused shall enjoy the right . . . to have the Assistance of Counsel for his defense." On June 6, 1983, the date upon which the Supreme Court granted the State's writ of certiorari in *Strickland*, the strength of the Sixth Amendment's right to counsel diminished. Some brief historical context is necessary to understand how.

At the time of its ratification in 1791, the Sixth Amendment was understood to minimally provide a criminal defendant with the right to retain a private attorney. A more difficult question loomed for more than a century: Does the Sixth Amendment require state governments to provide an attorney when the defendant cannot afford one?

The Warren Court sought to answer that question in the affirmative by steadily and dramatically expanding the right to counsel. The journey specifically began with the Supreme Court's 1963 ruling in *Gideon v. Wainwright*. *Gideon* promised counsel at state expense to indigent defendants charged with a felony. Writing for the majority on March 18, 1963, Justice Black reasoned, "[A]ny person haled into court, who is too poor to hire a lawyer, cannot be assured a fair trial unless counsel is provided for him." Moreover, Justice Black added, "The right of one charged with crime to counsel may not be deemed fundamental and essential to fair trials in some countries, but it is in ours."

If *Gideon* was not a clear manifestation of the Warren Court's intent to expand and strengthen the right to counsel, the Court then decided *Douglas v. California*. Remarkably, on the same day as *Gideon*, a majority of the Court relied on the Fourteenth Amendment to conclude that *Gideon* entitles an indigent defendant to counsel at state expense in order to prosecute his first appeal as of right.

Gideon and *Douglas* aside, the Warren Court more generally spent from 1956–1969 expanding indigent access to justice—particularly in the right-to-counsel area. By coalescing the Sixth Amendment, the Due Process Clause, the Fifth Amendment, and the Equal Protection Clause, the Warren Court issued a number of rulings that dramatically expanded indigent defendants' right to counsel. Creating the Warren Court's vision of that broadly conceived right took six years—from 1961–1967. But once complete, the Warren Court's right to counsel included access not only to attorneys at trial, in the interrogation room, at lineups, and on appeal—among other procedural phases—but it also extended more generally to things an attorney might need, like a trial transcript.

Despite the litany of Supreme Court right-to-counsel holdings, the law prior to *Strickland* was unclear as to what constituted constitutionally adequate criminal defense—a question distinct from that of *when* indigent defendants are entitled to counsel. The Supreme Court itself admitted that the issue presented in *Strickland* was novel.

Enter David Washington.

STRICKLAND V. WASHINGTON

466 U.S. 668
Supreme Court of the United States
January 10, 1984, Argued; May 14, 1984, Decided
No. 82-1554

JUSTICE O'CONNOR delivered the opinion of the Court.

This case requires us to consider the proper standards for judging a criminal defendant's contention that the Constitution requires a conviction or death sentence to be set aside because counsel's assistance at the trial or sentencing was ineffective.

I

A

During a 10-day period in September 1976, respondent planned and committed three groups of crimes, which included three brutal stabbing murders, torture, kidnaping, severe assaults, attempted murders, attempted extortion, and theft. After his two accomplices were arrested, respondent surrendered to police and voluntarily gave a lengthy statement confessing to the third of the criminal episodes. The State of Florida indicted respondent for kidnaping and murder and appointed an experienced criminal lawyer to represent him.

Counsel actively pursued pretrial motions and discovery. He cut his efforts short, however, and he experienced a sense of hopelessness about the case, when he learned that, against his specific advice, respondent had also confessed to the first two murders. By the date set for trial, respondent was subject to indictment for three counts of first-degree murder and multiple counts of robbery, kidnaping for ransom, breaking and entering and assault, attempted murder, and conspiracy to commit robbery. Respondent waived his right to a jury trial, again acting against counsel's advice, and pleaded guilty to all charges, including the three capital murder charges.

In the plea colloquy, respondent told the trial judge that, although he had committed a string of burglaries, he had no significant prior criminal record and that at the time of his criminal spree he was under extreme stress caused by his inability to support his family. He also stated, however, that he accepted responsibility for the crimes. The trial judge told respondent that he had "a great deal of respect for people who are willing to step forward and admit their responsibility" but that he was making no statement at all about his likely sentencing decision.

Counsel advised respondent to invoke his right under Florida law to an advisory jury at his capital sentencing hearing. Respondent rejected the advice and waived the right. He chose instead to be sentenced by the trial judge without a jury recommendation.

In preparing for the sentencing hearing, counsel spoke with respondent about his background. He also spoke on the telephone with respondent's wife and mother, though he did not follow up on the one unsuccessful effort to meet with them. He did not otherwise seek out character witnesses for respondent. Nor did he request a psychiatric examination, since his conversations with his client gave no indication that respondent had psychological problems.

Counsel decided not to present and hence not to look further for evidence concerning respondent's character and emotional state. That decision reflected trial counsel's sense of hopelessness about overcoming the evidentiary effect of respondent's confessions to the gruesome crimes. It also reflected the judgment that it was advisable to rely on the plea colloquy for evidence about respondent's background and about his claim of emotional stress: the plea colloquy communicated sufficient information about these subjects, and by forgoing the opportunity to present new evidence on these subjects, counsel prevented the State from cross-examining respondent on his claim and from putting on psychiatric evidence of its own.

Counsel also excluded from the sentencing hearing other evidence he thought was potentially damaging. He successfully moved to exclude respondent's "rap sheet." Because he judged that a presentence report might prove more detrimental than helpful, as it would have included respondent's criminal history and thereby would have undermined the claim of no significant history of criminal activity, he did not request that one be prepared.

At the sentencing hearing, counsel's strategy was based primarily on the trial judge's remarks at the plea colloquy as well as on his reputation as a sentencing judge who thought it important for a convicted defendant to own up to his crime. Counsel argued that respondent's remorse and acceptance of responsibility justified sparing him from the death penalty. Counsel also argued that respondent had no history of criminal activity and that respondent committed the crimes under extreme mental or emotional disturbance, thus coming within the statutory list of mitigating circumstances. He further argued that respondent should be spared death because he had surrendered, confessed, and offered to testify against a codefendant and because respondent was fundamentally a good person who had briefly gone badly wrong in extremely stressful circumstances. The State put on evidence and witnesses largely for the purpose of describing the details of the crimes. Counsel did not cross-examine the medical experts who testified about the manner of death of respondent's victims.

The trial judge found several aggravating circumstances with respect to each of the three murders. He found that all three murders were especially heinous, atrocious, and cruel, all involving repeated stabbings. All three murders were committed in the course of at least one other dangerous and violent felony, and since all involved robbery, the murders were for pecuniary gain. All three murders were committed to avoid arrest for the accompanying crimes and to hinder law enforcement. In the course of one of the murders, respondent knowingly subjected numerous persons to a grave risk of death by deliberately stabbing and shooting the murder victim's sisters-in-law, who sustained severe—in one case, ultimately fatal—injuries.

With respect to mitigating circumstances, the trial judge made the same findings for all three capital murders. First, although there was no admitted evidence of prior convictions, respondent had stated that he had engaged in a course of stealing. In any case, even if respondent had no significant history of criminal activity, the aggravating circumstances "would still clearly far outweigh" that mitigating factor. Second, the judge found that, during all three crimes, respondent was not suffering from extreme mental or emotional disturbance and could appreciate the criminality of his acts. Third, none of the victims was a participant in, or consented to, respondent's conduct. Fourth, respondent's participation in the crimes was neither minor nor the result of duress or domination by an accomplice. Finally, respondent's age (26) could not be considered a factor in mitigation, especially when viewed in light of respondent's planning of the crimes and disposition of the proceeds of the various accompanying thefts.

In short, the trial judge found numerous aggravating circumstances and no (or a single comparatively insignificant) mitigating circumstance. With respect to each of the three convictions for capital murder, the trial judge concluded: "A careful consideration of all matters presented to the court impels the conclusion that there are insufficient mitigating circumstances ... to outweigh the aggravating circumstances." He therefore sentenced respondent to death on each of the three counts of murder and to prison terms for the other crimes. The Florida Supreme Court upheld the convictions and sentences on direct appeal.

B

Respondent subsequently sought collateral relief in state court on numerous grounds, among them that counsel had rendered ineffective assistance at the sentencing proceeding. Respondent challenged counsel's assistance in six respects. He asserted that counsel was ineffective because he failed to move for a continuance to prepare for sentencing, to request a psychiatric report, to investigate and present character witnesses, to seek a presentence investigation report, to present meaningful arguments to the sentencing judge, and to investigate the medical examiner's reports or cross-examine the medical experts. In support of the claim, respondent submitted 14 affidavits from friends, neighbors, and relatives stating that they would have testified if asked to do so. He also submitted one psychiatric report and one psychological report stating that respondent, though not under the influence of extreme mental or emotional disturbance, was "chronically frustrated and depressed because of his economic dilemma" at the time of his crimes.

The trial court denied relief without an evidentiary hearing, finding that the record evidence conclusively showed that the ineffectiveness claim was meritless. Four of the assertedly prejudicial errors required little discussion. First, there were no grounds to request a continuance, so there was no error in not requesting one when respondent pleaded guilty. Second, failure to request a presentence investigation was not a serious error because the trial judge had discretion not to grant such a request and because any presentence investigation would have resulted in admission of respondent's "rap sheet" and thus would have undermined his assertion of no significant history of criminal activity. Third, the argument and memorandum given to the sentencing judge were "admirable" in light of the overwhelming aggravating circumstances and absence of mitigating circumstances. Fourth, there was no error in failure to examine the medical examiner's reports or to cross-examine the medical witnesses testifying on the manner of death of respondent's victims, since respondent admitted that the victims died in the ways shown by the unchallenged medical evidence.

The trial court dealt at greater length with the two other bases for the ineffectiveness claim. The court pointed out that a psychiatric examination of respondent was conducted by state order soon after respondent's initial arraignment. That report states that there was no indication of major mental illness at the time of the crimes. Moreover, both the reports submitted in the collateral proceeding state that, although respondent was "chronically frustrated and depressed because of his economic dilemma," he was not under the influence of extreme mental or emotional disturbance. All three reports thus directly undermine the contention made at the sentencing hearing that respondent was suffering from extreme mental or emotional disturbance during his crime spree. Accordingly, counsel could reasonably decide not to seek psychiatric reports; indeed, by relying solely on the plea colloquy to support the emotional disturbance contention, counsel denied the State an opportunity to rebut his claim with psychiatric testimony. In any event, the aggravating circumstances were so overwhelming that no substantial prejudice resulted from the absence at sentencing of the psychiatric evidence offered in the collateral attack.

The court rejected the challenge to counsel's failure to develop and to present character evidence for much the same reasons. The affidavits submitted in the collateral proceeding showed nothing more than that certain persons would have testified that respondent was basically a good person who was worried about his family's financial problems. Respondent himself had already testified along those lines at the plea colloquy. Moreover, respondent's admission of a course of stealing rebutted many of the factual allegations in the affidavits. For those reasons, and because the sentencing judge had stated that the death sentence would be appropriate even if respondent had no significant prior criminal history, no substantial prejudice resulted from the absence at sentencing of the character evidence offered in the collateral attack.

* * * [T]he trial court concluded that respondent had not shown that counsel's assistance reflected any substantial and serious deficiency measurably below that of competent counsel that was likely to have affected the outcome of the sentencing proceeding. * * * The Florida Supreme Court affirmed the denial of relief. * * *

C

Respondent next filed a petition for a writ of habeas corpus in the United States District Court for the Southern District of Florida. He advanced numerous grounds for relief, among them ineffective assistance of counsel based on the same errors, except for the failure to move for a continuance, as those he had identified in state court. The District Court held an evidentiary hearing to inquire into trial counsel's efforts to investigate and to present mitigating circumstances. Respondent offered the affidavits and reports he had submitted in the state collateral proceedings; he also called his trial counsel to testify. The State of Florida, over respondent's objection, called the trial judge to testify.

* * * Relying in part on the trial judge's testimony but also on the same factors that led the state courts to find no prejudice, the District Court concluded that "there does not appear to be a likelihood, or even a significant possibility," that any errors of trial counsel had affected the outcome of the sentencing proceeding. * * * The court accordingly denied the petition for a writ of habeas corpus.

On appeal, a panel of the United States Court of Appeals for the Fifth Circuit affirmed in part, vacated in part, and remanded with instructions to apply to the particular facts the framework for analyzing ineffectiveness claims that it developed in its opinion. The panel decision was itself vacated when Unit B of the former Fifth Circuit, now the Eleventh Circuit, decided to rehear the case *en banc*. The full Court of Appeals developed its own framework for analyzing ineffective assistance claims and reversed the judgment of the District Court and remanded the case for new factfinding under the newly announced standards. * * *

D

Petitioners, who are officials of the State of Florida, filed a petition for a writ of certiorari seeking review of the decision of the Court of Appeals. The petition presents a type of Sixth Amendment claim that this Court has not previously considered in any generality. The Court has considered Sixth Amendment claims based on actual or constructive denial of the assistance of counsel altogether, as well as claims based on state interference with the ability of counsel to render effective assistance to the accused. With the exception of *Cuyler v. Sullivan*, 446 U.S. 335 (1980), however, which involved a claim that counsel's assistance was rendered ineffective by a conflict of interest, the Court has never directly and fully addressed a claim of "actual ineffectiveness" of counsel's assistance in a case going to trial. * * *

II

In a long line of cases that includes *Powell v. Alabama*, 287 U.S. 45 (1932), *Johnson v. Zerbst*, 304 U.S. 458 (1938), and *Gideon v. Wainwright*, 372 U.S. 335 (1963), this Court has recognized that the Sixth Amendment right to counsel exists, and is needed, in order to protect the fundamental right to a fair trial. The Constitution guarantees a fair trial through the Due Process Clauses, but it defines the basic elements of a fair trial largely through the several provisions of the Sixth Amendment, including the Counsel Clause[.]

* * * The Sixth Amendment recognizes the right to the assistance of counsel because it envisions counsel's playing a role that is critical to the ability of the adversarial system to produce just results. An accused is entitled to be assisted by an attorney, whether retained or appointed, who plays the role necessary to ensure that the trial is fair. * * *

The Court has not elaborated on the meaning of the constitutional requirement of effective assistance in the latter class of cases—that is, those presenting claims of "actual ineffectiveness." In giving meaning to the requirement, however, we must take its purpose—to ensure a fair trial—as the guide. The benchmark for judging any claim of ineffectiveness must be whether counsel's conduct so undermined the proper functioning of the adversarial process that the trial cannot be relied on as having produced a just result. * * *

III

A convicted defendant's claim that counsel's assistance was so defective as to require reversal of a conviction or death sentence has two components. First, the defendant must show that counsel's performance was deficient. This requires showing that counsel made errors so serious that counsel was not functioning as the "counsel" guaranteed the defendant by the Sixth Amendment. Second, the defendant must show that the deficient performance prejudiced the defense. This requires showing that counsel's errors were so serious as to deprive the defendant of a fair trial, a trial whose result is reliable. Unless a defendant makes both showings, it cannot be said that the conviction or death sentence resulted from a breakdown in the adversary process that renders the result unreliable.

A

* * * [T]he proper standard for attorney performance is that of reasonably effective assistance. * * * When a convicted defendant complains of the ineffectiveness of counsel's assistance, the defendant must show that counsel's representation fell below an objective standard of reasonableness.

More specific guidelines are not appropriate. The Sixth Amendment refers simply to "counsel," not specifying particular requirements of effective assistance. It relies instead on the legal profession's maintenance of standards sufficient to justify the law's presumption that counsel will fulfill the role in the adversary process that the Amendment envisions. The proper measure of attorney performance remains simply reasonableness under prevailing professional norms.

Representation of a criminal defendant entails certain basic duties. Counsel's function is to assist the defendant, and hence counsel owes the client a duty of loyalty, a duty to avoid conflicts of interest. * * * These basic duties neither exhaustively define the obligations of counsel nor form a checklist for judicial evaluation of attorney performance. In any case presenting an ineffectiveness claim, the performance inquiry must be whether counsel's assistance was reasonable considering all the circumstances. Prevailing norms of practice as reflected in American Bar Association standards and the like are guides to determining what is reasonable, but they are only guides. * * *

Judicial scrutiny of counsel's performance must be highly deferential. * * * A fair assessment of attorney performance requires that every effort be made to eliminate the distorting effects of hindsight, to reconstruct the circumstances of counsel's challenged conduct, and to evaluate the conduct from counsel's perspective at the time. Because of the difficulties inherent in making the evaluation, a court must indulge a strong presumption that counsel's conduct falls within the wide range of reasonable professional assistance; that is, the defendant must overcome the presumption that, under the circumstances, the challenged action "might be considered sound trial strategy." * * *

Thus, a court deciding an actual ineffectiveness claim must judge the reasonableness of counsel's challenged conduct on the facts of the particular case, viewed as of the time of counsel's conduct. A convicted defendant making a claim of ineffective assistance must identify the acts or omissions of counsel that are alleged not to have been the result of reasonable professional judgment. The court must then determine whether, in light of all the circumstances, the identified acts or omissions were outside the wide range of professionally competent assistance. In making that determination, the court should keep in mind that counsel's function, as elaborated in prevailing professional norms, is to make the adversarial testing process work in the particular case. At the same time, the court should recognize that counsel is strongly presumed to have rendered adequate assistance and made all significant decisions in the exercise of reasonable professional judgment. * * *

B

An error by counsel, even if professionally unreasonable, does not warrant setting aside the judgment of a criminal proceeding if the error had no effect on the judgment. The purpose of the Sixth Amendment guarantee of counsel is to ensure that a defendant has the assistance necessary to justify reliance on the outcome of the proceeding. Accordingly, any deficiencies in counsel's performance must be prejudicial to the defense in order to constitute ineffective assistance under the Constitution.

In certain Sixth Amendment contexts, prejudice is presumed. Actual or constructive denial of the assistance of counsel altogether is legally presumed to result in prejudice. So are various kinds of state interference with counsel's assistance. * * * One type of actual ineffectiveness claim warrants a similar, though more limited, presumption of prejudice. In *Cuyler v. Sullivan*, the Court held that prejudice is presumed when counsel is burdened by an actual conflict of interest. In those circumstances, counsel breaches the duty of loyalty, perhaps the most basic of counsel's duties. * * * [T]he rule is not quite the per se rule of prejudice that exists for the Sixth Amendment claims mentioned above. Prejudice is presumed only if the defendant demonstrates that counsel "actively represented conflicting interests" and that "an actual conflict of interest adversely affected his lawyer's performance." *Cuyler v. Sullivan.*

Conflict of interest claims aside, actual ineffectiveness claims alleging a deficiency in attorney performance are subject to a general requirement that the defendant affirmatively prove prejudice. * * * Even if a defendant shows that particular errors of counsel were unreasonable, therefore, the defendant must show that they actually had an adverse effect on the defense.

It is not enough for the defendant to show that the errors had some conceivable effect on the outcome of the proceeding. * * * On the other hand, we believe that a defendant need not show that counsel's deficient conduct more likely than not altered the outcome in the case. * * * Accordingly, * * * [t]he defendant must show that there is a reasonable probability that, but for counsel's unprofessional errors, the result of the proceeding would have been different. A reasonable probability is a probability sufficient to undermine confidence in the outcome.

In making the determination whether the specified errors resulted in the required prejudice, a court should presume, absent challenge to the judgment on grounds of evidentiary insufficiency, that the judge or jury acted according to law. * * * When a defendant challenges a conviction, the question is whether there is a reasonable probability that, absent the errors, the factfinder would have had a reasonable doubt respecting guilt. When a defendant challenges a death sentence such as the one at issue in this case, the question is whether there is a reasonable probability that, absent the errors, the sentencer—including an appellate court, to the extent it independently reweighs the evidence—would have concluded that the balance of aggravating and mitigating circumstances did not warrant death.

In making this determination, a court hearing an ineffectiveness claim must consider the totality of the evidence before the judge or jury. * * *

V

Having articulated general standards for judging ineffectiveness claims, we think it useful to apply those standards to the facts of this case in order to illustrate the meaning of the general principles. * * * Application of the governing principles is not difficult in this case. The facts as described above make clear that the conduct of respondent's counsel at and before respondent's sentencing proceeding cannot be found unreasonable. They also make clear that, even assuming the challenged conduct of counsel was unreasonable, respondent suffered insufficient prejudice to warrant setting aside his death sentence.

With respect to the performance component, the record shows that respondent's counsel made a strategic choice to argue for the extreme emotional distress mitigating circumstance and to rely as fully as possible on respondent's acceptance of responsibility for his crimes. Although counsel understandably felt hopeless about respondent's prospects nothing in the record indicates, as one possible reading of the District Court's opinion suggests that counsel's sense of hopelessness distorted his professional judgment. Counsel's strategy choice was well within the range of professionally reasonable judgments, and the decision not to seek more character or psychological evidence than was already in hand was likewise reasonable.

The trial judge's views on the importance of owning up to one's crimes were well known to counsel. The aggravating circumstances were utterly overwhelming. Trial counsel could reasonably surmise from his conversations with respondent that character and psychological evidence would be of little help. Respondent had already been able to mention at the plea colloquy the substance of what there was to know about his financial and emotional troubles. Restricting testimony on respondent's character to what had come in at the plea colloquy ensured that contrary character and psychological evidence and respondent's criminal history, which counsel had successfully moved to exclude, would not come in. On these facts, there can be little question, even without application of the presumption of adequate performance, that trial counsel's defense, though unsuccessful, was the result of reasonable professional judgment.

With respect to the prejudice component, the lack of merit of respondent's claim is even more stark. The evidence that respondent says his trial counsel should have offered at the sentencing hearing would barely have altered the sentencing profile presented to the sentencing judge. As the state courts and District Court found, at most this evidence shows that numerous people who knew respondent thought he was generally a good person and that a psychiatrist and a psychologist believed he was under considerable emotional stress that did not rise to the level of extreme disturbance. Given the overwhelming aggravating factors, there is no reasonable probability that the omitted evidence would have changed the conclusion that the aggravating circumstances outweighed the mitigating circumstances and, hence, the sentence imposed. Indeed, admission of the evidence respondent now offers might even have been harmful to his case: his "rap sheet" would probably have been admitted into evidence, and the psychological reports would have directly contradicted respondent's claim that the mitigating circumstance of extreme emotional disturbance applied to his case.

Our conclusions on both the prejudice and performance components of the ineffectiveness inquiry do not depend on the trial judge's testimony at the District Court hearing. We therefore need not consider the general admissibility of that testimony, although, as noted, that testimony is irrelevant to the prejudice inquiry. Moreover, the prejudice question is resolvable, and hence the ineffectiveness claim can be rejected, without regard to the evidence presented at the District Court hearing. The state courts properly concluded that the ineffectiveness claim was meritless without holding an evidentiary hearing.

Failure to make the required showing of either deficient performance or sufficient prejudice defeats the ineffectiveness claim. Here there is a double failure. More generally, respondent has made no showing that the justice of his sentence was rendered unreliable by a breakdown in the adversary process caused by deficiencies in counsel's assistance. Respondent's sentencing proceeding was not fundamentally unfair.

We conclude, therefore, that the District Court properly declined to issue a writ of habeas corpus. The judgment of the Court of Appeals is accordingly

Reversed.

JUSTICE BRENNAN, concurring in part and dissenting in part.

I join the Court's opinion but dissent from its judgment. Adhering to my view that the death penalty is in all circumstances cruel and unusual punishment forbidden by the Eighth and Fourteenth Amendments, I would vacate respondent's death sentence and remand the case for further proceedings.

* * * I join the Court's opinion because I believe that the standards it sets out today will both provide helpful guidance to courts considering claims of actual ineffectiveness of counsel and also permit those courts to continue their efforts to achieve progressive development of this area of the law. * * * I believe these standards are sufficiently precise to permit meaningful distinctions between those attorney derelictions that deprive defendants of their constitutional rights and those that do not; at the same time, the standards are sufficiently flexible to accommodate the wide variety of situations giving rise to claims of this kind. * * *

That the Court rejects the ineffective-assistance claim in this case should not, of course, be understood to reflect any diminution in commitment to the principle that "the fundamental respect for humanity underlying the Eighth Amendment ... requires consideration of the character and record of the individual offender and the circumstances of the particular offense as a constitutionally indispensable part of the process of inflicting the penalty of death." I am satisfied that the standards announced today will go far towards assisting lower federal courts and state courts in discharging their constitutional duty to ensure that every criminal defendant receives the effective assistance of counsel guaranteed by the Sixth Amendment.

JUSTICE MARSHALL, dissenting.

* * * Today, for the first time, this Court attempts to synthesize and clarify those standards. For the most part, the majority's efforts are unhelpful. Neither of its two principal holdings seems to me likely to improve the adjudication of Sixth Amendment claims. And, in its zeal to survey comprehensively this field of doctrine, the majority makes many other generalizations and suggestions that I find unacceptable. Most importantly, the majority fails to take adequate account of the fact that the locus of this case is a capital sentencing proceeding. Accordingly, I join neither the Court's opinion nor its judgment.

* * * My objection to the performance standard adopted by the Court is that it is so malleable that, in practice, it will either have no grip at all or will yield excessive variation in the manner in which the Sixth Amendment is interpreted and applied by different courts. To tell lawyers and the lower courts that counsel for a criminal defendant must behave "reasonably" and must act like "a reasonably competent attorney" is to tell them almost nothing. * * *

Is a "reasonably competent attorney" a reasonably competent adequately paid retained lawyer or a reasonably competent appointed attorney? It is also a fact that the quality of representation available to ordinary defendants in different parts of the country varies significantly. Should the standard of performance mandated by the Sixth Amendment vary by locale? The majority offers no clues as to the proper responses to these questions. * * *

I object to the prejudice standard adopted by the Court for two independent reasons. First, it is often very difficult to tell whether a defendant convicted after a trial in which he was ineffectively represented would have fared better if his lawyer had been competent. Seemingly impregnable cases can sometimes be dismantled by good defense counsel. On the basis of a cold record, it may be impossible for a reviewing court confidently to ascertain how the government's evidence and arguments would have stood up against rebuttal and cross-examination by a shrewd, well-prepared lawyer. The difficulties of estimating prejudice after the fact are exacerbated by the possibility that evidence of injury to the defendant may be missing from the record precisely because of the incompetence of defense counsel. In view of all these impediments to a fair evaluation of the probability that the outcome of a trial was affected by ineffectiveness of counsel, it seems to me senseless to impose on a defendant whose lawyer has been shown to have been incompetent the burden of demonstrating prejudice.

Second and more fundamentally, the assumption on which the Court's holding rests is that the only purpose of the constitutional guarantee of effective assistance of counsel is to reduce the chance that innocent persons will be convicted. In my view, the guarantee also functions to ensure that convictions are obtained only through fundamentally fair procedures. The majority contends that the Sixth Amendment is not violated when a manifestly guilty defendant is convicted after a trial in which he was represented by a manifestly ineffective attorney. I cannot agree. Every defendant is entitled to a trial in which his interests are vigorously and conscientiously advocated by an able lawyer. A proceeding in which the defendant does not receive meaningful assistance in meeting the forces of the State does not, in my opinion, constitute due process. * * *

Even if I were inclined to join the majority's two central holdings, I could not abide the manner in which the majority elaborates upon its rulings. Particularly regrettable are the majority's discussion of the "presumption" of reasonableness to be accorded lawyers' decisions and its attempt to prejudge the merits of claims previously rejected by lower courts using different legal standards.

* * * The majority suggests that, "[for] purposes of describing counsel's duties," a capital sentencing proceeding "need not be distinguished from an ordinary trial." I cannot agree.

The Court has repeatedly acknowledged that the Constitution requires stricter adherence to procedural safeguards in a capital case than in other cases. * * *

The views expressed in the preceding section oblige me to dissent from the majority's disposition of the case before us. It is undisputed that respondent's trial counsel made virtually no investigation of the possibility of obtaining testimony from respondent's relatives, friends, or former employers pertaining to respondent's character or background. Had counsel done so, he would have found several persons willing and able to testify that, in their experience, respondent was a responsible, nonviolent man, devoted to his family, and active in the affairs of his church. Respondent contends that his lawyer could have and should have used that testimony to "humanize" respondent, to counteract the impression conveyed by the trial that he was little more than a cold-blooded killer. Had this evidence been admitted, respondent argues, his chances of obtaining a life sentence would have been significantly better.

Measured against the standards outlined above, respondent's contentions are substantial. Experienced members of the death-penalty bar have long recognized the crucial importance of adducing evidence at a sentencing proceeding that establishes the defendant's social and familial connections. The State makes a colorable—though in my view not compelling—argument that defense counsel in this case might have made a reasonable "strategic" decision not to present such evidence at the sentencing hearing on the assumption that an unadorned acknowledgment of respondent's responsibility for his crimes would be more likely to appeal to the trial judge, who was reputed to respect persons who accepted responsibility for their actions. But however justifiable such a choice might have been after counsel had fairly assessed the potential strength of the mitigating evidence available to him, counsel's failure to make any significant effort to find out what evidence might be garnered from respondent's relatives and acquaintances surely cannot be described as "reasonable." Counsel's failure to investigate is particularly suspicious in light of his candid admission that respondent's confessions and conduct in the course of the trial gave him a feeling of "hopelessness" regarding the possibility of saving respondent's life.

That the aggravating circumstances implicated by respondent's criminal conduct were substantial does not vitiate respondent's constitutional claim; judges and juries in cases involving behavior at least as egregious have shown mercy, particularly when afforded an opportunity to see other facets of the defendant's personality and life. Nor is respondent's contention defeated by the possibility that the material his counsel turned up might not have been sufficient to establish a statutory mitigating circumstance under Florida law; Florida sentencing judges and the Florida Supreme Court sometimes refuse to impose death sentences in cases "in which, even though statutory mitigating circumstances do not outweigh statutory aggravating circumstances, the addition of nonstatutory mitigating circumstances tips the scales in favor of life imprisonment."

If counsel had investigated the availability of mitigating evidence, he might well have decided to present some such material at the hearing. If he had done so, there is a significant chance that respondent would have been given a life sentence. In my view, those possibilities, conjoined with the unreasonableness of counsel's failure to investigate, are more than sufficient to establish a violation of the Sixth Amendment and to entitle respondent to a new sentencing proceeding.

I respectfully dissent.

QUESTIONS, COMMENTS, CONCERNS?

1. **Assessing Syed's claims.** Of the *Strickland* claims Syed asserted in his Petition for Post-Conviction Relief, repeated on page one of Casefile Document 1, which seem most persuasive and why?

2. **Qualifying *Strickland* concerns.** In that list of *Strickland* claims, notice what seems to missing—the fact that Gutierrez was likely laboring through trial while suffering from the effects of multiple sclerosis. Do you think a lawyer suffering from multiple sclerosis could stand as the basis for an independent *Strickland* claim? Your answer to that question should make you also think, or rethink, how you might answer similar questions about a defense lawyer who, while representing a defendant, suffers from mental illness, alcoholism, or drug dependency.

3. **"Just result" vs. "fair trial."** Notice the *Strickland* Court's seemingly inconsistent approach to the Sixth Amendment. At one point, Justice O'Connor suggests that counsel's role is to assist in producing a "just result," whereas, at another point, she suggests the proper role for the Sixth Amendment is to produce a "fair trial." Well, which is it? Answering that question seems important because, in Syed's case, the result may well be "just"

if he is, in fact, guilty, but that hardly *also* implies that his counsel's performance makes that result "fair."

The Supreme Court's decision in *Weaver v. Massachusetts*, 137 S. Ct. 1899 (2017), suggests a resolution. At Kentel Weaver's murder trial, the trial court closed off the courtroom to the public during jury selection. Although Weaver's trial counsel did not object, Weaver argued following his conviction that his lawyer's failure to object to the courtroom closure violated *Strickland*. The Massachusetts Supreme Judicial Court partially agreed. It held that the courtroom closure violated Weaver's Sixth Amendment right to a public trial and that counsel's failure to object constituted deficient performance. Although a violation of the Sixth Amendment right to a public trial constitutes structural error, the Massachusetts court concluded that Weaver failed to demonstrate prejudice as a result of counsel's performance.

The Supreme Court affirmed. It agreed that Weaver was unable to show how his trial counsel's failure to object to the trial court's closure of the courtroom prejudiced the outcome. In that sense, *Weaver* is not particularly notable. But a closer look at *Weaver* suggests the Court's willingness to view *Strickland* prejudice as contextually dependent. Speaking for a majority of the Court, Justice Kennedy wrote the following in dicta:

> [T]he concept of prejudice is defined in different ways depending on the context in which it appears. In the ordinary *Strickland* case, prejudice means "a reasonable probability that, but for counsel's unprofessional errors, the result of the proceeding would have been different." But the *Strickland* Court cautioned that the prejudice inquiry is not meant to be applied in a "mechanical" fashion. For when a court is evaluating an ineffective-assistance claim, *the ultimate inquiry must concentrate on "the fundamental fairness of the proceeding."*

Weaver, 137 S. Ct. at 1911 (emphasis added). That language suggests a potential expansion of *Strickland's* prejudice test to include a fundamental *un*fairness inquiry. That is, the *Weaver* formulation of prejudice advances an inquiry different from *Strickland's* exclusive focus on whether counsel's deficient performance affected the outcome. One wonders whether David Washington's ineffective assistance claim comes out differently if the original *Strickland* Court had focused more prominently on "fundamental fairness."

4.   *Strickland* **and new evidence.** Compare the list of *Strickland* claims in Casefile Document 1 to what remains in Syed's Motion to Re-Open Post-Conviction Proceedings. In what way has Syed's *Strickland* claim narrowed in that motion? [See Casefile Document 2, at 7.] How would you state that claim? And in what ways do Syed's new lawyers think his *Strickland* claim is based on new evidence?

5.   **Assessing "trial strategy."** Notice some fascinating exhibits appended to Casefile Document 2. They include, among others, a handwritten note from the omitted alibi witness, Asia McLain, alongside a follow-up letter

she sent to him when Syed went to prison. The handwritten letter seems most persuasive given that it was dated March 1, 1999. Can you think of a credible reason why Gutierrez would *not* have pursued an alibi defense for Syed or, at a minimum, reached out to Asia McLain? If so, does that reason qualify as the type of "trial strategy" discussed in Justice O'Connor's majority opinion? And, if that's the case, is *Strickland* tacitly permitting negligent behavior from defense lawyers?

6. **Considering the Syed exhibits.** Consider again the exhibits to Casefile Document 2. Attached at exhibit 6 is a letter from Syed's parents asking Gutierrez to include "newly discovered evidence provided by Ms. Asia McClain" in a motion for new trial. Does Gutierrez at that moment face a conflict? That is, if she abides by the parents' wishes, would she have to admit that she was ineffective?

7. **The evolution of Syed's *Strickland* claims.** What new *Strickland* claim emerges from Syed's filing in Casefile Document 3? As you consider the cell tower evidence, which element of *Strickland* seems most implicated: deficient performance or prejudice?

8. **Parsing multiple *Strickland* claims.** With now two viable *Strickland* claims emerging after Casefile Document 3, how would the claims relate to one another? Does one go to performance and the other to prejudice? Or, rather, must Syed prove both elements on each claim individually in order to prevail?

9. **The Circuit Court changes its mind.** In Casefile Document 5, the Circuit Court for Baltimore County agrees that Gutierrez should have investigated Asia McLain as a viable alibi witness. But recall Casefile Document 1, when the same court denied Syed's alibi witness *Strickland* claim. Can you articulate what changed? In other words, what did counsel for Syed do to change the same court's mind?

10. **The interplay between *Strickland* elements.** In many ways, the Circuit Court's holding in Casefile Document 5 on prejudice perfectly illustrates why so many complain about the *Strickland* standard. The *Strickland* detractors have a point. If Syed has proven that Gutierrez provided ineffective assistance, why should he *also* have to prove that that assistance prejudiced his defense? Why doesn't ineffective assistance automatically prejudice a defendant's defense? What does the Circuit Court say?

11. **Syed's new trial.** The Circuit Court ultimately grants Syed a new trial based on his second *Strickland* claim—the so-called "cell tower" claim. [See Casefile Document 5.] What should Gutierrez have done differently during Syed's trial? How did her inaction both produce ineffective assistant *and* prejudice Syed's case?

12. **The State's initial appeal.** In a lengthy 105-page opinion, the Court of Special Appeals of Maryland in 2018 affirmed the Circuit Court's grant of a new trial—but on different grounds. You may not have time amongst the demands of this and other classes to read the full opinion, but take a minute

to answer these two questions. First, what did the Court of Special Appeals find problematic about Gutierrez's representation of Syed? Second, what happened to the cell tower deficiency that the Circuit Court focused on? [See Casefile Document 7.]

13. The State's further appeal. In 2019, the Court of Appeals of Maryland, Maryland's highest court, reversed the Court of Special Appeals. [See Casefile Document 8.] Although the Court of Appeals agreed that Gutierrez provided deficient performance by failing to investigate the alibi witness, it concluded that Syed was not prejudiced by that deficiency. It noted in particular, "the State's case against Respondent could not have been substantially undermined merely by the alibi testimony of Ms. McClain because of the substantial direct and circumstantial evidence pointing to Mr. Syed's guilt." *Id.* at 35. Syed then filed a petition for writ of certiorari in the Supreme Court, but it was denied on November 25, 2019. *Syed v. Maryland,* 140 S. Ct. 562 (2019).

14. A curveball no one saw coming leads to Syed's release. Seemingly out of nowhere, the prosecution on September 15, 2022, moved to vacate Syed's conviction in large part because the state at the time of trial failed to turn over information about the possible involvement of two alternative suspects. [Casefile Document 9.] The state's motion also called into question the reliability of the incoming call evidence and further questioned the veracity of Jay Wilds' testimony. *Id.* at 12–17. Days later, on September 19, 2022, the Circuit Court for Baltimore County granted the state's motion. [Casefile Document 10.] Syed was released the same day. Julia Jester & David K. Li, *Conviction of Adnan Syed in 'Serial' podcast case is overturned and judge orders him released,* NBCNEWS.COM (Sept. 19, 2022), https://www.nbcnews.com/news/us-news/judge-tosses-conviction-adnan-syed-serial-case-orders-released-rcna48313.

A Postscript to *Strickland*[6]

Despite the Supreme Court and two prior appellate courts making much of the fact that Tunkey "excluded Washington's 'rap sheet,'" there was in fact no "rap sheet" to exclude. Washington had no criminal history. How then did Washington's non-existent "rap sheet" take on a life of its own? Here's the rest of the story.

Washington testified at his change of plea hearing, "I have been living right here in Dade County for eleven years and up until September of this year [1976] I never was arrested in Dade County for anything. You fault me for the crimes I committed, but you got to go a little further back and see why I did commit these crimes." He also added: "I never been in Dade County Jail, nothing but a traffic violation." Moreover, Washington said that killing Pridgen was "the first time [he] committed a crime."

---

[6] This subsection reprints with permission a portion of Brian Gallini, *The Historical Case for Abandoning* Strickland, 94 NEB. L. REV. 302 (2015). All footnotes are omitted.

Yet at the end of the state's case, it nevertheless sought to introduce "the defendant's rap sheet." Tunkey objected, noting "I would like to amplify that I object to [the state's] comment that [it] wants to introduce a so-called rap sheet[.]" The sentencing court sustained Tunkey's objection, telling the state that "[t]here is an appropriate manner for establishing other convictions and this is not it[.]" The sentencing court in pronouncing sentence later said the following about Washington's criminal history:

> While there was no evidence admitted of prior convictions of the defendant, he readily admitted that he had carried on a course of burglaries and had stolen property for a significant period of time, thus eliminating Section 921.141(6)(a), Florida Statutes, as a mitigating circumstance. The court finds, however, that even if the defendant were considered to have had no significant history of prior criminal activity, that the aggravating circumstances of this case would still clearly far outweigh this factor of mitigation.

Confusion about Washington's criminal history continued during his statutorily required 1978 direct appeal from his death sentences to the Supreme Court of Florida when, despite resisting his follow-up appointment, Tunkey remained as the attorney of record. In relevant part, Tunkey argued that the sentencing court failed to consider Washington's absence of criminal history as a mitigating factor. In rejecting Tunkey's argument and affirming Washington's death sentences, the Florida Supreme Court reasoned as follows:

> It appears from the record, and was recognized by the trial judge, that appellant had carried on a course of burglaries and had stolen property for a significant period of time. In his confession in the Birk case appellant stated he had committed a series of burglaries throughout Dade County and sold the stolen merchandise to Katrina Birk and her husband. He reiterated in open court that he was selling "hot merchandise" to Katrina Birk.

Whether, as the Florida Supreme Court believed, Washington admitted "a course of burglaries" and "reiterated in open court" that he was selling stolen merchandise to the Birks seems debatable. Although an investigating detective, Detective Simmons, testified at Washington's sentencing hearing that he believed Washington committed several neighborhood burglaries, Washington himself did not admit as much during his plea hearing. Rather, at that time, he indicated to the court his belief that the Birks were a ripe target for a robbery because, in his words, "they dealt with hot merchandise." Washington added, "They had a little shop set up. It was more hot merchandise into this place than it was legal merchandise." Contrary to both Detective Simmons and Washington, local newspapers reported that the Birks "ran frequent yard sales" rather than a fencing operation.

Confusion about Washington's criminal history persisted when Shapiro appealed the trial court's order denying his motion for post-conviction relief to the Florida Supreme Court. The Florida Supreme Court rejected Shapiro's complaint that Tunkey failed to proffer evidence of Washington's "good character and his emotional and economic stress" prior to the killings because in part Washington had already relayed to the sentencing court that "this was his *first encounter with the law*." Yet confusingly, in the same opinion, the court praised Tunkey's success in "preventing the introduction of appellant's 'rap sheet.' "

Clarity about Washington's criminal history did not emerge after Shapiro filed a writ of habeas corpus in federal district court on April 6, the same day the Florida Supreme Court denied relief and the Court stayed Washington's execution. During the hearing on Shapiro's federal habeas writ, Shapiro asked Tunkey point blank whether Washington had a "rap sheet." The pair had the following exchange:

> Shapiro: Did you make any other effort to determine whether [Washington] had ever been within the custody of the Department of Corrections or any other custodial facility in Florida?

> Tunkey: As part of the discovery material which I had, I had been given a copy of the FBI rap sheet by the prosecuting attorneys. I think it might be part of the record. But in any event, my recollection is that *even that revealed a lack of any convictions and certainly incarcerations*. That is my recollection.

Further evidence about the absence of any rap sheet came from an independent psychological examination performed by Dr. Jamal A. Amin on April 20, 1981. The report, filed in support of Washington's federal habeas petition, noted the following: "Despite the instability and acts of violence against him [growing up], there are no reports of prior crimes of violence nor of any drug or alcohol use by Mr. Washington, normal outlets under such stress."

Despite substantial ambiguity about the existence of Washington's criminal history, *Strickland* nonetheless highlighted for the Supreme Court in his opening brief that "defense counsel successfully excluded the Defendant's 'rap sheet.' " But Justice Powell's clerk, Cammie R. Robinson, remained skeptical about references to Washington's supposed rap sheet. In a bench memorandum she authored for Justice Powell dated December 30, 1983, she wrote, in response to Washington's claim that Tunkey prejudicially failed to request a sentencing hearing, that "such a request likely would have done more harm than good." To support her conclusion, she wrote, "any presentence report would have included [defendant's] 'rap sheet' and would have put before the judge all of defendant's prior criminal activities." Yet in a troubling but telling footnote, Robinson admitted the following: "I have not found any reference describing what if any prior criminal acts were committed by defendant."

Despite its ambiguous existence, the so-called "rap sheet" played a major role in Justice O'Connor's majority opinion in *Strickland*. She highlighted its existence four separate times. First, at the outset of the opinion, she indicated that Tunkey "successfully moved to exclude respondent's '*rap sheet.*'" Second, in justifying Tunkey's failure to request a presentence report, Justice O'Connor noted that "any presentence investigation would have resulted in admission of respondent's '*rap sheet*' and thus would have undermined his assertion of no significant history of criminal activity." Third, in Part V, she observed: "Restricting testimony on respondent's character to what had come in at the plea colloquy ensured that contrary character and psychological evidence and respondent's criminal history, which counsel had successfully moved to exclude, would not come in." Finally, also in Part V, Justice O'Connor took aim at Washington's claim that Tunkey should have introduced character or psychological evidence on his behalf, noting that "admission of the evidence respondent now offers might even have been harmful to his case: his '*rap sheet*' would probably have been admitted into evidence[.]"

It is disheartening to think that one of the most famous (and disappointing) cases in Supreme Court history was built in large part on a lawyer's effort to exclude a document that never existed.

C. ILLUSTRATIVE *STRICKLAND* DAMAGE

McFARLAND V. STATE
928 S.W.2d 482
Court of Criminal Appeals of Texas
February 21, 1996, Delivered
No. 71557

Appellant was convicted of the offense of capital murder, specifically murder in the course of a robbery. * * * Punishment was assessed * * * at death. Appeal to this Court is automatic. * * * We will affirm. * * *

Ineffective Assistance of Counsel

* * * [A]ppellant argues that he was rendered ineffective assistance of counsel. He points to various individual examples of deficiencies in his counsel's performance to prove that the representation by trial counsel fell below an objective standard of reasonableness and was prejudicial. He then argues that the totality of the incidents prejudiced him to such a degree that he was denied a fair trial. After a careful review of the record, and considering the strict standards for determining that counsel was ineffective, we cannot say appellant was rendered ineffective assistance.

The standard for testing claims of ineffective assistance of counsel was announced in *Strickland v. Washington*, 466 U.S. 668 (1984). * * * [Ed. note: The court engaged in a lengthy summary of *Strickland*.]

* * * Appellant contends * * * that he received ineffective assistance of counsel because Benn slept through parts of the trial. * * * [But] appellant had two attorneys. Appellant was never without counsel. Additionally, Melamed stated at the motion for new trial hearing that he was prepared to do everything in the case. Although we do not condone Benn's behavior, viewing the totality of circumstances, appellant fails to make any showing that he was not effectively represented at trial by Melamed.[20] Therefore, because appellant has failed to show that he was prejudiced to the extent that the result of his trial would have been different,[21] [this] point of error * * * is overruled. * * *

Right to Counsel

* * * [A]ppellant contends that his "Constitutional right to counsel of his choice" was violated when the trial court appointed Melamed to assist retained-counsel Benn. Appellant argues that he refused to sign the order appointing counsel and testified at the motion for new trial hearing that he did not want to sign the order without conferring with Benn. No further objections to Melamed's appointment or representation appear in the record.

Appellant had his counsel-of-choice in Benn.[22] He does not claim that Melamed impaired his defense in any manner nor did he object, after presumably consulting with Benn, to Melamed's representation. The record shows that Benn was 72 years old at the time of trial and was prone to take afternoon naps. The record further indicates that Melamed conducted himself reasonably and provided effective counsel. Where a trial court deems, as in the instant case, that retained counsel may need assistance, it is acceptable to appoint additional counsel, and does not violate a defendant's right to counsel of choice. Both the state and federal constitutions guarantee a right to effective assistance of counsel. Appointment of additional counsel in this case insured appellant that right. [These] points of error * * * are overruled. * * *

JUDGE BAIRD dissenting.

---

[20] We might also view Melamed's decision to allow Benn to sleep as a strategic move on his part. At the new trial hearing, Melamed stated that he believed that the jury might have sympathy for appellant because of Benn's "naps."

[21] Appellant argues that we should ignore the prejudice-prong of the *Strickland* test in this instance. *Strickland* states that in some instances prejudice shall be presumed, such as when the actual or constructive denial of counsel *altogether*. If appellant did not have co-counsel we might be inclined to agree. However, this is not the situation here.

[22] We note that the trial court did not appoint Melamed to replace Benn. The trial court did not designate that appointed counsel would take over as first chair nor did the trial court specify to what extent Melamed should participate. These decisions were made by counsel.

* * * [A]ppellant contends he was denied effective assistance of counsel because his attorney, John Benn, slept during trial. The State contends Benn's sleeping did not affect the outcome of the trial because appellant was represented by two attorneys. The Majority agrees with the State, holding appellant "failed to show that he was prejudiced to the extent that the result of his trial would have been different . . . ." For the following reasons, I respectfully dissent.

I.

In *Strickland v. Washington*, the Supreme Court * * * recognized situations where prejudice should be presumed once trial counsel's deficient representation is shown. * * * Appellant contends the instant case is one where prejudice should be presumed.

II.

After his arrest, appellant retained the services of John Benn, an attorney for forty-two years. However, while in a holding cell, appellant was visited by Sandy Melamed who stated he was going to be appellant's attorney. When Melamed asked appellant to "sign some papers," appellant refused and asked to speak to Benn. The transcript includes a Request for Appointment of Counsel and Order of Court. Although the request purports to have been sworn to before a Harris County deputy district clerk, appellant did not execute this request. Instead, there appears a notation that appellant refused to sign the Request for Appointment of Counsel. In spite of this the trial judge found appellant "executed an affidavit stating he is without counsel and is too poor to employ counsel . . . ." The trial judge appointed Melamed to represent appellant.

Both attorneys understood Benn was to be lead counsel. After his appointment, Melamed contacted Benn to determine "if he wanted to have a discussion about who would do what." However, Benn wanted no such discussion. According to Benn, the attorneys' joint preparation for trial was "three or four hours."[3] As the trial began, Benn indicated after the State's examination of each witness whether he wished to cross-examine that witness. If not, Melamed handled the cross-examination. The attorneys did not discuss the witnesses' examinations.

Benn testified his preparation for appellant's trial consisted of "reading the State's case and briefing a few points of law on evidence." Benn could not remember the number of times he visited appellant, but believes it was fewer than five.[4] Benn prepared no motions, made no request for the issuance of subpoenas, and did not seek to talk to any witnesses, nor did he contact any of the co-defendants in appellant's extraneous offenses.

---

[3] Melamed testified that he and Benn did not discuss the case "very often."

[4] Appellant testified that Benn visited him once at the Harris County Jail and once in the courtroom holding cell.

Because of the circumstances in which he was appointed, and because of Benn's unwillingness to discuss the case with him, Melamed testified he felt he had to be prepared "to do everything." However, Melamed further testified he felt constrained to obtain an agreement from Benn and appellant on any decision. Melamed testified his preparation for appellant's trial consisted of a seven hour review of the State's files, visiting appellant once in the Harris County Jail, and conferring with appellant on the telephone and during trial. Melamed attempted to contact a list of witnesses provided by appellant but was not successful.[5] Melamed prepared and filed several motions in appellant's behalf and made a request to have a subpoena issued for several witnesses but did not speak to any of the State's witnesses or the co-defendants in appellant's extraneous offenses.

Finally, the uncontroverted evidence before us establishes that Benn slept during appellant's trial. Appellant and Melamed testified Benn slept. Indeed, Benn testified:

Q. Do you have an illness that has caused you to sleep?

A. I'm 72 years old. I customarily take a short nap in the afternoon.

Q. Did you inform your client that you had to take a nap during the afternoon?

A. No, I did not. I had capable co-counsel all the time with me.

Melamed testified that as Benn slept at trial, he thought perhaps the jury would feel sorry for appellant.

III.

I find the majority's suggestion that it was somehow reasonable trial strategy for appellant's lead counsel to take a "short nap" during trial utterly ridiculous. The possibility of jury sympathy can never be a reasonable alternative to effective representation. A sleeping counsel is unprepared to present evidence, to cross-examine witnesses, and to present any coordinated effort to evaluate evidence and present a defense. In my view, a sleeping attorney is no attorney at all. In such situations prejudice should be presumed.

Even if prejudice could not be presumed in this case, I believe appellant satisfied his burden under *Strickland*. There can be no doubt that Benn's representation fell below any objective standard of reasonableness. And I believe the representation appellant received in this case was sufficient to "undermine the confidence in the outcome."

---

[5] The trial judge appointed an investigator to assist Melamed, but the investigator was not asked to locate these witnesses.

* * * [A]s the *Gideon* Court recognized, the assistance of counsel is essential to the fair administration of justice. The trial judge had so little confidence in Benn's ability to represent appellant that Melamed was appointed to assist Benn. But Benn remained the lead attorney. And considering the lack of communication between Benn and Melamed, the lack of preparation for trial, and the uncontroverted evidence of Benn's sleeping, I have no confidence in the hand that guided appellant's representation. Stated differently, I have no confidence that appellant was represented by counsel with adequate skill or knowledge to prepare his defenses, if any, and to prevent his conviction upon incompetent or irrelevant evidence.

In my view, Melamed's presence did not excuse or rehabilitate Benn's incompetent representation. Melamed's preparation for this trial consisted of only a seven hour review of the State's files. He visited appellant once before trial and prepared some pretrial motions. Such preparation cannot be what the Sixth Amendment contemplates for a capital murder trial where the death penalty is possible. Neither attorney interviewed a witness and neither attorney reviewed the extraneous offenses that were to be later admitted. Benn decided which witnesses he would cross-examine and he informed Melamed of his decision only after the State's examination. Thus, Melamed's preparation for cross-examination of his witnesses could not have been effective because he did not know which witnesses he was to question. And considering the role to which he was relegated, Melamed was in no position to put forth a coordinated defense strategy. Even more disturbing, Benn could sleep during the direct examination and still elect to conduct cross-examination. It seems to me that Melamed's belief the jury might feel sympathy for appellant was more a desperate hope than reasonable trial strategy.[7]

IV.

I believe appellant has established that he received ineffective assistance of counsel and is entitled to a new trial. However, because the majority holds a defendant may receive effective representation from slumbering counsel, I respectfully dissent.

QUESTIONS, COMMENTS, CONCERNS?

1. Mental illness. The result in *McFarland* is hardly anomalous. *Strickland* has been relied on by other courts in a variety of striking scenarios. In *Johnson v. Norris*, 207 F.3d 515 (8th Cir. 2000), for example, the Eighth Circuit upheld a defendant's death sentence despite his counsel suffering from

---

[7]   I focus on Benn's representation of appellant because Benn was the lead counsel. But even assuming it is possible that second counsel's representation may somehow allay the harm caused by the lead counsel's sleeping, such is not the case here. Clearly the circumstances in the instant case, such as Benn's refusal to discuss the case and his continued control over the case, prevented Melamed from assuming control and insuring competent representation.

bipolar disorder. Counsel's conduct included "lying to the petitioner about his experience in capital cases, submitting a false application for malpractice insurance, being unprepared to present the petitioner's case, and appearing confused during trial." Although the court recognized that counsel's conduct included "unprofessional behavior," it nonetheless held that defendant could not demonstrate prejudice, i.e., that the result would have been different.

2. Alcohol use. In *People v. Garrison*, 765 P.2d 419 (Cal. 1989), defendant successfully proved that his lawyer suffered from alcoholism during his murder trial. Specifically, counsel "consumed large amounts of alcohol each day of the trial." Counsel also "drank in the morning, during court recesses, and throughout the evening." On the second day of jury selection, counsel was even "arrested for driving to the courthouse with a .27 percent blood-alcohol content." Despite seemingly shocking facts, the Supreme Court of California concluded, "Our review of the facts indicates that [counsel] did a fine job in this case."

3. Drug use. In *Young v. Zant*, 727 F.2d 1489 (11th Cir. 1984), another death penalty defendant claimed that he received ineffective assistance of counsel because his counsel took "huge grey pills" during the trial. Yet, fatal to defendant's *Strickland* claim, the record "fail[ed] to support any claim that [counsel's] handling of the trial was affected by his drug use." To the contrary, the court said that counsel "presented a vigorous and capable defense."

D. AN ALTERNATIVE TO *STRICKLAND*?

Unsurprisingly, very few lawyers are satisfied with the *Strickland* standard. This section closes with an alternative approach: *United States v. Cronic*, decided on the same day as *Strickland*. The section begins with a brief look at how *Cronic* might apply as a supplement to *Strickland* litigation before finishing with a heavily excerpted look at the *Cronic* opinion itself.

STARVED OF MONEY FOR TOO LONG, PUBLIC DEFENDER OFFICES ARE SUING—AND STARTING TO WIN[7]
Lorelei Laird, ABA Journal, January 2017

In November 2015, word spread through New Orleans' Lower 9th Ward that people were DJing and shooting a music video at the neighborhood's Bunny Friend Park. Soon, several hundred people were packed into the one-square-block park, held in by a chain-link fence.

But when two groups started to fire guns at each other through the crowd, the merriment turned to chaos. Witnesses said people ran from one side of the park to the other, toppling part of the fence as they scrambled to get away. No one died, but 17 people were injured, including a 10-year-old boy. The city was outraged. Within a week, the New Orleans police had

---

[7] Ed. note: what follows is an excerpt.

arrested their first suspect, 32-year-old Joseph "Moe" Allen, based on eyewitness identification.

Allen was charged with 17 counts of attempted first-degree murder—but his family insisted that he'd been in Houston at the time, shopping for baby clothes with his pregnant wife. They hired a private defense attorney, who was able to track down security camera footage to prove it. The day prosecutors dropped the charges, Allen's family and defense lawyer Kevin Boshea celebrated with a press conference on the courthouse steps.

Watching this in the news, Orleans Parish Chief District Defender Derwyn Bunton was happy to see the exoneration—and the good work from a fellow defense lawyer—but also concerned about what it might mean for his office.

After years of cuts, his budget was down from $9 million to about $6 million, and he had just eight investigators for 21,000 cases per year. If Allen had been represented by a public defender, Bunton was sure an investigator would have sought out the security footage—but those videos typically are erased and overwritten within a few weeks. With such high caseloads, the PD investigator likely might not have gotten there in time, and Allen could have wrongly gone to prison.

"So I said, 'We will not be complicit in that kind of injustice,' " Bunton says. "And we began to refuse cases at limits and at points where we could not ethically, constitutionally or within standards handle those cases."

That meant putting certain serious cases on a waiting list—trying to find alternative counsel or asking defendants to wait until a public defender was free. Just days later, the American Civil Liberties Union and the ACLU of Louisiana sued, arguing that this violates defendants' Sixth Amendment right to counsel and 14th Amendment right to due process and equal protection of the laws. Although the official defendants are Bunton and Louisiana State Public Defender James T. Dixon Jr., the complaint places the blame squarely on the Louisiana government.

That lawsuit might be the most high-profile indigent defense case of 2016. But it has competition. Indigent defense advocates are increasingly suing regarding inadequate funding for public defenders. Although past efforts have yielded decidedly mixed results, the latest round has seen some victories.

"There's always been an enormous amount of litigation about public defense," says Norman Lefstein, a professor at Indiana University's Robert H. McKinney School of Law in Indianapolis and author of *Securing Reasonable Caseloads: Ethics and Law in Public Defense,* published by the ABA in 2011.

At least five lawsuits have reached successful decisions or settlements over the past five years—with a powerful ally in the Department of Justice.

More are coming. In 2016, at least six states were sued—two in state supreme courts—regarding funding of indigent defense.

A *Cronic* Issue

More than 50 years ago, the U.S. Supreme Court ruled in *Gideon v. Wainwright* that the Sixth Amendment requires appointed counsel for people who can't afford an attorney on their own and face felony charges. In *Argersinger v. Hamlin* in 1972, the court extended that right to counsel to those charged with any crime punishable with imprisonment.

But the justices left it up to the states to determine how—and how much—to pay for indigent defense.

"The *Gideon* decision was a huge unfunded mandate," says Lefstein, a special adviser to the ABA's Standing Committee on Legal Aid and Indigent Defendants and a past chair of the Criminal Justice Section. "Supreme Court decisions don't come with a legislative appropriation."

Because not much political upside to helping criminal defendants exists, many jurisdictions end up with a perennial funding problem. In 1983 and 2003, the ABA's standing committee marked the 20th and 40th anniversaries of Gideon with hearings on indigent defense funding. In both cases, the committee heard about extreme funding shortfalls, excessive caseloads and insufficient pay. Four years later, in 2007, the Bureau of Justice Statistics found that only about a quarter of county-based public defender offices reported having enough attorneys to handle their caseloads.

This has real consequences for defendants. Numerous studies that stretch from the 1980s to recent years show that public defenders meet with clients less quickly, file fewer motions, plea-bargain more often, and get charges dismissed less often than private attorneys do.

That's reflected in the complaints for many of the recent indigent defense funding lawsuits. In *Tucker v. Idaho*, the ACLU of Idaho says plaintiff Tracy Tucker was jailed for three months pending trial, partly because his public defender was not present when it was time to argue for a reduction in bail.

From jail, he tried unsuccessfully to call his public defender 50 times. Two of the three meetings he did get with the attorney were in courtroom hallways with no privacy. Tucker's attorney hadn't conducted any meaningful investigation into the case 10 days before trial on a felony domestic violence charge, the complaint reads.

This matters because the majority of defendants—a 2014 study put it at 80 percent—use some kind of indigent defense. That means most Americans charged with a crime are at risk of bad outcomes partly caused by the quality of representation that they can afford.

But in the past few years, several developments have encouraged hope among indigent defense advocates. Chief among those developments, advocates say, is the increasing involvement of the DOJ. Since 2013, the department has filed at least five statements of interest and at least two amicus briefs in lawsuits that argued that local public defender funding is inadequate.

"That's a big difference, [when] the nation's top law enforcement agency says that the people suing the states are on the right side of history," says David Carroll, executive director of the Sixth Amendment Center in Boston.

In addition, Carroll says, people who challenge indigent defense funding have started to rely on a 1984 Supreme Court decision, *U.S. v. Cronic*, which dealt with ineffective assistance of counsel. When legal observers think of ineffective assistance of counsel, he says, they most often think of *Strickland v. Washington*, the 1984 case that established standards for when attorneys have been so ineffective that their client's Sixth Amendment right to counsel has been violated. But *Strickland* deals with single defendants who bring post-conviction motions over completed trials. That makes it a poor tool for challenges to entire indigent defense systems and a favorite tool of defendants in those challenges.

But these days, Carroll says, plaintiffs increasingly look to *Cronic*. Decided on the same day as *Strickland*, *Cronic* lays out tests for when circumstances are so bad that courts may presume there will be ineffective assistance of counsel in the future.

The court said you can presume ineffectiveness if there were no counsel at all at a critical stage of the trial, or if there were a complete "breakdown in the adversarial process that would justify a presumption" of an unreliable conviction. The court referred to the situation in *Powell v. Alabama*, in which an out-of-state lawyer had less than a week to prepare for a death penalty trial, as an example of such a time. Then the court gave counterexamples of situations in which limited time did not create a presumption of ineffective assistance. The language is so unclear that it means whatever the trial judge wants it to mean.

Although the case is more than 30 years old, Carroll says it might not have been on attorneys' radars because the criminal defendant in *Cronic* lost his ineffective assistance claim. But in 2010, the DOJ filed a statement of interest in *Hurrell-Harring v. State of New York*, a systemic challenge to indigent defense as it was then practiced in much of New York. In that statement, Carroll says, the department explained the tests created by *Cronic's* line of cases: Courts may consider "structural limitations" to representation, such as underfunding of an indigent defense office, and absence of the "traditional markers of representation," such as meaningful attorney-client contact.

"The focus on *Cronic* is opening up a lot of different possibilities because courts are deciding—rightfully in my mind—that the types of systemic deficiencies we see around the country are *Cronic* violations," Carroll says. "And it really is, I think, largely due to the Department of Justice clarifying what *Cronic* means."

Perhaps because of that, observers say a few lawsuits are starting to see success in the courts. One of the most important such cases is *Hurrell-Harring*, arguably a direct predecessor to many of the currently pending crop of lawsuits.

In *Hurrell-Harring*, the New York Civil Liberties Union sued on behalf of 20 indigent defendants, arguing that the state's failure to adequately fund or oversee their local indigent defense offices violated their Sixth Amendment rights by leaving them with extremely poor representation. For example, the attorney for lead plaintiff Kimberly Hurrell-Harring advised her to plead guilty to a felony that could have been a misdemeanor. The attorney later was disbarred for falsifying documents when he couldn't keep up with his workload.

The New York Court of Appeals, the state's highest court, ruled in 2010 that the plaintiffs could sue regarding systematic problems that amounted to constructive denial of counsel. It expressly cited *Cronic* and rejected the defendants' argument that plaintiffs should bring individual *Strickland* claims after conviction.

Hurrell-Harring settled on the eve of trial in 2014, with an agreement that the state would, among other things, fully fund and staff indigent defense in the five defendant counties. In summer 2016, the state of New York passed a law that extended that decision to every county, requiring full funding from the state by 2023. According to Robert Perry, legislative director for the NYCLU, current indigent defense costs in New York total $460 million to $480 million, suggesting that the state would pay that much if it assumed full responsibility for indigent defense spending. Gov. Andrew Cuomo has yet to sign this.

"We think it's of historic significance," Perry says. "This bill essentially takes the framework of the settlement in *Hurrell-Harring* and treats it something as a template for statewide reform of public defense services."

Similar lawsuits are now popping up around the country. In addition to the New Orleans litigation, indigent defense lawsuits are pending in the Idaho Supreme Court; Fresno, California; Luzerne County, Pennsylvania; and the state of Utah.

In fact, Utah has a state lawsuit filed by the ACLU of Utah and a federal lawsuit from private attorney Mike Studebaker. Typically, these cases cite the Sixth and 14th Amendments, state constitutions and sometimes statutory rights. "Eventually, my hope is that we will get one of these cases before the United States Supreme Court," Lefstein says. * * *

UNITED STATES V. CRONIC

466 U.S. 648
Supreme Court of the United States
January 10, 1984, Argued; May 14, 1984, Decided
No. 82-660

JUSTICE STEVENS delivered the opinion of the Court.

Respondent and two associates were indicted on mail fraud charges involving the transfer of over $9,400,000 in checks between banks in Tampa, Fla., and Norman, Oklahoma, during a 4-month period in 1975. Shortly before the scheduled trial date, respondent's retained counsel withdrew. The court appointed a young lawyer with a real estate practice to represent respondent, but allowed him only 25 days for pretrial preparation, even though it had taken the Government over four and one-half years to investigate the case and it had reviewed thousands of documents during that investigation. The two codefendants agreed to testify for the Government; respondent was convicted on 11 of the 13 counts in the indictment and received a 25-year sentence.

The Court of Appeals reversed the conviction because it concluded that respondent did not "have the Assistance of Counsel for his defence" that is guaranteed by the Sixth Amendment to the Constitution. This conclusion was not supported by a determination that respondent's trial counsel had made any specified errors, that his actual performance had prejudiced the defense, or that he failed to exercise "the skill, judgment, and diligence of a reasonably competent defense attorney"; instead the conclusion rested on the premise that no such showing is necessary "when circumstances hamper a given lawyer's preparation of a defendant's case." The question presented by the Government's petition for certiorari is whether the Court of Appeals has correctly interpreted the Sixth Amendment.

I

The indictment alleged a "check kiting" scheme. At the direction of respondent, his codefendant Cummings opened a bank account in the name of Skyproof Manufacturing, Inc. (Skyproof) at a bank in Tampa, Fla, and codefendant Merritt opened two accounts, one in his own name and one in the name of Skyproof, at banks in Norman, Okla.[4] Knowing that there were insufficient funds in either account, the defendants allegedly drew a series of checks and wire transfers on the Tampa account aggregating $ 4,841,073.95, all of which were deposited in Skyproof's Norman bank account during the period between June 23, 1975, and October 16, 1975;

---

[4] Skyproof, according to the indictment, was largely a facade and pretense to permit the withdrawal of large sums of money from these banks.

during approximately the same period they drew checks on Skyproof's Norman account for deposits in Tampa aggregating $ 4,600,881.39. The process of clearing the checks involved the use of the mails. By "kiting" insufficient funds checks between the banks in those two cities, defendants allegedly created false or inflated balances in the accounts. After outlining the overall scheme, Count I of the indictment alleged the mailing of two checks each for less than $ 1,000 early in May. Each of the additional 12 counts realleged the allegations in Count I except its reference to the two specific checks, and then added an allegation identifying other checks issued and mailed at later dates.

At trial the Government proved that Skyproof's checks were issued and deposited at the times and places, and in the amounts, described in the indictment. Having made plea bargains with defendants Cummings and Merritt, who had actually handled the issuance and delivery of the relevant written instruments, the Government proved through their testimony that respondent had conceived and directed the entire scheme, and that he had deliberately concealed his connection with Skyproof because of prior financial and tax problems.

After the District Court ruled that a prior conviction could be used to impeach his testimony, respondent decided not to testify. Counsel put on no defense. By cross-examination of Government witnesses, however, he established that Skyproof was not merely a sham, but actually was an operating company with a significant cash flow, though its revenues were not sufficient to justify as large a "float" as the record disclosed. Cross-examination also established the absence of written evidence that respondent had any control over Skyproof, or personally participated in the withdrawals or deposits.

The 4-day jury trial ended on July 17, 1980, and respondent was sentenced on August 28, 1980. His counsel perfected a timely appeal, which was docketed on September 11, 1980. Two months later respondent filed a motion to substitute a new attorney in the Court of Appeals, and also filed a motion in the District Court seeking to vacate his conviction on the ground that he had newly discovered evidence of perjury by officers of the Norman bank, and that the Government knew or should have known of that perjury. In that motion he also challenged the competence of his trial counsel.[6] The District Court refused to entertain the motion while the appeal was pending. The Court of Appeals denied the motion to substitute the attorney designated by respondent, but did appoint still another

---

[6] During trial, in response to questions from the bench, respondent expressed his satisfaction with counsel's performance. However, in his motion for new trial, respondent attacked counsel's performance and explained his prior praise of counsel through an affidavit of a psychologist who indicated that he had advised respondent to praise trial counsel in order to ameliorate the lawyer's apparent lack of self-confidence.

attorney to handle the appeal. Later it allowed respondent's motion to supplement the record with material critical of trial counsel's performance.

The Court of Appeals reversed the conviction because it inferred that respondent's constitutional right to the effective assistance of counsel had been violated. * * *

III

While the Court of Appeals purported to apply a standard of reasonable competence, it did not indicate that there had been an actual breakdown of the adversarial process during the trial of this case. Instead it concluded that the circumstances surrounding the representation of respondent mandated an inference that counsel was unable to discharge his duties.

In our evaluation of that conclusion, we begin by recognizing that the right to the effective assistance of counsel is recognized not for its own sake, but because of the effect it has on the ability of the accused to receive a fair trial. Absent some effect of challenged conduct on the reliability of the trial process, the Sixth Amendment guarantee is generally not implicated. Moreover, because we presume that the lawyer is competent to provide the guiding hand that the defendant needs, the burden rests on the accused to demonstrate a constitutional violation. There are, however, circumstances that are so likely to prejudice the accused that the cost of litigating their effect in a particular case is unjustified.

Most obvious, of course, is the complete denial of counsel. The presumption that counsel's assistance is essential requires us to conclude that a trial is unfair if the accused is denied counsel at a critical stage of his trial. Similarly, if counsel entirely fails to subject the prosecution's case to meaningful adversarial testing, then there has been a denial of Sixth Amendment rights that makes the adversary process itself presumptively unreliable. * * *

Circumstances of that magnitude may be present on some occasions when although counsel is available to assist the accused during trial, the likelihood that any lawyer, even a fully competent one, could provide effective assistance is so small that a presumption of prejudice is appropriate without inquiry into the actual conduct of the trial. *Powell v. Alabama*, 287 U.S. 45 (1932), was such a case. * * * *Powell* was * * * a case in which the surrounding circumstances made it so unlikely that any lawyer could provide effective assistance that ineffectiveness was properly presumed without inquiry into actual performance at trial.

But every refusal to postpone a criminal trial will not give rise to such a presumption. * * * Thus, only when surrounding circumstances justify a presumption of ineffectiveness can a Sixth Amendment claim be sufficient without inquiry into counsel's actual performance at trial.

The Court of Appeals did not find that respondent was denied the presence of counsel at a critical stage of the prosecution. Nor did it find, based on the actual conduct of the trial, that there was a breakdown in the adversarial process that would justify a presumption that respondent's conviction was insufficiently reliable to satisfy the Constitution. The dispositive question in this case therefore is whether the circumstances surrounding respondent's representation * * * justified such a presumption.

IV

* * * Respondent places special stress on the disparity between the duration of the Government's investigation and the period the District Court allowed to newly appointed counsel for trial preparation. The lawyer was appointed to represent respondent on June 12, 1980, and on June 19, filed a written motion for a continuance of the trial that was then scheduled to begin on June 30. Although counsel contended that he needed at least 30 days for preparation, the District Court reset the trial for July 14—thus allowing 25 additional days for preparation.

Neither the period of time that the Government spent investigating the case, nor the number of documents that its agents reviewed during that investigation, is necessarily relevant to the question whether a competent lawyer could prepare to defend the case in 25 days. The Government's task of finding and assembling admissible evidence that will carry its burden of proving guilt beyond a reasonable doubt is entirely different from the defendant's task in preparing to deny or rebut a criminal charge. Of course, in some cases the rebuttal may be equally burdensome and time consuming, but there is no necessary correlation between the two. In this case, the time devoted by the Government to the assembly, organization, and summarization of the thousands of written records evidencing the two streams of checks flowing between the banks in Florida and Oklahoma unquestionably simplified the work of defense counsel in identifying and understanding the basic character of the defendants' scheme. When a series of repetitious transactions fit into a single mold, the number of written exhibits that are needed to define the pattern may be unrelated to the time that is needed to understand it.

The significance of counsel's preparation time is further reduced by the nature of the charges against respondent. Most of the Government's case consisted merely of establishing the transactions between the two banks. A competent attorney would have no reason to question the authenticity, accuracy, or relevance of this evidence—there could be no dispute that these transactions actually occurred. As respondent appears to recognize, the only bona fide jury issue open to competent defense counsel on these facts was whether respondent acted with intent to defraud. When there is no reason to dispute the underlying historical facts, the period of 25 days to consider the question whether those facts justify an inference of criminal intent is not so short that it even arguably justifies a presumption that no lawyer could provide the respondent with the effective assistance of counsel required by the Constitution.

That conclusion is not undermined by the fact that respondent's lawyer was young, that his principal practice was in real estate, or that this was his first jury trial. Every experienced criminal defense attorney once tried his first criminal case. Moreover, a lawyer's experience with real estate transactions might be more useful in preparing to try a criminal case involving financial transactions than would prior experience in handling, for example, armed robbery prosecutions. The character of a particular lawyer's experience may shed light in an evaluation of his actual performance, but it does not justify a presumption of ineffectiveness in the absence of such an evaluation. * * *

The judgment is reversed, and the case is remanded for further proceedings consistent with this opinion.

It is so ordered.

JUSTICE MARSHALL concurs in the judgment.

QUESTIONS, COMMENTS, CONCERNS?

1. **A *Cronic* civil cause of action.** On September 28, 2016, the Pennsylvania Supreme Court, in *Kuren v. Luzerne Cnty.*, 146 A.3d 715 (Pa. 2016), held that "there is a cognizable cause of action whereby a class of indigent defendants may seek relief for a widespread, systematic and constructive denial of counsel when alleged deficiencies in funding and resources provided by the county deny indigent defendants their constitutional right to counsel." Stated more plainly, the court recognized that indigent defendants have a right to challenge systemic deficiencies at the beginning of a case *before* having to suffer from actual or constructive denial of counsel.

2. ***Cronic* as a source of class action litigation.** As note 1 suggests, *Cronic*'s impact has been most pervasive in the civil context. In *Hurrell-Harring v. New York*, 930 N.E.2d 217 (N.Y. 2010), the New York Civil Liberties Union (NYCLU), on November 8, 2007, filed a class action lawsuit on behalf of twenty named indigent criminal defendants. The suit alleged that New York failed to provide funding and resources to its public defense system, which in turn, threated indigent defendants' right to effective assistance of counsel. After years of litigation, the parties reached a settlement agreement in 2014— just before trial was set to commence. Among other provisions, the settlement required New York to allocate increased financial resources to its public defender system, particularly to assist with the use of investigators and experts alongside improved training for lawyers representing indigent defendants.

3. Other *Cronic* examples. Still other civil class actions relying on *Cronic* exist. Consider *Wilbur v. City of Mount Vernon*, filed on June 11, 2011, where three indigent defendants sued two cities in the State of Washington for failing to monitor and oversee the public defense system. The system in place shockingly called for the two cities to contract with two attorneys to handle all public defense cases, which called upon each attorney to handle an excess of 1,000 cases per year. A federal district court would ultimately side with the plaintiffs, holding that "the system is broken to such an extent that confidential attorney/client communications are rare, the individual defendant is not represented in any meaningful way, and actual innocence could conceivably go unnoticed and unchampioned." *Wilbur v. City of Mt. Vernon*, 989 F. Supp. 2d 1122 (W.D. Wash. 2013).

4. Developing a professional philosophy. Now that you have studied the impact that your decisions as a lawyer have on the outcome of a case, take a few moments to think about a philosophy for how you might handle a criminal case. In doing so, reflect on the values, guiding principles, and well-being practices that you believe are foundational to providing your client(s) with quality legal representation.

To begin, assume you are a criminal defense lawyer:

- How do you justify defending someone like John Wayne Gacy who (as you will learn in Chapter 4) was one of America's most prolific and notorious serial killers?

- Imagine that you obtain a not-guilty verdict for a defendant like Gacy but later learn that the defendant did, in fact, commit the crimes for which he was accused. How do you go forward knowing that you successfully advocated on the defendant's behalf?

By contrast, assume you are a prosecutor:

- How do you balance your duty to the State with your duty to exercise prosecutorial discretion?

- How do you prosecute conduct that you personally do not believe is criminal? Imagine, for example, that you believe abortion should be legal, but you work as a prosecutor in a state that has categorically outlawed abortion in the wake of *Dobbs v. Jackson Women's Health Organization*, 142 S. Ct. 2228 (2022). How do you grapple with prosecuting a woman who received an abortion?

- Assume that you obtain a guilty verdict against a defendant for possession and distribution of a large amount of cocaine. Assume further that the defendant is eighteen-years-old and has no criminal record. What sentence is appropriate? What if a mandatory minimum sentence applies that you believe is too high?

No matter how you resolve these (and related) difficult questions, please recognize the importance of adopting a personal philosophy to guide your answers. It should be written and brief—perhaps just a sentence or two—and should be flexible but firm. That is, it should be flexible enough to adapt to your growth as a person and professional, but firm enough in principle that there is consistency in its foundation no matter how you might change over the years. You should also keep it in a place where you'll see it. Want an example? Email me, and I'll share mine with you.

CHAPTER 2

FOURTH AMENDMENT REMEDIES

■ ■ ■

I. MEET ALEX LEVIN[1]

On February 20, 2015, the Honorable Theresa Buchanan, United States Magistrate Judge for the Eastern District of Virginia, issued a search warrant allowing the Federal Bureau of Investigation to launch the most extensive hacking operation in U.S. history: Operation "Pacifier." The investigation began after FBI Special Agents operating in the District of Maryland connected to the internet via an anonymous server and gained access to a pornographic website called "Playpen."

"The Onion Router"

Playpen operated on an anonymous online network known as "Tor," which stands for "the Onion Router." Tor was originally deployed as a project of the U.S. Naval Research Laboratory, with a primary purpose of protecting government communications. The Tor software, which is now available to the public at large, protects user privacy by routing communications around a distributed network of relay computers, thereby masking a user's IP address with a virtually untraceable one. Use of the Tor software in that manner—to protect an internet user's privacy from network surveillance and traffic analysis—is perfectly legal. But oftentimes users rely on Tor software to engage scrupulously in unlawful internet activity. Enter Playpen.

"Playpen"

Playpen, an anonymous message board, primarily existed to advertise and distribute child pornography. According to the FBI, Playpen had a total of 158,094 members and 95,148 posts spanning across 9,333 total topics. The website furnished a number of chat room forums on subjects such as: Jailbait-Boy or Jailbait-Girl (referring to an underage but post-pubescent minor); Pre-teen Videos; Toddlers; and Family Incest. After reviewing the content of these forums, the FBI found that the majority hosted discussions

---

[1] The following introduction is compiled from a series of materials from the record. *See, e.g.,* Application for Search Warrant at 21–23 (1:15 cr-10271) (Feb. 20, 2015); Criminal Complaint (1:15 cr-10271) (Aug. 8, 2015); Indictment (1:15 cr-10271) (Sep. 9, 2015); Defendants Motion to Suppress (1:15 cr-10271) (Feb. 2, 2016).

Remember that you have access to the filings relevant to this chapter in your online repository.

as well as images depicting child pornography and child erotica of prepubescent children.

Upon further investigation into the site, agents discovered that many of the forum posts contained references to a private messaging function offered by the site. Users utilized the message service to privately discuss topics related to child pornography, including one post which stated: "Yes, I can help if you are a teen boy and want to fuck your little sister. Write me a private message." Based on their observations, agents concluded that Playpen was "[d]edicated to the advertisement and distribution of child pornography, the discussion of matters pertinent to child sexual abuse, including methods and tactics offenders use to abuse children, as well as methods and tactics offenders use to avoid law enforcement detection while perpetrating online child sexual exploitation."

NIT Warrant

Although the FBI was aware that Playpen was operating as a channel for the distribution of child pornography, the Tor network prevented agents from connecting any specific individual with the criminal activity. As a result, FBI agents sought a warrant, in the United States District Court of the Eastern District of Virginia, to deploy a "Network Investigative Technique" (NIT) allowing them to hack into each individual computer connected to Playpen's host server. The FBI requested that it be allowed to maintain administrative control of Playpen from a government-controlled computer server in Virginia for thirty days, and to deploy the NIT technique described below.

During normal internet browsing, websites send content to visitors and the user's computer downloads that content and uses it to display the web page. In the case of Playpen, the site followed the common practice of maintaining a "cookie" on users' computers. A cookie exists as a simple text file containing bits of information such as a user's username and password. Cookies are commonly used to keep a user logged into a website between multiple visits without requiring the user re-enter his or her login credentials. Cookies are also used to store site preferences and other data.

The NIT Warrant sought to allow the FBI to augment the content of the files downloaded to the user's computer with a malware virus that would download directly to the computer—bypassing the Tor network's anonymous server. As a result, the NIT malware would reveal to the government: (1) the IP address of the computer used to access Playpen; (2) the operating system running on that computer; and (3) the physical location of the equipment that connects the computer to the internet. United States Magistrate Judge Theresa Buchanan reviewed and approved the warrant on February 20, 2015.

Enter Alex Levin

Ten days earlier, on February 10, 2015, a profile named "Manakaralupa" was registered on Playpen. The NIT and website statistics revealed that, between February 10, 2015, and March 4, 2015, the user Manakaralupa had been actively logged into the website for a total of two hours, nineteen minutes, and thirty-five seconds. On March 4, Manakaralupa accessed a forum titled, "Strawberry Shortcake Reuped on 03/04/2015," which contained in part a link to an image of a picture collage that depicted a pre-pubescent female (between the ages of five and seven) posed in a variety of positions focusing on the child's vagina and anus. One picture in the collage showed a penis placed against the child's mouth.

According to the data obtained pursuant to the NIT warrant, Manakaralupa accessed Playpen from the IP address 108.20.181.106. The FBI was able to use publicly available information to determine that this IP address was operated by the Internet Service Provider (ISP) Verizon. The NIT also allowed the FBI to learn that Manakaralupa's computer included the host and login names, "Alex-PC" and "Alex." In response to an administrative subpoena, Verizon provided the name of the individual affiliated with this IP address, Alex Levin, and the address where he received internet service, 64 Plymouth Drive, Apartment C, Norwood, Massachusetts. Based on this information, United States Magistrate Judge Marianne B. Bowler issued a search warrant for a residence located at that address on August 11, 2015. The warrant was executed shortly after at 6:00 a.m. the following day.

While executing the search warrant, law enforcement encountered Alex Levin, the sole occupant of the residence. After being read his *Miranda* warnings, Levin told officers that he owned two HP laptops, a cell phone, and two tablet computers. A subsequent forensic review of one of Levin's HP laptops revealed seven videos and one still image that appeared to depict pre-pubescent females and males engaging in sexual intercourse and masturbation. Levin was later indicted for illegally possessing child pornography in violation of 18 U.S.C. § 2252A(a)(5)(B).

The Suppression Issue

On February 19, 2016, Levin filed a motion to suppress all evidence obtained from the Government's search of his computer pursuant to the NIT Warrant, as well as all evidence, including digital images seized from his home on August 12, 2015. Levin argued that the NIT warrant exceeded the authority granted by Fed. R. Crim. P. 41 and 28 U.S.C. § 636(a), which authorizes a magistrate judge to issue a search warrant *only* for a location within his or her judicial district. The NIT warrant, Levin reasoned, authorized a search in Massachusetts, but was authorized by a judge sitting in Virginia. Levin further argued that, because the Virginia judge did not have jurisdictional authority to issue the NIT warrant, the search of Levin's computer was unlawful. Levin therefore concluded that suppression of the evidence obtained pursuant to the NIT warrant was required to remedy the government's illegal search.

In response to Levin's motion, the Government argued in the relevant part that, even if the NIT Warrant was deficient, the evidence seized pursuant to that warrant and the subsequent residential warrant remained admissible under the good-faith exception to the exclusionary rule. The Government reasoned that the officers who executed the NIT and residential warrants acted in good faith and reasonably relied on warrants issued by federal magistrate judges.

A suppression hearing occurred on March 25, 2016, before the Honorable William Young, United States District Judge for the District of Massachusetts. At first, it appeared that the district court was inclined to rule in favor of the Government. Before hearing the arguments of counsel, the court commented to defense counsel, "I must tell you, I don't see a basis for suppression. I'm groping for something less than suppression. If there's any suggestion, though I haven't been able to come up with one? I wrestle with the good faith exception, that's where my mind is. I very much want to hear your argument."

In response, counsel for Levin commented, "I've never encountered an instance where this court has shied away from being the first to enter an order that no other judge has seen fit to issue." The court ultimately agreed with Levin that the NIT Warrant violated the territorial restrictions on the issuing magistrate judge's authority. Accordingly, it granted Levin's motion and suppressed the media files seized from his home on August 12, 2015.

The district court's use of the exclusionary rule as the proper remedy for the government's Fourth Amendment violation in Levin's case was controversial to say the least. Of particular concern to the government, the ruling threatened the viability of the other Operation Playpen prosecutions, of which there were hundreds.

But Levin and the many other Operation Playpen defendants were not out of the woods yet. As we will learn, use of the exclusionary rule as a Fourth Amendment remedy is decreasing considerably. That fact was surely on the government's mind when it appealed the district court's order to the U.S. Court of Appeals for the First Circuit. The First Circuit had to answer the question we will consider throughout this chapter: is exclusion *always* the proper remedy for a Fourth Amendment violation?

II. INTRODUCTION TO THE FOURTH AMENDMENT'S TEXT (& ACCOMPANYING DEBATES)

Many students read the Fourth Amendment and consider the text to be fairly simple. But nothing could be further from the truth. Studying the Fourth Amendment can take up nearly sixty percent of an investigative criminal procedure course—sometimes more. It may seem ridiculous now but the continued evolution of Fourth Amendment jurisprudence threatens to consume an entire semester of coursework. Luckily, this is a fascinating area of the law, albeit one that is exceptionally confusing.

To get started, let's read the text of the amendment before breaking it down and studying the legal implications. The Fourth Amendment provides as follows:

The right of the people to be secure in their persons, houses, papers, and effects, against unreasonable searches and seizures, shall not be violated, and no Warrants shall issue, but upon probable cause, supported by Oath or affirmation, and particularly describing the place to be searched, and the persons or things to be seized.

Let's begin by dividing the amendment's text into two sections. The first section we'll refer to as the "reasonableness clause" ("The right of the people to be secure in their persons, houses, papers, and effects, against unreasonable searches and seizures, shall not be violated"). The second clause we'll refer to as the "warrant clause" ("no Warrants shall issue, but upon probable cause, supported by Oath or affirmation, and particularly describing the place to be searched, and the persons or things to be seized").

The *two* clauses raise *three* primary questions that largely inform this Casebook's organization: first, how should we define the Fourth Amendment's terms? Second, how are we to understand the relationship between the reasonableness and warrant clauses? Finally, what is the remedy for a Fourth Amendment violation? In the following sections, we will investigate each of these questions and the implications they have for our current study and future practice of law.

Question 1:   How should we define the Fourth Amendment's terms?

This first question essentially raises a definitional debate. Professor Joshua Dressler has observed that the Amendment does indicate what the reasonableness clause prohibits.[2] Indeed, the text provides for who is covered ("the people"); what is covered ("persons, houses, papers, and effects"); and what the Amendment protects ("to be secure . . . against

---

[2]   *See* JOSHUA DRESSLER & ALAN C. MICHAELS, UNDERSTANDING CRIMINAL PROCEDURE, VOL. 1: INVESTIGATION 52 (LexisNexis 2013).

unreasonable searches and seizures"). Notably, the reasonableness clause fails to define any of its core terms.

The second clause, the Warrant Clause, provides the parameters governing the issuance of warrants. Specifically, a valid warrant requires: (1) probable cause (to search or seize); (2) oath or affirmation on the part of the affiant; and (3) a particular description of the person to be seized or the place to be searched. Like the Reasonableness Clause, the Warrant Clause does not define its key terms. Collectively among the two clauses, we should be aware that there understandably exists substantial debate about how best to define Fourth Amendment terms like "search," "seizure," and "probable cause."

> *Question 2:   How are we to understand the relationship between the Reasonableness and Warrant Clauses? (Has the Fourth Amendment been violated?)*

Assuming the Fourth Amendment applies to particular government conduct, the next question is whether that conduct violates the Amendment. This question, however, raises an even larger question: is a warrant necessary? Assuming the presence of probable cause for law enforcement's actions, the Amendment provides no guidance on whether officers need a warrant to search a person/property or seize that person/property.[3] Whether a warrant is required depends on whether the Fourth Amendment categorically imposes a warrant requirement or, instead, the Amendment merely requires that warrantless searches be "reasonable." That, in turn, begs the question of whether there exists any connection between the Fourth Amendment's Reasonableness and Warrant Clauses.

The Supreme Court's early Fourth Amendment jurisprudence unequivocally suggested that searches conducted without a warrant were presumptively "unreasonable." The Court reaffirmed that position in its 1967 decision, *Katz v. United States*, observing that "searches conducted outside the judicial process, without prior approval by judge or magistrate, are per se unreasonable under the Fourth Amendment—subject only to a few specifically established and well-delineated exceptions." Although the Court in the following two decades approved of more exceptions to the search warrant "requirement," it continued to periodically highlight the Fourth Amendment's Warrant Clause as the predominant clause.

Amid the discussion of exceptions to the warrant "requirement," the Court also began exploring a new analytical path. In *Terry v. Ohio*, a case decided one year after *Katz*, the Court observed that "the central inquiry under the Fourth Amendment [is] the reasonableness in all the circumstances of the particular governmental invasion of a citizen's

---

[3]   This subsection reprints with permission a portion of Brian Gallini, *Step Out of the Car: License, Registration, and DNA Please*, 62 ARK. L. REV. 475 (2009). All footnotes are omitted.

personal security." That shift in Fourth Amendment analysis, suggesting that the Reasonableness Clause governs, took hold in a number of subsequent cases. Perhaps Justice Scalia summed up the tension best by noting that the Court's Fourth Amendment jurisprudence has "lurched back and forth between imposing a categorical warrant requirement and looking to reasonableness alone."

In the Court's 2009 decision, *Arizona v. Gant*, the majority quoted from *Katz* and again noted that "searches conducted outside the judicial process, without prior approval by judge or magistrate, are per se unreasonable under the Fourth Amendment—subject only to a few specifically established and well-delineated exceptions." But the idea that the Court's reliance on that *Katz* language signals a return to viewing the Warrant Clause as supreme seems unlikely. Indeed, the Court's steady trend—*Gant* notwithstanding—is toward viewing reasonableness as the "touchstone" of constitutionality. The view is arguably best reflected in the following excerpt from the Court's 1991 decision, *California v. Acevedo*:

> To the extent that the [warrant-requirement] rule protects privacy, its protection is minimal. Law enforcement officers may seize a container and hold it until they obtain a search warrant. "Since the police, by hypothesis, have probable cause to seize the property, *we can assume that a warrant will be routinely forthcoming in the overwhelming majority of cases.*"

Given the modern Court's apparent willingness to dispense with the requirement of a neutral arbiter, it seems the "reasonableness" test, at least for the moment, is the Court's preferred analytical approach to the presence—or absence—of a warrant.

Under the reasonableness test, the Supreme Court analyzes the law by balancing its intrusion on an individual's liberty interests as against the law's promotion of legitimate governmental interests. In practice, "the reasonableness standard usually requires, at a minimum, that the facts upon which an intrusion is based be capable of measurement against 'an objective standard,' whether this be probable cause or a less stringent test." Wholly apart from the presence of a warrant, then, the Court still requires law enforcement to possess at least some objective, individualized suspicion to justify the infringement of a person's Fourth Amendment rights.

Question 3: What is the remedy for a Fourth Amendment violation?

The third and final Fourth Amendment question is simple: what's the remedy for a Fourth Amendment violation? Although the question is simply stated, simple is not always easy. By comparison to the Fifth Amendment, the Fourth Amendment's text contains no express remedy for its violation. That, however, does not mean that no Fourth Amendment remedy exists. As we will see, the Court's view over time has swung from interpreting the Fourth Amendment as providing a robust exclusionary remedy to more modernly questioning whether, in fact, such a remedy is constitutionally required.

Casebook Organization

With this introduction in mind, the Casebook proceeds by breaking the Fourth Amendment materials into three distinct parts. The materials open by first considering the remedy question (question three), by then taking up when the Fourth Amendment applies (question one), and by closing with when the Fourth Amendment is violated (question two). You may wonder: why cover the remedy question *first*? The answer is that we can more easily move through questions one and two once we have a firm understanding of what's ultimately at stake—the remedy—in Fourth Amendment litigation. From a big picture standpoint, then, you might conceptualize our study of the Fourth Amendment as follows:

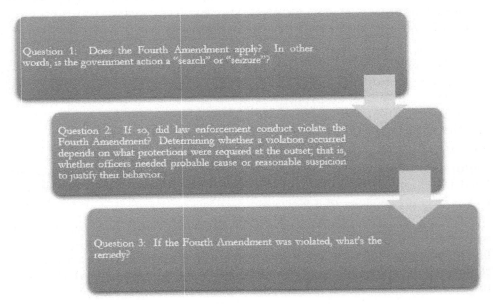

Question 1: Does the Fourth Amendment apply? In other words, is the government action a "search" or "seizure"?

Question 2: If so, did law enforcement conduct violate the Fourth Amendment? Determining whether a violation occurred depends on what protections were required at the outset; that is, whether officers needed probable cause or reasonable suspicion to justify their behavior.

Question 3: If the Fourth Amendment was violated, what's the remedy?

III.   THE RISE OF THE EXCLUSIONARY RULE

Fourth Amendment questions so often arise in the context of suppression hearings. In a criminal case, defense counsel often files a motion to suppress (i.e., exclude) evidence seized by law enforcement during the preceding investigation. Oftentimes, the result of a suppression motion determines a criminal case's outcome. Consider a routine drug possession case. Officer Smith hears over his police radio that a bright red 2017 Ford F-150 was stolen minutes ago in the vicinity near his beat. Three minutes later, Officer Smith pulls over a 2015 maroon Ford F-250 and sees cocaine in plain view during the ensuing traffic stop. Is the cocaine admissible against the defendant? That depends on the constitutionality of

Officer Smith's traffic stop. The defense, by filing a pretrial motion to suppress, will argue that the stop of the defendant's truck was unconstitutional. If successful, the cocaine will be suppressed, and the defendant will walk free. But if the motion fails, the defense has little left to argue because factual guilt is now established. The point, though, is that motions to suppress are often all or nothing propositions, and the remedy for a successful motion—exclusion—fuels the litigation.

The idea that the Fourth Amendment implicitly contains exclusion as a remedy emerged in 1914. In *Weeks v. United States*, 232 U.S. 383 (1914), the Supreme Court considered the admissibility of contraband against the defendant following two warrantless searches of his home: one by state police and a subsequent search by a Deputy United States Marshal. A unanimous Court held that, as to the federal search, the warrantless entry into the defendant's home was unconstitutional and, moreover, that the evidence seized from his home should be suppressed. The Court reasoned that failure "[t]o sanction such proceedings would be to affirm by judicial decision a manifest neglect if not an open defiance of the prohibitions of the Constitution, intended for the protection of the people against such unauthorized action." Notably, the Court's holding reached only the warrantless federal search; the Court's holding did not address the warrantless *state* search. As a result, contraband seized by state officials remained admissible against the defendant in a state prosecution.

Then, in 1949, the Supreme Court first considered whether *Weeks* should apply to the states in *Wolf v. Colorado*, 338 U.S. 25 (1949). Writing for a majority of the Court, Justice Frankfurter held that, although the Fourth Amendment contains *a* remedy, exclusion is not necessarily *the* remedy. Exclusion therefore remained a remedy confined solely to federal prosecutions. Of course, states could, at their discretion, adopt the exclusionary rule, and some did just that; indeed, at the time of *Wolf*, the Court observed that sixteen states had adopted the exclusionary rule after *Weeks*.

The Vinson Court (1946–1953) seemingly recognized the merits of exclusion just three years later in *Rochin v. California*, 342 U.S. 165 (1952). In *Rochin*, state officers entered the defendant's home where they personally watched the defendant swallow two capsules. Officers responded by jumping on the defendant in an effort to recover the capsules, but they were unsuccessful. The officers then handcuffed the defendant, took him to the hospital, and ordered a doctor to force the defendant to take a solution causing him to vomit. After the defendant vomited, the officers recovered two capsules containing morphine. The capsules were later introduced against the defendant, over objection, at his trial for possession of morphine.

Interestingly, Justice Frankfurter again wrote for a majority of the Court, but this time held that the morphine was inadmissible. He reasoned that the Fourteenth Amendment's Due Process Clause—not the Fourth Amendment—mandated exclusion because "[t]his is conduct that shocks the conscience. Illegally breaking into the privacy of the petitioner, the struggle to open his mouth and remove what was there, the forcible extraction of his stomach's contents—this course of proceeding by agents of the government to obtain evidence is bound to offend even hardened sensibilities." Until 1961, when the Court issued *Mapp v. Ohio*, our next case and one of the most famous criminal procedure cases in the Casebook, state defense lawyers had only *Rochin* to rely on as a remedy for Fourth Amendment violations committed by state actors. But still no specific remedy existed to address Fourth Amendment violations committed by state-level law enforcement.

Court personnel would change considerably in the interim time between 1952 and 1961. Critically, four members of the *Wolf* majority were no longer on the Court (Chief Justice Vinson, and Associate Justices Reed, Jackson, and Burton). One member of the 1961 Court who was not on the Court at the time of *Wolf* was Associate Justice Tom C. Clark. Appointed to the Court in 1949 just after *Wolf*, Justice Clark replaced Justice Frank Murphy who died unexpectedly that year (*Wolf* was published just a month before Justice Murphy passed). But *Mapp* itself still seemed an unlikely candidate to dramatically alter the Fourth Amendment jurisprudential landscape. Years after *Mapp*, Justice Potter Stewart would write:

> The jurisdictional statement in *Mapp v. Ohio* raised questions as to the constitutionality of the instructions to the jury, the sentence imposed, the statute upon which the conviction was based, and, finally, the conduct of the police. This last issue was limited solely to the constitutionality of the police behavior under the "shock the conscience" standard delineated in the 1952 stomach pump case, *Rochin v. California*.[4]

That is, no one asked the Court to overrule *Wolf*. In hindsight, though, perhaps Justice Clark's role in *Mapp* was preordained—or at least his views were. In reflective comments made years after the decision, Justice Clark in 1977 said:

> I couldn't understand why *Wolf v. Colorado* said that the Fourth Amendment applied to the states, but it just didn't seem to go all the way—in fact it was just an empty gesture, sort of like what Chief Justice Hughes used to say: No use to have a Constitution— it's pretty, got all sorts of nice fringes around it, but it doesn't mean anything, just a piece of paper—unless you really live by it

---

[4] Potter Stewart, *The Road to* Mapp v. Ohio *and Beyond: The Origins, Development and Future of the Exclusionary Rule in Search-and-Seizure Cases*, 83 COLUM. L. REV. 1365, 1367 (1983).

and enforce it. And so that's true with *Mapp* and the fourth amendment.[5]

How the *Mapp* Court went from considering the application of *Rochin* to overruling *Wolf* remains largely a mystery. Following oral argument on *Mapp*, the Justices agreed in conference that the police behavior in *Mapp* violated the First and Fourteenth Amendments.[6] One version of the story (of which there are several) goes like this:

> [N]o sooner had Clark left the conference room where he had agreed to write the opinion of the Court overturning Mapp's conviction on First Amendment grounds, than he turned to Justices Black and Brennan, who were standing in the elevator with him, and asked: "[W]ouldn't this be a good case to apply the exclusionary rule and do what *Wolf* didn't do?"[7]

A second meeting took place, this time with Chief Justice Warren and Justices Douglas and Brennen, who together sought to persuade Justice Black to join them in using *Mapp* as a vehicle to overrule *Wolf*.[8] Together, perhaps, those meetings form the basis of Justice Stewart's suspicions that a "rump caucus" took place post-conference.[9] When the draft came out roughly one month after the Court's conference, Justices Douglas and Brennan were predictably excited.

---

[5] Paul R. Baier, *Justice Clark, the Voice of the Past, and the Exclusionary Rule*, 64 TEX. L. REV. 415, 419 (1985).

[6] Stewart, *The Road to* Mapp v. Ohio *and* Beyond, 83 COLUM. L. REV. at 1367.

[7] Yale Kamisar, Mapp v. Ohio: *The First Shot Fired in the Warren Court's Criminal Procedure "Revolution," in* CRIMINAL PROCEDURE STORIES: AN IN-DEPTH LOOK AT LEADING CRIMINAL PROCEDURE CASES 50 (Carol Steiker ed. 2006) (citing BERNARD SHWARTZ, SUPER CHIEF 393 (1983)).

[8] *Id.* (citing ROGER K. NEWMAN, HUGO BLACK: A BIOGRAPHY 555–56 (1994)).

[9] Stewart, *The Road to* Mapp v. Ohio *and* Beyond, 83 COLUM. L. REV. at 1368.

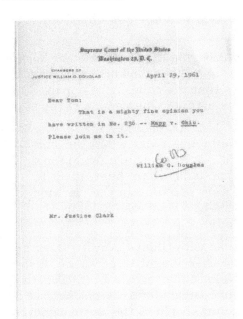

There's more to be said about *Mapp*, and Dollree Mapp in particular, but for now it suffices to say that *Mapp* is simultaneously a famous (infamous?), controversial, historically important, and fascinating decision.

MAPP V. OHIO

367 U.S. 643
Supreme Court of the United States
March 29, 1961, Argued; June 19, 1961, Decided
No. 236

MR. JUSTICE CLARK delivered the opinion of the Court.

Appellant stands convicted of knowingly having had in her possession and under her control certain lewd and lascivious books, pictures, and photographs in violation of § 2905.34 of Ohio's Revised Code.[1] As officially stated in the syllabus to its opinion, the Supreme Court of Ohio found that her conviction was valid though "based primarily upon the introduction in evidence of lewd and lascivious books and pictures unlawfully seized during an unlawful search of defendant's home . . . ."

---

[1]   The statute provides in pertinent part that

No person shall knowingly . . . have in his possession or under his control an obscene, lewd, or lascivious book [or] . . . picture . . . .

Whoever violates this section shall be fined not less than two hundred nor more than two thousand dollars or imprisoned not less than one nor more than seven years, or both.

On May 23, 1957, three Cleveland police officers arrived at appellant's residence in that city pursuant to information that "a person [was] hiding out in the home, who was wanted for questioning in connection with a recent bombing, and that there was a large amount of policy paraphernalia being hidden in the home." Miss Mapp and her daughter by a former marriage lived on the top floor of the two-family dwelling. Upon their arrival at that house, the officers knocked on the door and demanded entrance but appellant, after telephoning her attorney, refused to admit them without a search warrant. They advised their headquarters of the situation and undertook a surveillance of the house.

The officers again sought entrance some three hours later when four or more additional officers arrived on the scene. When Miss Mapp did not come to the door immediately, at least one of the several doors to the house was forcibly opened[2] and the policemen gained admittance. Meanwhile Miss Mapp's attorney arrived, but the officers, having secured their own entry, and continuing in their defiance of the law, would permit him neither to see Miss Mapp nor to enter the house. It appears that Miss Mapp was halfway down the stairs from the upper floor to the front door when the officers, in this highhanded manner, broke into the hall. She demanded to see the search warrant. A paper, claimed to be a warrant, was held up by one of the officers. She grabbed the "warrant" and placed it in her bosom. A struggle ensued in which the officers recovered the piece of paper and as a result of which they handcuffed appellant because she had been "belligerent" in resisting their official rescue of the "warrant" from her person. Running roughshod over appellant, a policeman "grabbed" her, "twisted [her] hand," and she "yelled [and] pleaded with him" because "it was hurting." Appellant, in handcuffs, was then forcibly taken upstairs to her bedroom where the officers searched a dresser, a chest of drawers, a closet and some suitcases. They also looked into a photo album and through personal papers belonging to the appellant. The search spread to the rest of the second floor including the child's bedroom, the living room, the kitchen and a dinette. The basement of the building and a trunk found therein were also searched. The obscene materials for possession of which she was ultimately convicted were discovered in the course of that widespread search.

At the trial no search warrant was produced by the prosecution, nor was the failure to produce one explained or accounted for. At best, "There is, in the record, considerable doubt as to whether there ever was any warrant for the search of defendant's home." The Ohio Supreme Court believed a "reasonable argument" could be made that the conviction should

---

[2]   A police officer testified that "we did pry the screen door to gain entrance"; the attorney on the scene testified that a policeman "tried . . . to kick in the door" and then "broke the glass in the door and somebody reached in and opened the door and let them in"; the appellant testified that "The back door was broken."

be reversed "because the 'methods' employed to obtain the [evidence] . . . were such as to 'offend "a sense of justice,"'" but the court found determinative the fact that the evidence had not been taken "from defendant's person by the use of brutal or offensive physical force against defendant."

The State says that even if the search were made without authority, or otherwise unreasonably, it is not prevented from using the unconstitutionally seized evidence at trial, citing *Wolf v. Colorado*, 338 U.S. 25 (1949)[.] * * * On this appeal, * * * it is urged once again that we review that holding.[3]

I.

* * * [I]n the year 1914, in [*Weeks v. United States*, 232 U.S. 383 (1914)], this Court "for the first time" held that "in a federal prosecution the Fourth Amendment barred the use of evidence secured through an illegal search and seizure." *Wolf v. Colorado*. This Court has ever since required of federal law officers a strict adherence to that command which this Court has held to be a clear, specific, and constitutionally required— even if judicially implied—deterrent safeguard without insistence upon which the Fourth Amendment would have been reduced to "a form of words." It meant, quite simply, that "conviction by means of unlawful seizures and enforced confessions . . . should find no sanction in the judgments of the courts . . . ," *Weeks v. United States*, and that such evidence "shall not be used at all." [*Silverthorne Lumber Co. v. United States*, 251 U.S. 385, 392 (1920).]

There are in the cases of this Court some passing references to the *Weeks* rule as being one of evidence. But the plain and unequivocal language of *Weeks*—and its later paraphrase in *Wolf*—to the effect that the *Weeks* rule is of constitutional origin, remains entirely undisturbed. * * *

II.

In 1949, 35 years after Weeks was announced, this Court, in *Wolf v. Colorado, supra*, again for the first time, discussed the effect of the Fourth Amendment upon the States through the operation of the Due Process Clause of the Fourteenth Amendment. * * * [A]fter declaring that the "security of one's privacy against arbitrary intrusion by the police" is "implicit in 'the concept of ordered liberty' and as such enforceable against the States through the Due Process Clause," and announcing that it "stoutly adhere[d]" to the *Weeks* decision, the Court decided that the *Weeks* exclusionary rule would not then be imposed upon the States as "an essential ingredient of the right." The Court's reasons for not considering

---

[3]   Other issues have been raised on this appeal but, in the view we have taken of the case, they need not be decided. Although appellant chose to urge what may have appeared to be the surer ground for favorable disposition and did not insist that *Wolf* be overruled, the amicus curiae, who was also permitted to participate in the oral argument, did urge the Court to overrule *Wolf*.

essential to the right to privacy, as a curb imposed upon the States by the Due Process Clause, that which decades before had been posited as part and parcel of the Fourth Amendment's limitation upon federal encroachment of individual privacy, were bottomed on factual considerations.

While they are not basically relevant to a decision that the exclusionary rule is an essential ingredient of the Fourth Amendment as the right it embodies is vouchsafed against the States by the Due Process Clause, we will consider the current validity of the factual grounds upon which *Wolf* was based.

* * * While in 1949, prior to the *Wolf* case, almost two-thirds of the States were opposed to the use of the exclusionary rule, now, despite the *Wolf* case, more than half of those since passing upon it, by their own legislative or judicial decision, have wholly or partly adopted or adhered to the *Weeks* rule. Significantly, among those now following the rule is California, which, according to its highest court, was "compelled to reach that conclusion because other remedies have completely failed to secure compliance with the constitutional provisions . . . ." In connection with this California case, we note that the second basis elaborated in *Wolf* in support of its failure to enforce the exclusionary doctrine against the States was that "other means of protection" have been afforded "the right to privacy." The experience of California that such other remedies have been worthless and futile is buttressed by the experience of other States. The obvious futility of relegating the Fourth Amendment to the protection of other remedies has, moreover, been recognized by this Court since *Wolf*. * * *

It, therefore, plainly appears that the factual considerations supporting the failure of the *Wolf* Court to include the *Weeks* exclusionary rule when it recognized the enforceability of the right to privacy against the States in 1949, while not basically relevant to the constitutional consideration, could not, in any analysis, now be deemed controlling.

III.

Some five years after *Wolf*, in answer to a plea made here Term after Term that we overturn its doctrine on applicability of the *Weeks* exclusionary rule, this Court indicated that such should not be done until the States had "adequate opportunity to adopt or reject the [*Weeks*] rule." * * * Today we once again examine *Wolf's* constitutional documentation of the right to privacy free from unreasonable state intrusion, and, after its dozen years on our books, are led by it to close the only courtroom door remaining open to evidence secured by official lawlessness in flagrant abuse of that basic right, reserved to all persons as a specific guarantee against that very same unlawful conduct. We hold that all evidence obtained by searches and seizures in violation of the Constitution is, by that same authority, inadmissible in a state court.

IV.

Since the Fourth Amendment's right of privacy has been declared enforceable against the States through the Due Process Clause of the Fourteenth, it is enforceable against them by the same sanction of exclusion as is used against the Federal Government. Were it otherwise, then just as without the *Weeks* rule the assurance against unreasonable federal searches and seizures would be "a form of words," valueless and undeserving of mention in a perpetual charter of inestimable human liberties, so too, without that rule the freedom from state invasions of privacy would be so ephemeral and so neatly severed from its conceptual nexus with the freedom from all brutish means of coercing evidence as not to merit this Court's high regard as a freedom "implicit in the concept of ordered liberty." * * * [I]n extending the substantive protections of due process to all constitutionally unreasonable searches—state or federal—it was logically and constitutionally necessary that the exclusion doctrine—an essential part of the right to privacy—be also insisted upon as an essential ingredient of the right newly recognized by the *Wolf* case. In short, the admission of the new constitutional right by *Wolf* could not consistently tolerate denial of its most important constitutional privilege, namely, the exclusion of the evidence which an accused had been forced to give by reason of the unlawful seizure. To hold otherwise is to grant the right but in reality to withhold its privilege and enjoyment. Only last year the Court itself recognized that the purpose of the exclusionary rule "is to deter—to compel respect for the constitutional guaranty in the only effectively available way—by removing the incentive to disregard it."

Indeed, we are aware of no restraint, similar to that rejected today, conditioning the enforcement of any other basic constitutional right. The right to privacy, no less important than any other right carefully and particularly reserved to the people, would stand in marked contrast to all other rights declared as "basic to a free society." *Wolf v. Colorado, supra,* at 27. This Court has not hesitated to enforce as strictly against the States as it does against the Federal Government the rights of free speech and of a free press, the rights to notice and to a fair, public trial, including, as it does, the right not to be convicted by use of a coerced confession, however logically relevant it be, and without regard to its reliability. * * * We find that, as to the Federal Government, the Fourth and Fifth Amendments and, as to the States, the freedom from unconscionable invasions of privacy and the freedom from convictions based upon coerced confessions do enjoy an "intimate relation" in their perpetuation of "principles of humanity and civil liberty [secured] ... only after years of struggle," *Bram v. United States,* 168 U.S. 532, 543–544 (1897). * * * The philosophy of each Amendment and of each freedom is complementary to, although not dependent upon, that of the other in its sphere of influence—the very least that together they assure in either sphere is that no man is to be convicted on unconstitutional evidence. *Cf. Rochin v. California,* 342 U.S. 165, 173 (1952).

V.

Moreover, our holding that the exclusionary rule is an essential part of both the Fourth and Fourteenth Amendments is not only the logical dictate of prior cases, but it also makes very good sense. There is no war between the Constitution and common sense. Presently, a federal prosecutor may make no use of evidence illegally seized, but a State's attorney across the street may, although he supposedly is operating under the enforceable prohibitions of the same Amendment. Thus the State, by admitting evidence unlawfully seized, serves to encourage disobedience to the Federal Constitution which it is bound to uphold. * * *

Federal-state cooperation in the solution of crime under constitutional standards will be promoted, if only by recognition of their now mutual obligation to respect the same fundamental criteria in their approaches. * * *

There are those who say, as did Justice (then Judge) Cardozo, that under our constitutional exclusionary doctrine "the criminal is to go free because the constable has blundered." In some cases this will undoubtedly be the result. But * * * "there is another consideration—the imperative of judicial integrity." The criminal goes free, if he must, but it is the law that sets him free. Nothing can destroy a government more quickly than its failure to observe its own laws, or worse, its disregard of the charter of its own existence. * * * Nor can it lightly be assumed that, as a practical matter, adoption of the exclusionary rule fetters law enforcement. * * *

The ignoble shortcut to conviction left open to the State tends to destroy the entire system of constitutional restraints on which the liberties of the people rest. Having once recognized that the right to privacy embodied in the Fourth Amendment is enforceable against the States, and that the right to be secure against rude invasions of privacy by state officers is, therefore, constitutional in origin, we can no longer permit that right to remain an empty promise. Because it is enforceable in the same manner and to like effect as other basic rights secured by the Due Process Clause, we can no longer permit it to be revocable at the whim of any police officer who, in the name of law enforcement itself, chooses to suspend its enjoyment. Our decision, founded on reason and truth, gives to the individual no more than that which the Constitution guarantees him, to the police officer no less than that to which honest law enforcement is entitled, and, to the courts, that judicial integrity so necessary in the true administration of justice.

The judgment of the Supreme Court of Ohio is reversed and the cause remanded for further proceedings not inconsistent with this opinion.

Reversed and remanded.

MR. JUSTICE BLACK, concurring.

[Omitted.]

MR. JUSTICE DOUGLAS, concurring.

[Omitted.]

Memorandum of MR. JUSTICE STEWART.

* * * I express no view as to the merits of the constitutional issue which the Court today decides. I would, however, reverse the judgment in this case, because I am persuaded that the provision of § 2905.34 of the Ohio Revised Code, upon which the petitioner's conviction was based, is, in the words of MR. JUSTICE HARLAN, not "consistent with the rights of free thought and expression assured against state action by the Fourteenth Amendment."

MR. JUSTICE HARLAN, whom MR. JUSTICE FRANKFURTER and MR. JUSTICE WHITTAKER join, dissenting.

In overruling the *Wolf* case the Court, in my opinion, has forgotten the sense of judicial restraint which, with due regard for stare decisis, is one element that should enter into deciding whether a past decision of this Court should be overruled. Apart from that I also believe that the *Wolf* rule represents sounder Constitutional doctrine than the new rule which now replaces it.

I.

From the Court's statement of the case one would gather that the central, if not controlling, issue on this appeal is whether illegally state-seized evidence is Constitutionally admissible in a state prosecution, an issue which would of course face us with the need for re-examining *Wolf*. However, such is not the situation. For, although that question was indeed raised here and below among appellant's subordinate points, the new and pivotal issue brought to the Court by this appeal is whether § 2905.34 of the Ohio Revised Code making criminal the mere knowing possession or control of obscene material, and under which appellant has been convicted, is consistent with the rights of free thought and expression assured against state action by the Fourteenth Amendment. That was the principal issue which was decided by the Ohio Supreme Court, which was tendered by appellant's Jurisdictional Statement, and which was briefed and argued in this Court.

In this posture of things, I think it fair to say that five members of this Court have simply "reached out" to overrule *Wolf*. With all respect for the views of the majority, and recognizing that stare decisis carries different weight in Constitutional adjudication than it does in nonconstitutional decision, I can perceive no justification for regarding this case as an appropriate occasion for re-examining *Wolf*.

* * * It seems to me that justice might well have been done in this case without overturning a decision on which the administration of criminal law in many of the States has long justifiably relied. * * *

II.

* * * I would not impose upon the States this federal exclusionary remedy. The reasons given by the majority for now suddenly turning its back on Wolf seem to me notably unconvincing.

First, it is said that "the factual grounds upon which *Wolf* was based" have since changed, in that more States now follow the *Weeks* exclusionary rule than was so at the time *Wolf* was decided. While that is true, a recent survey indicates that at present one-half of the States still adhere to the common-law non-exclusionary rule, and one, Maryland, retains the rule as to felonies. But in any case surely all this is beside the point, as the majority itself indeed seems to recognize. Our concern here, as it was in Wolf, is not with the desirability of that rule but only with the question whether the States are Constitutionally free to follow it or not as they may themselves determine, and the relevance of the disparity of views among the States on this point lies simply in the fact that the judgment involved is a debatable one. Moreover, the very fact on which the majority relies, instead of lending support to what is now being done, points away from the need of replacing voluntary state action with federal compulsion.

The preservation of a proper balance between state and federal responsibility in the administration of criminal justice demands patience on the part of those who might like to see things move faster among the States in this respect. Problems of criminal law enforcement vary widely from State to State. * * * For us the question remains, as it has always been, one of state power, not one of passing judgment on the wisdom of one state course or another. In my view this Court should continue to forbear from fettering the States with an adamant rule which may embarrass them in coping with their own peculiar problems in criminal law enforcement.

Further, we are told that imposition of the *Weeks* rule on the States makes "very good sense," in that it will promote recognition by state and federal officials of their "mutual obligation to respect the same fundamental criteria" in their approach to law enforcement, and will avoid "needless conflict between state and federal courts." * * *

An approach which regards the issue as one of achieving procedural symmetry or of serving administrative convenience surely disfigures the boundaries of this Court's functions in relation to the state and federal courts. * * * I do not believe that the Fourteenth Amendment empowers this Court to mould state remedies effectuating the right to freedom from "arbitrary intrusion by the police" to suit its own notions of how things should be done * * *. * * *

I regret that I find so unwise in principle and so inexpedient in policy a decision motivated by the high purpose of increasing respect for Constitutional rights. But in the last analysis I think this Court can increase respect for the Constitution only if it rigidly respects the limitations which the Constitution places upon it, and respects as well the principles inherent in its own processes. In the present case I think we exceed both, and that our voice becomes only a voice of power, not of reason.

* * *

A Postscript to *Mapp*

The public response to Justice Clark's opinion in *Mapp* was less than positive. The *New York Times* blamed *Mapp* for a forty percent decline in convictions and guilty pleas in New York County drug cases.[10] President Truman, who appointed Justice Clark, was rumored to have called the Clark appointment his "biggest mistake" as President.[11]

Dollree Mapp

---

[10] Leonard E. Ryan, *Narcotics Case Convictions Drop Since Ban on Illegal Searches*, N.Y. TIMES, Sept. 19. 1962, at 35.

[11] MERLE MILLER, PLAIN SPEAKING AN ORAL BIOGRAPHY OF HARRY S. TRUMAN 225 (1973).

For her part, Dollree Mapp was twenty-eight years old, living with her daughter, on the top floor of the two-family dwelling when officers came to bang on her door that day.[12] As the opinion relays, officers were acting on a tip that a suspect in a recent bombing was hiding out at the dwelling. It turns out that it was Don King who called in the tip because it was his house that had been bombed.[13] Yes, *that* Don King: the famous boxing promoter perhaps best known for promoting former undisputed heavyweight champion Mike Tyson. Back then, in 1957, King ran "one of Cleveland's largest racketeering operations" before making a name for himself in boxing.

Mapp's ties to boxing were not limited to King. While in Cleveland, she met and married Jimmy Bivins, an American heavyweight boxer.[14] The pair had a daughter together, Barbara, who died in 2002, but Mapp divorced Bivens because, she said, he was physically abusive.[15] Following her divorce, Mapp was briefly engaged to another heavyweight prizefighter, Archie Moore, who interestingly fought and defeated Bivens three times.[16] Mapp would later sue Moore for breach of promise when he terminated their engagement.[17]

Of course, as you know, officers never found bombing materials. Rather, the allegedly criminal materials Mapp possessed were sexually explicit drawings and books that, according to Mapp, belonged to a previous boarder.[18]

Mapp's run-ins with the law were, however, still not done. In 1968, she would move from Cleveland to Queens, New York, where she was convicted in 1971 for possession of narcotics.[19] She served time in prison in the New York State Correctional Institution, but Governor Hugh Carey commuted her sentence on December 31, 1980.[20] Public records are spotty, but Mapp

---

[12] Yale Kamisar, Mapp v. Ohio: *The First Shot Fired in the Warren Court's Criminal Procedure "Revolution," in* CRIMINAL PROCEDURE STORIES: AN IN-DEPTH LOOK AT LEADING CRIMINAL PROCEDURE CASES 47 (Carol Steiker ed. 2006).

[13] Elaine Woo, *Dollree Mapp dies at 91; arrest led to landmark search warrant ruling,* LOS ANGELES TIMES, Dec. 13, 2014, http://www.latimes.com/local/obituaries/la-me-dollree-mapp-2014 1214-story.html.

[14] Associated Press, *Woman who changed the face of civil rights and made it illegal for police to search without a warrant dies aged 91,* DAILYMAIL.COM (Dec. 14, 2014), http://www.dailymail. co.uk/news/article-2873820/Woman-changed-face-civil-rights-illegal-police-search-without-warrant-dies-aged-91.html.

[15] *Id.*

[16] William Yardley, *Dollree Mapp, Who Defied Police Search in Landmark Case, is Dead,* N.Y. TIMES, Dec. 9, 2014, at A33; *Jimmy Bivens,* BOXREC.COM, boxrec.com/boxer/9974 (last visited June 20, 2017).

[17] Yardley, *supra.*

[18] *Id.*

[19] *Id.*

[20] *Id.*

was born in 1923 or 1924, and passed away in December 2014 at age 90 or 91.

Now, the Court suppressed Mapp's illicit drawings (i.e., the evidence obtained from law enforcement's primary illegality (unlawfully intruding into Miss Mapp's home without a search warrant), but what *else* might the exclusionary rule suppress? After all, law enforcement has knowledge of Mapp's drawings, even if the state cannot rely on the drawings themselves. Would the exclusionary rule preclude an officer testifying about his knowledge of the illicit materials? The next case answers that question and helps us understand the potential reach of the exclusionary rule.

SILVERTHORNE LUMBER CO. v. UNITED STATES

251 U.S. 385
Supreme Court of the United States
Argued December 12, 1919; January 26, 1920
No. 358

MR. JUSTICE HOLMES delivered the opinion of the court.

This is a writ of error brought to reverse a judgment of the District Court fining the Silverthorne Lumber Company two hundred and fifty dollars for contempt of court and ordering Frederick W. Silverthorne to be imprisoned until he should purge himself of a similar contempt. The contempt in question was a refusal to obey subpoenas and an order of Court to produce books and documents of the company before the grand jury to be used in regard to alleged violation of the statutes of the United States by the said Silverthorne and his father. One ground of the refusal was that the order of the Court infringed the rights of the parties under the Fourth Amendment of the Constitution of the United States.

The facts are simple. An indictment upon a single specific charge having been brought against the two Silverthornes mentioned, they both were arrested at their homes early in the morning of February 25, 1919, and were detained in custody a number of hours. While they were thus detained representatives of the Department of Justice and the United States marshal without a shadow of authority went to the office of their company and made a clean sweep of all the books, papers and documents found there. All the employees were taken or directed to go to the office of the District Attorney of the United States to which also the books * * * were taken at once. An application was made as soon as might be to the District Court for a return of what thus had been taken unlawfully. It was opposed by the District Attorney so far as he had found evidence against the plaintiffs in error, and it was stated that the evidence so obtained was before the grand jury. Color had been given by the District Attorney to the approach of those concerned in the act by an invalid subpoena for certain documents relating to the charge in the indictment then on file. Thus the case is not that of knowledge acquired through the wrongful act of a stranger, but it must be assumed that the Government planned or at all events ratified the whole performance. Photographs and copies of material papers were made and a new indictment was framed based upon the knowledge thus obtained. The District Court ordered a return of the originals but impounded the photographs and copies. Subpoenas to produce the originals then were served and on the refusal of the plaintiffs in error to produce them the Court made an order that the subpoenas should be complied with, although it had found that all the papers had been seized in violation of the parties' constitutional rights. The refusal to obey this order is the contempt alleged. The Government now, while in form repudiating and condemning the illegal seizure, seeks to maintain its right to avail itself of the knowledge obtained by that means which otherwise it would not have had.

The proposition could not be presented more nakedly. It is that although of course its seizure was an outrage which the Government now regrets, it may study the papers before it returns them, copy them, and then may use the knowledge that it has gained to call upon the owners in a more regular form to produce them; that the protection of the Constitution covers the physical possession but not any advantages that the Government can gain over the object of its pursuit by doing the forbidden act. *Weeks v. United States*, 232 U.S. 383, to be sure, had established that laying the papers directly before the grand jury was unwarranted, but it is taken to mean only that two steps are required instead of one. In our opinion such is not the law. It reduces the Fourth Amendment to a form of words. 232 U.S. 393. The essence of a provision forbidding the acquisition of evidence in a certain way is that not merely evidence so acquired shall not be used before the Court but that it shall not be used at all. Of course this does not mean that the facts thus obtained become sacred and inaccessible. If knowledge of them is gained from an independent source they may be proved like any others, but the knowledge gained by the Government's own wrong cannot be used by it in the way proposed. The numerous decisions, like *Adams v. New York*, 192 U.S. 585, holding that a collateral inquiry into the mode in which evidence has been got will not be allowed when the question is raised for the first time at the trial, are no authority in the present proceeding, as is explained in *Weeks v. United States*, 232 U.S. 383, 394, 395. Whether some of those decisions have gone too far or have given wrong reasons it is unnecessary to inquire; the principle applicable to the present case seems to us plain. * * * In *Linn v. United States*, 251 Fed. Rep. 476, 480, it was thought that a different rule applied to a corporation, on the ground that it was not privileged from producing its books and papers. But the rights of a corporation against unlawful search and seizure are to be protected even if the same result might have been achieved in a lawful way.

Judgment reversed.

THE CHIEF JUSTICE and MR. JUSTICE PITNEY dissent.

QUESTIONS, COMMENTS, CONCERNS?

1. **Structuring the exclusionary rule.** As a starting point to considering an exclusionary rule problem, it's important to identify the primary illegality; that is, the fundamental police conduct that constitutes a violation of the defendant's Fourth Amendment rights. It's likewise important to identify the "fruit" of that initial illegality. For example, let's take a routine warrantless search of a defendant's home that uncovers drug paraphernalia. Assume for purposes of this exercise that the search was unconstitutional and that the defendant has filed a motion to suppress. Can you see that law enforcement's primary illegality was the unconstitutional search? That means the exclusionary rule would prevent the prosecution from later introducing the drugs into its case-in-chief should the case go to trial. Can you also identify that the fruit of the government's unlawful search is their *knowledge* that the defendant's home contained drugs? The reach of the exclusionary rule also keeps out that fruit. As a result, absent the application of an exception to the exclusionary rule, law enforcement cannot testify at trial about their knowledge that defendant's home contained contraband.

2. **Identify the primary illegality and fruit in Levin.** With note 1 in mind, can you identify what *Mapp* would exclude from the government's case-in-chief as an initial illegality in Alex Levin's case? What would also be suppressed as the fruit of that illegality pursuant to *Silverthorne Lumber*? Look carefully at Casefile Document 6, particularly Attachment B, which outlines information to be seized.

3. **Phrasing the remedy.** Compare how you would identify the evidence obtained from law enforcement's primary illegality and the fruit to how Levin described items to be suppressed in his Motion to Suppress Evidence. [See Casefile Document 7.] Is there a better way, in your opinion, to phrase the relief requested by Levin's motion?

4. **A concern.** Notice that the government, in its Application for an Order Authorizing Interception of Electronic Communications [see Casefile Document 4], seeks to assume administrative control over the Playpen website. Think about that for a moment—the plan was for the FBI to run a child pornography site for thirty days. As for supporting rationale, look specifically at page 30. The Application suggests that "[s]uch a tactic is necessary in order to locate and apprehend the TARGET SUBJECTS who are engaging in the continuing sexual abuse and exploitation of children, and to locate and rescue children from the imminent harm of ongoing abuse and exploitation." But surely there had to be another way that did not involve in the FBI becoming an active criminal participant in order to uncover the identities of the website's users. Can you think of another way? Surely, it's bad policy for the government to be actively involved in providing child pornography.

IV. THE DECLINE OF THE EXCLUSIONARY RULE

The *Mapp* precedent reigned until the exclusionary rule began to unravel in 1974.[21] Once again, a dramatic change in Court personnel was a major contributing factor. In hindsight, the exclusionary rule was a predictable target in the 70s given the wake left behind by the Warren Court. Although Earl Warren served as Chief Justice from 1953 until 1969, commentators often refer to the "Warren Court" to mean the time spanning from 1961, when Justice Arthur Goldberg replaced Justice Felix Frankfurter, to 1969, when Chief Justice Warren retired. During that period, the Court issued rulings on several controversial issues related to indigent criminal defense in trial and appellate representation, marital privacy, and state voting rights.

Those decisions, including *Mapp*, sparked national public outcry. "Impeach Earl Warren" signs littered the countryside, and the Court endured criticism from prominent critics like the American Bar Association, the National Association of Attorneys General, and Judge Learned Hand of the U.S. Court of Appeals for the Second Circuit. Even Congress joined the fray by refusing to authorize a pay increase for the Justices and by seeking to limit the Court's jurisdiction.

Chief Justice Warren initially announced his retirement on June 13, 1968, and to replace him, President Lyndon B. Johnson nominated sitting Associate Justice Abe Fortas. Yet, the Senate filibustered Justice Fortas's confirmation due to his questionable off-bench conduct—most notably, his acceptance of a $20,000 fee from a friend who was under investigation for violating federal securities laws. Warren therefore remained as Chief for one additional year because Johnson's term as President was set to expire before he could consider another nominee. When Chief Justice Burger finally filled Warren's position on June 23, 1969, he was anxious to distance his tenure from Warren's legacy.

Chief Justice Burger was not the lone new Justice. By the time of *United Staters v. Calandra*, our next case, the only Warren Court era Justices still on the court were Douglas and Brennan. In addition to Nixon appointing Warren Burger in 1969 to replace Earl Warren, Nixon would also appoint Harry Blackmun in 1970 to replace Abe Fortas; Lewis Powell in 1971 to replace Hugo Black; and William Rehnquist in 1971 to replace John Harlan. That block of four Justices often voted together, especially on criminal procedure issues. Collectively, once on the Supreme Court, Chief Justice Burger and his new colleagues began to reverse the course set by

---

[21] This introductory discussion is drawn with permission from portions of Brian Gallini, Schneckloth v. Bustamonte: *History's Unspoken Fourth Amendment Anomaly*, 79 TENN. L. REV. 233, 240–42, 281–82 (2012). All footnotes are omitted.

the Warren Court. This pattern most noticeably began during the 1972–73 term—the term immediately preceding *Calandra*.

But the Burger Court's work on the exclusionary rule was hardly finished. *Calandra* aside, the Burger Court would lay claim to issuing *United States v. Leon* in 1984—the second case we'll read in this block of materials. As you'll see, *Leon* relied on a "good faith" exception to the exclusionary rule. That good faith rationale not only pervaded into a number of subsequent Burger Court exclusionary rule cases, but also underlies the prevailing modern rationale of the rule. The modern Court has even gone as far as making clear that it fundamentally dislikes the exclusionary rule. In *Hudson v. Michigan*, 547 U.S. 586 (2006), for example, the Court declined to suppress cocaine and drugs found in Booker T. Hudson's home, despite the fact that officers violated the "knock and announce" rule while executing a search warrant for his home. In doing so, the *Hudson* Court made clear that the exclusionary rule rests on tenuous footing:

> Suppression of evidence, however, has always been our last resort, not our first impulse. The exclusionary rule generates "substantial social costs," which sometimes include setting the guilty free and the dangerous at large. We have therefore been "cautio[us] against expanding" it and "have repeatedly emphasized that the rule's 'costly toll' upon truth-seeking and law enforcement objectives presents a high obstacle for those urging [its] application." We have rejected "[i]ndiscriminate application" of the rule and have held it to be applicable only "where its remedial objectives are thought most efficaciously served"—that is, "where its deterrence benefits outweigh its 'substantial social costs.' "

Id. at 591. Our final opinion in this block, *Davis v. United States*, nicely summarizes the many good faith exclusionary rule cases while simultaneously making clear what the Roberts Court thinks of the exclusionary rule. Spoiler alert: the *Mapp* rationale is not prominent in *Davis*.

At this point, we should be asking what's left of the exclusionary rule. Quite apart from the applicability of any exception to the exclusionary rule, it now appears quite clear from *Davis* that the application of the exclusionary rule is hardly a given. To the contrary, courts should consider the applicability of the exclusionary rule on a case-by-case basis. In particular, post-*Davis* lower courts should first inquire whether the officer's behavior in question was objectively reasonable. If so, the exclusionary rule should not apply because there is nothing to deter.

Consider *Heien v. North Carolina*, 574 U.S. 54 (2014). In *Heien*, an officer stopped a vehicle that the defendant was traveling in because it had a broken taillight. During the stop, the defendant consented to a search of the vehicle, which uncovered drugs. Following the defendant's conviction for two counts of trafficking cocaine, the state court of appeals, held that the traffic stop was unconstitutional. The court reasoned that North Carolina law required only one working brake light. But the North Carolina Supreme Court reversed and held that reasonable suspicion necessary to make a stop may exist despite an officer's reasonable mistake of law. The Supreme Court agreed, noting that it was "objectively reasonable for an officer in [this officer's] position to think that Heien's faulty right brake light was a violation of North Carolina law. And because the mistake of law was reasonable, there was reasonable suspicion justifying the stop." *Id.* at 540.

Stated succinctly, the purpose of this introductory block is to demonstrate that you should first consider whether the exclusionary rule itself applies to your facts before considering whether an exception to that rule applies.

UNITED STATES V. CALANDRA

414 U.S. 338
Supreme Court of the United States
October 11, 1973, Argued; January 8, 1974, Decided
No. 72-734

MR. JUSTICE POWELL delivered the opinion of the Court.

This case presents the question whether a witness summoned to appear and testify before a grand jury may refuse to answer questions on the ground that they are based on evidence obtained from an unlawful search and seizure. The issue is of considerable importance to the administration of criminal justice.

I

On December 11, 1970, federal agents obtained a warrant authorizing a search of respondent John Calandra's place of business, the Royal Machine & Tool Co. in Cleveland, Ohio. The warrant was issued in connection with an extensive investigation of suspected illegal gambling operations. It specified that the object of the search was the discovery and seizure of bookmaking records and wagering paraphernalia. A master affidavit submitted in support of the application for the warrant contained information derived from statements by confidential informants to the Federal Bureau of Investigation (FBI), from physical surveillance conducted by FBI agents, and from court-authorized electronic surveillance.

The Royal Machine & Tool Co. occupies a two-story building. The first floor consists of about 13,000 square feet, and houses industrial machinery and inventory. The second floor contains a general office area of about 1,500 square feet and a small office occupied by Calandra, president of the company, and his secretary. On December 15, 1970, federal agents executed the warrant directed at Calandra's place of business and conducted a thorough, four-hour search of the premises. The record reveals that the agents spent more than three hours searching Calandra's office and files.

Although the agents found no gambling paraphernalia, one discovered, among certain promissory notes, a card indicating that Dr. Walter Loveland had been making periodic payments to Calandra. The agent stated in an affidavit that he was aware that the United States Attorney's office for the Northern District of Ohio was investigating possible violations of 18 U.S.C. §§ 892, 893, and 894, dealing with extortionate credit transactions, and that Dr. Loveland had been the victim of a "loansharking" enterprise then under investigation. The agent concluded that the card bearing Dr. Loveland's name was a loansharking record and therefore had it seized along with various other items, including books and records of the company, stock certificates, and address books.

On March 1, 1971, a special grand jury was convened in the Northern District of Ohio to investigate possible loansharking activities in violation of federal laws. The grand jury subpoenaed Calandra in order to ask him questions based on the evidence seized during the search of his place of business on December 15, 1970. Calandra appeared before the grand jury on August 17, 1971, but refused to testify, invoking his Fifth Amendment privilege against self-incrimination. The Government then requested the District Court to grant Calandra transactional immunity pursuant to 18 U.S.C. § 2514. Calandra requested and received a postponement of the hearing on the Government's application for the immunity order so that he could prepare a motion to suppress the evidence seized in the search.

Calandra later moved pursuant to Fed. Rule Crim. Proc. 41 (e) for suppression and return of the seized evidence on the grounds that the affidavit supporting the warrant was insufficient and that the search exceeded the scope of the warrant. On August 27, the District Court held a hearing at which Calandra stipulated that he would refuse to answer questions based on the seized materials. On October 1, the District Court entered its judgment ordering the evidence suppressed and returned to Calandra and further ordering that Calandra need not answer any of the grand jury's questions based on the suppressed evidence. * * *

The Court of Appeals for the Sixth Circuit affirmed, holding that the District Court had properly entertained the suppression motion and that the exclusionary rule may be invoked by a witness before the grand jury to bar questioning based on evidence obtained in an unlawful search and seizure. * * *

III

In the instant case, the Court of Appeals held that the exclusionary rule of the Fourth Amendment limits the grand jury's power to compel a witness to answer questions based on evidence obtained from a prior unlawful search and seizure. The exclusionary rule was adopted to effectuate the Fourth Amendment right of all citizens "to be secure in their persons, houses, papers, and effects, against unreasonable searches and seizures . . . ." Under this rule, evidence obtained in violation of the Fourth Amendment cannot be used in a criminal proceeding against the victim of the illegal search and seizure. *Weeks v. United States*, 232 U.S. 383 (1914); *Mapp v. Ohio*, 367 U.S. 643 (1961). This prohibition applies as well to the fruits of the illegally seized evidence. * * * *Silverthorne Lumber Co. v. United States*, 251 U.S. 385 (1920).

* * * [T]he rule's prime purpose is to deter future unlawful police conduct and thereby effectuate the guarantee of the Fourth Amendment against unreasonable searches and seizures[.] * * * In sum, the rule is a judicially created remedy designed to safeguard Fourth Amendment rights generally through its deterrent effect, rather than a personal constitutional right of the party aggrieved.

Despite its broad deterrent purpose, the exclusionary rule has never been interpreted to proscribe the use of illegally seized evidence in all proceedings or against all persons. As with any remedial device, the application of the rule has been restricted to those areas where its remedial objectives are thought most efficaciously served. The balancing process implicit in this approach is expressed in the contours of the standing requirement. Thus, standing to invoke the exclusionary rule has been confined to situations where the Government seeks to use such evidence to incriminate the victim of the unlawful search. This standing rule is premised on a recognition that the need for deterrence and hence the rationale for excluding the evidence are strongest where the Government's unlawful conduct would result in imposition of a criminal sanction on the victim of the search.

IV

In deciding whether to extend the exclusionary rule to grand jury proceedings, we must weigh the potential injury to the historic role and functions of the grand jury against the potential benefits of the rule as applied in this context. It is evident that this extension of the exclusionary rule would seriously impede the grand jury. Because the grand jury does not finally adjudicate guilt or innocence, it has traditionally been allowed to pursue its investigative and accusatorial functions unimpeded by the evidentiary and procedural restrictions applicable to a criminal trial. Permitting witnesses to invoke the exclusionary rule before a grand jury would precipitate adjudication of issues hitherto reserved for the trial on the merits and would delay and disrupt grand jury proceedings. Suppression hearings would halt the orderly progress of an investigation and might necessitate extended litigation of issues only tangentially related to the grand jury's primary objective. * * * In sum, we believe that allowing a grand jury witness to invoke the exclusionary rule would unduly interfere with the effective and expeditious discharge of the grand jury's duties.

Against this potential damage to the role and functions of the grand jury, we must weigh the benefits to be derived from this proposed extension of the exclusionary rule. Suppression of the use of illegally seized evidence against the search victim in a criminal trial is thought to be an important method of effectuating the Fourth Amendment. But it does not follow that the Fourth Amendment requires adoption of every proposal that might deter police misconduct. * * *

Any incremental deterrent effect which might be achieved by extending the rule to grand jury proceedings is uncertain at best. Whatever deterrence of police misconduct may result from the exclusion of illegally seized evidence from criminal trials, it is unrealistic to assume that application of the rule to grand jury proceedings would significantly further that goal. Such an extension would deter only police investigation consciously directed toward the discovery of evidence solely for use in a grand jury investigation. The incentive to disregard the requirement of the Fourth Amendment solely to obtain an indictment from a grand jury is substantially negated by the inadmissibility of the illegally seized evidence in a subsequent criminal prosecution of the search victim. For the most part, a prosecutor would be unlikely to request an indictment where a conviction could not be obtained. We therefore decline to embrace a view that would achieve a speculative and undoubtedly minimal advance in the deterrence of police misconduct at the expense of substantially impeding the role of the grand jury. * * *

V

Respondent also argues that each and every question based on evidence obtained from an illegal search and seizure constitutes a fresh and independent violation of the witness' constitutional rights. * * * [But] [q]uestions based on illegally obtained evidence are only a derivative use of the product of a past unlawful search and seizure. They work no new Fourth Amendment wrong. Whether such derivative use of illegally obtained evidence by a grand jury should be proscribed presents a question, not of rights, but of remedies.

In the usual context of a criminal trial, the defendant is entitled to the suppression of, not only the evidence obtained through an unlawful search and seizure, but also any derivative use of that evidence. The prohibition of the exclusionary rule must reach such derivative use if it is to fulfill its function of deterring police misconduct. In the context of a grand jury proceeding, we believe that the damage to that institution from the unprecedented extension of the exclusionary rule urged by respondent outweighs the benefit of any possible incremental deterrent effect. Our conclusion necessarily controls both the evidence seized during the course of an unlawful search and seizure and any question or evidence derived therefrom (the fruits of the unlawful search).[10] The same considerations of logic and policy apply to both the fruits of an unlawful search and seizure and derivative use of that evidence, and we do not distinguish between them. * * *

Reversed.

MR. JUSTICE BRENNAN, with whom MR. JUSTICE DOUGLAS and MR. JUSTICE MARSHALL join, dissenting.

The Court holds that the exclusionary rule in search-and-seizure cases does not apply to grand jury proceedings because the principal objective of the rule is "to deter future unlawful police conduct," ante and "it is unrealistic to assume that application of the rule to grand jury proceedings would significantly further that goal." This downgrading of the exclusionary rule to a determination whether its application in a particular type of proceeding furthers deterrence of future police misconduct reflects a startling misconception, unless it is a purposeful rejection, of the historical objective and purpose of the rule.

The commands of the Fourth Amendment are, of course, directed solely to public officials. Necessarily, therefore, only official violations of those commands could have created the evil that threatened to make the Amendment a dead letter. But curtailment of the evil, if a consideration at all, was at best only a hoped-for effect of the exclusionary rule, not its ultimate objective. Indeed, there is no evidence that the possible deterrent effect of the rule was given any attention by the judges chiefly responsible for its formulation. Their concern as guardians of the Bill of Rights was to fashion an enforcement tool to give content and meaning to the Fourth Amendment's guarantees. * * * In *Terry v. Ohio*, 392 U.S. 1, 12–13 (1968), Mr. Chief Justice Warren said for the Court:

The rule also serves another vital function—'the imperative of judicial integrity.' *Elkins v. United States*, 364 U.S. 206, 222 (1960). Courts which sit under our Constitution cannot and will

---

[10] It should be noted that, even absent the exclusionary rule, a grand jury witness may have other remedies to redress the injury to his privacy and to prevent a further invasion in the future. He may be entitled to maintain a cause of action for damages against the officers who conducted the unlawful search. *Bivens v. Six Unknown Fed. Narcotics Agents*, 403 U.S. 388 (1971). He may also seek return of the illegally seized property, and exclusion of the property and its fruits from being used as evidence against him in a criminal trial. *Go-Bart Importing Co. v. United States*, 282 U.S. 344 (1931). In these circumstances, we cannot say that such a witness is necessarily left remediless in the face of an unlawful search and seizure.

not be made party to lawless invasions of the constitutional rights of citizens by permitting unhindered governmental use of the fruits of such invasions.

* * * Thus, the Court seriously errs in describing the exclusionary rule as merely "a judicially created remedy designed to safeguard Fourth Amendment rights generally through its deterrent effect . . . ." Rather, the exclusionary rule is "part and parcel of the Fourth Amendment's limitation upon [governmental] encroachment of individual privacy," *Mapp v. Ohio*, [367 U.S. 643, 651 (1961)], and "an essential part of both the Fourth and Fourteenth Amendments," *id.*, at 657, that "gives to the individual no more than that which the Constitution guarantees him, to the police officer no less than that to which honest law enforcement is entitled, and, to the courts, that judicial integrity so necessary in the true administration of justice." *Id.*, at 660.

This *Mapp* summation crystallizes the series of decisions that developed the rule and with which today's holding is plainly at war. For the first time, the Court today discounts to the point of extinction the vital function of the rule to insure that the judiciary avoid even the slightest appearance of sanctioning illegal government conduct. This rejection of "the imperative of judicial integrity" openly invites "the conviction that all government is staffed by . . . hypocrites[, a conviction] easy to instill and difficult to erase." When judges appear to become "accomplices in the willful disobedience of a Constitution they are sworn to uphold," we imperil the very foundation of our people's trust in their Government on which our democracy rests. The exclusionary rule is needed to make the Fourth Amendment something real * * *.

Silverthorne plainly controls this case. Respondent, like plaintiffs in error in *Silverthorne*, seeks to avoid furnishing the grand jury with evidence that he would not have been called upon to supply but for the unlawful search and seizure. * * *

* * * [T]o allow Calandra to be subjected to questions derived from the illegal search of his office and seizure of his files is "to thwart the [Fourth and Fourteenth Amendments' protection] of . . . individual privacy . . . and to entangle the courts in the illegal acts of Government agents." [Gelbard v. United States, 408 U.S. 41, 51 (1972).] "And for a court, on petition of the executive department, to sentence a witness, who is [himself] the victim of the illegal [search and seizure], to jail for refusal to participate in the exploitation of that [conduct in violation of the explicit command of the Fourth Amendment] is to stand our whole system of criminal justice on its head." *In re Evans*, 452 F.2d 1239, 1252 (1971) (Wright, J., concurring). * * *

To be sure, the exclusionary rule does not "provide that illegally seized evidence is inadmissible against anyone for any purpose." *Alderman v.*

United States, 394 U.S. 165, 175 (1969). But clearly there is a crucial distinction between withholding its cover from individuals whose Fourth Amendment rights have not been violated—as has been done in the "standing" cases, *Alderman v. United States, supra*; *Jones v. United States*, 362 U.S. 257 (1960)—and withdrawing its cover from persons whose Fourth Amendment rights have in fact been abridged. * * *

Respondent does not seek vicariously to assert another's Fourth Amendment rights. He himself has been the victim of an illegal search and desires "to mend no one's privacy [but his] own." *Gelbard v. United States, supra*, at 63 (DOUGLAS, J., concurring). Respondent is told that he must look to damages to redress the concededly unconstitutional invasion of his privacy. In other words, officialdom may profit from its lawlessness if it is willing to pay a price.

In *Mapp*, the Court thought it had "close[d] the only courtroom door remaining open to evidence secured by official lawlessness" in violation of Fourth Amendment rights. The door is again ajar. As a consequence, I am left with the uneasy feeling that today's decision may signal that a majority of my colleagues have positioned themselves to reopen the door still further and abandon altogether the exclusionary rule in search-and-seizure cases; for surely they cannot believe that application of the exclusionary rule at trial furthers the goal of deterrence, but that its application in grand jury proceedings will not "significantly" do so. Unless we are to shut our eyes to the evidence that crosses our desks every day, we must concede that official lawlessness has not abated and that no empirical data distinguishes trials from grand jury proceedings. I thus fear that when next we confront a case of a conviction rested on illegally seized evidence, today's decision will be invoked to sustain the conclusion in that case also, that "it is unrealistic to assume" that application of the rule at trial would "significantly further" the goal of deterrence—though, if the police are presently undeterred, it is difficult to see how removal of the sanction of exclusion will induce more lawful official conduct. * * *

I dissent and would affirm the judgment of the Court of Appeals.

QUESTIONS, COMMENTS, CONCERNS?

1.   *Calandra's* **impact.** What does *Calandra* do to the exclusionary rule as a Fourth Amendment remedy? Is *Mapp* still good law?

UNITED STATES V. LEON

468 U.S. 897
Supreme Court of the United States
January 17, 1984, Argued; July 5, 1984, Decided
No. 82-1771

JUSTICE WHITE delivered the opinion of the Court.

This case presents the question whether the Fourth Amendment exclusionary rule should be modified so as not to bar the use in the prosecution's case in chief of evidence obtained by officers acting in reasonable reliance on a search warrant issued by a detached and neutral magistrate but ultimately found to be unsupported by probable cause. * * *

I

In August 1981, a confidential informant of unproven reliability informed an officer of the Burbank Police Department that two persons known to him as "Armando" and "Patsy" were selling large quantities of cocaine and methaqualone from their residence at 620 Price Drive in Burbank, Cal. The informant also indicated that he had witnessed a sale of methaqualone by "Patsy" at the residence approximately five months earlier and had observed at that time a shoebox containing a large amount of cash that belonged to "Patsy." He further declared that "Armando" and "Patsy" generally kept only small quantities of drugs at their residence and stored the remainder at another location in Burbank.

On the basis of this information, the Burbank police initiated an extensive investigation focusing first on the Price Drive residence and later on two other residences as well. Cars parked at the Price Drive residence were determined to belong to respondents Armando Sanchez, who had previously been arrested for possession of marihuana, and Patsy Stewart, who had no criminal record. During the course of the investigation, officers observed an automobile belonging to respondent Ricardo Del Castillo, who had previously been arrested for possession of 50 pounds of marihuana, arrive at the Price Drive residence. The driver of that car entered the house, exited shortly thereafter carrying a small paper sack, and drove away. A check of Del Castillo's probation records led the officers to respondent Alberto Leon, whose telephone number Del Castillo had listed as his employer's. Leon had been arrested in 1980 on drug charges, and a companion had informed the police at that time that Leon was heavily involved in the importation of drugs into this country. Before the current investigation began, the Burbank officers had learned that an informant had told a Glendale police officer that Leon stored a large quantity of methaqualone at his residence in Glendale. During the course of this investigation, the Burbank officers learned that Leon was living at 716 South Sunset Canyon in Burbank.

Subsequently, the officers observed several persons, at least one of whom had prior drug involvement, arriving at the Price Drive residence and leaving with small packages; observed a variety of other material activity at the two residences as well as at a condominium at 7902 Via Magdalena; and witnessed a variety of relevant activity involving respondents' automobiles. The officers also observed respondents Sanchez and Stewart board separate flights for Miami. The pair later returned to Los Angeles together, consented to a search of their luggage that revealed only a small amount of marihuana, and left the airport. Based on these and other observations summarized in the affidavit, Officer Cyril Rombach of the Burbank Police Department, an experienced and well-trained narcotics investigator, prepared an application for a warrant to search 620 Price Drive, 716 South Sunset Canyon, 7902 Via Magdalena, and automobiles registered to each of the respondents for an extensive list of items believed to be related to respondents' drug-trafficking activities. Officer Rombach's extensive application was reviewed by several Deputy District Attorneys.

A facially valid search warrant was issued in September 1981 by a State Superior Court Judge. The ensuing searches produced large quantities of drugs at the Via Magdalena and Sunset Canyon addresses and a small quantity at the Price Drive residence. Other evidence was discovered at each of the residences and in Stewart's and Del Castillo's automobiles. Respondents were indicted by a grand jury in the District Court for the Central District of California and charged with conspiracy to possess and distribute cocaine and a variety of substantive counts.

The respondents then filed motions to suppress the evidence seized pursuant to the warrant.[1] The District Court held an evidentiary hearing and, while recognizing that the case was a close one, granted the motions to suppress in part. It concluded that the affidavit was insufficient to establish probable cause, but did not suppress all of the evidence as to all of the respondents because none of the respondents had standing to challenge all of the searches. In response to a request from the Government, the court made clear that Officer Rombach had acted in good faith, but it rejected the Government's suggestion that the Fourth Amendment exclusionary rule should not apply where evidence is seized in reasonable, good-faith reliance on a search warrant.

---

[1] Respondent Leon moved to suppress the evidence found on his person at the time of his arrest and the evidence seized from his residence at 716 South Sunset Canyon. Respondent Stewart's motion covered the fruits of searches of her residence at 620 Price Drive and the condominium at 7902 Via Magdalena and statements she made during the search of her residence. Respondent Sanchez sought to suppress the evidence discovered during the search of his residence at 620 Price Drive and statements he made shortly thereafter. He also joined Stewart's motion to suppress evidence seized from the condominium. Respondent Del Castillo apparently sought to suppress all of the evidence seized in the searches. App. 78–80. The respondents also moved to suppress evidence seized in the searches of their automobiles.

The District Court denied the Government's motion for reconsideration and a divided panel of the Court of Appeals for the Ninth Circuit affirmed. * * *

II

* * * The Fourth Amendment contains no provision expressly precluding the use of evidence obtained in violation of its commands, and an examination of its origin and purposes makes clear that the use of fruits of a past unlawful search or seizure "[works] no new Fourth Amendment wrong." *United States v. Calandra*, 414 U.S. 338, 354 (1974). The wrong condemned by the Amendment is "fully accomplished" by the unlawful search or seizure itself, *ibid.*, and the exclusionary rule is neither intended nor able to "cure the invasion of the defendant's rights which he has already suffered." The rule thus operates as "a judicially created remedy designed to safeguard Fourth Amendment rights generally through its deterrent effect, rather than a personal constitutional right of the party aggrieved." *United States v. Calandra.*

Whether the exclusionary sanction is appropriately imposed in a particular case, our decisions make clear, is "an issue separate from the question whether the Fourth Amendment rights of the party seeking to invoke the rule were violated by police conduct." Only the former question is currently before us, and it must be resolved by weighing the costs and benefits of preventing the use in the prosecution's case in chief of inherently trustworthy tangible evidence obtained in reliance on a search warrant issued by a detached and neutral magistrate that ultimately is found to be defective.

The substantial social costs exacted by the exclusionary rule for the vindication of Fourth Amendment rights have long been a source of concern. * * * Particularly when law enforcement officers have acted in objective good faith or their transgressions have been minor, the magnitude of the benefit conferred on such guilty defendants offends basic concepts of the criminal justice system. Indiscriminate application of the exclusionary rule, therefore, may well "[generate] disrespect for the law and administration of justice." Accordingly, "[as] with any remedial device, the application of the rule has been restricted to those areas where its remedial objectives are thought most efficaciously served." *United States v. Calandra.* * * *

Close attention to those remedial objectives has characterized our recent decisions concerning the scope of the Fourth Amendment exclusionary rule. The Court has, to be sure, not seriously questioned, "in the absence of a more efficacious sanction, the continued application of the rule to suppress evidence from the [prosecution's] case where a Fourth Amendment violation has been substantial and deliberate. . . ." Nevertheless, the balancing approach that has evolved in various contexts—including criminal trials—"forcefully [suggests] that the exclusionary rule be more generally modified to permit the introduction of evidence obtained in the reasonable good-faith belief that a search or seizure was in accord with the Fourth Amendment." * * *

As yet, we have not recognized any form of good-faith exception to the Fourth Amendment exclusionary rule. But the balancing approach that has evolved during the years of experience with the rule provides strong support for the modification currently urged upon us. As we discuss below, our evaluation of the costs and benefits of suppressing reliable physical evidence seized by officers reasonably relying on a warrant issued by a detached and neutral magistrate leads to the conclusion that such evidence should be admissible in the prosecution's case in chief.

III

A

Because a search warrant "provides the detached scrutiny of a neutral magistrate, which is a more reliable safeguard against improper searches than the hurried judgment of a law enforcement officer 'engaged in the often competitive enterprise of ferreting out crime,'" we have expressed a strong preference for warrants and declared that "in a doubtful or marginal case a search under a warrant may be sustainable where without one it would fall." Reasonable minds frequently may differ on the question whether a particular affidavit establishes probable cause, and we have thus concluded that the preference for warrants is most appropriately effectuated by according "great deference" to a magistrate's determination.

Deference to the magistrate, however, is not boundless. It is clear, first, that the deference accorded to a magistrate's finding of probable cause does not preclude inquiry into the knowing or reckless falsity of the affidavit on which that determination was based. Second, the courts must also insist that the magistrate purport to "perform his 'neutral and detached' function and not serve merely as a rubber stamp for the police." A magistrate failing to "manifest that neutrality and detachment demanded of a judicial officer when presented with a warrant application" and who acts instead as "an adjunct law enforcement officer" cannot provide valid authorization for an otherwise unconstitutional search.

Third, reviewing courts will not defer to a warrant based on an affidavit that does not "provide the magistrate with a substantial basis for determining the existence of probable cause." "Sufficient information must be presented to the magistrate to allow that official to determine probable cause; his action cannot be a mere ratification of the bare conclusions of others." Even if the warrant application was supported by more than a "bare bones" affidavit, a reviewing court may properly conclude that, notwithstanding the deference that magistrates deserve, the warrant was invalid because the magistrate's probable-cause determination reflected an improper analysis of the totality of the circumstances, or because the form of the warrant was improper in some respect.

Only in the first of these three situations, however, has the Court set forth a rationale for suppressing evidence obtained pursuant to a search warrant; in the other areas, it has simply excluded such evidence without considering whether Fourth Amendment interests will be advanced. To the extent that proponents of exclusion rely on its behavioral effects on judges and magistrates in these areas, their reliance is misplaced. First, the exclusionary rule is designed to deter police misconduct rather than to punish the errors of judges and magistrates. Second, there exists no evidence suggesting that judges and magistrates are inclined to ignore or subvert the Fourth Amendment or that lawlessness among these actors requires application of the extreme sanction of exclusion.

Third, and most important, we discern no basis, and are offered none, for believing that exclusion of evidence seized pursuant to a warrant will have a significant deterrent effect on the issuing judge or magistrate. Many of the factors that indicate that the exclusionary rule cannot provide an effective "special" or "general" deterrent for individual offending law enforcement officers of the note apply as well to judges or magistrates. And, to the extent that the rule is thought to operate as a "systemic" deterrent on a wider audience, it clearly can have no such effect on individuals empowered to issue search warrants. Judges and magistrates are not adjuncts to the law enforcement team; as neutral judicial officers, they have no stake in the outcome of particular criminal prosecutions. The threat of exclusion thus cannot be expected significantly to deter them. Imposition of the exclusionary sanction is not necessary meaningfully to inform judicial officers of their errors, and we cannot conclude that admitting evidence obtained pursuant to a warrant while at the same time declaring that the warrant was somehow defective will in any way reduce judicial officers' professional incentives to comply with the Fourth Amendment, encourage them to repeat their mistakes, or lead to the granting of all colorable warrant requests.

B

If exclusion of evidence obtained pursuant to a subsequently invalidated warrant is to have any deterrent effect, therefore, it must alter the behavior of individual law enforcement officers or the policies of their departments. One could argue that applying the exclusionary rule in cases where the police failed to demonstrate probable cause in the warrant application deters future inadequate presentations or "magistrate shopping" and thus promotes the ends of the Fourth Amendment. Suppressing evidence obtained pursuant to a technically defective warrant supported by probable cause also might encourage officers to scrutinize more closely the form of the warrant and to point out suspected judicial errors. We find such arguments speculative and conclude that suppression of evidence obtained pursuant to a warrant should be ordered only on a case-by-case basis and only in those unusual cases in which exclusion will further the purposes of the exclusionary rule.

We have frequently questioned whether the exclusionary rule can have any deterrent effect when the offending officers acted in the objectively reasonable belief that their conduct did not violate the Fourth Amendment. * * * But even assuming that the rule effectively deters some police misconduct and provides incentives for the law enforcement profession as a whole to conduct itself in accord with the Fourth Amendment, it cannot be expected, and should not be applied, to deter objectively reasonable law enforcement activity. * * *[20] * * *

This is particularly true, we believe, when an officer acting with objective good faith has obtained a search warrant from a judge or magistrate and acted within its scope. In most such cases, there is no police illegality and thus nothing to deter. It is the magistrate's responsibility to determine whether the officer's allegations establish probable cause and, if so, to issue a warrant comporting in form with the requirements of the Fourth Amendment. In the ordinary case, an officer cannot be expected to question the magistrate's probable-cause determination or his judgment that the form of the warrant is technically sufficient. "[Once] the warrant issues, there is literally nothing more the policeman can do in seeking to comply with the law." Penalizing the officer for the magistrate's error, rather than his own, cannot logically contribute to the deterrence of Fourth Amendment violations.

C

We conclude that the marginal or nonexistent benefits produced by suppressing evidence obtained in objectively reasonable reliance on a subsequently invalidated search warrant cannot justify the substantial costs of exclusion. We do not suggest, however, that exclusion is always inappropriate in cases where an officer has obtained a warrant and abided by its terms. "[Searches] pursuant to a warrant will rarely require any deep inquiry into reasonableness," for "a warrant issued by a magistrate normally suffices to establish" that a law enforcement officer has "acted in good faith in conducting the search." Nevertheless, the officer's reliance on the magistrate's probable-cause determination and on the technical sufficiency of the warrant he issues must be objectively reasonable,[23] and

---

[20] We emphasize that the standard of reasonableness we adopt is an objective one. Many objections to a good-faith exception assume that the exception will turn on the subjective good faith of individual officers. "Grounding the modification in objective reasonableness, however, retains the value of the exclusionary rule as an incentive for the law enforcement profession as a whole to conduct themselves in accord with the Fourth Amendment." The objective standard we adopt, moreover, requires officers to have a reasonable knowledge of what the law prohibits. * * *

[23] * * * [W]e also eschew inquiries into the subjective beliefs of law enforcement officers who seize evidence pursuant to a subsequently invalidated warrant. Although we have suggested that,

it is clear that in some circumstances the officer will have no reasonable grounds for believing that the warrant was properly issued.

Suppression therefore remains an appropriate remedy if the magistrate or judge in issuing a warrant was misled by information in an affidavit that the affiant knew was false or would have known was false except for his reckless disregard of the truth. *Franks v. Delaware*, 438 U.S. 154 (1978). The exception we recognize today will also not apply in cases where the issuing magistrate wholly abandoned his judicial role in the manner condemned in *Lo-Ji Sales, Inc. v. New York*, 442 U.S. 319 (1979); in such circumstances, no reasonably well trained officer should rely on the warrant. Nor would an officer manifest objective good faith in relying on a warrant based on an affidavit "so lacking in indicia of probable cause as to render official belief in its existence entirely unreasonable." Finally, depending on the circumstances of the particular case, a warrant may be so facially deficient—i.e., in failing to particularize the place to be searched or the things to be seized—that the executing officers cannot reasonably presume it to be valid. * * *

IV

When the principles we have enunciated today are applied to the facts of this case, it is apparent that the judgment of the Court of Appeals cannot stand. * * *

In the absence of an allegation that the magistrate abandoned his detached and neutral role, suppression is appropriate only if the officers were dishonest or reckless in preparing their affidavit or could not have harbored an objectively reasonable belief in the existence of probable cause. Only respondent Leon has contended that no reasonably well trained police officer could have believed that there existed probable cause to search his house; significantly, the other respondents advance no comparable argument. Officer Rombach's application for a warrant clearly was supported by much more than a "bare bones" affidavit. The affidavit related the results of an extensive investigation and, as the opinions of the divided panel of the Court of Appeals make clear, provided evidence sufficient to create disagreement among thoughtful and competent judges as to the existence of probable cause. Under these circumstances, the officers' reliance on the magistrate's determination of probable cause was

---

"[on] occasion, the motive with which the officer conducts an illegal search may have some relevance in determining the propriety of applying the exclusionary rule," we believe that "sending state and federal courts on an expedition into the minds of police officers would produce a grave and fruitless misallocation of judicial resources." Accordingly, our good-faith inquiry is confined to the objectively ascertainable question whether a reasonably well trained officer would have known that the search was illegal despite the magistrate's authorization. In making this determination, all of the circumstances—including whether the warrant application had previously been rejected by a different magistrate—may be considered.

objectively reasonable, and application of the extreme sanction of exclusion is inappropriate.

Accordingly, the judgment of the Court of Appeals is

Reversed.

JUSTICE BLACKMUN, concurring.

[Omitted.]

JUSTICE BRENNAN, with whom JUSTICE MARSHALL joins, dissenting.*

Ten years ago in *United States v. Calandra*, 414 U.S. 338 (1974), I expressed the fear that the Court's decision "may signal that a majority of my colleagues have positioned themselves to reopen the door [to evidence secured by official lawlessness] still further and abandon altogether the exclusionary rule in search-and-seizure cases." Since then, in case after case, I have witnessed the Court's gradual but determined strangulation of the rule. It now appears that the Court's victory over the Fourth Amendment is complete. * * *

I   * * *

A

At bottom, the Court's decision turns on the proposition that the exclusionary rule is merely a " 'judicially created remedy designed to safeguard Fourth Amendment rights generally through its deterrent effect, rather than a personal constitutional right.' " The germ of that idea is found in *Wolf v. Colorado*, 338 U.S. 25 (1949), and although I had thought that such a narrow conception of the rule had been forever put to rest by our decision in *Mapp v. Ohio*, 367 U.S. 643 (1961), it has been revived by the present Court and reaches full flower with today's decision. The essence of this view, as expressed initially in the Calandra opinion and as reiterated today, is that the sole "purpose of the Fourth Amendment is to prevent unreasonable governmental intrusions into the privacy of one's person, house, papers, or effects. The wrong condemned is the unjustified governmental invasion of these areas of an individual's life. That wrong . . . is *fully accomplished* by the original search without probable cause." This reading of the Amendment implies that its proscriptions are directed solely at those government agents who may actually invade an individual's constitutionally protected privacy. The courts are not subject to any direct constitutional duty to exclude illegally obtained evidence, because the question of the admissibility of such evidence is not addressed by the Amendment. This view of the scope of the Amendment relegates the judiciary to the periphery. Because the only constitutionally cognizable injury has already been "fully accomplished" by the police by the time a case comes before the courts, the Constitution is not itself violated if the

---

*   [This opinion applies also to No. 82-963, *Massachusetts v. Sheppard* * * *.]

judge decides to admit the tainted evidence. Indeed, the most the judge can do is wring his hands and hope that perhaps by excluding such evidence he can deter future transgressions by the police.

Such a reading appears plausible, because, as critics of the exclusionary rule never tire of repeating, the Fourth Amendment makes no express provision for the exclusion of evidence secured in violation of its commands. A short answer to this claim, of course, is that many of the Constitution's most vital imperatives are stated in general terms and the task of giving meaning to these precepts is therefore left to subsequent judicial decisionmaking in the context of concrete cases. * * *

A more direct answer may be supplied by recognizing that the Amendment, like other provisions of the Bill of Rights, restrains the power of the government as a whole; it does not specify only a particular agency and exempt all others. The judiciary is responsible, no less than the executive, for ensuring that constitutional rights are respected.

When that fact is kept in mind, the role of the courts and their possible involvement in the concerns of the Fourth Amendment comes into sharper focus. Because seizures are executed principally to secure evidence, and because such evidence generally has utility in our legal system only in the context of a trial supervised by a judge, it is apparent that the admission of illegally obtained evidence implicates the same constitutional concerns as the initial seizure of that evidence. Indeed, by admitting unlawfully seized evidence, the judiciary becomes a part of what is in fact a single governmental action prohibited by the terms of the Amendment. Once that connection between the evidence-gathering role of the police and the evidence-admitting function of the courts is acknowledged, the plausibility of the Court's interpretation becomes more suspect. Certainly nothing in the language or history of the Fourth Amendment suggests that a recognition of this evidentiary link between the police and the courts was meant to be foreclosed. It is difficult to give any meaning at all to the limitations imposed by the Amendment if they are read to proscribe only certain conduct by the police but to allow other agents of the same government to take advantage of evidence secured by the police in violation of its requirements. The Amendment therefore must be read to condemn not only the initial unconstitutional invasion of privacy—which is done, after all, for the purpose of securing evidence—but also the subsequent use of any evidence so obtained.

The Court evades this principle by drawing an artificial line between the constitutional rights and responsibilities that are engaged by actions of the police and those that are engaged when a defendant appears before the courts. According to the Court, the substantive protections of the Fourth Amendment are wholly exhausted at the moment when police unlawfully invade an individual's privacy and thus no substantive force remains to those protections at the time of trial when the government seeks to use evidence obtained by the police.

I submit that such a crabbed reading of the Fourth Amendment casts aside the teaching of those Justices who first formulated the exclusionary rule, and rests ultimately on an impoverished understanding of judicial responsibility in our constitutional scheme. For my part, "[the] right of the people to be secure in their persons, houses, papers, and effects, against unreasonable searches and seizures" comprises a personal right to exclude all evidence secured by means of unreasonable searches and seizures. The right to be free from the initial invasion of privacy and the right of exclusion are coordinate components of the central embracing right to be free from unreasonable searches and seizures.

Such a conception of the rights secured by the Fourth Amendment was unquestionably the original basis of what has come to be called the exclusionary rule when it was first formulated in *Weeks v. United States*, 232 U.S. 383 (1914). * * *

What [the *Weeks* Court understood], ignored by the present Court, [is] that seizures are generally executed for the purpose of bringing "proof to the aid of the Government," that the utility of such evidence in a criminal prosecution arises ultimately in the context of the courts, and that the courts therefore cannot be absolved of responsibility for the means by which evidence is obtained. As the Court in Weeks clearly recognized, the obligations cast upon government by the Fourth Amendment are not confined merely to the police. In the words of Justice Holmes: "If the search and seizure are unlawful as invading personal rights secured by the Constitution those rights would be infringed yet further if the evidence were allowed to be used." * * *

That conception of the rule, in my view, is more faithful to the meaning and purpose of the Fourth Amendment and to the judiciary's role as the guardian of the people's constitutional liberties. In contrast to the present Court's restrictive reading, the Court in *Weeks* recognized that, if the Amendment is to have any meaning, police and the courts cannot be regarded as constitutional strangers to each other; because the evidence-gathering role of the police is directly linked to the evidence-admitting function of the courts, an individual's Fourth Amendment rights may be undermined as completely by one as by the other.

B

From the foregoing, it is clear why the question whether the exclusion of evidence would deter future police misconduct was never considered a relevant concern in the early cases * * *. In those formative decisions, the Court plainly understood that the exclusion of illegally obtained evidence was compelled not by judicially fashioned remedial purposes, but rather by a direct constitutional command. A new phase in the history of the rule, however, opened with the Court's decision in *Wolf v. Colorado*, 338 U.S. 25 (1949). * * *

Twelve years later, in *Mapp v. Ohio*, 367 U.S. 643 (1961), * * * the Court restored the original understanding of the *Weeks* case by overruling the holding of *Wolf* and repudiating its rationale. * * * Rejection of the *Wolf* approach was constitutionally required, the Court explained, because "the admission of the new constitutional right by *Wolf* could not consistently tolerate denial of its most important constitutional privilege, namely, the exclusion of the evidence which an accused had been forced to give by reason of the unlawful seizure. To hold otherwise is to grant the right but in reality to withhold its privilege and enjoyment." * * *

Despite this clear pronouncement, however, the Court since *Calandra* has gradually pressed the deterrence rationale for the rule back to center stage. * * *

In addition, the Court's decisions over the past decade have made plain that the entire enterprise of attempting to assess the benefits and costs of the exclusionary rule in various contexts is a virtually impossible task for the judiciary to perform honestly or accurately. Although the Court's language in those cases suggests that some specific empirical basis may support its analyses, the reality is that the Court's opinions represent inherently unstable compounds of intuition, hunches, and occasional pieces of partial and often inconclusive data. * * *

By remaining within its redoubt of empiricism and by basing the rule solely on the deterrence rationale, the Court has robbed the rule of legitimacy. * * * Rather than seeking to give effect to the liberties secured by the Fourth Amendment through guesswork about deterrence, the Court should restore to its proper place the principle framed 70 years ago in *Weeks* that an individual whose privacy has been invaded in violation of the Fourth Amendment has a right grounded in that Amendment to prevent the government from subsequently making use of any evidence so obtained. * * *

III

Even if I were to accept the Court's general approach to the exclusionary rule, I could not agree with today's result. There is no question that in the hands of the present Court the deterrence rationale has proved to be a powerful tool for confining the scope of the rule. In *Calandra*, for example, the Court concluded that the "speculative and undoubtedly minimal advance in the deterrence of police misconduct," was insufficient to outweigh the "expense of substantially impeding the role of the grand jury." * * *

* * * At the outset, the Court suggests that society has been asked to pay a high price—in terms either of setting guilty persons free or of

impeding the proper functioning of trials—as a result of excluding relevant physical evidence in cases where the police, in conducting searches and seizing evidence, have made only an "objectively reasonable" mistake concerning the constitutionality of their actions. But what evidence is there to support such a claim?

Significantly, the Court points to none, and, indeed, as the Court acknowledges, recent studies have demonstrated that the "costs" of the exclusionary rule—calculated in terms of dropped prosecutions and lost convictions—are quite low. Contrary to the claims of the rule's critics that exclusion leads to "the release of countless guilty criminals," these studies have demonstrated that federal and state prosecutors very rarely drop cases because of potential search and seizure problems. For example, a 1979 study prepared at the request of Congress by the General Accounting Office reported that only 0.4% of all cases actually declined for prosecution by federal prosecutors were declined primarily because of illegal search problems. Report of the Comptroller General of the United States, Impact of the Exclusionary Rule on Federal Criminal Prosecutions 14 (1979). If the GAO data are restated as a percentage of all arrests, the study shows that only 0.2% of all felony arrests are declined for prosecution because of potential exclusionary rule problems. Of course, these data describe only the costs attributable to the exclusion of evidence in all cases; the costs due to the exclusion of evidence in the narrower category of cases where police have made objectively reasonable mistakes must necessarily be even smaller. The Court, however, ignores this distinction and mistakenly weighs the aggregated costs of exclusion in all cases, irrespective of the circumstances that led to exclusion, against the potential benefits associated with only those cases in which evidence is excluded because police reasonably but mistakenly believe that their conduct does not violate the Fourth Amendment. When such faulty scales are used, it is little wonder that the balance tips in favor of restricting the application of the rule.

What then supports the Court's insistence that this evidence be admitted? Apparently, the Court's only answer is that even though the costs of exclusion are not very substantial, the potential deterrent effect in these circumstances is so marginal that exclusion cannot be justified. The key to the Court's conclusion in this respect is its belief that the prospective deterrent effect of the exclusionary rule operates only in those situations in which police officers, when deciding whether to go forward with some particular search, have reason to know that their planned conduct will violate the requirements of the Fourth Amendment. * * *

* * * But what the Court overlooks is that the deterrence rationale for the rule is not designed to be, nor should it be thought of as, a form of "punishment" of individual police officers for their failures to obey the restraints imposed by the Fourth Amendment. Instead, the chief deterrent

function of the rule is its tendency to promote institutional compliance with Fourth Amendment requirements on the part of law enforcement agencies generally. Thus, as the Court has previously recognized, "over the long term, [the] demonstration [provided by the exclusionary rule] that our society attaches serious consequences to violation of constitutional rights is thought to encourage those who formulate law enforcement policies, and the officers who implement them, to incorporate Fourth Amendment ideals into their value system." It is only through such an institutionwide mechanism that information concerning Fourth Amendment standards can be effectively communicated to rank-and-file officers.

If the overall educational effect of the exclusionary rule is considered, application of the rule to even those situations in which individual police officers have acted on the basis of a reasonable but mistaken belief that their conduct was authorized can still be expected to have a considerable long-term deterrent effect. If evidence is consistently excluded in these circumstances, police departments will surely be prompted to instruct their officers to devote greater care and attention to providing sufficient information to establish probable cause when applying for a warrant, and to review with some attention the form of the warrant that they have been issued, rather than automatically assuming that whatever document the magistrate has signed will necessarily comport with Fourth Amendment requirements.

After today's decisions, however, that institutional incentive will be lost. Indeed, the Court's "reasonable mistake" exception to the exclusionary rule will tend to put a premium on police ignorance of the law. Armed with the assurance provided by today's decisions that evidence will always be admissible whenever an officer has "reasonably" relied upon a warrant, police departments will be encouraged to train officers that if a warrant has simply been signed, it is reasonable, without more, to rely on it. Since in close cases there will no longer be any incentive to error on the side of constitutional behavior, police would have every reason to adopt a "let's-wait-until-it's-decided" approach in situations in which there is a question about a warrant's validity or the basis for its issuance.

Moreover, the good-faith exception will encourage police to provide only the bare minimum of information in future warrant applications. The police will now know that if they can secure a warrant, so long as the circumstances of its issuance are not "entirely unreasonable," all police conduct pursuant to that warrant will be protected from further judicial review. The clear incentive that operated in the past to establish probable cause adequately because reviewing courts would examine the magistrate's judgment carefully, has now been so completely vitiated that the police need only show that it was not "entirely unreasonable" under the circumstances of a particular case for them to believe that the warrant they were issued was valid. The long-run effect unquestionably will be to undermine the integrity of the warrant process. * * *

I dissent.

JUSTICE STEVENS, concurring in the judgment in No. 82-963, and dissenting in No. 82-1771.

[Omitted.]

QUESTIONS, COMMENTS, CONCERNS?

1. ***Leon*'s reliance on *Calandra*.** How does the *Leon* Court take advantage of *Calandra*'s holding to justify creating a "good faith" exception to the exclusionary rule?

2. **Levin's fundamental argument.** Notice the primary argument Levin proffers in his motion to suppress. [See Casefile Document 7.] In pertinent part, he contends that magistrate judges may "issue a search warrant *only* for a location within the judicial district itself[.]" *Id.* at 6. Recall that a magistrate in the Eastern District of Virginia issued the NIT Warrant. [See Casefile Document 5.] That warrant, in turn, led the FBI to discover that Levin was using the Playpen server. As a result, the FBI obtained a search warrant for Levin's residence in Massachusetts. [See Casefile Document 6.] Against that backdrop, does your opinion change on the government's primary illegality? In other words, did the government first act unconstitutionally when it searched Levin's home or, earlier, when it obtained Levin's name as a result of the NIT Warrant?

3. **The implications of Levin's argument.** Notice the potentially wide-reaching implications of Levin's assertions. If the government obtained the NIT Warrant unconstitutionally, which other Playpen users could argue that the government obtained their identities unlawful?

4. **The government's response.** The government primarily argues that it sought the NIT Warrant from a magistrate judge who sat within the jurisdiction of the U.S. District where the Playpen website operated. [Casefile Document 8, at 14–20.] Moreover, the government asserts, it had no choice but to focus on Virginia because "[t]he site was designed to hide the identity and location of its users, so the government had no way to know where the defendant was without using the NIT authorized by the warrant." The government concludes that the fact that it focused on obtaining a warrant where the website was established meant that it lawfully learned about *every* user accessing the website. If accepted, does this argument make it lawful for the government to pursue defendants across the country—in any state—based on just the NIT Warrant?

5. ***Leon* & Levin.** Look again at Casefile Document 8. How does the government suggest that *Leon* applies to the NIT Warrant? Compare the government's *Leon* argument to the *Leon* case itself. Did the government miss an opportunity to more broadly argue the "good faith reliance" logic of *Leon*?

DAVIS v. UNITED STATES

564 U.S. 229
Supreme Court of the United States
March 21, 2011, Argued; June 16, 2011, Decided
No. 09-11328

JUSTICE ALITO delivered the opinion of the Court.

The Fourth Amendment protects the right to be free from "unreasonable searches and seizures," but it is silent about how this right is to be enforced. To supplement the bare text, this Court created the exclusionary rule, a deterrent sanction that bars the prosecution from introducing evidence obtained by way of a Fourth Amendment violation. The question here is whether to apply this sanction when the police conduct a search in compliance with binding precedent that is later overruled. Because suppression would do nothing to deter police misconduct in these circumstances, and because it would come at a high cost to both the truth and the public safety, we hold that searches conducted in objectively reasonable reliance on binding appellate precedent are not subject to the exclusionary rule.

I

The question presented arises in this case as a result of a shift in our Fourth Amendment jurisprudence on searches of automobiles incident to arrests of recent occupants.

A

Under this Court's decision in *Chimel v. California*, 395 U.S. 752, 89 (1969), a police officer who makes a lawful arrest may conduct a warrantless search of the arrestee's person and the area "within his immediate control." This rule "may be stated clearly enough," but in the early going after *Chimel* it proved difficult to apply, particularly in cases that involved searches "inside [of] automobile[s] after the arrestees [we]re no longer in [them]." *See New York v. Belton*, 453 U.S. 454, 458–459 (1981). A number of courts upheld the constitutionality of vehicle searches that were "substantially contemporaneous" with occupants' arrests. Other courts disapproved of automobile searches incident to arrests, at least absent some continuing threat that the arrestee might gain access to the vehicle and "destroy evidence or grab a weapon." In *New York v. Belton*, this Court granted certiorari to resolve the conflict.

In *Belton*, a police officer conducting a traffic stop lawfully arrested four occupants of a vehicle and ordered the arrestees to line up, unhandcuffed, along the side of the thruway. The officer then searched the vehicle's passenger compartment and found cocaine inside a jacket that lay on the backseat. This Court upheld the search as reasonable incident to the occupants' arrests. In an opinion that repeatedly stressed the need for a "straightforward," "workable rule" to guide police conduct, the Court announced "that when a policeman has made a lawful custodial arrest of the occupant of an automobile, he may, as a contemporaneous incident of that arrest, search the passenger compartment of that automobile."

For years, *Belton* was widely understood to have set down a simple, bright-line rule. Numerous courts read the decision to authorize automobile searches incident to arrests of recent occupants, regardless of whether the arrestee in any particular case was within reaching distance of the vehicle at the time of the search. Even after the arrestee had stepped out of the vehicle and had been subdued by police, the prevailing understanding was that *Belton* still authorized a substantially contemporaneous search of the automobile's passenger compartment. * * *

[Things changed when] [t]his Court granted certiorari in [*Arizona v. Gant*, 552 U.S. 1230 (2008)] * * *. [There], the Court adopted a new, two-part rule under which an automobile search incident to a recent occupant's arrest is constitutional (1) if the arrestee is within reaching distance of the vehicle during the search, or (2) if the police have reason to believe that the vehicle contains "evidence relevant to the crime of arrest."

B

The search at issue in this case took place a full two years before this Court announced its new rule in Gant. On an April evening in 2007, police officers in Greenville, Alabama, conducted a routine traffic stop that eventually resulted in the arrests of driver Stella Owens (for driving while intoxicated) and passenger Willie Davis (for giving a false name to police). The police handcuffed both Owens and Davis, and they placed the arrestees in the back of separate patrol cars. The police then searched the passenger compartment of Owens' vehicle and found a revolver inside Davis' jacket pocket.

Davis was indicted in the Middle District of Alabama on one count of possession of a firearm by a convicted felon. In his motion to suppress the revolver, Davis acknowledged that the officers' search fully complied with "existing Eleventh Circuit precedent." Like most courts, the Eleventh Circuit had long read *Belton* to establish a bright-line rule authorizing substantially contemporaneous vehicle searches incident to arrests of recent occupants. Davis recognized that the District Court was obligated to follow this precedent, but he raised a Fourth Amendment challenge to preserve "the issue for review" on appeal. The District Court denied the motion, and Davis was convicted on the firearms charge.

While Davis' appeal was pending, this Court decided *Gant*. The Eleventh Circuit, in the opinion below, applied *Gant's* new rule and held that the vehicle search incident to Davis' arrest "violated [his] Fourth Amendment rights." As for whether this constitutional violation warranted suppression, the Eleventh Circuit viewed that as a separate issue that turned on "the potential of exclusion to deter wrongful police conduct." The court concluded that "penalizing the [arresting] officer" for following binding appellate precedent would do nothing to "dete[r] . . . Fourth Amendment violations." It therefore declined to apply the exclusionary rule and affirmed Davis' conviction. We granted certiorari.

II

The Fourth Amendment protects the "right of the people to be secure in their persons, houses, papers, and effects, against unreasonable searches and seizures." The Amendment says nothing about suppressing evidence obtained in violation of this command. That rule—the exclusionary rule—is a "prudential" doctrine, created by this Court to "compel respect for the constitutional guaranty." *Elkins v. United States,* 364 U.S. 206, 217 (1960); *see Weeks v. United States,* 232 U.S. 383 (1914); *Mapp v. Ohio,* 367 U.S. 643 (1961). Exclusion is "not a personal constitutional right," nor is it designed to "redress the injury" occasioned by an unconstitutional search. The rule's sole purpose, we have repeatedly held, is to deter future Fourth Amendment violations. *E.g.,* * * * *United States v. Leon,* 468 U.S. 897, 909, 921, n. 22 (1984) * * *. Our cases have thus limited the rule's operation to situations in which this purpose is "thought most efficaciously served." *United States v. Calandra,* 414 U.S. 338, 348 (1974). * * *

Real deterrent value is a "necessary condition for exclusion," but it is not "a sufficient" one. *Hudson v. Michigan,* 547 U.S. 586, 596 (2006). The analysis must also account for the "substantial social costs" generated by the rule. *Leon, supra,* at 907. Exclusion exacts a heavy toll on both the judicial system and society at large. It almost always requires courts to ignore reliable, trustworthy evidence bearing on guilt or innocence. And its bottom-line effect, in many cases, is to suppress the truth and set the criminal loose in the community without punishment. Our cases hold that society must swallow this bitter pill when necessary, but only as a "last resort." *Hudson, supra,* at 591. For exclusion to be appropriate, the deterrence benefits of suppression must outweigh its heavy costs.

Admittedly, there was a time when our exclusionary-rule cases were not nearly so discriminating in their approach to the doctrine. "Expansive dicta" in several decisions, suggested that the rule was a self-executing mandate implicit in the Fourth Amendment itself. *See* * * * *Mapp, supra,* at 655 ("[A]ll evidence obtained by searches and seizures in violation of the Constitution is, by that same authority, inadmissible in a state court"). * * * In time, however, we came to acknowledge the exclusionary rule for what it undoubtedly is—a "judicially created remedy" of this Court's own making. *Calandra, supra,* at 348. We abandoned the old, "reflexive" application of the doctrine, and imposed a more rigorous weighing of its costs and deterrence benefits. In a line of cases beginning with *Leon,* 468

U.S. 897, we also recalibrated our cost-benefit analysis in exclusion cases to focus the inquiry on the "flagrancy of the police misconduct" at issue.

The basic insight of the *Leon* line of cases is that the deterrence benefits of exclusion "var[y] with the culpability of the law enforcement conduct" at issue. When the police exhibit "deliberate," "reckless," or "grossly negligent" disregard for Fourth Amendment rights, the deterrent value of exclusion is strong and tends to outweigh the resulting costs. But when the police act with an objectively "reasonable good-faith belief" that their conduct is lawful, *Leon, supra*, at 90, or when their conduct involves only simple, "isolated" negligence, the " 'deterrence rationale loses much of its force,' " and exclusion cannot "pay its way." *Leon, supra*, at 919, 908, n.6.

The Court has over time applied this "good-faith" exception across a range of cases. *Leon* itself, for example, held that the exclusionary rule does not apply when the police conduct a search in "objectively reasonable reliance" on a warrant later held invalid. The error in such a case rests with the issuing magistrate, not the police officer, and "punish[ing] the errors of judges" is not the office of the exclusionary rule.

Other good-faith cases have sounded a similar theme. *Illinois v. Krull*, 480 U.S. 340 (1987), extended the good-faith exception to searches conducted in reasonable reliance on subsequently invalidated statutes. *Id.*, at 349–350 ("legislators, like judicial officers, are not the focus of the rule"). In [*Arizona v. Evans*], the Court applied the good-faith exception in a case where the police reasonably relied on erroneous information concerning an arrest warrant in a database maintained by judicial employees. [514 U.S. 1, 14 (1995)]. Most recently, in [*Herring v. United States*], we extended *Evans* in a case where police employees erred in maintaining records in a warrant database. "[I]solated," "nonrecurring" police negligence, we determined, lacks the culpability required to justify the harsh sanction of exclusion. [*Herring*, 555 U.S. 135, 137 (2009).]

III

The question in this case is whether to apply the exclusionary rule when the police conduct a search in objectively reasonable reliance on binding judicial precedent. At the time of the search at issue here, we had not yet decided *Gant*, and the Eleventh Circuit had interpreted our decision in *Belton* to establish a bright-line rule authorizing the search of a vehicle's passenger compartment incident to a recent occupant's arrest. The search incident to Davis' arrest in this case followed the Eleventh Circuit's * * * precedent to the letter. Although the search turned out to be unconstitutional under *Gant*, all agree that the officers' conduct was in strict compliance with then-binding Circuit law and was not culpable in any way.

Under our exclusionary-rule precedents, this acknowledged absence of police culpability dooms Davis' claim. Police practices trigger the harsh sanction of exclusion only when they are deliberate enough to yield "meaningfu[l]" deterrence, and culpable enough to be "worth the price paid by the justice system." *Herring*, 555 U.S., at 144. The conduct of the officers here was neither of these things. The officers who conducted the search did not violate Davis' Fourth Amendment rights deliberately, recklessly, or with gross negligence. Nor does this case involve any "recurring or systemic negligence" on the part of law enforcement. *Ibid.* The police acted in strict compliance with binding precedent, and their behavior was not wrongful. Unless the exclusionary rule is to become a strict-liability regime, it can have no application in this case.

Indeed, in 27 years of practice under *Leon's* good-faith exception, we have "never applied" the exclusionary rule to suppress evidence obtained as a result of nonculpable, innocent police conduct. * * * About all that exclusion would deter in this case is conscientious police work. * * * An officer who conducts a search in reliance on binding appellate precedent does no more than " 'ac[t] as a reasonable officer would and should act' " under the circumstances. *Leon*, 468 U.S., at 920. The deterrent effect of exclusion in such a case can only be to discourage the officer from " 'do[ing] his duty.' "

That is not the kind of deterrence the exclusionary rule seeks to foster. We have stated before, and we reaffirm today, that the harsh sanction of exclusion "should not be applied to deter objectively reasonable law enforcement activity." Evidence obtained during a search conducted in reasonable reliance on binding precedent is not subject to the exclusionary rule.

IV

* * * Davis argues that Fourth Amendment precedents of this Court will be effectively insulated from challenge under a good-faith exception for reliance on appellate precedent. But this argument is overblown. For one thing, it is important to keep in mind that this argument applies to an exceedingly small set of cases. Decisions overruling this Court's Fourth Amendment precedents are rare. Indeed, it has been more than 40 years since the Court last handed down a decision of the type to which Davis refers. *Chimel v. California*, 395 U.S. 752 (overruling *United States v. Rabinowitz*, 339 U.S. 56 (1950), and *Harris v. United States*, 331 U.S. 145 (1947)). And even in those cases, Davis points out that no fewer than eight separate doctrines may preclude a defendant who successfully challenges an existing precedent from getting any relief. Moreover, as a practical matter, defense counsel in many cases will test this Court's Fourth Amendment precedents in the same way that *Belton* was tested in *Gant*— by arguing that the precedent is distinguishable.

At most, Davis' argument might suggest that—to prevent Fourth Amendment law from becoming ossified—the petitioner in a case that results in the overruling of one of this Court's Fourth Amendment precedents should be given the benefit of the victory by permitting the suppression of evidence in that one case. Such a result would undoubtedly be a windfall to this one random litigant. But the exclusionary rule is "not a personal constitutional right." It is a "judicially created" sanction, *Calandra*, 414 U.S., at 348, specifically designed as a "windfall" remedy to deter future Fourth Amendment violations. The good-faith exception is a judicially created exception to this judicially created rule. Therefore, in a future case, we could, if necessary, recognize a limited exception to the good-faith exception for a defendant who obtains a judgment overruling one of our Fourth Amendment precedents.

But this is not such a case. Davis did not secure a decision overturning a Supreme Court precedent; the police in his case reasonably relied on binding Circuit precedent. That sort of blameless police conduct, we hold, comes within the good-faith exception and is not properly subject to the exclusionary rule.

    * * *

It is one thing for the criminal "to go free because the constable has blundered." It is quite another to set the criminal free because the constable has scrupulously adhered to governing law. Excluding evidence in such cases deters no police misconduct and imposes substantial social costs. We therefore hold that when the police conduct a search in objectively reasonable reliance on binding appellate precedent, the exclusionary rule does not apply. The judgment of the Court of Appeals for the Eleventh Circuit is affirmed.

JUSTICE SOTOMAYOR, concurring in the judgment.

[Omitted.]

JUSTICE BREYER, with whom JUSTICE GINSBURG joins, dissenting.

In 2009, in *Arizona v. Gant*, this Court held that a police search of an automobile without a warrant violates the Fourth Amendment if the police have previously removed the automobile's occupants and placed them securely in a squad car. The present case involves these same circumstances, and it was pending on appeal when this Court decided *Gant*. Because *Gant* represents a "shift" in the Court's Fourth Amendment jurisprudence, we must decide whether and how *Gant's* new rule applies here. * * *

I agree with the Court about whether *Gant's* new rule applies. It does apply. * * * The Court goes on, however, to decide how *Gant's* new rule will apply. And here it adds a fatal twist. While conceding that, like the search in *Gant*, this search violated the Fourth Amendment, it holds that, unlike

Gant, this defendant is not entitled to a remedy. That is because the Court finds a new "good faith" exception which prevents application of the normal remedy for a Fourth Amendment violation, namely, suppression of the illegally seized evidence. *Weeks v. United States*, 232 U.S. 383 (1914); *Mapp v. Ohio*, 367 U.S. 643 (1961). Leaving Davis with a right but not a remedy, the Court "keep[s] the word of promise to our ear" but "break[s] it to our hope."

* * * Perhaps more important, the Court's rationale for creating its new "good faith" exception threatens to undermine well-settled Fourth Amendment law. The Court correctly says that pre-*Gant* Eleventh Circuit precedent had held that a *Gant*-type search was constitutional; hence the police conduct in this case, consistent with that precedent, was "innocent." *Ante*, at 240, 180 L. Ed. 2d, at 296. But the Court then finds this fact sufficient to create a new "good faith" exception to the exclusionary rule. It reasons that the "sole purpose" of the exclusionary rule "is to deter future Fourth Amendment violations." The "deterrence benefits of exclusion vary with the culpability of the law enforcement conduct at issue." Those benefits are sufficient to justify exclusion where "police exhibit deliberate, reckless, or grossly negligent disregard for Fourth Amendment rights." But those benefits do not justify exclusion where, as here, the police act with "simple, isolated negligence" or an "objectively reasonable good-faith belief that their conduct is lawful."

If the Court means what it says, what will happen to the exclusionary rule, a rule that the Court adopted nearly a century ago for federal courts, *Weeks v. United States*, and made applicable to state courts a half century ago through the Fourteenth Amendment, *Mapp v. Ohio*. The Court has thought of that rule not as punishment for the individual officer or as reparation for the individual defendant but more generally as an effective way to secure enforcement of the Fourth Amendment's commands. *Weeks*, *supra*, at 393 (without the exclusionary rule, the Fourth Amendment would be "of no value," and "might as well be stricken from the Constitution"). This Court has deviated from the "suppression" norm in the name of "good faith" only a handful of times and in limited, atypical circumstances: where a magistrate has erroneously issued a warrant, *United States v. Leon*, 468 U.S. 897 (1984); where a database has erroneously informed police that they have a warrant, *Arizona v. Evans*, *supra*, *Herring v. United States*, 555 U.S. 135 (2009); and where an unconstitutional statute purported to authorize the search, *Illinois v. Krull*, 480 U.S. 340 (1987). *See Herring*, *supra*, at 142 ("good faith" exception inaptly named).

The fact that such exceptions are few and far between is understandable. Defendants frequently move to suppress evidence on Fourth Amendment grounds. In many, perhaps most, of these instances the police, uncertain of how the Fourth Amendment applied to the particular factual circumstances they faced, will have acted in objective good faith. Yet, in a significant percentage of these instances, courts will find that the police were wrong. And, unless the police conduct falls into one of the exceptions previously noted, courts have required the suppression of the evidence seized. 1 W. LaFave, Search and Seizure § 1.3, pp. 103–104 (4th ed. 2004) ("good faith" exception has not yet been applied to warrantless searches and seizures beyond the "rather special situations" of *Evans*, *Herring*, and *Krull*). *See* Valdes, *Frequency and Success: An Empirical Study of Criminal Law Defenses, Federal Constitutional Evidentiary Claims, and Plea Negotiations*, 153 U. Pa. L. Rev. 1709, 1728 (2005) (suppression motions are filed in approximately 7% of criminal cases; approximately 12% of suppression motions are successful); LaFave, *supra*, at 64 ("Surely many more Fourth Amendment violations result from carelessness than from intentional constitutional violations"); Stewart, *The Road to Mapp v. Ohio and Beyond: The Origins, Development and Future of the Exclusionary Rule in Search-and-Seizure Cases*, 83 Colum. L. Rev. 1365, 1389 (1983) ("[T]he vast majority of fourth amendment violations . . . [are] motivated by commendable zeal, not condemnable malice").

But an officer who conducts a search that he believes complies with the Constitution but which, it ultimately turns out, falls just outside the Fourth Amendment's bounds is no more culpable than an officer who follows erroneous "binding precedent." Nor is an officer more culpable where circuit precedent is simply suggestive rather than "binding," where it only describes how to treat roughly analogous instances, or where it just does not exist. Thus, if the Court means what it now says, if it would place determinative weight upon the culpability of an individual officer's conduct, and if it would apply the exclusionary rule only where a Fourth Amendment violation was "deliberate, reckless, or grossly negligent," then the "good faith" exception will swallow the exclusionary rule. Indeed, our broad dicta in *Herring*—dicta the Court repeats and expands upon today— may already be leading lower courts in this direction. Today's decision will doubtless accelerate this trend.

Any such change (which may already be underway) would affect not "an exceedingly small set of cases," but a very large number of cases, potentially many thousands each year. since the exclusionary rule is often the only sanction available for a Fourth Amendment violation, the Fourth Amendment would no longer protect ordinary Americans from "unreasonable searches and seizures." *See Wolf v. Colorado*, 338 U.S. 25, 41 (1949) (Murphy, J., dissenting) (In many circumstances, "there is but one alternative to the rule of exclusion. That is no sanction at all") (overruled by *Mapp v. Ohio*, *supra*; *Herring*, *supra*, at 152 (Ginsburg, J., dissenting) (the exclusionary rule is "an essential auxiliary" to the Fourth Amendment). It would become a watered-down Fourth Amendment, offering its protection against only those searches and seizures that are egregiously unreasonable.

III

In sum, I fear that the Court's opinion will undermine the exclusionary rule. * * *

For these reasons, with respect, I dissent.

QUESTIONS, COMMENTS, CONCERNS?

1.   **Leon and Davis.** Recall that the *Leon* good faith exception to the exclusionary rule is based on a search warrant. Is the Court's holding in *Davis* similarly predicated on an officer first obtaining a search warrant? If not, how does *Davis* seem to broaden *Leon*?

2.   **Davis and the exclusionary rule.** As the introductory materials made clear, *Davis* seems to further weaken exclusion as an appropriate remedy for a Fourth Amendment violation. It's fair then to ask what *other* remedy a defendant has for a Fourth Amendment violation? Surely, the Court does not think a criminal defendant has the funds necessary to pursue a civil suit against the police, right?

3.   **Davis and Levin.** Look back one more time at the government's response to Levin's motion to suppress [See Casefile Document 8]. It seems the government missed an opportunity to incorporate the logic of *Davis*. Although the government suggests that the "extreme remedy of suppression" is not appropriate, it does not rely on the cost-benefit analysis to argue that the exclusionary rule is an inappropriate remedy. This seems like a particularly good argument given that a violation of Federal Rule of Criminal Procedure 41 is not necessarily the same thing as a Fourth Amendment violation, right? Notice the district court is particularly concerned about this issue. [See Casefile Document 9, at 7.]

4.   **Considering suppression.** After *Davis*, what are the analytical steps Judge Young should undertake in determining whether to apply the exclusionary rule? More specifically, how might Judge Young properly incorporate *Leon*'s cost-benefit analysis in Levin's case?

V. EXCEPTIONS TO EXCLUSION

We've now learned that the exclusionary rule generally excludes both the primary evidence obtained by law enforcement following an unconstitutional search or seizure alongside any fruits of that evidence. For example, in a routine drug case where law enforcement seized drugs unconstitutionally, the exclusionary rule suppresses both the drugs (evidence obtained from the primary illegality) and law enforcement's knowledge of the drugs (fruit). We've also learned that *Leon* provides a good faith exception to the exclusionary rule.

We consider next the varied exceptions to exclusion. *Leon*'s creation of a "good faith" exception is of course one such exception. But understand that *Leon* both created an exception to the exclusionary rule *and* a groundbreaking analytical framework that subsequent Courts would rely on to further weaken the exclusionary rule in other contexts. In fact, the Court expanded *Leon* on the very day it was decided—in *Massachusetts v. Sheppard*. As the companion case to *Leon*, *Sheppard* helps us see *Leon* in action while ideally tightening our doctrinal understanding of the "good faith" exception.

As *Davis* summarizes, the *Leon-Sheppard* rationale would go on to impact exclusionary rule decisions in a variety of other contexts. In 1987, for instance, the Court in *Illinois v. Krull*, 480 U.S. 340, 349–51 (1987), held that the exclusionary rule does not apply to an officer's good faith reliance on a statute later held unconstitutional. By analogy to *Leon*, the Court reasoned in part that "application of the exclusionary rule to suppress evidence obtained by an officer acting in objectively reasonable reliance on a statute would have as little deterrent effect on the officer's actions as would the exclusion of evidence when an officer acts in objectively reasonable reliance on a warrant." *Id.* at 349.

Then, in *Arizona v. Evans*, 514 U.S. 1 (1995), the Court considered whether to suppress marijuana found during an automobile search—a search conducted after the officer who stopped Evans learned that he had an outstanding arrest warrant. Unknown to the officer, however, the warrant had been previously quashed and only remained on his record due to a clerical error. In declining to suppress the marijuana, the Court once again turned to *Leon*: "There is no indication that the arresting officer was not acting objectively reasonably when he relied upon the police computer record. Application of the *Leon* framework supports a categorical exception to the exclusionary rule for clerical errors of court employees." *Id.* at 15–16.

Similar logic pervaded when the Court considered *Herring v. United States*, 555 U.S. 135 (2009). In *Herring*, officers apprehended the defendant pursuant to a faulty arrest warrant that should have been recalled months earlier. Due to a negligent bookkeeping error, the warrant remained in the system, and Herring was arrested. Following the arrest, officers found drugs in Herring's pocket along with a gun under the seat of his truck. The trial court declined Herring's motion to suppress, and both the Eleventh Circuit and Supreme Court affirmed. Again relying on *Leon*, the Court held that law enforcement's bookkeeping error was insufficiently culpable to justify application of the exclusionary rule. Rather, "[t]o trigger the exclusionary rule, police conduct must be sufficiently deliberate that exclusion can meaningfully deter it, and sufficiently culpable that such deterrence is worth the price paid by the justice system." *Id.* at 144.

The *Leon-Sheppard* exception is exceptionally powerful: Evidence admitted pursuant to *Leon-Sheppard* (and related rationale) is primary evidence obtained from the original illegality. Evidence excluded would be the fruits from law enforcement's unconstitutional behavior. For instance, if law enforcement conducted an unlawful search of the defendant's residence and uncovered drugs, the drugs themselves—not law enforcement's knowledge of them (the fruit)—are admissible if *Leon-Sheppard* applies. Again, in such situations the exception is incredibly powerful.

Following our reading of *Sheppard*, as stated above, we consider three other exceptions: attenuation, independent source, and inevitable discovery. These three exceptions often apply to so-called "fruits" cases where the fruits of illegal behavior can be introduced despite the initial illegality of a search. In the easiest of exclusionary rule cases, the challenged evidence has a direct relationship to the primary illegality. That, for example, is at issue when an unlawful search produces drugs, and the defendant thereafter seeks to suppress those drugs.

Sometimes, however, the challenged evidence is secondary in nature. Consider the immediately preceding hypothetical: What if the prosecution sought to have an officer testify that he *knew* that defendant produced unlawful drugs? Although, as noted above, the exclusionary rule ordinarily operates to exclude the direct product of unconstitutional police behavior (the primary illegality—the drugs) alongside any secondary evidence (the fruits—the officer's knowledge of those drugs), these final three exceptions typically apply to the secondary evidence (again, the fruits). In other words, in these final exceptions, we consider when, despite an initial illegality, the prosecution may nonetheless introduce the "fruits" of that evidence against the defendant.

A. GOOD FAITH REVISITED (*LEON* IN ACTION)

MASSACHUSETTS V. SHEPPARD
468 U.S. 981
Supreme Court of the United States
January 17, 1984, Argued; July 5, 1984, Decided
No. 82-963

JUSTICE WHITE delivered the opinion of the Court.

This case involves the application of the rules articulated today in *United States v. Leon* to a situation in which police officers seize items pursuant to a warrant subsequently invalidated because of a technical error on the part of the issuing judge.

I

The badly burned body of Sandra Boulware was discovered in a vacant lot in the Roxbury section of Boston at approximately 5 a. m., Saturday, May 5, 1979. An autopsy revealed that Boulware had died of multiple compound skull fractures caused by blows to the head. After a brief investigation, the police decided to question one of the victim's boyfriends, Osborne Sheppard. Sheppard told the police that he had last seen the victim on Tuesday night and that he had been at a local gaming house (where card games were played) from 9 p.m. Friday until 5 a.m. Saturday. He identified several people who would be willing to substantiate the latter claim.

By interviewing the people Sheppard had said were at the gaming house on Friday night, the police learned that although Sheppard was at the gaming house that night, he had borrowed an automobile at about 3 o'clock Saturday morning in order to give two men a ride home. Even though the trip normally took only 15 minutes, Sheppard did not return with the car until nearly 5 a. m.

On Sunday morning, police officers visited the owner of the car Sheppard had borrowed. He consented to an inspection of the vehicle. Bloodstains and pieces of hair were found on the rear bumper and within the trunk compartment. In addition, the officers noticed strands of wire in the trunk similar to wire strands found on and near the body of the victim. The owner of the car told the officers that when he last used the car on Friday night, shortly before Sheppard borrowed it, he had placed articles in the trunk and had not noticed any stains on the bumper or in the trunk.

On the basis of the evidence gathered thus far in the investigation, Detective Peter O'Malley drafted an affidavit designed to support an application for an arrest warrant and a search warrant authorizing a search of Sheppard's residence. The affidavit set forth the results of the investigation and stated that the [items] police wished to search for[.] * * *

Detective O'Malley showed the affidavit to the District Attorney, the District Attorney's first assistant, and a sergeant, who all concluded that it set forth probable cause for the search and the arrest.

Because it was Sunday, the local court was closed, and the police had a difficult time finding a warrant application form. Detective O'Malley finally found a warrant form previously in use in the Dorchester District. The form was entitled "Search Warrant—Controlled Substance G.L. c. 276 §§ 1 through 3A." Realizing that some changes had to be made before the form could be used to authorize the search requested in the affidavit, Detective O'Malley deleted the subtitle "controlled substance" with a typewriter. He also substituted "Roxbury" for the printed "Dorchester" and typed Sheppard's name and address into blank spaces provided for that information. However, the reference to "controlled substance" was not deleted in the portion of the form that constituted the warrant application and that, when signed, would constitute the warrant itself.

Detective O'Malley then took the affidavit and the warrant form to the residence of a judge who had consented to consider the warrant application.

The judge examined the affidavit and stated that he would authorize the search as requested. Detective O'Malley offered the warrant form and stated that he knew the form as presented dealt with controlled substances. He showed the judge where he had crossed out the subtitles. After unsuccessfully searching for a more suitable form, the judge informed O'Malley that he would make the necessary changes so as to provide a proper search warrant. The judge then took the form, made some changes on it, and dated and signed the warrant. However, he did not change the substantive portion of the warrant, which continued to authorize a search for controlled substances; nor did he alter the form so as to incorporate the affidavit. The judge returned the affidavit and the warrant to O'Malley, informing him that the warrant was sufficient authority in form and content to carry out the search as requested. O'Malley took the two documents and, accompanied by other officers, proceeded to Sheppard's residence. The scope of the ensuing search was limited to the items listed in the affidavit, and several incriminating pieces of evidence were discovered. Sheppard was then charged with first-degree murder.

At a pretrial suppression hearing, the trial judge concluded that the warrant failed to conform to the commands of the Fourth Amendment because it did not particularly describe the items to be seized. The judge ruled, however, that the evidence could be admitted notwithstanding the defect in the warrant because the police had acted in good faith in executing what they reasonably thought was a valid warrant. At the subsequent trial, Sheppard was convicted.

On appeal, Sheppard argued that the evidence obtained pursuant to the defective warrant should have been suppressed. The Supreme Judicial Court of Massachusetts agreed. * * * We granted certiorari and set the case for argument in conjunction with *United States v. Leon.*

II

Having already decided that the exclusionary rule should not be applied when the officer conducting the search acted in objectively reasonable reliance on a warrant issued by a detached and neutral magistrate that subsequently is determined to be invalid, the sole issue before us in this case is whether the officers reasonably believed that the search they conducted was authorized by a valid warrant. There is no dispute that the officers believed that the warrant authorized the search that they conducted. Thus, the only question is whether there was an objectively reasonable basis for the officers' mistaken belief. * * *

The officers in this case took every step that could reasonably be expected of them. Detective O'Malley prepared an affidavit which was reviewed and approved by the District Attorney. He presented that affidavit to a neutral judge. The judge concluded that the affidavit established probable cause to search Sheppard's residence, and informed

O'Malley that he would authorize the search as requested. O'Malley then produced the warrant form and informed the judge that it might need to be changed. He was told by the judge that the necessary changes would be made. He then observed the judge make some changes and received the warrant and the affidavit. At this point, a reasonable police officer would have concluded, as O'Malley did, that the warrant authorized a search for the materials outlined in the affidavit.

Sheppard contends that since O'Malley knew the warrant form was defective, he should have examined it to make sure that the necessary changes had been made. However, that argument is based on the premise that O'Malley had a duty to disregard the judge's assurances that the requested search would be authorized and the necessary changes would be made. Whatever an officer may be required to do when he executes a warrant without knowing beforehand what items are to be seized,[6] we refuse to rule that an officer is required to disbelieve a judge who has just advised him, by word and by action, that the warrant he possesses authorizes him to conduct the search he has requested. In Massachusetts, as in most jurisdictions, the determinations of a judge acting within his jurisdiction, even if erroneous, are valid and binding until they are set aside under some recognized procedure. If an officer is required to accept at face value the judge's conclusion that a warrant form is invalid, there is little reason why he should be expected to disregard assurances that everything is all right, especially when he has alerted the judge to the potential problems.

In sum, the police conduct in this case clearly was objectively reasonable and largely error-free. An error of constitutional dimensions may have been committed with respect to the issuance of the warrant, but it was the judge, not the police officers, who made the critical mistake. * * * Suppressing evidence because the judge failed to make all the necessary clerical corrections despite his assurances that such changes would be made will not serve the deterrent function that the exclusionary rule was designed to achieve. Accordingly, federal law does not require the exclusion of the disputed evidence in this case. The judgment of the Supreme Judicial Court is therefore reversed, and the case is remanded for further proceedings not inconsistent with this opinion.

It is so ordered.

---

[6] Normally, when an officer who has not been involved in the application stage receives a warrant, he will read it in order to determine the object of the search. In this case, Detective O'Malley, the officer who directed the search, knew what items were listed in the affidavit presented to the judge, and he had good reason to believe that the warrant authorized the seizure of those items. Whether an officer who is less familiar with the warrant application or who has unalleviated concerns about the proper scope of the search would be justified in failing to notice a defect like the one in the warrant in this case is an issue we need not decide. We hold only that it was not unreasonable for the police in this case to rely on the judge's assurances that the warrant authorized the search they had requested.

[For opinion of JUSTICE STEVENS concurring in the judgment, see his opinion in *Leon*.]

[For dissenting opinion of JUSTICE BRENNAN, see his opinion in *Leon*.]

QUESTIONS, COMMENTS, CONCERNS?

1.   ***Leon* or *Sheppard*.** In its response to Levin's motion to suppress, the government cites to *Sheppard*, but seemingly does little more. [See Casefile Document 8.] Does *Leon* stand alone as one argument to justify the government obtaining knowledge of Levin's address, whereas *Sheppard* provides the government with a separate independent argument? Or, rather, do *Leon* and *Sheppard* work together such that they are essentially one good faith doctrine?

2.   **Approaching oral argument.** You now have a complete overview of the "good faith" exception to the Fourth Amendment's exclusionary rule. You've also had an opportunity to read Levin's motion to suppress alongside the government's response. As the government, how would you approach preparing for oral argument? Turn your attention now to Casefile Document 9, the transcript from the hearing on Levin's motion to suppress. Consider what seems like a problematic exchange on page 12 between the district court and the government during the hearing about five minutes into the government's argument:

THE COURT: Your strongest argument is—

MR. TOBIN: Please.

THE COURT: —is—if you want—it seems to me your strongest argument is, in this developing area, the agents acted in good faith.

MR. TOBIN: Oh, I agree, Judge, I'm saving the best for last.

THE COURT: Well, in about 5 minutes. Go ahead.

What just happened there? Keep in mind that the court gave the parties each about ten minutes. It seems like the government led with a handful of unpersuasive arguments. How would you have avoided making a similar mistake?

3.   **Approaching oral argument *redux*.** Return to Casefile Document 9. Notice that, during the government's argument about "good faith," it never once, beyond merely mentioning *Leon*, ties its argument to *Leon*, *Sheppard*, *Davis*, or any other Supreme Court exclusionary rule case. Is the government's casual use of "good faith" to blame? Even if the government meant that phrasing as a short-hand, it seemingly did so at its peril. After all, it's counsel's job to educate the court. Where did the government educate the court on the applicable law here? Look at page 16 of the transcript for some insight. The government seems to pay the price. The court asks the government to research how many NIT warrants have ever been issued. But the number of warrants on a particular topic was not relevant to the *Leon* Court, was it?

4.   Reaching a resolution. Look now at the Judge Young's order. [See Casefile Document 10.] As you'll see, the court holds first that the issuing magistrate did not, in fact, have jurisdiction to issue the NIT Warrant. The court then secondarily holds that *Leon* cannot save the warrant. Notice, as it relates to the *Leon* question, how the court frames the issue: "[w]hether the good-faith exception applies where a warrant was void is a question of first impression in this Circuit, and an unresolved question more broadly." *Id.* At 24. What does the court mean (look at the bottom of page twenty-five for help)? How should that impact the *Leon* analysis?

5.   Reaching a resolution *redux.* Think back on the cases you've read so far. Collectively, do they suggest that the modern Supreme Court is moving toward or away from *Mapp*? The trend seems clear, right? Given that trend, how can the district court justify its decision *not* to apply *Leon* to the Levin fact pattern?

6.   The policy problem. Given the district court's decision, what should the FBI have done differently at the outset when investigating Levin? At least according to the district court, the NIT Warrant was an inappropriate approach. How would the district court suggest that the government approach future cases involving child pornography servers? [See Casefile Document 10, at 34–38.]

7.   The result of the district court's order. By the time of Levin's motion, the government had made more than 800 worldwide arrests of defendants who used Playpen to obtain child pornography.[22] Not unlike many possession cases, those defendants, like Levin, had few viable legal arguments. They and their legal teams were therefore acutely interested in the results of Levin's motion to suppress. After all, if Levin won, presumably all of the defendants identified pursuant to the NIT Warrant would likewise file successful motions to suppress. Consequently, the district court's decision had wide-ranging implications. But the district court's order was not the end of the story.

8.   The rest of the story. The First Circuit reversed the district court on appeal. [See Casefile Document 11.] According to the First Circuit, *Leon* applied to Levin's case. In what ways does the First Circuit's opinion differ analytically from the district court's approach? In particular, how does the First Circuit apply the Supreme Court's cost-benefit analysis?

B. ATTENUATION

Attenuation, like other exceptions to the exclusionary rule, serves to limit suppression as an outcome in criminal prosecutions. Pursuant to the attenuation doctrine, as described by one lower court, "exclusion is

---

[22] *See* Stephanie Barry, *Holyoke grandfather, owner of 'How to practice child love' manual pleads guilty to receipt of child porn*, MASSLIVE.COM (Jan. 30, 2018), http://www.masslive.com/news/index.ssf/2018/01/holyoke_grandfather_owner_of_h.html; Stephanie Barry, *Local child porn cases may hang in the balance pending federal appeals decision*, MASSLIVE.COM (May 10, 2017), http://www.masslive.com/news/index.ssf/2017/05/local_child_porn_cases_may_han.html.

improper when the connection between the illegality and the discovery of the challenged evidence has 'become so attenuated as to dissipate the taint.' "[23] Traditionally, attenuation "only applies to derivative evidence because the nexus between an illegal search and direct or primary evidence (e.g., evidence seized from the pocket of a person illegally arrested) 'is both proximate and strong, not 'remote' or 'attenuated.' "[24]

WONG SUN V. UNITED STATES

371 U.S. 471
Supreme Court of the United States
March 29 and April 2, 1962, Argued; January 14, 1963, Decided
No. 36

MR. JUSTICE BRENNAN delivered the opinion of the Court.

* * * About 2 a. m. on the morning of June 4, 1959, federal narcotics agents in San Francisco, after having had one Hom Way under surveillance for six weeks, arrested him and found heroin in his possession. Hom Way, who had not before been an informant, stated after his arrest that he had bought an ounce of heroin the night before from one known to him only as "Blackie Toy," proprietor of a laundry on Leavenworth Street.

About 6 a. m. that morning six or seven federal agents went to a laundry at 1733 Leavenworth Street. The sign above the door of this establishment said "Oye's Laundry." It was operated by the petitioner James Wah Toy. There is, however, nothing in the record which identifies James Wah Toy and "Blackie Toy" as the same person. The other federal officers remained nearby out of sight while Agent Alton Wong, who was of Chinese ancestry, rang the bell. When petitioner Toy appeared and opened the door, Agent Wong told him that he was calling for laundry and dry cleaning. Toy replied that he didn't open until 8 o'clock and told the agent to come back at that time. Toy started to close the door. Agent Wong thereupon took his badge from his pocket and said, "I am a federal narcotics agent." Toy immediately "slammed the door and started running" down the hallway through the laundry to his living quarters at the back where his wife and child were sleeping in a bedroom. Agent Wong and the other federal officers broke open the door and followed Toy down the hallway to the living quarters and into the bedroom. Toy reached into a nightstand drawer. Agent Wong thereupon drew his pistol, pulled Toy's hand out of the drawer, placed him under arrest and handcuffed him. There was nothing in the drawer and a search of the premises uncovered no narcotics.

---

[23] *People v. Frazier*, 733 N.W.2d 713, 726 (Mich. 2007) (quoting *Wong Sun v. United States*, 371 U.S. 471, 487 (1963)).

[24] Tracey Maclin & Jennifer Rader, *The Exclusionary Rule: No More Chipping Away: The Roberts Court Uses an Axe to Take Out the Fourth Amendment Exclusionary Rule*, 81 MISS. L.J. 1183, 1218 (2012).

One of the agents said to Toy ". . . [Hom Way] says he got narcotics from you." Toy responded, "No, I haven't been selling any narcotics at all. However, I do know somebody who has." When asked who that was, Toy said, "I only know him as Johnny. I don't know his last name." However, Toy described a house on Eleventh Avenue where he said Johnny lived; he also described a bedroom in the house where he said "Johnny kept about a piece"[2] of heroin, and where he and Johnny had smoked some of the drug the night before. The agents left immediately for Eleventh Avenue and located the house. They entered and found one Johnny Yee in the bedroom. After a discussion with the agents, Yee took from a bureau drawer several tubes containing in all just less than one ounce of heroin, and surrendered them. Within the hour Yee and Toy were taken to the Office of the Bureau of Narcotics. Yee there stated that the heroin had been brought to him some four days earlier by petitioner Toy and another Chinese known to him only as "Sea Dog."

Toy was questioned as to the identity of "Sea Dog" and said that "Sea Dog" was Wong Sun. Some agents, including Agent Alton Wong, took Toy to Wong Sun's neighborhood where Toy pointed out a multifamily dwelling where he said Wong Sun lived. Agent Wong rang a downstairs door bell and a buzzer sounded, opening the door. The officer identified himself as a narcotics agent to a woman on the landing and asked "for Mr. Wong." The woman was the wife of petitioner Wong Sun. She said that Wong Sun was "in the back room sleeping." Alton Wong and some six other officers climbed the stairs and entered the apartment. One of the officers went into the back room and brought petitioner Wong Sun from the bedroom in handcuffs. A thorough search of the apartment followed, but no narcotics were discovered.

Petitioner Toy and Johnny Yee were arraigned before a United States Commissioner on June 4 on a complaint charging a violation of 21 U.S.C. § 174. Later that day, each was released on his own recognizance. Petitioner Wong Sun was arraigned on a similar complaint filed the next day and was also released on his own recognizance. Within a few days, both petitioners and Yee were interrogated at the office of the Narcotics Bureau by Agent William Wong, also of Chinese ancestry.[4] The agent advised each of the three of his right to withhold information which might be used against him, and stated to each that he was entitled to the advice of counsel, though it does not appear that any attorney was present during the questioning of any of the three. The officer also explained to each that no promises or offers of immunity or leniency were being or could be made.

---

[2] A "piece" is approximately one ounce.

[4] Because neither statement was ever signed, the blanks in which the dates were to have been inserted were never filled in. The heading of Toy's statement suggests that it was made on June 5, although Agent William Wong at the trial suggested he had only talked informally with Toy on that date, the formal statement not being made until June 9. The agent also testified that Wong Sun's statement was made June 9, although a rubber-stamp date beneath the agent's own signature at the foot of the statement reads, "June 15, 1959."

The agent interrogated each of the three separately. After each had been interrogated the agent prepared a statement in English from rough notes. The agent read petitioner Toy's statement to him in English and interpreted certain portions of it for him in Chinese. Toy also read the statement in English aloud to the agent, said there were corrections to be made, and made the corrections in his own hand. Toy would not sign the statement, however; in the agent's words "he wanted to know first if the other persons involved in the case had signed theirs." Wong Sun had considerable difficulty understanding the statement in English and the agent restated its substance in Chinese. Wong Sun refused to sign the statement although he admitted the accuracy of its contents.

Hom Way did not testify at petitioners' trial. The Government offered Johnny Yee as its principal witness but excused him after he invoked the privilege against self-incrimination and flatly repudiated the statement he had given to Agent William Wong. That statement was not offered in evidence nor was any testimony elicited from him identifying either petitioner as the source of the heroin in his possession, or otherwise tending to support the charges against the petitioners.

The statute expressly provides that proof of the accused's possession of the drug will support a conviction under the statute unless the accused satisfactorily explains the possession. The Government's evidence tending to prove the petitioners' possession (the petitioners offered no exculpatory testimony) consisted of four items which the trial court admitted over timely objections that they were inadmissible as "fruits" of unlawful arrests or of attendant searches: (1) the statements made orally by petitioner Toy in his bedroom at the time of his arrest; (2) the heroin surrendered to the agents by Johnny Yee; (3) petitioner Toy's pretrial unsigned statement; and (4) petitioner Wong Sun's similar statement. The dispute below and here has centered around the correctness of the rulings of the trial judge allowing these items in evidence.

* * * The Court of Appeals * * * held that the four items of proof were not the "fruits" of the illegal arrests and that they were therefore properly admitted in evidence. * * *

We believe that significant differences between the cases of the two petitioners require separate discussion of each. We shall first consider the case of petitioner Toy.

I

The Court of Appeals found there was neither reasonable grounds nor probable cause for Toy's arrest. Giving due weight to that finding, we think it is amply justified by the facts clearly shown on this record. * * *

It is conceded that the officers made no attempt to obtain a warrant for Toy's arrest. The simple fact is that on the sparse information at the officers' command, no arrest warrant could have issued * * *. * * * Thus we conclude that the Court of Appeals' finding that the officers' uninvited entry into Toy's living quarters was unlawful and that the bedroom arrest which followed was likewise unlawful, was fully justified on the evidence. It remains to be seen what consequences flow from this conclusion.

II

It is conceded that Toy's declarations in his bedroom are to be excluded if they are held to be "fruits" of the agents' unlawful action. * * *

The exclusionary rule has traditionally barred from trial physical, tangible materials obtained either during or as a direct result of an unlawful invasion. It follows from our holding in *Silverman v. United States*, 365 U.S. 505, that the Fourth Amendment may protect against the overhearing of verbal statements as well as against the more traditional seizure of "papers and effects." Similarly, testimony as to matters observed during an unlawful invasion has been excluded in order to enforce the basic constitutional policies. Thus, verbal evidence which derives so immediately from an unlawful entry and an unauthorized arrest as the officers' action in the present case is no less the "fruit" of official illegality than the more common tangible fruits of the unwarranted intrusion. Nor do the policies underlying the exclusionary rule invite any logical distinction between physical and verbal evidence. Either in terms of deterring lawless conduct by federal officers, or of closing the doors of the federal courts to any use of evidence unconstitutionally obtained, the danger in relaxing the exclusionary rules in the case of verbal evidence would seem too great to warrant introducing such a distinction.

The Government argues that Toy's statements to the officers in his bedroom, although closely consequent upon the invasion which we hold unlawful, were nevertheless admissible because they resulted from "an intervening independent act of a free will." This contention, however, takes insufficient account of the circumstances. Six or seven officers had broken the door and followed on Toy's heels into the bedroom where his wife and child were sleeping. He had been almost immediately handcuffed and arrested. Under such circumstances it is unreasonable to infer that Toy's response was sufficiently an act of free will to purge the primary taint of the unlawful invasion. * * *

III

We now consider whether the exclusion of Toy's declarations requires also the exclusion of the narcotics taken from Yee, to which those declarations led the police. The prosecutor candidly told the trial court that "we wouldn't have found those drugs except that Mr. Toy helped us to." Hence this is not the case envisioned by this Court where the exclusionary rule has no application because the Government learned of the evidence "from an independent source," *Silverthorne Lumber Co. v. United States*,

251 U.S. 385, 392; nor is this a case in which the connection between the lawless conduct of the police and the discovery of the challenged evidence has "become so attenuated as to dissipate the taint." We need not hold that all evidence is "fruit of the poisonous tree" simply because it would not have come to light but for the illegal actions of the police. Rather, the more apt question in such a case is "whether, granting establishment of the primary illegality, the evidence to which instant objection is made has been come at by exploitation of that illegality or instead by means sufficiently distinguishable to be purged of the primary taint." We think it clear that the narcotics were "come at by the exploitation of that illegality" and hence that they may not be used against Toy.

IV

It remains only to consider Toy's unsigned statement. We need not decide whether, in light of the fact that Toy was free on his own recognizance when he made the statement, that statement was a fruit of the illegal arrest. Since we have concluded that his declarations in the bedroom and the narcotics surrendered by Yee should not have been admitted in evidence against him, the only proofs remaining to sustain his conviction are his and Wong Sun's unsigned statements. Without scrutinizing the contents of Toy's ambiguous recitals, we conclude that no reference to Toy in Wong Sun's statement constitutes admissible evidence corroborating any admission by Toy. * * * [Ed. note: the Court then discussed non-constitutional supporting rationale to explain why Toy's unsigned statement was not admissible.]

V

We turn now to the case of the other petitioner, Wong Sun. We have no occasion to disagree with the finding of the Court of Appeals that his arrest, also, was without probable cause or reasonable grounds. At all events no evidentiary consequences turn upon that question. For Wong Sun's unsigned confession was not the fruit of that arrest, and was therefore properly admitted at trial. On the evidence that Wong Sun had been released on his own recognizance after a lawful arraignment, and had returned voluntarily several days later to make the statement, we hold that the connection between the arrest and the statement had "become so attenuated as to dissipate the taint." The fact that the statement was unsigned, whatever bearing this may have upon its weight and credibility, does not render it inadmissible; Wong Sun understood and adopted its substance, though he could not comprehend the English words. The petitioner has never suggested any impropriety in the interrogation itself which would require the exclusion of this statement.

We must then consider the admissibility of the narcotics surrendered by Yee. Our holding, *supra*, that this ounce of heroin was inadmissible against Toy does not compel a like result with respect to Wong Sun. The exclusion of the narcotics as to Toy was required solely by their tainted relationship to information unlawfully obtained from Toy, and not by any official impropriety connected with their surrender by Yee. The seizure of this heroin invaded no right of privacy of person or premises which would entitle Wong Sun to object to its use at his trial.

[Ed. note: the Court then discussed reasons unrelated to the fruits doctrine that entitled Wong Sun to a new trial.]

The judgment of the Court of Appeals is reversed and the case is remanded to the District Court for further proceedings consistent with this opinion.

It is so ordered.

APPENDIX TO OPINION OF THE COURT.

[Omitted.]

MR. JUSTICE DOUGLAS, concurring.

[Omitted.]

MR. JUSTICE CLARK, with whom MR. JUSTICE HARLAN, MR. JUSTICE STEWART and MR. JUSTICE WHITE join, dissenting.

[Omitted.]

QUESTIONS, COMMENTS, CONCERNS?

1. **When does attenuation apply?** One very real challenge presented by *Wong Sun* is trying to understand when to apply the attenuation doctrine. Many courts, including the Supreme Court in one of the cases we read below, *Utah v. Strieff*, 579 U.S. 232 (2016), consider a list of factors that originated in *Brown v. Illinois*, 422 U.S. 590 (1975). A recent federal district court aptly summarized those factors and their role in the attenuation analysis:

> First, the Court looks to the "temporal proximity" between the unconstitutional conduct and the discovery of evidence to determine how closely the discovery of evidence followed the unconstitutional search. This factor often favors suppressing the evidence unless "substantial time" elapses between an unlawful act and the time the evidence is obtained. The Supreme Court has previously concluded that a time span of "less than two hours" between the unconstitutional arrest and the confession was too short an interval, and, therefore, counseled in favor of suppressing the evidence.
>
> Second, the Court considers "the presence of intervening circumstances." The Supreme Court found sufficient intervening circumstances to admit the evidence in *Segura v. United States*, 468 U.S. 796 (1984) * * *. There, agents had probable cause to believe that apartment occupants were dealing cocaine. They sought a warrant. In the meantime, they entered the apartment, arrested the occupant,

and discovered evidence of drug activity during their security sweep. The next evening, they obtained a search warrant. The Supreme Court deemed the evidence admissible, notwithstanding the illegal search, because the information supporting the warrant was "wholly unconnected with the entry and was known to the agents well before the initial entry." The Supreme Court suggested that "the existence of a valid warrant favors finding that the connection between unlawful conduct and the discovery of evidence is 'sufficiently attenuated to dissipate the taint.' "

Third, and "particularly" significant under the Supreme Court's analysis, the Court examines "the purpose and flagrancy of the official misconduct." The exclusionary rule exists to deter police misconduct. The third factor reflects this rationale by favoring exclusion "only when the police misconduct is most in need of deterrence—that is, when it is purposeful or flagrant." Mere negligence in violating the Fourth Amendment "hardly rise[s] to a purposeful or flagrant violation."

United States v. Ramos, 194 F. Supp. 3d 1134, 1162–63 (D.N.M. 2016).

2.   Comment. *Wong Sun* is one of the hardest cases in the Casebook. Below are a handful of questions to make sure that you understand the case. As you consider the questions, be sure to compare who the police seized contraband from alongside who the prosecution seeks to introduce contraband against. That comparison is important because of the standing doctrine. That is, a defendant cannot seek to suppress contraband unless law enforcement's unconstitutional action violated his personal rights. As the Supreme Court in *Rakas v. Illinois* explained, one must show that "the disputed search and seizure has infringed an interest of the defendant which the Fourth Amendment was designed to protect." 439 U.S. 128, 140 (1978).

3.   Question. Can the drugs found on Yee be used against Toy?

4.   Question. Is Wong Sun's pretrial unsigned statement to narcotics agents—made after his arraignment and release on personal recognizance—admissible against him?

5.   Question. Are the drugs surrendered by Yee admissible against Wong Sun?

UNITED STATES V. CECCOLINI

435 U.S. 268
Supreme Court of the United States
Argued December 5, 1977; March 21, 1978; As Amended
No. 76-1151

MR. JUSTICE REHNQUIST delivered the opinion of the Court.

In December 1974, Ronald Biro, a uniformed police officer on assignment to patrol school crossings, entered respondent's place of business, the Sleepy Hollow Flower Shop, in North Tarrytown, N.Y. He went behind the customer counter and, in the words of Ichabod Crane, one of Tarrytown's more illustrious inhabitants of days gone past, "tarried," spending his short break engaged in conversation with his friend Lois Hennessey, an employee of the shop. During the course of the conversation he noticed an envelope with money sticking out of it lying on the drawer of the cash register behind the counter. Biro picked up the envelope and, upon examining its contents, discovered that it contained not only money but policy slips. He placed the envelope back on the register and, without telling Hennessey what he had seen, asked her to whom the envelope belonged. She replied that the envelope belonged to respondent Ceccolini, and that he had instructed her to give it to someone.

The next day, Officer Biro mentioned his discovery to North Tarrytown detectives who in turn told Lance Emory, an FBI agent. This very ordinary incident in the lives of Biro and Hennessey requires us, over three years later, to decide whether Hennessey's testimony against respondent Ceccolini should have been suppressed in his trial for perjury. Respondent was charged with that offense because he denied that he knew anything of, or was in any way involved with, gambling operations. Respondent was found guilty after a bench trial in the United States District Court for the Southern District of New York, but immediately after the finding of guilt the District Court granted respondent's motion to "suppress" the testimony of Hennessey because the court concluded that the testimony was a "fruit of the poisonous tree"; assuming respondent's motion for a directed verdict included a motion to set aside the verdict of guilty, the District Court granted the motion because it concluded that without Hennessey's testimony there was insufficient evidence of respondent's guilt. The Government appealed these rulings to the Court of Appeals for the Second Circuit. [The Second Circuit affirmed.] * * *

II

The "road" to which the Court of Appeals analogized the train of events from Biro's discovery of the policy slips to Hennessey's testimony at respondent's trial for perjury is one of literally thousands of such roads traveled periodically between an original investigative discovery and the ultimate trial of the accused. The constitutional question under the Fourth Amendment was phrased in *Wong Sun v. United States*, 371 U.S. 471 (1963), as whether "the connection between the lawless conduct of the police and the discovery of the challenged evidence has 'become so attenuated as to dissipate the taint.'" * * *

* * * We * * * reaffirm the holding of *Wong Sun, supra*, at 485, that "verbal evidence which derives so immediately from an unlawful entry and an unauthorized arrest as the officers' action in the present case is no less the 'fruit' of official illegality than the more common tangible fruits of the

unwarranted intrusion." We are of the view, however, that cases decided since *Wong Sun* significantly qualify its further observation that "the policies underlying the exclusionary rule [do not] invite any logical distinction between physical and verbal evidence." Rather, at least in a case such as this, where not only was the alleged "fruit of the poisonous tree" the testimony of a live witness, but unlike *Wong Sun* the witness was not a putative defendant, an examination of our cases persuades us that the Court of Appeals was simply wrong in concluding that if the road were uninterrupted, its length was immaterial. Its length, we hold, is material, as are certain other factors enumerated below to which the court gave insufficient weight.

* * * We have limited the standing requirement in the exclusionary rule context because the "additional benefits of extending the . . . rule" to persons other than the ones subject to the illegal search are outweighed by the "further encroachment upon the public interest in prosecuting those accused of crime and having them acquitted or convicted on the basis of all the evidence which exposes the truth." Even in situations where the exclusionary rule is plainly applicable, we have declined to adopt a "per se or 'but for' rule" that would make inadmissible any evidence, whether tangible or live-witness testimony, which somehow came to light through a chain of causation that began with an illegal arrest.

Evaluating the standards for application of the exclusionary rule to live-witness testimony in light of this balance, we are first impelled to conclude that the degree of free will exercised by the witness is not irrelevant in determining the extent to which the basic purpose of the exclusionary rule will be advanced by its application. This is certainly true when the challenged statements are made by a putative defendant after arrest, and *a fortiori* is true of testimony given by nondefendants.

The greater the willingness of the witness to freely testify, the greater the likelihood that he or she will be discovered by legal means and, concomitantly, the smaller the incentive to conduct an illegal search to discover the witness. Witnesses are not like guns or documents which remain hidden from view until one turns over a sofa or opens a filing cabinet. Witnesses can, and often do, come forward and offer evidence entirely of their own volition. And evaluated properly, the degree of free will necessary to dissipate the taint will very likely be found more often in the case of live-witness testimony than other kinds of evidence. The time, place and manner of the initial questioning of the witness may be such that any statements are truly the product of detached reflection and a desire to be cooperative on the part of the witness. And the illegality which led to the discovery of the witness very often will not play any meaningful part in the witness' willingness to testify. * * *

Another factor which not only is relevant in determining the usefulness of the exclusionary rule in a particular context, but also seems to us to differentiate the testimony of all live witnesses even putative defendants from the exclusion of the typical documentary evidence, is that such exclusion would perpetually disable a witness from testifying about relevant and material facts, regardless of how unrelated such testimony might be to the purpose of the originally illegal search or the evidence discovered thereby. Rules which disqualify knowledgeable witnesses from testifying at trial are, in the words of Professor McCormick, "serious obstructions to the ascertainment of truth"; accordingly, "[f]or a century the course of legal evolution has been in the direction of sweeping away these obstructions." * * *

In short, since the cost of excluding live-witness testimony often will be greater, a closer, more direct link between the illegality and that kind of testimony is required.

This is not to say, of course, that live-witness testimony is always or even usually more reliable or dependable than inanimate evidence. Indeed, just the opposite may be true. But a determination that the discovery of certain evidence is sufficiently unrelated to or independent of the constitutional violation to permit its introduction at trial is not a determination which rests on the comparative reliability of that evidence. Attenuation analysis, appropriately concerned with the differences between live-witness testimony and inanimate evidence, can consistently focus on the factors enumerated above with respect to the former, but on different factors with respect to the latter. * * *

III

Viewing this case in the light of the principles just discussed, we hold that the Court of Appeals erred in holding that the degree of attenuation was not sufficient to dissipate the connection between the illegality and the testimony. The evidence indicates overwhelmingly that the testimony given by the witness was an act of her own free will in no way coerced or even induced by official authority as a result of Biro's discovery of the policy slips. Nor were the slips themselves used in questioning Hennessey. Substantial periods of time elapsed between the time of the illegal search and the initial contact with the witness, on the one hand, and between the latter and the testimony at trial on the other. While the particular knowledge to which Hennessey testified at trial can be logically traced back to Biro's discovery of the policy slips, both the identity of Hennessey and her relationship with the respondent were well known to those investigating the case. There is, in addition, not the slightest evidence to suggest that Biro entered the shop or picked up the envelope with the intent of finding tangible evidence bearing on an illicit gambling operation, much less any suggestion that he entered the shop and searched with the intent of finding a willing and knowledgeable witness to testify against respondent. Application of the exclusionary rule in this situation could not have the slightest deterrent effect on the behavior of an officer such as Biro. The cost of permanently silencing Hennessey is too great for an evenhanded system of law enforcement to bear in order to secure such a speculative and very likely negligible deterrent effect.

Obviously no mathematical weight can be assigned to any of the factors which we have discussed, but just as obviously they all point to the conclusion that the exclusionary rule should be invoked with much greater reluctance where the claim is based on a causal relationship between a constitutional violation and the discovery of a live witness than when a similar claim is advanced to support suppression of an inanimate object. The judgment of the Court of Appeals is accordingly

Reversed.

MR. JUSTICE BLACKMUN took no part in the consideration or decision of this case.

MR. CHIEF JUSTICE BURGER, concurring in the judgment.

[Omitted.]

MR. JUSTICE MARSHALL, with whom MR. JUSTICE BRENNAN joins, dissenting.

[Omitted.]

QUESTIONS, COMMENTS, CONCERNS?

1.   Question. The *Wong Sun* Court commented, "Nor do the policies underlying the exclusionary rule invite any logical distinction between physical and verbal evidence." Witnesses are physical evidence, right? If so, why is this language from *Wong Sun* inapplicable in *Ceccolini*?

2.   Question. Why is the *Ceccolini* Court more reluctant to automatically apply the exclusionary rule in the context of live witnesses?

UTAH V. STRIEFF
579 U.S. 232
Supreme Court of the United States
February 22, 2016, Argued; June 20, 2016, Decided
No. 14-1373

JUSTICE THOMAS delivered the opinion of the Court.

To enforce the Fourth Amendment's prohibition against "unreasonable searches and seizures," this Court has at times required courts to exclude evidence obtained by unconstitutional police conduct. [But] [i]n some cases * * * the link between the unconstitutional conduct and the discovery of the evidence is too attenuated to justify suppression. The question in this case is whether this attenuation doctrine applies when an officer makes an unconstitutional investigatory stop; learns during that stop that the suspect is subject to a valid arrest warrant; and proceeds to arrest the suspect and seize incriminating evidence during a search incident to that arrest. * * *

I

This case began with an anonymous tip. In December 2006, someone called the South Salt Lake City police's drug-tip line to report "narcotics activity" at a particular residence. Narcotics detective Douglas Fackrell investigated the tip. Over the course of about a week, Officer Fackrell conducted intermittent surveillance of the home. He observed visitors who left a few minutes after arriving at the house. These visits were sufficiently frequent to raise his suspicion that the occupants were dealing drugs.

One of those visitors was respondent Edward Strieff. Officer Fackrell observed Strieff exit the house and walk toward a nearby convenience store. In the store's parking lot, Officer Fackrell detained Strieff, identified himself, and asked Strieff what he was doing at the residence.

As part of the stop, Officer Fackrell requested Strieff's identification, and Strieff produced his Utah identification card. Officer Fackrell relayed Strieff's information to a police dispatcher, who reported that Strieff had an outstanding arrest warrant for a traffic violation. Officer Fackrell then arrested Strieff pursuant to that warrant. When Officer Fackrell searched Strieff incident to the arrest, he discovered a baggie of methamphetamine and drug paraphernalia.

The State charged Strieff with unlawful possession of methamphetamine and drug paraphernalia. Strieff moved to suppress the evidence, arguing that the evidence was inadmissible because it was derived from an unlawful investigatory stop. At the suppression hearing, the prosecutor conceded that Officer Fackrell lacked reasonable suspicion for the stop but argued that the evidence should not be suppressed because the existence of a valid arrest warrant attenuated the connection between the unlawful stop and the discovery of the contraband.

The trial court agreed with the State and admitted the evidence. * * * Strieff conditionally pleaded guilty to reduced charges of attempted possession of a controlled substance and possession of drug paraphernalia, but reserved his right to appeal the trial court's denial of the suppression motion. The Utah Court of Appeals affirmed.

The Utah Supreme Court reversed. * * * We granted certiorari to resolve disagreement about how the attenuation doctrine applies where an unconstitutional detention leads to the discovery of a valid arrest warrant. * * *

II

A

The Fourth Amendment protects "[t]he right of the people to be secure in their persons, houses, papers, and effects, against unreasonable searches and seizures." * * * In the 20th century * * * the exclusionary rule—the rule that often requires trial courts to exclude unlawfully seized evidence in a criminal trial—became the principal judicial remedy to deter Fourth Amendment violations.

Under the Court's precedents, the exclusionary rule encompasses both the "primary evidence obtained as a direct result of an illegal search or seizure" and, relevant here, "evidence later discovered and found to be derivative of an illegality," the so-called " 'fruit of the poisonous tree.' " But the significant costs of this rule have led us to deem it "applicable only . . . where its deterrence benefits outweigh its substantial social costs." *Hudson v. Michigan*, 547 U.S. 586, 591 (2006) (internal quotation marks omitted). "Suppression of evidence . . . has always been our last resort, not our first impulse." *Ibid.*

We have accordingly recognized several exceptions to the rule. * * * [A]t issue here * * * is the attenuation doctrine: Evidence is admissible when the connection between unconstitutional police conduct and the evidence is remote or has been interrupted by some intervening circumstance, so that "the interest protected by the constitutional guarantee that has been violated would not be served by suppression of the evidence obtained." *Hudson, supra,* at 593.

B

Turning to the application of the attenuation doctrine to this case, we first address a threshold question: whether this doctrine applies at all to a case like this, where the intervening circumstance that the State relies on is the discovery of a valid, pre-existing, and untainted arrest warrant. [It does.] The attenuation doctrine evaluates the causal link between the government's unlawful act and the discovery of evidence, which often has nothing to do with a defendant's actions. And the logic of our prior attenuation cases is not limited to independent acts by the defendant.

It remains for us to address whether the discovery of a valid arrest warrant was a sufficient intervening event to break the causal chain between the unlawful stop and the discovery of drug-related evidence on Strieff's person. The three factors articulated in *Brown v. Illinois*, 422 U.S. 590 (1975), guide our analysis. First, we look to the "temporal proximity" between the unconstitutional conduct and the discovery of evidence to determine how closely the discovery of evidence followed the unconstitutional search. *Id.*, at 603. Second, we consider "the presence of intervening circumstances." *Id.*, at 603–604. Third, and "particularly" significant, we examine "the purpose and flagrancy of the official misconduct." *Id.*, at 604. In evaluating these factors, we assume without deciding (because the State conceded the point) that Officer Fackrell lacked reasonable suspicion to initially stop Strieff. And, because we ultimately conclude that the warrant breaks the causal chain, we also have no need to decide whether the warrant's existence alone would make the initial stop constitutional even if Officer Fackrell was unaware of its existence.

1

The first factor, temporal proximity between the initially unlawful stop and the search, favors suppressing the evidence. Our precedents have declined to find that this factor favors attenuation unless "substantial time" elapses between an unlawful act and when the evidence is obtained. Here, however, Officer Fackrell discovered drug contraband on Strieff's person only minutes after the illegal stop. As the Court explained in *Brown*, such a short time interval counsels in favor of suppression; there, we found that the confession should be suppressed, relying in part on the "less than two hours" that separated the unconstitutional arrest and the confession.

In contrast, the second factor, the presence of intervening circumstances, strongly favors the State. * * * [We have previously] suggested that the existence of a valid warrant favors finding that the connection between unlawful conduct and the discovery of evidence is "sufficiently attenuated to dissipate the taint." That principle applies here.

In this case, the warrant was valid, it predated Officer Fackrell's investigation, and it was entirely unconnected with the stop. And once Officer Fackrell discovered the warrant, he had an obligation to arrest Strieff. * * * Officer Fackrell's arrest of Strieff thus was a ministerial act that was independently compelled by the pre-existing warrant. And once Officer Fackrell was authorized to arrest Strieff, it was undisputedly lawful to search Strieff as an incident of his arrest to protect Officer Fackrell's safety.

Finally, the third factor, "the purpose and flagrancy of the official misconduct," *Brown, supra,* at 604, also strongly favors the State. The exclusionary rule exists to deter police misconduct. The third factor of the attenuation doctrine reflects that rationale by favoring exclusion only when the police misconduct is most in need of deterrence—that is, when it is purposeful or flagrant.

Officer Fackrell was at most negligent. In stopping Strieff, Officer Fackrell made two good-faith mistakes. First, he had not observed what time Strieff entered the suspected drug house, so he did not know how long Strieff had been there. Officer Fackrell thus lacked a sufficient basis to conclude that Strieff was a short-term visitor who may have been consummating a drug transaction. Second, because he lacked confirmation that Strieff was a short-term visitor, Officer Fackrell should have asked

Strieff whether he would speak with him, instead of demanding that Strieff do so. Officer Fackrell's stated purpose was to "find out what was going on [in] the house." Nothing prevented him from approaching Strieff simply to ask. But these errors in judgment hardly rise to a purposeful or flagrant violation of Strieff's Fourth Amendment rights. * * *

Moreover, there is no indication that this unlawful stop was part of any systemic or recurrent police misconduct. To the contrary, all the evidence suggests that the stop was an isolated instance of negligence that occurred in connection with a bona fide investigation of a suspected drug house. Officer Fackrell saw Strieff leave a suspected drug house. And his suspicion about the house was based on an anonymous tip and his personal observations.

Applying these factors, we hold that the evidence discovered on Strieff's person was admissible because the unlawful stop was sufficiently attenuated by the pre-existing arrest warrant. Although the illegal stop was close in time to Strieff's arrest, that consideration is outweighed by two factors supporting the State. The outstanding arrest warrant for Strieff's arrest is a critical intervening circumstance that is wholly independent of the illegal stop. The discovery of that warrant broke the causal chain between the unconstitutional stop and the discovery of evidence by compelling Officer Fackrell to arrest Strieff. And, it is especially significant that there is no evidence that Officer Fackrell's illegal stop reflected flagrantly unlawful police misconduct.

2

* * * Strieff argues that, because of the prevalence of outstanding arrest warrants in many jurisdictions, police will engage in dragnet searches if the exclusionary rule is not applied. We think that this outcome is unlikely. Such wanton conduct would expose police to civil liability. And in any event, the *Brown* factors take account of the purpose and flagrancy of police misconduct. Were evidence of a dragnet search presented here, the application of the *Brown* factors could be different. But there is no evidence that the concerns that Strieff raises with the criminal justice system are present in South Salt Lake City, Utah.

     * * *

We hold that the evidence Officer Fackrell seized as part of his search incident to arrest is admissible because his discovery of the arrest warrant attenuated the connection between the unlawful stop and the evidence seized from Strieff incident to arrest. The judgment of the Utah Supreme Court, accordingly, is reversed.

It is so ordered.

JUSTICE SOTOMAYOR, with whom JUSTICE GINSBURG joins as to Parts I, II, and III, dissenting.

The Court today holds that the discovery of a warrant for an unpaid parking ticket will forgive a police officer's violation of your Fourth Amendment rights. Do not be soothed by the opinion's technical language: This case allows the police to stop you on the street, demand your identification, and check it for outstanding traffic warrants—even if you are doing nothing wrong. If the officer discovers a warrant for a fine you forgot to pay, courts will now excuse his illegal stop and will admit into evidence anything he happens to find by searching you after arresting you on the warrant. Because the Fourth Amendment should prohibit, not permit, such misconduct, I dissent. * * *

II

It is tempting in a case like this, where illegal conduct by an officer uncovers illegal conduct by a civilian, to forgive the officer. After all, his instincts, although unconstitutional, were correct. But a basic principle lies at the heart of the Fourth Amendment: Two wrongs don't make a right. *See Weeks v. United States*, 232 U.S. 383, 392 (1914). When "lawless police conduct" uncovers evidence of lawless civilian conduct, this Court has long required later criminal trials to exclude the illegally obtained evidence. * * * *Mapp v. Ohio*, 367 U.S. 643, 655 (1961). For example, if an officer breaks into a home and finds a forged check lying around, that check may not be used to prosecute the homeowner for bank fraud. We would describe the check as " 'fruit of the poisonous tree.' " *Wong Sun v. United States*, 371 U.S. 471, 488 (1963). Fruit that must be cast aside includes not only evidence directly found by an illegal search but also evidence "come at by exploitation of that illegality." *Ibid.*

This "exclusionary rule" removes an incentive for officers to search us without proper justification. * * * But when courts admit illegally obtained evidence as well, they reward "manifest neglect if not an open defiance of the prohibitions of the Constitution." *Weeks*, 232 U.S., at 394.

Applying the exclusionary rule, the Utah Supreme Court correctly decided that Strieff's drugs must be excluded because the officer exploited his illegal stop to discover them. The officer found the drugs only after learning of Strieff's traffic violation; and he learned of Strieff's traffic violation only because he unlawfully stopped Strieff to check his driver's license.

The court also correctly rejected the State's argument that the officer's discovery of a traffic warrant unspoiled the poisonous fruit. The State analogizes finding the warrant to one of our earlier decisions, *Wong Sun v. United States*. There, an officer illegally arrested a person who, days later, voluntarily returned to the station to confess to committing a crime. Even though the person would not have confessed "but for the illegal actions of the police," we noted that the police did not exploit their illegal arrest to obtain the confession. Because the confession was obtained by "means sufficiently distinguishable" from the constitutional violation, we held that it could be admitted into evidence. The State contends that the search incident to the warrant-arrest here is similarly distinguishable from the illegal stop.

But *Wong Sun* explains why Strieff's drugs must be excluded. We reasoned that a Fourth Amendment violation may not color every investigation that follows but it certainly stains the actions of officers who exploit the infraction. We distinguished evidence obtained by innocuous means from evidence obtained by exploiting misconduct after considering a variety of factors: whether a long time passed, whether there were "intervening circumstances," and whether the purpose or flagrancy of the misconduct was "calculated" to procure the evidence. *Brown v. Illinois*, 422 U.S. 590, 603–604 (1975).

These factors confirm that the officer in this case discovered Strieff's drugs by exploiting his own illegal conduct. The officer did not ask Strieff to volunteer his name only to find out, days later, that Strieff had a warrant against him. The officer illegally stopped Strieff and immediately ran a warrant check. The officer's discovery of a warrant was not some intervening surprise that he could not have anticipated. Utah lists over 180,000 misdemeanor warrants in its database, and at the time of the arrest, Salt Lake County had a "backlog of outstanding warrants" so large that it faced the "potential for civil liability." The officer's violation was also calculated to procure evidence. His sole reason for stopping Strieff, he acknowledged, was investigative—he wanted to discover whether drug activity was going on in the house Strieff had just exited.

The warrant check, in other words, was not an "intervening circumstance" separating the stop from the search for drugs. It was part and parcel of the officer's illegal "expedition for evidence in the hope that something might turn up." *Brown*, 422 U.S., at 605. Under our precedents, because the officer found Strieff's drugs by exploiting his own constitutional violation, the drugs should be excluded.

III

* * * Most striking about the Court's opinion is its insistence that the event here was "isolated," with "no indication that this unlawful stop was part of any systemic or recurrent police misconduct." Respectfully, nothing about this case is isolated.

Outstanding warrants are surprisingly common. When a person with a traffic ticket misses a fine payment or court appearance, a court will issue a warrant. When a person on probation drinks alcohol or breaks curfew, a court will issue a warrant. The States and Federal Government maintain databases with over 7.8 million outstanding warrants, the vast majority of which appear to be for minor offenses. Even these sources may not track the "staggering" numbers of warrants, " 'drawers and drawers' " full, that many cities issue for traffic violations and ordinance infractions. The county in this case has had a "backlog" of such warrants. The Department of Justice recently reported that in the town of Ferguson, Missouri, with a population of 21,000, 16,000 people had outstanding warrants against them.

Justice Department investigations across the country have illustrated how these astounding numbers of warrants can be used by police to stop people without cause. In a single year in New Orleans, officers "made nearly 60,000 arrests, of which about 20,000 were of people with outstanding traffic or misdemeanor warrants from neighboring parishes for such infractions as unpaid tickets." In the St. Louis metropolitan area, officers "routinely" stop people—on the street, at bus stops, or even in court—for no reason other than "an officer's desire to check whether the subject had a municipal arrest warrant pending." In Newark, New Jersey, officers stopped 52,235 pedestrians within a 4-year period and ran warrant checks on 39,308 of them. The Justice Department analyzed these warrant-checked stops and reported that "approximately 93% of the stops would have been considered unsupported by articulated reasonable suspicion."

I do not doubt that most officers act in "good faith" and do not set out to break the law. That does not mean these stops are "isolated instance[s] of negligence," however. Many are the product of institutionalized training procedures. The New York City Police Department long trained officers to, in the words of a District Judge, "stop and question first, develop reasonable suspicion later." The Utah Supreme Court described as " 'routine procedure' or 'common practice' " the decision of Salt Lake City police officers to run warrant checks on pedestrians they detained without reasonable suspicion. In the related context of traffic stops, one widely followed police manual instructs officers looking for drugs to "run at least a warrants check on all drivers you stop. Statistically, narcotics offenders are . . . more likely to fail to appear on simple citations, such as traffic or trespass violations, leading to the issuance of bench warrants. Discovery of an outstanding warrant gives you cause for an immediate custodial arrest and search of the suspect."

The majority does not suggest what makes this case "isolated" from these and countless other examples. Nor does it offer guidance for how a defendant can prove that his arrest was the result of "widespread" misconduct. Surely it should not take a federal investigation of Salt Lake County before the Court would protect someone in Strieff's position. * * *

* * *

I dissent.

JUSTICE KAGAN, with whom JUSTICE GINSBURG joins, dissenting.

[Omitted.]

QUESTIONS, COMMENTS, CONCERNS?

1. **Comment.** Justice Sotomayor's dissent left its mark. Shortly after the opinion was released, Justin Driver, a law professor at the University of Chicago, commented that the dissent is "the strongest indication we have yet that the Black Lives Matter movement has made a difference at the Supreme Court—at least with one justice." Adam Liptak, *Supreme Court Says Police May Use Evidence Found After Illegal Stops*, N.Y. TIMES (June 20, 2016), https://www.nytimes.com/2016/06/21/us/supreme-court-says-police-may-use-evidence-found-after-illegal-stops.html. Another prominent media outlet, *The Atlantic*, referred to the dissent as "thundering" and one that addressed race and racism in an unusual level of detail. Matt Ford, *Justice Sotomayor's Ringing Dissent*, THEATLANTIC.COM (June 20, 2016), https://www.theatlantic.com/politics/archive/2016/06/utah-strieff-sotomayor/487922/.

2. **Beyond the Fourth Amendment.** Although *Wong Sun*, *Ceccolini*, and *Strieff* are Fourth Amendment cases, courts apply the attenuation doctrine as an exception to the Fifth and Sixth Amendment exclusionary rules. *E.g.*, *United States v. Kimball*, 884 F.2d 1274, 1279–80 (9th Cir. 1989) (Sixth Amendment); *United States v. Ahmed Khalfan Ghailani*, 743 F. Supp. 2d 261, 275–78 (S.D.N.Y. 2010) (Fifth Amendment).

3. **Burden of proof.** The prosecution bears the burden of proof at an attenuation hearing. *E.g.*, *People v. Bates*, 642 N.E.2d 774, 775 (Ill. App. Ct. 1994). In the Fourth Amendment context, the state must prove attenuation by a preponderance of the evidence. *E.g.*, *United States v. Hassanshahi*, 75 F. Supp. 3d 101, 110 (D.D.C. 2014). In the Fifth Amendment context, "[t]he prosecution must establish by a preponderance of the evidence that the defendant made the statement voluntarily in order for a challenged statement to be admitted." *People v. Medina*, 25 P.3d 1216, 1222 (Colo. 2001). The precise burden in the Sixth Amendment context is less than clear, although courts agree the burden remains with the prosecution. *United States v. Hall*, 419 F. Supp. 2d 279, 290 (E.D.N.Y. 2005); *United States v. Reyes*, 934 F. Supp. 546, 550 (S.D.N.Y. 1996).

C. INDEPENDENT SOURCE

Pursuant to the independent source exception to the exclusionary rule, unconstitutionally obtained evidence may nonetheless be admitted into evidence if the prosecution can prove by a preponderance that a genuinely independent origin exists for the evidence. Unlike the attenuation exception's traditional application just to derivative evidence, the independent source doctrine generally applies to *all* evidence acquired independently from investigators' unconstitutional activity.

The difficulty with the independent source cases, though, is determining what constitutes a "genuinely independent origin" for obtaining the challenged evidence. Oftentimes that question arises in the context of police seeking a search warrant to obtain evidence they have already seen pursuant to an unconstitutional warrantless action. It's possible that such overly zealous officers were motivated to obtain the search warrant only because of what they unlawfully saw. In that situation, the independent source exception would not apply because the officers' efforts to obtain a search warrant was not *genuinely independent* of their unconstitutional action.

But practically speaking, how would a reviewing court *actually* know if an officer's acquisition of a search warrant constitutes an independent source for challenged evidence rather than a purposeful effort to avoid the exclusionary rule? One lower court approaches that critical inquiry by asking two questions:

> First, was the magistrate's decision to issue the warrant affected by, or in reliance on, information obtained from an illegal search? Second, was the officer's decision to seek a warrant prompted by what he had seen during the illegal search? The second question is often re-worded as "would the officer have sought the warrant regardless of the illegal search?" If the answers to these questions are such that the magistrate did not rely on information found in an illegal search, and the officer's illegal search did not prompt the decision to obtain a warrant, then the challenged evidence has an independent source, and is admissible at trial. The reason is that excluding evidence that has a source independent of any police error or illegality would put the police in a worse position than they would have been without the error or illegality.

United States v. Hanhardt, 155 F. Supp. 2d 840, 847 (N.D. Ill. 2001).

MURRAY V. UNITED STATES

487 U.S. 533
Supreme Court of the United States
December 8, 1987, Argued; June 27, 1988, Decided
No. 86-995

JUSTICE SCALIA delivered the opinion of the Court.

* * * In these consolidated cases we are faced with the question whether, again assuming evidence obtained pursuant to an independently obtained search warrant, the portion of such evidence that had been observed in plain view at the time of a prior illegal entry must be suppressed.

I

Both cases arise out of the conviction of petitioner Michael F. Murray, petitioner James D. Carter, and others for conspiracy to possess and distribute illegal drugs. Insofar as relevant for our purposes, the facts are as follows: Based on information received from informants, federal law enforcement agents had been surveilling petitioner Murray and several of his co-conspirators. At about 1:45 p.m. on April 6, 1983, they observed Murray drive a truck and Carter drive a green camper, into a warehouse in South Boston. When the petitioners drove the vehicles out about 20 minutes later, the surveilling agents saw within the warehouse two individuals and a tractor-trailer rig bearing a long, dark container. Murray and Carter later turned over the truck and camper to other drivers, who were in turn followed and ultimately arrested, and the vehicles lawfully seized. Both vehicles were found to contain marijuana.

After receiving this information, several of the agents converged on the South Boston warehouse and forced entry. They found the warehouse unoccupied, but observed in plain view numerous burlap-wrapped bales that were later found to contain marijuana. They left without disturbing the bales, kept the warehouse under surveillance, and did not reenter it until they had a search warrant. In applying for the warrant, the agents did not mention the prior entry, and did not rely on any observations made during that entry. When the warrant was issued—at 10:40 p.m., approximately eight hours after the initial entry—the agents immediately reentered the warehouse and seized 270 bales of marijuana and notebooks listing customers for whom the bales were destined.

Before trial, petitioners moved to suppress the evidence found in the warehouse. The District Court denied the motion * * *. The First Circuit affirmed * * *. * * *

II

The exclusionary rule prohibits introduction into evidence of tangible materials seized during an unlawful search, *Weeks v. United States*, 232 U.S. 383 (1914), and of testimony concerning knowledge acquired during an unlawful search, *Silverman v. United States*, 365 U.S. 505 (1961). Beyond that, the exclusionary rule also prohibits the introduction of derivative evidence, both tangible and testimonial, that is the product of the primary evidence, or that is otherwise acquired as an indirect result of the unlawful search, up to the point at which the connection with the unlawful search becomes "so attenuated as to dissipate the taint," *Nardone v. United States*, 308 U.S. 338, 341 (1939). *See Wong Sun v. United States*, 371 U.S. 471, 484–485 (1963).

Almost simultaneously with our development of the exclusionary rule, in the first quarter of this century, we also announced what has come to be known as the "independent source" doctrine. *See Silverthorne Lumber Co. v. United States*, 251 U.S. 385, 392 (1920). That doctrine, which has been applied to evidence acquired not only through Fourth Amendment violations but also through Fifth and Sixth Amendment violations, has recently been described as follows:

> [T]he interest of society in deterring unlawful police conduct and the public interest in having juries receive all probative evidence of a crime are properly balanced by putting the police in the same, not a worse, position that they would have been in if no police error or misconduct had occurred. . . . When the challenged evidence has an independent source, exclusion of such evidence would put the police in a worse position than they would have been in absent any error or violation.

Nix v. Williams, 467 U.S. 431, 443 (1984)

The dispute here is over the scope of this doctrine. * * *

Our cases have used the concept of "independent source" in a more general and a more specific sense. The more general sense identifies all evidence acquired in a fashion untainted by the illegal evidence-gathering activity. Thus, where an unlawful entry has given investigators knowledge of facts x and y, but fact z has been learned by other means, fact z can be said to be admissible because derived from an "independent source." This is how we used the term in *Segura v. United States*, 468 U.S. 796 (1984). In that case, agents unlawfully entered the defendant's apartment and remained there until a search warrant was obtained. The admissibility of what they discovered while waiting in the apartment was not before us, but we held that the evidence found for the first time during the execution of the valid and untainted search warrant was admissible because it was discovered pursuant to an "independent source," *id.*, at 813–814.

The original use of the term, however, and its more important use for purposes of these cases, was more specific. It was originally applied in the exclusionary rule context, by Justice Holmes, with reference to that particular category of evidence acquired by an untainted search which is identical to the evidence unlawfully acquired—that is, in the example just given, to knowledge of facts x and y derived from an independent source:

> The essence of a provision forbidding the acquisition of evidence in a certain way is that not merely evidence so acquired shall not be used before the Court but that it shall not be used at all. Of course this does not mean that the facts thus obtained become sacred and inaccessible. If knowledge of them is gained from an independent source they may be proved like any others.

Silverthorne Lumber, supra, at 392. * * *

Petitioners' asserted policy basis for excluding evidence which is initially discovered during an illegal search, but is subsequently acquired through an independent and lawful source, is that a contrary rule will remove all deterrence to, and indeed positively encourage, unlawful police searches. As petitioners see the incentives, law enforcement officers will routinely enter without a warrant to make sure that what they expect to be on the premises is in fact there. If it is not, they will have spared themselves the time and trouble of getting a warrant; if it is, they can get the warrant and use the evidence despite the unlawful entry. We see the incentives differently. An officer with probable cause sufficient to obtain a search warrant would be foolish to enter the premises first in an unlawful manner. By doing so, he would risk suppression of all evidence on the premises, both seen and unseen, since his action would add to the normal burden of convincing a magistrate that there is probable cause the much more onerous burden of convincing a trial court that no information gained from the illegal entry affected either the law enforcement officers' decision to seek a warrant or the magistrate's decision to grant it. *See* Part III, *infra*. Nor would the officer without sufficient probable cause to obtain a search warrant have any added incentive to conduct an unlawful entry, since whatever he finds cannot be used to establish probable cause before a magistrate.[2]

It is possible to read petitioners' briefs as asserting the more narrow position that the "independent source" doctrine does apply to independent acquisition of evidence previously derived indirectly from the unlawful search, but does not apply to what they call "primary evidence," that is, evidence acquired during the course of the search itself. In addition to finding no support in our precedent, *see Silverthorne Lumber*, 251 U.S., at 392 (referring specifically to evidence seized during an unlawful search), this strange distinction would produce results bearing no relation to the policies of the exclusionary rule. It would mean, for example, that the government's knowledge of the existence and condition of a dead body, knowledge lawfully acquired through independent sources, would have to be excluded if government agents had previously observed the body during an unlawful search of the defendant's apartment; but not if they had observed a notation that the body was buried in a certain location, producing consequential discovery of the corpse.

---

[2]   JUSTICE MARSHALL argues, in effect, that where the police cannot point to some historically verifiable fact demonstrating that the subsequent search pursuant to a warrant was wholly unaffected by the prior illegal search—*e.g.,* that they had already sought the warrant before entering the premises—we should adopt a *per se* rule of inadmissibility. We do not believe that such a prophylactic exception to the independent source rule is necessary. To say that a district court must be satisfied that a warrant would have been sought without the illegal entry is not to give dispositive effect to police officers' assurances on the point. Where the facts render those assurances implausible, the independent source doctrine will not apply.

We might note that there is no basis for pointing to the present cases as an example of a "search first, warrant later" mentality. The District Court found that the agents entered the warehouse "in an effort to apprehend any participants who might have remained inside and to guard against the destruction of possibly critical evidence." While they may have misjudged the existence of sufficient exigent circumstances to justify the warrantless entry (the Court of Appeals did not reach that issue and neither do we), there is nothing to suggest that they went in merely to see if there was anything worth getting a warrant for.

III

To apply what we have said to the present cases: Knowledge that the marijuana was in the warehouse was assuredly acquired at the time of the unlawful entry. But it was also acquired at the time of entry pursuant to the warrant, and if that later acquisition was not the result of the earlier entry there is no reason why the independent source doctrine should not apply. Invoking the exclusionary rule would put the police (and society) not in the same position they would have occupied if no violation occurred, but in a worse one.

We think this is also true with respect to the tangible evidence, the bales of marijuana. * * * It seems to us * * * that reseizure of tangible evidence already seized is no more impossible than rediscovery of intangible evidence already discovered. * * * [W]hile the government should not profit from its illegal activity, neither should it be placed in a worse position than it would otherwise have occupied. So long as a later, lawful seizure is genuinely independent of an earlier, tainted one (which may well be difficult to establish where the seized goods are kept in the police's possession) there is no reason why the independent source doctrine should not apply.

The ultimate question, therefore, is whether the search pursuant to warrant was in fact a genuinely independent source of the information and tangible evidence at issue here. This would not have been the case if the agents' decision to seek the warrant was prompted by what they had seen during the initial entry,[3] or if information obtained during that entry was presented to the Magistrate and affected his decision to issue the warrant. [Ed. note: The Court then addressed deficient fact-finding; particularly, that the district court did not "explicitly find that the agents would have sought a warrant if they had not earlier entered the warehouse."] * * *

Accordingly, we vacate the judgment and remand these cases to the Court of Appeals with instructions that it remand to the District Court for determination whether the warrant-authorized search of the warehouse was an independent source of the challenged evidence in the sense we have described.

It is so ordered.

---

[3]   JUSTICE MARSHALL argues that "the relevant question [is] whether, even if the initial entry uncovered no evidence, the officers would return immediately with a warrant to conduct a second search." We do not see how this is "relevant" at all. To determine whether the warrant was independent of the illegal entry, one must ask whether it would have been sought even if what actually happened had not occurred—not whether it would have been sought if something else had happened. That is to say, what counts is whether the actual illegal search had any effect in producing the warrant, not whether some hypothetical illegal search would have aborted the warrant. Only that much is needed to assure that what comes before the court is not the product of illegality; to go further than that would be to expand our existing exclusionary rule.

JUSTICE MARSHALL, with whom JUSTICE STEVENS and JUSTICE O'CONNOR join, dissenting.

The Court today holds that the "independent source" exception to the exclusionary rule may justify admitting evidence discovered during an illegal warrantless search that is later "rediscovered" by the same team of investigators during a search pursuant to a warrant obtained immediately after the illegal search. I believe the Court's decision, by failing to provide sufficient guarantees that the subsequent search was, in fact, independent of the illegal search, emasculates the Warrant Clause and undermines the deterrence function of the exclusionary rule. I therefore dissent.

This Court has stated frequently that the exclusionary rule is principally designed to deter violations of the Fourth Amendment. *See, e.g., United States v. Leon*, 468 U.S. 897, 906 (1984); *Elkins v. United States*, 364 U.S. 206, 217 (1960). By excluding evidence discovered in violation of the Fourth Amendment, the rule "compel[s] respect for the constitutional guaranty in the only effectively available way, by removing the incentive to disregard it." *Id.*, at 217. The Court has crafted exceptions to the exclusionary rule when the purposes of the rule are not furthered by the exclusion. As the Court today recognizes, the independent source exception to the exclusionary rule "allows admission of evidence that has been discovered by means wholly independent of any constitutional violation." *Nix v. Williams*, 467 U.S. 431, 443 (1984); *see Silverthorne Lumber Co. v. United States*, 251 U.S. 385, 392 (1920). The independent source exception, like the inevitable discovery exception, is primarily based on a practical view that under certain circumstances the beneficial deterrent effect that exclusion will have on future constitutional violations is too slight to justify the social cost of excluding probative evidence from a criminal trial. *See Nix v. Williams, supra*, at 444–446; *cf. United States v. Leon, supra*, 906–909. When the seizure of the evidence at issue is "wholly independent of" the constitutional violation, then exclusion arguably will have no effect on a law enforcement officer's incentive to commit an unlawful search.[1]

* * * In holding that the independent source exception may apply to the facts of these cases, I believe the Court loses sight of the practical moorings of the independent source exception and creates an affirmative incentive for unconstitutional searches. This holding can find no justification in the purposes underlying both the exclusionary rule and the independent source exception.

---

[1]   The clearest case for the application of the independent source exception is when a wholly separate line of investigation, shielded from information gathered in an illegal search, turns up the same evidence through a separate, lawful search. Under these circumstances, there is little doubt that the lawful search was not connected to the constitutional violation. The exclusion of such evidence would not significantly add to the deterrence facing the law enforcement officers conducting the illegal search, because they would have little reason to anticipate the separate investigation leading to the same evidence.

The factual setting of the instant case is straightforward. [Ed. note: Justice Marshall then briefly recounted the facts.]

Under the circumstances of these cases, the admission of the evidence "reseized" during the second search severely undermines the deterrence function of the exclusionary rule. Indeed, admission in these cases affirmatively encourages illegal searches. The incentives for such illegal conduct are clear. Obtaining a warrant is inconvenient and time consuming. Even when officers have probable cause to support a warrant application, therefore, they have an incentive first to determine whether it is worthwhile to obtain a warrant. Probable cause is much less than certainty, and many "confirmatory" searches will result in the discovery that no evidence is present, thus saving the police the time and trouble of getting a warrant. If contraband is discovered, however, the officers may later seek a warrant to shield the evidence from the taint of the illegal search. The police thus know in advance that they have little to lose and much to gain by forgoing the bother of obtaining a warrant and undertaking an illegal search.

The Court, however, "see[s] the incentives differently." Under the Court's view, today's decision does not provide an incentive for unlawful searches, because the officer undertaking the search would know that "his action would add to the normal burden of convincing a magistrate that there is probable cause the much more onerous burden of convincing a trial court that no information gained from the illegal entry affected either the law enforcement officers' decision to seek a warrant or the magistrate's decision to grant it." The Court, however, provides no hint of why this risk would actually seem significant to the officers. Under the circumstances of these cases, the officers committing the illegal search have both knowledge and control of the factors central to the trial court's determination. First, it is a simple matter, as was done in these cases, to exclude from the warrant application any information gained from the initial entry so that the magistrate's determination of probable cause is not influenced by the prior illegal search. Second, today's decision makes the application of the independent source exception turn entirely on an evaluation of the officers' intent. It normally will be difficult for the trial court to verify, or the defendant to rebut, an assertion by officers that they always intended to obtain a warrant, regardless of the results of the illegal search.[2] The

---

[2]   Such an intent-based rule is of dubious value for other reasons as well. First, the intent of the officers prior to the illegal entry often will be of little significance to the relevant question: whether, even if the initial entry uncovered no evidence, the officers would return immediately with a warrant to conduct a second search. Officers who have probable cause to believe contraband is present genuinely might intend later to obtain a warrant, but after the illegal search uncovers no such contraband, those same officers might decide their time is better spent than to return with a warrant. In addition, such an intent rule will be difficult to apply. The Court fails to describe how a trial court will properly evaluate whether the law enforcement officers fully intended to obtain a warrant regardless of what they discovered during the illegal search. The obvious question

testimony of the officers conducting the illegal search is the only direct evidence of intent, and the defendant will be relegated simply to arguing that the officers should not be believed. Under these circumstances, the litigation risk described by the Court seems hardly a risk at all; it does not significantly dampen the incentive to conduct the initial illegal search.[3]

The strong Fourth Amendment interest in eliminating these incentives for illegal entry should cause this Court to scrutinize closely the application of the independent source exception to evidence obtained under the circumstances of the instant cases; respect for the constitutional guarantee requires a rule that does not undermine the deterrence function of the exclusionary rule. When, as here, the same team of investigators is involved in both the first and second search, there is a significant danger that the "independence" of the source will in fact be illusory, and that the initial search will have affected the decision to obtain a warrant notwithstanding the officers' subsequent assertions to the contrary. It is therefore crucial that the factual premise of the exception—complete independence—be clearly established before the exception can justify admission of the evidence. I believe the Court's reliance on the intent of the law enforcement officers who conducted the warrantless search provides insufficient guarantees that the subsequent legal search was unaffected by the prior illegal search.

To ensure that the source of the evidence is genuinely independent, the basis for a finding that a search was untainted by a prior illegal search must focus, as with the inevitable discovery doctrine, on "demonstrated historical facts capable of ready verification or impeachment." *Nix v. Williams*, 467 U.S., at 445, n.5. In the instant cases, there are no "demonstrated historical facts" capable of supporting a finding that the subsequent warrant search was wholly unaffected by the prior illegal search. The same team of investigators was involved in both searches. The warrant was obtained immediately after the illegal search, and no effort was made to obtain a warrant prior to the discovery of the marijuana during the illegal search. The only evidence available that the warrant search was wholly independent is the testimony of the agents who conducted the illegal search. Under these circumstances, the threat that the subsequent search was tainted by the illegal search is too great to allow

---

is whose intent is relevant? Intentions clearly may differ both among supervisory officers and among officers who initiate the illegal search.

  [3] The litigation risk facing these law enforcement officers may be contrasted with the risk faced by the officer in *Nix v. Williams*, 467 U.S. 431 (1984). *Nix* involved an application of the inevitable discovery exception to the exclusionary rule. In that case, the Court stressed that an officer "who is faced with the opportunity to obtain evidence illegally will rarely, if ever, be in a position to calculate whether the evidence sought would inevitably be discovered." Unlike the officer in *Nix*, who had no way of knowing about the progress of a wholly separate line of investigation that already had begun at the time of his unconstitutional conduct, the officers in the instant cases, at least under the Court's analysis, have complete knowledge and control over the factors relevant to the determination of "independence."

for the application of the independent source exception.[4] The Court's contrary holding lends itself to easy abuse, and offers an incentive to bypass the constitutional requirement that probable cause be assessed by a neutral and detached magistrate before the police invade an individual's privacy. * * *

In sum, under circumstances as are presented in these cases, when the very law enforcement officers who participate in an illegal search immediately thereafter obtain a warrant to search the same premises, I believe the evidence discovered during the initial illegal entry must be suppressed. Any other result emasculates the Warrant Clause and provides an intolerable incentive for warrantless searches. I respectfully dissent.

JUSTICE STEVENS, dissenting.

[Omitted.]

QUESTIONS, COMMENTS, CONCERNS?

1. **Application to primary violations.** Although the independent source doctrine primarily applies as a "fruits" exception, *Murray* makes clear that the exception *also* applies to evidence initially uncovered as a result of the initial illegality itself.

2. **Beyond the Fourth Amendment.** The independent source doctrine, like the other "fruits" exceptions, applies beyond the Fourth Amendment to violations of the Fifth and Sixth Amendments. *E.g., Kastigar v. United States*, 406 U.S. 441, 460–61 (1972) (Fifth Amendment); *Norman v. State*, 976 A.2d 843, 858 (Del. 2009) (Sixth Amendment).

3. **Burden of proof.** The burden of proof is on the prosecution to demonstrate that the challenged evidence came from an independent source. In the Fourth, Fifth, and Sixth Amendment contexts, the prosecution must generally prove by a preponderance of the evidence that an independent source exists for any unlawfully obtained evidence. *E.g., United States ex rel. Conroy v. Bombard*, 426 F. Supp. 97, 106 (S.D.N.Y. 1976) (Fourth Amendment); *United States v. Seiffert*, 501 F.2d 974, 982 (5th Cir. 1974) (Fifth Amendment); *United States v. Holland*, 59 F. Supp. 2d 492, 511 (D. Md. 1998).

---

[4]   To conclude that the initial search had no effect on the decision to obtain a warrant, and thus that the warrant search was an "independent source" of the challenged evidence, one would have to assume that even if the officers entered the premises and discovered no contraband, they nonetheless would have gone to the Magistrate, sworn that they had probable cause to believe that contraband was in the building, and then returned to conduct another search. Although such a scenario is possible, I believe it is more plausible to believe that the officers would not have chosen to return immediately to the premises with a warrant to search for evidence had they not discovered evidence during the initial search.

D. INEVITABLE DISCOVERY

The inevitable discovery exception, according to the Supreme Court below in *Nix*, is "closely related" to the independent source doctrine. The inevitable discovery doctrine admits unlawfully obtained evidence if police would have inevitably obtained the evidence by lawful investigative methods. The prosecution bears the burden of proving by a preponderance of the evidence that the inevitable discovery exception applies in any given case.

Some lower courts, however, view the inevitable discovery exception as either too broad or are concerned that the preponderance standard—more likely than not—is not sufficiently demanding. Accordingly, those courts have required the prosecution to prove that police were actively engaged in a separate line of lawful investigation before the unconstitutional search. Consider, for example, how the inevitable discovery doctrine works in Wisconsin:

> To [prove inevitable discovery], the prosecution must demonstrate: (1) a reasonable probability that the evidence in question would have been discovered by lawful means but for the police misconduct; (2) that the leads making discovery inevitable were possessed by the government at the time of the misconduct; and (3) that prior to the unlawful search the government also was actively pursuing some alternate line of investigation.

State v. Jackson, 882 N.W.2d 422, 437 (Wisc. 2016) (internal citation and quotation marks omitted).

Lower court approaches aside, always keep the inevitable discovery doctrine in mind as a powerful tool for admitting unconstitutionally obtained evidence.

NIX V. WILLIAMS

467 U.S. 431
Supreme Court of the United States
January 18, 1984, Argued; June 11, 1984, Decided
No. 82-1651

CHIEF JUSTICE BURGER delivered the opinion of the Court.[25]

We granted certiorari to consider whether, at respondent Williams' second murder trial in state court, evidence pertaining to the discovery and

---

25 Without intending to do so, Robert Williams had a substantial impact on the law; indeed, *Nix* is his second trip to the Supreme Court. His story is a fascinating one and one that we will study in substantially more detail when we read the predecessor to *Nix*: *Brewer v. Williams*. *Brewer* had both a historic and lasting impact on the Sixth Amendment. But more on that later. Following the Supreme Court's decision in *Brewer*, Williams received a second trial where he was again convicted of first degree murder. His appellate efforts once more made their way to the Supreme Court.

condition of the victim's body was properly admitted on the ground that it would ultimately or inevitably have been discovered even if no violation of any constitutional or statutory provision had taken place.

I

A

On December 24, 1968, 10-year-old Pamela Powers disappeared from a YMCA building in Des Moines, Iowa, where she had accompanied her parents to watch an athletic contest. Shortly after she disappeared, Williams was seen leaving the YMCA carrying a large bundle wrapped in a blanket; a 14-year-old boy who had helped Williams open his car door reported that he had seen "two legs in it and they were skinny and white."

Williams' car was found the next day 160 miles east of Des Moines in Davenport, Iowa. Later several items of clothing belonging to the child, some of Williams' clothing, and an army blanket like the one used to wrap the bundle that Williams carried out of the YMCA were found at a rest stop on Interstate 80 near Grinnell, between Des Moines and Davenport. A warrant was issued for Williams' arrest.

Police surmised that Williams had left Pamela Powers or her body somewhere between Des Moines and the Grinnell rest stop where some of the young girl's clothing had been found. On December 26, the Iowa Bureau of Criminal Investigation initiated a large-scale search. Two hundred volunteers divided into teams began the search 21 miles east of Grinnell, covering an area several miles to the north and south of Interstate 80. They moved westward from Poweshiek County, in which Grinnell was located, into Jasper County. Searchers were instructed to check all roads, abandoned farm buildings, ditches, culverts, and any other place in which the body of a small child could be hidden.

Meanwhile, Williams surrendered to local police in Davenport, where he was promptly arraigned. Williams contacted a Des Moines attorney who arranged for an attorney in Davenport to meet Williams at the Davenport police station. Des Moines police informed counsel they would pick Williams up in Davenport and return him to Des Moines without questioning him. Two Des Moines detectives then drove to Davenport, took Williams into custody, and proceeded to drive him back to Des Moines.

During the return trip, one of the policemen, Detective Leaming, began a conversation with Williams, saying:

> I want to give you something to think about while we're traveling down the road. . . . They are predicting several inches of snow for tonight, and I feel that you yourself are the only person that knows where this little girl's body is . . . and if you get a snow on top of it you yourself may be unable to find it. And since we will be going right past the area [where the body is] on the way into Des Moines,

I feel that we could stop and locate the body, that the parents of this little girl should be entitled to a Christian burial for the little girl who was snatched away from them on Christmas [Eve] and murdered. . . . [After] a snow storm [we may not be] able to find it at all.

Leaming told Williams he knew the body was in the area of Mitchellville—a town they would be passing on the way to Des Moines. He concluded the conversation by saying: "I do not want you to answer me. . . . Just think about it. . . ."

Later, as the police car approached Grinnell, Williams asked Leaming whether the police had found the young girl's shoes. After Leaming replied that he was unsure, Williams directed the police to a point near a service station where he said he had left the shoes; they were not found. As they continued the drive to Des Moines, Williams asked whether the blanket had been found and then directed the officers to a rest area in Grinnell where he said he had disposed of the blanket; they did not find the blanket. At this point Leaming and his party were joined by the officers in charge of the search. As they approached Mitchellville, Williams, without any further conversation, agreed to direct the officers to the child's body.

The officers directing the search had called off the search at 3 p. m., when they left the Grinnell Police Department to join Leaming at the rest area. At that time, one search team near the Jasper County-Polk County line was only two and one-half miles from where Williams soon guided Leaming and his party to the body. The child's body was found next to a culvert in a ditch beside a gravel road in Polk County, about two miles south of Interstate 80, and essentially within the area to be searched.

B

First Trial

[Ed. note: Following Williams' conviction for first-degree murder at the first trial, the Supreme Court in *Brewer v. Williams* held, on Sixth Amendment grounds, that Leaming's interrogation of Williams violated the latter's right to counsel. We cover the *Brewer* decision in depth in Chapter 10.]

C

Second Trial

At Williams' second trial in 1977 in the Iowa court, the prosecution did not offer Williams' statements into evidence, nor did it seek to show that Williams had directed the police to the child's body. However, evidence of the condition of her body as it was found, articles and photographs of her clothing, and the results of post mortem medical and chemical tests on the body were admitted. The trial court concluded that the State had proved by a preponderance of the evidence that, if the search had not been suspended and Williams had not led the police to the victim, her body would have been discovered *"within a short time"* in essentially the same condition as it was actually found. The trial court also ruled that if the police had not located the body, "the search would clearly have been taken up again where it left off, given the extreme circumstances of this case and the body would [have] been found *in short order."*

In finding that the body would have been discovered in essentially the same condition as it was actually found, the court noted that freezing temperatures had prevailed and tissue deterioration would have been suspended. The challenged evidence was admitted and the jury again found Williams guilty of first-degree murder; he was sentenced to life in prison.

On appeal, the Supreme Court of Iowa again affirmed. 285 N.W.2d 248 (1979). That court held that there was in fact a "hypothetical independent source" exception to the exclusionary rule[.] * * * In 1980 Williams renewed his attack on the state-court conviction by seeking a writ of habeas corpus in the United States District Court for the Southern District of Iowa. * * * The District Court denied Williams' petition.

The Court of Appeals for the Eighth Circuit reversed; an equally divided court denied rehearing *en banc*. That court assumed, without deciding, that there is an inevitable discovery exception to the exclusionary rule and that the Iowa Supreme Court correctly stated that exception to require proof that the police did not act in bad faith and that the evidence would have been discovered absent any constitutional violation. In reversing the District Court's denial of habeas relief, the Court of Appeals stated:

> We hold that the State has not met the first requirement. It is therefore unnecessary to decide whether the state courts' finding that the body would have been discovered anyway is fairly supported by the record. It is also unnecessary to decide whether the State must prove the two elements of the exception by clear and convincing evidence, as defendant argues, or by a preponderance of the evidence, as the state courts held.

* * * We granted the State's petition for certiorari and we reverse.

II

A

The Iowa Supreme Court correctly stated that the "vast majority" of all courts, both state and federal, recognize an inevitable discovery exception to the exclusionary rule. We are now urged to adopt and apply the so-called ultimate or inevitable discovery exception to the exclusionary rule.

Williams contends that evidence of the body's location and condition is "fruit of the poisonous tree," i.e., the "fruit" or product of Detective Leaming's plea to help the child's parents give her "a Christian burial," which this Court had already held equated to interrogation. He contends that admitting the challenged evidence violated the Sixth Amendment whether it would have been inevitably discovered or not. Williams also contends that, if the inevitable discovery doctrine is constitutionally permissible, it must include a threshold showing of police good faith.

B

The doctrine requiring courts to suppress evidence as the tainted "fruit" of unlawful governmental conduct had its genesis in *Silverthorne Lumber Co. v. United States*, 251 U.S. 385 (1920); there, the Court held that the exclusionary rule applies not only to the illegally obtained evidence itself, but also to other incriminating evidence derived from the primary evidence. The holding of *Silverthorne* was carefully limited, however, for the Court emphasized that such information does not automatically become "sacred and inaccessible." *Id.*, at 392. "If knowledge of [such facts] is gained from an *independent source*, they may be proved like any others. . . ." *Ibid.* (emphasis added).

Wong Sun v. United States, 371 U.S. 471 (1963), extended the exclusionary rule to evidence that was the indirect product or "fruit" of unlawful police conduct, but there again the Court emphasized that evidence that has been illegally obtained need not always be suppressed[.] * * * The Court [in doing so] pointedly negated the kind of good-faith requirement advanced by the Court of Appeals in reversing the District Court.

Although *Silverthorne* and *Wong Sun* involved violations of the Fourth Amendment, the "fruit of the poisonous tree" doctrine has not been limited to cases in which there has been a Fourth Amendment violation. The Court has applied the doctrine where the violations were of the Sixth Amendment as well as of the Fifth Amendment.

The core rationale consistently advanced by this Court for extending the exclusionary rule to evidence that is the fruit of unlawful police conduct has been that this admittedly drastic and socially costly course is needed to deter police from violations of constitutional and statutory protections. This Court has accepted the argument that the way to ensure such protections is to exclude evidence seized as a result of such violations notwithstanding the high social cost of letting persons obviously guilty go unpunished for their crimes. On this rationale, the prosecution is not to be put in a better position than it would have been in if no illegality had transpired.

By contrast, the derivative evidence analysis ensures that the prosecution is not put in a worse position simply because of some earlier police error or misconduct. The independent source doctrine allows admission of evidence that has been discovered by means wholly independent of any constitutional violation. That doctrine, although closely related to the inevitable discovery doctrine, does not apply here; Williams' statements to Leaming indeed led police to the child's body, but that is not the whole story. The independent source doctrine teaches us that the interest of society in deterring unlawful police conduct and the public interest in having juries receive all probative evidence of a crime are properly balanced by putting the police in the same, not a worse, position that they would have been in if no police error or misconduct had occurred. When the challenged evidence has an independent source, exclusion of such evidence would put the police in a worse position than they would have been in absent any error or violation. There is a functional similarity between these two doctrines in that exclusion of evidence that would inevitably have been discovered would also put the government in a worse position, because the police would have obtained that evidence if no misconduct had taken place. Thus, while the independent source exception would not justify admission of evidence in this case, its rationale is wholly consistent with and justifies our adoption of the ultimate or inevitable discovery exception to the exclusionary rule.

It is clear that the cases implementing the exclusionary rule "begin with the premise that the challenged evidence is in some sense the product of illegal governmental activity." Of course, this does not end the inquiry. If the prosecution can establish by a preponderance of the evidence that the information ultimately or inevitably would have been discovered by lawful means—here the volunteers' search—then the deterrence rationale has so little basis that the evidence should be received. Anything less would reject logic, experience, and common sense.

The requirement that the prosecution must prove the absence of bad faith, imposed here by the Court of Appeals, would place courts in the position of withholding from juries relevant and undoubted truth that would have been available to police absent any unlawful police activity. Of course, that view would put the police in a worse position than they would have been in if no unlawful conduct had transpired. And, of equal importance, it wholly fails to take into account the enormous societal cost of excluding truth in the search for truth in the administration of justice. Nothing in this Court's prior holdings supports any such formalistic, pointless, and punitive approach.

* * * More than a half century ago, Judge, later Justice, Cardozo made his seminal observation that under the exclusionary rule "[the] criminal is to go free because the constable has blundered." Prophetically, he went on to consider "how far-reaching in its effect upon society" the exclusionary rule would be when "[the] pettiest peace officer would have it in his power

through overzeal or indiscretion to confer immunity upon an offender for crimes the most flagitious."

Someday, Cardozo speculated, some court might press the exclusionary rule to the outer limits of its logic—or beyond—and suppress evidence relating to the "body of a murdered" victim because of the means by which it was found. Cardozo's prophecy was fulfilled in *Killough v. United States*, 315 F.2d 241, 245 (1962) (en banc). But when, as here, the evidence in question would inevitably have been discovered without reference to the police error or misconduct, there is no nexus sufficient to provide a taint and the evidence is admissible.

C

The Court of Appeals did not find it necessary to consider whether the record fairly supported the finding that the volunteer search party would ultimately or inevitably have discovered the victim's body. However, three courts independently reviewing the evidence have found that the body of the child inevitably would have been found by the searchers. Williams challenges these findings, asserting that the record contains only the "post hoc rationalization" that the search efforts would have proceeded two and one-half miles into Polk County where Williams had led police to the body.

When that challenge was made at the suppression hearing preceding Williams' second trial, the prosecution offered the testimony of Agent Ruxlow of the Iowa Bureau of Criminal Investigation. Ruxlow had organized and directed some 200 volunteers who were searching for the child's body. The searchers were instructed "to check all the roads, the ditches, any culverts. . . . If they came upon any abandoned farm buildings, they were instructed to go onto the property and search those abandoned farm buildings or any other places where a small child could be secreted." Ruxlow testified that he marked off highway maps of Poweshiek and Jasper Counties in grid fashion, divided the volunteers into teams of four to six persons, and assigned each team to search specific grid areas. Ruxlow also testified that, if the search had not been suspended because of Williams' promised cooperation, it would have continued into Polk County, using the same grid system. Although he had previously marked off into grids only the highway maps of Poweshiek and Jasper Counties, Ruxlow had obtained a map of Polk County, which he said he would have marked off in the same manner had it been necessary for the search to continue.

The search had commenced at approximately 10 a. m. and moved westward through Poweshiek County into Jasper County. At approximately 3 p. m., after Williams had volunteered to cooperate with the police, Detective Leaming, who was in the police car with Williams, sent word to Ruxlow and the other Special Agent directing the search to meet him at the Grinnell truck stop and the search was suspended at that time. Ruxlow also stated that he was "under the impression that there was a possibility" that Williams would lead them to the child's body at that time. The search was not resumed once it was learned that Williams had led the police to the body, which was found two and one-half miles from where the search had stopped in what would have been the easternmost grid to be searched in Polk County. There was testimony that it would have taken an additional three to five hours to discover the body if the search had continued; the body was found near a culvert, one of the kinds of places the teams had been specifically directed to search.

On this record it is clear that the search parties were approaching the actual location of the body, and we are satisfied, along with three courts earlier, that the volunteer search teams would have resumed the search had Williams not earlier led the police to the body and the body inevitably would have been found. The evidence asserted by Williams as newly discovered, i.e., certain photographs of the body and deposition testimony of Agent Ruxlow made in connection with the federal habeas proceeding, does not demonstrate that the material facts were inadequately developed in the suppression hearing in state court or that Williams was denied a full, fair, and adequate opportunity to present all relevant facts at the suppression hearing.

The judgment of the Court of Appeals is reversed, and the case is remanded for further proceedings consistent with this opinion.

It is so ordered.

JUSTICE WHITE, concurring.

[Omitted.]

JUSTICE STEVENS, concurring in the judgment.

[Omitted.]

JUSTICE BRENNAN, with whom JUSTICE MARSHALL joins, dissenting.

* * * To the extent that today's decision adopts this "inevitable discovery" exception to the exclusionary rule, it simply acknowledges a doctrine that is akin to the "independent source" exception first recognized by the Court in *Silverthorne Lumber Co. v. United States*, 251 U.S. 385, 392 (1920). *See* * * * *Wong Sun v. United States*, 371 U.S. 471, 487 (1963). In particular, the Court concludes that unconstitutionally obtained evidence may be admitted at trial if it inevitably would have been discovered in the same condition by an independent line of investigation that was already being pursued when the constitutional violation occurred. As has every Federal Court of Appeals previously addressing this issue, I agree that in these circumstances the "inevitable discovery" exception to the exclusionary rule is consistent with the requirements of the Constitution.

In its zealous efforts to emasculate the exclusionary rule, however, the Court loses sight of the crucial difference between the "inevitable discovery" doctrine and the "independent source" exception from which it is derived. When properly applied, the "independent source" exception allows the prosecution to use evidence only if it was, in fact, obtained by fully lawful means. It therefore does no violence to the constitutional protections that the exclusionary rule is meant to enforce. The "inevitable discovery" exception is likewise compatible with the Constitution, though it differs in one key respect from its next of kin: specifically, the evidence sought to be introduced at trial has not actually been obtained from an independent source, but rather would have been discovered as a matter of course if independent investigations were allowed to proceed.

In my view, this distinction should require that the government satisfy a heightened burden of proof before it is allowed to use such evidence. The inevitable discovery exception necessarily implicates a hypothetical finding that differs in kind from the factual finding that precedes application of the independent source rule. To ensure that this hypothetical finding is narrowly confined to circumstances that are functionally equivalent to an independent source, and to protect fully the fundamental rights served by the exclusionary rule, I would require clear and convincing evidence before concluding that the government had met its burden of proof on this issue. Increasing the burden of proof serves to impress the factfinder with the importance of the decision and thereby reduces the risk that illegally obtained evidence will be admitted. Because the lower courts did not impose such a requirement, I would remand this case for application of this heightened burden of proof by the lower courts in the first instance. I am therefore unable to join either the Court's opinion or its judgment.

QUESTIONS, COMMENTS, CONCERNS?

1.   **Beyond the Sixth(?) Amendment.** Notice that *Nix* is technically a Sixth Amendment case. Officers in *Nix* deliberately elicited incriminating statements from Williams in violation of his Sixth Amendment right to counsel. But what's important for purposes of this chapter is that the inevitable discovery doctrine broadly applies beyond the Sixth Amendment to both the Fourth and Fifth Amendments. *E.g., United States v. Heath*, 455 F.3d 52, 55 (2d Cir. 2006) (Fourth Amendment); *United States v. Martinez-Gallegos*, 807 F.2d 868, 870 (9th Cir. 1987) (Fifth Amendment).

2.   **Burden of proof.** As *Nix* indicates, the inevitable discovery doctrine admits unlawfully obtained evidence if the prosecution can establish by a preponderance that police would have inevitably discovered the evidence through lawful means. Some courts also require the prosecution to prove that it "was actively pursuing a substantial, alternative line of investigation at the time of the constitutional violation." *United States v. Conner*, 127 F.3d 663, 667 (8th Cir. 1997).

3.   **Levin and other exceptions.** Could any exception, apart from *Leon*, apply in favor of the government to Levin's case? Specifically, does

the government have any argument in favor of applying the doctrines of attenuation, independent source, or inevitable discovery?

CHAPTER 3

FOURTH AMENDMENT APPLICABILITY

■ ■ ■

I. THE THRESHOLD QUESTION: DOES THE FOURTH AMENDMENT APPLY?

As you now know, *Weeks, Mapp, Leon*, etc., dealt with the question of what remedy, if any, is available when members of law enforcement violate the Fourth Amendment. We step back to ask the threshold question: when do the protections of the Fourth Amendment apply?

Recall the reasonableness clause of the Fourth Amendment: "The right of the people to be secure in their persons, houses, papers, and effects, against unreasonable searches and seizures, shall not be violated[.]" Evaluating the text, we can draw a handful of important conclusions. To begin, the Fourth Amendment applies only to governmental action that qualifies as a "search" or a "seizure." Oftentimes, the cases characterize this textual consideration as governmental conduct that "intrudes upon" or is an "infringement of" Fourth Amendment interests. Whether governmental conduct "intrudes upon" or constitutes an "infringement of" Fourth Amendment interests says nothing about whether that intrusion or infringement is also a *violation* of the Fourth Amendment. Stated differently, the fact that governmental conduct implicates the Fourth Amendment does not necessarily mean that the conduct also violates the Fourth Amendment. Determining whether a Fourth Amendment violation has occurred is a separate analysis that we cover later in later chapters.

Notice one more broadly important issue: citizens have no Fourth Amendment protection from governmental conduct that is *not* a "search" or "seizure." That may seem obvious reading the Amendment, but it's a powerful observation. If the challenged conduct does not come within the ambit of the Fourth Amendment (i.e., the conduct does not qualify as a "search" or "seizure"), no further analysis is necessary.

Below are introductory comments on what constitutes a "search" and a "seizure" for purposes of the Fourth Amendment. Also below is a quick introduction to the concept of "standing"—a particularly tricky topic.

Search

The Supreme Court has crafted two tests for determining what constitutes a "search." First, in *Katz v. United States*, 389 U.S. 347 (1967), the Court established that a search occurs when governmental action infringes on a person's reasonable expectation of privacy that society would recognize as reasonable. This test—known as the reasonable expectation of privacy test—has broad applicability.

Three factors are particularly relevant to determining whether a search occurs under the reasonable expectation of privacy test: (1) the size or nature of the property, (2) the defendant's efforts, if any, to protect their privacy, and (3) the nature of the government intrusion (greater vs. lesser). Beginning with the first factor, it matters for Fourth Amendment purposes *where* the police investigate. The police are entitled to walk along public thoroughfares without infringing on any Fourth Amendment interest.

But let's assume an officer walks onto a person's property. Whether this constitutes a search depends on the nature of the property itself. For example, consider a multi-acre farm like this:

Does the Fourth Amendment prevent an officer from investigating this property without a search warrant? Although this is a complex question, the answer usually depends on whether the property constitutes "curtilage" or an "open field." Fourth Amendment protections extend to the curtilage of a home, but not to an open field.

Turning to the second factor—the defendant's effort to protect their privacy—the more a defendant seeks to shield an item or property from public view, the more likely it is that Fourth Amendment protections extend to that property or item. By contrast, what a defendant "knowingly exposes" to the public receives no Fourth Amendment protection. On some level, this makes sense: the homeowner who erects a privacy fence around his yard receives more Fourth Amendment protection than his neighbor whose yard has no fence. Before moving on, you should be aware that the Supreme Court has held that a defendant has no reasonable expectation of privacy in contraband regardless of their efforts to protect the contraband from public view.

Finally, the third factor is the nature of the government's intrusion. This factor turns on a straightforward question: how intrusive is the government's conduct? For now, it suffices for you to know that the more intrusive the government's conduct is, the more likely the conduct constitutes a Fourth Amendment "search."

Apart from the reasonable expectation of privacy test, the Supreme Court has more recently created the "constitutional trespass" test. The test is fairly simple: Law enforcement conduct that constitutes a common law trespass on a textually protected "person, paper, house, or effect" is a Fourth Amendment "search." That conduct qualifies as a search regardless of whether it would or would not satisfy the reasonable expectation of privacy test.

How then are we to know which test to apply? Begin with the constitutional trespass test. If the police investigative technique infringes upon a textually protected Fourth Amendment place or space, then the analysis is complete; that technique is a "search." If, however, the investigative technique occurred outside of a textually protected area (or if there is no trespass on a textually protected area), then apply the reasonable expectation of privacy test.

Seizure

Fourth Amendment seizures take one of two forms: seizures of property and seizures of people. A seizure of property happens when police "meaningfully interfere" with the defendant's possessory interests in that property.

Seizures of people are substantially more complicated. At the outset, note that not every police-citizen encounter constitutes a seizure. Nothing to prevent an officer from approaching an individual to ask, for example, where they are walking or who they recently visited. Colloquially called "walk and talks," such investigative methods do not invoke Fourth Amendment protections.

Things change, however, if the officer restricts an individual's freedom of movement. An ordinary police-citizen encounter can therefore become a "seizure" of the person when the officer restricts the person's freedom of movement in a way that, objectively, the citizen does not feel free to leave. Separately, a police-citizen encounter becomes a seizure when the officer uses a "showing of force" or a "showing of authority" to restrain a person's freedom of movement. Before we move on, please note that not every seizure of a person constitutes an arrest. As we'll learn later, a person can be "seized" for purposes of the Fourth Amendment without the seizure constituting an arrest.

Standing

The essential premise of standing is that Fourth Amendment rights (like Fifth and Sixth Amendment rights) are *personal* in nature and may not be raised on behalf of others. Thus, to have standing to challenge government conduct on Fourth Amendment grounds, a defendant must demonstrate that the conduct infringed on his or her Fourth Amendment rights, not the Fourth Amendment rights of others.

The Supreme Court for a time viewed standing as a separate, threshold facet of analyzing Fourth Amendment challenges. But that changed in *Rakas v. Illinois*, 439 U.S. 128 (1978). As Professor Richard A. Williamson observed shortly after the Court issued *Rakas*:

> Resolution of the "standing" problem in fourth amendment cases . . . required a court to rule regarding the "scope" of the amendment by identifying the class of persons entitled to the protections provided thereunder. Previous fourth amendment standing decisions can be viewed as rulings implicating the substantive "scope" of the amendment. The *Rakas* decision did not change the basic inquiry; but merely dropped the label "standing" as description of the process involved.[1]

Post *Rakas*, then, a defendant has Fourth Amendment standing to challenge a "search" when he demonstrates that he had a legitimate or reasonable expectation of privacy in the invaded space or place. In the seizure context, a defendant has Fourth Amendment standing when the challenged police conduct intruded on his liberty or possessory interests. In sum, standing is just another way of asking our threshold question: does the person bringing the challenge have an interest the Fourth Amendment was designed to protect?

II. WHAT IS A FOURTH AMENDMENT "SEARCH"?

A. MEET ROSS ULBRICHT[2]

Silk Road was launched in January 2011 as the first modern "darknet market"—a market on a carefully hidden commercial website specializing in permitting encrypted sales of both legal and illegal goods and services.

---

[1] Richard A. Williamson, *Fourth Amendment Standing and Expectations of Privacy:* Rakas v. Illinois *and New Directions for Some Old Concepts*, 31 FLA. L. REV. 831, 832 n.7 (1979).

[2] Remember that you have access to the filings relevant to this chapter in your online repository.

Like the "Playpen" website outlined in Chapter 2, Silk Road could only be accessed via the Tor network, effectively concealing both the IP addresses of Silk Road users and the website's server.

Operating as a type of Amazon Marketplace for illicit materials, Silk Road users were able to buy and sell drugs, fake ID's, passports, guns, and other illegal items with almost complete anonymity. Throughout its operation, Silk Road conducted nearly $15 million in illicit transactions annually, with its operator and founder Ross Ulbricht collecting nearly $80 million in commissions.

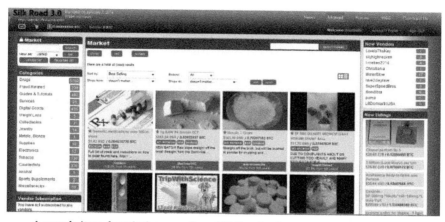

A sample item description page from Silk Road—the anonymous marketplace

After earning a bachelor's degree in physics from the University of Texas at Dallas in 2006, Ulbricht enrolled in a master's degree program at Pennsylvania State University where he became increasingly interested in the libertarian political philosophy of Ludwig von Mises. According to von Mises's philosophy, a citizen must obtain economic freedom to be politically and morally free. Ulbricht, desiring economic freedom, set out "to use economic theory as a means to abolish the use of coercion and aggression amongst mankind." To that end, he drew up plans "to create a website where people could buy anything anonymously, with no trail whatsoever that could lead back to [the user]." Silk Road was born, with Ulbricht selling his own psilocybin mushrooms as a starter product.

During the course of its investigation into Silk Road, the government executed a total of fourteen search warrants of various physical devices containing electronically stored information that connected Ulbricht to the Silk Road operation. In support of each warrant, the government provided an affidavit containing, among other things, the following statement:

> Earlier this year [(2013)], the FBI located the server hosting the Silk Road website in a foreign country [(Iceland)]. Through a Mutual Legal Assistance Treaty request, the FBI received an

image of the contents of the Silk Road Web Server on or about July 29, 2013.

Although no warrant was obtained to search Silk Road's Iceland server, an FBI forensic team was able to examine the server's data and obtain information crucial to the issuance of fourteen search warrants and a warrant for Ulbricht's arrest.

Ross Ulbricht

In October 2013, Ulbricht was arrested by FBI agents while working at the Glen Park branch of the San Francisco Public Library. Agents were concerned, however, that Ulbricht might encrypt or delete data on his laptop upon seeing their approach. Two agents therefore distracted Ulbricht by posing as quarreling lovers. With Ulbricht preoccupied, a third agent inserted a flash drive into Ulbricht's computer that cloned the computer's data. On August 21, 2014, the government charged Ulbricht by superseding indictment with seven crimes: Narcotics Trafficking, Distribution of Narcotics by Means of the Internet, Narcotics Trafficking Conspiracy, Continuing Criminal Enterprise, Conspiracy to Commit and Aid and Abet Computer Hacking, Conspiracy to Traffic in Fraudulent Identification Documents, and Money Laundering Conspiracy.

That same month, Ulbricht filed a lengthy motion to suppress all evidence obtained from the fourteen individual search warrants. Ulbricht theorized that each of the warrants were issued based on evidence illegally obtained from the government's warrantless search of Silk Road's Iceland server. He reasoned that it was impossible to know whether the FBI lawfully or unlawfully gained access to the Iceland server because the Government had failed to disclose how agents located the server in the first place. Nevertheless, Ulbricht maintained that agents likely found the server through a controversial practice known as "parallel construction," which he described as

a practice by the National Security Agency and the Drug Enforcement Administration by which the former provides the latter with information about non-national security criminal activity collected via NSA electronic surveillance, and the latter transmits the substance of the information to federal and/or local law enforcement agencies, sometimes without disclosing the origin of the information, and always with the condition that the NSA's involvement cannot be disclosed to defendants, their counsel, or even courts.

[See Casefile Document 1, at 30.] Ulbricht pointedly suggested that, "given the massive breadth of the NSA's dragnet electronic surveillance, this case is a prime candidate for parallel construction, particularly in light of Silk Road's exclusive operation on the Internet, and its use of both the Tor network and Bitcoin." *Id.* at 32. Accordingly, Ulbricht concluded that the government should be compelled to disclose how the FBI became aware of the Iceland server and that agents were required to obtain a search warrant before accessing that server.

In response, the government argued that Ulbricht had merely "conjure[d] up a bogeyman" in the National Security Agency, suggesting without proof that it was responsible for locating the Silk Road server. That response included a declaration from former FBI computer forensic examiner Christopher Tarbell who claimed that a flaw in Silk Road's configuration led to a "leak" of the server's information. The leak, in turn, allowed FBI agents to use publicly available information to locate the site's host server.

Although Ulbricht's court filings reflect his view that his case presented landmark Fourth Amendment electronic search issues, the government had a different argument entirely. Eleven days after the government filed its initial response to Ulbricht's motion to suppress, it filed a brief four-page supplemental brief arguing that Ulbricht lacked Fourth Amendment standing to challenge the search of the Iceland server in the first place. The government reasoned that Ulbricht failed to prove that he held a personal property or possessory interest in the Iceland server. Ulbricht countered that he was not required to establish standing to challenge the search of the Iceland server, but the district court ordered Ulbricht to file an affidavit outlining his personal property interest in the server. No such affidavit was ever filed.

On October 10, 2014, the district court denied Ulbricht's motion to suppress for lack of standing. The court, however, recognized that the standing doctrine appeared "to place Ulbricht in a catch-22." That is, although, the government had the burden to prove a connection between Ulbricht and Silk Road, Ulbricht had "to concede such a connection" existed to have standing to bring his Fourth Amendment challenges. The court admitted that it did not know whether Ulbricht had "made a tactical choice" because he was "between a rock and a hard place" or whether Ulbricht truly had "no personal privacy interest in the servers at issue."

Regardless, the court concluded that it could not analyze the substantive Fourth Amendment issued raised by Ulbricht because he had failed to establish standing.

After a jury trial, Ross Ulbricht was convicted on all seven counts and sentenced to life in prison without the possibility of parole. In 2017, the U.S. Court of Appeals for the Second Circuit affirmed his conviction and sentence.

B. THE REASONABLE EXPECTATION OF PRIVACY TEST

We move now into the law governing what constitutes a Fourth Amendment "search." The test announced in *Katz v. United States*, 389 U.S. 347 (1967), was a watershed moment in Fourth Amendment jurisprudence. And decades later, it remains one of the most fundamentally important Fourth Amendment decisions ever decided by the Supreme Court.

Before reading *Katz*, you might be interested to know that Charlie Katz was a professional gambler.[3] He placed bets on wide-array of sporting events, both for himself and on behalf of others.[4] He had his own system for ranking teams and predicting outcomes, though he specialized in basketball games.[5] By February 1965, Katz was living on the Sunset Strip in a poolside hotel room where he conducted a portion of his business with out-of-state bookmakers.[6]

An anonymous tip turned the FBI onto Katz.[7] In an effort to overhear his conversations, agents placed a recorder on top of the roof of the telephone booth Katz would later occupy.[8] The tape recorder would ultimately pick up only Katz's side of the conversation, which typically sounded like some version of the following: "Give me Temple minus ten and a half for a dime. Pass. Pass. Pass. Pass. Pass. Pass. Give me Duquesne minus 7 for a nickel."[9] According to the record, a "dime" equaled $1000 whereas a nickel meant $500.[10]

Although the tapes from the telephone booth were not the sole evidence against Katz, they played a major role in agents acquiring and executing a search warrant in Katz's hotel room.[11] That search, in turn,

---

[3]   David A. Slansky, Katz v. United States: *The Limits of Aphorism, in* CRIMINAL PROCEDURE STORIES 224 (Carol S. Steiker ed., 2006).

[4]   *Id.*

[5]   *Id.*

[6]   *Id.*

[7]   *Id.*

[8]   *Id.*

[9]   *Id.* at 225.

[10]   *Id.*

[11]   *Id.* at 225–26.

turned up a variety of incriminating materials, "including 148 pages of coded, handwritten notes about college basketball teams."[12] Katz would also make a handful of incriminating statements, including a promise that he would help lead agents to "the big fellows."[13]

KATZ V. UNITED STATES
389 U.S. 347
Supreme Court of the United States
October 17, 1967, Argued; December 18, 1967, Decided
No. 35

MR. JUSTICE STEWART delivered the opinion of the Court.

The petitioner was convicted in the District Court for the Southern District of California under an eight-count indictment charging him with transmitting wagering information by telephone from Los Angeles to Miami and Boston, in violation of a federal statute. At trial the Government was permitted, over the petitioner's objection, to introduce evidence of the petitioner's end of telephone conversations, overheard by FBI agents who had attached an electronic listening and recording device to the outside of the public telephone booth from which he had placed his calls. In affirming his conviction, the Court of Appeals rejected the contention that the recordings had been obtained in violation of the Fourth Amendment, because "there was no physical entrance into the area occupied by [the petitioner]." We granted certiorari in order to consider the constitutional questions thus presented.

The petitioner has phrased those questions as follows:

A. Whether a public telephone booth is a constitutionally protected area so that evidence obtained by attaching an electronic listening recording device to the top of such a booth is obtained in violation of the right to privacy of the user of the booth.

B. Whether physical penetration of a constitutionally protected area is necessary before a search and seizure can be said to be violative of the Fourth Amendment to the United States Constitution.

We decline to adopt this formulation of the issues. In the first place, the correct solution of Fourth Amendment problems is not necessarily promoted by incantation of the phrase "constitutionally protected area." Secondly, the Fourth Amendment cannot be translated into a general constitutional "right to privacy." That Amendment protects individual privacy against certain kinds of governmental intrusion, but its protections go further, and often have nothing to do with privacy at all. Other

---

[12] *Id.* at 226.

[13] *Id.*

provisions of the Constitution protect personal privacy from other forms of governmental invasion. But the protection of a person's general right to privacy—his right to be let alone by other people—is, like the protection of his property and of his very life, left largely to the law of the individual States.

Because of the misleading way the issues have been formulated, the parties have attached great significance to the characterization of the telephone booth from which the petitioner placed his calls. The petitioner has strenuously argued that the booth was a "constitutionally protected area." The Government has maintained with equal vigor that it was not. But this effort to decide whether or not a given "area," viewed in the abstract, is "constitutionally protected" deflects attention from the problem presented by this case.[9] For the Fourth Amendment protects people, not places. What a person knowingly exposes to the public, even in his own home or office, is not a subject of Fourth Amendment protection. But what he seeks to preserve as private, even in an area accessible to the public, may be constitutionally protected.

The Government stresses the fact that the telephone booth from which the petitioner made his calls was constructed partly of glass, so that he was as visible after he entered it as he would have been if he had remained outside. But what he sought to exclude when he entered the booth was not the intruding eye—it was the uninvited ear. He did not shed his right to do so simply because he made his calls from a place where he might be seen. No less than an individual in a business office, in a friend's apartment, or in a taxicab, a person in a telephone booth may rely upon the protection of the Fourth Amendment. One who occupies it, shuts the door behind him, and pays the toll that permits him to place a call is surely entitled to assume that the words he utters into the mouthpiece will not be broadcast to the world. To read the Constitution more narrowly is to ignore the vital role that the public telephone has come to play in private communication.

The Government contends, however, that the activities of its agents in this case should not be tested by Fourth Amendment requirements, for the surveillance technique they employed involved no physical penetration of the telephone booth from which the petitioner placed his calls. It is true that the absence of such penetration was at one time thought to foreclose further Fourth Amendment inquiry, for that Amendment was thought to limit only searches and seizures of tangible property. But "the premise that property interests control the right of the Government to search and seize has been discredited." * * * Indeed, we have expressly held that the Fourth Amendment governs not only the seizure of tangible items, but extends as well to the recording of oral statements, overheard without any "technical

---

[9]   It is true that this Court has occasionally described its conclusions in terms of "constitutionally protected areas," but we have never suggested that this concept can serve as a talismanic solution to every Fourth Amendment problem.

trespass under . . . local property law." *Silverman v. United States*, 365 U.S. 505, 511. Once this much is acknowledged, and once it is recognized that the Fourth Amendment protects people—and not simply "areas"—against unreasonable searches and seizures, it becomes clear that the reach of that Amendment cannot turn upon the presence or absence of a physical intrusion into any given enclosure.

We conclude that * * * the "trespass" doctrine there enunciated can no longer be regarded as controlling. The Government's activities in electronically listening to and recording the petitioner's words violated the privacy upon which he justifiably relied while using the telephone booth and thus constituted a "search and seizure" within the meaning of the Fourth Amendment. The fact that the electronic device employed to achieve that end did not happen to penetrate the wall of the booth can have no constitutional significance.

The question remaining for decision, then, is whether the search and seizure conducted in this case complied with constitutional standards. In that regard, the Government's position is that its agents acted in an entirely defensible manner: They did not begin their electronic surveillance until investigation of the petitioner's activities had established a strong probability that he was using the telephone in question to transmit gambling information to persons in other States, in violation of federal law. Moreover, the surveillance was limited, both in scope and in duration, to the specific purpose of establishing the contents of the petitioner's unlawful telephonic communications. The agents confined their surveillance to the brief periods during which he used the telephone booth,[14] and they took great care to overhear only the conversations of the petitioner himself.

Accepting this account of the Government's actions as accurate, it is clear that this surveillance was so narrowly circumscribed that a duly authorized magistrate, properly notified of the need for such investigation, specifically informed of the basis on which it was to proceed, and clearly apprised of the precise intrusion it would entail, could constitutionally have authorized, with appropriate safeguards, the very limited search and seizure that the Government asserts in fact took place. * * *

The Government urges that * * * because they did no more here than they might properly have done with prior judicial sanction, we should retroactively validate their conduct. That we cannot do. It is apparent that the agents in this case acted with restraint. Yet the inescapable fact is that this restraint was imposed by the agents themselves, not by a judicial

---

[14] Based upon their previous visual observations of the petitioner, the agents correctly predicted that he would use the telephone booth for several minutes at approximately the same time each morning. The petitioner was subjected to electronic surveillance only during this predetermined period. Six recordings, averaging some three minutes each, were obtained and admitted in evidence. They preserved the petitioner's end of conversations concerning the placing of bets and the receipt of wagering information.

officer. They were not required, before commencing the search, to present their estimate of probable cause for detached scrutiny by a neutral magistrate. They were not compelled, during the conduct of the search itself, to observe precise limits established in advance by a specific court order. Nor were they directed, after the search had been completed, to notify the authorizing magistrate in detail of all that had been seized. In the absence of such safeguards, this Court has never sustained a search upon the sole ground that officers reasonably expected to find evidence of a particular crime and voluntarily confined their activities to the least intrusive means consistent with that end. Searches conducted without warrants have been held unlawful "notwithstanding facts unquestionably showing probable cause," for the Constitution requires "that the deliberate, impartial judgment of a judicial officer . . . be interposed between the citizen and the police . . . ." *Wong Sun v. United States*, 371 U.S. 471, 481– 482. "Over and again this Court has emphasized that the mandate of the [Fourth] Amendment requires adherence to judicial processes," and that searches conducted outside the judicial process, without prior approval by judge or magistrate, are per se unreasonable under the Fourth Amendment—subject only to a few specifically established and well-delineated exceptions.

* * * The Government * * * argues that surveillance of a telephone booth should be exempted from the usual requirement of advance authorization by a magistrate upon a showing of probable cause. We cannot agree. * * *

* * * [B]ypassing a neutral predetermination of the scope of a search leaves individuals secure from Fourth Amendment violations "only in the discretion of the police."

These considerations do not vanish when the search in question is transferred from the setting of a home, an office, or a hotel room to that of a telephone booth. Wherever a man may be, he is entitled to know that he will remain free from unreasonable searches and seizures. The government agents here ignored "the procedure of antecedent justification . . . that is central to the Fourth Amendment," a procedure that we hold to be a constitutional precondition of the kind of electronic surveillance involved in this case. Because the surveillance here failed to meet that condition, and because it led to the petitioner's conviction, the judgment must be reversed.

It is so ordered.

MR. JUSTICE MARSHALL took no part in the consideration or decision of this case.

MR. JUSTICE DOUGLAS, with whom MR. JUSTICE BRENNAN joins, concurring.

[Omitted.]

MR. JUSTICE HARLAN, concurring.

I join the opinion of the Court, which I read to hold only (a) that an enclosed telephone booth is an area where, like a home, and unlike a field, a person has a constitutionally protected reasonable expectation of privacy; (b) that electronic as well as physical intrusion into a place that is in this sense private may constitute a violation of the Fourth Amendment; and (c) that the invasion of a constitutionally protected area by federal authorities is, as the Court has long held, presumptively unreasonable in the absence of a search warrant.

As the Court's opinion states, "the Fourth Amendment protects people, not places." The question, however, is what protection it affords to those people. Generally, as here, the answer to that question requires reference to a "place." My understanding of the rule that has emerged from prior decisions is that there is a twofold requirement, first that a person have exhibited an actual (subjective) expectation of privacy and, second, that the expectation be one that society is prepared to recognize as "reasonable." Thus a man's home is, for most purposes, a place where he expects privacy, but objects, activities, or statements that he exposes to the "plain view" of outsiders are not "protected" because no intention to keep them to himself has been exhibited. On the other hand, conversations in the open would not be protected against being overheard, for the expectation of privacy under the circumstances would be unreasonable.

The critical fact in this case is that "one who occupies it, [a telephone booth] shuts the door behind him, and pays the toll that permits him to place a call is surely entitled to assume" that his conversation is not being intercepted. The point is not that the booth is "accessible to the public" at other times, but that it is a temporarily private place whose momentary occupants' expectations of freedom from intrusion are recognized as reasonable.

In *Silverman v. United States*, 365 U.S. 505, we held that eavesdropping accomplished by means of an electronic device that penetrated the premises occupied by petitioner was a violation of the Fourth Amendment. That case established that interception of conversations reasonably intended to be private could constitute a "search and seizure," and that the examination or taking of physical property was not required. This view of the Fourth Amendment was followed in *Wong Sun v. United States*, 371 U.S. 471, at 485, and *Berger v. New York*, 388 U.S. 41, at 51.

Finally, I do not read the Court's opinion to declare that no interception of a conversation one-half of which occurs in a public telephone booth can be reasonable in the absence of a warrant. As elsewhere under the Fourth Amendment, warrants are the general rule, to which the legitimate needs of law enforcement may demand specific exceptions. It will be time enough to consider any such exceptions when an appropriate occasion presents itself, and I agree with the Court that this is not one.

MR. JUSTICE WHITE, concurring.

[Omitted.]

MR. JUSTICE BLACK, dissenting.

[Omitted.]

QUESTIONS, COMMENTS, CONCERNS?

1.   **Justice Harlan's concurrence.** As you will see in subsequent cases in this chapter, the two-part test outlined in Justice Harlan's concurrence has become one major part of the law on defining what constitutes a Fourth Amendment "search." That is, generally speaking, a defendant must demonstrate both a "subjective" and "objective" privacy interest in the item or place searched. Remember, though, that Justice Harlan's test addresses only the threshold question of whether police conduct qualifies as a "search." Whether the conduct *violates* the Fourth Amendment is a separate question.

2.   **The international Fourth Amendment.** How should the Fourth Amendment apply overseas? Consider the government's response on page 9 of its Memorandum of Law in Opposition to Defendant's Motion to Suppress Evidence. [See Casefile Document 2.] As a matter of policy, should the United States Government be required to obtain a warrant to search the contents of a computer server located abroad? Does your answer depend on the government's level of direction and supervision over international authorities during a foreign search?

3.   **Lawyering and tactics.** What was your general reaction to Ulbricht's motion to suppress? [See Casefile Document 1.] In particular, was it effective in your opinion for Ulbricht to spend approximately twenty-seven pages outlining the background law before addressing the merits? Ulbricht certainly did not lack for a well-known attorney in Joshua L. Dratel. Before representing Ulbricht, Dratel largely made a name for himself representing terror suspects including Bin Laden's personal secretary, Wadih El-Hage, and David Hicks, an Australian accused of fighting for the Taliban. Kiran Nazish, *With Distancing, and a Zeal for Fair Trials, a Lawyer Defends Terrorism Suspects*, N.Y. TIMES (May 29, 2014), https://www.nytimes.com/2014/05/29/nyregion/with-distancing-and-a-zeal-for-fair-trials-a-lawyer-defends-terrorism-suspects.html. When he was initially retained to defend Ulbricht, Dratel boldly described the government's case as comprised of "naked allegations." Andy Greenberg, *Alleged Silk Road Creator's New Lawyer Defended Guantanamo Detainee, NSA Target*, FORBES.COM (Oct. 16, 2013), https://www.forbes.com/sites/andygreenberg/2013/10/16/alleged-silk-road-creators-new-lawyer-defended-guantanamo-detainee-nsa-target/#636c8d2a502c.

4. What constitutes the search? As you review Ulbricht's suppression arguments, keep in mind that Ulbricht must demonstrate that the investigative technique used by the government to identify the Silk Road servers constitutes a Fourth Amendment search. How effective is he in applying the background law to the facts? Did Ulbricht persuade you that *Katz* applies to the government's investigative technique such that it amounted to a Fourth Amendment "search"? And a related question, how does Ulbricht's argument that the government improperly relied on the practice of "parallel construction" relate to his search argument? Is there a better way for Ulbricht to have articulated his argument?

5. What if no search occurred? In its response, the government asserts that Ulbricht had no "legitimate expectation of privacy" in the Silk Road server. What happens if the government's argument is successful? That is, what if Ulbricht is unable to demonstrate that the government's conduct in obtaining access to the Silk Road Servers overseas does not qualify as a "search" within the meaning of the Fourth Amendment?

* * *

With the *Katz* test now in mind, the question shifts to its application. The coming sections and subsections are organized by the three factors critical to the test's application: (1) the size or nature of the property; (2) the defendant's effort to protect his or her privacy; and (3) the nature of the governmental intrusion. We begin with the first factor.

1. Size or Nature of Property

In the context of real property, the first factor generally turns on a narrow question: whether police intruded onto the curtilage of a home or an open field. As we will learn in more detail below, a home and its surrounding curtilage are protected by the Fourth Amendment. Open fields, however, receive no such protection. As the contrast between *Oliver v. United States* (open fields) and *United States v. Dunn* (curtilage) reflects, determining whether property is curtilage or an open field is often a challenging task.

a) Open Fields

OLIVER V. UNITED STATES

466 U.S. 170
Supreme Court of the United States
November 9, 1983, Argued; April 17, 1984, Decided[14]
No. 82-15

JUSTICE POWELL delivered the opinion of the Court.

The "open fields" doctrine, first enunciated by this Court in *Hester v. United States*, 265 U.S. 57 (1924), permits police officers to enter and search a field without a warrant. We granted certiorari in these cases to clarify confusion that has arisen as to the continued vitality of the doctrine.

I

No. 82-15. Acting on reports that marihuana was being raised on the farm of petitioner Oliver, two narcotics agents of the Kentucky State Police went to the farm to investigate.[1] Arriving at the farm, they drove past petitioner's house to a locked gate with a "No Trespassing" sign. A footpath led around one side of the gate. The agents walked around the gate and along the road for several hundred yards, passing a barn and a parked camper. At that point, someone standing in front of the camper shouted: "No hunting is allowed, come back up here." The officers shouted back that they were Kentucky State Police officers, but found no one when they returned to the camper. The officers resumed their investigation of the farm and found a field of marihuana over a mile from petitioner's home.

Petitioner was arrested and indicted for "[manufacturing]" a "controlled substance." After a pretrial hearing, the District Court suppressed evidence of the discovery of the marihuana field. Applying *Katz v. United States*, 389 U.S. 347, 357 (1967), the court found that petitioner had a reasonable expectation that the field would remain private because petitioner "had done all that could be expected of him to assert his privacy in the area of farm that was searched." * * *

The Court of Appeals for the Sixth Circuit, sitting en banc, reversed the District Court. The court concluded that *Katz*, upon which the District Court relied, had not impaired the vitality of the open fields doctrine of *Hester.* * * *[3] We granted certiorari.

---

[14] Together with No. 82-1273, *Maine v. Thornton*, on certiorari to the Supreme Judicial Court of Maine.

[1] It is conceded that the police did not have a warrant authorizing the search, that there was no probable cause for the search, and that no exception to the warrant requirement is applicable.

[3] The four dissenting judges contended that the open fields doctrine did not apply where, as in this case, "reasonable [efforts] [have] been made to exclude the public." To that extent, the dissent considered that *Katz v. United States* implicitly had overruled previous holdings of this Court. The dissent then concluded that petitioner had established a "reasonable expectation of

No. 82-1273. After receiving an anonymous tip that marihuana was being grown in the woods behind respondent Thornton's residence, two police officers entered the woods by a path between this residence and a neighboring house. They followed a footpath through the woods until they reached two marihuana patches fenced with chicken wire. Later, the officers determined that the patches were on the property of respondent, obtained a warrant to search the property, and seized the marihuana. On the basis of this evidence, respondent was arrested and indicted.

The trial court granted respondent's motion to suppress the fruits of the second search. The warrant for this search was premised on information that the police had obtained during their previous warrantless search, that the court found to be unreasonable. "No Trespassing" signs and the secluded location of the marihuana patches evinced a reasonable expectation of privacy. Therefore, the court held, the open fields doctrine did not apply.

The Maine Supreme Judicial Court affirmed. * * * We granted certiorari.

II

The rule announced in *Hester v. United States* was founded upon the explicit language of the Fourth Amendment. That Amendment indicates with some precision the places and things encompassed by its protections. As Justice Holmes explained for the Court in his characteristically laconic style: "[The] special protection accorded by the Fourth Amendment to the people in their 'persons, houses, papers, and effects,' is not extended to the open fields. The distinction between the latter and the house is as old as the common law." *Hester v. United States*, 265 U.S., at 59.

Nor are the open fields "effects" within the meaning of the Fourth Amendment. * * * We conclude, as did the Court in deciding *Hester v. United States*, that the government's intrusion upon the open fields is not one of those "unreasonable searches" proscribed by the text of the Fourth Amendment.

III

This interpretation of the Fourth Amendment's language is consistent with the understanding of the right to privacy expressed in our Fourth Amendment jurisprudence. Since *Katz v. United States*, 389 U.S. 347 (1967), the touchstone of Amendment analysis has been the question whether a person has a "constitutionally protected reasonable expectation of privacy." *Id.*, at 360 (Harlan, J., concurring). The Amendment does not protect the merely subjective expectation of privacy, but only those

---

privacy" under the *Katz* standard. Judge Lively also wrote separately to argue that the open fields doctrine applied only to lands that could be viewed by the public.

"[expectations] that society is prepared to recognize as 'reasonable.' " *Id.*, at 361.

A

No single factor determines whether an individual legitimately may claim under the Fourth Amendment that a place should be free of government intrusion not authorized by warrant. In assessing the degree to which a search infringes upon individual privacy, the Court has given weight to such factors as the intention of the Framers of the Fourth Amendment, the uses to which the individual has put a location, and our societal understanding that certain areas deserve the most scrupulous protection from government invasion. These factors are equally relevant to determining whether the government's intrusion upon open fields without a warrant or probable cause violates reasonable expectations of privacy and is therefore a search proscribed by the Amendment.

In this light, the rule of *Hester v. United States, supra*, that we reaffirm today, may be understood as providing that an individual may not legitimately demand privacy for activities conducted out of doors in fields, except in the area immediately surrounding the home. This rule is true to the conception of the right to privacy embodied in the Fourth Amendment. The Amendment reflects the recognition of the Framers that certain enclaves should be free from arbitrary government interference. * * *

In contrast, open fields do not provide the setting for those intimate activities that the Amendment is intended to shelter from government interference or surveillance. There is no societal interest in protecting the privacy of those activities, such as the cultivation of crops, that occur in open fields. Moreover, as a practical matter these lands usually are accessible to the public and the police in ways that a home, an office, or commercial structure would not be. It is not generally true that fences or "No Trespassing" signs effectively bar the public from viewing open fields in rural areas. And both petitioner Oliver and respondent Thornton concede that the public and police lawfully may survey lands from the air. For these reasons, the asserted expectation of privacy in open fields is not an expectation that "society recognizes as reasonable."

The historical underpinnings of the open fields doctrine also demonstrate that the doctrine is consistent with respect for "reasonable expectations of privacy." As Justice Holmes, writing for the Court, observed in *Hester*, the common law distinguished "open fields" from the "curtilage," the land immediately surrounding and associated with the home. The distinction implies that only the curtilage, not the neighboring open fields, warrants the Fourth Amendment protections that attach to the home. At common law, the curtilage is the area to which extends the intimate activity associated with the "sanctity of a man's home and the privacies of life," and therefore has been considered part of the home itself for Fourth Amendment purposes. Thus, courts have extended Fourth Amendment protection to the curtilage; and they have defined the curtilage, as did the common law, by reference to the factors that determine whether an individual reasonably may expect that an area immediately adjacent to the home will remain private. Conversely, the common law implies, as we reaffirm today, that no expectation of privacy legitimately attaches to open fields.

We conclude, from the text of the Fourth Amendment and from the historical and contemporary understanding of its purposes, that an individual has no legitimate expectation that open fields will remain free from warrantless intrusion by government officers.

B

Petitioner Oliver and respondent Thornton contend, to the contrary, that the circumstances of a search sometimes may indicate that reasonable expectations of privacy were violated; and that courts therefore should analyze these circumstances on a case-by-case basis. The language of the Fourth Amendment itself answers their contention.

Nor would a case-by-case approach provide a workable accommodation between the needs of law enforcement and the interests protected by the Fourth Amendment. Under this approach, police officers would have to guess before every search whether landowners had erected fences sufficiently high, posted a sufficient number of warning signs, or located contraband in an area sufficiently secluded to establish a right of privacy. * * * This Court repeatedly has acknowledged the difficulties created for courts, police, and citizens by an ad hoc, case-by-case definition of Fourth Amendment standards to be applied in differing factual circumstances. The ad hoc approach not only makes it difficult for the policeman to discern the scope of his authority, it also creates a danger that constitutional rights will be arbitrarily and inequitably enforced.

IV

In any event, while the factors that petitioner Oliver and respondent Thornton urge the courts to consider may be relevant to Fourth Amendment analysis in some contexts, these factors cannot be decisive on the question whether the search of an open field is subject to the Amendment. Initially, we reject the suggestion that steps taken to protect privacy establish that expectations of privacy in an open field are legitimate. It is true, of course, that petitioner Oliver and respondent Thornton, in order to conceal their criminal activities, planted the marihuana upon secluded land and erected fences and "No Trespassing" signs around the property. And it may be that because of such precautions, few members of the public stumbled upon the marihuana crops seized by the police. Neither of these suppositions demonstrates, however, that the expectation of privacy was legitimate in the sense required by the Fourth Amendment. The test of legitimacy is not whether the individual chooses to conceal assertedly "private" activity. Rather, the correct inquiry is whether the government's intrusion infringes upon the personal and societal values protected by the Fourth Amendment. As we have explained, we find no basis for concluding that a police inspection of open fields accomplishes such an infringement.

Nor is the government's intrusion upon an open field a "search" in the constitutional sense because that intrusion is a trespass at common law. The existence of a property right is but one element in determining whether expectations of privacy are legitimate. * * *

The common law may guide consideration of what areas are protected by the Fourth Amendment by defining areas whose invasion by others is wrongful. The law of trespass, however, forbids intrusions upon land that the Fourth Amendment would not proscribe. For trespass law extends to instances where the exercise of the right to exclude vindicates no legitimate privacy interest.[15] Thus, in the case of open fields, the general rights of property protected by the common law of trespass have little or no relevance to the applicability of the Fourth Amendment.

V

We conclude that the open fields doctrine, as enunciated in *Hester*, is consistent with the plain language of the Fourth Amendment and its historical purposes. Moreover, Justice Holmes' interpretation of the Amendment in *Hester* accords with the "reasonable expectation of privacy" analysis developed in subsequent decisions of this Court. We therefore affirm *Oliver v. United States*; *Maine v. Thornton* is reversed and remanded for further proceedings not inconsistent with this opinion.

It is so ordered.

JUSTICE WHITE, concurring in part and concurring in the judgment.

[Omitted.]

JUSTICE MARSHALL, with whom JUSTICE BRENNAN and JUSTICE STEVENS join, dissenting.

In each of these consolidated cases, police officers, ignoring clearly visible "No Trespassing" signs, entered upon private land in search of

---

[15] The law of trespass recognizes the interest in possession and control of one's property and for that reason permits exclusion of unwanted intruders. But it does not follow that the right to exclude conferred by trespass law embodies a privacy interest also protected by the Fourth Amendment. To the contrary, the common law of trespass furthers a range of interests that have nothing to do with privacy and that would not be served by applying the strictures of trespass law to public officers. Criminal laws against trespass are prophylactic: they protect against intruders who poach, steal livestock and crops, or vandalize property. And the civil action of trespass serves the important function of authorizing an owner to defeat claims of prescription by asserting his own title. In any event, unlicensed use of property by others is presumptively unjustified, as anyone who wishes to use the property is free to bargain for the right to do so with the property owner. For these reasons, the law of trespass confers protections from intrusion by others far broader than those required by Fourth Amendment interests.

evidence of a crime. At a spot that could not be seen from any vantage point accessible to the public, the police discovered contraband, which was subsequently used to incriminate the owner of the land. In neither case did the police have a warrant authorizing their activities. * * *

* * *

A clear, easily administrable rule [should have emerged from these consolidated cases]: Private land marked in a fashion sufficient to render entry thereon a criminal trespass under the law of the State in which the land lies is protected by the Fourth Amendment's proscription of unreasonable searches and seizures. One of the advantages of the foregoing rule is that it draws upon a doctrine already familiar to both citizens and government officials. In each jurisdiction, a substantial body of statutory and case law defines the precautions a landowner must take in order to avail himself of the sanctions of the criminal law. The police know that body of law, because they are entrusted with responsibility for enforcing it against the public; it therefore would not be difficult for the police to abide by it themselves.

By contrast, the doctrine announced by the Court today is incapable of determinate application. Police officers, making warrantless entries upon private land, will be obliged in the future to make on-the-spot judgments as to how far the curtilage extends, and to stay outside that zone. In addition, we may expect to see a spate of litigation over the question of how much improvement is necessary to remove private land from the category of "unoccupied or undeveloped area" to which the "open fields exception" is now deemed applicable.

The Court's holding not only ill serves the need to make constitutional doctrine "workable for application by rank-and-file, trained police officers," it withdraws the shield of the Fourth Amendment from privacy interests that clearly deserve protection. By exempting from the coverage of the Amendment large areas of private land, the Court opens the way to investigative activities we would all find repugnant.[21]

The Fourth Amendment, properly construed, embodies and gives effect to our collective sense of the degree to which men and women, in civilized society, are entitled "to be let alone" by their governments. The Court's opinion bespeaks and will help to promote an impoverished vision of that fundamental right.

I dissent.

---

[21] Perhaps the most serious danger in the decision today is that, if the police are permitted routinely to engage in such behavior, it will gradually become less offensive to us all. As Justice Brandeis once observed: "Our Government is the potent, the omnipresent teacher. For good or for ill, it teaches the whole people by its example. Crime is contagious. If the Government becomes a lawbreaker, it breeds contempt for law. . . ."

b) Curtilage

UNITED STATES V. DUNN

480 U.S. 294
Supreme Court of the United States
January 20, 1987, Argued; March 3, 1987, Decided
No. 85-998

JUSTICE WHITE delivered the opinion of the Court.

We granted the Government's petition for certiorari to decide whether the area near a barn, located approximately 50 yards from a fence surrounding a ranch house, is, for Fourth Amendment purposes, within the curtilage of the house. The Court of Appeals for the Fifth Circuit held that the barn lay within the house's curtilage, and that the District Court should have suppressed certain evidence obtained as a result of law enforcement officials' intrusion onto the area immediately surrounding the barn. We conclude that the barn and the area around it lay outside the curtilage of the house, and accordingly reverse the judgment of the Court of Appeals.

I

Respondent Ronald Dale Dunn and a codefendant, Robert Lyle Carpenter, were convicted by a jury of conspiring to manufacture phenylacetone and amphetamine, and to possess amphetamine with intent to distribute * * *. Respondent was also convicted of manufacturing these two controlled substances and possessing amphetamine with intent to distribute. The events giving rise to respondent's apprehension and conviction began in 1980 when agents from the Drug Enforcement Administration (DEA) discovered that Carpenter had purchased large quantities of chemicals and equipment used in the manufacture of amphetamine and phenylacetone. DEA agents obtained warrants from a Texas state judge authorizing installation of miniature electronic transmitter tracking devices, or "beepers," in an electric hot plate stirrer, a drum of acetic anhydride, and a container holding phenylacetic acid, a precursor to phenylacetone. All of these items had been ordered by Carpenter. On September 3, 1980, Carpenter took possession of the electric hot plate stirrer, but the agents lost the signal from the "beeper" a few days later. The agents were able to track the "beeper" in the container of chemicals, however, from October 27, 1980, until November 5, 1980, on which date Carpenter's pickup truck, which was carrying the container, arrived at respondent's ranch. Aerial photographs of the ranch property showed Carpenter's truck backed up to a barn behind the ranch house. The agents also began receiving transmission signals from the "beeper" in the hot plate stirrer that they had lost in early September and determined that the stirrer was on respondent's ranch property.

Respondent's ranch comprised approximately 198 acres and was completely encircled by a perimeter fence. The property also contained several interior fences, constructed mainly of posts and multiple strands of barbed wire. The ranch residence was situated 1/2 mile from a public road. A fence encircled the residence and a nearby small greenhouse. Two barns were located approximately 50 yards from this fence. The front of the larger of the two barns was enclosed by a wooden fence and had an open overhang. Locked, waist-high gates barred entry into the barn proper, and netting material stretched from the ceiling to the top of the wooden gates.

On the evening of November 5, 1980, law enforcement officials made a warrantless entry onto respondent's ranch property. A DEA agent accompanied by an officer from the Houston Police Department crossed over the perimeter fence and one interior fence. Standing approximately midway between the residence and the barns, the DEA agent smelled what he believed to be phenylacetic acid, the odor coming from the direction of the barns. The officers approached the smaller of the barns—crossing over a barbed wire fence—and, looking into the barn, observed only empty boxes. The officers then proceeded to the larger barn, crossing another barbed wire fence as well as a wooden fence that enclosed the front portion of the barn. The officers walked under the barn's overhang to the locked wooden gates and, shining a flashlight through the netting on top of the gates, peered into the barn. They observed what the DEA agent thought to be a phenylacetone laboratory. The officers did not enter the barn. At this point the officers departed from respondent's property, but entered it twice more on November 6 to confirm the presence of the phenylacetone laboratory.

On November 6, 1980, at 8:30 p.m., a Federal Magistrate issued a warrant authorizing a search of respondent's ranch. DEA agents and state law enforcement officials executed the warrant on November 8, 1980.[2] The officers arrested respondent and seized chemicals and equipment, as well as bags of amphetamines they discovered in a closet in the ranch house.

* * * [Ed. note: the Court then recounted a complex procedural history.] The Government * * * submitted a supplement to its petition for certiorari, revising the question presented to whether the barn lay within the curtilage of the house. We granted the petition * * *.

II

* * * Drawing upon the Court's own cases and the cumulative experience of the lower courts that have grappled with the task of defining the extent of a home's curtilage, we believe that curtilage questions should be resolved with particular reference to four factors: the proximity of the area claimed to be curtilage to the home, whether the area is included

---

[2]   Prior to the actual search of the barn and ranch house, the agents entered the property for further observations.

within an enclosure surrounding the home, the nature of the uses to which the area is put, and the steps taken by the resident to protect the area from observation by people passing by.[4] We do not suggest that combining these factors produces a finely tuned formula that, when mechanically applied, yields a "correct" answer to all extent-of-curtilage questions. Rather, these factors are useful analytical tools only to the degree that, in any given case, they bear upon the centrally relevant consideration—whether the area in question is so intimately tied to the home itself that it should be placed under the home's "umbrella" of Fourth Amendment protection. Applying these factors to respondent's barn and to the area immediately surrounding it, we have little difficulty in concluding that this area lay outside the curtilage of the ranch house.

First. The record discloses that the barn was located 50 yards from the fence surrounding the house and 60 yards from the house itself. Standing in isolation, this substantial distance supports no inference that the barn should be treated as an adjunct of the house.

Second. It is also significant that respondent's barn did not lie within the area surrounding the house that was enclosed by a fence. We noted in *Oliver* that "for most homes, the boundaries of the curtilage will be clearly marked; and the conception defining the curtilage—as the area around the home to which the activity of home life extends—is a familiar one easily understood from our daily experience." Viewing the physical layout of respondent's ranch in its entirety, it is plain that the fence surrounding the residence serves to demark a specific area of land immediately adjacent to the house that is readily identifiable as part and parcel of the house. Conversely, the barn—the front portion itself enclosed by a fence—and the area immediately surrounding it, stands out as a distinct portion of respondent's ranch, quite separate from the residence.

Third. It is especially significant that the law enforcement officials possessed objective data indicating that the barn was not being used for intimate activities of the home. The aerial photographs showed that the truck Carpenter had been driving that contained the container of phenylacetic acid was backed up to the barn, "apparently," in the words of the Court of Appeals, "for the unloading of its contents." When on respondent's property, the officers' suspicion was further directed toward the barn because of "a very strong odor" of phenylacetic acid. As the DEA

---

[4] We decline the Government's invitation to adopt a "bright-line rule" that "the curtilage should extend no farther than the nearest fence surrounding a fenced house." Fencing configurations are important factors in defining the curtilage, * * * the primary focus is whether the area in question harbors those intimate activities associated with domestic life and the privacies of the home. Application of the Government's "first fence rule" might well lead to diminished Fourth Amendment protection in those cases where a structure lying outside a home's enclosing fence was used for such domestic activities. And, in those cases where a house is situated on a large parcel of property and has no nearby enclosing fence, the Government's rule would serve no utility; a court would still be required to assess the various factors outlined above to define the extent of the curtilage.

agent approached the barn, he "could hear a motor running, like a pump motor of some sort. . . ." Furthermore, the officers detected an "extremely strong" odor of phenylacetic acid coming from a small crack in the wall of the barn. Finally, as the officers were standing in front of the barn, immediately prior to looking into its interior through the netting material, "the smell was very, very strong . . . [and the officers] could hear the motor running very loudly." When considered together, the above facts indicated to the officers that the use to which the barn was being put could not fairly be characterized as so associated with the activities and privacies of domestic life that the officers should have deemed the barn as part of respondent's home.

Fourth. Respondent did little to protect the barn area from observation by those standing in the open fields. Nothing in the record suggests that the various interior fences on respondent's property had any function other than that of the typical ranch fence; the fences were designed and constructed to corral livestock, not to prevent persons from observing what lay inside the enclosed areas.

III

* * * Respondent asserts that he possessed an expectation of privacy, independent from his home's curtilage, in the barn and its contents, because the barn is an essential part of his business. Respondent overlooks the significance of *Oliver v. United States*, 466 U.S. 170 (1984).

We may accept, for the sake of argument, respondent's submission that his barn enjoyed Fourth Amendment protection and could not be entered and its contents seized without a warrant. But it does not follow on the record before us that the officers' conduct and the ensuing search and seizure violated the Constitution. *Oliver* reaffirmed the precept * * * that an open field is neither a "house" nor an "effect," and, therefore, "the government's intrusion upon the open fields is not one of those 'unreasonable searches' proscribed by the text of the Fourth Amendment." The Court expressly rejected the argument that the erection of fences on an open field—at least of the variety involved in those cases and in the present case—creates a constitutionally protected privacy interest. "[The] term 'open fields' may include any unoccupied or undeveloped area outside of the curtilage. An open field need be neither 'open' nor a 'field' as those terms are used in common speech." It follows that no constitutional violation occurred here when the officers crossed over respondent's ranch-style perimeter fence, and over several similarly constructed interior fences, prior to stopping at the locked front gate of the barn. As previously mentioned, the officers never entered the barn, nor did they enter any other structure on respondent's premises. Once at their vantage point, they merely stood, outside the curtilage of the house and in the open fields upon which the barn was constructed, and peered into the barn's open front. And, standing as they were in the open fields, the Constitution did not forbid them to observe the phenylacetone laboratory located in respondent's barn. This conclusion flows naturally from our previous decisions.

Under *Oliver* * * *, there is no constitutional difference between police observations conducted while in a public place and while standing in the open fields. Similarly, the fact that the objects observed by the officers lay within an area that we have assumed, but not decided, was protected by the Fourth Amendment does not affect our conclusion. * * *

The officers lawfully viewed the interior of respondent's barn, and their observations were properly considered by the Magistrate in issuing a search warrant for respondent's premises. Accordingly, the judgment of the Court of Appeals is reversed.

It is so ordered.

JUSTICE SCALIA, concurring in part.

[Omitted.]

JUSTICE BRENNAN, with whom JUSTICE MARSHALL joins, dissenting.

The Government agents' intrusions upon Ronald Dunn's privacy and property violated the Fourth Amendment for two reasons. First, the barnyard invaded by the agents lay within the protected curtilage of Dunn's farmhouse. Second, the agents infringed upon Dunn's reasonable expectation of privacy in the barn and its contents. Our society is not so exclusively urban that it is unable to perceive or unwilling to preserve the expectation of farmers and ranchers that barns and their contents are protected from (literally) unwarranted government intrusion.

* * *

Today's decision has an unforeseen consequence. In narrowing the meaning given to the concept of curtilage, the Court also narrows the scope of searches permissible under a warrant authorizing a search of building premises. Police officers often proceed as if a warrant that authorizes a search of the premises or the dwelling also authorizes a search of any outbuildings (such as garages, barns, sheds, smokehouses) because such buildings are commonly deemed within the curtilage. * * * After today, reliance upon this general rule is illegitimate, and warrants must specify that a search of the farmer's outbuildings is also contemplated.

* * *

The Fourth Amendment prohibits police activity which, if left unrestricted, would jeopardize individuals' sense of security or would too heavily burden those who wished to guard their privacy.[13] In this case, in

---

13 As Professor Amsterdam has observed, "[the] question is not whether you or I must draw the blinds before we commit a crime. It is whether you and I must discipline ourselves to draw the blinds every time we enter a room, under pain of surveillance if we do not."

order to look inside respondent's barn, the DEA agents traveled one-half mile off a public road over respondent's fenced-in property, crossed over three additional wooden and barbed wire fences, stepped under the eaves of the barn, and then used a flashlight to peer through otherwise opaque fishnetting. For the police habitually to engage in such surveillance— without a warrant—is constitutionally intolerable. Because I believe that farmers' and ranchers' expectations of privacy in their barns and other outbuildings are expectations society would regard as reasonable, and because I believe that sanctioning the police behavior at issue here does violence to the purpose and promise of the Fourth Amendment, I dissent.

QUESTIONS, COMMENTS, CONCERNS?

1.   **Open field vs. curtilage.** Applying the *Dunn* factors can lead to uneven results. Consider *United States v. Titemore*, 437 F.3d 251 (2d Cir. 2006), where an officer approached the rear of David Titemore's home at night and walked onto an outdoor porch. The officer walked up to the home's back entrance, which included both a sliding-glass door and a screen door. That night, the sliding-glass door was open, but the screen door was closed. The officer shined his flashlight through the screen without opening it and saw a rifle next to where Titemore was sitting and watching television. Titemore, as a convicted felon, was later charged with unlawful possession of the rifle. His motion to suppress was denied so he pleaded guilty, but reserved his right to appeal. The Second Circuit affirmed, holding that the officer entered onto an "open field," and therefore no search occurred. The court reasoned as follows:

> First, while the sliding-glass door and porch are connected to the house and, in this respect, would tend to support a finding that they are within the curtilage of the home, they also constitute part of a principal entranceway, which has associated with it a diminished expectation of privacy. Second, viewing the features of the property "within the larger context of the total property," we agree with the district court that the porch area and lawn were not completely enclosed, and thus separated from the public, because no fence was present * * *. Third, the evidence established that the sliding-glass door was in fact a primary entrance visible to and used by the public. The porch, door, and lawn * * * were visible from [two public roads]. Three steps led up to the porch, indicating that it was a means of ingress and egress. And there was also a doorbell, albeit one that was not working, which would suggest to visitors that they could visit the home from the porch. Fourth, the record evidence showed that no steps were taken to shield the sliding-glass door and porch from outside observation. The door, visible from both roads, was open, radiating light from the television set out onto the lawn, and the porch was not enclosed, as the trooper could observe from the roadway.

2.   Considering the role of a fence. In open fields cases, there can be no denying that building a fence around the property helps—to an extent. In *United States v. Taylor*, 458 F.3d 1201 (11th Cir. 2006), officers responded to Warren Taylor's rural home after they received a 911 call, and the caller hung up. Deputy Sheriff James Robinson drove to the caller's address—Taylor's residence—to conduct a "welfare check." Taylor's residence sat on about five acres and included a house, barn, and pond all fenced at the perimeter with an open field/livestock fence. Deputy Robinson approached the home and knocked on the door, but no one answered. Taylor then emerged from a nearby structure on the property. As Robinson went to meet Taylor, Robinson noticed fresh footprints leading from a pond on the property to a nearby camper. Robinson followed the footprints and saw "a green military-style pack in the grass line of the pond water, within reach of the edge of the pond." Upon retrieving the pack, Robinson discovered shotgun shells, and a subsequent search of the pond produced a shotgun. Taylor was charged with felon in possession of a firearm.

The district court denied Taylor's motion to suppress. On appeal, the Eleventh Circuit affirmed, holding that the pond was *not* within the home's curtilage. Applying the *Dunn* factors, the court reasoned that: (1) the pond was sixty yards away from the home and separated from the home by other structures; (2) the pond was not associated with any intimate activity of the home; (3) the perimeter fence was not sufficient to enclose the pond within the home's curtilage; and (4) the perimeter fence did not create an expectation of privacy on all five acres.

3.   Even a real privacy fence might not help. Consider the so-called "flyover cases" where law enforcement takes to the air via helicopter or airplane to learn about contraband inside a defendant's fence. *E.g., Florida v. Riley*, 488 U.S. 445 (1989); *California v. California v. Ciraolo*, 476 U.S. 207 (1986). Without reading those cases (yet), what's your guess? Do you think that a "search" occurs when police rely on planes, helicopters, or drones to look above a person's fence?

4.   What about an apartment building? It seems clear that living in an apartment complex comes with some unquantifiable reduction in the occupants' Fourth Amendment protections. In a handful of cases, lower courts have declined suppression motions arising from police entry into parking garages attached to apartment complexes. In *State v. Dumstrey*, 859 N.W.2d 138 (Wis. Ct. App. 2014), for example, an officer followed Brett Dumstrey into the parking garage of his apartment complex, blocked the garage door, and arrested Dumstrey for driving while intoxicated. The court held that the parking garage was not curtilage. It reasoned that the garage was a common area where Dumstrey had a "lack of complete dominion and control and inability to exclude others, including the landlord and dozens of tenants and their invitees[.]"

Similar considerations have led lower courts to hold that a resident has no reasonable expectation of privacy in the hallway of an apartment building, *United States v. Nohara*, 3 F.3d 1239 (9th Cir. 1993), the back porch of an apartment building, *People v. Lyles*, 772 N.E.2d 962 (Ill. App. Ct. 2002), the stairwell of an apartment building, *Commonwealth v. Reed*, 851 A.2d 958 (Pa. Super. Ct. 2004), or a basement storage locker in a multiunit dwelling that other residents could access, *United States v. McGrane*, 746 F.2d 632 (8th Cir. 1984).

c) Activities Within the Home

KYLLO V. UNITED STATES
533 U.S. 27
Supreme Court of the United States
February 20, 2001, Argued; June 11, 2001, Decided
No. 99-8508

JUSTICE SCALIA delivered the opinion of the Court.

This case presents the question whether the use of a thermal-imaging device aimed at a private home from a public street to detect relative amounts of heat within the home constitutes a "search" within the meaning of the Fourth Amendment.

I

In 1991 Agent William Elliott of the United States Department of the Interior came to suspect that marijuana was being grown in the home belonging to petitioner Danny Kyllo, part of a triplex on Rhododendron Drive in Florence, Oregon. Indoor marijuana growth typically requires high-intensity lamps. In order to determine whether an amount of heat was emanating from petitioner's home consistent with the use of such lamps, at 3:20 a.m. on January 16, 1992, Agent Elliott and Dan Haas used an Agema Thermovision 210 thermal imager to scan the triplex. Thermal imagers detect infrared radiation, which virtually all objects emit but which is not visible to the naked eye. The imager converts radiation into images based on relative warmth—black is cool, white is hot, shades of gray connote relative differences; in that respect, it operates somewhat like a video camera showing heat images. The scan of Kyllo's home took only a few minutes and was performed from the passenger seat of Agent Elliott's vehicle across the street from the front of the house and also from the street in back of the house. The scan showed that the roof over the garage and a side wall of petitioner's home were relatively hot compared to the rest of the home and substantially warmer than neighboring homes in the triplex. Agent Elliott concluded that petitioner was using halide lights to grow marijuana in his house, which indeed he was. Based on tips from informants, utility bills, and the thermal imaging, a Federal Magistrate Judge issued a warrant authorizing a search of petitioner's home, and the agents found an indoor growing operation involving more than 100 plants. Petitioner was indicted on one count of manufacturing marijuana * * *. He unsuccessfully moved to suppress the evidence seized from his home and then entered a conditional guilty plea.

[Ed. note: The Court recounted the case's procedural history.] A divided Court of Appeals * * * held that petitioner had shown no subjective expectation of privacy because he had made no attempt to conceal the heat escaping from his home and even if he had, there was no objectively reasonable expectation of privacy because the imager "did not expose any intimate details of Kyllo's life," only "amorphous 'hot spots' on the roof and exterior wall." We granted certiorari.

II

* * * "At the very core" of the Fourth Amendment "stands the right of a man to retreat into his own home and there be free from unreasonable governmental intrusion." With few exceptions, the question whether a warrantless search of a home is reasonable and hence constitutional must be answered no.

On the other hand, the antecedent question of whether or not a Fourth Amendment "search" has occurred is not so simple under our precedent. The permissibility of ordinary visual surveillance of a home used to be clear because, well into the 20th century, our Fourth Amendment jurisprudence was tied to common-law trespass. * * * We have since decoupled violation of a person's Fourth Amendment rights from trespassory violation of his property, but the lawfulness of warrantless visual surveillance of a home has still been preserved. * * *

One might think that the new validating rationale would be that examining the portion of a house that is in plain public view, while it is a "search" despite the absence of trespass, is not an "unreasonable" one under the Fourth Amendment. But in fact we have held that visual observation is no "search" at all—perhaps in order to preserve somewhat more intact our doctrine that warrantless searches are presumptively unconstitutional. In assessing when a search is not a search, we have applied somewhat in reverse the principle first enunciated in *Katz v. United States*, 389 U.S. 347 (1967). * * *

The present case involves officers on a public street engaged in more than naked-eye surveillance of a home. We have previously reserved judgment as to how much technological enhancement of ordinary perception from such a vantage point, if any, is too much. * * *

III

It would be foolish to contend that the degree of privacy secured to citizens by the Fourth Amendment has been entirely unaffected by the advance of technology. * * * The question we confront today is what limits there are upon this power of technology to shrink the realm of guaranteed privacy.

The *Katz* test—whether the individual has an expectation of privacy that society is prepared to recognize as reasonable—has often been criticized as circular, and hence subjective and unpredictable. While it may be difficult to refine *Katz* when the search of areas such as telephone booths, automobiles, or even the curtilage and uncovered portions of residences are at issue, in the case of the search of the interior of homes—the prototypical and hence most commonly litigated area of protected privacy—there is a ready criterion, with roots deep in the common law, of the minimal expectation of privacy that exists, and that is acknowledged to be reasonable. To withdraw protection of this minimum expectation would be to permit police technology to erode the privacy guaranteed by the Fourth Amendment. We think that obtaining by sense-enhancing technology any information regarding the interior of the home that could not otherwise have been obtained without physical "intrusion into a constitutionally protected area," constitutes a search—at least where (as here) the technology in question is not in general public use. This assures preservation of that degree of privacy against government that existed when the Fourth Amendment was adopted. On the basis of this criterion, the information obtained by the thermal imager in this case was the product of a search.

The Government maintains, however, that the thermal imaging must be upheld because it detected "only heat radiating from the external surface of the house." The dissent makes this its leading point, contending that there is a fundamental difference between what it calls "off-the-wall" observations and "through-the-wall surveillance." * * * We rejected such a mechanical interpretation of the Fourth Amendment in *Katz*, where the eavesdropping device picked up only sound waves that reached the exterior of the phone booth. Reversing that approach would leave the homeowner at the mercy of advancing technology—including imaging technology that could discern all human activity in the home. While the technology used in the present case was relatively crude, the rule we adopt must take account of more sophisticated systems that are already in use or in development. * * *

The Government also contends that the thermal imaging was constitutional because it did not "detect private activities occurring in private areas." * * * In the home, our cases show, all details are intimate details, because the entire area is held safe from prying government eyes. * * * These were intimate details because they were details of the home, just as was the detail of how warm—or even how relatively warm—Kyllo was heating his residence.

Limiting the prohibition of thermal imaging to "intimate details" would not only be wrong in principle; it would be impractical in application, failing to provide "a workable accommodation between the needs of law enforcement and the interests protected by the Fourth Amendment." *Oliver v. United States*, 466 U.S. 170, 181 (1984). To begin with, there is no necessary connection between the sophistication of the surveillance equipment and the "intimacy" of the details that it observes—which means that one cannot say (and the police cannot be assured) that use of the relatively crude equipment at issue here will always be lawful. The Agema Thermovision 210 might disclose, for example, at what hour each night the lady of the house takes her daily sauna and bath—a detail that many would consider "intimate"; and a much more sophisticated system might detect nothing more intimate than the fact that someone left a closet light on. We could not, in other words, develop a rule approving only that through-the-wall surveillance which identifies objects no smaller than 36 by 36 inches, but would have to develop a jurisprudence specifying which home activities are "intimate" and which are not. And even when (if ever) that jurisprudence were fully developed, no police officer would be able to know in advance whether his through-the-wall surveillance picks up "intimate" details—and thus would be unable to know in advance whether it is constitutional.

* * *

We have said that the Fourth Amendment draws "a firm line at the entrance to the house." That line, we think, must be not only firm but also bright—which requires clear specification of those methods of surveillance that require a warrant. While it is certainly possible to conclude from the videotape of the thermal imaging that occurred in this case that no "significant" compromise of the homeowner's privacy has occurred, we must take the long view, from the original meaning of the Fourth Amendment forward.

* * *

Where, as here, the Government uses a device that is not in general public use, to explore details of the home that would previously have been unknowable without physical intrusion, the surveillance is a "search" and is presumptively unreasonable without a warrant.

Since we hold the Thermovision imaging to have been an unlawful search, it will remain for the District Court to determine whether, without the evidence it provided, the search warrant issued in this case was supported by probable cause—and if not, whether there is any other basis for supporting admission of the evidence that the search pursuant to the warrant produced.

The judgment of the Court of Appeals is reversed; the case is remanded for further proceedings consistent with this opinion.

It is so ordered.

JUSTICE STEVENS, with whom THE CHIEF JUSTICE, JUSTICE O'CONNOR, and JUSTICE KENNEDY join, dissenting.

* * *

There is no need for the Court to craft a new rule to decide this case, as it is controlled by established principles from our Fourth Amendment jurisprudence. One of those core principles, of course, is that "searches and seizures *inside a home* without a warrant are presumptively unreasonable." *Payton v. New York*, 445 U.S. 573, 586 (1980) (emphasis added). But it is equally well settled that searches and seizures of property in plain view are presumptively reasonable. Whether that property is residential or commercial, the basic principle is the same: " 'What a person knowingly exposes to the public, even in his own home or office, is not a subject of Fourth Amendment protection.' " That is the principle implicated here.

While the Court "takes the long view" and decides this case based largely on the potential of yet-to-be-developed technology that might allow "through-the-wall surveillance," this case involves nothing more than off-the-wall surveillance by law enforcement officers to gather information exposed to the general public from the outside of petitioner's home. * * *

Indeed, the ordinary use of the senses might enable a neighbor or passerby to notice the heat emanating from a building, particularly if it is vented, as was the case here. Additionally, any member of the public might notice that one part of a house is warmer than another part or a nearby building if, for example, rainwater evaporates or snow melts at different rates across its surfaces. Such use of the senses would not convert into an unreasonable search if, instead, an adjoining neighbor allowed an officer onto her property to verify her perceptions with a sensitive thermometer. Nor, in my view, does such observation become an unreasonable search if made from a distance with the aid of a device that merely discloses that the exterior of one house, or one area of the house, is much warmer than another. Nothing more occurred in this case.

* * * Heat waves, like aromas that are generated in a kitchen, or in a laboratory or opium den, enter the public domain if and when they leave a building. A subjective expectation that they would remain private is not only implausible but also surely not "one that society is prepared to recognize as 'reasonable.' " *Katz*, 389 U.S. at 361 (Harlan, J., concurring).

To be sure, the homeowner has a reasonable expectation of privacy concerning what takes place within the home, and the Fourth Amendment's protection against physical invasions of the home should apply to their functional equivalent. But the equipment in this case did not penetrate the walls of petitioner's home, and while it did pick up "details of the home" that were exposed to the public, it did not obtain "any information regarding the *interior* of the home." In the Court's own words, based on what the thermal imager "showed" regarding the outside of petitioner's home, the officers "concluded" that petitioner was engaging in illegal activity inside the home. It would be quite absurd to characterize their thought processes as "searches," regardless of whether they inferred (rightly) that petitioner was growing marijuana in his house, or (wrongly) that "the lady of the house [was taking] her daily sauna and bath." * * *

Since what was involved in this case was nothing more than drawing inferences from off-the-wall surveillance, rather than any "through-the-wall" surveillance, the officers' conduct did not amount to a search and was perfectly reasonable.

   * * *

I respectfully dissent.

2.   Defendant's Effort to Protect Their Privacy

We now move to the second major factor associated with the *Katz* reasonable expectation of privacy test—the defendant's effort to protect his privacy. Some effort by the defendant to protect a privacy interest in the challenged evidence is important because, we learn quickly, the defendant cannot have a reasonable expectation of privacy in: (1) movements, property, or information knowingly exposed to the public; (2) information willingly communicated to a private third party; and (3) contraband. We begin by considering the "knowing exposure" doctrine, which has far-reaching implications.

a)   *Knowing Exposure*

CALIFORNIA V. GREENWOOD
486 U.S. 35
Supreme Court of the United States
January 11, 1988, Argued; May 16, 1988, Decided
No. 86-684

JUSTICE WHITE delivered the opinion of the Court.

The issue here is whether the Fourth Amendment prohibits the warrantless search and seizure of garbage left for collection outside the curtilage of a home. We conclude, in accordance with the vast majority of lower courts that have addressed the issue, that it does not.

I

In early 1984, Investigator Jenny Stracner of the Laguna Beach Police Department received information indicating that respondent Greenwood might be engaged in narcotics trafficking. Stracner learned that a criminal suspect had informed a federal drug enforcement agent in February 1984 that a truck filled with illegal drugs was en route to the Laguna Beach address at which Greenwood resided. In addition, a neighbor complained of heavy vehicular traffic late at night in front of Greenwood's single-family home. The neighbor reported that the vehicles remained at Greenwood's house for only a few minutes.

Stracner sought to investigate this information by conducting a surveillance of Greenwood's home. She observed several vehicles make brief stops at the house during the late-night and early morning hours, and she followed a truck from the house to a residence that had previously been under investigation as a narcotics-trafficking location.

On April 6, 1984, Stracner asked the neighborhood's regular trash collector to pick up the plastic garbage bags that Greenwood had left on the curb in front of his house and to turn the bags over to her without mixing their contents with garbage from other houses. The trash collector cleaned his truck bin of other refuse, collected the garbage bags from the street in front of Greenwood's house, and turned the bags over to Stracner. The officer searched through the rubbish and found items indicative of narcotics use. She recited the information that she had gleaned from the trash search in an affidavit in support of a warrant to search Greenwood's home.

Police officers encountered both respondents at the house later that day when they arrived to execute the warrant. The police discovered quantities of cocaine and hashish during their search of the house. Respondents were arrested on felony narcotics charges. They subsequently posted bail.

The police continued to receive reports of many late-night visitors to the Greenwood house. On May 4, Investigator Robert Rahaeuser obtained Greenwood's garbage from the regular trash collector in the same manner as had Stracner. The garbage again contained evidence of narcotics use.

Rahaeuser secured another search warrant for Greenwood's home based on the information from the second trash search. The police found more narcotics and evidence of narcotics trafficking when they executed the warrant. Greenwood was again arrested.

The Superior Court dismissed the charges against respondents on the authority of *People v. Krivda,* 5 Cal. 3d 357 (1971), which held that warrantless trash searches violate the Fourth Amendment and the California Constitution. The court found that the police would not have had probable cause to search the Greenwood home without the evidence obtained from the trash searches.

The Court of Appeal affirmed. * * * The California Supreme Court denied the State's petition for review of the Court of Appeal's decision. We granted certiorari * * *.

II

The warrantless search and seizure of the garbage bags left at the curb outside the Greenwood house would violate the Fourth Amendment only if respondents manifested a subjective expectation of privacy in their garbage that society accepts as objectively reasonable. Respondents do not disagree with this standard.

They assert, however, that they had, and exhibited, an expectation of privacy with respect to the trash that was searched by the police: The trash, which was placed on the street for collection at a fixed time, was contained in opaque plastic bags, which the garbage collector was expected to pick up, mingle with the trash of others, and deposit at the garbage dump. The trash was only temporarily on the street, and there was little likelihood that it would be inspected by anyone.

It may well be that respondents did not expect that the contents of their garbage bags would become known to the police or other members of the public. An expectation of privacy does not give rise to Fourth Amendment protection, however, unless society is prepared to accept that expectation as objectively reasonable.

Here, we conclude that respondents exposed their garbage to the public sufficiently to defeat their claim to Fourth Amendment protection. It is common knowledge that plastic garbage bags left on or at the side of a public street are readily accessible to animals, children, scavengers, snoops, and other members of the public. Moreover, respondents placed their refuse at the curb for the express purpose of conveying it to a third party, the trash collector, who might himself have sorted through respondents' trash or permitted others, such as the police, to do so. Accordingly, * * * respondents could have had no reasonable expectation of privacy in the inculpatory items that they discarded.

Furthermore, as we have held, the police cannot reasonably be expected to avert their eyes from evidence of criminal activity that could have been observed by any member of the public. Hence, "what a person knowingly exposes to the public, even in his own home or office, is not a subject of Fourth Amendment protection." *Katz v. United States.* * * *

* * * [W]e held in *California v. Ciraolo*, that the police were not required by the Fourth Amendment to obtain a warrant before conducting surveillance of the respondent's fenced backyard from a private plane flying at an altitude of 1,000 feet. We concluded that the respondent's expectation that his yard was protected from such surveillance was unreasonable because "any member of the public flying in this airspace who glanced down could have seen everything that these officers observed."

Our conclusion that society would not accept as reasonable respondents' claim to an expectation of privacy in trash left for collection in an area accessible to the public is reinforced by the unanimous rejection of similar claims by the Federal Courts of Appeals. * * * In addition, of those state appellate courts that have considered the issue, the vast majority have held that the police may conduct warrantless searches and seizures of garbage discarded in public areas.

* * *

The judgment of the California Court of Appeal is therefore reversed, and this case is remanded for further proceedings not inconsistent with this opinion.

It is so ordered.

JUSTICE KENNEDY took no part in the consideration or decision of this case.

JUSTICE BRENNAN, with whom JUSTICE MARSHALL joins, dissenting.

* * * Scrutiny of another's trash is contrary to commonly accepted notions of civilized behavior. I suspect, therefore, that members of our society will be shocked to learn that the Court, the ultimate guarantor of liberty, deems unreasonable our expectation that the aspects of our private lives that are concealed safely in a trash bag will not become public.

I

"A container which can support a reasonable expectation of privacy may not be searched, even on probable cause, without a warrant." *United States v. Jacobsen*, 466 U.S. 109, 120, n. 17 (1984) (citations omitted). Thus, as the Court observes, if Greenwood had a reasonable expectation that the contents of the bags that he placed on the curb would remain private, the warrantless search of those bags violated the Fourth Amendment.

The Framers of the Fourth Amendment understood that "unreasonable searches" of "paper[s] and effects"—no less than "unreasonable searches" of "person[s] and houses"—infringe privacy. As early as 1878, this Court acknowledged that the contents of "letters and sealed packages . . . in the mail are as fully guarded from examination and inspection . . . as if they were retained by the parties forwarding them in their own domiciles." In short, so long as a package is "closed against inspection," the Fourth Amendment protects its contents, "wherever they may be," and the police must obtain a warrant to search it just "as is required when papers are subjected to search in one's own household."

With the emergence of the reasonable-expectation-of-privacy analysis, *see Katz v. United States*, 389 U.S. 347, 361 (1967) (Harlan, J., concurring), we have reaffirmed this fundamental principle. * * * [Indeed,] [o]ur precedent * * * leaves no room to doubt that had respondents been carrying their personal effects in opaque, sealed plastic bags—identical to the ones they placed on the curb—their privacy would have been protected from warrantless police intrusion.

II

Respondents deserve no less protection just because Greenwood used the bags to discard rather than to transport his personal effects. Their contents are not inherently any less private, and Greenwood's decision to discard them, at least in the manner in which he did, does not diminish his expectation of privacy.

A trash bag, like any of the above-mentioned containers, "is a common repository for one's personal effects" and, even more than many of them, is "therefore . . . inevitably associated with the expectation of privacy." "Almost every human activity ultimately manifests itself in waste products . . . ." A single bag of trash testifies eloquently to the eating, reading, and recreational habits of the person who produced it. A search of trash, like a search of the bedroom, can relate intimate details about sexual practices, health, and personal hygiene. Like rifling through desk drawers or intercepting phone calls, rummaging through trash can divulge the target's financial and professional status, political affiliations and inclinations, private thoughts, personal relationships, and romantic interests. It cannot be doubted that a sealed trash bag harbors telling evidence of the "intimate activity associated with the 'sanctity of a man's home and the privacies of life,' " which the Fourth Amendment is designed to protect.

* * * Most of us, I believe, would be incensed to discover a meddler—whether a neighbor, a reporter, or a detective—scrutinizing our sealed trash containers to discover some detail of our personal lives. * * *

Beyond a generalized expectation of privacy, many municipalities, whether for reasons of privacy, sanitation, or both, reinforce confidence in the integrity of sealed trash containers by "prohibit[ing] anyone, except authorized employees of the Town . . . , to rummage into, pick up, collect, move or otherwise interfere with articles or materials placed on . . . any public street for collection." In fact, the California Constitution, as interpreted by the State's highest court, guarantees a right of privacy in trash vis-a-vis government officials.

That is not to deny that isolated intrusions into opaque, sealed trash containers occur. When, acting on their own, "animals, children, scavengers, snoops, [or] other members of the public," actually rummage through a bag of trash and expose its contents to plain view, "police cannot reasonably be expected to avert their eyes from evidence of criminal activity that could have been observed by any member of the public." * * *

Had Greenwood flaunted his intimate activity by strewing his trash all over the curb for all to see, or had some nongovernmental intruder invaded his privacy and done the same, I could accept the Court's conclusion that an expectation of privacy would have been unreasonable. * * *

III

In holding that the warrantless search of Greenwood's trash was consistent with the Fourth Amendment, the Court paints a grim picture of our society. It depicts a society in which local authorities may command their citizens to dispose of their personal effects in the manner least protective of the "sanctity of [the] home and the privacies of life," and then monitor them arbitrarily and without judicial oversight—a society that is not prepared to recognize as reasonable an individual's expectation of privacy in the most private of personal effects sealed in an opaque container and disposed of in a manner designed to commingle it imminently and inextricably with the trash of others. The American society with which I am familiar "chooses to dwell in reasonable security and freedom from surveillance," and is more dedicated to individual liberty and more sensitive to intrusions on the sanctity of the home than the Court is willing to acknowledge.

I dissent.

QUESTIONS, COMMENTS, CONCERNS?

1.   Subjective or objective expectation? The Court describes respondents' privacy efforts as follows: "The trash, which was placed on the street for collection at a fixed time, was contained in opaque plastic bags, which the garbage collector was expected to pick up, mingle with the trash of others, and deposit at the garbage dump. The trash was only temporarily on the street, and there was little likelihood that it would be inspected by anyone." Does the Court agree that, by configuring their trash in this manner, the respondents manifested at least a *subjective* expectation of privacy?

2.   Concern with the objective standard. Notice that the Court describes the objective standard in terms of what *society* is prepared to recognize as reasonable. Yet society is not who searched respondents' garbage; rather, it was the police. Do you see the problem? There seems to be a difference between defining a privacy interest in relation to *society* as opposed to the police. That is, I suspect you would feel differently about a member of the public rummaging through your garbage than you may feel about a police officer searching your trash.

3.   Rethinking the "knowing exposure" rationale. The *Greenwood* Court in large measure relies on the "knowing exposure" language that originated in *Katz*. The Court phrased its reliance as follows: "we conclude that respondents exposed their garbage to the public sufficiently to defeat their claim to Fourth Amendment protection." That language, however, relies on respondents exposing their garbage to the *public*? Should a standard that relies on the public apply, though, when it's actually a member of law enforcement who searched the trash? Respondents surely did not knowingly expose the contents of their garbage to the police, right?

4. **Knowing exposure and Ulbricht.** Consider the Declaration of Christopher Tarbell, filed in support of the government's opposition to Ulbricht's motion to suppress. [See Casefile Document 3.] In his declaration, Tarbell clarifies that the government learned about the Silk Road server due to a "leak" in the Tor network. Does *Greenwood* provide precedent to support an argument that, by not properly hiding the IP address for the computer hosting the Silk Road server, Ulbricht knowingly exposed the server to the public? *If he knew there was a "leak" he'd patch it*

b) Assumption of the Risk

UNITED STATES V. WHITE

401 U.S. 745
Supreme Court of the United States
November 10, 1969, Argued; April 5, 1971, Decided
No. 13

MR. JUSTICE WHITE announced the judgment of the Court and an opinion in which THE CHIEF JUSTICE, MR. JUSTICE STEWART, and MR. JUSTICE BLACKMUN join.

In 1966, respondent James A. White was tried and convicted under two consolidated indictments charging various illegal transactions in narcotics * * *. The issue before us is whether the Fourth Amendment bars from evidence the testimony of governmental agents who related certain conversations which had occurred between defendant White and a government informant, Harvey Jackson, and which the agents overheard by monitoring the frequency of a radio transmitter carried by Jackson and concealed on his person. On four occasions the conversations took place in Jackson's home; each of these conversations was overheard by an agent concealed in a kitchen closet with Jackson's consent and by a second agent outside the house using a radio receiver. Four other conversations—one in respondent's home, one in a restaurant, and two in Jackson's car—were overheard by the use of radio equipment. The prosecution was unable to locate and produce Jackson at the trial and the trial court overruled objections to the testimony of the agents who conducted the electronic surveillance. The jury returned a guilty verdict and defendant appealed. * * *

I * * *

Katz v. United States * * * swept away doctrines that electronic eavesdropping is permissible under the Fourth Amendment unless physical invasion of a constitutionally protected area produced the challenged evidence. * * * The Court of Appeals understood *Katz* to render inadmissible against White the agents' testimony concerning conversations that Jackson broadcast to them. We cannot agree. *Katz* involved no revelation to the Government by a party to conversations with the defendant nor did the

Court indicate in any way that a defendant has a justifiable and constitutionally protected expectation that a person with whom he is conversing will not then or later reveal the conversation to the police.

Hoffa v. United States, 385 U.S. 293 (1966), which was left undisturbed by *Katz*, held that however strongly a defendant may trust an apparent colleague, his expectations in this respect are not protected by the Fourth Amendment when it turns out that the colleague is a government agent regularly communicating with the authorities. In these circumstances, "no interest legitimately protected by the Fourth Amendment is involved," for that amendment affords no protection to "a wrongdoer's misplaced belief that a person to whom he voluntarily confides his wrongdoing will not reveal it." No warrant to "search and seize" is required in such circumstances, nor is it when the Government sends to defendant's home a secret agent who conceals his identity and makes a purchase of narcotics from the accused, or when the same agent, unbeknown to the defendant, carries electronic equipment to record the defendant's words and the evidence so gathered is later offered in evidence.

* * *

Concededly a police agent who conceals his police connections may write down for official use his conversations with a defendant and testify concerning them, without a warrant authorizing his encounters with the defendant and without otherwise violating the latter's Fourth Amendment rights. *Hoffa v. United States*, 385 U.S., at 300–303. For constitutional purposes, no different result is required if the agent instead of immediately reporting and transcribing his conversations with defendant, either (1) simultaneously records them with electronic equipment which he is carrying on his person, (2) or carries radio equipment which simultaneously transmits the conversations either to recording equipment located elsewhere or to other agents monitoring the transmitting frequency. If the conduct and revelations of an agent operating without electronic equipment do not invade the defendant's constitutionally justifiable expectations of privacy, neither does a simultaneous recording of the same conversations made by the agent or by others from transmissions received from the agent to whom the defendant is talking and whose trustworthiness the defendant necessarily risks.

Our problem is not what the privacy expectations of particular defendants in particular situations may be or the extent to which they may in fact have relied on the discretion of their companions. Very probably, individual defendants neither know nor suspect that their colleagues have gone or will go to the police or are carrying recorders or transmitters. Otherwise, conversation would cease and our problem with these encounters would be nonexistent or far different from those now before us. Our problem, in terms of the principles announced in *Katz*, is what expectations of privacy are constitutionally "justifiable"—what expectations the Fourth Amendment will protect in the absence of a warrant. So far, the law permits the frustration of actual expectations of privacy by permitting authorities to use the testimony of those associates who for one reason or another have determined to turn to the police, as well as by authorizing the use of informants in the manner exemplified by *Hoffa* * * *. If the law gives no protection to the wrongdoer whose trusted accomplice is or becomes a police agent, neither should it protect him when that same agent has recorded or transmitted the conversations which are later offered in evidence to prove the State's case.

Inescapably, one contemplating illegal activities must realize and risk that his companions may be reporting to the police. If he sufficiently doubts their trustworthiness, the association will very probably end or never materialize. But if he has no doubts, or allays them, or risks what doubt he has, the risk is his. In terms of what his course will be, what he will or will not do or say, we are unpersuaded that he would distinguish between probable informers on the one hand and probable informers with transmitters on the other. Given the possibility or probability that one of his colleagues is cooperating with the police, it is only speculation to assert that the defendant's utterances would be substantially different or his sense of security any less if he also thought it possible that the suspected colleague is wired for sound. At least there is no persuasive evidence that the difference in this respect between the electronically equipped and the unequipped agent is substantial enough to require discrete constitutional recognition, particularly under the Fourth Amendment which is ruled by fluid concepts of "reasonableness."

Nor should we be too ready to erect constitutional barriers to relevant and probative evidence which is also accurate and reliable. An electronic recording will many times produce a more reliable rendition of what a defendant has said than will the unaided memory of a police agent. It may also be that with the recording in existence it is less likely that the informant will change his mind, less chance that threat or injury will suppress unfavorable evidence and less chance that cross-examination will confound the testimony. Considerations like these obviously do not favor the defendant, but we are not prepared to hold that a defendant who has no constitutional right to exclude the informer's unaided testimony nevertheless has a Fourth Amendment privilege against a more accurate version of the events in question.

It is thus untenable to consider the activities and reports of the police agent himself, though acting without a warrant, to be a "reasonable" investigative effort and lawful under the Fourth Amendment but to view the same agent with a recorder or transmitter as conducting an "unreasonable" and unconstitutional search and seizure. Our opinion is currently shared by Congress and the Executive Branch, and the American Bar Association. It is also the result reached by prior cases in this Court.

No different result should obtain where, as in * * * the instant case, the informer disappears and is unavailable at trial; for the issue of whether specified events on a certain day violate the Fourth Amendment should not be determined by what later happens to the informer. His unavailability at trial and proffering the testimony of other agents may raise evidentiary problems or pose issues of prosecutorial misconduct with respect to the informer's disappearance, but they do not appear critical to deciding whether prior events invaded the defendant's Fourth Amendment rights. * * *

The judgment of the Court of Appeals is reversed.

It is so ordered.

MR. JUSTICE BLACK * * * concurs in the judgment of the Court for the reasons set forth in his dissent in *Katz v. United States*, 389 U.S. 347, 364 (1967).

MR. JUSTICE BRENNAN, concurring in the result.

[Omitted.]

MR. JUSTICE DOUGLAS, dissenting.

I

The issue in this case is clouded and concealed by the very discussion of it in legalistic terms. What the ancients knew as "eavesdropping," we now call "electronic surveillance"; but to equate the two is to treat man's first gunpowder on the same level as the nuclear bomb. Electronic surveillance is the greatest leveler of human privacy ever known. How most forms of it can be held "reasonable" within the meaning of the Fourth Amendment is a mystery. To be sure, the Constitution and Bill of Rights are not to be read as covering only the technology known in the 18th century. Otherwise its concept of "commerce" would be hopeless when it comes to the management of modern affairs. At the same time the concepts of privacy which the Founders enshrined in the Fourth Amendment vanish completely when we slavishly allow an all-powerful government, proclaiming law and order, efficiency, and other benign purposes, to penetrate all the walls and doors which men need to shield them from the pressures of a turbulent life around them and give them the health and strength to carry on. * * *

Today no one perhaps notices because only a small, obscure criminal is the victim. But every person is the victim, for the technology we exalt today is everyman's master. * * *

APPENDIX I TO OPINION OF DOUGLAS, J., DISSENTING

[Omitted.]

MR. JUSTICE HARLAN, dissenting. * * *

* * * We deal here with the constitutional validity of instantaneous third-party electronic eavesdropping, conducted by federal law enforcement officers, without any prior judicial approval of the technique utilized, but with the consent and cooperation of a participant in the conversation, and where the substance of the matter electronically overheard is related in a federal criminal trial by those who eavesdropped as direct, not merely corroborative, evidence of the guilt of the nonconsenting party. The magnitude of the issue at hand is evidenced not simply by the obvious doctrinal difficulty of weighing such activity in the Fourth Amendment balance, but also, and more importantly, by the prevalence of police utilization of this technique. * * *

The impact of the practice of third-party bugging, must, I think, be considered such as to undermine that confidence and sense of security in dealing with one another that is characteristic of individual relationships between citizens in a free society. * * *

Authority is hardly required to support the proposition that words would be measured a good deal more carefully and communication inhibited if one suspected his conversations were being transmitted and transcribed. Were third-party bugging a prevalent practice, it might well smother that spontaneity—reflected in frivolous, impetuous, sacrilegious, and defiant discourse—that liberates daily life. Much off-hand exchange is easily forgotten and one may count on the obscurity of his remarks, protected by the very fact of a limited audience, and the likelihood that the listener will either overlook or forget what is said, as well as the listener's inability to reformulate a conversation without having to contend with a documented record. All these values are sacrificed by a rule of law that permits official monitoring of private discourse limited only by the need to locate a willing assistant.

Finally, it is too easy to forget—and, hence, too often forgotten—that the issue here is whether to interpose a search warrant procedure between law enforcement agencies engaging in electronic eavesdropping and the public generally. By casting its "risk analysis" solely in terms of the expectations and risks that "wrongdoers" or "one contemplating illegal activities" ought to bear, the plurality opinion, I think, misses the mark entirely. * * * Interposition of a warrant requirement is designed not to shield "wrongdoers," but to secure a measure of privacy and a sense of personal security throughout our society.

The Fourth Amendment does, of course, leave room for the employment of modern technology in criminal law enforcement, but in the stream of current developments in Fourth Amendment law I think it must be held that third-party electronic monitoring, subject only to the self-restraint of law enforcement officials, has no place in our society. * * *

I would * * * affirm the judgment below.

MR. JUSTICE MARSHALL, dissenting.

[Omitted.]

QUESTIONS, COMMENTS, CONCERNS?

1. **Court composition matters.** *White* is the first post-*Katz* "what counts as a search" case. The *White* plurality expressly relies on Justice Harlan's reasonable expectation of privacy test, yet Justice Harlan dissents. Notice also that Justice Stewart, the author of the *Katz* majority opinion, joined the plurality. What might account for some of these oddities? Although only four years have passed since *Katz*, two members of the Court have retired— Chief Justice Burger replaced Chief Justice Warren, and Justice Blackmun replaced Justice Fortas. Both new members are in the plurality.

2. **Implications of *White*.** Does the Court hold that no search occurred when White's friend, Harvey Jackson, relayed their conversation to agents, or when Jackson recorded those conversations, or when Jackson consented to have an agent listen in his closet—or all the above? Does or should it matter that Jackson, as informant, was essentially acting as a government agent at the time he recorded his conversation with White? What does *Hoffa* say about that? And finally, does it matter that the conversations between White and Jackson occurred in Jackson's home, not White's?

3. **False friend scenarios.** Consider how *White-Hoffa* would resolve the following scenarios. For each, answer the question of whether the government conduct is a Fourth Amendment search as it relates to White, not Jackson.

a) Jackson is house-sitting for White. Before White returns home, Jackson consents to placing an agent in White's closet. Jackson and White share a conversation that incriminates White. S

b) Jackson visits White in his home wearing a wire that electronically transmits the content of their conversations back to listening agents. N S

c) Jackson and White converse on a bench in a public park. Unbeknownst to them, police have placed a listening device under the bench and record their conversation. White makes incriminating statements. NS

d) The same as scenario (c) except that Jackson consents to investigators' placement of the device under the park bench.

c) Contraband

ILLINOIS V. CABALLES

543 U.S. 405
Supreme Court of the United States
November 10, 2004, Argued; January 24, 2005, Decided
No. 03-923

JUSTICE STEVENS delivered the opinion of the Court.

Illinois State Trooper Daniel Gillette stopped respondent for speeding on an interstate highway. When Gillette radioed the police dispatcher to report the stop, a second trooper, Craig Graham, a member of the Illinois State Police Drug Interdiction Team, overheard the transmission and immediately headed for the scene with his narcotics-detection dog. When they arrived, respondent's car was on the shoulder of the road and respondent was in Gillette's vehicle. While Gillette was in the process of writing a warning ticket, Graham walked his dog around respondent's car. The dog alerted at the trunk. Based on that alert, the officers searched the trunk, found marijuana, and arrested respondent. The entire incident lasted less than 10 minutes.

Respondent was convicted of a narcotics offense and sentenced to 12 years' imprisonment and a $256,136 fine. The trial judge denied his motion to suppress the seized evidence and to quash his arrest. He held that the officers had not unnecessarily prolonged the stop and that the dog alert was sufficiently reliable to provide probable cause to conduct the search. Although the Appellate Court affirmed, the Illinois Supreme Court reversed, concluding that because the canine sniff was performed without any " 'specific and articulable facts' " to suggest drug activity, the use of the dog "unjustifiably enlarg[ed] the scope of a routine traffic stop into a drug investigation."

The question on which we granted certiorari is narrow: "Whether the Fourth Amendment requires reasonable, articulable suspicion to justify using a drug-detection dog to sniff a vehicle during a legitimate traffic stop." * * *

Official conduct that does not "compromise any legitimate interest in privacy" is not a search subject to the Fourth Amendment. We have held that any interest in possessing contraband cannot be deemed "legitimate," and thus, governmental conduct that only reveals the possession of contraband "compromises no legitimate privacy interest." This is because the expectation "that certain facts will not come to the attention of the authorities" is not the same as an interest in "privacy that society is prepared to consider reasonable." In *United States v. Place*, 462 U.S. 696 (1983), we treated a canine sniff by a well-trained narcotics-detection dog as "sui generis" because it "discloses only the presence or absence of narcotics, a contraband item." Respondent likewise concedes that "drug sniffs are designed, and if properly conducted are generally likely, to reveal only the presence of contraband." Although respondent argues that the error rates, particularly the existence of false positives, call into question the premise that drug-detection dogs alert only to contraband, the record contains no evidence or findings that support his argument. Moreover, respondent does not suggest that an erroneous alert, in and of itself, reveals any legitimate private information, and, in this case, the trial judge found that the dog sniff was sufficiently reliable to establish probable cause to conduct a full-blown search of the trunk.

Accordingly, the use of a well-trained narcotics-detection dog—one that "does not expose noncontraband items that otherwise would remain hidden from public view," *Place*, 462 U.S., at 707—during a lawful traffic stop, generally does not implicate legitimate privacy interests. In this case, the dog sniff was performed on the exterior of respondent's car while he was lawfully seized for a traffic violation. Any intrusion on respondent's privacy expectations does not rise to the level of a constitutionally cognizable infringement.

This conclusion is entirely consistent with our recent decision that the use of a thermal-imaging device to detect the growth of marijuana in a home constituted an unlawful search. *Kyllo v. United States*, 533 U.S. 27 (2001). Critical to that decision was the fact that the device was capable of detecting lawful activity—in that case, intimate details in a home, such as "at what hour each night the lady of the house takes her daily sauna and bath." The legitimate expectation that information about perfectly lawful activity will remain private is categorically distinguishable from respondent's hopes or expectations concerning the nondetection of contraband in the trunk of his car. A dog sniff conducted during a concededly lawful traffic stop that reveals no information other than the location of a substance that no individual has any right to possess does not violate the Fourth Amendment.

The judgment of the Illinois Supreme Court is vacated, and the case is remanded for further proceedings not inconsistent with this opinion.

It is so ordered.

THE CHIEF JUSTICE took no part in the decision of this case.

JUSTICE SOUTER, dissenting.

I would hold that using the dog for the purposes of determining the presence of marijuana in the car's trunk was a search unauthorized as an incident of the speeding stop and unjustified on any other ground. I would accordingly affirm the judgment of the Supreme Court of Illinois, and I respectfully dissent.

In *United States v. Place*, 462 U.S. 696 (1983), we categorized the sniff of the narcotics-seeking dog as "sui generis" under the Fourth Amendment and held it was not a search. The classification rests not only upon the limited nature of the intrusion, but on a further premise that experience has shown to be untenable, the assumption that trained sniffing dogs do not err. What we have learned about the fallibility of dogs in the years since *Place* was decided would itself be reason to call for reconsidering *Place's* decision against treating the intentional use of a trained dog as a search. The portent of this very case, however, adds insistence to the call, for an uncritical adherence to *Place* would render the Fourth Amendment indifferent to suspicionless and indiscriminate sweeps of cars in parking garages and pedestrians on sidewalks; if a sniff is not preceded by a seizure subject to Fourth Amendment notice, it escapes Fourth Amendment review entirely unless it is treated as a search. We should not wait for these developments to occur before rethinking *Place's* analysis, which invites such untoward consequences.

At the heart both of *Place* and the Court's opinion today is the proposition that sniffs by a trained dog are *sui generis* because a reaction by the dog in going alert is a response to nothing but the presence of contraband. Hence, the argument goes, because the sniff can only reveal the presence of items devoid of any legal use, the sniff "does not implicate legitimate privacy interests" and is not to be treated as a search.

The infallible dog, however, is a creature of legal fiction. * * * [T]heir supposed infallibility is belied by judicial opinions describing well-trained animals sniffing and alerting with less than perfect accuracy, whether owing to errors by their handlers, the limitations of the dogs themselves, or even the pervasive contamination of currency by cocaine. Indeed, a study cited by Illinois in this case for the proposition that dog sniffs are "generally reliable" shows that dogs in artificial testing situations return false positives anywhere from 12.55 to 60% of the time, depending on the length of the search. In practical terms, the evidence is clear that the dog that alerts hundreds of times will be wrong dozens of times.

Once the dog's fallibility is recognized, however, that ends the justification claimed in *Place* for treating the sniff as *sui generis* under the Fourth Amendment: the sniff alert does not necessarily signal hidden contraband, and opening the container or enclosed space whose emanations the dog has sensed will not necessarily reveal contraband or any other evidence of crime. This is not, of course, to deny that a dog's reaction may provide reasonable suspicion, or probable cause, to search the container or enclosure; the Fourth Amendment does not demand certainty of success to justify a search for evidence or contraband. The point is simply that the sniff and alert cannot claim the certainty that *Place* assumed, both in treating the deliberate use of sniffing dogs as *sui generis* and then taking that characterization as a reason to say they are not searches subject to

Fourth Amendment scrutiny. And when that aura of uniqueness disappears, there is no basis in *Place's* reasoning, and no good reason otherwise, to ignore the actual function that dog sniffs perform. They are conducted to obtain information about the contents of private spaces beyond anything that human senses could perceive, even when conventionally enhanced. * * * And given the fallibility of the dog, the sniff is the first step in a process that may disclose "intimate details" without revealing contraband, just as a thermal-imaging device might do, as described in *Kyllo v. United States*, 533 U.S. 27 (2001).

* * * I would treat the dog sniff as the familiar search it is in fact, subject to scrutiny under the Fourth Amendment.

JUSTICE GINSBURG, with whom JUSTICE SOUTER joins, dissenting.

[Omitted.]

3.   Nature of the Government Intrusion

We now move to the "nature of the government intrusion"—the third factor associated with the reasonable expectation of privacy test. In many ways, this is the simplest of the three factors to conceptualize because we simply consider the extent of the government's intrusion on the defendant's privacy interest. But simple is not always easy. The Court's opinion in *Smith v. Maryland*, in particular, raises significant questions about citizens' relationships to third party servicers, like cell phone providers, alongside the information that citizens convey to those servicers.

a)   Greater Intrusion

FLORIDA V. RILEY

488 U.S. 445
Supreme Court of the United States
October 3, 1988, Argued; January 23, 1989, Decided
No. 87-764

JUSTICE WHITE announced the judgment of the Court and delivered an opinion, in which THE CHIEF JUSTICE, JUSTICE SCALIA, and JUSTICE KENNEDY join.

On certification to it by a lower state court, the Florida Supreme Court addressed the following question: "Whether surveillance of the interior of a partially covered greenhouse in a residential backyard from the vantage point of a helicopter located 400 feet above the greenhouse constitutes a 'search' for which a warrant is required under the Fourth Amendment and Article I, § 12 of the Florida Constitution." The court answered the question in the affirmative, and we granted the State's petition for certiorari challenging that conclusion.

Respondent Riley lived in a mobile home located on five acres of rural property. A greenhouse was located 10 to 20 feet behind the mobile home. Two sides of the greenhouse were enclosed. The other two sides were not enclosed but the contents of the greenhouse were obscured from view from surrounding property by trees, shrubs, and the mobile home. The greenhouse was covered by corrugated roofing panels, some translucent and some opaque. At the time relevant to this case, two of the panels, amounting to approximately 10% of the roof area, were missing. A wire fence surrounded the mobile home and the greenhouse, and the property was posted with a "DO NOT ENTER" sign.

This case originated with an anonymous tip to the Pasco County Sheriff's office that marijuana was being grown on respondent's property. When an investigating officer discovered that he could not see the contents of the greenhouse from the road, he circled twice over respondent's property in a helicopter at the height of 400 feet. With his naked eye, he was able to see through the openings in the roof and one or more of the open sides of the greenhouse and to identify what he thought was marijuana growing in the structure. A warrant was obtained based on these observations, and the ensuing search revealed marijuana growing in the greenhouse. Respondent was charged with possession of marijuana under Florida law. The trial court granted his motion to suppress; the Florida Court of Appeals reversed but certified the case to the Florida Supreme Court, which quashed the decision of the Court of Appeals and reinstated the trial court's suppression order.

We agree with the State's submission that our decision in *California v. Ciraolo*, 476 U.S. 207 (1986), controls this case. There, acting on a tip, the police inspected the backyard of a particular house while flying in a fixed-wing aircraft at 1,000 feet. With the naked eye the officers saw what they concluded was marijuana growing in the yard. A search warrant was obtained on the strength of this airborne inspection, and marijuana plants were found. The trial court refused to suppress this evidence, but a state appellate court held that the inspection violated the Fourth and Fourteenth Amendments to the United States Constitution, and that the warrant was therefore invalid. We in turn reversed, holding that the inspection was not a search subject to the Fourth Amendment. We recognized that the yard was within the curtilage of the house, that a fence shielded the yard from observation from the street, and that the occupant had a subjective expectation of privacy. We held, however, that such an expectation was not reasonable and not one "that society is prepared to honor." Our reasoning was that the home and its curtilage are not necessarily protected from inspection that involves no physical invasion. " 'What a person knowingly exposes to the public, even in his own home or office, is not a subject of Fourth Amendment protection.' " *Id.*, at 213, quoting *Katz v. United States*, 389 U.S. 347, 351 (1967). As a general proposition, the police may see what may be seen "from a public vantage point where [they have] a right to be." Thus the police, like the public, would have been free to inspect the backyard garden from the street if their view had been unobstructed. They were likewise free to inspect the yard from the vantage point of an aircraft flying in the navigable airspace as this plane was. "In an age where private and commercial flight in the public airways is routine, it is unreasonable for respondent to expect that his marijuana plants were constitutionally protected from being observed with the naked eye from an altitude of 1,000 feet. The Fourth Amendment simply does not require the police traveling in the public airways at this altitude to obtain a warrant in order to observe what is visible to the naked eye." *Id.*, at 215.

We arrive at the same conclusion in the present case. In this case, as in *Ciraolo*, the property surveyed was within the curtilage of respondent's home. Riley no doubt intended and expected that his greenhouse would not be open to public inspection, and the precautions he took protected against ground-level observation. Because the sides and roof of his greenhouse were left partially open, however, what was growing in the greenhouse was subject to viewing from the air. Under the holding in *Ciraolo*, Riley could not reasonably have expected the contents of his greenhouse to be immune from examination by an officer seated in a fixed-wing aircraft flying in navigable airspace at an altitude of 1,000 feet or, as the Florida Supreme Court seemed to recognize, at an altitude of 500 feet, the lower limit of the navigable airspace for such an aircraft. Here, the inspection was made from a helicopter, but as is the case with fixed-wing planes, "private and commercial flight [by helicopter] in the public airways is routine" in this country, *Ciraolo*, and there is no indication that such flights are unheard of in Pasco County, Florida.[2] Riley could not reasonably have expected that his greenhouse was protected from public or official observation from a helicopter had it been flying within the navigable airspace for fixed-wing aircraft.

Nor on the facts before us, does it make a difference for Fourth Amendment purposes that the helicopter was flying at 400 feet when the officer saw what was growing in the greenhouse through the partially open roof and sides of the structure. We would have a different case if flying at that altitude had been contrary to law or regulation. But helicopters are not bound by the lower limits of the navigable airspace allowed to other aircraft.[3] Any member of the public could legally have been flying over

---

[2]   The first use of the helicopter by police was in New York in 1947, and today every State in the country uses helicopters in police work. As of 1980, there were 1,500 such aircraft used in police work. More than 10,000 helicopters, both public and private, are registered in the United States. And there are an estimated 31,697 helicopter pilots.

[3]   While Federal Aviation Administration regulations permit fixed-wing aircraft to be operated at an altitude of 1,000 feet while flying over congested areas and at an altitude of 500 feet above the surface in other than congested areas, helicopters may be operated at less than the minimums for fixed-wing aircraft "if the operation is conducted without hazard to persons or

Riley's property in a helicopter at the altitude of 400 feet and could have observed Riley's greenhouse. The police officer did no more. This is not to say that an inspection of the curtilage of a house from an aircraft will always pass muster under the Fourth Amendment simply because the plane is within the navigable airspace specified by law. But it is of obvious importance that the helicopter in this case was not violating the law, and there is nothing in the record or before us to suggest that helicopters flying at 400 feet are sufficiently rare in this country to lend substance to respondent's claim that he reasonably anticipated that his greenhouse would not be subject to observation from that altitude. Neither is there any intimation here that the helicopter interfered with respondent's normal use of the greenhouse or of other parts of the curtilage. As far as this record reveals, no intimate details connected with the use of the home or curtilage were observed, and there was no undue noise, and no wind, dust, or threat of injury. In these circumstances, there was no violation of the Fourth Amendment.

The judgment of the Florida Supreme Court is accordingly reversed. * * *

JUSTICE O'CONNOR, concurring in the judgment.

[Omitted.]

JUSTICE BRENNAN, with whom JUSTICE MARSHALL and JUSTICE STEVENS join, dissenting. * * *

The opinion for a plurality of the Court reads almost as if *Katz v. United States*, 389 U.S. 347 (1967), had never been decided. Notwithstanding the disclaimers of its final paragraph, the opinion relies almost exclusively on the fact that the police officer conducted his surveillance from a vantage point where, under applicable Federal Aviation Administration regulations, he had a legal right to be. *Katz* teaches, however, that the relevant inquiry is whether the police surveillance "violated the privacy upon which [the defendant] justifiably relied,"—or, as Justice Harlan put it, whether the police violated an "expectation of privacy . . . that society is prepared to recognize as 'reasonable.' " The result of that inquiry in any given case depends ultimately on the judgment "whether, if the particular form of surveillance practiced by the police is permitted to go unregulated by constitutional restraints, the amount of privacy and freedom remaining to citizens would be diminished to a compass inconsistent with the aims of a free and open society."

The plurality undertakes no inquiry into whether low-level helicopter surveillance by the police of activities in an enclosed backyard is consistent

property on the surface. In addition, each person operating a helicopter shall comply with routes or altitudes specifically prescribed for helicopters by the [FAA] Administrator."

with the "aims of a free and open society." Instead, it summarily concludes that Riley's expectation of privacy was unreasonable because "[a]ny member of the public could legally have been flying over Riley's property in a helicopter at the altitude of 400 feet and could have observed Riley's greenhouse." This observation is, in turn, based solely on the fact that the police helicopter was within the airspace within which such craft are allowed by federal safety regulations to fly. * * *

It is a curious notion that the reach of the Fourth Amendment can be so largely defined by administrative regulations issued for purposes of flight safety.[2] It is more curious still that the plurality relies to such an extent on the legality of the officer's act, when we have consistently refused to equate police violation of the law with infringement of the Fourth Amendment. But the plurality's willingness to end its inquiry when it finds that the officer was in a position he had a right to be in is misguided for an even more fundamental reason. Finding determinative the fact that the officer was where he had a right to be is, at bottom, an attempt to analogize surveillance from a helicopter to surveillance by a police officer standing on a public road and viewing evidence of crime through an open window or a gap in a fence. In such a situation, the occupant of the home may be said to lack any reasonable expectation of privacy in what can be seen from that road—even if, in fact, people rarely pass that way.

The police officer positioned 400 feet above Riley's backyard was not, however, standing on a public road. The vantage point he enjoyed was not one any citizen could readily share. His ability to see over Riley's fence depended on his use of a very expensive and sophisticated piece of machinery to which few ordinary citizens have access. In such circumstances it makes no more sense to rely on the legality of the officer's position in the skies than it would to judge the constitutionality of the wiretap in *Katz* by the legality of the officer's position outside the telephone booth. The simple inquiry whether the police officer had the legal right to be in the position from which he made his observations cannot suffice, for we cannot assume that Riley's curtilage was so open to the observations of passersby in the skies that he retained little privacy or personal security to be lost to police surveillance. The question before us must be not whether the police were where they had a right to be, but whether public observation of Riley's curtilage was so commonplace that Riley's expectation of privacy in his backyard could not be considered reasonable. To say that an invasion of Riley's privacy from the skies was not impossible is most emphatically not the same as saying that his expectation of privacy

---

[2] The plurality's use of the FAA regulations as a means for determining whether Riley enjoyed a reasonable expectation of privacy produces an incredible result. Fixed-wing aircraft may not be operated below 500 feet (1,000 feet over congested areas), while helicopters may be operated below those levels. Therefore, whether Riley's expectation of privacy is reasonable turns on whether the police officer at 400 feet above his curtilage is seated in an airplane or a helicopter. This cannot be the law.

within his enclosed curtilage was not "one that society is prepared to recognize as 'reasonable.' " *Katz*, 389 U.S., at 361 (Harlan, J., concurring). While, as we held in *Ciraolo*, air traffic at elevations of 1,000 feet or more may be so common that whatever could be seen with the naked eye from that elevation is unprotected by the Fourth Amendment, it is a large step from there to say that the Amendment offers no protection against low-level helicopter surveillance of enclosed curtilage areas. * * *

Perhaps the most remarkable passage in the plurality opinion is its suggestion that the case might be a different one had any "intimate details connected with the use of the home or curtilage [been] observed." What, one wonders, is meant by "intimate details"? If the police had observed Riley embracing his wife in the backyard greenhouse, would we then say that his reasonable expectation of privacy had been infringed? Where in the Fourth Amendment or in our cases is there any warrant for imposing a requirement that the activity observed must be "intimate" in order to be protected by the Constitution?

It is difficult to avoid the conclusion that the plurality has allowed its analysis of Riley's expectation of privacy to be colored by its distaste for the activity in which he was engaged. It is indeed easy to forget, especially in view of current concern over drug trafficking, that the scope of the Fourth Amendment's protection does not turn on whether the activity disclosed by a search is illegal or innocuous. But we dismiss this as a "drug case" only at the peril of our own liberties. * * * As Professor Amsterdam has eloquently written: "The question is not whether you or I must draw the blinds before we commit a crime. It is whether you and I must discipline ourselves to draw the blinds every time we enter a room, under pain of surveillance if we do not." * * *

The issue in this case is, ultimately, "how tightly the fourth amendment permits people to be driven back into the recesses of their lives by the risk of surveillance." The Court today approves warrantless helicopter surveillance from an altitude of 400 feet. * * * I find considerable cause for concern in the fact that a plurality of four Justices would remove virtually all constitutional barriers to police surveillance from the vantage point of helicopters. The Fourth Amendment demands that we temper our efforts to apprehend criminals with a concern for the impact on our fundamental liberties of the methods we use. I hope it will be a matter of concern to my colleagues that the police surveillance methods they would sanction were among those described 40 years ago in George Orwell's dread vision of life in the 1980's:

> The black-mustachio'd face gazed down from every commanding corner. There was one on the house front immediately opposite. BIG BROTHER IS WATCHING YOU, the caption said . . . . In the far distance a helicopter skimmed down between the roofs,

hovered for an instant like a bluebottle, and darted away again with a curving flight. It was the Police Patrol, snooping into people's windows.

Who can read this passage without a shudder, and without the instinctive reaction that it depicts life in some country other than ours? I respectfully dissent.

JUSTICE BLACKMUN, dissenting.

[Omitted.]

QUESTIONS, COMMENTS, CONCERNS?

1.   **More on *Ciraolo*.** The *Riley* Court relied, in part, on *California v. Ciraolo*, 476 U.S. 207 (1986), where police received an anonymous tip that respondent was growing marijuana in his backyard. Respondent erected a six-foot outer fence and ten-foot inner fence to completely enclose his yard. In response, police "secured a private plane and flew over respondent's house at an altitude of 1,000 feet, within navigable airspace[.]" While in flight, "officers readily identified marijuana plants 8 feet to 10 feet in height growing in a 15-by 25-foot plot in respondent's yard; they photographed the area with a standard 35mm camera." Based on the tip and photographs, police secured and executed a search warrant for respondent's property where they seized seventy-three marijuana plants. Respondent challenged the warrantless aerial observation of his yard on Fourth Amendment grounds. The Supreme Court, however, held that no Fourth Amendment search occurred. The Court reasoned that "[a]ny member of the public flying in this airspace who glanced down could have seen everything that these officers observed." The Court also commented that respondent's "10-foot fence might not shield these plants from the eyes of a citizen or a policeman perched on the top of a truck or a two-level bus."

2.   **Aerial surveillance and "industrial curtilage."** In *Dow Chemical v. United States*, 476 U.S. 227 (1986), company officials denied the EPA an opportunity to make an on-site inspection of two powerplants at the Dow property. In response, the EPA, without informing Dow, "employed a commercial aerial photographer, using a standard floor-mounted, precision aerial mapping camera, to take photographs of the facility from altitudes of 12,000, 3,000, and 1,200 feet. At all times the aircraft was lawfully within navigable airspace." Dow later sued the EPA claiming that the warrantless photography violated the Fourth Amendment. The Supreme Court disagreed, recognizing that "[t]he narrow issue raised by Dow's claim * * * concerns aerial observation of a 2,000-acre outdoor manufacturing facility *without* physical entry." As a result, the Court held that the EPA surveyed only "open fields" and took photographs that "are not so revealing of intimate details as to raise constitutional concerns." It reasoned that the photos were "limited to an outline of the facility's buildings and equipment" and they recorded no intimate

company details like "confidential discussions of chemical formulae or other trade secrets[.]"

b) Lesser Intrusion

SMITH V. MARYLAND
442 U.S. 735
Supreme Court of the United States
March 28, 1979, Argued; June 20, 1979, Decided
No. 78-5374

MR. JUSTICE BLACKMUN delivered the opinion of the Court.

This case presents the question whether the installation and use of a pen register[1] constitutes a "search" within the meaning of the Fourth Amendment * * *.

I

On March 5, 1976, in Baltimore, Md., Patricia McDonough was robbed. She gave the police a description of the robber and of a 1975 Monte Carlo automobile she had observed near the scene of the crime. After the robbery, McDonough began receiving threatening and obscene phone calls from a man identifying himself as the robber. On one occasion, the caller asked that she step out on her front porch; she did so, and saw the 1975 Monte Carlo she had earlier described to police moving slowly past her home. On March 16, police spotted a man who met McDonough's description driving a 1975 Monte Carlo in her neighborhood. By tracing the license plate number, police learned that the car was registered in the name of petitioner, Michael Lee Smith.

The next day, the telephone company, at police request, installed a pen register at its central offices to record the numbers dialed from the telephone at petitioner's home. The police did not get a warrant or court order before having the pen register installed. The register revealed that on March 17 a call was placed from petitioner's home to McDonough's phone. On the basis of this and other evidence, the police obtained a warrant to search petitioner's residence. The search revealed that a page in petitioner's phone book was turned down to the name and number of Patricia McDonough; the phone book was seized. Petitioner was arrested, and a six-man lineup was held on March 19. McDonough identified petitioner as the man who had robbed her.

---

[1] "A pen register is a mechanical device that records the numbers dialed on a telephone by monitoring the electrical impulses caused when the dial on the telephone is released. It does not overhear oral communications and does not indicate whether calls are actually completed." A pen register is "usually installed at a central telephone facility [and] records on a paper tape all numbers dialed from [the] line" to which it is attached.

Petitioner was indicted in the Criminal Court of Baltimore for robbery. By pretrial motion, he sought to suppress "all fruits derived from the pen register" on the ground that the police had failed to secure a warrant prior to its installation. The trial court denied the suppression motion, holding that the warrantless installation of the pen register did not violate the Fourth Amendment. Petitioner then waived a jury, and the case was submitted to the court on an agreed statement of facts. The pen register tape (evidencing the fact that a phone call had been made from petitioner's phone to McDonough's phone) and the phone book seized in the search of petitioner's residence were admitted into evidence against him. Petitioner was convicted and was sentenced to six years. He appealed to the Maryland Court of Special Appeals, but the Court of Appeals of Maryland issued a writ of certiorari to the intermediate court in advance of its decision in order to consider whether the pen register evidence had been properly admitted at petitioner's trial.

The Court of Appeals affirmed the judgment of conviction, holding that "there is no constitutionally protected reasonable expectation of privacy in the numbers dialed into a telephone system and hence no search within the fourth amendment is implicated by the use of a pen register installed at the central offices of the telephone company." Because there was no "search," the court concluded, no warrant was needed. * * * Certiorari was granted in order to resolve indications of conflict in the decided cases as to the restrictions imposed by the Fourth Amendment on the use of pen registers.

II

A

* * * Consistently with *Katz [v. United States]*, this Court uniformly has held that the application of the Fourth Amendment depends on whether the person invoking its protection can claim a "justifiable," a "reasonable," or a "legitimate expectation of privacy" that has been invaded by government action. This inquiry, as Mr. Justice Harlan aptly noted in his *Katz* concurrence, normally embraces two discrete questions. The first is whether the individual, by his conduct, has "exhibited an actual (subjective) expectation of privacy,"—whether, in the words of the *Katz* majority, the individual has shown that "he seeks to preserve [something] as private." The second question is whether the individual's subjective expectation of privacy is "one that society is prepared to recognize as 'reasonable,' "—whether, in the words of the *Katz* majority, the individual's expectation, viewed objectively, is "justifiable" under the circumstances.

B

In applying the *Katz* analysis to this case, it is important to begin by specifying precisely the nature of the state activity that is challenged. The activity here took the form of installing and using a pen register. Since the pen register was installed on telephone company property at the telephone company's central offices, petitioner obviously cannot claim that his "property" was invaded or that police intruded into a "constitutionally protected area." Petitioner's claim, rather, is that, notwithstanding the absence of a trespass, the State, as did the Government in *Katz*, infringed a "legitimate expectation of privacy" that petitioner held. Yet a pen register differs significantly from the listening device employed in *Katz*, for pen registers do not acquire the contents of communications. This Court recently noted:

> Indeed, a law enforcement official could not even determine from the use of a pen register whether a communication existed. These devices do not hear sound. They disclose only the telephone numbers that have been dialed—a means of establishing communication. Neither the purport of any communication between the caller and the recipient of the call, their identities, nor whether the call was even completed is disclosed by pen registers.

Given a pen register's limited capabilities, therefore, petitioner's argument that its installation and use constituted a "search" necessarily rests upon a claim that he had a "legitimate expectation of privacy" regarding the numbers he dialed on his phone.

This claim must be rejected. First, we doubt that people in general entertain any actual expectation of privacy in the numbers they dial. All telephone users realize that they must "convey" phone numbers to the telephone company, since it is through telephone company switching equipment that their calls are completed. All subscribers realize, moreover, that the phone company has facilities for making permanent records of the numbers they dial, for they see a list of their long-distance (toll) calls on their monthly bills. In fact, pen registers and similar devices are routinely used by telephone companies "for the purposes of checking billing operations, detecting fraud, and preventing violations of law." Electronic equipment is used not only to keep billing records of toll calls, but also "to keep a record of all calls dialed from a telephone which is subject to a special rate structure." Pen registers are regularly employed "to determine whether a home phone is being used to conduct a business, to check for a defective dial, or to check for overbilling." Although most people may be oblivious to a pen register's esoteric functions, they presumably have some awareness of one common use: to aid in the identification of persons making annoying or obscene calls. Most phone books tell subscribers, on a page entitled "Consumer Information," that the company "can frequently help in identifying to the authorities the origin of unwelcome and troublesome calls." Telephone users, in sum, typically know that they must convey numerical information to the phone company; that the phone company has facilities for recording this information; and that the phone company does in fact record this information for a variety of legitimate business purposes. Although subjective expectations cannot be scientifically gauged, it is too much to believe that telephone subscribers, under these circumstances, harbor any general expectation that the numbers they dial will remain secret.

Petitioner argues, however, that, whatever the expectations of telephone users in general, he demonstrated an expectation of privacy by his own conduct here, since he "[used] the telephone in his house to the exclusion of all others." But the site of the call is immaterial for purposes of analysis in this case. Although petitioner's conduct may have been calculated to keep the contents of his conversation private, his conduct was not and could not have been calculated to preserve the privacy of the number he dialed. Regardless of his location, petitioner had to convey that number to the telephone company in precisely the same way if he wished to complete his call. The fact that he dialed the number on his home phone rather than on some other phone could make no conceivable difference, nor could any subscriber rationally think that it would.

Second, even if petitioner did harbor some subjective expectation that the phone numbers he dialed would remain private, this expectation is not "one that society is prepared to recognize as 'reasonable.'" *Katz v. United States*, 389 U.S., at 361. This Court consistently has held that a person has no legitimate expectation of privacy in information he voluntarily turns over to third parties. * * *

This analysis dictates that petitioner can claim no legitimate expectation of privacy here. When he used his phone, petitioner voluntarily conveyed numerical information to the telephone company and "exposed" that information to its equipment in the ordinary course of business. In so doing, petitioner assumed the risk that the company would reveal to police the numbers he dialed. The switching equipment that processed those numbers is merely the modern counterpart of the operator who, in an earlier day, personally completed calls for the subscriber. Petitioner concedes that if he had placed his calls through an operator, he could claim no legitimate expectation of privacy. We are not inclined to hold that a different constitutional result is required because the telephone company has decided to automate. * *-*

We therefore conclude that petitioner in all probability entertained no actual expectation of privacy in the phone numbers he dialed, and that, even if he did, his expectation was not "legitimate." The installation and use of a pen register, consequently, was not a "search," and no warrant was required. The judgment of the Maryland Court of Appeals is affirmed.

It is so ordered.

MR. JUSTICE POWELL took no part in the consideration or decision of this case.

MR. JUSTICE STEWART, with whom MR. JUSTICE BRENNAN joins, dissenting.

* * * [W]e have squarely held that the user of even a public telephone is entitled "to assume that the words he utters into the mouthpiece will not be broadcast to the world." *Katz v. United States.*

The central question in this case is whether a person who makes telephone calls from his home is entitled to make a similar assumption about the numbers he dials. What the telephone company does or might do with those numbers is no more relevant to this inquiry than it would be in a case involving the conversation itself. It is simply not enough to say, after *Katz,* that there is no legitimate expectation of privacy in the numbers dialed because the caller assumes the risk that the telephone company will disclose them to the police.

I think that the numbers dialed from a private telephone—like the conversations that occur during a call—are within the constitutional protection recognized in *Katz*. It seems clear to me that information obtained by pen register surveillance of a private telephone is information in which the telephone subscriber has a legitimate expectation of privacy. The information captured by such surveillance emanates from private conduct within a person's home or office—locations that without question are entitled to Fourth and Fourteenth Amendment protection. Further, that information is an integral part of the telephonic communication that under *Katz* is entitled to constitutional protection, whether or not it is captured by a trespass into such an area.

The numbers dialed from a private telephone—although certainly more prosaic than the conversation itself—are not without "content." Most private telephone subscribers may have their own numbers listed in a publicly distributed directory, but I doubt there are any who would be happy to have broadcast to the world a list of the local or long distance numbers they have called. This is not because such a list might in some sense be incriminating, but because it easily could reveal the identities of the persons and the places called, and thus reveal the most intimate details of a person's life.

I respectfully dissent.

MR. JUSTICE MARSHALL, with whom MR. JUSTICE BRENNAN joins, dissenting.

* * * Applying the standards set forth in *Katz v. United States,* 389 U.S. 347, 361 (1967) (Harlan, J., concurring), the Court first determines that telephone subscribers have no subjective expectations of privacy concerning the numbers they dial. To reach this conclusion, the Court posits that individuals somehow infer from the long-distance listings on their phone bills, and from the cryptic assurances of "help" in tracing obscene calls included in "most" phone books, that pen registers are regularly used for recording local calls. But even assuming, as I do not, that individuals "typically know" that a phone company monitors calls for internal reasons, it does not follow that they expect this information to be made available to the public in general or the government in particular. Privacy is not a discrete commodity, possessed absolutely or not at all. Those who disclose certain facts to a bank or phone company for a limited business purpose need not assume that this information will be released to other persons for other purposes.

The crux of the Court's holding, however, is that whatever expectation of privacy petitioner may in fact have entertained regarding his calls, it is not one "society is prepared to recognize as 'reasonable.' " Ante, at 743. In so ruling, the Court determines that individuals who convey information to third parties have "assumed the risk" of disclosure to the government. This analysis is misconceived in two critical respects.

Implicit in the concept of assumption of risk is some notion of choice. At least in the third-party consensual surveillance cases, which first incorporated risk analysis into Fourth Amendment doctrine, the defendant presumably had exercised some discretion in deciding who should enjoy his confidential communications. *See, e.g.,* * * * *United States v. White, supra,* at 751–752 (plurality opinion). By contrast here, unless a person is prepared to forgo use of what for many has become a personal or professional necessity, he cannot help but accept the risk of surveillance. It is idle to speak of "assuming" risks in contexts where, as a practical matter, individuals have no realistic alternative.

More fundamentally, to make risk analysis dispositive in assessing the reasonableness of privacy expectations would allow the government to define the scope of Fourth Amendment protections. For example, law enforcement officials, simply by announcing their intent to monitor the content of random samples of first-class mail or private phone conversations, could put the public on notice of the risks they would thereafter assume in such communications. Yet, although acknowledging this implication of its analysis, the Court is willing to concede only that, in some circumstances, a further "normative inquiry would be proper." No meaningful effort is made to explain what those circumstances might be, or why this case is not among them.

In my view, whether privacy expectations are legitimate within the meaning of *Katz* depends not on the risks an individual can be presumed to accept when imparting information to third parties, but on the risks he should be forced to assume in a free and open society. By its terms, the constitutional prohibition of unreasonable searches and seizures assigns to the judiciary some prescriptive responsibility. As Mr. Justice Harlan, who formulated the standard the Court applies today, himself recognized: "[since] it is the task of the law to form and project, as well as mirror and reflect, we should not . . . merely recite . . . risks without examining the desirability of saddling them upon society." *United States v. White, supra*, at 786 (dissenting opinion). In making this assessment, courts must evaluate the "intrinsic character" of investigative practices with reference to the basic values underlying the Fourth Amendment. And for those "extensive intrusions that significantly jeopardize [individuals'] sense of security . . . , more than self-restraint by law enforcement officials is required." *United States v. White*, 401 U.S., at 786 (Harlan, J., dissenting).

The use of pen registers, I believe, constitutes such an extensive intrusion. To hold otherwise ignores the vital role telephonic communication plays in our personal and professional relationships, *see Katz v. United States*, 389 U.S., at 352, as well as the First and Fourth Amendment interests implicated by unfettered official surveillance. Privacy in placing calls is of value not only to those engaged in criminal activity. The prospect of unregulated governmental monitoring will undoubtedly prove disturbing even to those with nothing illicit to hide. Many individuals, including members of unpopular political organizations or journalists with confidential sources, may legitimately wish to avoid disclosure of their personal contacts. Permitting governmental access to telephone records on less than probable cause may thus impede certain forms of political affiliation and journalistic endeavor that are the hallmark of a truly free society. Particularly given the Government's previous reliance on warrantless telephonic surveillance to trace reporters' sources and monitor protected political activity, I am unwilling to insulate use of pen registers from independent judicial review.

Just as one who enters a public telephone booth is "entitled to assume that the words he utters into the mouthpiece will not be broadcast to the world," *Katz v. United States, supra*, at 352, so too, he should be entitled to assume that the numbers he dials in the privacy of his home will be recorded, if at all, solely for the phone company's business purposes. Accordingly, I would require law enforcement officials to obtain a warrant before they enlist telephone companies to secure information otherwise beyond the government's reach.

QUESTIONS, COMMENTS, CONCERNS?

1. **Thinking through *Smith*.** The *Smith* Court makes clear that "a person has no legitimate expectation of privacy in information he voluntarily turns over to third parties." Think about that statement, made by the Court in 1979, in today's world. Consider how much material you turn over to third parties—e.g., your Google searches, your text messages, your credit card statements. Are there any meaningful limits on *Smith's* third-party doctrine?

2. ***Smith* and Ulbricht from the defendant's perspective.** Return to Ulbricht's motion to suppress. [See Casefile Document 1.] Turn in particular to pages 37–48 of that motion. On page 39, Ulbricht argues in part that the

pen-trap revealed more than identifying information. The pen-trap was designed "to track Mr. Ulbricht's internet activity, coupled with his physical location, in an effort to connect him to access to the administrative section of the Silk Road Servers at particular times on particular dates." But *Smith* seems to permit exactly what Ulbricht complains about, right? In other words, has Ulbricht, by using an internet service, voluntarily disclosed the very information he contends is private? Does Ulbricht deal effectively with the wide-ranging applicability of *Smith* to his case?

3.   ***Smith* and Ulbricht from the government's perspective.** The government asserts that *Smith* is directly on point because the government sought to use the pen register solely to "collect routing data with respect to a user's Internet activity[.]" [See Casefile Document 2, at 20.] But how would the analysis change if, instead, the government used the pen register to collect information about Ulbricht's geolocation?

4.   ***Smith* and Ulbricht from the court's perspective.** How does the district court resolve the parties' arguments about the applicability of *Smith*? [See Casefile Document 7, at 33.]

CARPENTER V. UNITED STATES

138 S. Ct. 2206
Supreme Court of the United States
November 29, 2017, Argued; June 22, 2018, Decided
No. 16-402

Judges: ROBERTS, C.J., delivered the opinion of the Court, in which GINSBURG, BREYER, SOTOMAYOR, and KAGAN, JJ., joined. KENNEDY, J., filed a dissenting opinion, in which THOMAS and ALITO, JJ., joined. THOMAS, J., filed a dissenting opinion. ALITO, J., filed a dissenting opinion, in which THOMAS, J., joined. GORSUCH, J., filed a dissenting opinion.

CHIEF JUSTICE ROBERTS delivered the opinion of the Court.

This case presents the question whether the Government conducts a search under the Fourth Amendment when it accesses historical cell phone records that provide a comprehensive chronicle of the user's past movements.

I

A

There are 396 million cell phone service accounts in the United States—for a Nation of 326 million people. Cell phones perform their wide and growing variety of functions by connecting to a set of radio antennas called "cell sites." Although cell sites are usually mounted on a tower, they can also be found on light posts, flagpoles, church steeples, or the sides of buildings. Cell sites typically have several directional antennas that divide the covered area into sectors.

Cell phones continuously scan their environment looking for the best signal, which generally comes from the closest cell site. Most modern devices, such as smartphones, tap into the wireless network several times a minute whenever their signal is on, even if the owner is not using one of the phone's features. Each time the phone connects to a cell site, it generates a time-stamped record known as cell-site location information (CSLI). The precision of this information depends on the size of the geographic area covered by the cell site. The greater the concentration of cell sites, the smaller the coverage area. As data usage from cell phones has increased, wireless carriers have installed more cell sites to handle the traffic. That has led to increasingly compact coverage areas, especially in urban areas.

Wireless carriers collect and store CSLI for their own business purposes, including finding weak spots in their network and applying "roaming" charges when another carrier routes data through their cell sites. In addition, wireless carriers often sell aggregated location records to data brokers, without individual identifying information of the sort at issue here. While carriers have long retained CSLI for the start and end of incoming calls, in recent years phone companies have also collected location information from the transmission of text messages and routine data connections. Accordingly, modern cell phones generate increasingly vast amounts of increasingly precise CSLI.

B

In 2011, police officers arrested four men suspected of robbing a series of Radio Shack and (ironically enough) T-Mobile stores in Detroit. One of the men confessed that, over the previous four months, the group (along with a rotating cast of getaway drivers and lookouts) had robbed nine different stores in Michigan and Ohio. The suspect identified 15 accomplices who had participated in the heists and gave the FBI some of their cell phone numbers; the FBI then reviewed his call records to identify additional numbers that he had called around the time of the robberies.

Based on that information, the prosecutors applied for court orders under the Stored Communications Act to obtain cell phone records for petitioner Timothy Carpenter and several other suspects. That statute, as amended in 1994, permits the Government to compel the disclosure of certain telecommunications records when it "offers specific and articulable facts showing that there are reasonable grounds to believe" that the records sought "are relevant and material to an ongoing criminal investigation." 18 U.S.C. § 2703(d). Federal Magistrate Judges issued two orders directing Carpenter's wireless carriers—MetroPCS and Sprint—to disclose "cell/site sector [information] for [Carpenter's] telephone[ ] at call origination and at call termination for incoming and outgoing calls" during the four-month period when the string of robberies occurred. The first order sought 152 days of cell-site records from MetroPCS, which produced records spanning 127 days. The second order requested seven days of CSLI from Sprint, which produced two days of records covering the period when Carpenter's phone was "roaming" in northeastern Ohio. Altogether the Government obtained 12,898 location points cataloging Carpenter's movements—an average of 101 data points per day.

Carpenter was charged with six counts of robbery and an additional six counts of carrying a firearm during a federal crime of violence. Prior to trial, Carpenter moved to suppress the cell-site data provided by the wireless carriers. He argued that the Government's seizure of the records violated the Fourth Amendment because they had been obtained without a warrant supported by probable cause. The District Court denied the motion.

At trial, seven of Carpenter's confederates pegged him as the leader of the operation. In addition, FBI agent Christopher Hess offered expert testimony about the cell-site data. Hess explained that each time a cell phone taps into the wireless network, the carrier logs a time-stamped record of the cell site and particular sector that were used. With this information, Hess produced maps that placed Carpenter's phone near four of the charged robberies. In the Government's view, the location records clinched the case: They confirmed that Carpenter was "right where the . . . robbery was at the exact time of the robbery." Carpenter was convicted on all but one of the firearm counts and sentenced to more than 100 years in prison.

The Court of Appeals for the Sixth Circuit affirmed. The court held that Carpenter lacked a reasonable expectation of privacy in the location information collected by the FBI because he had shared that information with his wireless carriers. Given that cell phone users voluntarily convey cell-site data to their carriers as "a means of establishing communication," the court concluded that the resulting business records are not entitled to Fourth Amendment protection.

We granted certiorari.

II

A

The Fourth Amendment protects "[t]he right of the people to be secure in their persons, houses, papers, and effects, against unreasonable searches and seizures." The "basic purpose of this Amendment," our cases have recognized, "is to safeguard the privacy and security of individuals against arbitrary invasions by governmental officials." * * * As technology has enhanced the Government's capacity to encroach upon areas normally guarded from inquisitive eyes, this Court has sought to "assure[ ] preservation of that degree of privacy against government that existed when the Fourth Amendment was adopted." *Kyllo v. United States*, 533 U.S. 27, 34 (2001). * * *

* * * [I]n *Riley* [*v. California*, 573 U.S. 373 (2014)], the Court recognized the "immense storage capacity" of modern cell phones in holding that police officers must generally obtain a warrant before searching the contents of a phone. We explained that while the general rule allowing warrantless searches incident to arrest "strikes the appropriate balance in the context of physical objects, neither of its rationales has much force with respect to" the vast store of sensitive information on a cell phone.

B

The case before us involves the Government's acquisition of wireless carrier cell-site records revealing the location of Carpenter's cell phone whenever it made or received calls. This sort of digital data—personal location information maintained by a third party—does not fit neatly under existing precedents. Instead, requests for cell-site records lie at the intersection of two lines of cases, both of which inform our understanding of the privacy interests at stake.

The first set of cases addresses a person's expectation of privacy in his physical location and movements. In *United States v. Knotts*, 460 U.S. 276 (1983), we considered the Government's use of a "beeper" to aid in tracking a vehicle through traffic. Police officers in that case planted a beeper in a container of chloroform before it was purchased by one of Knotts's co-conspirators. The officers (with intermittent aerial assistance) then followed the automobile carrying the container from Minneapolis to Knotts's cabin in Wisconsin, relying on the beeper's signal to help keep the vehicle in view. The Court concluded that the "augment[ed]" visual surveillance did not constitute a search because "[a] person traveling in an automobile on public thoroughfares has no reasonable expectation of privacy in his movements from one place to another." Since the movements of the vehicle and its final destination had been "voluntarily conveyed to anyone who wanted to look," Knotts could not assert a privacy interest in the information obtained.

This Court in *Knotts*, however, was careful to distinguish between the rudimentary tracking facilitated by the beeper and more sweeping modes of surveillance. The Court emphasized the "limited use which the government made of the signals from this particular beeper" during a discrete "automotive journey." Significantly, the Court reserved the question whether "different constitutional principles may be applicable" if "twenty-four hour surveillance of any citizen of this country [were] possible."

Three decades later, the Court considered more sophisticated surveillance of the sort envisioned in *Knotts* and found that different principles did indeed apply. In *United States v. Jones*, FBI agents installed a GPS tracking device on Jones's vehicle and remotely monitored the vehicle's movements for 28 days. The Court decided the case based on the Government's physical trespass of the vehicle. At the same time, five Justices agreed that related privacy concerns would be raised by, for example, "surreptitiously activating a stolen vehicle detection system" in Jones's car to track Jones himself, or conducting GPS tracking of his cell phone. Since GPS monitoring of a vehicle tracks "every movement" a person makes in that vehicle, the concurring Justices concluded that "longer term GPS monitoring in investigations of most offenses impinges on expectations of privacy"—regardless whether those movements were disclosed to the public at large.

In a second set of decisions, the Court has drawn a line between what a person keeps to himself and what he shares with others. We have previously held that "a person has no legitimate expectation of privacy in information he voluntarily turns over to third parties." *Smith* [*v. Maryland*, 442 U.S. 735, 741, 743–44 (1979)]. That remains true "even if the information is revealed on the assumption that it will be used only for a limited purpose." *United States v. Miller*, 425 U.S. 435, 443 (1976). As a result, the Government is typically free to obtain such information from the recipient without triggering Fourth Amendment protections.

This third-party doctrine largely traces its roots to *Miller*. While investigating Miller for tax evasion, the Government subpoenaed his banks, seeking several months of canceled checks, deposit slips, and monthly statements. The Court rejected a Fourth Amendment challenge to the records collection. For one, Miller could "assert neither ownership nor possession" of the documents; they were "business records of the banks." For another, the nature of those records confirmed Miller's limited expectation of privacy, because the checks were "not confidential communications but negotiable instruments to be used in commercial transactions," and the bank statements contained information "exposed to [bank] employees in the ordinary course of business." The Court thus concluded that Miller had "take[n] the risk, in revealing his affairs to another, that the information [would] be conveyed by that person to the Government."

Three years later, *Smith* applied the same principles in the context of information conveyed to a telephone company. The Court ruled that the Government's use of a pen register—a device that recorded the outgoing phone numbers dialed on a landline telephone—was not a search. Noting the pen register's "limited capabilities," the Court "doubt[ed] that people in general entertain any actual expectation of privacy in the numbers they dial." Telephone subscribers know, after all, that the numbers are used by the telephone company "for a variety of legitimate business purposes," including routing calls. And at any rate, the Court explained, such an expectation "is not one that society is prepared to recognize as reasonable."

When Smith placed a call, he "voluntarily conveyed" the dialed numbers to the phone company by "expos[ing] that information to its equipment in the ordinary course of business." Once again, we held that the defendant "assumed the risk" that the company's records "would be divulged to police."

III

The question we confront today is how to apply the Fourth Amendment to a new phenomenon: the ability to chronicle a person's past movements through the record of his cell phone signals. Such tracking partakes of many of the qualities of the GPS monitoring we considered in Jones. Much like GPS tracking of a vehicle, cell phone location information is detailed, encyclopedic, and effortlessly compiled.

At the same time, the fact that the individual continuously reveals his location to his wireless carrier implicates the third-party principle of *Smith* and *Miller*. But while the third-party doctrine applies to telephone numbers and bank records, it is not clear whether its logic extends to the qualitatively different category of cell-site records. After all, when *Smith* was decided in 1979, few could have imagined a society in which a phone goes wherever its owner goes, conveying to the wireless carrier not just dialed digits, but a detailed and comprehensive record of the person's movements.

We decline to extend *Smith* and *Miller* to cover these novel circumstances. Given the unique nature of cell phone location records, the fact that the information is held by a third party does not by itself overcome the user's claim to Fourth Amendment protection. Whether the Government employs its own surveillance technology as in *Jones* or leverages the technology of a wireless carrier, we hold that an individual maintains a legitimate expectation of privacy in the record of his physical movements as captured through CSLI. The location information obtained from Carpenter's wireless carriers was the product of a search.[3]

A

A person does not surrender all Fourth Amendment protection by venturing into the public sphere. To the contrary, "what [one] seeks to preserve as private, even in an area accessible to the public, may be constitutionally protected." *Katz* [*v. United States*, 389 U.S. 347, 351–352 (1967)]. A majority of this Court has already recognized [in *Jones*] that

---

[3] The parties suggest as an alternative to their primary submissions that the acquisition of CSLI becomes a search only if it extends beyond a limited period. *See* Reply Brief 12 (proposing a 24-hour cutoff); Brief for United States 55–56 (suggesting a seven-day cutoff). As part of its argument, the Government treats the seven days of CSLI requested from Sprint as the pertinent period, even though Sprint produced only two days of records. * * * [W]e need not decide whether there is a limited period for which the Government may obtain an individual's historical CSLI free from Fourth Amendment scrutiny, and if so, how long that period might be. It is sufficient for our purposes today to hold that accessing seven days of CSLI constitutes a Fourth Amendment search.

individuals have a reasonable expectation of privacy in the whole of their physical movements. Prior to the digital age, law enforcement might have pursued a suspect for a brief stretch, but doing so "for any extended period of time was difficult and costly and therefore rarely undertaken." For that reason, "society's expectation has been that law enforcement agents and others would not—and indeed, in the main, simply could not—secretly monitor and catalogue every single movement of an individual's car for a very long period."

Allowing government access to cell-site records contravenes that expectation. Although such records are generated for commercial purposes, that distinction does not negate Carpenter's anticipation of privacy in his physical location. Mapping a cell phone's location over the course of 127 days provides an all-encompassing record of the holder's whereabouts. As with GPS information, the time-stamped data provides an intimate window into a person's life, revealing not only his particular movements, but through them his "familial, political, professional, religious, and sexual associations." These location records "hold for many Americans the 'privacies of life.'" *Riley*, 134 S. Ct. 2473. And like GPS monitoring, cell phone tracking is remarkably easy, cheap, and efficient compared to traditional investigative tools. With just the click of a button, the Government can access each carrier's deep repository of historical location information at practically no expense.

In fact, historical cell-site records present even greater privacy concerns than the GPS monitoring of a vehicle we considered in *Jones*. Unlike the bugged container in *Knotts* or the car in *Jones*, a cell phone—almost a "feature of human anatomy," *Riley*, 134 S. Ct. 2473—tracks nearly exactly the movements of its owner. While individuals regularly leave their vehicles, they compulsively carry cell phones with them all the time. A cell phone faithfully follows its owner beyond public thoroughfares and into private residences, doctor's offices, political headquarters, and other potentially revealing locales. Accordingly, when the Government tracks the location of a cell phone it achieves near perfect surveillance, as if it had attached an ankle monitor to the phone's user.

Moreover, the retrospective quality of the data here gives police access to a category of information otherwise unknowable. In the past, attempts to reconstruct a person's movements were limited by a dearth of records and the frailties of recollection. With access to CSLI, the Government can now travel back in time to retrace a person's whereabouts, subject only to the retention polices of the wireless carriers, which currently maintain records for up to five years. Critically, because location information is continually logged for all of the 400 million devices in the United States—not just those belonging to persons who might happen to come under investigation—this newfound tracking capacity runs against everyone.

Unlike with the GPS device in *Jones*, police need not even know in advance whether they want to follow a particular individual, or when.

Whoever the suspect turns out to be, he has effectively been tailed every moment of every day for five years, and the police may—in the Government's view—call upon the results of that surveillance without regard to the constraints of the Fourth Amendment. Only the few without cell phones could escape this tireless and absolute surveillance. * * *

At any rate, the rule the Court adopts "must take account of more sophisticated systems that are already in use or in development." While the records in this case reflect the state of technology at the start of the decade, the accuracy of CSLI is rapidly approaching GPS-level precision. As the number of cell sites has proliferated, the geographic area covered by each cell sector has shrunk, particularly in urban areas. In addition, with new technology measuring the time and angle of signals hitting their towers, wireless carriers already have the capability to pinpoint a phone's location within 50 meters.

Accordingly, when the Government accessed CSLI from the wireless carriers, it invaded Carpenter's reasonable expectation of privacy in the whole of his physical movements.

B

The Government's primary contention to the contrary is that the third-party doctrine governs this case. In its view, cell-site records are fair game because they are "business records" created and maintained by the wireless carriers. The Government (along with Justice Kennedy) recognizes that this case features new technology, but asserts that the legal question nonetheless turns on a garden-variety request for information from a third-party witness.

The Government's position fails to contend with the seismic shifts in digital technology that made possible the tracking of not only Carpenter's location but also everyone else's, not for a short period but for years and years. Sprint Corporation and its competitors are not your typical witnesses. Unlike the nosy neighbor who keeps an eye on comings and goings, they are ever alert, and their memory is nearly infallible. There is a world of difference between the limited types of personal information addressed in *Smith* and *Miller* and the exhaustive chronicle of location information casually collected by wireless carriers today. The Government thus is not asking for a straightforward application of the third-party doctrine, but instead a significant extension of it to a distinct category of information.

The third-party doctrine partly stems from the notion that an individual has a reduced expectation of privacy in information knowingly shared with another. But the fact of "diminished privacy interests does not mean that the Fourth Amendment falls out of the picture entirely." *Riley*, 134 S. Ct. 2473. *Smith* and *Miller*, after all, did not rely solely on the act of sharing. Instead, they considered "the nature of the particular documents sought" to determine whether "there is a legitimate 'expectation of privacy' concerning their contents." *Miller*, 425 U.S., at 442. *Smith* pointed out the limited capabilities of a pen register; as explained in *Riley*, telephone call logs reveal little in the way of "identifying information." *Miller* likewise noted that checks were "not confidential communications but negotiable instruments to be used in commercial transactions." In mechanically applying the third-party doctrine to this case, the Government fails to appreciate that there are no comparable limitations on the revealing nature of CSLI.

The Court has in fact already shown special solicitude for location information in the third-party context. In *Knotts*, the Court relied on *Smith* to hold that an individual has no reasonable expectation of privacy in public movements that he "voluntarily conveyed to anyone who wanted to look." But when confronted with more pervasive tracking, five Justices agreed [in *Jones*] that longer term GPS monitoring of even a vehicle traveling on public streets constitutes a search. Justice Gorsuch wonders why "someone's location when using a phone" is sensitive, and Justice Kennedy assumes that a person's discrete movements "are not particularly private." Yet this case is not about "using a phone" or a person's movement at a particular time. It is about a detailed chronicle of a person's physical presence compiled every day, every moment, over several years. Such a chronicle implicates privacy concerns far beyond those considered in *Smith* and *Miller*.

Neither does the second rationale underlying the third-party doctrine—voluntary exposure—hold up when it comes to CSLI. Cell phone location information is not truly "shared" as one normally understands the term. In the first place, cell phones and the services they provide are "such a pervasive and insistent part of daily life" that carrying one is indispensable to participation in modern society. Second, a cell phone logs a cell-site record by dint of its operation, without any affirmative act on the part of the user beyond powering up. Virtually any activity on the phone generates CSLI, including incoming calls, texts, or e-mails and countless other data connections that a phone automatically makes when checking for news, weather, or social media updates. Apart from disconnecting the phone from the network, there is no way to avoid leaving behind a trail of location data. As a result, in no meaningful sense does the user voluntarily "assume[ ] the risk" of turning over a comprehensive dossier of his physical movements. *Smith*, 442 U S., at 745.

We therefore decline to extend *Smith* and *Miller* to the collection of CSLI. Given the unique nature of cell phone location information, the fact that the Government obtained the information from a third party does not overcome Carpenter's claim to Fourth Amendment protection. The Government's acquisition of the cell-site records was a search within the meaning of the Fourth Amendment.

* * *

Our decision today is a narrow one. We do not express a view on matters not before us: real-time CSLI or "tower dumps" (a download of information on all the devices that connected to a particular cell site during a particular interval). We do not disturb the application of *Smith* and *Miller* or call into question conventional surveillance techniques and tools, such as security cameras. Nor do we address other business records that might incidentally reveal location information. Further, our opinion does not consider other collection techniques involving foreign affairs or national security. As Justice Frankfurter noted when considering new innovations in airplanes and radios, the Court must tread carefully in such cases, to ensure that we do not "embarrass the future."

IV

Having found that the acquisition of Carpenter's CSLI was a search, we also conclude that the Government must generally obtain a warrant supported by probable cause before acquiring such records. Although the "ultimate measure of the constitutionality of a governmental search is 'reasonableness,'" our cases establish that warrantless searches are typically unreasonable where "a search is undertaken by law enforcement officials to discover evidence of criminal wrongdoing." Thus, "[i]n the absence of a warrant, a search is reasonable only if it falls within a specific exception to the warrant requirement."

The Government acquired the cell-site records pursuant to a court order issued under the Stored Communications Act, which required the Government to show "reasonable grounds" for believing that the records were "relevant and material to an ongoing investigation." 18 U.S.C. § 2703(d). That showing falls well short of the probable cause required for a warrant. The Court usually requires "some quantum of individualized suspicion" before a search or seizure may take place. Under the standard in the Stored Communications Act, however, law enforcement need only show that the cell-site evidence might be pertinent to an ongoing investigation—a "gigantic" departure from the probable cause rule, as the Government explained below. Consequently, an order issued under Section 2703(d) of the Act is not a permissible mechanism for accessing historical cell-site records. Before compelling a wireless carrier to turn over a subscriber's CSLI, the Government's obligation is a familiar one—get a warrant.

Justice Alito contends that the warrant requirement simply does not apply when the Government acquires records using compulsory process. Unlike an actual search, he says, subpoenas for documents do not involve the direct taking of evidence; they are at most a "constructive search" conducted by the target of the subpoena. Given this lesser intrusion on personal privacy, Justice Alito argues that the compulsory production of records is not held to the same probable cause standard. In his view, this Court's precedents set forth a categorical rule—separate and distinct from the third-party doctrine—subjecting subpoenas to lenient scrutiny without regard to the suspect's expectation of privacy in the records.

But this Court has never held that the Government may subpoena third parties for records in which the suspect has a reasonable expectation of privacy. Almost all of the examples Justice Alito cites contemplated requests for evidence implicating diminished privacy interests or for a corporation's own books. The lone exception, of course, is *Miller*, where the Court's analysis of the third-party subpoena merged with the application of the third-party doctrine.

Justice Alito overlooks the critical issue. At some point, the dissent should recognize that CSLI is an entirely different species of business record—something that implicates basic Fourth Amendment concerns about arbitrary government power much more directly than corporate tax or payroll ledgers. When confronting new concerns wrought by digital technology, this Court has been careful not to uncritically extend existing precedents. * * *

This is certainly not to say that all orders compelling the production of documents will require a showing of probable cause. The Government will be able to use subpoenas to acquire records in the overwhelming majority of investigations. We hold only that a warrant is required in the rare case where the suspect has a legitimate privacy interest in records held by a third party.

Further, even though the Government will generally need a warrant to access CSLI, case-specific exceptions may support a warrantless search of an individual's cell-site records under certain circumstances. "One well-recognized exception applies when ' "the exigencies of the situation" make the needs of law enforcement so compelling that [a] warrantless search is objectively reasonable under the Fourth Amendment.' " *Kentucky v. King*, 563 U.S. 452, 460 (2011). Such exigencies include the need to pursue a fleeing suspect, protect individuals who are threatened with imminent harm, or prevent the imminent destruction of evidence.

As a result, if law enforcement is confronted with an urgent situation, such fact-specific threats will likely justify the warrantless collection of CSLI. Lower courts, for instance, have approved warrantless searches related to bomb threats, active shootings, and child abductions. Our decision today does not call into doubt warrantless access to CSLI in such circumstances. While police must get a warrant when collecting CSLI to assist in the mine-run criminal investigation, the rule we set forth does not limit their ability to respond to an ongoing emergency.

* * *

As Justice Brandeis explained in his famous dissent, the Court is obligated—as "[s]ubtler and more far-reaching means of invading privacy have become available to the Government"—to ensure that the "progress of science" does not erode Fourth Amendment protections. Here the progress of science has afforded law enforcement a powerful new tool to carry out its important responsibilities. At the same time, this tool risks Government encroachment of the sort the Framers, "after consulting the lessons of history," drafted the Fourth Amendment to prevent.

We decline to grant the state unrestricted access to a wireless carrier's database of physical location information. In light of the deeply revealing nature of CSLI, its depth, breadth, and comprehensive reach, and the inescapable and automatic nature of its collection, the fact that such information is gathered by a third party does not make it any less deserving of Fourth Amendment protection. The Government's acquisition of the cell-site records here was a search under that Amendment.

The judgment of the Court of Appeals is reversed, and the case is remanded for further proceedings consistent with this opinion.

It is so ordered.

JUSTICE KENNEDY, with whom JUSTICE THOMAS and JUSTICE ALITO join, dissenting.

[Omitted.]

JUSTICE THOMAS, dissenting.

This case should not turn on "whether" a search occurred. It should turn, instead, on *whose* property was searched. The Fourth Amendment guarantees individuals the right to be secure from unreasonable searches of "*their* persons, houses, papers, and effects." (Emphasis added.) In other words, "each person has the right to be secure against unreasonable searches . . . in his own person, house, papers, and effects." By obtaining the cell-site records of MetroPCS and Sprint, the Government did not search Carpenter's property. He did not create the records, he does not maintain them, he cannot control them, and he cannot destroy them. Neither the terms of his contracts nor any provision of law makes the records his. The records belong to MetroPCS and Sprint. * * *

The * * * fundamental problem with the Court's opinion, however, is its use of the "reasonable expectation of privacy" test, which was first articulated by Justice Harlan in *Katz v. United States*, 389 U.S. 347, 360–361 (1967) (concurring opinion). The *Katz* test has no basis in the text or history of the Fourth Amendment. And, it invites courts to make judgments about policy, not law. Until we confront the problems with this test, *Katz* will continue to distort Fourth Amendment jurisprudence. I respectfully dissent. * * *

In shifting the focus of the Fourth Amendment from property to privacy, the *Katz* test * * * reads the words "persons, houses, papers, and effects" out of the text. At its broadest formulation, the *Katz* test would find a search "*wherever* an individual may harbor a reasonable 'expectation of privacy.'" The Court today, for example, does not ask whether cell-site location records are "persons, houses, papers, [or] effects" within the meaning of the Fourth Amendment. Yet "persons, houses, papers, and effects" cannot mean "anywhere" or "anything." *Katz's* catchphrase that "the Fourth Amendment protects people, not places," is not a serious attempt to reconcile the constitutional text. The Fourth Amendment obviously protects people; "[t]he question . . . is what protection it affords to those people." The Founders decided to protect the people from unreasonable searches and seizures of four specific things—persons, houses, papers, and effects. They identified those four categories as "the objects of privacy protection to which the Constitution would extend, leaving further expansion to the good judgment . . . of the people through their representatives in the legislature." * * *

"[P]ersons, houses, papers, and effects" are not the only words that the *Katz* test reads out of the Fourth Amendment. The Fourth Amendment specifies that the people have a right to be secure from unreasonable searches of "their" persons, houses, papers, and effects. * * *

Carpenter attempts to argue that the cell-site records are, in fact, his "papers," but his arguments are unpersuasive. Carpenter stipulated below that the cell-site records are the business records of Sprint and MetroPCS. He cites no property law in his briefs to this Court, and he does not explain how he has a property right in the companies' records under the law of any jurisdiction at any point in American history. * * *

Instead of property, tort, or contract law, Carpenter relies on the federal Telecommunications Act of 1996 to demonstrate that the cell site records are his papers. The Telecommunications Act generally bars cell-phone companies from disclosing customers' cell site location information to the public. This is sufficient to make the records his, Carpenter argues, because the Fourth Amendment merely requires him to identify a source of "positive law" that "protects against access by the public without consent."

Carpenter is mistaken. To come within the text of the Fourth Amendment, Carpenter must prove that the cell-site records are his; positive law is potentially relevant only insofar as it answers that question. The text of the Fourth Amendment cannot plausibly be read to mean "any violation of positive law" any more than it can plausibly be read to mean "any violation of a reasonable expectation of privacy."

Thus, the Telecommunications Act is insufficient because it does not give Carpenter a property right in the cell-site records. * * * Any property rights remain with the companies. * * *

* * *

In several recent decisions, this Court has declined to apply the *Katz* test because it threatened to narrow the original scope of the Fourth Amendment. But as today's decision demonstrates, *Katz* can also be invoked to expand the Fourth Amendment beyond its original scope. This Court should not tolerate errors in either direction. * * * Whether the rights they ratified are too broad or too narrow by modern lights, this Court has no authority to unilaterally alter the document they approved.

Because the *Katz* test is a failed experiment, this Court is dutybound to reconsider it. Until it does, I agree with my dissenting colleagues' reading of our precedents. Accordingly, I respectfully dissent.

JUSTICE ALITO, with whom JUSTICE THOMAS joins, dissenting.

[Omitted.]

JUSTICE GORSUCH, dissenting.

In the late 1960s this Court suggested for the first time that a search triggering the Fourth Amendment occurs when the government violates an "expectation of privacy" that "society is prepared to recognize as 'reasonable.'" *Katz v. United States*, 389 U.S. 347, 361 (1967) (Harlan, J., concurring). Then, in a pair of decisions in the 1970s applying the *Katz* test, the Court held that a "reasonable expectation of privacy" doesn't attach to information shared with "third parties." *See Smith v. Maryland*, 442 U.S. 735, 743–744 (1979); *United States v. Miller*, 425 U.S. 435, 443 (1976). By these steps, the Court came to conclude, the Constitution does nothing to limit investigators from searching records you've entrusted to your bank, accountant, and maybe even your doctor.

What's left of the Fourth Amendment? Today we use the Internet to do most everything. Smartphones make it easy to keep a calendar, correspond with friends, make calls, conduct banking, and even watch the game. Countless Internet companies maintain records about us and, increasingly, for us. Even our most private documents—those that, in other eras, we would have locked safely in a desk drawer or destroyed—now reside on third party servers. *Smith* and *Miller* teach that the police can review all of this material, on the theory that no one reasonably expects any of it will be kept private. But no one believes that, if they ever did.

What to do? It seems to me we could respond in at least three ways. The first is to ignore the problem, maintain *Smith* and *Miller*, and live with the consequences. If the confluence of these decisions and modern technology means our Fourth Amendment rights are reduced to nearly nothing, so be it. The second choice is to set *Smith* and *Miller* aside and try again using the *Katz* "reasonable expectation of privacy" jurisprudence that produced them. The third is to look for answers elsewhere.

*

Start with the first option. *Smith* held that the government's use of a pen register to record the numbers people dial on their phones doesn't infringe a reasonable expectation of privacy because that information is freely disclosed to the third party phone company. *Miller* held that a bank account holder enjoys no reasonable expectation of privacy in the bank's records of his account activity. That's true, the Court reasoned, "even if the information is revealed on the assumption that it will be used only for a limited purpose and the confidence placed in the third party will not be betrayed." Today the Court suggests that *Smith* and *Miller* distinguish between kinds of information disclosed to third parties and require courts to decide whether to "extend" those decisions to particular classes of information, depending on their sensitivity. But * * * no balancing test of this kind can be found in *Smith* and *Miller*. Those cases announced a categorical rule: Once you disclose information to third parties, you forfeit any reasonable expectation of privacy you might have had in it. And even if *Smith* and *Miller* did permit courts to conduct a balancing contest of the kind the Court now suggests, it's still hard to see how that would help the petitioner in this case. Why is someone's location when using a phone so much more sensitive than who he was talking to (*Smith*) or what financial transactions he engaged in (*Miller*)? I do not know and the Court does not say.

The problem isn't with the Sixth Circuit's application of *Smith* and *Miller* but with the cases themselves. Can the government demand a copy of all your e-mail from Google or Microsoft without implicating your Fourth Amendment rights? Can it secure your DNA from 23andMe without a warrant or probable cause? *Smith* and *Miller* say yes it can—at least without running afoul of *Katz*. But that result strikes most lawyers and judges today—me included—as pretty unlikely. In the years since its adoption, countless scholars, too, have come to conclude that the "third-party doctrine is not only wrong, but horribly wrong." The reasons are obvious. * * * People often do reasonably expect that information they entrust to third parties, especially information subject to confidentiality agreements, will be kept private. Meanwhile, if the third party doctrine is supposed to represent a normative assessment of when a person should expect privacy, the notion that the answer might be "never" seems a pretty unattractive societal prescription. * * *

In the end, what do *Smith* and *Miller* add up to? A doubtful application of *Katz* that lets the government search almost whatever it wants whenever it wants. The Sixth Circuit had to follow that rule and faithfully did just that, but it's not clear why we should.

*

There's a second option. What if we dropped *Smith* and *Miller's* third party doctrine and retreated to the root *Katz* question whether there is a "reasonable expectation of privacy" in data held by third parties? Rather than solve the problem with the third party doctrine, I worry this option only risks returning us to its source. After all, it was *Katz* that produced *Smith* and *Miller* in the first place.

Katz's problems start with the text and original understanding of the Fourth Amendment, as Justice Thomas thoughtfully explains today. The Amendment's protections do not depend on the breach of some abstract "expectation of privacy" whose contours are left to the judicial imagination. Much more concretely, it protects your "person," and your "houses, papers, and effects." Nor does your right to bring a Fourth Amendment claim depend on whether a judge happens to agree that your subjective expectation to privacy is a "reasonable" one. Under its plain terms, the Amendment grants you the right to invoke its guarantees whenever one of your protected things (your person, your house, your papers, or your effects) is unreasonably searched or seized. Period. * * *

Even taken on its own terms, *Katz* has never been sufficiently justified. In fact, we still don't even know what its "reasonable expectation of privacy" test is. Is it supposed to pose an empirical question (what privacy expectations do people actually have) or a normative one (what expectations should they have)? Either way brings problems. If the test is supposed to be an empirical one, it's unclear why judges rather than legislators should conduct it. Legislators are responsive to their constituents and have institutional resources designed to help them discern and enact majoritarian preferences. Politically insulated judges come armed with only the attorneys' briefs, a few law clerks, and their own idiosyncratic experiences. They are hardly the representative group you'd expect (or want) to be making empirical judgments for hundreds of millions of people. Unsurprisingly, too, judicial judgments often fail to reflect public views. * * *

Maybe, then, the *Katz* test should be conceived as a normative question. But if that's the case, why (again) do judges, rather than legislators, get to determine whether society should be prepared to recognize an expectation of privacy as legitimate? Deciding what privacy interests should be recognized often calls for a pure policy choice, many times between incommensurable goods—between the value of privacy in a particular setting and society's interest in combating crime. Answering questions like that calls for the exercise of raw political will belonging to legislatures, not the legal judgment proper to courts. * * *

My concerns about *Katz* come with a caveat. Sometimes, I accept, judges may be able to discern and describe existing societal norms. That is particularly true when the judge looks to positive law rather than intuition for guidance on social norms. So there may be some occasions where *Katz* is capable of principled application—though it may simply wind up approximating the more traditional option I will discuss in a moment. Sometimes it may also be possible to apply *Katz* by analogizing from precedent when the line between an existing case and a new fact pattern is short and direct. But so far this Court has declined to tie itself to any significant restraints like these.

As a result, *Katz* has yielded an often unpredictable—and sometimes unbelievable—jurisprudence. *Smith* and *Miller* are only two examples; there are many others. Take *Florida v. Riley*, 488 U.S. 445 (1989), which says that a police helicopter hovering 400 feet above a person's property invades no reasonable expectation of privacy. Try that one out on your neighbors. Or *California v. Greenwood*, 486 U.S. 35 (1988), which holds that a person has no reasonable expectation of privacy in the garbage he puts out for collection. In that case, the Court said that the homeowners forfeited their privacy interests because "[i]t is common knowledge that plastic garbage bags left on or at the side of a public street are readily accessible to animals, children, scavengers, snoops, and other members of the public." But the habits of raccoons don't prove much about the habits of the country. I doubt, too, that most people spotting a neighbor rummaging through their garbage would think they lacked reasonable grounds to confront the rummager. Making the decision all the stranger, California state law expressly protected a homeowner's property rights in discarded trash. Yet rather than defer to that as evidence of the people's habits and reasonable expectations of privacy, the Court substituted its own curious judgment.

Resorting to *Katz* in data privacy cases threatens more of the same. Just consider. * * * The Court declines to say whether there is any sufficiently limited period of time "for which the Government may obtain an individual's historical [location information] free from Fourth Amendment scrutiny." But then it tells us that access to seven days' worth of information does trigger Fourth Amendment scrutiny—even though here the carrier "produced only two days of records." Why is the relevant fact the seven days of information the government asked for instead of the two days of information the government actually saw? Why seven days instead of ten or three or one? And in what possible sense did the government "search" five days' worth of location information it was never even sent? We do not know.

Later still, the Court adds that it can't say whether the Fourth Amendment is triggered when the government collects "real-time CSLI or 'tower dumps' (a download of information on all the devices that connected to a particular cell site during a particular interval)." But what distinguishes historical data from real-time data, or seven days of a single person's data from a download of everyone's data over some indefinite period of time? Why isn't a tower dump the paradigmatic example of "too permeating police surveillance" and a dangerous tool of "arbitrary" authority—the touchstones of the majority's modified *Katz* analysis? On what possible basis could such mass data collection survive the Court's test while collecting a single person's data does not? Here again we are left to guess. At the same time, though, the Court offers some firm assurances. It tells us its decision does not "call into question conventional surveillance techniques and tools, such as security cameras." That, however, just raises more questions for lower courts to sort out about what techniques qualify as "conventional" and why those techniques would be okay even if they lead to "permeating police surveillance" or "arbitrary police power."

Nor is this the end of it. After finding a reasonable expectation of privacy, the Court says there's still more work to do. Courts must determine whether to "extend" *Smith* and *Miller* to the circumstances before them. So apparently *Smith* and *Miller* aren't quite left for dead; they just no longer have the clear reach they once did. How do we measure their new reach? The Court says courts now must conduct a second *Katz*-like balancing inquiry, asking whether the fact of disclosure to a third party outweighs privacy interests in the "category of information" so disclosed. But how are lower courts supposed to weigh these radically different interests? Or assign values to different categories of information? All we know is that historical cell-site location information (for seven days, anyway) escapes *Smith* and *Miller's* shorn grasp, while a lifetime of bank or phone records does not. As to any other kind of information, lower courts will have to stay tuned.

In the end, our lower court colleagues are left with two amorphous balancing tests, a series of weighty and incommensurable principles to consider in them, and a few illustrative examples that seem little more than the product of judicial intuition. In the Court's defense, though, we have arrived at this strange place not because the Court has misunderstood *Katz*. Far from it. We have arrived here because this is where *Katz* inevitably leads.

*

There is another way. From the founding until the 1960s, the right to assert a Fourth Amendment claim didn't depend on your ability to appeal to a judge's personal sensibilities about the "reasonableness" of your expectations or privacy. It was tied to the law. The Fourth Amendment protects "the right of the people to be secure in their persons, houses, papers and effects, against unreasonable searches and seizures." True to those words and their original understanding, the traditional approach asked if a house, paper or effect was yours under law. No more was needed to trigger the Fourth Amendment. Though now often lost in *Katz's* shadow, this traditional understanding persists. *Katz* only "supplements, rather than displaces the traditional property-based understanding of the Fourth Amendment."

Beyond its provenance in the text and original understanding of the Amendment, this traditional approach comes with other advantages. Judges are supposed to decide cases based on "democratically legitimate sources of law"—like positive law or analogies to items protected by the enacted Constitution—rather than "their own biases or personal policy preferences." A Fourth Amendment model based on positive legal rights "carves out significant room for legislative participation in the Fourth Amendment context," too, by asking judges to consult what the people's representatives have to say about their rights. Nor is this approach hobbled by *Smith* and *Miller*, for those cases are just limitations on *Katz*, addressing only the question whether individuals have a reasonable expectation of privacy in materials they share with third parties. Under this more traditional approach, Fourth Amendment protections for your papers and effects do not automatically disappear just because you share them with third parties.

Given the prominence *Katz* has claimed in our doctrine, American courts are pretty rusty at applying the traditional approach to the Fourth Amendment. We know that if a house, paper, or effect is yours, you have a Fourth Amendment interest in its protection. But what kind of legal interest is sufficient to make something yours? And what source of law determines that? Current positive law? The common law at 1791, extended by analogy to modern times? Both? Much work is needed to revitalize this area and answer these questions. I do not begin to claim all the answers today, but (unlike with *Katz*) at least I have a pretty good idea what the questions are. And it seems to me a few things can be said.

First, the fact that a third party has access to or possession of your papers and effects does not necessarily eliminate your interest in them. Ever hand a private document to a friend to be returned? Toss your keys to a valet at a restaurant? Ask your neighbor to look after your dog while you travel? You would not expect the friend to share the document with others; the valet to lend your car to his buddy; or the neighbor to put Fido up for adoption. Entrusting your stuff to others is a bailment. A bailment is the "delivery of personal property by one person (the bailor) to another (the bailee) who holds the property for a certain purpose." A bailee normally owes a legal duty to keep the item safe, according to the terms of the parties' contract if they have one, and according to the "implication[s] from their conduct" if they don't. A bailee who uses the item in a different way than he's supposed to, or against the bailor's instructions, is liable for conversion. This approach is quite different from *Smith* and *Miller's* (counter)-intuitive approach to reasonable expectations of privacy; where those cases extinguish Fourth Amendment interests once records are given to a third party, property law may preserve them.

Our Fourth Amendment jurisprudence already reflects this truth. In *Ex parte Jackson*, 96 U.S. 727, 24 L. Ed. 877 (1878), this Court held that sealed letters placed in the mail are "as fully guarded from examination and inspection, except as to their outward form and weight, as if they were retained by the parties forwarding them in their own domiciles." The reason, drawn from the Fourth Amendment's text, was that "[t]he constitutional guaranty of the right of the people to be secure in their papers against unreasonable searches and seizures extends to *their papers*, thus closed against inspection, *wherever they may be*." It did not matter that letters were bailed to a third party (the government, no less). The sender enjoyed the same Fourth Amendment protection as he does "when papers are subjected to search in one's own household."

These ancient principles may help us address modern data cases too. Just because you entrust your data—in some cases, your modern-day papers and effects—to a third party may not mean you lose any Fourth Amendment interest in its contents. Whatever may be left of *Smith* and *Miller*, few doubt that e-mail should be treated much like the traditional mail it has largely supplanted—as a bailment in which the owner retains a vital and protected legal interest.

Second, I doubt that complete ownership or exclusive control of property is always a necessary condition to the assertion of a Fourth Amendment right. Where houses are concerned, for example, individuals can enjoy Fourth Amendment protection without fee simple title. Both the text of the Amendment and the common law rule support that conclusion. "People call a house 'their' home when legal title is in the bank, when they rent it, and even when they merely occupy it rent free." That rule derives from the common law. That is why tenants and resident family members—though they have no legal title—have standing to complain about searches of the houses in which they live.

Another point seems equally true: just because you have to entrust a third party with your data doesn't necessarily mean you should lose all Fourth Amendment protections in it. Not infrequently one person comes into possession of someone else's property without the owner's consent. Think of the finder of lost goods or the policeman who impounds a car. The law recognizes that the goods and the car still belong to their true owners, for "where a person comes into lawful possession of the personal property of another, even though there is no formal agreement between the property's owner and its possessor, the possessor will become a constructive bailee when justice so requires." At least some of this Court's decisions have already suggested that use of technology is functionally compelled by the demands of modern life, and in that way the fact that we store data with third parties may amount to a sort of involuntary bailment too.

Third, positive law may help provide detailed guidance on evolving technologies without resort to judicial intuition. State (or sometimes federal) law often creates rights in both tangible and intangible things. In the context of the Takings Clause we often ask whether those state-created rights are sufficient to make something someone's property for constitutional purposes. A similar inquiry may be appropriate for the Fourth Amendment. Both the States and federal government are actively legislating in the area of third party data storage and the rights users enjoy. State courts are busy expounding common law property principles in this area as well. If state legislators or state courts say that a digital record has the attributes that normally make something property, that may supply a sounder basis for judicial decisionmaking than judicial guesswork about societal expectations.

Fourth, while positive law may help establish a person's Fourth Amendment interest there may be some circumstances where positive law cannot be used to defeat it. *Ex parte Jackson* reflects that understanding. There this Court said that "[n]o law of Congress" could authorize letter carriers "to invade the secrecy of letters." So the post office couldn't impose a regulation dictating that those mailing letters surrender all legal interests in them once they're deposited in a mailbox. If that is right, *Jackson* suggests the existence of a constitutional floor below which Fourth Amendment rights may not descend. Legislatures cannot pass laws declaring your house or papers to be your property except to the extent the police wish to search them without cause. As the Court has previously explained, "we must 'assur[e] preservation of that degree of privacy against government that existed when the Fourth Amendment was adopted.' " Nor does this mean protecting only the specific rights known at the founding; it means protecting their modern analogues too. So, for example, while thermal imaging was unknown in 1791, this Court has recognized that using that technology to look inside a home constitutes a Fourth Amendment "search" of that "home" no less than a physical inspection might.

Fifth, this constitutional floor may, in some instances, bar efforts to circumvent the Fourth Amendment's protection through the use of subpoenas. No one thinks the government can evade *Jackson's* prohibition on opening sealed letters without a warrant simply by issuing a subpoena to a postmaster for "all letters sent by John Smith" or, worse, "all letters sent by John Smith concerning a particular transaction." So the question courts will confront will be this: What other kinds of records are sufficiently similar to letters in the mail that the same rule should apply?

It may be that, as an original matter, a subpoena requiring the recipient to produce records wasn't thought of as a "search or seizure" by the government implicating the Fourth Amendment, but instead as an act of compelled self-incrimination implicating the Fifth Amendment. But the common law of searches and seizures does not appear to have confronted a case where private documents equivalent to a mailed letter were entrusted to a bailee and then subpoenaed. As a result, "[t]he common-law rule regarding subpoenas for documents held by third parties entrusted with information from the target is . . . unknown and perhaps unknowable." Given that (perhaps insoluble) uncertainty, I am content to adhere to *Jackson* and its implications for now. * * *

＊

What does all this mean for the case before us? To start, I cannot fault the Sixth Circuit for holding that *Smith* and *Miller* extinguish any *Katz*-based Fourth Amendment interest in third party cell-site data. That is the plain effect of their categorical holdings. Nor can I fault the Court today for its implicit but unmistakable conclusion that the rationale of *Smith* and *Miller* is wrong; indeed, I agree with that. The Sixth Circuit was powerless to say so, but this Court can and should. At the same time, I do not agree with the Court's decision today to keep *Smith* and *Miller* on life support and supplement them with a new and multilayered inquiry that seems to be only *Katz*-squared. Returning there, I worry, promises more trouble than help. Instead, I would look to a more traditional Fourth Amendment approach. Even if *Katz* may still supply one way to prove a Fourth Amendment interest, it has never been the only way. Neglecting more traditional approaches may mean failing to vindicate the full protections of the Fourth Amendment.

Our case offers a cautionary example. It seems to me entirely possible a person's cell-site data could qualify as his papers or effects under existing law. Yes, the telephone carrier holds the information. But 47 U.S.C. § 222 designates a customer's cell-site location information as "customer proprietary network information" (CPNI) and gives customers certain rights to control use of and access to CPNI about themselves. The statute generally forbids a carrier to "use, disclose, or permit access to individually identifiable" CPNI without the customer's consent, except as needed to provide the customer's telecommunications services. It also requires the carrier to disclose CPNI "upon affirmative written request by the customer, to any person designated by the customer." Congress even afforded customers a private cause of action for damages against carriers who violate the Act's terms. Plainly, customers have substantial legal interests in this information, including at least some right to include, exclude, and control its use. Those interests might even rise to the level of a property right.

The problem is that we do not know anything more. Before the district court and court of appeals, Mr. Carpenter pursued only a *Katz* "reasonable expectations" argument. He did not invoke the law of property or any analogies to the common law, either there or in his petition for certiorari. Even in his merits brief before this Court, Mr. Carpenter's discussion of his positive law rights in cell-site data was cursory. He offered no analysis, for example, of what rights state law might provide him in addition to those supplied by § 222. In these circumstances, I cannot help but conclude—reluctantly—that Mr. Carpenter forfeited perhaps his most promising line of argument.

Unfortunately, too, this case marks the second time this Term that individuals have forfeited Fourth Amendment arguments based on positive law by failing to preserve them. Litigants have had fair notice since at least *United States v. Jones*, 565 U.S. 400 (2012) and *Florida v. Jardines*, 569 U.S. 1 (2013) that arguments like these may vindicate Fourth Amendment interests even where *Katz* arguments do not. Yet the arguments have gone unmade, leaving courts to the usual *Katz* handwaving. These omissions do not serve the development of a sound or fully protective Fourth Amendment jurisprudence.

QUESTIONS, COMMENTS, CONCERNS?

1.   **The reach of *Carpenter*.** Does *any* accessing of historical cell-site records count as a search? Or is short-term warrantless surveillance permitted? Regardless of your answers to those questions, does *Carpenter*'s reasoning about tracking a person's physical location apply just to physical location tracking or does it apply more broadly?

2.   **The remains of the third-party doctrine.** What's the status of the third-party doctrine? In dissent, Justice Gorsuch indicates that *Carpenter* puts *Smith* "on life support." Do you agree with Justice Gorsuch's characterization?

3.   ***Carpenter*'s application to other technologies.** Cell phones, of course, are not the only electronic devices capable of collecting personal information. Consider, for example, newer technologies like drones and smart homes. Each of these devices has the ability to provide insights and clues into criminal activity. How might *Carpenter* apply in those contexts? In answering this question, consider the competing interests between the freedom from surveillance against the cost of hampering criminal investigations.

4.   ***Carpenter*'s application to Ross Ulbricht.** Does *Carpenter* apply to the government's warrantless identification of the Silk Road servers? Does your answer depend on the amount of data the government acquired in the process? Chief Justice Roberts, writing for the majority, seemingly places

significance on this point: "Mapping a cell phone's location over the course of 127 days provides an all-encompassing record of the holder's whereabouts."

5. *Carpenter* **& bailments.** Must litigants in post-*Carpenter* cases now brief and prepare for an entirely separate property rights line of thinking involving bailments and trespass in order to win the vote of Justices Gorsuch (and possibly Justice Thomas). At a minimum, perhaps we should all have paid more attention to the chapter on bailments in our first-year property courses.

6. *Carpenter* **& the quality of lawyering.** *Carpenter* provides the first opportunity for us to read the writing of Justice Gorsuch. He appears refreshingly direct, yet not overly formalistic. Notice for example his outright criticism of *California v. Greenwood* (trash case) and *Florida v. Riley* (police flyover). Notice also how his opinion closes: by expressing frustration that the litigants failed to make a constitutional trespass argument. Specifically, he comments that litigants' failure to do so underserves "the development of a sound or fully protective Fourth Amendment jurisprudence." Apart from the obvious responsive comment that Justice Gorsuch was disappointed with the lawyering in *Carpenter*, it is interesting to think of his perspective—that lawyers bear as much responsibility to develop the law as the Supreme Court. We are reminded—again—about why Chapter 1 included a significant section dedicated to *Strickland v. Washington* and the importance of lawyering.

C. THE CONSTITUTIONAL TRESPASS TEST

Police conduct that constitutes a "constitutional trespass" is also a search. That is, wholly apart from the *Katz* test, the constitutional trespass test provides an alternative means for a defendant to claim Fourth Amendment protection. As noted in the introductory materials, the test is fairly simple: Law enforcement conduct that constitutes a physical trespass on a textually protected area (i.e., "person, paper, house, or effect") is a Fourth Amendment "search." We begin this section with *United States v. Jones*, where the Court first established the constitutional trespass test.

UNITED STATES V. JONES
565 U.S. 400
Supreme Court of the United States
November 8, 2011, Argued; January 23, 2012, Decided
No. 10-1259

JUSTICE SCALIA delivered the opinion of the Court.

We decide whether the attachment of a Global-Positioning-System (GPS) tracking device to an individual's vehicle, and subsequent use of that device to monitor the vehicle's movements on public streets, constitutes a search or seizure within the meaning of the Fourth Amendment.

I

In 2004 respondent Antoine Jones, owner and operator of a nightclub in the District of Columbia, came under suspicion of trafficking in narcotics and was made the target of an investigation by a joint Federal Bureau Investigation and Metropolitan Police Department task force. Officers employed various investigative techniques, including visual surveillance of the nightclub, installation of a camera focused on the front door of the club, and a pen register and wiretap covering Jones's cellular phone.

Based in part on information gathered from these sources, in 2005 the Government applied to the United States District Court for the District of Columbia for a warrant authorizing the use of an electronic tracking device on the Jeep Grand Cherokee registered to Jones's wife. A warrant issued, authorizing installation of the device in the District of Columbia and within 10 days.

On the 11th day, and not in the District of Columbia but in Maryland,[1] agents installed a GPS tracking device on the undercarriage of the Jeep while it was parked in a public parking lot. Over the next 28 days, the Government used the device to track the vehicle's movements, and once had to replace the device's battery when the vehicle was parked in a different public lot in Maryland. By means of signals from multiple satellites, the device established the vehicle's location within 50 to 100 feet, and communicated that location by cellular phone to a Government computer. It relayed more than 2,000 pages of data over the 4-week period.

The Government ultimately obtained a multiple-count indictment charging Jones and several alleged co-conspirators with, as relevant here, conspiracy to distribute and possess with intent to distribute five kilograms or more of cocaine and 50 grams or more of cocaine base * * *. Before trial, Jones filed a motion to suppress evidence obtained through the GPS device. The District Court granted the motion only in part, suppressing the data obtained while the vehicle was parked in the garage adjoining Jones's residence. * * * Jones's trial in October 2006 produced a hung jury on the conspiracy count.

In March 2007, a grand jury returned another indictment, charging Jones and others with the same conspiracy. The Government introduced at trial the same GPS-derived locational data admitted in the first trial, which connected Jones to the alleged conspirators' stash house that contained $850,000 in cash, 97 kilograms of cocaine, and 1 kilogram of cocaine base. The jury returned a guilty verdict, and the District Court sentenced Jones to life imprisonment.

---

[1]   In this litigation, the Government has conceded noncompliance with the warrant and has argued only that a warrant was not required.

The United States Court of Appeals for the District of Columbia Circuit reversed the conviction because of admission of the evidence obtained by warrantless use of the GPS device which, it said, violated the Fourth Amendment. * * * We granted certiorari.

II

A

The Fourth Amendment provides in relevant part that "[t]he right of the people to be secure in their persons, houses, papers, and effects, against unreasonable searches and seizures, shall not be violated." It is beyond dispute that a vehicle is an "effect" as that term is used in the Amendment. We hold that the Government's installation of a GPS device on a target's vehicle,[2] and its use of that device to monitor the vehicle's movements, constitutes a "search."

It is important to be clear about what occurred in this case: The Government physically occupied private property for the purpose of obtaining information. We have no doubt that such a physical intrusion would have been considered a "search" within the meaning of the Fourth Amendment when it was adopted. * * *

Consistent with this understanding, our Fourth Amendment jurisprudence was tied to common-law trespass, at least until the latter half of the 20th century. * * *

Our later cases, of course, have deviated from that exclusively property-based approach. In *Katz v. United States*, 389 U.S. 347, 351 (1967), we said that "the Fourth Amendment protects people, not places," and found a violation in attachment of an eavesdropping device to a public telephone booth. Our later cases have applied the analysis of Justice Harlan's concurrence in that case, which said that a violation occurs when government officers violate a person's "reasonable expectation of privacy."

The Government contends that the Harlan standard shows that no search occurred here, since Jones had no "reasonable expectation of privacy" in the area of the Jeep accessed by Government agents (its underbody) and in the locations of the Jeep on the public roads, which were visible to all. But we need not address the Government's contentions, because Jones's Fourth Amendment rights do not rise or fall with the *Katz* formulation. At bottom, we must "assur[e] preservation of that degree of privacy against government that existed when the Fourth Amendment was adopted." As explained, for most of our history the Fourth Amendment was

---

    [2]   As we have noted, the Jeep was registered to Jones's wife. The Government acknowledged, however, that Jones was "the exclusive driver." If Jones was not the owner he had at least the property rights of a bailee. The Court of Appeals concluded that the vehicle's registration did not affect his ability to make a Fourth Amendment objection, and the Government has not challenged that determination here. We therefore do not consider the Fourth Amendment significance of Jones's status.

understood to embody a particular concern for government trespass upon the areas ("persons, houses, papers, and effects") it enumerates. *Katz* did not repudiate that understanding. * * *

The Government contends that several of our post-*Katz* cases foreclose the conclusion that what occurred here constituted a search. It relies principally on two cases in which we rejected Fourth Amendment challenges to "beepers," electronic tracking devices that represent another form of electronic monitoring. The first case, [*United States v.*] *Knotts*, upheld against Fourth Amendment challenge the use of a "beeper" that had been placed in a container of chloroform, allowing law enforcement to monitor the location of the container. We said that there had been no infringement of Knotts' reasonable expectation of privacy since the information obtained—the location of the automobile carrying the container on public roads, and the location of the off-loaded container in open fields near Knotts' cabin—had been voluntarily conveyed to the public.[6] But as we have discussed, the *Katz* reasonable-expectation-of-privacy test has been added to, not substituted for, the common-law trespassory test. The holding in *Knotts* addressed only the former, since the latter was not at issue. The beeper had been placed in the container before it came into Knotts' possession, with the consent of the then-owner. Knotts did not challenge that installation, and we specifically declined to consider its effect on the Fourth Amendment analysis. *Knotts* would be relevant, perhaps, if the Government were making the argument that what would otherwise be an unconstitutional search is not such where it produces only public information. The Government does not make that argument, and we know of no case that would support it.

The second "beeper" case, *United States v. Karo*, 468 U.S. 705 (1984), does not suggest a different conclusion. There we addressed the question left open by *Knotts*, whether the installation of a beeper in a container amounted to a search or seizure. As in *Knotts*, at the time the beeper was installed the container belonged to a third party, and it did not come into possession of the defendant until later. Thus, the specific question we considered was whether the installation *"with the consent of the original owner* constitute[d] a search or seizure . . . when the container is delivered to a buyer having no knowledge of the presence of the beeper." We held not. The Government, we said, came into physical contact with the container only before it belonged to the defendant Karo; and the transfer of the container with the unmonitored beeper inside did not convey any information and thus did not invade Karo's privacy. That conclusion is perfectly consistent with the one we reach here. Karo accepted the

---

[6] *Knotts* noted the "limited use which the government made of the signals from this particular beeper," and reserved the question whether "different constitutional principles may be applicable" to "dragnet-type law enforcement practices" of the type that GPS tracking made possible here, ibid.

container as it came to him, beeper and all, and was therefore not entitled to object to the beeper's presence, even though it was used to monitor the container's location. Jones, who possessed the Jeep at the time the Government trespassorily inserted the information-gathering device, is on much different footing. * * *

Finally, the Government's position gains little support from our conclusion in *Oliver v. United States*, 466 U.S. 170 (1984), that officers' information-gathering intrusion on an "open field" did not constitute a Fourth Amendment search even though it was a trespass at common law. Quite simply, an open field, unlike the curtilage of a home, *see United States v. Dunn*, 480 U.S. 294, 300 (1987), is not one of those protected areas enumerated in the Fourth Amendment. The Government's physical intrusion on such an area—unlike its intrusion on the "effect" at issue here—is of no Fourth Amendment significance.[8]

B

The concurrence begins by accusing us of applying "18th-century tort law." That is a distortion. What we apply is an 18th-century guarantee against unreasonable searches, which we believe must provide at a minimum the degree of protection it afforded when it was adopted. The concurrence does not share that belief. It would apply exclusively *Katz's* reasonable-expectation-of-privacy test, even when that eliminates rights that previously existed.

The concurrence faults our approach for "present[ing] particularly vexing problems" in cases that do not involve physical contact, such as those that involve the transmission of electronic signals. We entirely fail to understand that point. For unlike the concurrence, which would make *Katz* the exclusive test, we do not make trespass the exclusive test. Situations involving merely the transmission of electronic signals without trespass would remain subject to *Katz* analysis. * * *

III

The Government argues in the alternative that even if the attachment and use of the device was a search, it was reasonable—and thus lawful—under the Fourth Amendment because "officers had reasonable suspicion, and indeed probable cause, to believe that [Jones] was a leader in a large-scale cocaine distribution conspiracy." We have no occasion to consider this argument. The Government did not raise it below, and the D. C. Circuit therefore did not address it. We consider the argument forfeited.

The judgment of the Court of Appeals for the D. C. Circuit is affirmed.

---

8   * * * The Fourth Amendment protects against trespassory searches only with regard to those items ("persons, houses, papers, and effects") that it enumerates. The trespass that occurred in *Oliver* may properly be understood as a "search," but not one "in the constitutional sense."

It is so ordered.

JUSTICE SOTOMAYOR, concurring.

I join the Court's opinion because I agree that a search within the meaning of the Fourth Amendment occurs, at a minimum, "[w]here, as here, the Government obtains information by physically intruding on a constitutionally protected area." * * *

Of course, the Fourth Amendment is not concerned only with trespassory intrusions on property. Rather, even in the absence of a trespass, "a Fourth Amendment search occurs when the government violates a subjective expectation of privacy that society recognizes as reasonable." In *Katz*, this Court enlarged its then-prevailing focus on property rights by announcing that the reach of the Fourth Amendment does not "turn upon the presence or absence of a physical intrusion." As the majority's opinion makes clear, however, *Katz's* reasonable-expectation-of-privacy test augmented, but did not displace or diminish, the common-law trespassory test that preceded it. Thus, "when the Government does engage in physical intrusion of a constitutionally protected area in order to obtain information, that intrusion may constitute a violation of the Fourth Amendment." *United States v. Knotts*, 460 U.S. 276, 286 (1983) (Brennan, J., concurring in judgment). * * * [T]he trespassory test applied in the majority's opinion reflects an irreducible constitutional minimum: When the government physically invades personal property to gather information, a search occurs. * * *

Nonetheless, * * * physical intrusion is now unnecessary to many forms of surveillance. With increasing regularity, the government will be capable of duplicating the monitoring undertaken in this case by enlisting factory- or owner-installed vehicle tracking devices or GPS-enabled smartphones. In cases of electronic or other novel modes of surveillance that do not depend upon a physical invasion on property, the majority opinion's trespassory test may provide little guidance. But "[s]ituations involving merely the transmission of electronic signals without trespass would remain subject to *Katz* analysis." * * *

Awareness that the government may be watching chills associational and expressive freedoms. And the government's unrestrained power to assemble data that reveal private aspects of identity is susceptible to abuse. The net result is that GPS monitoring—by making available at a relatively low cost such a substantial quantum of intimate information about any person whom the government, in its unfettered discretion, chooses to track—may "alter the relationship between citizen and government in a way that is inimical to democratic society."

* * * [I]t may be necessary to reconsider the premise that an individual has no reasonable expectation of privacy in information voluntarily disclosed to third parties. *E.g., Smith* [*v. Maryland*], 442 U.S., at 742. This

approach is ill suited to the digital age, in which people reveal a great deal of information about themselves to third parties in the course of carrying out mundane tasks. People disclose the phone numbers that they dial or text to their cellular providers; the URLs that they visit and the e-mail addresses with which they correspond to their Internet service providers; and the books, groceries, and medications they purchase to online retailers. * * * I for one doubt that people would accept without complaint the warrantless disclosure to the government of a list of every Web site they had visited in the last week, or month, or year. But whatever the societal expectations, they can attain constitutionally protected status only if our Fourth Amendment jurisprudence ceases to treat secrecy as a prerequisite for privacy. I would not assume that all information voluntarily disclosed to some member of the public for a limited purpose is, for that reason alone, disentitled to Fourth Amendment protection. *See Smith*, 442 U.S., at 749 (Marshall, J., dissenting) ("Privacy is not a discrete commodity, possessed absolutely or not at all. Those who disclose certain facts to a bank or phone company for a limited business purpose need not assume that this information will be released to other persons for other purposes"); *see also Katz*, 389 U.S., at 351–352 ("[W]hat [a person] seeks to preserve as private, even in an area accessible to the public, may be constitutionally protected").

Resolution of these difficult questions in this case is unnecessary, however, because the Government's physical intrusion on Jones' Jeep supplies a narrower basis for decision. I therefore join the majority's opinion.

JUSTICE ALITO, with whom JUSTICE GINSBURG, JUSTICE BREYER, and JUSTICE KAGAN join, concurring in the judgment.

[Omitted.]

QUESTIONS, COMMENTS, CONCERNS?

1. ***Jones* and *Smith*.** Reconsider *Smith* as a trespass case. Had *Jones* existed as precedent at the time of that case, could the *Smith* petitioner have relied on the "constitutional trespass" test to demonstrate that the attachment of a pen register is a "search"? Does *Jones* change the third-party doctrine?

2. ***Jones* and *Ulbricht*.** In light of *Jones*, could Ulbricht argue that the attachment of the trap and trace device to identify the source IP address of his internet communications constituted a "search"? For Ulbricht's opinion, scan his reply brief beginning with page 22. [See Casefile Document 5.] There, Ulbricht suggests that the government's investigative conduct "mirrors what the government collected in *Jones* via the GPS device employed in that case[.]" What's wrong with that logic?

FLORIDA V. JARDINES

569 U.S. 1
Supreme Court of the United States
October 31, 2012, Argued; March 26, 2013, Decided
No. 11-564

JUSTICE SCALIA delivered the opinion of the Court.

We consider whether using a drug-sniffing dog on a homeowner's porch to investigate the contents of the home is a "search" within the meaning of the Fourth Amendment.

I

In 2006, Detective William Pedraja of the Miami-Dade Police Department received an unverified tip that marijuana was being grown in the home of respondent Joelis Jardines. One month later, the Department and the Drug Enforcement Administration sent a joint surveillance team to Jardines' home. Detective Pedraja was part of that team. He watched the home for fifteen minutes and saw no vehicles in the driveway or activity around the home, and could not see inside because the blinds were drawn. Detective Pedraja then approached Jardines' home accompanied by Detective Douglas Bartelt, a trained canine handler who had just arrived at the scene with his drug-sniffing dog. The dog was trained to detect the scent of marijuana, cocaine, heroin, and several other drugs, indicating the presence of any of these substances through particular behavioral changes recognizable by his handler.

Detective Bartelt had the dog on a six-foot leash, owing in part to the dog's "wild" nature, and tendency to dart around erratically while searching. As the dog approached Jardines' front porch, he apparently sensed one of the odors he had been trained to detect, and began energetically exploring the area for the strongest point source of that odor. As Detective Bartelt explained, the dog "began tracking that airborne odor by . . . tracking back and forth," engaging in what is called "bracketing," "back and forth, back and forth." Detective Bartelt gave the dog "the full six feet of the leash plus whatever safe distance [he could] give him" to do this—he testified that he needed to give the dog "as much distance as I can." And Detective Pedraja stood back while this was occurring, so that he would not "get knocked over" when the dog was "spinning around trying to find" the source.

After sniffing the base of the front door, the dog sat, which is the trained behavior upon discovering the odor's strongest point. Detective Bartelt then pulled the dog away from the door and returned to his vehicle. He left the scene after informing Detective Pedraja that there had been a positive alert for narcotics.

On the basis of what he had learned at the home, Detective Pedraja applied for and received a warrant to search the residence. When the warrant was executed later that day, Jardines attempted to flee and was arrested; the search revealed marijuana plants, and he was charged with trafficking in cannabis.

At trial, Jardines moved to suppress the marijuana plants on the ground that the canine investigation was an unreasonable search. The trial court granted the motion, and the Florida Third District Court of Appeal reversed. On a petition for discretionary review, the Florida Supreme Court quashed the decision of the Third District Court of Appeal and approved the trial court's decision to suppress, holding (as relevant here) that the use of the trained narcotics dog to investigate Jardines' home was a Fourth Amendment search unsupported by probable cause, rendering invalid the warrant based upon information gathered in that search.

We granted certiorari, limited to the question of whether the officers' behavior was a search within the meaning of the Fourth Amendment.

II   * * *

A

* * * [W]hen it comes to the Fourth Amendment, the home is first among equals. At the Amendment's "very core" stands "the right of a man to retreat into his own home and there be free from unreasonable governmental intrusion." *Silverman v. United States*, 365 U.S. 505, 511 (1961). This right would be of little practical value if the State's agents could stand in a home's porch or side garden and trawl for evidence with impunity; the right to retreat would be significantly diminished if the police could enter a man's property to observe his repose from just outside the front window.

We therefore regard the area "immediately surrounding and associated with the home"—what our cases call the curtilage—as "part of the home itself for Fourth Amendment purposes." * * * While the boundaries of the curtilage are generally "clearly marked," the "conception defining the curtilage" is at any rate familiar enough that it is "easily understood from our daily experience." Here there is no doubt that the officers entered it: The front porch is the classic exemplar of an area adjacent to the home and "to which the activity of home life extends."

B

Since the officers' investigation took place in a constitutionally protected area, we turn to the question of whether it was accomplished through an unlicensed physical intrusion. While law enforcement officers need not "shield their eyes" when passing by the home "on public thoroughfares," an officer's leave to gather information is sharply circumscribed when he steps off those thoroughfares and enters the Fourth Amendments protected areas. *Entick v. Carrington*, 2 Wils. K. B. 275, 95 Eng. Rep. 807 (K. B. 1765), a case "undoubtedly familiar" to "every American statesman" at the time of the

Founding, *Boyd v. United States*, 116 U.S. 616, 626 (1886), states the general rule clearly: "[O]ur law holds the property of every man so sacred, that no man can set his foot upon his neighbour's close without his leave." As it is undisputed that the detectives had all four of their feet and all four of their companion's firmly planted on the constitutionally protected extension of Jardines' home, the only question is whether he had given his leave (even implicitly) for them to do so. He had not.

We have * * * recognized that "the knocker on the front door is treated as an invitation or license to attempt an entry, justifying ingress to the home by solicitors, hawkers and peddlers of all kinds." This implicit license typically permits the visitor to approach the home by the front path, knock promptly, wait briefly to be received, and then (absent invitation to linger longer) leave. Complying with the terms of that traditional invitation does not require fine-grained legal knowledge; it is generally managed without incident by the Nation's Girl Scouts and trick-or-treaters. Thus, a police officer not armed with a warrant may approach a home and knock, precisely because that is "no more than any private citizen might do." *Kentucky v. King*, 563 U.S. ___, ___, 131 S. Ct. 1849 (2011).

But introducing a trained police dog to explore the area around the home in hopes of discovering incriminating evidence is something else. There is no customary invitation to do that. An invitation to engage in canine forensic investigation assuredly does not inhere in the very act of hanging a knocker. To find a visitor knocking on the door is routine (even if sometimes unwelcome); to spot that same visitor exploring the front path with a metal detector, or marching his bloodhound into the garden before saying hello and asking permission, would inspire most of us to—well, call the police. The scope of a license—express or implied—is limited not only to a particular area but also to a specific purpose. Consent at a traffic stop to an officer's checking out an anonymous tip that there is a body in the trunk does not permit the officer to rummage through the trunk for narcotics. Here, the background social norms that invite a visitor to the front door do not invite him there to conduct a search.

* * * [As a result], [the officers'] behavior objectively reveals a purpose to conduct a search, which is not what anyone would think he had license to do.

III

The State argues that investigation by a forensic narcotics dog by definition cannot implicate any legitimate privacy interest. The State cites for authority our decisions in *United States v. Place*, 462 U.S. 696 (1983), *United States v. Jacobsen*, 466 U.S. 109 (1984), and *Illinois v. Caballes*, 543 U.S. 405 (2005), which held, respectively, that canine inspection of luggage in an airport, chemical testing of a substance that had fallen from a parcel in transit, and canine inspection of an automobile during a lawful traffic stop, do not violate the "reasonable expectation of privacy" described in *Katz*.

Just last Term, we considered an argument much like this. *Jones* held that tracking an automobile's whereabouts using a physically-mounted GPS receiver is a Fourth Amendment search. The Government argued that the *Katz* standard "show[ed] that no search occurred," as the defendant had "no 'reasonable expectation of privacy' " in his whereabouts on the public roads, *Jones*, 565 U.S., at ___—a proposition with at least as much support in our case law as the one the State marshals here. *See, e.g., United States v. Knotts*, 460 U.S. 276, 278 (1983). But because the GPS receiver had been physically mounted on the defendant's automobile (thus intruding on his "effects"), we held that tracking the vehicle's movements was a search: a person's "Fourth Amendment rights do not rise or fall with the *Katz* formulation." *Jones, supra*, at ___. The *Katz* reasonable-expectations test "has been added to, not substituted for," the traditional property-based understanding of the Fourth Amendment, and so is unnecessary to consider when the government gains evidence by physically intruding on constitutionally protected areas. *Jones, supra*, at ___.

Thus, we need not decide whether the officers' investigation of Jardines' home violated his expectation of privacy under *Katz*. One virtue of the Fourth Amendment's property-rights baseline is that it keeps easy cases easy. That the officers learned what they learned only by physically intruding on Jardines' property to gather evidence is enough to establish that a search occurred. * * *

The government's use of trained police dogs to investigate the home and its immediate surroundings is a "search" within the meaning of the Fourth Amendment. The judgment of the Supreme Court of Florida is therefore affirmed.

It is so ordered.

JUSTICE KAGAN, with whom JUSTICE GINSBURG and JUSTICE SOTOMAYOR join, concurring.

[Omitted.]

JUSTICE ALITO, with whom THE CHIEF JUSTICE, JUSTICE KENNEDY, and JUSTICE BREYER join, dissenting.

[Omitted.]

III. WHAT IS A FOURTH AMENDMENT "SEIZURE"?

A. MEET ALBERT JONES

Our next defendant, Albert Christopher Jones, is a routine drug offender who takes us into day-to-day criminal practice. His case would ultimately produce a surprising appellate result.

At roughly 6:00 p.m. on Friday, October 3, 2014, Jones was walking through a Washington, D.C. alley when he came upon two officers sitting in a marked car. Jones was holding a flattened Newport cigarette box and, when Jones neared the car, he dropped his hand with the box to his right side. One of the officers, Zachary Blier, then asked Jones, "Hey man how you doing?" Jones stopped. Officer Blier then began questioning Jones about where he was coming from, whether he had identification on him, and where he lived.

Although Officer Blier's partner remained in the vehicle, Officer Blier exited the vehicle. As he did, Officer Blier noticed Jones place the cigarette box behind his leg in an effort to conceal it. That, in turn, prompted Officer Blier to ask, "can I see that cigarette box?" Jones handed the box to Officer Blier who looked inside the box and discovered cocaine. Jones was placed under arrest, and following a search of his person, Officer Blier located a tan powder inside Jones's pants pocket that turned out to be opiates. The government filed a two-count information against Jones charging him with: (1) unlawful possession of cocaine, and (2) unlawful possession of heroin.

Jones's lawyer filed a motion to suppress. In the "factual background" section, she wrote that "[o]ne of the officers exited the police cruiser and order Mr. Jones to place the cigarette box on the hood of the car." Based largely on that fact, defense counsel argued that Jones was unreasonably "seized" without either probable cause or reasonable suspicion. Accordingly, she concluded, the search that produced the cocaine was unlawful, and the cocaine should be suppressed.

In the government's response, it argued that Jones's motion was both late-filed and failed to provide record support for its assertion that the officers "ordered" Jones to place the cigarette box onto the hood of the police cruiser. But that factual dispute aside, the government contended that "the officer had reasonable suspicion, or in the alternative, probable cause, to believe that the cigarette box was the instrumentality of a crime."

Following a hearing, the trial court denied Jones's motion. Jones entered a conditional plea of guilt, reserving the right to appeal the denial of his motion. On appeal, a majority of the District of Columbia Court of Appeals reversed, holding that Jones was unlawfully seized without reasonable suspicion or probable cause in violation of the Fourth Amendment. The court highlighted two critical facts. First, "the officer got out [of the cruiser] and planted himself in appellant's path in the straitened space (clearly but a few feet wide) between the vehicle and the alley wall." Second, Officer Blier asked his partner to perform a warrant check on Jones. The court reasoned that a warrant check "sends a strong signal to a reasonable person that the officer will not allow him to leave while the inquiry is in progress precisely because the outcome of the inquiry may necessitate the person's detention." Accordingly, the court ordered suppression of the cocaine and reversed Jones's conviction.

B. SEIZURES OF PEOPLE

UNITED STATES V. MENDENHALL
446 U.S. 544
Supreme Court of the United States
February 19, 1980, Argued; May 27, 1980, Decided
No. 78-1821

MR. JUSTICE STEWART announced the judgment of the Court and delivered an opinion, in which MR. JUSTICE REHNQUIST joined.

The respondent was brought to trial in the United States District Court for the Eastern District of Michigan on a charge of possessing heroin with intent to distribute it. She moved to suppress the introduction at trial of the heroin as evidence against her on the ground that it had been acquired from her through an unconstitutional search and seizure by agents of the Drug Enforcement Administration (DEA). The District Court denied the respondent's motion, and she was convicted after a trial upon stipulated facts. The Court of Appeals reversed, finding the search of the respondent's person to have been unlawful. We granted certiorari to consider whether any right of the respondent guaranteed by the Fourth Amendment was violated in the circumstances presented by this case.

I

At the hearing in the trial court on the respondent's motion to suppress, it was established how the heroin she was charged with possessing had been obtained from her. The respondent arrived at the Detroit Metropolitan Airport on a commercial airline flight from Los Angeles early in the morning on February 10, 1976. As she disembarked from the airplane, she was observed by two agents of the DEA, who were present at the airport for the purpose of detecting unlawful traffic in narcotics. After observing the respondent's conduct, which appeared to the agents to be characteristic of persons unlawfully carrying narcotics,[1] the

---

[1]   The agent testified that the respondent's behavior fit the so-called "drug courier profile"—an informally compiled abstract of characteristics thought typical of persons carrying illicit drugs. In this case the agents thought it relevant that (1) the respondent was arriving on a flight from

agents approached her as she was walking through the concourse, identified themselves as federal agents, and asked to see her identification and airline ticket. The respondent produced her driver's license, which was in the name of Sylvia Mendenhall, and, in answer to a question of one of the agents, stated that she resided at the address appearing on the license. The airline ticket was issued in the name of "Annette Ford." When asked why the ticket bore a name different from her own, the respondent stated that she "just felt like using that name." In response to a further question, the respondent indicated that she had been in California only two days. Agent Anderson then specifically identified himself as a federal narcotics agent and, according to his testimony, the respondent "became quite shaken, extremely nervous. She had a hard time speaking."

After returning the airline ticket and driver's license to her, Agent Anderson asked the respondent if she would accompany him to the airport DEA office for further questions. She did so, although the record does not indicate a verbal response to the request. The office, which was located up one flight of stairs about 50 feet from where the respondent had first been approached, consisted of a reception area adjoined by three other rooms. At the office the agent asked the respondent if she would allow a search of her person and handbag and told her that she had the right to decline the search if she desired. She responded: "Go ahead." She then handed Agent Anderson her purse, which contained a receipt for an airline ticket that had been issued to "F. Bush" three days earlier for a flight from Pittsburgh through Chicago to Los Angeles. The agent asked whether this was the ticket that she had used for her flight to California, and the respondent stated that it was.

A female police officer then arrived to conduct the search of the respondent's person. She asked the agents if the respondent had consented to be searched. The agents said that she had, and the respondent followed the policewoman into a private room. There the policewoman again asked the respondent if she consented to the search, and the respondent replied that she did. The policewoman explained that the search would require that the respondent remove her clothing. The respondent stated that she had a plane to catch and was assured by the policewoman that if she were carrying no narcotics, there would be no problem. The respondent then began to disrobe without further comment. As the respondent removed her clothing, she took from her undergarments two small packages, one of which appeared to contain heroin, and handed both to the policewoman. The agents then arrested the respondent for possessing heroin. * * *

Los Angeles, a city believed by the agents to be the place of origin for much of the heroin brought to Detroit; (2) the respondent was the last person to leave the plane, "appeared to be very nervous," and "completely scanned the whole area where [the agents] were standing"; (3) after leaving the plane the respondent proceeded past the baggage area without claiming any luggage; and (4) the respondent changed airlines for her flight out of Detroit.

II

* * * [T]he Government concedes that its agents had neither a warrant nor probable cause to believe that the respondent was carrying narcotics when the agents conducted a search of the respondent's person. It is the Government's position, however, that the search was conducted pursuant to the respondent's consent, and thus was excepted from the requirements of both a warrant and probable cause. * * * We must first consider, therefore, whether such conduct occurred, either on the concourse or in the DEA office at the airport.

A

* * * [A] person is "seized" only when, by means of physical force or a show of authority, his freedom of movement is restrained. Only when such restraint is imposed is there any foundation whatever for invoking constitutional safeguards. The purpose of the Fourth Amendment is not to eliminate all contact between the police and the citizenry, but "to prevent arbitrary and oppressive interference by enforcement officials with the privacy and personal security of individuals." As long as the person to whom questions are put remains free to disregard the questions and walk away, there has been no intrusion upon that person's liberty or privacy as would under the Constitution require some particularized and objective justification.

Moreover, characterizing every street encounter between a citizen and the police as a "seizure," while not enhancing any interest secured by the Fourth Amendment, would impose wholly unrealistic restrictions upon a wide variety of legitimate law enforcement practices. The Court has on other occasions referred to the acknowledged need for police questioning as a tool in the effective enforcement of the criminal laws. * * *

We conclude that a person has been "seized" within the meaning of the Fourth Amendment only if, in view of all of the circumstances surrounding the incident, a reasonable person would have believed that he was not free to leave.[6] Examples of circumstances that might indicate a seizure, even where the person did not attempt to leave, would be the threatening presence of several officers, the display of a weapon by an officer, some physical touching of the person of the citizen, or the use of language or tone of voice indicating that compliance with the officer's request might be compelled. In the absence of some such evidence, otherwise inoffensive contact between a member of the public and the police cannot, as a matter of law, amount to a seizure of that person.

On the facts of this case, no "seizure" of the respondent occurred. The events took place in the public concourse. The agents wore no uniforms and

---

[6] We agree with the District Court that the subjective intention of the DEA agent in this case to detain the respondent, had she attempted to leave, is irrelevant except insofar as that may have been conveyed to the respondent.

displayed no weapons. They did not summon the respondent to their presence, but instead approached her and identified themselves as federal agents. They requested, but did not demand to see the respondent's identification and ticket. Such conduct, without more, did not amount to an intrusion upon any constitutionally protected interest. The respondent was not seized simply by reason of the fact that the agents approached her, asked her if she would show them her ticket and identification, and posed to her a few questions. Nor was it enough to establish a seizure that the person asking the questions was a law enforcement official. In short, nothing in the record suggests that the respondent had any objective reason to believe that she was not free to end the conversation in the concourse and proceed on her way, and for that reason we conclude that the agents' initial approach to her was not a seizure.

Our conclusion that no seizure occurred is not affected by the fact that the respondent was not expressly told by the agents that she was free to decline to cooperate with their inquiry, for the voluntariness of her responses does not depend upon her having been so informed. We also reject the argument that the only inference to be drawn from the fact that the respondent acted in a manner so contrary to her self-interest is that she was compelled to answer the agents' questions. It may happen that a person makes statements to law enforcement officials that he later regrets, but the issue in such cases is not whether the statement was self-protective, but rather whether it was made voluntarily. * * *

B

Although we have concluded that the initial encounter between the DEA agents and the respondent on the concourse at the Detroit Airport did not constitute an unlawful seizure, it is still arguable that the respondent's Fourth Amendment protections were violated when she went from the concourse to the DEA office. Such a violation might in turn infect the subsequent search of the respondent's person.

The question whether the respondent's consent to accompany the agents was in fact voluntary or was the product of duress or coercion, express or implied, is to be determined by the totality of all the circumstances, and is a matter which the Government has the burden of proving. The respondent herself did not testify at the hearing. The Government's evidence showed that the respondent was not told that she had to go to the office, but was simply asked if she would accompany the officers. There were neither threats nor any show of force. The respondent had been questioned only briefly, and her ticket and identification were returned to her before she was asked to accompany the officers.

On the other hand, it is argued that the incident would reasonably have appeared coercive to the respondent, who was 22 years old and had not been graduated from high school. It is additionally suggested that the respondent, a female and a Negro, may have felt unusually threatened by the officers, who were white males. While these factors were not irrelevant, neither were they decisive, and the totality of the evidence in this case was plainly adequate to support the District Court's finding that the respondent voluntarily consented to accompany the officers to the DEA office.

C

Because the search of the respondent's person was not preceded by an impermissible seizure of her person, it cannot be contended that her apparent consent to the subsequent search was infected by an unlawful detention. There remains to be considered whether the respondent's consent to the search was for any other reason invalid. The District Court explicitly credited the officers' testimony and found that the "consent was freely and voluntarily given." There was more than enough evidence in this case to sustain that view. * * *

III

We conclude that the District Court's determination that the respondent consented to the search of her person "freely and voluntarily" was sustained by the evidence and that the Court of Appeals was, therefore, in error in setting it aside. Accordingly, the judgment of the Court of Appeals is reversed, and the case is remanded to that court for further proceedings.

It is so ordered.

MR. JUSTICE POWELL, with whom THE CHIEF JUSTICE and MR. JUSTICE BLACKMUN join, concurring in part and concurring in the judgment.

I join Parts I, II-B, II-C, and III of the Court's opinion. Because neither of the courts below considered the question, I do not reach the Government's contention that the agents did not "seize" the respondent within the meaning of the Fourth Amendment. In my view, we may assume for present purposes that the stop did constitute a seizure.[1] I would hold— as did the District Court—that the federal agents had reasonable suspicion that the respondent was engaging in criminal activity, and, therefore, that they did not violate the Fourth Amendment by stopping the respondent for routine questioning.

* * * The public has a compelling interest in detecting those who would traffic in deadly drugs for personal profit. Few problems affecting the

---

[1] MR. JUSTICE STEWART concludes in Part II-A that there was no "seizure" within the meaning of the Fourth Amendment. He reasons that such a seizure occurs "only if, in view of all of the circumstances surrounding the incident, a reasonable person would have believed that he was not free to leave." MR. JUSTICE STEWART also notes that " '[there] is nothing in the Constitution which prevents a policeman from addressing questions to anyone on the streets.' " I do not necessarily disagree with the views expressed in Part II-A. For me, the question whether the respondent in this case reasonably could have thought she was free to "walk away" when asked by two Government agents for her driver's license and ticket is extremely close.

health and welfare of our population, particularly our young, cause greater concern than the escalating use of controlled substances. Much of the drug traffic is highly organized and conducted by sophisticated criminal syndicates. The profits are enormous. And many drugs, including heroin, may be easily concealed. As a result, the obstacles to detection of illegal conduct may be unmatched in any other area of law enforcement.

To meet this pressing concern, the Drug Enforcement Administration since 1974 has assigned highly skilled agents to the Detroit Airport as part of a nationwide program to intercept drug couriers transporting narcotics between major drug sources and distribution centers in the United States. Federal agents have developed "drug courier profiles" that describe the characteristics generally associated with narcotics traffickers. For example, because the Drug Enforcement Administration believes that most drugs enter Detroit from one of four "source" cities (Los Angeles, San Diego, Miami, or New York), agents pay particular attention to passengers who arrive from those places. During the first 18 months of the program, agents watching the Detroit Airport searched 141 persons in 96 encounters. They found controlled substances in 77 of the encounters and arrested 122 persons. When two of these agents stopped the respondent in February 1976, they were carrying out a highly specialized law enforcement operation designed to combat the serious societal threat posed by narcotics distribution.

* * * In reviewing the factors that led the agents to stop and question the respondent, it is important to recall that a trained law enforcement agent may be "able to perceive and articulate meaning in given conduct which would be wholly innocent to the untrained observer." Among the circumstances that can give rise to reasonable suspicion are the agent's knowledge of the methods used in recent criminal activity and the characteristics of persons engaged in such illegal practices. Law enforcement officers may rely on the "characteristics of the area," and the behavior of a suspect who appears to be evading police contact. "In all situations the officer is entitled to assess the facts in light of his experience."

The two officers who stopped the respondent were federal agents assigned to the Drug Enforcement Administration. Agent Anderson, who initiated the stop and questioned the respondent, had 10 years of experience and special training in drug enforcement. He had been assigned to the Detroit Airport, known to be a crossroads for illicit narcotics traffic,[4] for over a year and he had been involved in approximately 100 drug-related arrests.

---

[4]   From 1975 through 1978, more than 135 pounds of heroin and 22 pounds of cocaine were seized at the Detroit Airport. In 1978, 1,536 dosage units of other dangerous drugs were discovered there.

The agents observed the respondent as she arrived in Detroit from Los Angeles. The respondent, who appeared very nervous, engaged in behavior that the agents believed was designed to evade detection. She deplaned only after all other passengers had left the aircraft. Agent Anderson testified that drug couriers often disembark last in order to have a clear view of the terminal so that they more easily can detect government agents. Once inside the terminal the respondent scanned the entire gate area and walked "very, very slowly" toward the baggage area. When she arrived there, she claimed no baggage. Instead, she asked a skycap for directions to the Eastern Airlines ticket counter located in a different terminal. Agent Anderson stood in line immediately behind the respondent at the ticket counter. Although she carried an American Airlines ticket for a flight from Detroit to Pittsburgh, she asked for an Eastern Airlines ticket. An airline employee gave her an Eastern Airlines boarding pass. Agent Anderson testified that drug couriers frequently travel without baggage and change flights en route to avoid surveillance. On the basis of these observations, the agents stopped and questioned the respondent.

* * * The specially trained agents acted pursuant to a well-planned, and effective, federal law enforcement program. They observed respondent engaging in conduct that they reasonably associated with criminal activity. Furthermore, the events occurred in an airport known to be frequented by drug couriers.[6] In light of all of the circumstances, I would hold that the agents possessed reasonable and articulable suspicion of criminal activity when they stopped the respondent in a public place and asked her for identification. * * *

MR. JUSTICE WHITE, with whom MR. JUSTICE BRENNAN, MR. JUSTICE MARSHALL, and MR. JUSTICE STEVENS join, dissenting.

The Court today concludes that agents of the Drug Enforcement Administration (DEA) acted lawfully in stopping a traveler changing planes in an airport terminal and escorting her to a DEA office for a strip-search of her person. This result is particularly curious because a majority of the Members of the Court refuse to reject the conclusion that Ms. Mendenhall was "seized," while a separate majority decline to hold that there were reasonable grounds to justify a seizure. * * *

I

* * * MR. JUSTICE STEWART believes that a "seizure" within the meaning of the Fourth Amendment occurs when an individual's freedom of movement is restrained by means of physical force or a show of authority.

---

[6] The results of the Drug Enforcement Agency's efforts at the Detroit Airport support the conclusion that considerable drug traffic flows through the Detroit Airport. Contrary to MR. JUSTICE WHITE'S apparent impression, I do not believe that these statistics establish by themselves the reasonableness of this search. Nor would reliance upon the "drug courier profile" necessarily demonstrate reasonable suspicion. Each case raising a Fourth Amendment issue must be judged on its own facts.

Although it is undisputed that Ms. Mendenhall was not free to leave after the DEA agents stopped her and inspected her identification, MR. JUSTICE STEWART concludes that she was not "seized" because he finds that, under the totality of the circumstances, a reasonable person would have believed that she was free to leave. While basing this finding on an alleged absence from the record of objective evidence indicating that Ms. Mendenhall was not free to ignore the officer's inquiries and continue on her way, MR. JUSTICE STEWART's opinion brushes off the fact that this asserted evidentiary deficiency may be largely attributable to the fact that the "seizure" question was never raised below. In assessing what the record does reveal, the opinion discounts certain objective factors that would tend to support a "seizure" finding,[3] while relying on contrary factors inconclusive even under its own illustrations of how a "seizure" may be established.[4] Moreover, although MR. JUSTICE STEWART's opinion purports to make its "seizure" finding turn on objective factors known to the person accosted, in distinguishing prior decisions holding that investigatory stops constitute "seizures," it does not rely on differences in the extent to which persons accosted could reasonably believe that they were free to leave. Even if one believes the Government should be permitted to raise the "seizure" question in this Court, the proper course would be to direct a remand to the District Court for an evidentiary hearing on the question, rather than to decide it in the first instance in this Court.

II

Assuming, as we should, that Ms. Mendenhall was "seized" within the meaning of the Fourth Amendment when she was stopped by the DEA agents, the legality of that stop turns on whether there were reasonable grounds for suspecting her of criminal activity at the time of the stop. * * *

At the time they stopped Ms. Mendenhall, the DEA agents' suspicion that she was engaged in criminal activity was based solely on their brief observations of her conduct at the airport. The officers had no advance information that Ms. Mendenhall, or anyone on her flight, would be carrying drugs. What the agents observed Ms. Mendenhall do in the airport was not "unusual conduct" which would lead an experienced officer reasonably to conclude that criminal activity was afoot, but rather the kind of behavior that could reasonably be expected of anyone changing planes in an airport terminal.

---

[3] Not the least of these factors is the fact that the DEA agents for a time took Ms. Mendenhall's plane ticket and driver's license from her. It is doubtful that any reasonable person about to board a plane would feel free to leave when law enforcement officers have her plane ticket.

[4] MR. JUSTICE STEWART notes, for example, that a "seizure" might be established even if the suspect did not attempt to leave, by the nature of the language or tone of voice used by the officers, factors that were never addressed at the suppression hearing, very likely because the "seizure" question was not raised.

None of the aspects of Ms. Mendenhall's conduct, either alone or in combination, were sufficient to provide reasonable suspicion that she was engaged in criminal activity. The fact that Ms. Mendenhall was the last person to alight from a flight originating in Los Angeles was plainly insufficient to provide a basis for stopping her. Nor was the fact that her flight originated from a "major source city," for the mere proximity of a person to areas with a high incidence of drug activity or to persons known to be drug addicts, does not provide the necessary reasonable suspicion for an investigatory stop. Under the circumstances of this case, the DEA agents' observations that Ms. Mendenhall claimed no luggage and changed airlines were also insufficient to provide reasonable suspicion. * * * Ms. Mendenhall's subsequent conduct negated any reasonable inference that she was traveling a long distance without luggage or changing her ticket to a different airline to avoid detection. Agent Anderson testified that he heard the ticket agent tell Ms. Mendenhall that her ticket to Pittsburgh already was in order and that all she needed was a boarding pass for the flight.[9] Thus it should have been plain to an experienced observer that Ms. Mendenhall's failure to claim luggage was attributable to the fact that she was already ticketed through to Pittsburgh on a different airline. Because Agent Anderson's suspicion that Ms. Mendenhall was transporting narcotics could be based only on "his inchoate and unparticularized suspicion or 'hunch,' " rather than "specific reasonable inferences which he is entitled to draw from the facts in light of his experience," he was not justified in "seizing" Ms. Mendenhall.

III

Whatever doubt there may be concerning whether Ms. Mendenhall's Fourth Amendment interests were implicated during the initial stages of her confrontation with the DEA agents, she undoubtedly was "seized" within the meaning of the Fourth Amendment when the agents escorted her from the public area of the terminal to the DEA office for questioning and a strip-search of her person. * * * [T]he nature of the intrusion to which Ms. Mendenhall was subjected when she was escorted by DEA agents to their office and detained there for questioning and a strip-search was so great that it "was in important respects indistinguishable from a traditional arrest." Although Ms. Mendenhall was not told that she was under arrest, she in fact was not free to refuse to go to the DEA office and was not told that she was. Furthermore, once inside the office, Ms. Mendenhall would not have been permitted to leave without submitting to a strip-search. * * *

The Court's suggestion that no Fourth Amendment interest possessed by Ms. Mendenhall was implicated because she consented to go to the DEA

---

[9]   Agent Anderson testified on cross-examination at the suppression hearing that he believed Ms. Mendenhall's failure to pick up luggage was suspicious only before he learned that she was changing planes.

office is * * * unsupported in the record. There was no evidence in the record to support the District Court's speculation * * * that Ms. Mendenhall accompanied "Agent Anderson to the airport DEA Office 'voluntarily in a spirit of apparent cooperation with the [agent's] investigation.'" Ms. Mendenhall did not testify at the suppression hearing and the officers presented no testimony concerning what she said, if anything, when informed that the officers wanted her to come with them to the DEA office. Indeed, the only testimony concerning what occurred between Agent Anderson's "request" and Ms. Mendenhall's arrival at the DEA office is the agent's testimony that if Ms. Mendenhall had wanted to leave at that point she would have been forcibly restrained. * * *

The Court recognizes that the Government has the burden of proving that Ms. Mendenhall consented to accompany the officers, but it nevertheless holds that the "totality of evidence was plainly adequate" to support a finding of consent. * * * While the Government need not prove that Ms. Mendenhall knew that she had a right to refuse to accompany the officers, it cannot rely solely on acquiescence to the officers' wishes to establish the requisite consent. * * *

Since the defendant was not present to testify at the suppression hearing, we can only speculate about her state of mind as her encounter with the DEA agents progressed from surveillance, to detention, to questioning, to seclusion in a private office, to the female officer's command to remove her clothing. Nevertheless, it is unbelievable that this sequence of events involved no invasion of a citizen's constitutionally protected interest in privacy. The rule of law requires a different conclusion.

Because Ms. Mendenhall was being illegally detained at the time of the search of her person, her suppression motion should have been granted in the absence of evidence to dissipate the taint.

QUESTIONS, COMMENTS, CONCERNS?

1.   **Charging document.** Notice that the prosecution charged Jones by information. [See Casefile Document 1.] Recall from Chapter 1 that an information is a formal criminal charge filed directly by the prosecution without grand jury involvement. In an information jurisdiction, a preliminary hearing will typically take place to determine whether sufficient evidence (probable cause) exists to justify additional criminal proceedings—like a trial.

2.   **Quality of lawyering.** In this brief casefile, compare Jones's motion to suppress with the government's opposition. [See Casefile Documents 2 & 3.] What key factual dispute exists between the parties? What could Jones's motion have done to eliminate the government's concern? What other concerns does the government raise about the motion's timeliness?

3.   ***Mendenhall* and *Jones*.** The *Jones* majority discusses *Mendenhall*, but also comments that D.C. precedent takes an "'earthy' and realistic

approach to such street encounters." [See Casefile Document 5.] What is the majority implicitly saying about the result in *Mendenhall*? Commentary aside, what *Mendenhall* factors most prominently contribute to the court's holding?

4. State approaches to the seizure analysis. Consider *State v. Sum*, 511 P.3d 92 (Wash. 2022). In *Sum*, Pierce County Deputy Sheriff Mark Rickerson was on patrol, driving his police cruiser through a neighborhood with "some problem houses," when he noticed a Honda Civic parked near the entrance of a church parking lot. Rickerson could see a man, later identified as Palla Sum, unconscious in the driver's seat of the Civic and decided to conduct "a social contact." On his approach, Rickerson observed another man inside the Civic who was sitting in the front passenger seat and also unconscious. Rickerson knocked on the driver's side window, awoke Sum, and asked him what he and his passenger were doing. Sum responded that they "were waiting for a friend." After Sum could not identify the Civic's owner, Rickerson asked Sum for identification. Sum asked why Rickerson wanted identification, and Rickerson answered that Sum and his passenger "were sitting in an area known for stolen vehicles" and that Sum "did not appear to know to whom the vehicle he was sitting in belonged." Sum then gave a false name and date of birth, and Rickerson returned to his cruiser to verify Sum's information.

Seeing an opportunity to escape, Sum drove off at a high rate of speed through a stop sign and several red lights before crashing into a nearby resident's front yard. There, Rickerson handcuffed Sum and read him his Miranda warnings. A later search of the Civic pursuant to a warrant revealed a pistol. On these facts, Sum was charged with unlawful possession of a firearm in the first degree, attempting to elude a pursuing police vehicle, and making a false or misleading statement to a public servant. The charging document identified Sum's race as "ASIAN/PACIFIC ISLANDER" and his ethnicity as "Non-Hispanic." In response, Sum moved to suppress the false name and birthday he provided, arguing that he was unlawfully seized when Rickerson asked for his identification while implying that Sum was under investigation for vehicle theft. The trial court denied Sum's motion, and Sum was convicted on all three counts. The Washington Court of Appeals affirmed the denial of Sum's motion to suppress, holding that Sum was not seized by Rickerson's "request for identification because 'merely asking for identification is properly characterized as a social contact.'"

The Washington Supreme Court reversed the lower courts' rulings, holding that Sum was unlawfully seized for purposes of Article I, Section 7 of the Washington Constitution when Rickerson explained why he wanted Sum's identification. The court began by explaining that the Washington Constitution provides greater protection to individual privacy rights than the Fourth Amendment. Under the Washington Constitution, the court continued, a seizure occurs, "when considering all the circumstances, an individual's freedom of movement is restrained and the individual would not believe [they are] free to leave or decline a request due to an officer's use of force or display of authority." The court then went on to recognize that, as a matter of state law, a suspect's race and ethnicity are relevant "circumstances" courts should consider when evaluating whether a suspect is seized. Considering the circumstances of Sum's case, including his race, the court concluded that Sum was seized for purposes of the Washington Constitution when Rickerson explained why he wanted Sum's identification. Because Rickerson lacked reasonable suspicion or probable cause to seize Sum, the court suppressed Sum's false statements under the State's exclusionary rule.

5.   Identifying when Jones was seized. The lawyers and court are focused generally on whether Jones was seized—in general—during his encounter with Officer Blier. That's certainly appropriate. But it's a bit more tactical—from the defense perspective—to think of the *Mendenhall* factors along a continuum where the defense might argue that defendant was seized at perhaps earlier points during the police-citizen encounter. In Jones's case, it's possible to argue (likely unsuccessfully) that he was seized at the time that Officer Blier rolled his window down and said, "hey, man, how you doing?" After all, Jones was walking along a narrow alleyway obstructed by a police cruiser. And who, really, would "feel free to terminate the encounter" with Officer Blier at that stage. *See United States v. Drayton*, 536 U.S. 194, 201 (2002).

Perhaps Jones was seized while Officer Blier engaged him in conversation. And if not then, perhaps when Officer Blier asked his partner to run Jones's name in the system. And if not then, perhaps when . . . . You get the point, right? The point is that there were several moments in time when Jones was arguably seized. From a defense prospective, chronologically framing a police-citizen encounter helps both to create multiple seizure arguments while forcing meaningful thought about the facts that may contribute to a seizure vs. non-seizure outcomes. Prosecutors, however, are wise to limit the conversation—and therefore the corresponding arguments—to a more general "was the defendant seized" analysis.

6.   Quality of lawyering (redux). Concerns about the quality of Jones's trial representation persisted at the appellate level. [See Casefile Document 5.] In Judge Fisher's dissent, he commented:

> Two days before trial, defense counsel filed an untimely and perfunctory motion to suppress which claimed that the police had unlawfully searched the cigarette box without consent after ordering appellant to place it on the police car. The motion did not mention a warrant check, much less assert that it had turned a consensual encounter into a seizure. This is important because neither the trial court nor the prosecutor was put on notice of the need to create a factual record illuminating that issue. The warrant check was mentioned in the testimony, but defense counsel did not argue that it was a factor which turned the encounter into a seizure. I see nothing to indicate that appellant was "detained" while the warrant check was completed.

In light of what you learned about *Strickland* in Chapter 1, did appellate counsel for Jones miss an opportunity to raise an important issue?

* * *

A Postscript to *Mendenhall*

Notice Justice Stewart's implicit acceptance of the so-called "drug courier profile" in his majority *Mendenhall* opinion. As you think through the implications of accepting the practice of profiling (a topic that will arise again later), consider the comments below from Judge Becton.[15] He observes in part that the proliferation of profiling has produced an abundance of criteria that arguably makes any citizen fit a drug profile:

1. *Reservations and Ticket Purchases*

In many cases drug agents testify without hesitation that drug couriers seldom make reservations, and that couriers instead prefer to purchase their airline tickets immediately before flight departure time. With no less resolve drug agents testify also that drug couriers often make recent or short-notice reservations. They also testify that a passenger's use of bogus or false telephone call-back numbers when making reservations is as significant as a passenger's failure to give any call-back number to the airline. Similarly, while DEA agents accept as profile factors the purchase of round-trip tickets and the purchase of one-way tickets, they treat with equal significance "paying for an airline ticket in currency of small denominations" and purchasing a ticket with large denominations of cash. Furthermore, the testimony of DEA agents indicates that the purchase of a "coach" ticket may be as salient a profile factor as the purchase of a "first-class" ticket.

2. *Airports and Flights*

When DEA agents first developed the drug courier profile, the "source city" designation became a preeminent profile factor. Drug agents routinely monitored incoming flights from source cities. When it became necessary, however, drug agents testified not only about the relevance of source cities but also about the significance of use cities, transshipment cities, hub cities, and cross-road cities. And, as expected, "outgoing flights" have become as important as "incoming flights." A greater inconsistency surfaces, however, when DEA agents testify about frequent, short turn-around trips to and from source cities. With little regard for consistency, DEA agents testify that each of the following constitutes a prominent profile factor: (1) Non-stop or direct flights to and from source cities; and (2) Circuitous routes or changing airlines or flights to and from source cities.

---

[15] This subsection reprints with permission a portion of Charles L. Becton, *The Drug Courier Profile, All Seems Infected That Th'Infected Spy, as All Looks Yellow to the Jaundic'd Eye*, 65 N.C. L. REV. 417, 438, 439–44 (1987). All footnotes are omitted.

3. *Nervousness and Associated Behavior*

Despite drug agents' testimony that they can detect "growing nervousness" or tell-tale eyes, there is no uniform or coherent list of profile factors relating to nervousness. Walking quickly is considered a prime behavior factor, but so is walking slowly. Walking in an unusual pattern through the terminal and rushing to the restroom after deplaning appear just as significant as leaving the terminal in a hurried and nervous manner. And although perspiring profusely, shortness of breath, and becoming nervous during an identification stop, comprise stock, boiler-plate profile factors—appearing "cool" and exhibiting a "calm demeanor"—also constitute profile factors.

4. *Significance of Luggage*

All air travelers fit at least one of the profile factors regarding the use of luggage. DEA agents deem it significant when air travelers check no luggage. They also consider the following as decisive profile factors: Continuing to stare at a suitcase after checking it; failing to claim luggage at the baggage claim area; switching baggage claim stubs; having a companion claim the luggage; and placing an identification tag on checked luggage that differs from other forms of identification. Similarly, DEA agents testify inconsistently regarding the amount of luggage an air traveler carries. Carrying no luggage is as noteworthy as carrying a small tote bag, a medium-size bag, two bulky garment bags, "two apparently heavy-laden suitcases," or four pieces of luggage. Furthermore, agents speak inconsistently regarding the significance of the manner in which air travelers handle their luggage or possessions. For example, both dissociative behavior towards a briefcase and holding a briefcase firmly appear as profile factors in the case law.

5. *Companions*

The following inconsistent profile factors regarding drug couriers and their companions appear repeatedly in drug profile cases: an individual traveling alone; two or more people traveling together; people who travel together, but attempt to appear separate; and people who disclaim knowledge of traveling companions.

6. *Personal Characteristics*

Depending on which case is read, a typical drug courier is either a black male, a female, a black female, an Hispanic person, or a young person who may be "sloppily dressed" or "smartly dressed." And, of course, the drug courier can have a Fu Manchu mustache or collar-length hair.

7. *Miscellany*

The topical heading "Miscellany," with its omnibus implications, dramatically illustrates how incongruous and fatuous drug courier profile factors have become. For example, drug agents treat the following drug courier profile factors with equal significance: being the first, or one of the first, passengers to deplane; being the last passenger to deplane; and deplaning from the middle. By way of further example, making a local telephone call immediately after deplaning constitutes a profile factor, as does making a long-distance telephone call. Similarly, drug agents have testified that leaving the airport by public transportation, especially taxi, private vehicle, limousine, or hotel courtesy van all constitute profile factors.

That some DEA agents commendably and candidly admit they stop air travelers when anything arouses their suspicions does not obviate the need to cross-examine agents about the bases of their suspicions. Rather, such admissions highlight the inconsistencies among the factors relied on by drug agents and invite careful analysis of the purported logic behind the drug courier profile.

BRENDLIN V. CALIFORNIA
551 U.S. 249
Supreme Court of the United States
April 23, 2007, Argued; June 18, 2007, Decided
No. 06-8120

JUSTICE SOUTER delivered the opinion of the Court.

When a police officer makes a traffic stop, the driver of the car is seized within the meaning of the Fourth Amendment. The question in this case is whether the same is true of a passenger. We hold that a passenger is seized as well and so may challenge the constitutionality of the stop.

I

Early in the morning of November 27, 2001, Deputy Sheriff Robert Brokenbrough and his partner saw a parked Buick with expired registration tags. In his ensuing conversation with the police dispatcher, Brokenbrough learned that an application for renewal of registration was being processed. The officers saw the car again on the road, and this time Brokenbrough noticed its display of a temporary operating permit with the number "11," indicating it was legal to drive the car through November. The officers decided to pull the Buick over to verify that the permit matched the vehicle, even though, as Brokenbrough admitted later, there was nothing unusual about the permit or the way it was affixed. Brokenbrough asked the driver, Karen Simeroth, for her license and saw a passenger in the front seat, petitioner Bruce Brendlin, whom he recognized as "one of the Brendlin brothers." He recalled that either Scott or Bruce Brendlin had dropped out of parole supervision and asked Brendlin to identify himself. Brokenbrough returned to his cruiser, called for backup, and verified that Brendlin was a parole violator with an outstanding no-bail warrant for his arrest. While he was in the patrol car, Brokenbrough saw Brendlin briefly open and then close the passenger door of the Buick. Once reinforcements arrived, Brokenbrough went to the passenger side of the Buick, ordered him out of the car at gunpoint, and declared him under arrest. When the police searched Brendlin incident to arrest, they found an orange syringe cap on his person. A patdown search of Simeroth revealed syringes and a plastic bag of a green leafy substance, and she was also formally arrested. Officers then searched the car and found tubing, a scale, and other things used to produce methamphetamine.

Brendlin was charged with possession and manufacture of methamphetamine, and he moved to suppress the evidence obtained in the searches of his person and the car as fruits of an unconstitutional seizure, arguing that the officers lacked probable cause or reasonable suspicion to make the traffic stop. He did not assert that his Fourth Amendment rights were violated by the search of Simeroth's vehicle, but claimed only that the traffic stop was an unlawful seizure of his person. The trial court denied the suppression motion after finding that the stop was lawful and Brendlin was not seized until Brokenbrough ordered him out of the car and formally arrested him. Brendlin pleaded guilty, subject to appeal on the suppression issue, and was sentenced to four years in prison.

The California Court of Appeal reversed the denial of the suppression motion, holding that Brendlin was seized by the traffic stop, which the court held unlawful. By a narrow majority, the Supreme Court of California reversed. * * *

We granted certiorari to decide whether a traffic stop subjects a passenger, as well as the driver, to Fourth Amendment seizure. * * *

II

A

* * * Justice Stewart in *United States v. Mendenhall*, 446 U.S. 544 (1980), * * * wrote that a seizure occurs if "in view of all of the circumstances surrounding the incident, a reasonable person would have believed that he was not free to leave." Later on, the Court adopted Justice Stewart's touchstone, but added that when a person "has no desire to leave" for reasons unrelated to the police presence, the "coercive effect of the encounter" can be measured better by asking whether "a reasonable person would feel free to decline the officers' requests or otherwise terminate the encounter." [*Florida v.*] Bostick, [501 U.S. 429], 435–436 (1991); *see also United States v. Drayton*, 536 U.S. 194, 202 (2002).

The law is settled that in Fourth Amendment terms a traffic stop entails a seizure of the driver "even though the purpose of the stop is limited and the resulting detention quite brief." And although we have not, until today, squarely answered the question whether a passenger is also seized, we have said over and over in dicta that during a traffic stop an officer seizes everyone in the vehicle, not just the driver. * * *

B

The State concedes that the police had no adequate justification to pull the car over, but argues that the passenger was not seized and thus cannot claim that the evidence was tainted by an unconstitutional stop. We resolve this question by asking whether a reasonable person in Brendlin's position when the car stopped would have believed himself free to "terminate the encounter" between the police and himself. *Bostick*, 501 U.S., at 436. We think that in these circumstances any reasonable passenger would have understood the police officers to be exercising control to the point that no one in the car was free to depart without police permission.

A traffic stop necessarily curtails the travel a passenger has chosen just as much as it halts the driver, diverting both from the stream of traffic to the side of the road, and the police activity that normally amounts to intrusion on "privacy and personal security" does not normally (and did not here) distinguish between passenger and driver. An officer who orders one particular car to pull over acts with an implicit claim of right based on fault of some sort, and a sensible person would not expect a police officer to allow people to come and go freely from the physical focal point of an investigation into faulty behavior or wrongdoing. If the likely wrongdoing is not the driving, the passenger will reasonably feel subject to suspicion owing to close association; but even when the wrongdoing is only bad driving, the passenger will expect to be subject to some scrutiny, and his attempt to leave the scene would be so obviously likely to prompt an objection from the officer that no passenger would feel free to leave in the first place. *Cf. Drayton, supra*, at 197–199, 203–204 (finding no seizure when police officers boarded a stationary bus and asked passengers for permission to search for drugs).[3]

It is also reasonable for passengers to expect that a police officer at the scene of a crime, arrest, or investigation will not let people move around in ways that could jeopardize his safety. In *Maryland v. Wilson*, 519 U.S. 408 (1997), we held that during a lawful traffic stop an officer may order a passenger out of the car as a precautionary measure, without reasonable suspicion that the passenger poses a safety risk. *Id.*, at 414–415; cf. *Pennsylvania v. Mimms*, 434 U.S. 106 (1977) (per curiam) (driver may be

---

[3] Of course, police may also stop a car solely to investigate a passenger's conduct. Accordingly, a passenger cannot assume, merely from the fact of a traffic stop, that the driver's conduct is the cause of the stop.

ordered out of the car as a matter of course). In fashioning this rule, we invoked our earlier statement that " '[t]he risk of harm to both the police and the occupants is minimized if the officers routinely exercise unquestioned command of the situation.' " What we have said in these opinions probably reflects a societal expectation of " 'unquestioned [police] command' " at odds with any notion that a passenger would feel free to leave, or to terminate the personal encounter any other way, without advance permission.

Our conclusion comports with the views of all nine Federal Courts of Appeals, and nearly every state court, to have ruled on the question. And the treatise writers share this prevailing judicial view that a passenger may bring a Fourth Amendment challenge to the legality of a traffic stop.

C

The contrary conclusion drawn by the Supreme Court of California, that seizure came only with formal arrest, reflects three premises as to which we respectfully disagree. First, the State Supreme Court reasoned that Brendlin was not seized by the stop because Deputy Sheriff Brokenbrough only intended to investigate Simeroth and did not direct a show of authority toward Brendlin. The court saw Brokenbrough's "flashing lights [as] directed at the driver," and pointed to the lack of record evidence that Brokenbrough "was even aware [Brendlin] was in the car prior to the vehicle stop." But that view of the facts ignores the objective *Mendenhall* test of what a reasonable passenger would understand. To the extent that there is anything ambiguous in the show of force (was it fairly seen as directed only at the driver or at the car and its occupants?), the test resolves the ambiguity, and here it leads to the intuitive conclusion that all the occupants were subject to like control by the successful display of authority. The State Supreme Court's approach, on the contrary, shifts the issue from the intent of the police as objectively manifested to the motive of the police for taking the intentional action to stop the car, and we have repeatedly rejected attempts to introduce this kind of subjectivity into Fourth Amendment analysis.

California defends the State Supreme Court's ruling on this point by citing our cases holding that seizure requires a purposeful, deliberate act of detention. * * * The intent that counts under the Fourth Amendment is the "intent [that] has been conveyed to the person confronted," and the criterion of willful restriction on freedom of movement is no invitation to look to subjective intent when determining who is seized. Our most recent cases are in accord on this point. * * *

Second, the Supreme Court of California assumed that Brendlin, "as the passenger, had no ability to submit to the deputy's show of authority" because only the driver was in control of the moving vehicle. But what may amount to submission depends on what a person was doing before the show of authority: a fleeing man is not seized until he is physically overpowered, but one sitting in a chair may submit to authority by not getting up to run away. Here, Brendlin had no effective way to signal submission while the car was still moving on the roadway, but once it came to a stop he could, and apparently did, submit by staying inside.

Third, the State Supreme Court shied away from the rule we apply today for fear that it "would encompass even those motorists following the vehicle subject to the traffic stop who, by virtue of the original detention, are forced to slow down and perhaps even come to a halt in order to accommodate that vehicle's submission to police authority." But an occupant of a car who knows that he is stuck in traffic because another car has been pulled over (like the motorist who cannot even make out why the road is suddenly clogged) would not perceive a show of authority as directed at him or his car. Such incidental restrictions on freedom of movement would not tend to affect an individual's "sense of security and privacy in traveling in an automobile." *Prouse*, 440 U.S., at 662. Nor would the consequential blockage call for a precautionary rule to avoid the kind of "arbitrary and oppressive interference by [law] enforcement officials with the privacy and personal security of individuals" that the Fourth Amendment was intended to limit.[6]

Indeed, the consequence to worry about would not flow from our conclusion, but from the rule that almost all courts have rejected. Holding that the passenger in a private car is not (without more) seized in a traffic stop would invite police officers to stop cars with passengers regardless of probable cause or reasonable suspicion of anything illegal. The fact that evidence uncovered as a result of an arbitrary traffic stop would still be admissible against any passengers would be a powerful incentive to run the kind of "roving patrols" that would still violate the driver's Fourth Amendment right.

Brendlin was seized from the moment Simeroth's car came to a halt on the side of the road, and it was error to deny his suppression motion on the ground that seizure occurred only at the formal arrest. It will be for the state courts to consider in the first instance whether suppression turns on any other issue. The judgment of the Supreme Court of California is vacated, and the case is remanded for further proceedings not inconsistent with this opinion.

It is so ordered.

---

[6]   California claims that, under today's rule, "all taxi cab and bus passengers would be 'seized' under the Fourth Amendment when the cab or bus driver is pulled over by the police for running a red light." But the relationship between driver and passenger is not the same in a common carrier as it is in a private vehicle, and the expectations of police officers and passengers differ accordingly. In those cases, as here, the crucial question would be whether a reasonable person in the passenger's position would feel free to take steps to terminate the encounter.

CALIFORNIA V. HODARI D.

499 U.S. 621
Supreme Court of the United States
January 14, 1991, Argued; April 23, 1991, Decided
No. 89-1632

JUSTICE SCALIA delivered the opinion of the Court.

Late one evening in April 1988, Officers Brian McColgin and Jerry Pertoso were on patrol in a high-crime area of Oakland, California. They were dressed in street clothes but wearing jackets with "Police" embossed on both front and back. Their unmarked car proceeded west on Foothill Boulevard, and turned south onto 63rd Avenue. As they rounded the corner, they saw four or five youths huddled around a small red car parked at the curb. When the youths saw the officers' car approaching they apparently panicked, and took flight. The respondent here, Hodari D., and one companion ran west through an alley; the others fled south. The red car also headed south, at a high rate of speed.

The officers were suspicious and gave chase. McColgin remained in the car and continued south on 63rd Avenue; Pertoso left the car, ran back north along 63rd, then west on Foothill Boulevard, and turned south on 62nd Avenue. Hodari, meanwhile, emerged from the alley onto 62nd and ran north. Looking behind as he ran, he did not turn and see Pertoso until the officer was almost upon him, whereupon he tossed away what appeared to be a small rock. A moment later, Pertoso tackled Hodari, handcuffed him, and radioed for assistance. Hodari was found to be carrying $ 130 in cash and a pager; and the rock he had discarded was found to be crack cocaine.

In the juvenile proceeding brought against him, Hodari moved to suppress the evidence relating to the cocaine. The court denied the motion without opinion. The California Court of Appeal reversed, holding that Hodari had been "seized" when he saw Officer Pertoso running towards him, that this seizure was unreasonable under the Fourth Amendment, and that the evidence of cocaine had to be suppressed as the fruit of that illegal seizure. The California Supreme Court denied the State's application for review. We granted certiorari.

As this case comes to us, the only issue presented is whether, at the time he dropped the drugs, Hodari had been "seized" within the meaning of the Fourth Amendment.[1] If so, respondent argues, the drugs were the fruit of that seizure and the evidence concerning them was properly

---

[1] California conceded below that Officer Pertoso did not have the "reasonable suspicion" required to justify stopping Hodari, see Terry v. Ohio, 392 U.S. 1 (1968). That it would be unreasonable to stop, for brief inquiry, young men who scatter in panic upon the mere sighting of the police is not self-evident, and arguably contradicts proverbial common sense. See Proverbs 28:1 ("The wicked flee when no man pursueth"). We do not decide that point here, but rely entirely upon the State's concession.

excluded. If not, the drugs were abandoned by Hodari and lawfully recovered by the police, and the evidence should have been admitted. * * *

We have long understood that the Fourth Amendment's protection against "unreasonable . . . seizures" includes seizure of the person * * *. From the time of the founding to the present, the word "seizure" has meant a "taking possession." For most purposes at common law, the word connoted not merely grasping, or applying physical force to, the animate or inanimate object in question, but actually bringing it within physical control. * * * To constitute an arrest, * * *—the quintessential "seizure of the person" under our Fourth Amendment jurisprudence—the mere grasping or application of physical force with lawful authority, whether or not it succeeded in subduing the arrestee, was sufficient. * * *

To say that an arrest is effected by the slightest application of physical force, despite the arrestee's escape, is not to say that for Fourth Amendment purposes there is a continuing arrest during the period of fugitivity. If, for example, Pertoso had laid his hands upon Hodari to arrest him, but Hodari had broken away and had then cast away the cocaine, it would hardly be realistic to say that that disclosure had been made during the course of an arrest. The present case, however, is even one step further removed. It does not involve the application of any physical force; Hodari was untouched by Officer Pertoso at the time he discarded the cocaine. * * * Hodari contends (and we accept as true for purposes of this decision) that Pertoso's pursuit qualified as a "show of authority" calling upon Hodari to halt. The narrow question before us is whether, with respect to a show of authority as with respect to application of physical force, a seizure occurs even though the subject does not yield. We hold that it does not.

The language of the Fourth Amendment, of course, cannot sustain respondent's contention. The word "seizure" readily bears the meaning of a laying on of hands or application of physical force to restrain movement, even when it is ultimately unsuccessful. ("She seized the purse-snatcher, but he broke out of her grasp.") It does not remotely apply, however, to the prospect of a policeman yelling "Stop, in the name of the law!" at a fleeing form that continues to flee. That is no seizure. Nor can the result respondent wishes to achieve be produced—indirectly, as it were—by suggesting that Pertoso's uncomplied-with show of authority was a common-law arrest, and then appealing to the principle that all common-law arrests are seizures. An arrest requires either physical force (as described above) or, where that is absent, submission to the assertion of authority. * * *

We do not think it desirable, even as a policy matter, to stretch the Fourth Amendment beyond its words and beyond the meaning of arrest, as respondent urges. Street pursuits always place the public at some risk, and compliance with police orders to stop should therefore be encouraged. Only a few of those orders, we must presume, will be without adequate basis, and since the addressee has no ready means of identifying the deficient ones it almost invariably is the responsible course to comply. Unlawful orders will not be deterred, moreover, by sanctioning through the exclusionary rule those of them that are not obeyed. Since policemen do not command "Stop!" expecting to be ignored, or give chase hoping to be outrun, it fully suffices to apply the deterrent to their genuine, successful seizures.

Respondent contends that his position is sustained by the so-called *Mendenhall* test, formulated by Justice Stewart's opinion in *United States v. Mendenhall*, 446 U.S. 544, 554 (1980) * * *: "[A] person has been 'seized' within the meaning of the Fourth Amendment only if, in view of all the circumstances surrounding the incident, a reasonable person would have believed that he was not free to leave." In seeking to rely upon that test here, respondent fails to read it carefully. It says that a person has been seized "only if," not that he has been seized "whenever"; it states a necessary, but not a sufficient, condition for seizure—or, more precisely, for seizure effected through a "show of authority." *Mendenhall* establishes that the test for existence of a "show of authority" is an objective one: not whether the citizen perceived that he was being ordered to restrict his movement, but whether the officer's words and actions would have conveyed that to a reasonable person. * * *

In sum, assuming that Pertoso's pursuit in the present case constituted a "show of authority" enjoining Hodari to halt, since Hodari did not comply with that injunction he was not seized until he was tackled. The cocaine abandoned while he was running was in this case not the fruit of a seizure, and his motion to exclude evidence of it was properly denied. We reverse the decision of the California Court of Appeal, and remand for further proceedings not inconsistent with this opinion.

It is so ordered.

JUSTICE STEVENS, with whom JUSTICE MARSHALL joins, dissenting.

* * * For the purposes of decision, the following propositions are not in dispute. First, when Officer Pertoso began his pursuit of respondent,[4] the officer did not have a lawful basis for either stopping or arresting respondent. Second, the officer's chase amounted to a "show of authority" as soon as respondent saw the officer nearly upon him. Third, the act of discarding the rock of cocaine was the direct consequence of the show of

---

[4]   The Court's gratuitous quotation from Proverbs 28:1 mistakenly assumes that innocent residents have no reason to fear the sudden approach of strangers. We have previously considered, and rejected, this ivory-towered analysis of the real world for it fails to describe the experience of many residents, particularly if they are members of a minority. It has long been "a matter of common knowledge that men who are entirely innocent do sometimes fly from the scene of a crime through fear of being apprehended as the guilty parties, or from an unwillingness to appear as witnesses. Nor is it true as an accepted axiom of criminal law that 'the wicked flee when no man pursueth, but the righteous are as bold as a lion.' "

authority. Fourth, as the Court correctly demonstrates, no common-law arrest occurred until the officer tackled respondent. Thus, the Court is quite right in concluding that the abandonment of the rock was not the fruit of a common-law arrest. * * *

[But] [t]he Court today takes a narrow view of "seizure," which is at odds with the broader view adopted by this Court almost 25 years ago. * * *

Whatever else one may think of today's decision, it unquestionably represents a departure from earlier Fourth Amendment case law. The notion that our prior cases contemplated a distinction between seizures effected by a touching on the one hand, and those effected by a show of force on the other hand, and that all of our repeated descriptions of the *Mendenhall* test stated only a necessary, but not a sufficient, condition for finding seizures in the latter category, is nothing if not creative lawmaking. Moreover, by narrowing the definition of the term seizure, instead of enlarging the scope of reasonable justifications for seizures, the Court has significantly limited the protection provided to the ordinary citizen by the Fourth Amendment. * * *

In this case the officer's show of force—taking the form of a head-on chase—adequately conveyed the message that respondent was not free to leave. * * * There was an interval of time between the moment that respondent saw the officer fast approaching and the moment when he was tackled, and thus brought under the control of the officer. The question is whether the Fourth Amendment was implicated at the earlier or the later moment.

Because the facts of this case are somewhat unusual, it is appropriate to note that the same issue would arise if the show of force took the form of a command to "freeze," a warning shot, or the sound of sirens accompanied by a patrol car's flashing lights. In any of these situations, there may be a significant time interval between the initiation of the officer's show of force and the complete submission by the citizen. At least on the facts of this case, the Court concludes that the timing of the seizure is governed by the citizen's reaction, rather than by the officer's conduct. One consequence of this conclusion is that the point at which the interaction between citizen and police officer becomes a seizure occurs, not when a reasonable citizen believes he or she is no longer free to go, but, rather, only after the officer exercises control over the citizen.

In my view, our interests in effective law enforcement and in personal liberty would be better served by adhering to a standard that "allows the police to determine in advance whether the conduct contemplated will implicate the Fourth Amendment." The range of possible responses to a police show of force, and the multitude of problems that may arise in determining whether, and at which moment, there has been "submission," can only create uncertainty and generate litigation. * * *

If an officer effects an arrest by touching a citizen, apparently the Court would accept the fact that a seizure occurred, even if the arrestee should thereafter break loose and flee. In such a case, the constitutionality of the seizure would be evaluated as of the time the officer acted. That category of seizures would then be analyzed in the same way as searches, namely, was the police action justified when it took place? It is anomalous, at best, to fashion a different rule for the subcategory of "show of force" arrests.

In cases within this new subcategory, there will be a period of time during which the citizen's liberty has been restrained, but he or she has not yet completely submitted to the show of force. A motorist pulled over by a highway patrol car cannot come to an immediate stop, even if the motorist intends to obey the patrol car's signal. * * * In an airport setting, may a drug enforcement agent now approach a group of passengers with his gun drawn, announce a "baggage search," and rely on the passengers' reactions to justify his investigative stops? The holding of today's majority fails to recognize the coercive and intimidating nature of such behavior and creates a rule that may allow such behavior to go unchecked. * * *

It is too early to know the consequences of the Court's holding. If carried to its logical conclusion, it will encourage unlawful displays of force that will frighten countless innocent citizens into surrendering whatever privacy rights they may still have. It is not too soon, however, to note the irony in the fact that the Court's own justification for its result is its analysis of the rules of the common law of arrest that antedated our decision[ ] in *Katz* * * *. Yet, even in those days the common law provided the citizen with protection against an attempt to make an unlawful arrest. The central message of *Katz* * * * was that the protection the Fourth Amendment provides to the average citizen is not rigidly confined by ancient common-law precept. The message that today's literal-minded majority conveys is that the common law, rather than our understanding of the Fourth Amendment as it has developed over the last quarter of a century, defines, and limits, the scope of a seizure. The Court today defines a seizure as commencing, not with egregious police conduct, but rather with submission by the citizen. Thus, it both delays the point at which "the Fourth Amendment becomes relevant" to an encounter and limits the range of encounters that will come under the heading of "seizure." Today's qualification of the Fourth Amendment means that innocent citizens may remain "secure in their persons . . . against unreasonable searches and seizures" only at the discretion of the police.

Some sacrifice of freedom always accompanies an expansion in the executive's unreviewable law enforcement powers. A court more sensitive to the purposes of the Fourth Amendment would insist on greater rewards to society before decreeing the sacrifice it makes today. * * *

I respectfully dissent.

QUESTIONS, COMMENTS, CONCERNS?

1. **Jones and show of force.** Reconsider the facts of Jones's case. Was it a "show of authority" for *Hodari D.* purposes when Officer Blier asked Jones, "hey, can I see that cigarette box?" [See Casefile Document 5.] Remember that, at that point, Officer Blier had exited his vehicle and was standing close to Jones where Jones would have to walk through a narrow space in the alley way to continue on his way.

2. **Jones and the surrounding neighborhood.** Officer Blier testified at the suppression hearing that he knew the area where Jones was walking "historically had a high volume of drug sales." [See Casefile Document 5.] What role should a citizen's neighborhood play in an officer's decision to stop and talk to the citizen? To search the citizen? And what do you make of Officer Blier's testimony that he "kn[e]w individuals commonly hide drugs and drug paraphernalia in Newport boxes"? Does that mean legitimate cigarette smokers who wander along the 2500 block of North Capital Street, Northeast, are automatically suspected of drug possession?

We take up the neighborhood question more directly in the next chapter, but for now it's worth considering whether testimony like Officer Blier's represents good policework based on training and experience or, instead, generalized stereotyping.

C. SEIZURES OF PROPERTY

UNITED STATES V. KARO
468 U.S. 705
Supreme Court of the United States
April 25, 1984, Argued; July 3, 1984, Decided
No. 83-850

JUSTICE WHITE delivered the opinion of the Court.

In *United States v. Knotts*, 460 U.S. 276 (1983), we held that the warrantless monitoring of an electronic tracking device ("beeper")[1] inside a container of chemicals did not violate the Fourth Amendment when it revealed no information that could not have been obtained through visual surveillance. In this case, we are called upon to address * * * whether installation of a beeper in a container of chemicals with the consent of the original owner constitutes a search or seizure within the meaning of the Fourth Amendment when the container is delivered to a buyer having no knowledge of the presence of the beeper * * *.

I

In August 1980 Agent Rottinger of the Drug Enforcement Administration (DEA) learned that respondents James Karo, Richard

---

[1] "A beeper is a radio transmitter, usually battery operated, which emits periodic signals that can be picked up by a radio receiver." *United States v. Knotts*, 460 U.S., at 277.

Horton, and William Harley had ordered 50 gallons of ether from Government informant Carl Muehlenweg of Graphic Photo Design in Albuquerque, N. M. Muehlenweg told Rottinger that the ether was to be used to extract cocaine from clothing that had been imported into the United States. The Government obtained a court order authorizing the installation and monitoring of a beeper in one of the cans of ether. With Muehlenweg's consent, agents substituted their own can containing a beeper for one of the cans in the shipment and then had all 10 cans painted to give them a uniform appearance.

On September 20, 1980, agents saw Karo pick up the ether from Muehlenweg. They then followed Karo to his house using visual and beeper surveillance. At one point later that day, agents determined by using the beeper that the ether was still inside the house, but they later determined that it had been moved undetected to Horton's house, where they located it using the beeper. Agent Rottinger could smell the ether from the public sidewalk near Horton's residence. Two days later, agents discovered that the ether had once again been moved, and, using the beeper, they located it at the residence of Horton's father. The next day, the beeper was no longer transmitting from Horton's father's house, and agents traced the beeper to a commercial storage facility.

Because the beeper equipment was not sensitive enough to allow agents to learn precisely which locker the ether was in, agents obtained a subpoena for the records of the storage company and learned that locker 143 had been rented by Horton. Using the beeper, agents confirmed that the ether was indeed in one of the lockers in the row containing locker 143, and using their noses they detected the odor of ether emanating from locker 143. On October 8 agents obtained an order authorizing installation of an entry tone alarm into the door jamb of the locker so they would be able to tell when the door was opened. While installing the alarm, agents observed that the cans containing ether were still inside. Agents ceased visual and beeper surveillance, relying instead on the entry tone alarm. However, on October 16 Horton retrieved the contents from the locker without sounding the alarm. Agents did not learn of the entry until the manager of the storage facility notified them that Horton had been there.

Using the beeper, agents traced the beeper can to another self-storage facility three days later. Agents detected the smell of ether coming from locker 15 and learned from the manager that Horton and Harley had rented that locker using an alias the same day that the ether had been removed from the first storage facility. The agents obtained an order authorizing the installation of an entry tone alarm in locker 15, but instead of installing that alarm, they obtained consent from the manager of the facility to install a closed-circuit video camera in a locker that had a view of locker 15. On February 6, 1981, agents observed, by means of the video camera, Gene Rhodes and an unidentified woman removing the cans from the locker and loading them onto the rear bed of Horton's pickup truck. Using both visual and beeper surveillance agents tracked the truck to Rhodes' residence where it was parked in the driveway. Agents then observed Rhodes and a woman bringing boxes and other items from inside the house and loading the items into the trunk of an automobile. Agents did not see any cans being transferred from the pickup.

At about 6 p. m. on February 6, the car and the pickup left the driveway and traveled along public highways to Taos. During the trip, the two vehicles were under both physical and electronic surveillance. When the vehicles arrived at a house in Taos rented by Horton, Harley, and Michael Steele, the agents did not maintain tight surveillance for fear of detection. When the vehicles left the Taos residence, agents determined, using the beeper monitor, that the beeper can was still inside the house. Again on February 7, the beeper revealed that the ether can was still on the premises. At one point, agents noticed that the windows of the house were wide open on a cold windy day, leading them to suspect that the ether was being used. On February 8, the agents applied for and obtained a warrant to search the Taos residence based in part on information derived through use of the beeper. The warrant was executed on February 10, 1981, and Horton, Harley, Steele, and Evan Roth were arrested, and cocaine and laboratory equipment were seized.

Respondents Karo, Horton, Harley, Steele, and Roth were indicted for conspiring to possess cocaine with intent to distribute it and with the underlying offense. Respondent Rhodes was indicted only for conspiracy to possess. The District Court granted respondents' pretrial motion to suppress the evidence seized from the Taos residence on the grounds that the initial warrant to install the beeper was invalid and that the Taos seizure was the tainted fruit of an unauthorized installation and monitoring of that beeper. * * * The Court of Appeals affirmed, except with respect to Rhodes, holding that a warrant was required to install the beeper in one of the 10 cans of ether and to monitor it in private dwellings and storage lockers. * * * We granted the Government's petition for certiorari, which raised the question whether a warrant was required to authorize either the installation of the beeper * * *.

II

Because the judgment below in favor of Karo rested in major part on the conclusion that the installation violated his Fourth Amendment rights and that any information obtained from monitoring the beeper was tainted by the initial illegality, we must deal with the legality of the warrantless installation. It is clear that the actual placement of the beeper into the can violated no one's Fourth Amendment rights. The can into which the beeper was placed belonged at the time to the DEA, and by no stretch of the imagination could it be said that respondents then had any legitimate expectation of privacy in it. The ether and the original 10 cans, on the other hand, belonged to, and were in the possession of, Muehlenweg, who had given his consent to any invasion of those items that occurred. Thus, even if there had been no substitution of cans and the agents had placed the beeper into one of the original 10 cans, Muehlenweg's consent was sufficient to validate the placement of the beeper in the can.

The Court of Appeals acknowledged that before Karo took control of the ether "the DEA and Muehlenweg presumably could do with the can and ether whatever they liked without violating Karo's rights." It did not hold that the actual placement of the beeper into the ether can violated the Fourth Amendment. Instead, it held that the violation occurred at the time the beeper-laden can was transferred to Karo. The court stated:

> All individuals have a legitimate expectation of privacy that objects coming into their rightful ownership do not have electronic devices attached to them, devices that would give law enforcement agents the opportunity to monitor the location of the objects at all times and in every place that the objects are taken, including inside private residences and other areas where the right to be free from warrantless governmental intrusion is unquestioned.

Not surprisingly, the Court of Appeals did not describe the transfer as * * * a "seizure," for plainly it is [not]. * * *

A "seizure" of property occurs when "there is some meaningful interference with an individual's possessory interests in that property." Although the can may have contained an unknown and unwanted foreign object, it cannot be said that anyone's possessory interest was interfered with in a meaningful way. At most, there was a technical trespass on the space occupied by the beeper. The existence of a physical trespass is only marginally relevant to the question of whether the Fourth Amendment has been violated, however, for an actual trespass is neither necessary nor sufficient to establish a constitutional violation. Of course, if the presence of a beeper in the can constituted a seizure merely because of its occupation of space, it would follow that the presence of any object, regardless of its nature, would violate the Fourth Amendment.

We conclude that no Fourth Amendment interest of Karo or of any other respondent was infringed by the installation of the beeper. * * *[3]

The judgment of the Court of Appeals is accordingly

Reversed.

---

[3] Despite this holding, warrants for the installation and monitoring of a beeper will obviously be desirable since it may be useful, even critical, to monitor the beeper to determine that it is actually located in a place not open to visual surveillance. * * *

JUSTICE O'CONNOR, with whom JUSTICE REHNQUIST joins, concurring in part and concurring in the judgment.

[Omitted.]

JUSTICE STEVENS, with whom JUSTICE BRENNAN and JUSTICE MARSHALL join, concurring in part and dissenting in part.

The beeper is a species of radio transmitter. Mounted inside a container, it has much in common with a microphone mounted on a person. It reveals the location of the item to which it is attached—the functional equivalent of a radio transmission saying "Now I am at ___."

The * * * question in this case is whether the beeper invaded any interest protected by the Fourth Amendment. * * *

I

The attachment of the beeper, in my judgment, constituted a "seizure." The owner of property, of course, has a right to exclude from it all the world, including the Government, and a concomitant right to use it exclusively for his own purposes. When the Government attaches an electronic monitoring device to that property, it infringes that exclusionary right; in a fundamental sense it has converted the property to its own use. Surely such an invasion is an "interference" with possessory rights; the right to exclude, which attached as soon as the can respondents purchased was delivered, had been infringed.[2] That interference is also "meaningful"; the character of the property is profoundly different when infected with an electronic bug than when it is entirely germ free.

Here * * *, by attaching a monitoring device to respondents' property, the agents usurped a part of a citizen's property—in this case a part of respondents' exclusionary rights in their tangible personal property. By attaching the beeper and using the container to conceal it, the Government in the most fundamental sense was asserting "dominion and control" over the property—the power to use the property for its own purposes. And "[asserting] dominion and control" is a "seizure" in the most basic sense of the term. * * *

Accordingly, I respectfully dissent.

---

[2] It makes no difference in this case that when the beeper was initially attached, the can had not yet been delivered to respondents. Once the delivery had been effected, the container was respondents' property from which they had the right to exclude all the world. It was at that point that the infringement of this constitutionally protected interest began.

IV. STANDING

RAKAS V. ILLINOIS

439 U.S. 128
Supreme Court of the United States
October 3, 1978, Argued; December 5, 1978, Decided
No. 77-5781

MR. JUSTICE REHNQUIST delivered the opinion of the Court.

Petitioners were convicted of armed robbery in the Circuit Court of Kankakee County, Ill., and their convictions were affirmed on appeal. At their trial, the prosecution offered into evidence a sawed-off rifle and rifle shells that had been seized by police during a search of an automobile in which petitioners had been passengers. Neither petitioner is the owner of the automobile and neither has ever asserted that he owned the rifle or shells seized. The Illinois Appellate Court held that petitioners lacked standing to object to the allegedly unlawful search and seizure and denied their motion to suppress the evidence. We granted certiorari * * *.

I

* * * A police officer on a routine patrol received a radio call notifying him of a robbery of a clothing store in Bourbonnais, Ill., and describing the getaway car. Shortly thereafter, the officer spotted an automobile which he thought might be the getaway car. After following the car for some time and after the arrival of assistance, he and several other officers stopped the vehicle. The occupants of the automobile, petitioners and two female companions, were ordered out of the car and, after the occupants had left the car, two officers searched the interior of the vehicle. They discovered a box of rifle shells in the glove compartment, which had been locked, and a sawed-off rifle under the front passenger seat. After discovering the rifle and the shells, the officers took petitioners to the station and placed them under arrest.

Before trial petitioners moved to suppress the rifle and shells seized from the car on the ground that the search violated the Fourth and Fourteenth Amendments. They conceded that they did not own the automobile and were simply passengers; the owner of the car had been the driver of the vehicle at the time of the search. Nor did they assert that they owned the rifle or the shells seized. The prosecutor challenged petitioners' standing to object to the lawfulness of the search of the car because neither the car, the shells nor the rifle belonged to them. The trial court agreed that petitioners lacked standing and denied the motion to suppress the evidence. * * * On appeal after petitioners' conviction, the Appellate Court of Illinois, Third Judicial District, affirmed the trial court's denial of petitioners' motion to suppress because it held that "without a proprietary or other similar interest in an automobile, a mere passenger therein lacks standing to challenge the legality of the search of the vehicle."

The Illinois Supreme Court denied petitioners leave to appeal.

II

Petitioners first urge us to relax or broaden the rule of standing enunciated in *Jones v. United States*, 362 U.S. 257 (1960), so that any criminal defendant at whom a search was "directed" would have standing to contest the legality of that search and object to the admission at trial of evidence obtained as a result of the search. Alternatively, petitioners argue that they have standing to object to the search under *Jones* because they were "legitimately on [the] premises" at the time of the search.

The concept of standing discussed in *Jones* focuses on whether the person seeking to challenge the legality of a search as a basis for suppressing evidence was himself the "victim" of the search or seizure.[2] Adoption of the so-called "target" theory advanced by petitioners would in effect permit a defendant to assert that a violation of the Fourth Amendment rights of a third party entitled him to have evidence suppressed at his trial. * * * We shall therefore consider in turn petitioners' target theory, the necessity for continued adherence to the notion of standing discussed in *Jones* as a concept that is theoretically distinct from the merits of a defendant's Fourth Amendment claim, and, finally, the proper disposition of petitioners' ultimate claim in this case.

A

We decline to extend the rule of standing in Fourth Amendment cases in the manner suggested by petitioners. As we stated in *Alderman v. United States*, 394 U.S. 165, 174 (1969), "Fourth Amendment rights are personal rights which, like some other constitutional rights, may not be vicariously asserted." A person who is aggrieved by an illegal search and seizure only through the introduction of damaging evidence secured by a search of a third person's premises or property has not had any of his Fourth Amendment rights infringed. And since the exclusionary rule is an attempt to effectuate the guarantees of the Fourth Amendment, it is proper to permit only defendants whose Fourth Amendment rights have been violated to benefit from the rule's protections. There is no reason to think that a party whose rights have been infringed will not, if evidence is used against him, have ample motivation to move to suppress it. * * *

---

[2] * * * There is an aspect of traditional standing doctrine that was not considered in *Jones* and which we do not question. It is the proposition that a party seeking relief must allege such a personal stake or interest in the outcome of the controversy as to assure the concrete adverseness which Art. III requires. Thus, a person whose Fourth Amendment rights were violated by a search or seizure, but who is not a defendant in a criminal action in which the illegally seized evidence is sought to be introduced, would not have standing to invoke the exclusionary rule to prevent use of that evidence in that action.

Conferring standing to raise vicarious Fourth Amendment claims would necessarily mean a more widespread invocation of the exclusionary rule during criminal trials. * * *

Each time the exclusionary rule is applied it exacts a substantial social cost for the vindication of Fourth Amendment rights. Relevant and reliable evidence is kept from the trier of fact and the search for truth at trial is deflected. Since our cases generally have held that one whose Fourth Amendment rights are violated may successfully suppress evidence obtained in the course of an illegal search and seizure, misgivings as to the benefit of enlarging the class of persons who may invoke that rule are properly considered when deciding whether to expand standing to assert Fourth Amendment violations.

B

* * * It should be emphasized that nothing we say here casts the least doubt on cases which recognize that, as a general proposition, the issue of standing involves two inquiries: first, whether the proponent of a particular legal right has alleged "injury in fact," and, second, whether the proponent is asserting his own legal rights and interests rather than basing his claim for relief upon the rights of third parties. But this Court's long history of insistence that Fourth Amendment rights are personal in nature has already answered many of these traditional standing inquiries, and we think that definition of those rights is more properly placed within the purview of substantive Fourth Amendment law than within that of standing.

Analyzed in these terms, the question is whether the challenged search and seizure violated the Fourth Amendment rights of a criminal defendant who seeks to exclude the evidence obtained during it. That inquiry in turn requires a determination of whether the disputed search and seizure has infringed an interest of the defendant which the Fourth Amendment was designed to protect. We are under no illusion that by dispensing with the rubric of standing used in *Jones* we have rendered any simpler the determination of whether the proponent of a motion to suppress is entitled to contest the legality of a search and seizure. But by frankly recognizing that this aspect of the analysis belongs more properly under the heading of substantive Fourth Amendment doctrine than under the heading of standing, we think the decision of this issue will rest on sounder logical footing.

C

Here petitioners, who were passengers occupying a car which they neither owned nor leased, seek to analogize their position to that of the defendant in *Jones v. United States*. In *Jones*, petitioner was present at the time of the search of an apartment which was owned by a friend. The friend had given Jones permission to use the apartment and a key to it, with which Jones had admitted himself on the day of the search. He had a suit and shirt at the apartment and had slept there "maybe a night," but his home was elsewhere. At the time of the search, Jones was the only occupant of the apartment because the lessee was away for a period of several days. Under these circumstances, this Court stated that while one wrongfully on the premises could not move to suppress evidence obtained as a result of searching them, "anyone legitimately on premises where a search occurs may challenge its legality." Petitioners argue that their occupancy of the automobile in question was comparable to that of Jones in the apartment and that they therefore have standing to contest the legality of the search— or as we have rephrased the inquiry, that they, like Jones, had their Fourth Amendment rights violated by the search.

* * * We think that *Jones* on its facts merely stands for the unremarkable proposition that a person can have a legally sufficient interest in a place other than his own home so that the Fourth Amendment protects him from unreasonable governmental intrusion into that place. In defining the scope of that interest, we adhere to the view expressed in *Jones* and echoed in later cases that arcane distinctions developed in property and tort law between guests, licensees, invitees, and the like, ought not to control. But the *Jones* statement that a person need only be "legitimately on premises" in order to challenge the validity of the search of a dwelling place cannot be taken in its full sweep beyond the facts of that case. * * *

D

Judged by the foregoing analysis, petitioners' claims must fail. They asserted neither a property nor a possessory interest in the automobile, nor an interest in the property seized. And as we have previously indicated, the fact that they were "legitimately on [the] premises" in the sense that they were in the car with the permission of its owner is not determinative of whether they had a legitimate expectation of privacy in the particular areas of the automobile searched. It is unnecessary for us to decide here whether the same expectations of privacy are warranted in a car as would be justified in a dwelling place in analogous circumstances. We have on numerous occasions pointed out that cars are not to be treated identically with houses or apartments for Fourth Amendment purposes. But here petitioners' claim is one which would fail even in an analogous situation in a dwelling place, since they made no showing that they had any legitimate expectation of privacy in the glove compartment or area under the seat of the car in which they were merely passengers. Like the trunk of an automobile, these are areas in which a passenger qua passenger simply would not normally have a legitimate expectation of privacy.

Jones v. United States, 362 U.S. 257 (1960) * * * involved significantly different factual circumstances. Jones not only had permission to use the apartment of his friend, but had a key to the apartment with which he admitted himself on the day of the search and kept possessions in the apartment. Except with respect to his friend, Jones had complete dominion and control over the apartment and could exclude others from it. * * * Jones could legitimately expect privacy in the areas which were the subject of the search and seizure each sought to contest. No such showing was made by these petitioners with respect to those portions of the automobile which were searched and from which incriminating evidence was seized.

III

The Illinois courts were therefore correct in concluding that it was unnecessary to decide whether the search of the car might have violated the rights secured to someone else by the Fourth and Fourteenth Amendments to the United States Constitution. Since it did not violate any rights of these petitioners, their judgment of conviction is

Affirmed.

MR. JUSTICE POWELL, with whom THE CHIEF JUSTICE joins, concurring.

[Omitted.]

MR. JUSTICE WHITE, with whom MR. JUSTICE BRENNAN, MR. JUSTICE MARSHALL, and MR. JUSTICE STEVENS join, dissenting.

[Omitted.]

QUESTIONS, COMMENTS, CONCERNS?

1. Standing and *Katz*. What does *Rakas* add to the requirement that a defendant demonstrate a subjective expectation of privacy in the place or item searched? Viewed in that manner, is standing really a separate threshold requirement? Some language from Justice Rehnquist is instructive. He wrote that the relevant inquiry requires a "determination of whether the disputed search and seizure has infringed an interest of the defendant which the Fourth Amendment was designed to protect." Roughly translated, a defendant may assert a violation of only *his* personal Fourth Amendment rights; that is, no vicarious standing exists. As a result, a defendant cannot claim that evidence seized in violation of his confederate's Fourth Amendment rights mandates suppression of that evidence in both of their criminal cases.

2. Standing and Ulbricht from the government's perspective. Just a few weeks after filing its response to Ulbricht's motion to suppress, the government filed a Supplemental Memorandum of Law in Opposition to Defendant's Motion to Suppress Evidence. [See Casefile Document 4.] In it, the government makes a powerful argument: "Ulbricht's motion fails to allege, much less prove, that he had any property or possessory interest in the SR Server, as required for him to move to suppress its contents." Think about that claim. Could Ulbricht demonstrate the requisite property or possessory interest in the Silk Road server without simultaneously admitting guilt?

3.   **Standing and Ulbricht from Ulbricht's perspective.** Consider Ulbricht's reply brief. [See Casefile Document 5.] At the time of that filing, the chief questions presented by Ulbricht's case included: (a) whether Ulbricht has standing to challenge the government's identification of the Silk Road server; (b) whether the government's reliance on a pen register constitutes a Fourth Amendment "search"; and (c) whether the government needed a warrant to have authorities in Iceland serve the server. In your opinion, what does Ulbricht's reply brief do to address these questions? Does he address the question we posed in the immediately preceding note? Pay particular attention to pages 18–21.

4.   **Standing and Ulbricht from the court's perspective.** Notice the district court is extremely concerned about Ulbricht's relationship to the Silk Road server alongside how that relationship impacts whether he has standing to challenge the government's investigative behavior. [See Casefile Document 6.] In an October 7, 2014 order, the district court invites Ulbricht to file an affidavit "demonstrating that he had a subjective expectation of privacy in any of the items seized and as to which his suppression motion relates." He ultimately filed no such document.

5.   **Standing and Ulbricht from the court's perspective (redux).** The district court concludes that Ulbricht's failure to demonstrate his interest in the Silk Road server is fatal to his motion to suppress. [See Casefile Document 7.] Notice that the court does not think filing a document demonstrating his interest in the server would be tantamount to an admission of guilt. At page 7 of the court's order denying Ulbricht's motion to suppress, the court noted that Ulbricht could have established standing "by submitting a sworn statement that could not be offered against him at trial as evidence of his guilt (though it could be used to impeach him should he take the witness stand)." Notice also the court's specific treatment of *Rakas* beginning on page 13 of its order and again on page 24. If Ulbricht had conceded a personal interest in the Silk Road server, how do you think the district court would have ruled on the motion to suppress?

6.   **Revisiting *Rakas*.** The Court recently revisited the limits of the standing doctrine. In *Byrd v. United States*, 138 S. Ct. 1518 (2018), Pennsylvania State Troopers pulled over a car driven by Terrence Byrd. During the ensuing traffic stop, the troopers learned that Byrd was driving a rented car, but that he was not listed as an authorized driver in the rental agreement. The troopers then, without Byrd's consent, searched the vehicle and found body armor alongside forty-nine bricks of heroin. Byrd was prosecuted in federal court and moved to suppress the evidence found in the vehicle. Both the district court and the Third Circuit denied the motion on the grounds that Byrd lacked standing to challenge the search because his name was not listed on the rental agreement. Stated differently, the lower courts found that that Byrd lacked a reasonable expectation of privacy in the car.

The Supreme Court disagreed. The Court unanimously held that Byrd had standing to challenge the troopers' search of the rented car, reasoning that

Byrd had the renter's permission to drive the car. The Court saw "no reason why the expectation of privacy that comes from lawful possession and control and the attendant right to exclude would differ depending on whether the car in question is rented or privately owned by someone other than the person in current possession of it[.]" The Court, however, observed that, wholly apart from the standing question, it remained an open question whether the troopers had probable cause to search the vehicle.

The Third Circuit never reached that question. In affirming Byrd's conviction on remand, the Third Circuit held, "The search in this case was authorized by binding precedent in this Circuit at the time it was conducted. Accordingly, the good-faith exception to the exclusionary rule applies[.]" *United States v. Byrd*, No, 16-1509, 2018 U.S. App. LEXIS 22058, at *4 (3d Cir. Aug. 8, 2018). Well, you win some and you lose some.

CHAPTER 4

JUSTIFICATIONS FOR SEARCHES, SEIZURES & OTHER LIMITED INTRUSIONS

■ ■ ■

I. INTRODUCTION

"Probable cause" is at the heart of the Fourth Amendment. Probable cause is the justification or quantum of suspicion generally necessary to support law enforcement acquiring a warrant, executing an arrest, and/or searching/seizing property. From this definition, we can discern three types of probable cause: (1) probable cause to search; (2) probable cause to arrest, and (3) probable cause to seize property. This section introduces the probable cause standard, defines each category of probable cause, and examines a few common issues that arise when conducting a probable cause inquiry.

The Supreme Court has never quantified the probable cause standard. Rather, the Court has called probable cause a "fluid concept," *Gates*, 462 U.S. at 232, that is "incapable of precise definition or quantification into percentages because it deals with probabilities and depends on the totality of the circumstances," *Maryland v. Pringle*, 540 U.S. 366, 371 (2003). Practically, probable cause is a standard less demanding than proof beyond a reasonable doubt that roughly translates into "a reasonable ground for belief of guilt," *Brinegar v. United States*, 338 U.S. 160, 175 (1949) (internal citation and quotation marks omitted), where more than a "bare suspicion" of guilt is necessary.

So, what kind of "circumstances" or facts may an officer rely on to establish probable cause to conduct a Fourth Amendment intrusion? Well, the Supreme Court has been careful to emphasize that the probable cause standard is an objective concept where the subjective motivations of an officer are irrelevant. An officer's belief that probable cause does or does *not* exist is irrelevant. That said, courts have shown a periodic willingness to consider some of the subjective attributes of a particular officer in some cases.

For now (and for outline purposes), you should know that officers may rely on two types of objective information and three subjective characteristics to establish probable cause to conduct a Fourth Amendment intrusion. The two types of objective information are: (1) direct information (i.e., what the officer learns through personal observation); and (2) reliable hearsay information (i.e., what an officer learns from a trustworthy informant). The subjective characteristics are: (1) an officer's particular knowledge or expertise,[1] (2) the officer's personal experience patrolling a specific area,[2] and (3) the number of years the officer has served in law enforcement.[3] Finally, note that an officer may rely on any combination of the above to develop probable cause to conduct a Fourth Amendment intrusion.

Recall that there are three—and only three—types of probable cause: probable cause to search, probable cause to arrest, and probable cause to seize property. First, in order to have probable cause to search, the police must have reliable information to reasonably believe that contraband or evidence of a crime will be found at the place of search when the search occurs. Second, for probable cause to arrest, police must have reliable information to reasonably believe that the arrestee is committing, is about to commit, or will commit a crime. Finally, probable cause to seize property exists when officers have reliable information to reasonably believe that the property to be seized is contraband or evidence of a crime.

Problematically, lawyers and the general public often toss around the term "probable cause" without connecting it to any particular Fourth Amendment intrusion. "Well, it depends if the officer had probable cause," is a good example. Please resist the temptation to discuss probable cause in that manner. Rather, you must specify whether the officer had probable cause to search, probable cause to arrest, or probable cause to seize property.

A few more problems to be mindful of in the probable cause context include staleness, informants, profiling, and neighborhoods. Each of those discrete topics present unique challenges to assessing whether probable cause supports a particular investigative technique.

Consider staleness first. Just because probable cause exists now does not mean it will exist forever: information in support of probable cause to arrest or search can become stale. Consider a trustworthy tip from an informant that drugs are in a particular residence. Police would be wise to hastily obtain and execute a search warrant at that property. That tip is valid only as long as the drugs remain at the informed location. But the moment the drugs move, the corresponding probable cause is stale.

Next, consider informants, a critical part of the first case we'll read in these materials. That case, *Illinois v. Gates*, 462 U.S. 213 (1983), deals with

---

[1]   *E.g., State v. Ellison*, 455 So. 2d 424, 431 (Fla. Ct. App. 1984).

[2]   *E.g., People v. Hanes*, 72 Cal. Rptr. 2d 212, 214 (Cal. App. Dep't Super. Ct. 1997).

[3]   *E.g., State v. Litke*, No. 2013AP1606-CR, 2014 Wisc. App. LEXIS 196, at *12 (Wisc. Ct. App. Mar. 11, 2014).

the problem of informants, known or unknown, and how to evaluate their role in the probable cause analysis. In this context, we should be mindful of an informant's: (1) basis of knowledge, and (2) veracity. In the basis of knowledge context, we are concerned about the role of hearsay; that is, how many levels of hearsay are involved in the informant's information? Hearsay is already in play anytime an informant contributes information. But if the informant *heard* the information being conveyed, now two levels of hearsay are involved.

When we discuss the veracity of an informant in the warrant context, we're asking why a reviewing magistrate should believe the informant. According to *Gates*, the affiant-officer can demonstrate informant veracity by showing the informant was "credible" or that his information was "reliable." An informant's credibility often turns on his "track record," i.e., an assertion that the informant's prior tips have led to arrests culminating in convictions. An informant is most often viewed as reliable when independent police work corroborates the tipster's information.

Next, consider profiling. Profiling also has a very real role in the formation of probable cause. When it comes to profiling, the Court has permitted the practice—at least *implicitly*. That matters because officers might rely on a "drug courier profile" as part of developing a basis to stop or detain someone (think *Mendenhall*). Whereas the drug courier profile is connected, at least in theory, to a pattern of behaviors and indicators that can be linked to a particular type of crime, a much more troubling and explicitly vague type of profiling practice has arisen that merits discussion.

Consider a common scenario: officers perform a traffic stop on the purported basis of investigating a traffic violation, though in actuality the officers seek to investigate some other more serious offense. That practice, formally called "a pretextual stop," is constitutional, so long as probable cause exists to believe that a traffic violation occurred. Study after study demonstrates that more of these stops happen to drivers of color. Moreover, concerns about racial profiling extend beyond an officer's decision to stop and into the duration of that stop, whether the officer issues the driver a ticket, whether the officer elects to search the vehicle, and whether the officer uses force at some point during the traffic encounter.

Whatever you might think of the practice of profiling, it's important to know that, in the context of a pretextual stop, the probable cause goes with the officers' *basis* for the stop (e.g., speeding)—not with what the officer hopes to learn *during* the stop (e.g., the suspect possesses drugs). The actual reason for the stop—the officer's hope to find evidence of a separate crime—is irrelevant as long as the pretext is legally sufficient.

Finally, as we'll see, a suspect's presence in a so-called "high crime neighborhood" plays a contributing role in establishing the presence of probable cause or, minimally, reasonable suspicion (more on that standard later).

How then does all of this work in practice? In short, the officer walking the beat will determine, based on objective information and certain subjective characteristics, that probable cause to arrest, search, or seize exists. Notice in this context that the officer makes a discretionary, on-the-spot decision, which lacks the benefit of independent judicial review. Alternatively, the officer may elect to obtain a warrant either to search, arrest, and/or seize property depending on the type of probable cause the officer has developed in the field.

II. PROBABLE CAUSE

A. MEET JOHN WAYNE GACY[4]

John Wayne Gacy, one of America's most prolific and notorious serial killers, was a man of many faces. Born March 17, 1942, in Chicago, Illinois, Gacy was one of three children parented by an abusive and alcoholic father. In 1963, Gacy graduated from Northwest Business College and, shortly thereafter, met his first wife, Marlynn Myers. The couple moved to Waterloo, Iowa, where Marlynn's father had purchased three Kentucky Fried Chicken restaurants. Gacy became the manager and joined the Jaycees, an organization that taught leadership and offered civic opportunities. Gacy rose to become vice president, and, meanwhile, Marlynn gave birth to two children.

But in 1968, Gacy was indicted for forcing the fifteen-year-old son of a Jaycee member to perform oral sex on him. Gacy was convicted and sentenced to ten years, after which Marlynn filed for divorce, won, and took the children with her. Although Gacy would never see the three of them again, he served only eighteen months of his sentence before being released on parole.

---

[4] Remember that you have access to the filings relevant to this chapter in your online repository.

Former First Lady Rosalynn Carter shakes hands with serial killer John Wayne Gacy

  Gacy set about remaking himself following prison. He moved home to Illinois and purchased a home in Cook County. In 1972, he remarried—this time to Carole Hoff who he had dated in high school. She and her two daughters moved into Gacy's home at 8213 West Summerdale Avenue where many of his murders would take place. In 1974, Gacy started his own construction business known as Painting, Decorating and Maintenance ("PDM") Contractors. From then until 1978, Gacy was a well-known community leader in part because of his work for the Democratic Party. Gacy was even photographed with First Lady Rosalynn Carter.

  Gacy's community work helped mask a much darker side of his life. Gacy killed his first victim, Jack McCoy, in 1972—the same year Gacy remarried—and buried him in the crawl space of his home under a layer of concrete. Following that killing, Gacy used his construction company to search for his next victims, choosing to hire a number of teenaged boys to work for him.

Gacy also identified victims through his membership in the "Jolly Joker" clown club, whose members would dress up as circus clowns and perform at fundraising events and parades in addition to entreating hospitalized children. By late 1975, Gacy had created his own performance characters known as "Pogo the Clown" and "Patches the Clown." But by that same time, Gacy and Hoff, his second wife, began to drift apart. Gacy had become an insomniac, and Hoff would find magazines depicting naked men around their house. When confronted, Gacy admitted the magazines were his and told Hoff that he preferred young men to women. Hoff filed for divorce, which became final on March 2, 1976.

With the divorce final and Hoff moving out, Gacy became a horrifically prolific killer. Between 1976 and 1978, Gacy would kill twenty-three teenage boys. Gacy buried his victims in the crawl space of his home, stacking them as many as three bodies high, until he actually filled his crawl space. He then began dumping his victims in along the Des Plains River as an alternative.

Gacy finally made a mistake in late 1978. On the afternoon of December 11th, Gacy visited Nisson's Pharmacy in Des Plaines, Illinois, to discuss a potential remodeling project with the store's owner, Phil Torf. In earshot of this discussion was a fifteen-year-old employee of Nisson's named Robert Piest. Piest overheard Gacy mentioning that PDM Contractors frequently hired teenage boys at a starting salary of $5 per hour—almost double the salary Piest earned at the pharmacy. After Gacy left the store, Piest told his mother that "some contractor wants to talk to me about a job," telling her he would return to the store shortly. Piest was never seen alive again.

When Piest failed to return to the store, Piest's family filed a missing person's report with the Des Plaines Police Department. During the investigation, Torf revealed that Gacy was most likely the contractor Piest had left the store to speak with. Gacy denied talking to Piest about any job and promised to come to the police station and give a full, written statement about their conversation. When Gacy arrived at the station later that day, he was suspiciously covered in mud, claiming he had just been involved in a car accident.

The Des Plaines police, convinced Gacy was behind Piest's disappearance, checked Gacy's criminal record and learned of his prison sentence in Iowa. As a result, police obtained a search warrant for Gacy's residence on December 13th. During the execution of the warrant, investigators quickly noticed a rancid odor coming from the crawl space of the home. But the smell was attributed to a faulty sewage line and was not pursued further.

Yet that initial search of Gacy's home would ultimately uncover vital clues and lead investigators to suspect that Piest was but one of many suspicious disappearances in which Gacy was involved. The search, for example, turned up a 1975 high school class ring engraved with the initials J.A.S., various driver's licenses of unknown teenage boys, handcuffs, books on homosexuality and pederasty, clothing too small for Gacy, a pistol, and a photo receipt from the pharmacy where Piest worked. During a review of the items seized from Gacy's home, investigators realized that the class ring had belonged to John Szyc, a young teenager who had disappeared a year earlier.[5] Investigators elected to assign a two-man surveillance team to follow Gacy while police continued their investigation.

The following day, December 14th, investigators received a phone call from a PDM employee and former roommate of Gacy's named Michael Rossi. Rossi suggested that Gacy might be involved in a number of other suspicious disappearances, including that of a former PDM employee Charles Hattula who was found drowned the previous year. Detectives also learned of a battery charge pending against Gacy, filed on July 15, 1978, in which the complainant reported that Gacy lured him into Gacy's car, chloroformed and raped him, and then dumped him in Lincoln Park, Chicago, with severe chest and facial burns as well as rectal bleeding.

By December 18th, Gacy was beginning to show signs of strain as a result of the constant surveillance. He was unshaven, tired, anxious, and drinking heavily. That day, Gacy drove to his lawyer's office in an attempt to prepare a $750,000 civil suit against the Des Plaines Police Department, demanding that they cease their constant surveillance. Meanwhile, police traced the serial number of the pharmacy photo receipt found during the search of Gacy's home to a young woman named Kim Byers, a co-worker of Piest's at Nisson's Pharmacy. Byers revealed that she had placed the receipt in a jacket she loaned to Piest on the day of his disappearance. That same evening, Michael Rossi gave a second statement to police in which he told investigators that, in the summer of 1977, Gacy instructed Rossi to spread ten bags of lime in the crawl space of his home. Another former roommate of Gacy's, David Cram, would also reveal that Gacy asked him to spread lime in the crawl space as well as dig trenches roughly the size of human graves. Armed with these new revelations, investigators began to

---

[5]   Officers later discovered a portable Motorola TV located in Gacy's bedroom that belonged to Szyc. Szyc's body was one of those found in Gacy's crawl space.

compile evidence for a second search warrant of Gacy's home—this time to include the crawl space.

On December 21, 1978, as investigators were preparing the second search warrant, Gacy began acting erratically. Upon leaving his lawyer's office early that morning, Gacy drove to a local Shell Station where he handed the young gas attendant a small bag of marijuana, stating, "The end is coming [for me]." The attendant immediately handed the marijuana over to the surveillance officers. Throughout that morning, Gacy drove to friends' and co-workers' homes, hugging them and, in some cases, confessing to raping and murdering over thirty young boys. Surveillance detectives, meanwhile, radioed in reports that caused police to fear that Gacy was contemplating suicide. In order to prevent Gacy from harming himself before police could establish probable cause to arrest him for murder, officers made the decision to arrest Gacy for possessing and distributing the marijuana he gave to the young gas attendant. At 4:30 p.m. that evening, Judge Marvin Peters signed a warrant to search Gacy's crawl space.

Armed with the warrant, police and evidence technicians drove to Gacy's home. But upon arrival, officers found that Gacy had unplugged his sump pump, which caused flooding to the crawl space. After draining the crawl space, evidence technician Daniel Genty entered the space and began digging. Within minutes, he discovered the partial remains of a human arm. Genty yelled out from under the crawl space, telling detectives they could now arrest Gacy for murder.

Authorities eventually discovered the remains of twenty-seven corpses in the crawl space plus two more under the garage and driveway. It would take more than a month for authorities to dig up the bodies found on Gacy's property.

B. DEFINING THE DOCTRINE

We move now into defining the probable cause doctrine. Keep in mind that, although *Illinois v. Gates* addresses the role of hearsay in the probable cause analysis, it also reforms the probable cause inquiry. As you read *Gates*, please consider an important question raised by Gacy's case that we consider in more detail later: whether the two-pronged approach in *Gates* applies to hearsay provided by confidential and known informants alike.

After *Gates*, we consider the constitutionality of so-called "anticipatory warrants." By way of preview, an anticipatory warrant is one that is based on evidence of a crime that will exist at a place or time in the future. An anticipatory warrant may be relevant, for instance, in the context of a scheduled controlled drug purchase that has yet to occur. Consider also by way of example law enforcement's ability to prove that a parcel containing cocaine has been mailed to a defendant, but has not yet been delivered. Finally, we close this section by considering whether the "alert" of a well-trained drug dog establishes probable cause to search.

ILLINOIS V. GATES

462 U.S. 213
Supreme Court of the United States
October 13, 1982, Argued; June 8, 1983, Decided
No. 81-430

JUSTICE REHNQUIST delivered the opinion of the Court.

Respondents Lance and Susan Gates were indicted for violation of state drug laws after police officers, executing a search warrant, discovered marihuana and other contraband in their automobile and home. Prior to trial, the Gateses moved to suppress evidence seized during this search. The Illinois Supreme Court affirmed the decisions of lower state courts granting the motion. It held that the affidavit submitted in support of the State's application for a warrant to search the Gateses' property was inadequate under this Court's decisions in *Aguilar v. Texas*, 378 U.S. 108 (1964) and *Spinelli v. United States*, 393 U.S. 410 (1969).

We granted certiorari to consider the application of the Fourth Amendment to a magistrate's issuance of a search warrant on the basis of a partially corroborated anonymous informant's tip. * * *

II

* * * [T]he question presented in the State's * * * petition for certiorari * * * [is] whether respondents' rights under the Fourth and Fourteenth Amendments were violated by the search of their car and house. A chronological statement of events usefully introduces the issues at stake. Bloomingdale, Ill., is a suburb of Chicago located in Du Page County. On May 3, 1978, the Bloomingdale Police Department received by mail an anonymous handwritten letter which read as follows:

> This letter is to inform you that you have a couple in your town who strictly make their living on selling drugs. They are Sue and Lance Gates, they live on Greenway, off Bloomingdale Rd. in the condominiums. Most of their buys are done in Florida. Sue his wife drives their car to Florida, where she leaves it to be loaded up with drugs, then Lance flys down and drives it back. Sue flys back after she drops the car off in Florida. May 3 she is driving down there again and Lance will be flying down in a few days to drive it back. At the time Lance drives the car back he has the trunk loaded with over $100,000.00 in drugs. Presently they have over $100,000.00 worth of drugs in their basement.

> They brag about the fact they never have to work, and make their entire living on pushers.

> I guarantee if you watch them carefully you will make a big catch. They are friends with some big drugs dealers, who visit their house often.

Lance & Susan Gates

Greenway

in Condominiums

The letter was referred by the Chief of Police of the Bloomingdale Police Department to Detective Mader who decided to pursue the tip. Mader learned from the office of the Illinois Secretary of State that an Illinois driver's license had been issued to one Lance Gates, residing at a stated address in Bloomingdale. He contacted a confidential informant whose examination of certain financial records revealed a more recent address for the Gateses, and he also learned from a police officer assigned to O'Hare Airport that "L. Gates" had made a reservation on Eastern Airlines Flight 245 to West Palm Beach, Fla., scheduled to depart from Chicago on May 5 at 4:15 p.m.

Mader then made arrangements with an agent of the Drug Enforcement Administration for surveillance of the May 5 Eastern Airlines flight. The agent later reported to Mader that Gates had boarded the flight, and that federal agents in Florida had observed him arrive in West Palm Beach and take a taxi to the nearby Holiday Inn. They also reported that Gates went to a room registered to one Susan Gates and that, at 7 o'clock the next morning, Gates and an unidentified woman left the motel in a Mercury bearing Illinois license plates and drove northbound on an interstate highway frequently used by travelers to the Chicago area. In addition, the DEA agent informed Mader that the license plate number on the Mercury was registered to a Hornet station wagon owned by Gates. The agent also advised Mader that the driving time between West Palm Beach and Bloomingdale was approximately 22 to 24 hours.

Mader signed an affidavit setting forth the foregoing facts and submitted it to a judge of the Circuit Court of Du Page County, together with a copy of the anonymous letter. The judge of that court thereupon issued a search warrant for the Gateses' residence and for their automobile. The judge, in deciding to issue the warrant, could have determined that the modus operandi of the Gateses had been substantially corroborated. As the anonymous letter predicted, Lance Gates had flown from Chicago to West Palm Beach late in the afternoon of May 5th, had checked into a hotel room registered in the name of his wife, and, at 7 o'clock the following morning, had headed north, accompanied by an unidentified woman, out of West Palm Beach on an interstate highway used by travelers from South Florida to Chicago in an automobile bearing a license plate issued to him.

At 5:15 a.m. on March 7, only 36 hours after he had flown out of Chicago, Lance Gates and his wife returned to their home in Bloomingdale, driving the car in which they had left West Palm Beach some 22 hours earlier. The Bloomingdale police were awaiting them, searched the trunk of the Mercury, and uncovered approximately 350 pounds of marihuana. A search of the Gateses' home revealed marihuana, weapons, and other contraband. The Illinois Circuit Court ordered suppression of all these items on the ground that the affidavit submitted to the Circuit Judge failed to support the necessary determination of probable cause to believe that the Gateses' automobile and home contained the contraband in question. This decision was affirmed in turn by the Illinois Appellate Court and by a divided vote of the Supreme Court of Illinois.

The Illinois Supreme Court concluded—and we are inclined to agree—that, standing alone, the anonymous letter sent to the Bloomingdale Police Department would not provide the basis for a magistrate's determination that there was probable cause to believe contraband would be found in the Gateses' car and home. The letter provides virtually nothing from which one might conclude that its author is either honest or his information reliable; likewise, the letter gives absolutely no indication of the basis for the writer's predictions regarding the Gateses' criminal activities. Something more was required, then, before a magistrate could conclude that there was probable cause to believe that contraband would be found in the Gateses' home and car.

The Illinois Supreme Court also properly recognized that Detective Mader's affidavit might be capable of supplementing the anonymous letter with information sufficient to permit a determination of probable cause. In holding that the affidavit in fact did not contain sufficient additional information to sustain a determination of probable cause, the Illinois court applied a "two-pronged test," derived from our decision in *Spinelli v. United States*, 393 U.S. 410 (1969).[3] The Illinois Supreme Court, like some others, apparently understood *Spinelli* as requiring that the anonymous letter satisfy each of two independent requirements before it could be relied on. According to this view, the letter, as supplemented by Mader's affidavit, first had to adequately reveal the "basis of knowledge" of the letter writer—the particular means by which he or she came by the information given in

---

[3]   In *Spinelli*, police officers observed Mr. Spinelli going to and from a particular apartment in which the telephone company said contained two telephones with stated numbers. The officers also were "informed by a confidential reliable informant that William Spinelli [was engaging in illegal gambling activities]" at the apartment and that he used two phones with numbers corresponding to those possessed by the police. The officers submitted an affidavit with this information to a magistrate and obtained a warrant to search Spinelli's apartment. We held that the magistrate could have made his determination of probable cause only by "abdicating his constitutional function." The Government's affidavit contained absolutely no information regarding the informant's reliability. Thus, it did not satisfy Aguilar's requirement that such affidavits contain "some of the underlying circumstances" indicating that "the informant . . . was 'credible' " or that "his information [was] 'reliable.' " In addition, the tip failed to satisfy Aguilar's requirement that it detail "some of the underlying circumstances from which the informant concluded that . . . narcotics were where he claimed they were." We also held that if the tip concerning Spinelli had contained "sufficient detail" to permit the magistrate to conclude "that he [was] relying on something more substantial than a casual rumor circulating in the underworld or an accusation based merely on an individual's general reputation," then he properly could have relied on it; we know, however, that the tip lacked the requisite detail to permit this "self-verifying detail" analysis.

the report. Second, it had to provide facts sufficiently establishing either the "veracity" of the affiant's informant or, alternatively, the "reliability" of the informant's report in this particular case.

The Illinois court, alluding to an elaborate set of legal rules that have developed among various lower courts to enforce the "two-pronged test,"[4] found that the test had not been satisfied. First, the "veracity" prong was not satisfied because "[there] was simply no basis [for concluding] that the anonymous person [who wrote the letter to the Bloomingdale Police Department] was credible." The court indicated that corroboration by police of details contained in the letter might never satisfy the "veracity" prong, and in any event, could not do so if, as in the present case, only "innocent" details are corroborated. In addition, the letter gave no indication of the basis of its writer's knowledge of the Gateses' activities. The Illinois court understood *Spinelli* as permitting the detail contained in a tip to be used to infer that the informant had a reliable basis for his or her statements, but it thought that the anonymous letter failed to provide sufficient detail to permit such an inference. Thus, it concluded that no showing of probable cause had been made.

We agree with the Illinois Supreme Court that an informant's "veracity," "reliability," and "basis of knowledge" are all highly relevant in determining the value of his or her report. We do not agree, however, that these elements should be understood as entirely separate and independent requirements to be rigidly exacted in every case, which the opinion of the Supreme Court of Illinois would imply. Rather, as detailed below, they should be understood simply as closely intertwined issues that may usefully illuminate the commonsense, practical question of whether there is "probable cause" to believe that contraband or evidence is located in a particular place.

III

This totality-of-the-circumstances approach is far more consistent with our prior treatment of probable cause than is any rigid demand that specific "tests" be satisfied by every informant's tip. Perhaps the central teaching of our decisions, bearing on the probable-cause standard, is that it is a "practical, nontechnical conception." "In dealing with probable cause, ... as the very name implies, we deal with probabilities. These are not

---

[4] In summary, these rules posit that the "veracity" prong of the *Spinelli* test has two "spurs"—the informant's "credibility" and the "reliability" of his or her information. Various interpretations are advanced for the meaning of the "reliability" spur of the "veracity" prong. Both the "basis of knowledge" prong and the "veracity" prong are treated as entirely separate requirements that must be independently satisfied in every case in order to sustain a determination of probable cause. Some ancillary doctrines are relied on to satisfy certain foregoing requirements. For example, the "self-verifying detail" of a tip may satisfy the "basis of knowledge" requirement although not the "credibility" spur of the "veracity" prong. Conversely, corroboration would seem not capable of supporting the "basis of knowledge" prong but only the "veracity" prong. * * *

technical; they are the factual and practical considerations of everyday life on which reasonable and prudent men, not legal technicians, act." * * *

* * * [P]robable cause is a fluid concept—turning on the assessment of probabilities in particular factual contexts—not readily, or even usefully, reduced to a neat set of legal rules. Informants' tips doubtless come in many shapes and sizes from many different types of persons. * * *

Moreover, the "two-pronged test" directs analysis into two largely independent channels: the informant's "veracity" or "reliability" and his "basis of knowledge." There are persuasive arguments against according these two elements such independent status. Instead, they are better understood as relevant considerations in the totality-of-the-circumstances analysis that traditionally has guided probable-cause determinations: a deficiency in one may be compensated for, in determining the overall reliability of a tip, by a strong showing as to the other or by some other indicia of reliability.

If, for example, a particular informant is known for the unusual reliability of his predictions of certain types of criminal activities in a locality, his failure, in a particular case, to thoroughly set forth the basis of his knowledge surely should not serve as an absolute bar to a finding of probable cause based on his tip. Likewise, if an unquestionably honest citizen comes forward with a report of criminal activity—which if fabricated would subject him to criminal liability—we have found rigorous scrutiny of the basis of his knowledge unnecessary. Conversely, even if we entertain some doubt as to an informant's motives, his explicit and detailed description of alleged wrongdoing, along with a statement that the event was observed firsthand, entitles his tip to greater weight than might otherwise be the case. Unlike a totality-of-the-circumstances analysis, which permits a balanced assessment of the relative weights of all the various indicia of reliability (and unreliability) attending an informant's tip, the "two-pronged test" has encouraged an excessively technical dissection of informants' tips with undue attention being focused on isolated issues that cannot sensibly be divorced from the other facts presented to the magistrate. * * *

We also have recognized that affidavits "are normally drafted by nonlawyers in the midst and haste of a criminal investigation. Technical requirements of elaborate specificity once exacted under common law pleadings have no proper place in this area." Likewise, search and arrest warrants long have been issued by persons who are neither lawyers nor judges and who certainly do not remain abreast of each judicial refinement of the nature of "probable cause." The rigorous inquiry into the *Spinelli* prongs and the complex superstructure of evidentiary and analytical rules that some have seen implicit in our *Spinelli* decision cannot be reconciled with the fact that many warrants are—quite properly—issued on the basis of nontechnical, common-sense judgments of laymen applying a standard less demanding than those used in more formal legal proceedings. Likewise, given the informal, often hurried context in which it must be applied, the "built-in subtleties" of the "two-pronged test" are particularly unlikely to assist magistrates in determining probable cause.

Similarly, we have repeatedly said that after-the-fact scrutiny by courts of the sufficiency of an affidavit should not take the form of de novo review. A magistrate's "determination of probable cause should be paid great deference by reviewing courts." * * *

If the affidavits submitted by police officers are subjected to the type of scrutiny some courts have deemed appropriate, police might well resort to warrantless searches with the hope of relying on consent or some other exception to the Warrant Clause that might develop at the time of the search. In addition, the possession of a warrant by officers conducting an arrest or search greatly reduces the perception of unlawful or intrusive police conduct by assuring "the individual whose property is searched or seized of the lawful authority of the executing officer, his need to search, and the limits of his power to search." Reflecting this preference for the warrant process, the traditional standard for review of an issuing magistrate's probable-cause determination has been that so long as the magistrate had a "substantial basis for . . . [concluding]" that a search would uncover evidence of wrongdoing, the Fourth Amendment requires no more. We think reaffirmation of this standard better serves the purpose of encouraging recourse to the warrant procedure and is more consistent with our traditional deference to the probable-cause determinations of magistrates than is the "two-pronged test."

Finally, * * * [t]he strictures that inevitably accompany the "two-pronged test" cannot avoid seriously impeding the task of law enforcement. If, as the Illinois Supreme Court apparently thought, that test must be rigorously applied in every case, anonymous tips would be of greatly diminished value in police work. * * * As a result, anonymous tips seldom could survive a rigorous application of either of the *Spinelli* prongs. Yet, such tips, particularly when supplemented by independent police investigation, frequently contribute to the solution of otherwise "perfect crimes." While a conscientious assessment of the basis for crediting such tips is required by the Fourth Amendment, a standard that leaves virtually no place for anonymous citizen informants is not.

For all these reasons, we conclude that it is wiser to abandon the "two-pronged test" established by our decisions in *Aguilar* and *Spinelli*. In its place, we reaffirm the totality-of-the-circumstances analysis that traditionally has informed probable-cause determinations. The task of the issuing magistrate is simply to make a practical, common-sense decision whether, given all the circumstances set forth in the affidavit before him, including the "veracity" and "basis of knowledge" of persons supplying hearsay information, there is a fair probability that contraband or evidence of a crime will be found in a particular place. And the duty of a reviewing court is simply to ensure that the magistrate had a "substantial basis for . . . [concluding]" that probable cause existed. We are convinced that this flexible, easily applied standard will better achieve the accommodation of public and private interests that the Fourth Amendment requires than does the approach that has developed from *Aguilar* and *Spinelli.* * * *

IV.

Our decisions, applying the totality-of-the-circumstances analysis, * * * have consistently recognized the value of corroboration of details of an informant's tip by independent police work. * * *

Our decision in *Draper v. United States,* 358 U.S. 307 (1959), * * * is the classic case on the value of corroborative efforts of police officials. There, an informant named Hereford reported that Draper would arrive in Denver on a train from Chicago on one of two days and that he would be carrying a quantity of heroin. The informant also supplied a fairly detailed physical description of Draper and predicted that he would be wearing a light-colored raincoat, brown slacks, and black shoes and would be walking "real fast." Hereford gave no indication of the basis for his information.[12]

On one of the stated dates, police officers observed a man matching this description exit a train arriving from Chicago; his attire and luggage matched Hereford's report, and he was walking rapidly. We explained in *Draper* that, by this point in his investigation, the arresting officer "had personally verified every facet of the information given him by Hereford except whether petitioner had accomplished his mission and had the three ounces of heroin on his person or in his bag. And surely, with every other bit of Hereford's information being thus personally verified, [the officer] had 'reasonable grounds' to believe that the remaining unverified bit of Hereford's information—that Draper would have the heroin with him— was likewise true."

The showing of probable cause in the present case was fully as compelling as that in *Draper.* Even standing alone, the facts obtained through the independent investigation of Mader and the DEA at least suggested that the Gateses were involved in drug trafficking. In addition to being a popular vacation site, Florida is well known as a source of

---

[12] The tip in *Draper* might well not have survived the rigid application of the "two-pronged test" that developed following *Spinelli.* The only reference to Hereford's reliability was that he had "been engaged as a 'special employee' of the Bureau of Narcotics at Denver for about six months, and from time to time gave information to [the police for] small sums of money, and that [the officer] had always found the information given by Hereford to be accurate and reliable." Likewise, the tip gave no indication of how Hereford came by his information. At most, the detailed and accurate predictions in the tip indicated that however Hereford obtained his information, it was reliable.

narcotics and other illegal drugs. Lance Gates' flight to West Palm Beach, his brief, overnight stay in a motel, and apparent immediate return north to Chicago in the family car, conveniently awaiting him in West Palm Beach, is as suggestive of a prearranged drug run, as it is of an ordinary vacation trip.

In addition, the judge could rely on the anonymous letter, which had been corroborated in major part by Mader's efforts—just as had occurred in *Draper*.[13] The Supreme Court of Illinois reasoned that *Draper* involved an informant who had given reliable information on previous occasions, while the honesty and reliability of the anonymous informant in this case were unknown to the Bloomingdale police. While this distinction might be an apt one at the time the Police Department received the anonymous letter, it became far less significant after Mader's independent investigative work occurred. The corroboration of the letter's predictions that the Gateses' car would be in Florida, that Lance Gates would fly to Florida in the next day or so, and that he would drive the car north toward Bloomingdale all indicated, albeit not with certainty, that the informant's other assertions also were true. "[Because] an informant is right about some things, he is more probably right about other facts," *Spinelli*, 393 U.S. at 427 (WHITE, J., concurring)—including the claim regarding the Gateses' illegal activity. This may well not be the type of "reliability" or "veracity" necessary to satisfy some views of the "veracity prong" of *Spinelli*, but we think it suffices for the practical, common-sense judgment called for in making a probable-cause determination. It is enough, for purposes of assessing probable cause, that "[corroboration] through other sources of information reduced the chances of a reckless or prevaricating tale," thus providing "a substantial basis for crediting the hearsay."

Finally, the anonymous letter contained a range of details relating not just to easily obtained facts and conditions existing at the time of the tip, but to future actions of third parties ordinarily not easily predicted. The letter writer's accurate information as to the travel plans of each of the Gateses was of a character likely obtained only from the Gateses

---

[13] The Illinois Supreme Court thought that the verification of details contained in the anonymous letter in this case amounted only to "[the] corroboration of innocent activity" and that this was insufficient to support a finding of probable cause. We are inclined to agree, however, with the observation of Justice Moran in his dissenting opinion that "[in] this case, just as in *Draper*, seemingly innocent activity became suspicious in light of the initial tip." And it bears noting that all of the corroborating detail established in *Draper* was of entirely innocent activity—a fact later pointed out by [two subsequent Supreme Court cases].

This is perfectly reasonable. As discussed previously, probable cause requires only a probability or substantial chance of criminal activity, not an actual showing of such activity. By hypothesis, therefore, innocent behavior frequently will provide the basis for a showing of probable cause; to require otherwise would be to *sub silentio* impose a drastically more rigorous definition of probable cause than the security of our citizens demands. We think the Illinois court attempted a too rigid classification of the types of conduct that may be relied upon in seeking to demonstrate probable cause. In making a determination of probable cause, the relevant inquiry is not whether particular conduct is "innocent" or "guilty" but the degree of suspicion that attaches to particular types of noncriminal acts.

themselves or from someone familiar with their not-entirely-ordinary travel plans. If the informant had access to accurate information of this type, a magistrate could properly conclude that it was not unlikely that he or she also had access to reliable information of the Gateses' alleged illegal activities. * * * It is apparent, therefore, that the judge issuing the warrant had a "substantial basis for . . . [concluding]" that probable cause to search the Gateses' home and car existed. The judgment of the Supreme Court of Illinois therefore must be

Reversed.

JUSTICE WHITE, concurring in the judgment.

[Omitted.]

JUSTICE BRENNAN, with whom JUSTICE MARSHALL joins, dissenting.

* * * I write separately to dissent from the Court's unjustified and ill-advised rejection of the two-prong test for evaluating the validity of a warrant based on hearsay announced in *Aguilar v. Texas*, 378 U.S. 108 (1964) and refined in *Spinelli v. United States*, 393 U.S. 410 (1969).

I

* * * Findings of probable cause, and attendant intrusions, should not be authorized unless there is some assurance that the information on which they are based has been obtained in a reliable way by an honest or credible person. As applied to police officers, the rules focus on the way in which the information was acquired. As applied to informants, the rules focus both on the honesty or credibility of the informant and on the reliability of the way in which the information was acquired. Insofar as it is more complicated, an evaluation of affidavits based on hearsay involves a more difficult inquiry. This suggests a need to structure the inquiry in an effort to insure greater accuracy. The standards announced in *Aguilar*, as refined by *Spinelli*, fulfill that need. The standards inform the police of what information they have to provide and magistrates of what information they should demand. The standards also inform magistrates of the subsidiary findings they must make in order to arrive at an ultimate finding of probable cause. *Spinelli*, properly understood, directs the magistrate's attention to the possibility that the presence of self-verifying detail might satisfy *Aguilar's* basis of knowledge prong and that corroboration of the details of a tip might satisfy *Aguilar's* veracity prong. By requiring police to provide certain crucial information to magistrates and by structuring magistrates' probable-cause inquiries, *Aguilar* and *Spinelli* assure the magistrate's role as an independent arbiter of probable cause, insure greater accuracy in probable-cause determinations, and advance the substantive value identified above. * * *

II

At the heart of the Court's decision to abandon *Aguilar* and *Spinelli* appears to be its belief that "the direction taken by decisions following *Spinelli* poorly serves '[the] most basic function of any government': 'to provide for the security of the individual and of his property.'" This conclusion rests on the judgment that *Aguilar* and *Spinelli* "seriously [impede] the task of law enforcement," ante at 237, and render anonymous tips valueless in police work. Surely, the Court overstates its case. But of particular concern to all Americans must be that the Court gives virtually no consideration to the value of insuring that findings of probable cause are based on information that a magistrate can reasonably say has been obtained in a reliable way by an honest or credible person. I share JUSTICE WHITE's fear that the Court's rejection of *Aguilar* and *Spinelli* and its adoption of a new totality-of-the-circumstances test "may foretell an evisceration of the probable-cause standard . . . ." * * *

JUSTICE STEVENS, with whom JUSTICE BRENNAN joins, dissenting.

[Omitted.]

QUESTIONS, COMMENTS, CONCERNS?

1. Evaluating the probable cause standard: officer's state of mind. In *Arkansas v. Sullivan*, 532 U.S. 769 (2001), officers stopped respondent for speeding and improperly tinted windows. During the stop, one officer realized that that he was aware of "intelligence on [respondent] regarding narcotics." The officer arrested respondent for speeding, driving without his registration and insurance documentation, carrying a weapon (a roofing hatchet), and improper window tinting. During a search of respondent's person incident to his arrest, officers discovered methamphetamine and suspected drug paraphernalia. Respondent was ultimately charged with various state-law drug offenses, unlawful possession of a weapon, and speeding. Respondent contended that his arrest was unlawful because the original basis for the arrest was merely a pretext to search his vehicle for drugs. The Supreme Court disagreed and upheld the validity of respondent's arrest. It reasoned that individual motivations of an officer are irrelevant to the probable cause analysis.

2. Quantifying probable cause. In *Maryland v. Pringle*, 540 U.S. 366 (2003), an officer stopped a vehicle for speeding in the early hours of morning. The officer searched the car, which was carrying three men, and found "$763 of rolled-up cash from the glove compartment and five glassine baggies of cocaine from between the back-seat armrest and the back seat." Although all three men denied ownership, the officer arrested all three. Pringle, one of the three men, challenged his arrest, contending that the officer lacked probable cause to believe that the contraband belonged specifically to him. The Supreme Court disagreed, observing, "The probable-cause standard is incapable of precise definition or quantification into percentages because it deals with probabilities and depends on the totality of the circumstances." Against that backdrop, the Court held that it was an "entirely reasonable inference from these facts that any or all three of the occupants had knowledge of, and exercised dominion and control over, the cocaine." The Court reasoned that "a reasonable officer could conclude that there was probable cause to believe Pringle committed the crime of possession of cocaine, either solely or jointly."

3.   Evaluating the probable cause standard (redux): reliance on a confidential informant. On a January morning in 1964, petitioner in *McCray v. Illinois*, 386 U.S. 300 (1967), was arrested for possession of narcotics. The arresting officers, who later testified at a suppression hearing, indicated that petitioner's arrest was based on conversations they had with an unidentified informant. That informant relayed that petitioner was selling narcotics; the informant even told the officers where they could find petitioner and, later, the informant pointed petitioner out to the officers. Although petitioner admitted that probable cause existed to support his arrest, he claimed that he had a constitutional right to know the informant's identity. In rejecting petitioner's contention, the Supreme Court held that, when the question of probable cause for an arrest or search is at issue, nothing in the Constitution requires disclosure of an informant's identity. Rather, probable cause may appropriately be based on hearsay so long as the information is both "credible" and "reliable." Were the rule otherwise, the Court reasoned, it would hamper the government's efforts in enforcing drug laws.

4.   A note on the Gacy casefile. As you have likely noticed, the briefs filed in Gacy's case are long—very long. Both Gacy's appellate brief and the state's responsive brief are more than three-hundred pages. [Casefile Documents 1 & 2.] Yes, you read that correctly. In an effort to structure our conversation, please focus only on the first three issues raised by Gacy's brief, [Casefile Document 1, at 3–50], and the state's arguments in response to those issues, [Casefile Document 2, at 1–59]. Before embarking on our Gacy conversation, though, please pause to note that Gacy's brief raises thirty-nine appellate issues. [Casefile Document 1, at 3–5.] How effective do you think it is to raise so many issues? Does it heighten Gacy's chances of receiving a new trial or resentencing? Or does it distract the appellate court and invite it to focus on collateral issues rather than Gacy's best issues?

5.   Understanding the timeline. Before we dive into the probable cause issues raised by Gacy's case, let's focus on the relevant timeline. Here, to help you navigate the casefile, are the critical times associated with law enforcements acquisition of the first two search warrants in Gacy's case:

December 11, 1978

- *~8:30 pm:* Robert Piest, a fifteen-year-old boy, disappears from his job at Nissen's Pharmacy. While at work, and just before disappearing, Piest told a co-worker at the pharmacy, "Come watch the register, that contractor guy wants to talk to me; I'll be right back."

December 12, 1978

- *Evening:* Officers visit Gacy's home. Gacy tells officers that he was at the pharmacy the previous day, but could not remember talking to any boys. He promises to come to the station to give a formal statement.

December 13, 1978

- *~3:30 am:* Gacy comes to the station to give a formal statement, but the officer in charge of the investigation was gone. Gacy leaves the station with plans to return later in the day.

- *Officer Joseph Kozenzak obtains a search warrant:* Officer Kozenzak obtains a search warrant for Gacy's home and three vehicles that Gacy owned.

- *Police execute the search warrant:* Officers execute the warrant on Gacy's home—while Gacy returns to the police station to give a formal statement. During the search, officers find: (1) a photo receipt from the Nissen Pharmacy, and (2) a class ring from Maine West High School with the initials "J.A.S." The ring belonged to John Szyc, another murder victim. They also photographed Gacy's recreation room, including a picture of a television that, police would learn later, belonged to a different victim.

December 15

- *Surveillance:* Police decide to put Gacy under twenty-four-hour surveillance.

December 19

- *An afternoon invitation:* Gacy invites one of the surveillance officers into his home. Officer Robert Schultz comes into the home and uses the bathroom. While doing so, the furnace turns on, and Schultz smells a strong odor of what he associates with the smell of decaying human bodies.

December 21

- *Gacy is arrested:* In view of surveillance officers, Gacy passes marijuana to a young gas station attendant. Officers arrest Gacy and take him to the police station.

- *~7:00 pm:* Officers execute a second search warrant on Gacy's home and discover human remains in the crawl space.

6. Probable cause for the December 13 search warrant. Gacy contends that no probable cause existed to support this first search warrant. That warrant provides four major pieces of information to establish probable cause to search Gacy's home for evidence of unlawful restraint. *First*, Piest's co-worker, Kim Byers, told Detective Kozenzak that Piest approached her and said, "Come watch the register, that contractor guy wants to talk to me, I'll be right back." [Casefile Document 2, at 16.] *Second*, the victim's mother, Elizabeth Piest, told Detective Kozenzak that, when she arrived at Nissen's to pick up Piest from work, he asked if she would "wait a few minutes while he spoke to a subject about a summer construction job." *Id.* at 16–17. *Third*, Gacy was present at the store on two occasions on December 11. *Id.* at 17. *Finally*, Gacy "was arrested and convicted in Waterloo, Iowa in 1968 for Sodomy and sentenced to 10 yrs. In prison. The Sodomy arrest involved 15 and 16 year old youths." *Id.*

Gacy makes a handful of core arguments about why the warrant lacks probable cause. First, he contends that it fails to connect Gacy to "that contractor guy." [Casefile Document 1, at 25.] Second, he asserts that Kozenzak does not clarify how he knew that Gacy was at Nissen's on two occasions on December 11. *Id.* at 25–26. Third, he argues that the warrant's allegations "would not lead a reasonable person to conclude that a crime had been committed." *Id.* at 28. Specifically, he says, "The described activities were innocent activities which had to be presumed to be innocent for the purpose of establishing probable cause." *Id.* Finally, Gacy claims that the warrant fails to assert that "evidence of the unlawful restraint would be found in defendant's residence or vehicles." *Id.* at 30.

The state appellate brief responds by imploring the appellate court to read the warrant "as a whole." [Casefile Document 2, at 20.] After all, says the state, "[t]he question is not whether the affidavit is a masterpiece of writing, the question is whether taken as a whole it supplies probable cause when read in a common sense and realistic fashion." *Id.* at 22.

Applying *Gates*, which was not yet published at the time Detective Kozenzak secured the first search warrant, did probable cause exist to believe that evidence of "unlawful restraint" would be present at Gacy's home on December 13? [*See* Casefile Document 4, at 1178–79 (resolving Gacy's probable cause arguments about the first search warrant).] Compared to *Aguilar-Spinelli*, can you see how *Gates* makes resolving Gacy's probable cause arguments easier?

7. Probable cause for the December 21 search warrant. Recall that officers executed the second search warrant of Gacy's home on December 21. The affidavit in support of the second warrant, also authored by Detective Kozenzak, included the following language:

> On December 21, 1978 I had occasion to speak to Officer Robert Schultz, Star #215 of the Des Plaines police department. Officer Shultz has been a Des Plaines police officer for the past eight and one-half years. He told me that on Tuesday, December 19, 1978 at 7:30 p.m., he was at the John Gacy residence at 8213 W. Summerdale, Norridge, Ill. on surveillance assignment. At that time, John Gacy approached Officer Schultz's police vehicle and asked him if he would like to enter his residence. Officer Schultz responded in the affirmative and entered the Gacy residence via the kitchen entrance

with Mr. Gacy. Once inside Officer Schultz immediately detected an odor similar to that of a putrified human body. Officer Schultz further indicated that during his tenure as a Des Plaines police officer, he had smelled the odor of at least forty (40) putrified human bodies, and that the odor he detected in the Gacy residence smelled similar to the odor of putrified bodies he has smelled in the past.

[Casefile Document 1, at 43.] On appeal, Gacy contends that there are "no facts demonstrating that Schultz had been trained in detecting particular odors." *Id.* at 45. Gacy adds, "Evidence that Schultz, in fact, lacked the ability to differentiate the odor of a putrified human body from the odor of other decaying objects is reflected in his two day delay in bringing his discovery to the attention of his supervisors." *Id.* at 46.

A few questions emerge from Gacy's arguments. First, the state argues that "an experienced officer detecting the odor of decaying human flesh in the house where there was valid reason to believe Robert Piest had been was more than sufficient, standing alone, to show probable cause and to convince a reasonably prudent man that the issuance of a search warrant was proper." [Casefile Document 2, at 47.] Do you agree? Second, what do you make of the delay? Do you agree with Gacy that Schultz's delay in telling his superiors about the smell in Gacy's home alters the probable cause analysis? As you consider your answer to that question, remember that officers had already been in Gacy's home during execution of the first search warrant, yet no one reported a peculiar odor. Finally, is Schultz an "informant" for *Gates* purposes? That is, given that Detective Kozenzak is relying on hearsay information (what Schultz told him), must the magistrate evaluate Schultz's "veracity" and "basis of knowledge"? [*See* Casefile Document 4, at 1179–80 (resolving Gacy's probable cause arguments about the second search warrant).]

8. Revisiting the second warrant: does the December 13 warrant taint the December 21 warrant? Apart from the second search warrant's reliance on the odor in Gacy's house, it also expressly relies on what officers found while executing the first search warrant. In particular, the affidavit in support of the second warrant expressly highlights that officers found "a customer receipt no. 361119 from a film developing envelope with the name and address of Nissen's Pharmacy stamped on it in ink. Further investigation revealed that this receipt has last been in the possession of Robert Piest immediately prior to the time he disappeared." [Casefile Document 2, at 45.]

Gacy correctly notes that the first search warrant made no mention of a receipt. [Casefile Document 1, at 40.] He therefore asserts that law enforcement's seizure of the receipt was unlawful because it was outside the scope of the first search warrant. *Id.* Assume for a moment that the court accepts Gacy's argument about the first warrant, thereby rendering its execution unconstitutional. Would the second search warrant's reliance on the receipt found during the execution of the first search warrant taint officers' discovery of human remains at Gacy's home during the execution of the second warrant? Even if it was improper for the second warrant to rely on the receipt, could a suppression court excise out that problematic portion and hold that probable cause exists solely based on Schultz smelling human decay at Gacy's home?

9. *Gates* **and "known informants."** Gacy argues extensively that *Aguilar*'s two-part inquiry into the "veracity" and "basis of knowledge" for hearsay information applies to the first search warrant. [Casefile Document 1, at 24.] By way of example, Gacy contends that "Kozenczak's complaint did not set forth the basis of the conclusion that Piest left the store to meet John W. Gacy." *Id.* Moreover, he says, the affidavit (what Gacy calls "the complaint") "did not provide the magistrate with the facts and underlying circumstances from which Byers concluded that the 'contractor guy' Piest went out to meet was in fact John W. Gacy." *Id.* at 25. Gacy's concerns on this topic culminate with the following:

> According to the complaint, Piest did not say he was going to see Gacy. Did Byers describe the man she thought was Gacy? Did Byers know Gacy? Had she previously been introduced to him? Did she know he was a contractor? Had she seen Piest go outside and actually meet Gacy? These questions were not answered by the mere conclusory statement that Piest went to meet with Gacy.

Id. The state responds with a simple argument: there is no need to evaluate the "basis of knowledge" and "veracity" of known informants. In particular, it asserts, "when the person supplying the information is a private citizen as opposed to an undisclosed police informant, the requirement of prior reliability (basis for crediting hearsay) does not exist." [Casefile Document 2, at 21.] The appellate court agreed with the state because "it is readily apparent from the affidavit from whom the hearsay information contained in the complaint was obtained." [Casefile Document 3, at 1177.]

Do you agree with the state and the appellate court? Specifically, does the *Gates* opinion distinguish between "known" and "unknown" informants for purposes of the veracity and basis of knowledge inquiries? Or, instead, is *Gates* concerned more generally with evaluating *all* hearsay information included in a search warrant affidavit?

Lower courts since *Gates* have generally assumed that *Gates* address all informants—known and unknown alike—who provide hearsay information. *E.g., United States v. DeQuasie*, 373 F.3d 509, 518 (4th Cir. 2004) ("[W]hen an effort is made to establish probable cause for the issuance of a search warrant based on hearsay from an informant, 'it is necessary to consider all the circumstances set forth in the affidavit, including the veracity and basis of knowledge of persons supplying hearsay information.'" (internal citation omitted)). Knowing that the appellate court was likely wrong, does that change your opinion on whether probable cause existed to support the first (i.e., December 13) warrant in Gacy's case?

UNITED STATES V. GRUBBS

547 U.S. 90
Supreme Court of the United States
January 18, 2006, Argued; March 21, 2006, Decided
No. 04-1414

JUSTICE SCALIA delivered the opinion of the Court.

Federal law enforcement officers obtained a search warrant for respondent's house on the basis of an affidavit explaining that the warrant would be executed only after a controlled delivery of contraband to that location. We address two challenges to the constitutionality of this anticipatory warrant.

I

Respondent Jeffrey Grubbs purchased a videotape containing child pornography from a Web site operated by an undercover postal inspector. Officers from the Postal Inspection Service arranged a controlled delivery of a package containing the videotape to Grubbs' residence. A postal inspector submitted a search warrant application to a Magistrate Judge for the Eastern District of California, accompanied by an affidavit describing the proposed operation in detail. The affidavit stated:

> Execution of this search warrant will not occur unless and until the parcel has been received by a person(s) and has been physically taken into the residence .... At that time, and not before, this search warrant will be executed by me and other United States Postal inspectors, with appropriate assistance from other law enforcement officers in accordance with this warrant's command.

In addition to describing this triggering condition, the affidavit referred to two attachments, which described Grubbs' residence and the items officers would seize. These attachments, but not the body of the affidavit, were incorporated into the requested warrant. The affidavit concluded:

> Based upon the foregoing facts, I respectfully submit there exists probable cause to believe that the items set forth in Attachment B to this affidavit and the search warrant, will be found [at Grubbs' residence], which residence is further described at Attachment A.

The Magistrate Judge issued the warrant as requested. Two days later, an undercover postal inspector delivered the package. Grubbs' wife signed for it and took the unopened package inside. The inspectors detained Grubbs as he left his home a few minutes later, then entered the house and commenced the search. Roughly 30 minutes into the search, Grubbs was provided with a copy of the warrant, which included both attachments but not the supporting affidavit that explained when the warrant would be executed. Grubbs consented to interrogation by the postal inspectors and admitted ordering the videotape. He was placed under arrest and various items were seized, including the videotape.

A grand jury for the Eastern District of California indicted Grubbs on one count of receiving a visual depiction of a minor engaged in sexually explicit conduct. He moved to suppress the evidence seized during the search of his residence, arguing as relevant here that the warrant was invalid because it failed to list the triggering condition. After an evidentiary hearing, the District Court denied the motion. Grubbs pleaded guilty but reserved his right to appeal the denial of his motion to suppress.

The Court of Appeals for the Ninth Circuit reversed. * * * [I]t held that "the particularity requirement of the Fourth Amendment applies with full force to the conditions precedent to an anticipatory search warrant." An anticipatory warrant defective for that reason may be "cur[ed]" if the precedent conditions are set forth in an affidavit that is incorporated in the warrant and "presented to the person whose property is being searched." Because the postal inspectors "failed to present the affidavit—the only document in which the triggering conditions were listed"—to Grubbs or his wife, the "warrant was . . . inoperative, and the search was illegal." We granted certiorari.

II

Before turning to the Ninth Circuit's conclusion that the warrant at issue here ran afoul of the Fourth Amendment's particularity requirement, we address the antecedent question whether anticipatory search warrants are categorically unconstitutional. An anticipatory warrant is "a warrant based upon an affidavit showing probable cause that at some future time (but not presently) certain evidence of crime will be located at a specified place." Most anticipatory warrants subject their execution to some condition precedent other than the mere passage of time—a so-called "triggering condition." The affidavit at issue here, for instance, explained that "[e]xecution of th[e] search warrant will not occur unless and until the parcel [containing child pornography] has been received by a person(s) and has been physically taken into the residence." If the government were to execute an anticipatory warrant before the triggering condition occurred, there would be no reason to believe the item described in the warrant could be found at the searched location; by definition, the triggering condition which establishes probable cause has not yet been satisfied when the warrant is issued. Grubbs argues that for this reason anticipatory warrants contravene the Fourth Amendment's provision that "no Warrants shall issue, but upon probable cause."

We reject this view, as has every Court of Appeals to confront the issue. Probable cause exists when "there is a fair probability that contraband or evidence of a crime will be found in a particular place." *Illinois v. Gates,*

462 U.S. 213, 238 (1983). Because the probable-cause requirement looks to whether evidence will be found when the search is conducted, all warrants are, in a sense, "anticipatory." In the typical case where the police seek permission to search a house for an item they believe is already located there, the magistrate's determination that there is probable cause for the search amounts to a prediction that the item will still be there when the warrant is executed.[2] The anticipatory nature of warrants is even clearer in the context of electronic surveillance. When police request approval to tap a telephone line, they do so based on the probability that, during the course of the surveillance, the subject will use the phone to engage in crime-related conversations. The relevant federal provision requires a judge authorizing "interception of wire, oral, or electronic communications" to determine that "there is probable cause for belief that particular communications concerning [one of various listed offenses] will be obtained through such interception." Thus, when an anticipatory warrant is issued, "the fact that the contraband is not presently located at the place described in the warrant is immaterial, so long as there is probable cause to believe that it will be there when the search warrant is executed."

Anticipatory warrants are, therefore, no different in principle from ordinary warrants. They require the magistrate to determine (1) that it is now probable that (2) contraband, evidence of a crime, or a fugitive will be on the described premises (3) when the warrant is executed. It should be noted, however, that where the anticipatory warrant places a condition (other than the mere passage of time) upon its execution, the first of these determinations goes not merely to what will probably be found if the condition is met. (If that were the extent of the probability determination, an anticipatory warrant could be issued for every house in the country, authorizing search and seizure if contraband should be delivered—though for any single location there is no likelihood that contraband will be delivered.) Rather, the probability determination for a conditioned anticipatory warrant looks also to the likelihood that the condition will occur and, thus, that a proper object of seizure will be on the described premises. In other words, for a conditioned anticipatory warrant to comply with the Fourth Amendment's requirement of probable cause, two prerequisites of probability must be satisfied. It must be true not only that if the triggering condition occurs "there is a fair probability that contraband or evidence of a crime will be found in a particular place" but also that there is probable cause to believe the triggering condition will occur. The supporting affidavit must provide the magistrate with sufficient information to evaluate both aspects of the probable-cause determination.

---

[2] For this reason, probable cause may cease to exist after a warrant is issued. The police may learn, for instance, that contraband is no longer located at the place to be searched. Or the probable-cause showing may have grown "stale" in view of the time that has passed since the warrant was issued.

In this case, the occurrence of the triggering condition—successful delivery of the videotape to Grubbs' residence—would plainly establish probable cause for the search. In addition, the affidavit established probable cause to believe the triggering condition would be satisfied. Although it is possible that Grubbs could have refused delivery of the videotape he had ordered, that was unlikely. The Magistrate therefore "had a 'substantial basis for . . . conclud[ing]' that probable cause existed."

III

The Ninth Circuit invalidated the anticipatory search warrant at issue here because the warrant failed to specify the triggering condition. The Fourth Amendment's particularity requirement, it held, "applies with full force to the conditions precedent to an anticipatory search warrant."

The Fourth Amendment, however, does not set forth some general "particularity requirement." It specifies only two matters that must be "particularly describ[ed]" in the warrant: "the place to be searched" and "the persons or things to be seized." We have previously rejected efforts to expand the scope of this provision to embrace unenumerated matters. In *Dalia v. United States*, 441 U.S. 238 (1979), we considered an order authorizing the interception of oral communications by means of a "bug" installed by the police in the petitioner's office. The petitioner argued that, if a covert entry is necessary to install such a listening device, the authorizing order must "explicitly set forth its approval of such entries before the fact." This argument fell before the "precise and clear" words of the Fourth Amendment: "Nothing in the language of the Constitution or in this Court's decisions interpreting that language suggests that, in addition to the [requirements set forth in the text], search warrants also must include a specification of the precise manner in which they are to be executed." The language of the Fourth Amendment is likewise decisive here; its particularity requirement does not include the conditions precedent to execution of the warrant. * * *

* * *

* * * The judgment of the Court of Appeals is reversed, and the case is remanded for further proceedings consistent with this opinion.

It is so ordered.

JUSTICE ALITO took no part in the consideration or decision of this case.

JUSTICE SOUTER, with whom JUSTICE STEVENS and JUSTICE GINSBURG join, concurring in part and concurring in the judgment.

[Omitted.]

QUESTIONS, COMMENTS, CONCERNS?

1.   **Gacy & good faith.** Even on January 25, 1983, the idea of *United States v. Leon* (Chapter 2) was on the minds of savvy prosecutors. Remember that Gacy argued that, for a variety of reasons, the first (i.e., December 13) search warrant was invalid. As a closing argument in response to Gacy's contentions, the state argued as follows: "it should be noted that all searches in this case were formed by the officers in good faith reliance on search warrants which they had every reason to believe were valid." [Casefile Document 2, at 42.] *Leon* would not come out for another year—on July 5, 1984—but the Gacy fact pattern reminds us that *Leon*'s good faith rationale consistently serves as a powerful backup argument for prosecutors in a variety of suppression contexts. Can you see any reason why, even if Gacy successfully argued for the invalidity of the first warrant, *Leon* would not save admission of the class ring and Nissen's Pharmacy receipt? In many ways, Gacy's case also illustrates why we studied *Leon* so early in the course—we should be mindful of *Leon*'s potential applicability throughout our Fourth Amendment journey.

2.   **Gacy, independent source, and inevitably discovery.** Although it never explicitly created an independent point-heading, the state's brief periodically injects independent source and inevitable discovery concepts into its filing. Consider a couple of examples:

- "Evidence leading to Gacy's conviction of the murders of Robert Piest and John Szyc was independently obtained and would have come to light had the first warrant never existed." [Casefile Document 2, at 37.]

- "Szyc's body was found in the crawl space under the Gacy house following the discovery of other human remains pursuant to the execution of the second search warrant. This body would have been found and identified had the first warrant never been executed." *Id.* at 41.

Given the increasing focus investigators placed on Gacy, do you agree that law enforcement would have inevitably discovered the mass graves under his home?

FLORIDA V. HARRIS

568 U.S. 237
Supreme Court of the United States
October 31, 2012, Argued; February 19, 2013, Decided
No. 11-817

JUSTICE KAGAN delivered the opinion of the Court.

In this case, we consider how a court should determine if the "alert" of a drug-detection dog during a traffic stop provides probable cause to search a vehicle. The Florida Supreme Court held that the State must in every case present an exhaustive set of records, including a log of the dog's performance in the field, to establish the dog's reliability. We think that demand inconsistent with the "flexible, common-sense standard" of probable cause. *Illinois v. Gates*, 462 U.S. 213, 239 (1983).

I

William Wheetley is a K-9 Officer in the Liberty County, Florida Sheriff's Office. On June 24, 2006, he was on a routine patrol with Aldo, a German shepherd trained to detect certain narcotics (methamphetamine, marijuana, cocaine, heroin, and ecstasy). Wheetley pulled over respondent Clayton Harris's truck because it had an expired license plate. On approaching the driver's-side door, Wheetley saw that Harris was "visibly nervous," unable to sit still, shaking, and breathing rapidly. Wheetley also noticed an open can of beer in the truck's cup holder. Wheetley asked Harris for consent to search the truck, but Harris refused. At that point, Wheetley retrieved Aldo from the patrol car and walked him around Harris's truck for a "free air sniff." Aldo alerted at the driver's-side door handle—signaling, through a distinctive set of behaviors, that he smelled drugs there.

Wheetley concluded, based principally on Aldo's alert, that he had probable cause to search the truck. His search did not turn up any of the drugs Aldo was trained to detect. But it did reveal 200 loose pseudoephedrine pills, 8,000 matches, a bottle of hydrochloric acid, two containers of antifreeze, and a coffee filter full of iodine crystals—all ingredients for making methamphetamine. Wheetley accordingly arrested Harris, who admitted after proper Miranda warnings that he routinely "cooked" methamphetamine at his house and could not go "more than a few days without using" it. The State charged Harris with possessing pseudoephedrine for use in manufacturing methamphetamine.

While out on bail, Harris had another run-in with Wheetley and Aldo. This time, Wheetley pulled Harris over for a broken brake light. Aldo again sniffed the truck's exterior, and again alerted at the driver's-side door handle. Wheetley once more searched the truck, but on this occasion discovered nothing of interest.

Harris moved to suppress the evidence found in his truck on the ground that Aldo's alert had not given Wheetley probable cause for a search. At the hearing on that motion, Wheetley testified about both his and Aldo's training in drug detection. In 2004, Wheetley (and a different dog) completed a 160-hour course in narcotics detection offered by the Dothan, Alabama Police Department, while Aldo (and a different handler) completed a similar, 120-hour course given by the Apopka, Florida Police Department. That same year, Aldo received a one-year certification from Drug Beat, a private company that specializes in testing and certifying K-9 dogs. Wheetley and Aldo teamed up in 2005 and went through another,

40-hour refresher course in Dothan together. They also did four hours of training exercises each week to maintain their skills. Wheetley would hide drugs in certain vehicles or buildings while leaving others "blank" to determine whether Aldo alerted at the right places. According to Wheetley, Aldo's performance in those exercises was "really good." The State introduced "Monthly Canine Detection Training Logs" consistent with that testimony: They showed that Aldo always found hidden drugs and that he performed "satisfactorily" (the higher of two possible assessments) on each day of training.

On cross-examination, Harris's attorney chose not to contest the quality of Aldo's or Wheetley's training. She focused instead on Aldo's certification and his performance in the field, particularly the two stops of Harris's truck. Wheetley conceded that the certification (which, he noted, Florida law did not require) had expired the year before he pulled Harris over. Wheetley also acknowledged that he did not keep complete records of Aldo's performance in traffic stops or other field work; instead, he maintained records only of alerts resulting in arrests. But Wheetley defended Aldo's two alerts to Harris's seemingly narcotics-free truck: According to Wheetley, Harris probably transferred the odor of methamphetamine to the door handle, and Aldo responded to that "residual odor."

The trial court concluded that Wheetley had probable cause to search Harris's truck and so denied the motion to suppress. Harris then entered a no-contest plea while reserving the right to appeal the trial court's ruling. An intermediate state court summarily affirmed.

The Florida Supreme Court reversed, holding that Wheetley lacked probable cause to search Harris's vehicle under the Fourth Amendment. "[W]hen a dog alerts," the court wrote, "the fact that the dog has been trained and certified is simply not enough to establish probable cause." To demonstrate a dog's reliability, the State needed to produce a wider array of evidence:

> [T]he State must present . . . the dog's training and certification records, an explanation of the meaning of the particular training and certification, field performance records (including any unverified alerts), and evidence concerning the experience and training of the officer handling the dog, as well as any other objective evidence known to the officer about the dog's reliability.

The court particularly stressed the need for "evidence of the dog's performance history," including records showing "how often the dog has alerted in the field without illegal contraband having been found." That data, the court stated, could help to expose such problems as a handler's tendency (conscious or not) to "cue [a] dog to alert" and "a dog's inability to distinguish between residual odors and actual drugs." Accordingly, an officer like Wheetley who did not keep full records of his dog's field performance could never have the requisite cause to think "that the dog is a reliable indicator of drugs." * * *

We granted certiorari and now reverse.

II

A police officer has probable cause to conduct a search when "the facts available to [him] would 'warrant a [person] of reasonable caution in the belief'" that contraband or evidence of a crime is present. * * * All we have required is the kind of "fair probability" on which "reasonable and prudent [people,] not legal technicians, act."

In evaluating whether the State has met this practical and commonsensical standard, we have consistently looked to the totality of the circumstances. * * * Probable cause, we [have] emphasized, is "a fluid concept—turning on the assessment of probabilities in particular factual contexts—not readily, or even usefully, reduced to a neat set of legal rules."

The Florida Supreme Court flouted this established approach to determining probable cause. To assess the reliability of a drug-detection dog, the court created a strict evidentiary checklist, whose every item the State must tick off. Most prominently, an alert cannot establish probable cause under the Florida court's decision unless the State introduces comprehensive documentation of the dog's prior "hits" and "misses" in the field. (One wonders how the court would apply its test to a rookie dog.) No matter how much other proof the State offers of the dog's reliability, the absent field performance records will preclude a finding of probable cause. That is the antithesis of a totality-of-the-circumstances analysis. * * *

Making matters worse, the decision below treats records of a dog's field performance as the gold standard in evidence, when in most cases they have relatively limited import. Errors may abound in such records. If a dog on patrol fails to alert to a car containing drugs, the mistake usually will go undetected because the officer will not initiate a search. Field data thus may not capture a dog's false negatives. Conversely (and more relevant here), if the dog alerts to a car in which the officer finds no narcotics, the dog may not have made a mistake at all. The dog may have detected substances that were too well hidden or present in quantities too small for the officer to locate. Or the dog may have smelled the residual odor of drugs previously in the vehicle or on the driver's person. Field data thus may markedly overstate a dog's real false positives. * * *

For that reason, evidence of a dog's satisfactory performance in a certification or training program can itself provide sufficient reason to trust his alert. If a bona fide organization has certified a dog after testing his reliability in a controlled setting, a court can presume (subject to any conflicting evidence offered) that the dog's alert provides probable cause to search. The same is true, even in the absence of formal certification, if the dog has recently and successfully completed a training program that evaluated his proficiency in locating drugs. After all, law enforcement units have their own strong incentive to use effective training and certification programs, because only accurate drug-detection dogs enable officers to locate contraband without incurring unnecessary risks or wasting limited time and resources.

A defendant, however, must have an opportunity to challenge such evidence of a dog's reliability, whether by cross-examining the testifying officer or by introducing his own fact or expert witnesses. The defendant, for example, may contest the adequacy of a certification or training program, perhaps asserting that its standards are too lax or its methods faulty. So too, the defendant may examine how the dog (or handler) performed in the assessments made in those settings. Indeed, evidence of the dog's (or handler's) history in the field, although susceptible to the kind of misinterpretation we have discussed, may sometimes be relevant, as the Solicitor General acknowledged at oral argument. And even assuming a dog is generally reliable, circumstances surrounding a particular alert may undermine the case for probable cause—if, say, the officer cued the dog (consciously or not), or if the team was working under unfamiliar conditions.

In short, a probable-cause hearing focusing on a dog's alert should proceed much like any other. The court should allow the parties to make their best case, consistent with the usual rules of criminal procedure. And the court should then evaluate the proffered evidence to decide what all the circumstances demonstrate. If the State has produced proof from controlled settings that a dog performs reliably in detecting drugs, and the defendant has not contested that showing, then the court should find probable cause. If, in contrast, the defendant has challenged the State's case (by disputing the reliability of the dog overall or of a particular alert), then the court should weigh the competing evidence. In all events, the court should not prescribe, as the Florida Supreme Court did, an inflexible set of evidentiary requirements. The question—similar to every inquiry into probable cause—is whether all the facts surrounding a dog's alert, viewed through the lens of common sense, would make a reasonably prudent person think that a search would reveal contraband or evidence of a crime. A sniff is up to snuff when it meets that test.

III

And here, Aldo's did. The record in this case amply supported the trial court's determination that Aldo's alert gave Wheetley probable cause to search Harris's truck.

The State, as earlier described, introduced substantial evidence of Aldo's training and his proficiency in finding drugs. The State showed that two years before alerting to Harris's truck, Aldo had successfully completed a 120-hour program in narcotics detection, and separately obtained a certification from an independent company. And although the certification expired after a year, the Sheriff's Office required continuing training for Aldo and Wheetley. The two satisfied the requirements of another, 40-hour training program one year prior to the search at issue. And Wheetley worked with Aldo for four hours each week on exercises designed to keep their skills sharp. Wheetley testified, and written records confirmed, that in those settings Aldo always performed at the highest level.

Harris, as also noted above, declined to challenge in the trial court any aspect of Aldo's training. To be sure, Harris's briefs in this Court raise questions about that training's adequacy—for example, whether the programs simulated sufficiently diverse environments and whether they used enough blind testing (in which the handler does not know the location of drugs and so cannot cue the dog). Similarly, Harris here queries just how well Aldo performed in controlled testing. But Harris never voiced those doubts in the trial court, and cannot do so for the first time here. As the case came to the trial court, Aldo had successfully completed two recent drug-detection courses and maintained his proficiency through weekly training exercises. Viewed alone, that training record—with or without the prior certification—sufficed to establish Aldo's reliability.

And Harris's cross-examination of Wheetley, which focused on Aldo's field performance, failed to rebut the State's case. Harris principally contended in the trial court that because Wheetley did not find any of the substances Aldo was trained to detect, Aldo's two alerts must have been false. But we have already described the hazards of inferring too much from the failure of a dog's alert to lead to drugs, and here we doubt that Harris's logic does justice to Aldo's skills. Harris cooked and used methamphetamine on a regular basis; so as Wheetley later surmised, Aldo likely responded to odors that Harris had transferred to the driver's-side door handle of his truck. A well-trained drug-detection dog should alert to such odors; his response to them might appear a mistake, but in fact is not. And still more fundamentally, we do not evaluate probable cause in hindsight, based on what a search does or does not turn up. For the reasons already stated, Wheetley had good cause to view Aldo as a reliable detector of drugs. And no special circumstance here gave Wheetley reason to discount Aldo's usual dependability or distrust his response to Harris's truck.

Because training records established Aldo's reliability in detecting drugs and Harris failed to undermine that showing, we agree with the trial court that Wheetley had probable cause to search Harris's truck. We accordingly reverse the judgment of the Florida Supreme Court.

It is so ordered.

QUESTIONS, COMMENTS, CONCERNS?

1.   **The rest of the Gacy story.** Shortly after officers discovered human remains on December 21, Gacy would tell police that he had thrown four additional corpses into the Des Planes River. Gacy was convicted on thirty-three counts of murder, one count of sexual assault, and one count of indecent liberties with a child. He was executed by lethal injection at the age of fifty-two on May 10, 1994. For his last meal, Gacy asked for fried shrimp, French fries, and, you guessed it, a bucket of original recipe KFC. Gacy's last words were, "Kiss my ass."

The impact of Gacy's crimes and trial has reverberated for years. Gacy's trial attorney, Sam Amirante, published a book in 2012 called *Defending a Monster*, which in part detailed the personal struggles he faced while representing Gacy. And while awaiting execution, Gacy became a prolific painter. After his death, the topic of displaying his artwork has become a controversial one. CNN Wire Staff, *Controversial Serial Killer's Paintings Go On Display in Las Vegas*, CNN.COM (May 13, 2011), http://www.cnn.com/2011/US/05/13/serial.killer.art/index.html.

Conversations about Gacy and his legacy continue to this day. For example, some have likened Bill Cosby's ability to hide his sinister side to Gacy's. John Blake, *He Was Seen As a Hero. Then They Discovered He Was Something Else*, CNN.COM (May 12, 2018), https://www.cnn.com/2018/05/12/us/public-private-double-life/index.html. The mother of a Gacy victim has been searching for her boy's remains for forty years. Larry Portash, *Mother of Boy Thought to be Gacy Victim Hoping New Information Leads to Answers*, WGNTV.COM (Apr. 30, 2018), http://wgntv.com/2018/04/30/mother-of-boy-thought-to-be-gacy-victim-hoping-new-information-leads-to-answers/.

And finally, an adult came forward telling a story that he could have been Gacy's first victim. Burt Constable, *Man Says He Could Have Been John Wayne Gacy's first victim*, PJSTAR.COM (May 5, 2018), https://www.pjstar.com/story/news/crime/2018/05/06/man-says-he-could-have/12301664007/.

C.   PROBABLE CAUSE TO DO WHAT?

The next case, *Whren v. United States*, makes constitutional what is now known as the "pretextual stop." In a pretextual stop, an officer executes a traffic stop for something innocuous—like failure to use a signal while changing lanes—but actually suspects that the driver unlawfully possesses a controlled substance. The lawful traffic stop serves as a pretext to enable officers to explore their suspicions about the driver's involvement in other criminal activity. In that scenario, the officer's probable cause goes with the traffic *stop*—not the officer's suspicion about the driver's involvement with drugs. *Whren*, policy concerns aside (of which there are many), serves as an important reminder to always understand that probable cause must be specifically linked to a specific governmental action—probable cause to *search*, probable cause to *arrest*, or probable cause to *seize* property.

WHREN V. UNITED STATES

517 U.S. 806
Supreme Court of the United States
April 17, 1996, Argued; June 10, 1996, Decided
No. 95-5841

JUSTICE SCALIA delivered the opinion of the Court.

In this case we decide whether the temporary detention of a motorist who the police have probable cause to believe has committed a civil traffic violation is inconsistent with the Fourth Amendment's prohibition against unreasonable seizures unless a reasonable officer would have been motivated to stop the car by a desire to enforce the traffic laws.

I

On the evening of June 10, 1993, plainclothes vice-squad officers of the District of Columbia Metropolitan Police Department were patrolling a "high drug area" of the city in an unmarked car. Their suspicions were aroused when they passed a dark Pathfinder truck with temporary license plates and youthful occupants waiting at a stop sign, the driver looking down into the lap of the passenger at his right. The truck remained stopped at the intersection for what seemed an unusually long time—more than 20 seconds. When the police car executed a U-turn in order to head back toward the truck, the Pathfinder turned suddenly to its right, without signaling, and sped off at an "unreasonable" speed. The policemen followed, and in a short while overtook the Pathfinder when it stopped behind other traffic at a red light. They pulled up alongside, and Officer Ephraim Soto stepped out and approached the driver's door, identifying himself as a police officer and directing the driver, petitioner Brown, to put the vehicle in park. When Soto drew up to the driver's window, he immediately observed two large plastic bags of what appeared to be crack cocaine in petitioner Whren's hands. Petitioners were arrested, and quantities of several types of illegal drugs were retrieved from the vehicle.

Petitioners were charged in a four-count indictment with violating various federal drug laws * * *. At a pretrial suppression hearing, they challenged the legality of the stop and the resulting seizure of the drugs. They argued that the stop had not been justified by probable cause to believe, or even reasonable suspicion, that petitioners were engaged in illegal drug-dealing activity; and that Officer Soto's asserted ground for approaching the vehicle—to give the driver a warning concerning traffic violations—was pretextual. The District Court denied the suppression motion, concluding that "the facts of the stop were not controverted" and "there was nothing to really demonstrate that the actions of the officers were contrary to a normal traffic stop."

Petitioners were convicted of the counts at issue here. The Court of Appeals affirmed the convictions, holding with respect to the suppression issue that, "regardless of whether a police officer subjectively believes that the occupants of an automobile may be engaging in some other illegal behavior, a traffic stop is permissible as long as a reasonable officer in the same circumstances could have stopped the car for the suspected traffic violation." We granted certiorari.

II

The Fourth Amendment guarantees "the right of the people to be secure in their persons, houses, papers, and effects, against unreasonable searches and seizures." Temporary detention of individuals during the stop of an automobile by the police, even if only for a brief period and for a limited purpose, constitutes a "seizure" of "persons" within the meaning of this provision. An automobile stop is thus subject to the constitutional imperative that it not be "unreasonable" under the circumstances. As a general matter, the decision to stop an automobile is reasonable where the police have probable cause to believe that a traffic violation has occurred.

Petitioners accept that Officer Soto had probable cause to believe that various provisions of the District of Columbia traffic code had been violated. *See* 18 D.C. Mun. Regs. §§ 2213.4 (1995) ("An operator shall . . . give full time and attention to the operation of the vehicle"); 2204.3 ("No person shall turn any vehicle . . . without giving an appropriate signal"); 2200.3 ("No person shall drive a vehicle . . . at a speed greater than is reasonable and prudent under the conditions"). They argue, however, that "in the unique context of civil traffic regulations" probable cause is not enough. Since, they contend, the use of automobiles is so heavily and minutely regulated that total compliance with traffic and safety rules is nearly impossible, a police officer will almost invariably be able to catch any given motorist in a technical violation. This creates the temptation to use traffic stops as a means of investigating other law violations, as to which no probable cause or even articulable suspicion exists. Petitioners, who are both black, further contend that police officers might decide which motorists to stop based on decidedly impermissible factors, such as the race of the car's occupants. To avoid this danger, they say, the Fourth Amendment test for traffic stops should be, not the normal one (applied by the Court of Appeals) of whether probable cause existed to justify the stop; but rather, whether a police officer, acting reasonably, would have made the stop for the reason given.

A

Petitioners contend that the standard they propose is consistent with our past cases' disapproval of police attempts to use valid bases of action against citizens as pretexts for pursuing other investigatory agendas. * * * But only an undiscerning reader would regard these cases as endorsing the principle that ulterior motives can invalidate police conduct that is justifiable on the basis of probable cause to believe that a violation of law has occurred. * * *

We think these cases foreclose any argument that the constitutional reasonableness of traffic stops depends on the actual motivations of the individual officers involved. We of course agree with petitioners that the Constitution prohibits selective enforcement of the law based on considerations such as race. But the constitutional basis for objecting to intentionally discriminatory application of laws is the Equal Protection Clause, not the Fourth Amendment. Subjective intentions play no role in ordinary, probable-cause Fourth Amendment analysis.

B

Recognizing that we have been unwilling to entertain Fourth Amendment challenges based on the actual motivations of individual officers, petitioners disavow any intention to make the individual officer's subjective good faith the touchstone of "reasonableness." They insist that the standard they have put forward—whether the officer's conduct deviated materially from usual police practices, so that a reasonable officer in the same circumstances would not have made the stop for the reasons given—is an "objective" one.

But although framed in empirical terms, this approach is plainly and indisputably driven by subjective considerations. Its whole purpose is to prevent the police from doing under the guise of enforcing the traffic code what they would like to do for different reasons. Petitioners' proposed standard may not use the word "pretext," but it is designed to combat nothing other than the perceived "danger" of the pretextual stop, albeit only indirectly and over the run of cases. Instead of asking whether the individual officer had the proper state of mind, the petitioners would have us ask, in effect, whether (based on general police practices) it is plausible to believe that the officer had the proper state of mind.

Why one would frame a test designed to combat pretext in such fashion that the court cannot take into account actual and admitted pretext is a curiosity that can only be explained by the fact that our cases have foreclosed the more sensible option. If those cases were based only upon the evidentiary difficulty of establishing subjective intent, petitioners' attempt to root out subjective vices through objective means might make sense. But they were not based only upon that or indeed even principally upon that. Their principal basis—which applies equally to attempts to reach subjective intent through ostensibly objective means—is simply that the Fourth Amendment's concern with "reasonableness" allows certain actions to be taken in certain circumstances, whatever the subjective intent. But even if our concern had been only an evidentiary one, petitioners' proposal would by no means assuage it. Indeed, it seems to us somewhat easier to figure out the intent of an individual officer than to plumb the collective consciousness of law enforcement in order to determine whether a "reasonable officer" would have been moved to act upon the traffic violation. While police manuals and standard procedures may sometimes provide objective assistance, ordinarily one would be reduced to speculating about the hypothetical reaction of a hypothetical constable— an exercise that might be called virtual subjectivity.

Moreover, police enforcement practices, even if they could be practicably assessed by a judge, vary from place to place and from time to time. We cannot accept that the search and seizure protections of the Fourth Amendment are so variable, and can be made to turn upon such trivialities. The difficulty is illustrated by petitioners' arguments in this case. Their claim that a reasonable officer would not have made this stop is based largely on District of Columbia police regulations which permit plainclothes officers in unmarked vehicles to enforce traffic laws "only in the case of a violation that is so grave as to pose an immediate threat to the safety of others." This basis of invalidation would not apply in jurisdictions that had a different practice. And it would not have applied even in the District of Columbia, if Officer Soto had been wearing a uniform or patrolling in a marked police cruiser. * * *

III.

In what would appear to be an elaboration on the "reasonable officer" test, petitioners argue that the balancing inherent in any Fourth Amendment inquiry requires us to weigh the governmental and individual interests implicated in a traffic stop such as we have here. That balancing, petitioners claim, does not support investigation of minor traffic infractions by plainclothes police in unmarked vehicles; such investigation only minimally advances the government's interest in traffic safety, and may indeed retard it by producing motorist confusion and alarm—a view said to be supported by the Metropolitan Police Department's own regulations generally prohibiting this practice. And as for the Fourth Amendment interests of the individuals concerned, petitioners point out that our cases acknowledge that even ordinary traffic stops entail "a possibly unsettling show of authority;" that they at best "interfere with freedom of movement, are inconvenient, and consume time" and at worst "may create substantial anxiety." That anxiety is likely to be even more pronounced when the stop is conducted by plainclothes officers in unmarked cars.

It is of course true that in principle every Fourth Amendment case, since it turns upon a "reasonableness" determination, involves a balancing of all relevant factors. With rare exceptions not applicable here, however, the result of that balancing is not in doubt where the search or seizure is based upon probable cause. * * *

Where probable cause has existed, the only cases in which we have found it necessary actually to perform the "balancing" analysis involved searches or seizures conducted in an extraordinary manner, unusually harmful to an individual's privacy or even physical interests—such as, for example, seizure by means of deadly force, unannounced entry into a home, entry into a home without a warrant, or physical penetration of the body. The making of a traffic stop out of uniform does not remotely qualify as such an extreme practice, and so is governed by the usual rule that probable cause to believe the law has been broken "outbalances" private interest in avoiding police contact.

Petitioners urge as an extraordinary factor in this case that the "multitude of applicable traffic and equipment regulations" is so large and so difficult to obey perfectly that virtually everyone is guilty of violation, permitting the police to single out almost whomever they wish for a stop. But we are aware of no principle that would allow us to decide at what point a code of law becomes so expansive and so commonly violated that infraction itself can no longer be the ordinary measure of the lawfulness of enforcement. And even if we could identify such exorbitant codes, we do not know by what standard (or what right) we would decide, as petitioners would have us do, which particular provisions are sufficiently important to merit enforcement.

For the run-of-the-mine case, which this surely is, we think there is no realistic alternative to the traditional common-law rule that probable cause justifies a search and seizure.

* * *

Here the District Court found that the officers had probable cause to believe that petitioners had violated the traffic code. That rendered the stop reasonable under the Fourth Amendment, the evidence thereby discovered admissible, and the upholding of the convictions by the Court of Appeals for the District of Columbia Circuit correct. The judgment is

Affirmed.

QUESTIONS, COMMENTS, CONCERNS?

1. **Reasonable suspicion and pretextual stops.** Although *Whren* contemplates the role of probable cause to support a pretextual traffic stop, *Whren* seemingly applies in the lower courts to support traffic stops supported merely by reasonable suspicion. *See, e.g., United States v. Johnson,* 734 F.3d 270, 275 (4th Cir. 2013); *United States v. Diaz,* No. 2:16-cr-00055-DCN, 2018 U.S. Dist. LEXIS 58775, at *16–17 (D.S.C. Apr. 6, 2018); *State v. Ochoa,* 206 P.3d 143, 152 (N.M. Ct. App. 2008).

Since the 1980s, more than twenty states have decriminalized minor traffic violations as civil or noncriminal offenses. Courts in these jurisdictions that apply a reasonable suspicion standard to evaluate the constitutionality of initiated routine traffic stops are doing so even when the underlying traffic violation is not a crime. *See* Jordan Blair Woods, *Decriminalization, Police Authority, and Routine Traffic Stops*, 62 UCLA L. REV. 672, 712 (2015).

2.   What did the *Whren* Court know about the vice officers? Recall some of the relevant facts in *Whren*: "plainclothes vice-squad officers of the District of Columbia Metropolitan Police Department were patrolling a 'high drug area' of the city in an unmarked car." Think about that: vice-squad officers—officers typically tasked with monitoring crimes like prostitution, gambling, and narcotics—stopped petitioner's Pathfinder for *traffic violations*. Is traffic enforcement an appropriate task for vice-squad officers? That aside, the *Whren* Court named just one of the vice-squad officers involved in the traffic stop—Officer Ephraim Soto. Dig a bit deeper and you'll learn that Soto was accompanied that night by Homer Littlejohn. *United States v. Whren*, 53 F.3d 371, 372 (D.C. 1995).

Dig deeper still and the plot thickens. Soto and Littlejohn were members of the 6th District Vice Unit who, along with Anthony McGee and Lonnie Moses Jr., would in 2000 be accused of planting evidence, harassing citizens, and lying on the witness stand—among other infractions. Jason Cherkis, *Rough Justice: How Four Vice Officers Served as Judge and Jury on the Streets of the MPD's 6th District*, WASHINGTONCITYPAPER.COM (Jan. 7, 2000), https://www. washingtoncitypaper.com/news/article/13019154/rough-justice.

Littlejohn was later indicted for lying to a grand jury in 2003, although he was acquitted. Jason Cherkis, *Officer Acquitted of Lying*, WASHINGTONCITY PAPER.COM (Mar. 12, 2004), https://www.washingtoncitypaper.com/news/ article/13028617/officer-acquitted-of-lying; Jason Cherkis, *Stand and Deliver*, WASHINGTONCITYPAPER.COM (Dec. 19, 2003), https://www.washingtoncity paper.com/news/article/13028160/stand-and-deliver.

One wonders what, if anything, the Supreme Court knew in 1996 about the 6th District Vice Unit at the time it unanimously agreed on *Whren*. Does *Whren* come out differently if the Court knew about the 6th District Vice Unit's indiscretions?

III.   REASONABLE SUSPICION

A.   INTRODUCTION

As we discussed at the outset of this chapter, probable cause is at the heart of the Fourth Amendment. We also saw that probable cause serves as the justification for arrest just as it serves as the primary justification for searches (warrantless or otherwise). Prior to 1968 and the Court's opinion in *Terry v. Ohio*, 392 U.S. 1 (1968), probable cause was the *only* justification available to support those Fourth Amendment actions. Thus, in the pre-*Terry* context of seizures, the Fourth Amendment permitted just two scenarios: first, an ordinary police-citizen encounter, which is *not* a seizure and, second, an arrest. There was, in other words, no intermediate step between a police-citizen encounter and an arrest. Similarly, in the pre-*Terry* context of warrantless searches that originated based on police-citizen encounters, officers could only search a citizen following arrest. The search itself was a full search of the person of the arrestee.

Practically, then, officers pre-*Terry* had only one choice when interacting with a citizen: arrest or not. That, in turn, required the officer to make an on-the-spot determination about the existence or absence of probable cause to arrest. Consider the pre-*Terry* officer's choice expressed in this simple illustration:

Pre-Terry Seizures

Police-citizen encounter   Arrest

|————————————————————————————►|

Fourth Amendment inapplicable   Probable cause required

Pre-Terry (Warrantless) Searches

Police-citizen encounter   Search incident to arrest

|————————————————————————————►|

Fourth Amendment inapplicable   Probable cause to arrest required

Terry established that both seizures and searches can vary in their levels of intrusiveness. In the context of seizures, *Terry* recognized that, although all arrests are Fourth Amendment seizures, not all Fourth Amendment seizures constitute arrests. Thus, somewhat confusingly, there now exists an entirely separate category of Fourth Amendment seizures—called *Terry* stops—that are both not arrests and do not require probable cause as a supporting justification.

Terry also altered the search landscape. As a result of *Terry*, many police-citizen encounters that do not produce arrests and corresponding searches incident to those arrests are permissible in the absence of a warrant or probable cause. Those interactions, colloquially called *Terry* "frisks," permit an officer to perform a limited pat down of the suspect's outer clothing for weapons in the interest of officer safety. Each new limited seizure (the stop) and search (the frisk) is justified, *Terry* teaches, by the presence of a new, less-demanding standard: reasonable suspicion ("RS").

Collectively, after *Terry*, there are (for searches and seizures alike) police-citizen encounters that can mature into something *less* than either an arrest or full-blown search. Practically, that translates into an increase in an officer's choices during a police-citizen encounter. Consider the doctrinal changes brought about by *Terry* via these illustrations:

Post-Terry Seizures

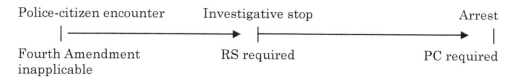

Post-Terry (Warrantless) Searches

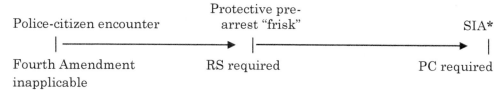

* Search incident to arrest

Terry is perhaps best known by its other name: "stop and frisk." Be warned, that title is misleading. Doctrinally, it's critical for you to keep the stop separate from the frisk. The officer who has reasonable suspicion to execute a *Terry* stop does not necessarily have the same suspicion to conduct a frisk. Regardless of the temptation to conduct a frisk following *every* stop, the *Terry* majority contemplated a separation between the two. An officer should therefore only conduct a frisk if, during the stop, "nothing in the initial stages of the encounter serves to dispel [the officer's] reasonable fear for his own or others' safety." *Terry*, 392 U.S. at 30. Stated more simply, an officer must have reasonable suspicion to support the stop (a concern that criminal activity is afoot) and separate reasonable suspicion to support the frisk (a concern that the citizen may be armed and dangerous).

Beyond its doctrinal impact, *Terry* is, for two main reasons, one of the most significant historical opinions in this Casebook. First, *Terry* is a dramatically misunderstood opinion. As the New York litigation in our Casefile for this chapter demonstrates, *Terry* is often blamed for permitting expansive and unchecked police discretion. That discretion, in turn, can lead to police abuse, that is, routinely stopping and frisking citizens who live in minority communities. But contrary to the modern controversy surrounding police stop and frisk policies, the *Terry* doctrine was created, perhaps to your surprise, as a way to *limit*—not expand—police discretion.

Step back for a moment to consider what was happening—and how much was happening—in America around the time of *Terry*. Recall that *Terry* was argued in 1967, just as U.S. military involvement in Vietnam increased.[6] As criticism of that involvement also increased, so too did the conflict itself. The conflict peaked with the Viet Cong Tet Offensive, and Americans grew increasingly concerned about whether the war could be won following the Tet Offensive. Yet the public was also deeply concerned about poverty, civil rights, the threat of nuclear war, and environmental issues. The division in American popular thought was perhaps best illustrated by the 1968 election of Richard Nixon as President, who earned only 43.5 % of the popular vote.

Even as the Vietnam War began to deescalate at the close of the decade, societal chaos continued. On April 4, 1968, months before *Terry* was decided, Dr. Martin Luther King's assassination in Memphis sparked rioting in the city and required the aid of 4,000 National Guardsmen. Collectively, the social tensions arising from the Vietnam War and the civil rights movement gave rise to mass demonstrations and protests unlike any the country had ever seen. For example, nearly 150 American cities experienced civil unrest in the summer of 1967 alone. Law enforcement officials were often uncertain as to the appropriate responses and measures of force to use in light of these unprecedented civil disturbances. In short, the police were encountering citizens outside of the custodial context in unprecedented numbers and concerns grew over the police response: to simply arrest everyone.

Terry was drafted against that tenuous political backdrop as a response to the growing concern about unchecked police discretion. Although Chief Justice Warren is credited with authoring the majority opinion, Justice Brennan's biographers tell a captivating behind-the-scenes story about how it was Brennan who ghost-wrote Warren's majority opinion:

> During the justices' private conference discussion of *Terry*, Brennan helped move his colleagues toward the view that any stop and frisk had to be supported by probable cause, as if there were an arrest and search being carried out. Because of his active role at the conference, Brennan was concerned when Warren decided to write the decision rather than assigning it to him.

> Brennan was further disappointed when Warren circulated his draft in January; it focused largely on the frisk rather than the initial question of whether the officer had justification to stop the suspect. Brennan sent Warren a long memo raising the concern that it would be difficult to control police conduct at the stage of the frisk, especially in a case in which a weapon was found, and that a probable-cause standard had to be imposed to justify the

---

[6] Portions of this paragraph and the subsequent paragraph are adapted from Brian Gallini, Schneckloth v. Bustamonte: *History's Unspoken Fourth Amendment Anomaly*. This article was published originally at 79 TENN. L. REV. 233, 239–40 (2012), and this portion, edited by the Author, appears by permission of the Tennessee Law Review Association, Inc.

initial stop of an individual. Other justices weighed in, and Warren's redraft did little to clarify the problem. Then Brennan took the highly unusual step of taking the comments of various other justices and Warren's draft and quietly writing his own version of the opinion. Despite the long, easy working relationship between the two men, Brennan was quite solicitous when he sent his version privately to Warren in mid-March, noting, "I hope you won't think me presumptuous to submit my thoughts in this form."

Two aspects of Brennan's new draft stood out, most of which Warren used as the core of the final opinion. First, Brennan expressed a deep concern that the tone of Warren's original drafts would encourage police to stop and frisk individuals freely, and so inflame civil rights passions against the police. As Brennan's law clerk Raymond Fisher later wrote in the annual term history, the chief justice's opinion was "written in a rhetoric almost embarrassingly sympathetic to the plight of the policeman." Brennan felt this approach would be likely to compound "the 'crime in the streets' alarms being sounded in this election year in the Congress, the White House and every Governor's office," as he wrote Warren.

Brennan also notably abandoned the use of probable cause as the required threshold for police to stop and frisk. Instead, he turned to the first clause of the Fourth Amendment, which prohibits "unreasonable searches." He said the reasonableness standard was the right measure, because probable cause was intended to provide an independent assessment by a judge prior to police activity; this was simply not a feasible approach to the immediacy of the stop-and-frisk situation.

The requirement that an officer have only "reasonable suspicion" and not probable cause for a stop and frisk became the rule adopted by the Court in the *Terry* case. It is one that remains controversial, since it gives law enforcement considerable leeway to justify stopping, questioning, and searching individuals on the street. Indeed, Brennan foresaw the controversy in his March 14 letter to Warren, but apparently viewed it as the more practical alternative. "In this lies the terrible risk that police will conjure up 'suspicious circumstances' and courts will credit their versions,' Brennan told Warren. Injecting the dimension of contemporary civil rights strife, Brennan added, "It will not take much of this to aggravate the already white hot resentment of ghetto Negroes against the police—and the Court will become the scapegoat."

SETH STERN & STEPHEN WERMIEL, JUSTICE BRENNAN: LIBERAL CHAMPION 299–300 (2010). Some of the concern about the role of race shows through in Chief Justice Warren's final majority opinion, where he notes the "wholesale harassment by certain elements of the police community, of which minority groups, particularly Negroes, frequently complain[.]" *Terry*, 392 U.S. at 14.

Terry is known for one more thing: designing the stop and frisk doctrine by categorically declining to apply the Warrant Clause. This new type of police-citizen encounter, said the Court, constituted "an entire rubric of police conduct—necessarily swift action predicated upon the on-the-spot observations of the officer on the beat—which historically has not been, and as a practical matter could not be, subjected to the warrant procedure." *Id.* at 20. The *Terry* Court's decision to exempt stop and frisk from the Warrant Clause fueled the existing debate about whether the Fourth Amendment presumptively *requires* a warrant or, rather, whether police action—warrant-based or warrantless—must simply be reasonable. It is less than clear, however, that the *Terry* Court meant to reignite that familiar debate or, rather, meant to confine notions of reasonableness solely to the stop and frisk context.[7] Indeed, just a year earlier in *Katz v. United States*, this same Warren Court wrote that "searches conducted outside the judicial process, without prior approval by judge or magistrate, are per se unreasonable under the Fourth Amendment—subject only to a few specifically established and well-delineated exceptions."[8] Thus, it's more than an ironic twist that the modern Supreme Court has often relied on *Terry*'s reasonableness analysis to assume that no warrant requirement exists. Rather, "the ultimate measure of the constitutionality of a governmental search is 'reasonableness.' "[9]

B. THE NEW YORK STOP & FRISK LITIGATION[10]

David Floyd, an African-American man, claimed that on February 27, 2008, he was walking on a path adjacent to his home in the Bronx, New York, when he encountered the tenant who lived in the basement apartment of his building. The tenant claimed that he was locked out of his apartment and asked Floyd for help because Floyd's godmother owned the building. Floyd claimed that he retrieved seven to ten keys from his

---

[7] Robert Berkley Harper, *Has the Replacement of "Probable Cause" with "Reasonable Suspicion" Resulted in the Creation of the Best of All Possible Worlds*, 22 AKRON L. REV. 13, 44 (1988) ("[T]he balancing test should only be used in those rare situations where there is a threat of irreversible physical danger to society which would require unfettered and immediate police action.").

[8] 389 U.S. 347, 357 (1967).

[9] *Maryland v. King*, 569 U.S. 435, 447 (2013) (internal citation and quotation marks omitted).

[10] Please note an absence from the Floyd litigation casefile in this chapter. Plaintiff's Response to Defendant's Motion for Summary Judgment was filed under seal and is therefore not included.

apartment, after which he and the tenant attempted to open the tenant's door. But before the two could get the door open, three NYPD officers approached them and asked the two what they were doing. They then instructed Floyd and the tenant to stop trying to open the door and proceeded to frisk them. The officers claimed that they stopped Floyd because they believed Floyd was committing a burglary. The officers sought to justify stopping Floyd by arguing that his behavior was suspicious and fit a pattern of recent burglaries for that time of day in Floyd's neighborhood.

Since 2002, police have conducted more than five million stops and street interrogations of New York City residents. Although New York City officials celebrated its controversial approach to stop-and-frisk as the reason the City's crime rate dropped, research conducted by the ACLU reflects that nearly nine out of ten stop-and-frisks failed to uncover contraband.[11] More troublingly, nearly 90 percent of those stopped were either Black or Hispanic.

But given the volume of stops by the NYPD, determining the constitutional legitimacy of each one became a nearly impossible task. The task of assessing the legitimacy of the NYPD's policy was made more complicated by the number of stops that did not produce criminal charges. A whopping four million residents fell in that category and were left without a judicial remedy to challenge the constitutionality of the NYPD's *Terry* policy.

The Center for Constitutional Rights turned to federal civil court seeking to challenge the NYPD's *Terry* practices. On January 31, 2008, the Center filed a lawsuit in the United States District Court for the Southern District of New York based on § 1983 of the Civil Rights Act, which allows citizens to sue state officials for violating constitutional rights. The Center's suit alleged that the NYPD's use of stop-and-frisk violated both the Fourth Amendment and the Equal Protection Clause of the Fourteenth Amendment of the United States Constitution. The suit was later certified as a class action lawsuit on behalf of New York City's minority citizens, with David Floyd listed as the named plaintiff.

As it turned out, a report from the New York State Attorney General's Office in early 1999 placed the City on notice that police were implementing the stop-and-frisk program in a racially skewed manner. In response, the City of New York adopted a reporting policy requiring each officer to prepare a "UF-250" form (pictured on the following page) for each of the officers' *Terry* stops. According to "UF-250" data, the NYPD conducted over 4.4 million *Terry* stops between January 2004 and June 2012. The number of stops per year rose sharply from 314,000 in 2004 to a high of 686,000 in 2011.

---

[11] NYCLU Stop-and-Frisk Data, NYCLU.ORG, https://www.nyclu.org/en/stop-and-frisk-data (last visited June 26, 2022).

The data further reflected that 52% of all stops were followed by a protective frisk for weapons. That frisk, however, revealed a weapon only 1.5% of the time. In 8% of all stops, officers searched the detained person's clothing based on the officer feeling an object during the frisk that he or she suspected to be a weapon. But only 9% of those searches disclosed a weapon and only 14% produced contraband. Collectively, only 6% of all stops produced an arrest and another 6% resulted in a summons. The remaining 88% of the 4.4 million stops produced no further law enforcement action.

The plaintiffs in *Floyd v. City of New York* claimed that this "UF-250" data established a clear racial bias in New York City's stop-and-frisk practices. The *Floyd* plaintiffs highlighted that in 52% of the 4.4 million stops, the individual stopped was Black and 31% of those stopped was Hispanic. By comparison, Whites represented just 10% of all *Terry* stops despite 2010 census data demonstrating that New York City's resident population was roughly 23% Black, 29% Hispanic, and 33% White. Alarmingly, 23% of the stops of Black individuals and 24% of the stops of Hispanics also involved officer use of force. The number for Whites was just 17%.

Still other troubling statistics emerged from the UF-250 data. For example, weapons were seized in just 1.0% of stops involving Blacks, 1.1% of the stops of Hispanics, and 1.4% of the stops of Whites. Weapons aside, contraband was seized in only 1.8% of the stops of Blacks, 1.7% of the stops of Hispanics, and 2.3% of the stops of Whites. And between 2004 and 2009, the percentage of stops where the officer failed to state a specific suspected crime rose from 11% to 36%.

When the *Floyd* case reached trial in 2013, evidence revealed that, in the years following 1999, New York City Officials as high as Mayors Giuliani and Bloomberg began pressuring NYPD supervisors to increase the number of *Terry* stops. Supervisors, in turn, pressured their officers to meet certain stop-and-frisk quotas, but failed to provide any adequate monitoring or supervision of the justification for those stops. Many officers testified that they were instructed to effectuate a certain number of stops or arrests or to issue a certain number of summonses per month. The *Floyd* plaintiffs also introduced evidence that the Patrolmen's Benevolent Association filed a labor grievance on behalf of six patrol officers and one sergeant who were transferred out of their precinct for allegedly failing to meet a ten summons-per-month quota. One officer even testified that he witnessed fellow officers stop civilians without reasonable suspicion and issue summonses without probable cause. He further testified that, on several occasions, he and his fellow officers were ordered by their supervisor to fill out UF-250 forms for *Terry* stops they did not conduct or observe and issue criminal summonses for incidents they did not observe.

APPENDIX B
Blank UF-250 Form

The UF-250 Form

After nearly six years of litigation—including a nine-week trial—United States District Judge Shira A. Scheindlin held that New York City's approach to stop-and-frisk violated the Fourth and Fourteenth Amendments to the United States Constitution. The court further held that the UF-250 forms used unreliable and subjective factors to justify the large number of stops. The court noted that officers had increasingly developed "scripts" for checking off stop factors in order to justify stopping individuals. Most troublingly, observed the court, was that the average number of stop factors checked on UF-250's increased and so too did officers' reliance on largely unverifiable subjective stop factors, like "Furtive Movements," "Evasive Response," "High Crime Area," and "Actions Indicative of Engaging in Violent Crimes."

In addition to the subjective nature of the New York stop-and-frisk procedure, the court found that NYPD supervisors, in their attempt to monitor and increase the number of stops, instituted policies to address the quantity of stops, but failed to oversee the constitutionality of those stops. The court therefore concluded that imposing numerical performance goals for enforcement activities, without providing effective safeguards, could permit an officer to execute a *Terry* stop in order to meet a performance goal, rather than because a violation of the law has either occurred, or is imminent.

In the aftermath, the court ordered the City of New York Police Department to adopt a written policy to specify when and under what circumstances an officer is allowed to conduct a *Terry* stop. Although the United States Court of Appeals for the Second Circuit initially blocked the order requiring changes to the stop-and-frisk program (and removed Judge Scheindlin from the case), the Court of Appeals ultimately declined to stay the district court's order. For some reason, the city then elected to drop its appeal. Since the *Floyd* litigation, the number of *Terry* stops in New York City has steadily decreased from a record high of 685,725 stops in 2011, to only 22,929 stops in 2015.

C. DEFINING THE DOCTRINE

We next consider the Supreme Court's landmark case in *Terry v. Ohio*. Remember, as noted earlier, *Terry* created an entirely new approach to policing on the street. Its specific creation of a "stop" provides officers with a basis to seize individuals—for a limited time—based on a degree of suspicion less than probable cause. And, correspondingly, the Court's creation of a "frisk" allowed officers to conduct a limited "search" of individuals in certain circumstances—also premised on a degree of suspicion less than probable cause. The case was and is momentous for so many reasons, one of which is that, prior to 1968, police-citizen encounters could produce only two results pursuant to Fourth Amendment doctrine: a "full blown" seizure or, instead, no seizure at all. *Terry* creates a middle-ground.

TERRY V. OHIO
392 U.S. 1
Supreme Court of the United States
December 12, 1967, Argued; June 10, 1968, Decided
No. 67

MR. CHIEF JUSTICE WARREN delivered the opinion of the Court.

This case presents serious questions concerning the role of the Fourth Amendment in the confrontation on the street between the citizen and the policeman investigating suspicious circumstances.

Petitioner Terry was convicted of carrying a concealed weapon and sentenced to the statutorily prescribed term of one to three years in the penitentiary.[1] Following the denial of a pretrial motion to suppress, the prosecution introduced in evidence two revolvers and a number of bullets

---

[1]   Ohio Rev. Code § 2923.01 (1953) provides in part that "no person shall carry a pistol, bowie knife, dirk, or other dangerous weapon concealed on or about his person." An exception is made for properly authorized law enforcement officers.

seized from Terry and a codefendant, Richard Chilton,[2] by Cleveland Police Detective Martin McFadden. At the hearing on the motion to suppress this evidence, Officer McFadden testified that while he was patrolling in plain clothes in downtown Cleveland at approximately 2:30 in the afternoon of October 31, 1963, his attention was attracted by two men, Chilton and Terry, standing on the corner of Huron Road and Euclid Avenue. He had never seen the two men before, and he was unable to say precisely what first drew his eye to them. However, he testified that he had been a policeman for 39 years and a detective for 35 and that he had been assigned to patrol this vicinity of downtown Cleveland for shoplifters and pickpockets for 30 years. He explained that he had developed routine habits of observation over the years and that he would "stand and watch people or walk and watch people at many intervals of the day." He added: "Now, in this case when I looked over they didn't look right to me at the time."

His interest aroused, Officer McFadden took up a post of observation in the entrance to a store 300 to 400 feet away from the two men. "I get more purpose to watch them when I seen their movements," he testified. He saw one of the men leave the other one and walk southwest on Huron Road, past some stores. The man paused for a moment and looked in a store window, then walked on a short distance, turned around, and walked back toward the corner, pausing once again to look in the same store window. He rejoined his companion at the corner, and the two conferred briefly. Then the second man went through the same series of motions, strolling down Huron Road, looking in the same window, walking on a short distance, turning back, peering in the store window again, and returning to confer with the first man at the corner. The two men repeated this ritual alternately between five and six times apiece—in all, roughly a dozen trips. At one point, while the two were standing together on the corner, a third man approached them and engaged them briefly in conversation. This man then left the two others and walked west on Euclid Avenue. Chilton and Terry resumed their measured pacing, peering, and conferring. After this had gone on for 10 to 12 minutes, the two men walked off together, heading west on Euclid Avenue, following the path taken earlier by the third man.

By this time, Officer McFadden had become thoroughly suspicious. He testified that after observing their elaborately casual and oft-repeated reconnaissance of the store window on Huron Road, he suspected the two

---

[2]   Terry and Chilton were arrested, indicted, tried, and convicted together. They were represented by the same attorney, and they made a joint motion to suppress the guns. After the motion was denied, evidence was taken in the case against Chilton. This evidence consisted of the testimony of the arresting officer and of Chilton. It was then stipulated that this testimony would be applied to the case against Terry, and no further evidence was introduced in that case. The trial judge considered the two cases together, rendered the decisions at the same time, and sentenced the two men at the same time. They prosecuted their state court appeals together through the same attorney, and they petitioned this Court for certiorari together. Following the grant of the writ upon this joint petition, Chilton died. Thus, only Terry's conviction is here for review.

men of "casing a job, a stick-up," and that he considered it his duty as a police officer to investigate further. He added that he feared "they may have a gun." Thus, Officer McFadden followed Chilton and Terry and saw them stop in front of Zucker's store to talk to the same man who had conferred with them earlier on the street corner. Deciding that the situation was ripe for direct action, Officer McFadden approached the three men, identified himself as a police officer and asked for their names. At this point, his knowledge was confined to what he had observed. He was not acquainted with any of the three men by name or by sight, and he had received no information concerning them from any other source. When the men "mumbled something" in response to his inquiries, Officer McFadden grabbed petitioner Terry, spun him around so that they were facing the other two, with Terry between McFadden and the others, and patted down the outside of his clothing. In the left breast pocket of Terry's overcoat Officer McFadden felt a pistol. He reached inside the overcoat pocket, but was unable to remove the gun. At this point, keeping Terry between himself and the others, the officer ordered all three men to enter Zucker's store. As they went in, he removed Terry's overcoat completely, removed a .38-caliber revolver from the pocket, and ordered all three men to face the wall with their hands raised. Officer McFadden proceeded to pat down the outer clothing of Chilton and the third man, Katz. He discovered another revolver in the outer pocket of Chilton's overcoat, but no weapons were found on Katz. The officer testified that he only patted the men down to see whether they had weapons, and that he did not put his hands beneath the outer garments of either Terry or Chilton until he felt their guns. So far as appears from the record, he never placed his hands beneath Katz' outer garments. Officer McFadden seized Chilton's gun, asked the proprietor of the store to call a police wagon, and took all three men to the station where Chilton and Terry were formally charged with carrying concealed weapons.

On the motion to suppress the guns the * * * court denied the defendants' motion on the ground that Officer McFadden, on the basis of his experience, "had reasonable cause to believe . . . that the defendants were conducting themselves suspiciously, and some interrogation should be made of their action." Purely for his own protection, the court held, the officer had the right to pat down the outer clothing of these men, who he had reasonable cause to believe might be armed. The court distinguished between an investigatory "stop" and an arrest, and between a "frisk" of the outer clothing for weapons and a full-blown search for evidence of crime. The frisk, it held, was essential to the proper performance of the officer's investigatory duties, for without it "the answer to the police officer may be a bullet, and a loaded pistol discovered during the frisk is admissible."

After the court denied their motion to suppress, Chilton and Terry waived jury trial and pleaded not guilty. The court adjudged them guilty, and the Court of Appeals * * * affirmed. The Supreme Court of Ohio dismissed their appeal on the ground that no "substantial constitutional question" was involved. We granted certiorari * * *. * * *

I.

* * * Unquestionably petitioner was entitled to the protection of the Fourth Amendment as he walked down the street in Cleveland. The question is whether in all the circumstances of this on-the-street encounter, his right to personal security was violated by an unreasonable search and seizure.

We would be less than candid if we did not acknowledge that this question thrusts to the fore difficult and troublesome issues regarding a sensitive area of police activity—issues which have never before been squarely presented to this Court. Reflective of the tensions involved are the practical and constitutional arguments pressed with great vigor on both sides of the public debate over the power of the police to "stop and frisk"— as it is sometimes euphemistically termed—suspicious persons.

On the one hand, it is frequently argued that in dealing with the rapidly unfolding and often dangerous situations on city streets, the police are in need of an escalating set of flexible responses, graduated in relation to the amount of information they possess. For this purpose, it is urged that distinctions should be made between a "stop" and an "arrest" (or a "seizure" of a person), and between a "frisk" and a "search." Thus, it is argued, the police should be allowed to "stop" a person and detain him or her briefly for questioning upon suspicion that he or she may be connected with criminal activity. Upon suspicion that the person may be armed, the police should have the power to "frisk" him or her for weapons. If the "stop" and the "frisk" give rise to probable cause to believe that the suspect has committed a crime, then the police should be empowered to make a formal "arrest," and a full incident "search" of the person. This scheme is justified in part upon the notion that a "stop" and a "frisk" amount to a mere "minor inconvenience and petty indignity," which can properly be imposed upon the citizen in the interest of effective law enforcement on the basis of a police officer's suspicion.

On the other side the argument is made that the authority of the police must be strictly circumscribed by the law of arrest and search as it has developed to date in the traditional jurisprudence of the Fourth Amendment. It is contended with some force that there is not—and cannot be—a variety of police activity which does not depend solely upon the voluntary cooperation of the citizen and yet which stops short of an arrest based upon probable cause to make such an arrest. * * * This, it is argued, can only serve to exacerbate police-community tensions in the crowded centers of our Nation's cities.

In this context we approach the issues in this case mindful of the limitations of the judicial function in controlling the myriad daily situations in which policemen and citizens confront each other on the street. The State has characterized the issue here as "the right of a police officer . . . to make an on-the-street stop, interrogate and pat down for weapons (known in street vernacular as 'stop and frisk')." But this is only partly accurate. For the issue is not the abstract propriety of the police conduct, but the admissibility against petitioner of the evidence uncovered by the search and seizure. Ever since its inception, the rule excluding evidence seized in violation of the Fourth Amendment has been recognized as a principal mode of discouraging lawless police conduct. * * *

The exclusionary rule has its limitations, however, as a tool of judicial control. It cannot properly be invoked to exclude the products of legitimate police investigative techniques on the ground that much conduct which is closely similar involves unwarranted intrusions upon constitutional protections. Moreover, in some contexts the rule is ineffective as a deterrent. Street encounters between citizens and police officers are incredibly rich in diversity. They range from wholly friendly exchanges of pleasantries or mutually useful information to hostile confrontations of armed men involving arrests, or injuries, or loss of life. Moreover, hostile confrontations are not all of a piece. Some of them begin in a friendly enough manner, only to take a different turn upon the injection of some unexpected element into the conversation. Encounters are initiated by the police for a wide variety of purposes, some of which are wholly unrelated to a desire to prosecute for crime. * * *

Proper adjudication of cases in which the exclusionary rule is invoked demands a constant awareness of these limitations. The wholesale harassment by certain elements of the police community—of which minority groups, particularly Negroes, frequently complain,[11] will not be stopped by the exclusion of any evidence from any criminal trial. Yet a rigid and unthinking application of the exclusionary rule, in futile protest against practices which it can never be used effectively to control, may exact a high toll in human injury and frustration of efforts to prevent crime. No judicial opinion can comprehend the protean variety of the street encounter, and we can only judge the facts of the case before us. Nothing we say today is to be taken as indicating approval of police conduct outside the legitimate investigative sphere. Under our decision, courts still retain

---

[11] The President's Commission on Law Enforcement and Administration of Justice found that "in many communities, field interrogations are a major source of friction between the police and minority groups." It was reported that the friction caused by "misuse of field interrogations" increases "as more police departments adopt 'aggressive patrol' in which officers are encouraged routinely to stop and question persons on the street who are unknown to them, who are suspicious, or whose purpose for being abroad is not readily evident." While the frequency with which "frisking" forms a part of field interrogation, practice varies tremendously with the locale, the objective of the interrogation, and the particular officer; it cannot help but be a severely exacerbating factor in police-community tensions. This is particularly true in situations where the "stop and frisk" of youths or minority group members is "motivated by the officers' perceived need to maintain the power image of the beat officer, an aim sometimes accomplished by humiliating anyone who attempts to undermine police control of the streets."

their traditional responsibility to guard against police conduct which is overbearing or harassing, or which trenches upon personal security without the objective evidentiary justification which the Constitution requires. When such conduct is identified, it must be condemned by the judiciary and its fruits must be excluded from evidence in criminal trials. * * *

* * * [W]e turn our attention to the quite narrow question posed by the facts before us: whether it is always unreasonable for a policeman to seize a person and subject him to a limited search for weapons unless there is probable cause for an arrest. Given the narrowness of this question, we have no occasion to canvass in detail the constitutional limitations upon the scope of a policeman's power when he confronts a citizen without probable cause to arrest him.

II.

Our first task is to establish at what point in this encounter the Fourth Amendment becomes relevant. That is, we must decide whether and when Officer McFadden "seized" Terry and whether and when he conducted a "search." There is some suggestion in the use of such terms as "stop" and "frisk" that such police conduct is outside the purview of the Fourth Amendment because neither action rises to the level of a "search" or "seizure" within the meaning of the Constitution. We emphatically reject this notion. It is quite plain that the Fourth Amendment governs "seizures" of the person which do not eventuate in a trip to the station house and prosecution for crime—"arrests" in traditional terminology. It must be recognized that whenever a police officer accosts an individual and restrains his freedom to walk away, he has "seized" that person. And it is nothing less than sheer torture of the English language to suggest that a careful exploration of the outer surfaces of a person's clothing all over his or her body in an attempt to find weapons is not a "search." Moreover, it is simply fantastic to urge that such a procedure performed in public by a policeman while the citizen stands helpless, perhaps facing a wall with his hands raised, is a "petty indignity." It is a serious intrusion upon the sanctity of the person, which may inflict great indignity and arouse strong resentment, and it is not to be undertaken lightly.

The danger in the logic which proceeds upon distinctions between a "stop" and an "arrest," or "seizure" of the person, and between a "frisk" and a "search" is twofold. It seeks to isolate from constitutional scrutiny the initial stages of the contact between the policeman and the citizen. And by suggesting a rigid all-or-nothing model of justification and regulation under the Amendment, it obscures the utility of limitations upon the scope, as well as the initiation, of police action as a means of constitutional regulation. * * *

The distinctions of classical "stop-and-frisk" theory thus serve to divert attention from the central inquiry under the Fourth Amendment—the reasonableness in all the circumstances of the particular governmental invasion of a citizen's personal security. "Search" and "seizure" are not talismans. We therefore reject the notions that the Fourth Amendment does not come into play at all as a limitation upon police conduct if the officers stop short of something called a "technical arrest" or a "full-blown search."

In this case, there can be no question, then, that Officer McFadden "seized" petitioner and subjected him to a "search" when he took hold of him and patted down the outer surfaces of his clothing. We must decide whether at that point it was reasonable for Officer McFadden to have interfered with petitioner's personal security as he did.[16] And in determining whether the seizure and search were "unreasonable" our inquiry is a dual one—whether the officer's action was justified at its inception and whether it was reasonably related in scope to the circumstances which justified the interference in the first place.

III.

If this case involved police conduct subject to the Warrant Clause of the Fourth Amendment, we would have to ascertain whether "probable cause" existed to justify the search and seizure which took place. However, that is not the case. We do not retreat from our holdings that the police must, whenever practicable, obtain advance judicial approval of searches and seizures through the warrant procedure * * *. But we deal here with an entire rubric of police conduct—necessarily swift action predicated upon the on-the-spot observations of the officer on the beat—which historically has not been, and as a practical matter could not be, subjected to the warrant procedure. Instead, the conduct involved in this case must be tested by the Fourth Amendment's general proscription against unreasonable searches and seizures.

Nonetheless, the notions which underlie both the warrant procedure and the requirement of probable cause remain fully relevant in this context. In order to assess the reasonableness of Officer McFadden's conduct as a general proposition, it is necessary "first to focus upon the governmental interest which allegedly justifies official intrusion upon the constitutionally protected interests of the private citizen," for there is "no ready test for determining reasonableness other than by balancing the

---

[16] We thus decide nothing today concerning the constitutional propriety of an investigative "seizure" upon less than probable cause for purposes of "detention" and/or interrogation. Obviously, not all personal intercourse between policemen and citizens involves "seizures" of persons. Only when the officer, by means of physical force or show of authority, has in some way restrained the liberty of a citizen may we conclude that a "seizure" has occurred. We cannot tell with any certainty upon this record whether any such "seizure" took place here prior to Officer McFadden's initiation of physical contact for purposes of searching Terry for weapons, and we thus may assume that up to that point no intrusion upon constitutionally protected rights had occurred.

need to search [or seize] against the invasion which the search [or seizure] entails." And in justifying the particular intrusion the police officer must be able to point to specific and articulable facts which, taken together with rational inferences from those facts, reasonably warrant that intrusion. The scheme of the Fourth Amendment becomes meaningful only when it is assured that at some point the conduct of those charged with enforcing the laws can be subjected to the more detached, neutral scrutiny of a judge who must evaluate the reasonableness of a particular search or seizure in light of the particular circumstances. And in making that assessment, it is imperative that the facts be judged against an objective standard: would the facts available to the officer at the moment of the seizure or the search "warrant a man of reasonable caution in the belief" that the action taken was appropriate? Anything less would invite intrusions upon constitutionally guaranteed rights based on nothing more substantial than inarticulate hunches, a result this Court has consistently refused to sanction. * * *

Applying these principles to this case, we consider first the nature and extent of the governmental interests involved. One general interest is of course that of effective crime prevention and detection; it is this interest which underlies the recognition that a police officer may in appropriate circumstances and in an appropriate manner approach a person for purposes of investigating possibly criminal behavior even though there is no probable cause to make an arrest. It was this legitimate investigative function Officer McFadden was discharging when he decided to approach petitioner and his companions. He had observed Terry, Chilton, and Katz go through a series of acts, each of them perhaps innocent in itself, but which taken together warranted further investigation. There is nothing unusual in two men standing together on a street corner, perhaps waiting for someone. Nor is there anything suspicious about people in such circumstances strolling up and down the street, singly or in pairs. Store windows, moreover, are made to be looked in. But the story is quite different where, as here, two men hover about a street corner for an extended period of time, at the end of which it becomes apparent that they are not waiting for anyone or anything; where these men pace alternately along an identical route, pausing to stare in the same store window roughly 24 times; where each completion of this route is followed immediately by a conference between the two men on the corner; where they are joined in one of these conferences by a third man who leaves swiftly; and where the two men finally follow the third and rejoin him a couple of blocks away. It would have been poor police work indeed for an officer of 30-years' experience in the detection of thievery from stores in this same neighborhood to have failed to investigate this behavior further.

The crux of this case, however, is not the propriety of Officer McFadden's taking steps to investigate petitioner's suspicious behavior, but rather, whether there was justification for McFadden's invasion of Terry's personal security by searching him for weapons in the course of that investigation. We are now concerned with more than the governmental interest in investigating crime; in addition, there is the more immediate interest of the police officer in taking steps to assure himself that the person with whom he is dealing is not armed with a weapon that could unexpectedly and fatally be used against him. * * * Virtually all of these deaths and a substantial portion of the injuries are inflicted with guns and knives.[21]

In view of these facts, we cannot blind ourselves to the need for law enforcement officers to protect themselves and other prospective victims of violence in situations where they may lack probable cause for an arrest. When an officer is justified in believing that the individual whose suspicious behavior he is investigating at close range is armed and presently dangerous to the officer or to others, it would appear to be clearly unreasonable to deny the officer the power to take necessary measures to determine whether the person is in fact carrying a weapon and to neutralize the threat of physical harm.

We must still consider, however, the nature and quality of the intrusion on individual rights which must be accepted if police officers are to be conceded the right to search for weapons in situations where probable cause to arrest for crime is lacking. Even a limited search of the outer clothing for weapons constitutes a severe, though brief, intrusion upon cherished personal security, and it must surely be an annoying, frightening, and perhaps humiliating experience. * * *

Our evaluation of the proper balance that has to be struck in this type of case leads us to conclude that there must be a narrowly drawn authority to permit a reasonable search for weapons for the protection of the police officer, where he has reason to believe that he is dealing with an armed and dangerous individual, regardless of whether he has probable cause to arrest the individual for a crime. The officer need not be absolutely certain that the individual is armed; the issue is whether a reasonably prudent man in the circumstances would be warranted in the belief that his safety or that of others was in danger. And in determining whether the officer acted reasonably in such circumstances, due weight must be given, not to his inchoate and unparticularized suspicion or "hunch," but to the specific reasonable inferences which he is entitled to draw from the facts in light of his experience.

---

[21] Fifty-seven law enforcement officers were killed in the line of duty in this country in 1966, bringing the total to 335 for the seven-year period beginning with 1960. Also in 1966, there were 23,851 assaults on police officers, 9,113 of which resulted in injuries to the policemen. Fifty-five of the 57 officers killed in 1966 died from gunshot wounds, 41 of them inflicted by handguns easily secreted about the person. The remaining two murders were perpetrated by knives. * * *

IV.

We must now examine the conduct of Officer McFadden in this case to determine whether his search and seizure of petitioner were reasonable, both at their inception and as conducted. He had observed Terry, together with Chilton and another man, acting in a manner he took to be preface to a "stick-up." We think on the facts and circumstances Officer McFadden detailed before the trial judge a reasonably prudent man would have been warranted in believing petitioner was armed and thus presented a threat to the officer's safety while he was investigating his suspicious behavior. The actions of Terry and Chilton were consistent with McFadden's hypothesis that these men were contemplating a daylight robbery—which, it is reasonable to assume, would be likely to involve the use of weapons—and nothing in their conduct from the time he first noticed them until the time he confronted them and identified himself as a police officer gave him sufficient reason to negate that hypothesis. Although the trio had departed the original scene, there was nothing to indicate abandonment of an intent to commit a robbery at some point. Thus, when Officer McFadden approached the three men gathered before the display window at Zucker's store, he had observed enough to make it quite reasonable to fear that they were armed, and nothing in their response to his hailing them, identifying himself as a police officer, and asking their names served to dispel that reasonable belief. We cannot say his decision at that point to seize Terry and pat his clothing for weapons was the product of a volatile or inventive imagination or was undertaken simply as an act of harassment; the record evidences the tempered act of a policeman who in the course of an investigation had to make a quick decision as to how to protect himself and others from possible danger, and took limited steps to do so. * * * The sole justification of the search in the present situation is the protection of the police officer and others nearby, and it must therefore be confined in scope to an intrusion reasonably designed to discover guns, knives, clubs, or other hidden instruments for the assault of the police officer.

The scope of the search in this case presents no serious problem in light of these standards. Officer McFadden patted down the outer clothing of petitioner and his two companions. He did not place his hands in their pockets or under the outer surface of their garments until he had felt weapons, and then he merely reached for and removed the guns. He never did invade Katz' person beyond the outer surfaces of his clothes, since he discovered nothing in his pat-down which might have been a weapon. Officer McFadden confined his search strictly to what was minimally necessary to learn whether the men were armed and to disarm them once he discovered the weapons. He did not conduct a general exploratory search for whatever evidence of criminal activity he might find.

V.

We conclude that the revolver seized from Terry was properly admitted in evidence against him. At the time he seized petitioner and searched him for weapons, Officer McFadden had reasonable grounds to believe that petitioner was armed and dangerous, and it was necessary for the protection of himself and others to take swift measures to discover the true facts and neutralize the threat of harm if it materialized. The policeman carefully restricted his search to what was appropriate to the discovery of the particular items which he sought. Each case of this sort will, of course, have to be decided on its own facts. We merely hold today that where a police officer observes unusual conduct which leads him reasonably to conclude in light of his experience that criminal activity may be afoot and that the persons with whom he is dealing may be armed and presently dangerous, where in the course of investigating this behavior he identifies himself as a policeman and makes reasonable inquiries, and where nothing in the initial stages of the encounter serves to dispel his reasonable fear for his own or others' safety, he is entitled for the protection of himself and others in the area to conduct a carefully limited search of the outer clothing of such persons in an attempt to discover weapons which might be used to assault him. Such a search is a reasonable search under the Fourth Amendment, and any weapons seized may properly be introduced in evidence against the person from whom they were taken.

Affirmed.

MR. JUSTICE BLACK concurs in the judgment and the opinion except where the opinion quotes from and relies upon this Court's opinion in *Katz v. United States* and the concurring opinion in *Warden v. Hayden.*

MR. JUSTICE HARLAN, concurring.

[Omitted.]

MR. JUSTICE WHITE, concurring.

I join the opinion of the Court, reserving judgment, however, on some of the Court's general remarks about the scope and purpose of the exclusionary rule which the Court has fashioned in the process of enforcing the Fourth Amendment.

Also, although the Court puts the matter aside in the context of this case, I think an additional word is in order concerning the matter of interrogation during an investigative stop. There is nothing in the Constitution which prevents a policeman from addressing questions to anyone on the streets. Absent special circumstances, the person approached may not be detained or frisked but may refuse to cooperate and go on his way. However, given the proper circumstances, such as those in this case, it seems to me the person may be briefly detained against his will while pertinent questions are directed to him. Of course, the person stopped is not obliged to answer, answers may not be compelled, and refusal to answer furnishes no basis for an arrest, although it may alert the officer to the need for continued observation. In my view, it is temporary detention, warranted by the circumstances, which chiefly justifies the protective frisk for weapons. Perhaps the frisk itself, where proper, will have beneficial results whether questions are asked or not. If weapons are found, an arrest will follow. If none are found, the frisk may nevertheless serve preventive ends because of its unmistakable message that suspicion has been aroused. But if the investigative stop is sustainable at all, constitutional rights are not necessarily violated if pertinent questions are asked and the person is restrained briefly in the process.

MR. JUSTICE DOUGLAS, dissenting.

[Omitted.]

QUESTIONS, COMMENTS, CONCERNS?

1. ***Terry* and completed felonies.** In *United States v. Hensley*, 469 U.S. 221 (1985), six days after an armed robbery at a tavern in a suburb of Cincinnati, officers interviewed an informant who relayed that respondent Hensley drove the getaway car. Based on that information, officers issued a "wanted flyer" to police departments in the Cincinnati metropolitan area. Hensley was stopped in a nearby town pursuant to the flyer while driving, and officers executed a traffic stop. During the stop, Hensley and his passenger were ordered out of the vehicle, after which a search produced three handguns. Hensley was indicted for being a convicted felon in possession of firearms. He moved to suppress the weapons, arguing that *Terry* did not permit investigatory stops based on completed offenses. The Supreme Court disagreed, holding that, "if police have a reasonable suspicion, grounded in specific and articulable facts, that a person they encounter was involved in or is wanted in connection with a completed felony, then a *Terry* stop may be made to investigate that suspicion." In this case, the Court reasoned, officers were justified in relying on the wanted flyer to stop Hensley for the purpose of checking his identification.

2. ***Terry* and minor traffic violations.** In *Arizona v. Johnson*, 555 U.S. 323 (2009), officers on patrol in an area suspected for Crips gang activity pulled over a vehicle carrying three occupants (including respondent Johnson) "after a license plate check revealed that the vehicle's registration had been suspended for an insurance-related violation." Such an infraction, pursuant to Arizona law, was civil in nature and merited a fine only. During the stop, three officers approached the vehicle. One officer, Trevizo, noticed that Johnson was wearing clothing consistent with Crips membership and was carrying a police scanner. Trevizo ordered Johnson out of the car and patted him down, which revealed the butt of a weapon. Johnson was charged with felon-in-possession and moved to suppress, claiming that the vehicle stop was unlawful. The Supreme Court disagreed, holding that "[a] lawful roadside stop begins when a vehicle is pulled over for investigation of a traffic violation." The Court

further held that officers may properly investigate matters outside the basis for the stop—in this case, gang activity because "[a]n officer's inquiries into matters unrelated to the justification for the traffic stop . . . do not convert the encounter into something other than a lawful seizure, so long as those inquiries do not measurably extend the duration of the stop."

3.   The disputed policy. In your review of the Floyd complaint, what exactly is the problematic NYPD policy? [*See* Casefile Document 1.] Is there one? This seems an important point; the City contends that there is no "written or other formal policy that requires or even permits the stopping, questioning and/or frisking of persons without sufficient reasonable suspicion." [Casefile Document 2, at 13.] Other potentially problematic NYPD policies include the City's use of the UF-250 form to report each officer's *Terry* stop. Does that form cabin the *Terry* analysis?

And what about the NYPD's development and use of a Racial Profiling Policy? That policy, as relayed by the district court, "prohibits the use of race, color, ethnicity or national origin as a determinative factor in taking law enforcement action[.]" [Casefile Document 5, at 19.] Could Floyd be arguing that the NYPD violated its own policy?

Policies aside, its seems that Floyd's real complaint surrounds the NYPD's implementation practices. How would you, on behalf of Floyd, incorporate those practices to clearly articulate the NYPD's unconstitutional behavior?

4.   *Terry* stops vs. arrests. Floyd alleges that, despite an extreme number of *Terry* stops of minority citizens, officers ultimately conducted very few arrests. [Casefile Document 1, at 24–25.] But *Terry* is created in part to permit exactly this type of law enforcement investigative tactic, right? Surely, Floyd is not arguing that minority citizens who were stopped should *also* have been arrested.

5.   Stops vs. frisks. Does Floyd contend that the NYPD followed an unconstitutional policy for *Terry* stops or frisks? Or both? [*See* Casefile Document 1.]

6.   Quantifying reasonable suspicion. When an officer elects to stop an individual, does reasonable suspicion require the officer to be certain that criminal activity is afoot? If not, can we quantify the reasonable suspicion standard? Must an officer by 75% sure? 50%? 25%? The judiciary has never said, though the Supreme Court has indicated that the level of suspicion needed for reasonable suspicion is "considerably less than proof of wrongdoing by a preponderance of the evidence." *United States v. Sokolow*, 490 U.S. 1, 7 (1989). If officers are not held to a percentage of success associated with their *Terry* stops, does it matter, as Floyd highlights, that only 2% of *Terry* stops by the NYPD of minority citizens produced a weapon? [*See* Casefile Document 1, at 27.]

7.   What if the judiciary *did* quantify reasonable suspicion? In a 1982 study, Professor C.M.A. McCauliff surveyed 164 federal judges and asked how they would quantify the reasonable suspicion standard on a scale of 0 percent to 100 percent. C.M.A. McCauliff, *Burdens of Proof: Degrees of Belief,*

Quanta of Evidence, or Constitutional Guarantees?, 35 VAND. L. REV. 1293, 1325, n.184 (1982). Tabulating the responses reflected an average percentage of 29.59. *Id.* at 1332.

8. **Stop *and* frisk as opposed to stop *then* frisk.** The district court in its *Floyd* opinion held that reasonable suspicion supported both the officers' initial stop of Floyd and their ensuing frisk. The court reasoned that the officers were "aware of a midday burglary pattern in the neighborhood" and they watched " 'two Black men trying to unlock the front door of a house in the middle of the afternoon using keys.' " [Casefile Document 5, at 55.] But what about the frisk? The court wrote, "In addition, because the officers suspected that Floyd and his neighbor were committing the violent crime of burglary, they were justified in frisking the two men to ensure the officers' own safety," *Id.*

But as noted above, *Terry* contemplates that an officer must have reasonable suspicion to support the stop (a concern that criminal activity is afoot) and *separate* reasonable suspicion to support the frisk (a concern that the suspect is armed and dangerous). Recall that *Terry* indicates that a frisk is appropriate only if "nothing in the initial stages of the encounter serves to dispel his reasonable fear for his own or others' safety[.]" 392 U.S. at 30. Has the district court in *Floyd* properly applied *Terry* to Floyd's frisk?

9. ***Terry* and training.** Floyd's complaint alleges that the NYPD failed to adequately train its officers, which, in part, contributed to violating citizens' Fourth Amendment rights. [Casefile Document 1, at 30 at ¶¶ 119–20.] Should officers separately receive *Terry*-specific training? As you will read in a moment, the officer in *Terry*, Officer McFadden, executed what turned out to be a lawful stop despite never having—in his thirty-nine years as an officer—observed anyone "casing a place for a stickup."

* * *

A Postscript to *Terry*

Defense counsel for John Terry, the Honorable Louis Stokes, reflected in 1998 on his experience defending Terry. Stokes recalled:

> I knew Terry before he got into this particular difficulty. Terry was sort of a "hanger on." He was more of a petty criminal than anything else. Also, he was addicted to drugs.

> I knew Terry from his hanging around with another person whom I represented, a fellow by the name of Billy Cox. Billy Cox was a rather notorious individual around Cleveland. I represented Billy Cox in a couple of murder cases and knew Terry from his hanging around Billy Cox, because Terry liked to be around the more notorious type of individuals in the community. After his arrest, Terry called me. I went down to see him, and he asked me if I would represent both him and Chilton. Both of them were able at that time to retain me. Later on, it was determined they were both

really indigent. Not only could they not afford me, they could not afford to take this case up to the United States Supreme Court.

Once it was apparent that we had a case that was destined to go all the way, I realized the importance of it. I decided that if it meant that I would have to pay the expenses of getting this case up to the United States Supreme Court, I would do that.

Louis Stokes, *Representing John W. Terry*, 72 ST. JOHN'S L. REV. 727, 727–28 (1998). About Officer McFadden, Stokes remembered the following:

He was a real character—a tall, stately guy, and basically a good policeman. "Mac," as we called him, was really a guy that we really liked. He was straight. One thing about him—as a police officer, he came straight down the line. You did not have to worry about him misrepresenting what the facts were. He would come straight down the line, and as a defense lawyer I could appreciate that.

When I put him on as my witness on the motion to suppress, I, of course, did not know what he would say. All I could rely upon was what my clients had told me. I could not believe his testimony as it came out of his mouth on the stand. He said to us that he had seen these two fellows standing across the street from him, and he described them as being two Negroes, and then he talked of the white fellow who came up to them and talked with them. Then he went on down the street. Mac then admitted to us they weren't doing anything, except one of the black fellows would leave the other one, walk down the street a little bit, turn around, peer into the window at either the United Airlines or the jewelry store window, then walk back up to where the other fellow was. Then the other fellow would take a walk in a similar manner.

He was asked specifically what attracted him to them. On one occasion he said, "Well, to tell the truth, I just didn't like 'em.' " He was asked how long he'd been a police officer. "Thirty nine years." How long had he been a detective? "Thirty five years." What did he think they were doing? "Well," he said, "I suspected that they were casing a joint for the purpose of robbing it." "Well," he was asked, "have you ever in your thirty-nine years as a police officer, thirty-five as a detective, had the opportunity to observe anybody casing a place for a stickup?" He said, "No, I haven't." "Have you ever arrested anybody for that purpose?" "No, I haven't." "Then what attracted you to them?" He indicated he just didn't like them. He suspected they might be up to a stickup. That also is the reason why he thought they might have guns.

At any rate, the fact situation was that he then followed them down the street. After he saw this white fellow, Katz, come up, talk with them and then go down the street on Euclid Avenue, he then saw the two of them make one more trip up and down Huron Road.

And then the two of them walked. We asked, "Did they run down the street? Did they act suspicious or anything?" "No, they walked at a normal gait." "What did you do?" "I followed behind them."

When they got in front of Zucker's store, the three of them—two black males and a white male—were just standing there doing nothing. He said, "I went over to them and identified myself as a police officer. I said, 'What are your names?' " In one place in the record he says, "They mumbled something." At another place in the record, he says, "They gave it to me quick."

Then he was asked, "What did you do at that point?" He said, "I grabbed Terry, spun him around," and then, when he couldn't get the gun out of the top coat, he then took the whole top coat off of him. Then he took the gun out of Terry's pocket. That's when he ordered the three of them into the store. As he walked into the store, he said that he told the store personnel, "Call the wagon." He testified that that meant they were under arrest.

Id. at 729–30. That same year, former Cleveland prosecutor Reuben M. Payne had an opportunity to reflect on McFadden as an officer. He noted:

[McFadden] was an exceptional police officer. He had been on the force for thirty-nine years at the time of the Terry incident. Two years after joining the police force, his talents as an able, capable, and intelligent police officer were sufficient to earn him a promotion to detective. For approximately thirteen years, he handled cases that came through the detective bureau with excellent results. McFadden was injured and then assigned to light duty patrol in the downtown Cleveland area. He was often referred to as a "door shaker." A door shaker was a police officer assigned for benefit of the merchants in the heavy populated downtown area. His duties were to prevent petty thieveries and robberies, and to observe all persons who may be contemplating the commission of a robbery, pickpockets or boosters. He had an uncanny memory for faces and people who had been responsible for previous criminal activity. He would stand for hours observing people, their actions, and conduct.

I do not recall a case that McFadden brought to the court wherein the matter was thrown out or the defendant acquitted. There were many arrests and convictions in the performance of his job. He had an ability to enunciate the facts, describe clearly what took place, and was renowned for the number of arrests and convictions made in the performance of his duty. He had a keen sense of intuition * * *. McFadden was an exceptional, outstanding police officer.

Reuben M. Payne, *Detective McFadden Had a Right to Protect Himself*, 72 ST. JOHN'S L. REV. 733, 733–34 (1998).

D. *TERRY* & INFORMANTS

This section explores the role that informants—known and unknown—play in the reasonable suspicion calculus. Just like informants can help officers establish probable cause, so too can they contribute to establishing reasonable suspicion. In this context, though, the presence or absence of reasonable suspicion goes initially to support the *Terry* "stop," bit not necessarily to the frisk.

ADAMS V. WILLIAMS

407 U.S. 143
Supreme Court of the United States
April 10, 1972, Argued; June 12, 1972, Decided
No. 70-283

MR. JUSTICE REHNQUIST delivered the opinion of the Court.

Respondent Robert Williams was convicted in a Connecticut state court of illegal possession of a handgun found during a "stop and frisk," as well as of possession of heroin that was found during a full search incident to his weapons arrest. * * *

Police Sgt. John Connolly was alone early in the morning on car patrol duty in a high-crime area of Bridgeport, Connecticut. At approximately 2:15 a.m. a person known to Sgt. Connolly approached his cruiser and informed him that an individual seated in a nearby vehicle was carrying narcotics and had a gun at his waist.

After calling for assistance on his car radio, Sgt. Connolly approached the vehicle to investigate the informant's report. Connolly tapped on the car window and asked the occupant, Robert Williams, to open the door. When Williams rolled down the window instead, the sergeant reached into the car and removed a fully loaded revolver from Williams' waistband. The gun had not been visible to Connolly from outside the car, but it was in precisely the place indicated by the informant. Williams was then arrested by Connolly for unlawful possession of the pistol. A search incident to that arrest was conducted after other officers arrived. They found substantial quantities of heroin on Williams' person and in the car, and they found a machete and a second revolver hidden in the automobile.

Respondent contends that the initial seizure of his pistol, upon which rested the later search and seizure of other weapons and narcotics, was not justified by the informant's tip to Sgt. Connolly. He claims that absent a more reliable informant, or some corroboration of the tip, the policeman's actions were unreasonable under the standards set forth in *Terry v. Ohio.*

[Ed. note: The Court reviewed the *Terry* decision.] * * * Applying these principles to the present case, we believe that Sgt. Connolly acted justifiably in responding to his informant's tip. The informant was known to him personally and had provided him with information in the past. This is a stronger case than obtains in the case of an anonymous telephone tip. The informant here came forward personally to give information that was immediately verifiable at the scene. Indeed, under Connecticut law, the informant might have been subject to immediate arrest for making a false complaint had Sgt. Connolly's investigation proved the tip incorrect. Thus, while the Court's decisions indicate that this informant's unverified tip may have been insufficient for a narcotics arrest or search warrant, the information carried enough indicia of reliability to justify the officer's forcible stop of Williams.

In reaching this conclusion, we reject respondent's argument that reasonable cause for a stop and frisk can only be based on the officer's personal observation, rather than on information supplied by another person. Informants' tips, like all other clues and evidence coming to a policeman on the scene, may vary greatly in their value and reliability. One simple rule will not cover every situation. Some tips, completely lacking in indicia of reliability, would either warrant no police response or require further investigation before a forcible stop of a suspect would be authorized. But in some situations—for example, when the victim of a street crime seeks immediate police aid and gives a description of his assailant, or when a credible informant warns of a specific impending crime—the subtleties of the hearsay rule should not thwart an appropriate police response.

While properly investigating the activity of a person who was reported to be carrying narcotics and a concealed weapon and who was sitting alone in a car in a high-crime area at 2:15 in the morning, Sgt. Connolly had ample reason to fear for his safety.[3] When Williams rolled down his window, rather than complying with the policeman's request to step out of the car so that his movements could more easily be seen, the revolver allegedly at Williams' waist became an even greater threat. Under these circumstances the policeman's action in reaching to the spot where the gun was thought to be hidden constituted a limited intrusion designed to insure his safety, and we conclude that it was reasonable. The loaded gun seized as a result of this intrusion was therefore admissible at Williams' trial.

---

[3]   Figures reported by the Federal Bureau of Investigation indicate that 125 policemen were murdered in 1971, with all but five of them having been killed by gunshot wounds. According to one study, approximately 30% of police shootings occurred when a police officer approached a suspect seated in an automobile.

Once Sgt. Connolly had found the gun precisely where the informant had predicted, probable cause existed to arrest Williams for unlawful possession of the weapon. * * * Under the circumstances surrounding Williams' possession of the gun seized by Sgt. Connolly, the arrest on the weapons charge was supported by probable cause, and the search of his person and of the car incident to that arrest was lawful. The fruits of the search were therefore properly admitted at Williams' trial, and the Court of Appeals erred in reaching a contrary conclusion.

Reversed.

MR. JUSTICE DOUGLAS, with whom MR. JUSTICE MARSHALL concurs, dissenting.

[Omitted.]

MR. JUSTICE BRENNAN, dissenting.

[Omitted.]

ALABAMA V. WHITE

496 U.S. 325
Supreme Court of the United States
April 17, 1990, Argued; June 11, 1990, Decided
No. 89-789

MR. JUSTICE WHITE delivered the opinion of the Court.

Based on an anonymous telephone tip, police stopped respondent's vehicle. A consensual search of the car revealed drugs. The issue is whether the tip, as corroborated by independent police work, exhibited sufficient indicia of reliability to provide reasonable suspicion to make the investigatory stop. We hold that it did.

On April 22, 1987, at approximately 3 p.m., Corporal B. H. Davis of the Montgomery Police Department received a telephone call from an anonymous person, stating that Vanessa White would be leaving 235-C Lynwood Terrace Apartments at a particular time in a brown Plymouth station wagon with the right taillight lens broken, that she would be going to Dobey's Motel, and that she would be in possession of about an ounce of cocaine inside a brown attaché case. Corporal Davis and his partner, Corporal P. A. Reynolds, proceeded to the Lynwood Terrace Apartments. The officers saw a brown Plymouth station wagon with a broken right taillight in the parking lot in front of the 235 building. The officers observed respondent leave the 235 building, carrying nothing in her hands, and enter the station wagon. They followed the vehicle as it drove the most direct route to Dobey's Motel. When the vehicle reached the Mobile Highway, on which Dobey's Motel is located, Corporal Reynolds requested a patrol unit to stop the vehicle. The vehicle was stopped at approximately 4:18 p.m., just short of Dobey's Motel. Corporal Davis asked respondent to step to the rear of her car, where he informed her that she had been stopped because she was suspected of carrying cocaine in the vehicle. He asked if they could look for cocaine and respondent said they could look. The officers found a locked brown attaché case in the car and, upon request, respondent provided the combination to the lock. The officers found marijuana in the attaché case and placed respondent under arrest. During processing at the station, the officers found three milligrams of cocaine in respondent's purse.

Respondent was charged in Montgomery County court with possession of marijuana and possession of cocaine. The trial court denied respondent's motion to suppress, and she pleaded guilty to the charges, reserving the right to appeal the denial of her suppression motion. The Court of Criminal Appeals of Alabama held that the officers did not have the reasonable suspicion necessary under *Terry v. Ohio*, 392 U.S. 1 (1968), to justify the investigatory stop of respondent's car and that the marijuana and cocaine were fruits of respondent's unconstitutional detention. * * * The Supreme Court of Alabama denied the State's petition for writ of certiorari * * *. * * * We now reverse. * * *

[The Court reviewed both *Adams* and *Gates*.] The opinion in *Gates* recognized that an anonymous tip alone seldom demonstrates the informant's basis of knowledge or veracity inasmuch as ordinary citizens generally do not provide extensive recitations of the basis of their everyday observations and given that the veracity of persons supplying anonymous tips is "by hypothesis largely unknown, and unknowable." This is not to say that an anonymous caller could never provide the reasonable suspicion necessary for a *Terry* stop. But the tip in *Gates* was not an exception to the general rule, and the anonymous tip in this case is like the one in *Gates*: "[it] provides virtually nothing from which one might conclude that [the caller] is either honest or his information reliable; likewise, the [tip] gives absolutely no indication of the basis for the [caller's] predictions regarding [Vanessa White's] criminal activities." By requiring "something more," as *Gates* did, ibid., we merely apply what we said in *Adams*: "Some tips, completely lacking in indicia of reliability, would either warrant no police response or require further investigation before a forcible stop of a suspect would be authorized." Simply put, a tip such as this one, standing alone, would not " 'warrant a man of reasonable caution in the belief' that [a stop] was appropriate." *Terry, supra.*

As there was in *Gates*, however, in this case there is more than the tip itself. The tip was not as detailed, and the corroboration was not as complete, as in *Gates*, but the required degree of suspicion was likewise not as high. * * *

Reasonable suspicion is a less demanding standard than probable cause not only in the sense that reasonable suspicion can be established with information that is different in quantity or content than that required to establish probable cause, but also in the sense that reasonable suspicion can arise from information that is less reliable than that required to show probable cause. * * * Reasonable suspicion, like probable cause, is dependent upon both the content of information possessed by police and its degree of reliability. Both factors—quantity and quality—are considered in the "totality of the circumstances—the whole picture," that must be taken into account when evaluating whether there is reasonable suspicion. Thus, if a tip has a relatively low degree of reliability, more information will be required to establish the requisite quantum of suspicion than would be required if the tip were more reliable. The *Gates* Court applied its totality of the circumstances approach in this manner, taking into account the facts known to the officers from personal observation, and giving the anonymous tip the weight it deserved in light of its indicia of reliability as established through independent police work. The same approach applies in the reasonable suspicion context, the only difference being the level of suspicion that must be established. Contrary to the court below, we conclude that when the officers stopped respondent, the anonymous tip had been sufficiently corroborated to furnish reasonable suspicion that respondent was engaged in criminal activity and that the investigative stop therefore did not violate the Fourth Amendment.

It is true that not every detail mentioned by the tipster was verified, such as the name of the woman leaving the building or the precise apartment from which she left; but the officers did corroborate that a woman left the 235 building and got into the particular vehicle that was described by the caller. With respect to the time of departure predicted by the informant, Corporal Davis testified that the caller gave a particular time when the woman would be leaving, but he did not state what that time was. He did testify that, after the call, he and his partner proceeded to the Lynwood Terrace Apartments to put the 235 building under surveillance. Given the fact that the officers proceeded to the indicated address immediately after the call and that respondent emerged not too long thereafter, it appears from the record before us that respondent's departure from the building was within the time frame predicted by the caller. As for the caller's prediction of respondent's destination, it is true that the officers stopped her just short of Dobey's Motel and did not know whether she would have pulled in or continued on past it. But given that the four-mile route driven by respondent was the most direct route possible to Dobey's Motel, but nevertheless involved several turns, we think respondent's destination was significantly corroborated.

The Court's opinion in *Gates* gave credit to the proposition that because an informant is shown to be right about some things, he is probably right about other facts that he has alleged, including the claim that the object of the tip is engaged in criminal activity. Thus, it is not unreasonable to conclude in this case that the independent corroboration by the police of significant aspects of the informer's predictions imparted some degree of reliability to the other allegations made by the caller.

We think it also important that, as in *Gates*, "the anonymous [tip] contained a range of details relating not just to easily obtained facts and conditions existing at the time of the tip, but to future actions of third parties ordinarily not easily predicted." The fact that the officers found a car precisely matching the caller's description in front of the 235 building is an example of the former. Anyone could have "predicted" that fact because it was a condition presumably existing at the time of the call. What was important was the caller's ability to predict respondent's future behavior, because it demonstrated inside information—a special familiarity with respondent's affairs. The general public would have had no way of knowing that respondent would shortly leave the building, get in the described car, and drive the most direct route to Dobey's Motel. Because only a small number of people are generally privy to an individual's itinerary, it is reasonable for police to believe that a person with access to such information is likely to also have access to reliable information about that individual's illegal activities. When significant aspects of the caller's predictions were verified, there was reason to believe not only that the caller was honest but also that he was well informed, at least well enough to justify the stop.

Although it is a close case, we conclude that under the totality of the circumstances the anonymous tip, as corroborated, exhibited sufficient indicia of reliability to justify the investigatory stop of respondent's car. We therefore reverse the judgment of the Court of Criminal Appeals of Alabama and remand for further proceedings not inconsistent with this opinion.

So ordered.

JUSTICE STEVENS, with whom JUSTICE BRENNAN and JUSTICE MARSHALL join, dissenting.

Millions of people leave their apartments at about the same time every day carrying an attaché case and heading for a destination known to their neighbors. Usually, however, the neighbors do not know what the briefcase contains. An anonymous neighbor's prediction about somebody's time of departure and probable destination is anything but a reliable basis for assuming that the commuter is in possession of an illegal substance— particularly when the person is not even carrying the attaché case described by the tipster.

The record in this case does not tell us how often respondent drove from the Lynwood Terrace Apartments to Dobey's Motel; for all we know, she may have been a room clerk or telephone operator working the evening shift. It does not tell us whether Officer Davis made any effort to ascertain the informer's identity, his reason for calling, or the basis of his prediction about respondent's destination. Indeed, for all that this record tells us, the tipster may well have been another police officer who had a "hunch" that respondent might have cocaine in her attaché case.

Anybody with enough knowledge about a given person to make her the target of a prank, or to harbor a grudge against her, will certainly be able to formulate a tip about her like the one predicting Vanessa White's excursion. In addition, under the Court's holding, every citizen is subject to being seized and questioned by any officer who is prepared to testify that the warrantless stop was based on an anonymous tip predicting whatever conduct the officer just observed. Fortunately, the vast majority of those in our law enforcement community would not adopt such a practice. But the Fourth Amendment was intended to protect the citizen from the overzealous and unscrupulous officer as well as from those who are conscientious and truthful. This decision makes a mockery of that protection.

I respectfully dissent.

FLORIDA V. J.L.

529 U.S. 266
Supreme Court of the United States
February 29, 2000, Argued; March 28, 2000, Decided
No. 98-1993

JUSTICE GINSBURG delivered the opinion of the Court.

The question presented in this case is whether an anonymous tip that a person is carrying a gun is, without more, sufficient to justify a police officer's stop and frisk of that person. We hold that it is not.

I

On October 13, 1995, an anonymous caller reported to the Miami-Dade Police that a young black male standing at a particular bus stop and wearing a plaid shirt was carrying a gun. So far as the record reveals, there is no audio recording of the tip, and nothing is known about the informant. Sometime after the police received the tip—the record does not say how long—two officers were instructed to respond. They arrived at the bus stop about six minutes later and saw three black males "just hanging out [there]." One of the three, respondent J. L., was wearing a plaid shirt. Apart from the tip, the officers had no reason to suspect any of the three of illegal conduct. The officers did not see a firearm, and J. L. made no threatening or otherwise unusual movements. One of the officers approached J. L., told him to put his hands up on the bus stop, frisked him, and seized a gun from J. L.'s pocket. The second officer frisked the other two individuals, against whom no allegations had been made, and found nothing.

J. L., who was at the time of the frisk "10 days shy of his 16th birthday," was charged under state law with carrying a concealed firearm without a license and possessing a firearm while under the age of 18. He moved to suppress the gun as the fruit of an unlawful search, and the trial court granted his motion. The intermediate appellate court reversed, but the Supreme Court of Florida quashed that decision and held the search invalid under the Fourth Amendment.

* * * We granted certiorari and now affirm the judgment of the Florida Supreme Court.

II

Our "stop and frisk" decisions begin with *Terry v. Ohio*, 392 U.S. 1 (1968). [Ed. note: The Court briefly reviewed the *Terry* decision.] * * *

In the instant case, the officers' suspicion that J. L. was carrying a weapon arose not from any observations of their own but solely from a call made from an unknown location by an unknown caller. Unlike a tip from a known informant whose reputation can be assessed and who can be held responsible if her or his allegations turn out to be fabricated, *see Adams v. Williams*, "an anonymous tip alone seldom demonstrates the informant's basis of knowledge or veracity," *Alabama v. White*. As we have recognized, however, there are situations in which an anonymous tip, suitably corroborated, exhibits "sufficient indicia of reliability to provide reasonable suspicion to make the investigatory stop." The question we here confront is whether the tip pointing to J. L. had those indicia of reliability.

[Ed. note: The Court then summarized its decision in *Alabama v. White*.] * * * The tip in the instant case lacked the moderate indicia of reliability present in White and essential to the Court's decision in that case. The anonymous call concerning J. L. provided no predictive information and therefore left the police without means to test the informant's knowledge or credibility. That the allegation about the gun turned out to be correct does not suggest that the officers, prior to the frisks, had a reasonable basis for suspecting J. L. of engaging in unlawful conduct: The reasonableness of official suspicion must be measured by what the officers knew before they conducted their search. All the police had to go on in this case was the bare report of an unknown, unaccountable informant who neither explained how he knew about the gun nor supplied any basis for believing he had inside information about J. L. If *White* was a close case on the reliability of anonymous tips, this one surely falls on the other side of the line.

Florida contends that the tip was reliable because its description of the suspect's visible attributes proved accurate: There really was a young black male wearing a plaid shirt at the bus stop. * * *

An accurate description of a subject's readily observable location and appearance is of course reliable in this limited sense: It will help the police correctly identify the person whom the tipster means to accuse. Such a tip, however, does not show that the tipster has knowledge of concealed criminal activity. The reasonable suspicion here at issue requires that a tip be reliable in its assertion of illegality, not just in its tendency to identify a determinate person.

A second major argument advanced by Florida and the United States as amicus is, in essence, that the standard *Terry* analysis should be modified to license a "firearm exception." Under such an exception, a tip alleging an illegal gun would justify a stop and frisk even if the accusation would fail standard pre-search reliability testing. We decline to adopt this position.

Firearms are dangerous, and extraordinary dangers sometimes justify unusual precautions. Our decisions recognize the serious threat that armed criminals pose to public safety; *Terry*'s rule, which permits protective police searches on the basis of reasonable suspicion rather than demanding that officers meet the higher standard of probable cause, responds to this very concern. But an automatic firearm exception to our established reliability analysis would rove too far. Such an exception would enable any person seeking to harass another to set in motion an intrusive, embarrassing police search of the targeted person simply by placing an anonymous call falsely reporting the target's unlawful carriage of a gun. Nor could one securely confine such an exception to allegations involving firearms. Several Courts of Appeals have held it per se foreseeable for people carrying significant amounts of illegal drugs to be carrying guns as well. If police officers may properly conduct *Terry* frisks on the basis of bare-boned tips about guns, it would be reasonable to maintain under the above-cited decisions that the police should similarly have discretion to frisk based on bare-boned tips about narcotics. As we clarified when we made indicia of reliability critical in *Adams* and *White*, the Fourth Amendment is not so easily satisfied.

The facts of this case do not require us to speculate about the circumstances under which the danger alleged in an anonymous tip might be so great as to justify a search even without a showing of reliability. We do not say, for example, that a report of a person carrying a bomb need bear the indicia of reliability we demand for a report of a person carrying a firearm before the police can constitutionally conduct a frisk. Nor do we hold that public safety officials in quarters where the reasonable expectation of Fourth Amendment privacy is diminished, such as airports, and schools, cannot conduct protective searches on the basis of information insufficient to justify searches elsewhere.

* * * [W]e hold that an anonymous tip lacking indicia of reliability of the kind contemplated in *Adams* and *White* does not justify a stop and frisk whenever and however it alleges the illegal possession of a firearm.

The judgment of the Florida Supreme Court is affirmed.

It is so ordered.

JUSTICE KENNEDY, with whom THE CHIEF JUSTICE joins, concurring.

[Omitted.]

NAVARETTE V. CALIFORNIA
572 U.S. 393
Supreme Court of the United States
January 21, 2014, Argued; April 22, 2014, Decided
No. 12-9490

JUSTICE THOMAS delivered the opinion of the Court.

After a 911 caller reported that a vehicle had run her off the road, a police officer located the vehicle she identified during the call and executed a traffic stop. We hold that the stop complied with the Fourth Amendment because, under the totality of the circumstances, the officer had reasonable suspicion that the driver was intoxicated.

I

On August 23, 2008, a Mendocino County 911 dispatch team for the California Highway Patrol (CHP) received a call from another CHP dispatcher in neighboring Humboldt County. The Humboldt County dispatcher relayed a tip from a 911 caller, which the Mendocino County team recorded as follows: "Showing southbound Highway 1 at mile marker 88, Silver Ford 150 pickup. Plate of 8-David-94925. Ran the reporting party off the roadway and was last seen approximately five [minutes] ago." The Mendocino County team then broadcast that information to CHP officers at 3:47 p.m.

A CHP officer heading northbound toward the reported vehicle responded to the broadcast. At 4:00 p.m., the officer passed the truck near mile marker 69. At about 4:05 p.m., after making a U-turn, he pulled the truck over. A second officer, who had separately responded to the broadcast, also arrived on the scene. As the two officers approached the truck, they smelled marijuana. A search of the truck bed revealed 30 pounds of marijuana. The officers arrested the driver, petitioner Lorenzo Prado Navarette, and the passenger, petitioner José Prado Navarette.

Petitioners moved to suppress the evidence, arguing that the traffic stop violated the Fourth Amendment because the officer lacked reasonable suspicion of criminal activity. Both the magistrate who presided over the suppression hearing and the Superior Court disagreed.[1] Petitioners pleaded guilty to transporting marijuana and were sentenced to 90 days in jail plus three years of probation.

The California Court of Appeal affirmed, concluding that the officer had reasonable suspicion to conduct an investigative stop. * * * The California Supreme Court denied review. We granted certiorari and now affirm.

II

The Fourth Amendment permits brief investigative stops—such as the traffic stop in this case—when a law enforcement officer has "a particularized and objective basis for suspecting the particular person stopped of criminal activity." The "reasonable suspicion" necessary to justify such a stop "is dependent upon both the content of information possessed by police and its degree of reliability." The standard takes into account "the totality of the circumstances—the whole picture." Although a mere " 'hunch' " does not create reasonable suspicion, the level of suspicion the standard requires is "considerably less than proof of wrongdoing by a preponderance of the evidence," and "obviously less" than is necessary for probable cause.

A

These principles apply with full force to investigative stops based on information from anonymous tips. We have firmly rejected the argument "that reasonable cause for a[n investigative stop] can only be based on the officer's personal observation, rather than on information supplied by another person." Of course, "an anonymous tip alone seldom demonstrates the informant's basis of knowledge or veracity." That is because "ordinary citizens generally do not provide extensive recitations of the basis of their everyday observations," and an anonymous tipster's veracity is " 'by hypothesis largely unknown, and unknowable.' " But under appropriate circumstances, an anonymous tip can demonstrate "sufficient indicia of reliability to provide reasonable suspicion to make [an] investigatory stop."

Our decisions in *Alabama v. White*, 496 U.S. 325 (1990), and *Florida v. J. L.*, 529 U.S. 266 (2000), are useful guides. * * *

B

The initial question in this case is whether the 911 call was sufficiently reliable to credit the allegation that petitioners' truck "ran the [caller] off the roadway." Even assuming for present purposes that the 911 call was

---

[1] At the suppression hearing, counsel for petitioners did not dispute that the reporting party identified herself by name in the 911 call recording. Because neither the caller nor the Humboldt County dispatcher who received the call was present at the hearing, however, the prosecution did not introduce the recording into evidence. The prosecution proceeded to treat the tip as anonymous, and the lower courts followed suit.

anonymous, *see* n. 1, *supra*, we conclude that the call bore adequate indicia of reliability for the officer to credit the caller's account. The officer was therefore justified in proceeding from the premise that the truck had, in fact, caused the caller's car to be dangerously diverted from the highway.

By reporting that she had been run off the road by a specific vehicle— a silver Ford F-150 pickup, license plate 8D94925—the caller necessarily claimed eyewitness knowledge of the alleged dangerous driving. That basis of knowledge lends significant support to the tip's reliability. This is in contrast to *J. L.*, where the tip provided no basis for concluding that the tipster had actually seen the gun. Even in *White*, where we upheld the stop, there was scant evidence that the tipster had actually observed cocaine in the station wagon. We called *White* a "close case" because "[k]nowledge about a person's future movements indicates some familiarity with that person's affairs, but having such knowledge does not necessarily imply that the informant knows, in particular, whether that person is carrying hidden contraband." A driver's claim that another vehicle ran her off the road, however, necessarily implies that the informant knows the other car was driven dangerously.

There is also reason to think that the 911 caller in this case was telling the truth. Police confirmed the truck's location near mile marker 69 (roughly 19 highway miles south of the location reported in the 911 call) at 4:00 p.m. (roughly 18 minutes after the 911 call). That timeline of events suggests that the caller reported the incident soon after she was run off the road. That sort of contemporaneous report has long been treated as especially reliable. * * * There was no indication that the tip in *J. L.* (or even in *White*) was contemporaneous with the observation of criminal activity or made under the stress of excitement caused by a startling event, but those considerations weigh in favor of the caller's veracity here.

Another indicator of veracity is the caller's use of the 911 emergency system. A 911 call has some features that allow for identifying and tracing callers, and thus provide some safeguards against making false reports with immunity. As this case illustrates, *see* n. 1, *supra*, 911 calls can be recorded, which provides victims with an opportunity to identify the false tipster's voice and subject him to prosecution. The 911 system also permits law enforcement to verify important information about the caller. In 1998, the Federal Communications Commission (FCC) began to require cellular carriers to relay the caller's phone number to 911 dispatchers. Beginning in 2001, carriers have been required to identify the caller's geographic location with increasing specificity. And although callers may ordinarily block call recipients from obtaining their identifying information, FCC regulations exempt 911 calls from that privilege. None of this is to suggest that tips in 911 calls are per se reliable. Given the foregoing technological and regulatory developments, however, a reasonable officer could conclude that a false tipster would think twice before using such a system. The caller's use of the 911 system is therefore one of the relevant circumstances that, taken together, justified the officer's reliance on the information reported in the 911 call.

C

Even a reliable tip will justify an investigative stop only if it creates reasonable suspicion that "criminal activity may be afoot." We must therefore determine whether the 911 caller's report of being run off the roadway created reasonable suspicion of an ongoing crime such as drunk driving as opposed to an isolated episode of past recklessness. We conclude that the behavior alleged by the 911 caller, "viewed from the standpoint of an objectively reasonable police officer, amount[s] to reasonable suspicion" of drunk driving. The stop was therefore proper.

Reasonable suspicion depends on "the factual and practical considerations of everyday life on which reasonable and prudent men, not legal technicians, act." Under that commonsense approach, we can appropriately recognize certain driving behaviors as sound indicia of drunk driving. Indeed, the accumulated experience of thousands of officers suggests that these sorts of erratic behaviors are strongly correlated with drunk driving. Of course, not all traffic infractions imply intoxication. Unconfirmed reports of driving without a seatbelt or slightly over the speed limit, for example, are so tenuously connected to drunk driving that a stop on those grounds alone would be constitutionally suspect. But a reliable tip alleging the dangerous behaviors discussed above generally would justify a traffic stop on suspicion of drunk driving.

The 911 caller in this case reported more than a minor traffic infraction and more than a conclusory allegation of drunk or reckless driving. Instead, she alleged a specific and dangerous result of the driver's conduct: running another car off the highway. That conduct bears too great a resemblance to paradigmatic manifestations of drunk driving to be dismissed as an isolated example of recklessness. Running another vehicle off the road suggests lane-positioning problems, decreased vigilance, impaired judgment, or some combination of those recognized drunk driving cues. And the experience of many officers suggests that a driver who almost strikes a vehicle or another object—the exact scenario that ordinarily causes "running [another vehicle] off the roadway"—is likely intoxicated. As a result, we cannot say that the officer acted unreasonably under these circumstances in stopping a driver whose alleged conduct was a significant indicator of drunk driving.

* * * It is true that the reported behavior might also be explained by, for example, a driver responding to "an unruly child or other distraction." But we have consistently recognized that reasonable suspicion "need not rule out the possibility of innocent conduct."

Nor did the absence of additional suspicious conduct, after the vehicle was first spotted by an officer, dispel the reasonable suspicion of drunk driving. It is hardly surprising that the appearance of a marked police car would inspire more careful driving for a time. Extended observation of an allegedly drunk driver might eventually dispel a reasonable suspicion of intoxication, but the 5-minute period in this case hardly sufficed in that regard. Of course, an officer who already has such a reasonable suspicion need not surveil a vehicle at length in order to personally observe suspicious driving. Once reasonable suspicion of drunk driving arises, "[t]he reasonableness of the officer's decision to stop a suspect does not turn on the availability of less intrusive investigatory techniques." This would be a particularly inappropriate context to depart from that settled rule, because allowing a drunk driver a second chance for dangerous conduct could have disastrous consequences.

III

Like *White*, this is a "close case." As in that case, the indicia of the 911 caller's reliability here are stronger than those in *J. L.*, where we held that a bare-bones tip was unreliable. Although the indicia present here are different from those we found sufficient in *White*, there is more than one way to demonstrate "a particularized and objective basis for suspecting the particular person stopped of criminal activity." Under the totality of the circumstances, we find the indicia of reliability in this case sufficient to provide the officer with reasonable suspicion that the driver of the reported vehicle had run another vehicle off the road. That made it reasonable under the circumstances for the officer to execute a traffic stop. We accordingly affirm.

It is so ordered.

JUSTICE SCALIA, with whom JUSTICE GINSBURG, JUSTICE SOTOMAYOR, and JUSTICE KAGAN join, dissenting.

[Omitted.]

E. OTHER *TERRY* SCENARIOS

Apart from the interplay between informants and *Terry*, there exist separate concerns about the role of reasonable suspicion in other scenarios unconsidered by the original *Terry* Court. For example, in *Illinois v. Wardlow*, we evaluate how the neighborhood a citizen lives in makes the existence of reasonable suspicion more or less likely. Then, in *United States v. Montero-Camargo*, we consider how a number of innocuous circumstances—when considered together—can establish reasonable suspicion to conduct an investigative stop of a vehicle.

ILLINOIS V. WARDLOW

528 U.S. 119
Supreme Court of the United States
November 2, 1999, Argued; January 12, 2000, Decided
No. 98-1036

CHIEF JUSTICE REHNQUIST delivered the opinion of the Court. * * *

On September 9, 1995, Officers Nolan and Harvey were working as uniformed officers in the special operations section of the Chicago Police Department. The officers were driving the last car of a four car caravan converging on an area known for heavy narcotics trafficking in order to investigate drug transactions. The officers were traveling together because they expected to find a crowd of people in the area, including lookouts and customers.

As the caravan passed 4035 West Van Buren, Officer Nolan observed respondent Wardlow standing next to the building holding an opaque bag. Respondent looked in the direction of the officers and fled. Nolan and Harvey turned their car southbound, watched him as he ran through the gangway and an alley, and eventually cornered him on the street. Nolan then exited his car and stopped respondent. He immediately conducted a protective pat-down search for weapons because in his experience it was common for there to be weapons in the near vicinity of narcotics transactions. During the frisk, Officer Nolan squeezed the bag respondent was carrying and felt a heavy, hard object similar to the shape of a gun. The officer then opened the bag and discovered a .38-caliber handgun with five live rounds of ammunition. The officers arrested Wardlow.

The Illinois trial court denied respondent's motion to suppress, finding the gun was recovered during a lawful stop and frisk. Following a stipulated bench trial, Wardlow was convicted of unlawful use of a weapon by a felon. The Illinois Appellate Court reversed Wardlow's conviction, concluding that the gun should have been suppressed because Officer Nolan did not have reasonable suspicion sufficient to justify an investigative stop pursuant to *Terry v. Ohio.*

The Illinois Supreme Court agreed. * * * We granted certiorari and now reverse.[1]

This case, involving a brief encounter between a citizen and a police officer on a public street, is governed by the analysis we first applied in *Terry.* In *Terry,* we held that an officer may, consistent with the Fourth Amendment, conduct a brief, investigatory stop when the officer has a reasonable, articulable suspicion that criminal activity is afoot. While "reasonable suspicion" is a less demanding standard than probable cause and requires a showing considerably less than preponderance of the

---

[1] The state courts have differed on whether unprovoked flight is sufficient grounds to constitute reasonable suspicion.

evidence, the Fourth Amendment requires at least a minimal level of objective justification for making the stop. The officer must be able to articulate more than an "inchoate and unparticularized suspicion or 'hunch'" of criminal activity.[2]

Nolan and Harvey were among eight officers in a four car caravan that was converging on an area known for heavy narcotics trafficking, and the officers anticipated encountering a large number of people in the area, including drug customers and individuals serving as lookouts. It was in this context that Officer Nolan decided to investigate Wardlow after observing him flee. An individual's presence in an area of expected criminal activity, standing alone, is not enough to support a reasonable, particularized suspicion that the person is committing a crime. But officers are not required to ignore the relevant characteristics of a location in determining whether the circumstances are sufficiently suspicious to warrant further investigation. Accordingly, we have previously noted the fact that the stop occurred in a "high crime area" among the relevant contextual considerations in a *Terry* analysis. *Adams v. Williams.*

In this case, moreover, it was not merely respondent's presence in an area of heavy narcotics trafficking that aroused the officers' suspicion but his unprovoked flight upon noticing the police. Our cases have also recognized that nervous, evasive behavior is a pertinent factor in determining reasonable suspicion. Headlong flight—wherever it occurs— is the consummate act of evasion: It is not necessarily indicative of wrongdoing, but it is certainly suggestive of such. In reviewing the propriety of an officer's conduct, courts do not have available empirical studies dealing with inferences drawn from suspicious behavior, and we cannot reasonably demand scientific certainty from judges or law enforcement officers where none exists. Thus, the determination of reasonable suspicion must be based on commonsense judgments and inferences about human behavior. We conclude Officer Nolan was justified in suspecting that Wardlow was involved in criminal activity, and, therefore, in investigating further.

Such a holding is entirely consistent with our decision in *Florida v. Royer*, 460 U.S. 491 (1983), where we held that when an officer, without reasonable suspicion or probable cause, approaches an individual, the individual has a right to ignore the police and go about his business. And any "refusal to cooperate, without more, does not furnish the minimal level of objective justification needed for a detention or seizure." But unprovoked flight is simply not a mere refusal to cooperate. Flight, by its very nature, is not "going about one's business"; in fact, it is just the opposite. Allowing officers confronted with such flight to stop the fugitive and investigate

---

[2]   We granted certiorari solely on the question of whether the initial stop was supported by reasonable suspicion. Therefore, we express no opinion as to the lawfulness of the frisk independently of the stop.

further is quite consistent with the individual's right to go about his business or to stay put and remain silent in the face of police questioning.

Respondent and amici also argue that there are innocent reasons for flight from police and that, therefore, flight is not necessarily indicative of ongoing criminal activity. This fact is undoubtedly true, but does not establish a violation of the Fourth Amendment. Even in *Terry*, the conduct justifying the stop was ambiguous and susceptible of an innocent explanation. The officer observed two individuals pacing back and forth in front of a store, peering into the window and periodically conferring. All of this conduct was by itself lawful, but it also suggested that the individuals were casing the store for a planned robbery. *Terry* recognized that the officers could detain the individuals to resolve the ambiguity.

In allowing such detentions, *Terry* accepts the risk that officers may stop innocent people. Indeed, the Fourth Amendment accepts that risk in connection with more drastic police action; persons arrested and detained on probable cause to believe they have committed a crime may turn out to be innocent. The *Terry* stop is a far more minimal intrusion, simply allowing the officer to briefly investigate further. If the officer does not learn facts rising to the level of probable cause, the individual must be allowed to go on his way. But in this case the officers found respondent in possession of a handgun, and arrested him for violation of an Illinois firearms statute. No question of the propriety of the arrest itself is before us.

The judgment of the Supreme Court of Illinois is reversed, and the cause is remanded for further proceedings not inconsistent with this opinion.

It is so ordered.

JUSTICE STEVENS, with whom JUSTICE SOUTER, JUSTICE GINSBURG, and JUSTICE BREYER join, concurring in part and dissenting in part.

The State of Illinois asks this Court to announce a "bright-line rule," authorizing the temporary detention of anyone who flees at the mere sight of a police officer. Respondent counters by asking us to adopt the opposite per se rule—that the fact that a person flees upon seeing the police can never, by itself, be sufficient to justify a temporary investigative stop of the kind authorized by *Terry v. Ohio.* * * *

Although I agree with the Court's rejection of the per se rules proffered by the parties, unlike the Court, I am persuaded that in this case the brief testimony of the officer who seized respondent does not justify the conclusion that he had reasonable suspicion to make the stop. Before discussing the specific facts of this case, I shall comment on the parties' requests for a per se rule.

I

* * * The question in this case concerns "the degree of suspicion that attaches to" a person's flight—or, more precisely, what "commonsense conclusions" can be drawn respecting the motives behind that flight. A pedestrian may break into a run for a variety of reasons—to catch up with a friend a block or two away, to seek shelter from an impending storm, to arrive at a bus stop before the bus leaves, to get home in time for dinner, to resume jogging after a pause for rest, to avoid contact with a bore or a bully, or simply to answer the call of nature—any of which might coincide with the arrival of an officer in the vicinity. A pedestrian might also run because he or she has just sighted one or more police officers. In the latter instance, the State properly points out "that the fleeing person may be, inter alia, (1) an escapee from jail; (2) wanted on a warrant, (3) in possession of contraband, (i.e. drugs, weapons, stolen goods, etc.); or (4) someone who has just committed another type of crime." In short, there are unquestionably circumstances in which a person's flight is suspicious, and undeniably instances in which a person runs for entirely innocent reasons.[3]

Given the diversity and frequency of possible motivations for flight, it would be profoundly unwise to endorse either per se rule. The inference we can reasonably draw about the motivation for a person's flight, rather, will depend on a number of different circumstances. Factors such as the time of day, the number of people in the area, the character of the neighborhood, whether the officer was in uniform, the way the runner was dressed, the direction and speed of the flight, and whether the person's behavior was otherwise unusual might be relevant in specific cases. This number of variables is surely sufficient to preclude either a bright-line rule that always justifies, or that never justifies, an investigative stop based on the sole fact that flight began after a police officer appeared nearby. * * *

Even assuming we know that a person runs because he sees the police, the inference to be drawn may still vary from case to case. * * * [A] reasonable person may conclude that an officer's sudden appearance indicates nearby criminal activity. And where there is criminal activity there is also a substantial element of danger—either from the criminal or from a confrontation between the criminal and the police. These

---

[3]   *Compare, e.g.,* Proverbs 28:1 ("The wicked flee when no man pursueth: but the righteous are as bold as a lion") *with* Proverbs 22:3 ("A shrewd man sees trouble coming and lies low; the simple walk into it and pay the penalty").

I have rejected reliance on the former proverb in the past, because its "ivory-towered analysis of the real world" fails to account for the experiences of many citizens of this country, particularly those who are minorities. *See California v. Hodari D.,* 499 U.S. 621, 630, n.4 (1991) (STEVENS, J., dissenting). That this pithy expression fails to capture the total reality of our world, however, does not mean it is inaccurate in all instances.

considerations can lead to an innocent and understandable desire to quit the vicinity with all speed.[6]

Among some citizens, particularly minorities and those residing in high crime areas, there is also the possibility that the fleeing person is entirely innocent, but, with or without justification, believes that contact with the police can itself be dangerous, apart from any criminal activity associated with the officer's sudden presence. For such a person, unprovoked flight is neither "aberrant" nor "abnormal." Moreover, these concerns and fears are known to the police officers themselves,[9] and are validated by law enforcement investigations into their own practices.[10] Accordingly, the evidence supporting the reasonableness of these beliefs is too pervasive to be dismissed as random or rare, and too persuasive to be disparaged as inconclusive or insufficient. In any event, just as we do not require "scientific certainty" for our commonsense conclusion that

---

[6] Statistical studies of bystander victimization are rare. One study attributes this to incomplete recordkeeping and a lack of officially compiled data. Nonetheless, that study, culling data from newspaper reports in four large cities over an 11-year period, found "substantial increases in reported bystander killings and woundings in all four cities." From 1986 to 1988, for example, the study identified 250 people who were killed or wounded in bystander shootings in the four survey cities. Most significantly for the purposes of the present case, the study found that such incidents "rank at the top of public outrage." The saliency of this phenomenon, in turn, "violates the routine assumptions" of day-to-day affairs, and, "with enough frequency . . . it shapes the conduct of daily life."

[9] The Chief of the Washington, D. C., Metropolitan Police Department, for example, confirmed that "sizeable percentages of Americans today—especially Americans of color—still view policing in the United States to be discriminatory, if not by policy and definition, certainly in its day-to-day application." And a recent survey of 650 Los Angeles Police Department officers found that 25% felt that "racial bias (prejudice) on the part of officers toward minority citizens currently exists and contributes to a negative interaction between police and the community."

[10] New Jersey's Attorney General, in a recent investigation into allegations of racial profiling on the New Jersey Turnpike, concluded that "minority motorists have been treated differently [by New Jersey State Troopers] than non-minority motorists during the course of traffic stops on the New Jersey Turnpike." "The problem of disparate treatment is real—not imagined," declared the Attorney General. Not surprisingly, the report concluded that this disparate treatment "engenders feelings of fear, resentment, hostility, and mistrust by minority citizens." Recently, the United States Department of Justice, citing this very evidence, announced that it would appoint an outside monitor to oversee the actions of the New Jersey State Police and ensure that it enacts policy changes advocated by the Interim Report, and keeps records on racial statistics and traffic stops.

Likewise, the Massachusetts Attorney General investigated similar allegations of egregious police conduct toward minorities. The report stated:

> We conclude that Boston police officers engaged in improper, and unconstitutional, conduct in the 1989–90 period with respect to stops and searches of minority individuals . . . . Although we cannot say with precision how widespread this illegal conduct was, we believe that it was sufficiently common to justify changes in certain Department practices.

Perhaps the most disturbing evidence was that the scope of a number of *Terry* searches went far beyond anything authorized by that case and indeed, beyond anything that we believe would be acceptable under the federal and state constitutions even where probable cause existed to conduct a full search incident to an arrest. Forcing young men to lower their trousers, or otherwise searching inside their underwear, on public streets or in public hallways, is so demeaning and invasive of fundamental precepts of privacy that it can only be condemned in the strongest terms. The fact that not only the young men themselves, but independent witnesses complained of strip searches, should be deeply alarming to all members of this community.

unprovoked flight can sometimes indicate suspicious motives, neither do we require scientific certainty to conclude that unprovoked flight can occur for other, innocent reasons.[12] * * *

II

Guided by that totality-of-the-circumstances test, the Court concludes that Officer Nolan had reasonable suspicion to stop respondent. In this respect, my view differs from the Court's. * * *

Officer Nolan and his partner were in the last of the four patrol cars that "were all caravanning eastbound down Van Buren." Nolan first observed respondent "in front of 4035 West Van Buren." Wardlow "looked in our direction and began fleeing." Nolan then "began driving southbound down the street observing [respondent] running through the gangway and the alley southbound," and observed that Wardlow was carrying a white, opaque bag under his arm. After the car turned south and intercepted respondent as he "ran right towards us," Officer Nolan stopped him and conducted a "protective search," which revealed that the bag under respondent's arm contained a loaded handgun.

This terse testimony is most noticeable for what it fails to reveal. Though asked whether he was in a marked or unmarked car, Officer Nolan could not recall the answer. He was not asked whether any of the other three cars in the caravan were marked, or whether any of the other seven officers were in uniform. Though he explained that the size of the caravan was because "normally in these different areas there's an enormous amount of people, sometimes lookouts, customers," Officer Nolan did not testify as to whether anyone besides Wardlow was nearby 4035 West Van Buren. Nor is it clear that that address was the intended destination of the caravan. As the Appellate Court of Illinois interpreted the record, "it appears that the officers were simply driving by, on their way to some unidentified location, when they noticed defendant standing at 4035 West Van Buren." Officer Nolan's testimony also does not reveal how fast the officers were driving. It does not indicate whether he saw respondent notice the other patrol cars. And it does not say whether the caravan, or any part of it, had already passed Wardlow by before he began to run.

Indeed, the Appellate Court thought the record was even "too vague to support the inference that . . . defendant's flight was related to his expectation of police focus on him." Presumably, respondent did not react to the first three cars, and we cannot even be sure that he recognized the occupants of the fourth as police officers. The adverse inference is based

---

[12] As a general matter, local courts often have a keener and more informed sense of local police practices and events that may heighten these concerns at particular times or locations. Thus, a reviewing court may accord substantial deference to a local court's determination that fear of the police is especially acute in a specific location or at a particular time.

entirely on the officer's statement: "He looked in our direction and began fleeing."

No other factors sufficiently support a finding of reasonable suspicion. Though respondent was carrying a white, opaque bag under his arm, there is nothing at all suspicious about that. Certainly the time of day—shortly after noon—does not support Illinois' argument. Nor were the officers "responding to any call or report of suspicious activity in the area." * * *

The State, along with the majority of the Court, relies as well on the assumption that this flight occurred in a high crime area. Even if that assumption is accurate, it is insufficient because even in a high crime neighborhood unprovoked flight does not invariably lead to reasonable suspicion. On the contrary, because many factors providing innocent motivations for unprovoked flight are concentrated in high crime areas, the character of the neighborhood arguably makes an inference of guilt less appropriate, rather than more so. Like unprovoked flight itself, presence in a high crime neighborhood is a fact too generic and susceptible to innocent explanation to satisfy the reasonable suspicion inquiry. * * *

I therefore respectfully dissent from the Court's judgment to reverse the court below.

QUESTIONS, COMMENTS, CONCERNS?

1.   **Defining "high crime".** In your opinion, does the majority in *Wardlow* give a satisfactory definition of what constitutes a "high crime" neighborhood? Remember that the respondent in *Wardlow* lived in Chicago. Since *Wardlow*, Chicago has experienced a spike in homicides. Yuliana Romanyshyn, *Chicago Homicide Rate Compared: Most Big Cities Don't Recover From Spikes Right Away*, THE CHICAGO TRIBUNE (Sept. 26, 2017), https://www.chicagotribune.com/data/ct-homicide-spikes-comparison-htmlstory.html. Does that make it a *higher* crime neighborhood than in *Wardlow*?

In an effort to more concretely define the quantum of evidence necessary to establish that an area is, indeed, properly characterized as "high crime," the First Circuit compiled a list of factors considered important by other lower courts:

> (1) the nexus between the type of crime most prevalent or common in the area and the type of crime suspected in the instant case; (2) limited geographic boundaries of the "area" or "neighborhood" being evaluated; and (3) temporal proximity between evidence of heightened criminal activity and the date of the stop or search at issue. Evidence on these issues could include a mix of objective data and the testimony of police officers, describing their experiences in the area.

United States v. Wright, 485 F.3d 45, 53–54 (1st Cir. 2007).

2. **Defining "high crime" redux.** What qualifies as a "high crime" neighborhood outside of Chicago? What types of crimes qualify? Is *Wardlow* relative? That is, do *all* neighborhoods have a "high crime" section for *Wardlow* purposes? Considered one of the safest cities in America, Ann Arbor, Michigan, is about three and one-half hours east of Chicago. With just 193 violent crimes per 100,000 residents, does Ann Arbor too have a "high crime" section? Leanna Garfield, *The 33 Safest American Cities to Live In*, BUSINESS INSIDER (Mar. 7, 2018), https://www.businessinsider.com/safest-cities-america-us-2017-8.

3. **High crime and the *Floyd* litigation.** In many ways, the *Floyd* litigation demonstrates *Wardlow's* deficiencies. Return to Floyd's initial complaint, particularly the preliminary statement. [Casefile Document 1, at 2.] Recall that Floyd challenges the NYPD's *Terry* policy on the basis that officers were unconstitutionally stopping and frisking citizens on the basis of "race and/or national origin, not reasonable suspicion[.]"*Id.* But what if the area where Floyd was stopped—Beach Avenue in his Bronx neighborhood— was a "high crime" neighborhood? *See id.* at 23 at ¶ 100. Consider that Floyd was walking home and, presumably, was passing other homes along his walk. Consider also that, compared with, for example, Manhattan, the Bronx would experience more burglary claims in 2010 (remember Floyd was stopped in 2007 and again in 2008). *Crime & Safety Report: Comparing Neighborhoods*, DNA INFO.COM, http://lawschool.westlaw.com/shared/westlawRedirect.aspx?task= find&cite=528+U.S.+119&appflag=67.12 (last visited Apr. 9, 2018). Assuming the applicability of the 2010 data to Floyd's case, is the Bronx sufficiently "high crime" in the burglary sense that officers could stop Floyd? The City of New York certainly thought Floyd's neighborhood alongside the prospect of a burglary mattered. Consider a relevant portion of its motion for summary judgment:

> The officers observed plaintiff in a neighborhood where a pattern of midday burglaries had been occurring and saw his bag. * * * Based on the totality of the circumstances, it was not unreasonable for the officers to stop Floyd on suspicion of burglary and frisk him for safety concerns.

[Casefile Document 2 at 3.] Persuaded?

4. **Floyd and *Whren*.** By issuing a unanimous opinion, the *Whren* Court seemingly made clear that the Fourth Amendment is not an appropriate source of law to litigate racially disparate law enforcement practices. In light of *Whren*, how can Floyd prove a violation of the Fourth Amendment?

UNITED STATES V. MONTERO-CAMARGO

208 F.3d 1122
United States Court of Appeals for the Ninth Circuit
December 16, 1999, Argued and Submitted; April 11, 2000, Filed
Nos. 97-50643, 97-50645

REINHARDT, CIRCUIT JUDGE:

The question before us is whether Border Patrol agents had reasonable suspicion to stop German Espinoza Montero-Camargo and Lorenzo Sanchez-Guillen. The defendants, who were driving separate automobiles in tandem, made U-turns on a highway at the only place where the view of the agents manning a permanent stationary checkpoint was obstructed. Following the turns, the two cars, both bearing Mexicali license plates, stopped briefly in an area that is often used as a drop-off and pick-up point for undocumented aliens and contraband. The U-turns occurred shortly after the cars passed a sign stating that the previously closed Border Patrol facility was now open. Based on these and other factors, the district court concluded that the stop, which occurred some fifty miles north of the Mexican border, was justified, as did the majority of the three judge panel that considered the question. We took the case en banc to reconsider the reasonable suspicion question. Although we affirm the result reached by both the district court and the panel majority, we reject some of the factors on which they relied.

FACTS

On the afternoon of October 15, 1996, a passing driver told border patrol agents at the Highway 86 permanent stationary checkpoint in El Centro, California, that two cars heading north, with Mexicali license plates,[1] had just made U-turns on the highway shortly before the checkpoint. Upon receiving the tip, two Border Patrol Agents, Brian Johnson and Carl Fisher, got into separate marked patrol cars and headed south to investigate. Approximately one minute later (and about one mile from the checkpoint), the two agents saw a blue Chevrolet Blazer and a red Nissan sedan, both with Mexicali plates, pull off the shoulder and re-enter the highway heading south.

According to the agents, the area where they first observed the cars is used by lawbreakers to drop off and pick up undocumented aliens and illegal drugs, while evading inspection. Its use for such purposes is due in part to the fact that the view of that part of the highway area from the Border Patrol checkpoint is blocked. The location, according to Agent Johnson, is the only place where it is feasible to turn around both safely and with impunity. After that point, the road narrows and is in plain view

---

[1]   Border Patrol Agent Brian Johnson testified that Beja California or Mexicali plates are distinctive orange plates with a darker letter background and "Front BC" embossed on the bottom of the plate.

of the checkpoint. The highway itself runs through the open desert and there is a fence on either side.

Both agents testified that almost all of the stops made by the Border Patrol at the turnaround site resulted in the discovery of "a violation of some sort . . ." involving either illegal aliens or narcotics. In contrast, Agent Johnson said that similar stops made in connection with turnarounds near other checkpoints did not result in arrests nearly as frequently. He attributed the difference to the fact that travelers routinely miss their turnoffs to camping sites near those other checkpoints. Before the northbound Highway 86 checkpoint, however, there are no exits, driveways, or roads nearby that a driver might accidentally pass by. In fact, the only exit off of Highway 86 in that area is a private driveway to the Elmore Ranch, some two miles from the turnaround point.

The place where the agents saw that the vehicles had stopped following the U-turn was a deserted area on the side of the southbound highway located opposite the large sign on the northbound side advising drivers that the checkpoint was open. As Agent Johnson testified, the sign was the first indication to northbound drivers that the Border Patrol's facility was operational. The checkpoint in question had been closed for some time and had reopened only a day or two earlier.

At the suppression hearing, Agent Johnson testified that the majority of people going through the El Centro checkpoint are Hispanic. This demographic makeup is typical of the larger region of which the city El Centro is a part. In Imperial County, where El Centro is located, Hispanics make up roughly 73% of the population. Agent Johnson also testified that as he pulled behind the Blazer, he noted that both the driver and the passenger appeared to be Hispanic. Johnson stated that when the driver and passenger noticed him behind them, the passenger picked up a newspaper and began reading. This, according to Agent Johnson, further aroused his suspicions. Johnson then stopped the Blazer, identified himself as a Border Patrol agent, and asked about the citizenship of the two occupants. In response to Johnson's inquiries, the driver, Lorenzo Sanchez-Guillen, and his passenger, Sylvia Renteria-Wolff, showed Agent Johnson I–586 cards, which allow Mexican citizens to travel up to 25 miles inside the United States for no longer than 72 hours at a time. As the Blazer had been stopped approximately 50 miles from the border, Johnson then brought the two occupants to the checkpoint for processing.

In the meantime, Agent Fisher continued to follow the second car, a red Nissan sedan. According to Fisher, when he and Agent Johnson first drew near the two cars, the Nissan began to accelerate. As Fisher caught up with the vehicle, he could see that the second driver also appeared to be Hispanic. Fisher ultimately pulled the Nissan over after following it for approximately four miles. Appellant German Espinoza Montero-Camargo was the driver. After stopping the car, Agent Fisher, with the aid of Agent Johnson, who had returned to help him, searched the trunk and found two large bags of marijuana. A subsequent search of the Blazer back at the checkpoint turned up a loaded .32 caliber pistol in the glove compartment and an ammunition clip that fit the pistol in the passenger's purse.

Montero-Camargo, Sanchez-Guillen, and Renteria-Wolff were charged with conspiracy to possess marijuana with intent to distribute in violation of 21 U.S.C. §§ 846 and 841(a)(1), as well as possession of marijuana with intent to distribute in violation of 21 U.S.C. § 841(a)(1). Sanchez-Guillen was also charged with being an illegal alien in possession of ammunition in violation of 18 U.S.C. § 922(g)(5) and § 924(a)(2) and aiding and abetting the carrying of a firearm during the commission of a drug trafficking crime in violation of 18 U.S.C. § 924(c)(1) and (2). The three defendants filed a pre-trial motion to suppress on the ground that the vehicle stop was not based on reasonable suspicion. When the district court denied the motion, Montero-Camargo entered a conditional guilty plea to conspiracy to possess and possession of marijuana with the intent to distribute; he reserved the right to challenge on appeal two of the district court's determinations, including the denial of the motion to suppress.[7] Sanchez-Guillen went to trial, and a jury convicted him of conspiracy to possess and possession of marijuana with the intent to distribute, as well as being an illegal alien in possession of ammunition. He raises a number of issues on appeal.[8]

In denying the motion to suppress, the district court conceded that the government's case "was somewhat weak," but concluded that, upon considering "all the factors that the officers had in their possession at the time that each of them made the stops, . . . there was a sufficient founded suspicion to make an investigatory stop." Those factors, as the district court categorized them, included: 1) the tip about a U-turn made in the middle of the highway just before the checkpoint by two cars with Mexican license plates; 2) the alleged driving in tandem and the Mexicali license plates which supported the inference drawn by the officers that these were the two cars identified by the tipster; 3) the area in question, which, based on the officers' experience with previous stops, is "a notorious spot where smugglers turn around to avoid inspection" just before the first sign indicating that the checkpoint was in fact open; 4) the fact that the occupants of both cars appeared to be of Hispanic descent; and 5) the fact that the passenger in the Blazer picked up a newspaper as the Border Patrol car approached. The district judge concluded that when these factors

---

[7]   Renteria-Wolff, whose conviction is not at issue in this appeal and who is not a party to it, pled guilty to being an illegal alien in possession of ammunition, in violation of 18 U.S.C. § 922(g)(5) and 924(a)(2).

[8]   Because we consider here only the reasonable suspicion issue and reach the same result as the panel majority, the panel opinion is reinstated as to all other issues.

were considered in light of the officers' experience, they supported a finding of reasonable suspicion.

On appeal, Montero-Camargo and Sanchez-Guillen argued that the district court erred in denying the motion to suppress. The panel majority agreed, however, with the district court's conclusion. It did so by listing, without further explication, a number of factors, including: apparent avoidance of a checkpoint, tandem driving, Mexicali license plates, the Hispanic appearance of the vehicles' occupants, the behavior of Renteria-Wolff, the agent's prior experience during stops after similar turnarounds, and the pattern of criminal activity at the remote spot where the two cars stopped. Although we reach the same result as both the district judge and the panel majority, we do so on the basis of a more selective set of factors.

ANALYSIS

1. The Reasonable Suspicion Calculus

The Fourth Amendment "applies to all seizures of the person, including seizures that involve only a brief detention short of traditional arrest." Accordingly, the Fourth Amendment requires that such seizures be, at a minimum, "reasonable." In order to satisfy the Fourth Amendment's strictures, an investigatory stop by the police may be made only if the officer in question has "a reasonable suspicion supported by articulable facts that criminal activity may be afoot . . . ."

Like probable cause determinations, the reasonable suspicion analysis is "not 'readily, or even usefully, reduced to a neat set of legal rules' " and, also like probable cause, takes into account the totality of the circumstances. Although the level of suspicion required for a brief investigatory stop is less demanding than that for probable cause, the Fourth Amendment nevertheless requires an objective justification for such a stop. As a result, the officer in question "must be able to articulate more than an 'inchoate and unparticularized suspicion' or 'hunch' of criminal activity." Rather, reasonable suspicion exists when an officer is aware of specific, articulable facts which, when considered with objective and reasonable inferences, form a basis for particularized suspicion.

The requirement of particularized suspicion encompasses two elements. First, the assessment must be based upon the totality of the circumstances. Second, that assessment must arouse a reasonable suspicion that the particular person being stopped has committed or is about to commit a crime. Accordingly, we have rejected profiles that are "likely to sweep many ordinary citizens into a generality of suspicious appearance . . . ."

* * * In *United States v. Sokolow*, [490 U.S. 1, 7 (1989),] the Supreme Court held that: "[i]n making a determination of probable cause the relevant inquiry is not whether particular conduct is 'innocent' or 'guilty,'

but the degree of suspicion that attaches to particular types of 'noncriminal acts.' That principle applies equally well to the reasonable suspicion inquiry." In short, conduct that is not necessarily indicative of criminal activity may, in certain circumstances, be relevant to the reasonable suspicion calculus. At the same time, however, innocuous conduct does not justify an investigatory stop unless there is other information or surrounding circumstances of which the police are aware, which, when considered along with the otherwise innocuous conduct, tend to indicate criminal activity has occurred or is about to take place.

In all circumstances, "the officer is entitled to assess the facts in light of his experience in detecting illegal entry and smuggling." Nevertheless, "[w]hile an officer may evaluate the facts supporting reasonable suspicion in light of his experience, experience may not be used to give the officers unbridled discretion in making a stop." In other words, an officer's experience may furnish the background against which the relevant facts are to be assessed, as long as the inferences he draws are objectively reasonable; but "experience" does not in itself serve as an independent factor in the reasonable suspicion analysis.

2.   *The Factors Considered by the District Court*

As noted above, the district court based its determination that reasonable suspicion existed on a series of factors: 1) the U-turn made before the checkpoint by the two cars; 2) the driving in tandem and the Mexicali license plates; 3) the area at which the U-turn occurred included a well-known drop-off point for smugglers; 4) the Hispanic appearance of the three defendants; and 5) Renteria-Wolff's picking up the newspaper after glancing back at the patrol cars. Although we agree with the district court that reasonable suspicion did exist to justify an investigatory stop, we conclude that some of the factors on which the district court relied are not relevant or appropriate to the reasonable suspicion analysis. We begin by considering the factors in that category, before turning to address those which the district court properly considered.

In concluding that reasonable suspicion existed, both the district court and the panel majority relied in part upon the Hispanic appearance of the three defendants. We hold that they erred in doing so. We first note that Agent Johnston testified at the suppression hearing that the majority of people who pass through the El Centro checkpoints are Hispanic, and thus, presumably have a Hispanic appearance.

As we stressed earlier, reasonable suspicion requires particularized suspicion. Where, as here, the majority (or any substantial number) of people share a specific characteristic, that characteristic is of little or no probative value in such a particularized and context-specific analysis. As we put it in [*United States v.*] *Rodriguez*, [976 F.2d 592 (9th Cir. 1992),] "[w]e are not prepared to approve the wholesale seizure of miscellaneous persons . . . in the absence of well-founded suspicion based on particular, individualized, and objectively observable factors which indicate that the person is engaged in criminal activity."

The likelihood that in an area in which the majority-or even a substantial part-of the population is Hispanic, any given person of Hispanic ancestry is in fact an alien, let alone an illegal alien, is not high enough to make Hispanic appearance a relevant factor in the reasonable suspicion calculus. As we have previously held, factors that have such a low probative value that no reasonable officer would have relied on them to make an investigative stop must be disregarded as a matter of law. Moreover, as we explain below, Hispanic appearance is not, in general, an appropriate factor.

* * * According to the U.S. Census Bureau, as of January 1, 2000, that population group stands at nearly 34 million. Furthermore, Hispanics are heavily concentrated in certain states in which minorities are becoming if not the majority, then at least the single largest group, either in the state as a whole or in a significant number of counties. According to the same data, California has the largest Hispanic population of any state-estimated at 10,112,986 in 1998, while Texas has approximately 6 million. As of this year, minorities-Hispanics, Asians, blacks and Native Americans-comprise half of California's residents; by 2021, Hispanics are expected to be the Golden State's largest group, making up about 40% of the state's population. Today, in Los Angeles County, which is by far the state's biggest population center, Hispanics already constitute the largest single group.

One area where Hispanics are heavily in the majority is El Centro, the site of the vehicle stop. As Agent Johnson acknowledged, the majority of the people who pass through the El Centro checkpoint are Hispanic. His testimony is in turn corroborated by more general demographic data from that area. The population of Imperial County, in which El Centro is located, is 73% Hispanic. In Imperial County, as of 1998, Hispanics accounted for 105,355 of the total population of 144,051. More broadly, according to census data, five Southern California counties are home to more than a fifth of the nation's Hispanic population. During the current decade, Hispanics will become the single largest population group in Southern California, and by 2040, will make up 59% of Southern California's population. Accordingly, Hispanic appearance is of little or no use in determining which particular individuals among the vast Hispanic populace should be stopped by law enforcement officials on the lookout for illegal aliens. Reasonable suspicion requires particularized suspicion, and in an area in which a large number of people share a specific characteristic, that characteristic casts too wide a net to play any part in a particularized reasonable suspicion determination.

* * * We decide no broad constitutional questions here. Rather, we are confronted with the narrow question of how to square the Fourth Amendment's requirement of individualized reasonable suspicion with the fact that the majority of the people who pass through the checkpoint in question are Hispanic. In order to answer that question, we conclude that, at this point in our nation's history, and given the continuing changes in our ethnic and racial composition, Hispanic appearance is, in general, of such little probative value that it may not be considered as a relevant factor where particularized or individualized suspicion is required. Moreover, we conclude, for the reasons we have indicated, that it is also not an appropriate factor.

We now turn to another factor on which the United States relies, namely Renteria-Wolff's behavior. Both the district court judge as well as the panel majority concluded that Renteria-Wolff's behavior—more specifically, her picking up a newspaper after glancing at the patrol car in the rear-view mirror—was a relevant factor in the reasonable suspicion analysis. We disagree. In general, although eye contact, or the lack thereof, may be considered as a factor establishing reasonable suspicion, we have noted that whether the contact is suspicious or not "is highly subjective and must be evaluated in light of the circumstances of each case." The skepticism with which this factor is treated is in large part due to the fact that reliance upon "suspicious" looks can so easily devolve into a case of damned if you do, equally damned if you don't. Accordingly, we have noted that that factor is "of questionable value . . . generally."

In this case, Agent Johnson testified that, as he approached the Blazer from behind, he observed that Renteria-Wolff appeared to glance quickly in the rear view mirror before picking up a newspaper and reading it. It is unclear from the record whether Johnson could in fact have seen such a glance as he drove up behind the Blazer. In any event, it is a common, if not universal, practice for drivers and passengers alike to take note of a law enforcement vehicle coming up behind them. In fact, the most law-abiding of citizens frequently adjust their driving accordingly.

Further, we give no weight to the fact that Sylvia Renteria-Wolff picked up a newspaper after glancing at the patrol car. Agent Johnson did not suggest that by this action she sought to conceal her face so that he would not recognize her. Had Renteria-Wolff continued to keep her eyes on the patrol car behind them after her initial glance, Agent Johnson might well have found it equally suspicious-because she paid too much, rather than too little attention to him. It is, in fact, difficult to imagine what Renteria-Wolff could have done at that point that might not have appeared suspicious to a Border Patrol agent.

* * * We recognize that in its recent decision in [*Illinois v.*] *Wardlow*, [528 U.S. 119 (2000),] the Supreme Court noted that evasive behavior may

be a "pertinent factor in determining reasonable suspicion." However, nothing in Wardlow—or the three Supreme Court cases it cites to illustrate that proposition—runs contrary to our conclusion that Renteria-Wolff's conduct provides no basis for reasonable suspicion. The three earlier cases all involved obvious, unambiguous attempts to evade contact with law enforcement officials-conduct very different from what was observed by the Border Patrol agent as he followed the car in which Renteria-Wolff was riding. In the first case, namely [United States v.] Brignoni-Ponce, [422 U.S. 873 (1975),] the Supreme Court categorized evasive behavior as "obvious attempts to evade officers" or to hide. In the second case, Sokolow, the Court held that evidence that the suspect took an evasive or erratic path through an airport in an apparent attempt to avoid police might also be relevant to the reasonable suspicion determination. In the third, Florida v. Rodriguez, 469 U.S. 1, 6 (1984) (per curiam), the Supreme Court held that articulable suspicion existed where three men spoke furtively among themselves after seeing officers approaching them, where one was twice overheard during that conversation urging the others to "get out of here," and where one of the three, Rodriguez, in fact turned around and attempted to flee. As noted above, all three cases described actual—and obvious—attempts to evade or to hide from law enforcement officers. Moreover, Wardlow itself, of course, involved headlong flight, which the Court termed "the consummate act of evasion . . . ." We do not mean to suggest that these cases establish the outer parameters for what is evasive behavior. Rather, we conclude only that glancing in a rear view mirror and then picking up a newspaper to read is not. Such actions are simply not the sort of evasive conduct that the Supreme Court has held is properly part of the reasonable suspicion calculus, nor did the officers suggest that it was the type of behavior they had observed in the past when wrongdoing was afoot. Accordingly, we conclude that, like Hispanic appearance, Renteria-Wolff's behavior was not a relevant or appropriate factor to consider in determining reasonable suspicion.

The question then is what factors are both relevant and appropriate to the reasonable suspicion analysis in this case. Those factors are, in a certain sense, interwoven, and they draw their significance, in part, from one another. The first of these factors to consider is the U-turn or turnaround. In United States v. Ogilvie, 527 F.2d 330, 332 (9th Cir. 1975), this Court held that "turning off the highway and turning around [are] not in themselves suspicious . . . ." Accordingly, "the proximity of the turn to the checkpoint, regardless of the legality of the checkpoint, [is] not a sufficient foundation on which to rest reasonable suspicion."

In the panel decision, the majority and the dissenting judge disagreed as to whether Ogilvie prohibited reliance on the U-turn in this case. We side with the majority and conclude that it does not. Ogilvie simply holds that a turnaround alone is not enough in and of itself to create reasonable suspicion. Indeed, in subsequent decisions, this Court has made it clear that a turnaround combined with other factors may be considered as part of a reasonable suspicion analysis. Even more so, a U-turn.

In concluding that the U-turn in this case constitutes a significant factor, we note a number of circumstances that combine to make it so, some of which also constitute independent factors in the reasonable suspicion analysis. First, a U-turn on a highway is very different from reversing direction by using a designated highway exit. The use of a highway exit is both frequent and legal; in contrast, a U-turn on a highway is unusual and often illegal. While it is not clear whether the U-turn here was legal, the other surrounding circumstances render the reversal-in-direction one that may properly be given significant weight in our reasonable suspicion analysis. One of those circumstances is the fact that the two cars made their U-turn and immediately stopped at the side of the highway in an isolated, desert area frequently used to drop off or pick up undocumented aliens or contraband. Another is that the U-turn occurred just after a sign indicating that an upcoming checkpoint had been re-opened. Finally, it is highly unlikely that the reason for the U-turn was that the cars had accidentally passed their exit point. There is only one turn-off anywhere in the area before the checkpoint, and that turn-off leads to a private road rather than one that members of the general public might use.

We also rely on the characteristics of the area in which the cars stopped after the reversal-in-direction as an independent factor. We note initially that an individual's presence in a high crime area is not enough to support reasonable, particularized suspicion that the individual in question has committed or is about to commit a crime. Still, "officers are not required to ignore the relevant characteristics of a location in determining whether the circumstances are sufficiently suspicious to warrant further investigation."

The citing of an area as "high-crime" requires careful examination by the court, because such a description, unless properly limited and factually based, can easily serve as a proxy for race or ethnicity. District courts must carefully examine the testimony of police officers in cases such as this, and make a fair and forthright evaluation of the evidence they offer, regardless of the consequences. We must be particularly careful to ensure that a "high crime" area factor is not used with respect to entire neighborhoods or communities in which members of minority groups regularly go about their daily business, but is limited to specific, circumscribed locations where particular crimes occur with unusual regularity. In this case, the "high crime" area is in an isolated and unpopulated spot in the middle of the desert. Thus, the likelihood of an innocent explanation for the defendants' presence and actions is far less than if the stop took place in a residential or business area.

Finally, we consider the tandem driving as well as the Mexicali license plates. The panel majority treated the two as independent factors giving rise to reasonable suspicion. In contrast, the district court took a different approach, relying on the "tandem driving" and Mexicali license plates solely for the purposes of linking the cars described by the tipster to the ones observed by the Border Patrol officers. We conclude that, under the circumstances present here, both occurrences may be given some direct weight in the reasonable suspicion analysis. They do not, however, constitute substantial factors, either singly or collectively.

With respect to tandem driving, we have held that two or more cars traveling together, although not sufficient in itself to establish reasonable suspicion, may nonetheless "be indicative of illegal smuggling activity." However, the circumstances of the tandem driving will in the end determine whether that factor is relevant. While two cars driving together is intrinsically innocuous, here the fact that the two cars not only turned around in tandem in the middle of a highway, but then pulled off the shoulder together and stopped where criminal activity often took place, makes the tandem driving relevant. The fact that the cars had Mexicali license plates may also provide some additional weight, given all the other circumstances. While having Mexican plates is ordinarily of no significance, where the criminal act suspected involves border-crossing, the presence of foreign license plates may be afforded some weight in determining whether a stop is reasonable.

CONCLUSION

In this case, the two cars driven in tandem by Montero-Camargo and Sanchez-Guillen made U-turns on a highway, at a place where the view of the border officials was obstructed, and stopped briefly at a locale historically used for illegal activities, before proceeding back in the direction from which they had come. The U-turn occurred at a location where it was unlikely that the cars would have reversed directions because they had missed an exit. Moreover, the vehicles in question bore Mexicali license plates and the U-turn occurred just after a sign indicating that a Border Patrol checkpoint that had been closed for some time was now open. We conclude that these factors, although not overwhelming, are sufficient to constitute reasonable suspicion for the stop. In reaching that result, however, we firmly reject any reliance upon the Hispanic appearance or ethnicity of the defendants. We also do not consider Renteria-Wolff's behavior in glancing at the Border Patrol car in the rear view mirror and then picking up and reading a newspaper.

In affirming the district court's ruling, we note that the agents' initial decision to investigate the tip and to pursue the two vehicles was made without any knowledge on their part of the defendants' ethnicity or Hispanic appearance. Agents Johnson and Fisher observed that appearance only when the officers subsequently caught up with the defendants' cars. Moreover, the agents had enough information to justify the stop before they became aware of the defendants' likely ethnicity. Under these circumstances, there is no need to remand the matter to the district court for reconsideration of its decision. Instead, we AFFIRM the district court's denial of the motion to suppress.

KOZINSKI, CIRCUIT JUDGE, WITH WHOM JUDGES T.G. NELSON, KLEINFELD AND SILVERMAN JOIN, CONCURRING:

[Omitted.]

QUESTIONS, COMMENTS, CONCERNS?

1. **_Terry_'s relevance to "suspicionless" searches.** In _Maryland v. King_, 569 U.S. 435 (2013), Alonzo King was arrested for first-degree and second-degree assault in Wicomico County, Maryland. As part of the routine booking procedure for serious offenses, and in accordance with state law, officers took a sample of King's DNA by applying a buccal swab to the inside of his cheek. King's DNA was later used to connect him to a rape that had occurred six years earlier in Salisbury, Maryland. King moved to suppress the DNA match on the grounds that Maryland's DNA collection law violated the Fourth Amendment. The trial court denied King's motion, and a jury convicted King of rape. On appeal, the Maryland Court of Appeals struck down the law as unconstitutional, concluding that the suspicionless DNA swab constituted an unlawful search under the Fourth Amendment.

The Supreme Court granted certiorari and reversed the decision of the Maryland Court of Appeals. As a threshold matter, the Court recognized that the use of "a buccal swab on the inner tissues of a person's cheek in order to obtain DNA samples is a search" for purposes of the Fourth Amendment. The Court then went on to hold that such a search—even in the absence of reasonable suspicion—comports with the Fourth Amendment so long as it occurs as part of a routine booking procedure. In reaching this conclusion, the Court reasoned that the government interest in identifying an arrestee outweighs the minimal intrusion of a cheek swab.

It would be reasonable to ask why _King_ is organized in the _Terry_ materials when _King_ itself required no additional suspicion—beyond the probable cause to arrest—to justify a separate search of the arrestee's mouth. Well, that's the point—that that separate search (i.e., use of a buccal swab) is investigative in nature and the Court required no additional suspicion. But as Justice Scalia noted in dissent, "[w]henever this Court has allowed a suspicionless search, it has insisted upon a justifying motive apart from the investigation of crime." It is _absence_, then, of reasonable suspicion to justify the buccal swab that is particularly notable—and "scary" according to Justice Scalia—in _King_.

One final comment on _King_: Federal courts have upheld statutory provisions allowing for DNA collection from: (1) individuals on supervised release, _United States v. Lujan_, 504 F.3d 1003, 1006–07 (9th Cir. 2007); (2)

parolees, *Banks v. Gonzales*, 415 F. Supp. 2d 1248, 1261 (N.D. Okla. 2006); and (3) convicted felons, *United States v. Kincade*, 379 F.3d 813, 839 (9th Cir. 2004) (en banc). In doing so, each court has thematically relied on the status of the offenders to justify its holdings—i.e., that convicted persons and parolees have a reduced expectation of privacy. What made—and makes—*King* so controversial is that *arrestees* have no similar diminishment of their reasonable expectation of privacy.

IV. THE STANDARDS FACE OFF: PROBABLE CAUSE VS. REASONABLE SUSPICION

Before closing out this chapter, we ask a challenging question: when must officers have probable cause to support a seizure as opposed to merely reasonable suspicion? Or phrased another way, we consider how long officers can "seize" a suspect during an investigatory detention before that seizure matures into a de facto arrest requiring probable cause. The Court's jurisprudence on this topic is hardly a model of clarity, but the question is important. If the officer has detained the suspect beyond the length of a permissible investigatory detention without probable cause, then that suspect has a new and separate Fourth Amendment basis for later seeking to suppress any incriminating evidence derived from the encounter. Recall from Chapter 2 that the Fourth Amendment can serve to suppress a wide-range of evidence, including statements.

DUNAWAY V. NEW YORK
442 U.S. 200
Supreme Court of the United States
March 21, 1979, Argued; June 5, 1979, Decided
No. 78-5066

MR. JUSTICE BRENNAN delivered the opinion of the Court. * * *

I

On March 26, 1971, the proprietor of a pizza parlor in Rochester, N.Y., was killed during an attempted robbery. On August 10, 1971, Detective Anthony Fantigrossi of the Rochester Police was told by another officer that an informant had supplied a possible lead implicating petitioner in the crime. Fantigrossi questioned the supposed source of the lead—a jail inmate awaiting trial for burglary—but learned nothing that supplied "enough information to get a warrant" for petitioner's arrest. Nevertheless, Fantigrossi ordered other detectives to "pick up" petitioner and "bring him in." Three detectives located petitioner at a neighbor's house on the morning of August 11. Petitioner was taken into custody; although he was not told he was under arrest, he would have been physically restrained if he had attempted to leave. He was driven to police headquarters in a police car and placed in an interrogation room, where he was questioned by officers after being given the warnings required by *Miranda v. Arizona*, 384 U.S. 436 (1966). Petitioner waived counsel and eventually made statements and drew sketches that incriminated him in the crime. * * *

II

We * * * consider whether the Rochester police violated the Fourth and Fourteenth Amendments when, without probable cause to arrest, they took petitioner into custody, transported him to the police station, and detained him there for interrogation.

* * * There can be little doubt that petitioner was "seized" in the Fourth Amendment sense when he was taken involuntarily to the police station. And respondent State concedes that the police lacked probable cause to arrest petitioner before his incriminating statement during interrogation. Nevertheless respondent contends that the seizure of petitioner did not amount to an arrest and was therefore permissible under the Fourth Amendment because the police had a "reasonable suspicion" that petitioner possessed "intimate knowledge about a serious and unsolved crime." We disagree.

Before *Terry v. Ohio*, 392 U.S. 1 (1968), the Fourth Amendment's guarantee against unreasonable seizures of persons was analyzed in terms of arrest, probable cause for arrest and warrants based on such probable cause. The basic principles were relatively simple and straightforward: The term "arrest" was synonymous with those seizures governed by the Fourth Amendment. While warrants were not required in all circumstances, the requirement of probable cause, as elaborated in numerous precedents, was treated as absolute. * * * The standard of probable cause thus represented the accumulated wisdom of precedent and experience as to the minimum justification necessary to make the kind of intrusion involved in an arrest "reasonable" under the Fourth Amendment. The standard applied to all arrests, without the need to "balance" the interests and circumstances involved in particular situations.

Terry for the first time recognized an exception to the requirement that Fourth Amendment seizures of persons must be based on probable cause. That case involved a brief, on-the-spot stop on the street and a frisk for weapons, a situation that did not fit comfortably within the traditional concept of an "arrest." Nevertheless, the Court held that even this type of "necessarily swift action predicated upon the on-the-spot observations of the officer on the beat" constituted a "serious intrusion upon the sanctity of the person, which may inflict great indignity and arouse strong resentment," and therefore "must be tested by the Fourth Amendment's general proscription against unreasonable searches and seizures." However, since the intrusion involved in a "stop and frisk" was so much less severe than that involved in traditional "arrests," the Court declined to stretch the concept of "arrest"—and the general rule requiring probable cause to make arrests "reasonable" under the Fourth Amendment—to cover such intrusions. Instead, the Court treated the stop-and-frisk intrusion as a *sui generis* "rubric of police conduct." And to determine the justification necessary to make this specially limited intrusion "reasonable" under the Fourth Amendment, the Court balanced the limited violation of individual privacy involved against the opposing interests in crime prevention and detection and in the police officer's safety. As a consequence, the Court established "a narrowly drawn authority to permit a reasonable search for weapons for the protection of the police officer, where he has reason to believe that he is dealing with an armed and dangerous individual, regardless of whether he has probable cause to arrest the individual for a crime." Thus, *Terry* departed from traditional Fourth Amendment analysis in two respects. First, it defined a special category of Fourth Amendment "seizures" so substantially less intrusive than arrests that the general rule requiring probable cause to make Fourth Amendment "seizures" reasonable could be replaced by a balancing test. Second, the application of this balancing test led the Court to approve this narrowly defined less intrusive seizure on grounds less rigorous than probable cause, but only for the purpose of a pat-down for weapons.

Because *Terry* involved an exception to the general rule requiring probable cause, this Court has been careful to maintain its narrow scope. *Terry* itself involved a limited, on-the-street frisk for weapons.[12] Two subsequent cases which applied *Terry* also involved limited weapons frisks. * * *

In contrast to the brief and narrowly circumscribed intrusions involved in those cases, the detention of petitioner was in important respects indistinguishable from a traditional arrest. Petitioner was not questioned briefly where he was found. Instead, he was taken from a neighbor's home to a police car, transported to a police station, and placed in an interrogation room. He was never informed that he was "free to go"; indeed, he would have been physically restrained if he had refused to accompany the officers or had tried to escape their custody. The application of the Fourth Amendment's requirement of probable cause does not depend on whether an intrusion of this magnitude is termed an "arrest" under state law. The mere facts that petitioner was not told he was under arrest, was not "booked," and would not have had an arrest record if the interrogation had proved fruitless, while not insignificant for all purposes, obviously do not make petitioner's seizure even roughly analogous to the narrowly defined intrusions involved in *Terry* and its progeny. Indeed, any "exception" that could cover a seizure as intrusive, as that in this case, would threaten to swallow the general rule that Fourth Amendment seizures are "reasonable" only if based on probable cause. * * *

---

[12] *Terry* specifically declined to address "the constitutional propriety of an investigative 'seizure' upon less than probable cause for purposes of 'detention' and/or interrogation." * * *

* * * [D]etention for custodial interrogation—regardless of its label—intrudes so severely on interests protected by the Fourth Amendment as necessarily to trigger the traditional safeguards against illegal arrest. We accordingly hold that the Rochester police violated the Fourth and Fourteenth Amendments when, without probable cause, they seized petitioner and transported him to the police station for interrogation. * * *

Reversed.

MR. JUSTICE POWELL took no part in the consideration or decision of this case.

MR. JUSTICE WHITE, concurring.

[Omitted.]

MR. JUSTICE STEVENS, concurring.

[Omitted.]

MR. JUSTICE REHNQUIST, with whom THE CHIEF JUSTICE joins, dissenting.

[Omitted.]

QUESTIONS, COMMENTS, CONCERNS?

1.   **Less intrusive means.** In *Florida v. Royer*, 460 U.S. 491 (1983), two detectives at Miami Airport believed that Royer fit a "drug courier profile." Royer had paid cash for a one-way ticket to New York and, when the detectives approached him before the flight, Royer produced his license and an airline ticket issued under an assumed name. The detectives told Royer they suspected him of transporting narcotics. Without returning his ticket or license, the detectives asked Royer to accompany them to a separate room adjacent to the airport concourse. The room was small, equipped with a desk and two chairs, and Royer was alone in there with the two officers. A detective then retrieved Royer's luggage from the airline and brought it to the room. Royer consented to a search of his luggage, which uncovered marijuana.

One of the detectives later admitted at a suppression hearing that he did not have probable cause to arrest Royer until he saw the marijuana. A plurality of the Supreme Court held that Royer's detention was not a legitimate *Terry* stop because, "[a]s a practical matter, Royer was under arrest." It reasoned that the detectives had other less intrusive means available to verify or dispel their suspicion. For example, said the Court, the detectives could have: (1) returned Royer's ticket and driver's license and told him he was free to leave before asking for his consent, (2) asked for consent to search his luggage on the concourse rather than in a private room, or (3) relied on the use of a trained narcotics dog.

UNITED STATES V. SOKOLOW

490 U.S. 1
Supreme Court of the United States
January 10, 1989, Argued; April 3, 1989, Decided
No. 87-1295

CHIEF JUSTICE REHNQUIST delivered the opinion of the Court.

Respondent Andrew Sokolow was stopped by Drug Enforcement Administration (DEA) agents upon his arrival at Honolulu International Airport. The agents found 1,063 grams of cocaine in his carry-on luggage. * * *

This case involves a typical attempt to smuggle drugs through one of the Nation's airports. On a Sunday in July 1984, respondent went to the United Airlines ticket counter at Honolulu Airport, where he purchased two round-trip tickets for a flight to Miami leaving later that day. The tickets were purchased in the names of "Andrew Kray" and "Janet Norian" and had open return dates. Respondent paid $2,100 for the tickets from a large roll of $20 bills, which appeared to contain a total of $4,000. He also gave the ticket agent his home telephone number. The ticket agent noticed that respondent seemed nervous; he was about 25 years old; he was dressed in a black jumpsuit and wore gold jewelry; and he was accompanied by a woman, who turned out to be Janet Norian. Neither respondent nor his companion checked any of their four pieces of luggage.

After the couple left for their flight, the ticket agent informed Officer John McCarthy of the Honolulu Police Department of respondent's cash purchase of tickets to Miami. Officer McCarthy determined that the telephone number respondent gave to the ticket agent was subscribed to a "Karl Herman," who resided at 348-A Royal Hawaiian Avenue in Honolulu. Unbeknownst to McCarthy (and later to the DEA agents), respondent was Herman's roommate. The ticket agent identified respondent's voice on the answering machine at Herman's number. Officer McCarthy was unable to find any listing under the name "Andrew Kray" in Hawaii. McCarthy subsequently learned that return reservations from Miami to Honolulu had been made in the names of Kray and Norian, with their arrival scheduled for July 25, three days after respondent and his companion had left. He also learned that Kray and Norian were scheduled to make stopovers in Denver and Los Angeles.

On July 25, during the stopover in Los Angeles, DEA agents identified respondent. He "appeared to be very nervous and was looking all around the waiting area." Later that day, at 6:30 p.m., respondent and Norian arrived in Honolulu. As before, they had not checked their luggage. Respondent was still wearing a black jumpsuit and gold jewelry. The couple proceeded directly to the street and tried to hail a cab, where Agent Richard Kempshall and three other DEA agents approached them. Kempshall displayed his credentials, grabbed respondent by the arm, and moved him back onto the sidewalk. Kempshall asked respondent for his airline ticket and identification; respondent said that he had neither. He told the agents that his name was "Sokolow," but that he was traveling under his mother's maiden name, "Kray."

Respondent and Norian were escorted to the DEA office at the airport. There, the couple's luggage was examined by "Donker," a narcotics detector dog, which alerted on respondent's brown shoulder bag. The agents arrested respondent. He was advised of his constitutional rights and declined to make any statements. The agents obtained a warrant to search the shoulder bag. They found no illicit drugs, but the bag did contain several suspicious documents indicating respondent's involvement in drug trafficking. The agents had Donker reexamine the remaining luggage, and this time the dog alerted on a medium-sized Louis Vuitton bag. By now, it was 9:30 p.m., too late for the agents to obtain a second warrant. They allowed respondent to leave for the night, but kept his luggage. The next morning, after a second dog confirmed Donker's alert, the agents obtained a warrant and found 1,063 grams of cocaine inside the bag.

Respondent was indicted for possession with the intent to distribute cocaine * * *. The United States District Court for Hawaii denied his motion to suppress the cocaine and other evidence seized from his luggage, finding that the DEA agents had a reasonable suspicion that he was involved in drug trafficking when they stopped him at the airport. Respondent then entered a conditional plea of guilty to the offense charged.

The United States Court of Appeals for the Ninth Circuit reversed respondent's conviction by a divided vote, holding that the DEA agents did not have a reasonable suspicion to justify the stop. * * * We granted certiorari to review the decision of the Court of Appeals, 486 U.S. 1042 (1988), because of its serious implications for the enforcement of the federal narcotics laws. We now reverse.

The Court of Appeals held that the DEA agents seized respondent when they grabbed him by the arm and moved him back onto the sidewalk. 831 F. 2d, at 1416. The Government does not challenge that conclusion, and we assume—without deciding—that a stop occurred here. Our decision, then, turns on whether the agents had a reasonable suspicion that respondent was engaged in wrongdoing when they encountered him on the sidewalk. In *Terry v. Ohio*, 392 U.S. 1, 30 (1968), we held that the police can stop and briefly detain a person for investigative purposes if the officer has a reasonable suspicion supported by articulable facts that criminal activity "may be afoot," even if the officer lacks probable cause.

The officer, of course, must be able to articulate something more than an "inchoate and unparticularized suspicion or 'hunch.'" The Fourth Amendment requires "some minimal level of objective justification" for making the stop. That level of suspicion is considerably less than proof of wrongdoing by a preponderance of the evidence. We have held that probable cause means "a fair probability that contraband or evidence of a crime will be found," *Illinois v. Gates*, 462 U.S. 213, 238 (1983), and the level of suspicion required for a *Terry* stop is obviously less demanding than that for probable cause.

The concept of reasonable suspicion, like probable cause, is not "readily, or even usefully, reduced to a neat set of legal rules." *Gates, supra.* * * * In evaluating the validity of a stop such as this, we must consider "the totality of the circumstances—the whole picture." * * *

The rule enunciated by the Court of Appeals, in which evidence available to an officer is divided into evidence of "ongoing criminal behavior," on the one hand, and "probabilistic" evidence, on the other, is not in keeping with the quoted statements from our decisions. It also seems to us to draw a sharp line between types of evidence, the probative value of which varies only in degree. The Court of Appeals classified evidence of traveling under an alias, or evidence that the suspect took an evasive or erratic path through an airport, as meeting the test for showing "ongoing criminal activity." But certainly instances are conceivable in which traveling under an alias would not reflect ongoing criminal activity: for example, a person who wished to travel to a hospital or clinic for an operation and wished to conceal that fact. One taking an evasive path through an airport might be seeking to avoid a confrontation with an angry acquaintance or with a creditor. This is not to say that each of these types of evidence is not highly probative, but they do not have the sort of ironclad significance attributed to them by the Court of Appeals.

On the other hand, the factors in this case that the Court of Appeals treated as merely "probabilistic" also have probative significance. Paying $2,100 in cash for two airplane tickets is out of the ordinary, and it is even more out of the ordinary to pay that sum from a roll of $20 bills containing nearly twice that amount of cash. Most business travelers, we feel confident, purchase airline tickets by credit card or check so as to have a record for tax or business purposes, and few vacationers carry with them thousands of dollars in $20 bills. We also think the agents had a reasonable ground to believe that respondent was traveling under an alias; the evidence was by no means conclusive, but it was sufficient to warrant consideration. While a trip from Honolulu to Miami, standing alone, is not a cause for any sort of suspicion, here there was more: surely few residents of Honolulu travel from that city for 20 hours to spend 48 hours in Miami during the month of July.

Any one of these factors is not by itself proof of any illegal conduct and is quite consistent with innocent travel. But we think taken together they amount to reasonable suspicion. * * *

We do not agree with respondent that our analysis is somehow changed by the agents' belief that his behavior was consistent with one of the DEA's "drug courier profiles."[6] A court sitting to determine the existence of reasonable suspicion must require the agent to articulate the factors leading to that conclusion, but the fact that these factors may be set forth in a "profile" does not somehow detract from their evidentiary significance as seen by a trained agent.

Respondent also contends that the agents were obligated to use the least intrusive means available to verify or dispel their suspicions that he was smuggling narcotics. In respondent's view, the agents should have simply approached and spoken with him, rather than forcibly detaining him. * * * The reasonableness of the officer's decision to stop a suspect does not turn on the availability of less intrusive investigatory techniques. Such a rule would unduly hamper the police's ability to make swift, on-the-spot decisions—here, respondent was about to get into a taxicab—and it would require courts to "indulge in 'unrealistic second-guessing.'"

We hold that the agents had a reasonable basis to suspect that respondent was transporting illegal drugs on these facts. The judgment of the Court of Appeals is therefore reversed, and the case is remanded for further proceedings consistent with our decision.

It is so ordered.

JUSTICE MARSHALL, with whom JUSTICE BRENNAN joins, dissenting.

[Omitted.]

UNITED STATES V. SHARPE

470 U.S. 675
Supreme Court of the United States
November 27, 1984, Argued; March 20, 1985, Decided
No. 83-529

CHIEF JUSTICE BURGER delivered the opinion of the Court.

* * * On the morning of June 9, 1978, Agent Cooke of the Drug Enforcement Administration (DEA) was on patrol in an unmarked vehicle on a coastal road near Sunset Beach, North Carolina, an area under surveillance for suspected drug trafficking. At approximately 6:30 a.m., Cooke noticed a blue pickup truck with an attached camper shell traveling on the highway in tandem with a blue Pontiac Bonneville. Respondent Savage was driving the pickup, and respondent Sharpe was driving the Pontiac. The Pontiac also carried a passenger, Davis, the charges against whom were later dropped. Observing that the truck was riding low in the

---

[6]   Agent Kempshall testified that respondent's behavior "had all the classic aspects of a drug courier." Since 1974, the DEA has trained narcotics officers to identify drug smugglers on the basis of the sort of circumstantial evidence at issue here.

rear and that the camper did not bounce or sway appreciably when the truck drove over bumps or around curves, Agent Cooke concluded that it was heavily loaded. A quilted material covered the rear and side windows of the camper.

Cooke's suspicions were sufficiently aroused to follow the two vehicles for approximately 20 miles as they proceeded south into South Carolina. He then decided to make an "investigative stop" and radioed the State Highway Patrol for assistance. Officer Thrasher, driving a marked patrol car, responded to the call. Almost immediately after Thrasher caught up with the procession, the Pontiac and the pickup turned off the highway and onto a campground road.[1] Cooke and Thrasher followed the two vehicles as the latter drove along the road at 55 to 60 miles an hour, exceeding the speed limit of 35 miles an hour. The road eventually looped back to the highway, onto which Savage and Sharpe turned and continued to drive south.

At this point, all four vehicles were in the middle lane of the three right-hand lanes of the highway. Agent Cooke asked Officer Thrasher to signal both vehicles to stop. Thrasher pulled alongside the Pontiac, which was in the lead, turned on his flashing light, and motioned for the driver of the Pontiac to stop. As Sharpe moved the Pontiac into the right lane, the pickup truck cut between the Pontiac and Thrasher's patrol car, nearly hitting the patrol car, and continued down the highway. Thrasher pursued the truck while Cooke pulled up behind the Pontiac.

Cooke approached the Pontiac and identified himself. He requested identification, and Sharpe produced a Georgia driver's license bearing the name of Raymond J. Pavlovich. Cooke then attempted to radio Thrasher to determine whether he had been successful in stopping the pickup truck, but he was unable to make contact for several minutes, apparently because Thrasher was not in his patrol car. Cooke radioed the local police for assistance, and two officers from the Myrtle Beach Police Department arrived about 10 minutes later. Asking the two officers to "maintain the situation," Cooke left to join Thrasher.

In the meantime, Thrasher had stopped the pickup truck about one-half mile down the road. After stopping the truck, Thrasher had approached it with his revolver drawn, ordered the driver, Savage, to get out and assume a "spread eagled" position against the side of the truck, and patted him down. Thrasher then holstered his gun and asked Savage for his driver's license and the truck's vehicle registration. Savage produced his own Florida driver's license and a bill of sale for the truck bearing the name of Pavlovich. In response to questions from Thrasher concerning the ownership of the truck, Savage said that the truck belonged to a friend and

---

[1]   Officer Thrasher testified that the respondents' vehicles turned off the highway "[about] one minute" after he joined the procession.

that he was taking it to have its shock absorbers repaired. When Thrasher told Savage that he would be held until the arrival of Cooke, whom Thrasher identified as a DEA agent, Savage became nervous, said that he wanted to leave, and requested the return of his driver's license. Thrasher replied that Savage was not free to leave at that time.

Agent Cooke arrived at the scene approximately 15 minutes after the truck had been stopped. Thrasher handed Cooke Savage's license and the bill of sale for the truck; Cooke noted that the bill of sale bore the same name as Sharpe's license. Cooke identified himself to Savage as a DEA agent and said that he thought the truck was loaded with marijuana. Cooke twice sought permission to search the camper, but Savage declined to give it, explaining that he was not the owner of the truck. Cooke then stepped on the rear of the truck and, observing that it did not sink any lower, confirmed his suspicion that it was probably overloaded. He put his nose against the rear window, which was covered from the inside, and reported that he could smell marijuana. Without seeking Savage's permission, Cooke removed the keys from the ignition, opened the rear of the camper, and observed a large number of burlap-wrapped bales resembling bales of marihuana that Cooke had seen in previous investigations. Agent Cooke then placed Savage under arrest and left him with Thrasher.

Cooke returned to the Pontiac and arrested Sharpe and Davis. Approximately 30 to 40 minutes had elapsed between the time Cooke stopped the Pontiac and the time he returned to arrest Sharpe and Davis. Cooke assembled the various parties and vehicles and led them to the Myrtle Beach police station. That evening, DEA agents took the truck to the Federal Building in Charleston, South Carolina. Several days later, Cooke supervised the unloading of the truck, which contained 43 bales weighing a total of 2,629 pounds. Acting without a search warrant, Cooke had eight randomly selected bales opened and sampled. Chemical tests showed that the samples were marihuana. * * *

Sharpe and Savage were charged with possession of a controlled substance with intent to distribute it * * *. The United States District Court for the District of South Carolina denied respondents' motion to suppress the contraband, and respondents were convicted. * * *

II

A

The Fourth Amendment is not, of course, a guarantee against all searches and seizures, but only against unreasonable searches and seizures. The authority and limits of the Amendment apply to investigative stops of vehicles such as occurred here. In *Terry v. Ohio*, 392 U.S. 1 (1968), we adopted a dual inquiry for evaluating the reasonableness of an investigative stop. Under this approach, we examine "whether the officer's action was justified at its inception, and whether it was reasonably related in scope to the circumstances which justified the interference in the first place." * * *

Admittedly, [our prior cases], considered together, may in some instances create difficult line-drawing problems in distinguishing an investigative stop from a de facto arrest. Obviously, if an investigative stop continues indefinitely, at some point it can no longer be justified as an investigative stop. But our cases impose no rigid time limitation on *Terry* stops. While it is clear that "the brevity of the invasion of the individual's Fourth Amendment interests is an important factor in determining whether the seizure is so minimally intrusive as to be justifiable on reasonable suspicion," we have emphasized the need to consider the law enforcement purposes to be served by the stop as well as the time reasonably needed to effectuate those purposes. Much as a "bright line" rule would be desirable, in evaluating whether an investigative detention is unreasonable, common sense and ordinary human experience must govern over rigid criteria. * * *

* * * [W]e [have] expressly rejected the suggestion that we adopt a hard-and-fast time limit for a permissible *Terry* stop:

> We understand the desirability of providing law enforcement authorities with a clear rule to guide their conduct. Nevertheless, we question the wisdom of a rigid time limitation. Such a limit would undermine the equally important need to allow authorities to graduate their responses to the demands of any particular situation.

The Court of Appeals' decision would effectively establish a per se rule that a 20-minute detention is too long to be justified under the *Terry* doctrine. Such a result is clearly and fundamentally at odds with our approach in this area.

B

In assessing whether a detention is too long in duration to be justified as an investigative stop, we consider it appropriate to examine whether the police diligently pursued a means of investigation that was likely to confirm or dispel their suspicions quickly, during which time it was necessary to detain the defendant. A court making this assessment should take care to consider whether the police are acting in a swiftly developing situation, and in such cases the court should not indulge in unrealistic second-guessing. A creative judge engaged in *post hoc* evaluation of police conduct can almost always imagine some alternative means by which the objectives of the police might have been accomplished. But "[the] fact that the protection of the public might, in the abstract, have been accomplished by 'less intrusive' means does not, by itself, render the search unreasonable." The question is not simply whether some other alternative was available but whether the police acted unreasonably in failing to recognize or to pursue it.

We readily conclude that, given the circumstances facing him, Agent Cooke pursued his investigation in a diligent and reasonable manner. During most of Savage's 20-minute detention, Cooke was attempting to contact Thrasher and enlisting the help of the local police who remained with Sharpe while Cooke left to pursue Officer Thrasher and the pickup. Once Cooke reached Officer Thrasher and Savage, he proceeded expeditiously: within the space of a few minutes, he examined Savage's driver's license and the truck's bill of sale, requested (and was denied) permission to search the truck, stepped on the rear bumper and noted that the truck did not move, confirming his suspicion that it was probably overloaded. He then detected the odor of marihuana.

Clearly this case does not involve any delay unnecessary to the legitimate investigation of the law enforcement officers. Respondents presented no evidence that the officers were dilatory in their investigation. The delay in this case was attributable almost entirely to the evasive actions of Savage, who sought to elude the police as Sharpe moved his Pontiac to the side of the road.[6] Except for Savage's maneuvers, only a short and certainly permissible pre-arrest detention would likely have taken place. The somewhat longer detention was simply the result of a "[graduated] . . . [response] to the demands of [the] particular situation."

We reject the contention that a 20-minute stop is unreasonable when the police have acted diligently and a suspect's actions contribute to the added delay about which he complains. The judgment of the Court of Appeals is reversed, and the case is remanded for further proceedings consistent with this opinion.

Reversed and remanded.

JUSTICE BLACKMUN, concurring.

[Omitted.]

JUSTICE MARSHALL, concurring in the judgment.

[Omitted.]

JUSTICE BRENNAN, dissenting.

The respondent William Sharpe and his passenger were pulled over to the side of the highway, concededly without probable cause, and held for more than 30 minutes, much of that time in the back seat of a police cruiser,

---

[6]   Even if it could be inferred that Savage was not attempting to elude the police when he drove his car between Thrasher's patrol car and Sharpe's Pontiac—in the process nearly hitting the patrol car—such an assumption would not alter our analysis or our conclusion. The significance of Savage's actions is that, whether innocent or purposeful, they made it necessary for Thrasher and Cooke to split up, placed Thrasher and Cooke out of contact with each other, and required Cooke to enlist the assistance of local police before he could join Thrasher and Savage.

before they ultimately were arrested and informed of the charges against them. In the meantime, the respondent Donald Savage was stopped one-half mile down the road, also according to the Court without probable cause. He was ordered out of his pickup truck at gunpoint, spread-eagled and frisked, and questioned by the detaining patrolman, Kenneth Thrasher, about a suspected shipment of marihuana in his vehicle. Although Savage repeatedly asked to be released, Thrasher held him for almost 15 minutes until DEA Agent Luther Cooke, the officer who had stopped Sharpe back up the road, could arrive and sniff the vehicle's windows to determine whether he could smell the suspected marihuana. As Thrasher later conceded, Savage "was under custodial arrest" the entire time.

The Court today concludes that these lengthy detentions constituted reasonable investigative stops within the meaning of *Terry v. Ohio*, 392 U.S. 1 (1968). * * *

I dissent. * * *

* * * I agree with the Court that the constitutional propriety of these detentions is governed by *Terry* and its progeny. These precedents lead inexorably to the conclusion that the investigative actions at issue here violated the Fourth Amendment. * * *

* * * Assuming that Savage did not break away from the officers by taking "evasive actions" to "elude" them—in which instance this is not a *Terry* case at all—the Government has not demonstrated why two trained law enforcement officers driving in separate vehicles, both equipped with flashing lights, could not have carried out a stop of a Pontiac and a pickup truck in such a manner as to ensure that both vehicles would be stopped together. Reasonable methods for bringing about the proximate stop of two vehicles readily come to mind; such methods would have been particularly important if, as the Court assumes, both officers knew that only Cooke was capable of carrying out the investigation. * * *

The record strongly suggests that the delay may have been attributable in large measure to the poor investigative coordination and botched communications on the part of the DEA. Drug enforcement agents were swarming throughout the immediate area on the morning that Savage and Sharpe were detained, conducting numerous roadblocks and "profile stops" of campers and recreational vehicles similar to Savage's. Even accepting the Court's dubious premise that a highway patrolman is somehow incapable of carrying out a simple investigative stop, it is clear that Cooke had followed Sharpe and Savage for over 30 minutes and, knowing that a multiple-vehicle stop was in the offing, should have obtained assistance from other DEA agents. This was, in fact, precisely what he attempted to do. He repeatedly tried to contact the area DEA headquarters but complained over his police radio that "I can't raise anybody else right now." He asked the local police dispatcher to telephone the DEA office to "ask them if anybody there has any contact with me on my DEA frequency." The dispatcher reported that the line was busy; local police units had to be sent out to headquarters "to tell these people to get off the telephone." Once the units arrived, it was learned that "[there's] no one there. They're all down at the Mar Vista Motel." Additional units had to be sent to the motel to "get those people out of the sack." Agents apparently were eventually located at the motel and at Don's Pancake House, ibid., for by the time that Cooke returned to the Pontiac to complete the arrests there were several other DEA agents waiting to assist him. In the meantime, of course, Cooke had had to request Thrasher as a local backup.

Far from demonstrating that these investigative stops were carried out in the most "expeditious way" using all "reasonably available" investigative methods, the record in this case therefore strongly suggests custodial detentions more accurately characterized as resulting from hopelessly bungled communications and from Thrasher's unwillingness to tread on Cooke's investigative turf. I do not mean to suggest that Cooke and Thrasher bore the entire blame for these delays; it was not Cooke's fault that his DEA backups apparently were sleeping or eating breakfast rather than monitoring their radios for his calls, and Thrasher might well have felt that it was not his place to carry out an investigation he apparently was fully capable of conducting. But constitutional rights should not so easily be balanced away simply because the individual officers may have subjectively been acting in good faith, especially where an objective evaluation of the facts suggests an unnecessarily intrusive exercise of police power. * * *

We must remember the Fourth Amendment values at stake here. * * * *Terry's* brevity requirement * * * functions as an important constitutional safeguard that prevents an investigative stop from being transformed into a custodial detention merely because "the law enforcement purposes to be served by the stop" are considered important. Absent a rigorously enforced brevity requirement, the *Terry* rationale "would threaten to swallow the general rule that Fourth Amendment seizures are 'reasonable' only if based on probable cause." *Dunaway v. New York.* * * *

In this connection, I am particularly disturbed by the Court's suggestion that it might be constitutionally reasonable for a highway patrolman to hold a motorist on *Terry* suspicion pending the arrival of an officer with more "training and experience." * * *

The Court today has * * * failed * * * to acknowledge the evidence of bungling, miscommunication, and reasonable investigative alternatives, and pronounced simply that the individual officers "acted diligently." Thus the Court has moved a step or two further in what appears to be "an emerging tendency on the part of the Court to convert the *Terry* decision into a general statement that the Fourth Amendment requires only that any seizure be reasonable"—a balancing process in which the judicial thumb apparently will be planted firmly on the law enforcement side of the scales.

* * * I dissent.

JUSTICE STEVENS, dissenting.

[Omitted.]

UNITED STATES V. MONTOYA DE HERNANDEZ

473 U.S. 531
Supreme Court of the United States
April 24, 1985, Argued; July 1, 1985, Decided
No. 84-755

JUSTICE REHNQUIST delivered the opinion of the Court.

Respondent Rosa Elvira Montoya de Hernandez was detained by customs officials upon her arrival at the Los Angeles Airport on a flight from Bogota, Colombia. She was found to be smuggling 88 cocaine-filled balloons in her alimentary canal, and was convicted after a bench trial of various federal narcotics offenses. A divided panel of the United States Court of Appeals for the Ninth Circuit reversed her convictions, holding that her detention violated the Fourth Amendment to the United States Constitution because the customs inspectors did not have a "clear indication" of alimentary canal smuggling at the time she was detained. Because of a conflict in the decisions of the Courts of Appeals on this question and the importance of its resolution to the enforcement of customs laws, we granted certiorari. We now reverse.

Respondent arrived at Los Angeles International Airport shortly after midnight, March 5, 1983, on Avianca Flight 080, a direct 10-hour flight from Bogota, Colombia. Her visa was in order so she was passed through Immigration and proceeded to the customs desk. At the customs desk she encountered Customs Inspector Talamantes, who reviewed her documents and noticed from her passport that she had made at least eight recent trips to either Miami or Los Angeles. Talamantes referred respondent to a secondary customs desk for further questioning. At this desk Talamantes and another inspector asked respondent general questions concerning herself and the purpose of her trip. Respondent revealed that she spoke no English and had no family or friends in the United States. She explained in Spanish that she had come to the United States to purchase goods for her husband's store in Bogota. The customs inspectors recognized Bogota as a "source city" for narcotics. Respondent possessed $5,000 in cash, mostly $50 bills, but had no billfold. She indicated to the inspectors that she had no appointments with merchandise vendors, but planned to ride around Los Angeles in taxicabs visiting retail stores such as J. C. Penney and K-Mart, in order to buy goods for her husband's store with the $5,000.

Respondent admitted that she had no hotel reservations, but stated that she planned to stay at a Holiday Inn. Respondent could not recall how her airline ticket was purchased. When the inspectors opened respondent's one small valise, they found about four changes of "cold weather" clothing. Respondent had no shoes other than the high-heeled pair she was wearing. Although respondent possessed no checks, waybills, credit cards, or letters of credit, she did produce a Colombian business card and a number of old receipts, waybills, and fabric swatches displayed in a photo album.

At this point Talamantes and the other inspector suspected that respondent was a "balloon swallower," one who attempts to smuggle narcotics into this country hidden in her alimentary canal. Over the years Inspector Talamantes had apprehended dozens of alimentary canal smugglers arriving on Avianca Flight 080.

The inspectors requested a female customs inspector to take respondent to a private area and conduct a patdown and strip search. During the search the female inspector felt respondent's abdomen area and noticed a firm fullness, as if respondent were wearing a girdle. The search revealed no contraband, but the inspector noticed that respondent was wearing two pairs of elastic underpants with a paper towel lining the crotch area.

When respondent returned to the customs area and the female inspector reported her discoveries, the inspector in charge told respondent that he suspected she was smuggling drugs in her alimentary canal. Respondent agreed to the inspector's request that she be x-rayed at a hospital but in answer to the inspector's query stated that she was pregnant. She agreed to a pregnancy test before the x ray. Respondent withdrew the consent for an x ray when she learned that she would have to be handcuffed en route to the hospital. The inspector then gave respondent the option of returning to Colombia on the next available flight, agreeing to an x ray, or remaining in detention until she produced a monitored bowel movement that would confirm or rebut the inspectors' suspicions. Respondent chose the first option and was placed in a customs office under observation. She was told that if she went to the toilet she would have to use a wastebasket in the women's restroom, in order that female customs inspectors could inspect her stool for balloons or capsules carrying narcotics. The inspectors refused respondent's request to place a telephone call.

Respondent sat in the customs office, under observation, for the remainder of the night. During the night customs officials attempted to place respondent on a Mexican airline that was flying to Bogota via Mexico City in the morning. The airline refused to transport respondent because she lacked a Mexican visa necessary to land in Mexico City. Respondent was not permitted to leave, and was informed that she would be detained until she agreed to an xray or her bowels moved. She remained detained in the customs office under observation, for most of the time curled up in a chair leaning to one side. She refused all offers of food and drink, and refused to use the toilet facilities. The Court of Appeals noted that she exhibited symptoms of discomfort consistent with "heroic efforts to resist the usual calls of nature."

At the shift change at 4:00 o'clock the next afternoon, almost 16 hours after her flight had landed, respondent still had not defecated or urinated or partaken of food or drink. At that time customs officials sought a court order authorizing a pregnancy test, an x ray, and a rectal examination. The Federal Magistrate issued an order just before midnight that evening, which authorized a rectal examination and involuntary x ray, provided that the physician in charge considered respondent's claim of pregnancy. Respondent was taken to a hospital and given a pregnancy test, which later turned out to be negative. Before the results of the pregnancy test were known, a physician conducted a rectal examination and removed from respondent's rectum a balloon containing a foreign substance. Respondent was then placed formally under arrest. By 4:10 a.m. respondent had passed 6 similar balloons; over the next four days she passed 88 balloons containing a total of 528 grams of 80% pure cocaine hydrochloride.

After a suppression hearing the District Court admitted the cocaine in evidence against respondent. She was convicted of possession of cocaine with intent to distribute and unlawful importation of cocaine.

A divided panel of the United States Court of Appeals for the Ninth Circuit reversed respondent's convictions. * * *

The Fourth Amendment commands that searches and seizures be reasonable. What is reasonable depends upon all of the circumstances surrounding the search or seizure and the nature of the search or seizure itself. The permissibility of a particular law enforcement practice is judged by "balancing its intrusion on the individual's Fourth Amendment interests against its promotion of legitimate governmental interests." * * *

We have not previously decided what level of suspicion would justify a seizure of an incoming traveler for purposes other than a routine border search. * * *

We hold that the detention of a traveler at the border, beyond the scope of a routine customs search and inspection, is justified at its inception if customs agents, considering all the facts surrounding the traveler and her trip, reasonably suspect that the traveler is smuggling contraband in her alimentary canal.

The "reasonable suspicion" standard has been applied in a number of contexts and effects a needed balance between private and public interests when law enforcement officials must make a limited intrusion on less than probable cause. It thus fits well into the situations involving alimentary canal smuggling at the border: this type of smuggling gives no external signs and inspectors will rarely possess probable cause to arrest or search, yet governmental interests in stopping smuggling at the border are high indeed. Under this standard officials at the border must have a "particularized and objective basis for suspecting the particular person" of alimentary canal smuggling.

The facts, and their rational inferences, known to customs inspectors in this case clearly supported a reasonable suspicion that respondent was an alimentary canal smuggler. We need not belabor the facts, including respondent's implausible story, that supported this suspicion. The trained customs inspectors had encountered many alimentary canal smugglers and certainly had more than an "inchoate and unparticularized suspicion or 'hunch,' " *Terry, supra,* that respondent was smuggling narcotics in her alimentary canal. The inspectors' suspicion was a " 'common-sense [conclusion] about human behavior' upon which 'practical people,'— including government officials, are entitled to rely."

The final issue in this case is whether the detention of respondent was reasonably related in scope to the circumstances which justified it initially. In this regard, we have cautioned that courts should not indulge in "unrealistic second-guessing," *United States v. Sharpe,* 470 U.S. 675, 686 (1985), and we have noted that "creative [judges], engaged in post hoc evaluations of police conduct can almost always imagine some alternative means by which the objectives of the police might have been accomplished." But "[the] fact that the protection of the public might, in the abstract, have been accomplished by 'less intrusive' means does not, in itself, render the search unreasonable." Authorities must be allowed "to graduate their response to the demands of any particular situation." Here, respondent was detained incommunicado for almost 16 hours before inspectors sought a warrant; the warrant then took a number of hours to procure, through no apparent fault of the inspectors. This length of time undoubtedly exceeds any other detention we have approved under reasonable suspicion. But we have also consistently rejected hard-and-fast time limits. Instead, "common sense and ordinary human experience must govern over rigid criteria." *Sharpe, supra.*

The rudimentary knowledge of the human body which judges possess in common with the rest of humankind tells us that alimentary canal smuggling cannot be detected in the amount of time in which other illegal activity may be investigated through brief *Terry*-type stops. It presents few, if any external signs; a quick frisk will not do, nor will even a strip search. In the case of respondent the inspectors had available, as an alternative to simply awaiting her bowel movement, an x ray. They offered her the alternative of submitting herself to that procedure. But when she refused that alternative, the customs inspectors were left with only two practical alternatives: detain her for such time as necessary to confirm their suspicions, a detention which would last much longer than the typical *Terry* stop, or turn her loose into the interior carrying the reasonably suspected contraband drugs.

The inspectors in this case followed this former procedure. They no doubt expected that respondent, having recently disembarked from a 10-hour direct flight with a full and stiff abdomen, would produce a bowel movement without extended delay. But her visible efforts to resist the call of nature, which the court below labeled "heroic," disappointed this expectation and in turn caused her humiliation and discomfort. Our prior cases have refused to charge police with delays in investigatory detention attributable to the suspect's evasive actions, and that principle applies here as well. Respondent alone was responsible for much of the duration and discomfort of the seizure.

Under these circumstances, we conclude that the detention in this case was not unreasonably long. It occurred at the international border, where the Fourth Amendment balance of interests leans heavily to the Government. * * *

Respondent's detention was long, uncomfortable, indeed, humiliating; but both its length and its discomfort resulted solely from the method by which she chose to smuggle illicit drugs into this country. * * * Her detention for the period of time necessary to either verify or dispel the suspicion was not unreasonable. The judgment of the Court of Appeals is therefore

Reversed.

JUSTICE STEVENS, concurring in the judgment.

[Omitted.]

JUSTICE BRENNAN, with whom JUSTICE MARSHALL joins, dissenting.

We confront a "disgusting and saddening episode" at our Nation's border. Shortly after midnight on March 5, 1983, the respondent Rosa Elvira Montoya de Hernandez was detained by customs officers because she fit the profile of an "alimentary canal smuggler."[2] This profile did not of course give the officers probable cause to believe that De Hernandez was smuggling drugs into the country, but at most a "reasonable suspicion" that

---

[2] Specifically, De Hernandez "had paid cash for her ticket, came from a source port of embarcation, carried $5,000 in U.S. currency, had made many trips of short duration into the United States, had no family or friends in the United States, had only one small piece of luggage, had no confirmed hotel reservations, did not speak English, and said she was planning to go shopping using taxis for transportation."

she might be engaged in such an attempt. After a thorough strip search failed to uncover any contraband, De Hernandez agreed to go to a local hospital for an abdominal x ray to resolve the matter. When the officers approached with handcuffs at the ready to lead her away, however, "she crossed her arms by her chest and began stepping backwards shaking her head negatively," protesting: "You are not going to put those on me. That is an insult to my character."

Stymied in their efforts, the officers decided on an alternative course: they would simply lock De Hernandez away in an adjacent manifest room "until her peristaltic functions produced a monitored bowel movement." The officers explained to De Hernandez that she could not leave until she had excreted by squatting over a wastebasket pursuant to the watchful eyes of two attending matrons. De Hernandez responded "I will not submit to your degradation and I'd rather die." She was locked away with the matrons.

De Hernandez remained locked up in the room for almost 24 hours. Three shifts of matrons came and went during this time. The room had no bed or couch on which she could lie, but only hard chairs and a table. The matrons told her that if she wished to sleep, she could lie down on the hard, uncarpeted floor. De Hernandez instead "sat in her chair clutching her purse," "occasionally putting her head down on the table to nap." Most of the time, she simply wept and pleaded "to go home." She repeatedly begged for permission "to call my husband and tell him what you are doing to me." Permission was denied. Sobbing, she insisted that she had to "make a phone call home so that she could talk to her children and to let them know that everything was all right." Permission again was denied. In fact, the matrons considered it highly "unusual" that "each time someone entered the search room, she would take out two small pictures of her children and show them to the person." De Hernandez also demanded that her attorney be contacted. Once again, permission was denied. As far as the outside world knew, Rosa de Hernandez had simply vanished. And although she already had been stripped and searched and probed, the customs officers decided about halfway through her ordeal to repeat that process—"to ensure the safety of the surveilling officers. The result was again negative."

After almost 24 hours had passed, someone finally had the presence of mind to consult a Magistrate and to obtain a court order for an x ray and a body-cavity search. De Hernandez, "very agitated," was handcuffed and led away to the hospital. A rectal examination disclosed the presence of a cocaine-filled balloon. At approximately 3:15 in the morning of March 6, *almost 27 hours after her initial detention,* De Hernandez was formally placed under arrest and advised of her *Miranda* rights. Over the course of the next four days she excreted a total of 88 balloons. * * *

The issue * * * is simply this: Does the Fourth Amendment permit an international traveler, citizen or alien, to be subjected to the sort of treatment that occurred in this case without the sanction of a judicial officer and based on nothing more than the "reasonable suspicion" of low-ranking investigative officers that something might be amiss? The Court today concludes that the Fourth Amendment grants such sweeping and unmonitored authority to customs officials. * * *

I dissent. Indefinite involuntary incommunicado detentions "for investigation" are the hallmark of a police state, not a free society. In my opinion, Government officials may no more confine a person at the border under such circumstances for purposes of criminal investigation than they may within the interior of the country. The nature and duration of the detention here may well have been tolerable for spoiled meat or diseased animals, but not for human beings held on simple suspicion of criminal activity. I believe such indefinite detentions can be "reasonable" under the Fourth Amendment only with the approval of a magistrate. I also believe that such approval can be given only upon a showing of probable cause. * * *

In my opinion, allowing the Government to hold someone in indefinite, involuntary, incommunicado isolation without probable cause and a judicial warrant violates our constitutional charter whether the purpose is to extract ransom or to investigate suspected criminal activity. Nothing in the Fourth Amendment permits an exception for such actions at the Nation's border. It is tempting, of course, to look the other way in a case that so graphically illustrates the "veritable national crisis" caused by narcotics trafficking. But if there is one enduring lesson in the long struggle to balance individual rights against society's need to defend itself against lawlessness, it is that "[it] is easy to make light of insistence on scrupulous regard for the safeguards of civil liberties when invoked on behalf of the unworthy. It is too easy. History bears testimony that by such disregard are the rights of liberty extinguished, heedlessly at first, then stealthily, and brazenly in the end."

I dissent.

RODRIGUEZ V. UNITED STATES

575 U.S. 348
Supreme Court of the United States
January 21, 2015, Argued; April 21, 2015, Decided
No. 13-9972

JUSTICE GINSBURG delivered the opinion of the Court.

In *Illinois v. Caballes*, 543 U.S. 405 (2005), this Court held that a dog sniff conducted during a lawful traffic stop does not violate the Fourth Amendment's proscription of unreasonable seizures. This case presents the question whether the Fourth Amendment tolerates a dog sniff conducted after completion of a traffic stop. We hold that a police stop exceeding the time needed to handle the matter for which the stop was made violates the Constitution's shield against unreasonable seizures. * * *

I

Just after midnight on March 27, 2012, police officer Morgan Struble observed a Mercury Mountaineer veer slowly onto the shoulder of Nebraska State Highway 275 for one or two seconds and then jerk back onto the road. Nebraska law prohibits driving on highway shoulders and on that basis, Struble pulled the Mountaineer over at 12:06 a.m. Struble is a K-9 officer with the Valley Police Department in Nebraska, and his dog Floyd was in his patrol car that night. Two men were in the Mountaineer: the driver, Dennys Rodriguez, and a front-seat passenger, Scott Pollman.

Struble approached the Mountaineer on the passenger's side. After Rodriguez identified himself, Struble asked him why he had driven onto the shoulder. Rodriguez replied that he had swerved to avoid a pothole. Struble then gathered Rodriguez's license, registration, and proof of insurance, and asked Rodriguez to accompany him to the patrol car. Rodriguez asked if he was required to do so, and Struble answered that he was not. Rodriguez decided to wait in his own vehicle.

After running a records check on Rodriguez, Struble returned to the Mountaineer. Struble asked passenger Pollman for his driver's license and began to question him about where the two men were coming from and where they were going. Pollman replied that they had traveled to Omaha, Nebraska, to look at a Ford Mustang that was for sale and that they were returning to Norfolk, Nebraska. Struble returned again to his patrol car, where he completed a records check on Pollman, and called for a second officer. Struble then began writing a warning ticket for Rodriguez for driving on the shoulder of the road.

Struble returned to Rodriguez's vehicle a third time to issue the written warning. By 12:27 or 12:28 a.m., Struble had finished explaining the warning to Rodriguez, and had given back to Rodriguez and Pollman the documents obtained from them. As Struble later testified, at that point, Rodriguez and Pollman "had all their documents back and a copy of the written warning. I got all the reason[s] for the stop out of the way[,] . . . took care of all the business."

Nevertheless, Struble did not consider Rodriguez "free to leave." Although justification for the traffic stop was "out of the way," Struble asked for permission to walk his dog around Rodriguez's vehicle. Rodriguez said no. Struble then instructed Rodriguez to turn off the ignition, exit the vehicle, and stand in front of the patrol car to wait for the second officer. Rodriguez complied. At 12:33 a.m., a deputy sheriff arrived. Struble retrieved his dog and led him twice around the Mountaineer. The dog alerted to the presence of drugs halfway through Struble's second pass. All told, seven or eight minutes had elapsed from the time Struble issued the written warning until the dog indicated the presence of drugs. A search of the vehicle revealed a large bag of methamphetamine.

Rodriguez was indicted in the United States District Court for the District of Nebraska on one count of possession with intent to distribute 50 grams or more of methamphetamine. He moved to suppress the evidence seized from his car on the ground, among others, that Struble had prolonged the traffic stop without reasonable suspicion in order to conduct the dog sniff. * * *

The District Court * * * denied Rodriguez's motion to suppress. * * * The Eighth Circuit affirmed. * * *

We granted certiorari to resolve a division among lower courts on the question whether police routinely may extend an otherwise-completed traffic stop, absent reasonable suspicion, in order to conduct a dog sniff.

II

A seizure for a traffic violation justifies a police investigation of that violation. "[A] relatively brief encounter," a routine traffic stop is "more analogous to a so-called 'Terry stop' . . . than to a formal arrest." Like a Terry stop, the tolerable duration of police inquiries in the traffic-stop context is determined by the seizure's "mission"—to address the traffic violation that warranted the stop, and attend to related safety concerns. Because addressing the infraction is the purpose of the stop, it may "last no longer than is necessary to effectuate th[at] purpose." Authority for the seizure thus ends when tasks tied to the traffic infraction are—or reasonably should have been—completed. * * *

Beyond determining whether to issue a traffic ticket, an officer's mission includes "ordinary inquiries incident to [the traffic] stop." Typically such inquiries involve checking the driver's license, determining whether there are outstanding warrants against the driver, and inspecting the automobile's registration and proof of insurance. These checks serve the same objective as enforcement of the traffic code: ensuring that vehicles on the road are operated safely and responsibly.

A dog sniff, by contrast, is a measure aimed at "detect[ing] evidence of ordinary criminal wrongdoing." Candidly, the Government acknowledged at oral argument that a dog sniff, unlike the routine measures just mentioned, is not an ordinary incident of a traffic stop. Lacking the same close connection to roadway safety as the ordinary inquiries, a dog sniff is not fairly characterized as part of the officer's traffic mission. * * *

The Government argues that an officer may "incremental[ly]" prolong a stop to conduct a dog sniff so long as the officer is reasonably diligent in pursuing the traffic-related purpose of the stop, and the overall duration of the stop remains reasonable in relation to the duration of other traffic stops involving similar circumstances. The Government's argument, in effect, is that by completing all traffic-related tasks expeditiously, an officer can earn bonus time to pursue an unrelated criminal investigation. The reasonableness of a seizure, however, depends on what the police in fact do. In this regard, the Government acknowledges that "an officer always has to be reasonably diligent." How could diligence be gauged other than by noting what the officer actually did and how he did it? If an officer can complete traffic-based inquiries expeditiously, then that is the amount of "time reasonably required to complete [the stop's] mission." As we said in *Caballes* and reiterate today, a traffic stop "prolonged beyond" that point is "unlawful." The critical question, then, is not whether the dog sniff occurs before or after the officer issues a ticket, * * * but whether conducting the sniff "prolongs"—i.e., adds time to—"the stop."

* * *

For the reasons stated, the judgment of the United States Court of Appeals for the Eighth Circuit is vacated, and the case is remanded for further proceedings consistent with this opinion.

It is so ordered.

JUSTICE KENNEDY, dissenting.

[Omitted.]

JUSTICE THOMAS, with whom JUSTICE ALITO joins, and with whom JUSTICE KENNEDY joins as to all but Part III, dissenting. * * *

I

* * * Because Rodriguez does not dispute that Officer Struble had probable cause to stop him, the only question is whether the stop was otherwise executed in a reasonable manner. I easily conclude that it was. Approximately 29 minutes passed from the time Officer Struble stopped Rodriguez until his narcotics-detection dog alerted to the presence of drugs. That amount of time is hardly out of the ordinary for a traffic stop by a single officer of a vehicle containing multiple occupants even when no dog sniff is involved. During that time, Officer Struble conducted the ordinary activities of a traffic stop—he approached the vehicle, questioned Rodriguez about the observed violation, asked Pollman about their travel plans, ran serial warrant checks on Rodriguez and Pollman, and issued a written warning to Rodriguez. And when he decided to conduct a dog sniff, he took the precaution of calling for backup out of concern for his safety.

As *Caballes* makes clear, the fact that Officer Struble waited until after he gave Rodriguez the warning to conduct the dog sniff does not alter this analysis. Because "the use of a well-trained narcotics-detection dog . . . generally does not implicate legitimate privacy interests," "conducting a dog sniff would not change the character of a traffic stop that is lawful at its inception and otherwise executed in a reasonable manner." The stop here was "lawful at its inception and otherwise executed in a reasonable manner." As in *Caballes*, "conducting a dog sniff [did] not change the character of [the] traffic stop," and thus no Fourth Amendment violation occurred.

II   * * *

* * * [T]he majority's inquiry elides the distinction between traffic stops based on probable cause and those based on reasonable suspicion. * * *

Traffic stops can be initiated based on probable cause or reasonable suspicion. Although the Court has commented that a routine traffic stop is "more analogous to a so-called '*Terry* stop' than to a formal arrest," it has rejected the notion "that a traffic stop supported by probable cause may not exceed the bounds set by the Fourth Amendment on the scope of a *Terry* stop."

Although all traffic stops must be executed reasonably, our precedents make clear that traffic stops justified by reasonable suspicion are subject to additional limitations that those justified by probable cause are not. A traffic stop based on reasonable suspicion, like all *Terry* stops, must be "justified at its inception" and "reasonably related in scope to the circumstances which justified the interference in the first place." It also "cannot continue for an excessive period of time or resemble a traditional arrest." By contrast, a stop based on probable cause affords an officer considerably more leeway. In such seizures, an officer may engage in a warrantless arrest of the driver, a warrantless search incident to arrest of the driver, and a warrantless search incident to arrest of the vehicle if it is reasonable to believe evidence relevant to the crime of arrest might be found there.

The majority casually tosses this distinction aside. It asserts that the traffic stop in this case, which was undisputedly initiated on the basis of probable cause, can last no longer than is in fact necessary to effectuate the mission of the stop. And, it assumes that the mission of the stop was merely to write a traffic ticket, rather than to consider making a custodial arrest. In support of that durational requirement, it relies primarily on cases involving *Terry* stops.

The only case involving a traffic stop based on probable cause that the majority cites for its rule is *Caballes*. But, that decision provides no support for today's restructuring of our Fourth Amendment jurisprudence. In *Caballes*, the Court made clear that, in the context of a traffic stop supported by probable cause, "a dog sniff would not change the character of a traffic stop that is lawful at its inception and otherwise executed in a reasonable manner." To be sure, the dissent in *Caballes* would have "appl[ied] *Terry*'s reasonable-relation test . . . to determine whether the canine sniff impermissibly expanded the scope of the initially valid seizure of *Caballes*." But even it conceded that the *Caballes* majority had "implicitly [rejected] the application of *Terry* to a traffic stop converted, by calling in a dog, to a drug search."

By strictly limiting the tasks that define the durational scope of the traffic stop, the majority accomplishes today what the *Caballes* dissent could not: strictly limiting the scope of an officer's activities during a traffic stop justified by probable cause. In doing so, it renders the difference between probable cause and reasonable suspicion virtually meaningless in this context. That shift is supported neither by the Fourth Amendment nor by our precedents interpreting it. And, it results in a constitutional framework that lacks predictability. Had Officer Struble arrested, handcuffed, and taken Rodriguez to the police station for his traffic violation, he would have complied with the Fourth Amendment. But because he made Rodriguez wait for seven or eight extra minutes until a dog arrived, he evidently committed a constitutional violation. Such a view of the Fourth Amendment makes little sense.

* * *

I would conclude that the police did not violate the Fourth Amendment here. Officer Struble possessed probable cause to stop Rodriguez for driving on the shoulder, and he executed the subsequent stop in a reasonable manner. Our decision in *Caballes* requires no more. The majority's holding to the contrary is irreconcilable with *Caballes* and a number of other routine police practices, distorts the distinction between traffic stops justified by probable cause and those justified by reasonable suspicion, and abandons reasonableness as the touchstone of the Fourth Amendment. I respectfully dissent.

JUSTICE ALITO, dissenting.

This is an unnecessary, impractical, and arbitrary decision. * * *

* * * The Court refuses to address the real Fourth Amendment question: whether the stop was unreasonably prolonged. Instead, the Court latches onto the fact that Officer Struble delivered the warning prior to the dog sniff and proclaims that the authority to detain based on a traffic stop ends when a citation or warning is handed over to the driver. The Court thus holds that the Fourth Amendment was violated, not because of the length of the stop, but simply because of the sequence in which Officer Struble chose to perform his tasks.

This holding is not only arbitrary; it is perverse since Officer Struble chose that sequence for the purpose of protecting his own safety and possibly the safety of others. Without prolonging the stop, Officer Struble could have conducted the dog sniff while one of the tasks that the Court regards as properly part of the traffic stop was still in progress, but that sequence would have entailed unnecessary risk. At approximately 12:19 a.m., after collecting Pollman's driver's license, Officer Struble did two things. He called in the information needed to do a records check on Pollman (a step that the Court recognizes was properly part of the traffic stop), and he requested that another officer report to the scene. Officer Struble had decided to perform a dog sniff but did not want to do that without another officer present. When occupants of a vehicle who know that their vehicle contains a large amount of illegal drugs see that a drug-sniffing dog has alerted for the presence of drugs, they will almost certainly realize that the police will then proceed to search the vehicle, discover the drugs, and make arrests. Thus, it is reasonable for an officer to believe that an alert will increase the risk that the occupants of the vehicle will attempt to flee or perhaps even attack the officer.

In this case, Officer Struble was concerned that he was outnumbered at the scene, and he therefore called for backup and waited for the arrival of another officer before conducting the sniff. As a result, the sniff was not completed until seven or eight minutes after he delivered the warning. But Officer Struble could have proceeded with the dog sniff while he was waiting for the results of the records check on Pollman and before the arrival of the second officer. The drug-sniffing dog was present in Officer Struble's car. If he had chosen that riskier sequence of events, the dog sniff would have been completed before the point in time when, according to the Court's analysis, the authority to detain for the traffic stop ended. Thus, an action that would have been lawful had the officer made the unreasonable decision to risk his life became unlawful when the officer made the reasonable decision to wait a few minutes for backup. Officer Struble's error—apparently—was following prudent procedures motivated by legitimate safety concerns. The Court's holding therefore makes no practical sense. And nothing in the Fourth Amendment, which speaks of reasonableness, compels this arbitrary line.

The rule that the Court adopts will do little good going forward. It is unlikely to have any appreciable effect on the length of future traffic stops. Most officers will learn the prescribed sequence of events even if they cannot fathom the reason for that requirement. (I would love to be the proverbial fly on the wall when police instructors teach this rule to officers who make traffic stops.)

For these reasons and those set out in Justice Thomas's opinion, I respectfully dissent.

CHAPTER 5

WARRANTS

■ ■ ■

I. INTRODUCTION

Warrants come in one of two forms—arrest and search. An arrest warrant is a document, approved by judge (usually a magistrate), that authorizes law enforcement to arrest someone for committing a crime. A search warrant, by contrast, is a document approved by a judge that authorizes law enforcement to search property and seize evidence of a crime. The two warrants might be issued separately or together (e.g., an arrest warrant might be included with a search warrant). If the two warrants are issued together, the document or supporting affidavit must establish both probable cause for the search and probable cause for the arrest.

From a constitutional perspective, a valid warrant—either arrest or search—contains four basic requirements: (1) it is supported by probable cause; (2) it includes an oath, affirmation, or sworn testimony, typically by an officer, setting forth the underlying facts and circumstances giving rise to probable cause; (3) it describes the person (arrest) or property to be seized (search) with particularity; and (4) it is issued by a neutral and detached magistrate.

From a form perspective, arrest warrants typically must include the defendant's name, describe the offense charged, and be signed by a magistrate. There is no statute of limitations on arrest warrants so, once issued, the defendant who ignores an arrest warrant does himself no favors; indeed, it's possible that the defendant who dodges an arrest warrant could become a fugitive. That said, law enforcement must make reasonable efforts to locate the named individual. The warrant, once issued, enables officers to arrest the named person essentially anywhere—their residence, place of business, or in public.

Practically, arrest warrants are rare. Although the Supreme Court has expressed a preference for the use of arrest warrants,[1] arrests for a felony do not require a warrant. As you'll read, arrest warrants are required for in-home arrests, absent consent or emergency circumstances. Beyond that, however, the vast majority of arrests are warrantless arrests in public.

---

[1]   *Gerstein v. Pugh*, 420 U.S. 103, 113 (1975).

Whereas the arrest warrant focuses exclusively on seizing and detaining people, a search warrant can fill a number of diverse functions. For example, a search warrant might be issued for contraband, evidence of a crime, or even the subject of an arrest warrant. A search warrant should identify any person or property to be seized and generally must be executed within a particular time during daylight hours. The warrant must then be returned to the issuing magistrate within a limited timeframe. The warrant return should include an inventory of the seized property—both physical and electronic.

Evidence seized pursuant to a defective warrant is subject to suppression. A defendant can challenge a warrant in one of two basic ways. First, the defendant can argue that the warrant is facially invalid. To succeed, the defendant must show that the four corners of the warrant lack some basic constitutional requirement. In the search context, the advantage of this argument is that evidence seized pursuant to a facially invalid warrant is not subject to *Leon*'s good faith exception.

Second, under *Franks v. Delaware*, 438 U.S. 154 (1978), a defendant may challenge a warrant by asserting that it contains a false statement from the affiant. To succeed, the defendant must make a "substantial preliminary showing" that: (1) the affiant made a false statement or material omission in the warrant; (2) the affiant made the false statement "knowingly and intentionally" or with reckless disregard for the truth; and (3) the false statement was necessary for the magistrate's probable cause determination. That showing entitles the defendant to an evidentiary hearing where the defendant must prove his allegations by a preponderance of the evidence. If successful, the warrant is void and the fruits of the search are excluded from evidence at the criminal trial.

II. REQUIREMENTS FOR A VALID WARRANT

We move now to considering each requirement for a valid warrant— one at a time. First, recall that a warrant must be issued by a neutral and detached magistrate. Second, the warrant must describe the person (in the case of an arrest) or property to be seized (in the case of search) with particularity. Third, warrants must be, according to the Fourth Amendment "supported by Oath or affirmation." And finally, probable cause must exist to support the warrant. Note that we do not cover probable cause below given our recent coverage of the topic in Chapter 4.

A. NEUTRAL & DETACHED MAGISTRATE

We begin by briefly considering the requirement that all warrants be issued by a neutral and detached magistrate. Notice that this requirement is not textually required by the Fourth Amendment. The basic idea, though, is that warrants must be issued by an independent member of the judicial branch and not by, for example, the Attorney General—who actively investigates and prosecutes crime. *Coolidge v. New Hampshire*, 403 U.S. 443, 450 (1971). Membership in the judiciary, as our next cases discuss, does not necessarily satisfy the neutral and detached requirement.

By the way, before reading *Shadwick v. Tampa*, you might be interested in a definition for the amorphous term "magistrate." A magistrate is "[a] local official who possesses whatever power is specified in the appointment or statutory grant of authority."[2] The term is alternatively defined as "[a] judicial officer with strictly limited jurisdiction and authority, often on the local level and often restricted to criminal cases."[3]

At the state level, for example, magistrate judges in Iowa must be attorneys.[4] They "have jurisdiction over simple misdemeanors, county and municipal infractions, small claims, evictions, and certain involuntary commitment matters. Magistrates have authority to issue search warrants and conduct preliminary hearings."[5] By contrast, at the federal level a United States magistrate is appointed by a majority vote of the federal district judges of the particular district. Pursuant to 28 U.S.C. § 631 (LexisNexis 2018), full-time magistrate judges serve terms of eight years, unlike federal district and appellate judges who have lifetime tenure.

SHADWICK V. TAMPA

407 U.S. 345
Supreme Court of the United States
April 10, 1972, Argued; June 19, 1972, Decided
No. 71-5445

MR. JUSTICE POWELL delivered the opinion of the Court.

The charter of Tampa, Florida, authorizes the issuance of certain arrest warrants by clerks of the Tampa Municipal Court.[1] The sole question

---

[2] *Magistrate*, BLACK'S LAW DICTIONARY 970 (8th ed. 2004).

[3] *Id.*

[4] Iowa Code § 602.6404 (2022).

[5] IOWA JUD. BRANCH, GUIDE TO IOWA'S COURT SYSTEM 3 (2022).

[1] The relevant Florida statute and Tampa charter provisions are set forth below.

1. Section 168.04 of Fla. Stat. (1965) reads as follows:

The clerk may administer an oath to and take affidavit of any person charging another with an offense by breach of an ordinance, and may issue a warrant to the marshal to have the accused person arrested and brought before the mayor for trial. The marshal may, in the absence of the mayor and clerk from the police station, administer oaths to affidavits of complaints and issue warrants for the arrest of persons complained against.

2. Section 495 of the Charter of the City of Tampa enacted by the legislature of the State of Florida in Section 17, Chapter 5363, Laws of Florida 1903, reads as follows:

The Chief of Police, or any policeman of the City of Tampa, may arrest, without warrant, any person violating any of the ordinances of said city, committed in the presence of such officer, and when knowledge of the violation of any ordinance of said city shall come to said chief of police or policeman, not committed in his presence, he shall at once make affidavit, before the judge or clerk of the municipal court, against the person charged with in this case is whether these clerks qualify as neutral and detached magistrates for purposes of the Fourth Amendment. We hold that they do.

Appellant was arrested for impaired driving on a warrant issued by a clerk of the municipal court. He moved the court to quash the warrant on the ground that it was issued by a nonjudicial officer in violation of the Fourth and Fourteenth Amendments. When the motion was denied, he initiated proceedings in the Florida courts by means of that State's writ of common-law certiorari. The state proceedings culminated in the holding of the Florida Supreme Court that "the clerk and deputy clerks of the municipal court of the City of Tampa are neutral and detached 'magistrates' . . . for the purpose of issuing arrest warrants within the requirements of the United States Constitution . . . ." * * *

I

A clerk of the municipal court is appointed by the city clerk from a classified list of civil servants and assigned to work in the municipal court. The statute does not specify the qualifications necessary for this job, but no law degree or special legal training is required. The clerk's duties are to receive traffic fines, prepare the court's dockets and records, fill out commitment papers and perform other routine clerical tasks. Apparently, he may issue subpoenas. He may not, however, sit as a judge, and he may not issue a search warrant or even a felony or misdemeanor arrest warrant for violations of state laws. The only warrants he may issue are for the arrest of those charged with having breached municipal ordinances of the city of Tampa.

Appellant, contending that the Fourth Amendment requires that warrants be issued by "judicial officers," argues that even this limited warrant authority is constitutionally invalid. He reasons that warrant applications of whatever nature cannot be assured the discerning, independent review compelled by the Fourth Amendment when the review is performed by less than a judicial officer. It is less than clear, however, as to who would qualify as a "judicial officer" under appellant's theory. There is some suggestion in appellant's brief that a judicial officer must be a lawyer or the municipal court judge himself. A more complete portrayal of appellant's position would be that the Tampa clerks are disqualified as judicial officers not merely because they are not lawyers or judges, but because they lack the institutional independence associated with the

---

such violation, whereupon said judge or clerk shall issue a warrant for the arrest of such person.

3. Section 160 of the Charter of the City of Tampa enacted by the legislature of the State of Florida in Section 1, Chapter 61–2915, Laws of Florida 1961, reads as follows:

The city clerk of the City of Tampa, with the approval of the mayor, may appoint one or more deputies, such deputy or deputies to be selected from the approved classified list of the city civil service, and to have and exercise the same powers as the city clerk himself, including but not limited to the issuance of warrants. One or more of such deputies may be designated as clerks of the municipal court.

judiciary in that they are members of the civil service, appointed by the city clerk, "an executive official," and enjoy no statutorily specified tenure in office.

II.

Past decisions of the Court have mentioned review by a "judicial officer" prior to issuance of a warrant. In some cases, the term "judicial officer" appears to have been used interchangeably with that of "magistrate." In others, it was intended simply to underscore the now accepted fact that someone independent of the police and prosecution must determine probable cause. The very term "judicial officer" implies, of course, some connection with the judicial branch. But it has never been held that only a lawyer or judge could grant a warrant, regardless of the court system or the type of warrant involved. In *Jones [v. United States]*, the Court implied that United States Commissioners, many of whom were not lawyers or judges, were nonetheless "independent judicial officers."

The Court frequently has employed the term "magistrate" to denote those who may issue warrants. Historically, a magistrate has been defined broadly as "a public civil officer, possessing such power, legislative, executive or judicial, as the government appointing him may ordain," or, in a narrower sense "an inferior judicial officer, such as a justice of the peace." More recent definitions have not much changed.[7]

An examination of the Court's decisions reveals that the terms "magistrate" and "judicial officer" have been used interchangeably. Little attempt was made to define either term, to distinguish the one from the other, or to advance one as the definitive Fourth Amendment requirement. We find no commandment in either term, however, that all warrant authority must reside exclusively in a lawyer or judge. Such a requirement would have been incongruous when even within the federal system warrants were until recently widely issued by nonlawyers.

To attempt to extract further significance from the above terminology would be both unnecessary and futile. The substance of the Constitution's warrant requirements does not turn on the labeling of the issuing party. The warrant traditionally has represented an independent assurance that a search and arrest will not proceed without probable cause to believe that a crime has been committed and that the person or place named in the warrant is involved in the crime. Thus, an issuing magistrate must meet

---

[7]   In *Compton [v. Alabama]*, a notary public was deemed a "magistrate," but the Court has nowhere indicated that the term denotes solely a lawyer or judge.

Webster's Dictionary (2d ed. 1957), defines magistrate as "[a] person clothed with power as a public civil officer; a public civil officer invested with executive or judicial powers . . ." or, more narrowly, "[a] magistrate of a class having summary, often criminal, jurisdiction, as a justice of the peace, or one of certain officials having a similar jurisdiction . . ." Random House Dictionary (1966) defines magistrate as (1) "a civil officer charged with the administration of the law" and (2) "a minor judicial officer, as a justice of the peace or a police justice, having jurisdiction to try minor criminal cases and to conduct preliminary examinations of persons charged with serious crimes."

two tests. He must be neutral and detached, and he must be capable of determining whether probable cause exists for the requested arrest or search. This Court long has insisted that inferences of probable cause be drawn by "a neutral and detached magistrate instead of being judged by the officer engaged in the often competitive enterprise of ferreting out crime." * * * If, on the other hand, detachment and capacity do conjoin, the magistrate has satisfied the Fourth Amendment's purpose.

III

The requisite detachment is present in the case at hand. Whatever else neutrality and detachment might entail, it is clear that they require severance and disengagement from activities of law enforcement. There has been no showing whatever here of partiality, or affiliation of these clerks with prosecutors or police. The record shows no connection with any law enforcement activity or authority which would distort the independent judgment the Fourth Amendment requires. Appellant himself expressly refused to allege anything to that effect. The municipal court clerk is assigned not to the police or prosecutor but to the municipal court judge for whom he does much of his work. In this sense, he may well be termed a "judicial officer." While a statutorily specified term of office and appointment by someone other than "an executive authority" might be desirable, the absence of such features is hardly disqualifying. Judges themselves take office under differing circumstances. Some are appointed, but many are elected by legislative bodies or by the people. Many enjoy but limited terms and are subject to re-appointment or re-election. Most depend for their salary level upon the legislative branch. We will not elevate requirements for the independence of a municipal clerk to a level higher than that prevailing with respect to many judges. The clerk's neutrality has not been impeached: he is removed from prosecutor or police and works within the judicial branch subject to the supervision of the municipal court judge.

Appellant likewise has failed to demonstrate that these clerks lack capacity to determine probable cause. The clerk's authority extends only to the issuance of arrest warrants for breach of municipal ordinances. We presume from the nature of the clerk's position that he would be able to deduce from the facts on an affidavit before him whether there was probable cause to believe a citizen guilty of impaired driving, breach of peace, drunkenness, trespass, or the multiple other common offenses covered by a municipal code. There has been no showing that this is too difficult a task for a clerk to accomplish. Our legal system has long entrusted nonlawyers to evaluate more complex and significant factual data than that in the case at hand. Grand juries daily determine probable cause prior to rendering indictments, and trial juries assess whether guilt is proved beyond a reasonable doubt. The significance and responsibility of these lay judgments betray any belief that the Tampa clerks could not determine probable cause for arrest.

We decide today only that clerks of the municipal court may constitutionally issue the warrants in question. * * *

What we do reject * * * is any *per se* invalidation of a state or local warrant system on the ground that the issuing magistrate is not a lawyer or judge. Communities may have sound reasons for delegating the responsibility of issuing warrants to competent personnel other than judges or lawyers.[10] Many municipal courts face stiff and unrelenting caseloads. A judge pressured with the docket before him may give warrant applications more brisk and summary treatment than would a clerk. All this is not to imply that a judge or lawyer would not normally provide the most desirable review of warrant requests. But our federal system warns of converting desirable practice into constitutional commandment. It recognizes in plural and diverse state activities one key to national innovation and vitality. States are entitled to some flexibility and leeway in their designation of magistrates, so long as all are neutral and detached and capable of the probable-cause determination required of them.

We affirm the judgment of the Florida Supreme Court.

Affirmed.

QUESTIONS, COMMENTS, CONCERNS?

1. **Particularity and revisiting the "neutral and detached" requirement.** In *Lo-Ji Sales, Inc. v. New York*, 442 U.S. 319 (1979), an investigator from the New York State Police purchased two reels of film from defendant's "adult" bookstore. After viewing the films, he concluded that they violated the state's obscenity laws and took them to a Town Justice to obtain a search warrant for defendant's store. The Town Justice viewed both films and agreed that they were obscene. The investigator signed an affidavit before the Town Justice who then issued a warrant authorizing the search of petitioner's store and the seizure of other copies of the two films. The investigator's affidavit also asserted that "similar" films and "printed matter portraying similar activities could be found on the premises[.]" The affidavit also requested that the justice join in the execution of the warrant so that the justice might determine independently if any other items of the store violated the obscenity law. The Town Justice agreed to participate in the search.

When the search party converged on the bookstore, they conducted a search that lasted nearly six hours. They seized numerous materials, and defendant was charged with obscenity in the second degree. Following defendant's guilty plea and appeal, the Supreme Court reversed. It held that the warrant was invalid because: (1) it failed at the outset to satisfy the

---

[10] Some communities, such as those in rural or sparsely settled areas, may have a shortage of available lawyers and judges and must entrust responsibility for issuing warrants to other qualified persons. The Federal Magistrates Act, for example, explicitly makes provision for nonlawyers to be appointed in those communities where members of the bar are not available.

particularity requirement, and (2) it was not issued by a neutral and detached magistrate.

As to the particularity holding, the Court reasoned, "Except for the specification of copies of the two films previously purchased, the warrant did not purport to 'particularly describe the things to be seized.'" As for the role of the Town Justice, the Court commented that he "allowed himself to become a member, if not the leader, of the search party which was essentially a police operation. Once in the store, he conducted a generalized search under authority of an invalid warrant; he was not acting as a judicial officer but as an adjunct law enforcement officer."

UNITED STATES V. PARKER
373 F.3d 770
United States Court of Appeals for the Sixth Circuit
April 22, 2004, Argued; June 28, 2004, Decided; June 28, 2004, Filed
No. 03-5303

PATRICK J. DUGGAN, DISTRICT JUDGE.

In this interlocutory appeal, the government challenges the district court's decision to suppress evidence seized at the residence of Barbara Jean Sutton and Peter Jansen Sutton (collectively the "Suttons") pursuant to two search warrants. The district court concluded that the trial commissioner who issued the search warrants was not neutral and detached because she also served as an administrative assistant at the county jail. The court therefore held that the search warrants were invalid. The district court additionally ruled that the exception to the exclusionary rule set forth in *United States v. Leon*, 468 U.S. 897 (1984), is inapplicable under these circumstances. The government filed appeal, challenging the district court's decision. For the reasons that follow, we affirm.

I.   Standard of Review

This court reviews the district court's findings of fact in a suppression hearing under the clearly erroneous standard, while the district court's conclusions of law are reviewed *de novo*.

II.   Factual Background

On July 21 and 24, 2001, law enforcement officers in Ohio County, Kentucky, seized seventy-one firearms, marijuana, cocaine, methamphetamine, drug paraphernalia, explosive materials, and allegedly stolen personal property pursuant to two search warrants executed for the Suttons' residence. Ohio County Trial Commissioner Michelle Madison ("Madison") signed both warrants.[1] Judge Renona C. Browning ("Judge Browning"), District Judge for Kentucky's 38th Judicial District, swore in

---

[1]   The only district judge for Ohio County was not in the district when the warrants were signed.

Madison as a trial commissioner for Ohio County several weeks earlier, on July 2, 2001. Madison was married to Judge Browning's brother, who died on September 2, 2000.

On June 25, 2001, Judge Browning had written Kentucky Supreme Court Chief Justice Joseph E. Lambert, requesting the appointment of a temporary trial commissioner for Ohio County based on a district judge vacancy. In her letter, Judge Browning advised Chief Justice Lambert that she had been unable to find an attorney in the county interested in this responsibility but that Madison agreed to take the position if it became available. Judge Browning informed Chief Justice Lambert that Madison was an employee of the Ohio County Detention Center and that her "duties at the jail are bookkeeping, finance officer, purchasing agent and general lieutenant." On June 29, 2001, Chief Justice Lambert signed an order approving the appointment of a temporary trial commissioner for Ohio County pursuant to Kentucky Supreme Court Rule 5.010 and Section 113(5) of the Kentucky Constitution; although he did not specifically approve the appointment of Madison.

Although there was some indication in the record that Madison's title at the detention center was "Chief Lieutenant Deputy Jailer," the district court concluded that her duties were similar to those of an administrative assistant. The court further found that Madison served at the pleasure of a law enforcement agent, as the Ohio County Jailer hired and could fire her. The court determined that Madison's job responsibilities included the following: handling the purchase orders for all jail bills; assisting the jailer with the yearly budget; keeping track of expenditures for the jail; billing surrounding counties for housing their inmates; maintaining the records of the jail's commissary account; handling the jailer's correspondence; and purchasing jail supplies. Madison additionally handled inmates' work release requests by obtaining information from the prisoners and completing work release forms. She assisted inmates with their child support obligations, helped inmates obtain legal representation, and facilitated inmates' drug rehabilitation placements. Unlike the county's deputy jailers, Madison did not carry a weapon; nor did she wear a badge or uniform. She never arrested anyone, did not participate in the ongoing training required of deputy jailers, and was not on the regular rotation of duties for monitoring prisoners.

Based on the evidence seized at the Suttons' residence, a federal grand jury returned a five-count indictment against the Defendants on September 4, 2002.

III. Applicable Law and Analysis

It is a long established requirement that, to be valid under the Fourth Amendment, a search warrant must be issued by a neutral and detached magistrate. *Shadwick v. City of Tampa*, 407 U.S. 345, 350 (1972). * * *

Following *Shadwick*, several courts have upheld search warrants issued by individuals connected to the judiciary. *See, e.g., United States v. Mitro*, 880 F.2d 1480 (1st Cir. 1989) (approving state warrant issued by assistant district court clerk); *United States v. Martinez-Zayas*, 857 F.2d 122 (3d Cir. 1988) (upholding warrant issued by municipal court bail commissioner); *United States v. Comstock*, 805 F.2d 1194 (5th Cir. 1986) (upholding warrant issued by justice of the peace). Similarly, this court upheld a search warrant issued by a judicial commissioner in Shelby County, Tennessee, despite the defendant's claim that the county's judicial commissioners could not be considered neutral and detached because they were appointed by a local legislative authority which also set the terms of their office and compensation. *United States v. Pennington*, 328 F.3d 215 (6th Cir. 2003). * * *

The government relies on *Pennington*, as well as this court's unpublished opinion in *United States v. King*, to argue that Madison's position at the county jail did not, by itself, contravene her neutrality and detachment as a trial commissioner. In *King*, the defendant moved to suppress evidence seized from his home pursuant to a search warrant, claiming that the warrant was invalid because the issuing judicial commissioner was married to a deputy sheriff who worked as a corrections officer at the county jail and because the couple occasionally socialized with other deputies and their spouses. We upheld the warrant, concluding that the judicial commissioner's social life was insufficient to demonstrate an engagement with law enforcement that would render her lacking in neutrality and detachment.

In this case, the district court concluded that Madison was engaged in law enforcement. This court agrees and therefore finds *King* and *Pennington* distinguishable. Unlike the judicial commissioner in *King*, Madison's connection to law enforcement was not limited to her social interactions or relationships with law enforcement officials. Unlike the judicial commissioner in *Pennington*, Madison's connection to the executive branch extended beyond her appointment by an executive official.

The district court found that Madison was employed by and worked for a law enforcement agency. Not only was she hired by the Jailer, a law enforcement official, but the Jailer served as her immediate and only supervisor. While Madison's daily duties may have been different than those of a deputy jailer, her work was performed at and for the Ohio County jail. Furthermore, Madison interacted with and assisted prisoners.

It also appears that Madison has an interest in the outcome of proceedings before her because of her work as the "chief lieutenant deputy jailor" for financial matters, including the collection of fees and billings for housing inmates and for trying to secure the financial stability of the jail. * * * In the case before us, Madison oversees the jail's budget and is in charge of its financial transactions. Madison's agency stands to gain financially in the form of bookings, administrative fees from arrests and per diem lodging. Madison explained that for arrestees for which she would issue an arrest warrant in her county as trial commissioner, as jailor she would collect various fees for the jail: "if someone comes in and they make bond and they're being released, they can pay the booking fee; the deputies can write them a receipt and accept that money and put it into our safe." * * * Madison may have a financial interest in the outcome of cases before her because she can issue warrants for the arrest of persons who would then pay fees to Madison as the jail's financial officer and whose lodging may be reimbursed by other government agencies. This set of incentives reinforces our conclusion that Madison's ability to act as a neutral and objective magistrate is questionable.

Based on these factual findings, which this court finds the record supports, we conclude that Madison was not sufficiently disengaged from activities of law enforcement to satisfy the Fourth Amendment's neutral and detached requirement.

In *Leon*, the Supreme Court carved out a good-faith exception to the exclusionary rule when officers act in reasonable reliance on a search warrant issued by a neutral and detached magistrate that is subsequently found to be invalid. However, as a matter of first impression among the Circuit Courts, this court held in 2001 that *Leon* is inapplicable when a warrant is signed by an individual lacking the legal authority necessary to issue warrants. *United States v. Scott*, 260 F.3d 512 (6th Cir. 2001). The court reasoned that the Supreme Court, in carving out a good-faith exception in *Leon*, "presupposed that the warrant was issued by a magistrate or judge clothed in the proper legal authority." The *Scott* court held that a search warrant issued by an individual who is not neutral and detached is void *ab initio*. As Madison's appointment as a trial commissioner was unlawful due to her engagement with law enforcement activities, *Scott* controls this case. Thus this court concludes that the district court properly declined to apply *Leon's* good-faith exception in this case.

* * * [I]t is a violation of the Fourth Amendment to authorize individuals insufficiently detached from law enforcement to issue warrants. In other words, such individuals never could be legally authorized to issue warrants. Therefore, because Madison was not a neutral and detached magistrate, the search warrants she signed were void from the beginning.

Accordingly, the district court's decision is AFFIRMED.

QUESTIONS, COMMENTS, CONCERNS?

1. **A primer on standards of review.** Notice that the court in *Parker* begins its discussion by reviewing the applicable standard of review. At the appellate court level, save for the Supreme Court, that's common practice. A standard of review generally denotes the strictness by which an appellate court evaluates a trial court's decision. There are roughly four standards of review that are worth your being familiar with: "*de novo*," "clearly erroneous," "substantial evidence," and "abuse of discretion." The first, *de novo*, is the standard applied to lower court rulings of law, and it accords essentially no deference to the lower court. The clearly erroneous standard involves slightly more deference and most often applies to district court factual findings. According to a past definition from the Supreme Court, "A finding is 'clearly erroneous' when although there is evidence to support it, the reviewing court on the entire evidence is left with the definite and firm conviction that a mistake has been committed." *United States v. U.S. Gypsum Co.*, 333 U.S. 364, 395 (1948).

Still more deferential is the third standard, substantial evidence, which the Supreme Court has applied to jury factual findings. In *Universal Camera Corp. v. NLRB*, 340 U.S. 474, 477 (1951), the Court defined substantial evidence as "such relevant evidence as a reasonable mind might accept as adequate to support a conclusion." The final standard, abuse of discretion, is the most deferential and applies, for example, to lower court decisions on the admission of evidence. The Supreme Court has previously recognized that a district court abuses its discretion when it makes a "clear error of judgment." *Citizens to Preserve Overton Park, Inc. v. Volpe*, 401 U.S. 402, 416 (1971).

Thus, you might lay out the varied standards of review, from the strictest to most deferential as follows:

De novo ⟶ clearly ⟶ substantial ⟶ abuse of
           erroneous   evidence   discretion

2. **Standards of review and the U.S. Supreme Court.** Standards of review are largely inapplicable to the Supreme Court. When the Court takes a case on *certiorari*, the consequence is that it is accepting the case to determine whether a legal (i.e., non-factual) error occurred below.

Some commentators nonetheless periodically confuse standards of review with judicial review at the Supreme Court level. The former is irrelevant whereas the latter may be highly relevant. For example, the Court is concerned with "judicial review" (assuming there is a requisite basis for jurisdiction—which must be stated in a brief to the Supreme Court) when reviewing the constitutionality of a statute or other law.

3. **Avoiding *Leon*.** Notice the considerable benefit to defense attorneys in arguing that a neutral and detached magistrate did not issue the challenged warrant: *Leon*'s good faith rule does not apply.

B. PARTICULARITY

We move next to the Fourth Amendment's requirement that "no Warrants shall issue" without "particularly describing the place to be searched, and the persons or things to be seized." The particularity requirement "was the founding generation's response to the reviled 'general warrants' and 'writs of assistance' of the colonial era, which allowed British officers to rummage through homes in an unrestrained search for evidence of criminal activity." *Riley v. California*, 573 U.S. 373, 403 (2014). Thus, the core purpose of the particularity requirement is to prevent "the seizure of one thing under a warrant describing another." *Marron v. United States*, 275 U.S. 192, 196 (1927).

GROH V. RAMIREZ

540 U.S. 551
Supreme Court of the United States
November 4, 2003, Argued; February 24, 2004, Decided
No. 02-811

JUSTICE STEVENS delivered the opinion of the Court. * * *

I

Respondents, Joseph Ramirez and members of his family, live on a large ranch in Butte-Silver Bow County, Montana. Petitioner, Jeff Groh, has been a Special Agent for the Bureau of Alcohol, Tobacco and Firearms (ATF) since 1989. In February 1997, a concerned citizen informed petitioner that on a number of visits to respondents' ranch the visitor had seen a large stock of weaponry, including an automatic rifle, grenades, a grenade launcher, and a rocket launcher. Based on that information, petitioner prepared and signed an application for a warrant to search the ranch. The application stated that the search was for "any automatic firearms or parts to automatic weapons, destructive devices to include but not limited to grenades, grenade launchers, rocket launchers, and any and all receipts pertaining to the purchase or manufacture of automatic weapons or explosive devices or launchers." Petitioner supported the application with a detailed affidavit, which he also prepared and executed, that set forth the basis for his belief that the listed items were concealed on the ranch. Petitioner then presented these documents to a Magistrate, along with a warrant form that petitioner also had completed. The Magistrate signed the warrant form.

Although the application particularly described the place to be searched and the contraband petitioner expected to find, the warrant itself was less specific; it failed to identify any of the items that petitioner intended to seize. In the portion of the form that called for a description of the "person or property" to be seized, petitioner typed a description of respondents' two-story blue house rather than the alleged stockpile of firearms.[2] The warrant did not incorporate by reference the itemized list contained in the application. It did, however, recite that the Magistrate was satisfied the affidavit established probable cause to believe that contraband was concealed on the premises, and that sufficient grounds existed for the warrant's issuance.

The day after the Magistrate issued the warrant, petitioner led a team of law enforcement officers, including both federal agents and members of the local sheriff's department, in the search of respondents' premises. Although respondent Joseph Ramirez was not home, his wife and children were. Petitioner states that he orally described the objects of the search to Mrs. Ramirez in person and to Mr. Ramirez by telephone. According to Mrs. Ramirez, however, petitioner explained only that he was searching for " 'an explosive device in a box.' " At any rate, the officers' search uncovered no illegal weapons or explosives. When the officers left, petitioner gave Mrs. Ramirez a copy of the search warrant, but not a copy of the application, which had been sealed. The following day, in response to a request from respondents' attorney, petitioner faxed the attorney a copy of the page of the application that listed the items to be seized. No charges were filed against the Ramirezes.

Respondents sued petitioner * * * raising eight claims, including violation of the Fourth Amendment. The District Court entered summary judgment for all defendants. The court found no Fourth Amendment violation, because it considered the case comparable to one in which the warrant contained an inaccurate address, and in such a case, the court reasoned, the warrant is sufficiently detailed if the executing officers can locate the correct house. * * *

The Court of Appeals affirmed the judgment with respect to all defendants and all claims, with the exception of respondents' Fourth Amendment claim against petitioner. On that claim, the court held that the warrant was invalid because it did not "describe with particularity the place to be searched and the items to be seized," and that oral statements by petitioner during or after the search could not cure the omission. * * * We granted certiorari.

II.

The warrant was plainly invalid. The Fourth Amendment states unambiguously that "no Warrants shall issue, but upon probable cause, supported by Oath or affirmation, and particularly describing the place to be searched, and *the persons or things to be seized.*" (Emphasis added.) The warrant in this case complied with the first three of these requirements: It

---

[2]   The warrant stated: "[T]here is now concealed [on the specified premises] a certain person or property, namely [a] single dwelling residence two story in height which is blue in color and has two additions attached to the east. The front entrance to the residence faces in a southerly direction."

was based on probable cause and supported by a sworn affidavit, and it described particularly the place of the search. On the fourth requirement, however, the warrant failed altogether. Indeed, petitioner concedes that "the warrant . . . was deficient in particularity because it provided no description of the type of evidence sought."

The fact that the application adequately described the "things to be seized" does not save the warrant from its facial invalidity. The Fourth Amendment by its terms requires particularity in the warrant, not in the supporting documents. And for good reason: "The presence of a search warrant serves a high function," and that high function is not necessarily vindicated when some other document, somewhere, says something about the objects of the search, but the contents of that document are neither known to the person whose home is being searched nor available for her inspection. We do not say that the Fourth Amendment prohibits a warrant from cross-referencing other documents. Indeed, most Courts of Appeals have held that a court may construe a warrant with reference to a supporting application or affidavit if the warrant uses appropriate words of incorporation, and if the supporting document accompanies the warrant. But in this case the warrant did not incorporate other documents by reference, nor did either the affidavit or the application (which had been placed under seal) accompany the warrant. Hence, we need not further explore the matter of incorporation.

Petitioner argues that even though the warrant was invalid, the search nevertheless was "reasonable" within the meaning of the Fourth Amendment. He notes that a Magistrate authorized the search on the basis of adequate evidence of probable cause, that petitioner orally described to respondents the items to be seized, and that the search did not exceed the limits intended by the Magistrate and described by petitioner. Thus, petitioner maintains, his search of respondents' ranch was functionally equivalent to a search authorized by a valid warrant.

We disagree. This warrant did not simply omit a few items from a list of many to be seized, or misdescribe a few of several items. Nor did it make what fairly could be characterized as a mere technical mistake or typographical error. Rather, in the space set aside for a description of the items to be seized, the warrant stated that the items consisted of a "single dwelling residence . . . blue in color." In other words, the warrant did not describe the items to be seized at all. In this respect the warrant was so obviously deficient that we must regard the search as "warrantless" within the meaning of our case law. "We are not dealing with formalities." Because "'the right of a man to retreat into his own home and there be free from unreasonable governmental intrusion'" stands "'[a]t the very core' of the Fourth Amendment," our cases have firmly established the "'basic principle of Fourth Amendment law' that searches and seizures inside a home without a warrant are presumptively unreasonable." Thus, "absent exigent circumstances, a warrantless entry to search for weapons or contraband is unconstitutional even when a felony has been committed and there is probable cause to believe that incriminating evidence will be found within." * * *

Petitioner asks us to hold that a search conducted pursuant to a warrant lacking particularity should be exempt from the presumption of unreasonableness if the goals served by the particularity requirement are otherwise satisfied. He maintains that the search in this case satisfied those goals—which he says are "to prevent general searches, to prevent the seizure of one thing under a warrant describing another, and to prevent warrants from being issued on vague or dubious information,"—because the scope of the search did not exceed the limits set forth in the application. But unless the particular items described in the affidavit are also set forth in the warrant itself (or at least incorporated by reference, and the affidavit present at the search), there can be no written assurance that the Magistrate actually found probable cause to search for, and to seize, every item mentioned in the affidavit. In this case, for example, it is at least theoretically possible that the Magistrate was satisfied that the search for weapons and explosives was justified by the showing in the affidavit, but not convinced that any evidentiary basis existed for rummaging through respondents' files and papers for receipts pertaining to the purchase or manufacture of such items. Or, conceivably, the Magistrate might have believed that some of the weapons mentioned in the affidavit could have been lawfully possessed and therefore should not be seized. The mere fact that the Magistrate issued a warrant does not necessarily establish that he agreed that the scope of the search should be as broad as the affiant's request. Even though petitioner acted with restraint in conducting the search, "the inescapable fact is that this restraint was imposed by the agents themselves, not by a judicial officer."

We have long held, moreover, that the purpose of the particularity requirement is not limited to the prevention of general searches. A particular warrant also "assures the individual whose property is searched or seized of the lawful authority of the executing officer, his need to search, and the limits of his power to search."

Petitioner argues that even if the goals of the particularity requirement are broader than he acknowledges, those goals nevertheless were served because he orally described to respondents the items for which he was searching. Thus, he submits, respondents had all of the notice that a proper warrant would have accorded. But this case presents no occasion even to reach this argument, since respondents, as noted above, dispute petitioner's account. According to Mrs. Ramirez, petitioner stated only that he was looking for an " 'explosive device in a box.' " Because this dispute is before us on petitioner's motion for summary judgment, "[t]he evidence of the nonmovant is to be believed, and all justifiable inferences are to be drawn in [her] favor." The posture of the case therefore obliges us to credit Mrs. Ramirez's account, and we find that petitioner's description of " 'an explosive device in a box' " was little better than no guidance at all.

It is incumbent on the officer executing a search warrant to ensure the search is lawfully authorized and lawfully conducted. Because petitioner did not have in his possession a warrant particularly describing the things he intended to seize, proceeding with the search was clearly "unreasonable" under the Fourth Amendment. The Court of Appeals correctly held that the search was unconstitutional. * * *

Accordingly, the judgment of the Court of Appeals is affirmed.

It is so ordered.

JUSTICE KENNEDY, with whom THE CHIEF JUSTICE joins, dissenting.

[Omitted.]

JUSTICE THOMAS, with whom JUSTICE SCALIA joins, and with whom THE CHIEF JUSTICE joins as to Part III, dissenting.

[Omitted.]

QUESTIONS, COMMENTS, CONCERNS?

1. Technology and particularity. At first blush, the particularity requirement presents as straightforward. But beware—constitutional questions surrounding the particularity requirement have grown in complexity when applied to seizures of electronic devices. Does a search warrant authorizing the seizure of a suspect's computer simultaneously authorize investigators to search the computer's entire hard drive, including all folders and files found inside? Similar questions arise in the context of search warrants written for smart phones.

For instance, is a search warrant requesting permission to seize "[r]ecords and documents stored on computers" sufficiently particular? No said the Ohio Supreme Court in the context of a search warrant that sought defendant's computer records to assist a prosecution for crimes that included "retaliation, criminal trespassing, criminal damaging, and possession of criminal tools." *State v. Castagnola*, 46 N.E.3d 638, 657 (Ohio 2015). The plain language of the warrant, said the *Castagnola* court, "demonstrates that there is no limitation on what records and documents were to be searched for in Castagnola's computer." In concluding that the warrant failed the constitutional particularity requirement, the court reasoned as follows:

> Courts addressing the particularity requirement of the Fourth Amendment are concerned with two issues. The first issue is whether the warrant provides sufficient information to "guide and control" the judgment of the executing officer in what to seize. The second issue is whether the category as specified is too broad in that it includes items that should not be seized.

A search warrant that includes broad categories of items to be seized may nevertheless be valid when the description is "as specific as the circumstances and the nature of the activity under investigation permit." Warrants that fail to describe the items to be seized with as much specificity as the government's knowledge and the circumstances allow are "invalidated by their substantial failure to specify as nearly as possible the distinguishing characteristics of the goods to be seized."

Because computers can store a large amount of information "there is a greater potential for the 'intermingling' of documents and a consequent invasion of privacy when police execute a search for evidence on a computer. * * * Officers must be clear as to what it is they are seeking on the computer and conduct the search in a way that avoids searching files of types not identified in the warrant." "[P]ractical accuracy rather than technical precision" is the operative consideration.

Here, the search warrant did not contain any description or qualifiers of the "records and documents stored on the computer" that the searcher was permitted to look for. The next section of the search warrant, which delineated that if any records and documents were seized, those items would be used to prosecute Castagnola for the crimes of retaliation, criminal trespassing, criminal damaging, and possession of criminal tools, added nothing to narrow the search. As written, this search warrant failed to address both concerns that courts consider when determining whether a warrant satisfies the particularity requirement of the Fourth Amendment.

First, as evidenced by the testimony of the BCI analyst, the language of the search warrant did not "guide and control" her judgment as to what was to be seized on the computer. She indicated that Castagnola's computer was brought in for a case involving "menacing, threatening, and intimidation." The analyst read the case synopsis and the search-warrant affidavit and then looked at all the information on the hard drive "looking for any evidence of intimidation of David Maistros * * * and anything associated with that." Therefore, the determination on what to seize was within her discretion.

Second, the broad language of this search warrant clearly included items that were not subject to seizure. The search warrant permitted her to examine every record or document on Castagnola's computer in order to find any evidence of the alleged crimes. In processing the hard drive, she testified, she was going through the "documents, images, videos." * * *

In this case, the detective believed that Castagnola had found Maistros's address online and that evidence of the online search would be useful in the prosecution of the alleged offenses. The detective testified at the suppression hearing that in addition to a general Google or online-white-pages search for Maistros's name, he believed that Castagnola may have searched a clerk of courts' website for information about Maistros because Castagnola had mentioned * * * that he had discovered that Maistros had received a parking ticket years earlier. The detective also testified that from his previous experience, he knew that an online search would create "a cookie, which will tell you where [the persons who have used the computer] have been, what searches they have done, things of that nature."

Under the Fourth Amendment, these details regarding the records or documents stored on the computer should have been included in the search warrant to guide and control the searcher and to sufficiently narrow the category of records or documents subject to seizure. Moreover, this degree of specificity was required, since the circumstances and the nature of the activity under investigation permitted the affiant to be this specific.

In urging this court to find that the search warrant sufficiently particularized the items to be searched for, the state provides a breadth of authority rejecting the notion that a search warrant must contain a restrictive protocol, methodology, or other strategy for conducting the search in order to satisfy the Fourth Amendment. We agree that the Fourth Amendment does not require a search warrant to specify restrictive search protocols, but we also recognize that the Fourth Amendment does prohibit a "sweeping comprehensive search of a computer's hard drive." The logical balance of these principles leads to the conclusion that officers must describe what they believe will be found on a computer with as much specificity as possible under the circumstances. This will enable the searcher to narrow his or her search to only the items to be seized. Adherence to this requirement is especially important when, as here, the person conducting the search is not the affiant.

* * * We understand that police and magistrates are not required to do the impossible. However, the specific evidence sought must be clearly stated * * *.

2. Gacy and particularity. Return for a moment to the case of John Wayne Gacy in Chapter 4. Recall that Officer Joseph Kozenzak obtained the first warrant to search Gacy's home on December 13, 1978—two days after the victim Robert Piest went missing. In pertinent part, that search warrant sought to search for and seize the following: "Light blue down filled ski jacket with hood, tan levi type pants, brown wedge suede lace type shoes, tan T-shirt, and a brown leather wallet along with hair samples, blood stained clothing, dried blood samples." [Gacy Casefile Document 2, at 16.] Gacy's appellate brief asserted, in part, that such a request lacked particularity:

The search warrant described the items to be seized as to type and color. But there is no indication as to the alleged owner of the clothing or items. There is no mention of any sizes, styles or manufacturers. There is absolutely no explanation given in the complaint and warrant as to why the items to be seized were evidence of crime. Were the police looking for the clothes worn or items possessed by John Gacy or Robert Piest on the night in question? One could not determine such from a reading of the complaint and warrant.

[Gacy Casefile Document 1, at 34.] Recall the *Groh* Court's concern that the warrant at issue in that case "did not describe the items to be seized at all." In particular, the *Groh* warrant, "in the space set aside for a description of the items to be seized, the warrant stated that the items consisted of a 'single dwelling residence . . . blue in color.' " The absence of particularity permits law enforcement to, in essence, conduct a general search. But by comparison, would you agree that the Gacy search warrant is far more detailed and therefore satisfies the constitutional requirement for particularity? [*See* Gacy Casefile Document 4, at 1179 (providing the appellate court's response to Gacy's particularity argument).]

3.   **Gacy and scope of search.** Stay for a moment in the Gacy Casefile. Recall that the first search warrant, issued on December 13, 1978, authorized law enforcement to search for and seize the following: "Light blue down jacket and hood, tan colored Levi Pants—Brown wedge type suede shoes—law type—brown leather wallet—Levi T-shirt, along with hair samples, blood stained clothing and dried blood samples." [Gacy Casefile Document 1, at 33.] Based on the wording of that search warrant, where may officers go in Gacy's home to search for those items? That matters because, as you will further recall, police found a high school ring with the initials J.A.S. and a film receipt from Nissen Pharmacy during the execution of the December 13 search warrant.

In *United States v. Ross*, the Supreme Court helpfully defined and illustrated the scope of a valid warrant to search a premises:

> A lawful search of fixed premises generally extends to the entire area in which the object of the search may be found and is not limited by the possibility that separate acts of entry or opening may be required to complete the search. Thus, a warrant that authorizes an officer to search a home for illegal weapons also provides authority to open closets, chests, drawers, and containers in which the weapon might be found. A warrant to open a footlocker to search for marihuana would also authorize the opening of packages found inside. A warrant to search a vehicle would support a search of every part of the vehicle that might contain the object of the search.

456 U.S. 798, 820–21 (1982). Based on the *Ross* language, is there anywhere in Gacy's home where officers could *not* go in order to locate the items listed in the December 13 warrant? Based on your answer to that question, are you concerned, as Gacy was, that the authority to search granted by that warrant "was so broad as to constitute an impermissible general search"? [Gacy Casefile Document 1, at 37.]

C. OATH OR AFFIRMATION

The Fourth Amendment requires that "no Warrants shall issue" unless they are "supported by Oath or affirmation." Stated simply, the Fourth Amendment requires the affiant to swear that probable cause supports the requested warrant. As a result, the absence of sworn testimony in support of a warrant application voids the warrant. But what happens when an officer's testimony under oath does not happen in the physical presence of the magistrate? Our next case considers that question.

CLAY V. STATE

391 S.W.3d 94
Court of Criminal Appeals of Texas
January 9, 2013, Delivered; January 9, 2013, Filed
No. PD-0579-12

Opinion by: PRICE.

Must a law-enforcement officer seeking to obtain a search warrant * * * swear out the affidavit in support of that warrant in the physical presence of the magistrate or may he do so telephonically, as happened in this case? We granted the appellant's petition for discretionary review to address that question. We hold that the warrant affidavit in this particular case was properly sworn out, and we affirm the judgment of the court of appeals.

FACTS AND PROCEDURAL POSTURE

On June 29, 2008, the appellant was arrested and charged with misdemeanor driving while intoxicated. She filed a pre-trial motion to suppress evidence obtained as a result of the execution of a search warrant to draw her blood for forensic testing. The parties proceeded on stipulated facts, without conducting an evidentiary hearing. The stipulated facts establish that the appellant was stopped by State Trooper J. Ortega for traveling 80 miles per hour in a 70 mile-per-hour zone. When probable cause to suspect the appellant of driving while intoxicated arose in the course of the stop, Ortega placed the appellant under arrest and requested that she provide a breath specimen for testing. The appellant refused, so Ortega filled out an affidavit for a search warrant to obtain a specimen of her blood. Ortega then called Hill County Court at Law Judge A. Lee Harris on the telephone. Ortega and Harris "each recognized the other's voice[,]" and in the course of the telephone conversation, Ortega "swore to and signed" the search warrant affidavit. It is specifically stipulated that Ortega did not sign the warrant affidavit "in the physical presence of Judge Harris" and that "Judge Harris did not physically witness" Ortega sign the warrant affidavit. Ortega faxed the warrant affidavit to Judge Harris, who signed and dated the jurat. Judge Harris then signed a search warrant authorizing the blood draw and faxed it back to Ortega, who had the appellant's blood drawn accordingly.

The trial court denied the appellant's motion to suppress. The appellant pled guilty pursuant to a negotiated plea agreement, and her punishment was assessed at three days' incarceration in the county jail (with three days' credit for time already served) and a fine of $1,500. The trial court certified her right to appeal. On appeal, the appellant argued that the search warrant was invalid because the affidavit in support of the warrant was not sworn to in the physical presence of the magistrate, as she contends is required by Article 18.01 of the Code of Criminal Procedure. The Tenth Court of Appeals disagreed, holding that "a face-to-face meeting between the trooper and the judge was not required and the making of the oath over the telephone did not invalidate the search warrant." At least one other court of appeals has reached the opposite result on comparable facts, albeit in an unpublished opinion. We granted the appellant's petition for discretionary review to resolve this issue.

THE ISSUE

By statute, an evidentiary search warrant may issue in Texas for the extraction of blood for forensic testing. The issuance of such a search warrant is governed by, inter alia, Article 18.01(b) of the Code of Criminal Procedure, which provides:

> (b) No search warrant shall issue for any purpose in this state unless sufficient facts are first presented to satisfy the issuing magistrate that probable cause does in fact exist for its issuance. A sworn affidavit setting forth substantial facts establishing probable cause shall be filed in every instance in which a search warrant is requested. Except as provided by [another Article not pertinent here], the affidavit is public information if executed, and the magistrate's clerk shall make a copy of the affidavit available for public inspection in the clerk's office during normal business hours.

Whether an investigating officer may apply for a search warrant by swearing out a supporting affidavit over the telephone is not specifically addressed in Article 18.01(b), or in any other provision of the Code of Criminal Procedure. We are therefore confronted with a case of first impression—just as we were half a dozen years ago in *Smith v. State*.

In *Smith*, the officer seeking a search warrant swore out his probable cause affidavit in the physical presence of the magistrate, but, although he was under oath when he did so, he neglected to actually sign the affidavit. The question before us was whether either the Fourth Amendment to the United States Constitution or Article 18.01(b) requires that an affidavit in support of a search warrant include the signature of the affiant. With respect to Article 18.01(b), we observed that the purpose of the signature on an affidavit is to memorialize the fact that the affiant took an oath. While an oath is both constitutionally and statutorily indispensable, we held, a signature memorializing that the affiant swore out the affidavit is not, and the affidavit may still suffice to support the issuance of a search warrant if the record indicates that "the affidavit was solemnized by other means." We expressly held "that the failure to sign the warrant affidavit does not invalidate the warrant if other evidence proves that the affiant personally swore to the truth of the facts in the affidavit before the issuing magistrate." We went on to observe,

> Although the affiant's signature on an affidavit serves as an important memorialization of the officer's act of swearing before the magistrate, it is that act of swearing, not the signature itself, that is essential. It is important, too, that the law retain some flexibility in the face of technological advances. For example, the federal courts and some state courts, now permit telephonic search warrants, and one can foresee the day in which search warrants might be obtained via e-mail or a recorded video conference with a magistrate located many miles away. In a state as large as Texas, such innovations should not be foreclosed by the requirement of a signed affidavit if the officer's oath can be memorialized by other, equally satisfactory, means. We leave those potential future changes to the Texas Legislature, but we should not stand in the way of the future by declaring that all affidavits, which are properly sworn to but unsigned, are necessarily invalid.[14]

Not surprisingly, both the appellant and the State find sufficient latitude in this passage from *Smith* to suggest support for their respective positions in this case.

For its part, the State relies upon *Smith's* emphasis on the need to construe the statute with sufficient "flexibility" to account for "technological advances" and points to our express allusion to those jurisdictions that have legislated specific procedures governing telephonic application for search warrants. The appellant counters that such innovations are properly left to the legislative branch, not the judicial— that, while it would be a proper exercise of our judicial function for us to hold that telephonic search warrants do not offend the Fourth Amendment (or, for that matter, Article I, Section 9 of the Texas Constitution), we would have no occasion to do so unless and until the Texas Legislature should authorize them, as have most of the other jurisdictions to which we alluded in Smith.

---

[14] We note that in 2011, since our opinion in Smith, the federal authority to issue telephonic warrants was re-codified in Rule 41, allowing a magistrate judge to "consider information communicated by telephone or other reliable electronic means when . . . deciding whether to issue a warrant[.]" Fed. R. Crim. P. 41(a).

We agree with the appellant that whether telephonic search warrants are permissible in Texas depends upon the parameters of the statute as it currently reads. Our job is to faithfully construe statutory language, never to enlarge upon it. We cannot, simply for the sake of keeping pace with the technology, stretch the meaning of the statute beyond the bounds of what its language will tolerate. Article 18.01(b) requires a "sworn affidavit." In *Smith*, we held that a "sworn affidavit" need not contain the affiant's signature before it may support a search warrant, so long as there is other evidence to show "that the affiant personally swore to the truth of the facts in the affidavit before the issuing magistrate." And indeed, this Court has held for the better part of a hundred years that, before a written statement in support of a search warrant will constitute a "sworn affidavit," the necessary oath must be administered "before" a magistrate or other qualified officer. In the name of flexibility, can it reasonably be said that an oath administered over the telephone satisfies the requirement that, to be a "sworn affidavit" for purposes of Article 18.01(b), a writing must be sworn to "personally . . . before the issuing magistrate" or other qualified oath-giver? As presently written, does Article 18.01(b) allow for the granting of a search warrant based upon an affidavit that is sworn to over the telephone, inasmuch as the one thing we held in Smith to be "essential," namely the oath, is not administered in the corporal presence of the magistrate or other official authorized to administer it?

ANALYSIS

The statutory requirement of a "sworn affidavit" serves two important functions: to solemnize and to memorialize. That the affidavit must be sworn to fulfills the constitutional requirement that it be executed under oath or affirmation so as "to impress upon the swearing individual an appropriate sense of obligation to tell the truth." That it must be in writing serves the additional objective that the sum total of the information actually provided to the issuing magistrate in support of his probable cause determination be memorialized in some enduring way to facilitate later judicial review. Article 18.01(b)'s requirement that the memorialization take the form of a written affidavit was satisfied in this case by the fact that Ortega drafted a written affidavit and faxed it to Judge Harris, so that the issuing magistrate had a document to be "filed" as required. On the particular facts of this case, then, the only remaining question is whether Ortega's written affidavit was properly "sworn" to, in contemplation of Article 18.01(b), when Judge Harris administered the oath to Ortega over the telephone rather than face to face.

There is apparently no Fourth Amendment impediment to administering the oath or affirmation telephonically. The Federal Rules of Criminal Procedure have authorized telephonic applications for a search warrant since 1977, and the federal courts long ago rejected the specific argument "that for constitutional purposes an oath or affirmation is invalid merely because it is taken over the telephone[,]" elaborating that "[t]he moral, religious and legal significance of the undertaking remains the same whether the oath taker and the witness communicate face-to-face or over the telephone." Following the federal lead, many states now provide for telephonic search warrant applications by statute or rule, and many of those provisions expressly permit the obligatory oath to be administered over the telephone. At least one state's highest appellate court has refused to suppress evidence based upon a warrant application that was made, and the oath administered, orally over the telephone—even in the face of a statute that requires a written affidavit. Another state's highest court has held, in light of express statutory language requiring an affidavit to be "sworn to before" the issuing magistrate, that the telephonic application for a search warrant was invalid, but the court nevertheless refused to suppress the fruit of the search because the police officers acted in good faith. Yet another highest state court has recently held, however, in construing a statute that explicitly requires an "affidavit sworn to before the magistrate," that an oath administered over the telephone "complies with the literal terms of the statute such that there was no defect in the warrant." Our statute neither facially provides for, nor explicitly prohibits, administration of the oath telephonically.

We do not think that it impermissibly enlarges upon the statutory language to construe Article 18.01(b) to permit the administration of the oath over the telephone—at least under the circumstances of the present case. Article 18.01(b) simply requires a "sworn affidavit." While our case law has historically defined an affidavit to be a writing sworn to "before" the oath-administering authority, most of those cases pre-date the advent of our most modern electronic means of communication, and none expressly addresses the question whether an oath administered over the telephone qualifies as an oath "before" the magistrate. As the State points out, the last edition of Black's Law Dictionary to have included a definition of the word "before" provides: "In the presence of; under the official purview of; as in a magistrate's jurat, 'before me personally appeared,' etc." This definition suggests that there may exist circumstances under which a search warrant affiant could validly present himself "before" an issuing magistrate—that is to say, "under the official purview of" that issuing magistrate—without the necessity of presenting himself corporally.

The numerous states that now provide for telephonic application for search warrants certainly assume as much. Several of the state regulatory schemes emphasize the importance of the magistrate's ability to verify the identity of the telephonic warrant applicant and/or his affiants for purposes of administering the oath. The obvious intent behind such a requirement is to maximize the solemnizing efficacy of the telephonic oath to compensate for the absence of face-to-face administration. An officer who adequately identifies himself to an issuing magistrate over the telephone and who then deliberately swears out a false affidavit would almost certainly subject himself to prosecution for perjury. In any event, he would surely perceive the gravity of the enterprise and "an appropriate sense of obligation to tell the truth."

That is the posture of the present case. As the court of appeals observed,

> In this instance, the personal familiarity of the trooper and the judge with each other's voice provides very strong indicia of truthfulness, trustworthiness, and reliability so as to call upon Trooper Ortega's "sense of moral duty to tell the truth and instill in him a sense of seriousness and responsibility."

We agree. We see no compelling reason to construe the "sworn affidavit" contemplated by Article 18.01(b) necessarily to require that the oath always be administered in the corporal presence of the magistrate, so long as sufficient care is taken in the individual case to preserve the same or an equivalent solemnizing function to that which corporal presence accomplishes. Only the Legislature is free to amend or supplement Article 18.01(b) to specifically and comprehensively regulate the process of obtaining search warrants by telephonic or other electronic means, as so many other states have now done. Until that time, the question of whether the circumstances of an individual telephonic warrant application will suffice to satisfy the solemnizing function of the oath requirement under Article 18.01(b) will have to be resolved on a case-by-case basis.

CONCLUSION

Because Ortega and Judge Harris recognized one another's voices on the telephone at the time Ortega swore out his warrant affidavit, it was properly solemnized. And because Ortega reduced the affidavit to writing and faxed it to Judge Harris for filing, the basis for probable cause was properly memorialized. Under these circumstances, we hold that Article 18.01(b)'s requirement of a "sworn affidavit" was satisfied. Accordingly, we affirm the judgment of the court of appeals.

MEYERS, J., filed a dissenting opinion.

[Omitted.]

D. OTHER CHALLENGES TO THE FACIAL VALIDITY OF A WARRANT

We consider next how else, other than the constitutional requirements discussed earlier, a defendant might challenge the facial validity of a warrant. A so-called *Franks* challenge, which derives its name from our next case, enables a defendant to challenge false statements and material omissions included in the affidavit supporting the warrant.

FRANKS V. DELAWARE

438 U.S. 154
Supreme Court of the United States
February 27, 1978, Argued; June 26, 1978, Decided
No. 77–5176

MR. JUSTICE BLACKMUN delivered the opinion of the Court. * * *

I

The controversy over the veracity of the search warrant affidavit in this case arose in connection with petitioner Jerome Franks' state conviction for rape, kidnaping, and burglary. On Friday, March 5, 1976, Mrs. Cynthia Bailey told police in Dover, Del., that she had been confronted in her home earlier that morning by a man with a knife, and that he had sexually assaulted her. She described her assailant's age, race, height, build, and facial hair, and gave a detailed description of his clothing as consisting of a white thermal undershirt, black pants with a silver or gold buckle, a brown leather three-quarter-length coat, and a dark knit cap that he wore pulled down around his eyes.

That same day, petitioner Franks coincidentally was taken into custody for an assault involving a 15-year-old girl, Brenda B. _____, six days earlier. After his formal arrest, and while awaiting a bail hearing in Family Court, petitioner allegedly stated to Robert McClements, the youth officer accompanying him, that he was surprised the bail hearing was "about Brenda B. _____. I know her. I thought you said Bailey. I don't know her." At the time of this statement, the police allegedly had not yet recited to petitioner his rights under *Miranda v. Arizona.*

On the following Monday, March 8, Officer McClements happened to mention the courthouse incident to a detective, Ronald R. Brooks, who was working on the Bailey case. On March 9, Detective Brooks and Detective Larry D. Gray submitted a sworn affidavit to a Justice of the Peace in Dover, in support of a warrant to search petitioner's apartment.

In paragraph 8 of the affidavit's "probable cause page" mention was made of petitioner's statement to McClements. In paragraph 10, it was noted that the description of the assailant given to the police by Mrs. Bailey included the above-mentioned clothing. Finally, the affidavit also described the attempt made by police to confirm that petitioner's typical outfit matched that of the assailant. Paragraph 15 recited: "On Tuesday, 3/9/76, your affiant contacted Mr. James Williams and Mr. Wesley Lucas of the Delaware Youth Center where Jerome Franks is employed and did have personal conversation with both these people." Paragraphs 16 and 17 respectively stated: "Mr. James Williams revealed to your affiant that the normal dress of Jerome Franks does consist of a white knit thermal undershirt and a brown leather jacket," and "Mr. Wesley Lucas revealed to your affiant that in addition to the thermal undershirt and jacket, Jerome Franks often wears a dark green knit hat."

The warrant was issued on the basis of this affidavit. Pursuant to the warrant, police searched petitioner's apartment and found a white thermal undershirt, a knit hat, dark pants, and a leather jacket, and, on petitioner's kitchen table, a single-blade knife. All these ultimately were introduced in evidence at trial.

Prior to the trial, however, petitioner's counsel filed a written motion to suppress the clothing and the knife found in the search; this motion alleged that the warrant on its face did not show probable cause and that the search and seizure were in violation of the Fourth and Fourteenth Amendments. At the hearing on the motion to suppress, defense counsel orally amended the challenge to include an attack on the veracity of the warrant affidavit; he also specifically requested the right to call as witnesses Detective Brooks, Wesley Lucas of the Youth Center, and James D. Morrison, formerly of the Youth Center. Counsel asserted that Lucas and Morrison would testify that neither had been personally interviewed by the warrant affiants, and that, although they might have talked to another police officer, any information given by them to that officer was "somewhat different" from what was recited in the affidavit. Defense counsel charged that the misstatements were included in the affidavit not inadvertently, but in "bad faith." Counsel also sought permission to call Officer McClements and petitioner as witnesses, to seek to establish that petitioner's courthouse statement to police had been obtained in violation of petitioner's *Miranda* rights, and that the search warrant was thereby tainted as the fruit of an illegally obtained confession.

* * * The motion to suppress was denied, and the clothing and knife were admitted as evidence at the ensuing trial. Petitioner was convicted. In a written motion for judgment of acquittal and/or new trial, petitioner repeated his objection to the admission of the evidence, stating that he "should have been allowed to impeach the Affidavit used in the Search Warrant to show purposeful misrepresentation of information contained therein." The motion was denied, and petitioner was sentenced to two consecutive terms of 25 years each and an additional consecutive life sentence.

On appeal, the Supreme Court of Delaware affirmed. * * * Franks' petition for certiorari presented only the issue whether the trial court had erred in refusing to consider his allegation of misrepresentation in the warrant affidavit. * * * [W]e granted certiorari. * * *

III

Whether the Fourth and Fourteenth Amendments, and the derivative exclusionary rule made applicable to the States under *Mapp v. Ohio*, 367 U.S. 643 (1961), ever mandate that a defendant be permitted to attack the veracity of a warrant affidavit after the warrant has been issued and executed, is a question that encounters conflicting values. * * * [That's why] the rule announced today has a limited scope, both in regard to when exclusion of the seized evidence is mandated, and when a hearing on allegations of misstatements must be accorded. But neither do the considerations cited by respondent and others have a fully controlling weight; we conclude that they are insufficient to justify an absolute ban on post-search impeachment of veracity. On this side of the balance, also, there are pressing considerations:

First, a flat ban on impeachment of veracity could denude the probable-cause requirement of all real meaning. The requirement that a warrant not issue "but upon probable cause, supported by Oath or affirmation," would be reduced to a nullity if a police officer was able to use deliberately falsified allegations to demonstrate probable cause, and, having misled the magistrate, then was able to remain confident that the ploy was worthwhile. It is this specter of intentional falsification that, we think, has evoked such widespread opposition to the flat nonimpeachment rule from the commentators, from the American Law Institute in its Model Code of Pre-Arraignment Procedure, from the federal courts of appeals, and from state courts. On occasion, of course, an instance of deliberate falsity will be exposed and confirmed without a special inquiry either at trial, or at a hearing on the sufficiency of the affidavit. A flat nonimpeachment rule would bar re-examination of the warrant even in these cases.

Second, the hearing before the magistrate not always will suffice to discourage lawless or reckless misconduct. The pre-search proceeding is necessarily *ex parte*, since the subject of the search cannot be tipped off to the application for a warrant lest he destroy or remove evidence. The usual reliance of our legal system on adversary proceedings itself should be an indication that an *ex parte* inquiry is likely to be less vigorous. The magistrate has no acquaintance with the information that may contradict the good faith and reasonable basis of the affiant's allegations. The pre-search proceeding will frequently be marked by haste, because of the understandable desire to act before the evidence disappears; this urgency will not always permit the magistrate to make an extended independent examination of the affiant or other witnesses.

Third, the alternative sanctions of a perjury prosecution, administrative discipline, contempt, or a civil suit are not likely to fill the gap. *Mapp v. Ohio*, implicitly rejected the adequacy of these alternatives. * * *

Fourth, allowing an evidentiary hearing, after a suitable preliminary proffer of material falsity, would not diminish the importance and solemnity of the warrant-issuing process. It is the *ex parte* nature of the initial hearing, rather than the magistrate's capacity, that is the reason for the review. A magistrate's determination is presently subject to review before trial as to sufficiency without any undue interference with the dignity of the magistrate's function. Our reluctance today to extend the rule of exclusion beyond instances of deliberate misstatements, and those of reckless disregard, leaves a broad field where the magistrate is the sole protection of a citizen's Fourth Amendment rights, namely, in instances where police have been merely negligent in checking or recording the facts relevant to a probable-cause determination.

Fifth, the claim that a post-search hearing will confuse the issue of the defendant's guilt with the issue of the State's possible misbehavior is footless. The hearing will not be in the presence of the jury. An issue extraneous to guilt already is examined in any probable-cause determination or review of probable cause. Nor, if a sensible threshold showing is required and sensible substantive requirements for suppression are maintained, need there be any new large-scale commitment of judicial resources; many claims will wash out at an early stage, and the more substantial ones in any event would require judicial resources for vindication if the suggested alternative sanctions were truly to be effective. The requirement of a substantial preliminary showing would suffice to prevent the misuse of a veracity hearing for purposes of discovery or obstruction. And because we are faced today with only the question of the integrity of the affiant's representations as to his own activities, we need not decide, and we in no way predetermine, the difficult question whether a reviewing court must ever require the revelation of the identity of an informant once a substantial preliminary showing of falsity has been made. *McCray v. Illinois*, 386 U.S. 300 (1967), the Court's earlier disquisition in this area, concluded only that the Due Process Clause of the Fourteenth Amendment did not require the State to expose an informant's identity routinely, upon a defendant's mere demand, when there was ample evidence in the probable-cause hearing to show that the informant was reliable and his information credible.

Sixth and finally, as to the argument that the exclusionary rule should not be extended to a "new" area, we cannot regard any such extension really to be at issue here. Despite the deep skepticism of Members of this Court as to the wisdom of extending the exclusionary rule to collateral areas, such as civil or grand jury proceedings, the Court has not questioned, in the absence of a more efficacious sanction, the continued application of the rule to suppress evidence from the State's case where a Fourth Amendment violation has been substantial and deliberate. We see no principled basis for distinguishing between the question of the sufficiency of an affidavit, which also is subject to a post-search re-examination, and the question of its integrity.

IV

* * * There is, of course, a presumption of validity with respect to the affidavit supporting the search warrant. To mandate an evidentiary hearing, the challenger's attack must be more than conclusory and must be supported by more than a mere desire to cross-examine. There must be allegations of deliberate falsehood or of reckless disregard for the truth, and those allegations must be accompanied by an offer of proof. They should point out specifically the portion of the warrant affidavit that is claimed to be false; and they should be accompanied by a statement of supporting reasons. Affidavits or sworn or otherwise reliable statements of witnesses should be furnished, or their absence satisfactorily explained. Allegations of negligence or innocent mistake are insufficient. The deliberate falsity or reckless disregard whose impeachment is permitted today is only that of the affiant, not of any nongovernmental informant. Finally, if these requirements are met, and if, when material that is the subject of the alleged falsity or reckless disregard is set to one side, there remains sufficient content in the warrant affidavit to support a finding of probable cause, no hearing is required. On the other hand, if the remaining content is insufficient, the defendant is entitled, under the Fourth and Fourteenth Amendments, to his hearing. Whether he will prevail at that hearing is, of course, another issue.

Because of Delaware's absolute rule, its courts did not have occasion to consider the proffer put forward by petitioner Franks. Since the framing of suitable rules to govern proffers is a matter properly left to the States, we decline ourselves to pass on petitioner's proffer. The judgment of the Supreme Court of Delaware is reversed, and the case is remanded for further proceedings not inconsistent with this opinion.

APPENDIX A TO OPINION OF THE COURT

[Omitted.]

APPENDIX B TO OPINION OF THE COURT

[Omitted.]

MR. JUSTICE REHNQUIST, with whom THE CHIEF JUSTICE joins, dissenting.

[Omitted.]

QUESTIONS, COMMENTS, CONCERNS?

1.   **Ulbricht (redux).** Go back to the casefile of Chapter 3 and reconsider pages 36–37 of Ross Ulbricht's motion to suppress. [*See* Ulbricht Casefile Document 1.] How might *Franks* have helped Ulbricht's argument that the government failed to disclose critical information concerning how federal agents learned about the Silk Road server? How does the government respond in its opposition? [*See* Ulbricht Casefile Document 2, at 16–17.]

2. ***Franks* in action.** In *United States v. Ippolito*, 774 F.2d 1482 (9th Cir. 1985), the FBI applied for a wiretap warrant against Ippolito. The application stated that none of the criminal informants that would be helpful to the case were willing to testify, thus requiring the need for a wiretap warrant. It was later discovered that one informant, Hanophy, was actually willing to testify and continue investigating undercover, but was told to say he was unwilling by FBI Agents so that his refusal could be used to demonstrate the necessity of a wiretap.

The Ninth Circuit applied *Franks* and held that the government made intentionally false or misleading statements in the application for the warrant. Absent the false statements, the court reasoned, the Government would not have been able to demonstrate the necessity for a wiretap and, as such, would not have received the warrant. Thus, the Ninth Circuit upheld the district court's decision to suppress evidence obtained pursuant to the wiretap warrant.

UNITED STATES V. JACOBS

986 F.2d 1231
United States Court of Appeals for the Eighth Circuit
October 16, 1992, Submitted; March 1, 1993, Filed
No. 92-2170SI

RICHARD S. ARNOLD, CHIEF JUDGE.

The defendant appeals from his conviction * * * for possession with intent to distribute cocaine. The basis for this conviction was laid when Iowa City Police Officer Michael Brotherton received a tip from a Phoenix, Arizona, police officer that a Federal Express package addressed to the defendant appeared to be suspicious. After obtaining a search warrant, a team of officers from the Johnson County Multi-jurisdictional Task Force (an Iowa drug-interdiction unit) opened the package at the Federal Express office in Iowa City. After finding that the package contained drugs, the officers resealed the package and delivered it to the defendant at his residence. Shortly thereafter, the officers executed a second search warrant at the residence and took the defendant into custody.

The defendant was charged with possession with intent to distribute cocaine, as well as several firearms offenses. At a pre-trial suppression hearing, and again during trial, the defendant attempted to exclude the evidence found in the Federal Express package and in his residence on the ground that it was the fruit of an illegal search. The District Court overruled the defendant's objection, and a jury found him guilty of the drug offense.

On appeal, the defendant raises several arguments challenging the search of the Federal Express package. Initially, he asserts that a canine sniff conducted at the Federal Express office violated his Fourth Amendment rights because the police did not have a reasonable, articulable suspicion that the package contained drugs. In addition, the defendant, relying upon *Franks v. Delaware*, 438 U.S. 154 (1978), claims that Officer Brotherton included a deliberate falsehood and deliberately omitted relevant information in his warrant application. Finally, the defendant argues that his Fourth Amendment rights were violated when the police failed to inform the magistrate judge that a second canine sniff had yielded negative results.

I.

The focus of this appeal arises out of events occurring on November 20 and 21, 1991. On the evening of November 20, 1991, Officer Brotherton and another police officer received a tip from Officer Billingsley in Phoenix, Arizona. He told the officers that a package being shipped to the defendant via Federal Express was suspicious. Specifically, Billingsley told Brotherton that the well-wrapped, three-pound package was delivered to the Federal Express office just before the company shipped its packages, by a person (other than the sender) who did not know the local zip code. In addition, the cost of mailing was paid in cash. On the basis of this information, as well as Brotherton's allegation that the defendant was involved in the distribution of drugs, the Iowa City police decided to examine the package, and if it was indeed suspicious, to obtain a search warrant and open it.

On the morning of November 21, 1991, the Task Force split into two groups. Officer Brotherton took a warrant application and went to a magistrate judge's office. The remainder of the group proceeded to the Iowa City Federal Express office to intercept the package and conduct a canine sniff. Officer Brotherton maintained contact with this group via a cellular telephone.

At the Federal Express office, six to eight packages, including the package addressed to the defendant, were isolated in a room. The police then brought in a drug dog, "Turbo," to conduct a canine sniff. "Turbo" examined all of the packages and showed an interest in the defendant's package by pushing it around with his nose and scratching it twice. This action did not amount to an official "alert," however, so the dog's handler was not sure that the package contained drugs. Officer Henderson, a Task Force member at the Federal Express office, called Brotherton in the magistrate judge's chambers to relay this information. He told Brotherton that "the dog had showed an interest in the package, but had not given a full alert to the package." Brotherton then typed on the warrant application that "the Johnson County Drug Dog, 'Turbo' was presented with 8 different packages including the package being sent to Ron Jacobs. The Canine exhibited an interest in only that particular package addressed to Ron Jacobs."

After Henderson's call, the police requested that a second dog examine the package. This dog failed to alert or show an interest in the defendant's package. In a second phone call to Brotherton, Officer Henderson learned that the warrant had already been issued. Henderson informed Brotherton that a second dog had arrived, and that the team was going to wait for this dog to conduct a sniff before executing the warrant. Neither the magistrate judge or, apparently, Officer Brotherton was informed of the results of the second sniff.

After receiving the search warrant, the Task Force, despite the results of the second sniff, decided to open the package. Upon opening the package, the police discovered cocaine. They then rewrapped the package and delivered it to the defendant's residence. Approximately fifteen minutes after this delivery, the police executed a second search warrant at the defendant's residence. There, the police found the Federal Express package, additional quantities of drugs, several guns, drug paraphernalia, and a large sum of money.

The defendant's primary argument on appeal is that the police violated the Supreme Court's holding in *Franks v. Delaware, supra,* by their actions in obtaining the search warrant. The defendant's attack under *Franks* is two-fold: (1) that by including and emphasizing the word "interest" in the warrant application, the police told a deliberate falsehood; and (2) that by failing to include Henderson's statement that "Turbo" had not alerted to the package, Brotherton deliberately omitted vital information necessary to the magistrate judge's determination of probable cause. In addition, the defendant also asserts that the officers' failure to notify Brotherton and the magistrate judge of the results of the second canine sniff rendered the search warrant affidavit misleading in violation of *Franks.*

II.

[Ed. note: the court preliminarily reviewed *Franks v. Delaware.*] * * *As support for his argument that the police included a deliberate falsehood in the warrant application, the defendant points to Brotherton's statement that "the Canine exhibited an interest in only that particular package addressed to Ron Jacobs." The defendant argues that by underlining "interest," Brotherton was attempting to mislead the magistrate judge by emphasizing the word in such a fashion as to equate it with the term of art "alert." As the testimony at trial indicated, "Turbo" did not "alert" to the package, as it was trained to do if drugs were present. As a result, the dog's handler could not say with certainty that drugs were present. The defendant argues that Brotherton was attempting to brush over this fact by emphasizing the word "interest" in a manner designed to influence the magistrate judge's thinking. We disagree.

While the defendant's interpretation of these actions is plausible, we find it equally likely that by underlining the word "interest," Officer

Brotherton was indicating, at least to some readers, that an alert did not occur. He could have been attempting to show the magistrate judge that, while the dog was attracted to the package, it did not give the response it was trained to give in the presence of drugs. In any event, we will not engage in speculation about the officer's intention in underlining the word "interest." Suffice it to say that this issue could be resolved equally well in favor of the police as in favor of the defendant.

III.

The defendant's argument that the police violated *Franks* by omitting key information from the warrant application is more forceful. First, he argues that by omitting "Turbo's" failure to alert, Officer Brotherton was deliberately misleading the magistrate judge. Secondly, the defendant argues that the failure to notify Brotherton and the magistrate judge that the second canine sniff was negative further violated *Franks* by depriving the magistrate judge of key information necessary to a determination of probable cause.

Officer Brotherton correctly informed the magistrate judge that the dog had shown an interest in the Jacobs package, but neglected to include Henderson's statement that no alert had occurred. In order for this omission to be a violation of *Franks* * * *, the defendant must make two showings. The first is a showing that the police omitted the information with the intent to make, or in reckless disregard of whether they made, the affidavit misleading. In the present case, "Turbo's" failure to alert was omitted from the affidavit. Because of the highly relevant nature of the omitted information, we hold the omission occurred at least with reckless disregard of its effect upon the affidavit. Brotherton knew that the dog had failed to alert to the box before he submitted the affidavit to the magistrate judge, yet he did not include this information. Any reasonable person would have known that this was the kind of thing the judge would wish to know.

* * * [T]he failure to include the information and a reckless disregard for its consequences may be inferred from the fact that the information was omitted. However, in order for this inference to be valid, the defendant must show that the omitted material would be " 'clearly critical' to the finding of probable cause." The omission of the fact that the dog failed to alert to the package satisfies this criterion.

Having shown that relevant information was recklessly omitted from the warrant application, Jacobs must further show that the affidavit, if supplemented with the omitted information, would not be sufficient to support a finding of probable cause. "Only if the affidavit as supplemented by the omitted material could not have supported the existence of probable cause" will suppression be warranted.

In this case, if the warrant application were reworked to include the omitted phrase, it would read something like this: "The dog had showed an interest in the [defendant's] package, but had not given a full alert to the package." We hold that such an application, on its face, would not support probable cause. The evidence in support of probable cause would be limited to the information that Officer Brotherton received from Officer Billingsley in Phoenix, plus the fact that the dog had shown an interest in the package, but had not alerted to it. Without an alert, the police clearly lacked the probable cause necessary to open the package. While the information received from Officer Billingsley, plus the fact that the dog showed an interest in the package, might have provided reasonable suspicion that it contained contraband, more is needed to overcome the defendant's Fourth Amendment right to privacy in its contents. In this case, the failure to inform the magistrate judge that the dog had not given its trained response when confronted with a package containing drugs, coupled with the dog handler's admission that he could not say with certainty that drugs were in the package, causes us to hold that the warrant would not have been supported by probable cause, if the omitted material had been included.

IV.

* * * [T]he government argues that the actions of the police should be excused under the objective-reasonableness exception of *United States v. Leon*, 468 U.S. 897 (1984). This argument fails for two reasons. First, under *Leon*, a *Franks* violation is not excused. Second, even if the violation of *Franks* could be protected under *Leon*, we could not find that the officers acted reasonably when they executed this warrant. At the time the warrant was executed, not only did the officers know that "Turbo" had failed to alert to the package, they were also aware that a second dog called in to verify this conclusion had not even shown the amount of interest that "Turbo" exhibited. Nevertheless, the officers executed the warrant, ignoring the obvious negative finding obtained during the second sniff. This is indefensible. Not only was the warrant deficient under *Franks*, this further information should have alerted the officers that they lacked probable cause to examine the package. Furthermore, we think the officers had a duty to provide the magistrate judge with any information which would undercut the warrant's validity. The officers could not simply rest on a warrant they had already received when this information came to light. We feel confident that if the magistrate judge had been aware of the full scope of the investigation, the application for a warrant would not have been granted. The facts surrounding the second sniff, if not sufficient to invalidate the warrant (already invalidated, anyway, without reference to the second sniff), are clearly sufficient to negative any "good faith" defense, in the *Leon* sense.

The judgment of the District Court is reversed, and the cause remanded for further proceedings consistent with this opinion.

III. ARREST WARRANTS

A. MEET ROBERT DURST[6]

In February 2015, HBO launched its hit docuseries *The Jinx: The Life and Deaths of Robert Durst*. *The Jinx* producers promised to solve the mystery of the December 2000 execution-style murder of Robert Durst's longtime friend Susan Berman in Benedict Canyon, California. What no one could have anticipated, however, was that just before the airing of the final episode of *The Jinx*, Durst was arrested for Berman's murder.

Given that it occurred in the week leading up to the final episode of *The Jinx*, the timing of Durst's arrest was odd. Although the fifth episode of *The Jinx*, which aired the Sunday before Durst's arrest, drew only 446,000 viewers, documentary producers during that episode revealed their intention to confront Durst with what they considered to be damning evidence linking him to Berman's murder. The episode left viewers to anxiously wonder how Durst would react. Meanwhile, California investigators were, as Durst's defense attorneys later said, "crafting a dramatic moment of their own." Durst was arrested on March 14, 2015, pursuant to an arrest warrant authored—perhaps hastily—by the Los Angeles Police Department. After Durst's arrest, more than 800,000 viewers tuned in to watch the dramatic conclusion to "*The Jinx*," during which Durst appeared to confess to murdering Berman on camera in a moment when he failed to realize that his microphone was still on.

Robert Durst

Robert Durst was born on April 12, 1943, into one of New York City's oldest family-run commercial and residential real estate companies. As heir to the Durst Organization, which as of 2014 owned and managed more than 8.5 million square feet of real estate in Midtown Manhattan, Durst owns a nearly $43 million share of the family's trust. Despite his extreme wealth, however, Durst styled himself as a member of the hippie counterculture in the late 1960s. While enrolled in graduate school at UCLA in 1965, Durst became a follower of Beatles guru Maharishi Mahesh Yogi. After meeting his future wife, Kathleen McCormack (whose later disappearance would spark rumors of foul play), Durst abandoned the hippie UCLA lifestyle, moved back to New York, and became a real estate developer in his father's business.

Susan Berman & the Disappearance of Kathleen McCormack

Susan Berman was born on May 18, 1945. As the daughter of Davie "Davie the Jew" Berman, a prominent Las Vegas mob figure, Berman became known as a "Mafia Princess," and authored several memoirs

---

[6] Remember that you have access to the filings relevant to this chapter in your online repository.

detailing her life as a mobster's daughter. Berman received a bachelor's degree in 1967 from UCLA, during which time she met and became good friends with Robert Durst. The two would remain close despite Durst moving back to New York in 1969.

In February 1982, Durst walked into a Manhattan police station to file a missing person report on his wife, Kathleen McCormack Durst. Durst maintained that he put McCormack on a train to New York City from Upstate New York where he and his wife owned a home. McCormack was returning to the couple's penthouse in the city, where she was staying while studying to become a pediatrician at the Albert Einstein College of Medicine. Durst claimed that he knew she arrived safely, but asserted that he never heard from her again. When the tabloids swarmed Durst's home in upstate New York, Berman stood alongside Durst as his de facto publicist, even signing a sworn statement attesting to Durst's version of events. To this date, McCormack's body has never been recovered.

The Murder of Susan Berman

On December 24, 2000, Berman, was found murdered execution style in her home in Benedict Canyon, California. There was no apparent motive behind her murder, but investigators were quick to identify Durst as a person of interest because he recently gave Berman more than $25,000 and authorities learned that Durst was in Northern California days before her death. Although Durst confirmed to LAPD that he sent Berman $25,000, he declined to be further questioned. Curiously, investigators also received a handwritten note postmarked after Berman's body was discovered, advising police that they would find a "cadaver" at Berman's address.

The Jinx: The Final Drama

In the fifth episode of "The Jinx," broadcast on March 8, 2015, the show's producers revealed that they recently discovered a letter written by Durst to Berman authored more than a year before her death. The producers theorized that the address written on the note's envelope, when compared against the address written in the "cadaver" note, could be used to link Durst to Berman's murder. In particular, both the "cadaver" note and Durst's letter to Berman were written in seemingly identical handwriting and both misspelled Beverly Hills as "Beverley Hills." The fifth episode ended in what Durst's defense attorney referred to as "a made-for-TV cliffhanger" with Durst's note being placed in a safe deposit box "as [producers] schemed to confront Durst with it and a copy of the 'cadaver' note."

On March 11, 2015, shortly after the broadcast of episode five, and just four days before the dramatic finale was to air, LAPD obtained a warrant to arrest Durst for the murder of Berman. In the arrest warrant and supporting affidavit, LAPD detective Luis Romero detailed how the Cold Case Homicide Unit recently conducted a forensic analysis on the "cadaver" note, which revealed that Durst authored the note. Although the affidavit acknowledged the existence of the HBO series, it made no mention of the envelope and confrontation teased by "The Jinx" producers:

> Your affiant is aware of recent national media attention regarding Robert Durst as a possible suspect in the murder of Susan Berman. The media attention has coincided with an HBO series which has detailed Robert Durst's life and the speculation that he is a suspect in the disappearance of his wife and the murder of Susan Berman.

On March 14th, the day before the "The Jinx" dramatic finale, Durst was arrested in a New Orleans hotel lobby.

B. THE NEED FOR AN ARREST WARRANT

In our next pair of cases, we consider when officers need a warrant to make an arrest. As you will come to quickly see, arrest warrants are unnecessary in a large majority of cases. As Professor Yale Kamisar has noted, "the percentage of arrests made pursuant to an arrest warrant is astonishingly small. For example, five years after *Mapp*, of 171,288 arrests made by the New York City police, 'only 366 were made pursuant to an arrest warrant.' "[7]

UNITED STATES V. WATSON

423 U.S. 411
Supreme Court of the United States
October 8, 1975, Argued; January 26, 1976, Decided
No. 74-538

MR. JUSTICE WHITE delivered the opinion of the Court.

This case presents questions under the Fourth Amendment as to the legality of a warrantless arrest and of an ensuing search of the arrestee's automobile carried out with his purported consent.

I

The relevant events began on August 17, 1972, when an informant, one Khoury, telephoned a postal inspector informing him that respondent Watson was in possession of a stolen credit card and had asked Khoury to cooperate in using the card to their mutual advantage. On five to 10 previous occasions Khoury had provided the inspector with reliable information on postal inspection matters, some involving Watson. Later that day Khoury delivered the card to the inspector. On learning that Watson had agreed to furnish additional cards, the inspector asked Khoury to arrange to meet with Watson. Khoury did so, a meeting being scheduled

---

[7] Yale Kamisar, *The Writings of John Barker Waite and Thomas Davies on the Search and Seizure Exclusionary Rule*, 100 MICH. L. REV. 1821, 1847 n.113 (2002).

for August 22. Watson canceled that engagement, but at noon on August 23, Khoury met with Watson at a restaurant designated by the latter. Khoury had been instructed that if Watson had additional stolen credit cards, Khoury was to give a designated signal. The signal was given, the officers closed in, and Watson was forthwith arrested. He was removed from the restaurant to the street where he was given the warnings required by *Miranda v. Arizona*, 384 U.S. 436 (1966). A search having revealed that Watson had no credit cards on his person, the inspector asked if he could look inside Watson's car, which was standing within view. Watson said, "Go ahead," and repeated these words when the inspector cautioned that "[i]f I find anything, it is going to go against you." Using keys furnished by Watson, the inspector entered the car and found under the floor mat an envelope containing two credit cards in the names of other persons. These cards were the basis for two counts of a four-count indictment charging Watson with possessing stolen mail * * *.

Prior to trial, Watson moved to suppress the cards, claiming that his arrest was illegal for want of probable cause and an arrest warrant and that his consent to search the car was involuntary and ineffective because he had not been told that he could withhold consent. The motion was denied, and Watson was convicted of illegally possessing the two cards seized from his car.

A divided panel of the Court of Appeals for the Ninth Circuit reversed * * *. We granted certiorari.

II

* * * Contrary to the Court of Appeals' view, Watson's arrest was not invalid because executed without a warrant. * * *

"The usual rule is that a police officer may arrest without warrant one believed by the officer upon reasonable cause to have been guilty of a felony. . . ." * * *

The cases construing the Fourth Amendment * * * reflect the ancient common-law rule that a peace officer was permitted to arrest without a warrant for a misdemeanor or felony committed in his presence as well as for a felony not committed in his presence if there was reasonable ground for making the arrest. This has also been the prevailing rule under state constitutions and statutes. * * *

The balance struck by the common law in generally authorizing felony arrests on probable cause, but without a warrant, has survived substantially intact. It appears in almost all of the States in the form of express statutory authorization. * * *

* * * Law enforcement officers may find it wise to seek arrest warrants where practicable to do so, and their judgments about probable cause may be more readily accepted where backed by a warrant issued by a

magistrate. But we decline to transform this judicial preference into a constitutional rule when the judgment of the Nation * * * has for so long been to authorize warrantless public arrests on probable cause rather than to encumber criminal prosecutions with endless litigation with respect to the existence of exigent circumstances, whether it was practicable to get a warrant, whether the suspect was about to flee, and the like.

Watson's arrest did not violate the Fourth Amendment, and the Court of Appeals erred in holding to the contrary. * * *

So ordered.

MR. JUSTICE STEVENS took no part in the consideration or decision of this case.

MR. JUSTICE POWELL, concurring.

[Omitted.]

MR. JUSTICE STEWART, concurring in the result.

[Omitted.]

MR. JUSTICE MARSHALL, with whom MR. JUSTICE BRENNAN joins, dissenting.

[Omitted.]

QUESTIONS, COMMENTS, CONCERNS?

1.   **Durst in context.** The Durst casefile is complicated to say the least. His case essentially operates as a comprehensive review of the material you have covered to this point alongside a preview of what's coming. Although you may focus on a variety of other topics in class, the Durst block of discussion questions will focus largely on the presence of the two warrants—both arrest and search—alongside the varied challenges Durst makes specifically to those warrants. We revisit Durst in Chapter 6 to consider how the "inventory exception" to the Fourth Amendment's warrant requirement applies to his case.

2.   **Durst and quality of lawyering.** Compare the motion to suppress filed on behalf of Durst [Durst Casefile Document 3] and the motion filed on behalf of Albert Jones in Chapter 3 [Jones Casefile Document 2]. Did Jones and Durst receive the same type of zealous advocacy?

PAYTON V. NEW YORK

445 U.S. 573
Supreme Court of the United States
March 26, 1979, Argued; October 9, 1979, Reargued; April 15, 1980, Decided[8]
No. 78-5420

MR. JUSTICE STEVENS delivered the opinion of the Court.

These appeals challenge the constitutionality of New York statutes that authorize police officers to enter a private residence without a warrant and with force, if necessary, to make a routine felony arrest. * * *

I

On January 14, 1970, after two days of intensive investigation, New York detectives had assembled evidence sufficient to establish probable cause to believe that Theodore Payton had murdered the manager of a gas station two days earlier. At about 7:30 a. m. on January 15, six officers went to Payton's apartment in the Bronx, intending to arrest him. They had not obtained a warrant. Although light and music emanated from the apartment, there was no response to their knock on the metal door. They summoned emergency assistance and, about 30 minutes later, used crowbars to break open the door and enter the apartment. No one was there. In plain view, however, was a .30-caliber shell casing that was seized and later admitted into evidence at Payton's murder trial.

In due course Payton surrendered to the police, was indicted for murder, and moved to suppress the evidence taken from his apartment. The trial judge held that the warrantless and forcible entry was authorized by the New York Code of Criminal Procedure, and that the evidence in plain view was properly seized. He found that exigent circumstances justified the officers' failure to announce their purpose before entering the apartment as required by the statute. He had no occasion, however, to decide whether those circumstances also would have justified the failure to obtain a warrant, because he concluded that the warrantless entry was adequately supported by the statute without regard to the circumstances. The Appellate Division, First Department, summarily affirmed.

On March 14, 1974, Obie Riddick was arrested for the commission of two armed robberies that had occurred in 1971. He had been identified by the victims in June 1973, and in January 1974 the police had learned his address. They did not obtain a warrant for his arrest. At about noon on March 14, a detective, accompanied by three other officers, knocked on the door of the Queens house where Riddick was living. When his young son opened the door, they could see Riddick sitting in bed covered by a sheet. They entered the house and placed him under arrest. Before permitting him to dress, they opened a chest of drawers two feet from the bed in search

---

[8]   Together with No. 78-5421, *Riddick v. New York*, also on appeal from the same court.

of weapons and found narcotics and related paraphernalia. Riddick was subsequently indicted on narcotics charges. At a suppression hearing, the trial judge held that the warrantless entry into his home was authorized by the revised New York statute, and that the search of the immediate area was reasonable * * *. The Appellate Division, Second Department, affirmed the denial of the suppression motion.

The New York Court of Appeals, in a single opinion, affirmed the convictions of both Payton and Riddick. * * *

II

It is familiar history that indiscriminate searches and seizures conducted under the authority of "general warrants" were the immediate evils that motivated the framing and adoption of the Fourth Amendment. Indeed, as originally proposed in the House of Representatives, the draft contained only one clause, which directly imposed limitations on the issuance of warrants, but imposed no express restrictions on warrantless searches or seizures. As it was ultimately adopted, however, the Amendment contained two separate clauses, the first protecting the basic right to be free from unreasonable searches and seizures and the second requiring that warrants be particular and supported by probable cause. * * *

It is thus perfectly clear that the evil the Amendment was designed to prevent was broader than the abuse of a general warrant. Unreasonable searches or seizures conducted without any warrant at all are condemned by the plain language of the first clause of the Amendment. * * *

The simple language of the Amendment applies equally to seizures of persons and to seizures of property. Our analysis in this case may therefore properly commence with rules that have been well established in Fourth Amendment litigation involving tangible items. * * * And we have long adhered to the view that the warrant procedure minimizes the danger of needless intrusions of that sort.

It is a "basic principle of Fourth Amendment law" that searches and seizures inside a home without a warrant are presumptively unreasonable. Yet it is also well settled that objects such as weapons or contraband found in a public place may be seized by the police without a warrant. The seizure of property in plain view involves no invasion of privacy and is presumptively reasonable, assuming that there is probable cause to associate the property with criminal activity.

* * * [But a]bsent exigent circumstances, a warrantless entry to search for weapons or contraband is unconstitutional even when a felony has been committed and there is probable cause to believe that incriminating evidence will be found within. * * * [T]he constitutional protection afforded to the individual's interest in the privacy of his own home is equally

applicable to a warrantless entry for the purpose of arresting a resident of the house; for it is inherent in such an entry that a search for the suspect may be required before he can be apprehended. * * * [A]n entry to arrest and an entry to search for and to seize property implicate the same interest in preserving the privacy and the sanctity of the home, and justify the same level of constitutional protection. * * *

The majority of the New York Court of Appeals, however, suggested that there is a substantial difference in the relative intrusiveness of an entry to search for property and an entry to search for a person. * * *

But the critical point is that any differences in the intrusiveness of entries to search and entries to arrest are merely ones of degree rather than kind. The two intrusions share this fundamental characteristic: the breach of the entrance to an individual's home. The Fourth Amendment protects the individual's privacy in a variety of settings. In none is the zone of privacy more clearly defined than when bounded by the unambiguous physical dimensions of an individual's home—a zone that finds its roots in clear and specific constitutional terms: "The right of the people to be secure in their . . . houses . . . shall not be violated." That language unequivocally establishes the proposition that "[at] the very core [of the Fourth Amendment] stands the right of a man to retreat into his own home and there be free from unreasonable governmental intrusion." In terms that apply equally to seizures of property and to seizures of persons, the Fourth Amendment has drawn a firm line at the entrance to the house. Absent exigent circumstances, that threshold may not reasonably be crossed without a warrant. * * *

IV

The parties have argued at some length about the practical consequences of a warrant requirement as a precondition to a felony arrest in the home. In the absence of any evidence that effective law enforcement has suffered in those States that already have such a requirement, we are inclined to view such arguments with skepticism. More fundamentally, however, such arguments of policy must give way to a constitutional command that we consider to be unequivocal.

Finally, we note the State's suggestion that only a search warrant based on probable cause to believe the suspect is at home at a given time can adequately protect the privacy interests at stake, and since such a warrant requirement is manifestly impractical, there need be no warrant of any kind. We find this ingenious argument unpersuasive. It is true that an arrest warrant requirement may afford less protection than a search warrant requirement, but it will suffice to interpose the magistrate's determination of probable cause between the zealous officer and the citizen. If there is sufficient evidence of a citizen's participation in a felony to persuade a judicial officer that his arrest is justified, it is constitutionally reasonable to require him to open his doors to the officers of the law. Thus, for Fourth Amendment purposes, an arrest warrant founded on probable cause implicitly carries with it the limited authority to enter a dwelling in which the suspect lives when there is reason to believe the suspect is within.

Because no arrest warrant was obtained in either of these cases, the judgments must be reversed and the cases remanded to the New York Court of Appeals for further proceedings not inconsistent with this opinion.

It is so ordered.

MR. JUSTICE BLACKMUN, concurring.

[Omitted.]

MR. JUSTICE WHITE, with whom THE CHIEF JUSTICE and MR. JUSTICE REHNQUIST join, dissenting.

* * * Today's decision rests, in large measure, on the premise that warrantless arrest entries constitute a particularly severe invasion of personal privacy. I do not dispute that the home is generally a very private area or that the common law displayed a special "reverence . . . for the individual's right of privacy in his house." However, the Fourth Amendment is concerned with protecting people, not places, and no talismanic significance is given to the fact that an arrest occurs in the home rather than elsewhere. It is necessary in each case to assess realistically the actual extent of invasion of constitutionally protected privacy. * * * The inquiry in the present case, therefore, is whether the incremental intrusiveness that results from an arrest's being made in the dwelling is enough to support an inflexible constitutional rule requiring warrants for such arrests whenever exigent circumstances are not present.

Today's decision ignores the carefully crafted restrictions on the common-law power of arrest entry and thereby overestimates the dangers inherent in that practice. At common law, absent exigent circumstances, entries to arrest could be made only for felony. Even in cases of felony, the officers were required to announce their presence, demand admission, and be refused entry before they were entitled to break doors. Further, it seems generally accepted that entries could be made only during daylight hours. And, in my view, the officer entering to arrest must have reasonable grounds to believe, not only that the arrestee has committed a crime, but also that the person suspected is present in the house at the time of the entry.

These four restrictions on home arrests—felony, knock and announce, daytime, and stringent probable cause—constitute powerful and complementary protections for the privacy interests associated with the home. The felony requirement guards against abusive or arbitrary enforcement and ensures that invasions of the home occur only in case of the most serious crimes. The knock-and-announce and daytime requirements protect individuals against the fear, humiliation, and embarrassment of being roused from their beds in states of partial or complete undress. And these requirements allow the arrestee to surrender at his front door, thereby maintaining his dignity and preventing the officers from entering other rooms of the dwelling. The stringent probable-cause requirement would help ensure against the possibility that the police would enter when the suspect was not home, and, in searching for him, frighten members of the family or ransack parts of the house, seizing items in plain view. In short, these requirements, taken together, permit an individual suspected of a serious crime to surrender at the front door of his dwelling and thereby avoid most of the humiliation and indignity that the Court seems to believe necessarily accompany a house arrest entry. Such a front-door arrest, in my view, is no more intrusive on personal privacy than the public warrantless arrests which we found to pass constitutional muster in *Watson*.

All of these limitations on warrantless arrest entries are satisfied on the facts of the present cases. The arrests here were for serious felonies—murder and armed robbery—and both occurred during daylight hours. The authorizing statutes required that the police announce their business and demand entry; neither Payton nor Riddick makes any contention that these statutory requirements were not fulfilled. And it is not argued that the police had no probable cause to believe that both Payton and Riddick were in their dwellings at the time of the entries. Today's decision, therefore, sweeps away any possibility that warrantless home entries might be permitted in some limited situations other than those in which exigent circumstances are present. The Court substitutes, in one sweeping decision, a rigid constitutional rule in place of the common-law approach, evolved over hundreds of years, which achieved a flexible accommodation between the demands of personal privacy and the legitimate needs of law enforcement.

A rule permitting warrantless arrest entries would not pose a danger that officers would use their entry power as a pretext to justify an otherwise invalid warrantless search. A search pursuant to a warrantless arrest entry will rarely, if ever, be as complete as one under authority of a search warrant. If the suspect surrenders at the door, the officers may not enter other rooms. Of course, the suspect may flee or hide, or may not be at home, but the officers cannot anticipate the first two of these possibilities and the last is unlikely given the requirement of probable cause to believe that the suspect is at home. Even when officers are justified in searching other rooms, they may seize only items within the arrestee's possession or immediate control or items in plain view discovered during the course of a search reasonably directed at discovering a hiding suspect. Hence a warrantless home entry is likely to uncover far less evidence than a search conducted under authority of a search warrant. Furthermore, an arrest entry will inevitably tip off the suspects and likely result in destruction or removal of evidence not uncovered during the arrest. I therefore cannot believe that the police would take the risk of losing valuable evidence through a pretextual arrest entry rather than applying to a magistrate for a search warrant.

* * * Accordingly, I respectfully dissent.

MR. JUSTICE REHNQUIST, dissenting.

[Omitted.]

QUESTIONS, COMMENTS, CONCERNS?

1.   **Organizing federal and state cooperation.** Let's pause to collect and orient ourselves in the Durst casefile. Recall that the FBI in *New Orleans* had an arrest warrant for Durst authored by the Robbery-Homicide Division, Task Force, in *Los Angeles*. That type of federal-state collaboration in a high-profile case like Durst's is common. Title 18 U.S.C. § 3052 contemplates that type of partnership by authorizing FBI special agents and officials of the FBI to make arrests, carry firearms, and serve warrants.

2.   *Watson* **as opposed to** *Payton.* The parties agree that Durst was arrested in the lobby of the J.W. Marriott Hotel in New Orleans. Is a hotel lobby a private or public area for arrest warrant purposes? Could the FBI have arrested Durst *without* a warrant?

3.   **Durst and** *Franks.* Durst raises a *Franks* challenge to the Los Angeles arrest warrant. [Casefile Document 3, at 9.] Chief among his supporting arguments is that the affiant, Detective Romero, omitted two key pieces of information: (1) a different handwriting analyst concluded that another suspect, Nyle Brenner, authored the "cadaver" note; and (2) Durst did not previously testify that he was in Los Angeles at the time of Susan Berman's death. Take a moment to review what Durst must prove as part of his *Franks* challenge. If he succeeds at this stage, does Durst earn suppression of the evidence obtained pursuant to the warrant or, rather, does he receive an evidentiary hearing on the warrant's deficiencies?

4.   **The government responds to Durst's** *Franks* **challenge.** Consider how the government responds to Durst's *Franks* challenge. [See Casefile Document 4.] The government notes in part, that, "by March 2015 [when the arrest warrant for Durst was drafted], investigators viewed Brenner as a dead-end lead; any early suspicion about him had long evaporated and was, therefore, immaterial for probable cause to arrest Durst." [Casefile Document 4, at 46.] Do you accept the government's argument that it had no obligation to include information about Nyle Brenner because, in the government's view, he was no longer a suspect in Berman's death?

If you do accept the government's argument, are you worried about the argument's implications? That is, if accepted, the argument could perhaps enable the government to eliminate information from warrant affidavits about alternative suspects. Then, if confronted about it later, the government could simply say it eliminated that individual as a suspect. Is that a concern?

5. The district court weighs in. The U.S. District Court for the Eastern District of Louisiana denied Durst's motion to suppress. [Casefile Document 6.] On the subject of the *Franks* issue, the court relied on the "excise" portion of the *Franks* decision. What exactly is that? And more generally, what is your opinion of the court's analysis of the *Franks* issue? [Casefile Document 6, at 12.] Finally, notice an oddity: a *Louisiana* federal court made a determination about what was (and was not) material to the probable cause determination made by a *California* state court.

C. EXECUTING AN ARREST WARRANT

STEAGALD V. UNITED STATES

451 U.S. 204
Supreme Court of the United States
January 14, 1981, Argued; April 21, 1981, Decided
No. 79-6777

JUSTICE MARSHALL delivered the opinion of the Court.

The issue in this case is whether, under the Fourth Amendment, a law enforcement officer may legally search for the subject of an arrest warrant in the home of a third party without first obtaining a search warrant. Concluding that a search warrant must be obtained absent exigent circumstances or consent, we reverse the judgment of the United States Court of Appeals for the Fifth Circuit affirming petitioner's conviction.

I

In early January 1978, an agent of the Drug Enforcement Administration (DEA) was contacted in Detroit, Mich., by a confidential informant who suggested that he might be able to locate Ricky Lyons, a federal fugitive wanted on drug charges. On January 14, 1978, the informant called the agent again, and gave him a telephone number in the Atlanta, Ga., area where, according to the informant, Ricky Lyons could be reached during the next 24 hours. On January 16, 1978, the agent called fellow DEA Agent Kelly Goodowens in Atlanta and relayed the information he had obtained from the informant. Goodowens contacted Southern Bell Telephone Co., and secured the address corresponding to the telephone number obtained by the informant. Goodowens also discovered that Lyons was the subject of a 6-month-old arrest warrant.

Two days later, Goodowens and 11 other officers drove to the address supplied by the telephone company to search for Lyons. The officers observed two men standing outside the house to be searched. These men were Hoyt Gaultney and petitioner Gary Steagald. The officers approached with guns drawn, frisked both men, and, after demanding identification, determined that neither man was Lyons. Several agents proceeded to the house. Gaultney's wife answered the door and informed the agents that she was alone in the house. She was told to place her hands against the wall and was guarded in that position while one agent searched the house. Ricky Lyons was not found, but during the search of the house the agent observed what he believed to be cocaine. Upon being informed of this discovery, Agent Goodowens sent an officer to obtain a search warrant and in the meantime conducted a second search of the house, which uncovered additional incriminating evidence. During a third search conducted pursuant to a search warrant, the agents uncovered 43 pounds of cocaine. Petitioner was arrested and indicted on federal drug charges.

Prior to trial, petitioner moved to suppress all evidence uncovered during the various searches on the ground that it was illegally obtained because the agents had failed to secure a search warrant before entering the house. Agent Goodowens testified at the suppression hearing that there had been no "physical hinderance" preventing him from obtaining a search warrant and that he did not do so because he believed that the arrest warrant for Ricky Lyons was sufficient to justify the entry and search. The District Court agreed with this view and denied the suppression motion. Petitioner was convicted and renewed his challenge to the search in his appeal. A divided Court of Appeals for the Fifth Circuit affirmed the District Court's denial of petitioner's suppression motion. Because the issue presented by this case is an important one that has divided the Circuits, we granted certiorari. * * *

III

The question before us is a narrow one. The search at issue here took place in the absence of consent or exigent circumstances. Except in such special situations, we have consistently held that the entry into a home to conduct a search or make an arrest is unreasonable under the Fourth Amendment unless done pursuant to a warrant. * * * Here, of course, the agents had a warrant—one authorizing the arrest of Ricky Lyons. However, the Fourth Amendment claim here is not being raised by Ricky Lyons. Instead, the challenge to the search is asserted by a person not named in the warrant who was convicted on the basis of evidence uncovered during a search of his residence for Ricky Lyons. Thus, the narrow issue before us is whether an arrest warrant—as opposed to a search warrant—is adequate to protect the Fourth Amendment interests of persons not named in the warrant, when their homes are searched without their consent and in the absence of exigent circumstances.

The purpose of a warrant is to allow a neutral judicial officer to assess whether the police have probable cause to make an arrest or conduct a search. * * * However, while an arrest warrant and a search warrant both serve to subject the probable-cause determination of the police to judicial review, the interests protected by the two warrants differ. An arrest warrant is issued by a magistrate upon a showing that probable cause exists to believe that the subject of the warrant has committed an offense and thus the warrant primarily serves to protect an individual from an unreasonable seizure. A search warrant, in contrast, is issued upon a showing of probable cause to believe that the legitimate object of a search is located in a particular place, and therefore safeguards an individual's interest in the privacy of his home and possessions against the unjustified intrusion of the police.

Thus, whether the arrest warrant issued in this case adequately safeguarded the interests protected by the Fourth Amendment depends upon what the warrant authorized the agents to do. To be sure, the warrant embodied a judicial finding that there was probable cause to believe that Ricky Lyons had committed a felony, and the warrant therefore authorized the officers to seize Lyons. However, the agents sought to do more than use the warrant to arrest Lyons in a public place or in his home; instead, they relied on the warrant as legal authority to enter the home of a third person based on their belief that Ricky Lyons might be a guest there. Regardless of how reasonable this belief might have been, it was never subjected to the detached scrutiny of a judicial officer. Thus, while the warrant in this case may have protected Lyons from an unreasonable seizure, it did absolutely nothing to protect petitioner's privacy interest in being free from an unreasonable invasion and search of his home. Instead, petitioner's only protection from an illegal entry and search was the agent's personal determination of probable cause. In the absence of exigent circumstances, we have consistently held that such judicially untested determinations are not reliable enough to justify an entry into a person's home to arrest him without a warrant, or a search of a home for objects in the absence of a search warrant. We see no reason to depart from this settled course when the search of a home is for a person rather than an object.[7]

A contrary conclusion—that the police, acting alone and in the absence of exigent circumstances, may decide when there is sufficient justification for searching the home of a third party for the subject of an arrest warrant—would create a significant potential for abuse. Armed solely with an arrest warrant for a single person, the police could search all the homes

---

[7]   * * * Because an arrest warrant authorizes the police to deprive a person of his liberty, it necessarily also authorizes a limited invasion of that person's privacy interest when it is necessary to arrest him in his home. This analysis, however, is plainly inapplicable when the police seek to use an arrest warrant as legal authority to enter the home of a third party to conduct a search. Such a warrant embodies no judicial determination whatsoever regarding the person whose home is to be searched. Because it does not authorize the police to deprive the third person of his liberty, it cannot embody any derivative authority to deprive this person of his interest in the privacy of his home. Such a deprivation must instead be based on an independent showing that a legitimate object of a search is located in the third party's home. We have consistently held, however, that such a determination is the province of the magistrate, and not that of the police officer.

of that individual's friends and acquaintances. Moreover, an arrest warrant may serve as the pretext for entering a home in which the police have a suspicion, but not probable cause to believe, that illegal activity is taking place. The Government recognizes the potential for such abuses but contends that existing remedies—such as motions to suppress illegally procured evidence and damages actions for Fourth Amendment violations—provide adequate means of redress. We do not agree. * * * [I]f suppression motions and damages actions were sufficient to implement the Fourth Amendment's prohibition against unreasonable searches and seizures, there would be no need for the constitutional requirement that in the absence of exigent circumstances a warrant must be obtained for a home arrest or a search of a home for objects. We have instead concluded that in such cases the participation of a detached magistrate in the probable-cause determination is an essential element of a reasonable search or seizure, and we believe that the same conclusion should apply here.

In sum, two distinct interests were implicated by the search at issue here—Ricky Lyons' interest in being free from an unreasonable seizure and petitioner's interest in being free from an unreasonable search of his home. Because the arrest warrant for Lyons addressed only the former interest, the search of petitioner's home was no more reasonable from petitioner's perspective than it would have been if conducted in the absence of any warrant. Since warrantless searches of a home are impermissible absent consent or exigent circumstances, we conclude that the instant search violated the Fourth Amendment.

IV   * * *

A

The Government contends that at common law an officer could forcibly enter the home of a third party to execute an arrest warrant. * * *

The Fourth Amendment was intended partly to protect against the abuses of the general warrants that had occurred in England and of the writs of assistance used in the Colonies. The general warrant specified only an offense—typically seditious libel—and left to the discretion of the executing officials the decision as to which persons should be arrested and which places should be searched. Similarly, the writs of assistance used in the Colonies noted only the object of the search—any uncustomed goods—and thus left customs officials completely free to search any place where they believed such goods might be. The central objectionable feature of both warrants was that they provided no judicial check on the determination of the executing officials that the evidence available justified an intrusion into any particular home. An arrest warrant, to the extent that it is invoked as authority to enter the homes of third parties, suffers from the same infirmity. Like a writ of assistance, it specifies only the object of a search—

in this case, Ricky Lyons—and leaves to the unfettered discretion of the police the decision as to which particular homes should be searched. We do not believe that the Framers of the Fourth Amendment would have condoned such a result.

B

The Government also suggests that practical problems might arise if law enforcement officers are required to obtain a search warrant before entering the home of a third party to make an arrest. The basis of this concern is that persons, as opposed to objects, are inherently mobile, and thus officers seeking to effect an arrest may be forced to return to the magistrate several times as the subject of the arrest warrant moves from place to place. We are convinced, however, that a search warrant requirement will not significantly impede effective law enforcement efforts.

First, the situations in which a search warrant will be necessary are few. As noted in *Payton v. New York*, an arrest warrant alone will suffice to enter a suspect's own residence to effect his arrest. Furthermore, if probable cause exists, no warrant is required to apprehend a suspected felon in a public place. *United States v. Watson*, 423 U.S. 411 (1976). Thus, the subject of an arrest warrant can be readily seized before entering or after leaving the home of a third party.[14] Finally, the exigent-circumstances doctrine significantly limits the situations in which a search warrant would be needed. For example, a warrantless entry of a home would be justified if the police were in "hot pursuit" of a fugitive. Thus, to the extent that searches for persons pose special problems, we believe that the exigent-circumstances doctrine is adequate to accommodate legitimate law enforcement needs.

Moreover, in those situations in which a search warrant is necessary, the inconvenience incurred by the police is simply not that significant. First, if the police know of the location of the felon when they obtain an arrest warrant, the additional burden of obtaining a search warrant at the same time is miniscule. The inconvenience of obtaining such a warrant does not increase significantly when an outstanding arrest warrant already exists. In this case, for example, Agent Goodowens knew the address of the house to be searched two days in advance and planned the raid from the federal courthouse in Atlanta where, we are informed, three fulltime magistrates were on duty. In routine search cases such as this, the short time required to obtain a search warrant from a magistrate will seldom hinder efforts to apprehend a felon. Finally, if a magistrate is not nearby, a telephonic search warrant can usually be obtained.

---

[14] Indeed, the "inherent mobility" of persons noted by the Government suggests that in most situations the police may avoid altogether the need to obtain a search warrant simply by waiting for a suspect to leave the third person's home before attempting to arrest that suspect.

Whatever practical problems remain, however, cannot outweigh the constitutional interests at stake. Any warrant requirement impedes to some extent the vigor with which the Government can seek to enforce its laws, yet the Fourth Amendment recognizes that this restraint is necessary in some cases to protect against unreasonable searches and seizures. We conclude that this is such a case. The additional burden imposed on the police by a warrant requirement is minimal. In contrast, the right protected—that of presumptively innocent people to be secure in their homes from unjustified, forcible intrusions by the Government—is weighty. Thus, in order to render the instant search reasonable under the Fourth Amendment, a search warrant was required.

Accordingly, the judgment of the Court of Appeals is reversed, and the case is remanded to that court for further proceedings consistent with this opinion.

So ordered.

THE CHIEF JUSTICE concurs in the judgment.

JUSTICE REHNQUIST, with whom JUSTICE WHITE joins, dissenting.

* * * In determining the reasonableness of dispensing with the requirement of a separate search warrant in this case, I believe that the existence of a valid arrest warrant is highly relevant.

The government's interests in the warrantless entry of a third-party dwelling to execute an arrest warrant are compelling. The basic problem confronting police in such situations is the inherent mobility of the fugitive. By definition, the police have probable cause to believe that the fugitive is in a dwelling which is not his home. He may stay there for a week, a day, or 10 minutes. Fugitives from justice tend to be mobile, and police officers will generally have no way of knowing whether the subject of an arrest warrant will be at the dwelling when they return from seeking a search warrant. Imposition of a search warrant requirement in such circumstances will frustrate the compelling interests of the government and indeed the public in the apprehension of those subject to outstanding arrest warrants.

The Court's responses to these very real concerns are singularly unpersuasive. It first downplays them by stating that "the situations in which a search warrant will be necessary are few," because no search warrant is necessary to arrest a suspect at his home and, if the suspect is at another's home, the police need only wait until he leaves, since no search warrant is needed to arrest him in a public place. Ibid. These beguilingly simple answers to a serious law enforcement problem simply will not wash. Criminals who know or suspect they are subject to arrest warrants would not be likely to return to their homes, and while "[the] police could reduce the likelihood of escape by staking out all possible exits . . . the costs of such a stakeout seem excessive in an era of rising crime and scarce police resources." The Court's ivory tower misconception of the realities of the apprehension of fugitives from justice reaches its apogee when it states: "In routine search cases such as this, the short time required to obtain a search warrant from a magistrate will seldom hinder efforts to apprehend a felon." The cases we are considering are not "routine search cases." They are cases Of attempted arrest, pursuant to a warrant, when the object of the arrest may flee at any time—including the "short time" during which the police are endeavoring to obtain a search warrant.

At the same time the interference with the Fourth Amendment privacy interests of those whose homes are entered to apprehend the felon is not nearly as significant as suggested by the Court. The arrest warrant serves some of the functions a separate search warrant would. It assures the occupants that the police officer is present on official business. The arrest warrant also limits the scope of the search, specifying what the police may search for (i.e., the subject of the arrest warrant). No general search is permitted, but only a search of those areas in which the object of the search might hide. Indeed, there may be no intrusion on the occupant's privacy at all, since if present the suspect will have the opportunity to voluntarily surrender at the door. Even if the suspect does not surrender but secretes himself within the house, the occupant can limit the search by pointing him out to the police. It is important to remember that the contraband discovered during the entry and search for Lyons was in plain view and was discovered during a "sweep search" for Lyons, not a probing of drawers or cabinets for contraband.

Because the burden on law enforcement officers to obtain a separate search warrant before entering the dwelling of a third party to execute a concededly valid arrest warrant is great and carries with it a high possibility that the fugitive named in the arrest warrant will escape apprehension, I would conclude that the application of the traditional "reasonableness" standard of the Fourth Amendment does not require a separate search warrant in a case such as this. * * *

QUESTIONS, COMMENTS, CONCERNS?

1. **What's permissible after executing the arrest warrant?** Without learning more *yet*, what do you imagine officers may permissibly do after arresting a suspect? Remember that after arresting Durst, the FBI acquired his room key. [Casefile Document 2, at 3.] It also learned that Durst was staying twenty-three floors up in Room 2303. Agents escorted Durst back to his room and searched it—all on the basis of his arrest. Does that seem permissible or do you think the Fourth Amendment should protect Durst in other ways? After all, an arrest is a Fourth Amendment "seizure," and a hotel room search is, of course, a "search."

2.   *Payton* and search warrants. Notice that *Steagald* extends *Payton*'s reach. Although *Payton*'s holding is premised on arrest warrants, *Steagald* makes clear that *Payton* also applies to search warrants. Citing *Payton*, the *Steagald* Court commented, "Except in such special situations, we have consistently held that the entry into a home to conduct a search or make an arrest is unreasonable under the Fourth Amendment unless done pursuant to a warrant." Given *Payton*'s applicability to in-home *searches*, how does the FBI justify searching Durst's hotel room post-arrest despite not having a search warrant? [*See* Casefile Document 4.]

3.   *Steagald* or *Payton* in a hotel. Is a hotel room a citizen's "home" during the totality of their stay or, rather, are they "temporary visitors"? The answer to that matters because if Durst, for example, is merely a temporary visitor at the JW Marriott, then presumably the warrant for his arrest would be sufficient for the FBI to search his room, right? But if a hotel room is properly his "home," then *Payton* would apply and require officers to have an in-home search warrant.

4.   Revisiting *Rakas*. Recall our discussion of standing in Chapter 3. The government contends that Durst has no standing to challenge the search of his hotel room because he checked in under an alias. [Casefile Document 4.] In your opinion, does a change to a person's name alter their expectation of privacy?

5.   Precision and probable cause. Durst raises a number of arguments in his motion to suppress, including that the government's evidence in support of probable cause to search his hotel room was "stale." [Casefile Document 3, at 33.] In pertinent part, Durst maintains that "[t]here were no facts of recent vintage to support a conclusion that evidence of a December 2000 homicide in Los Angeles could be found in Durst's New Orleans hotel room in March 2015." [Casefile Document 3, at 34.] That's a relatively narrow view of the probable cause inquiry—that the government must possess probable cause to believe that evidence of Durst's involvement in a 2000 homicide would be present in his hotel room in March 2015. The government, by contrast, frames the inquiry more broadly, asserting that probable cause existed to believe that Durst had "incriminating evidence with him." [Casefile Document 4, at 29.] Which side makes the more persuasive argument?

Regardless of your answer, you should note that both sides are arguing what the probable cause goes *with*; that is, what standard the government should be held to in order to search Durst's hotel room. Too often lawyers, judges, officers, and, yes, students talk about probable cause in isolation by merely asking "whether probable cause existed." But that's not enough; the probable cause must go *with* specific government action triggering Fourth Amendment protection. More particularly, there must exist probable cause to search, as in the case of searching Durst's hotel room, or seize, as in the case of Durst's arrest.

Does the district court actually resolve Durst's staleness argument as it relates to the *search* (not arrest) warrant? [*See* Casefile Document 6.]

6. Revisiting the independent source rule and *Murray*. Boy, Durst's case looks an awful lot like our independent source case—*Murray v. United States*. You remember *Murray* from Chapter 2, right? In short, law enforcement agents warrantlessly forced their way into defendant's warehouse and saw marijuana. The agents left the marijuana undisturbed, but kept the warehouse under surveillance. Through their continued surveillance, the agents developed an independent factual basis for believing that the warehouse contained marijuana. Relying solely on those facts, the agents applied for and received a warrant to search the warehouse. The agents then executed the warrant and seized the marijuana.

Writing for a majority of the Supreme Court, Justice Scalia held that the marijuana was admissible because the warrant was based solely on the facts agents obtained through their lawful surveillance and not on the facts agents learned through their unlawful search.

Justice Marshall dissented. He noted, "When, as here, the same team of investigators is involved in both the first and second search, there is a significant danger that the 'independence' of the source will in fact be illusory, and that the initial search will have affected the decision to obtain a warrant notwithstanding the officers' subsequent assertions to the contrary." *Murray v. United States*, 487 U.S. 533, 548–49 (1988) (Marshall, J., dissenting).

Justice Marshall's concerns appear on full display in Durst's case. Notice that, in the federal case, Durst was charged with felon in possession of a firearm—not murder of Susan Berman. [Casefile Document 2, at 1.] The key evidence against Durst, then, is the revolver in his jacket pocket. The FBI learned about that revolver during the "inventory" search of Durst's hotel room when, according to the FBI agent, Durst volunteered that he had a revolver in his jacket hanging in the closet. But shortly thereafter, the LAPD asked the FBI to cease the inventory search, after which the LAPD obtained a search warrant for Durst's hotel room and "rediscovered" the revolver. [Casefile Document 2, at 5.]

Compare certain parts of Durst's motion to suppress with the government's response. *Compare* Casefile Document 3, at 36–43, *with* Casefile Document 4, at 19–22. In relevant part, Durst points to the significant overlap in the evidence obtained by the FBI before the search warrant, the evidence requested from the warrant application, and the evidence found during execution of the search warrant. [Casefile Document 3, at 40.] The government's arguably most persuasive response included the following argument: "It makes no sense to characterize the second search of the hotel room as a "confirmatory search" because the LAPD was interested in finding evidence about Durst's flight and Berman's murder, not evidence of the firearm upon which this prosecution is based." [Casefile Document 4, at 22.] Does the government's argument fall apart when we recall that federal and state authorities were working together to investigate Durst? The incentive for the LAPD to seek a warrant that specifically requests a firearm seemingly rises, right?

In denying Durst's motion to suppress, the district court applied the independent source exception. It noted that it credited the LAPD's assertion that law enforcement "was already planning on obtaining a search warrant for whatever location where Durst was located and whatever personal property he had with him when found." [Casefile Document 6, at 9.] But couldn't every law enforcement agency raise the same argument in every similar case to insulate itself from suppression and ensure application of the independent source rule?

IV. SEARCH WARRANTS

A. SEARCHING THE AVERY SALVAGE YARD[9]

As the investigation into Teresa Halbach's October 31, 2005, disappearance intensified, officers began to focus on Steven Avery; more specifically, they focused on the Avery property—a roughly forty-acre salvage yard that included multiple structures and roughly 4,000 vehicles.

An aerial view of the Avery salvage yard containing approximately
nineteen buildings and nearly 4,000 vehicles

On November 3, 2005, just days after Halbach's disappearance, Sergeant Andrew Colborn called dispatch to ask about a license plate number (SWH582) and stated the year and make of the car (1999 Toyota RAV4) during the conversation. Dispatch confirmed that the car belonged to Teresa Halbach. Strangely, however, Halbach's car had not actually been found yet.

The next day, Manitowoc County detective James Lenk received a request from one of the lead investigators, Mark Weigert, to go re-interview

---

[9]   Remember that you have access to the filings relevant to this chapter in your online repository.

Avery at his home (Sergeant Colborn previously questioned Steven Avery). At that time, Lenk obtained consent from Avery to search Avery's home— a trailer. Lenk and a Manitowoc County detective, Dave Remiker, searched Avery's trailer for approximately five minutes.

Then, on November 5, at roughly 9:00 a.m., Pamela Sturm (Halbach's second cousin) and her daughter, Nikole Sturm, met members of a search party at an old farmhouse that Halbach was renting. They were given a camera and sent out to look for Halbach.

At 9:50 am, Pamela and Nikole arrived at the Avery salvage yard. They received permission to search the property from Earl Avery, Steven's brother, and discovered Teresa's RAV four just forty minutes later. The above picture depicts the RAV4 as it appeared when discovered by Pamela and Nikole.

Investigators arrived at the Avery salvage yard at approximately 10:54 a.m. and decided by roughly 1:04 p.m. that afternoon to obtain a warrant to search the salvage yard. By 3:00 p.m., investigators had obtained a signed search warrant from Judge Jerome Fox. In reliance on that warrant, police conducted several searches of Avery's trailer and detached garage between November 5 and November 9.

The exterior of Avery's trailer

A view of Avery's garage and trailer

Before considering those searches, consider first Avery's trailer in more detail (although evidence was later uncovered in the garage, this section focuses on his trailer). As depicted by the below diagram, the single-floor trailer contained two bedrooms, a bathroom, living room, dining room, and kitchen. In total, the trailer was roughly 700 square feet.

Here is a breakdown of each entry including durations:

Date	Number of trailer entries & duration of search	Number of garage entries & duration of search
November 5	3 entries; 2:50 total	1 entry; 0:03 total
November 6	2 entries; 0:58 total	1 entry; 1:47 total
November 7	1 entry; 0:07 total	No garage search
November 8*	1 entry; 3:53 total	1 entry; 0:26
November 9	2 entries; 0:30 total	1 entry; 0:19

Based on the November 5 warrant, officers searched Avery's trailer eight times and searched his garage four times. The most important search, of course, occurred on November 8 when Lenk found a key to the RAV4 in Avery's trailer. Including the consent search, officers entered Avery's trailer eight times before discovering the key. The key would later be introduced against Avery at his trial for murdering Halbach. Avery was ultimately convicted of that murder and sentenced to life in prison without parole.

B. IS THERE A SEARCH WARRANT REQUIREMENT?

Recall our introductory conversation in Chapter 2 about whether the Fourth Amendment contains a warrant requirement. Remember that, assuming the presence of probable cause for law enforcement's actions, the Amendment provides no guidance on whether officers are required to obtain a warrant to search a person/property or seize that person/property. Whether a warrant is required depends on whether the Fourth Amendment categorically imposes a warrant requirement or, instead, the Amendment merely requires that warrantless searches be "reasonable."

As noted in Chapter 2, the Supreme Court's early Fourth Amendment caselaw clearly seemed to indicate that the Amendment includes a warrant requirement. *E.g., Katz v. United States*, 389 U.S. 347 (1967). Even post-*Katz*, the Court spoke in terms of a "warrant requirement." The Court referred to "exceptions" to that warrant requirement when approving warrantless searches and seizures. A few years after *Katz*, in *United States v. United States District Court for the Eastern District of Michigan*, the Court summarized this approach:

> It is true that there have been some exceptions to the warrant requirement. But those exceptions are few in number and carefully delineated; in general, they serve the legitimate needs of law enforcement officers to protect their own well-being and preserve evidence from destruction. Even while carving out those exceptions, the Court has reaffirmed the principle that the "police must, whenever practicable, obtain advance judicial approval of searches and seizures through the warrant procedure."

407 U.S. 297, 318 (1972).

Things, as you now know, shifted in *Terry*. Today, the modern Court no longer views the Fourth Amendment as requiring a warrant, but rather, merely requiring that law enforcement conduct be "reasonable." As Justice Thomas once jested:

> [T]he Court has vacillated between imposing a categorical warrant requirement and applying a general reasonableness standard. The Court has most frequently held that warrantless searches are presumptively unreasonable, but has also found a plethora of exceptions to presumptive unreasonableness. That is, our cases stand for the illuminating proposition that warrantless searches are per se unreasonable, except, of course, when they are not.

540 U.S. 551, 572–73 (2004) (Thomas, J., dissenting). Given the tension in the Court's jurisprudence, it is perhaps more accurate to say that the Fourth Amendment expresses a warrant *preference*. *E.g., United States v. Ventresca*, 380 U.S. 102, 105–06 (1965). Indeed, it seems uncontroversial to any member of the Court—at any time in its life—to say that, where convenient, an officer should obtain a warrant. Doing so, of course, provides the benefit of neutral and detached magistrate review.

In an effort to present the material as clearly as possible, the Casebook follows the view that the Fourth Amendment has a search warrant requirement. This view allows us to delineate more clearly the varying contexts where the Supreme Court has held that no search warrant is requirement.

C. EXECUTING & RETURNING A SEARCH WARRANT

We now turn to the basic components of executing and returning a search warrant. After obtaining a search warrant that meets the basic constitutional requirements outlined above, the question turns to execution. Officers may generally execute a search warrant any time of day within a set period of time (authorized by the warrant or by rule) and must ordinarily "knock and announce" their presence. *Wilson v. Arkansas*, 514 U.S. 927, 930 (1995). Should law enforcement seek to dispense either with the daytime and/or knock and announce components, the affiant must demonstrate beforehand to the magistrate that a reasonable suspicion exists to believe that following those general rules could endanger the safety of officers or others. *Richards v. Wisconsin*, 520 U.S. 385, 395–96 (1997).

Once inside a structure or vehicle, officers may seize only the items described with particularity in the search warrant and those that satisfy the plain view exception (which we cover in Chapter 6). To safely execute the warrant, the Supreme Court has authorized law enforcement to temporarily detain residents while the premises are searched, *Michigan v. Summers*, 452 U.S. 692, 704–05 (1981), and use "reasonable force" to maintain detention of those individuals, *Muehler v. Mena*, 544 U.S. 93, 98–99 (2005). That same authority, however, does not automatically also permit officers to *search* an individual who happens to be present at a premises where officers are executing a search warrant. *Ybarra v. Illinois*, 444 U.S. 85, 91 (1979).

A special situation arises when officers develop probable cause to believe that a suspect has placed contraband inside a home, but do not yet have a warrant to search the home. In that case, the Supreme Court authorizes officers to "freeze the scene"—i.e., refuse to permit the suspect(s) to reenter the premises until officers may diligently obtain a search warrant. *Illinois v. McArthur*, 531 U.S. 326, 337 (2001). No matter the scenario, if information becomes available to the officers during the search that requires them to narrow or abandon their search—despite what the warrant authorizes—then that information trumps the warrant's terms. *Maryland v. Garrison*, 480 U.S. 79, 88 (1987).

After executing a search warrant, officers must file a return of search with the issuing court within a reasonable time, but usually no later than ten days after executing the warrant. Oftentimes, officers will attach a property receipt to the return in order to provide a detailed description of the seized items.

Despite the Supreme Court's activity in this area, unanswered questions persist. For example, the Supreme Court has not addressed how long officers can spend inside the premises while executing a search warrant. Also unanswered is the question of how many entries law enforcement can make pursuant to one search warrant. Finally, there exists a question of whether any penalty—e.g., exclusion—attaches to an officer's failure to file a return of search. We take up some of those questions below.

UNITED STATES V. BANKS

540 U.S. 31
Supreme Court of the United States
October 15, 2003, Argued; December 2, 2003, Decided
No. 02-473

JUSTICE SOUTER delivered the opinion of the Court.

Officers executing a warrant to search for cocaine in respondent Banks's apartment knocked and announced their authority. The question is whether their 15-to-20-second wait before a forcible entry satisfied the Fourth Amendment * * *. We hold that it did.

I

With information that Banks was selling cocaine at home, North Las Vegas Police Department officers and Federal Bureau of Investigation agents got a warrant to search his two-bedroom apartment. As soon as they arrived there, about 2 o'clock on a Wednesday afternoon, officers posted in front called out "police search warrant" and rapped hard enough on the door to be heard by officers at the back door. There was no indication whether anyone was home, and after waiting for 15 to 20 seconds with no answer, the officers broke open the front door with a battering ram. Banks was in the shower and testified that he heard nothing until the crash of the door, which brought him out dripping to confront the police. The search produced weapons, crack cocaine, and other evidence of drug dealing.

In response to drug and firearms charges, Banks moved to suppress evidence, arguing that the officers executing the search warrant waited an unreasonably short time before forcing entry, and so violated both the Fourth Amendment * * *. The District Court denied the motion, and Banks pleaded guilty, reserving his right to challenge the search on appeal.

A divided panel of the Ninth Circuit reversed and ordered suppression of the evidence found. * * *

We granted certiorari to consider how to go about applying the standard of reasonableness to the length of time police with a warrant must wait before entering without permission after knocking and announcing their intent in a felony case. * * *

II

There has never been a dispute that these officers were obliged to knock and announce their intentions when executing the search warrant, an obligation they concededly honored. Despite this agreement, we start with a word about standards for requiring or dispensing with a knock and announcement, since the same criteria bear on when the officers could legitimately enter after knocking.

The Fourth Amendment says nothing specific about formalities in exercising a warrant's authorization, speaking to the manner of searching as well as to the legitimacy of searching at all simply in terms of the right to be "secure . . . against unreasonable searches and seizures." Although the notion of reasonable execution must therefore be fleshed out, we have done that case by case, largely avoiding categories and protocols for searches. Instead, we have treated reasonableness as a function of the facts of cases so various that no template is likely to produce sounder results than examining the totality of circumstances in a given case; it is too hard to invent categories without giving short shrift to details that turn out to be important in a given instance, and without inflating marginal ones. We have, however, pointed out factual considerations of unusual, albeit not dispositive, significance.

In *Wilson v. Arkansas*, 514 U.S. 927 (1995), we held that the common law knock-and-announce principle is one focus of the reasonableness enquiry; and we subsequently decided that although the standard generally requires the police to announce their intent to search before entering closed premises, the obligation gives way when officers "have a reasonable suspicion that knocking and announcing their presence, under the particular circumstances, would be dangerous or futile, or . . . would inhibit the effective investigation of the crime by, for example, allowing the destruction of evidence," *Richards v. Wisconsin*, 520 U.S. 385, 394 (1997). When a warrant applicant gives reasonable grounds to expect futility or to suspect that one or another such exigency already exists or will arise instantly upon knocking, a magistrate judge is acting within the Constitution to authorize a "no-knock" entry.[2] And even when executing a warrant silent about that, if circumstances support a reasonable suspicion of exigency when the officers arrive at the door, they may go straight in.

Since most people keep their doors locked, entering without knocking will normally do some damage, a circumstance too common to require a heightened justification when a reasonable suspicion of exigency already justifies an unwarned entry. We have accordingly held that police in exigent circumstances may damage premises so far as necessary for a no-knock entrance without demonstrating the suspected risk in any more

---

[2] Some States give magistrate judges the authority to issue "no-knock" warrants, and some do not.

detail than the law demands for an unannounced intrusion simply by lifting the latch. *United States v. Ramirez*, 523 U.S. 65, 70–71 (1998). Either way, it is enough that the officers had a reasonable suspicion of exigent circumstances.[3]

III

Like *Ramirez*, this case turns on the significance of exigency revealed by circumstances known to the officers, for the only substantive difference between the two situations goes to the time at which the officers reasonably anticipated some danger calling for action without delay.[4] Whereas the *Ramirez* Magistrate Judge found in advance that the customary warning would raise an immediate risk that a wanted felon would elude capture or pose a threat to the officers, here the Government claims that a risk of losing evidence arose shortly after knocking and announcing. Although the police concededly arrived at Banks's door without reasonable suspicion of facts justifying a no-knock entry, they argue that announcing their presence started the clock running toward the moment of apprehension that Banks would flush away the easily disposable cocaine, prompted by knowing the police would soon be coming in. While it was held reasonable for the police in *Ramirez* to enter forcibly upon arrival, the Government argues it was equally reasonable for the officers to go in with force here as soon as the danger of disposal had ripened.

Banks does not, of course, deny that exigency may develop in the period beginning when officers with a warrant knock to be admitted, and the issue comes down to whether it was reasonable to suspect imminent loss of evidence after the 15 to 20 seconds the officers waited prior to forcing their way. Though we agree * * * that this call is a close one, we think that after 15 or 20 seconds without a response, police could fairly suspect that cocaine would be gone if they were reticent any longer. Courts of Appeals have, indeed, routinely held similar wait times to be reasonable in drug cases with similar facts including easily disposable evidence (and some courts have found even shorter ones to be reasonable enough).[5]

---

[3] The standard for a no-knock entry stated in Richards applies on reasonable suspicion of exigency or futility. Because the facts here go to exigency, not futility, we speak of that alone.

[4] *Ramirez* and *Richards*, our cases addressing the role of exigency in assessing the reasonableness of a no-knock entry, involved searches by warrant for evidence of a felony, as does this case. In a different context governed by the Fourth Amendment, we have held that the risk of losing evidence of a minor offense is insufficient to make it reasonable to enter a dwelling to make a warrantless arrest. *See Welsh v. Wisconsin*, 466 U.S. 740 (1984). Courts of Appeals have applied *Welsh* to warrantless entries simply to search for evidence, considering the gravity of the offense in determining whether exigent circumstances exist. We intimate nothing here about such warrantless entry cases. Nor do we express a view on the significance of the existence of a warrant in evaluating whether exigency justifies action in knock-and-announce cases when the reason for the search is a minor offense.

[5] Several Courts of Appeals have explicitly taken into account the risk of disposal of drug evidence as a factor in evaluating the reasonableness of waiting time. *See, e.g., United States v. Goodson*, 165 F.3d 610, 612, 614 (8th Cir. 1999) (holding a 20-second wait after a loud announcement at a one-story ranch reasonable); *United States v. Spikes*, 158 F.3d 913, 925–927

A look at Banks's counterarguments shows why these courts reached sensible results, for each of his reasons for saying that 15 to 20 seconds was too brief rests on a mistake about the relevant enquiry: the fact that he was actually in the shower and did not hear the officers is not to the point, and the same is true of the claim that it might have taken him longer than 20 seconds if he had heard the knock and headed straight for the door. As for the shower, it is enough to say that the facts known to the police are what count in judging reasonable waiting time, and there is no indication that the police knew that Banks was in the shower and thus unaware of an impending search that he would otherwise have tried to frustrate.

And the argument that 15 to 20 seconds was too short for Banks to have come to the door ignores the very risk that justified prompt entry. True, if the officers were to justify their timing here by claiming that Banks's failure to admit them fairly suggested a refusal to let them in, Banks could at least argue that no such suspicion can arise until an occupant has had time to get to the door, a time that will vary with the size of the establishment, perhaps five seconds to open a motel room door, or several minutes to move through a townhouse. In this case, however, the police claim exigent need to enter, and the crucial fact in examining their actions is not time to reach the door but the particular exigency claimed. On the record here, what matters is the opportunity to get rid of cocaine, which a prudent dealer will keep near a commode or kitchen sink. The significant circumstances include the arrival of the police during the day, when anyone inside would probably have been up and around, and the sufficiency of 15 to 20 seconds for getting to the bathroom or the kitchen to start flushing cocaine down the drain. That is, when circumstances are exigent because a pusher may be near the point of putting his drugs beyond reach, it is imminent disposal, not travel time to the entrance, that governs when the police may reasonably enter; since the bathroom and kitchen are usually in the interior of a dwelling, not the front hall, there is no reason generally to peg the travel time to the location of the door, and no reliable basis for giving the proprietor of a mansion a longer wait than the resident of a bungalow, or an apartment like Banks's. And 15 to 20 seconds does not

---

(6th Cir. 1998) (holding a 15-to-30-second wait in midmorning after a loud announcement reasonable); *United States v. Spriggs*, 996 F.2d 320, 322–323 (D.C. Cir. 1993) (holding a 15-second wait after a reasonably audible announcement at 7:45 a.m. on a weekday reasonable); *United States v. Garcia*, 983 F.2d 1160, 1168 (1st Cir. 1993) (holding a 10-second wait after a loud announcement reasonable); *United States v. Jones*, 133 F.3d 358, 361–362 (5th Cir. 1998) (relying specifically on the concept of exigency, holding a 15-to-20-second wait reasonable). *See also United States v. Chavez-Miranda*, 306 F.3d 973, 981–982, n.7 (9th Cir. 2002) ("Banks appears to be a departure from our prior decisions. . . . [W]e have found a 10 to 20 second wait to be reasonable in similar circumstances, albeit when the police heard sounds after the knock and announcement"); *United States v. Jenkins*, 175 F.3d 1208, 1215 (10th Cir. 1999) (holding a 14-to-20-second wait at 10 a.m. reasonable); *United States v. Markling*, 7 F.3d 1309, 1318–1319 (7th Cir. 1993) (holding a 7-second wait at a small motel room reasonable when officers acted on a specific tip that the suspect was likely to dispose of the drugs).

seem an unrealistic guess about the time someone would need to get in a position to rid his quarters of cocaine.

Once the exigency had matured, of course, the officers were not bound to learn anything more or wait any longer before going in, even though their entry entailed some harm to the building. *Ramirez* held that the exigent need of law enforcement trumps a resident's interest in avoiding all property damage, and there is no reason to treat a post-knock exigency differently from the no-knock counterpart in *Ramirez* itself.

IV

Our emphasis on totality analysis necessarily rejects positions taken on each side of this case. *Ramirez*, for example, cannot be read with the breadth the Government espouses, as "reflect[ing] a general principle that the need to damage property in order to effectuate an entry to execute a search warrant should not be part of the analysis of whether the entry itself was reasonable." At common law, the knock-and-announce rule was traditionally "justified in part by the belief that announcement generally would avoid 'the destruction or breaking of any house . . . by which great damage and inconvenience might ensue.' " One point in making an officer knock and announce, then, is to give a person inside the chance to save his door. That is why, in the case with no reason to suspect an immediate risk of frustration or futility in waiting at all, the reasonable wait time may well be longer when police make a forced entry, since they ought to be more certain the occupant has had time to answer the door. It is hard to be more definite than that, without turning the notion of a reasonable time under all the circumstances into a set of sub-rules * * *. Suffice it to say that the need to damage property in the course of getting in is a good reason to require more patience than it would be reasonable to expect if the door were open. Police seeking a stolen piano may be able to spend more time to make sure they really need the battering ram. * * *

V

* * * [I]n a case like this, where the officers knocked and announced their presence, and forcibly entered after a reasonable suspicion of exigency had ripened, their entry satisfied * * * the Fourth Amendment, even without refusal of admittance.

The judgment of the Court of Appeals is reversed.

So ordered.

QUESTIONS, COMMENTS, CONCERNS?

1. **The missing knock and announce remedy.** Describing "knock and announce" as a requirement seems disingenuous. In *Hudson v. Michigan*, 547 U.S. 586 (2006), officers executed a search warrant on Booker T. Hudson's home without knocking and announcing their presence. Writing for a slim,

five-member majority of the Court, Justice Scalia declined to apply the exclusionary rule to the evidence found inside Hudson's home. He reasoned that the social costs of applying the exclusionary rule to knock-and-announce violations is considerable, while the incentive to commit such violations is minimal "and the extant deterrences against them are substantial[.]" The take away: Evidence obtained in violation of the knock and announce requirement is not subject to the Fourth Amendment's exclusionary rule.

2. **A temporary seizure of *property* pending search warrant execution.** In *Illinois v. McArthur*, 531 U.S. 326 (2001), officers had probable cause to believe Charles McArthur had hidden marijuana in his home. As a result, they prevented McArthur from entering his home for about two hours while police obtained a search warrant. After obtaining the warrant, officers entered McArthur's home and discovered contraband. The Court upheld investigators' decision to briefly seize McArthur's home without a warrant. It reasoned that the brief seizure was not unreasonable considering the prospect that McArthur could have destroyed evidence within the home had he gained entry.

3. **A temporary seizure of *people* pending search warrant execution.** In *Michigan v. Summers*, 452 U.S. 692 (1981), Detroit police officers were about to execute a residential search warrant when they encountered respondent leaving the premises. The officers required respondent to reenter and remain inside the house while they executed the warrant. The Supreme Court held that "a warrant to search for contraband founded on probable cause implicitly carries with it the limited authority to detain the occupants of the premises while a proper search is conducted." Accordingly, law enforcement's temporary detention of respondent did not constitute an unconstitutional seizure.

4. **Does a search warrant for a public premises permit the warrantless search of all persons present?** No said the Court in *Ybarra v. Illinois*, 444 U.S. 85 (1979). In *Ybarra*, police obtained a warrant to search a tavern and the tavern owner for evidence of heroin possession. During the warrant's execution, officers conducted a "cursory search for weapons" on *all* of the tavern's patrons. While patting down one of the patrons, Ventura Ybarra, an officer felt "a cigarette pack with objects in it," but did not automatically remove it from Ybarra's pocket. After patting down the other patrons, the officer returned to Ybarra, retrieved the pack, looked inside, and found heroin. The Supreme Court suppressed the heroin, holding that the warrantless search of Ybarra's person violated the Fourth Amendment. The Court reasoned that, although the search warrant gave the officers authority to search the tavern and its owner, the warrant did not allow the officers "to invade the constitutional protections possessed individually by the tavern's customers." Each patron on the premises, the Court explained, was entitled to individualized Fourth Amendment protection.

5. **Good faith and search warrant execution.** In *Maryland v. Garrison*, 480 U.S. 79 (1987), Baltimore police applied for a warrant to search

the person of Lawrence McWebb and "the premises known as 2036 Park Avenue third floor apartment." While executing the warrant, officers learned that the third floor was actually divided into two apartments and that they were inside the wrong apartment. The officers discovered their mistake only after finding drugs and cash belonging to respondent Garrison. The Supreme Court declined to suppress the contraband, reasoning that the officers reasonably relied on a warrant that they believed authorized the search of the entire third floor.

6. **Avery and particularity.** Recall *Lo-Ji Sales* and *Groh v. Ramirez* from earlier in this chapter. You'll remember that both cases recognized that, per the Fourth Amendment's plain language, a search warrant must state with particularity the place to be searched and the things to be seized. *Groh* specifically commented "that the purpose of the particularity requirement is not limited to the prevention of general searches. A particular warrant also 'assures the individual whose property is searched or seized of the lawful authority of the executing officer, his need to search, and the limits of his power to search.'" With that language in mind, turn to the first search warrant issued for the Avery compound. [Casefile Document 1.] Pay special attention to paragraph 3, which in pertinent part states: "On the property, there are numerous outbuildings and vehicles, those that are operational and also junked and scrapped vehicles, associated with the salvage yard business." That paragraph goes on to list six categories of evidence, but the warrant does not connect those categories to a specific building or junked car. Does that create a particularity problem? Law enforcement must state, with particularity, its desire to search a vehicle parked in a resident's driveway. Why would the Avery salvage yard be treated differently?

Now look at the first two paragraphs of the warrant—the paragraphs that list the trailers for Avery and Barbara Janda (Steven Avery's sister and Brendan's mother). Does listing those two properties specifically mean that other buildings on the Avery compound remain private? Is paragraph three supposed to be a catch-all that would permit searching those other buildings?

7. **The first Avery warrant and probable cause.** Where is the probable cause to search the various things listed in the November 5, 2005 search warrant? [*See* Casefile Document 1.] Of course, by November 5, officers were investigating Halbach's disappearance, but does the warrant make clear why Halbach might be connected to Avery's trailer (as opposed to another building on the property)? And perhaps more problematically, why have officers included Janda's home? Does the affidavit attached to the November 5 warrant provide any insight?

8. ***Franks* and Avery.** The November 5, 2005 search warrant omits two key facts. First, it omits that, on November 4, 2005, officers searched Avery's trailer pursuant to consent, but found nothing. It seems misleading to leave out the results of the consent search because the inference to be drawn by the November 5 warrant is that there is incriminating evidence in the trailer. That is, if the previous consent search of the trailer did not turn up

evidence, why is there now probable cause to believe evidence is inside the trailer?

Second, the warrant omits the fact Sergeant Andrew Colborn knew to call dispatch to ask about a license plate number that dispatch confirms belonged to Teresa Halbach. How did Colborn know to ask for *that* license plate before the RAV4 was actually discovered? He was unable to provide a satisfactory answer at trial.

Based on these omissions, should the defense have argued *Franks*? And if *Franks* applied, could the prosecution seek to excise the problematic material in order to save the warrant?

9. Avery and suppression. If Avery were to succeed in arguing absence of particularity, absence of probable cause, or the applicability of *Franks*, what would the remedy be? Could he argue for suppression of everything seized pursuant to the November 5 warrant *and* the November 9 warrant. [*See* Casefile Document 2.] Would *Leon* help the prosecution save the warrants or any evidence obtained pursuant to the warrants? *Leon* aside, what other exception to the exclusionary rule might apply?

UNITED STATES V. KESZTHELYI

308 F.3d 557
United States Court of Appeals for the Sixth Circuit
June 12, 2002, Argued; October 17, 2002, Decided and Filed
No. 00-6630

MOORE, CIRCUIT JUDGE.

Defendant-Appellant Rudolph Keszthelyi appeals the district court's denial of his motion to suppress evidence seized during three searches of his house * * *. Defendant contends * * * that the warrant authorizing the initial search of his residence was invalid due to material factual omissions in the warrant affidavit. Defendant also argues that his Fourth Amendment rights were violated when law enforcement agents conducted a second search of his home without obtaining a new search warrant. * * * For the reasons stated below, we AFFIRM.

I. FACTS AND PROCEDURE * * *

A. Background and Investigation

Keszthelyi migrated from South Africa to the United States in October of 1992 on a work visa. Keszthelyi settled in Chattanooga, Tennessee, where he began employment with a company called E & R Products. This company produced various woodwork products, including customized van interiors. In 1994, Keszthelyi purchased E & R Products and obtained a business license, which was in effect from 1994 to 1995. There is no record of E & R Products operating after 1995. Keszthelyi's visa expired in 1995, but he continued to remain in the United States illegally.

In December of 1998, the Chattanooga Police Department ("CPD"), the Drug Enforcement Agency ("DEA"), and the Bureau of Alcohol, Tobacco, and Firearms ("ATF") initiated an undercover investigation to identify individuals selling cocaine in Chattanooga night clubs. Keszthelyi, a suspected cocaine dealer, was the primary target of this investigation. ATF Special Agent Jeff Harwood worked undercover, posing as a successful Nashville businessman named Jeff Harris who was on probation for prior drug arrests. Harwood frequented night clubs in Chattanooga in an effort to befriend targets of the investigation. Harwood was wired and monitored by a control agent during these activities. Over the course of the investigation, Harwood made a number of controlled purchases of cocaine from the defendant Keszthelyi. Sometime after July 18, 1999, Harwood returned to Nashville and ceased to be involved in the investigation.

On October 8, 1999, law enforcement authorities obtained a warrant to search Keszthelyi's home from a magistrate judge. The warrant instructed the officers to search the home "on or before October 18, 1999 (not to exceed 10 days)." Agent James Isom of the DEA submitted an affidavit in support of the warrant. A substantial portion of the affidavit described a number of controlled purchases of cocaine from the defendant made by a confidential informant identified as CI-4. The affidavit explains that in August of 1999, CI-4 was apprehended leaving Keszthelyi's residence, at which time he informed law enforcement officials that he had just purchased a gram of cocaine from the defendant and had been buying one to two grams per week from Keszthelyi for approximately one year. CI-4 agreed to cooperate with the investigation at that time. In August, September, and October of 1999, CI-4 engaged in six controlled purchases of cocaine from the defendant in quantities ranging from one to five grams. These transactions were electronically monitored and observed by law enforcement agents. Three of these purchases occurred at Keszthelyi's residence. The final purchase at his residence occurred on October 7, 1999, the day before the warrant was issued.

In addition to the information concerning CI-4, Agent Isom's affidavit described two controlled purchases of cocaine made by Agent Harwood while working undercover. The affidavit also noted the statements of three other confidential informants, identified as CI-1, CI-2, and CI-3, describing Keszthelyi's cocaine distribution activities. Finally, the affidavit described the results of an extensive financial investigation of Keszthelyi, which revealed that the defendant had made cash deposits into multiple bank accounts totaling $240,034 over five years and had made a number of very expensive purchases despite having no appreciable legitimate income.

Law enforcement agents arrested Keszthelyi at approximately 3:00 p.m. on October 8, 1999. On that day, agents waited for Keszthelyi to leave his residence and arrested him in his vehicle as he was driving away from his home. Agents searched the vehicle at that time and found four grams of cocaine hidden inside the defendant's garage door opener. Shortly after arresting the defendant, agents commenced a search of Keszthelyi's home pursuant to the search warrant obtained earlier that day. Agents found a loaded semi-automatic pistol inside a night table in Keszthelyi's bedroom and a loaded pistol-gripped shotgun in the bedroom closet. Agents discovered approximately $1000 cash in the pocket of a jacket hanging in the bedroom closet. Agents also found a digital scale, electronic surveillance equipment set up to monitor the exterior of the house, business records, several boxes of ammunition, a digital pager, numerous bottles of pills, a box of syringes, and various other items. No cocaine was found on the premises. The agents concluded their search and left the property at approximately 5:00 p.m.

On October 9, Agent Isom, who had not participated in the initial search of Keszthelyi's residence, telephoned the U.S. Attorney's office about returning to the residence to continue the search. Isom stated that he "felt very strongly that there was something there that had not been located" during the initial search. The decision was made to re-enter the residence and continue the search without obtaining a new search warrant. During the second search of defendant's residence, Isom noticed that the oven in defendant's kitchen was moveable. He moved the oven and discovered a plastic bottle containing approximately one ounce of cocaine.

After Keszthelyi's arrest, law enforcement agents interviewed a number of additional witnesses, including three confidential informants identified as W-1, W-2, and W-3. Witnesses W-1, W-2, and W-3 were known to the police before October 8, 1999, but the investigation team waited to interview them until after Keszthelyi was in custody in order to ensure that Keszthelyi would not influence them. These witnesses informed the agents that they had purchased cocaine from Keszthelyi, and stated that Keszthelyi had buried money on his property.

On October 11, Agent Isom obtained a new warrant to search defendant's property once again. The affidavit in support of the new warrant summarized the information contained in the first affidavit, and added information concerning the cocaine and other evidence seized from the defendant's car and home on October 8 and 9, as well as the information obtained from W-1, W-2, and W-3. Pursuant to the warrant, agents searched Keszthelyi's home again on October 11, 1999, but no money or drugs were found.

B. Suppression Proceedings

In the district court, Keszthelyi moved to suppress all evidence seized as a result of the three searches of his home. Keszthelyi argued that the affidavit in support of the first warrant was insufficient to demonstrate probable cause, and that the affidavit contained material omissions concerning allegations of misconduct on the part of Agent Harwood.

Keszthelyi further objected that the search of October 9, 1999, could not be permitted under the auspices of the initial warrant, and that the search of October 11, 1999, was not supported by new probable cause.

A suppression hearing was held on March 20, 2000. Defense counsel called Agent Harwood and questioned him about allegations that Harwood became involved in a sexual relationship with Kim Brogdon, a target of the investigation and ex-girlfriend of the defendant, during his participation in the undercover investigation. Harwood testified that he was not sexually involved with Brogdon during the investigation, but that he did begin a sexual relationship with her after his involvement in the investigation ended. Harwood stated that Brogdon spent the night at his undercover apartment several times, but Harwood denied having sexual intercourse with her on any of those occasions.

Defense counsel also asked Harwood whether he had ever used drugs while working undercover. In particular, defense counsel cited suspicious circumstances surrounding a drug purchase made by Harwood on February 13, 1999, at the South Beach Nightclub. Evidence surrounding that transaction showed that Harwood paid $300 for a quantity of cocaine. Although $300 would have been the normal price for one-eighth of an ounce of cocaine, Harwood only turned over one-sixteenth of an ounce to his control agents. Law enforcement records also showed that the cocaine was not turned over to the DEA until several days after it was purchased. Harwood testified that he did not use any of the cocaine, and that it would have been his normal practice immediately to turn the drugs over to his control agent.

According to Harwood, an internal affairs investigation concerning charges of his drug use and improper relationship with Brogdon was launched in January 2000. Harwood denied any wrongdoing and was unaware of the current status of the investigation.

Agent Isom also testified at the suppression hearing. Isom testified at length about the information gathered in support of the warrant affidavit, including the investigation surrounding the confidential informant identified as CI-4 and the alleged improprieties of Agent Harwood. Isom stated that he personally observed the controlled purchases made by CI-4. Isom also stated that Agent Harwood had no connection to any activities involving CI-4. Isom testified that he did not know whether Brogdon and Harwood became involved romantically before Harwood's undercover assignment ended.

The district court denied Keszthelyi's motion to suppress. * * *

II. ANALYSIS

A. Fourth Amendment Objections

1. Search on October 8, 1999

Keszthelyi's first assignment of error alleges that Agent Isom's affidavit was insufficient to establish probable cause for the search warrant issued on October 8, 1999. The defendant alleges that Agent Isom omitted material facts concerning Agent Harwood's misconduct from the affidavit in violation of *Franks v. Delaware*. * * * On appellate review of the district court's ruling on a *Franks* challenge, we review de novo the district court's legal conclusions, and we review the district court's findings of fact for clear error. [Ed. note: the Court then discussed *Franks* in detail.] * * *

Assuming that Keszthelyi could show that Agent Isom intentionally or recklessly omitted facts relating to Agent Harwood's misconduct, the unaffected portions of the affidavit were more than sufficient to establish probable cause. * * * At most, inclusion of information about Agent Harwood's alleged misconduct would have undermined the reliability of the information generated by Harwood himself. Thus, the magistrate may have disbelieved the information provided in paragraphs 7, 8, 9, 11, and 12 of the affidavit, which relate to two controlled purchases by Agent Harwood and Harwood's account of various statements made by others implicating Keszthelyi in cocaine trafficking. Harwood's misconduct would not discredit information relating to the six controlled purchases made by CI-4, three of which occurred at Keszthelyi's residence. The uncontradicted evidence at the suppression hearing established that Harwood played no role in the development of CI-4. The controlled purchases by CI-4 were electronically monitored and recorded by the police. Such evidence offers strong support for a finding of probable cause. The magistrate judge's probable cause determination was further supported by the statements of CI-1, CI-2, and CI-3, as well as the independent investigation of Keszthelyi's finances. Taken together, this untainted information was sufficient to establish probable cause to believe that contraband would be found in Keszthelyi's home. We therefore affirm the district court's decision denying Keszthelyi's motion to suppress the fruits of the search on October 8, 1999.

2. Search on October 9, 1999

Keszthelyi next challenges the constitutionality of the second entry into and search of his home on October 9, 1999. Keszthelyi argues that once the police terminated their search on October 8, any return to the premises constituted a new search and required officers to obtain a new warrant. The government contends that the second search was a reasonable continuation of the October 8 search, and therefore was authorized by the October 8 warrant. In the alternative, the government contends that even if the October 9 search was invalid, the evidence discovered during that search should not be suppressed because it would have been discovered inevitably during the third search of defendant's residence on October 11, 1999. We agree with the defendant that the October 9 search was not a reasonable continuation of the October 8 search. We nevertheless agree with the government that the cocaine inevitably would have been discovered during the October 11 search and should not be suppressed.

a. The Reasonable Continuation Rule

Most of the federal courts of appeals to have considered the question, including the Sixth Circuit, have held that a single search warrant may authorize more than one entry into the premises identified in the warrant, as long as the second entry is a reasonable continuation of the original search. * * *

Two aspects of the reasonable continuation rule [are critical]. First, the subsequent entry must indeed be a continuation of the original search, and not a new and separate search. Thus, other courts * * * have appropriately cast the legal question as whether subsequent entries ostensibly carried out under a single warrant are properly characterized as reasonable continuations of the original search or as separate searches requiring separate warrants. Second, the decision to conduct a second entry to continue the search must be reasonable under the totality of the circumstances.

(1) Continuation v. New Search

Guided by the foregoing discussion, we conclude that the October 9 search of Keszthelyi's residence satisfies neither aspect of the reasonable continuation rule. First, we conclude that the October 9 search was a separate search, requiring its own authorization by either a separate warrant or a recognized exception to the warrant requirement, rather than a continuation of the original search on October 8, 1999. We note that a search conducted pursuant to a lawful warrant may last as long, and be as thorough, as reasonably necessary to fully execute the warrant. Thus, law enforcement agents generally may continue to search the premises described in the warrant until they are satisfied that all available evidence has been located. Once the execution of a warrant is complete, however, the authority conferred by the warrant terminates. In the instant case, law enforcement agents searched Keszthelyi's residence on October 8, 1999, until they were content that all available evidence had been located. The testimony at the suppression hearing did not indicate that any aspect of the search was left incomplete when the agents terminated the search at approximately 5:00 p.m., or that the agents were unable to search any area specified in the warrant during the October 8 search. It is undisputed that the agents could have stayed longer if they believed that any evidence remained in the house. Agent Isom admitted that the search conducted on October 8 was a thorough one, and that drug detection dogs were used to attempt to locate narcotics. The thoroughness of the original search is underscored by the range of items seized at that time, including electronic surveillance equipment, business records, various bottles of pills, and even defendant's last will and testament. Thus, we think that when the agents terminated their search of the defendant's residence on October 8, 1999, the search was complete and the warrant was fully executed. If the agents desired to conduct an additional search after that time, we think they were required to apply for a new warrant or identify a valid exception to the warrant requirement authorizing re-entry.

(2) Fourth Amendment Reasonableness

Even if we were to assume that the second entry into defendant's home on October 9, 1999, was a "continuation" of the original search, the continuation search would nevertheless fail the Fourth Amendment's reasonableness requirement. We acknowledge that "it is generally left to the discretion of the executing officers to determine the details of how best to proceed with the performance of a search authorized by warrant." It is always the case, however, that "the manner in which a warrant is executed is subject to later judicial review as to its reasonableness." The reasonableness of a search under the Fourth Amendment is determined by "balanc[ing] the nature and quality of the intrusion on the individual's Fourth Amendment interests against the importance of the governmental interests alleged to justify the intrusion." Reasonableness depends upon "whether the totality of the circumstances justifie[s] a particular sort of search or seizure."

In the instant case, we conclude that the circumstances did not justify the second entry and search of defendant's residence on October 9, 1999. Initially we note that here, unlike many of the cases in which continuation searches were approved, nothing impaired the ability of the agents to execute fully the warrant at the time of their initial entry. Agent Isom's decision to conduct two complete searches of the defendant's residence over a period of two days, therefore, was in no sense necessary or important to the successful execution of the search warrant.

Moreover, the government has not shown that, at the time of the second search, the agents possessed a reasonable basis for believing that undiscovered evidence remained in the defendant's home. the reasonableness of the second search. In the instant case, agents thoroughly searched the defendant's residence for drugs on October 8, 1999. Despite the assistance of trained drug-detection dogs, the agents found no cocaine at that time. Other than the agents' expectation that more evidence would be found, the government has not shown any basis for believing at the time that the first search was deficient in any respect. Agent Isom testified merely that he "felt that we had just not found something inside of that residence." If law enforcement agents could resume an already-completed search based only on a "feeling" that evidence remained on the property, there would be no limit to the number of official intrusions that could be carried out pursuant to a warrant.

Finally, we note that the government took no steps to limit the scope or intrusiveness of the second search of defendant's residence. Upon re-entering the defendant's home on October 9, 1999, the agents conducted another complete search of the property. Agent Isom testified that more than five agents participated in the second search, which by all accounts was just as thorough as the first. In this respect, the instant case is distinguishable from those cases which have upheld limited continuation searches carried out for narrowly defined purposes, such as to recover a specific piece of evidence inadvertently left behind during the initial search. Similarly, the instant case contrasts sharply with cases * * * in which the police arguably were able to ameliorate the impairment of a suspect's Fourth Amendment interests by conducting two entries rather than one.

Based upon the foregoing considerations, we conclude that the second search of the defendant's residence was unreasonable. The government's interest in conducting a second search was minimal, since the agents were able to execute fully the warrant during their initial entry and little objective basis existed for believing that evidence escaped the first search. In contrast, the second search of defendant's residence significantly intruded upon Keszthelyi's protected property and privacy interests. Absent some reasonable justification or showing of necessity, we do not think that law enforcement agents may, under the authority of a single warrant, conduct a thorough search of a private residence on one day, and then return the next day to begin the whole process again.

[Ed. note: The court then applied the inevitable discovery doctrine, noting: "we think the evidence clearly supports the district court's conclusion that a new warrant to search the defendant's residence inevitably would have been obtained, and that the cocaine behind defendant's oven inevitably would have been discovered, even in the absence of the illegal search on October 9, 1999."]

* * *Based upon the foregoing analysis, we AFFIRM * * *.

BOGGS, CIRCUIT JUDGE, concurring.

[Omitted.]

QUESTIONS, COMMENTS, CONCERNS?

1. **Putting *Keszthelyi* in context for Avery.** In total, law enforcement in Avery's case would rely on the November 5, 2005 warrant to justify a total of eight entries into his trailer and four entries into his garage. From those entries, it seems the most important piece of evidence at issue is

the key to the RAV4 found in Avery's trailer. Officers found the key on their eighth entry. Detective James Lenk would contend later that he found the key in plain view.

2. **Parsing Avery's motion to suppress.** Review Avery's motion to suppress. [Casefile Document 3.] Now, consider two sets of questions. First, what does Avery contend should be suppressed? Is the motion sufficiently precise on the question of exclusion?

Second, when does Avery think the November 5 search warrant was fully executed? Are there other arguments missing from Avery's motion that you would have included?

3. **Considering the state's response.** Move to the state's response to Avery's motion. [Casefile Document 4.] The state initially contends that "[t]here was one warrant and there was only one search; one search that took seven days and thirty minutes to complete." The problem with that argument, besides being a run-on sentence, is that the state acquired a subsequent warrant on November 9. Surely the state has a better argument, right?

Consider some other questions the state needs to answer: first, in your opinion, does the state adequately address the question of whether the November 5 warrant authorized the search of specific buildings or, alternatively, the *entire* Avery property? Second, even if this was not one single search, what arguments does the state fall back on? Are there other arguments missing from the state's motion that you would have included?

4. **Who gets the better of the fight?** Before turning to the Circuit Court's order, who do you think go the better of the arguments—Avery or the state? In particular, which side in your opinion best applied the law governing the reasonable continuation rule—most importantly *Keszthelyi* as compared to *Squillacote*?

5. **The Circuit Court's resolution.** Why does the Circuit Court ultimately deny Avery's motion to suppress? [*See* Casefile Document 5.] In your opinion, how sound is the court's analysis of the reasonable continuation issue? Relatedly, how does the court apply that analysis to admit the controversial RAV4 key? And finally, reasonable continuation aside, how does the inevitable discovery rule apply? Notice that, in discussing the inevitable discovery rule, the court talks about "the evidence." The court should be more precise, though, right? After all, it's difficult to tell if the court's analysis of "the evidence" is sufficiently specific to apply to the RAV4 key.

STATE V. SVEUM

787 N.W.2d 317
Supreme Court of Wisconsin
March 2, 2010, Argued; July 20, 2010, Filed
No. 2008AP658-CR

JUDGES: PATIENCE DRAKE ROGGENSACK, J. N. PATRICK CROOKS, J. (concurring). ANNETTE KINGSLAND ZIEGLER, J. (concurring). SHIRLEY S. ABRAHAMSON, C.J. (dissenting). BRADLEY, J., joins dissent.

PATIENCE DRAKE ROGGENSACK, J. We review a decision of the court of appeals affirming the circuit court's judgment convicting Michael A. Sveum (Sveum) of aggravated stalking and denying Sveum's post-conviction motion for a new trial. In upholding the judgment of conviction, the court of appeals affirmed the circuit court's denial of Sveum's motion to suppress evidence obtained from a Global Positioning System (GPS) tracking device, which law enforcement attached to Sveum's car. Our focus is on whether the circuit court erred in its denial of Sveum's suppression motion. * * *

We * * * [conclude] that the order authorizing law enforcement to install and monitor a GPS tracking device on Sveum's vehicle constituted a valid warrant and that the officers' execution of the warrant was reasonable. Accordingly, we affirm the decision of the court of appeals.

I. BACKGROUND

In 1996, "Sveum was charged with stalking and harassing Jamie Johnson [(Johnson)], his former girlfriend." "He was also charged with violating a harassment injunction for contacting [Johnson] personally and by telephone" and "criminal damage to property." Sveum was convicted of all charges, which the court of appeals affirmed. He was sentenced to 11 years of probation for the stalking conviction that commenced upon serving three consecutive, three-year prison terms for the remaining three convictions. Sveum remained in confinement until his mandatory release date of July 2, 2002, when he was released on probation and parole.

In March 2003, Johnson reported to the police that she believed Sveum was stalking her again. On April 22, 2003, Detective Mary Ricksecker (Ricksecker) requested circuit court authorization to install and monitor an electronic device on Sveum's vehicle. Specifically, she requested to attach a GPS tracking device to Sveum's vehicle, a 1980 black Chevy Beretta Coup with a Wisconsin license plate number of 754 ELL and a Vehicle Identification Number (VIN) of 1G1LZ14A2LY130646, and to monitor the tracking device "inside such private and public areas." She further requested "permission to obtain a key to operate the motor vehicle, if necessary" and "to use the same methods to retrieve the device." Finally, she requested "that the order be authorized for a period of time not to exceed 60 days from the date the order is signed."

Ricksecker filed an affidavit in support of this request, alleging that GPS monitoring of Sveum's vehicle "could provide relevant information to the criminal investigation of the crime of stalking." * * *

On the same day Ricksecker requested authorization, the circuit court issued an order granting her request to install and monitor a GPS tracking device on Sveum's vehicle. The court concluded that "[b]ased on the information provided in the affidavit submitted by Detective Ricksecker, the court finds that there is probable cause to believe that the installation of a tracking device in the below listed vehicle is relevant to an on-going criminal investigation and that the vehicle is being used in the commission of a crime of stalking . . ." The court ordered the following:

1.   The State[']s request to install and monitor a tracking device on the below listed vehicle is granted based on the authority granted in [United States v. Karo, 468 U.S. 705 (1984)].

2.   The Madison Police Department is authorized to place an electronic tracking device on a 1990 black Beretta with a license plate number of 754 ELL and a VIN of 1G1LZ14A2LY130646, and they are hereby authorized to surreptitiously enter and reenter the vehicle and any buildings and structures containing the vehicle or any premises on which the vehicle is located to install, use, maintain and conduct surveillance and monitoring of the location and movement of a mobile electronic tracking device in the vehicle and any and all places within or outside the jurisdiction of Iowa or Dane County, including but not limited to private residence and other locations not open to visual surveillance; to accomplish the installation, agents are authorized to obtain and use a key to operate and move the vehicle for a required time to a concealed location and are authorized to open the engine compartment and trunk areas of the vehicle to install the device.

3.   It is further ordered that the Madison Police Department shall remove the electronic tracking device as soon as practicable after the objectives of the surveillance are accomplished or not later than 60 days from the date the order is signed unless extended by this court or another court of competent jurisdiction.

In the early morning hours of April 23, 2003, Ricksecker and three other law enforcement officers located Sveum's vehicle parked in the driveway of 2426 Valley Road, Cross Plains. A battery-powered GPS tracking device was attached to the "undercarriage" of Sveum's vehicle with magnetic equipment and tape. The officers did not open the engine compartment or trunk area of the vehicle while installing the GPS. Because of the limited battery life of the GPS, the officers replaced the GPS twice. Both replacement devices were attached to Sveum's vehicle in the same manner in which the first was attached, i.e., to the undercarriage of the vehicle with magnetic equipment and tape while parked in the driveway of 2426 Valley Road, Cross Plains. The third and final GPS was removed from Sveum's vehicle on May 27, 2003.

Upon removal of the GPS devices, the stored information on each of the GPS devices was downloaded and then stored on a disk. The information from the disk was put on a map so the officers could see where Sveum's vehicle had traveled.

The GPS device revealed data incriminating Sveum. The GPS data indicated that on April 25, 2003, Sveum's vehicle traveled to a location 468 feet from Johnson's residence, and his vehicle remained there from 8:14 p.m. to 9:08 p.m. Sveum's vehicle then traveled to a shopping mall near Mineral Point Road and the Beltline Highway and remained there from 9:16 p.m. to 9:19 p.m. Phone records indicated that at 9:17 p.m. Johnson received a hang-up call from a pay phone located near the shopping mall where Sveum's vehicle was. Additionally, the GPS data demonstrated that on April 26, 2003, Sveum's vehicle traveled to a location 277 feet from Johnson's residence and remained there from 8:28 p.m. to 9:43 p.m.

Based, in part, on the above-described tracking data from the GPS devices, the police obtained two additional search warrants. One warrant authorized the police to search the premises located at 2426 Valley Road, Cross Plains and Sveum's vehicle. The search revealed evidence incriminating Sveum, including photos of Johnson, a handwritten chronological log recording sightings of Johnson and letters sent to his sister, Renee Sveum, asking for information about Johnson. The other warrant authorized the police to search the premises located at 6685 County Trunk Highway K, Renee Sveum's residence, which did not reveal any incriminating evidence.

On August 4, 2003, the State filed a complaint charging Sveum with aggravated stalking as a party to a crime contrary to Wis. Stat. § 940.32(3)(b) (2001–02) and Wis. Stat. § 930.05 (2001–02). Sveum filed a motion to suppress all information obtained from the GPS device, arguing that it was unlawfully obtained in violation of the Fourth Amendment. The circuit court denied the motion on the grounds that installing and monitoring the GPS device was not a search. * * *

The case proceeded to trial where a jury found Sveum guilty of the charged offense. On February 6, 2007, the court entered a judgment of conviction and sentenced Sveum to seven years and six months in prison followed by five years of extended supervision. * * * The court of appeals affirmed. * * * Sveum petitioned this court for review, which we granted. We now affirm the decision of the court of appeals. * * *

III. DISCUSSION

[Ed. note: following a lengthy discussion, the court concluded that the warrant was constitutionally valid.] * * * Even if a court determines that a search warrant is constitutionally valid, the manner in which the warrant was executed remains subject to judicial review. * * * Whether a search was reasonably ordered and executed is [ ] informed by the Wisconsin Statutes. For example, Wis. Stat. § 968.12(1) defines the parameters of a search warrant. Section 968.12 codifies the Warrant Clause's requirements and provides part of the framework for a circuit court's action; § 968.12(1) provides:

> A search warrant is an order signed by a judge directing a law enforcement officer to conduct a search of a designated person, a designated object or a designated place for the purpose of seizing designated property or kinds of property. A judge shall issue a search warrant if probable cause is shown.

* * * [T]he data seized from the GPS device was not subject to suppression.

The officers entered the driveway to install the GPS device in Sveum's vehicle. Installation was achieved simply, by attaching the device with magnets and tape to the vehicle's undercarriage. Maintenance of the GPS device included replacing the device twice, due to its limited battery life. Both replacement devices were installed in the same manner as the first. After monitoring Sveum's vehicle for 35 days, the officers removed the GPS device. Execution in this manner stayed well within the confines of the authority granted by the order, which authorized law enforcement to "install, use, [and] maintain" a GPS tracking device on Sveum's vehicle and to subsequently "remove" such device.

Additionally, "[t]here is no indication that [law enforcement's] intrusion went beyond what was necessary to install and remove the equipment." Indeed, the officers did not enter any building, including Sveum's home, nor did they access the passenger compartment or the trunk of the vehicle during installation, maintenance and removal of the GPS device. Additionally, the officers replaced the GPS devices only as was necessary and in the same minimally intrusive manner as the initial installation.

Sveum raises several arguments, which he contends demonstrate that the order was not reasonably executed. Specifically, Sveum argues that the officers violated his Fourth Amendment rights by * * * performing a search that exceeded the scope of the order * * *. * * * He argues this is so because each day the officers monitored Sveum's vehicle using the GPS device constituted a separate intrusion requiring a new search warrant. * * * [W]e disagree.

In *United States v. Squillacote*, 221 F.3d 542 (4th Cir. 2000), the United States Court of Appeals for the Fourth Circuit rejected an argument similar to Sveum's. In *Squillacote*, pursuant to an investigation of suspected "espionage-related activities," a search warrant was issued authorizing the search of the defendants' home for a period of not more than 10 days. The search extended over six days. The defendants argued that the evidence seized pursuant to the warrant "must [ ] be suppressed because the government did not obtain a new warrant for each successive day of searching."

The court rejected this argument reasoning that due to the complex, ongoing nature of the espionage-related activities and the nature of the evidence sought "the search was necessarily extensive and exhaustive." Because "the search could not have been completed in a single day" and because it viewed "the subsequent entries [ ] not [as] separate searches requiring separate warrants, but instead [as] [ ] reasonable continuations of the original search" the government was not required to obtain additional warrants for each day the search continued.

We similarly conclude that the complex, ongoing nature of stalking justified the 35 days of GPS surveillance on a single search warrant. Evidence sufficient to demonstrate Sveum's stalking required, inter alia, data demonstrating Sveum engaged in "a series of 2 or more acts carried out over time," inducing Johnson to fear bodily injury or death. See § 940.32(1)(a), (2)(c). A search obtaining this type of evidence could not have been completed in a single day. Moreover, the daily, continuous monitoring of the GPS device on Sveum's vehicle "were not separate searches requiring separate warrants, but instead were simply reasonable continuations of the original search." *Squillacote*, 221 F.3d at 557. Accordingly, the officers were not required to obtain additional search warrants for each day the GPS monitoring continued. * * *

By the Court.—The decision of the court of appeals is affirmed.

N. PATRICK CROOKS, J. (concurring).

[Omitted.]

ANNETTE KINGSLAND ZIEGLER, J. (concurring).

[Omitted.]

SHIRLEY S. ABRAHAMSON, C.J. (dissenting).

[Omitted.]

QUESTIONS, COMMENTS, CONCERNS?

1. *Sveum* **inapplicable to Avery.** Note that *Sveum* came out after Avery and the state argued over the scope of the November 2005 searches.

2. Materials forgotten but listed in a warrant. In *United States v. Carter*, 854 F.2d 1102 (8th Cir. 1988), a police officer located defendant at a motel. After defendant gave the officer consent to search the room, the officer made a protective sweep and saw cocaine on a table. He placed defendant under arrest and obtained a search warrant for the room. After police executed the warrant, defendant contended that $4,000 hidden under the mattress was not inventoried as seized property. Several hours later, the officer returned and found the money. Defendant later challenged the return search and argued that the money should be suppressed. The Eighth Circuit disagreed. The court reasoned that, because the warrant listed money as an item to be seized and the officer returned for the money several shortly after executing the warrant, the warrant's authority "had not expired and therefore the return search was not beyond the scope of the Fourth Amendment."

3. Materials forgotten but listed in a warrant (redux). In *United States v. Kaplan*, 895 F.2d 618 (9th Cir. 1990), FBI agents returned to Dr. Kaplan's office with a duly authorized search warrant naming specific files to be obtained the day after his arrest for unlawfully prescribing controlled substances. After executing the warrant and leaving the office, agents realized that they had not seized all records named in the warrant. Two hours and ten minutes after executing the warrant, an agent returned to Kaplan's office and obtained the remaining files. Kaplan challenged this return search as unconstitutional. The Ninth Circuit held that the return search did not violate the Fourth Amendment under the continuation doctrine.

4. How long is too long for a subsequent search? In *United States v. Gerber*, 994 F.2d 1556 (11th Cir. 1993), defendant committed an armed robbery and confessed to his roommate. His roommate contacted the FBI and provided corroborating evidence. The FBI obtained a warrant for the defendant's arrest and a search warrant containing a particularized description of the car based on an eyewitness account. The warrants were issued in the late afternoon on Thursday, September 12, 1991. The search warrant was drafted to expire on Friday, September 13, 1991.

After the defendant's arrest, the agents impounded his car to search it pursuant to the warrant. During the search on September 13, the agents found multiple pieces of evidence. However, the agents could not locate the hood release lever to enable them to search under the hood. The agents decided to wait until the next business day, Monday, to obtain the assistance of a mechanic. On Monday, September 16, the agents resumed their search of the vehicle with the help of a mechanic and discovered more evidence. The agents were not aware that the search warrant expired the previous Friday.

The district court granted the defendant's motion to suppress the evidence found under the hood of the car writing, "There is no suggestion here that the warrant was improperly issued. The government was simply careless in executing the warrant several days late, and the exclusionary rule was fashioned to deter such mistakes." On appeal, the court reversed the district court's decision, reasoning that the Monday search "was reasonable and well founded on probable cause."

UNITED STATES V. DUDEK

530 F.2d 684
United States Court of Appeals for the Sixth Circuit
October 2, 1975, Cause Argued; February 12, 1976, Decided; February 12, 1976, Filed
No. 75-1547

JUDGES: EDWARDS and ENGEL, CIRCUIT JUDGES, and HARVEY

EDWARDS, CIRCUIT JUDGE.

In this case the government appeals from an order granting a motion to suppress evidence entered by the United States District Court in the Northern District of Ohio, Eastern Division.

Appellee was charged with transporting and receiving firearms and ammunition in interstate commerce without being licensed to do so, in violation of 18 U.S.C. § 922(a)(1) (1970). He was also charged with knowingly receiving and possessing said firearms being a felon, in violation of 18 U.S.C. App. § 1202(a)(1) (1970) and conspiracy to violate the laws above in violation of 18 U.S.C. § 371 (1970).

The motion to suppress evidence was made prior to trial on the basis of the fact that the search warrant issued by an Ohio state judge was not "promptly" returned after the search and that the inventory had not been properly "verified." In these respects appellee relies upon Ohio law, particularly Rule 41 of the Ohio Rules of Criminal Procedure.

The language in Ohio Rule 41(D) which is particularly relevant to this appeal is as follows:[2]

> *(D) Execution and return with inventory.* The officer taking property under the warrant shall give to the person from whom or from whose premises the property was taken a copy of the warrant and a receipt for the property taken, or shall leave the copy and receipt at the place from which the property was taken. The return shall be made promptly and shall be accompanied by a written inventory of any property taken. The inventory shall be made in the presence of the applicant for the warrant and the person from whose possession or premises the property was taken, if they are present, or in the presence of at least one credible person other than the applicant for the warrant or the person from whose possession or premises the property was taken, and shall be verified by the officer. The judge shall upon request deliver a copy of the inventory to the person from whom or from whose

---

[2] This rule is an exact copy of Rule 41(D) Fed. R. Crim. P. except that the Ohio rule refers to Judge rather than Federal Magistrate.

premises the property was taken and to the applicant for the warrant. . . .

The government concedes in this case that the return of the warrant was not made "promptly" and that the inventory was not "verified" in accordance with the terms of the rule just quoted. The record discloses that the inventory was filled out at the plant where the seizures were made and in the presence of one of the partners in charge. It was not signed by the officer in charge or returned to the court which issued it for nearly eleven months. It was filed with the court two weeks before this trial. The defendant-appellee does not assert any prejudice from the late filing or the failure to verify.

The factual circumstances surrounding the failures referred to above are shown in the following colloquy between the District Judge and the officer in charge of the execution of the search warrant:

THE COURT: Now, so that I understand you, you came back and you said you tried to make the return to the Clerk's office when?

THE WITNESS: That afternoon.

THE COURT: On the 15th?

THE WITNESS: Yes, sir.

THE COURT: And they were closed?

THE WITNESS: Yes, sir.

. . . .

THE COURT: How long did you keep the warrants that had the inventories fastened to them?

THE WITNESS: About three or four days.

THE COURT: And you didn't make any further attempt to take them to the Clerk's office or take them to the Judge because you return them to the person who issued it?

THE WITNESS: Well, like I previously stated, your Honor, they were in the file and the file was taken to the Chief's office.

THE COURT: Well, now, for three or four days, you said, they were with you?

THE WITNESS: Yes, sir, they were.

THE COURT: And you did not take them anywhere?

THE WITNESS: No, sir, I didn't.

THE COURT: Anybody inform you of the statutes of Ohio that require that you make a return of the inventory in three days?

THE WITNESS: Yes, sir, I was aware that they had to be taken back, but it's just that at the time, what was going on and the work involved—I don't know what to say. It was oversight or—but we didn't have very much help with the inventory and we had people calling from all over, West Virginia, Pennsylvania, asking about it, and every call that came in either my partner or I had to take and clarify and bring people in, let them view the merchandise, take them to the Water Department, to the basement or upstairs.

THE COURT: In other words, you were constantly dealing with his merchandise?

THE WITNESS: Yes, sir, we were, seven to ten days after the search.

THE COURT: When the file was taken from your office, was it taken from you, personally?

THE WITNESS: I brought it down to the Chief's office.

THE COURT: He told you to bring it down?

THE WITNESS: Yes, sir.

THE COURT: Did you advise him a return had not been made yet?

THE WITNESS: No, sir, I did not, your Honor.

* * * Counsel for the government in its appeal argues that the inventory was complete, that the fact that it was not properly signed or filed did not prejudice defendant's interest in any way, that under federal law the return of the inventory provisions would be directory only and prejudice would have to be shown before suppression could be regarded as an appropriate remedy. The government, of course, argues that federal law controls.

Appellee argues vigorously that the state has a right to establish a higher standard in enforcing search procedures than the federal one if it wishes to do so. * * * This appeal then appears to present three possible questions:

I   Under Ohio law does the failure of state officers, executing a valid state search warrant, to file a timely return and a properly verified inventory require suppression of the fruits of the search, where defendant suffers no prejudice from such failure and the omission was inadvertent?

II   In a federal prosecution, if the search had been conducted by federal officers, would the failure to file a timely return and verified inventory, as required by FED. R. CRIM. P. 41(d), be grounds for exclusion of the fruits of the search, where defendant suffers no prejudice and the omission was inadvertent?

III Assuming that the evidence in question would be suppressed in an Ohio prosecution, should the fruits of the state search nonetheless be admissible in a federal prosecution?

I

* * * While we find no Ohio Supreme Court case dealing with our present issues, there is a recent (as yet unpublished) decision of the Court of Appeals of Franklin County, Ohio, *Ohio v. Moretti*, Nos. 73AP-440, 441, 442 (Ct. App. of Franklin County, Ohio, Apr. 9, 1974), *cert. denied*, 420 U.S. 928 (1975), which holds that suppression of evidence is not called for where an officer failed to file an inventory. The carefully reasoned opinion of Judge Whiteside, citing previous unpublished Ohio Court of Appeals decisions, held:

> Thus, the question is whether a failure of a police officer to file the inventory will vitiate an otherwise lawful search and seizure pursuant to a search warrant. There is no statutory, or constitutional, exclusionary rule requiring exclusion of evidence lawfully seized pursuant to a search warrant because of the failure of a police officer to file an inventory thereof. Nor do we think that such an exclusionary rule should be judicially imposed. To impose such an exclusionary rule would be an unwarranted extension of the exclusionary rule imposed for violations of the constitutional prohibition against unlawful searches and seizures.

> In this instance, there is a lawful search and seizure, but the complaint is that there was a failure to comply with a subsequent related requirement which does not constitute part of the search and seizure but is to be performed only once the search and seizure is completed. We do not condone the failure of the police officer to perform his statutory duty. However, there is no reason to penalize the public because of the failure of a police officer to perform this type of duty. There is no prejudice to the defendant that is inherent in the failure of the officer to file an inventory. Unlike the case of an unlawful search and seizure in violation of constitutional safeguards, the failure of an officer to file an inventory does not violate any fundamental rights of the defendants.

> The failure of the officer to file an inventory may give rise to problems concerning admissibility of evidence if a question arises as to the identity of the property seized pursuant to a search warrant, but a per se exclusionary rule is neither required nor warranted. The purpose of the per se exclusionary rule imposed, with respect to illegally obtained evidence, is to discourage the obtaining of evidence by unlawful means. The old rule permitting illegally obtained evidence to be used against a defendant at trial

has been described as placing "a judicial stamp of approval on the use of unlawful means to justify an end result."

Here, there is no unlawfully obtained evidence. The evidence was lawfully obtained, and the question is whether the state should be denied the use of such lawfully obtained evidence because of the failure of a police officer to comply with a statutory requirement in connection with the identification and preservation of such lawfully obtained evidence. No reason for imposing such a per se exclusionary rule has been advanced. Most of the cases refuse to do so, and we do likewise.

II

The issue with which we are currently concerned has been answered in similar fashion by this court and other Courts of Appeals in the context of federally authorized searches and federal prosecutions. Clearly, failure to follow the requirements of Rule 41 of the Federal Rules of Criminal Procedure pertaining to inventory of objects seized and a prompt return to the court has been held not to require invalidation of an otherwise properly issued and executed search warrant or the suppression of evidence acquired under it. * * * [T]his [has] circuit said:

> * * * The failure of the officer to whom a search warrant is directed to make a return thereof cannot invalidate the search or seizure made by authority of such warrant. If the officer neglects to do this, he can be required to make return of the writ at any later time, or if the person whose premises were searched or whose property was seized is injured in any way by the failure to make this return, the officer failing to make such return is liable to him in damages. The making of the return is merely a ministerial act, to be performed after the warrant is executed. * * *

III

This leads then directly to consideration of whether the fruits of the state search in this case should be admitted in a federal prosecution, even if the Ohio Supreme Court (which has not passed on the question) were to hold the evidence inadmissible under state law. * * *

[W]e hold that the failure to make a prompt return and to verify the inventory in this case have no relation at all to the command of the Fourth Amendment which bars unreasonable searches and seizures. Both of these failures to comply with Ohio's Rule 41 pertain to requirements of that rule which came into play after the search and seizure was completed. The requirement of verification of the inventory of items seized is doubtless designed to allow for proper identification of property taken by the police under the warrant and to protect the owner's rights therein. The requirement of prompt return serves, among other purposes, to make sure that the warrant and its affidavit are available to counsel for inspection in preparation for trial.

We note, as appellee urges us to, that the language of Ohio's Rule 41 (like that of the federal counterpart) is mandatory. And we entertain no doubt that it was meant to be followed. There are, however, many possible methods of vindicating the inventory and return sections of the rule other than suppression of the lawfully seized evidence. Possible remedies might include a judicial writ to compel performance of the neglected acts. Additionally, a trial court might grant an adjournment to counsel who, because of delay in filing the return, had been deprived of opportunity to inspect the affidavit and search warrant. And if there were a dispute over whether an item tendered as evidence had actually been seized on the premises concerned as authorized by the warrant, failure to verify the inventory might justify the trial court in indulging a presumption unfavorable to the government. We do not need to decide these matters or to carry this speculation further, for no contentions of prejudice to appellee are presented by this record.

We hold that nonconstitutional, nonprejudicial and inadvertent failures to follow the post-search and seizure requirements of Ohio's rule which are involved here do not require application of the federal exclusionary rule.

The order of the District Court suppressing evidence is vacated and the case is remanded for further proceedings.

QUESTIONS, COMMENTS, CONCERNS?

1. **Dudek and Avery.** Look again at the November 5, 2005 warrant. Notice on the second page the following sentence: "NOW, THEREFORE, in the name of the State of Wisconsin, you are commanded forthwith to search the said premises for said things, and if the same or any portion thereof are found, to bring the same, and the persons(s) in whose possession the same are found, and return this warrant within *forty-eight hours* of service, before the said Court, to be dealt with according to law." [Casefile Document 1, at 2 (emphasis added).] Now compare that to the "RETURN OF OFFICER" just a few pages later and pay special attention to the date: November 10, 2005. Does *Dudek* provide an unexplored remedy for Avery?

2. **Comparing the warrant to the return.** Now, compare the list in the November 10 return to the list of items requested by the November 5 warrant. It looks at several points as though officers exceeded the scope of the November 5 warrant and seized things outside of what the warrant requested. Is that a ministerial issue only or, rather, could Avery rely on that disconnect to demonstrate the type of prejudice seemingly contemplated by *Dudek*?

3. **The rest of the Avery story.** Avery was convicted following a jury trial of the first-degree intentional homicide of Teresa Halbach. He was

sentenced to life in prison without the possibility of parole. The Court of Appeals of Wisconsin relied in part on *Sveum* and affirmed the Circuit Court's denial of Avery's motion to suppress. *State v. Avery*, 804 N.W.2d 216 (Wis. Ct. App. 2011). Avery remains in prison, although he has retained new counsel who is actively pursuing various grounds for a new trial.

CHAPTER 6

SEARCH WARRANT "EXCEPTIONS" & WHEN SEARCH WARRANTS ARE NOT REQUIRED

■ ■ ■

I. INTRODUCTION[1]

As we have discussed in some depth, there is ongoing debate over whether the Fourth Amendment prohibits warrantless searches and seizures absent certain exceptions or, instead, whether the Fourth Amendment imposes no warrant requirement so long as law enforcement's conduct is "reasonable." Regardless of how that debate is resolved, if it ever is, we can say with overwhelming confidence that the Supreme Court does not require officers to obtain warrants for *every* investigative action.

Over the past several decades, the Court has permitted a broad array of warrantless law enforcement activity. This chapter highlights the seven most prominent examples—often referred to as "exceptions" to the warrant requirement. They are, in order of presentation, as follows:

1. Exigent circumstances
2. Searches incident to arrest
3. Consent
4. Automobile exception
5. Plain sense seizures
6. Inventory searches
7. Special needs, emergency, and administrative searches

Consider organizing the law governing each "exception" by answering the following five questions:

1. What is the general rule?
2. What are the specific justification requirements?
3. What are the scope requirements?

---

[1] Remember that you have access to the all of the filings relevant to this chapter in your online repository. Keep in mind there are several casefiles associated with this chapter.

4.   What are the timing requirements?

5.   What is the general rationale?

Before we go further, let's cover some background on each question, other than the first.

Justification. The crux of this question is what standard governs the police behavior at issue. Stated differently, we're typically trying to identify the quantum of suspicion, if any, that officers must have in order to engage in the challenged warrantless conduct. In some cases, officers might need probable cause, whereas in others they might need only reasonable suspicion. There are other cases where officers need no suspicion whatsoever to conduct a warrantless search.

Scope. This core inquiry here is how far each exception extends. Sometimes, scope can be limited temporally (e.g., consent searches). It can also be limited spatially (e.g., automobile exception searches). Broadly speaking, scope issues break down into four categories: persons, areas, vehicles, and containers. For example, if an officer is searching a person, can the officer reach inside that person's pockets? What about if the person is wearing a backpack; can the officer open and search it? And the question on *everyone's* mind—what about searching cell phones? Can an officer warrantless search a phone found on an arrestee?

Timing. The timing question is perhaps the easiest to conceptualize. We're simply asking when the warrantless search may/must occur. Simple, however, is not always easy. It's simple, yes, to understand that timing concerns arise in the context of warrantless investigative actions, but the Supreme Court seemingly never explains, with precision, how long an officer has to perform the warrantless act.

Simple fact patterns can therefore get complicated quickly. Consider a straightforward consent scenario: an officer knocks on the door of a single family home. The homeowner answers. The officer asks the homeowner for consent to search the home, and the homeowner replies, "Sure." The officer then leaves after receiving an urgent radio call and returns thirty minutes later. Is the homeowner's consent still valid? Again, in the context of timing, simple is not necessarily easy.

General rationale. Here we ask "why" the Court permits officers to conduct the challenged investigative activity without a warrant. Perhaps there is a concern that, if officers took the time to obtain a warrant, the officers or others could be harmed. Maybe there is concern that evidence could be damaged or destroyed, /or that the target of the search itself could get away. Regardless of the particular concern, the Court's underlying rationale for permitting the challenged investigative action often informs the required justification, underlying scope, and permissible timing. Thus, this question is the "glue" that helps us understand the other questions.

II. EXIGENT CIRCUMSTANCES

A. INTRODUCTION

"Exigent circumstances" is the most pervasive exception to the warrant requirement. Given the frequency with which the terms are used, though, it can be easy to get caught up using them without considering their meaning. Broadly speaking, exigent circumstances conveys an emergency situation. The idea is that, due to the situation, law enforcement does not have time to obtain a warrant and therefore must conduct the challenged activity without one.

Because the concept of exigent circumstances is, by definition, broad, the legal issue in many cases often focuses on whether the factual circumstances presented should be categorized as an exigency that justifies warrantless action. As a result, it is important to know what factual circumstances qualify as accepted exigencies. The Supreme Court's decision in *Minnesota v. Olson*, 495 U.S. 91 (1990), is instructive on that question.

In *Olson*, police suspected that Joseph Ecker had just robbed a gas station and fatally shot the station's manager in the process. Further suspecting that he had a partner, the police drove to Ecker's home where they were met at the same time by an Oldsmobile vehicle. Upon seeing the police, the Oldsmobile's driver, Ecker, took "evasive action," but spun the vehicle out of control. Ecker and another person exited the vehicle and began to flee on foot. Police captured Ecker, but his passenger got escaped.

The next morning, police received a call from an informant who told them that the passenger, Robert Olson, was hiding at a particular address with two women. Police dispatched several officers who surrounded the home. Then, "[w]ithout seeking permission and with weapons drawn, the police entered the upper unit and found respondent hiding in a closet." Olson shortly thereafter made an inculpatory statement.

Olson filed a motion to suppress his statement, which the trial court denied. The Supreme Court of Minnesota reversed, holding that no exigent circumstances existed to justify the officers' entry. The suspect was, after all, surrounded and would have been apprehended had he attempted to flee. The Supreme Court affirmed, noting that it was "not inclined to disagree with [the Minnesota Supreme Court's] fact-specific application of the proper legal standard." Importantly, for our purposes, the Court approved of the Minnesota Supreme Court's definition of exigent circumstances:

> The Minnesota Supreme Court applied essentially the correct standard in determining whether exigent circumstances existed. The court observed that "a warrantless intrusion may be justified

by hot pursuit of a fleeing felon, or imminent destruction of evidence, or the need to prevent a suspect's escape, or the risk of danger to the police or to other persons inside or outside the dwelling." The court also apparently thought that in the absence of hot pursuit there must be at least probable cause to believe that one or more of the other factors justifying the entry were present and that in assessing the risk of danger, the gravity of the crime and likelihood that the suspect is armed should be considered.

Note the Court's use of "probable cause" in that last sentence. The Court is telling us that, in order for exigent circumstances to apply, police must possess probable cause to believe that one of the listed circumstances is present. Accordingly, regardless of whether a warrant is required, probable cause is *always* required for application of an exigency—no matter the category of exigency.

B. MEET O.J. SIMPSON

On June 15, 1995, jurors sat and watched as former NFL football player and movie star O.J. Simpson attempted to fit his hands into a pair of cashmere-lined leather gloves. To the dismay of prosecutors, the gloves did not fit. The moment handed Simpson's defense attorneys Johnnie Cochran and Robert Shapiro perhaps one of the most well-known defense theories in history: "If it doesn't fit, you must acquit." And the jury did acquit. On October 3, 1995, an estimated 100 million people nationwide tuned in to watch the dramatic "not guilty" ending to the trial of the century.

A Primer on O.J. Simpson

    Orenthal James "O.J." Simpson, nicknamed "The Juice," was born on
July 9, 1947, in San Francisco, California. Growing up, Simpson lived with
his mother, Eunice Simpson, and father, Jimmy Lee Simpson, in the
housing projects of the Potrero Hill neighborhood. Simpson grew up
resenting his father who, as a well-known "drag queen" in the San
Francisco Bay area, had little time to spare for O.J. By his early teenage
years, Simpson began to slack off in school, focusing instead on his
membership in a street gang known as the Persian Warriors. According to
Simpson's childhood sweetheart and future first wife, Marguerite L.
Whitley, Simpson was "really an awful person then." But after a third

arrest and a meeting with hall of fame baseball player Willie Mays, Simpson turned his attention to high school sports rather than street life.

Simpson attended Galileo High School in San Francisco where he played football for the Galileo Lions. Although Simpson was an All-City football player at Galileo, his less than mediocre grades kept him from attracting the attention of college recruiters. As such, Simpson enrolled at City College of San Francisco in 1965, where he played as both running back and defensive back and was named to the Junior College All-American Team. His efforts earned him a full scholarship to play football at the University of Southern California. In 1968, during his senior year, Simpson rushed for 1,709 yards and 22 touchdowns, and won the Heisman Trophy by the largest margin of victory in history.

By 1969, Simpson was well on his way to becoming a household name. Drafted by the Buffalo Bills the first round of the 1969 NFL Draft, Simpson would go on to earn a record-breaking 11,236 yards and 75 touchdowns throughout his pro career. He would also establish himself in the film and television industry, starring in six major motion pictures before retiring from the NFL in 1979. After retiring, Simpson grew his fame further by becoming a commentator for Monday Night Football and The NFL on NBC.

In 1977, Simpson met his second wife: eighteen-year-old Nicole Brown, a waitress at a private night club called "The Daisy." Although Simpson was still married to his first wife Marguerite, Simpson and Brown began dating. The two married in 1985, roughly five years after Simpson's divorce from Marguerite and his retirement from football. The marriage between Brown and Simpson lasted nearly seven years, during which time Simpson pleaded no contest to spousal abuse in 1989. Brown filed for divorce on February 25, 1992, citing irreconcilable differences.

The Crime

From 1992 to 1994, Brown and Simpson would frequent an upscale Italian restaurant, known as the Mezzaluna Trattoria, in Brentwood, California. Among the staff at the Mezzaluna was a waiter and aspiring restaurateur named Ronald Goldman. In May 1994, Brown and Goldman struck up a relationship that would blossom into a close friendship over the next six weeks. Friends of Brown and Goldman maintained that the relationship was always platonic.

On June 13, 1994, at approximately 12:10 a.m., Nicole Brown and Ronald Goldman were found stabbed to death on the front walkway of Brown's residence. Once Los Angeles Detectives arrived on scene, they observed bloody footprints and found a blue knit hat and a left-handed brown leather glove with blood stains near the foot of Goldman's body. As detectives surveyed the interior of the home, they discovered Brown's and Simpson's two young children hiding inside.

Detectives next drove to Simpson's home at 360 N. Rockingham Place, which was approximately two miles from Brown's home. Simpson's home was fully enclosed by walls and fences, and visitors could enter only through two electronically controlled gates. Detectives made numerous attempts to contact someone inside the home, but were unsuccessful. Detective Mark Fuhrman decided to climb an exterior wall and manually open the electronic gates after police found blood on the door of a white Ford Bronco parked just outside Simpson's home.

Inside the compound, detectives discovered that the rear of the property contained a single-story guest house where Simpson's friend, Brian Kaelin, was living. Kaelin told police that a couple days ago, at roughly 10:45 p.m. on June 11, he heard a loud disturbance that he believed was caused by a regular California earthquake. Detective Fuhrman elected to investigate the area where Kaelin said the sounds had originated. Detective Fuhrman proceeded to the exterior of the guest house and discovered a blood stained brown leather glove that appeared to be the right-handed match to the glove found at the murder scene. Later DNA testing would reveal that the glove contained genetic markers of Nicole Brown, Ron Goldman, and O.J. Simpson.

On June 17, 1994, after failing to turn himself over to police, Simpson engaged police in a low speed pursuit in a white 1993 Ford Bronco (different from the one found at Simpson's home, which was impounded prior to the chase). TV stations interrupted coverage of the 1994 NBA Finals to broadcast the incident live, with an estimated 95 million people tuned in to watch the chase and Simpson's ultimate arrest. The chase kicked off what became known as the "trial of the century."

The Suppression Motion

Although the infamous bloody glove would give Simpson's "dream team" defense counsel a mantra that helped win the case, Simpson's lawyers originally sought to prevent the prosecution from using the right-handed glove entirely. On June 29, 1994, Simpson filed a motion to suppress virtually all of the evidence uncovered as a result of the search outside his home on the morning of June 13. Simpson argued that he manifested a reasonable expectation of privacy in his property by surrounding it with a fence and locked gates. Moreover, he contended that detectives had no evidence of any threat to life, health, or property to justify a warrantless entry onto his property. The State of California, in response, highlighted two facts: the presence of blood on the Ford Bronco and Simpson's unaccompanied children at the murder scene. Based on those two facts, the prosecution argued that "it would be difficult to imagine a greater dereliction of duty had the officers . . . failed to further their investigation . . . by climbing over the wall."

On July 8, 1994, Judge Kathleen Kennedy-Powell heard arguments on Simpson's motion to suppress. After several hours, Judge Kennedy-Powell commended both the prosecution and the defense, saying that both gave "an excellent presentation," and acknowledged that "there is no set formula to establish when an exigent circumstance does exist and when it doesn't." Judge Kennedy-Powell nonetheless denied Simpson's motion. She reasoned that the detectives were not interested in searching the premises, but rather were focused on the prospect of further injury or death were they to delay entry to the property by obtaining a search warrant.

C. THE CASES

KENTUCKY V. KING

563 U.S. 452
Supreme Court of the United States
January 12, 2011, Argued; May 16, 2011, Decided
No. 09-1272

JUSTICE ALITO delivered the opinion of the Court.

It is well established that "exigent circumstances," including the need to prevent the destruction of evidence, permit police officers to conduct an otherwise permissible search without first obtaining a warrant. In this case, we consider whether this rule applies when police, by knocking on the door of a residence and announcing their presence, cause the occupants to attempt to destroy evidence. The Kentucky Supreme Court held that the exigent circumstances rule does not apply in the case at hand because the police should have foreseen that their conduct would prompt the occupants to attempt to destroy evidence. We reject this interpretation of the exigent circumstances rule. The conduct of the police prior to their entry into the apartment was entirely lawful. They did not violate the Fourth Amendment or threaten to do so. In such a situation, the exigent circumstances rule applies.

I

A

This case concerns the search of an apartment in Lexington, Kentucky. Police officers set up a controlled buy of crack cocaine outside an apartment complex. Undercover Officer Gibbons watched the deal take place from an unmarked car in a nearby parking lot. After the deal occurred, Gibbons radioed uniformed officers to move in on the suspect. He told the officers that the suspect was moving quickly toward the breezeway of an apartment building, and he urged them to "hurry up and get there" before the suspect entered an apartment.

In response to the radio alert, the uniformed officers drove into the nearby parking lot, left their vehicles, and ran to the breezeway. Just as they entered the breezeway, they heard a door shut and detected a very strong odor of burnt marijuana. At the end of the breezeway, the officers saw two apartments, one on the left and one on the right, and they did not know which apartment the suspect had entered. Gibbons had radioed that the suspect was running into the apartment on the right, but the officers did not hear this statement because they had already left their vehicles. Because they smelled marijuana smoke emanating from the apartment on the left, they approached the door of that apartment.

Officer Steven Cobb, one of the uniformed officers who approached the door, testified that the officers banged on the left apartment door "as loud as [they] could" and announced, " 'This is the police' " or " 'Police, police, police.' " Cobb said that "[a]s soon as [the officers] started banging on the door," they "could hear people inside moving," and "[i]t sounded as [though] things were being moved inside the apartment." These noises, Cobb testified, led the officers to believe that drug-related evidence was about to be destroyed.

At that point, the officers announced that they "were going to make entry inside the apartment." Cobb then kicked in the door, the officers entered the apartment, and they found three people in the front room: respondent Hollis King, respondent's girlfriend, and a guest who was smoking marijuana.[1] The officers performed a protective sweep of the apartment during which they saw marijuana and powder cocaine in plain view. In a subsequent search, they also discovered crack cocaine, cash, and drug paraphernalia.

Police eventually entered the apartment on the right. Inside, they found the suspected drug dealer who was the initial target of their investigation.

B

In the Fayette County Circuit Court, a grand jury charged respondent with trafficking in marijuana, first-degree trafficking in a controlled substance, and second-degree persistent felony offender status. Respondent filed a motion to suppress the evidence from the warrantless search, but the Circuit Court denied the motion. The Circuit Court concluded that the officers had probable cause to investigate the marijuana odor * * * Respondent then entered a conditional guilty plea, reserving his right to appeal the denial of his suppression motion. The court sentenced respondent to 11 years' imprisonment.

The Kentucky Court of Appeals affirmed. * * * The Supreme Court of Kentucky reversed. * * *

---

[1] Respondent's girlfriend leased the apartment, but respondent stayed there part of the time, and his child lived there. Based on these facts, Kentucky conceded in state court that respondent has Fourth Amendment standing to challenge the search.

To determine whether police impermissibly created the exigency, the Supreme Court of Kentucky announced a two-part test. First, the court held, police cannot "deliberately creat[e] the exigent circumstances with the bad faith intent to avoid the warrant requirement." Second, even absent bad faith, the court concluded, police may not rely on exigent circumstances if "it was reasonably foreseeable that the investigative tactics employed by the police would create the exigent circumstances." Although the court found no evidence of bad faith, it held that exigent circumstances could not justify the search because it was reasonably foreseeable that the occupants would destroy evidence when the police knocked on the door and announced their presence.

We granted certiorari.

II

A

The text of the [Fourth] Amendment * * * expressly imposes two requirements. First, all searches and seizures must be reasonable. Second, a warrant may not be issued unless probable cause is properly established and the scope of the authorized search is set out with particularity.

Although the text of the Fourth Amendment does not specify when a search warrant must be obtained, this Court has inferred that a warrant must generally be secured. "It is a 'basic principle of Fourth Amendment law,'" we have often said, "'that searches and seizures inside a home without a warrant are presumptively unreasonable.' But we have also recognized that this presumption may be overcome in some circumstances because "the ultimate touchstone of the Fourth Amendment is 'reasonableness.' Accordingly, the warrant requirement is subject to certain reasonable exceptions.

One well-recognized exception applies when "'the exigencies of the situation' make the needs of law enforcement so compelling that [a] warrantless search is objectively reasonable under the Fourth Amendment."

This Court has identified several exigencies that may justify a warrantless search of a home. Under the "emergency aid" exception, for example, "officers may enter a home without a warrant to render emergency assistance to an injured occupant or to protect an occupant from imminent injury." Police officers may enter premises without a warrant when they are in hot pursuit of a fleeing suspect. And—what is relevant here—the need "to prevent the imminent destruction of evidence" has long been recognized as a sufficient justification for a warrantless search.[3]

---

[3] Preventing the destruction of evidence may also justify dispensing with Fourth Amendment requirements in other contexts. *See, e.g., Richards v. Wisconsin*, 520 U.S. 385, 395–396 (1997) (failure to comply with the knock-and-announce requirement was justified because "the

B

Over the years, lower courts have developed an exception to the exigent circumstances rule, the so-called "police-created exigency" doctrine. Under this doctrine, police may not rely on the need to prevent destruction of evidence when that exigency was "created" or "manufactured" by the conduct of the police.

In applying this exception for the "creation" or "manufacturing" of an exigency by the police, courts require something more than mere proof that fear of detection by the police caused the destruction of evidence. An additional showing is obviously needed because, as the Eighth Circuit has recognized, "in some sense the police always create the exigent circumstances." That is to say, in the vast majority of cases in which evidence is destroyed by persons who are engaged in illegal conduct, the reason for the destruction is fear that the evidence will fall into the hands of law enforcement. Destruction of evidence issues probably occur most frequently in drug cases because drugs may be easily destroyed by flushing them down a toilet or rinsing them down a drain. Persons in possession of valuable drugs are unlikely to destroy them unless they fear discovery by the police. Consequently, a rule that precludes the police from making a warrantless entry to prevent the destruction of evidence whenever their conduct causes the exigency would unreasonably shrink the reach of this well-established exception to the warrant requirement.

Presumably for the purpose of avoiding such a result, the lower courts have held that the police-created exigency doctrine requires more than simple causation, but the lower courts have not agreed on the test to be applied. * * *

III

A

Despite the welter of tests devised by the lower courts, the answer to the question presented in this case follows directly and clearly from the principle that permits warrantless searches in the first place. As previously noted, warrantless searches are allowed when the circumstances make it reasonable, within the meaning of the Fourth Amendment, to dispense with the warrant requirement. Therefore, the answer to the question before us is that the exigent circumstances rule justifies a warrantless search when the conduct of the police preceding the exigency is reasonable in the same sense. Where, as here, the police did not create the exigency by engaging or threatening to engage in conduct that violates the Fourth

---

circumstances . . . show[ed] that the officers had a reasonable suspicion that [a suspect] might destroy evidence if given further opportunity to do so"); *Schmerber v. California*, 384 U.S. 757, 770–771 (1966) (warrantless testing for blood-alcohol content was justified based on potential destruction of evidence) * * *.

Amendment, warrantless entry to prevent the destruction of evidence is reasonable and thus allowed.[4] * * *

B

Some lower courts have adopted a rule that is similar to the one that we recognize today. But others, including the Kentucky Supreme Court, have imposed additional requirements that are unsound and that we now reject.

Bad faith. Some courts, including the Kentucky Supreme Court, ask whether law enforcement officers 'deliberately created the exigent circumstances with the bad faith intent to avoid the warrant requirement.'

This approach is fundamentally inconsistent with our Fourth Amendment jurisprudence. "Our cases have repeatedly rejected" a subjective approach, asking only whether "the circumstances, viewed objectively, justify the action." Indeed, we have never held, outside limited contexts such as an "inventory search or administrative inspection . . . , that an officer's motive invalidates objectively justifiable behavior under the Fourth Amendment."

The reasons for looking to objective factors, rather than subjective intent, are clear. Legal tests based on reasonableness are generally objective, and this Court has long taken the view that "evenhanded law enforcement is best achieved by the application of objective standards of conduct, rather than standards that depend upon the subjective state of mind of the officer."

Reasonable foreseeability. Some courts, again including the Kentucky Supreme Court, hold that police may not rely on an exigency if 'it was reasonably foreseeable that the investigative tactics employed by the police would create the exigent circumstances.' Courts applying this test have invalidated warrantless home searches on the ground that it was reasonably foreseeable that police officers, by knocking on the door and announcing their presence, would lead a drug suspect to destroy evidence.

Contrary to this reasoning, however, we have rejected the notion that police may seize evidence without a warrant only when they come across the evidence by happenstance. * * *

Adoption of a reasonable foreseeability test would also introduce an unacceptable degree of unpredictability. For example, whenever law enforcement officers knock on the door of premises occupied by a person who may be involved in the drug trade, there is some possibility that the

---

[4]   There is a strong argument to be made that, at least in most circumstances, the exigent circumstances rule should not apply where the police, without a warrant or any legally sound basis for a warrantless entry, threaten that they will enter without permission unless admitted. In this case, however, no such actual threat was made, and therefore we have no need to reach that question.

occupants may possess drugs and may seek to destroy them. Under a reasonable foreseeability test, it would be necessary to quantify the degree of predictability that must be reached before the police-created exigency doctrine comes into play. * * *

Probable cause and time to secure a warrant. Some courts, in applying the police-created exigency doctrine, fault law enforcement officers if, after acquiring evidence that is sufficient to establish probable cause to search particular premises, the officers do not seek a warrant but instead knock on the door and seek either to speak with an occupant or to obtain consent to search.

This approach unjustifiably interferes with legitimate law enforcement strategies. There are many entirely proper reasons why police may not want to seek a search warrant as soon as the bare minimum of evidence needed to establish probable cause is acquired. Without attempting to provide a comprehensive list of these reasons, we note a few.

First, the police may wish to speak with the occupants of a dwelling before deciding whether it is worthwhile to seek authorization for a search. They may think that a short and simple conversation may obviate the need to apply for and execute a warrant. Second, the police may want to ask an occupant of the premises for consent to search because doing so is simpler, faster, and less burdensome than applying for a warrant. A consensual search also "may result in considerably less inconvenience" and embarrassment to the occupants than a search conducted pursuant to a warrant. Third, law enforcement officers may wish to obtain more evidence before submitting what might otherwise be considered a marginal warrant application. Fourth, prosecutors may wish to wait until they acquire evidence that can justify a search that is broader in scope than the search that a judicial officer is likely to authorize based on the evidence then available. And finally, in many cases, law enforcement may not want to execute a search that will disclose the existence of an investigation because doing so may interfere with the acquisition of additional evidence against those already under suspicion or evidence about additional but as yet unknown participants in a criminal scheme.

We have said that "[l]aw enforcement officers are under no constitutional duty to call a halt to criminal investigation the moment they have the minimum evidence to establish probable cause." Faulting the police for failing to apply for a search warrant at the earliest possible time after obtaining probable cause imposes a duty that is nowhere to be found in the Constitution.

Standard or good investigative tactics. Finally, some lower court cases suggest that law enforcement officers may be found to have created or manufactured an exigency if the court concludes that the course of their investigation was "contrary to standard or good law enforcement practices (or to the policies or practices of their jurisdictions)." This approach fails to provide clear guidance for law enforcement officers and authorizes courts to make judgments on matters that are the province of those who are responsible for federal and state law enforcement agencies.

C

Respondent argues for a rule that differs from those discussed above, but his rule is also flawed. Respondent contends that law enforcement officers impermissibly create an exigency when they "engage in conduct that would cause a reasonable person to believe that entry is imminent and inevitable." In respondent's view, relevant factors include the officers' tone of voice in announcing their presence and the forcefulness of their knocks. But the ability of law enforcement officers to respond to an exigency cannot turn on such subtleties.

Police officers may have a very good reason to announce their presence loudly and to knock on the door with some force. A forceful knock may be necessary to alert the occupants that someone is at the door. Furthermore, unless police officers identify themselves loudly enough, occupants may not know who is at their doorstep. Officers are permitted—indeed, encouraged—to identify themselves to citizens, and "in many circumstances this is cause for assurance, not discomfort." Citizens who are startled by an unexpected knock on the door or by the sight of unknown persons in plain clothes on their doorstep may be relieved to learn that these persons are police officers. Others may appreciate the opportunity to make an informed decision about whether to answer the door to the police.

If respondent's test were adopted, it would be extremely difficult for police officers to know how loudly they may announce their presence or how forcefully they may knock on a door without running afoul of the police-created exigency rule. And in most cases, it would be nearly impossible for a court to determine whether that threshold had been passed. The Fourth Amendment does not require the nebulous and impractical test that respondent proposes.

D

For these reasons, we conclude that the exigent circumstances rule applies when the police do not gain entry to premises by means of an actual or threatened violation of the Fourth Amendment. This holding provides ample protection for the privacy rights that the Amendment protects.

When law enforcement officers who are not armed with a warrant knock on a door, they do no more than any private citizen might do. And whether the person who knocks on the door and requests the opportunity to speak is a police officer or a private citizen, the occupant has no obligation to open the door or to speak. And even if an occupant chooses to open the door and speak with the officers, the occupant need not allow the officers to enter the premises and may refuse to answer any questions at any time.

Occupants who choose not to stand on their constitutional rights but instead elect to attempt to destroy evidence have only themselves to blame for the warrantless exigent-circumstances search that may ensue.

IV

We now apply our interpretation of the police-created exigency doctrine to the facts of this case. * * *

We * * * assume for purposes of argument that an exigency existed. We decide only the question on which the Kentucky Supreme Court ruled and on which we granted certiorari: Under what circumstances do police impermissibly create an exigency? * * *

In this case, we see no evidence that the officers either violated the Fourth Amendment or threatened to do so prior to the point when they entered the apartment. Officer Cobb testified without contradiction that the officers "banged on the door as loud as [they] could" and announced either " 'Police, police, police' " or " 'This is the police.' " This conduct was entirely consistent with the Fourth Amendment, and we are aware of no other evidence that might show that the officers either violated the Fourth Amendment or threatened to do so (for example, by announcing that they would break down the door if the occupants did not open the door voluntarily).

Respondent argues that the officers "demanded" entry to the apartment, but he has not pointed to any evidence in the record that supports this assertion. He relies on a passing statement made by the trial court in its opinion denying respondent's motion to suppress. In recounting the events that preceded the search, the judge wrote that the officers "banged on the door of the apartment on the back left of the breezeway identifying themselves as police officers and demanding that the door be opened by the persons inside." However, at a later point in this opinion, the judge stated that the officers "initially knock[ed] on the door of the apartment unit and await[ed] the response or consensual entry." This later statement is consistent with the testimony at the suppression hearing and with the findings of the state appellate courts. There is no evidence of a "demand" of any sort, much less a demand that amounts to a threat to violate the Fourth Amendment. If there is contradictory evidence that has not been brought to our attention, the state court may elect to address that matter on remand.

Finally, respondent claims that the officers "explained to [the occupants that the officers] were going to make entry inside the apartment," but the record is clear that the officers did not make this statement until after the exigency arose. As Officer Cobb testified, the officers "knew that there was possibly something that was going to be destroyed inside the apartment," and "*[a]t that point,* . . . [they] explained . . . [that they]* were going to make entry." Given that this announcement was made after the exigency arose, it could not have created the exigency.

* * *

* * * The judgment of the Kentucky Supreme Court is reversed, and the case is remanded for further proceedings not inconsistent with this opinion.

It is so ordered.

JUSTICE GINSBURG, dissenting.

[Omitted.]

QUESTIONS, COMMENTS, CONCERNS?

1.   **A "police created" exigency.** In footnote four, the *King* Court says, "There is a strong argument to be made that, at least in most circumstances, the exigent circumstances rule should not apply where the police, without a warrant or any legally sound basis for a warrantless entry, threaten that they will enter without permission unless admitted." What does that look like exactly? Are we to assume that when the police approach a residence and yell "police, police" they are not implicitly threatening to enter without permission? After all, most would assume that, if the police are knocking on their door, that is the functional equivalent of a demand to enter. Even if you disagree, does the analysis after the Court's comment now turn on whether police say while knocking "it's the police" as opposed to "open up, it's the police"? The former appears appropriate whereas the later may constitute the type of threat the Court is concerned about.

In her dissenting opinion omitted above, Justice Ginsburg wrote that any exigency "must exist, I would rule, when the police come on the scene, not subsequent to their arrival, prompted by their own conduct." *Kentucky v. King,* 563 U.S. 452, 473 (2011) (Ginsburg, J., dissenting). Would her approach eliminate this note's concern?

2.   **Exigencies and warrant execution.** In *Richards v. Wisconsin,* 520 U.S. 385 (1997), officers secured a standard search warrant—as opposed to a "no-knock" warrant—for Richards' hotel room. The warrant obligated officers to knock and announce their presence before entering the room. On their arrival, an officer dressed as a hotel maintenance man knocked on Richards' door. Richards answered, but noticed other officers standing behind the "maintenance man." He therefore slammed the door, and officers forcibly entered the room, where they found cash and cocaine. Richards moved to suppress the evidence, but the state courts rejected his motion on the grounds that officers were justified in forcefully entering the room out of concern that Richards would "destroy evidence" or try to escape.

The Supreme Court agreed that it was appropriate for officers to dispense with the knock and announce requirement. It recognized that, "[i]n order to justify a 'no-knock' entry, the police must have a reasonable suspicion that knocking and announcing their presence, under the particular circumstances, would be dangerous or futile, or that it would inhibit the effective investigation of the crime by, for example, allowing the destruction of evidence." Applying that standard, the Court had no trouble concluding that officers had reasonable suspicion to dispense with the knock-and-announce requirement. The Court reasoned that Richards reacted hastily after noticing the officers at his door and that the drugs were "easily disposable."

3.   No "murder scene" exigency. In *Mincey v. Arizona*, 437 U.S. 385 (1978), an undercover officer, Barry Headricks, got into a shootout with Rufus Mincey during a controlled drug buy gone wrong. After the shooting, which killed Headricks and wounded Mincey, officers entered Mincey's apartment, "thinking that other persons in the apartment might have been injured," and "looked about quickly for other victims." That entry matured into a four-day-long warrantless search of Mincey's apartment. Mincey moved to suppress evidence found during the search, but the motion was denied. The Arizona Supreme Court affirmed the denial of Mincey's motion, holding that a "warrantless search of the scene of a homicide—or of a serious personal injury with likelihood of death where there is reason to suspect foul play—does not violate the Fourth Amendment to the United States Constitution where the law enforcement officers were legally on the premises in the first instance." The Supreme Court, however, disagreed, holding that "the 'murder scene exception' created by the Arizona Supreme Court is inconsistent with the Fourth and Fourteenth Amendments—that the warrantless search of Mincey's apartment was not constitutionally permissible simply because a homicide had recently occurred there."

The Court reaffirmed *Mincey* years later in *Thompson v. Louisiana*, 469 U.S. 17 (1984). In *Thompson*, investigators performed a roughly two-hour warrantless search of a home where a recent murder had occurred. Following petitioner's indictment for murder, she moved to suppress incriminating items discovered during the search. The trial court granted in part and denied in part the motion. After the case made its way through the state appellate process, the Supreme Court, relying on *Mincey*, held that the search was unconstitutional. Quoting *Mincey*, the Court reasoned that, although officers may warrantlessly enter a premises if they "reasonably believe that a person is in need of immediate aid" or "if there are other victims or if a killer is still on the premises," a warrantless search of a home is inappropriate merely because a homicide recently occurred there.

4.   Gacy and exigent circumstances. Before we dive into O.J. Simpson's Casefile, return for a moment to the case of John Wayne Gacy from Chapter 4. Consider the facts of Gacy's case in light of *Olson*. By way of brief summary, remember that, on December 13, 1978, officers had information that Robert Piest, a fifteen-year-old boy, had disappeared two days earlier. They also suspected that Gacy was seen at the victim's place of employment,

Nissen's Pharmacy, around the time of Piest's disappearance. Moreover, police knew that Gacy's criminal history included a conviction and ten-year prison sentence for a sex crime involving victims who were roughly the same age as Piest. Could exigent circumstances justify a warrantless intrusion into Gacy's home on December 13? As you answer that question, consider whether the two-day interval between when officers approached Gacy (December 13) and when Piest disappeared (December 11) strengthens or weakens the state's case to enter Gacy's home based on exigent circumstances.

5.   Why did police _immediately_ think of Simpson? Notice that officers went to O.J. Simpson's home right after discovering the dead bodies of Nicole Simpson and Ronald Goldman. Why is that? The state contends that "[d]etectives followed up by going to Defendant's residence for the purposes of (i) death notification, (ii) placement of Defendant SIMPSON's two children who were now in police protective custody, and (iii) a concern for the welfare of the defendant and/or other individuals associated with the SIMPSONS." [Casefile Document 3, at 5.] But in another portion of its opposition to Simpson's motion to suppress, the state acknowledges that it knew at the time officers went to Simpson's home that he "had been embroiled in previous domestic violence situations, one of these resulting in the arrest of Defendant SIMPSON." _Id. Id._

Judge Kennedy-Powell would ultimately accept the state's rationale. She wrote:

> The person who is the next of kin to those children is the defendant. He's their father. He's the person that logically would be the one that would be called upon to take action, to take custody of those children. So I don't find anything improper—in terms of the police conduct— with the idea that they are going to go to the Simpson home.

[Casefile Document 4, at 2.] Maybe that logic is right. But if police think at the time they approached Simpson's home that he is already a suspect, are they creating an exigency in violation of _King_ in doing so? After all, remember that police upon arrival "attempted to contact the occupants of the residence by ringing the gate bell for approximately ten (10) minutes." [Casefile Document 3, at 18.]

6.   _Olson_ and Simpson. Reviewing the category of available exigencies from _Olson_, which one—exactly—does the prosecution contend applies? It seems hard to pin down. The state lists numerous possibilities throughout its opposition to Simpson's motion to suppress. At the outset, and as noted above, the state asserts that officers went to Simpson's home in part out of "a concern for the welfare of the defendant and/or other individuals associated with the SIMPSONS." [Casefile Document 3, at 5.] Later, the state adds that, upon arriving, officers rang the gate bell for roughly ten minutes and received no response. _Id._ at 18. Did police have probable cause to believe that _Olson_ exigency exists at that moment?

What about after observing blood on the 1994 Ford Bronco parked at the curb near Simpson's home? As you consider your answer, note that, in addition to seeing blood, officers looked through the truck's window and saw "a package with a label indicating a return address to O.J. Simpson Enterprises." *Id.* at 19. A subsequent registration check of the car also reflected that it was a rental. Based on this new information, do police have probable cause to believe an exigency exists now? If so, is it a different *Olson* exigency from the one that may have existed earlier—when no one responded to police ringing the gate bell? The state implicitly takes the position that multiple exigencies existed. It states, "Detective Fuhrman entered the property by climbing over the wall to determine *whether there were additional victims or hostages.*" *Id.* (emphasis added). Does the municipal court resolve, to your satisfaction, which exigency permitted Detective Fuhrman to climb over the gate and enter Simpson's property? [*See* Casefile Document 4, at 5.]

    7. Did police "search" the Bronco? Think about where the rental Bronco was parked (at the curb near Simpson's home). Was it constitutionally permissible for officers to approach the vehicle? If it was, could officers lawfully observe it and look inside? *Id.* at 3. If so, what doctrine made their doing so constitutional? And would your answer change if you knew that police used a flashlight to look inside the Bronco in order to see the return address on the package?

    Citing *Rakas v. Illinois* (Chapter 3), the state frames the issue, in part, by arguing that Simpson lacks standing to contest officers' "observations of the exterior of the 1994 Ford Bronco." [Casefile Document 3, at 3.] Is standing the right way to frame the issue? Or, instead, is the better argument that no Fourth Amendment "search" occurred when officers approached and looked inside the vehicle?

MISSOURI V. MCNEELY

569 U.S. 141
Supreme Court of the United States
January 9, 2013, Argued; April 17, 2013, Decided
No. 11-1425

JUSTICE SOTOMAYOR announced the judgment of the Court and delivered the opinion of the Court with respect to Parts I, II-A, II-B, and IV, and an opinion with respect to Parts II-C and III, in which JUSTICE SCALIA, JUSTICE GINSBURG, and JUSTICE KAGAN join.

    In *Schmerber v. California*, 384 U.S. 757 (1966), this Court upheld a warrantless blood test of an individual arrested for driving under the influence of alcohol because the officer "might reasonably have believed that he was confronted with an emergency, in which the delay necessary to obtain a warrant, under the circumstances, threatened the destruction of evidence." The question presented here is whether the natural metabolization of alcohol in the bloodstream presents a per se exigency that justifies an exception to the Fourth Amendment's warrant requirement for nonconsensual blood testing in all drunk-driving cases. * * *

I

While on highway patrol at approximately 2:08 a.m., a Missouri police officer stopped McNeely's truck after observing it exceed the posted speed limit and repeatedly cross the centerline. The officer noticed several signs that McNeely was intoxicated, including McNeely's bloodshot eyes, his slurred speech, and the smell of alcohol on his breath. McNeely acknowledged to the officer that he had consumed "a couple of beers" at a bar, and he appeared unsteady on his feet when he exited the truck. After McNeely performed poorly on a battery of field-sobriety tests and declined to use a portable breath-test device to measure his blood alcohol concentration (BAC), the officer placed him under arrest.

The officer began to transport McNeely to the station house. But when McNeely indicated that he would again refuse to provide a breath sample, the officer changed course and took McNeely to a nearby hospital for blood testing. The officer did not attempt to secure a warrant. Upon arrival at the hospital, the officer asked McNeely whether he would consent to a blood test. Reading from a standard implied consent form, the officer explained to McNeely that under state law refusal to submit voluntarily to the test would lead to the immediate revocation of his driver's license for one year and could be used against him in a future prosecution. McNeely nonetheless refused. The officer then directed a hospital lab technician to take a blood sample, and the sample was secured at approximately 2:35 a.m. Subsequent laboratory testing measured McNeely's BAC at 0.154 percent, which was well above the legal limit of 0.08 percent.

McNeely was charged with driving while intoxicated (DWI) * * *.[1] He moved to suppress the results of the blood test, arguing in relevant part that, under the circumstances, taking his blood for chemical testing without first obtaining a search warrant violated his rights under the Fourth Amendment. The trial court agreed. * * * On appeal, the Missouri Court of Appeals stated an intention to reverse but transferred the case directly to the Missouri Supreme Court.

The Missouri Supreme Court affirmed. * * * Finding that this was "unquestionably a routine DWI case" in which no factors other than the natural dissipation of blood-alcohol suggested that there was an emergency, the court held that the nonconsensual warrantless blood draw violated McNeely's Fourth Amendment right to be free from unreasonable searches of his person.

We granted certiorari to resolve a split of authority on the question whether the natural dissipation of alcohol in the bloodstream establishes a per se exigency that suffices on its own to justify an exception to the

---

[1]   As a result of his two prior drunk-driving convictions, McNeely was charged with a class D felony under Missouri law, which carries a maximum imprisonment term of four years.

warrant requirement for nonconsensual blood testing in drunk-driving investigations. * * *

II

A

* * * Our cases have held that a warrantless search of the person is reasonable only if it falls within a recognized exception. * * *

* * * "One well-recognized exception," and the one at issue in this case, "applies when the exigencies of the situation make the needs of law enforcement so compelling that a warrantless search is objectively reasonable under the Fourth Amendment." *Kentucky v. King*, 563 U.S. ___, ___, 131 S. Ct. 1849, 1856 (2011). A variety of circumstances may give rise to an exigency sufficient to justify a warrantless search, including law enforcement's need to provide emergency assistance to an occupant of a home, engage in "hot pursuit" of a fleeing suspect, or enter a burning building to put out a fire and investigate its cause. As is relevant here, we have also recognized that in some circumstances law enforcement officers may conduct a search without a warrant to prevent the imminent destruction of evidence. While these contexts do not necessarily involve equivalent dangers, in each a warrantless search is potentially reasonable because "there is compelling need for official action and no time to secure a warrant."

To determine whether a law enforcement officer faced an emergency that justified acting without a warrant, this Court looks to the totality of circumstances. We apply this "finely tuned approach" to Fourth Amendment reasonableness in this context because the police action at issue lacks "the traditional justification that . . . a warrant . . . provides." Absent that established justification, "the fact-specific nature of the reasonableness inquiry," demands that we evaluate each case of alleged exigency based "on its own facts and circumstances."[3] * * *

B

The State properly recognizes that the reasonableness of a warrantless search under the exigency exception to the warrant requirement must be evaluated based on the totality of the circumstances. But the State nevertheless seeks a per se rule for blood testing in drunk-driving cases. The State contends that whenever an officer has probable cause to believe an individual has been driving under the influence of alcohol, exigent circumstances will necessarily exist because BAC evidence is inherently evanescent. As a result, the State claims that so long as the officer has

---

[3] We have recognized a limited class of traditional exceptions to the warrant requirement that apply categorically and thus do not require an assessment of whether the policy justifications underlying the exception, which may include exigency-based considerations, are implicated in a particular case. By contrast, the general exigency exception, which asks whether an emergency existed that justified a warrantless search, naturally calls for a case-specific inquiry.

probable cause and the blood test is conducted in a reasonable manner, it is categorically reasonable for law enforcement to obtain the blood sample without a warrant.

It is true that as a result of the human body's natural metabolic processes, the alcohol level in a person's blood begins to dissipate once the alcohol is fully absorbed and continues to decline until the alcohol is eliminated. Testimony before the trial court in this case indicated that the percentage of alcohol in an individual's blood typically decreases by approximately 0.015 percent to 0.02 percent per hour once the alcohol has been fully absorbed. More precise calculations of the rate at which alcohol dissipates depend on various individual characteristics (such as weight, gender, and alcohol tolerance) and the circumstances in which the alcohol was consumed. Regardless of the exact elimination rate, it is sufficient for our purposes to note that because an individual's alcohol level gradually declines soon after he stops drinking, a significant delay in testing will negatively affect the probative value of the results. * * *

But it does not follow that we should depart from careful case-by-case assessment of exigency and adopt the categorical rule proposed by the State and its amici. In those drunk-driving investigations where police officers can reasonably obtain a warrant before a blood sample can be drawn without significantly undermining the efficacy of the search, the Fourth Amendment mandates that they do so. We do not doubt that some circumstances will make obtaining a warrant impractical such that the dissipation of alcohol from the bloodstream will support an exigency justifying a properly conducted warrantless blood test. That, however, is a reason to decide each case on its facts, * * * not to accept the "considerable overgeneralization" that a per se rule would reflect.

The context of blood testing is different in critical respects from other destruction-of-evidence cases in which the police are truly confronted with a " 'now or never' " situation. In contrast to, for example, circumstances in which the suspect has control over easily disposable evidence, BAC evidence from a drunk-driving suspect naturally dissipates over time in a gradual and relatively predictable manner. Moreover, because a police officer must typically transport a drunk-driving suspect to a medical facility and obtain the assistance of someone with appropriate medical training before conducting a blood test, some delay between the time of the arrest or accident and the time of the test is inevitable regardless of whether police officers are required to obtain a warrant. This reality undermines the force of the State's contention * * * that we should recognize a categorical exception to the warrant requirement because BAC evidence "is actively being destroyed with every minute that passes." * * *

The State's proposed per se rule also fails to account for advances in the 47 years since *Schmerber* was decided that allow for the more expeditious processing of warrant applications, particularly in contexts like drunk-driving investigations where the evidence offered to establish probable cause is simple. The Federal Rules of Criminal Procedure were amended in 1977 to permit federal magistrate judges to issue a warrant based on sworn testimony communicated by telephone. As amended, the law now allows a federal magistrate judge to consider "information communicated by telephone or other reliable electronic means." Fed. Rule Crim. Proc. 4.1. States have also innovated. Well over a majority of States allow police officers or prosecutors to apply for search warrants remotely through various means, including telephonic or radio communication, electronic communication such as e-mail, and video conferencing. And in addition to technology-based developments, jurisdictions have found other ways to streamline the warrant process, such as by using standard-form warrant applications for drunk-driving investigations.

We by no means claim that telecommunications innovations have, will, or should eliminate all delay from the warrant-application process. Warrants inevitably take some time for police officers or prosecutors to complete and for magistrate judges to review. Telephonic and electronic warrants may still require officers to follow time-consuming formalities designed to create an adequate record, such as preparing a duplicate warrant before calling the magistrate judge. And improvements in communications technology do not guarantee that a magistrate judge will be available when an officer needs a warrant after making a late-night arrest. But technological developments that enable police officers to secure warrants more quickly, and do so without undermining the neutral magistrate judge's essential role as a check on police discretion, are relevant to an assessment of exigency. That is particularly so in this context, where BAC evidence is lost gradually and relatively predictably.

Of course, there are important countervailing concerns. While experts can work backwards from the BAC at the time the sample was taken to determine the BAC at the time of the alleged offense, longer intervals may raise questions about the accuracy of the calculation. For that reason, exigent circumstances justifying a warrantless blood sample may arise in the regular course of law enforcement due to delays from the warrant application process. But adopting the State's per se approach would improperly ignore the current and future technological developments in warrant procedures, and might well diminish the incentive for jurisdictions "to pursue progressive approaches to warrant acquisition that preserve the protections afforded by the warrant while meeting the legitimate interests of law enforcement."

In short, while the natural dissipation of alcohol in the blood may support a finding of exigency in a specific case, as it did in *Schmerber*, it does not do so categorically. Whether a warrantless blood test of a drunk-driving suspect is reasonable must be determined case by case based on the totality of the circumstances. * * *

III

* * * [T]he State and its amici point to the compelling governmental interest in combating drunk driving and contend that prompt BAC testing, including through blood testing, is vital to pursuit of that interest. They argue that is particularly so because, in addition to laws that make it illegal to operate a motor vehicle under the influence of alcohol, all 50 States and the District of Columbia have enacted laws that make it per se unlawful to operate a motor vehicle with a BAC of over 0.08 percent.[8] To enforce these provisions, they reasonably assert, accurate BAC evidence is critical.

"No one can seriously dispute the magnitude of the drunken driving problem or the States' interest in eradicating it." Certainly we do not. While some progress has been made, drunk driving continues to exact a terrible toll on our society.

But the general importance of the government's interest in this area does not justify departing from the warrant requirement without showing exigent circumstances that make securing a warrant impractical in a particular case. To the extent that the State and its amici contend that applying the traditional Fourth Amendment totality-of-the-circumstances analysis to determine whether an exigency justified a warrantless search will undermine the governmental interest in preventing and prosecuting drunk-driving offenses, we are not convinced.

As an initial matter, States have a broad range of legal tools to enforce their drunk-driving laws and to secure BAC evidence without undertaking warrantless nonconsensual blood draws. For example, all 50 States have adopted implied consent laws that require motorists, as a condition of operating a motor vehicle within the State, to consent to BAC testing if they are arrested or otherwise detained on suspicion of a drunk-driving offense. Such laws impose significant consequences when a motorist withdraws consent; typically the motorist's driver's license is immediately suspended or revoked, and most States allow the motorist's refusal to take a BAC test to be used as evidence against him in a subsequent criminal prosecution.

It is also notable that a majority of States either place significant restrictions on when police officers may obtain a blood sample despite a suspect's refusal (often limiting testing to cases involving an accident resulting in death or serious bodily injury) or prohibit nonconsensual blood

---

[8]   Pursuant to congressional directive, the NHTSA conditions federal highway grants on States' adoption of laws making it a per se offense to operate a motor vehicle with a BAC of 0.08 percent or greater. Several federal prohibitions on drunk driving also rely on the 0.08 percent standard. In addition, 32 States and the District of Columbia have adopted laws that impose heightened penalties for operating a motor vehicle at or above a BAC of 0.15 percent.

tests altogether. Among these States, several lift restrictions on nonconsensual blood testing if law enforcement officers first obtain a search warrant or similar court order. We are aware of no evidence indicating that restrictions on nonconsensual blood testing have compromised drunk-driving enforcement efforts in the States that have them. And in fact, field studies in States that permit nonconsensual blood testing pursuant to a warrant have suggested that, although warrants do impose administrative burdens, their use can reduce breath-test-refusal rates and improve law enforcement's ability to recover BAC evidence.

To be sure, "States [may] choos[e] to protect privacy beyond the level that the Fourth Amendment requires." But wide-spread state restrictions on nonconsensual blood testing provide further support for our recognition that compelled blood draws implicate a significant privacy interest. They also strongly suggest that our ruling today will not "severely hamper effective law enforcement."

IV

The State argued before this Court that the fact that alcohol is naturally metabolized by the human body creates an exigent circumstance in every case. The State did not argue that there were exigent circumstances in this particular case because a warrant could not have been obtained within a reasonable amount of time. In his testimony before the trial court, the arresting officer did not identify any other factors that would suggest he faced an emergency or unusual delay in securing a warrant. He testified that he made no effort to obtain a search warrant before conducting the blood draw even though he was "sure" a prosecuting attorney was on call and even though he had no reason to believe that a magistrate judge would have been unavailable. The officer also acknowledged that he had obtained search warrants before taking blood samples in the past without difficulty. He explained that he elected to forgo a warrant application in this case only because he believed it was not legally necessary to obtain a warrant. Based on this testimony, the trial court concluded that there was no exigency and specifically found that, although the arrest took place in the middle of the night, "a prosecutor was readily available to apply for a search warrant and a judge was readily available to issue a warrant."[11]

The Missouri Supreme Court in turn affirmed that judgment, holding first that the dissipation of alcohol did not establish a per se exigency, and second that the State could not otherwise satisfy its burden of establishing

---

[11] No findings were made by the trial court concerning how long a warrant would likely have taken to issue under the circumstances. The minimal evidence presented on this point was not uniform. A second patrol officer testified that in a typical DWI case, it takes between 90 minutes and 2 hours to obtain a search warrant following an arrest. McNeely, however, also introduced an exhibit documenting six recent search warrant applications for blood testing in Cape Girardeau County that had shorter processing times.

exigent circumstances. In petitioning for certiorari to this Court, the State challenged only the first holding; it did not separately contend that the warrantless blood test was reasonable regardless of whether the natural dissipation of alcohol in a suspect's blood categorically justifies dispensing with the warrant requirement.

Here and in its own courts the State based its case on an insistence that a driver who declines to submit to testing after being arrested for driving under the influence of alcohol is always subject to a nonconsensual blood test without any precondition for a warrant. That is incorrect.

Although the Missouri Supreme Court referred to this case as "unquestionably a routine DWI case," the fact that a particular drunk-driving stop is "routine" in the sense that it does not involve " 'special facts,' " such as the need for the police to attend to a car accident, does not mean a warrant is required. Other factors present in an ordinary traffic stop, such as the procedures in place for obtaining a warrant or the availability of a magistrate judge, may affect whether the police can obtain a warrant in an expeditious way and therefore may establish an exigency that permits a warrantless search. The relevant factors in determining whether a warrantless search is reasonable, including the practical problems of obtaining a warrant within a timeframe that still preserves the opportunity to obtain reliable evidence, will no doubt vary depending upon the circumstances in the case.

Because this case was argued on the broad proposition that drunk-driving cases present a per se exigency, the arguments and the record do not provide the Court with an adequate analytic framework for a detailed discussion of all the relevant factors that can be taken into account in determining the reasonableness of acting without a warrant. It suffices to say that the metabolization of alcohol in the bloodstream and the ensuing loss of evidence are among the factors that must be considered in deciding whether a warrant is required. No doubt, given the large number of arrests for this offense in different jurisdictions nationwide, cases will arise when anticipated delays in obtaining a warrant will justify a blood test without judicial authorization, for in every case the law must be concerned that evidence is being destroyed. But that inquiry ought not to be pursued here where the question is not properly before this Court. Having rejected the sole argument presented to us challenging the Missouri Supreme Court's decision, we affirm its judgment.

* * *

We hold that in drunk-driving investigations, the natural dissipation of alcohol in the bloodstream does not constitute an exigency in every case sufficient to justify conducting a blood test without a warrant.

The judgment of the Missouri Supreme Court is affirmed.

It is so ordered.

JUSTICE KENNEDY, concurring in part.

[Omitted]

CHIEF JUSTICE ROBERTS, with whom JUSTICE BREYER and JUSTICE ALITO join, concurring in part and dissenting in part.

A police officer reading this Court's opinion would have no idea—no idea—what the Fourth Amendment requires of him, once he decides to obtain a blood sample from a drunk driving suspect who has refused a breathalyzer test. I have no quarrel with the Court's "totality of the circumstances" approach as a general matter; that is what our cases require. But the circumstances in drunk driving cases are often typical, and the Court should be able to offer guidance on how police should handle cases like the one before us.

In my view, the proper rule is straightforward. Our cases establish that there is an exigent circumstances exception to the warrant requirement. That exception applies when there is a compelling need to prevent the imminent destruction of important evidence, and there is no time to obtain a warrant. The natural dissipation of alcohol in the bloodstream constitutes not only the imminent but ongoing destruction of critical evidence. That would qualify as an exigent circumstance, except that there may be time to secure a warrant before blood can be drawn. If there is, an officer must seek a warrant. If an officer could reasonably conclude that there is not, the exigent circumstances exception applies by its terms, and the blood may be drawn without a warrant.

I

* * * [The Fourth Amendment's] language does not state that warrants are required prior to searches, but this Court has long held that warrants must generally be obtained. *See Kentucky v. King*, 563 U.S. ___, ___, 131 S. Ct. 1849, 1856 (2011). We have also held that bodily intrusions like blood draws constitute searches and are subject to the warrant requirement. *See Schmerber v. California*, 384 U.S. 757, 767, 770 (1966).

However, "the ultimate touchstone of the Fourth Amendment is 'reasonableness,'" and thus "the warrant requirement is subject to certain reasonable exceptions," *King*, 563 U.S., at ___, 131 S. Ct. 1849, 1856. One of those exceptions is known as the "exigent circumstances exception," which "applies when the exigencies of the situation make the needs of law enforcement so compelling that a warrantless search is objectively reasonable under the Fourth Amendment." *Ibid.* (internal quotation marks and alterations omitted).

Within the exigent circumstances exception, we have identified several sets of exigent circumstances excusing the need for a warrant. For example, there is an emergency aid exception to the warrant requirement. * * * There is also a fire exception to the warrant requirement. * * * And there is a hot pursuit exception to the warrant requirement as well. * * * In each of these cases, the requirement that we base our decision on the "totality of the circumstances" has not prevented us from spelling out a general rule for the police to follow.

The exigency exception most on point here is the one for imminent destruction of evidence. We have affirmed on several occasions that "law enforcement officers may make a warrantless entry onto private property . . . to prevent the imminent destruction of evidence." * * *

As an overarching principle, we have held that if there is a "compelling need for official action and no time to secure a warrant," the warrant requirement may be excused. The question here is whether and how this principle applies in the typical case of a police officer stopping a driver on suspicion of drunk driving.

II

A

The reasonable belief that critical evidence is being destroyed gives rise to a compelling need for blood draws in cases like this one. Here, in fact, there is not simply a belief that any alcohol in the bloodstream will be destroyed; it is a biological certainty. Alcohol dissipates from the bloodstream at a rate of 0.01 percent to 0.025 percent per hour. Evidence is literally disappearing by the minute. That certainty makes this case an even stronger one than usual for application of the exigent circumstances exception.

And that evidence is important. A serious and deadly crime is at issue. According to the Department of Transportation, in 2011, one person died every 53 minutes due to drinking and driving. No surprise then that drinking and driving is punished severely, including with jail time. McNeely, for instance, faces up to four years in prison.

Evidence of a driver's blood alcohol concentration (BAC) is crucial to obtain convictions for such crimes. All 50 States and the District of Columbia have laws providing that it is per se illegal to drive with a BAC of 0.08 percent or higher. Most States also have laws establishing additional penalties for drivers who drive with a "high BAC," often defined as 0.15 percent or above. BAC evidence clearly matters. And when drivers refuse breathalyzers, as McNeely did here, a blood draw becomes necessary to obtain that evidence.

The need to prevent the imminent destruction of BAC evidence is no less compelling because the incriminating alcohol dissipates over a limited period of time, rather than all at once. As noted, the concentration of alcohol can make a difference not only between guilt and innocence, but between different crimes and different degrees of punishment. The officer is unlikely to know precisely when the suspect consumed alcohol or how much; all he knows is that critical evidence is being steadily lost. Fire can spread gradually, but that does not lessen the need and right of the officers to respond immediately.

McNeely contends that there is no compelling need for a warrantless blood draw, because if there is some alcohol left in the blood by the time a warrant is obtained, the State can use math and science to work backwards and identify a defendant's BAC at the time he was driving. But that's not good enough. We have indicated that exigent circumstances justify warrantless entry when drugs are about to be flushed down the toilet. We have not said that, because there could well be drug paraphernalia elsewhere in the home, or because a defendant's co-conspirator might testify to the amount of drugs involved, the drugs themselves are not crucial and there is no compelling need for warrantless entry.

The same approach should govern here. There is a compelling need to search because alcohol—the nearly conclusive evidence of a serious crime—is dissipating from the bloodstream. The need is no less compelling because the police might be able to acquire second-best evidence some other way.

B

For exigent circumstances to justify a warrantless search, however, there must also be "no time to secure a warrant." In this respect, obtaining a blood sample from a suspected drunk driver differs from other exigent circumstances cases.

Importantly, there is typically delay between the moment a drunk driver is stopped and the time his blood can be drawn. Drunk drivers often end up in an emergency room, but they are not usually pulled over in front of one. In most exigent circumstances situations, police are just outside the door to a home. Inside, evidence is about to be destroyed, a person is about to be injured, or a fire has broken out. Police can enter promptly and must do so to respond effectively to the emergency. But when police pull a person over on suspicion of drinking and driving, they cannot test his blood right away. There is a time-consuming obstacle to their search, in the form of a trip to the hospital and perhaps a wait to see a medical professional. In this case, for example, approximately 25 minutes elapsed between the time the police stopped McNeely and the time his blood was drawn.

As noted, the fact that alcohol dissipates gradually from the bloodstream does not diminish the compelling need for a search—critical evidence is still disappearing. But the fact that the dissipation persists for some time means that the police—although they may not be able to do anything about it right away—may still be able to respond to the ongoing destruction of evidence later on.

There might, therefore, be time to obtain a warrant in many cases. As the Court explains, police can often request warrants rather quickly these days. At least 30 States provide for electronic warrant applications. In many States, a police officer can call a judge, convey the necessary information, and be authorized to affix the judge's signature to a warrant. Utah has an e-warrant procedure where a police officer enters information into a system, the system notifies a prosecutor, and upon approval the officer forwards the information to a magistrate, who can electronically return a warrant to the officer. Judges have been known to issue warrants in as little as five minutes. And in one county in Kansas, police officers can e-mail warrant requests to judges' iPads; judges have signed such warrants and e-mailed them back to officers in less than 15 minutes. The police are presumably familiar with the mechanics and time involved in the warrant process in their particular jurisdiction.

III

A

In a case such as this, applying the exigent circumstances exception to the general warrant requirement of the Fourth Amendment seems straightforward: If there is time to secure a warrant before blood can be drawn, the police must seek one. If an officer could reasonably conclude that there is not sufficient time to seek and receive a warrant, or he applies for one but does not receive a response before blood can be drawn, a warrantless blood draw may ensue.

Requiring police to apply for a warrant if practicable increases the likelihood that a neutral, detached judicial officer will review the case, helping to ensure that there is probable cause for any search and that any search is reasonable. We have already held that forced blood draws can be constitutional—that such searches can be reasonable—but that does not change the fact that they are significant bodily intrusions. Requiring a warrant whenever practicable helps ensure that when blood draws occur, they are indeed justified.

At the same time, permitting the police to act without a warrant to prevent the imminent destruction of evidence is well established in Fourth Amendment law. There is no reason to preclude application of that exception in drunk driving cases simply because it may take the police some time to be able to respond to the undoubted destruction of evidence, or because the destruction occurs continuously over an uncertain period.

And that is so even in situations where police have requested a warrant but do not receive a timely response. An officer who reasonably concluded there was no time to secure a warrant may have blood drawn from a suspect upon arrival at a medical facility. There is no reason an officer should be in a worse position, simply because he sought a warrant prior to his arrival at the hospital. * * *

* * *

Because the Missouri courts did not apply the rule I describe above, and because this Court should not do so in the first instance, I would vacate and remand for further proceedings in the Missouri courts.

JUSTICE THOMAS, dissenting.

[Omitted.]

QUESTIONS, COMMENTS, CONCERNS?

1. **Restricting the scope of an exigency—place and time.** *McNeely*, at its core, is a scope case. That is, it recognizes that an exigency can only last for so long. As the Court observes, "It suffices to say that the metabolization of alcohol in the bloodstream and the ensuing loss of evidence are among the factors that must be considered in deciding whether a warrant is required."

In her order denying Simpson's motion to suppress, Judge Kennedy-Powell more generally summarizes the scope component of the exigent circumstances doctrine: "the search involved must be strictly circumscribed by the exigencies which justify its initiation." [Casefile Document 4, at 2.] That comment essentially breaks into two parts: exigencies are limited both by where police can search (the place) and for how long (time).

Consider first the "place" where police can search. For example, if police enter a home out of concern that suspects will destroy evidence, officers can search only the areas of the home where probable cause exists to believe that evidence will be found. Accordingly, the area where police can enter differs if they are concerned about the destruction of drugs as opposed to flat-screen televisions.

As for the temporal component, any warrantless search supported by exigent circumstances must end when the exigency itself ends. Thus, in the former example involving a search for drugs, the police must stop searching once they secure those drugs. Note also that another exception to the warrant requirement may permit additional warrantless investigation even after the initially exigency expires.

These scope concerns came to life in *Warden v. Hayden*, 387 U.S. 294 (1967), when an armed robber took $363 from the Diamond Cab Company in Baltimore, Maryland, and fled. Two cab drivers followed the assailant to a home and relayed the home's location to police. Officers arrived at the address within minutes and made a warrantless entry. They spread out across the first and second floors and the cellar in search of the suspect. Officers found the suspect—Hayden—in an upstairs bedroom pretending to sleep. Meanwhile, an officer in the cellar heard running water in a cellar bathroom and discovered a shotgun and pistol hiding in the flush tank. Another officer in the cellar found Hayden's clothing in a washing machine.

The Supreme Court approved of both the warrantless entry and warrantless search for the robber. As to the entry, the Court noted that "[s]peed here was essential, and only a thorough search of the house for persons and weapons could have insured that Hayden was the only man present and that the police had control of all weapons which could be used against them or to effect an escape." As for the search and seizure of the weapons and clothing, the Court reasoned, "The permissible scope of a search must, therefore, at the least, be as broad as may reasonably be necessary to prevent the dangers that the suspect at large in the house may resist or escape."

2.   **Simpson and the geographic scope of the exigency.** Assume that Detective Fuhrman could lawfully hop over the gate and enter Simpson's property. With the state's "additional victims or hostages" exigency theory in mind, where are officers now permitted to search? That matters, of course, because Detective Fuhrman found the bloody right-handed glove while on the Simpson property—the apparent match to the left-handed glove found at the murder scene. Recall what led to Detective Fuhrman locating the bloody glove: (1) Detective Fuhrman climbs over the gate; (2) he walks to the rear of the Simpson property; (3) he knocks on the door of a guest house; (4) the guest house's occupant, Brian Kaelin, told Fuhrman that he heard an "earthquake" noise from the "south wall area behind his room"; and (5) Fuhrman discovered the glove at "the south wall area of the exterior of the guest house." [Casefile Document 3, at 7–8.] Does the claimed exigency permit Detective Fuhrman to lawfully walk through the Simpson property, knock on the door of a different interior home, and ultimately walk around otherwise private areas of the full property? Those questions are of course also relevant to application of Detective Fuhrman's plain view seizure of the bloody glove. But more on that later.

Unrelated to the law, do you find it odd that Kaelin, after hearing the "earthquake" sound, which he also thought could be a "prowler outside his residence," "went outside to investigate the noise" but otherwise did nothing. *Id.* at 8. That is, is it odd that Kaelin did not think the noise significant enough to justify calling the police, but the police themselves rely on that noise, in part, as an exigency justifying the continued investigation of Simpson's property?

3.   **Simpson and the temporal scope of the exigency.** Assume one more time that Detective Fuhrman could lawfully hop over the gate and enter Simpson's property. With the state's "additional victims or hostages" exigency theory in mind, how long were he and his officers now permitted to search? Recall that Kaelin told detectives that Simpson's daughter also lived on the premises. [*See* Casefile Document 3, at 6.] Recall further that detectives spoke with Simpson's daughter, Arnelle Simpson, who consented to a search of the main house, which she unlocked. Has the exigency terminated at that point? That is, is the exigency over once police learn that both Kaelin and Arnelle Simpson are safe? It seems a critical question because, if so, the exigency terminated before Detective Fuhrman found the bloody right-handed glove. Do Simpson's attorneys make any "scope of exigency" arguments in their motion to suppress? [*See* Casefile Document 2.] After reviewing that motion, do you agree that the media properly dubbed Simpson's attorneys "the dream team"?

4.   Simpson and the independent source exception. Toward the end of her order denying Simpson's motion to suppress, Judge Kennedy-Powell commented as follows:

> Contrary to the suggestions in [the] defense['s] argument that this ruling allowing the officers' conduct, or finding that it was reasonable and there were exigent circumstances, would mean the end of the 4th Amendment and the Constitution and anarchy, I disagree. And I think one only needs to look as far as the fact that *a short time after the glove was discovered, that the officers did in fact obtain a search warrant* and apparently many other items of evidence were recovered, none of which are going to be offered during the course of this particular proceeding.

[Casefile Document 4, at 9 (emphasis added).] Could her comment about the officers obtaining a search warrant shortly after finding the glove be a thinly-veiled reference to the independent source exception (think: *Murray v. United States* from Chapter 2)? If in fact no exigent circumstances existed, could the independent source exception have saved admission of the bloody glove? What about the inevitable discovery doctrine (think: *Nix v. Williams* also from Chapter 2)?

UNITED STATES V. CARABALLO

831 F.3d 95
United States Court of Appeals for the Second Circuit
January 27, 2016, Argued; August 1, 2016, Decided
Docket No. 12-3839-cr (L), 14-4203-cr (Con)

CALABRESI, CIRCUIT JUDGE:

Early in the summer of 2011, Brattleboro police made a series of controlled purchases of narcotics from Frank Caraballo. After the body of Melissa Barratt, an associate of Caraballo's, was discovered on the morning of July 29, 2011, the officers investigating her death asked Sprint, Caraballo's cell-phone provider, to track the GPS coordinates of Caraballo's cell phone over a two-hour period. Sprint complied with the officers' request, and Caraballo was located and apprehended later that day. Caraballo contends that the "pinging" of his cell phone was a search that violated the Fourth Amendment and that, as a result, the District Court's failure to suppress evidence recovered upon his arrest requires reversal of his conviction. Because we conclude that the circumstances justified the officers' warrantless identification of the GPS coordinates of Caraballo's phone, we AFFIRM the judgment of the District Court.

BACKGROUND

The Scene. At approximately 10:45 a.m. on July 29, 2011, officers of the Vermont State Police responded to a report of a woman's body near the town limits of Brattleboro, Vermont. This area was "off the beaten path," in a wooded area approximately 30 yards from the road. When the officers arrived, they found the woman's body. She had a gunshot wound to the back of the head and was on the ground in a kneeling position with her hands clasped in front of her. Based on the body's position, it was apparent that the woman had not committed suicide. Moreover, the lack of a blood trail indicated that she had been shot there. The officers inferred that the homicide had taken place that morning based on a report from a nearby construction crew of a gunshot-like sound earlier in the morning.[2] As a result, the officers "suspected that the woman was a victim of a homicide and that her assailant could still be armed."

The officers identified the woman as Melissa Barratt. Barratt had recently come to the attention of Vermont State Police when she was arrested in Brattleboro for selling drugs on May 31, 2011. At the time, Barratt had told her arresting officers that she was "extremely nervous and afraid of Frank Caraballo," with whom she worked dealing drugs. In particular, she stated that "if he knew that she was talking to [the officer], he would hurt her, kill her." This, she indicated, was not an idle threat, as she knew Caraballo to have access to multiple firearms, and to have committed assault or even homicide on previous occasions. Though the arresting officers sought to have Barratt cooperate with them in an investigation of Caraballo, she refused, largely out of fear that she would "basically be killed" if she did so. The officers at the scene subsequently learned that Barratt had continued to work for Caraballo after her release.

Moreover, the investigating officers knew that, after Barratt's arrest, Brattleboro police had conducted an investigation of Caraballo's drug operation. Through June and July, police completed "at least three recent controlled buys of narcotics" with Caraballo, and these sales required the participation of multiple undercover agents and confidential informants. Through these sales, the police knew two phone numbers that Caraballo had used in connection with his operation. They were similarly aware that Caraballo had no residence in Vermont, but instead traveled to and from Massachusetts and stayed in hotels.

In sum, the officers found themselves in a difficult position. They had found a woman who was the subject of a "coldblooded execution." Their primary suspect was a man whom the victim had told them not only had a significant propensity for violence but also possessed a number of firearms. In addition, the investigation of Caraballo had separately indicated that he had taken over the drug operation of his brother, Michael, and was as such "armed and dealing drugs."

The officers also believed that the local police who had infiltrated Caraballo's drug operation could be harmed if they came into contact with

---

[2]   It was later learned that Barratt had been killed a day earlier on July 28, 2011.

him. As one officer testified, referring particularly to agents and informants involved in the investigation of Caraballo's drug operation:

> I was concerned that if there was information leaked before the homicide occurred we did not know what extent that information was. We knew that we had our narcotics officers in deep working with their [confidential informants] investigating Frank Caraballo. And we were concerned that if there was some sort of information leaked we weren't sure if he was going to be going after any sort of [informants] or narcotic officers at that point.

Thus, the officers' belief was that it was necessary to obtain Caraballo's location or "potentially someone [was] going to get hurt or killed."

The officers were also assertedly concerned for the possible destruction or dissipation of evidence. Consistent with this, one officer testified that "access to the potential assailant shortly after the homicide was likely to yield important and irreplaceable evidence" such as gunshot residue and DNA. This evidence would likely dissipate or be destroyed if the assailant was not "promptly apprehended."

The Officers' Response. The officers considered various methods for tracking down Caraballo. These included a) having a confidential informant contact him, and b) posting police on major roadways to identify his vehicle as it left the state. They also thought of obtaining a search warrant, and, pursuant to that warrant, asking Sprint, Caraballo's cell carrier, to determine the position of the cell phones associated with Caraballo's drug business. As discussed below, Sprint could determine the location of those phones through their global positioning system ("GPS"). The officers, however, viewed the time that it would take to secure this information by search warrant prohibitory. This was because, "in the absence of exigent circumstances," the provider's slow compliance with the warrant would "likely . . . involve 'a huge delay of getting the information.'"[3]

Cell phones like Caraballo's can be located in two ways. First, cell phones create a record of their location based on the cell towers near them (called "cell-site" location data or information). Cell phones automatically generate this data when turned on; having phones in constant communication with the network enables calls to be routed appropriately. This process can generate a historical log of a phone's movements, though only with limited precision (here, with a margin for error of about 5,000 meters).

---

[3] The District Court found that, although the officers' past experience suggested it would take only "six hours before a warrant could be obtained from a state court judge," it would take much more time—"several days or weeks"—before a cell phone provider would provide location data pursuant to this request.

Second, the position of a cell phone can be determined based on its GPS location, which is generated by triangulating the cell phone's position by reference to three or more network satellites. By contrast with cell-site data, this information is generated only at the specific command of a Sprint operator—an action called "pinging"—and is quite precise (here, within a range of 8 to 46 meters). If fewer than three satellites are in contact with a phone at the time of a request, however, the ping produces only the phone's less precise, cell-tower location.

The investigating officers believed that applicable law permitted them to request a warrantless search of a phone's GPS location "if there was an emergency involving a threat of serious bodily injury or death."[4] They had little experience with this procedure; one officer testified to having requested such information without a warrant "on two previous occasions: one involving a kidnapping and the other involving a missing person." Concluding that this was "a legitimate emergency," the officers decided to request that Sprint locate Caraballo's phones through their GPS without securing a warrant. This approach was endorsed by the county's state attorney, who agreed that such a search "was appropriate and it was probably the best action to take."

The officers then contacted Sprint, which had them fill out a standard form to request the relevant GPS data. This form was submitted at 3:20 p.m., and it explained the exigency by stating that a "[m]ale with phones is suspect in possible homicide." Sprint's practice was to provide location information as soon as possible whenever law enforcement submitted such an emergency request form. Accordingly, Sprint accepted the form and agreed to help the officers locate Caraballo's phones. As agreed, the officers would call Sprint to initiate each search, or "ping," of the location of Caraballo's phone. The results of each "ping" would then be immediately conveyed back to them by a Sprint representative.

Caraballo is Apprehended. Sprint's attempts to ping Caraballo's phones began at 3:43 p.m.. Although one of Caraballo's phones was unresponsive, a ping of another phone hit at 4:03 p.m., revealing that this phone was in the Brattleboro area. The officers had Sprint continue to ping this phone—thirteen times in all, with nine providing GPS coordinates and four providing cell-site location information. Through this process they determined that the phone was being transported north on Interstate 91 and had ceased moving at the town center of Springfield, Vermont. The officers then notified local police about Caraballo and, after local police observed Caraballo's car at a nearby McDonald's, the officers pinged his

---

[4] 18 U.S.C. § 2702(c)(4) authorizes cell-phone carriers to provide "a record or other information pertaining to a subscriber to or customer of such service . . . to a governmental entity, if the provider, in good faith, believes that an emergency involving danger of death or serious physical injury to any person requires disclosure without delay of information relating to the emergency."

phone two final times, at 5:11 p.m. and 5:20 p.m., to confirm this identification.

From that point on, the officers relied on visual surveillance to track Caraballo. Believing that they had sufficient probable cause to arrest Caraballo for the earlier-mentioned narcotics offenses, police stopped his car and arrested him. Upon arrest, Caraballo made a number of statements to police that the Government would subsequently offer at trial.

Procedural History. The Government brought two separate cases against Caraballo. On September 7, 2011, Caraballo was indicted on one count of conspiring to distribute at least 28 grams of cocaine base * * * and on five counts of distributing cocaine base * * *. Caraballo pleaded guilty to the distribution counts in May 2012, and the Government dismissed the conspiracy count. On September 13, 2012, the District Court sentenced Caraballo to 200 months' imprisonment on each distribution count to run concurrently, with a lifetime of supervised release. An appeal by Caraballo concerning the sentence in this case is dealt with in a summary order that is issued together with this opinion.

Subsequently, on December 5, 2012, Caraballo was indicted on: (1) one count of conspiring to distribute at least 280 grams of cocaine base * * *; (2) one count of possessing a firearm in furtherance of a drug trafficking crime and of causing the death of Barratt by discharging a firearm * * *; (3) one count of possessing a firearm in furtherance of a drug trafficking crime * * *; and (4) one count of being a felon in possession of a firearm * * *.

Prior to trial on this indictment, Caraballo moved to suppress the evidence recovered following his arrest. * * * The Government responded by arguing, in relevant part, that * * * no warrant was necessary for any such search because the officers' actions were justified by exigent circumstances * * *.

The District Court denied Caraballo's motion to suppress. First, the Court found that the officers' actions did not constitute a "search" under the Fourth Amendment. Caraballo, it said, lacked a subjective expectation of privacy in the GPS location of his phone, because his contract with Sprint put him "on notice that disclosure of his real time location information to law enforcement [might] occur in the event of an 'emergency.' " Second, and in the alternative, the District Court held that "exigent circumstances alone rendered the warrantless search of Defendant's cell phone location reasonable" and therefore permissible under the Fourth Amendment. * * *

Caraballo proceeded to trial, and was convicted of the first three counts. * * * The Court subsequently sentenced Caraballo to a total term of forty years' imprisonment to run concurrently with the September 13, 2012 drug sentence.

Caraballo appealed.

DISCUSSION

As we have repeatedly held, "the warrant requirement of the Fourth Amendment must yield in those situations in which exigent circumstances require law enforcement officers to act without delay." In such circumstances, "the exigencies of the situation make the needs of law enforcement so compelling that [a] warrantless search is objectively reasonable under the Fourth Amendment." *Kentucky v. King*, 563 U.S. 452, 460 (2011). In the circumstances of this case, we conclude that exigent circumstances justified the police in pinging Caraballo's phone and thereby determining his location.

* * * [W]e begin by discussing briefly the District Court's alternative grounds for not suppressing the evidence derived from the pinging.

The District Court concluded that Caraballo lacked a subjective expectation of privacy in his phone given the terms of Sprint's service agreement and noted that, in any event, such an expectation "is not one society is prepared to accept as reasonable." * * * Because we conclude that exigent circumstances justified the officers' pinging of Caraballo's phone, we need not today resolve this important and complex Fourth Amendment question.

* * * The "core question" in applying the exigent-circumstances doctrine is "whether the facts, as they appeared at the moment of entry, would lead a reasonable, experienced officer to believe that there was an urgent need to render aid or take action." The relevant facts might evidence "the need to prevent the imminent destruction of evidence in individual cases, to pursue a fleeing suspect, and to assist persons who are seriously injured or are threatened with imminent injury." In addressing this question, however, we are "cognizant of the Supreme Court's admonition that exceptions to the warrant requirement are few in number and carefully delineated and that the police bear a heavy burden when attempting to demonstrate an urgent need that might justify warrantless searches or arrests." Moreover, we have cautioned that "general knowledge, without more, cannot support a finding of exigency" because that inquiry must rely on the particular circumstances that create exigency specific to each case.

Exigent-circumstances determinations typically consider [the following factors]:

(1) the gravity or violent nature of the offense with which the suspect is to be charged; (2) whether the suspect is reasonably believed to be armed; (3) a clear showing of probable cause . . . to believe that the suspect committed the crime; (4) strong reason to believe that the suspect is in the premises being entered; (5) a

likelihood that the suspect will escape if not swiftly apprehended; and (6) the peaceful circumstances of the entry.

Such factors, however, are "illustrative, not exhaustive," as the determination is an "objective one that turns on [an] examination of the totality of the circumstances" of each individual case.

Significantly, in making an exigency determination, we have also considered the degree to which the officers, in conducting the search, intruded on a defendant's privacy interests. Thus * * * whether the entry was forceful or peaceful can affect our finding:

> [T]hat the entry, though not consented, is made peaceably [is relevant]. Forcible entry may in some instances be justified. But the fact that entry was not forcible aids in showing reasonableness of police attitude and conduct. The police, by identifying their mission, give the person an opportunity to surrender himself without a struggle and thus to avoid the invasion of privacy involved in entry into the home.

We read this language to mean that the greater the invasion of privacy, e.g., of a person's home, and the clearer the restrictions on police behavior in the absence of exigency, the more stringent the requirements that the search be urgently undertaken in order for the exigency exception to apply. In this respect, exigency analysis incorporates both principles of objectively proper officer behavior and the degree of privacy invasion involved. * * *

Applying the above principles to the case before us makes clear that exigent circumstances justified the officers' pinging of Caraballo's phone following their discovery of Barratt's body.

The Government identifies two possible sources of exigency to justify the officers' pinging of Caraballo's phone. First, the Government contends that the officers reasonably believed that Caraballo posed an imminent threat to law enforcement, particularly those undercover agents and confidential informants involved in the investigation of Caraballo. Second, the Government argues that the delay associated with securing a warrant could result in the imminent destruction or dissipation of evidence. In the circumstances of this case, we conclude that the first source of exigency suffices to support the officers' limited intrusion in Caraballo's privacy from the pinging.

The first two * * * factors strongly indicate that the officers' actions were reasonable. First, Barratt's killing was brutal: she was found with a gunshot wound to the back of her head, "kneeling . . . [with] her hands folded." And, the position of Barratt's body, together with the location of the gunshot, made it apparent that this was "a coldblooded execution." Second, the officers had good reason to believe that Caraballo was armed:

not only had Barratt been killed by gunshot, but Barratt also had told police, upon her earlier arrest, that Caraballo had "access to guns," including "shotguns, Tech 9s and other types of weapons."

As to the third factor, though the officers thought they lacked probable cause to arrest Caraballo on Barratt's murder, they properly considered him their "primary suspect." At the time of Barratt's arrest, she told officers that "she was involved in drug activity in Brattleboro with [Caraballo], that 'she was extremely nervous and afraid of [Caraballo]' and that 'if he knew that she was talking to [the officers], he would hurt her, kill her." Given that Barratt perceived herself to be in significant danger from Caraballo for speaking with police, and given her role in his organization, officers had strong reasons to link Caraballo to Barratt's death. Though this * * * factor does not itself support exigency, it does not cut strongly against it.

More important, however, the officers had specific reasons to think that Caraballo would commit acts of violence against undercover agents and confidential informants. The mere fact of a brutal killing does not necessarily suggest that other violence, either against officers in the field or against civilians, will follow. But here, Barratt's statement that Caraballo would "kill her" if she were speaking to police took on special significance. As one officer testified, her murder suggested that the police's investigation of Caraballo's drug operation had been discovered. And, as the District Court noted, the informants "knew [Caraballo] well enough to contact him" by phone and were "likely to be individuals who had encountered [him] on more than a single, remote, or passing occasion." Accordingly, "[i]f the motive for the Barratt homicide was to silence a cooperator, it could extend to the confidential informants as well."

Given this specific threat, then, it was not clearly erroneous for the District Court to conclude that the officers had a "legitimate, good faith belief that [Caraballo] must be apprehended immediately to ensure that confidential informants and undercover narcotics agents would not be exposed to an imminent risk of death or serious bodily injury."

Finally, officers did not have a reasonable opportunity to secure a warrant for the search. Although it would take only six hours to obtain a warrant, the officers' experience led them to believe that Sprint would respond much less quickly—to the tune of days or weeks—if pinging were sought through the warrant process. The odds that Caraballo would come into contact with an undercover officer or confidential informant—and potentially kill that person—over this period could reasonably seem to the officers to be anything but remote.

At the same time, and significantly, the degree of the officers' intrusion into Caraballo's privacy was relatively slight. First of all, the officers showed due regard for applicable law in conducting their search. In the words of the District Court, the officers "held a good faith, reasonable belief that there was a serious and imminent threat to human life and that *federal law authorized a warrantless cell phone pinging in those circumstances.*" Indeed, not only was this belief consistent with the officers' limited experience with pinging, but it was also endorsed by the county's state attorney, who viewed the course of action as "appropriate." * * *

Finally, the officers' pinging was "strictly circumscribed" to finding Caraballo as quickly as possible. It took place over a very short period of time (less than two hours) and ceased immediately upon the officers confirming that the identified vehicle was Caraballo's. And although, given its precision, pinging can provide data "that reflects a wealth of detail about her familial, political, professional, religious, and sexual associations," the officers did not attempt to elicit such facts here. They used the GPS coordinates only to trace Caraballo's path generally toward Brattleboro, and then confirmed that a particular car was Caraballo's after it had been identified by local police. Thus, the officers' use of this information was no more expansive than necessary to address the exigency that they perceived existed.

CONCLUSION

The officers reasonably believed that Caraballo posed an exigent threat to the undercover officers and confidential informants involved in his drug operation. This threat justified the pinging of Caraballo's phone, a) which at most constituted a limited intrusion into his privacy interests, b) which objectively could be viewed as plausibly consistent with existing law and c) which the officers used in the most limited way to achieve their necessary aim. Accordingly, and for the reasons given in an accompanying summary order that deals with the other issues that Caraballo has raised in this appeal, we AFFIRM the judgment of the District Court.

QUESTIONS, COMMENTS, CONCERNS?

1. **Did police "search" Caraballo's phone?** Notice that the district court in *Caraballo* held that Caraballo had no reasonable expectation of privacy in the real-time GPS location of his cell phone. As a result, no Fourth Amendment "search" occurred when officers investigating Barratt's death asked Sprint to track the GPS coordinates of Caraballo's cell phone over a two-hour period. As you saw, the Second Circuit declined to reach the question of whether Sprint tracking Caraballo's cell phone constituted a search. Recall *United States v. White* (Chapter 3). Did Caraballo knowingly expose his location to Sprint—a third party?

2. ***Caraballo* and Simpson.** Although Simpson is not a cell phone case, the state argued that Detective Fuhrman climbing over the security gate did not constitute a "search" because Simpson "had no reasonable expectation of privacy in the common areas" of his home. [Casefile Document 3, at 21.] The core of the state's argument was as follows:

> Security systems, guards, walls, or no trespassing signs cannot
> protect an area from police entry, if occupants within that area must
> reasonably expect to encounter strangers there. They may have a
> reasonable expectation of security in that area, but not a reasonable
> expectation of privacy. As long as homes with guest houses, duplexes,
> triplexes, fourplexes, motels, hotels, apartment houses, rooming
> houses, condominiums, public storage facilities and other multi-unit
> enclaves permit each tenant to invite in people who are strangers to
> the other occupants, they cannot claim Fourth Amendment
> protection from police entry of their common areas. Neither the
> landlord nor the tenants can reasonably expect privacy in these
> common areas.

Id. at 21–22. To properly evaluate the merit of the state's argument, we must
first ask a review question: was the gated space separating the public road
from the enclosures on Simpson's property "curtilage" or an "open field."
Applying the factors from *United States v. Dunn* (Chapter 3), surely that space
is curtilage, right? And more specifically, it is curtilage in a way that the
common area of a rental complex is not. The state's argument would seemingly
treat the open areas of *all* multi-structure dwellings the same for Fourth
Amendment purposes. But the Fourth Amendment protection provided to
tenants in the common areas of a condominium complex surely differs from the
Fourth Amendment interest Simpson has in the interior space of his gated
compound, right?

The state would also have you believe that, because a tenant can "invite
in people who are strangers to the occupants," a member of law enforcement
can warrantlessly climb over the gate of an enclosed home. Exigent
circumstances aside, does that logic mean that no Fourth Amendment "search"
occurred when Detective Fuhrman climbed over Simpson's gate?

3.   Exigent circumstances and "minor offenses." In *Welsh v.
Wisconsin*, 466 U.S. 740 (1984), Edward Welsh was driving his car erratically
when he swerved off the road. Welsh walked away from the car, and a passerby
called the police. When the police arrived, the witness stated that the driver
was "either very inebriated or very sick." Police checked the registration of the
abandoned vehicle, obtained Welsh's address, and proceeded to his home at
roughly 9 p.m. Without a warrant, police entered the home, found Welsh in an
upstairs bedroom, and arrested him for driving a vehicle under the influence
of an intoxicant. Once at the station, Welsh refused to submit to a breath-
analysis test.

Welsh was charged with violating Wisconsin's DUI statute—a
noncriminal, civil offense for first-time offenders. Welsh challenged his arrest,
arguing that officers needed a warrant to arrest him inside his home. The state
countered that exigent circumstances permitted the warrantless arrest. The
Supreme Court sided with Welsh, holding that "application of the exigent-
circumstances exception in the context of a home entry should rarely be

sanctioned when there is probable cause to believe that only a minor offense, such as the kind at issue in this case, has been committed."

4.   **Detective Fuhrman: a problematic witness.** Detective Fuhrman testified as a witness for the prosecution at O.J. Simpson's murder trial. Part of Simpson's defense strategy was to make his prosecution appear racially motivated. At the time of Simpson's trial in 1995, "Los Angeles was still reeling from a 1991 video showing city police beating black taxi driver Rodney King, an incident which led to the 1992 L.A. riots." Travis M. Andrews, *Fox News taps Mark Fuhrman, O.J. Simpson trial's racist cop, to analyze Simpson's parole hearing*, WASHINGTONPOST.COM (July 18, 2017), https://www. washingtonpost.com/news/morning-mix/wp/2017/07/18/fox-news-taps-mark-fuhrman-o-j-simpson-trials-racist-cop-to-analyze-simpsons-parole-hearing/.

One part of the defense strategy called for highlighting Fuhrman's past use of the n-word. After Fuhrman testified that he had not used the word for over ten ears, the defense entered into evidence "a recorded conversation between Fuhrman and screenwriter Laura Hart McKinny in which he used the n-word more than 40 times." *Id.* Fuhrman was later charged with perjury, to which he pleaded no contest, and sentenced to a three-year term of probation.

5.   **The rest of the Simpson story.** Following an eleven-month trial, a jury found Simpson not guilty on October 3, 1995. Goldman's family then filed a wrongful death civil suit against Simpson. The civil trial against Simpson began in October 1996 and culminated with a jury verdict finding Simpson liable for the wrongful death of Goldman in January 1997. The jury awarded more than thirty-three million dollars in damages. Simpson would default on his mortgage, be evicted, and the property's new owner demolished the home.

In many ways, Simpson's legal troubles have never ended. He was arrested in 2001 and again in 2002. Then, in 2007, he was arrested for armed robbery. He would be tried and convicted on that charge, for which he was sentenced in 2008 to thirty-three years in prison. Simpson would serve nine years of that sentence. He was released on parole on October 1, 2017. Amy Harmon & Christina Caron, *O.J. Simpson Is Freed on Parole in Nevada After 9 Years*, NYTIMES.COM (Oct. 1, 2017), https://www.nytimes.com/2017/10/01/us/oj-simpson-parole-nevada.html.

III. SEARCHES INCIDENT TO ARREST

A. INTRODUCTION

We move next to the "search incident to arrest" exception to the warrant requirement. The exception is powerful example of police authority. Stated simplistically, the doctrine enables the police—at the moment of arrest—to conduct a warrantless and suspicionless search of the person of the arrestee.

The search incident to arrest doctrine involves two separate and distinct Fourth Amendment intrusions: first is the arrest—a seizure of the person—and second is the search of the arrestee. Note that officers may not search the arrestee without the presence of a lawful arrest supported by probable cause. In other words, the probable cause must go to the arrest (the seizure). That's important because, absent an arrest, officers may not search citizens without a warrant *even if* they have probable cause to believe that the person is carrying contraband.

But the reverse is also true. That is, so long as probable cause exists to arrest, no separate suspicion is necessary to support the accompanying search. In Fourth Amendment terms, then, the search following an arrest is "suspicionless" in the sense that it does not require separate justification.

The cases below consider the search incident to arrest doctrine generally and in various fact-specific scenarios. The first case lays out the doctrine and parameters governing when and how an officer may constitutionally search an individual incident to an arrest. The three cases that follow consider the Supreme Court's treatment of the search incident to arrest doctrine in the context of the arrestee's home (*Maryland v. Buie*), car (*Arizona v. Gant*), and cell phone (*Riley v. California*). As each of those cases reflect, the search incident to arrest doctrine has expanded since its original inception.

B. MEET RICHARD KUKLINSKI

Richard Kuklinski, at 6′4″ and 275 lbs., towered over his defense attorney as he stood up to hear a New Jersey jury convict him on two counts of first-degree murder. For the prosecution, Kuklinski's 1988 conviction marked the end of a three-year investigation that uncovered more than two hundred murders across roughly a decade. At the center of these murders was Richard Kuklinski, the prolific mafia hitman. Known for freezing his victims in order to dispose of their bodies years later, Kuklinski earned the nickname, "The Iceman." To date, Kuklinski remains the most notorious mafia hitman in history.

Richard Kuklinski

Richard Kuklinski was born on April 11, 1935, in Jersey City, New Jersey. Growing up, Kuklinski hated his parents. His father, Stanislaw "Stanley" Kuklinski, was a Polish Immigrant railroad worker who would frequently get drunk and beat Kuklinski. Kuklinski's mother, Anna McNally, was the daughter of Catholic Irish Immigrants and believed that religious teachings ought to be administered by broom handle or other household objects. These abuses would instill a violent rage within Kuklinski who reported killing numerous neighborhood cats before the age of ten.

As a teenager, Kuklinski was a regular target for neighborhood bullies. Neighborhood schoolmates would call him "pollack" as they dished out weekly beatings. But on a cold evening in December 1948, Kuklinski decided that he was not going to be a victim anymore. He took a thick wooden clothes rack from his parents closet and waited in an alley for Charley Lane—one of his regular neighborhood bullies—to walk by. As Lane approached, Kuklinski emerged from the shadows and beat the teenager to death, claiming his first victim. According to Kuklinski, killing Lane led him to a profound realization: murder was the answer to all of life's problems.

By the late 1950s, Kuklinski worked as a warehouse worker in Jersey City, earning extra money on the side by hustling at pool. During that period, Kuklinski began to earn a violent reputation by, for example, chasing down and beating the drivers of cars that cut him off in traffic. He also would frequently resort to violent brawls if a disagreement broke out over a game of pool.

As the 1960s approached, Kuklinski began to court a secretary named Barbara Pedrici. The two married in September 1961 and would ultimately have three children. By the mid-1960s, Kuklinski took a job in a New York City film copying lab making copies of children's movies for retail sale. But Kuklinski quickly learned that his coworkers were also using the lab to illegally copy bootleg pornography. At the time, New York City was on the verge of "The Golden Age of Porn," which raised the demand for adult film shops to produce affordable pornographic films.

Kuklinski sought to join the criminal enterprise, but needed capital to purchase a share. After expressing his interest to coworkers, one employee agreed to introduce Kuklinski to a Gambino crime family loan shark by the name of Roy DeMeo. DeMeo was then one of the Gambino family's most feared enforcers who himself was rumored to have committed more than seventy mafia-related murders. Kuklinski secured a $65,000 loan from DeMeo and began distributing bootleg pornography. Kuklinski, however, underestimated the time it would take to liquidate the contraband and he defaulted on DeMeo's loan. One night while Kuklinski was at work, DeMeo showed up with two thugs and beat Kuklinski over the head with his own film reels. Kuklinski would pay the remaining debt in full within the week.

DeMeo was impressed by Kuklinski's ability to quickly pay off the remainder of the $65,000 loan. Considering his stature, DeMeo also viewed Kuklinski as a potential asset who could help DeMeo recover money from others who defaulted on their loans. In his new role, however, Kuklinski often went too far and inadvertently beat targets to death by accident. Recognizing that a defaulter would repay their loans, DeMeo appropriated Kuklinski's talents elsewhere: contract killing. Over the next decade, Kuklinski would become one of the mafia's most accomplished hitmen, claiming to have committed more than two hundred murders—including Jimmy Hoffa.

Kuklinski carried out his murders across the country in every way imaginable. If a victim was a suspected snitch, Kuklinski would leave the body in the street to warn other would-be cooperators about the consequences. Cars containing trunks full of bodies were frequently compacted and shipped to China so they could be made into steel and sold back to the United States. On one particular occasion, Kuklinski entered a victim's California hotel room brandishing a gun, causing the man to cry out to God asking that Kuklinski not murder him. Kuklinski then decided to lower the gun and told the man that he had thirty minutes to pray for God to come and save him. After the victim prayed for thirty-one minutes, Kuklinski shot him and left.

Robert Pronge and His Freezer

By the early 1980s, Kuklinski was charging $10,000 or more per assassination. Kuklinski during that period met another mafia hitman, Robert Pronge, who was an army-trained demolition expert. Pronge drove an ice cream truck as a cover for his hitman operation: earning him the name "Mr. Sofftee."

As a tandem, Kuklinski and Pronge carried out numerous mafia assassinations while sharing tips and tricks of their craft. In particular, Pronge told Kuklinski that he frequently froze the bodies of his victims in his ice cream truck freezer for disposal months later. Doing so, he explained, made it impossible for police and medical examiners to establish a time of death for the particular murder. Pronge also taught Kuklinski another trick involving cyanide, a deadly poison that rapidly dissipates upon ingestion into the human body. Pronge specifically taught Kuklinski that only 100 mgs. of cyanide (or half of an aspirin tablet) will kill an adult male and has a half-life of just one hour after ingestion. Thus, according to Pronge, the victim poisoned with cyanide would appear to a medical examiner to have suffered a heart attack. Kuklinski adopted Pronge's method, frequently poisoning his targets by putting cyanide on their food, pouring a cyanide-laced drink on their clothing, or spraying it into their face while pretending to sneeze.

Kuklinski's Downfall

As the 1980s progressed, DeMeo began to see Kuklinski as a threat. Kuklinski's prolific career had led Kuklinski to conduct contract killings for all five of the New York Crime Families. Moreover, DeMeo's own position in the Gambino Family was in jeopardy after a federal investigation began to focus on him. One night, while DeMeo and Kuklinski were having dinner at the Gemini Lounge, a notorious gangster hangout, DeMeo pulled an Uzi on Kuklinski. After Kuklinski calmly talked DeMeo down, Kuklinski left his prolific career as a mafia hitman to focus on other criminal endeavors.

Kuklinski began to advertise himself as a supplier of cheap contraband like guns, pornography, and bootleg VHS tapes. Kuklinski assembled a small crew, including Gary Smith and Daniel Deppner, in order to help build his new criminal enterprise. The enterprise was simple. Kuklinski offered to buy or sell videotapes in cash, although in actuality the plan was to kill the victim and steal whatever money they had with them to support the false transaction. Kuklinski killed the first victim of this scheme, George Malliband, on January 31, 1980, after Malliband met with Mr. Kuklinski to sell several videotapes. Malliband's body was found days later, stuffed in a fifty-five gallon drum. He had been carrying $27,000.

Then, in July 1981, a New Jersey store owner named Louis Masgay approached Kuklinski about buying a number of VHS tapes for his store. After arriving at the meeting with nearly $100,000 cash, Masgay was never seen alive again. Masgay's car was discovered three days later, but with no other evidence, his disappearance was treated as a missing persons case. The scheme continued with the disappearance of Paul Hoffman in April 1982. Hoffman was last seen carrying $22,000 in cash on his way to purchase a prescription drug from Kuklinski.

By late 1982, Kuklinski began to fear that his crew was preparing to turn him over to the police. Kuklinski began with Smith. Kuklinski called Deppner and Smith to meet him in Room 31 of the York Motel in North Bergen, New Jersey. Kuklinski showed up to the room with three hamburgers, one with pickles and the other two without. Kuklinski had poisoned the hamburger with the pickles. After feeding the burger to Smith, Smith doubled over and began to choke. Kuklinski would later remark that although most people who ingested cyanide would die immediately, Smith "had the constitution of a bull" and simply kept choking. As a result, Kuklinski and Deppner choked Smith to death and left his body to rot under the motel mattress. Four days would pass before the smell of Smith's body caused guests of Room 31 to discover him under the mattress. Deppner's body was found stuffed inside green garbage bags a year later by a cyclist riding through a wooded area of West Milford, New Jersey.

The Final Investigation

In September 1983, nearly two years after his disappearance, New Jersey State Police found Louis Masgay's body in Rockland County, New Jersey. Police found Masgay's body on the side of the road with two bullet wounds in the back of his head. During a subsequent autopsy, the medical examiner heard a crunching sound as he pressed on Masgay's abdomen. Further investigation revealed that Masgay's body cavity had ice crystals clustered around his heart and lungs, which lead the examiner to conclude that Masgay had been frozen. Masgay was also wearing the same clothing that he had on the day he disappeared. Masgay's wife would later tell police that Masgay planned to see a "Richard Kuklinski" on the day of his disappearance.

The New Jersey Attorney General's Office, already suspecting Kuklinski's involvement in the murders of Smith and Deppner, began to focus on Kuklinski. In 1986, three years after the discovery of Masgay's body, the Attorney General launched a joint task force operation known as "Operation Iceman." Led by prosecutor Bob Carroll, FBI Agent Paul Smith, and ATF Agent Dominic Polifrone, the operation required Polifrone to go undercover as a well-connected mobster by the name of Michael Provenzano. Polifrone was directed to spend time at a local restaurant where Kuklinski often visited in the hopes of attracting his attention. After boasting around the restaurant for months about his ability to obtain military-grade explosives, Kuklinski called Agent Polifrone to setup a meeting.

Over the next several weeks, Agent Polifrone befriended Kuklinski by pretending to be a fellow hitman. Kuklinski told Agent Polifrone about countless murders he committed, including those of Smith and Deppner. But because Polifrone began to suspect that Kuklinski was also planning to kill him, the Operation Iceman taskforce devised a plan for apprehending Kuklinski.

In December 1986, Polifrone approached Kuklinski about a murder-for-hire. Polifrone told Kuklinski that a "rich Jewish kid" who frequently bought cocaine from him would be carrying $80,000 cash at the time of his next drug purchase. Together, Agent Polifrone and Kuklinski agreed that Polifrone would supply Kuklinski with cyanide, which Kuklinski would use to poison the victim's sandwich. Then, when the victim came to make the drug deal, Kuklinski would feed him the sandwich, and both Polifrone and Kuklinski would split the $80,000.

On December 17, 1986, Agent Polifrone met Kuklinski at the Vince Lombardi Service Station just off the New Jersey Turnpike where Agent Polifrone gave Kuklinski a batch of imitation cyanide created by the New Jersey Crime Lab. Per the task force plan, Agent Smith was to show up acting as the wealthy buyer who would help make the arrest after Kuklinski fed him the sandwich.

But Kuklinski got suspicious. Kuklinski told Agent Polifrone that he wanted to take a walk. Suspecting that the cyanide was fake, Kuklinski attempted to poison a stray dog. When the dog survived, Kuklinski got in his car and drove home. Agent Polifrone and the rest of the task force followed. As the task force van approached Kuklinski's home, Kuklinski's car backed out of the driveway and sped toward them. Agent Polifrone and others jumped from the van and, standing in the middle of the street, drew their weapons. Kuklinski stopped the car. Agents arrested both him and Barbara, his wife, who was also in the car. A search incident to arrest revealed a firearm located under the front seat of Kuklinski's car. Further investigation revealed that Kuklinski had also laced a sandwich meant for Agent Polifrone with the fake cyanide. Kuklinski intended to kill him and keep the $80,000 for himself.

Kuklinski was charged in a twenty-five count indictment on February 26, 1987. [See Casefile Document 1.] Among the indictment's many charges were three counts of first-degree murder for the killings of Malliband, Masgay, and Hoffman. The indictment also charged Kuklinski with the possession of a weapon for unlawful purposes—a Beretta automatic pistol, caliber 6.35 millimeter, with serial number B85553. The Beretta was the same weapon found under the front seat of Kuklinski's car when he was arrested.

To pressure Kuklinski, prosecutors also indicted his wife, Barbara, on February 26, 1987. They charged her with possession of a weapon without a permit. [See Casefile Document 2.] The weapon in question was the same one included in Kuklinski's indictment—a Beretta automatic pistol, caliber 6.35 millimeter, with serial number B85553. Later that year, the state also charged Kuklinski's son, Dwayne, for possession of marijuana found in his car during a traffic stop. [See Casefile Document 3.] Then, in 1988, the state charged Dwayne for unlawfully possessing a switchblade knife and a cestus. [See Casefile Document 4.]

On May 25, 1988, in exchange for the state dropping all charges against his family, Kuklinski pleaded guilty to the two murder counts associated with Malliband and Masgay. [See Casefile Document 5.] He received two life terms with an order for him to serve thirty years on each count—to run consecutively—before becoming parole eligible. [See Casefile Document 6.] By the time of his plea, Kuklinski, now fifty-two years old, had already been tried and convicted on March 16, 1988, of murdering Smith and Deppner. During sentencing for those murders, the judge asked Kuklinski why he did it. Kuklinski replied, "it was due to business."

C. THE CASES

1. Establishing the Search Incident to Arrest Doctrine

UNITED STATES V. ROBINSON

414 U.S. 218
Supreme Court of the United States
October 9, 1973, Argued; December 11, 1973, Decided
No. 72-936

MR. JUSTICE REHNQUIST delivered the opinion of the Court.

Respondent Robinson was convicted in United States District Court for the District of Columbia of the possession and facilitation of concealment of heroin * * *. He was sentenced to concurrent terms of imprisonment for these offenses. * * *

On April 23, 1968, at approximately 11 p. m., Officer Richard Jenks, a 15-year veteran of the District of Columbia Metropolitan Police Department, observed the respondent driving a 1965 Cadillac near the intersection of 8th and C Streets, N. E., in the District of Columbia. Jenks, as a result of previous investigation following a check of respondent's operator's permit four days earlier, determined there was reason to believe that respondent was operating a motor vehicle after the revocation of his operator's permit. This is an offense defined by statute in the District of Columbia which carries a mandatory minimum jail term, a mandatory minimum fine, or both.

Jenks signaled respondent to stop the automobile, which respondent did, and all three of the occupants emerged from the car. At that point Jenks informed respondent that he was under arrest for "operating after revocation and obtaining a permit by misrepresentation." It was assumed by the Court of Appeals, and is conceded by the respondent here, that Jenks had probable cause to arrest respondent, and that he effected a full-custody arrest.

In accordance with procedures prescribed in police department instructions, Jenks then began to search respondent. He explained at a subsequent hearing that he was "face-to-face" with the respondent, and "placed [his] hands on [the respondent], my right-hand to his left breast like this (demonstrating) and proceeded to pat him down thus [with the right hand]." During this patdown, Jenks felt an object in the left breast pocket of the heavy coat respondent was wearing, but testified that he "couldn't tell what it was" and also that he "couldn't actually tell the size of it." Jenks then reached into the pocket and pulled out the object, which turned out to be a "crumpled up cigarette package." Jenks testified that at this point he still did not know what was in the package:

> As I felt the package I could feel objects in the package but I couldn't tell what they were. . . . I knew they weren't cigarettes.

The officer then opened the cigarette pack and found 14 gelatin capsules of white powder which he thought to be, and which later analysis proved to be, heroin. Jenks then continued his search of respondent to completion, feeling around his waist and trouser legs, and examining the remaining pockets. The heroin seized from the respondent was admitted into evidence at the trial which resulted in his conviction in the District Court. * * *

I

It is well settled that a search incident to a lawful arrest is a traditional exception to the warrant requirement of the Fourth

Amendment. This general exception has historically been formulated into two distinct propositions. The first is that a search may be made of the person of the arrestee by virtue of the lawful arrest. The second is that a search may be made of the area within the control of the arrestee.

Examination of this Court's decisions shows that these two propositions have been treated quite differently. The validity of the search of a person incident to a lawful arrest has been regarded as settled from its first enunciation, and has remained virtually unchallenged until the present case. The validity of the second proposition, while likewise conceded in principle, has been subject to differing interpretations as to the extent of the area which may be searched. * * *

Throughout the series of cases in which the Court has addressed the second proposition relating to a search incident to a lawful arrest—the permissible area beyond the person of the arrestee which such a search may cover—no doubt has been expressed as to the unqualified authority of the arresting authority to search the person of the arrestee. *Chimel v. California*, 395 U.S. 752 (1969). In *Chimel*, where the Court overruled *Rabinowitz* and *Harris* as to the area of permissible search incident to a lawful arrest, full recognition was again given to the authority to search the person of the arrestee:

> When an arrest is made, it is reasonable for the arresting officer to search the person arrested in order to remove any weapons that the latter might seek to use in order to resist arrest or effect his escape. Otherwise, the officer's safety might well be endangered, and the arrest itself frustrated. In addition, it is entirely reasonable for the arresting officer to search for and seize any evidence on the arrestee's person in order to prevent its concealment or destruction.

Three years after the decision in *Chimel, supra,* we upheld the validity of a search in which heroin had been taken from the person of the defendant after his arrest on a weapons charge, in *Adams v. Williams*, 407 U.S. 143 (1972). * * *

Last Term in *Cupp v. Murphy*, 412 U.S. 291, 295 (1973), we again reaffirmed the traditional statement of the authority to search incident to a valid arrest.

Thus the broadly stated rule, and the reasons for it, have been repeatedly affirmed in the decisions of this Court since *Weeks v. United States* * * * nearly 60 years ago. * * *

II

In its decision of this case, the Court of Appeals decided that even after a police officer lawfully places a suspect under arrest for the purpose of taking him into custody, he may not ordinarily proceed to fully search the prisoner. He must, instead, conduct a limited frisk of the outer clothing and remove such weapons that he may, as a result of that limited frisk, reasonably believe and ascertain that the suspect has in his possession. While recognizing that *Terry v. Ohio*, 392 U.S. 1 (1968), dealt with a permissible "frisk" incident to an investigative stop based on less than probable cause to arrest, the Court of Appeals felt that the principles of that case should be carried over to this probable-cause arrest for driving while one's license is revoked. Since there would be no further evidence of such a crime to be obtained in a search of the arrestee, the court held that only a search for weapons could be justified.

Terry v. Ohio, supra, did not involve an arrest for probable cause, and it made quite clear that the "protective frisk" for weapons which it approved might be conducted without probable cause. This Court's opinion explicitly recognized that there is a "distinction in purpose, character, and extent between a search incident to an arrest and a limited search for weapons." * * *

Terry, therefore, affords no basis to carry over to a probable-cause arrest the limitations this Court placed on a stop-and-frisk search permissible without probable cause. * * *

III   * * *

The Court of Appeals in effect determined that the only reason supporting the authority for a full search incident to lawful arrest was the possibility of discovery of evidence or fruits. Concluding that there could be no evidence or fruits in the case of an offense such as that with which respondent was charged, it held that any protective search would have to be limited by the conditions laid down in *Terry* for a search upon less than probable cause to arrest. Quite apart from the fact that *Terry* clearly recognized the distinction between the two types of searches, and that a different rule governed one than governed the other, we find additional reason to disagree with the Court of Appeals.

The justification or reason for the authority to search incident to a lawful arrest rests quite as much on the need to disarm the suspect in order to take him into custody as it does on the need to preserve evidence on his person for later use at trial. The standards traditionally governing a search incident to lawful arrest are not, therefore, commuted to the stricter *Terry* standards by the absence of probable fruits or further evidence of the particular crime for which the arrest is made.

Nor are we inclined, on the basis of what seems to us to be a rather speculative judgment, to qualify the breadth of the general authority to search incident to a lawful custodial arrest on an assumption that persons arrested for the offense of driving while their licenses have been revoked are less likely to possess dangerous weapons than are those arrested for other crimes. It is scarcely open to doubt that the danger to an officer is far greater in the case of the extended exposure which follows the taking of a suspect into custody and transporting him to the police station than in the case of the relatively fleeting contact resulting from the typical *Terry*-type stop. This is an adequate basis for treating all custodial arrests alike for purposes of search justification.

But quite apart from these distinctions, our more fundamental disagreement with the Court of Appeals arises from its suggestion that there must be litigated in each case the issue of whether or not there was present one of the reasons supporting the authority for a search of the person incident to a lawful arrest. We do not think the long line of authorities of this Court dating back to *Weeks*, or what we can glean from the history of practice in this country and in England, requires such a case-by-case adjudication. A police officer's determination as to how and where to search the person of a suspect whom he has arrested is necessarily a quick ad hoc judgment which the Fourth Amendment does not require to be broken down in each instance into an analysis of each step in the search. The authority to search the person incident to a lawful custodial arrest, while based upon the need to disarm and to discover evidence, does not depend on what a court may later decide was the probability in a particular arrest situation that weapons or evidence would in fact be found upon the person of the suspect. A custodial arrest of a suspect based on probable cause is a reasonable intrusion under the Fourth Amendment; that intrusion being lawful, a search incident to the arrest requires no additional justification. It is the fact of the lawful arrest which establishes the authority to search, and we hold that in the case of a lawful custodial arrest a full search of the person is not only an exception to the warrant requirement of the Fourth Amendment, but is also a "reasonable" search under that Amendment.

IV

The search of respondent's person conducted by Officer Jenks in this case and the seizure from him of the heroin, were permissible under established Fourth Amendment law. * * * Since it is the fact of custodial arrest which gives rise to the authority to search, it is of no moment that Jenks did not indicate any subjective fear of the respondent or that he did not himself suspect that respondent was armed. Having in the course of a lawful search come upon the crumpled package of cigarettes, he was entitled to inspect it; and when his inspection revealed the heroin capsules, he was entitled to seize them as "fruits, instrumentalities, or contraband" probative of criminal conduct. The judgment of the Court of Appeals holding otherwise is

Reversed.

MR. JUSTICE POWELL, concurring.

[Omitted.]

MR. JUSTICE MARSHALL, with whom MR. JUSTICE DOUGLAS and MR. JUSTICE BRENNAN join, dissenting.

[Omitted.]

2.   Accessing the Arrestee's Home

MARYLAND V. BUIE

494 U.S. 325
Supreme Court of the United States
December 4, 1989, Argued; February 28, 1990, Decided
No. 88-1369

JUSTICE WHITE delivered the opinion of the Court. * * *

I

On February 3, 1986, two men committed an armed robbery of a Godfather's Pizza restaurant in Prince George's County, Maryland. One of the robbers was wearing a red running suit. That same day, Prince George's County police obtained arrest warrants for respondent Jerome Edward Buie and his suspected accomplice in the robbery, Lloyd Allen. Buie's house was placed under police surveillance.

On February 5, the police executed the arrest warrant for Buie. They first had a police department secretary telephone Buie's house to verify that he was home. The secretary spoke to a female first, then to Buie himself. Six or seven officers proceeded to Buie's house. Once inside, the officers fanned out through the first and second floors. Corporal James Rozar announced that he would "freeze" the basement so that no one could come up and surprise the officers. With his service revolver drawn, Rozar twice shouted into the basement, ordering anyone down there to come out. When a voice asked who was calling, Rozar announced three times: "this is the police, show me your hands." Eventually, a pair of hands appeared around the bottom of the stairwell and Buie emerged from the basement. He was arrested, searched, and handcuffed by Rozar. Thereafter, Detective Joseph Frolich entered the basement "in case there was someone else" down there. He noticed a red running suit lying in plain view on a stack of clothing and seized it.

The trial court denied Buie's motion to suppress the running suit, stating in part: "The man comes out from a basement, the police don't know how many other people are down there. He is charged with a serious offense." The State introduced the running suit into evidence at Buie's trial. A jury convicted Buie of robbery with a deadly weapon and using a handgun in the commission of a felony.

The Court of Special Appeals of Maryland affirmed the trial court's denial of the suppression motion. The court stated that Detective Frolich did not go into the basement to search for evidence, but to look for the suspected accomplice or anyone else who might pose a threat to the officers on the scene. * * *

The Court of Appeals of Maryland reversed by a 4-to-3 vote. The court acknowledged that "when the intrusion is slight, as in the case of a brief stop and frisk on a public street, and the public interest in prevention of crime is substantial, reasonable articulable suspicion may be enough to pass constitutional muster". The court, however, stated that when the sanctity of the home is involved, the exceptions to the warrant requirement are few, and held: "To justify a protective sweep of a home, the government must show that there is probable cause to believe that " 'a serious and demonstrable potentiality for danger' " exists." The court went on to find that the State had not satisfied that probable-cause requirement. We granted certiorari.

II

* * * The issue in this case is what level of justification the Fourth Amendment required before Detective Frolich could legally enter the basement to see if someone else was there. * * *

III

It goes without saying that the Fourth Amendment bars only unreasonable searches and seizures. * * *

The *Terry [v. Ohio]* case is most instructive for present purposes. [Ed. note: The Court then summarized its holding in *Terry*.] * * *

The ingredients to apply the balance struck in *Terry* * * * are present in this case. Possessing an arrest warrant and probable cause to believe Buie was in his home, the officers were entitled to enter and to search anywhere in the house in which Buie might be found. Once he was found, however, the search for him was over, and there was no longer that particular justification for entering any rooms that had not yet been searched.

That Buie had an expectation of privacy in those remaining areas of his house, however, does not mean such rooms were immune from entry. In *Terry* * * * we were concerned with the immediate interest of the police officers in taking steps to assure themselves that the persons with whom they were dealing were not armed with, or able to gain immediate control of, a weapon that could unexpectedly and fatally be used against them. In the instant case, there is an analogous interest of the officers in taking steps to assure themselves that the house in which a suspect is being, or has just been, arrested is not harboring other persons who are dangerous and who could unexpectedly launch an attack. The risk of danger in the context of an arrest in the home is as great as, if not greater than, it is in an on-the-street or roadside investigatory encounter. A *Terry* * * * frisk occurs before a police-citizen confrontation has escalated to the point of arrest. A protective sweep, in contrast, occurs as an adjunct to the serious step of taking a person into custody for the purpose of prosecuting him for a crime. Moreover, unlike an encounter on the street or along a highway, an in-home arrest puts the officer at the disadvantage of being on his adversary's "turf." An ambush in a confined setting of unknown configuration is more to be feared than it is in open, more familiar surroundings.

We recognized in *Terry* that "even a limited search of the outer clothing for weapons constitutes a severe, though brief, intrusion upon cherished personal security, and it must surely be an annoying, frightening, and perhaps humiliating experience." But we permitted the intrusion, which was no more than necessary to protect the officer from harm. Nor do we here suggest, as the State does, that entering rooms not examined prior to the arrest is a *de minimis* intrusion that may be disregarded. We are quite sure, however, that the arresting officers are permitted in such circumstances to take reasonable steps to ensure their safety after, and while making, the arrest. That interest is sufficient to outweigh the intrusion such procedures may entail.

We agree with the State, as did the court below, that a warrant was not required.[1] We also hold that as an incident to the arrest the officers could, as a precautionary matter and without probable cause or reasonable suspicion, look in closets and other spaces immediately adjoining the place of arrest from which an attack could be immediately launched. Beyond that, however, we hold that there must be articulable facts which, taken together with the rational inferences from those facts, would warrant a reasonably prudent officer in believing that the area to be swept harbors an individual posing a danger to those on the arrest scene. This is no more and no less than was required in *Terry* and *Long*, and as in those cases, we think this balance is the proper one.

We should emphasize that such a protective sweep, aimed at protecting the arresting officers, if justified by the circumstances, is nevertheless not a full search of the premises, but may extend only to a cursory inspection of those spaces where a person may be found. The sweep lasts no longer than is necessary to dispel the reasonable suspicion of danger and in any event no longer than it takes to complete the arrest and depart the premises.

---

[1]   *Buie* suggests that because the police could have sought a warrant to search for dangerous persons in the house, they were constitutionally required to do so. But the arrest warrant gave the police every right to enter the home to search for *Buie*. Once inside, the potential for danger justified a standard of less than probable cause for conducting a limited protective sweep.

IV

Affirmance is not required by *Chimel v. California*, 395 U.S. 752 (1969), where it was held that in the absence of a search warrant, the justifiable search incident to an in-home arrest could not extend beyond the arrestee's person and the area from within which the arrestee might have obtained a weapon. First, *Chimel* was concerned with a full-blown search of the entire house for evidence of the crime for which the arrest was made, not the more limited intrusion contemplated by a protective sweep. Second, the justification for the search incident to arrest considered in *Chimel* was the threat posed by the arrestee, not the safety threat posed by the house, or more properly by unseen third parties in the house. To reach our conclusion today, therefore, we need not disagree with the Court's statement in *Chimel*, that "the invasion of privacy that results from a top-to-bottom search of a man's house [cannot be characterized] as 'minor,'" nor hold that "simply because some interference with an individual's privacy and freedom of movement has lawfully taken place, further intrusions should automatically be allowed despite the absence of a warrant that the Fourth Amendment would otherwise require". The type of search we authorize today is far removed from the "top-to-bottom" search involved in *Chimel*; moreover, it is decidedly not "automatic," but may be conducted only when justified by a reasonable, articulable suspicion that the house is harboring a person posing a danger to those on the arrest scene.

V

We conclude that by requiring a protective sweep to be justified by probable cause to believe that a serious and demonstrable potentiality for danger existed, the Court of Appeals of Maryland applied an unnecessarily strict Fourth Amendment standard. The Fourth Amendment permits a properly limited protective sweep in conjunction with an in-home arrest when the searching officer possesses a reasonable belief based on specific and articulable facts that the area to be swept harbors an individual posing a danger to those on the arrest scene. We therefore vacate the judgment below and remand this case to the Court of Appeals of Maryland for further proceedings not inconsistent with this opinion.

It is so ordered.

JUSTICE STEVENS, concurring.

[Omitted.]

JUSTICE KENNEDY, concurring.

[Omitted.]

JUSTICE BRENNAN, with whom JUSTICE MARSHALL joins, dissenting.

[Omitted.]

QUESTIONS, COMMENTS, CONCERNS?

1. ***Buie* and Kuklinski.** Does the warrantless arrest of Kuklinski just outside his home enable officers, pursuant to *Buie*, to enter his home in order to perform a protective sweep?

3.   Accessing the Arrestee's Car

ARIZONA V. GANT

556 U.S. 332
Supreme Court of the United States
October 7, 2008, Argued; April 21, 2009, Decided
No. 07-542

JUSTICE STEVENS delivered the opinion of the Court.

After Rodney Gant was arrested for driving with a suspended license, handcuffed, and locked in the back of a patrol car, police officers searched his car and discovered cocaine in the pocket of a jacket on the backseat. Because Gant could not have accessed his car to retrieve weapons or evidence at the time of the search, the Arizona Supreme Court held that the search-incident-to-arrest exception to the Fourth Amendment's warrant requirement, as defined in *Chimel v. California*, 395 U.S. 752 (1960), and applied to vehicle searches in *New York v. Belton*, 453 U.S. 454 (1981), did not justify the search in this case. We agree with that conclusion.

Under *Chimel*, police may search incident to arrest only the space within an arrestee's " 'immediate control,' " meaning "the area from within which he might gain possession of a weapon or destructible evidence." The safety and evidentiary justifications underlying *Chimel's* reaching-distance rule determine *Belton's* scope. Accordingly, we hold that *Belton* does not authorize a vehicle search incident to a recent occupant's arrest after the arrestee has been secured and cannot access the interior of the vehicle. Consistent with the holding in *Thornton v. United States*, 541 U.S. 615 (2004), and following the suggestion in Justice Scalia's opinion concurring in the judgment in that case, we also conclude that circumstances unique to the automobile context justify a search incident to arrest when it is reasonable to believe that evidence of the offense of arrest might be found in the vehicle.

I

On August 25, 1999, acting on an anonymous tip that the residence at 2524 North Walnut Avenue was being used to sell drugs, Tucson police officers Griffith and Reed knocked on the front door and asked to speak to the owner. Gant answered the door and, after identifying himself, stated that he expected the owner to return later. The officers left the residence and conducted a records check, which revealed that Gant's driver's license had been suspended and there was an outstanding warrant for his arrest for driving with a suspended license.

When the officers returned to the house that evening, they found a man near the back of the house and a woman in a car parked in front of it. After a third officer arrived, they arrested the man for providing a false name and the woman for possessing drug paraphernalia. Both arrestees were handcuffed and secured in separate patrol cars when Gant arrived. The officers recognized his car as it entered the driveway, and Officer Griffith confirmed that Gant was the driver by shining a flashlight into the car as it drove by him. Gant parked at the end of the driveway, got out of his car, and shut the door. Griffith, who was about 30 feet away, called to Gant, and they approached each other, meeting 10-to-12 feet from Gant's car. Griffith immediately arrested Gant and handcuffed him.

Because the other arrestees were secured in the only patrol cars at the scene, Griffith called for backup. When two more officers arrived, they locked Gant in the backseat of their vehicle. After Gant had been handcuffed and placed in the back of a patrol car, two officers searched his car: One of them found a gun, and the other discovered a bag of cocaine in the pocket of a jacket on the backseat.

Gant was charged with two offenses—possession of a narcotic drug for sale and possession of drug paraphernalia (i.e., the plastic bag in which the cocaine was found). He moved to suppress the evidence seized from his car on the ground that the warrantless search violated the Fourth Amendment. Among other things, Gant argued that Belton did not authorize the search of his vehicle because he posed no threat to the officers after he was handcuffed in the patrol car and because he was arrested for a traffic offense for which no evidence could be found in his vehicle. When asked at the suppression hearing why the search was conducted, Officer Griffith responded: "Because the law says we can do it."

The trial court rejected the State's contention that the officers had probable cause to search Gant's car for contraband when the search began, but it denied the motion to suppress. Relying on the fact that the police saw Gant commit the crime of driving without a license and apprehended him only shortly after he exited his car, the court held that the search was permissible as a search incident to arrest. A jury found Gant guilty on both drug counts, and he was sentenced to a 3-year term of imprisonment.

* * * [T]he Arizona Supreme Court concluded that the search of Gant's car was unreasonable within the meaning of the Fourth Amendment. The court's opinion discussed at length our decision in *[New York v.] Belton*, which held that police may search the passenger compartment of a vehicle and any containers therein as a contemporaneous incident of an arrest of the vehicle's recent occupant. The court distinguished *Belton* as a case concerning the permissible scope of a vehicle search incident to arrest and

concluded that it did not answer "the threshold question whether the police may conduct a search incident to arrest at all once the scene is secure." Relying on our earlier decision in *Chimel*, the court observed that the search-incident-to-arrest exception to the warrant requirement is justified by interests in officer safety and evidence preservation. When "the justifications underlying *Chimel* no longer exist because the scene is secure and the arrestee is handcuffed, secured in the back of a patrol car, and under the supervision of an officer," the court concluded, a "warrantless search of the arrestee's car cannot be justified as necessary to protect the officers at the scene or prevent the destruction of evidence." Accordingly, the court held that the search of Gant's car was unreasonable. * * *

The chorus that has called for us to revisit *Belton* includes courts, scholars, and Members of this Court who have questioned that decision's clarity and its fidelity to Fourth Amendment principles. We therefore granted the State's petition for certiorari.

II

Consistent with our precedent, our analysis begins, as it should in every case addressing the reasonableness of a warrantless search, with the basic rule that "searches conducted outside the judicial process, without prior approval by judge or magistrate, are per se unreasonable under the Fourth Amendment—subject only to a few specifically established and well-delineated exceptions." *Katz v. United States*, 389 U.S. 347, 357 (1967) (footnote omitted). Among the exceptions to the warrant requirement is a search incident to a lawful arrest. The exception derives from interests in officer safety and evidence preservation that are typically implicated in arrest situations.

* * * [Ed. note: the Court discussed its holding in *Chimel*.] In *Belton*, we considered *Chimel*'s application to the automobile context. A lone police officer in that case stopped a speeding car in which Belton was one of four occupants. While asking for the driver's license and registration, the officer smelled burnt marijuana and observed an envelope on the car floor marked "Supergold"—a name he associated with marijuana. Thus having probable cause to believe the occupants had committed a drug offense, the officer ordered them out of the vehicle, placed them under arrest, and patted them down. Without handcuffing the arrestees, the officer " 'split them up into four separate areas of the Thruway . . . so they would not be in physical touching area of each other' " and searched the vehicle, including the pocket of a jacket on the backseat, in which he found cocaine.

The New York Court of Appeals found the search unconstitutional, concluding that after the occupants were arrested the vehicle and its contents were "safely within the exclusive custody and control of the police." *State v. Belton*, 407 N.E.2d 420, 423 (1980). The State asked this Court to consider whether the exception recognized in *Chimel* permits an officer to search "a jacket found inside an automobile while the automobile's four occupants, all under arrest, are standing unsecured around the vehicle." We granted certiorari because "courts ha[d] found no workable definition of 'the area within the immediate control of the arrestee' when that area arguably includes the interior of an automobile."

* * * [W]e held that when an officer lawfully arrests "the occupant of an automobile, he may, as a contemporaneous incident of that arrest, search the passenger compartment of the automobile" and any containers therein. *Belton*, 453 U.S., at 460. That holding was based in large part on our assumption "that articles inside the relatively narrow compass of the passenger compartment of an automobile are in fact generally, even if not inevitably, within 'the area into which an arrestee might reach.' "

The Arizona Supreme Court read our decision in *Belton* as merely delineating "the proper scope of a search of the interior of an automobile" incident to an arrest. That is, when the passenger compartment is within an arrestee's reaching distance, *Belton* supplies the generalization that the entire compartment and any containers therein may be reached. On that view of *Belton*, the state court concluded that the search of Gant's car was unreasonable because Gant clearly could not have accessed his car at the time of the search. It also found that no other exception to the warrant requirement applied in this case.

Gant now urges us to adopt the reading of *Belton* followed by the Arizona Supreme Court.

III

Despite the textual and evidentiary support for the Arizona Supreme Court's reading of *Belton*, our opinion has been widely understood to allow a vehicle search incident to the arrest of a recent occupant even if there is no possibility the arrestee could gain access to the vehicle at the time of the search. * * *

Under this broad reading of *Belton*, a vehicle search would be authorized incident to every arrest of a recent occupant notwithstanding that in most cases the vehicle's passenger compartment will not be within the arrestee's reach at the time of the search. To read *Belton* as authorizing a vehicle search incident to every recent occupant's arrest would thus untether the rule from the justifications underlying the *Chimel* exception— a result clearly incompatible with our statement in *Belton* that it "in no way alters the fundamental principles established in the *Chimel* case regarding the basic scope of searches incident to lawful custodial arrests." Accordingly, we reject this reading of *Belton* and hold that the *Chimel* rationale authorizes police to search a vehicle incident to a recent occupant's arrest only when the arrestee is unsecured and within reaching distance of the passenger compartment at the time of the search.[4]

Although it does not follow from *Chimel*, we also conclude that circumstances unique to the vehicle context justify a search incident to a lawful arrest when it is "reasonable to believe evidence relevant to the crime of arrest might be found in the vehicle." In many cases, as when a recent occupant is arrested for a traffic violation, there will be no reasonable basis to believe the vehicle contains relevant evidence. But in others, including *Belton* and *Thornton*, the offense of arrest will supply a basis for searching the passenger compartment of an arrestee's vehicle and any containers therein.

Neither the possibility of access nor the likelihood of discovering offense-related evidence authorized the search in this case. Unlike in *Belton*, which involved a single officer confronted with four unsecured arrestees, the five officers in this case outnumbered the three arrestees, all of whom had been handcuffed and secured in separate patrol cars before the officers searched Gant's car. Under those circumstances, Gant clearly was not within reaching distance of his car at the time of the search. An evidentiary basis for the search was also lacking in this case. Whereas Belton and Thornton were arrested for drug offenses, Gant was arrested for driving with a suspended license—an offense for which police could not expect to find evidence in the passenger compartment of Gant's car. Because police could not reasonably have believed either that Gant could have accessed his car at the time of the search or that evidence of the offense for which he was arrested might have been found therein, the search in this case was unreasonable. * * *

VI

Police may search a vehicle incident to a recent occupant's arrest only if the arrestee is within reaching distance of the passenger compartment at the time of the search or it is reasonable to believe the vehicle contains evidence of the offense of arrest. When these justifications are absent, a search of an arrestee's vehicle will be unreasonable unless police obtain a warrant or show that another exception to the warrant requirement applies. The Arizona Supreme Court correctly held that this case involved an unreasonable search. Accordingly, the judgment of the State Supreme Court is affirmed.

It is so ordered.

---

[4] Because officers have many means of ensuring the safe arrest of vehicle occupants, it will be the rare case in which an officer is unable to fully effectuate an arrest so that a real possibility of access to the arrestee's vehicle remains. But in such a case a search incident to arrest is reasonable under the Fourth Amendment.

JUSTICE SCALIA, concurring.

To determine what is an "unreasonable" search within the meaning of the Fourth Amendment, we look first to the historical practices the Framers sought to preserve; if those provide inadequate guidance, we apply traditional standards of reasonableness. Since the historical scope of officers' authority to search vehicles incident to arrest is uncertain, traditional standards of reasonableness govern. It is abundantly clear that those standards do not justify what I take to be the rule set forth in *New York v. Belton*, 453 U.S. 454 (1981), and *Thornton*: that arresting officers may always search an arrestee's vehicle in order to protect themselves from hidden weapons. When an arrest is made in connection with a roadside stop, police virtually always have a less intrusive and more effective means of ensuring their safety—and a means that is virtually always employed: ordering the arrestee away from the vehicle, patting him down in the open, handcuffing him, and placing him in the squad car.

Law enforcement officers face a risk of being shot whenever they pull a car over. But that risk is at its height at the time of the initial confrontation; and it is not at all reduced by allowing a search of the stopped vehicle after the driver has been arrested and placed in the squad car. I observed in *Thornton* that the Government had failed to provide a single instance in which a formerly restrained arrestee escaped to retrieve a weapon from his own vehicle; Arizona and its amici have not remedied that significant deficiency in the present case.

It must be borne in mind that we are speaking here only of a rule automatically permitting a search when the driver or an occupant is arrested. Where no arrest is made, we have held that officers may search the car if they reasonably believe "the suspect is dangerous and . . . may gain immediate control of weapons." In the no-arrest case, the possibility of access to weapons in the vehicle always exists, since the driver or passenger will be allowed to return to the vehicle when the interrogation is completed. * * *

* * * In my view we should simply abandon the *Belton-Thornton* charade of officer safety and overrule those cases. I would hold that a vehicle search incident to arrest is *ipso facto* "reasonable" only when the object of the search is evidence of the crime for which the arrest was made, or of another crime that the officer has probable cause to believe occurred. Because respondent was arrested for driving without a license (a crime for which no evidence could be expected to be found in the vehicle), I would hold in the present case that the search was unlawful. * * *

No other Justice, however, shares my view that application of *Chimel* in this context should be entirely abandoned. It seems to me unacceptable for the Court to come forth with a 4-to-1-to-4 opinion that leaves the governing rule uncertain. * * * I therefore join the opinion of the Court.

JUSTICE BREYER, dissenting.

[Omitted.]

JUSTICE ALITO, with whom THE CHIEF JUSTICE and JUSTICE KENNEDY join, and with whom JUSTICE BREYER joins except as to Part II-E, dissenting.

Twenty-eight years ago, in *New York v. Belton*, 453 U.S. 454, 460 (1981), this Court held that "when a policeman has made a lawful custodial arrest of the occupant of an automobile, he may, as a contemporaneous incident of that arrest, search the passenger compartment of that automobile." Five years ago, in *Thornton v. United States*, 541 U.S. 615 (2004)—a case involving a situation not materially distinguishable from the situation here—the Court not only reaffirmed but extended the holding of *Belton*, making it applicable to recent occupants. Today's decision effectively overrules those important decisions, even though respondent Gant has not asked us to do so.

* * * I would follow *Belton*, and I therefore respectfully dissent.

I

Although the Court refuses to acknowledge that it is overruling *Belton* and *Thornton*, there can be no doubt that it does so. * * *

II

Because the Court has substantially overruled *Belton* and *Thornton*, the Court must explain why its departure from the usual rule of stare decisis is justified. I recognize that *stare decisis* is not an "inexorable command," and applies less rigidly in constitutional cases. But the Court has said that a constitutional precedent should be followed unless there is a " 'special justification' " for its abandonment. Relevant factors identified in prior cases include whether the precedent has engendered reliance, whether there has been an important change in circumstances in the outside world, whether the precedent has proved to be unworkable, whether the precedent has been undermined by later decisions, and whether the decision was badly reasoned. These factors weigh in favor of retaining the rule established in *Belton*. * * *

III

Respondent in this case has not asked us to overrule *Belton*, much less *Chimel*. Respondent's argument rests entirely on an interpretation of *Belton* that is plainly incorrect, an interpretation that disregards *Belton's* explicit delineation of its holding. I would therefore leave any reexamination of our prior precedents for another day, if such a reexamination is to be undertaken at all. In this case, I would simply apply *Belton* and reverse the judgment below.

QUESTIONS, COMMENTS, CONCERNS?

1. ***Gant*'s implications.** Two holdings emerge from *Gant*. First, at the outset of the majority opinion, Justice Stevens writes that it is no longer constitutional for police to search a recent occupant's vehicle incident to arrest after the arrestee has been secured. Can you imagine a scenario where a single officer can—or should—search the vehicle of an unsecured arrestee? Even if there is more than one officer present to help execute the arrest, when do you think an arrestee would remain "unsecured" such that other officers could search the arrestee's vehicle?

Second, the majority holds that "circumstances unique to the automobile context justify a search incident to arrest when it is reasonable to believe that evidence of the offense of arrest might be found in the vehicle." A few questions emerge from that holding. To begin, what kind of standard is "reasonable to believe"? Is that something different from reasonable suspicion or probable cause? And relatedly, what do you think falls within the ambit of "evidence of the offense of arrest"?

2. **A return to a search warrant "requirement"?** Did you catch that Justice Stevens quoted *Katz v. United States* (Chapter 3) in writing that "searches conducted outside the judicial process, without prior approval by judge or magistrate, are per se unreasonable under the Fourth Amendment— subject only to a few specifically established and well-delineated exceptions." Does the Court's reliance on that language signal a return to viewing the Fourth Amendment as requiring a search warrant?

3. ***Gant* and Kuklinski.** Recall that police searched Kuklinski's vehicle following his arrest and found a Beretta pistol under the front seat. In count seven of his February 26, 1987 indictment, the state charged Kuklinski with unlawful possession of a weapon with the purpose to use it unlawfully. [Casefile Document 1, at 11.] How does *Gant* apply to Kuklinski's arrest? Do the officers, at the time of arrest, need to state that they are arresting Kuklinski for murder to make it "reasonable to believe" that evidence of murder will be found in the vehicle"? And relatedly, do officers have reason to believe that Kuklinski would be armed given that his preferred method of killing involved poison?

4. ***Gant* and Barbara Kuklinski.** Does *Gant* legitimize the warrantless search of Kuklinski's vehicle as it relates to his wife, Barbara?

5. ***Gant* and double-dipping?** Recall that the state charged Barbara with unlawful possession of the same Beretta pistol referenced in count seven of Kuklinski's indictment. [Casefile Document 2.] Can officers permissibly charge both Kuklinski and his wife with unlawfully possessing the same weapon?

6. **Barbara and standing.** Does Barbara have standing to challenge the search of her husband's vehicle incident to *his* arrest? The issue was never litigated, but it's a compelling question. To perhaps heighten your interest, Kuklinski was apparently driving a vehicle with a single front bench seat.

7.   The rest of the Kuklinski story. Kuklinski died at the age of seventy in March 2006 after serving eighteen years of his sentence. Douglas Martin, *Richard Kuklinski, 70, a Killer of Many People and Many Ways, Dies*, N.Y. Times (Mar. 9, 2006), https://www.nytimes.com/2006/03/09/nyregion/ richard-kuklinski-70-a-killer-of-many-people-and-many-ways-dies.html.   His celebrity fame grew during his time in prison. He appeared in two HBO documentaries and was the subject of two books. Most recently, his life was featured in the 2012 film, *The Iceman*, starring Michael Shannon, Winona Ryder, and Ray Liotta.

Before his death, Kuklinski was diagnosed with a rare and incurable disease of the blood vessels. While lying in intensive care on his death bed, Kuklinski would see Barbara one final time. On the day of her final visit, Barbara signed a "do not resuscitate" order for Kuklinski despite Kuklinski previously asking doctors to revive him should he flatline. A week before Kuklinski's death, the hospital called Barbara to ask if she wanted to rescind the order. She declined. Adam Higginbotham, *Married to the Iceman*, Telegraph.co.uk (June 7, 2013), https://www.telegraph.co.uk/culture/film/99 59985/Married-to-The-Iceman.html.

4.   Accessing the Arrestee's Cell Phone

RILEY V. CALIFORNIA
573 U.S. 373
Supreme Court of the United States
April 29, 2014, Argued;[2] June 25, 2014, Decided
13-132, 13-212

Chief Justice Roberts delivered the opinion of the Court.

These two cases raise a common question: whether the police may, without a warrant, search digital information on a cell phone seized from an individual who has been arrested.

I

A

In the first case, petitioner David Riley was stopped by a police officer for driving with expired registration tags. In the course of the stop, the officer also learned that Riley's license had been suspended. The officer impounded Riley's car, pursuant to department policy, and another officer conducted an inventory search of the car. Riley was arrested for possession of concealed and loaded firearms when that search turned up two handguns under the car's hood.

An officer searched Riley incident to the arrest and found items associated with the "Bloods" street gang. He also seized a cell phone from

---

[2]   Together with No. 13-212, *United States v. Wurie*, on certiorari to the United States Court of Appeals for the First Circuit.

Riley's pants pocket. According to Riley's uncontradicted assertion, the phone was a "smart phone," a cell phone with a broad range of other functions based on advanced computing capability, large storage capacity, and Internet connectivity. The officer accessed information on the phone and noticed that some words (presumably in text messages or a contacts list) were preceded by the letters "CK"—a label that, he believed, stood for "Crip Killers," a slang term for members of the Bloods gang.

At the police station about two hours after the arrest, a detective specializing in gangs further examined the contents of the phone. The detective testified that he "went through" Riley's phone "looking for evidence, because . . . gang members will often video themselves with guns or take pictures of themselves with the guns." Although there was "a lot of stuff" on the phone, particular files that "caught [the detective's] eye" included videos of young men sparring while someone yelled encouragement using the moniker "Blood." The police also found photographs of Riley standing in front of a car they suspected had been involved in a shooting a few weeks earlier.

Riley was ultimately charged, in connection with that earlier shooting, with firing at an occupied vehicle, assault with a semiautomatic firearm, and attempted murder. The State alleged that Riley had committed those crimes for the benefit of a criminal street gang, an aggravating factor that carries an enhanced sentence. Prior to trial, Riley moved to suppress all evidence that the police had obtained from his cell phone. He contended that the searches of his phone violated the Fourth Amendment, because they had been performed without a warrant and were not otherwise justified by exigent circumstances. The trial court rejected that argument. At Riley's trial, police officers testified about the photographs and videos found on the phone, and some of the photographs were admitted into evidence. Riley was convicted on all three counts and received an enhanced sentence of 15 years to life in prison.

The California Court of Appeal affirmed. * * * The California Supreme Court denied Riley's petition for review, and we granted certiorari.

B

In the second case, a police officer performing routine surveillance observed respondent Brima Wurie make an apparent drug sale from a car. Officers subsequently arrested Wurie and took him to the police station. At the station, the officers seized two cell phones from Wurie's person. The one at issue here was a "flip phone," a kind of phone that is flipped open for use and that generally has a smaller range of features than a smart phone. Five to ten minutes after arriving at the station, the officers noticed that the phone was repeatedly receiving calls from a source identified as "my house" on the phone's external screen. A few minutes later, they opened the phone and saw a photograph of a woman and a baby set as the phone's wallpaper. They pressed one button on the phone to access its call log, then another button to determine the phone number associated with the "my house" label. They next used an online phone directory to trace that phone number to an apartment building.

When the officers went to the building, they saw Wurie's name on a mailbox and observed through a window a woman who resembled the woman in the photograph on Wurie's phone. They secured the apartment while obtaining a search warrant and, upon later executing the warrant, found and seized 215 grams of crack cocaine, marijuana, drug paraphernalia, a firearm and ammunition, and cash.

Wurie was charged with distributing crack cocaine, possessing crack cocaine with intent to distribute, and being a felon in possession of a firearm and ammunition. He moved to suppress the evidence obtained from the search of the apartment, arguing that it was the fruit of an unconstitutional search of his cell phone. The District Court denied the motion. Wurie was convicted on all three counts and sentenced to 262 months in prison.

A divided panel of the First Circuit reversed the denial of Wurie's motion to suppress and vacated Wurie's convictions for possession with intent to distribute and possession of a firearm as a felon. The court held that cell phones are distinct from other physical possessions that may be searched incident to arrest without a warrant, because of the amount of personal data cell phones contain and the negligible threat they pose to law enforcement interests.

We granted certiorari. * * *

III

These cases require us to decide how the search incident to arrest doctrine applies to modern cell phones, which are now such a pervasive and insistent part of daily life that the proverbial visitor from Mars might conclude they were an important feature of human anatomy. A smart phone of the sort taken from Riley was unheard of ten years ago; a significant majority of American adults now own such phones. Even less sophisticated phones like Wurie's, which have already faded in popularity since Wurie was arrested in 2007, have been around for less than 15 years. Both phones are based on technology nearly inconceivable just a few decades ago, when *Chimel* and *Robinson* were decided.

Absent more precise guidance from the founding era, we generally determine whether to exempt a given type of search from the warrant requirement "by assessing, on the one hand, the degree to which it intrudes upon an individual's privacy and, on the other, the degree to which it is needed for the promotion of legitimate governmental interests." Such a balancing of interests supported the search incident to arrest exception in

Robinson, and a mechanical application of *Robinson* might well support the warrantless searches at issue here.

But while *Robinson*'s categorical rule strikes the appropriate balance in the context of physical objects, neither of its rationales has much force with respect to digital content on cell phones. On the government interest side, *Robinson* concluded that the two risks identified in *Chimel*—harm to officers and destruction of evidence—are present in all custodial arrests. There are no comparable risks when the search is of digital data. In addition, *Robinson* regarded any privacy interests retained by an individual after arrest as significantly diminished by the fact of the arrest itself. Cell phones, however, place vast quantities of personal information literally in the hands of individuals. A search of the information on a cell phone bears little resemblance to the type of brief physical search considered in *Robinson.*

We therefore decline to extend *Robinson* to searches of data on cell phones, and hold instead that officers must generally secure a warrant before conducting such a search.

A

We first consider each *Chimel* concern in turn. In doing so, we do not overlook *Robinson*'s admonition that searches of a person incident to arrest, "while based upon the need to disarm and to discover evidence," are reasonable regardless of "the probability in a particular arrest situation that weapons or evidence would in fact be found." Rather than requiring the "case-by-case adjudication" that *Robinson* rejected, we ask instead whether application of the search incident to arrest doctrine to this particular category of effects would "untether the rule from the justifications underlying the *Chimel* exception".

1

Digital data stored on a cell phone cannot itself be used as a weapon to harm an arresting officer or to effectuate the arrestee's escape. Law enforcement officers remain free to examine the physical aspects of a phone to ensure that it will not be used as a weapon—say, to determine whether there is a razor blade hidden between the phone and its case. Once an officer has secured a phone and eliminated any potential physical threats, however, data on the phone can endanger no one.

Perhaps the same might have been said of the cigarette pack seized from Robinson's pocket. Once an officer gained control of the pack, it was unlikely that Robinson could have accessed the pack's contents. But unknown physical objects may always pose risks, no matter how slight, during the tense atmosphere of a custodial arrest. The officer in *Robinson* testified that he could not identify the objects in the cigarette pack but knew they were not cigarettes. Given that, a further search was a reasonable protective measure. No such unknowns exist with respect to digital data. As the First Circuit explained, the officers who searched Wurie's cell phone "knew exactly what they would find therein: data. They also knew that the data could not harm them."

The United States and California both suggest that a search of cell phone data might help ensure officer safety in more indirect ways, for example by alerting officers that confederates of the arrestee are headed to the scene. There is undoubtedly a strong government interest in warning officers about such possibilities, but neither the United States nor California offers evidence to suggest that their concerns are based on actual experience. The proposed consideration would also represent a broadening of *Chimel*'s concern that an arrestee himself might grab a weapon and use it against an officer "to resist arrest or effect his escape." And any such threats from outside the arrest scene do not "lurk[ ] in all custodial arrests." Accordingly, the interest in protecting officer safety does not justify dispensing with the warrant requirement across the board. To the extent dangers to arresting officers may be implicated in a particular way in a particular case, they are better addressed through consideration of case-specific exceptions to the warrant requirement, such as the one for exigent circumstances.

2

The United States and California focus primarily on the second *Chimel* rationale: preventing the destruction of evidence.

Both Riley and Wurie concede that officers could have seized and secured their cell phones to prevent destruction of evidence while seeking a warrant. That is a sensible concession. And once law enforcement officers have secured a cell phone, there is no longer any risk that the arrestee himself will be able to delete incriminating data from the phone.

The United States and California argue that information on a cell phone may nevertheless be vulnerable to two types of evidence destruction unique to digital data—remote wiping and data encryption. Remote wiping occurs when a phone, connected to a wireless network, receives a signal that erases stored data. This can happen when a third party sends a remote signal or when a phone is preprogrammed to delete data upon entering or leaving certain geographic areas (so-called "geofencing"). Encryption is a security feature that some modern cell phones use in addition to password protection. When such phones lock, data becomes protected by sophisticated encryption that renders a phone all but "unbreakable" unless police know the password.

As an initial matter, these broader concerns about the loss of evidence are distinct from *Chimel*'s focus on a defendant who responds to arrest by trying to conceal or destroy evidence within his reach. With respect to remote wiping, the Government's primary concern turns on the actions of third parties who are not present at the scene of arrest. And data encryption is even further afield. There, the Government focuses on the ordinary operation of a phone's security features, apart from any active attempt by a defendant or his associates to conceal or destroy evidence upon arrest.

We have also been given little reason to believe that either problem is prevalent. The briefing reveals only a couple of anecdotal examples of remote wiping triggered by an arrest. Similarly, the opportunities for officers to search a password-protected phone before data becomes encrypted are quite limited. Law enforcement officers are very unlikely to come upon such a phone in an unlocked state because most phones lock at the touch of a button or, as a default, after some very short period of inactivity. *See, e.g.,* iPhone User Guide for iOS 7.1 Software 10 (2014) (default lock after about one minute). This may explain why the encryption argument was not made until the merits stage in this Court, and has never been considered by the Courts of Appeals.

Moreover, in situations in which an arrest might trigger a remote-wipe attempt or an officer discovers an unlocked phone, it is not clear that the ability to conduct a warrantless search would make much of a difference. The need to effect the arrest, secure the scene, and tend to other pressing matters means that law enforcement officers may well not be able to turn their attention to a cell phone right away. Cell phone data would be vulnerable to remote wiping from the time an individual anticipates arrest to the time any eventual search of the phone is completed, which might be at the station house hours later. Likewise, an officer who seizes a phone in an unlocked state might not be able to begin his search in the short time remaining before the phone locks and data becomes encrypted.

In any event, as to remote wiping, law enforcement is not without specific means to address the threat. Remote wiping can be fully prevented by disconnecting a phone from the network. There are at least two simple ways to do this: First, law enforcement officers can turn the phone off or remove its battery. Second, if they are concerned about encryption or other potential problems, they can leave a phone powered on and place it in an enclosure that isolates the phone from radio waves. Such devices are commonly called "Faraday bags," after the English scientist Michael Faraday. They are essentially sandwich bags made of aluminum foil: cheap, lightweight, and easy to use. They may not be a complete answer to the problem, but at least for now they provide a reasonable response. In fact, a number of law enforcement agencies around the country already encourage the use of Faraday bags.

To the extent that law enforcement still has specific concerns about the potential loss of evidence in a particular case, there remain more targeted ways to address those concerns. If "the police are truly confronted with a 'now or never' situation,"—for example, circumstances suggesting that a defendant's phone will be the target of an imminent remote-wipe attempt—they may be able to rely on exigent circumstances to search the phone immediately. Or, if officers happen to seize a phone in an unlocked state, they may be able to disable a phone's automatic-lock feature in order to prevent the phone from locking and encrypting data. Such a preventive measure could be analyzed under the principles set forth in our decision in *[Illinois v.] McArthur*, which approved officers' reasonable steps to secure a scene to preserve evidence while they awaited a warrant.

B

The search incident to arrest exception rests not only on the heightened government interests at stake in a volatile arrest situation, but also on an arrestee's reduced privacy interests upon being taken into police custody. *Robinson* focused primarily on the first of those rationales. But it also quoted with approval then-Judge Cardozo's account of the historical basis for the search incident to arrest exception: "Search of the person becomes lawful when grounds for arrest and accusation have been discovered, and the law is in the act of subjecting the body of the accused to its physical dominion." Put simply, a patdown of Robinson's clothing and an inspection of the cigarette pack found in his pocket constituted only minor additional intrusions compared to the substantial government authority exercised in taking Robinson into custody.

The fact that an arrestee has diminished privacy interests does not mean that the Fourth Amendment falls out of the picture entirely. Not every search "is acceptable solely because a person is in custody." To the contrary, when "privacy-related concerns are weighty enough" a "search may require a warrant, notwithstanding the diminished expectations of privacy of the arrestee." One such example, of course, is *Chimel*. *Chimel* refused to "characteriz[e] the invasion of privacy that results from a top-to-bottom search of a man's house as 'minor.'" Because a search of the arrestee's entire house was a substantial invasion beyond the arrest itself, the Court concluded that a warrant was required.

Robinson is the only decision from this Court applying *Chimel* to a search of the contents of an item found on an arrestee's person. In an earlier case, this Court had approved a search of a zipper bag carried by an arrestee, but the Court analyzed only the validity of the arrest itself. Lower courts applying *Robinson* and *Chimel*, however, have approved searches of a variety of personal items carried by an arrestee. *See, e.g., United States v. Carrion*, 809 F.2d 1120, 1123, 1128 (5th Cir. 1987) (billfold and address book); *United States v. Watson*, 669 F.2d 1374, 1383–84 (11th Cir. 1982) (wallet); United States v. Lee, 501 F.2d 890, 892 (D.C. Cir. 1974) (purse).

The United States asserts that a search of all data stored on a cell phone is "materially indistinguishable" from searches of these sorts of physical items. That is like saying a ride on horseback is materially indistinguishable from a flight to the moon. Both are ways of getting from point A to point B, but little else justifies lumping them together. Modern cell phones, as a category, implicate privacy concerns far beyond those implicated by the search of a cigarette pack, a wallet, or a purse. A conclusion that inspecting the contents of an arrestee's pockets works no substantial additional intrusion on privacy beyond the arrest itself may make sense as applied to physical items, but any extension of that reasoning to digital data has to rest on its own bottom.

1

Cell phones differ in both a quantitative and a qualitative sense from other objects that might be kept on an arrestee's person. The term "cell phone" is itself misleading shorthand; many of these devices are in fact minicomputers that also happen to have the capacity to be used as a telephone. They could just as easily be called cameras, video players, rolodexes, calendars, tape recorders, libraries, diaries, albums, televisions, maps, or newspapers.

One of the most notable distinguishing features of modern cell phones is their immense storage capacity. Before cell phones, a search of a person was limited by physical realities and tended as a general matter to constitute only a narrow intrusion on privacy. Most people cannot lug around every piece of mail they have received for the past several months, every picture they have taken, or every book or article they have read—nor would they have any reason to attempt to do so. * * *

But the possible intrusion on privacy is not physically limited in the same way when it comes to cell phones. The current top-selling smart phone has a standard capacity of 16 gigabytes (and is available with up to 64 gigabytes). Sixteen gigabytes translates to millions of pages of text, thousands of pictures, or hundreds of videos. Cell phones couple that capacity with the ability to store many different types of information: Even the most basic phones that sell for less than $20 might hold photographs, picture messages, text messages, Internet browsing history, a calendar, a thousand-entry phone book, and so on. We expect that the gulf between physical practicability and digital capacity will only continue to widen in the future.

The storage capacity of cell phones has several interrelated consequences for privacy. First, a cell phone collects in one place many distinct types of information—an address, a note, a prescription, a bank statement, a video—that reveal much more in combination than any isolated record. Second, a cell phone's capacity allows even just one type of information to convey far more than previously possible. The sum of an individual's private life can be reconstructed through a thousand photographs labeled with dates, locations, and descriptions; the same cannot be said of a photograph or two of loved ones tucked into a wallet. Third, the data on a phone can date back to the purchase of the phone, or even earlier. A person might carry in his pocket a slip of paper reminding him to call Mr. Jones; he would not carry a record of all his communications with Mr. Jones for the past several months, as would routinely be kept on a phone.

Finally, there is an element of pervasiveness that characterizes cell phones but not physical records. Prior to the digital age, people did not typically carry a cache of sensitive personal information with them as they went about their day. Now it is the person who is not carrying a cell phone, with all that it contains, who is the exception. According to one poll, nearly three-quarters of smart phone users report being within five feet of their phones most of the time, with 12% admitting that they even use their phones in the shower. A decade ago police officers searching an arrestee might have occasionally stumbled across a highly personal item such as a diary. But those discoveries were likely to be few and far between. Today, by contrast, it is no exaggeration to say that many of the more than 90% of American adults who own a cell phone keep on their person a digital record of nearly every aspect of their lives—from the mundane to the intimate. Allowing the police to scrutinize such records on a routine basis is quite different from allowing them to search a personal item or two in the occasional case.

Although the data stored on a cell phone is distinguished from physical records by quantity alone, certain types of data are also qualitatively different. An Internet search and browsing history, for example, can be found on an Internet-enabled phone and could reveal an individual's private interests or concerns—perhaps a search for certain symptoms of disease, coupled with frequent visits to WebMD. Data on a cell phone can also reveal where a person has been. Historic location information is a standard feature on many smart phones and can reconstruct someone's specific movements down to the minute, not only around town but also within a particular building.

Mobile application software on a cell phone, or "apps," offer a range of tools for managing detailed information about all aspects of a person's life. There are apps for Democratic Party news and Republican Party news; apps for alcohol, drug, and gambling addictions; apps for sharing prayer requests; apps for tracking pregnancy symptoms; apps for planning your budget; apps for every conceivable hobby or pastime; apps for improving your romantic life. There are popular apps for buying or selling just about anything, and the records of such transactions may be accessible on the phone indefinitely. There are over a million apps available in each of the two major app stores; the phrase "there's an app for that" is now part of the popular lexicon. The average smart phone user has installed 33 apps, which together can form a revealing montage of the user's life.

In 1926, Learned Hand observed (in an opinion later quoted in *Chimel*) that it is "a totally different thing to search a man's pockets and use against him what they contain, from ransacking his house for everything which may incriminate him." If his pockets contain a cell phone, however, that is no longer true. Indeed, a cell phone search would typically expose to the government far more than the most exhaustive search of a house: A phone not only contains in digital form many sensitive records previously found in the home; it also contains a broad array of private information never found in a home in any form—unless the phone is.

2

To further complicate the scope of the privacy interests at stake, the data a user views on many modern cell phones may not in fact be stored on the device itself. Treating a cell phone as a container whose contents may be searched incident to an arrest is a bit strained as an initial matter. But the analogy crumbles entirely when a cell phone is used to access data located elsewhere, at the tap of a screen. That is what cell phones, with increasing frequency, are designed to do by taking advantage of "cloud computing." Cloud computing is the capacity of Internet-connected devices to display data stored on remote servers rather than on the device itself. Cell phone users often may not know whether particular information is stored on the device or in the cloud, and it generally makes little difference. Moreover, the same type of data may be stored locally on the device for one user and in the cloud for another.

The United States concedes that the search incident to arrest exception may not be stretched to cover a search of files accessed remotely—that is, a search of files stored in the cloud. Such a search would be like finding a key in a suspect's pocket and arguing that it allowed law enforcement to unlock and search a house. But officers searching a phone's data would not typically know whether the information they are viewing was stored locally at the time of the arrest or has been pulled from the cloud.

Although the Government recognizes the problem, its proposed solutions are unclear. It suggests that officers could disconnect a phone from the network before searching the device—the very solution whose feasibility it contested with respect to the threat of remote wiping. Alternatively, the Government proposes that law enforcement agencies "develop protocols to address" concerns raised by cloud computing. Probably a good idea, but the Founders did not fight a revolution to gain the right to government agency protocols. The possibility that a search might extend well beyond papers and effects in the physical proximity of an arrestee is yet another reason that the privacy interests here dwarf those in *Robinson*. * * *

IV

We cannot deny that our decision today will have an impact on the ability of law enforcement to combat crime. Cell phones have become important tools in facilitating coordination and communication among members of criminal enterprises, and can provide valuable incriminating information about dangerous criminals. Privacy comes at a cost.

Our holding, of course, is not that the information on a cell phone is immune from search; it is instead that a warrant is generally required before such a search, even when a cell phone is seized incident to arrest. Our cases have historically recognized that the warrant requirement is "an important working part of our machinery of government," not merely "an inconvenience to be somehow 'weighed' against the claims of police efficiency." Recent technological advances similar to those discussed here have, in addition, made the process of obtaining a warrant itself more efficient.

Moreover, even though the search incident to arrest exception does not apply to cell phones, other case-specific exceptions may still justify a warrantless search of a particular phone. "One well-recognized exception applies when ' "the exigencies of the situation" make the needs of law enforcement so compelling that [a] warrantless search is objectively reasonable under the Fourth Amendment.' " Such exigencies could include the need to prevent the imminent destruction of evidence in individual cases, to pursue a fleeing suspect, and to assist persons who are seriously injured or are threatened with imminent injury. * * * *

In light of the availability of the exigent circumstances exception, there is no reason to believe that law enforcement officers will not be able to address some of the more extreme hypotheticals that have been suggested: a suspect texting an accomplice who, it is feared, is preparing to detonate a bomb, or a child abductor who may have information about the child's location on his cell phone. The defendants here recognize—indeed, they stress—that such fact-specific threats may justify a warrantless search of cell phone data. The critical point is that, unlike the search incident to arrest exception, the exigent circumstances exception requires a court to examine whether an emergency justified a warrantless search in each particular case.

* * *

* * * Modern cell phones are not just another technological convenience. With all they contain and all they may reveal, they hold for many Americans "the privacies of life". The fact that technology now allows an individual to carry such information in his hand does not make the information any less worthy of the protection for which the Founders fought. Our answer to the question of what police must do before searching

a cell phone seized incident to an arrest is accordingly simple—get a warrant.

We reverse the judgment of the California Court of Appeal in No. 13-132 and remand the case for further proceedings not inconsistent with this opinion. We affirm the judgment of the First Circuit in No. 13-212.

It is so ordered.

JUSTICE ALITO, concurring in part and concurring in the judgment.

[Omitted.]

IV. CONSENT

A. INTRODUCTION[3]

One of the more popular warrantless search tools for the officer walking the beat is the consent search. Although no precise data exist on how often consent searches occur, one study reports that the two most commonly utilized warrantless searches are consent searches and searches incident to arrest. In that study, one detective estimated that consent serves as the basis for ninety-eight percent of all searches conducted. Police may request consent even if they do not need it, and at no point must an officer advise the citizen that they can refuse consent.

With this in mind, it would be an understatement to suggest that officers rely heavily on consent searches. Academics generally view the Supreme Court's current consent search doctrine with disdain. Courts and academics alike view consent searches as difficult to police given the pervasive discretion that officers have in deciding who to ask for consent to search. As a result of this discretion, allegations of racism pervade many state police officers' consent search practices.

Given the skepticism of current consent search practices—as opposed to the consent search doctrine itself—a simple question arises: how did we get here? Well, maybe it happened in 1969 when Warren Burger replaced Earl Warren as Chief Justice of the Supreme Court. At that time, many believed his "law and order" background foretold overruling the so-called Warren Court trilogy—*Gideon* (requiring that counsel be appointed for indigent defendants), *Mapp* (extending the exclusionary rule to the states), and *Miranda* (requiring officers to provide warnings to suspects subject to custodial interrogation). Because that never happened, a handful of important commentators and historians view the Burger Court's criminal procedure decisions as anticlimactic. That popular view, however, overlooks one of the Burger Court's primary anti-*Miranda* achievements:

---

[3] Portions of the discussion that follows are adapted with permission from Brian Gallini, Schneckloth v. Bustamonte: *History's Unspoken Fourth Amendment Anomaly,* 79 TENN. L. REV. 233 (2012). All footnotes are omitted.

Schneckloth v. Bustamonte. Schneckloth, our first case in these materials, remarkably made clear that the Fourth Amendment does not require officers to warn citizens of their right to refuse consent. But ironically, thanks to *Miranda*, suspects in the interrogation room are provided with a panoply of rights.

As we undertake the study of consent searches, there are numerous questions to keep in mind. Chief among them are what constitutes consent? Does a simple "yes" in response to an officer's request to search, for example, a home permit that officer to search the entire home for an indeterminate period of time? The facts of our next defendant's case, Zach Witman, are, in a word, heartbreaking. But the investigation into Witman's case also highlights the full array of challenges often presented by consent search cases.

B. MEET ZACH WITMAN

The Crime

On Friday, October 2, 1998, Susquehannock High School in Freedom Borough, Pennsylvania, was preparing for its homecoming football game. Among the high school students was fourteen-year-old Erynn Jeffery. When Jeffery got home from school that afternoon, she immediately called her best friend, Gregory Witman, to see if he wanted to accompany her to the game. But when Jeffery called the Witman home phone at 3:09 p.m., she was surprised when someone picked up the phone and immediately hung up. Because Jeffery and Greg spoke on the phone nearly every day after school, Jeffery was able to recognize that whoever hung up the phone did so from the flip style phone located in the kitchen because it made a distinct sound when hung up.

Jeffery assumed that Greg simply had not gotten off the bus from school yet. She therefore waited and called again at 3:15 p.m. This time, Greg's older brother, Zachary, who was home sick that day, answered. Zach informed Jeffery that Greg had not yet come home from school, but that he should be off the bus in a few minutes. After saying goodbye, Jeffery noticed that Zach was not speaking on the flip phone in the kitchen because it did not make a distinctive sound when Zach hung up. At 3:17 p.m., Zach Witman called 911 explaining that he had just come downstairs to find his brother brutally murdered.

Greg was pronounced dead by the York County Coroner at 4:25 p.m. on October 2, 1998. The coroner determined the time of death to be approximately 3:15 p.m. earlier that day. A subsequent autopsy revealed that Greg was stabbed approximately 100 times with a small 1¾ inch blade knife. Approximately sixty-five of those stab wounds were around Greg's neck, which nearly decapitated him. Ultimately, the medical examiner listed the cause and manner of death as homicide by multiple sharp force injuries.

The Investigation

On October 2, 1998, at approximately 3:17 p.m., York County dispatch received the call from Zach reporting that he had found Greg stabbed to death inside their home at #9 Albright Court, New Freedom Borough, Pennsylvania. As police and emergency vehicles rushed to the scene, Zach told the dispatcher that he came downstairs after hearing a commotion and found Greg lying dead in the laundry room with his throat cut. When emergency personnel arrived, they found a hysterical Zach with blood stains covering his sweatshirt and socks. They rushed Zach to the hospital for treatment. While on the way to the hospital, EMTs removed Zach's bloody sweatshirt and socks.

Police Chief Childs arrived on scene at approximately 3:30 p.m. and took control of the investigation. Fearing that someone might still be inside the home, Childs searched the interior of the house both upstairs and downstairs. Finding no one else, Childs directed Officer Boddington to follow Zach's ambulance and seize his clothing because he regarded the clothing as part of the crime scene. At the hospital, an EMT, assuming that Boddington had authority to seize them, handed over a bag containing Zach's bloody clothes. The EMT also gave Boddington the towel, alcohol swabs, and latex gloves used in Zach's treatment. Hospital personnel also retrieved Zach's clothing, sweatpants, and underwear from inside the ER examining room at Officer Boddington's request. At no point did law enforcement ask Zach for consent to seize his clothing.

Back at the crime scene, Detective Goodfellow, unaware that Childs had already conducted a security sweep, entered the Witman House with Chief Childs. Goodfellow made extensive plain view observations of the bloody scene downstairs. Based on the massive scale of the crime scene, Goodfellow called in the Crime Scene Identification Unit ("CSIU") to conduct a full forensic evaluation of the home. Goodfellow and Childs then left the home and waited for CSIU to arrive. As they waited, Childs called Zach's mother, Sue Witman, but did not ask for consent to search the house or yard, or to seize Zach's clothing. Instead, Childs explained to Mrs. Witman "what they were going to do as far as what we needed to do as far as processing the crime scene to obtain clues" assuming "that you know, she knew what I wanted to do and what the detective team was going to do." According to Childs, Mrs. Witman's only reply was to demand that the police find her son's killer, telling him "he better do his job."

A comprehensive search of the Witman residence began at 5:30 p.m. CSIU's processing of the home was extensive. Although no visible footprints or blood trails were observed, the search employed the use of Luminol, a prescriptive chemical designed to enhance the ability to see blood. The Luminol test commenced at approximately 12:30 p.m. on October 3. The Luminol revealed a trail of blood from the front door of the home, through the kitchen, and out into the back yard where a hot tub and gazebo were located. There, investigators discovered a mound of freshly disturbed dirt next to the gazebo where they recovered a bloody pen knife with a 1¾ inch blade and a bloody glove. In all, law enforcement seized forty-four items during the initial search of the Witman residence (including Zach's bloody clothing).

Zach's father, Ron Witman, arrived at the hospital at approximately 8:00 p.m. on October 2, several hours after the crime but before the Luminol test began. Detective Clancy told Mr. Witman about the search that was currently underway at his home. Mr. Witman replied, "go find Greg's killer" and "whatever it takes, do!" Detective Clancy then returned to the Witman residence and shared Mr. Witman's response with his fellow investigators.

The Motion

Days after the crime, on October 10, 1998, the Commonwealth filed a criminal complaint charging Zach with intentionally, knowingly, recklessly, or negligently causing the death of his brother, Greg Witman. Then, on February 16, 1999, Zach's defense attorney filed a motion to suppress all items seized during CSIU's warrantless search of the Witman residence alongside the clothing seized from Zach at the hospital by Officer Boddington. Addressing the search of the Witman home, Zach argued that Childs had already conducted a protective sweep to secure the home. Accordingly, Zach contended, CSIU was required to obtain a search warrant before investigating further. As for the hospital seizure, Zach asserted that Boddington unlawfully seized his clothing without either a search warrant or obtaining his or a parent's consent.

The Commonwealth responsively argued that Zach consented to police presence in his home because he called 911 requesting emergency assistance. It also argued that Zach, as a fifteen-year-old minor, did not have standing to challenge the home search because he did not have a proprietary or possessory interest in the premises or the items seized. Even if Zach had standing to challenge the search, the Commonwealth contended, police had consent to search the premises from Zach (through his call to 911) and his mother (through her acknowledgement of the policing presence at her home and instructing them to do their jobs).

In a forty-four-page opinion, Court of Common Pleas Judge John C. Uhler ruled that Zach had standing to challenge the search of his home. Specifically, the court held that Zach had a valid privacy interest in the home's contents that was not invalidated by his request for emergency assistance. As a result, said the court, the 911 phone call Zach made did not establish consent to search the home. The court moreover held that Mrs. Witman's comment for police to "do their job" was not an affirmative consent to search the residence, but instead a responsive acquiescence to Childs's explanation of how detectives would process the crime scene. The court, however, construed Mr. Witman's "whatever it takes, do" statement as providing valid consent to search the home. Thus, the court: (1) admitted all items that were seized in plain view during the protective sweep of the home, (2) admitted all items obtained after Mr. Witman's consent, and (3) suppressed items seized after the protective sweep but before Mr. Witman's consent.

Zach's trial for the murder of his brother began on May 8, 2003, after years of delays caused by appeals related to his suppression motion.

C. THE CASES

SCHNECKLOTH V. BUSTAMONTE

412 U.S. 218
Supreme Court of the United States
October 10, 1972, Argued; May 29, 1973, Decided
No. 71-732

MR. JUSTICE STEWART delivered the opinion of the Court.

* * * The constitutional question in the present case concerns the definition of "consent" in this Fourth and Fourteenth Amendment context.

I

The respondent was brought to trial in a California court upon a charge of possessing a check with intent to defraud. He moved to suppress the introduction of certain material as evidence against him on the ground that the material had been acquired through an unconstitutional search and seizure. In response to the motion, the trial judge conducted an evidentiary hearing where it was established that the material in question had been acquired by the State under the following circumstances:

While on routine patrol in Sunnyvale, California, at approximately 2:40 in the morning, Police Officer James Rand stopped an automobile when he observed that one headlight and its license plate light were burned out. Six men were in the vehicle. Joe Alcala and the respondent, Robert Bustamonte, were in the front seat with Joe Gonzales, the driver. Three older men were seated in the rear. When, in response to the policeman's question, Gonzales could not produce a driver's license, Officer Rand asked if any of the other five had any evidence of identification. Only Alcala produced a license, and he explained that the car was his brother's. After the six occupants had stepped out of the car at the officer's request and after two additional policemen had arrived, Officer Rand asked Alcala if he could search the car. Alcala replied, "Sure, go ahead." Prior to the search no one was threatened with arrest and, according to Officer Rand's uncontradicted testimony, it "was all very congenial at this time." Gonzales testified that Alcala actually helped in the search of the car, by opening the trunk and glove compartment. In Gonzales' words: "The police officer asked Joe [Alcala], he goes, 'Does the trunk open?' And Joe said, 'Yes.' He went to the car and got the keys and opened up the trunk." Wadded up under the left rear seat, the police officers found three checks that had previously been stolen from a car wash.

The trial judge denied the motion to suppress, and the checks in question were admitted in evidence at Bustamonte's trial. On the basis of this and other evidence he was convicted, and the California Court of Appeal for the First Appellate District affirmed the conviction. In agreeing that the search and seizure were constitutionally valid, the appellate court applied the standard earlier formulated by the Supreme Court of California in an opinion by then Justice Traynor: "Whether in a particular case an apparent consent was in fact voluntarily given or was in submission to an express or implied assertion of authority, is a question of fact to be determined in the light of all the circumstances." The appellate court found that "in the instant case the prosecution met the necessary burden of showing consent . . . since there were clearly circumstances from which the trial court could ascertain that consent had been freely given without coercion or submission to authority. Not only officer Rand, but Gonzales, the driver of the automobile, testified that Alcala's assent to the search of his brother's automobile was freely, even casually given. At the time of the request to search the automobile the atmosphere, according to Rand, was 'congenial' and there had been no discussion of any crime. As noted, Gonzales said Alcala even attempted to aid in the search." The California Supreme Court denied review.

Thereafter, the respondent sought a writ of habeas corpus in a federal district court. It was denied. On appeal, the Court of Appeals for the Ninth Circuit, relying on its prior decisions * * * set aside the District Court's order. The appellate court reasoned that a consent was a waiver of a person's Fourth and Fourteenth Amendment rights, and that the State was under an obligation to demonstrate, not only that the consent had been uncoerced, but that it had been given with an understanding that it could be freely and effectively withheld. Consent could not be found, the court held, solely from the absence of coercion and a verbal expression of assent. Since the District Court had not determined that Alcala had known that his consent could have been withheld and that he could have refused to have his vehicle searched, the Court of Appeals vacated the order denying the writ and remanded the case for further proceedings. We granted certiorari to determine whether the Fourth and Fourteenth Amendments require the showing thought necessary by the Court of Appeals.

II

* * * [T]he State concedes that "when a prosecutor seeks to rely upon consent to justify the lawfulness of a search, he has the burden of proving that the consent was, in fact, freely and voluntarily given."

The precise question in this case, then, is what must the prosecution prove to demonstrate that a consent was "voluntarily" given. And upon that question there is a square conflict of views between the state and federal courts that have reviewed the search involved in the case before us. * * *

A

The most extensive judicial exposition of the meaning of "voluntariness" has been developed in those cases in which the Court has had to determine the "voluntariness" of a defendant's confession for purposes of the Fourteenth Amendment. Almost 40 years ago, in *Brown v. Mississippi*, 297 U.S. 278, the Court held that a criminal conviction based upon a confession obtained by brutality and violence was constitutionally invalid under the Due Process Clause of the Fourteenth Amendment. In some 30 different cases decided during the era that intervened between *Brown* and *Escobedo v. Illinois*, 378 U.S. 478, the Court was faced with the necessity of determining whether in fact the confessions in issue had been "voluntarily" given. It is to that body of case law to which we turn for initial guidance on the meaning of "voluntariness" in the present context.

Those cases yield no talismanic definition of "voluntariness," mechanically applicable to the host of situations where the question has arisen. * * *

* * * "The ultimate test remains that which has been the only clearly established test in Anglo-American courts for two hundred years: the test of voluntariness. Is the confession the product of an essentially free and unconstrained choice by its maker? If it is, if he has willed to confess, it may be used against him. If it is not, if his will has been overborne and his capacity for self-determination critically impaired, the use of his confession offends due process."

In determining whether a defendant's will was over-borne in a particular case, the Court has assessed the totality of all the surrounding circumstances—both the characteristics of the accused and the details of the interrogation. Some of the factors taken into account have included the youth of the accused, his lack of education, or his low intelligence, the lack of any advice to the accused of his constitutional rights, the length of detention, the repeated and prolonged nature of the questioning, and the use of physical punishment such as the deprivation of food or sleep. In all of these cases, the Court determined the factual circumstances surrounding the confession, assessed the psychological impact on the accused, and evaluated the legal significance of how the accused reacted.

The significant fact about all of these decisions is that none of them turned on the presence or absence of a single controlling criterion; each reflected a careful scrutiny of all the surrounding circumstances. In none of them did the Court rule that the Due Process Clause required the prosecution to prove as part of its initial burden that the defendant knew he had a right to refuse to answer the questions that were put. While the state of the accused's mind, and the failure of the police to advise the accused of his rights, were certainly factors to be evaluated in assessing the "voluntariness" of an accused's responses, they were not in and of themselves determinative.

B

Similar considerations lead us to agree with the courts of California that the question whether a consent to a search was in fact "voluntary" or was the product of duress or coercion, express or implied, is a question of fact to be determined from the totality of all the circumstances. While knowledge of the right to refuse consent is one factor to be taken into account, the government need not establish such knowledge as the *sine qua non* of an effective consent. As with police questioning, two competing concerns must be accommodated in determining the meaning of a "voluntary" consent—the legitimate need for such searches and the equally important requirement of assuring the absence of coercion.

In situations where the police have some evidence of illicit activity, but lack probable cause to arrest or search, a search authorized by a valid consent may be the only means of obtaining important and reliable evidence. In the present case for example, while the police had reason to stop the car for traffic violations, the State does not contend that there was probable cause to search the vehicle or that the search was incident to a valid arrest of any of the occupants. Yet, the search yielded tangible evidence that served as a basis for a prosecution, and provided some assurance that others, wholly innocent of the crime, were not mistakenly brought to trial. And in those cases where there is probable cause to arrest or search, but where the police lack a warrant, a consent search may still be valuable. If the search is conducted and proves fruitless, that in itself may convince the police that an arrest with its possible stigma and embarrassment is unnecessary, or that a far more extensive search pursuant to a warrant is not justified. In short, a search pursuant to consent may result in considerably less inconvenience for the subject of the search, and, properly conducted, is a constitutionally permissible and wholly legitimate aspect of effective police activity.

But the Fourth and Fourteenth Amendments require that a consent not be coerced, by explicit or implicit means, by implied threat or covert force. For, no matter how subtly the coercion was applied, the resulting "consent" would be no more than a pretext for the unjustified police intrusion against which the Fourth Amendment is directed. * * *

* * * In examining all the surrounding circumstances to determine if in fact the consent to search was coerced, account must be taken of subtly coercive police questions, as well as the possibly vulnerable subjective state of the person who consents. Those searches that are the product of police coercion can thus be filtered out without undermining the continuing validity of consent searches. In sum, there is no reason for us to depart in the area of consent searches, from the traditional definition of "voluntariness."

The approach of the Court of Appeals for the Ninth Circuit finds no support in any of our decisions that have attempted to define the meaning of "voluntariness." Its ruling, that the State must affirmatively prove that the subject of the search knew that he had a right to refuse consent, would, in practice, create serious doubt whether consent searches could continue to be conducted. There might be rare cases where it could be proved from the record that a person in fact affirmatively knew of his right to refuse—such as a case where he announced to the police that if he didn't sign the consent form, "you [police] are going to get a search warrant;" or a case where by prior experience and training a person had clearly and convincingly demonstrated such knowledge. But more commonly where there was no evidence of any coercion, explicit or implicit, the prosecution would nevertheless be unable to demonstrate that the subject of the search in fact had known of his right to refuse consent.

The very object of the inquiry—the nature of a person's subjective understanding—underlines the difficulty of the prosecution's burden under the rule applied by the Court of Appeals in this case. Any defendant who was the subject of a search authorized solely by his consent could effectively frustrate the introduction into evidence of the fruits of that search by simply failing to testify that he in fact knew he could refuse to consent. And the near impossibility of meeting this prosecutorial burden suggests why this Court has never accepted any such litmus-paper test of voluntariness. * * *

One alternative that would go far toward proving that the subject of a search did know he had a right to refuse consent would be to advise him of that right before eliciting his consent. That, however, is a suggestion that has been almost universally repudiated by both federal and state courts, and, we think, rightly so. For it would be thoroughly impractical to impose on the normal consent search the detailed requirements of an effective warning. Consent searches are part of the standard investigatory techniques of law enforcement agencies. They normally occur on the highway, or in a person's home or office, and under informal and unstructured conditions. The circumstances that prompt the initial request to search may develop quickly or be a logical extension of investigative police questioning. The police may seek to investigate further suspicious circumstances or to follow up leads developed in questioning persons at the scene of a crime. These situations are a far cry from the structured atmosphere of a trial where, assisted by counsel if he chooses, a defendant is informed of his trial rights. And, while surely a closer question, these situations are still immeasurably far removed from "custodial interrogation" where, in *Miranda v. Arizona*, we found that the Constitution required certain now familiar warnings as a prerequisite to police interrogation. * * *

Consequently, we cannot accept the position of the Court of Appeals in this case that proof of knowledge of the right to refuse consent is a necessary prerequisite to demonstrating a "voluntary" consent. Rather, it is only by analyzing all the circumstances of an individual consent that it can be ascertained whether in fact it was voluntary or coerced. It is this careful sifting of the unique facts and circumstances of each case that is evidenced in our prior decisions involving consent searches. * * *

It is said, however, that a "consent" is a "waiver" of a person's rights under the Fourth and Fourteenth Amendments. The argument is that by allowing the police to conduct a search, a person "waives" whatever right he had to prevent the police from searching. It is argued that under the doctrine of *Johnson v. Zerbst*, 304 U.S. 458, 464 to establish such a "waiver" the State must demonstrate "an intentional relinquishment or abandonment of a known right or privilege."

But these standards were enunciated in *Johnson* in the context of the safeguards of a fair criminal trial. Our cases do not reflect an uncritical demand for a knowing and intelligent waiver in every situation where a person has failed to invoke a constitutional protection. * * *

Almost without exception, the requirement of a knowing and intelligent waiver has been applied only to those rights which the Constitution guarantees to a criminal defendant in order to preserve a fair trial. * * *

There is a vast difference between those rights that protect a fair criminal trial and the rights guaranteed under the Fourth Amendment. Nothing, either in the purposes behind requiring a "knowing" and "intelligent" waiver of trial rights, or in the practical application of such a requirement suggests that it ought to be extended to the constitutional guarantee against unreasonable searches and seizures.

A strict standard of waiver has been applied to those rights guaranteed to a criminal defendant to insure that he will be accorded the greatest possible opportunity to utilize every facet of the constitutional model of a fair criminal trial. Any trial conducted in derogation of that model leaves open the possibility that the trial reached an unfair result precisely

because all the protections specified in the Constitution were not provided.
* * *

The protections of the Fourth Amendment are of a wholly different order, and have nothing whatever to do with promoting the fair ascertainment of truth at a criminal trial. Rather, as Mr. Justice Frankfurter's opinion for the Court put it in *Wolf v. Colorado*, 338 U.S. 25, 27, the Fourth Amendment protects the "security of one's privacy against arbitrary intrusion by the police . . . ." * * * The Fourth Amendment "is not an adjunct to the ascertainment of truth." The guarantees of the Fourth Amendment stand "as a protection of quite different constitutional values—values reflecting the concern of our society for the right of each individual to be let alone. To recognize this is no more than to accord those values undiluted respect." * * *

In short, there is nothing in the purposes or application of the waiver requirements of *Johnson v. Zerbst* that justifies, much less compels, the easy equation of a knowing waiver with a consent search. To make such an equation is to generalize from the broad rhetoric of some of our decisions, and to ignore the substance of the differing constitutional guarantees. * * *

D   * * *

In this case, there is no evidence of any inherently coercive tactics—either from the nature of the police questioning or the environment in which it took place. Indeed, since consent searches will normally occur on a person's own familiar territory, the specter of incommunicado police interrogation in some remote station house is simply inapposite. There is no reason to believe, under circumstances such as are present here, that the response to a policeman's question is presumptively coerced; and there is, therefore, no reason to reject the traditional test for determining the voluntariness of a person's response. *Miranda*, of course, did not reach investigative questioning of a person not in custody, which is most directly analogous to the situation of a consent search, and it assuredly did not indicate that such questioning ought to be deemed inherently coercive.

It is also argued that the failure to require the Government to establish knowledge as a prerequisite to a valid consent, will relegate the Fourth Amendment to the special province of "the sophisticated, the knowledgeable and the privileged." We cannot agree. The traditional definition of voluntariness we accept today has always taken into account evidence of minimal schooling, low intelligence, and the lack of any effective warnings to a person of his rights; and the voluntariness of any statement taken under those conditions has been carefully scrutinized to determine whether it was in fact voluntarily given.

E

Our decision today is a narrow one. We hold only that when the subject of a search is not in custody and the State attempts to justify a search on the basis of his consent, the Fourth and Fourteenth Amendments require that it demonstrate that the consent was in fact voluntarily given, and not the result of duress or coercion, express or implied. Voluntariness is a question of fact to be determined from all the circumstances, and while the subject's knowledge of a right to refuse is a factor to be taken into account, the prosecution is not required to demonstrate such knowledge as a prerequisite to establishing a voluntary consent. Because the California court followed these principles in affirming the respondent's conviction, and because the Court of Appeals for the Ninth Circuit in remanding for an evidentiary hearing required more, its judgment must be reversed.

It is so ordered.

MR. JUSTICE BLACKMUN, concurring.

[Omitted.]

MR. JUSTICE POWELL, with whom THE CHIEF JUSTICE and MR. JUSTICE REHNQUIST join, concurring.

[Omitted.]

MR. JUSTICE DOUGLAS, dissenting.

[Omitted.]

MR. JUSTICE BRENNAN, dissenting.

[Omitted.]

MR. JUSTICE MARSHALL, dissenting.

Several years ago, MR. JUSTICE STEWART reminded us that "the Constitution guarantees . . . a society of free choice. Such a society presupposes the capacity of its members to choose." I would have thought that the capacity to choose necessarily depends upon knowledge that there is a choice to be made. But today the Court reaches the curious result that one can choose to relinquish a constitutional right—the right to be free of unreasonable searches—without knowing that he has the alternative of refusing to accede to a police request to search. I cannot agree, and therefore dissent. * * *

II

My approach to the case is straightforward and, to me, obviously required by the notion of consent as a relinquishment of Fourth Amendment rights. I am at a loss to understand why consent "cannot be taken literally to mean a 'knowing' choice." In fact, I have difficulty in comprehending how a decision made without knowledge of available alternatives can be treated as a choice at all.

If consent to search means that a person has chosen to forgo his right to exclude the police from the place they seek to search, it follows that his consent cannot be considered a meaningful choice unless he knew that he could in fact exclude the police. The Court appears, however, to reject even the modest proposition that, if the subject of a search convinces the trier of fact that he did not know of his right to refuse assent to a police request for permission to search, the search must be held unconstitutional. For it says only that "knowledge of the right to refuse consent is one factor to be taken into account." I find this incomprehensible. I can think of no other situation in which we would say that a person agreed to some course of action if he convinced us that he did not know that there was some other course he might have pursued. I would therefore hold, at a minimum, that the prosecution may not rely on a purported consent to search if the subject of the search did not know that he could refuse to give consent. * * *

The Court contends that if an officer paused to inform the subject of his rights, the informality of the exchange would be destroyed. I doubt that a simple statement by an officer of an individual's right to refuse consent would do much to alter the informality of the exchange, except to alert the subject to a fact that he surely is entitled to know. It is not without significance that for many years the agents of the Federal Bureau of Investigation have routinely informed subjects of their right to refuse consent, when they request consent to search. The reported cases in which the police have informed subjects of their right to refuse consent show, also, that the information can be given without disrupting the casual flow of events. What evidence there is, then, rather strongly suggests that nothing disastrous would happen if the police, before requesting consent, informed the subject that he had a right to refuse consent and that his refusal would be respected.

I must conclude, with some reluctance, that when the Court speaks of practicality, what it really is talking of is the continued ability of the police to capitalize on the ignorance of citizens so as to accomplish by subterfuge what they could not achieve by relying only on the knowing relinquishment of constitutional rights. Of course it would be "practical" for the police to ignore the commands of the Fourth Amendment, if by practicality we mean that more criminals will be apprehended, even though the constitutional rights of innocent people also go by the board. But such a practical advantage is achieved only at the cost of permitting the police to disregard the limitations that the Constitution places on their behavior, a cost that a constitutional democracy cannot long absorb.

I find nothing in the opinion of the Court to dispel my belief that, in such a case, as the Court of Appeals for the Ninth Circuit said, "under many circumstances a reasonable person might read an officer's 'May I' as the courteous expression of a demand backed by force of law." * * * Permitting searches in such circumstances, without any assurance at all that the subject of the search knew that, by his consent, he was relinquishing his constitutional rights, is something that I cannot believe is sanctioned by the Constitution.

III

The proper resolution of this case turns, I believe, on a realistic assessment of the nature of the interchange between citizens and the police, and of the practical import of allocating the burden of proof in one way rather than another. The Court seeks to escape such assessments by escalating its rhetoric to unwarranted heights, but no matter how forceful the adjectives the Court uses, it cannot avoid being judged by how well its image of these interchanges accords with reality. Although the Court says without real elaboration that it "cannot agree," the holding today confines the protection of the Fourth Amendment against searches conducted without probable cause to the sophisticated, the knowledgeable, and, I might add, the few. In the final analysis, the Court now sanctions a game of blindman's buff, in which the police always have the upper hand, for the sake of nothing more than the convenience of the police. But the guarantees of the Fourth Amendment were never intended to shrink before such an ephemeral and changeable interest. The Framers of the Fourth Amendment struck the balance against this sort of convenience and in favor of certain basic civil rights. It is not for this Court to restrike that balance because of its own views of the needs of law enforcement officers. I fear that that is the effect of the Court's decision today.

It is regrettable that the obsession with validating searches like that conducted in this case, so evident in the Court's hyperbole, has obscured the Court's vision of how the Fourth Amendment was designed to govern the relationship between police and citizen in our society. I believe that experience and careful reflection show how narrow and inaccurate that vision is, and I respectfully dissent.

QUESTIONS, COMMENTS, CONCERNS?

1.   **An introductory note on the Witman case and casefile.** As the topic heading for this portion of the chapter would suggest, we will focus on the extent to which Zach, Mrs. Witman, and Mr. Witman gave consent to search the Witman home and seize Zach's clothing at the hospital. Consent aside, we will also consider whether law enforcement was justified in searching the Witman property pursuant to exigent circumstances or pursuant to what the Commonwealth calls a "protective sweep." Our doing so will help us test the limits of the plain view doctrine (discussed later in this chapter).

One other note before we proceed. You will see that the suppression court's order addresses seventy-two pieces of evidence. [Casefile Document 8, at 1–2.] If you would, look at that order for a moment. To help narrow our conversation, the questions in this portion of the chapter will focus heavily on the admissibility of the following key items: "(15) Defendant's white socks taken from pink plastic bag obtained at the hospital"; "(16) Defendant's pants and underwear"; and "(26) NAPA knife wrapped in pair of dock socks [gloves] w/ blood on from buried under tree at rear of house[.]" *Id.* at 2–3. Rest assured that you do not need to parse out every piece of evidence at issue in the parties' filings.

2.   Does Witman's defense lawyer look familiar? Look at the name on the signature block at the end of Witman's initial motion to suppress. [*See* Casefile Document 2, at 13.] Remember Christina Gutierrez? You met her in Chapter 1; she was the controversial defense lawyer who represented Adnan Syed. You will recall that, in Syed's case, Gutierrez elected not to contact an alibi witness—a decision that would ultimately earn Syed a new trial. [Syed Casefile Document 7.] Notice also that the dates match up. That is, Gutierrez represented Witman and Syed *simultaneously*. That's not all. As it turns out, Gutierrez was also representing Hector Oscar Acosta-Martinez in Puerto Rico and Levi Pace in Alabama—both on murder charges. Colin Miller, *Cristina Gutierrez Was Involved in 4 1st Degree Murder Cases in 4 Different Jurisdictions in 1999/2000*, EVIDENCEPROF BLOG (July 30, 2015), http://lawprofessors.typepad.com/evidenceprof/2015/07/yesterday-i-postedan-entryabout-how-cristina-gutierrez-was-involved-in-three-first-degree-murder-cases-in-three-different-ju.html.

To be clear, Gutierrez was handling four different murder cases in four different jurisdictions at the same time. Perhaps not surprisingly given that workload alongside Gutierrez's serious illness, her work on Witman's case was problematically similar to the work she performed on Syed's case. Witman's parents would ultimately remove Gutierrez as Zach's attorney and sue her for misplaced funds. Arielle Dachille, *Adnan Syed's Lawyer Cristina Gutierrez Has a History of Tough Cases*, BUSTLE.COM (Dec. 5, 2014), https://www.bustle.com/articles/52323-adnan-syeds-lawyer-cristina-gutierrez-has-a-history-of-tough-cases.

3.   Understanding the timeline. Before we dive into the relevant legal issues raised by Witman's case, let's first be clear about the timeline. Here, to help you navigate the casefile, are the critical times when law enforcement investigated Zach and the Witman home *without* a search warrant:

October 2, 1998

- *3:17 p.m.*: Zach calls 911 requesting emergency assistance.

- *3:25 p.m.*: Officer Sean Siggins from the Southern Regional Police Department arrives at the Witman home. Officer Siggins briefly speaks to Zach and then walks to the doorway in the garage leading to the laundry room where he observes Greg's body on the floor.

- *3:30 p.m.*: Chief James Childs arrives on the scene. Among other activities, Chief Childs performs a security sweep of the home to determine whether others are inside.

- *3:45 p.m.*: Zach leaves for the hospital. Chief Childs instructs Officer Boddington to follow the ambulance and secure Zach's clothing. Chief Childs then reenters the home to show Detective Goodfellow what evidence he saw during his first entry.

  During the ambulance ride, Witman asks an EMT to remove his sweatshirt and socks. The EMT does so and places them inside a plastic bag.

- *Between 4:00 to 4:45 p.m.*: Mrs. Witman, arrives at home from work. According to subsequent testimony from Chief Childs, "She told me I better do my job and find out who did this."

- *4:30 p.m.*: The first member of the State Police crime scene unit arrives. That member photographs the outside of the Witman residence.

- *Between 5:15–5:30 p.m.*: Detective Clancy arrives at the hospital. Sometime around this period, Officer Boddington collects the plastic bag containing Zach's sweatshirt and socks.

- *5:30 p.m.*: Another member of the crime scene unit arrives with Trooper Woodcock, and a more detailed processing of the crime scene begins. Around this time, Chief Childs relays Mrs. Witman's "do your job" comment to Detective Goodfellow.

- *8:00 p.m.*: Mr. Witman arrives at the hospital. When told that police were at his home processing the scene, Mr. Witman tells Detective Clancy, "whatever it takes, do" and "Go find Greg's killer."

- *Between 8:30–9:00 p.m.*: Detective Clancy returns to the Witman home and relays Mr. Witman's remarks to the other investigators.

October 3, 1998

- *12:30 p.m.*: The State Police Lab brings Luminol to the crime scene to detect trails of blood not visible to the naked eye. The trails lead investigators to a crop of trees next to a Jacuzzi in the backyard. There, investigators find a knife and a pair of athletic gloves buried under a mound of dirt.

4.   **Consent by calling 911?** Based on the above timeline, law enforcement searched the Witman household on and off for roughly nine hours. We have seen that before, right? The Witman fact pattern—hours of warrantless searching predicated on a need to "process the scene"—looks a bit

like how officers approached the O.J. Simpson home, right? And we learned in the O.J. materials that both *Mincey v. Arizona*, 437 U.S. 385 (1978) and *Thompson v. Louisiana*, 469 U.S. 17 (1984) stand for the proposition that a recent homicide does not justify the warrantless search of a home. But, per *Thompson*, officers may make a warrantless entry on the premises if they "reasonably believe that a person is in need of immediate aid" or "if there are other victims or if a killer is still on the premises."

In many ways, the Commonwealth accepts that *Mincey v. Arizona* precludes justifying law enforcement's warrantless search of the Witman property—at least on a "murder scene" exception basis. [*See* Casefile Document 6, at 5–6.] Instead, the Commonwealth argues that, by calling 911 to request emergency aid for his brother, Zach implicitly consented to the search of his home. *Id.* at 20–21. In particular, says the Commonwealth, Zach "requested official help through 911 and not only did he open his home to the police, he directed them inside to aid his murdered brother and to get his mother's phone number." *Id.* at 21.

The Commonwealth's argument is simultaneously right and wrong. If you call 911, would you agree that you are consenting? Sure, but consenting to what *exactly*? You are minimally consenting to the presence of law enforcement in your home—after all, you called them. But, and this is where it gets tricky, you called the police to request *aid*—not to investigate crime. Consent terminates once the scene is secure, right?

Lower courts are split on the general question of whether a 911 call justifies the warrantless search of a home. *Compare Woodward v. Tucson*, No. CV-15-00077-TUC-RM, 2016 U.S. Dist. LEXIS 191336, at *24 (D. Ariz. Mar. 31, 2016) ("The clearly established law thus rejects Defendants' argument that consent can be inferred from a 911 call where the issue of consent to enter the apartment was never addressed."), *with Hubbard v. State*, 382 So.2d 577, 591 (Ala. App. 1979) (holding that defendant's call for emergency services supplied implicit consent). But little dispute exists among lower courts on the more specific issue of whether a defendant consents to a warrantless search after calling 911 and blaming a third party for the crime. As one court has observed:

> When a crime is reported to the police by an individual who owns or controls the premises to which the police are summoned, and that individual either states or suggests that it was committed by a third person, he or she implicitly consents to a search of the premises reasonably related to the routine investigation of the offense and the identification of the perpetrator.

State v. Fleischman, 754 P.2d 340, 344 (Ariz. Ct. App. 1988); *accord Zeigler v. State*, 402 So. 2d 365, 372 (Fla. 1981).

But many courts recognize that the implicit consent generated by 911 calls blaming a third party for a crime ends when the caller becomes a suspect. *E.g., State v. Flippo*, 575 S.E.2d 170, 183 (W. Va. 2002) ("If the person affirmatively revokes his/her implied consent or becomes a suspect during the investigation, the police must stop the search and obtain a warrant for the purpose of continuing the search."); *Brown v. State*, 856 S.W.2d 177, 182 (Tex. Crim. App. 1993) ("As long as the individual is not a suspect in the case or does nothing to revoke his consent, the police may search the premises for these purposes, and evidence obtained thereby is admissible.").

A critical issue, then, is when precisely Zach became a suspect in the death of his brother. In many ways, both the suppression court and appellate court fail to meaningfully analyze when Zach moved from victim to suspect. The suppression court, in any event, generally held that "placing an emergency call to the 911 dispatcher does not amount to consent for a general search of the residence." [Casefile Document 9, at 22.] The appellate court, by contrast, concluded that there was "no indication police suspected" Zach and therefore his 911 call provided consent to justify police's entire warrantless post-call investigation. [Casefile Document 10, at 337.] Do you see anywhere in the Casefile that adequately answers when Zach became a suspect? If not, is the appellate court's conclusion supportable?

As a closing comment on this issue, police suspicion about Zach's role in Greg's death was likely solidified by October 5, 1998, when police talked to an unnamed source. That source relayed that, two weeks before his death, Greg said he was afraid of Zach because the latter had a bad temper when he used drugs and that Greg planned to tell police about Zach's drug use. Rick Lee, *Zachary Witman murder case: Everything you need to know in case of fratricide*, YORK DAILY RECORD (Nov. 29, 2017), https://www.ydr.com/story/news/2017/ 11/29/zachary-gregory-witman-case-where-things-stand-mysterious-case- fratricide/863616001/.

5. Witman and exigent circumstances. Consent aside, exigent circumstances certainly existed at the time officers arrived at the Witman home. Applying what we learned from O.J. Simpson and *Warden v. Hayden*, 287 U.S. 294 (1967), officers minimally had a right to search for additional suspects and to secure the home. In this way, the Commonwealth's "protective sweep" argument is correct. The Commonwealth, to remind you, argued that Chief Childs' initial entry into the Witman home was appropriate to determine "whether there were any remaining victims inside the residence and to sweep for the alleged perpetrator or perpetrators." [Casefile Document 5, at 10.]

As we also learned from the O.J. Simpson casefile and *Minnesota v. Olson*, 495 U.S. 91 (1990) that officers may enter a home without a warrant when there is "the risk of danger" to "other persons inside or outside the dwelling." You will recall that Zach ostensibly called the police to seek emergency assistance for his brother. The police therefore certainly had a right, at the outset, to be present in his home.

But the Commonwealth is wrong to suggest that either a protective sweep or the rendering of emergency aid—after the expiration of those circumstances—also permits a nine-hour warrantless search of the Witman home. Remember, use of an exigency to support a warrantless search is "strictly circumscribed by the exigencies which justify its initiation." *Terry v.*

Ohio, 392 U.S. 1, 26 (1968). Accordingly, the exigencies in Zach's case terminated once law enforcement realized that Greg was dead *and* no other suspects were present in the home. What should law enforcement have done at that point to justify continuing to search the Witman home without a search warrant?

6. **Ambiguous consent.** Consider Mrs. Witman's comment that Chief Childs needed to "do [his] job and find out who did this." [Casefile Document 6, at 3.] The suppression court held that Mrs. Witman's statement "more closely resembles an acquiescence to a claim of lawful authority rather than unambiguous consent." [Casefile Document 9, at 22.] By contrast, the appellate court held that Mrs. Witman's statement constituted consent to search the home. [Casefile Document 10, at 338–39.] The appellate court reasoned that "the only logical meaning of the mother's statement is a directive to police to conduct their investigation." *Id.* at 338. What do you think—did Mrs. Witman consent to the search of her home? If so, how much of the home and for how long? Does or should police have any obligation to ask her any follow-up clarification questions?

What about Mr. Witman's "whatever it takes, do" statement? [Casefile Document 7, at 7.] The suppression court viewed his statement as unequivocal consent to search the Witman home. [*See* Casefile Document 9, at 25.] It therefore admitted all evidence obtained after 8 p.m. on October 2—when Mr. Witman made that statement. The appellate court's reversal aside, even the suppression court's order would therefore admit the knife and gloves against Zach. *Id.* at 32.

7. **The impact of refusing to consent.** Do you think an officer has reasonable suspicion or probable cause to search if a suspect *refuses* an officer's request to search?

8. **Limitations and the scope of consent.** Most often, consent is a binary proposition. That is, suspects reply either "yes" or "no" when an officer requests consent to search. But the law permits suspects to limit consent both spatially and temporally. *Florida v. Jimeno*, 500 U.S. 248, 252 (1991) ("A suspect may of course delimit as he chooses the scope of the search to which he consents."). The law also permits a suspect to withdraw consent. *E.g., United States v. Mitchell*, 82 F.3d 146, 151 (7th Cir. 1996) ("Consent to search may, of course, be withdrawn or limited by a criminal suspect").

9. **Right to refuse consent warnings.** Notice that, according to the Witman appellate court, Pennsylvania considers "knowledge of the right to refuse consent" as a factor in the *Schneckloth* voluntariness analysis. [Casefile Document 10, at 338.] The suppression court went one step further, asserting that, "[u]nder Pennsylvania law, the police were required to inform the subject of the search that they had a right to refuse consent." [Casefile Document 9, at 24 (emphasis omitted).]

Pennsylvania aside, other states have interpreted their own state's constitution to require that officers provide right to refuse consent warnings.

See, e.g., State v. Brown, 156 S.W.3d 722, 732 (Ark. 2004); *State v. Trainor*, 925 P.2d 818, 828 (Haw. 1996); *State v. Johnson*, 346 A.2d 66, 68 (N.J. 1975); *State v. Ferrier*, 960 P.2d 927, 934 (Wash. 1998). Providing consent warnings to citizens, however, has done little to change the rate of consent. Matthew Phillips, *Effective Warnings Before Consent Searches: Practice, Necessary, and Desirable*, 45 AM. CRIM. L. REV. 1185, 1205 (2008).

ILLINOIS V. RODRIGUEZ

497 U.S. 177
Supreme Court of the United States
March 20, 1990, Argued; June 21, 1990, Decided
No. 88-2018

JUSTICE SCALIA delivered the opinion of the Court.

In *United States v. Matlock*, 415 U.S. 164 (1974), this Court reaffirmed that a warrantless entry and search by law enforcement officers does not violate the Fourth Amendment's proscription of "unreasonable searches and seizures" if the officers have obtained the consent of a third party who possesses common authority over the premises. The present case presents an issue we expressly reserved in *Matlock*: Whether a warrantless entry is valid when based upon the consent of a third party whom the police, at the time of the entry, reasonably believe to possess common authority over the premises, but who in fact does not do so.

I

Respondent Edward Rodriguez was arrested in his apartment by law enforcement officers and charged with possession of illegal drugs. The police gained entry to the apartment with the consent and assistance of Gail Fischer, who had lived there with respondent for several months. The relevant facts leading to the arrest are as follows.

On July 26, 1985, police were summoned to the residence of Dorothy Jackson on South Wolcott in Chicago. They were met by Ms. Jackson's daughter, Gail Fischer, who showed signs of a severe beating. She told the officers that she had been assaulted by respondent Edward Rodriguez earlier that day in an apartment on South California Avenue. Fischer stated that Rodriguez was then asleep in the apartment, and she consented to travel there with the police in order to unlock the door with her key so that the officers could enter and arrest him. During this conversation, Fischer several times referred to the apartment on South California as "our" apartment, and said that she had clothes and furniture there. It is unclear whether she indicated that she currently lived at the apartment, or only that she used to live there.

The police officers drove to the apartment on South California, accompanied by Fischer. They did not obtain an arrest warrant for Rodriguez, nor did they seek a search warrant for the apartment. At the apartment, Fischer unlocked the door with her key and gave the officers permission to enter. They moved through the door into the living room, where they observed in plain view drug paraphernalia and containers filled with white powder that they believed (correctly, as later analysis showed) to be cocaine. They proceeded to the bedroom, where they found Rodriguez asleep and discovered additional containers of white powder in two open attaché cases. The officers arrested Rodriguez and seized the drugs and related paraphernalia.

Rodriguez was charged with possession of a controlled substance with intent to deliver. He moved to suppress all evidence seized at the time of his arrest, claiming that Fischer had vacated the apartment several weeks earlier and had no authority to consent to the entry. The Cook County Circuit Court granted the motion, holding that at the time she consented to the entry Fischer did not have common authority over the apartment. The Court concluded that Fischer was not a "usual resident" but rather an "infrequent visitor" at the apartment on South California, based upon its findings that Fischer's name was not on the lease, that she did not contribute to the rent, that she was not allowed to invite others to the apartment on her own, that she did not have access to the apartment when respondent was away, and that she had moved some of her possessions from the apartment. The Circuit Court also rejected the State's contention that, even if Fischer did not possess common authority over the premises, there was no Fourth Amendment violation if the police reasonably believed at the time of their entry that Fischer possessed the authority to consent.

The Appellate Court of Illinois affirmed the Circuit Court in all respects. The Illinois Supreme Court denied the State's petition for leave to appeal and we granted certiorari.

II

The Fourth Amendment generally prohibits the warrantless entry of a person's home, whether to make an arrest or to search for specific objects. *Payton v. New York*, 445 U.S. 573 (1980). The prohibition does not apply, however, to situations in which voluntary consent has been obtained, either from the individual whose property is searched, *see Schneckloth v. Bustamonte*, 412 U.S. 218 (1973), or from a third party who possesses common authority over the premises, *see United States v. Matlock, supra,* at 171. The State of Illinois contends that that exception applies in the present case.

As we stated in *Matlock*, "common authority" rests "on mutual use of the property by persons generally having joint access or control for most purposes . . . ." The burden of establishing that common authority rests upon the State. On the basis of this record, it is clear that burden was not sustained. The evidence showed that although Fischer, with her two small children, had lived with Rodriguez beginning in December 1984, she had moved out on July 1, 1985, almost a month before the search at issue here, and had gone to live with her mother. She took her and her children's clothing with her, though leaving behind some furniture and household effects. During the period after July 1 she sometimes spent the night at Rodriguez's apartment, but never invited her friends there, and never went there herself when he was not home. Her name was not on the lease nor did she contribute to the rent. She had a key to the apartment, which she said at trial she had taken without Rodriguez's knowledge (though she testified at the preliminary hearing that Rodriguez had given her the key). On these facts the State has not established that, with respect to the South California apartment, Fischer had "joint access or control for most purposes." To the contrary, the Appellate Court's determination of no common authority over the apartment was obviously correct.

III   * * *

The State contends that, even if Fischer did not in fact have authority to give consent, it suffices to validate the entry that the law enforcement officers reasonably believed she did. * * *

* * * [R]espondent asserts that permitting a reasonable belief of common authority to validate an entry would cause a defendant's Fourth Amendment rights to be "vicariously waived." We disagree.

We have been unyielding in our insistence that a defendant's waiver of his trial rights cannot be given effect unless it is "knowing" and "intelligent." We would assuredly not permit, therefore, evidence seized in violation of the Fourth Amendment to be introduced on the basis of a trial court's mere "reasonable belief"—derived from statements by unauthorized persons—that the defendant has waived his objection. But one must make a distinction between, on the one hand, trial rights that derive from the violation of constitutional guarantees and, on the other hand, the nature of those constitutional guarantees themselves. As we said in *Schneckloth*:

> There is a vast difference between those rights that protect a fair criminal trial and the rights guaranteed under the Fourth Amendment. Nothing, either in the purposes behind requiring a 'knowing' and 'intelligent' waiver of trial rights, or in the practical application of such a requirement suggests that it ought to be extended to the constitutional guarantee against unreasonable searches and seizures.

What Rodriguez is assured by the trial right of the exclusionary rule, where it applies, is that no evidence seized in violation of the Fourth Amendment will be introduced at his trial unless he consents. What he is assured by the Fourth Amendment itself, however, is not that no government search of his house will occur unless he consents; but that no such search will occur that is "unreasonable." U.S. Const., Amdt. 4. There are various elements, of course, that can make a search of a person's house "reasonable"—one of which is the consent of the person or his cotenant. The essence of respondent's argument is that we should impose upon this element a requirement that we have not imposed upon other elements that regularly compel government officers to exercise judgment regarding the facts: namely, the requirement that their judgment be not only responsible but correct.

The fundamental objective that alone validates all unconsented government searches is, of course, the seizure of persons who have committed or are about to commit crimes, or of evidence related to crimes. But "reasonableness," with respect to this necessary element, does not demand that the government be factually correct in its assessment that that is what a search will produce. Warrants need only be supported by "probable cause," which demands no more than a proper "assessment of probabilities in particular factual contexts . . . ." *Illinois v. Gates*, 462 U.S. 213, 232 (1983). If a magistrate, based upon seemingly reliable but factually inaccurate information, issues a warrant for the search of a house in which the sought-after felon is not present, has never been present, and was never likely to have been present, the owner of that house suffers one of the inconveniences we all expose ourselves to as the cost of living in a safe society; he does not suffer a violation of the Fourth Amendment.

Another element often, though not invariably, required in order to render an unconsented search "reasonable" is, of course, that the officer be authorized by a valid warrant. Here also we have not held that "reasonableness" precludes error with respect to those factual judgments that law enforcement officials are expected to make. In *Maryland v. Garrison*, 480 U.S. 79 (1987), a warrant supported by probable cause with respect to one apartment was erroneously issued for an entire floor that was divided (though not clearly) into two apartments. We upheld the search of the apartment not properly covered by the warrant. * * *

The ordinary requirement of a warrant is sometimes supplanted by other elements that render the unconsented search "reasonable." Here also we have not held that the Fourth Amendment requires factual accuracy. A warrant is not needed, for example, where the search is incident to an arrest. In *Hill v. California*, 401 U.S. 797 (1971), we upheld a search incident to an arrest, even though the arrest was made of the wrong person. * * *

It would be superfluous to multiply these examples. It is apparent that in order to satisfy the "reasonableness" requirement of the Fourth Amendment, what is generally demanded of the many factual determinations that must regularly be made by agents of the government— whether the magistrate issuing a warrant, the police officer executing a warrant, or the police officer conducting a search or seizure under one of the exceptions to the warrant requirement—is not that they always be correct, but that they always be reasonable. * * *

We see no reason to depart from this general rule with respect to facts bearing upon the authority to consent to a search. Whether the basis for such authority exists is the sort of recurring factual question to which law enforcement officials must be expected to apply their judgment; and all the Fourth Amendment requires is that they answer it reasonably. The Constitution is no more violated when officers enter without a warrant because they reasonably (though erroneously) believe that the person who has consented to their entry is a resident of the premises, than it is violated when they enter without a warrant because they reasonably (though erroneously) believe they are in pursuit of a violent felon who is about to escape.

Stoner v. California, 376 U.S. 483 (1964), is in our view not to the contrary. There, in holding that police had improperly entered the defendant's hotel room based on the consent of a hotel clerk, we stated that "the rights protected by the Fourth Amendment are not to be eroded . . . by unrealistic doctrines of 'apparent authority.'" It is ambiguous, of course, whether the word "unrealistic" is descriptive or limiting—that is, whether we were condemning as unrealistic all reliance upon apparent authority, or whether we were condemning only such reliance upon apparent authority as is unrealistic. Similarly ambiguous is the opinion's earlier statement that "there [is no] substance to the claim that the search was reasonable because the police, relying upon the night clerk's expressions of consent, had a reasonable basis for the belief that the clerk had authority to consent to the search." Was there no substance to it because it failed as a matter of law, or because the facts could not possibly support it? At one point the opinion does seem to speak clearly:

> It is important to bear in mind that it was the petitioner's constitutional right which was at stake here, and not the night clerk's nor the hotel's. It was a right, therefore, which only the petitioner could waive by word or deed, either directly or through an agent.

But as we have discussed, what is at issue when a claim of apparent consent is raised is not whether the right to be free of searches has been waived, but whether the right to be free of unreasonable searches has been violated. Even if one does not think the *Stoner* opinion had this subtlety in mind, the supposed clarity of its foregoing statement is immediately compromised [later in the opinion] * * *. In sum, we were correct in *Matlock*, when we regarded the present issue as unresolved.

As *Stoner* demonstrates, what we hold today does not suggest that law enforcement officers may always accept a person's invitation to enter premises. Even when the invitation is accompanied by an explicit assertion that the person lives there, the surrounding circumstances could conceivably be such that a reasonable person would doubt its truth and not act upon it without further inquiry. As with other factual determinations bearing upon search and seizure, determination of consent to enter must "be judged against an objective standard: would the facts available to the officer at the moment . . . 'warrant a man of reasonable caution in the belief'" that the consenting party had authority over the premises? *Terry v. Ohio*, 392 U.S. 1, 21–22 (1968). If not, then warrantless entry without further inquiry is unlawful unless authority actually exists. But if so, the search is valid.

* * *

In the present case, the Appellate Court found it unnecessary to determine whether the officers reasonably believed that Fischer had the authority to consent, because it ruled as a matter of law that a reasonable belief could not validate the entry. Since we find that ruling to be in error, we remand for consideration of that question. The judgment of the Illinois Appellate Court is reversed, and the case is remanded for further proceedings not inconsistent with this opinion.

So ordered.

JUSTICE MARSHALL, with whom JUSTICE BRENNAN and JUSTICE STEVENS join, dissenting.

Dorothy Jackson summoned police officers to her house to report that her daughter Gail Fischer had been beaten. Fischer told police that Ed Rodriguez, her boyfriend, was her assaulter. During an interview with Fischer, one of the officers asked if Rodriguez dealt in narcotics. Fischer did not respond. Fischer did agree, however, to the officers' request to let them into Rodriguez's apartment so that they could arrest him for battery. The police, without a warrant and despite the absence of an exigency, entered Rodriguez's home to arrest him. As a result of their entry, the police discovered narcotics that the State subsequently sought to introduce in a drug prosecution against Rodriguez.

* * *

Our prior cases discussing searches based on third-party consent have never suggested that such searches are "reasonable." In *United States v. Matlock*, this Court upheld a warrantless search conducted pursuant to the consent of a third party who was living with the defendant. The Court rejected the defendant's challenge to the search, stating that a person who permits others to have "joint access or control for most purposes . . . assume[s] the risk that [such persons] might permit the common area to be searched." 415 U.S. at 171, n.7 * * *. As the Court's assumption-of-risk analysis makes clear, third-party consent limits a person's ability to challenge the reasonableness of the search only because that person voluntarily has relinquished some of his expectation of privacy by sharing access or control over his property with another person.

A search conducted pursuant to an officer's reasonable but mistaken belief that a third party had authority to consent is thus on an entirely different constitutional footing from one based on the consent of a third party who in fact has such authority. Even if the officers reasonably believed that Fischer had authority to consent, she did not, and Rodriguez's expectation of privacy was therefore undiminished. Rodriguez accordingly can challenge the warrantless intrusion into his home as a violation of the Fourth Amendment. This conclusion flows directly from *Stoner v. California*, 376 U.S. 483 (1964). There, the Court required the suppression of evidence seized in reliance on a hotel clerk's consent to a warrantless search of a guest's room. The Court reasoned that the guest's right to be free of unwarranted intrusion "was a right . . . which only [he] could waive by word or deed, either directly or through an agent." Accordingly, the Court rejected resort to "unrealistic doctrines of 'apparent authority' " as a means of upholding the search to which the guest had not consented. * * *

Acknowledging that the third party in this case lacked authority to consent, the majority seeks to rely on cases suggesting that reasonable but mistaken factual judgments by police will not invalidate otherwise reasonable searches. The majority reads these cases as establishing a "general rule" that "what is generally demanded of the many factual determinations that must regularly be made by agents of the government—whether the magistrate issuing a warrant, the police officer executing a warrant, or the police officer conducting a search or seizure under one of the exceptions to the warrant requirement—is not that they always be correct, but that they always be reasonable."

The majority's assertion, however, is premised on the erroneous assumption that third-party consent searches are generally reasonable. The cases the majority cites thus provide no support for its holding. * * *

Our cases demonstrate that third-party consent searches are free from constitutional challenge only to the extent that they rest on consent by a party empowered to do so. The majority's conclusion to the contrary ignores the legitimate expectations of privacy on which individuals are entitled to rely. That a person who allows another joint access to his property thereby limits his expectation of privacy does not justify trampling the rights of a person who has not similarly relinquished any of his privacy expectation.

Instead of judging the validity of consent searches, as we have in the past, based on whether a defendant has in fact limited his expectation of privacy, the Court today carves out an additional exception to the warrant requirement for third-party consent searches without pausing to consider whether " 'the exigencies of the situation' make the needs of law enforcement so compelling that the warrantless search is objectively reasonable under the Fourth Amendment." Where this free-floating creation of "reasonable" exceptions to the warrant requirement will end, now that the Court has departed from the balancing approach that has long been part of our Fourth Amendment jurisprudence, is unclear. But by allowing a person to be subjected to a warrantless search in his home without his consent and without exigency, the majority has taken away some of the liberty that the Fourth Amendment was designed to protect.

QUESTIONS, COMMENTS, CONCERNS?

1. **Witman and standing.** The Commonwealth argues several times—and even on appeal—that Zach lacks standing to challenge the warrantless search of his own home. For example, the Commonwealth contends that, "as a minor, Zachary Witman did not have any proprietary or possessory interest in those premises, nor in the evidence seized by law enforcement officers; Zachary did not have a possessory interest in the blood or body of the deceased, Gregory Witman, nor in any of the other evidence obtained by law enforcement officers." [Casefile Document 5, at 5.] At most, said the Commonwealth, "[a]s a minor, the defendant's proprietary interest would be in his bedroom." *Id.* at 6. Applying your understanding of the standing doctrine, as taught by *Rakas v. Illinois* (Chapter 3), does the Commonwealth have a strong argument?

Witman counters with some strong arguments. He points in particular to *Minnesota v. Olson*, 495 U.S. 91 (1990). [Casefile Document 7, at 9–10.] Although we looked at *Olson* in the limited context of exigent circumstances, the full opinion held that an overnight guest has a reasonable expectation of privacy in the residence. The Court reasoned, "hosts will more likely than not respect the privacy interests of their guests, who are entitled to a legitimate expectation of privacy despite the fact that they have no legal interest in the premises and do not have the legal authority to determine who may or may not enter the household."

Olson aside, a handful of lower courts have assumed that a minor has standing to challenge the search of their parents' home. *E.g., Hannah v. Pinkston*, No. 94-1230-WEB, 1998 U.S. Dist. LEXIS 4730, *14 (D. Kan. Mar. 13, 1998); *In re M.*, 487 S.W.2d 502, 509 (Mo. 1972). Applying those cases and *Olson*, what do you think about the Commonwealth's standing argument now?

Neither the suppression court nor the appellate court in Witman's case was persuaded that standing was a worthwhile argument. As the suppression court observed, "[I]t is clear, though challenged by the Commonwealth, that the Defendant has standing to challenge the constitutionality of the search at issue. The place searched was the Defendant's home, in which he unquestionably had a reasonable expectation of privacy." [Casefile Document 9, at 12.] The Superior Court agreed: "[I]t is clear appellant had a legitimate expectation of privacy in the house in which he lived at the time he placed the 911 phone call." [Casefile Document 10, at 334.]

The Commonwealth's stubborn dedication to the Witman standing argument demonstrates an important point: as a litigator, sometimes it is best not to make every possible argument.

2. Capacity to consent. Notice that Witman's motion to suppress consistently mentions that he "was a 15 year old juvenile who did not give consent[.]" [Casefile Document 2, at 3–4.] Is he arguing that, at fifteen, he lacked capacity to consent? That argument has not fared well over the years. As a general rule, age is merely a factor in *Schneckloth*'s totality of the circumstances voluntariness analysis. Megan Annitto, *Consent Searches of Minors*, 38 N.Y.U. REV. L. & SOC. CHANGE 1, 33 (2014) (collecting cases and concluding that "the case law reveals that while age remains a consideration in some courts, many courts ignore it—particularly where a minor is over age fourteen").

Notice also in that same motion that Witman argues he was "in a highly agitated state" and that he therefore could not "give any consent to any searches or seizures." [Casefile Document 2, at 4.] Is Witman's condition at the hospital relevant to his capacity to consent? Applying *Rodriguez*, did objective facts exist to allow officers to believe that, his age and condition aside, Witman had authority over his home? As you think about the application of *Rodriguez* to Witman, you might also consider the role of *United States v. Matlock*—the case discussed in *Rodriguez*. For context, *Matlock* held that "the consent of one who possesses *common authority* over premises or effects is valid as against the absent, nonconsenting person with whom that authority is shared." 415 U.S. 164, 170 (1974) (emphasis added).

Notice that actual, common, and apparent consent arguments may often run together—as they do in Witman's case. After all, Witman had common authority to consent to the search of his parents' home. As a resident in that home, he also had capacity to give actual consent. Finally, in the minds of first responders, Witman minimally had apparent authority because he called 911 and answered the door on their arrival. The point is to always remember to consider all of the consent doctrines—actual, common, and apparent authority.

FERNANDEZ V. CALIFORNIA

571 U.S. 292
Supreme Court of the United States
November 13, 2013, Argued; February 25, 2014, Decided
No. 12-7822

JUSTICE ALITO delivered the opinion of the Court.

Our cases firmly establish that police officers may search jointly occupied premises if one of the occupants[1] consents. *See United States v. Matlock*, 415 U.S. 164 (1974). In *Georgia v. Randolph*, 547 U.S. 103, 126 S.

---

[1] We use the terms "occupant," "resident," and "tenant" interchangeably to refer to persons having "common authority" over premises within the meaning of *Matlock*. *See United States v. Matlock*, 415 U.S. 164, 171, n.7 (1974).

Ct. 1515, 164 L. Ed. 2d 208 (2006), we recognized a narrow exception to this rule, holding that the consent of one occupant is insufficient when another occupant is present and objects to the search. In this case, we consider whether *Randolph* applies if the objecting occupant is absent when another occupant consents. Our opinion in *Randolph* took great pains to emphasize that its holding was limited to situations in which the objecting occupant is physically present. We therefore refuse to extend *Randolph* to the very different situation in this case, where consent was provided by an abused woman well after her male partner had been removed from the apartment they shared.

I

A

The events involved in this case occurred in Los Angeles in October 2009. After observing Abel Lopez cash a check, petitioner Walter Fernandez approached Lopez and asked about the neighborhood in which he lived. When Lopez responded that he was from Mexico, Fernandez laughed and told Lopez that he was in territory ruled by the "D.F.S.," i.e., the "Drifters" gang. Petitioner then pulled out a knife and pointed it at Lopez' chest. Lopez raised his hand in self-defense, and petitioner cut him on the wrist.

Lopez ran from the scene and called 911 for help, but petitioner whistled, and four men emerged from a nearby apartment building and attacked Lopez. After knocking him to the ground, they hit and kicked him and took his cell phone and his wallet, which contained $400 in cash.

A police dispatch reported the incident and mentioned the possibility of gang involvement, and two Los Angeles police officers, Detective Clark and Officer Cirrito, drove to an alley frequented by members of the Drifters. A man who appeared scared walked by the officers and said: " '[T]he guy is in the apartment.' " The officers then observed a man run through the alley and into the building to which the man was pointing. A minute or two later, the officers heard sounds of screaming and fighting coming from that building.

After backup arrived, the officers knocked on the door of the apartment unit from which the screams had been heard. Roxanne Rojas answered the door. She was holding a baby and appeared to be crying. Her face was red, and she had a large bump on her nose. The officers also saw blood on her shirt and hand from what appeared to be a fresh injury. Rojas told the police that she had been in a fight. Officer Cirrito asked if anyone else was in the apartment, and Rojas said that her 4-year-old son was the only other person present.

After Officer Cirrito asked Rojas to step out of the apartment so that he could conduct a protective sweep, petitioner appeared at the door wearing only boxer shorts. Apparently agitated, petitioner stepped forward and said, " 'You don't have any right to come in here. I know my rights.' " Suspecting that petitioner had assaulted Rojas, the officers removed him from the apartment and then placed him under arrest. Lopez identified petitioner as his initial attacker, and petitioner was taken to the police station for booking.

Approximately one hour after petitioner's arrest, Detective Clark returned to the apartment and informed Rojas that petitioner had been arrested. Detective Clark requested and received both oral and written consent from Rojas to search the premises. In the apartment, the police found Drifters gang paraphernalia, a butterfly knife, clothing worn by the robbery suspect, and ammunition. Rojas' young son also showed the officers where petitioner had hidden a sawed-off shotgun.

B

Petitioner was charged with robbery, infliction of corporal injury on a spouse, cohabitant, or child's parent, possession of a firearm by a felon, possession of a short-barreled shotgun, and felony possession of ammunition.

Before trial, petitioner moved to suppress the evidence found in the apartment, but after a hearing, the court denied the motion. Petitioner then pleaded *nolo contendere* to the firearms and ammunition charges. On the remaining counts—for robbery and infliction of corporal injury—he went to trial and was found guilty by a jury. The court sentenced him to 14 years of imprisonment.

The California Court of Appeal affirmed. * * * The California Supreme Court denied the petition for review, and we granted certiorari.

II

A

* * * [C]ertain categories of permissible warrantless searches have long been recognized. Consent searches occupy one of these categories. "Consent searches are part of the standard investigatory techniques of law enforcement agencies" and are "a constitutionally permissible and wholly legitimate aspect of effective police activity." *Schneckloth v. Bustamonte*, 412 U.S. 218, 228 (1973). It would be unreasonable—indeed, absurd—to require police officers to obtain a warrant when the sole owner or occupant of a house or apartment voluntarily consents to a search. * * *

While it is clear that a warrantless search is reasonable when the sole occupant of a house or apartment consents, what happens when there are two or more occupants? Must they all consent? Must they all be asked? Is consent by one occupant enough? The Court faced that problem 40 years ago in *United States v. Matlock*, 415 U.S. 164 (1974).

[As *Matlock* held], "the consent of one who possesses common authority over premises or effects is valid as against the absent, nonconsenting person with whom that authority is shared."

In *Illinois v. Rodriguez*, 497 U.S. 177 (1990), the Court reaffirmed and extended the *Matlock* holding. * * * [There] [t]he Court * * * held that [a] warrantless entry was lawful because the police reasonably believed that [the consenting party] was a resident.

B

While consent by one resident of jointly occupied premises is generally sufficient to justify a warrantless search, we recognized a narrow exception to this rule in *Georgia v. Randolph*, 547 U.S. 103 (2006). In that case, * * * [we] reiterated the proposition that a person who shares a residence with others assumes the risk that "any one of them may admit visitors, with the consequence that a guest obnoxious to one may nevertheless be admitted in his absence by another." But the Court held that "a physically present inhabitant's express refusal of consent to a police search [of his home] is dispositive as to him, regardless of the consent of a fellow occupant."

The Court's opinion went to great lengths to make clear that its holding was limited to situations in which the objecting occupant is present. Again and again, the opinion of the Court stressed this controlling factor.

III

In this case, petitioner was not present when Rojas consented, but petitioner still contends that *Randolph* is controlling. He advances two main arguments. First, he claims that his absence should not matter since he was absent only because the police had taken him away. Second, he maintains that it was sufficient that he objected to the search while he was still present. Such an objection, he says, should remain in effect until the objecting party "no longer wishes to keep the police out of his home." Neither of these arguments is sound.

A

We first consider the argument that the presence of the objecting occupant is not necessary when the police are responsible for his absence. In *Randolph*, the Court suggested in dictum that consent by one occupant might not be sufficient if "there is evidence that the police have removed the potentially objecting tenant from the entrance for the sake of avoiding a possible objection." We do not believe the statement should be read to suggest that improper motive may invalidate objectively justified removal. Hence, it does not govern here.

The *Randolph* dictum is best understood not to require an inquiry into the subjective intent of officers who detain or arrest a potential objector but instead to refer to situations in which the removal of the potential objector is not objectively reasonable. As petitioner acknowledges, our Fourth Amendment cases "have repeatedly rejected" a subjective approach. * * *

Petitioner does not claim that the *Randolph* Court meant to break from this consistent practice, and we do not think that it did. And once it is recognized that the test is one of objective reasonableness, petitioner's argument collapses. He does not contest the fact that the police had reasonable grounds for removing him from the apartment so that they could speak with Rojas, an apparent victim of domestic violence, outside of petitioner's potentially intimidating presence. In fact, he does not even contest the existence of probable cause to place him under arrest. We therefore hold that an occupant who is absent due to a lawful detention or arrest stands in the same shoes as an occupant who is absent for any other reason.

* * * The *Randolph* holding unequivocally requires the presence of the objecting occupant in every situation other than the one mentioned in the dictum discussed above.

B

This brings us to petitioner's second argument, viz., that his objection, made at the threshold of the premises that the police wanted to search, remained effective until he changed his mind and withdrew his objection. This argument is inconsistent with *Randolph's* reasoning in at least two important ways. First, the argument cannot be squared with the "widely shared social expectations" or "customary social usage" upon which the *Randolph* holding was based. Explaining why consent by one occupant could not override an objection by a physically present occupant, the *Randolph* Court stated:

> [I]t is fair to say that a caller standing at the door of shared premises would have no confidence that one occupant's invitation was a sufficiently good reason to enter when a fellow tenant stood there saying, 'stay out.' Without some very good reason, no sensible person would go inside under those conditions.

It seems obvious that the calculus of this hypothetical caller would likely be quite different if the objecting tenant was not standing at the door. When the objecting occupant is standing at the threshold saying "stay out," a friend or visitor invited to enter by another occupant can expect at best an uncomfortable scene and at worst violence if he or she tries to brush past the objector. But when the objector is not on the scene (and especially when it is known that the objector will not return during the course of the visit), the friend or visitor is much more likely to accept the invitation to enter. Thus, petitioner's argument is inconsistent with *Randolph's* reasoning.

Second, petitioner's argument would create the very sort of practical complications that *Randolph* sought to avoid. * * * The rule that petitioner would have us adopt would produce a plethora of practical problems. For one thing, there is the question of duration. Petitioner argues that an objection, once made, should last until it is withdrawn by the objector, but such a rule would be unreasonable. Suppose that a husband and wife owned a house as joint tenants and that the husband, after objecting to a search of the house, was convicted and sentenced to a 15-year prison term. Under petitioner's proposed rule, the wife would be unable to consent to a search of the house 10 years after the date on which her husband objected. We refuse to stretch *Randolph* to such strange lengths.

Nor are we persuaded to hold that an objection lasts for a "reasonable" time. "[I]t is certainly unusual for this Court to set forth precise time limits governing police action," Maryland v. Shatzer, 559 U.S. 98, 110 (2010), and what interval of time would be reasonable in this context? A week? A month? A year? Ten years?

Petitioner's rule would also require the police and ultimately the courts to determine whether, after the passage of time, an objector still had "common authority" over the premises, and this would often be a tricky question. * * *

Another problem concerns the procedure needed to register a continuing objection. Would it be necessary for an occupant to object while police officers are at the door? If presence at the time of consent is not needed, would an occupant have to be present at the premises when the objection was made? Could an objection be made pre-emptively? * * *

Finally, there is the question of the particular law enforcement officers who would be bound by an objection. Would this set include just the officers who were present when the objection was made? Would it also apply to other officers working on the same investigation? Would it extend to officers who were unaware of the objection? How about officers assigned to different but arguably related cases? Would it be limited by law enforcement agency?

If *Randolph* is taken at its word—that it applies only when the objector is standing in the door saying "stay out" when officers propose to make a consent search—all of these problems disappear. * * *

C

Petitioner argues strenuously that his expansive interpretation of *Randolph* would not hamper law enforcement because in most cases where officers have probable cause to arrest a physically present objector they also have probable cause to search the premises that the objector does not want them to enter, but this argument misunderstands the constitutional status of consent searches. A warrantless consent search is reasonable and thus consistent with the Fourth Amendment irrespective of the availability of a warrant. Even with modern technological advances, the warrant procedure imposes burdens on the officers who wish to search, the magistrate who must review the warrant application, and the party willing to give consent. When a warrantless search is justified, requiring the police to obtain a warrant may "unjustifiably interfer[e] with legitimate law enforcement strategies." Such a requirement may also impose an unmerited burden on the person who consents to an immediate search, since the warrant application procedure entails delay. Putting the exception the Court adopted in *Randolph* to one side, the lawful occupant of a house or apartment should have the right to invite the police to enter the dwelling and conduct a search. Any other rule would trample on the rights of the occupant who is willing to consent. Such an occupant may want the police to search in order to dispel "suspicion raised by sharing quarters with a criminal." And an occupant may want the police to conduct a thorough search so that any dangerous contraband can be found and removed. In this case, for example, the search resulted in the discovery and removal of a sawed-off shotgun to which Rojas' 4-year-old son had access.

Denying someone in Rojas' position the right to allow the police to enter her home would also show disrespect for her independence. Having beaten Rojas, petitioner would bar her from controlling access to her own home until such time as he chose to relent. The Fourth Amendment does not give him that power. * * *

The judgment of the California Court of Appeal is affirmed.

It is so ordered.

JUSTICE SCALIA, concurring.

[Omitted.]

JUSTICE GINSBURG, with whom JUSTICE SOTOMAYOR and JUSTICE KAGAN join, dissenting.

[Omitted.]

QUESTIONS, COMMENTS, CONCERNS?

1.   *Fernandez* **and Witman.** Assume that Mr. Witman did not consent to a search of his home when he arrived at the hospital at 8:00 p.m. on October 2, 1998. Would he have an argument to challenge the warrantless search of his home that revealed, for example, unlawful narcotics found in the drawer of his bedside table on October 3? Remember that Mrs. Witman had advised officers earlier on the afternoon of October 2 to do their job and "find out who did this." Is Mrs. Witman's grant of consent, if you indeed agree that she clearly granted consent, overruled by Mr. Witman's subsequent objection? If not, does Mrs. Witman's comment permit officers to search the drawers of *Mr. Witman's* bedside table?

2.   The issue in Witman's case that everyone missed. Notice that the prosecution failed to argue the inevitable discovery exception. Although the suppression court and appellate court reached opposite conclusions on whether Mrs. Witman's comment granted consent to search the Witman home, both courts agreed that Mr. Witman's statement provided the requisite consent. [Casefile Document 9, at 22–25; Casefile Document 10, at 337–38.] The appellate court concluded as follows:

> Even had the consent of the mother not been valid, consent by the father to search the crime scene, which remained secured, would have led inevitably to the discovery of those items determined by the suppression court to have been improperly seized pursuant to mother's consent. As a result, these items would be properly admitted at trial on the basis of the "inevitable discovery" doctrine."

[Casefile Document 10, at 339.]

3.   The rest of the Witman story. After nearly four and a half years of pretrial motions, Zachary Witman was convicted by a jury for the murder of his brother Gregory in 2003. Zach, by the way, consented to these delays by waiving his right to a speedy trial. [Casefile Document 3, at 2.] Zach was sentenced to life without parole, but for years following his conviction, both he and his parents maintained his innocence. Rick Lee, *Zach Witman Still Insists He Didn't Kill Brother Gregory in 1998*, YORK DAILY RECORD (Dec. 17, 2010), https://www.ydr.com/story/archives/2010/12/17/zach-witman-take-a-second-look/73896372/. Given the media attention the case received, and continued to receive, many in the community likewise viewed Zach as innocent. *E.g.*, Lonnie Soury, *Zach Witman is innocent. Set him free now.*, YORK DAILY RECORD (Nov. 30, 2017), https://www.ydr.com/story/opinion/columnists/2017/11/30/zach-witman-innocent-set-him-free-now-column/909646001/.

At one point, on March 27, 2013, Zach's parents held a press conference, during which Mr. Witman read a letter from Zach. The letter read, in pertinent part, "I still believe that no one deserves to be treated the way I have been by the public and the media." Liz Evans Scolforo, *Retired NYC Homicide Cop Says Witman Fratricide Case Needs To Be Reopened*, YORKDISPATCH.COM (Mar. 27, 2013), https://www.yorkdispatch.com/story/archives/2013/03/27/retired-nyc-homicide-cop-says-witman-fratricide-case/75321200/. He added, "I feel let down by the people of York County . . . because they never even gave me a chance." *Id.*

But then the Supreme Court decided *Montgomery v. Louisiana*, 577 U.S. 190 (2016). *Montgomery* held that the Court's 2012 decision in *Miller v. Alabama*, 567 U.S. 460 (2012), applied retroactively. *Id.* at 736. *Miller*, for its part, held that sentencing juvenile offenders to a mandatory term of life in prison without parole violated the Eighth and Fourteenth Amendments. 567 U.S. at 470. *Montgomery* therefore mandated that Zach be resentenced.

While awaiting his resentencing, prosecutors approached Zach about a possible plea deal. According to a media report, "The prosecution offered

Witman a sentence that would make him eligible for parole in less than a year in exchange for his guilty plea to third-degree murder. Witman took the deal." Rick Lee, *Here's how Zachary Witman came to plead guilty to killing brother and earn shot at parole*, FLORIDATODAY.COM (Feb. 10, 2018), https://www.floridatoday.com/story/news/2018/02/10/how-zachary-witman-plead-guilty-plea-killing-brother-gregory-witman-parole/323139002/. During the hearing on his plea, Zach admitted in open court that he did, in fact, kill Greg. Zach was released on parole in May 2019. Liz Evans Scolforo, *Zachary Witman Released; Murdered 13-Year-Old Brother in 1988*, YORKDISPATCH.COM, https://www.yorkdispatch.com/story/news/crime/2019/05/21/zachary-witman-paroled-murdered-13-year-old-brother-1998/3752644002/ (last updated Sept. 26, 2021, 8:43 AM).

V. AUTOMOBILE EXCEPTION

A. INTRODUCTION

The question presented by the so-called "car cases" is when law enforcement can warrantlessly search a vehicle and its containers. For some time, the Supreme Court's jurisprudence governing the "automobile exception" was a genuine mess. The Court established the exception in *Carroll v. United States*, 267 U.S. 132 (1925), a prohibition-era decision holding that officers may search a car without a warrant so long as they have probable cause to believe that the car contains contraband. The right to search a vehicle pursuant to the automobile exception, as the *Carroll* Court made clear, does not depend on an officer's right to arrest an occupant of the vehicle. But *Carroll* left unclear exactly *when* a vehicle must be searched pursuant to the automobile exception.

The Court first addressed that issue nearly a half-century later in *Chambers v. Maroney*, 399 U.S. 42 (1970). In that case, officers stopped a blue compact station wagon based on a tip that its driver might be a suspect in a string of robberies. Following the stop, however, officers declined to immediately search the vehicle. Rather, the car was driven to the station where a subsequent stationhouse search of the car revealed incriminating items. In permitting admission of the discovered contraband against the defendant, the Supreme Court upheld the warrantless stationhouse vehicle search. It reasoned that the car remained "readily movable"—even though it was secured at the police station.

Just a year later, in *Coolidge v. New Hampshire*, 403 U.S. 443 (1971), a plurality of the Court retreated from the seemingly extreme position it took in *Chambers*. Roughly two hours after the arrest of the *Coolidge* defendant, police seized two of his cars—both parked in his driveway. Police then executed three warrantless searches of one of the two vehicles. The first search took place two days following defendant's arrest; the second took place one year later; and the third search took place fifteen months later. The Court declined to extend *Chambers* and held that evidence obtained from the three warrantless searches was inadmissible. *Carroll*, the Court reasoned, was inapplicable because no exigent circumstances were present.

In 1985, the Court again addressed the timing requirement of the automobile exception, this time retreating from its decision in *Coolidge* and returning to the position it took in *Chambers*. In *California v. Carney*, 471 U.S. 386 (1985), officers suspected that Charles Carney was using his motor home to exchange marijuana for sexual contacts with a minor. At law enforcement's request, a youth knocked on the door of the motor home. When Carney came to the door, investigators observed marijuana and related drug paraphernalia. Following Carney's arrest, officers searched the motor home and found additional contraband. The Supreme Court upheld the search.

In doing so, the Court summarized the general rationale underlying the automobile exception:

> When a vehicle is being used on the highways, or if it is readily capable of such use and is found stationary in a place not regularly used for residential purposes—temporary or otherwise—the two justifications for the vehicle exception come into play. First, the vehicle is obviously readily mobile by the turn of an ignition key, if not actually moving. Second, there is a reduced expectation of privacy stemming from its use as a licensed motor vehicle subject to a range of police regulation inapplicable to a fixed dwelling. At least in these circumstances, the overriding societal interests in effective law enforcement justify an immediate search before the vehicle and its occupants become unavailable.

Based on this rationale, the Court concluded that the automobile exception applied to Carney's motor home because Carney *could* use the home as a vehicle and move it "beyond the reach of the police."

The Court, however, acknowledged that some motor homes will constitute a home for Fourth Amendment purposes. In a footnote, of all places, the Court provided a non-exhaustive list of five factors relevant to the inquiry:

> Among the factors that might be relevant in determining whether a warrant would be required in such a circumstance is its location, whether the vehicle is readily mobile or instead, for instance, elevated on blocks, whether the vehicle is licensed, whether it is connected to utilities, and whether it has convenient access to a public road.

Finally, note that *Carroll*, *Chambers*, *Coolidge*, and *Carney* largely focus on answering the questions of "when" and "why." That is, these cases address when the automobile exception applies and provide supporting rationale for why the exception should apply. But they leave a critical question unanswered: Does the automobile exception allow officers to search a "container" found inside the car itself?

The Court considered that very question in *United States v. Chadwick*, 433 U.S. 1 (1977). In *Chadwick*, two suspects loaded a large double-locked footlocker leaking talcum powder onto a San Diego train bound for Boston. When the train arrived, federal agents were waiting. They watched three people move the footlocker by baggage cart to the open trunk of Chadwick's waiting automobile. While the trunk was still open and before the car's engine was started, agents arrested all three suspects and took possession of the footlocker. Agents searched the footlocker without a warrant an hour and a half later at a federal building and found marijuana. The Supreme Court suppressed the marijuana, holding that no exigency permitted the warrantless search of Chadwick's footlocker. The Court reasoned that its prior "ready mobility" rationale did not apply to the footlocker.

The Court extended *Chadwick* two years later in *Arkansas v. Sanders*, 442 U.S. 753 (1979). In *Sanders*, officers developed probable cause to believe that Lonnie Sanders would arrive on a flight to the Little Rock airport carrying a green suitcase filled with marijuana. When Sanders landed, officers watched as he placed the unlocked suitcase into a taxicab trunk. Unlike *Chadwick*, officers waited until the taxi departed and stopped it a few blocks away from the airport. During the stop, officers had the driver open the trunk. Officers then removed the suitcase, searched it, and discovered marijuana. The Court held that the warrantless search was unconstitutional, reasoning that "a suitcase taken from an automobile stopped on the highway is not necessarily attended by any lesser expectation of privacy than is associated with luggage taken from other locations."

A clear divide emerged after *Sanders*. On the one hand, the *Carroll-Chambers-Carney* line of cases permitted officers to search a car, but because of the *Chadwick-Sanders* line of cases, officers could not search containers found inside the car. *See Robbins v. California*, 453 U.S. 420 (1981).

In 1982, the Court further complicated the issue in *United States v. Ross*, 456 U.S. 798 (1982). In *Ross*, law enforcement stopped and searched the trunk of suspect's vehicle, believing that the suspect was selling drugs out of the trunk. During the stop, officers took suspect's keys, opened the trunk, and discovered a closed paper bag, inside of which they found drugs. The Supreme Court upheld the search. Focusing on the fact that officers had probable cause to stop the vehicle—as opposed to a container inside— Justice Stevens wrote for the majority that, "[i]f probable cause justifies the search of a lawfully stopped vehicle, it justifies the search of every part of the vehicle and its contents that may conceal the object of the search." After *Ross*, then, officers could access certain containers if they had probable cause to search a vehicle, but could not search a *specific* container if the officers' probable cause went only to that container—as opposed to the full vehicle.

Confused yet? The good news is that our first case in these materials, *California v. Acevedo*, cleans up much of the Court's convoluted automobile exception jurisprudence. The tale of two New York rappers, believe it or not, also helps illustrate the practical applicability of the modern automobile exception.

B. MEET MICHAEL GARRETT & PAUL RIVERA

Michael "Rab" Garrett and Paul "Paulie" Rivera together were members of the rap group TF Mafia. According to the 2009 TF Mafia album, titled *Bossilini*, "TF Mafia is a musical representation of a larger organization called Together Forever" ("TF"). An FBI investigation that began in 2012 would reveal that TF was actually a criminal enterprise—a modern day mafia—with wide-ranging criminal interests in drug trafficking, prostitution, money laundering, and murder. And, as it would turn out, music videos published by TF Mafia became a key piece of evidence against Garrett and Rivera at the pair's 2015 jury trial. But more on that later.

In its heyday, between 2007–2013, TF was based out of Rivera's tattoo shop in Brownsville, New York, though it grew a strong offshoot presence in Scranton, Pennsylvania. Rivera was the organization's founder, and Garrett grew to become a leader in the group. Although the investigation into TF was a complicated one involving multiple law enforcement agencies at the federal and state levels, the organization's downfall began with two seemingly routine traffic stops.

Michael Garrett's 2010 Traffic Stop

On September 1, 2010, New Jersey State Police Trooper Armando Rivas, a seven-year state police veteran, was patrolling Interstate I-80 in Hope, New Jersey. At roughly 10:30 p.m. that night, Rivas observed a black 2008 Mercedes with New York plates traveling westbound in the left lane. He watched as the car made what Rivas judged to be an unsafe lane change from the left lane to the center lane while failing to use a turn signal. Both an unsafe lane change and failure to use a signal when changing lanes are traffic violations under New Jersey law. On the basis of those violations, Rivas pulled the Mercedes over.

To begin the stop, Rivas exited his vehicle and approached the Mercedes from the passenger side. He then made conversation with the car's sole occupant, Michael Garrett, who said that he was on his way to a Mohegan Sun casino to attend an event as a DJ or rapper. Rivas explained why he stopped Garrett, requested Garrett's license and registration, and explained that he was going to return to his police vehicle to check Garrett's driving record. During that check, Rivas learned that Garrett was driving on a suspended license and that there was a traffic warrant out for Garrett's arrest. Rivas then arrested Garrett and called a tow truck to tow the Mercedes to a private lot.

As Rivas worked to detain Garrett, Trooper Rachel Trent arrived on the scene. The pair agreed that Rivas would transport Garrett to the station while Trent waited for the tow truck to arrive. As Garrett left, he asked Trent to retrieve three cell phones from his car and hold them for him, which she did. Once at the station, Rivas directed Garrett, pursuant to department protocol, to remove his shoes and belt before entering a holding cell. When Garrett complied, Rivas discovered a partially smoked marijuana cigarette in Garrett's left shoe.

Meanwhile, back at the scene of the traffic stop, a tow truck operator named Todd Unangst arrived. The federal district court summarized Unangst's testimony at a subsequent suppression hearing as follows:

> Mr. Unangst testified that with "higher-end" cars like Mr. Garrett's Mercedes, equipment called a "tow loop" is used to tow the vehicle without damaging the suspension or the frame of the vehicle. The tow loop screws into the front bumper, and the tow hook from the tow truck attaches to the tow loop instead of the front bumper itself. Mr. Unangst testified that in the course of his work as a tow truck operator, Mr. Unangst routinely used tow loops to tow high-end vehicles, which he understands to be the common practice among tow truck companies generally.

> As was his common practice, Mr. Unangst used a key to open the trunk and retrieve the tow loop from the Garrett Vehicle. Mr. Unangst testified that he did not recall exactly how he obtained the keys for the Garrett Vehicle, but he believed that either Trooper Trent handed him the keys for the Garrett Vehicle or the keys were left for him in or near the Garrett Vehicle. Mr. Unangst testified that the [police] did not direct him to open the trunk of the Garrett Vehicle.

> Mr. Unangst testified that when he opened the trunk of the Garrett Vehicle, he noticed that it smelled like marijuana. Mr. Unangst then lifted the floor mat of the trunk to search for the tow loop in the spare tire and tools chamber. After lifting up the floor mat, Mr. Unangst saw a bag that was approximately ten to twelve inches in length.

[Casefile Document 9, at 11–12.] The package Unangst saw was roughly ten to twelve inches long. He called for Trent to come over to the trunk and "check it out" because he thought the package looked "odd." Trent made a note of the package and directed Unangst to tow Garrett's vehicle to the police station rather than to Unangst's private lot, as was the original plan.

On his arrival to the police station, Trent retrieved the package and handed it to Rivas. Rivas would later describe the mysterious package as "a clear vacuum-sealed bag with a black bag inside of it." Rivas showed the package to Garrett who responsively told Rivas that the package was not his. Rivas then asked for consent to search the package, which Garrett denied. Garrett also denied Rivas's request for consent to search Garrett's Mercedes.

After looking more into Garrett's background and learning that he possessed an extensive criminal history, Rivas elected to call his superior, Detective Jeffrey Shotwell, for assistance. Shotwell took his turn looking at the mysterious package seized from Garrett's trunk. He observed that the vacuum-sealed package contained a dark-colored thin plastic bag. He also noticed that the package was sealed in a manner that kept air *inside* rather than to remove air. Shotwell suspected that air was left in the package to mask the smell of its contents.

Shotwell then decided to pick up the package. He felt its contents and detected that several small round packages were contained within the dark plastic bag. Believing that the package contained drugs, Shotwell conferred with a supervisor, and the pair elected to cut open the package. Upon doing so, Shotwell smelled a vinegar odor and, inside the dark plastic bag contained within the package, Shotwell saw that the dark plastic bag held five smaller clear plastic bags. Those five small interior plastic bags contained multi-colored balloons with heroin concealed inside. In total, officers would inventory 506 multi-colored balloons containing forty-five grams of heroin. A search of Garrett's car pursuant to a search warrant revealed a bag of marijuana, rolling papers, a digital camera, and another cell phone.

Paul Rivera's 2012 Traffic Stop

On the morning of January 18, 2012, Trooper Thomas Horan, a nine-year veteran of the Pennsylvania State Police, was patrolling Interstate 81 in Susquehanna County in Pennsylvania. At roughly 8:08 am, Horan was driving in the left lane behind a silver Honda Accord with New York plates. The Honda moved into the right lane to allow Horan to pass, but after Horan went by, the vehicle immediately moved back into the left lane. Horan then elected to pull over into an emergency turnaround area of the highway, allowing the Honda to pass him. Horan reentered the highway and observed the Honda still driving in the left lane for roughly two minutes without passing a vehicle. In Pennsylvania, remaining in the left lane when the right lane is available on a limited access highway is a traffic violation. Horan elected to stop the Honda for committing what is known as a "left-lane violation."

Horan began the traffic encounter by walking up to the passenger side of the Honda. A female passenger opened the front passenger window and Horan counted five occupants in the car. After asking for identification from all five people in the vehicle, Horan identified the driver as Paul Rivera, the front-seat passenger as Shelby Rivera, the back left-seat passenger as John Portalatin, the back middle-seat passenger as Kathryn Rivera, and the back right-seat passenger as a juvenile female. Horan explained to Rivera that he pulled the vehicle over for a left-lane violation. As they were talking, Horan noticed a marijuana smell and asked Rivera who owned the vehicle, to which Rivera replied that it belonged to "his boss," Michael Garrett.

Horan then returned to his patrol car and ran a records check for the vehicle's occupants. He learned that Rivera had an extensive criminal record. He also learned that the Honda was registered to a Honda dealer in Brooklyn, New York, not to Garrett. When Horan returned to the Honda, he asked Rivera for the car's registration, which Rivera did not have, and further asked where the group was going, to which Rivera gave differing answers. Given that both Rivera and Portalatin appeared excessively nervous to Horan, he elected to call for backup.

Veteran Trooper Paul Lindsay arrived on the scene at roughly 8:30 a.m. Lindsay also received inconsistent answers about where the group was traveling and observed nervous behavior from Rivera. Horan then gave Rivera a traffic citation for the left-lane violation, which Rivera appeared happy to receive. Horan suspected criminal activity based on Rivera's response alongside his collective interaction with Rivera and elected to request that a K9 unit report to the scene.

Trooper Gerald Powell and his dog "Johnny" arrived between thirty to thirty-five minutes later. While the group waited for Powell and Johnny, Horan asked Rivera for consent to search the vehicle, which Rivera denied. When Powell reported with Johnny, Horan and Lindsay ordered the Honda's occupants out of the car and instructed them to stand on the side of the road. During the ensuing dog sniff, Johnny alerted to the center console of the Honda by jumping into the car through either an open door or window. Horan then informed Rivera that he was going to seize the vehicle. At 9:29 a.m., the officers took Rivera and the vehicle's other occupants into custody and had the vehicle taken to the police station.

At roughly 12:40 p.m., Horan applied for a warrant to search the Honda. During the ensuing search, officers discovered a red plastic bag containing two vacuum-sealed packages in the spare tire wheel well of the Honda's trunk. Inside each of the vacuum-sealed plastic bags was a black plastic bag. One of the black plastic bags contained 6.105 ounces of crack cocaine. The other black plastic bag contained yet another clear plastic bag containing 170 additional bags of heroin (in total roughly 7.5 grams) marked "Monster Mash." All five of the vehicle's occupants were placed under arrest.

The State and Federal Authorities Discover a Shared Interest in TF Mafia

Following Rivera's arrest, he was charged for several state felonies and held in a pretrial detention facility. After a preliminary hearing held on April 3, 2012, Rivera began sending communications to various individuals, including the judge assigned to his case, indicating his desire to cooperate with federal law enforcement. In one detailed letter, Rivera explained that he was motivated to cooperate out of concern that he and other people were "in danger." The letter offered extensive details about Garrett's criminal activities and accused Garret of setting him up on January 18, 2012, by putting drugs in the trunk of the Honda without Rivera's knowledge.

At that time of Rivera's letters, the U.S. Attorney's Office for the Middle District of Pennsylvania had already begun investigating the activities of TF Mafia. Pennsylvania state authorities shared Rivera's letters with federal law enforcement, including the FBI and U.S. Attorney's office. After reading the letters, on August 30, 2012, Assistant U.S. Attorney William Houser and FBI Task Force Officer Daniel Mimnaugh, among others, visited Rivera to explore his willingness to cooperate.

During that visit, Rivera would sign a proffer agreement, waive his *Miranda* rights, and make numerous statements repeating what he wrote in his letters. He also made a number of new statements, including that he and Garrett were members of TF Mafia, that TF Mafia operations were often conducted in Rivera's Brooklyn tattoo shop, and that Rivera killed Robert "Crowbar" Barber for Garrett because Barber owed Garrett money. Rivera also indicated that he and Garrett co-owned TF Mafia Muzik LLC, which served as a repository for proceeds earned from illegal TF Mafia criminal enterprises. Rivera was transferred to federal custody months later in February 2013.

Garrett & Rivera Are Prosecuted

By the time the federal investigation was complete, Rivera and Garrett were charged jointly in a wide-ranging third superseding indictment filed on April 28, 2014. [Casefile Document 3.] The extensive indictment charged the pair with violating numerous federal statutes, including racketeering, racketeering conspiracy, interstate prostitution, sex trafficking of children, conspiracy to distribute narcotics, money laundering, conspiracy to commit murder in aid of racketeering, and witness tampering.

Garrett and Rivera retained separate counsel and filed separate suppression motions in June 2014. Garrett sought to suppress evidence found during the September 1, 2010 traffic stop, while Rivera sought to suppress evidence found during the January 18, 2012 traffic stop. The district court denied both motions in a comprehensive 100+ page order filed on February 4, 2015.

C. THE CASES

CALIFORNIA V. ACEVEDO

500 U.S. 565
Supreme Court of the United States
January 8, 1991, Argued; May 30, 1991, Decided
No. 89-1690

JUSTICE BLACKMUN delivered the opinion of the Court.

This case requires us once again to consider the so-called "automobile exception" to the warrant requirement of the Fourth Amendment and its application to the search of a closed container in the trunk of a car.

I

On October 28, 1987, Officer Coleman of the Santa Ana, Cal., Police Department received a telephone call from a federal drug enforcement agent in Hawaii. The agent informed Coleman that he had seized a package containing marijuana which was to have been delivered to the Federal Express Office in Santa Ana and which was addressed to J. R. Daza at 805 West Stevens Avenue in that city. The agent arranged to send the package to Coleman instead. Coleman then was to take the package to the Federal Express office and arrest the person who arrived to claim it.

Coleman received the package on October 29, verified its contents, and took it to the Senior Operations Manager at the Federal Express office. At about 10:30 a.m. on October 30, a man, who identified himself as Jamie Daza, arrived to claim the package. He accepted it and drove to his apartment on West Stevens. He carried the package into the apartment.

At 11:45 a.m., officers observed Daza leave the apartment and drop the box and paper that had contained the marijuana into a trash bin. Coleman at that point left the scene to get a search warrant. About 12:05 p.m., the officers saw Richard St. George leave the apartment carrying a blue knapsack which appeared to be half full. The officers stopped him as he was driving off, searched the knapsack, and found 1 ½ pounds of marijuana.

At 12:30 p.m., respondent Charles Steven Acevedo arrived. He entered Daza's apartment, stayed for about 10 minutes, and reappeared carrying a brown paper bag that looked full. The officers noticed that the bag was the size of one of the wrapped marijuana packages sent from Hawaii. Acevedo walked to a silver Honda in the parking lot. He placed the bag in the trunk of the car and started to drive away. Fearing the loss of evidence, officers in a marked police car stopped him. They opened the trunk and the bag, and found marijuana.[1]

Respondent was charged in state court with possession of marijuana for sale * * *. He moved to suppress the marijuana found in the car. The motion was denied. He then pleaded guilty but appealed the denial of the suppression motion.

The California Court of Appeal, Fourth District, concluded that the marijuana found in the paper bag in the car's trunk should have been suppressed. The court concluded that the officers had probable cause to believe that the paper bag contained drugs but lacked probable cause to suspect that Acevedo's car, itself, otherwise contained contraband. Because the officers' probable cause was directed specifically at the bag, the court held that the case was controlled by *United States v. Chadwick*, 433 U.S. 1 (1977), rather than by *United States v. Ross*, 456 U.S. 798 (1982). Although the court agreed that the officers could seize the paper bag, it held that, under *Chadwick*, they could not open the bag without first obtaining a warrant for that purpose. The court then recognized "the anomalous nature" of the dichotomy between the rule in *Chadwick* and the rule in *Ross*. That dichotomy dictates that if there is probable cause to search a car, then the entire car—including any closed container found therein—may be searched without a warrant, but if there is probable cause only as to a container in the car, the container may be held but not searched until a warrant is obtained.

The Supreme Court of California denied the State's petition for review. * * *

We granted certiorari to reexamine the law applicable to a closed container in an automobile, a subject that has troubled courts and law enforcement officers since it was first considered in *Chadwick*. * * *

V

[Ed. note: The Court provided a detailed historic overview of its car cases. In doing so, it clearly separated what it called the "*Carroll* cases" from the "*Chadwick-Sanders* line."]

The *Chadwick-Sanders* rule not only has failed to protect privacy but also has confused courts and police officers and impeded effective law enforcement. The conflict between the *Carroll* doctrine cases and the *Chadwick-Sanders* line has been criticized in academic commentary. One leading authority on the Fourth Amendment, after comparing *Chadwick* and *Sanders* with *Carroll* and its progeny, observed: "These two lines of authority cannot be completely reconciled, and thus how one comes out in

---

[1]   When Officer Coleman returned with a warrant, the apartment was searched and bags of marijuana were found there. We are here concerned, of course, only with what was discovered in the automobile.

the container-in-the-car situation depends upon which line of authority is used as a point of departure." 3 W. LAFAVE, SEARCH AND SEIZURE 53 (2d ed. 1987).

The discrepancy between the two rules has led to confusion for law enforcement officers. For example, when an officer, who has developed probable cause to believe that a vehicle contains drugs, begins to search the vehicle and immediately discovers a closed container, which rule applies? The defendant will argue that the fact that the officer first chose to search the container indicates that his probable cause extended only to the container and that *Chadwick* and *Sanders* therefore require a warrant. On the other hand, the fact that the officer first chose to search in the most obvious location should not restrict the propriety of the search. The *Chadwick* rule, as applied in *Sanders*, has devolved into an anomaly such that the more likely the police are to discover drugs in a container, the less authority they have to search it. We have noted the virtue of providing " ' "clear and unequivocal" guidelines to the law enforcement profession.' " The *Chadwick-Sanders* rule is the antithesis of a " 'clear and unequivocal' guideline."

* * *

The *Chadwick* dissenters predicted that the container rule would have "the perverse result of allowing fortuitous circumstances to control the outcome" of various searches. The rule also was so confusing that within two years after *Chadwick*, this Court found it necessary [in *Sanders*] to expound on the meaning of that decision and explain its application to luggage in general. Again, dissenters bemoaned the "inherent opaqueness" of the difference between the *Carroll* and *Chadwick* principles and noted "the confusion to be created for all concerned." Three years after *Sanders*, we returned in *Ross* to "this troubled area," in order to assert that *Sanders* had not cut back on *Carroll*.

Although we have recognized firmly that the doctrine of *stare decisis* serves profoundly important purposes in our legal system, this Court has overruled prior case on the comparatively rare occasion when it has bred confusion or been a derelict or led to anomalous results. *Sanders* was explicitly undermined in *Ross*, and the existence of the dual regimes for automobile searches that uncover containers has proved as confusing as the *Chadwick* and *Sanders* dissenters predicted. We conclude that it is better to adopt one clear-cut rule to govern automobile searches and eliminate the warrant requirement for closed containers set forth in *Sanders*.

VI

The interpretation of the *Carroll* doctrine set forth in *Ross* now applies to all searches of containers found in an automobile. In other words, the police may search without a warrant if their search is supported by probable cause. The Court in *Ross* put it this way:

> The scope of a warrantless search of an automobile . . . is not defined by the nature of the container in which the contraband is secreted. Rather, it is defined by the object of the search and the places in which there is probable cause to believe that it may be found.

It went on to note: "Probable cause to believe that a container placed in the trunk of a taxi contains contraband or evidence does not justify a search of the entire cab." We reaffirm that principle. In the case before us, the police had probable cause to believe that the paper bag in the automobile's trunk contained marijuana. That probable cause now allows a warrantless search of the paper bag. The facts in the record reveal that the police did not have probable cause to believe that contraband was hidden in any other part of the automobile and a search of the entire vehicle would have been without probable cause and unreasonable under the Fourth Amendment.

Our holding today neither extends the *Carroll* doctrine nor broadens the scope of the permissible automobile search delineated in *Carroll*, *Chambers*, and *Ross*. * * *

Until today, this Court has drawn a curious line between the search of an automobile that coincidentally turns up a container and the search of a container that coincidentally turns up in an automobile. The protections of the Fourth Amendment must not turn on such coincidences. We therefore interpret *Carroll* as providing one rule to govern all automobile searches. The police may search an automobile and the containers within it where they have probable cause to believe contraband or evidence is contained.

The judgment of the California Court of Appeal is reversed, and the case is remanded to that court for further proceedings not inconsistent with this opinion.

It is so ordered.

JUSTICE SCALIA, concurring in the judgment.

I agree with the dissent that it is anomalous for a briefcase to be protected by the "general requirement" of a prior warrant when it is being carried along the street, but for that same briefcase to become unprotected as soon as it is carried into an automobile. On the other hand, I agree with the Court that it would be anomalous for a locked compartment in an automobile to be unprotected by the "general requirement" of a prior warrant, but for an unlocked briefcase within the automobile to be protected. I join in the judgment of the Court because I think its holding is more faithful to the text and tradition of the Fourth Amendment, and if these anomalies in our jurisprudence are ever to be eliminated that is the direction in which we should travel.

The Fourth Amendment does not by its terms require a prior warrant for searches and seizures; it merely prohibits searches and seizures that are "unreasonable." What it explicitly states regarding warrants is by way of limitation upon their issuance rather than requirement of their use. * * *

Although the Fourth Amendment does not explicitly impose the requirement of a warrant, it is of course textually possible to consider that implicit within the requirement of reasonableness. For some years after the (still continuing) explosion in Fourth Amendment litigation that followed our announcement of the exclusionary rule in *Weeks v. United States*, 232 U.S. 383 (1914), our jurisprudence lurched back and forth between imposing a categorical warrant requirement and looking to reasonableness alone. * * * By the late 1960's, the preference for a warrant had won out, at least rhetorically.

The victory was illusory. Even before today's decision, the "warrant requirement" had become so riddled with exceptions that it was basically unrecognizable. In 1985, one commentator cataloged nearly 20 such exceptions, including "searches incident to arrest . . . automobile searches . . . border searches . . . administrative searches of regulated businesses . . . exigent circumstances . . . search[es] incident to nonarrest when there is probable cause to arrest . . . boat boarding for document checks . . . welfare searches . . . inventory searches . . . airport searches . . . school search[es]. . . ." Since then, we have added at least two more. *California v. Carney*, 471 U.S. 386 (1985) (searches of mobile homes); O'Connor v. Ortega, 480 U.S. 709 (1987) (searches of offices of government employees). Our intricate body of law regarding "reasonable expectation of privacy" has been developed largely as a means of creating these exceptions, enabling a search to be denominated not a Fourth Amendment "search" and therefore not subject to the general warrant requirement.

Unlike the dissent, therefore, I do not regard today's holding as some momentous departure, but rather as merely the continuation of an inconsistent jurisprudence that has been with us for years. Cases like *United States v. Chadwick*, 433 U.S. 1 (1977), and *Arkansas v. Sanders*, 442 U.S. 753 (1979), have taken the "preference for a warrant" seriously, while cases like *United States v. Ross*, 456 U.S. 798 (1982), and *Carroll v. United States*, 267 U.S. 132 (1925), have not. There can be no clarity in this area unless we make up our minds, and unless the principles we express comport with the actions we take.

In my view, the path out of this confusion should be sought by returning to the first principle that the "reasonableness" requirement of the Fourth Amendment affords the protection that the common law afforded. I have no difficulty with the proposition that that includes the requirement of a warrant, where the common law required a warrant * * *. But the supposed "general rule" that a warrant is always required does not appear to have any basis in the common law, and confuses rather than facilitates any attempt to develop rules of reasonableness in light of changed legal circumstances, as the anomaly eliminated and the anomaly created by today's holding both demonstrate.

And there are more anomalies still. Under our precedents (as at common law), a person may be arrested outside the home on the basis of probable cause, without an arrest warrant. *United States v. Watson*, 423 U.S. 411, 418–421 (1976). Upon arrest, the person, as well as the area within his grasp, may be searched for evidence related to the crime. *Chimel v. California*, *supra*, at 762–763. Under these principles, if a known drug dealer is carrying a briefcase reasonably believed to contain marijuana (the unauthorized possession of which is a crime), the police may arrest him and search his person on the basis of probable cause alone. And, under our precedents, upon arrival at the station house, the police may inventory his possessions, including the briefcase, even if there is no reason to suspect that they contain contraband. *Illinois v. Lafayette*, 462 U.S. 640 (1983). According to our current law, however, the police may not, on the basis of the same probable cause, take the less intrusive step of stopping the individual on the street and demanding to see the contents of his briefcase. That makes no sense *a priori*, and in the absence of any common-law tradition supporting such a distinction, I see no reason to continue it.

    * * *

I would reverse the judgment in the present case, not because a closed container carried inside a car becomes subject to the "automobile" exception to the general warrant requirement, but because the search of a closed container, outside a privately owned building, with probable cause to believe that the container contains contraband, and when it in fact does contain contraband, is not one of those searches whose Fourth Amendment reasonableness depends upon a warrant. For that reason I concur in the judgment of the Court.

JUSTICE WHITE, dissenting.

Agreeing as I do with most of JUSTICE STEVENS' opinion and with the result he reaches, I dissent and would affirm the judgment below.

JUSTICE STEVENS, with whom JUSTICE MARSHALL joins, dissenting.

    * * *

II

In its opinion today, the Court recognizes that the police did not have probable cause to search respondent's vehicle and that a search of anything but the paper bag that respondent had carried from Daza's apartment and placed in the trunk of his car would have been unconstitutional. Moreover, as I read the opinion, the Court assumes that the police could not have made a warrantless inspection of the bag before it was placed in the car. Finally, the Court also does not question the fact that, under our prior cases, it would have been lawful for the police to seize the container and detain it (and respondent) until they obtained a search warrant. Thus, all of the relevant facts that governed our decisions in Chadwick and Sanders are present here whereas the relevant fact that justified the vehicle search in Ross is not present.

The Court does not attempt to identify any exigent circumstances that would justify its refusal to apply the general rule against warrantless searches. Instead, it advances these three arguments: First, the rules identified in the foregoing cases are confusing and anomalous. Second, the rules do not protect any significant interest in privacy. And, third, the rules impede effective law enforcement. None of these arguments withstands scrutiny.

The "Confusion"

* * * The Court summarizes the alleged "anomaly" created by the coexistence of *Ross, Chadwick*, and *Sanders* with the statement that "the more likely the police are to discover drugs in a container, the less authority they have to search it." This juxtaposition is only anomalous, however, if one accepts the flawed premise that the degree to which the police are likely to discover contraband is correlated with their authority to search without a warrant. Yet, even proof beyond a reasonable doubt will not justify a warrantless search that is not supported by one of the exceptions to the warrant requirement. And, even when the police have a warrant or an exception applies, once the police possess probable cause, the extent to which they are more or less certain of the contents of a container has no bearing on their authority to search it.

To the extent there was any "anomaly" in our prior jurisprudence, the Court has "cured" it at the expense of creating a more serious paradox. For surely it is anomalous to prohibit a search of a briefcase while the owner is carrying it exposed on a public street yet to permit a search once the owner has placed the briefcase in the locked trunk of his car. One's privacy interest in one's luggage can certainly not be diminished by one's removing it from a public thoroughfare and placing it—out of sight—in a privately owned vehicle. Nor is the danger that evidence will escape increased if the luggage is in a car rather than on the street. In either location, if the police have probable cause, they are authorized to seize the luggage and to detain it until they obtain judicial approval for a search. Any line demarking an exception to the warrant requirement will appear blurred at the edges, but the Court has certainly erred if it believes that, by erasing one line and drawing another, it has drawn a clearer boundary.

The Privacy Argument

The Court's statement that *Chadwick* and *Sanders* provide only "minimal protection to privacy" is also unpersuasive. Every citizen clearly has an interest in the privacy of the contents of his or her luggage, briefcase, handbag or any other container that conceals private papers and effects from public scrutiny. That privacy interest has been recognized repeatedly in cases spanning more than a century.

Under the Court's holding today, the privacy interest that protects the contents of a suitcase or a briefcase from a warrantless search when it is in public view simply vanishes when its owner climbs into a taxicab. Unquestionably the rejection of the Sanders line of cases by today's decision will result in a significant loss of individual privacy.

To support its argument that today's holding works only a minimal intrusion on privacy, the Court suggests that "if the police know that they may open a bag only if they are actually searching the entire car, they may search more extensively than they otherwise would in order to establish the general probable cause required by *Ross*." * * * [T]his fear is unexplained and inexplicable. Neither evidence uncovered in the course of a search nor the scope of the search conducted can be used to provide post hoc justification for a search unsupported by probable cause at its inception. * * *

The Burden on Law Enforcement

The Court's suggestion that *Chadwick* and *Sanders* have created a significant burden on effective law enforcement is unsupported, inaccurate, and, in any event, an insufficient reason for creating a new exception to the warrant requirement.

Despite repeated claims that *Chadwick* and *Sanders* have "impeded effective law enforcement," the Court cites no authority for its contentions. Moreover, all evidence that does exist points to the contrary conclusion. In the years since *Ross* was decided, the Court has heard argument in 30 Fourth Amendment cases involving narcotics. In all but one, the government was the petitioner. All save two involved a search or seizure without a warrant or with a defective warrant. And, in all except three, the Court upheld the constitutionality of the search or seizure.

In the meantime, the flow of narcotics cases through the courts has steadily and dramatically increased. No impartial observer could criticize this Court for hindering the progress of the war on drugs. On the contrary, decisions like the one the Court makes today will support the conclusion that this Court has become a loyal foot soldier in the Executive's fight against crime.

Even if the warrant requirement does inconvenience the police to some extent, that fact does not distinguish this constitutional requirement from any other procedural protection secured by the Bill of Rights. It is merely a part of the price that our society must pay in order to preserve its freedom. * * *

It is too early to know how much freedom America has lost today. The magnitude of the loss is, however, not nearly as significant as the Court's willingness to inflict it without even a colorable basis for its rejection of prior law.

I respectfully dissent.

QUESTIONS, COMMENTS, CONCERNS?

1. **The reach of *Acevedo*'s probable cause.** Return to the September 1, 2010 traffic stop of Garret's Mercedes. Recall that Trent told Rivas about the mysterious vacuum-sealed bag in Garrett's trunk once Trent returned to the station. Assuming probable cause exists at that moment, it's important to think through the limits of that probable cause. Does probable cause exist to open the bag? If so, does that same probable cause permit opening the dark colored interior bag? And if that's the case, does that probable cause extend to opening the five additional plastic bags? And, if so, does that also extend to the 506 separate balloons?

Asked simply, does the probable cause to open Acevedo's paper bag permit opening all the varied layers of Garrett's complex vacuum-sealed package? It's an important question because it exposes the many unanswered questions left behind by *Acevedo*. At the outset, note that opening a paper bag is a binary proposition—there is either contraband in the bag or not. But if no contraband was found, could the police have continued to search Acevedo's car or does the probable cause terminate once police realize the bag is empty? If the police *could* continue to search Acevedo's vehicle, must they limit their search to the remainder of his trunk or are they permitted to search the passenger compartment too?

Notice the reverse concern also exists. That is, after finding contraband in Acevedo's trunk, must the police stop looking in his vehicle? Or, because they found contraband in the paper bag, are they entitled to infer that more contraband is present elsewhere in the car? Finally, notice that Garrett's case exposes another critical, unanswered question: how does *Acevedo* apply to closed containers within other closed containers found inside a vehicle?

2. **The reach of *Acevedo*'s probable cause (redux).** Recall the scene at the station as officers evaluated what to do with Garrett's suspicious package. Remember that Detective Shotwell "cut the package open." [Casefile Document 8, at 13.] How does *Acevedo* apply to an officer's decision to destroy the suspect's property? Does Shotwell's decision change the Fourth Amendment analysis in any manner? In other words, is Shotwell's election to cut the bag open sufficiently analogous to police opening Acevedo's brown bag?

In your opinion, does the district court's analysis of *Acevedo* resolve the questions raised by this note and the preceding note? [*See* Casefile Document 11, at 27–30.]

3.   Revisiting dog sniffs. We learned in Chapter 3 that a dog sniff of the exterior of a vehicle during a lawful traffic stop is not a "search" for purposes of the Fourth Amendment. Is that what happened during Rivera's stop? Consider the government's recitation of the incident:

> When the K-9 sniff search of the Rivera Vehicle was complete, Trooper Powell advised Trooper Horan that the dog had alerted to the center console. Specifically, during the search, the dog entered the Rivera Vehicle through either an open door or window.

[Casefile Document 8, at 24.] Does *Caballes* justify K9 Johnny physically entering Rivera's vehicle? If not, does that render Johnny's sniff a warrantless "search"? Assume for the moment that it does. How would that impact the result in Rivera's motion to suppress? Be clear about labeling the "fruit" and the "poisonous tree."

A couple final questions on the topic of Johnny entering Rivera's vehicle. Remember that the government claimed Johnny entered through "an open door or window." Also keep in mind that it's roughly 8 a.m. in January in Susquehanna County—the northeast corner of Pennsylvania. We can probably rule out an "open window." That begs the question about the car's doors. Remember that officers ordered Rivera and his passengers out of the vehicle before Johnny began his sniff. Could the occupants have closed the car doors upon exiting? If so, could officers have opened them back up before Johnny started his sniff?

4.   Revisiting standing. Remember that police confronted Garrett with the vacuum-sealed package at the station following his arrest. Recall also that Garrett was asked for consent to search the vacuum-sealed bag and that he denied that the package was his. [Casefile Document 8, at 10.] Following Garrett's motion to suppress, the government creatively argued that Garrett "made clear that he intended to abandon the bag for the purposes of the Fourth Amendment." [Casefile Document 6, at 46.] Garrett countered that, "[a]s owner and operator of the automobile," he had "standing to challenge the search of his car and all items within it." [Casefile Document 7, at 1.] Applying your understanding of *Rakas* and the standing doctrine from Chapter 3, which side has the better argument? Does the district court resolve the standing question? [*See* Casefile Document 11, at 5.]

5.   Garrett and returning to inevitable discovery. As a fall back, the government argued that, regardless of any other constitutional problems, the heroin seized from Garrett's vehicle is admissible pursuant to the inevitable discovery doctrine. [Casefile Document 6, at 50–51.] Applying your recollection of *Nix v. Williams* (Chapter 2), is this argument a slam dunk for the government? How does the district court rule on the inevitable discovery question? [*See* Casefile Document 11, at 30–34.]

WYOMING V. HOUGHTON

526 U.S. 295
Supreme Court of the United States
January 12, 1999, Argued; April 5, 1999, Decided
No. 98-184

JUSTICE SCALIA delivered the opinion of the Court.

This case presents the question whether police officers violate the Fourth Amendment when they search a passenger's personal belongings inside an automobile that they have probable cause to believe contains contraband.

I

In the early morning hours of July 23, 1995, a Wyoming Highway Patrol officer stopped an automobile for speeding and driving with a faulty brake light. There were three passengers in the front seat of the car: David Young (the driver), his girlfriend, and respondent. While questioning Young, the officer noticed a hypodermic syringe in Young's shirt pocket. He left the occupants under the supervision of two backup officers as he went to get gloves from his patrol car. Upon his return, he instructed Young to step out of the car and place the syringe on the hood. The officer then asked Young why he had a syringe; with refreshing candor, Young replied that he used it to take drugs.

At this point, the backup officers ordered the two female passengers out of the car and asked them for identification. Respondent falsely identified herself as "Sandra James" and stated that she did not have any identification. Meanwhile, in light of Young's admission, the officer searched the passenger compartment of the car for contraband. On the back seat, he found a purse, which respondent claimed as hers. He removed from the purse a wallet containing respondent's driver's license, identifying her properly as Sandra K. Houghton. When the officer asked her why she had lied about her name, she replied: "In case things went bad."

Continuing his search of the purse, the officer found a brown pouch and a black wallet-type container. Respondent denied that the former was hers, and claimed ignorance of how it came to be there; it was found to contain drug paraphernalia and a syringe with 60 ccs of methamphetamine. Respondent admitted ownership of the black container, which was also found to contain drug paraphernalia, and a syringe (which respondent acknowledged was hers) with 10 ccs of methamphetamine—an amount insufficient to support the felony conviction at issue in this case. The officer also found fresh needle-track marks on respondent's arms. He placed her under arrest.

The State of Wyoming charged respondent with felony possession of methamphetamine in a liquid amount greater than three-tenths of a gram. After a hearing, the trial court denied her motion to suppress all evidence obtained from the purse as the fruit of a violation of the Fourth and Fourteenth Amendments. The court held that the officer had probable cause to search the car for contraband, and, by extension, any containers therein that could hold such contraband. A jury convicted respondent as charged.

The Wyoming Supreme Court, by divided vote, reversed the conviction * * *. * * *

The court held that the search of respondent's purse violated the Fourth and Fourteenth Amendments because the officer "knew or should have known that the purse did not belong to the driver, but to one of the passengers," and because "there was no probable cause to search the passengers' personal effects and no reason to believe that contraband had been placed within the purse."

II

* * *

It is uncontested in the present case that the police officers had probable cause to believe there were illegal drugs in the car. *Carroll v. United States*, 267 U.S. 132 (1925), similarly involved the warrantless search of a car that law enforcement officials had probable cause to believe contained contraband—in that case, bootleg liquor. The Court concluded that the Framers would have regarded such a search as reasonable in light of legislation enacted by Congress from 1789 through 1799—as well as subsequent legislation from the Founding era and beyond—that empowered customs officials to search any ship or vessel without a warrant if they had probable cause to believe that it contained goods subject to a duty. Thus, the Court held that "contraband goods concealed and illegally transported in an automobile or other vehicle may be searched for without a warrant" where probable cause exists.

We have furthermore read the historical evidence to show that the Framers would have regarded as reasonable (if there was probable cause) the warrantless search of containers within an automobile. In [*United States v. Ross*, 456 U.S. 798 (1982)], we upheld as reasonable the warrantless search of a paper bag and leather pouch found in the trunk of the defendant's car by officers who had probable cause to believe that the trunk contained drugs. * * *

Ross summarized its holding as follows: "If probable cause justifies the search of a lawfully stopped vehicle, it justifies the search of *every part of the vehicle and its contents* that may conceal the object of the search." 456 U.S. at 825 (emphasis added). And our later cases describing *Ross* have characterized it as applying broadly to all containers within a car, without qualification as to ownership. *See, e.g., California v. Acevedo*, 500 U.S. 565, 572 (1991) ("This Court in *Ross* took the critical step of saying that closed containers in cars could be searched without a warrant because of their presence within the automobile"); *United States v. Johns*, 469 U.S. 478, 479–480 (1985) (*Ross* "held that if police officers have probable cause to search a lawfully stopped vehicle, they may conduct a warrantless search of any containers found inside that may conceal the object of the search").

To be sure, there was no passenger in *Ross*, and it was not claimed that the package in the trunk belonged to anyone other than the driver. Even so, if the rule of law that *Ross* announced were limited to contents belonging to the driver, or contents other than those belonging to passengers, one would have expected that substantial limitation to be expressed. And, more importantly, one would have expected that limitation to be apparent in the historical evidence that formed the basis for *Ross's* holding. In fact, however, nothing in the statutes *Ross* relied upon, or in the practice under those statutes, would except from authorized warrantless search packages belonging to passengers on the suspect ship, horse-drawn carriage, or automobile.

Finally, we must observe that the analytical principle underlying the rule announced in *Ross* is fully consistent—as respondent's proposal is not—with the balance of our Fourth Amendment jurisprudence. *Ross* concluded from the historical evidence that the permissible scope of a warrantless car search "is defined by the object of the search and the places in which there is probable cause to believe that it may be found." * * *

In sum, neither *Ross* itself nor the historical evidence it relied upon admits of a distinction among packages or containers based on ownership. When there is probable cause to search for contraband in a car, it is reasonable for police officers—like customs officials in the Founding era— to examine packages and containers without a showing of individualized probable cause for each one. A passenger's personal belongings, just like the driver's belongings or containers attached to the car like a glove compartment, are "in" the car, and the officer has probable cause to search for contraband in the car.

Even if the historical evidence, as described by *Ross*, were thought to be equivocal, we would find that the balancing of the relative interests weighs decidedly in favor of allowing searches of a passenger's belongings. Passengers, no less than drivers, possess a reduced expectation of privacy with regard to the property that they transport in cars, which "travel public thoroughfares," *Cardwell v. Lewis*, 417 U.S. 583, 590 (1974), "seldom serve as . . . the repository of personal effects," *ibid.* are subjected to police stop and examination to enforce "pervasive" governmental controls "as an everyday occurrence," *South Dakota v. Opperman*, 428 U.S. 364, 368 (1976), and, finally, are exposed to traffic accidents that may render all their contents open to public scrutiny. * * *

Whereas the passenger's privacy expectations are, as we have described, considerably diminished, the governmental interests at stake are substantial. Effective law enforcement would be appreciably impaired without the ability to search a passenger's personal belongings when there is reason to believe contraband or evidence of criminal wrongdoing is hidden in the car. As in all car-search cases, the "ready mobility" of an automobile creates a risk that the evidence or contraband will be permanently lost while a warrant is obtained. *California v. Carney*, 471 U.S. 386, 390 (1985). In addition, a car passenger * * * will often be engaged in a common enterprise with the driver, and have the same interest in concealing the fruits or the evidence of their wrongdoing. A criminal might be able to hide contraband in a passenger's belongings as readily as in other containers in the car—perhaps even surreptitiously, without the passenger's knowledge or permission. (This last possibility provided the basis for respondent's defense at trial; she testified that most of the seized contraband must have been placed in her purse by her traveling companions at one or another of various times, including the time she was "half asleep" in the car.)

To be sure, these factors favoring a search will not always be present, but the balancing of interests must be conducted with an eye to the generality of cases. To require that the investigating officer have positive reason to believe that the passenger and driver were engaged in a common enterprise, or positive reason to believe that the driver had time and occasion to conceal the item in the passenger's belongings, surreptitiously or with friendly permission, is to impose requirements so seldom met that a "passenger's property" rule would dramatically reduce the ability to find and seize contraband and evidence of crime. * * * When balancing the competing interests, our determinations of "reasonableness" under the Fourth Amendment must take account of these practical realities. We think they militate in favor of the needs of law enforcement, and against a personal-privacy interest that is ordinarily weak. * * *

     * * *

We hold that police officers with probable cause to search a car may inspect passengers' belongings found in the car that are capable of concealing the object of the search. The judgment of the Wyoming Supreme Court is reversed.

It is so ordered.

JUSTICE BREYER, concurring.

I join the Court's opinion with the understanding that history is meant to inform, but not automatically to determine, the answer to a Fourth Amendment question. I also agree with the Court that when a police officer has probable cause to search a car, say, for drugs, it is reasonable for that officer also to search containers within the car. If the police must establish a container's ownership prior to the search of that container (whenever, for example, a passenger says "that's mine"), the resulting uncertainty will destroy the workability of the bright-line rule set forth in *United States v. Ross*, 456 U.S. 798 (1982). At the same time, police officers with probable cause to search a car for drugs would often have probable cause to search containers regardless. Hence a bright-line rule will authorize only a limited number of searches that the law would not otherwise justify.

At the same time, I would point out certain limitations upon the scope of the bright-line rule that the Court describes. Obviously, the rule applies only to automobile searches. Equally obviously, the rule applies only to containers found within automobiles. And it does not extend to the search of a person found in that automobile. * * *

Less obviously, but in my view also important, is the fact that the container here at issue, a woman's purse, was found at a considerable distance from its owner, who did not claim ownership until the officer discovered her identification while looking through it. Purses are special containers. They are repositories of especially personal items that people generally like to keep with them at all times. So I am tempted to say that a search of a purse involves an intrusion so similar to a search of one's person that the same rule should govern both. However, given this Court's prior cases, I cannot argue that the fact that the container was a purse automatically makes a legal difference, for the Court has warned against trying to make that kind of distinction. But I can say that it would matter if a woman's purse, like a man's billfold, were attached to her person. It might then amount to a kind of "outer clothing," which under the Court's cases would properly receive increased protection. In this case, the purse was separate from the person, and no one has claimed that, under those circumstances, the type of container makes a difference. For that reason, I join the Court's opinion.

JUSTICE STEVENS, with whom JUSTICE SOUTER and JUSTICE GINSBURG join, dissenting.

After Wyoming's highest court decided that a state highway patrolman unlawfully searched Sandra Houghton's purse, the State of Wyoming petitioned for a writ of certiorari. The State asked that we consider the propriety of searching an automobile passenger's belongings when the government has developed probable cause to search the vehicle for contraband based on the driver's conduct. The State conceded that the trooper who searched Houghton's purse lacked a warrant, consent, or "probable cause specific to the purse or passenger." In light of our established preference for warrants and individualized suspicion, I would respect the result reached by the Wyoming Supreme Court and affirm its judgment.

In all of our prior cases applying the automobile exception to the Fourth Amendment's warrant requirement, either the defendant was the operator of the vehicle and in custody of the object of the search, or no question was raised as to the defendant's ownership or custody. In the only automobile case confronting the search of a passenger defendant—*United States v. Di Re*, 332 U.S. 581 (1948)—the Court held that the exception to the warrant requirement did not apply. 332 U.S. at 583–587 (addressing searches of the passenger's pockets and the space between his shirt and underwear, both of which uncovered counterfeit fuel rations). In *Di Re*, as here, the information prompting the search directly implicated the driver, not the passenger. Today, instead of adhering to the settled distinction between drivers and passengers, the Court fashions a new rule that is based on a distinction between property contained in clothing worn by a passenger and property contained in a passenger's briefcase or purse. In cases on both sides of the Court's newly minted test, the property is in a "container" (whether a pocket or a pouch) located in the vehicle. Moreover, unlike the Court, I think it quite plain that the search of a passenger's purse or briefcase involves an intrusion on privacy that may be just as serious as was the intrusion in *Di Re*.

Even apart from *Di Re*, the Court's rights-restrictive approach is not dictated by precedent. For example, in *United States v. Ross*, 456 U.S. 798 (1982), we were concerned with the interest of the driver in the integrity of "his automobile," and we categorically rejected the notion that the scope of a warrantless search of a vehicle might be "defined by the nature of the container in which the contraband is secreted." "Rather, it is defined by the object of the search and the places in which there is probable cause to believe that it may be found." We thus disapproved of a possible container-based distinction between a man's pocket and a woman's pocketbook. Ironically, while we concluded in *Ross* that "probable cause to believe that a container placed in the trunk of a taxi contains contraband or evidence does not justify a search of the entire cab," the rule the Court fashions would apparently permit a warrantless search of a passenger's briefcase if there is probable cause to believe the taxidriver had a syringe somewhere in his vehicle.

Nor am I persuaded that the mere spatial association between a passenger and a driver provides an acceptable basis for presuming that they are partners in crime or for ignoring privacy interests in a purse. Whether or not the Fourth Amendment required a warrant to search Houghton's purse, *cf. Carroll v. United States*, 267 U.S. 132, 153 (1925), at the very least the trooper in this case had to have probable cause to believe that her purse contained contraband. The Wyoming Supreme Court concluded that he did not.

Finally, in my view, the State's legitimate interest in effective law enforcement does not outweigh the privacy concerns at issue. I am as confident in a police officer's ability to apply a rule requiring a warrant or individualized probable cause to search belongings that are—as in this case—obviously owned by and in the custody of a passenger as is the Court in a "passenger-confederate[']s" ability to circumvent the rule. Certainly the ostensible clarity of the Court's rule is attractive. But that virtue is insufficient justification for its adoption. Moreover, a rule requiring a warrant or individualized probable cause to search passenger belongings is every bit as simple as the Court's rule; it simply protects more privacy.

I would decide this case in accord with what we have said about passengers and privacy, rather than what we might have said in cases where the issue was not squarely presented. * * *

* * * Instead of applying ordinary Fourth Amendment principles to this case, the majority extends the automobile warrant exception to allow searches of passenger belongings based on the driver's misconduct. Thankfully, the Court's automobile-centered analysis limits the scope of its holding. But it does not justify the outcome in this case.

I respectfully dissent.

QUESTIONS, COMMENTS, CONCERNS?

1.   **The passengers in Rivera's car.** Recall that there were five total people in Rivera's Honda at the time of the January 18, 2012 traffic stop. Fast-forward to about the mid-point of that stop, just after Horan asked for a K9 to come sniff Rivera's vehicle. [*See* Casefile Document 8, at 22.] Once K9 Johnny arrived, Horan and another officer ordered all five occupants to get out of the car and stand on the side of the road. *Id.* at 23. Assuming probable cause to search the Honda exists, does *Houghton* permit a K9 to sniff all areas of the Honda—i.e., where *all* of the occupants were sitting?

COLLINS V. VIRGINIA
138 S. Ct. 1663
Supreme Court of the United States
January 9, 2018, Argued; May 29, 2018, Decided
No. 16-1027

JUSTICE SOTOMAYOR delivered the opinion of the Court.

This case presents the question whether the automobile exception to the Fourth Amendment permits a police officer, uninvited and without a warrant, to enter the curtilage of a home in order to search a vehicle parked therein. It does not.

I

Officer Matthew McCall of the Albemarle County Police Department in Virginia saw the driver of an orange and black motorcycle with an extended frame commit a traffic infraction. The driver eluded Officer

McCall's attempt to stop the motorcycle. A few weeks later, Officer David Rhodes of the same department saw an orange and black motorcycle traveling well over the speed limit, but the driver got away from him, too. The officers compared notes and concluded that the two incidents involved the same motorcyclist.

Upon further investigation, the officers learned that the motorcycle likely was stolen and in the possession of petitioner Ryan Collins. After discovering photographs on Collins' Facebook profile that featured an orange and black motorcycle parked at the top of the driveway of a house, Officer Rhodes tracked down the address of the house, drove there, and parked on the street. It was later established that Collins' girlfriend lived in the house and that Collins stayed there a few nights per week.

From his parked position on the street, Officer Rhodes saw what appeared to be a motorcycle with an extended frame covered with a white tarp, parked at the same angle and in the same location on the driveway as in the Facebook photograph. Officer Rhodes, who did not have a warrant, exited his car and walked toward the house. He stopped to take a photograph of the covered motorcycle from the sidewalk, and then walked onto the residential property and up to the top of the driveway to where the motorcycle was parked. In order "to investigate further," Officer Rhodes pulled off the tarp, revealing a motorcycle that looked like the one from the speeding incident. He then ran a search of the license plate and vehicle identification numbers, which confirmed that the motorcycle was stolen. After gathering this information, Officer Rhodes took a photograph of the uncovered motorcycle, put the tarp back on, left the property, and returned to his car to wait for Collins.

Shortly thereafter, Collins returned home. Officer Rhodes walked up to the front door of the house and knocked. Collins answered, agreed to speak with Officer Rhodes, and admitted that the motorcycle was his and that he had bought it without title. Officer Rhodes then arrested Collins.

Collins was indicted by a Virginia grand jury for receiving stolen property. He filed a pretrial motion to suppress the evidence that Officer Rhodes had obtained as a result of the warrantless search of the motorcycle. Collins argued that Officer Rhodes had trespassed on the curtilage of the house to conduct an investigation in violation of the Fourth Amendment. The trial court denied the motion and Collins was convicted.

The Court of Appeals of Virginia affirmed. It assumed that the motorcycle was parked in the curtilage of the home and held that Officer Rhodes had probable cause to believe that the motorcycle under the tarp was the same motorcycle that had evaded him in the past. It further concluded that Officer Rhodes' actions were lawful under the Fourth Amendment even absent a warrant because "numerous exigencies justified both his entry onto the property and his moving the tarp to view the motorcycle and record its identification number."

The Supreme Court of Virginia affirmed on different reasoning. It explained that the case was most properly resolved with reference to the Fourth Amendment's automobile exception. Under that framework, it held that Officer Rhodes had probable cause to believe that the motorcycle was contraband, and that the warrantless search therefore was justified.

We granted certiorari and now reverse.

II

* * * This case arises at the intersection of two components of the Court's Fourth Amendment jurisprudence: the automobile exception to the warrant requirement and the protection extended to the curtilage of a home.

A

1

The Court has held that the search of an automobile can be reasonable without a warrant. * * *

The "ready mobility" of vehicles served as the core justification for the automobile exception for many years. Later cases then introduced an additional rationale based on "the pervasive regulation of vehicles capable of traveling on the public highways." * * *

In announcing each of these two justifications, the Court took care to emphasize that the rationales applied only to automobiles and not to houses, and therefore supported "treating automobiles differently from houses" as a constitutional matter.

When these justifications for the automobile exception "come into play," officers may search an automobile without having obtained a warrant so long as they have probable cause to do so.

2

Like the automobile exception, the Fourth Amendment's protection of curtilage has long been black letter law. "[W]hen it comes to the Fourth Amendment, the home is first among equals." To give full practical effect to that right, the Court considers curtilage—"the area 'immediately surrounding and associated with the home' "—to be " 'part of the home itself for Fourth Amendment purposes.' " * * *

When a law enforcement officer physically intrudes on the curtilage to gather evidence, a search within the meaning of the Fourth Amendment has occurred. Such conduct thus is presumptively unreasonable absent a warrant.

B

1

With this background in mind, we turn to the application of these doctrines in the instant case. As an initial matter, we decide whether the part of the driveway where Collins' motorcycle was parked and subsequently searched is curtilage.

According to photographs in the record, the driveway runs alongside the front lawn and up a few yards past the front perimeter of the house. The top portion of the driveway that sits behind the front perimeter of the house is enclosed on two sides by a brick wall about the height of a car and on a third side by the house. A side door provides direct access between this partially enclosed section of the driveway and the house. A visitor endeavoring to reach the front door of the house would have to walk partway up the driveway, but would turn off before entering the enclosure and instead proceed up a set of steps leading to the front porch. When Officer Rhodes searched the motorcycle, it was parked inside this partially enclosed top portion of the driveway that abuts the house.

The " 'conception defining the curtilage' is . . . familiar enough that it is 'easily understood from our daily experience.' " Just like the front porch, side garden, or area "outside the front window," the driveway enclosure where Officer Rhodes searched the motorcycle constitutes "an area adjacent to the home and 'to which the activity of home life extends,' " and so is properly considered curtilage.

2

In physically intruding on the curtilage of Collins' home to search the motorcycle, Officer Rhodes not only invaded Collins' Fourth Amendment interest in the item searched, i.e., the motorcycle, but also invaded Collins' Fourth Amendment interest in the curtilage of his home. The question before the Court is whether the automobile exception justifies the invasion of the curtilage.[2] The answer is no.

Applying the relevant legal principles to a slightly different factual scenario confirms that this is an easy case. Imagine a motorcycle parked inside the living room of a house, visible through a window to a passerby on the street. Imagine further that an officer has probable cause to believe that the motorcycle was involved in a traffic infraction. Can the officer, acting without a warrant, enter the house to search the motorcycle and confirm whether it is the right one? Surely not.

---

[2]   Helpfully, the parties have simplified matters somewhat by each making a concession. Petitioner concedes "for purposes of this appeal" that Officer Rhodes had probable cause to believe that the motorcycle was the one that had eluded him, and Virginia concedes that Officer Rhodes searched the motorcycle."

The reason is that the scope of the automobile exception extends no further than the automobile itself. Virginia asks the Court to expand the scope of the automobile exception to permit police to invade any space outside an automobile even if the Fourth Amendment protects that space. Nothing in our case law, however, suggests that the automobile exception gives an officer the right to enter a home or its curtilage to access a vehicle without a warrant. Expanding the scope of the automobile exception in this way would both undervalue the core Fourth Amendment protection afforded to the home and its curtilage and " 'untether' " the automobile exception " 'from the justifications underlying' " it.

The Court already has declined to expand the scope of other exceptions to the warrant requirement to permit warrantless entry into the home. The reasoning behind those decisions applies equally well in this context. For instance, under the plain-view doctrine, "any valid warrantless seizure of incriminating evidence" requires that the officer "have a lawful right of access to the object itself." A plain-view seizure thus cannot be justified if it is effectuated "by unlawful trespass." Had Officer Rhodes seen illegal drugs through the window of Collins' house, for example, assuming no other warrant exception applied, he could not have entered the house to seize them without first obtaining a warrant.

Similarly, it is a "settled rule that warrantless arrests in public places are valid," but, absent another exception such as exigent circumstances, officers may not enter a home to make an arrest without a warrant, even when they have probable cause. That is because being " 'arrested in the home involves not only the invasion attendant to all arrests but also an invasion of the sanctity of the home.' " Likewise, searching a vehicle parked in the curtilage involves not only the invasion of the Fourth Amendment interest in the vehicle but also an invasion of the sanctity of the curtilage.

Just as an officer must have a lawful right of access to any contraband he discovers in plain view in order to seize it without a warrant, and just as an officer must have a lawful right of access in order to arrest a person in his home, so, too, an officer must have a lawful right of access to a vehicle in order to search it pursuant to the automobile exception. The automobile exception does not afford the necessary lawful right of access to search a vehicle parked within a home or its curtilage because it does not justify an intrusion on a person's separate and substantial Fourth Amendment interest in his home and curtilage.

As noted, the rationales underlying the automobile exception are specific to the nature of a vehicle and the ways in which it is distinct from a house. The rationales thus take account only of the balance between the intrusion on an individual's Fourth Amendment interest in his vehicle and the governmental interests in an expedient search of that vehicle; they do not account for the distinct privacy interest in one's home or curtilage. To allow an officer to rely on the automobile exception to gain entry into a house or its curtilage for the purpose of conducting a vehicle search would unmoor the exception from its justifications, render hollow the core Fourth Amendment protection the Constitution extends to the house and its curtilage, and transform what was meant to be an exception into a tool with far broader application. Indeed, its name alone should make all this clear enough: It is, after all, an exception for automobiles.

Given the centrality of the Fourth Amendment interest in the home and its curtilage and the disconnect between that interest and the justifications behind the automobile exception, we decline Virginia's invitation to extend the automobile exception to permit a warrantless intrusion on a home or its curtilage.

III   * * *

* * * Virginia urges the Court to adopt a more limited rule regarding the intersection of the automobile exception and the protection afforded to curtilage. Virginia would prefer that the Court draw a bright line and hold that the automobile exception does not permit warrantless entry into "the physical threshold of a house or a similar fixed, enclosed structure inside the curtilage like a garage." Requiring officers to make "case-by-case curtilage determinations," Virginia reasons, unnecessarily complicates matters and "raises the potential for confusion and . . . error."

The Court, though, has long been clear that curtilage is afforded constitutional protection. As a result, officers regularly assess whether an area is curtilage before executing a search. Virginia provides no reason to conclude that this practice has proved to be unadministrable, either generally or in this context. Moreover, creating a carveout to the general rule that curtilage receives Fourth Amendment protection, such that certain types of curtilage would receive Fourth Amendment protection only for some purposes but not for others, seems far more likely to create confusion than does uniform application of the Court's doctrine.

In addition, Virginia's proposed rule rests on a mistaken premise about the constitutional significance of visibility. The ability to observe inside curtilage from a lawful vantage point is not the same as the right to enter curtilage without a warrant for the purpose of conducting a search to obtain information not otherwise accessible. So long as it is curtilage, a parking patio or carport into which an officer can see from the street is no less entitled to protection from trespass and a warrantless search than a fully enclosed garage.

Finally, Virginia's proposed bright-line rule automatically would grant constitutional rights to those persons with the financial means to afford residences with garages in which to store their vehicles but deprive those persons without such resources of any individualized consideration as to whether the areas in which they store their vehicles qualify as curtilage.

IV

For the foregoing reasons, we conclude that the automobile exception does not permit an officer without a warrant to enter a home or its curtilage in order to search a vehicle therein. We leave for resolution on remand whether Officer Rhodes' warrantless intrusion on the curtilage of Collins' house may have been reasonable on a different basis, such as the exigent circumstances exception to the warrant requirement. The judgment of the Supreme Court of Virginia is therefore reversed, and the case is remanded for further proceedings not inconsistent with this opinion.

It is so ordered.

JUSTICE THOMAS, concurring.

[Omitted.]

JUSTICE ALITO, dissenting. * * *

In this case, there is no dispute that the search of the motorcycle was governed by the Fourth Amendment, and therefore whether or not it occurred within the curtilage is not of any direct importance. The question before us is not whether there was a Fourth Amendment search but whether the search was reasonable. And the only possible argument as to why it might not be reasonable concerns the need for a warrant. For nearly a century, however, it has been well established that officers do not need a warrant to search a motor vehicle on public streets so long as they have probable cause. Thus, the issue here is whether there is any good reason why this same rule should not apply when the vehicle is parked in plain view in a driveway just a few feet from the street.

In considering that question, we should ask whether the reasons for the "automobile exception" are any less valid in this new situation. Is the vehicle parked in the driveway any less mobile? Are any greater privacy interests at stake? If the answer to those questions is "no," then the automobile exception should apply. And here, the answer to each question is emphatically "no." The tarp-covered motorcycle parked in the driveway could have been uncovered and ridden away in a matter of seconds. And Officer Rhodes's brief walk up the driveway impaired no real privacy interests.

In this case, the Court uses the curtilage concept in a way that is contrary to our decisions regarding other, exigency-based exceptions to the warrant requirement. Take, for example, the "emergency aid" exception. When officers reasonably believe that a person inside a dwelling has urgent need of assistance, they may cross the curtilage and enter the building without first obtaining a warrant. The same is true when officers reasonably believe that a person in a dwelling is destroying evidence. In both of those situations, we ask whether " 'the exigencies of the situation' make the needs of law enforcement so compelling that the warrantless search is objectively reasonable." We have not held that the need to cross the curtilage independently necessitates a warrant, and there is no good reason to apply a different rule here.

It is no answer to this argument that the emergency-aid and destruction-of-evidence exceptions require an inquiry into the practicality of obtaining a warrant in the particular circumstances of the case. Our precedents firmly establish that the motor-vehicle exception, unlike these other exceptions, "has no separate exigency requirement." It is settled that the mobility of a motor vehicle categorically obviates any need to engage in such a case-specific inquiry. Requiring such an inquiry here would mark a substantial alteration of settled Fourth Amendment law.

This does not mean, however, that a warrant is never needed when officers have probable cause to search a motor vehicle, no matter where the vehicle is located. While a case-specific inquiry regarding exigency would be inconsistent with the rationale of the motor-vehicle exception, a case-specific inquiry regarding the degree of intrusion on privacy is entirely appropriate when the motor vehicle to be searched is located on private property. After all, the ultimate inquiry under the Fourth Amendment is whether a search is reasonable, and that inquiry often turns on the degree of the intrusion on privacy. Thus, contrary to the opinion of the Court, an affirmance in this case would not mean that officers could perform a warrantless search if a motorcycle were located inside a house. In that situation, the intrusion on privacy would be far greater than in the present case, where the real effect, if any, is negligible.

I would affirm the decision below and therefore respectfully dissent.

QUESTIONS, COMMENTS, CONCERNS?

1.   A review of standing. Collins's girlfriend lived in the house where Officer Rhodes found the stolen motorcycle. Collins, says the Court, stayed there "a few nights per week." Does Collins have standing to challenge the entry onto his girlfriend's home or the search of the motorcycle, or both?

2.   Considering Justice Alito's dissent. Is Justice Alito asserting that the automobile exception applies even to vehicles seen by officers on private property? Does his analogous reliance on the exigent circumstances doctrine help or hurt his overarching argument?

3.   A controversial approach to proving Garrett and Rivera's guilt. During its existence, TF Mafia made a variety of music videos. [*See* Casefile Folder Labeled as 9 (containing four TF Mafia music videos).] Those videos depicted a lifestyle that, according to the government, was consistent with TF Mafia's involvement in criminal behavior. Accordingly, the government moved to introduce twenty total videos into evidence at Garrett's and Rivera's trial. Garrett and Rivera responded that the videos were produced solely "for entertainment purposes" and that the weapons, cash and drugs in the videos were merely "props." The district court held that the videos were admissible at trial. [Casefile Document 10.] That ruling, as the media documented, conflicted with a handful of other courts that declined to admit, for example, a rapper's lyrics against him as evidence in his criminal trial. Yohance Kyles, *Judge Rules Prosecutors Can Use Rap Videos as Evidence Against Alleged Brooklyn Drug Gang TF Mafia*, ALLHIPHOP.COM (Apr. 20, 2015), https://allhiphop.com/2015/04/20/judge-rules-prosecutors-can-use-rap-videos-as-evidence-against-alleged-brooklyn-drug-gang/; Sha Be Allah, *Brooklyn Gang TF Mafia Video is Ok As Evidence in Trial*, THESOURCE.COM (Apr. 20, 2015), http://thesource.com/2015/04/20/brooklyn-gang-tf-mafia-video-is-ok-as-evidence-in-trial/; John Marzulli, *Brooklyn Drug Gang's YouTube Hip-Hop Videos Can Be Used in Trial, Judge Rules*, NYDAILYNEWS.COM (Apr. 18, 2015), http://www.nydailynews.com/new-york/nyc-crime/exclusive-brooklyn-drug-gang-hip-hop-videos-trial-article-1.2189715.

4.   The rest of the Garrett and Rivera story. On June 25, 2015, following a seven-week trial, a jury convicted both Garrett and Rivera on all counts. Sentencing, however, became a protracted endeavor that lasted for more than a year. As the proceedings dragged on and both defendants awaited sentencing, Garrett died from a synthetic marijuana overdose on February 28, 2016, at the age of forty. John Marzulli, *Brooklyn Rapper Convicted of Murder Dies of Synthetic Marijuana Overdose in Federal Prison*, NYDAILYNEWS.COM (May 23, 2016), http://www.nydailynews.com/new-york/nyc-crime/rapper-convicted-murder-dies-synthetic-marijuana-overdose-article-1.2646093. The district court vacated Garrett's conviction posthumously. Meanwhile, Rivera, at the age of forty-nine, was sentenced to life in prison on December 29, 2016. [Casefile Document 12.] There is no parole in the federal system.

VI. PLAIN SENSE SEIZURES

A. INTRODUCTION

The plain view doctrine initially appears straightforward. After all, if officers see contraband, they can take it, right? Sort of. Often thought of as an "exception" to the need for a warrant to conduct a search of a person, house, paper, or effect, the plain view doctrine actually justifies warrantless *seizures* of contraband in plain view. In order for the doctrine to apply, police must observe contraband from a lawful vantage point and have a lawful right of access to the item itself. Thus, standing on its own, plain view cannot justify a warrantless a seizure—justification for the underlying search must also exist.

Officers might lawfully observe contraband in any number of scenarios. For instance, law enforcement might discover an illegal item during the execution of a search warrant or during an in-home arrest. Of course, it's also possible that officers could view an illegal item while engaged in a lawful warrantless search; that is, any scenario when a search warrant is not required. Finally, officers might view contraband in circumstances that raise no Fourth Amendment concern. The police officer walking the beat, for instance, might see unlawful activity from their vantage point on a public sidewalk.

Note that officers with lawful access to the place where contraband is found who observe that contraband from a lawful vantage point must also know that the item to be seized is, in fact, contraband. In other words, as the Supreme Court observed in *Arizona v. Hicks*, 480 U.S. 321 (1987), law enforcement must have probable cause to believe that the item to be seized is unlawful.

The plain view doctrine has spawned other corollary "plain sense" concepts. For example, there now exists the doctrines of "plain touch," "plain feel," "plain hearing," and "plain smell." Note, however, that the "plain hearing" and "plain smell" rules encompass police conduct that does not trigger Fourth Amendment protection.

B. MEET AARON HERNANDEZ

In spring 2010, the New England Patriots secured a record breaking tight-end duo through its draft of Rob Gronkowski and Aaron Hernandez. Together, Hernandez and Gronkowski became the first pair of tight-ends in NFL history to catch at least five touchdowns each in consecutive seasons for the same team. By 2011, the duo was setting tight-end records for yardage, receptions, and touchdowns, combining for 169 receptions, 2,237 yards, and 24 touchdowns. In recognition of their success, the Patriots offered the duo the largest contract extensions in NFL history— locking Hernandez and Gronkowski into five-year contracts that combined were worth more than $90 million.

Aaron Hernandez was born on November 6, 1989, in Bristol, Connecticut. Growing up, Hernandez's father Dennis always knew that Hernandez was going to be a great athlete, and he was right. In 2005, when Hernandez was only a junior at Bristol Central High School, Hernandez was rated the nation's number one tight-end recruit. But tragedy struck soon after Hernandez's junior year when his father passed away suddenly from complications following hernia surgery.

On the field, Hernandez seemed unaffected by his father's death. In his senior year of High School, Hernandez broke the state and national records for receptions and accepted a full scholarship to play for the University of Florida. As a junior in 2009, Hernandez led the Gators with sixty-eight receptions and five touchdowns and won the John Mackey Award given annually to the nation's best tight-end.

Off the field, Hernandez began to spiral. According to his mother, Terri, Hernandez became rebellious, stating that "he wasn't the same kid, the way he spoke to me. The shock of losing his dad, there was so much anger." In 2007, the Gainesville police department recommended that

Hernandez be charged with felony battery after he ruptured the eardrum of a restaurant employee who confronted Hernandez over his refusal to pay his bill. Hernandez was also questioned as a person of interest after five gunshots were fired into a car outside a Gainesville nightclub. Hernandez would ultimately invoke his right to counsel and refused to talk to the police. No charges were filed. Despite these incidents, the Patriots selected Hernandez in the fourth round of the NFL Draft and offered him a cautious contract that required Hernandez to "prove himself capable of keeping his nose clean to cash in."

On Monday, June 17, 2013, at approximately 5:37 p.m., the North Attleboro Police Department in Massachusetts responded to a 911 call reporting that a dead body had been found in the area of 344 John L. Dietsch Boulevard in North Attleboro. On their arrival, the responding officers found a deceased male, later identified as Odin L. Lloyd, lying on the ground with several apparent gunshot wounds. After searching Odin's pockets, officers located two sets of keys for a black 2013 Chevrolet Suburban bearing Enterprise Rent-A-Car labels. After inquiring with Enterprise, police discovered that the Suburban was currently being rented by one Aaron Hernandez of 22 Ronald C. Meyer Drive in North Attleboro.

Later that evening, officers traveled to Hernandez's home and attempted to make contact. While knocking on the door, the officers observed three large surveillance cameras permanently affixed to the exterior of Hernandez's home. Eventually, the officers were able to make contact with Hernandez who, upon learning that the officers were conducting a death investigation, slammed the door without asking about the identity of the decedent. Hernandez later emerged from the house and volunteered to have his girlfriend, Shayanna Jenkins, drive him to the police station so he could give a statement.

Although the police allowed Jenkins to drive Hernandez to the station, Jenkins immediately drove away after dropping Hernandez off. Officers followed Jenkins out of the parking lot and stopped her vehicle adjacent to the police department. As soon as the officers informed Jenkins that they were investigating Lloyd's death, Jenkins began to cry. Jenkins informed police that Lloyd was dating her sister, and that she had last seen Lloyd sitting with Hernandez in the black Suburban two days ago—on June 15, 2013. Jenkins also told police that Hernandez had recently installed a video surveillance system in his home and that the system recorded both the front of the residence as well as the street.

On Tuesday, June 18, 2013, investigators executed their first search warrant of Hernandez's residence. Police seized digital video evidence from the home's video surveillance system, which included a total of fourteen interior and exterior cameras. The video footage showed that, at approximately 1:00 a.m. on June 17th, 2013, Hernandez and two other males exited Hernandez's residence and left in a silver Nissan Altima (police later discovered that Hernandez rented the Altima from Enterprise-Rent-A-Car). The footage then revealed all three men returning to the residence at approximately 3:27 a.m. To appreciate the significance of that timeline, you may wish to pause and watch the video contained in the Aaron Hernandez Casefile. [*See* Casefile Video, listed as item #5.]

Police found a bottle of Vitamin Water, a piece of paper containing a colorful child's drawing, a piece of chewed blue bubble gum, and a spent .45 caliber bullet casing inside a dumpster at the Enterprise Rental. The Enterprise manager identified the items as being those she removed from the 2012 Nissan Altima that Hernandez returned on the morning of June 18, 2013.

On June 22, 2013, investigators sought a second search warrant for Hernandez's home, arguing that probable cause existed to believe that the persons responsible for the murder of Odin were traveling in the Nissan Altima rented by Hernandez and that Hernandez and the two unidentified males were present at the location and time of the murder of Lloyd. Specifically, the warrant sought to search and seize the following:

> Trace/Biological evidence, including blood, serums, skin, clothing, gunshot residue, fingerprints, firearms, ammunition, DNA, clothing as identified in Addendum 'A,' 'B,' and 'C,' shoes, footwear impressions, and any other evidence described in the affidavit to assist in the identification of a suspect or suspects, and that if any of the above evidence is found that it be seized as evidence and further analyzed and searched as necessary.

According to the handwritten Return on the warrant, several items were seized from Hernandez's home, including a white bath towel, a scale and a dish located in a safe, and a bottle of Vitamin Water.

Hernandez was arrested for Lloyd's murder days later—on June 26, 2013. A grand jury formally indicted him on August 22, 2013, and Hernandez was held without bail. On September 15, 2014, Hernandez filed a motion to suppress the bath towel, scale and safe, and bottle of Vitamin Water, arguing that they were outside the scope of the June 22 search warrant. Hernandez reasoned that the items were not admissible under the plain view exception because they were not specifically mentioned in the warrant.

The Commonwealth countered that the items were admissible under the plain view doctrine because police had a legally sufficient basis for inferring that they were plausibly related to criminal activity. In support of this argument, the Commonwealth pointed out that the seized bath towel was similar in appearance to a towel observed in video images of the occupants in Hernandez's vehicle on the night of the murder. It also highlighted that the seized Vitamin Water bottle was similar to the one found in the Enterprise dumpster. The Commonwealth further contended that the scale and dish constituted illegal drug paraphernalia. Collectively, the Commonwealth asserted that the seizure of each item was wholly consistent with application of the plain view doctrine.

On October 10, 2014, Judge E. Susan Garsh granted Hernandez's motion to suppress with respect to the towel, but otherwise denied the motion as to the other items seized from his home.

C. THE CASES

1. Plain View Seizure

HORTON V. CALIFORNIA

496 U.S. 128
Supreme Court of the United States
February 21, 1990, Argued; June 4, 1990, Decided
No. 88-7164

JUDGES: STEVENS, J., delivered the opinion of the Court, in which REHNQUIST, C. J., and WHITE, BLACKMUN, O'CONNOR, SCALIA, and KENNEDY, JJ. joined. BRENNAN, J., filed a dissenting opinion, in which MARSHALL, J., joined.

Opinion by: STEVENS

In this case we revisit an issue that was considered, but not conclusively resolved, in *Coolidge v. New Hampshire*, 403 U.S. 443 (1971): Whether the warrantless seizure of evidence of crime in plain view is prohibited by the Fourth Amendment if the discovery of the evidence was not inadvertent. We conclude that even though inadvertence is a characteristic of most legitimate "plain view" seizures, it is not a necessary condition.

I

Petitioner was convicted of the armed robbery of Erwin Wallaker, the treasurer of the San Jose Coin Club. When Wallaker returned to his home after the Club's annual show, he entered his garage and was accosted by two masked men, one armed with a machine gun and the other with an electrical shocking device, sometimes referred to as a "stun gun." The two men shocked Wallaker, bound and handcuffed him, and robbed him of jewelry and cash. During the encounter sufficient conversation took place to enable Wallaker subsequently to identify petitioner's distinctive voice. His identification was partially corroborated by a witness who saw the robbers leaving the scene, and by evidence that petitioner had attended the coin shows.

Sergeant LaRault, an experienced police officer, investigated the crime and determined that there was probable cause to search petitioner's home for the proceeds of the robbery and for the weapons used by the robbers. His affidavit for a search warrant referred to police reports that described the weapons as well as the proceeds, but the warrant issued by the Magistrate only authorized a search for the proceeds, including three specifically described rings.

Pursuant to the warrant, LaRault searched petitioner's residence, but he did not find the stolen properly. During the course of the search, however, he discovered the weapons in plain view and seized them. Specifically, he seized an Uzi machine gun, a .38 caliber revolver, two stun guns, a handcuff key, a San Jose Coin Club advertising brochure, and a few items of clothing identified by the victim.[1] LaRault testified that while he was searching for the rings, he also was interested in finding other evidence connecting petitioner to the robbery. Thus, the seized evidence was not discovered "inadvertently."

The trial court refused to suppress the evidence found in petitioner's home and, after a jury trial, petitioner was found guilty and sentenced to prison. The California Court of Appeal affirmed. It rejected petitioner's argument that our decision in *Coolidge* required suppression of the seized evidence that had not been listed in the warrant because its discovery was not inadvertent. * * * The California Supreme Court denied petitioner's request for review.

Because the California courts' interpretation of the "plain view" doctrine conflicts with the view of other courts, and because the unresolved issue is important, we granted certiorari.

II

* * * The right to security in person and property protected by the Fourth Amendment may be invaded in quite different ways by searches and seizures. A search compromises the individual interest in privacy; a seizure deprives the individual of dominion over his or her person or property. The "plain view" doctrine is often considered an exception to the general rule that warrantless searches are presumptively unreasonable, but this characterization overlooks the important difference between searches and seizures. If an article is already in plain view, neither its observation nor its seizure would involve any invasion of privacy. *Arizona v. Hicks*, 480 U.S. 321, 325 (1987); *Illinois v. Andreas*, 463 U.S. 765, 771 (1983). A seizure of the article, however, would obviously invade the owner's possessory interest. If "plain view" justifies an exception from an otherwise applicable warrant requirement, therefore, it must be an exception that is addressed to the concerns that are implicated by seizures rather than by searches.

---

[1] Although the officer viewed other handguns and rifles, he did not seize them because there was no probable cause to believe they were associated with criminal activity.

The criteria that generally guide "plain view" seizures were set forth in *Coolidge v. New Hampshire*, 403 U.S. 443 (1971). The Court held that the seizure of two automobiles parked in plain view on the defendant's driveway in the course of arresting the defendant violated the Fourth Amendment. Accordingly, particles of gun powder that had been subsequently found in vacuum sweepings from one of the cars could not be introduced in evidence against the defendant. The State endeavored to justify the seizure of the automobiles, and their subsequent search at the police station, on four different grounds, including the "plain view" doctrine. The scope of that doctrine as it had developed in earlier cases was fairly summarized in these three paragraphs from Justice Stewart's opinion:

> It is well established that under certain circumstances the police may seize evidence in plain view without a warrant. But it is important to keep in mind that, in the vast majority of cases, any evidence seized by the police will be in plain view, at least at the moment of seizure. The problem with the 'plain view' doctrine has been to identify the circumstances in which plain view has legal significance rather than being simply the normal concomitant of any search, legal or illegal.

> An example of the applicability of the 'plain view' doctrine is the situation in which the police have a warrant to search a given area for specified objects, and in the course of the search come across some other article of incriminating character. Where the initial intrusion that brings the police within plain view of such an article is supported, not by a warrant, but by one of the recognized exceptions to the warrant requirement, the seizure is also legitimate. Thus the police may inadvertently come across evidence while in 'hot pursuit' of a fleeing suspect. And an object that comes into view during a search incident to arrest that is appropriately limited in scope under existing law may be seized without a warrant. Finally, the 'plain view' doctrine has been applied where a police officer is not searching for evidence against the accused, but nonetheless inadvertently comes across an incriminating object.

> What the 'plain view' cases have in common is that the police officer in each of them had a prior justification for an intrusion in the course of which he came inadvertently across a piece of evidence incriminating the accused. The doctrine serves to supplement the prior justification—whether it be a warrant for another object, hot pursuit, search incident to lawful arrest, or some other legitimate reason for being present unconnected with a search directed against the accused—and permits the warrantless seizure. Of course, the extension of the original

justification is legitimate only where it is immediately apparent to the police that they have evidence before them; the 'plain view' doctrine may not be used to extend a general exploratory search from one object to another until something incriminating at last emerges.

Justice Stewart then described the two limitations on the doctrine that he found implicit in its rationale: First, "that plain view alone is never enough to justify the warrantless seizure of evidence"; and second, "that the discovery of evidence in plain view must be inadvertent." * * * It is, of course, an essential predicate to any valid warrantless seizure of incriminating evidence that the officer did not violate the Fourth Amendment in arriving at the place from which the evidence could be plainly viewed. There are, moreover, two additional conditions that must be satisfied to justify the warrantless seizure. First, not only must the item be in plain view, its incriminating character must also be "immediately apparent." * * * Second, not only must the officer be lawfully located in a place from which the object can be plainly seen, but he or she must also have a lawful right of access to the object itself. As the Solicitor General has suggested, Justice Harlan's vote in *Coolidge* may have rested on the fact that the seizure of the cars was accomplished by means of a warrantless trespass on the defendant's property. In all events, we are satisfied that the absence of inadvertence was not essential to the court's rejection of the State's "plain view" argument in *Coolidge*.

III

Justice Stewart concluded that the inadvertence requirement was necessary to avoid a violation of the express constitutional requirement that a valid warrant must particularly describe the things to be seized. He explained:

> The rationale of the exception to the warrant requirement, as just stated, is that a plain-view seizure will not turn an initially valid (and therefore limited) search into a 'general' one, while the inconvenience of procuring a warrant to cover an inadvertent discovery is great. But where the discovery is anticipated, where the police know in advance the location of the evidence and intend to seize it, the situation is altogether different. The requirement of a warrant to seize imposes no inconvenience whatever, or at least none which is constitutionally cognizable in a legal system that regards warrantless searches as 'per se unreasonable' in the absence of 'exigent circumstances.'

> If the initial intrusion is bottomed upon a warrant that fails to mention a particular object, though the police know its location and intend to seize it, then there is a violation of the express

constitutional requirement of 'Warrants . . . particularly describing . . . [the] things to be seized.'

We find two flaws in this reasoning. First, evenhanded law enforcement is best achieved by the application of objective standards of conduct, rather than standards that depend upon the subjective state of mind of the officer. The fact that an officer is interested in an item of evidence and fully expects to find it in the course of a search should not invalidate its seizure if the search is confined in area and duration by the terms of a warrant or a valid exception to the warrant requirement. If the officer has knowledge approaching certainty that the item will be found, we see no reason why he or she would deliberately omit a particular description of the item to be seized from the application for a search warrant. Specification of the additional item could only permit the officer to expand the scope of the search. On the other hand, if he or she has a valid warrant to search for one item and merely a suspicion concerning the second, whether or not it amounts to probable cause, we fail to see why that suspicion should immunize the second item from seizure if it is found during a lawful search for the first. * * *

Second, the suggestion that the inadvertence requirement is necessary to prevent the police from conducting general searches, or from converting specific warrants into general warrants, is not persuasive because that interest is already served by the requirements that no warrant issue unless it "particularly describes the place to be searched and the persons or things to be seized," and that a warrantless search be circumscribed by the exigencies which justify its initiation. Scrupulous adherence to these requirements serves the interests in limiting the area and duration of the search that the inadvertence requirement inadequately protects. Once those commands have been satisfied and the officer has a lawful right of access, however, no additional Fourth Amendment interest is furthered by requiring that the discovery of evidence be inadvertent. If the scope of the search exceeds that permitted by the terms of a validly issued warrant or the character of the relevant exception from the warrant requirement, the subsequent seizure is unconstitutional without more. * * *

In this case, the scope of the search was not enlarged in the slightest by the omission of any reference to the weapons in the warrant. Indeed, if the three rings and other items named in the warrant had been found at the outset—or petitioner had them in his possession and had responded to the warrant by producing them immediately—no search for weapons could have taken place. * * * As we have already suggested, by hypothesis the seizure of an object in plain view does not involve an intrusion on privacy.[11] If the interest in privacy has been invaded, the violation must have

---

[11] Even if the item is a container, its seizure does not compromise the interest in preserving the privacy of its contents because it may only be opened pursuant to either a search warrant, or one of the well-delineated exceptions to the warrant requirement.

occurred before the object came into plain view and there is no need for an inadvertence limitation on seizures to condemn it. The prohibition against general searches and general warrants serves primarily as a protection against unjustified intrusions on privacy. But reliance on privacy concerns that support that prohibition is misplaced when the inquiry concerns the scope of an exception that merely authorizes an officer with a lawful right of access to an item to seize it without a warrant.

In this case the items seized from petitioner's home were discovered during a lawful search authorized by a valid warrant. When they were discovered, it was immediately apparent to the officer that they constituted incriminating evidence. He had probable cause, not only to obtain a warrant to search for the stolen property, but also to believe that the weapons and handguns had been used in the crime he was investigating. The search was authorized by the warrant, the seizure was authorized by the "plain view" doctrine. The judgment is affirmed.

It is so ordered.

JUSTICE BRENNAN, with whom JUSTICE MARSHALL joins, dissenting.

I

* * * The plain view doctrine is an exception to the general rule that a seizure of personal property must be authorized by a warrant. As Justice Stewart explained in *Coolidge*, we accept a warrantless seizure when an officer is lawfully in a location and inadvertently sees evidence of a crime because of "the inconvenience of procuring a warrant" to seize this newly discovered piece of evidence. But "where the discovery is anticipated, where the police know in advance the location of the evidence and intend to seize it," the argument that procuring a warrant would be "inconvenient" loses much, if not all, of its force. Barring an exigency, there is no reason why the police officers could not have obtained a warrant to seize this evidence before entering the premises. The rationale behind the inadvertent discovery requirement is simply that we will not excuse officers from the general requirement of a warrant to seize if the officers know the location of evidence, have probable cause to seize it, intend to seize it, and yet do not bother to obtain a warrant particularly describing that evidence. To do so would violate "the express constitutional requirement of 'Warrants . . . particularly describing . . . [the] things to be seized,' " and would "fly in the face of the basic rule that no amount of probable cause can justify a warrantless seizure."

Although joined by only three other Members of the Court, Justice Stewart's discussion of the inadvertent discovery requirement has become widely accepted. Forty-six States and the District of Columbia and twelve United States Court of Appeals now require plain view seizures to be inadvertent. There has been no outcry from law enforcement officials that the inadvertent discovery requirement unduly burdens their efforts. Given that the requirement is inescapably rooted in the plain language of the Fourth Amendment, I cannot fathom the Court's enthusiasm for discarding this element of the plain view doctrine. * * *

III

The Fourth Amendment demands that an individual's possessory interest in property be protected from unreasonable governmental seizures, not just by requiring a showing of probable cause, but also by requiring a neutral and detached magistrate to authorize the seizure in advance. The Court today ignores the explicit language of the Fourth Amendment, which protects possessory interests in the same manner as it protects privacy interests, in order to eliminate a generally accepted element of the plain view doctrine that has caused no apparent difficulties for law enforcement officers. I am confident, however, that when confronted with more egregious police conduct than that found in this case, such as pretextual searches, the Court's interpretation of the Constitution will be less parsimonious than it is today. I respectfully dissent.

QUESTIONS, COMMENTS, CONCERNS?

1. **Garrett and plain view.** Return for a moment to the story of TF Mafia and the Rivera and Garrett casefile. Specifically, think again about Garrett's September 1, 2010 traffic stop. Remember that the tow truck operator opened Garrett's trunk, saw something he viewed as suspicious, and then called Trent over to look at it. [Rivera Casefile Document 8, at 8–9.] The government argued in opposing Garrett's motion to suppress that Trent saw the package in plain view. [Rivera Casefile Document 6, at 45.] Applying *Horton*, did Trent satisfy the requirements of the plain view doctrine? What did the district court think? [*See* Rivera Casefile Document 11, at 21–26.]

Now reconsider the story that the tow truck operator told. He testified that "[t]he top loop screws into the *front bumper* and serves as the place where the hook from the tow truck can be attached, rather than to the front bumper itself." [Rivera Casefile Document 8, at 8 (emphasis added).] If the toe loop screws are associated with the front bumper, what was the tow truck operator doing looking "for the tow loops in the same compartment as the spare tire in the *trunk* of the vehicle"? *Id.* (emphasis added). In light of that disconnect, did the police really have lawful access to Garrett's trunk? And, by the way, what exactly *are* tow loops anyway?

2. **Witman and plain view.** Now return for a moment to the heart-breaking case of Zach Witman. You will recall that Zach was accused of killing his brother on October 2, 1998. Zach called 911 requesting emergency assistance at 3:17 p.m. that day, and police arrived at the home by 3:25 p.m., at which time an officer saw Greg's body on the floor. Would the plain view doctrine support admission of the condition of Greg's body at Zach's later trial?

Then, at 3:30 p.m., Chief James Childs arrived on the scene and performed a security sweep of the home to determine whether other suspects or victims were still inside. During the sweep, Childs saw drops of blood on the kitchen floor. [Witman Casefile Document 9, at 4.] He also saw large amounts of blood on the hallway floor and, in addition, he saw a jacket, backpack, and key ring. *Id.* He would also see a towel on the floor in an upstairs bathroom. *Id.* Are any or all of those items admissible pursuant to the plain view doctrine? *See, e.g., id.* at 16–18 (providing suppression court's analysis); [Casefile Document 10, at 336–37 (providing appellate court's analysis)].

3. Gacy and plain view. Finally, return to the case of John Wayne Gacy from Chapter 4. Recall that, during the execution of the first search warrant for Gacy's home on December 13, 1978, officers found a receipt from Nissen's Pharmacy—among other items. About the receipt, though, the state wrote: "Upon examining the receipt it was apparent to the officer that it was evidence connecting Gacy to the disappearance of Piest and possible violence to him by Gacy." [Gacy Casefile Document 2, at 39.] After *Arizona v. Hicks*, 480 U.S. 321 (1987), which came out after Gacy's case, the critical question becomes what did the state mean by "examining"?

In *Hicks*, an officer, while executing a valid search warrant in respondent's apartment, moved a piece of stereo equipment to read its serial numbers. After doing so, the officer developed probable cause to believe equipment was stolen. The Supreme Court held that, by moving the stereo equipment, the officer committed an unconstitutional warrantless search. The Court reasoned that the ensuing seizure was not justified by the plain view doctrine because the incriminating character of the stereo equipment was not "immediately apparent." Stated differently, the plain view exception did not apply because the officer developed probable cause to believe the equipment was stolen only *after* he moved it.

Apply *Hicks* to the officer's "examination" of the receipt in Gacy's home on December 13. Assuming the officer picked up the receipt to examine it, did the officer violate *Hicks*? If so, what is the correct remedy and how might exclusion of the receipt impact issuance of the December 21 warrant? As you answer that question, remember that law enforcement relied, in part, on the receipt to obtain the December 21 warrant. [Gacy Casefile Document 2, at 45.]

4. *Horton* and the Hernandez warrant. Compare the search warrant in *Horton* to the June 22, 2013 Hernandez warrant. [*See* Casefile Document 1.] The *Horton* warrant authorized police to search for "proceeds, including three specifically described rings." Meanwhile, the Hernandez warrant was written much more broadly to include, "Trace / Biological evidence, including blood, serums, skin, clothing, gunshot residue, fingerprints, firearms, ammunition, DNA." Now, notice certain limiting language from *Horton*: "if the three rings and other items named in the warrant had been found at the outset—or petitioner had them in his possession and had responded to the warrant by producing them immediately—no search for weapons could have taken place." Does that language incentivize law enforcement to draft search warrants narrowly or broadly? Indeed, is it possible to find "Trace/Biological evidence" immediately or, in the words of the

Horton Court, "at the outset"? If not, when would a search of Hernandez's home end for *Horton* purposes?

5.   Hernandez's motion to suppress. As it relates to the seized towel, scale and dish in the safe, and Vitamin Water bottle, what exactly is Hernandez arguing as a basis for suppression? [*See* Casefile Document 2.] He contends, in part, that the seizure of these items fell outside "the scope authorized by the warrant." *Id.* at 1. But that happens in every plain view seizure, right? That is, officers seize something in plain view that they have probable cause to believe is contraband—but that is outside the scope of the warrant (or applicable warrant exception). What distinguishes Hernandez's argument, if anything?

6.   Plain view and inadvertence. Recall that, in *Horton*, Sergeant LaRault openly admitted that his discovery of the weapon in plain view while executing the search warrant of petitioner's home was "not inadvertent." As you know, the *Horton* Court abandoned any type of inadvertence requirement as part of the plain view doctrine.

But look at the Commonwealth's opposition to Hernandez's motion to suppress. [*See* Casefile Document 4.] How does the inadvertence requirement still apply in Massachusetts? *Id.* at 4. Why would a state be interested in retaining an inadvertence requirement? What purpose does the requirement serve?

As you consider that question, you may be wondering how the Supreme Court can reject a particular doctrine, but a state court elects to retain it. The answer is that "a State is free as a matter of its own law to impose greater restrictions on police activity than those this Court holds to be necessary upon federal constitutional standards." *Oregon v. Haas*, 420 U.S. 714, 719 (1975). Thus, in this context, Massachusetts has elected to retain a version of the inadvertence requirement, though *Horton* does not require it to do so.

7.   The incriminating character of evidence seized from Hernandez's home. *Horton* requires that the "incriminating character" of the evidence in plain view be "immediately apparent." How does the Commonwealth explain that the seized items—the towel, the Vitamin Water bottle, and the scale and dish—bore incriminating characteristics that, to the officers, were immediately apparent? [*See* Casefile Document 3, at 5.]

8.   Assessing the Superior Court's decision. The Superior Court granted in part and denied in part Hernandez's motion to suppress. [Casefile Document 4.] In particular, the court elected to suppress the towel. What *Horton* requirement did the Commonwealth fail to satisfy? *See id.* at 7. As for the other items—the Vitamin Water bottle and the scale and dish—what was different about them that justified denying their suppression? *See id.* at 7–8.

9.   Who was Odin Lloyd? At the time of his death, Lloyd was dating a sister of Hernandez's fiancée. Through that relationship, Lloyd began spending time with Hernandez. Their friendship made sense given that Lloyd was a linebacker for the Boston Bandits, a semipro football team. Before his death,

Lloyd received tickets to the Patriots games and spent time partying with Hernandez. But he also told his then-coach, Michael Branch, that, "[f]or an NFL guy, [Hernandez] parties a lot." Susan Candiotti, *A Year After Odin Lloyd's Death, Loved Ones Cling to Memories and Pain*, CNN.COM (Sept. 29, 2014), https://www.cnn.com/2014/06/17/justice/hernandez-odin-lloyd/index.html.

10. Hernandez's motive. Why did Hernandez kill Lloyd? Prosecutors wrestled with that question at Hernandez's murder trial. And appropriately so given that there were no obvious answers. Some of the more popular theories include that Hernandez was upset at Lloyd over two trivial incidents. The first involved Lloyd seeing guns and ammunition stored at Hernandez's apartment in Franklin, Massachusetts—his so-called "flop house." Hernandez was also apparently upset over an incident between the two at a nightclub earlier on the night of June 14, 2013. Susan Candiotti & Laura Dolan, *Source: Aaron Hernandez's Anger Over Two Trivial Incidents Linked to Killing*, CNN.COM (June 21, 2014), https://www.cnn.com/2014/06/21/justice/aaron-hernandez-motive/index.html.

Others theorized that Hernandez was bisexual and that Lloyd knew it. NBC Sports Boston Staff, *Report: Aaron Hernandez's Bisexuality Considered As Motive For Odin Lloyd Murder*, NBCSPORTS.COM (Apr. 21, 2017), http://www.nbcsports.com/boston/new-england-patriots/new-england-patriots-report-aaron-hernandez-bisexuality-considered-motive-odin-lloyd-murder. Additionally, some speculate that Lloyd insulted Hernandez by directing anti-gay slurs toward him. Christopher Brennan, *Aaron Hernandez's Hidden Bisexuality Investigated As Murder Motive*, NYDAILYNEWS.COM (Apr. 21, 2017), https://www.nydailynews.com/news/national/hernandez-lloyd-murder-stemmed-hidden-sexuality-report-article-1.3086678.

11. Aaron Hernandez: the rest of the story. Hernandez was tried and convicted on April 15, 2015, of murdering Lloyd. In Massachusetts, that conviction carries with it a mandatory life without parole sentence. Remarkably, Hernandez was also investigated and ultimately charged with two counts of first-degree murder in connection with a double homicide that took place in Boston back in 2012. A jury, however, would find him not guilty on both counts on April 14, 2017. But just days later, on April 19, 2017, a naked Hernandez hanged himself from his cell window using his bedsheets. Hernandez, who had written "John 3:16" on his forehead, tried to block officers from entering the cell by jamming the door with various items and pouring shampoo all over the cell's floor.

Hernandez also left three suicide notes in the cell where he was found. The first was to his fiancée, and the second was to his four-year-old daughter. Reports assert that the third note was intended for Kyle Kennedy, a twenty-two-year-old prisoner who was rumored to be Hernandez's boyfriend—a claim that Hernandez's fiancée disputes.

There are two final wrinkles. The contents of Hernandez's suicide note to his fiancée subsequently became public. It read, in part, as follows:

Tell my story fully but never think anything besides how much I love you. This was the supreme's, the almighty's plan, not mine! I love you! Let (redacted) know how much I love her! Look after (redacted) and (redacted) for me—those are my boys. (You're Rich)

John Breech, *Massachusetts Court Releases One of Aaron Hernandez's Three Suicide Notes*, CBSSPORTS.COM (May 5, 2017), https://www.cbssports.com/nfl/news/massachusetts-court-releases-one-of-aaron-hernandezs-three-suicide-notes/. Hernandez's reference to his fiancée being rich was apparently a nod to what was then a prison rumor. The rumor, which Hernandez evidently believed, was that if an inmate died while in prison with a pending appeal, then the court system would view him as not guilty. That, in turn, would enable his fiancée to collect life insurance proceeds. Turns out, the rumor was true. A Massachusetts judge vacated Hernandez's murder conviction on May 9, 2017. Eric Levenson & Holly Yan, *Aaron Hernandez's Murder Conviction Cleared After Suicide*, CNN.COM (May 9, 2017), https://www.cnn.com/2017/05/09/us/aaron-hernandez-murder-conviction-abated/index.html.

The second wrinkle surrounds what doctors learned about the condition of Hernandez's brain at the time of his suicide. According to a news article summarizing the findings of Boston University researchers, "Aaron Hernandez suffered the most severe case of chronic traumatic encephalopathy ever discovered in a person his age, damage that would have significantly affected his decision-making, judgment and cognition." Adam Kilgore, *Aaron Hernandez Suffered From Most Severe CTE Ever Found in a Person His Age*, WASHINGTONPOST.COM (Nov. 9, 2017), https://www.washingtonpost.com/sports/aaron-hernandez-suffered-from-most-severe-cte-ever-found-in-a-person-his-age/2017/11/09/fa7cd204-c57b-11e7-afe9-4f60b5a6c4a0_story.html?utm_term=.7dd1dc56b5dd. Chronic traumatic encephalopathy, otherwise known as CTE, is a brain disease that, in Hernandez, reached Stage 3—a stage never before seen in a brain younger than forty-six years old. *Id.*

2. Plain Feel

MINNESOTA V. DICKERSON

508 U.S. 366
Supreme Court of the United States
March 3, 1993, Argued; June 7, 1993, Decided
No. 91-2019

JUSTICE WHITE delivered the opinion of the Court.

In this case, we consider whether the Fourth Amendment permits the seizure of contraband detected through a police officer's sense of touch during a protective patdown search.

I

On the evening of November 9, 1989, two Minneapolis police officers were patrolling an area on the city's north side in a marked squad car. At about 8:15 p.m., one of the officers observed respondent leaving a 12-unit apartment building on Morgan Avenue North. The officer, having previously responded to complaints of drug sales in the building's hallways and having executed several search warrants on the premises, considered the building to be a notorious "crack house." According to testimony credited by the trial court, respondent began walking toward the police but, upon spotting the squad car and making eye contact with one of the officers, abruptly halted and began walking in the opposite direction. His suspicion aroused, this officer watched as respondent turned and entered an alley on the other side of the apartment building. Based upon respondent's seemingly evasive actions and the fact that he had just left a building known for cocaine traffic, the officers decided to stop respondent and investigate further.

The officers pulled their squad car into the alley and ordered respondent to stop and submit to a patdown search. The search revealed no weapons, but the officer conducting the search did take an interest in a small lump in respondent's nylon jacket. The officer later testified:

> As I pat-searched the front of his body, I felt a lump, a small lump, in the front pocket. I examined it with my fingers and it slid and it felt to be a lump of crack cocaine in cellophane.

The officer then reached into respondent's pocket and retrieved a small plastic bag containing one fifth of one gram of crack cocaine. Respondent was arrested and charged in Hennepin County District Court with possession of a controlled substance.

Before trial, respondent moved to suppress the cocaine. The trial court first concluded that the officers were justified under *Terry v. Ohio*, 392 U.S. 1 (1968), in stopping respondent to investigate whether he might be engaged in criminal activity. The court further found that the officers were justified in frisking respondent to ensure that he was not carrying a weapon. Finally, analogizing to the "plain-view" doctrine, under which officers may make a warrantless seizure of contraband found in plain view during a lawful search for other items, the trial court ruled that the officers' seizure of the cocaine did not violate the Fourth Amendment * * *.

His suppression motion having failed, respondent proceeded to trial and was found guilty.

On appeal, the Minnesota Court of Appeals reversed. The court agreed with the trial court that the investigative stop and protective patdown search of respondent were lawful under *Terry* because the officers had a reasonable belief based on specific and articulable facts that respondent was engaged in criminal behavior and that he might be armed and dangerous. The court concluded, however, that the officers had overstepped the bounds allowed by *Terry* in seizing the cocaine. In doing so, the Court of Appeals "decline[d] to adopt the plain feel exception" to the warrant requirement.

The Minnesota Supreme Court affirmed. Like the Court of Appeals, the State Supreme Court held that both the stop and the frisk of respondent were valid under *Terry*, but found the seizure of the cocaine to be unconstitutional. The court expressly refused "to extend the plain view doctrine to the sense of touch" on the grounds that "the sense of touch is inherently less immediate and less reliable than the sense of sight" and that "the sense of touch is far more intrusive into the personal privacy that is at the core of the Fourth Amendment." The court thus appeared to adopt a categorical rule barring the seizure of any contraband detected by an officer through the sense of touch during a patdown search for weapons. The court further noted that "even if we recognized a 'plain feel' exception, the search in this case would not qualify" because "the pat search of the defendant went far beyond what is permissible under *Terry*." As the State Supreme Court read the record, the officer conducting the search ascertained that the lump in respondent's jacket was contraband only after probing and investigating what he certainly knew was not a weapon.

We granted certiorari to resolve a conflict among the state and federal courts over whether contraband detected through the sense of touch during a patdown search may be admitted into evidence. We now affirm.

II

A

* * * The question presented today is whether police officers may seize nonthreatening contraband detected during a protective patdown search of the sort permitted by *Terry*. We think the answer is clearly that they may, so long as the officers' search stays within the bounds marked by *Terry*.

B

* * * Under [the plain view] doctrine, if police are lawfully in a position from which they view an object, if its incriminating character is immediately apparent, and if the officers have a lawful right of access to the object, they may seize it without a warrant. *See Horton v. California*, 496 U.S. 128, 136–137 (1990); *Texas v. Brown*, 460 U.S. 730, 739 (1983) (plurality opinion). If, however, the police lack probable cause to believe that an object in plain view is contraband without conducting some further search of the object—i.e., if "its incriminating character [is not] 'immediately apparent,'" *Horton, supra*, at 136—the plain-view doctrine cannot justify its seizure. *Arizona v. Hicks*, 480 U.S. 321 (1987).

We think that this doctrine has an obvious application by analogy to cases in which an officer discovers contraband through the sense of touch during an otherwise lawful search. The rationale of the plain-view doctrine is that if contraband is left in open view and is observed by a police officer from a lawful vantage point, there has been no invasion of a legitimate expectation of privacy and thus no "search" within the meaning of the Fourth Amendment—or at least no search independent of the initial intrusion that gave the officers their vantage point. The warrantless seizure of contraband that presents itself in this manner is deemed justified by the realization that resort to a neutral magistrate under such circumstances would often be impracticable and would do little to promote the objectives of the Fourth Amendment. The same can be said of tactile discoveries of contraband. If a police officer lawfully pats down a suspect's outer clothing and feels an object whose contour or mass makes its identity immediately apparent, there has been no invasion of the suspect's privacy beyond that already authorized by the officer's search for weapons; if the object is contraband, its warrantless seizure would be justified by the same practical considerations that inhere in the plain-view context. * * *

III

It remains to apply these principles to the facts of this case. Respondent has not challenged the finding made by the trial court and affirmed by both the Court of Appeals and the State Supreme Court that the police were justified under *Terry* in stopping him and frisking him for weapons. Thus, the dispositive question before this Court is whether the officer who conducted the search was acting within the lawful bounds marked by *Terry* at the time he gained probable cause to believe that the lump in respondent's jacket was contraband. The State District Court did not make precise findings on this point, instead finding simply that the officer, after feeling "a small, hard object wrapped in plastic" in respondent's pocket, "formed the opinion that the object . . . was crack . . . cocaine." The District Court also noted that the officer made "no claim that he suspected this object to be a weapon," a finding affirmed on appeal. The Minnesota Supreme Court, after "a close examination of the record," held that the officer's own testimony "belies any notion that he 'immediately' " recognized the lump as crack cocaine. Rather, the court concluded, the officer determined that the lump was contraband only after "squeezing, sliding and otherwise manipulating the contents of the defendant's pocket"—a pocket which the officer already knew contained no weapon.

Under the State Supreme Court's interpretation of the record before it, it is clear that the court was correct in holding that the police officer in this case overstepped the bounds of the "strictly circumscribed" search for weapons allowed under *Terry*. Where, as here, "an officer who is executing a valid search for one item seizes a different item," this Court rightly "has been sensitive to the danger . . . that officers will enlarge a specific authorization, furnished by a warrant or an exigency, into the equivalent of a general warrant to rummage and seize at will." Here, the officer's continued exploration of respondent's pocket after having concluded that it contained no weapon was unrelated to "the sole justification of the search [under *Terry*:] . . . the protection of the police officer and others nearby." It therefore amounted to the sort of evidentiary search that *Terry* expressly refused to authorize, and that we have condemned in subsequent cases.

Once again, the analogy to the plain-view doctrine is apt. In *Arizona v. Hicks*, 480 U.S. 321 (1987), this Court held invalid the seizure of stolen stereo equipment found by police while executing a valid search for other evidence. Although the police were lawfully on the premises, they obtained probable cause to believe that the stereo equipment was contraband only after moving the equipment to permit officers to read its serial numbers. The subsequent seizure of the equipment could not be justified by the plain-view doctrine, this Court explained, because the incriminating character of the stereo equipment was not immediately apparent; rather, probable cause to believe that the equipment was stolen arose only as a result of a further search—the moving of the equipment—that was not authorized by a search warrant or by any exception to the warrant requirement. The facts of this case are very similar. Although the officer was lawfully in a position to feel the lump in respondent's pocket, because *Terry* entitled him to place his hands upon respondent's jacket, the court below determined that the incriminating character of the object was not immediately apparent to him. Rather, the officer determined that the item was contraband only after conducting a further search, one not authorized by *Terry* or by any other exception to the warrant requirement. Because this further search of respondent's pocket was constitutionally invalid, the seizure of the cocaine that followed is likewise unconstitutional.

IV

For these reasons, the judgment of the Minnesota Supreme Court is

Affirmed.

JUSTICE SCALIA, concurring.

[Omitted.]

CHIEF JUSTICE REHNQUIST, with whom JUSTICE BLACKMUN and JUSTICE THOMAS join, concurring in part and dissenting in part.

[Omitted.]

QUESTIONS, COMMENTS, CONCERNS?

1.   **Garrett and plain feel.** Return for a moment to the story of TF Mafia and the Rivera and Garrett casefile. Specifically, think again about Garrett's September 1, 2010 traffic stop. Remember that night that Detective Shotwell made the decision to cut open the vacuum-sealed bag found in Garrett's trunk following the traffic stop. But before he did so, there was a critical moment where Shotwell picked up the bag. The government described the important facts as follows: "Upon picking up the package, Detective Shotwell felt that the package contained several small-sized, round packages

within the dark plastic bag, and immediately believed that the package contained illegal narcotics." [Rivera Casefile Document 8, at 12.] Does *Dickerson* permit Shotwell to "feel" Garrett's vacuum-sealed package without a warrant? [*See* Rivera Casefile Document 11, at 26–27.]

PENNSYLVANIA V. MIMMS
434 U.S. 106
Supreme Court of the United States
December 5, 1977
No. 76-1830

PER CURIAM.

* * * The facts are not in dispute. While on routine patrol, two Philadelphia police officers observed respondent Harry Mimms driving an automobile with an expired license plate. The officers stopped the vehicle for the purpose of issuing a traffic summons. One of the officers approached and asked respondent to step out of the car and produce his owner's card and operator's license. Respondent alighted, whereupon the officer noticed a large bulge under respondent's sports jacket. Fearing that the bulge might be a weapon, the officer frisked respondent and discovered in his waistband a .38-caliber revolver loaded with five rounds of ammunition. The other occupant of the car was carrying a .32-caliber revolver. Respondent was immediately arrested and subsequently indicted for carrying a concealed deadly weapon and for unlawfully carrying a firearm without a license. His motion to suppress the revolver was denied; and, after a trial at which the revolver was introduced into evidence, respondent was convicted on both counts.

As previously indicated, the Supreme Court of Pennsylvania reversed respondent's conviction, however, holding that the revolver should have been suppressed because it was seized contrary to the guarantees contained in the Fourth and Fourteenth Amendments to the United States Constitution. The Pennsylvania court did not doubt that the officers acted reasonably in stopping the car. It was also willing to assume, *arguendo*, that the limited search for weapons was proper once the officer observed the bulge under respondent's coat. But the court nonetheless thought the search constitutionally infirm because the officer's order to respondent to get out of the car was an impermissible "seizure." This was so because the officer could not point to "objective observable facts to support a suspicion that criminal activity was afoot or that the occupants of the vehicle posed a threat to police safety." Since this unconstitutional intrusion led directly to observance of the bulge and to the subsequent "pat down," the revolver was the fruit of an unconstitutional search, and, in the view of the Supreme Court of Pennsylvania, should have been suppressed.

We do not agree with this conclusion. * * *

In this case, unlike *Terry v. Ohio*, there is no question about the propriety of the initial restrictions on respondent's freedom of movement. Respondent was driving an automobile with expired license tags in violation of the Pennsylvania Motor Vehicle Code. Deferring for a moment the legality of the "frisk" once the bulge had been observed, we need presently deal only with the narrow question of whether the order to get out of the car, issued after the driver was lawfully detained, was reasonable and thus permissible under the Fourth Amendment. This inquiry must therefore focus not on the intrusion resulting from the request to stop the vehicle or from the later "pat-down," but on the incremental intrusion resulting from the request to get out of the car once the vehicle was lawfully stopped.

Placing the question in this narrowed frame, we look first to that side of the balance which bears the officer's interest in taking the action that he did. The State freely concedes the officer had no reason to suspect foul play from the particular driver at the time of the stop, there having been nothing unusual or suspicious about his behavior. It was apparently his practice to order all drivers out of their vehicles as a matter of course whenever they had been stopped for a traffic violation. The State argues that this practice was adopted as a precautionary measure to afford a degree of protection to the officer and that it may be justified on that ground. Establishing a face-to-face confrontation diminishes the possibility, otherwise substantial, that the driver can make unobserved movements; this, in turn, reduces the likelihood that the officer will be the victim of an assault.

We think it too plain for argument that the State's proffered justification—the safety of the officer—is both legitimate and weighty. * * * Indeed, it appears "that a significant percentage of murders of police officers occurs when the officers are making traffic stops."

The hazard of accidental injury from passing traffic to an officer standing on the driver's side of the vehicle may also be appreciable in some situations. Rather than conversing while standing exposed to moving traffic, the officer prudently may prefer to ask the driver of the vehicle to step out of the car and off onto the shoulder of the road where the inquiry may be pursued with greater safety to both.

Against this important interest we are asked to weigh the intrusion into the driver's personal liberty occasioned not by the initial stop of the vehicle, which was admittedly justified, but by the order to get out of the car. We think this additional intrusion can only be described as *de minimis*. The driver is being asked to expose to view very little more of his person than is already exposed. The police have already lawfully decided that the driver shall be briefly detained; the only question is whether he shall spend that period sitting in the driver's seat of his car or standing alongside it. Not only is the insistence of the police on the latter choice not a "serious intrusion upon the sanctity of the person," but it hardly rises to the level of a " 'petty indignity.' " *Terry v. Ohio, supra,* at 17. What is at most a mere inconvenience cannot prevail when balanced against legitimate concerns for the officer's safety.[6]

There remains the second question of the propriety of the search once the bulge in the jacket was observed. We have as little doubt on this point as on the first; the answer is controlled by *Terry v. Ohio, supra.* In that case we thought the officer justified in conducting a limited search for weapons once he had reasonably concluded that the person whom he had legitimately stopped might be armed and presently dangerous. Under the standard enunciated in that case—whether "the facts available to the officer at the moment of the seizure or the search 'warrant a man of reasonable caution in the belief' that the action taken was appropriate"— there is little question the officer was justified. The bulge in the jacket permitted the officer to conclude that Mimms was armed and thus posed a serious and present danger to the safety of the officer. In these circumstances, any man of "reasonable caution" would likely have conducted the "pat-down."

Respondent's motion to proceed in forma pauperis is granted. The petition for writ of certiorari is granted, the judgment of the Supreme Court of Pennsylvania is reversed, and the case is remanded for further proceedings not inconsistent with this opinion.

It is so ordered.

MR. JUSTICE MARSHALL, dissenting.

[Omitted.]

MR. JUSTICE STEVENS, with whom MR. JUSTICE BRENNAN and MR. JUSTICE MARSHALL join, dissenting.

[Omitted.]

QUESTIONS, COMMENTS, CONCERNS?

1. **Officer Safety and traffic stops.** The Supreme Court has stressed that traffic stops are "especially fraught with danger to police officers" and that, to mitigate that risk, officers need "unquestioning command of the situation." *Arizona v. Johnson,* 555 U.S. 323, 330 (2009) (first quoting *Michigan v. Long,* 463 U.S. 1032, 1047 (1997); then quoting *Maryland v. Wilson,* 519 U.S. 408, 414 (1997)). Some scholars, however, have challenged the idea that traffic stops are especially dangerous situations. In one study, Professor Jordan Blair Woods found that violence against law enforcement

---

6   * * * [W]e do not hold today that "whenever an officer has an occasion to speak with the driver of a vehicle, he may also order the driver out of the car." We hold only that once a motor vehicle has been lawfully detained for a traffic violation, the police officers may order the driver to get out of the vehicle without violating the Fourth Amendment's proscription of unreasonable searches and seizures.

officers during routine traffic stops is rare and that incidents that do involve violence are typically low-risk and do not involve weapons. *See* Jordan Blair Woods, *Policing, Danger Narratives, and Routine Traffic Stops*, 117 MICH. L. REV. 635, 712 (2019).

3.   Plain Smell

STATE V. SOUTH
885 P.2d 795
Court of Appeals of Utah
November 1, 1994, Filed
Case No. 930362-CA

GREENWOOD, JUDGE:

Defendants Jeffery Earl South and Dianna South appeal their convictions of possession of a controlled substance and possession of drug paraphernalia within 1000 feet of a church, class A misdemeanors * * *. Defendants argue that the search of their home violated their state and federal constitutional rights. * * * We reverse and remand * * *.

BACKGROUND

On March 15, 1992, Detective Dennis Simonson of the Logan City Police Department went to defendants' residence to investigate a reported theft of a cellular phone. Defendant Jeffery South met Detective Simonson at the door but refused to let him enter the premises. Detective Simonson detected a heavy odor of burnt marijuana coming from inside defendants' home and also on defendant Jeffery South's clothing.

Detective Simonson then obtained a search warrant and returned to defendants' home with three other police officers. Upon arrival, three of the officers, including Simonson, smelled burnt marijuana emanating from inside the house. The officers then served the search warrant upon defendants and proceeded to search the home. As a result of the search, the officers found controlled substances and drug paraphernalia, including one gram of marijuana, electrical clips, a book, and a scale. All the drug paraphernalia later tested positive for marijuana.

Defendants were charged with possession of a controlled substance and possession of drug paraphernalia within 1000 feet of a church. Prior to trial, defendants moved to suppress the evidence found in their home because the evidence was seized in an illegal search and seizure. Defendants argued that the search warrant was defective because it authorized only a search of the "persons of Jeffery Earl and Dianna South" and not a search of the premises. After a hearing, the trial court denied defendants' motion to suppress, ruling that although the search warrant was defective, the officers nevertheless had probable cause to conduct the search of the premises under the plain smell doctrine.

Defendants were subsequently convicted by a jury of possession of a controlled substance and possession of drug paraphernalia. At sentencing, the trial court found that the offenses were committed within 1000 feet of a church.

ISSUES ON APPEAL

On appeal, defendants argue that the search of their home was illegal because officers had neither a valid search warrant nor probable cause and exigent circumstances sufficient to conduct the search without a warrant. The State argues that the trial court erred in ruling that the search warrant did not permit a search of defendants' residence. Thus, we examine [two] issues: * * * [(1)] Does the plain smell of marijuana provide officers with probable cause to conduct a search of a private residence? [(2)] If so, may the residence be searched without first obtaining a valid warrant, absent exigent circumstances?

STANDARD OF REVIEW

In reviewing a trial court's ruling on a motion to suppress, we accord no deference to the trial court's legal conclusions and review them for correctness. However, we will disturb the trial court's underlying factual findings "only if those findings are clearly erroneous."

ANALYSIS * * *

Probable Cause Under Plain Smell Doctrine

In *State v. Naisbitt*, 827 P.2d 969 (Utah App. 1992) this court held that the odor of marijuana emanating from an automobile gave an officer probable cause to conduct a warrantless search of that automobile. In *Naisbitt* we stated that "the constitutional basis for this rule is that '[a] strong, emanating odor of marijuana comes within the "plain view" doctrine and need not be ignored by officers.' " Further, we noted that "objects in 'plain view' constitute one ... exception [to the warrant requirement], and may be seized without a warrant if the police officer is lawfully present and the evidence is clearly incriminating. This exception encompasses evidence within 'plain smell.' " Thus, we must determine if, based upon the plain smell doctrine, the odor of marijuana also establishes probable cause if it comes from a private residence.

Probable cause is defined as a "fair probability that contraband or evidence of a crime will be found." *Illinois v. Gates*, 462 U.S. 213, 238 (1983). Thus, in determining the existence of probable cause we focus on the suspicious nature of the circumstances involved. In examining this issue under the plain smell doctrine, we see no significant difference whether an odor of marijuana emanates from an automobile or from a private residence. In both situations an officer who is lawfully present could reasonably conclude that contraband or evidence of a crime may be discovered. Thus, we hold that the plain smell of marijuana emanating from a private residence provides law enforcement officials with probable cause to conduct a search of the premises.

Warrant Requirement Under Plain Smell Doctrine

We must next determine if the plain smell doctrine alone justifies a warrantless search of a private residence.

We must first clarify that the plain view doctrine and its corollary "plain smell" theory, do not in and of themselves provide an exception to the requirement of obtaining a valid search warrant. The *Naisbitt* decision relied on *State v. Bartley,* 784 P.2d 1231 (Utah App. 1989), which in turn, cites 1 Wayne R. LaFave, *Search and Seizure* § 2.2(a) (2d ed. 1987). LaFave's exposition differentiates between circumstances where seized items are inadvertently discovered during a prior valid intrusion, and those where the plain view or smell observation is noted without a prior intrusion into constitutionally protected space. Id. In the latter circumstances, the observation is lawful but seizure of the items observed or smelled poses a different question. LaFave notes the caution—" 'you can't touch everything you can see [or smell].' " Therefore, "in the absence of a search warrant, some recognized ground for warrantless seizure equally applicable outside plain view cases, must be present."

Consequently, in this case, whereas the smell of burnt marijuana provided the officers with probable cause to obtain a search warrant authorizing a search of the constitutionally protected home, it did not, alone, validate a warrantless search. Because the State argues that exigent circumstances justify the warrantless search in this case, we consider whether this exception to the warrant requirement applies. * * *

In *State v. Naisbitt,* 827 P.2d 969 (Utah App. 1992), this court held that the plain smell doctrine allowed officers to conduct a warrantless search of an automobile. Although *Naisbitt* did not discuss exigent circumstances, prior case law clearly establishes that under the automobile exception to the warrant requirement, exigent circumstances exist where " 'the car is movable, the occupants are alerted, and the car's contents may never be found again if a warrant must be obtained.' "

However, there is a significant difference between an exigent circumstances analysis involving an automobile and one involving a private residence. In their own homes, citizens enjoy a "heightened expectation of privacy." This is because "physical entry of the home is the chief evil against which the wording of the Fourth Amendment is directed." Further, the State's burden in demonstrating both probable cause and exigent circumstances is "particularly heavy" when entry into a private residence is involved.

In the instant case, the State asks us to hold that the plain smell doctrine automatically provides officers with exigent circumstances to justify a warrantless search of a home. The State argues that exigent circumstances can be demonstrated under the plain smell doctrine because marijuana is easily disposed of. The same argument has been made and rejected in a number of other jurisdictions. * * *

We * * * find the State's argument unpersuasive. Unlike an automobile, a home cannot simply be driven away with its contents which may " 'never be found again if a warrant must be obtained.' " Rather, the home will still be there when officers return with a search warrant. Further, officers can secure a home while a search warrant is obtained. As stated by the court in *Strange v. State*, 530 So. 2d 1336, 1340 (Miss. 1988), "No exigent circumstances existed, as, again, three of the officers could have secured the premises while a fourth complied with the Constitution and obtained a warrant." Therefore, the fact that the marijuana may be "removed, hidden, or destroyed is not, in and of itself, an exigent circumstance."

If we were to hold that the mere possibility that evidence may be destroyed constitutes an exigent circumstance, we would essentially undermine the exigent circumstance requirement since it is possible that most forms of evidence can be destroyed before officers return with a warrant. The State's concern that marijuana may be hidden or disposed of before officers obtain a warrant is outweighed by the concern that a warrant less search would violate the heightened expectation of privacy in a private home. Thus, we hold that although the plain smell doctrine provides officers probable cause to believe contraband or evidence of a crime may be found,[4] it does not automatically provide officers with exigent circumstances justifying a warrantless search of a private residence. Therefore, the trial court erred in denying defendants' motion to suppress because the evidence was seized during an unlawful search of their home.

CONCLUSION

The State's argument regarding the validity of the search warrant is not properly before this court. Further, although the officers had, under the plain smell doctrine, probable cause to search the defendants' home, they did not demonstrate exigent circumstances to conduct the search without a valid warrant. We therefore reverse and remand for proceedings consistent with this opinion.

QUESTIONS, COMMENTS, CONCERNS?

1. **Rivera and plain smell.** Return please for a moment to the story of TF Mafia and the Rivera and Garrett casefile. Specifically, think again about Rivera's January 18, 2012 traffic stop. After executing the stop, Trooper Horan detected an odor of marijuana. The government would argue, in opposition to

---

[4]   Therefore giving officers a basis on which to obtain a search warrant; which is exactly what they did in this case.

Rivera's motion to suppress, as follows: "The moment Trooper Horan smelled the marijuana, he had probable cause to search the vehicle as a matter of federal constitutional law." [Rivera Casefile Document 8, at 61.] Applying the plain smell doctrine from *South*, is the government's argument correct?

2. Gacy and plain smell. Return once more to the Gacy Casefile. Recall that the second search warrant, issued on December 21, 1978, relied in part on Officer Schultz smelling "an odor similar to that of a putrified human body." [Gacy Casefile Document 1, at 43.] Gacy contended that "[t]he facts furnished did not explain to the magistrate how Schultz differentiated one odor from another." *Id.* at 46. Does the plain smell doctrine contemplate a requirement for the state to demonstrate Schultz's ability to distinguish odors? The state responded to Gacy's argument by noting that Schultz "was familiar with the odor of decaying human bodies from his past experience with the police department." [Gacy Casefile Document 2, at 44.] Is that response sufficient to justify application of the plain smell doctrine?

4. Plain Hearing

UNITED STATES V. CAREY

836 F.3d 1092
United States Court of Appeals for the Ninth Circuit
May 6, 2016, Argued and Submitted, Pasadena, California; September 7, 2016, Filed
No. 14-50222

GOULD, CIRCUIT JUDGE:

Acting pursuant to the Wiretap Act, 18 U.S.C. §§ 2510–22, federal agents secured a wiretap order for a San Diego phone number based on evidence that Ignacio Escamilla Estrada (Escamilla) was using the number in a drug smuggling and distribution conspiracy. Agents monitoring the wiretap overheard drug-related phone conversations. At some point during a seven-day period, the agents realized that Escamilla was not using the phone. Agents continued listening, however, believing at least initially that the people speaking on the phone might have been part of the Escamilla conspiracy. The seven days of wiretap monitoring culminated in a traffic stop, and agents then confirmed that the persons on the phone had no connection to Escamilla.

Appellant Michael Carey was eventually identified as a speaker in some of the phone calls, and he was then charged with conspiracy to distribute cocaine. Carey moved to suppress the evidence obtained from the wiretaps, arguing that the government violated the Wiretap Act by never applying for a wiretap as to him or his coconspirators. The district court denied the motion, ruling that the government could rely on the Escamilla order to listen to Carey's conversations.

The Fourth Amendment provides an exception to the warrant or probable cause requirement when police see contraband in "plain view."

We adopt a similar principle today and hold that the police may use evidence obtained in "plain hearing" when they overhear speakers unrelated to the target conspiracy while listening to a valid wiretap, without having complied with the Wiretap Act requirements of probable cause and necessity as to those specific speakers. However, the agents must discontinue monitoring the wiretap once they know or reasonably should know that the phone calls only involved speakers outside the target conspiracy.

The district court did not apply these principles, and the record in this case does not show exactly when agents knew or should have known that the phone conversations did not involve Escamilla and his coconspirators. We vacate the district court's denial of Carey's motion to suppress and remand to the district court on an open record to determine what evidence was lawfully obtained in "plain hearing."

I

On March 5, 2010, the district court granted FBI Special Agent Christopher Melzer's application for a wiretap order for several phone numbers thought to be associated with a drug conspiracy led by Ignacio Escamilla Estrada (Escamilla). The phone number designated "T-14" was believed to belong to Escamilla. The wiretap of T-14 went live on March 5, although no calls were intercepted until March 10.

Starting on the 10th, the agents overheard "drug-related" calls, but at some point the agents realized that the person using T-14 was not Escamilla. The agents did not know who the people speaking on T-14 were, although Melzer initially "thought the callers and calls might still be affiliated with [the] known targets or part of the criminal activity [he] was investigating." Melzer consulted with federal prosecutors, and agents continued to monitor the calls.

On the morning of March 17, 2010, agents intercepted a call indicating that someone would be traveling with "invoices" (believed to be code for drug money). The agents coordinated with local police officers to execute a traffic stop on a car involved in the phone calls. Officers identified the driver as Adrian Madrid and searched the vehicle, finding cash and a cellphone tied to the T-14 number. Officers then obtained a search warrant for a related residence and found cocaine. Now knowing Madrid's identity, Melzer learned that there was an ongoing DEA/ICE investigation into Madrid and his associates. Melzer met with ICE and DEA agents, and they concluded that there was no "overlap" between the Madrid and Escamilla conspiracies.

Agents later identified Carey as a member of Madrid's conspiracy.[1] Carey was indicted in February 2011 for conspiracy to distribute cocaine in violation of 21 U.S.C. §§ 841(a)(1) and 846. He filed a motion to suppress "any and all evidence derived from the use of wiretaps," arguing that the government failed to comply with the Wiretap Act, 18 U.S.C. §§ 2510–22, with respect to Carey and his coconspirators. In Carey's view, the government instead had unlawfully "relie[d] on the validity of the Escamilla order to justify the independent and unrelated use of wiretap surveillance against Mr. Carey." * * *

The district court denied the motion to suppress, reasoning that the government had complied with the statute to obtain the wiretap order against Escamilla and holding that "[t]here was no requirement for a separate showing of necessity once the agents concluded that T-14 was not primarily used by Escamilla. The agents reasonably believed that the callers and calls might be affiliated with Escamilla or other offenses." Carey pled guilty in an agreement that preserved his right to appeal the denial of his motion to suppress. Carey's appeal was timely and we have jurisdiction under 28 U.S.C. § 1291. * * *

III

Turning to the question whether agents could lawfully use the Escamilla wiretap to listen to Carey's conversations, we note that there is a lack of Ninth Circuit precedent squarely on point. While the Wiretap Act allows officials to intercept and use calls "relating to offenses other than those specified in the order of authorization or approval," 18 U.S.C. § 2517(5), we have found no case in which this statutory provision was used to authorize officers to listen to people who were unaffiliated with the initial wiretap subjects. Carey cites several cases for the proposition that the necessity showing in a wiretap application must be specifically tailored to the target subjects, but none of these cases involves a situation in which a concededly valid wiretap order was used to obtain evidence of an unrelated person's crime.

Here the government showed necessity and probable cause for a wiretap of the target conspiracy. But what happens when a wiretap that is valid at its inception is later used to listen to someone who is not involved in the conspiracy under surveillance? It is that novel question to which we turn our attention.

The Seventh Circuit has addressed a similar situation in dicta. Writing for that court, then-Chief Judge Posner explained, "It is true that if government agents execute a valid wiretap order and in the course of

---

[1] Phone calls intercepted by the wiretap referred to "Garrocha," apparently Carey's nickname, but the record does not show when agents made that connection. The record also does not reveal how Carey's associate, Jose Antonio Hernandez-Gutierrez, ended up with Escamilla's phone number.

executing it discover that it was procured by a mistake and at the same time overhear incriminating conversations, the record of the conversations is admissible in evidence. It is just the 'plain view' doctrine translated from the visual to the oral dimension." *United States v. Ramirez*, 112 F.3d 849, 851 (7th Cir. 1997) (internal citations omitted). "But," the court continued, "once the mistake is discovered, the government cannot use the authority of the warrant, or of the [wiretap] order, to conduct a search or interception that they know is unsupported by probable cause or is otherwise outside the scope of the statute or the Constitution." We conclude that the Seventh Circuit's observations are persuasive. * * *

Having carefully reviewed the full record, including any portions filed under seal, we conclude that the provisions of the wiretap order persuasively indicate that the unknown people referred to in the wiretap order must be involved with the Escamilla conspiracy; the order does not authorize the wiretap of "others yet unknown" participating in a conspiracy "yet unknown." Moreover, the wiretap order could not authorize surveillance of an unknown conspiracy because the statute requires agents to demonstrate probable cause and necessity to procure a wiretap order. Agent Melzer's affidavit contained probable cause that "others yet unknown" were participating in the Escamilla conspiracy, but it understandably contained no information about unknown people engaged in drug trafficking outside the Escamilla conspiracy. * * *

In short, we see no reason to depart from principles requiring cessation of a wiretap once the government knows or reasonably should know that the person speaking on the tapped line is not involved in the target conspiracy. *See Ramirez*, 112 F.3d at 851–52. The government may use evidence obtained from a valid wiretap "[p]rior to the officers' discovery of [a] factual mistake" that causes or should cause them to realize that they are listening to phone calls "erroneously included within the terms of the" wiretap order. And once the officers know or should know they are listening to conversations outside the scope of the wiretap order, they must discontinue monitoring the wiretap until they secure a new wiretap order, if possible.

IV

Applying this rule to Carey's case, we first note that Carey does not challenge the validity of the wiretap order as to Escamilla, so the agents were justified in initially listening to the conversations on T-14. But because the order did not authorize agents to listen to Carey or his associates, the government may only use evidence obtained in accordance with the "plain hearing" doctrine discussed above.

The record does not indicate what evidence was obtained before the agents knew or should have known that they were listening to calls outside of the Escamilla conspiracy. Melzer's declaration stated, "Within that time frame [March 10–17], after an amount of time that I do not recall exactly, we concluded that the person using T-14 was not Ignacio Escamilla Estrada. We also did not know the identities of the persons calling T-14." While Melzer's declaration suggests that he "thought the callers and calls might still be affiliated with" the Escamilla conspiracy, the record does not show whether he continued or reasonably could have continued to hold that belief through March 17. In fact, at some point agents consulted with federal prosecutors about whether they could or should continue to intercept calls on the wiretap.

It is unclear how much of the government's wiretap evidence may fall outside of the "plain hearing" doctrine. Because the parties staked out polarized positions before the district court—the government arguing for all wiretap evidence, Carey for none of it—and because the district court adopted the government's position in denying the motion to suppress, the record lacks the findings necessary to determine what evidence was admissible against Carey. We vacate the district court's order denying the motion to suppress and remand on an open record to determine what evidence is admissible against Carey under the legal framework set forth above. * * *

VACATED AND REMANDED.

KOZINSKI, CIRCUIT JUDGE, dissenting:

[Omitted.]

VII.   INVENTORY SEARCHES

A. INTRODUCTION

The inventory search is another "exception" to the need for a warrant and, in the context of cars, presents a third opportunity for officers to search the passenger compartment of an automobile. Recall that police might also search a vehicle pursuant to the search incident to arrest doctrine (*Arizona v. Gant*) or automobile exception (*California v. Acevedo*).

But inventory searches of a vehicle operate differently. Whereas both the search incident to arrest doctrine and automobile exception require probable cause, an inventory search is a "suspicionless" search. Under *Gant*, police may search the passenger compartment of a vehicle following a lawful arrest "when it is reasonable to believe that evidence of the offense of arrest might be found in the vehicle." That arrest must, of course, be supported by probable cause. Under *Acevedo*, officers may search a vehicle and its containers where they have probable cause to believe contraband is located. The only limitation, if indeed that's the appropriate term, is that officers can search only where contraband or illegal items might be hidden. But again, officers must at least develop probable cause beforehand.

By contrast, an inventory search is suspicionless in the sense that no probable cause is necessary to support the warrantless vehicle search. Rather, the vehicle must be "lawfully impounded." A vehicle might be impounded following an arrest, or if the car is abandoned, or due to accrued parking violations. The vehicle search, which must follow "standard police procedures," is justified not by law enforcement's investigatory function, but rather law enforcement's administrative caretaking function. Thus, in the context of inventory searches, officers are not investigating crime and, as a result, do not need a search warrant.

The inventory search has three rationales: (1) protect the owner's property while it is in police custody, (2) protect the police from claims over stolen property, and (3) protect law enforcement from harm should the contents of the vehicle be dangerous.

As you'll see below, the concept of an inventory search extends also to arrestees. Following an arrest, if the arrestee will be incarcerated, even temporarily, then the arrestee is typically "booked." The booking process includes a second search of the arrestee and their belongings (the first being the search incident to arrest). The booking process may also involve things like fingerprinting, recording information about the arrestee's criminal and personal background, and photographing. Controversially, booking might even include, depending on the crime of arrest, taking a buccal swab inside the arrestee's mouth to obtain a DNA sample.

B. REVISITING ROBERT DURST

You no doubt recall meeting Robert Durst in Chapter 5. In that context, remember we focused on the arrest warrant that led to Durst's March 14, 2015 arrest in a New Orleans hotel lobby. We now return to Durst's case to focus on the factual events that occurred immediately after his arrest.

It was approximately 4:30 p.m. on March 14, 2015, when Durst was arrested by New Orleans based FBI agents. After his arrest, around 5:15 p.m., agents took Durst's room key from him. At that point, according to the affidavit in support of the criminal complaint, the following events took place:

> Special Agent Bender and I escorted DURST to room 2303 of the referenced hotel to inventory and itemize his belongings and to review the passport he stated was in his room. I again explained to DURST that I wished to inventory and itemize his belongings so that he could be provided a receipt and the same would be placed with NOPD for safekeeping. * * * DURST was frisked for Agent safety and asked to be seated in a hotel room chair where his left arm was cuffed to a room table again for Agent safety.

[Casefile Document 3, at 3.] Once at the hotel room, agents searched the room and Durst's personal items including his luggage and a jacket hanging in the closet. Inside the jacket, agents found a .38 caliber revolver with four live rounds and an expended casing in the cylinder. Agents also recovered the owner's manual for the weapon. It's important to note that the revolver is the subject of the Durst prosecution. [Casefile Document 3, at 1 (charging Durst with felon in possession of a firearm).]

Things get (more) interesting from here. At 6:30 p.m., Los Angeles *state* police officers contacted the arresting FBI agents to inform the agents that they were on their way to New Orleans from Houston. The FBI agents told state authorities that they had searched Durst's room and shared with the state officers that the search had produced a weapon. The state officers asked the agents to stop inventorying Durst's belongings and to secure his hotel room because they would be seeking a warrant for the room. *Id.* at 5.

At about 2:00 a.m. on March 15, 2015, the state officers applied for a warrant to search Durst's room before a Louisiana magistrate. That warrant sought, in part, to search for the following property:

> Any handgun or any miscellaneous gun pieces, ammunition, holsters, ammunition belts, gun clips, original box packaging, expended casings or pieces of lead, any photographs of firearms, or any paperwork showing the purchase, storage, disposition or dominion and control over guns and ammunition or any of the above items.

[Casefile Document 2, at 2.] A search of Durst's hotel room pursuant to the warrant again yielded the .38 caliber revolver that become the subject of Durst's federal prosecution.

Following the filing of a criminal complaint charging Durst with felon in possession of a firearm, Durst moved to suppress the weapon on June 4, 2015. As it related to the inventory portion of the motion, Durst argued in part that the warrantless search of Durst's hotel room did not qualify as an inventory search. Rather, said Durst, "[t]he agents' asserted need for an inventory was merely an excuse to gather evidence without a warrant." [Casefile Document 4, at 30.] The government, however, countered that the weapon was "admissible under the independent source doctrine because it was seized pursuant to a search warrant untainted by any prior, arguably illegal entry." [Casefile 5, at 4.] On October 6, 2015, the district court declined to suppress the .38.

C. THE CASES

FLORIDA V. WELLS

495 U.S. 1
Supreme Court of the United States
December 4, 1989, Argued; April 18, 1990, Decided
No. 88-1835

CHIEF JUSTICE REHNQUIST delivered the opinion of the Court.

A Florida Highway Patrol trooper stopped respondent Wells for speeding. After smelling alcohol on Wells' breath, the trooper arrested Wells for driving under the influence. Wells then agreed to accompany the trooper to the station to take a breathalyzer test. The trooper informed Wells that the car would be impounded and obtained Wells' permission to open the trunk. At the impoundment facility, an inventory search of the car turned up two marijuana cigarette butts in an ashtray and a locked suitcase in the trunk. Under the trooper's direction, employees of the facility forced open the suitcase and discovered a garbage bag containing a considerable amount of marijuana.

Wells was charged with possession of a controlled substance. His motion to suppress the marijuana on the ground that it was seized in violation of the Fourth Amendment to the United States Constitution was denied by the trial court. He thereupon pleaded nolo contendere to the charge but reserved his right to appeal the denial of the motion to suppress. On appeal, the Florida District Court of Appeal for the Fifth District held, inter alia, that the trial court erred in denying suppression of the marijuana found in the suitcase. Over a dissent, the Supreme Court of Florida affirmed. We granted certiorari and now affirm (although we disagree with part of the reasoning of the Supreme Court of Florida).

The Supreme Court of Florida relied on the opinions in *Colorado v. Bertine*, 479 U.S. 367 (1987); *id.*, at 376 (BLACKMUN, J., concurring). Referring to language in the *Bertine* concurrence and a footnote in the majority opinion, the court held that

> [i]n the absence of a policy specifically requiring the opening of closed containers found during a legitimate inventory search, *Bertine* prohibits us from countenancing the procedure followed in this instance.

According to the court, the record contained no evidence of any Highway Patrol policy on the opening of closed containers found during inventory searches. The court added, however:

> The police under *Bertine* must mandate either that all containers will be opened during an inventory search, or that no containers will be opened. There can be no room for discretion.

While this latter statement of the Supreme Court of Florida derived support from a sentence in the *Bertine* concurrence taken in isolation, we think it is at odds with the thrust of both the concurrence and the opinion of the Court in that case. We said in *Bertine*:

> Nothing in [*South Dakota v.*] *Opperman*[, 428 U.S. 364 (1976),] or [*Illinois v.*] *Lafayette*[, 462 U.S. 640 (1983),] prohibits the exercise of police discretion so long as that discretion is exercised according to standard criteria and on the basis of something other than suspicion of evidence of criminal activity.

Our view that standardized criteria, or established routine, *Illinois v. Lafayette*, 462 U.S. 640, 648 (1983), must regulate the opening of containers found during inventory searches is based on the principle that an inventory search must not be a ruse for a general rummaging in order to discover incriminating evidence. The policy or practice governing inventory searches should be designed to produce an inventory. The individual police officer must not be allowed so much latitude that inventory searches are turned into "a purposeful and general means of discovering evidence of crime," *Bertine, supra*, at 376 (BLACKMUN, J., concurring).

But in forbidding uncanalized discretion to police officers conducting inventory searches, there is no reason to insist that they be conducted in a totally mechanical "all or nothing" fashion. "[I]nventory procedures serve to protect an owner's property while it is in the custody of the police, to insure against claims of lost, stolen, or vandalized property, and to guard the police from danger." A police officer may be allowed sufficient latitude to determine whether a particular container should or should not be opened in light of the nature of the search and characteristics of the container itself. Thus, while policies of opening all containers or of opening no containers are unquestionably permissible, it would be equally permissible, for example, to allow the opening of closed containers whose contents officers determine they are unable to ascertain from examining the containers' exteriors. The allowance of the exercise of judgment based on concerns related to the purposes of an inventory search does not violate the Fourth Amendment.

In the present case, the Supreme Court of Florida found that the Florida Highway Patrol had no policy whatever with respect to the opening of closed containers encountered during an inventory search. We hold that absent such a policy, the instant search was not sufficiently regulated to satisfy the Fourth Amendment and that the marijuana which was found in the suitcase, therefore, was properly suppressed by the Supreme Court of Florida. Its judgment is therefore Affirmed.

JUSTICE BRENNAN, with whom JUSTICE MARSHALL joins, concurring in the judgment.

I agree with the Court that the judgment of the Florida Supreme Court should be affirmed because the Florida Highway Patrol had no policy at all with respect to opening closed containers. As the majority recognizes, the search was therefore unconstitutional under any reading of our cases. *See Colorado v. Bertine*, 479 U.S. 367, 374 (1987) (opening closed container found in a vehicle during an inventory search constitutional only because policy mandated opening of such containers). Our cases have required that inventory searches be "sufficiently regulated," so as to avoid the possibility that police will abuse their power to conduct such a search. *See South Dakota v. Opperman*, 428 U.S. 364, 384 (1976) (Powell, J., concurring) ("[N]o significant discretion is placed in the hands of the individual officer: he usually has no choice as to the subject of the search of its scope").

The facts of this case demonstrate a prime danger of insufficiently regulated inventory searches: police may use the excuse of an "inventory search" as a pretext for broad searches of vehicles and their contents. In this case, there was no evidence that the inventory search was done in accordance with any standardized inventory procedure. Although the State characterized the search as an inventory search in the trial court, it did not point to any standard policy governing inventory searches of vehicles (much less to any policy governing the opening of closed containers) until the case reached the Florida Supreme Court. At that time, which was after our decision in *Bertine, supra,* the Florida Highway Patrol entered the case as amicus curiae and argued that Chapter 16 of the "Florida Highway Patrol Forms and Procedural Manual" contained the standard policy that guided the conduct of the search in this case. The Florida Supreme Court concluded that the manual did not provide any policy for the opening of closed containers. But it now appears that the Florida Supreme Court may have been under the misapprehension that the manual was in effect at the time of the search in this case. The State conceded at oral argument before this Court that the manual was not in effect at the time of the search in this case, but argued nonetheless that the officer had performed the search according to "standard operating procedures" that were later incorporated into the Highway Patrol Manual. But the State did not offer any evidence at the suppression hearing to support a finding that Trooper Adams performed the inventory according to "standard operating procedures." Trooper Adams testified that he asked his immediate superior whether he should impound and inventory the car but that his superior left it to Adams' discretion, stating that he found nothing suspicious about the car. Trooper Adams testified that he "took it upon [himself] to go ahead and have the car towed." He also testified that he thought that opening the suitcase was part of a proper inventory but that he did not ask anyone else's opinion until after the search was completed. He testified "Well, I had to take my chances."

In addition, there was no evidence that an inventory was actually done in this case: [T]he State introduced neither an inventory sheet nor any testimony that the officer actually inventoried the items found in respondent's car. Rather, the testimony at the suppression hearing suggests that the officer used the need to "inventory" as an excuse to search for drugs. The testimony establishes that after arresting respondent for driving under the influence of alcohol and accompanying him to the station house, Trooper Adams returned to the impound lot to conduct the inventory search at 1:30 a.m. Grover Bryan, who assisted the state trooper with the inventory, testified at the hearing that Trooper Adams told him that "he wanted to inventory the car good, he wanted to go through it real good because he felt that there was drugs in it." According to Bryan, Adams' desire to inventory the car stemmed from the fact that there was a large amount of cash lying on the floor of the car when respondent was arrested. Bryan testified that Adams insisted that contraband would be found in the car because "[t]here ain't nobody runs around with that kind of money in the floorboard unless they're dealing drugs or something like that." When they finally found the locked suitcase in the trunk, Bryan testified that Adams "want[ed] in the suitcase" because he "had a strong suspicion there was drugs in that car and it was probably in that suitcase." The men then spent 10 minutes prying open the lock on the suitcase with two knives. Bryan testified that once they opened the suitcase and found a bag of marijuana inside, "[Adams] was quite excited. He said 'there it is.' "

The majority finds it unnecessary to recount these facts because it affirms the Florida Supreme Court on the narrow ground, clearly established by *Opperman* and *Bertine*, that police may not be given total discretion to decide whether to open closed containers found during an inventory search. With this much I agree. Like JUSTICE BLACKMUN, however, I cannot join the majority opinion because it goes on to suggest that a State may adopt an inventory policy that vests individual police officers with some discretion to decide whether to open such containers. This suggestion is pure dictum given the disposition of the case. But as JUSTICE BLACKMUN notes, there is a danger that this dictum will be relied on by lower courts in reviewing the constitutionality of particular inventory searches, or even by local policymakers drafting procedures for police to follow when performing inventories of impounded vehicles. Thus, I write separately to emphasize that the majority's suggestion is inconsistent with the reasoning underlying our inventory search cases and relies on a mischaracterization of the holding in *Bertine*.

Our cases clearly hold that an inventory search is reasonable under the Fourth Amendment only if it is done in accordance with standard procedures that limit the discretion of the police. *See Opperman*, 428 U.S., at 384 (Powell, J., concurring). In *Bertine*, the Court held that the police may open closed containers found within an impounded vehicle only if the inventory policy mandates the opening of all such containers. *See* 479 U.S., at 374, n.6 ("We emphasize that, in this case, the trial court found that the Police Department's procedures mandated the opening of closed containers and the listing of their contents"). Contrary to the majority's assertion today, *Bertine* did not establish that police may exercise discretion with respect to the opening of closed containers during an inventory search. The statement in *Bertine* that "[n]othing in *Opperman* . . . prohibits the exercise of police discretion so long as that discretion is exercised according to standard criteria," 479 U.S., at 375, was made in response to an argument that the inventory search was unconstitutional because the police had some discretion to determine whether to impound the car. The Court's conclusion that the opening of defendant's backpack was constitutional was clearly premised on the city's inventory policy that left no discretion to individual police officers as to the opening of containers found inside a car once it was impounded. JUSTICE BLACKMUN's concurrence in *Bertine* could not be clearer: "[I]t is permissible for police officers to open closed containers in an inventory search only if they are following standard police procedures that mandate the opening of such containers in every impounded vehicle."

Opening a closed container constitutes a great intrusion into the privacy of its owner even when the container is found in an automobile. For this reason, I continue to believe that in the absence of consent or exigency, police may not open a closed container found during an inventory search of an automobile.[2] In any event, in *Bertine*, the Court recognized that opening a container constitutes such a great intrusion that the discretion of the police to do so must be circumscribed sharply to guard against abuse. If the Court wishes to revisit that holding, it must wait for another case. Attempting to cast doubt on the vitality of the holding in *Bertine* in this otherwise easy case is not justified.

JUSTICE BLACKMUN, concurring in the judgment.

I agree with the Court that the judgment of the Supreme Court of Florida is to be affirmed. If our cases establish anything, it is that an individual police officer cannot be given complete discretion in choosing whether to search or to leave undisturbed containers and other items encountered during an inventory search. *See Colorado v. Bertine*, 479 U.S. 367, 374, n. 6 (1987); *South Dakota v. Opperman*, 428 U.S. 364 (1976). Here, given the complete discretion Florida Highway Patrol troopers

---

[2] The Court has recognized that an inventory search potentially can serve three governmental interests: protection of the owner's valuables, protection of the police from false claims of theft or damage, and protection of the police from danger. The Court has concluded that routine inventory searches are constitutional because these government interests outweigh an individual's diminished expectation of privacy in a car. I do not agree that these interests justify the opening of a closed container in which an individual retains a significant expectation of privacy. Indeed, I do not see how the treatment of the luggage in this case—prying open the lock with two knives—served any of these governmental interests.

enjoyed to open or not to open closed containers, the evidence in question properly was suppressed. I do not join the majority opinion, however, because, instead of ending the case at that point, it continues with language, unnecessary on the facts of this case, concerning the extent to which a policeman, under the Fourth Amendment, may be given discretion in conducting an inventory search.

The majority disagrees with the Florida Supreme Court's statement that a police department must have a policy which "mandate[s] either that all containers will be opened during an inventory search, or that no containers will be opened." The majority concludes that the Fourth Amendment does not impose such an "all or nothing" requirement. With this much I agree. A State, for example, consistent with the Fourth Amendment, probably could adopt a policy which requires the opening of all containers that are not locked, or a policy which requires the opening of all containers over or under a certain size, even though these policies do not call for the opening of all or no containers. In other words, a State has the discretion to choose a scheme that lies somewhere between the extremes identified by the Florida Supreme Court.

It is an entirely different matter, however, to say, as this majority does, that an individual policeman may be afforded discretion in conducting an inventory search. The exercise of discretion by an individual officer, especially when it cannot be measured against objective, standard criteria, creates the potential for abuse of Fourth Amendment rights our earlier inventory-search cases were designed to guard against. Thus, when the majority states that a "police officer may be allowed sufficient latitude to determine whether a particular container should or should not be opened in light of the nature of the search," and that it is permissible for a State "to allow the opening of closed containers whose contents officers determine they are unable to ascertain from examining the containers' exteriors," the majority is doing more than refuting the Florida Supreme Court's all-or-nothing approach; it is opining about a very different and important constitutional question not addressed by the state courts here and not raised by the circumstances of the case. Although the majority's statements on the issue perhaps are to be regarded as no more than dicta, they nonetheless are problematic inasmuch as they may be taken out of context or misinterpreted by policymakers and trial courts. Because, as noted above, the complete discretion afforded Florida policemen in this case renders the search at issue undeniably unconstitutional, I see no reason for the Court to say anything about precisely how much, if any, discretion an individual policeman constitutionally may exercise.

JUSTICE STEVENS, concurring in the judgment.

[Omitted.]

QUESTIONS, COMMENTS, CONCERNS?

1. Reconsidering Garrett's traffic stop. Return to the September 1, 2010 traffic stop of Michael Garrett's Mercedes. Recall that, following Garrett's arrest, the plan was for Trooper Rachel Trent to stay with Garrett's vehicle until a tow truck operator could tow the vehicle to a *private* lot. But once the tow operator saw a suspicious package in Garrett's trunk, plans changed, and Trent directed the tow truck operator to tow the vehicle back to the police station. Now, as you know, Garrett's vehicle was ultimately searched at the station pursuant to a search warrant. That search revealed a bag of marijuana, rolling papers, a digital camera, and a cell phone. But assume instead that officers searched the vehicle pursuant to the inventory exception. What would the government have to prove, pursuant to *Wells*, in order for the marijuana, rolling papers, camera, and cell phone to be admissible?

ILLINOIS V. LAFAYETTE

462 U.S. 640
Supreme Court of the United States
April 20, 1983, Argued; June 20, 1983, Decided
No. 81-1859

CHIEF JUSTICE BURGER delivered the opinion of the Court.

The question presented is whether, at the time an arrested person arrives at a police station, the police may, without obtaining a warrant, search a shoulder bag carried by that person.

I

On September 1, 1980, at about 10 p.m., Officer Maurice Mietzner of the Kankakee City Police arrived at the Town Cinema in Kankakee, Ill., in response to a call about a disturbance. There he found respondent involved in an altercation with the theater manager. He arrested respondent for disturbing the peace, handcuffed him, and took him to the police station. Respondent carried a purse-type shoulder bag on the trip to the station.

At the police station respondent was taken to the booking room; there, Officer Mietzner removed the handcuffs from respondent and ordered him to empty his pockets and place the contents on the counter. After doing so, respondent took a package of cigarettes from his shoulder bag and placed the bag on the counter. Mietzner then removed the contents of the bag, and found 10 amphetamine pills inside the plastic wrap of a cigarette package.

Respondent was subsequently charged with violating § 402(b) of the Illinois Controlled Substances Act on the basis of the controlled substances found in his shoulder bag. A pretrial suppression hearing was held at which the State argued that the search of the shoulder bag was a valid inventory search under *South Dakota v. Opperman*, 428 U.S. 364 (1976). Officer Mietzner testified that he examined the bag's contents because it was standard procedure to inventory "everything" in the possession of an arrested person. He testified that he was not seeking and did not expect to find drugs or weapons when he searched the bag, and he conceded that the shoulder bag was small enough that it could have been placed and sealed in a bag, container, or locker for protective purposes. After the hearing, but before any ruling, the State submitted a brief in which it argued for the first time that the search was valid as a delayed search incident to arrest. Thereafter, the trial court ordered the suppression of the amphetamine pills.

On appeal, the Illinois Appellate Court affirmed. It first held that the State had waived the argument that the search was incident to a valid arrest by failing to raise that argument at the suppression hearing. However, the court went on to discuss and reject the State's argument: "[Even] assuming, *arguendo*, that the State has not waived this argument, the stationhouse search of the shoulder bag did not constitute a valid search incident to a lawful arrest."

The state court also held that the search was not a valid inventory of respondent's belongings. * * *

The Illinois Supreme Court denied discretionary review. We granted certiorari because of the frequency with which this question confronts police and courts, and we reverse.

II

The question here is whether, consistent with the Fourth Amendment, it is reasonable for police to search the personal effects of a person under lawful arrest as part of the routine administrative procedure at a police station house incident to booking and jailing the suspect. The justification for such searches does not rest on probable cause, and hence the absence of a warrant is immaterial to the reasonableness of the search. Indeed, we have previously established that the inventory search constitutes a well-defined exception to the warrant requirement. *See South Dakota v. Opperman, supra.* * * *

A so-called inventory search is not an independent legal concept but rather an incidental administrative step following arrest and preceding incarceration. To determine whether the search of respondent's shoulder bag was unreasonable we must "[balance] its intrusion on the individual's Fourth Amendment interests against its promotion of legitimate governmental interests."

In order to see an inventory search in proper perspective, it is necessary to study the evolution of interests along the continuum from arrest to incarceration. We have held that immediately upon arrest an officer may lawfully search the person of an arrestee, *United States v. Robinson*, 414 U.S. 218 (1973); he may also search the area within the

arrestee's immediate control, *Chimel v. California*, 395 U.S. 752 (1969).
* * *

An arrested person is not invariably taken to a police station or confined; if an arrestee is taken to the police station, that is no more than a continuation of the custody inherent in the arrest status. Nonetheless, the factors justifying a search of the person and personal effects of an arrestee upon reaching a police station but prior to being placed in confinement are somewhat different from the factors justifying an immediate search at the time and place of arrest.

The governmental interests underlying a station-house search of the arrestee's person and possessions may in some circumstances be even greater than those supporting a search immediately following arrest. Consequently, the scope of a station-house search will often vary from that made at the time of arrest. Police conduct that would be impractical or unreasonable—or embarrassingly intrusive—on the street can more readily—and privately—be performed at the station. For example, the interests supporting a search incident to arrest would hardly justify disrobing an arrestee on the street, but the practical necessities of routine jail administration may even justify taking a prisoner's clothes before confining him, although that step would be rare. * * *

At the station house, it is entirely proper for police to remove and list or inventory property found on the person or in the possession of an arrested person who is to be jailed. A range of governmental interests supports an inventory process. It is not unheard of for persons employed in police activities to steal property taken from arrested persons; similarly, arrested persons have been known to make false claims regarding what was taken from their possession at the station house. A standardized procedure for making a list or inventory as soon as reasonable after reaching the station house not only deters false claims but also inhibits theft or careless handling of articles taken from the arrested person. Arrested persons have also been known to injure themselves—or others— with belts, knives, drugs, or other items on their person while being detained. Dangerous instrumentalities—such as razor blades, bombs, or weapons—can be concealed in innocent-looking articles taken from the arrestee's possession. The bare recital of these mundane realities justifies reasonable measures by police to limit these risks—either while the items are in police possession or at the time they are returned to the arrestee upon his release. Examining all the items removed from the arrestee's person or possession and listing or inventorying them is an entirely reasonable administrative procedure. It is immaterial whether the police actually fear any particular package or container; the need to protect against such risks arises independently of a particular officer's subjective concerns. Finally, inspection of an arrestee's personal property may assist the police in ascertaining or verifying his identity. In short, every consideration of orderly police administration benefiting both police and the public points toward the appropriateness of the examination of respondent's shoulder bag prior to his incarceration.

Our prior cases amply support this conclusion. In *South Dakota v. Opperman*, 428 U.S. 364 (1976), we upheld a search of the contents of the glove compartment of an abandoned automobile lawfully impounded by the police. We held that the search was reasonable because it served legitimate governmental interests that outweighed the individual's privacy interests in the contents of his car. Those measures protected the owner's property while it was in the custody of the police and protected police against possible false claims of theft. We found no need to consider the existence of less intrusive means of protecting the police and the property in their custody—such as locking the car and impounding it in safe storage under guard. Similarly, standardized inventory procedures are appropriate to serve legitimate governmental interests at stake here. * * *

Applying these principles, we hold that it is not "unreasonable" for police, as part of the routine procedure incident to incarcerating an arrested person, to search any container or article in his possession, in accordance with established inventory procedures.

The judgment of the Illinois Appellate Court is reversed, and the case is remanded for proceedings not inconsistent with this opinion.

It is so ordered.

JUSTICE MARSHALL, with whom JUSTICE BRENNAN joins, concurring in the judgment.

[Omitted.]

QUESTIONS, COMMENTS, CONCERNS?

1. **An organizational note.** You will no doubt recognize many of the documents in this Durst casefile as duplicates from the Chapter 5 Durst Casefile. But there are some notable, and important, differences. In particular, this casefile includes the search warrant for Durst's hotel room. You may also find interesting the inclusion of documents related to Durst's plea agreement and sentencing.

2. *Lafayette* **and Durst.** Does any reasonable application of the arrest inventory exception permit admission of the .38 caliber revolver found in Durst's hotel room? Would it change your answer if the arresting agents testified that, pursuant to FBI protocol, FBI agents are instructed to inventory the contents of hotel rooms when suspects are arrested at or near a hotel?

3. **The government's approach to the inventory exception.** Notice that the government took something of a controversial approach to arguing the inventory exception's application to Durst's case—the government took no position whatsoever. Rather, the government contended that "[t]he

independent source doctrine disposes of this issue regardless of whether an exception to the warrant requirement applies." [Casefile Document 5, at 10.] Is the government, in essence, conceding that the FBI unconstitutionally searched Durst's hotel room and seized the revolver? From a tactical standpoint, was it wise for the government not to make an inventory search argument? As you answer that question, consider how the district court responded to the litigants' arguments on the issue. [*See* Casefile Document 7, at 5–9.]

4. Durst and revisiting the independent source exception. Recall *Murray v. United States*, 487 U.S. 533 (1988), and the independent source doctrine from Chapter 2. Remember that federal law enforcement agents watched Murray and his confederate, James Carter, drive a green camper into a warehouse. When they drove out of the warehouse twenty minutes later and turned the vehicle over to other drivers, agents stopped the camper and found marijuana. After relaying that information back to agents at the warehouse, the warehouse agents unlawfully entered the warehouse and saw marijuana. They ultimately left the warehouse but keep it under surveillance. In applying for a warrant to search the warehouse, the agents did not rely on observations made during their unlawful entry. The Supreme Court, in holding the marijuana admissible, applied the independent source exception. Writing for the majority, Justice Scalia commented that, for the independent source exception to apply, the later lawful seizure must be "genuinely independent of an earlier, tainted one." *Id.* at 542.

Applying *Murray*, does the government have a strong independent source argument to gain admission of Durst's revolver? Notice that, as part of its argument, the government claims that "the events of this case are strikingly parallel to those described in *Murray v. United States*." [See Casefile Document 5, at 11.] There is no doubt similarity between the two cases, but it seems the government overlooks a critical difference. In Durst's case, the Los Angeles police were expressly told the results of the hotel room search and seemed to incorporate those results in their application to search Durst's hotel room. By contrast, agents in *Murray* "did not rely on any observations made during [their] entry." 487 U.S. at 536. With that difference in mind, was the Los Angeles police's search of Durst's hotel room "genuinely independent" of the FBI's prior (unlawful?) inventory search?

The district court declined to suppress the revolver by applying the independent source exception. In particular, the court commented, "Detective Whelan's affidavit was submitted to the Court and it shows that his department was already planning on obtaining a search warrant for whatever location where Durst was located and whatever personal property he had with him when found." [See Casefile Document 7, at 9.] Did the court get it right? If so, would *any* action by law enforcement in a similar future case merit suppression? Or, alternatively, will the independent source exception always save the evidence so long as a warrant application is planned?

5. The rest of Durst's gun case. After losing his motion to suppress, Durst, by then seventy-two, elected to plead guilty on April 27, 2016. [Casefile Document 9.] Durst was sentenced, pursuant to a plea agreement, to serve eighty-five months in federal prison. [Casefile Document 8, at 1.]

Interestingly, Durst's legal team was so confident in its motion to suppress that it declined a previous plea agreement that proposed a twenty-seven-month sentence for Durst. Charles V. Bagli, *Robert Durst Pleads Guilty in Gun Case, Setting up Possible Murder Trial*, NYTIMES.COM (Feb. 3, 2016), https://www.nytimes.com/2016/02/04/nyregion/robert-durst-gun-charges.html. As his lead attorney would say about the plea after losing the motion to suppress, "It's more than I wanted. It's kind of the price of poker." *Id.*

After the gun case, Durst was convicted with the murder of Susan Berman. Brian Melley, *Robert Durst Sentenced to Life in Best Friend's Murder*, HOUSTONPUBLICMEDIA.COM (Oct. 15, 2021, 6:55 AM), https://www.houston publicmedia.org/articles/news/criminal-justice/2021/10/15/411028/robert-durst-sentenced-to-life-in-best-friends-murder/. He was sentenced to life without parole on October 14, 2021. *Id.*

VIII. SPECIAL NEEDS, EMERGENCY & ADMINISTRATIVE SEARCHES

A. INTRODUCTION

Previous chapters of this casebook, with the exception of inventory searches, have focused on the Fourth Amendment's application to criminal investigations. That is, most police investigative efforts include a Fourth Amendment "search" or "seizure." And, as we've seen, when the Fourth Amendment applies to government conduct to search, for instance, police must ordinarily have a search warrant supported by probable cause to justify the particular investigative technique. Where no warrant is required, the Supreme Court has nonetheless made unmistakably clear that probable cause must ordinarily exist to justify law enforcement action. And even if probable cause is not required, individualized suspicion is minimally needed.

With the exception of some searches directed at students, none of that is true in the context of administrative searches. In this context, so the reasoning goes, police are acting outside their investigative capacity. When that happens, the Warrant Clause—and its inclusion of probable cause—is no longer relevant. The point here is that neither warrant rules nor individualized suspicion apply when police engage in non-criminal searches and seizures—sometimes premised on police "special needs" outside of traditional law enforcement. The sole question in such cases is whether law enforcement's behavior was "reasonable" because it is all that remains for purposes of the Fourth Amendment.

The line between criminal investigations and non-criminal administrative (again, often suspicionless) searches is admittedly thin. After all, a non-criminal administrative search could uncover evidence later used in a criminal prosecution. But understanding the constitutional difference between the two—criminal vs. non-criminal searches or seizures—has become increasingly important as the field of administrative searches continues to grow.

What began as a relatively narrow constitutional doctrine has expanded since its inception in *Camara v. Municipal Court*, 387 U.S. 523 (1967). The logic of *Camara*, provided below as the first case in this area, has since pervaded into the inspections of "closely regulated" businesses,[4] inspections of fire scenes,[5] visits into the homes of welfare beneficiaries,[6] searches of parolees and those on probation,[7] searches of public school students,[8] searches of public employees,[9] border searches,[10] vehicle inspections/checkpoints,[11] and searches of prisoners.[12] But rather than try to tackle all of those independent exceptions, this portion of the Casebook focuses on seemingly the most pressing constitutional questions surrounding checkpoints, border patrol, and school safety.

B. THE "CHECKPOINT OF THE STARS" & DANIEL ERICKSEN

At 9:00 a.m. on November 26, 2010, Willie Nelson's tour bus, the "Honeysuckle Rose III," rolled into the Border Patrol Checkpoint on Interstate 10 in Sierra Blanca, Texas. Border Patrol agents detected a suspicious smell wafting from inside the vehicle. After a search of the Honeysuckle uncovered six ounces (170 g) of marijuana hidden inside, Nelson was arrested for possession of marijuana and transported to Hudspeth County Jail. Mickey Raphael, Nelson's longtime harmonica player, told news outlets that the arrest did not particularly impact Nelson: "He said he feels great—he lost six ounces."

---

[4] *E.g., New York v. Burger*, 482 U.S. 691 (1987); *Marshall v. Barlow's, Inc.*, 436 U.S. 307 (1978).

[5] *E.g., Michigan v. Tyler*, 436 U.S. 499 (1978).

[6] *E.g., Wyman v. James*, 400 U.S. 309 (1971).

[7] *E.g., Samson v. California*, 547 U.S. 843 (2006).

[8] *See, e.g., Safford Unified Sch. Dist. #1 v. Redding*, 557 U.S. 364 (2009); *Vernonia Sch. Dist. 47J v. Acton*, 515 U.S. 646 (1995); *New Jersey v. T.L.O.*, 469 U.S. 325 (1985).

[9] *See, e.g., Skinner v. Railway Labor Executives' Association*, 489 U.S. 602 (1989); *National Treasury Employees Union v. Von Raab*, 489 U.S. 656 1989).

[10] *E.g., United States v. Ramsey*, 431 U.S. 606 (1977).

[11] *E.g., Mich. Dep't of State Police v. Sitz*, 496 U.S. 444 (1990); *Delaware v. Prouse*, 440 U.S. 648 (1979).

[12] *E.g., Hudson v. Palmer*, 468 U.S. 517 (1984).

Nelson's arrest joined his name on a growing list of traveling celebrities who have fallen victim to the Sierra Blanca Border Checkpoint—earning it the nickname the "checkpoint of the stars." From 2009 to 2015, in addition to Nelson, Snoop Dogg, Nelly, and Fiona Apple were all arrested for possession of marijuana after Sierra Blanca Border Patrol Agents searched their tour buses.

The "checkpoint of the stars" has long been the bane of marijuana smokers driving from Los Angeles to Texas. At its peak, Sierra Blanca Border Patrol agents made as many as twenty to thirty marijuana busts per day. More recently, Hudspeth County Sheriff Arvin West has refused to refer any more marijuana cases for state prosecution that stem from the checkpoint. West reasoned that housing so many inmates proved too costly.

Because of West's position, the pendulum has now swung in the opposite direction. That is, everyone from personal pot smokers to medium-size marijuana traffickers now routinely avoid jail time if stopped at the Sierra Blanca checkpoint. Although the Border Patrol does not release the numbers of individuals who have their narcotics confiscated but are not arrested, Chris Cabrera, a Border Patrol union representative in the Rio Grande Valley confirmed that traffickers who are caught with dozens of pounds of pot are routinely released.

Although these high-profile arrests offer some insight into Customs and Border Protection's border search practices, a deeper look into their procedures suggests some systemic concerns. Pursuant to documents obtained by the ACLU, Customs and Border Protection received roughly 142 civil rights complaints from 2011–14, the majority of which were filed between 2012–13. Of those complaints, 134 involved allegations of Fourth Amendment violations, including numerous reports of stops and searches undertaken by agents without any valid legal basis.

Numerous complainants describe agents making roving patrol stops on, at best, inconsistent grounds, including: motorists stopped for speeding, driving too slowly, driving with out-of-state license plates, driving vehicles "registered in another town," driving on less common routes, "turning around," and commuting to work early in the morning. Agents once told a woman, who demanded to know why she had been pulled over in Tucson Arizona, sixty miles from the border, "We'll think of something."

In response to these allegations, the Border Patrol argued that its interior checkpoints are an efficient and effective strategy to secure the border. But ACLU data has revealed that nine out of twenty-three of the Tucson Arizona Sector checkpoints reported no arrests of "deportable subjects" in 2013 and fifteen others reported fewer than ten arrests of "deportable subjects."

Conversely, the Yuma Arizona Sector saw 1,535 arrests of U.S. Citizens, as compared to only 197 arrests of "deportable subjects." In particular, one Yuma Sector checkpoint, located seventy-five miles from the border, reported only one non-citizen apprehension in three years while producing multiple civil rights complaints during the same period. Thus, whether these checkpoints serve to police the border or, rather, as a general "crime control" tool seems an unanswered and important question.

Enter Daniel Ericksen. Celebrities are not the only people who fall victim to Customs and Border Patrol's use of the border search exception. Since 2012, the U.S. Attorney's Office for the Eastern District of Michigan defended a particular Border Patrol stop at the Port Huron crossing at the Canadian border. That stop involved the arrest for possession of marijuana of Daniel Eriksen, the son of a Huntington Woods attorney. Since the arrest, Ericksen's father, Michael Ericksen, has filed two separate lawsuits against customs and border protection—both of which were appealed all the way to the United States Supreme Court (where certiorari was denied).

On June 22, 2012, twenty-one-year-old Daniel Ericksen was driving alone from Huntington Woods, Michigan, to Wooden Acres, a summer camp near Port Huron where Ericksen worked as a counselor. But Ericksen took a wrong turn on Interstate 94 and was routed to the Blue Water Bridge, which connects Michigan to Ontario, Canada. When Ericksen arrived at the border, he told the Border Patrol agent manning the toll booth that he did not intend to travel to Canada and was only at the checkpoint by accident. The agent then handed Ericksen a laminated Customs and Border Patrol card, which read on the front:

> You are being allowed to turn around without traveling to Canada. Please present this card, along with your identification to an open CBP inspection booth prior to departing. Thank you.

The back of the card provided:

> All persons, baggage, and merchandise arriving in the Customs territory of the United States or from places outside thereof are liable to inspection and search by a Customs official.

The agent then instructed Ericksen to make a U-turn, without entering Canada, and present the card at the inspection booth intercepting vehicles entering the country.

After turning around, Ericksen handed the inspection-booth agent his laminated card. Rather than allowing Ericksen to pass, the agent instructed Ericksen to proceed to a vehicle inspection point and exit his vehicle. Ericksen was then escorted to the station house to wait while Customs and Border Patrol Agent Joseph Vittorini searched his vehicle. During the search, Vittorini located a backpack in the truck. Inside the backpack was what appeared to be drug paraphernalia and a small quantity of marijuana.

Vittorini questioned Ericksen, who acknowledged that the marijuana belonged to him. Vittorini then proceeded to contact the Port Huron Police Department and Officer Thomas Rumely responded to the scene. Officer Rumley advised Ericksen of his *Miranda* rights, which Ericksen waived and again acknowledged that the marijuana was his. Ericksen was then arrested and transported to the Port Huron Police Department where he received a citation to appear in Port Huron District Court for possession of marijuana and possession of drug paraphernalia.

Ericksen filed a motion to suppress the search of his vehicle. He argued that because he had no intention of leaving the United States, the border search exception to the search warrant requirement did not apply. The Port

Huron District Court disagreed and held that Ericksen's intent was irrelevant. Rather, the court reasoned, Border Patrol Agents have the right to conduct routine searches and seizures of *all* vehicles at the border without probable cause or a warrant.

Ericksen appealed to the Circuit Court for the County of St. Clair. That court found Ericksen's argument "interesting" because Ericksen, after all, was forced to drive to the border after missing his exit. But the court ultimately held that no authority existed to create an exception to border searches. Accordingly, the court concluded that Ericksen's "intention of not wanting to be there is legally irrelevant."

Ericksen's presence in the legal system did not end there. Led by his father, Michael, Erickson filed not one but two civil suits against certain U.S. Customs and Border Protection agents claiming violations of his Fourth Amendment rights. Both lawsuits were dismissed.

C. THE CASES

1. Establishing the Doctrine

CAMARA V. MUNICIPAL COURT OF SAN FRANCISCO

387 U.S. 523
Supreme Court of the United States
February 15, 1967, Argued; June 5, 1967, Decided
No. 92

MR. JUSTICE WHITE delivered the opinion of the Court. * * *

Appellant brought this action in a California Superior Court alleging that he was awaiting trial on a criminal charge of violating the San Francisco Housing Code by refusing to permit a warrantless inspection of his residence, and that a writ of prohibition should issue to the criminal court because the ordinance authorizing such inspections is unconstitutional on its face. The Superior Court denied the writ, the District Court of Appeal affirmed, and the Supreme Court of California denied a petition for hearing. Appellant properly raised and had considered by the California courts the federal constitutional questions he now presents to this Court.

Though there were no judicial findings of fact in this prohibition proceeding, we shall set forth the parties' factual allegations. On November 6, 1963, an inspector of the Division of Housing Inspection of the San Francisco Department of Public Health entered an apartment building to make a routine annual inspection for possible violations of the city's Housing Code.[1] The building's manager informed the inspector that

---

[1] The inspection was conducted pursuant to § 86 (3) of the San Francisco Municipal Code, which provides that apartment house operators shall pay an annual license fee in part to defray

appellant, lessee of the ground floor, was using the rear of his leasehold as a personal residence. Claiming that the building's occupancy permit did not allow residential use of the ground floor, the inspector confronted appellant and demanded that he permit an inspection of the premises. Appellant refused to allow the inspection because the inspector lacked a search warrant.

The inspector returned on November 8, again without a warrant, and appellant again refused to allow an inspection. A citation was then mailed ordering appellant to appear at the district attorney's office. When appellant failed to appear, two inspectors returned to his apartment on November 22. They informed appellant that he was required by law to permit an inspection under § 503 of the Housing Code:

> Sec. 503 RIGHT TO ENTER BUILDING. Authorized employees of the City departments or City agencies, so far as may be necessary for the performance of their duties, shall, upon presentation of proper credentials, have the right to enter, at reasonable times, any building, structure, or premises in the City to perform any duty imposed upon them by the Municipal Code.

Appellant nevertheless refused the inspectors access to his apartment without a search warrant. Thereafter, a complaint was filed charging him with refusing to permit a lawful inspection in violation of § 507 of the Code.[2] Appellant was arrested on December 2 and released on bail. When his demurrer to the criminal complaint was denied, appellant filed this petition for a writ of prohibition.

Appellant has argued throughout this litigation that § 503 is contrary to the Fourth and Fourteenth Amendments in that it authorizes municipal officials to enter a private dwelling without a search warrant and without probable cause to believe that a violation of the Housing Code exists therein. Consequently, appellant contends, he may not be prosecuted under § 507 for refusing to permit an inspection unconstitutionally authorized by § 503. * * * [T]he District Court of Appeal held that § 503 does not violate Fourth Amendment rights because it "is part of a regulatory scheme which is essentially civil rather than criminal in nature, inasmuch as that section

---

the cost of periodic inspections of their buildings. The inspections are to be made by the Bureau of Housing Inspection "at least once a year and as often thereafter as may be deemed necessary." The permit of occupancy, which prescribes the apartment units which a building may contain, is not issued until the license is obtained.

  [2] "Sec. 507 PENALTY FOR VIOLATION. Any person, the owner or his authorized agent who violates, disobeys, omits, neglects, or refuses to comply with, or who resists or opposes the execution of any of the provisions of this Code, or any order of the Superintendent, the Director of Public Works, or the Director of Public Health made pursuant to this Code, shall be guilty of a misdemeanor and upon conviction thereof shall be punished by a fine not exceeding five hundred dollars ($ 500.00), or by imprisonment, not exceeding six (6) months or by both such fine and imprisonment, unless otherwise provided in this Code, and shall be deemed guilty of a separate offense for every day such violation, disobedience, omission, neglect or refusal shall continue."

creates a right of inspection which is limited in scope and may not be exercised under unreasonable conditions." * * * [W]e reverse.

I.   * * *

In *Frank v. Maryland*, this Court upheld the conviction of one who refused to permit a warrantless inspection of private premises for the purposes of locating and abating a suspected public nuisance. Although *Frank* can arguably be distinguished from this case on its facts,[4] the *Frank* opinion has generally been interpreted as carving out an additional exception to the rule that warrantless searches are unreasonable under the Fourth Amendment. The District Court of Appeal so interpreted *Frank* in this case, and that ruling is the core of appellant's challenge here. We proceed to a re-examination of the factors which persuaded the *Frank* majority to adopt this construction of the Fourth Amendment's prohibition against unreasonable searches.

To the *Frank* majority, municipal fire, health, and housing inspection programs "touch at most upon the periphery of the important interests safeguarded by the Fourteenth Amendment's protection against official intrusion," because the inspections are merely to determine whether physical conditions exist which do not comply with minimum standards prescribed in local regulatory ordinances. Since the inspector does not ask that the property owner open his doors to a search for "evidence of criminal action" which may be used to secure the owner's criminal conviction, historic interests of "self-protection" jointly protected by the Fourth and Fifth Amendments are said not to be involved, but only the less intense "right to be secure from intrusion into personal privacy."

We may agree that a routine inspection of the physical condition of private property is a less hostile intrusion than the typical policeman's search for the fruits and instrumentalities of crime. For this reason alone, *Frank* differed from the great bulk of Fourth Amendment cases which have been considered by this Court. But we cannot agree that the Fourth Amendment interests at stake in these inspection cases are merely "peripheral." It is surely anomalous to say that the individual and his private property are fully protected by the Fourth Amendment only when the individual is suspected of criminal behavior. For instance, even the most law-abiding citizen has a very tangible interest in limiting the circumstances under which the sanctity of his home may be broken by official authority, for the possibility of criminal entry under the guise of official sanction is a serious threat to personal and family security. And even accepting *Frank's* rather remarkable premise, inspections of the kind

---

[4] In *Frank*, the Baltimore ordinance required that the health inspector "have cause to suspect that a nuisance exists in any house, cellar or enclosure" before he could demand entry without a warrant, a requirement obviously met in Frank because the inspector observed extreme structural decay and a pile of rodent feces on the appellant's premises. Section 503 of the San Francisco Housing Code has no such "cause" requirement * * *.

we are here considering do in fact jeopardize "self-protection" interests of the property owner. Like most regulatory laws, fire, health, and housing codes are enforced by criminal processes. In some cities, discovery of a violation by the inspector leads to a criminal complaint. Even in cities where discovery of a violation produces only an administrative compliance order, refusal to comply is a criminal offense, and the fact of compliance is verified by a second inspection, again without a warrant. Finally, as this case demonstrates, refusal to permit an inspection is itself a crime, punishable by fine or even by jail sentence.

The *Frank* majority suggested, and appellee reasserts, two other justifications for permitting administrative health and safety inspections without a warrant. First, it is argued that these inspections are "designed to make the least possible demand on the individual occupant." The ordinances authorizing inspections are hedged with safeguards, and at any rate the inspector's particular decision to enter must comply with the constitutional standard of reasonableness even if he may enter without a warrant.[10] In addition, the argument proceeds, the warrant process could not function effectively in this field. The decision to inspect an entire municipal area is based upon legislative or administrative assessment of broad factors such as the area's age and condition. Unless the magistrate is to review such policy matters, he must issue a "rubber stamp" warrant which provides no protection at all to the property owner.

In our opinion, these arguments unduly discount the purposes behind the warrant machinery contemplated by the Fourth Amendment. Under the present system, when the inspector demands entry, the occupant has no way of knowing whether enforcement of the municipal code involved requires inspection of his premises, no way of knowing the lawful limits of the inspector's power to search, and no way of knowing whether the inspector himself is acting under proper authorization. These are questions which may be reviewed by a neutral magistrate without any reassessment of the basic agency decision to canvass an area. Yet, only by refusing entry and risking a criminal conviction can the occupant at present challenge the inspector's decision to search. And even if the occupant possesses sufficient fortitude to take this risk, as appellant did here, he may never learn any more about the reason for the inspection than that the law generally allows housing inspectors to gain entry. The practical effect of this system is to leave the occupant subject to the discretion of the official in the field. This is precisely the discretion to invade private property which we have consistently circumscribed by a requirement that a disinterested party

---

[10] The San Francisco Code requires that the inspector display proper credentials, that he inspect "at reasonable times," and that he not obtain entry by force, at least when there is no emergency. The Baltimore ordinance in Frank required that the inspector "have cause to suspect that a nuisance exists." Some cities notify residents in advance, by mail or posted notice, of impending area inspections. State courts upholding these inspections without warrants have imposed a general reasonableness requirement.

warrant the need to search. We simply cannot say that the protections provided by the warrant procedure are not needed in this context; broad statutory safeguards are no substitute for individualized review, particularly when those safeguards may only be invoked at the risk of a criminal penalty.

The final justification suggested for warrantless administrative searches is that the public interest demands such a rule: it is vigorously argued that the health and safety of entire urban populations is dependent upon enforcement of minimum fire, housing, and sanitation standards, and that the only effective means of enforcing such codes is by routine systematized inspection of all physical structures. Of course, in applying any reasonableness standard, including one of constitutional dimension, an argument that the public interest demands a particular rule must receive careful consideration. But we think this argument misses the mark. The question is not, at this stage at least, whether these inspections may be made, but whether they may be made without a warrant. For example, to say that gambling raids may not be made at the discretion of the police without a warrant is not necessarily to say that gambling raids may never be made. In assessing whether the public interest demands creation of a general exception to the Fourth Amendment's warrant requirement, the question is not whether the public interest justifies the type of search in question, but whether the authority to search should be evidenced by a warrant, which in turn depends in part upon whether the burden of obtaining a warrant is likely to frustrate the governmental purpose behind the search. It has nowhere been urged that fire, health, and housing code inspection programs could not achieve their goals within the confines of a reasonable search warrant requirement. Thus, we do not find the public need argument dispositive.

In summary, we hold that administrative searches of the kind at issue here are significant intrusions upon the interests protected by the Fourth Amendment, that such searches when authorized and conducted without a warrant procedure lack the traditional safeguards which the Fourth Amendment guarantees to the individual, and that the reasons put forth in *Frank v. Maryland* and in other cases for upholding these warrantless searches are insufficient to justify so substantial a weakening of the Fourth Amendment's protections. Because of the nature of the municipal programs under consideration, however, these conclusions must be the beginning, not the end, of our inquiry. The *Frank* majority gave recognition to the unique character of these inspection programs by refusing to require search warrants; to reject that disposition does not justify ignoring the question whether some other accommodation between public need and individual rights is essential.

II.

The Fourth Amendment provides that, "no Warrants shall issue, but upon probable cause." Borrowing from more typical Fourth Amendment cases, appellant argues not only that code enforcement inspection programs must be circumscribed by a warrant procedure, but also that warrants should issue only when the inspector possesses probable cause to believe that a particular dwelling contains violations of the minimum standards prescribed by the code being enforced. We disagree.

In cases in which the Fourth Amendment requires that a warrant to search be obtained, "probable cause" is the standard by which a particular decision to search is tested against the constitutional mandate of reasonableness. To apply this standard, it is obviously necessary first to focus upon the governmental interest which allegedly justifies official intrusion upon the constitutionally protected interests of the private citizen. For example, in a criminal investigation, the police may undertake to recover specific stolen or contraband goods. But that public interest would hardly justify a sweeping search of an entire city conducted in the hope that these goods might be found. Consequently, a search for these goods, even with a warrant, is "reasonable" only when there is "probable cause" to believe that they will be uncovered in a particular dwelling.

Unlike the search pursuant to a criminal investigation, the inspection programs at issue here are aimed at securing city-wide compliance with minimum physical standards for private property. The primary governmental interest at stake is to prevent even the unintentional development of conditions which are hazardous to public health and safety. Because fires and epidemics may ravage large urban areas, because unsightly conditions adversely affect the economic values of neighboring structures, numerous courts have upheld the police power of municipalities to impose and enforce such minimum standards even upon existing structures. In determining whether a particular inspection is reasonable—and thus in determining whether there is probable cause to issue a warrant for that inspection—the need for the inspection must be weighed in terms of these reasonable goals of code enforcement.

There is unanimous agreement among those most familiar with this field that the only effective way to seek universal compliance with the minimum standards required by municipal codes is through routine periodic inspections of all structures. It is here that the probable cause debate is focused, for the agency's decision to conduct an area inspection is unavoidably based on its appraisal of conditions in the area as a whole, not on its knowledge of conditions in each particular building. Appellee contends that, if the probable cause standard urged by appellant is adopted, the area inspection will be eliminated as a means of seeking compliance with code standards and the reasonable goals of code enforcement will be dealt a crushing blow.

In meeting this contention, appellant argues first, that his probable cause standard would not jeopardize area inspection programs because only a minute portion of the population will refuse to consent to such inspections, and second, that individual privacy in any event should be given preference to the public interest in conducting such inspections. The first argument, even if true, is irrelevant to the question whether the area inspection is reasonable within the meaning of the Fourth Amendment. The second argument is in effect an assertion that the area inspection is an unreasonable search. Unfortunately, there can be no ready test for determining reasonableness other than by balancing the need to search against the invasion which the search entails. But we think that a number of persuasive factors combine to support the reasonableness of area code-enforcement inspections. First, such programs have a long history of judicial and public acceptance. *See Frank v. Maryland*, 359 U.S., at 367–371. Second, the public interest demands that all dangerous conditions be prevented or abated, yet it is doubtful that any other canvassing technique would achieve acceptable results. Many such conditions—faulty wiring is an obvious example—are not observable from outside the building and indeed may not be apparent to the inexpert occupant himself. Finally, because the inspections are neither personal in nature nor aimed at the discovery of evidence of crime, they involve a relatively limited invasion of the urban citizen's privacy. Both the majority and the dissent in *Frank* emphatically supported this conclusion * * *.

Having concluded that the area inspection is a "reasonable" search of private property within the meaning of the Fourth Amendment, it is obvious that "probable cause" to issue a warrant to inspect must exist if reasonable legislative or administrative standards for conducting an area inspection are satisfied with respect to a particular dwelling. Such standards, which will vary with the municipal program being enforced, may be based upon the passage of time, the nature of the building (e.g., a multi-family apartment house), or the condition of the entire area, but they will not necessarily depend upon specific knowledge of the condition of the particular dwelling. It has been suggested that so to vary the probable cause test from the standard applied in criminal cases would be to authorize a "synthetic search warrant" and thereby to lessen the overall protections of the Fourth Amendment. But we do not agree. The warrant procedure is designed to guarantee that a decision to search private property is justified by a reasonable governmental interest. But reasonableness is still the ultimate standard. If a valid public interest justifies the intrusion contemplated, then there is probable cause to issue a suitably restricted search warrant. Such an approach neither endangers time-honored doctrines applicable to criminal investigations nor makes a nullity of the probable cause requirement in this area. It merely gives full recognition to the competing public and private interests here at stake and, in so doing, best fulfills the historic purpose behind the constitutional right to be free from unreasonable government invasions of privacy.

III.

Since our holding emphasizes the controlling standard of reasonableness, nothing we say today is intended to foreclose prompt inspections, even without a warrant, that the law has traditionally upheld in emergency situations. On the other hand, in the case of most routine area inspections, there is no compelling urgency to inspect at a particular time or on a particular day. Moreover, most citizens allow inspections of their property without a warrant. Thus, as a practical matter and in light of the Fourth Amendment's requirement that a warrant specify the property to be searched, it seems likely that warrants should normally be sought only after entry is refused unless there has been a citizen complaint or there is other satisfactory reason for securing immediate entry. Similarly, the requirement of a warrant procedure does not suggest any change in what seems to be the prevailing local policy, in most situations, of authorizing entry, but not entry by force, to inspect.

IV.

In this case, appellant has been charged with a crime for his refusal to permit housing inspectors to enter his leasehold without a warrant. There was no emergency demanding immediate access; in fact, the inspectors made three trips to the building in an attempt to obtain appellant's consent to search. Yet no warrant was obtained and thus appellant was unable to verify either the need for or the appropriate limits of the inspection. No doubt, the inspectors entered the public portion of the building with the consent of the landlord, through the building's manager, but appellee does not contend that such consent was sufficient to authorize inspection of appellant's premises. Assuming the facts to be as the parties have alleged, we therefore conclude that appellant had a constitutional right to insist that the inspectors obtain a warrant to search and that appellant may not constitutionally be convicted for refusing to consent to the inspection. It appears from the opinion of the District Court of Appeal that under these circumstances a writ of prohibition will issue to the criminal court under California law.

The judgment is vacated and the case is remanded for further proceedings not inconsistent with this opinion.

It is so ordered.

QUESTIONS, COMMENTS, CONCERNS?

1. *Camara* **starts a new brand of logic.** The *Camara* Court's creation of this modified probable cause standard for administrative searches is less relevant than its creation of a new "balancing approach" to the Fourth Amendment. It is that latter contribution that becomes so influential in the Court's subsequent special needs, emergency, and administrative search jurisprudence. Stated more precisely, the Court's new balancing approach matters in the context of criminal investigations where the Warrant Clause— and thus probable cause—are not at issue.

2. **Was the border patrol's search of Ericksen "administrative" or "investigative"?** Look at some of the *Camara* Court's logic, particularly this sentence: "[B]ecause the inspections are neither personal in nature nor aimed at the discovery of evidence of crime, they involve a relatively limited invasion of the urban citizen's privacy." From that logic we should see that, pursuant to the Court's new balancing approach, a search is more likely "administrative" in nature when its purpose is not to investigate crime. And when that's the case, the Warrant Clause drops out, thus rendering probable cause irrelevant.

Now apply the *Camara* Court's logic to Ericksen. We will learn more about the border search exception in the next two cases, but for now, a simple question: did Border Patrol Agents search Ericksen's car for "non-criminal" reasons? In other words, was the search of his vehicle "administrative" in nature?

As you consider those questions, recall that Border Patrol Agents did *not* stop Ericksen's friend, Ben Sofferin, or his mother, Lisa Ericksen. [Casefile Document 4, at 2.] How does the Fourth Amendment analysis change if you conclude that the Border Patrol was, in fact, looking for evidence of a crime when it stopped Ericksen?

2. Border Searches (vs. Patrols)

UNITED STATES V. FLORES-MONTANO

541 U.S. 149
Supreme Court of the United States
February 25, 2004, Argued; March 30, 2004, Decided
No. 02-1794

CHIEF JUSTICE REHNQUIST delivered the opinion of the Court.

Customs officials seized 37 kilograms—a little more than 81 pounds— of marijuana from respondent Manuel Flores-Montano's gas tank at the international border. The Court of Appeals for the Ninth Circuit, relying on an earlier decision by a divided panel of that court, *United States v. Molina-Tarazon*, 279 F.3d 709 (2002), held that the Fourth Amendment forbade the fuel tank search absent reasonable suspicion. We hold that the search in question did not require reasonable suspicion.

Respondent, driving a 1987 Ford Taurus station wagon, attempted to enter the United States at the Otay Mesa Port of Entry in southern California. A customs inspector conducted an inspection of the station wagon, and requested respondent to leave the vehicle. The vehicle was then taken to a secondary inspection station.

At the secondary station, a second customs inspector inspected the gas tank by tapping it, and noted that the tank sounded solid. Subsequently, the inspector requested a mechanic under contract with Customs to come to the border station to remove the tank. Within 20 to 30 minutes, the mechanic arrived. He raised the car on a hydraulic lift, loosened the straps and unscrewed the bolts holding the gas tank to the undercarriage of the vehicle, and then disconnected some hoses and electrical connections. After the gas tank was removed, the inspector hammered off bondo (a putty-like hardening substance that is used to seal openings) from the top of the gas tank. The inspector opened an access plate underneath the bondo and found 37 kilograms of marijuana bricks. The process took 15 to 25 minutes.

A grand jury for the Southern District of California indicted respondent on one count of unlawfully importing marijuana, and one count of possession of marijuana with intent to distribute. Relying on *Molina-Tarazon*, respondent filed a motion to suppress the marijuana recovered from the gas tank. In *Molina-Tarazon*, a divided panel of the Court of Appeals held, *inter alia*, that removal of a gas tank requires reasonable suspicion in order to be consistent with the Fourth Amendment.

The Government advised the District Court that it was not relying on reasonable suspicion as a basis for denying respondent's suppression motion, but that it believed *Molina-Tarazon* was wrongly decided. The District Court, relying on *Molina-Tarazon*, held that reasonable suspicion was required to justify the search and, accordingly, granted respondent's motion to suppress. The Court of Appeals, citing *Molina-Tarazon*, summarily affirmed the District Court's judgment. We granted certiorari and now reverse.

In *Molina-Tarazon*, the Court of Appeals decided a case presenting similar facts to the one at bar. It asked "whether [the removal and dismantling of the defendant's fuel tank] is a 'routine' border search for which no suspicion whatsoever is required." The Court of Appeals stated that "[i]n order to conduct a search that goes beyond the routine, an inspector must have reasonable suspicion," and the "critical factor" in determining whether a search is "routine" is the "degree of intrusiveness."

The Court of Appeals seized on language from our opinion in *United States v. Montoya de Hernandez*, 473 U.S. 531 (1985), in which we used the word "routine" as a descriptive term in discussing border searches. The Court of Appeals took the term "routine," fashioned a new balancing test, and extended it to searches of vehicles. * * * Complex balancing tests to determine what is a "routine" search of a vehicle, as opposed to a more "intrusive" search of a person, have no place in border searches of vehicles.

The Government's interest in preventing the entry of unwanted persons and effects is at its zenith at the international border. Time and again, we have stated that "searches made at the border, pursuant to the longstanding right of the sovereign to protect itself by stopping and examining persons and property crossing into this country, are reasonable simply by virtue of the fact that they occur at the border." *United States v. Ramsey*, 431 U.S. 606, 616 (1977). Congress, since the beginning of our Government, "has granted the Executive plenary authority to conduct routine searches and seizures at the border, without probable cause or a warrant, in order to regulate the collection of duties and to prevent the introduction of contraband into this country." *United States v. Montoya de Hernandez*, 473 U.S. 531, 537 (citing *Ramsey, supra,* at 616–617 (citing Act of July 31, 1789, ch 5, 1 Stat 29)). The modern statute that authorized the search in this case,[1] derived from a statute passed by the First Congress, and reflects the "impressive historical pedigree" of the Government's power and interest. It is axiomatic that the United States, as sovereign, has the inherent authority to protect, and a paramount interest in protecting, its territorial integrity.

That interest in protecting the borders is illustrated in this case by the evidence that smugglers frequently attempt to penetrate our borders with contraband secreted in their automobiles' fuel tank. Over the past 5 1/2 fiscal years, there have been 18,788 vehicle drug seizures at the southern California ports of entry. Of those 18,788, gas tank drug seizures have accounted for 4,619 of the vehicle drug seizures, or approximately 25%. In addition, instances of persons smuggled in and around gas tank compartments are discovered at the ports of entry of San Ysidro and Otay Mesa at a rate averaging 1 approximately every 10 days.

Respondent asserts two main arguments with respect to his Fourth Amendment interests. First, he urges that he has a privacy interest in his fuel tank, and that the suspicionless disassembly of his tank is an invasion of his privacy. But on many occasions, we have noted that the expectation of privacy is less at the border than it is in the interior. We have long recognized that automobiles seeking entry into this country may be searched. It is difficult to imagine how the search of a gas tank, which

---

[1] Section 1581(a) provides:

Any officer of the customs may at any time go on board of any vessel or vehicle at any place in the United States or within the customs waters or, as he may be authorized, within a customs-enforcement area established under the Anti-Smuggling Act, or at any other authorized place, without as well as within his district, and examine the manifest and other documents and papers and examine, inspect, and search the vessel or vehicle and every part thereof and any person, trunk, package, or cargo on board, and to this end may hail and stop such vessel or vehicle, and use all necessary force to compel compliance.

should be solely a repository for fuel, could be more of an invasion of privacy than the search of the automobile's passenger compartment.

Second, respondent argues that the Fourth Amendment "protects property as well as privacy," and that the disassembly and reassembly of his gas tank is a significant deprivation of his property interest because it may damage the vehicle. He does not, and on the record cannot, truly contend that the procedure of removal, disassembly, and reassembly of the fuel tank in this case or any other has resulted in serious damage to, or destruction of, the property. According to the Government, for example, in fiscal year 2003, 348 gas tank searches conducted along the southern border were negative (i.e., no contraband was found), the gas tanks were reassembled, and the vehicles continued their entry into the United States without incident.

Respondent cites not a single accident involving the vehicle or motorist in the many thousands of gas tank disassemblies that have occurred at the border. A gas tank search involves a brief procedure that can be reversed without damaging the safety or operation of the vehicle. If damage to a vehicle were to occur, the motorist might be entitled to recovery. While the interference with a motorist's possessory interest is not insignificant when the Government removes, disassembles, and reassembles his gas tank, it nevertheless is justified by the Government's paramount interest in protecting the border.[3]

For the reasons stated, we conclude that the Government's authority to conduct suspicionless inspections at the border includes the authority to remove, disassemble, and reassemble a vehicle's fuel tank. While it may be true that some searches of property are so destructive as to require a different result, this was not one of them. The judgment of the United States Court of Appeals for the Ninth Circuit is therefore reversed, and the case is remanded for further proceedings consistent with this opinion.

It is so ordered.

JUSTICE BREYER, concurring.

[Omitted.]

---

[3]   Respondent also argued that he has some sort of Fourth Amendment right not to be subject to delay at the international border and that the need for the use of specialized labor, as well as the hour actual delay here and the potential for even greater delay for reassembly are an invasion of that right. Respondent points to no cases indicating the Fourth Amendment shields entrants from inconvenience or delay at the international border.

The procedure in this case took about an hour (including the wait for the mechanic). At oral argument, the Government advised us that, depending on the type of car, a search involving the disassembly and reassembly of a gas tank may take one to two hours. We think it clear that delays of one to two hours at international borders are to be expected.

QUESTIONS, COMMENTS, CONCERNS?

1. **Removing the fuel tank from a vehicle.** The *Flores-Montano* Court paints quite the rosy picture of fuel tank removal. It suggests that the process takes "15 to 25 minutes" and consists of "rais[ing] the car on a hydraulic lift, loosen[ing] the straps and unscrew[ing] the bolts holding the gas tank to the undercarriage of the vehicle, and then disconnect[ing] some hoses and electrical connections." You could do that in between classes, right?

More seriously, some reasons may exist to be skeptical of this description. A casual web survey of sites describing how to remove a car's fuel tank suggest numerous additional, and sometimes different, steps involved in the process. For example, the mechanic should disconnect the car's battery before beginning, blow compressed air to remove debris from outside the fuel lines, and may need different tools to remove the hoses depending on the of tank attached to the vehicle. *How to Drop a Gas Tank*, WIKIHOW, https://www.wiki how.com/Drop-a-Gas-Tank (last visited May 11, 2018); Brady Klopfer, *How to Drop a Gas Tank*, YOURMECHANIC.COM (June 29, 2016), https://www.your mechanic.com/article/how-to-drop-a-gas-tank-by-brady-klopfer. Do these steps, omitted by the Court, alter the border search analysis?

2. **Damaging a vehicle while removing its fuel tank.** At one point, the *Flores-Montano* Court suggests that a search that is "so destructive"—even if conducted at the border—may "require a different result." Removal of a fuel tank, says the Court, does not meet that standard because 348 gas tank searches in fiscal year 2003 occurred "without incident." But what if the Border Patrol relies on a shoddy mechanic who damages the 349th fuel tank? The Court notes that damage to that vehicle "might" enable the driver to recover, but is that likely? Can you see anywhere in the Court's opinion that spells out *how* a driver could seek "recovery"? Perhaps the more interesting (and likely) question left unanswered is whether the driver whose vehicle is damaged *and* has contraband in the fuel tank could recover.

3. **The scope of border searches: "privacy interest" vs. "destructive" searches.** On the one hand, the Court notes that searching a fuel tank is justified because "the expectation of privacy is less at the border than it is in the interior." But on the other hand, the Court highlights that a "destructive" search may not fall within the scope of the border search exception. Well, which is it? On the privacy logic, is there an area of the car where agents could search that is *too private* but not destructive? Alternatively, could agents conduct an overly-destructive search to easily accessible non-private area of the vehicle? Assume both scenarios could extend the border search exception too far. If so, would the search automatically be unconstitutional or could the automobile exception admit any found contraband?

4. **If fuel tank removal is permissible, what *else* can authorities search?** Lower courts have extended the logic of *Flores-Montano* considerably. For example, the Ninth Circuit has held that reasonable suspicion is not necessary to permit slashing a vehicle's spare tire to enable searching inside.

United States v. Cortez-Rocha, 394 F.3d 1115, 1119 (9th Cir. 2005). The Ninth Circuit has similarly permitted the removal of a car's interior door panel, *United States v. Hernandez*, 424 F.3d 1056 (9th Cir. 2005), and the drilling of a hole in a pickup truck bed, *United States v. Chaudhry*, 424 F.3d 1051, 1053 (9th Cir. 2005).

An ongoing issue at the border, vehicles aside, is the extent to which agents may search *inside* the vehicle—particularly electronic devices inside the vehicle. On the one hand, the Ninth Circuit has permitted the search of an electronic storage device at the border by characterizing it as analogous to a "closed container." *United States v. Arnold*, 533 F.3d 1003, 1008 (9th Cir. 2008). After *Arnold*, the Ninth Circuit refined its approach in 2013 by holding that a "forensic" search of a computer at the border requires reasonable suspicion. *United States v. Cotterman*, 709 F.3d 952, 966 (9th Cir. 2013).

That view, however, is hardly uniform. In *United States v. Vergara*, 884 F.3d 1309, 1312 (11th Cir. 2018), the Eleventh Circuit recognized that "[t]he forensic searches of [defendant's] phones required neither a warrant nor probable cause." By contrast, the Fourth Circuit held that some suspicion is required for a forensic search of a cell phone seized by border patrol authorities. *United States v. Kolsuz*, No. 16-4687, 2018 U.S. App. LEXIS 12147, *27 (4th Cir. May 9, 2018).

5.   Ericksen and *Flores-Montano*. How does *Flores-Montano* apply to Ericksen? Note that Ericksen's motion to suppress expressly relies on *Flores-Montano*. [Casefile Document 2, at 5.] But does that reliance help? After all, unlike *Flores-Montano*, agents did not disassemble any portion of Ericksen's car, and they did not search for contraband in an electronic storage device. Admittedly, it is unclear how much time it took for agents to search Ericksen's vehicle at the secondary inspection area while he was detained. But even Ericksen himself does not highlight the detention's duration as constitutionally problematic. Note, however, that *Flores-Montano* makes a temporal assessment relevant. In footnote four, the Court observes, "We think it clear that delays of one to two hours at international borders are to be expected."

Back to Ericksen's argument. Delays at the border aside, perhaps something else is going on. The core of Ericksen's argument appears to be that his interaction at the border does not constitute international travel. As he states, "the *sine qua non* for the border-search exception is international travel. There is no rational basis for broadening the exception to encompass 'turn-around' traffic." [Casefile Document 2, at 6.] Does *Flores-Montano* suggest that a driver's intent to travel internationally matters for purposes of applying the border search exception? What did the suppression court think? [*See* Casefile Document 4, at 5.]

UNITED STATES V. ARVIZU

534 U.S. 266
Supreme Court of the United States
November 27, 2001, Argued; January 15, 2002, Decided
No. 00-1519

CHIEF JUSTICE REHNQUIST delivered the opinion of the Court. * * *

On an afternoon in January 1998, Agent Clinton Stoddard was working at a border patrol checkpoint along U.S. Highway 191 approximately 30 miles north of Douglas, Arizona. Douglas has a population of about 13,000 and is situated on the United States-Mexico border in the southeastern part of the State. Only two highways lead north from Douglas. Highway 191 leads north to Interstate 10, which passes through Tucson and Phoenix. State Highway 80 heads northeast through less populated areas toward New Mexico, skirting south and east of the portion of the Coronado National Forest that lies approximately 20 miles northeast of Douglas.[1]

The checkpoint is located at the intersection of 191 and Rucker Canyon Road, an unpaved east-west road that connects 191 and the Coronado National Forest. When the checkpoint is operational, border patrol agents stop the traffic on 191 as part of a coordinated effort to stem the flow of illegal immigration and smuggling across the international border. Agents use roving patrols to apprehend smugglers trying to circumvent the checkpoint by taking the backroads, including those roads through the sparsely populated area between Douglas and the national forest. Magnetic sensors, or "intrusion devices," facilitate agents' efforts in patrolling these areas. Directionally sensitive, the sensors signal the passage of traffic that would be consistent with smuggling activities.

Sensors are located along the only other northbound road from Douglas besides Highways 191 and 80: Leslie Canyon Road. Leslie Canyon Road runs roughly parallel to 191, about halfway between 191 and the border of the Coronado National Forest, and ends when it intersects Rucker Canyon Road. It is unpaved beyond the 10-mile stretch leading out of Douglas and is very rarely traveled except for use by local ranchers and forest service personnel. Smugglers commonly try to avoid the 191 checkpoint by heading west on Rucker Canyon Road from Leslie Canyon Road and thence to Kuykendall Cutoff Road, a primitive dirt road that leads north approximately 12 miles east of 191. From there, they can gain access to Tucson and Phoenix.

Around 2:15 p.m., Stoddard received a report via Douglas radio that a Leslie Canyon Road sensor had triggered. This was significant to Stoddard

---

[1] Coronado National Forest consists of 12 widely scattered sections of land covering 1,780,000 acres in southeastern Arizona and southwestern New Mexico. The section of the forest near Douglas includes the Chiricahua, Dragoon, and Peloncillo Mountain Ranges.

for two reasons. First, it suggested to him that a vehicle might be trying to circumvent the checkpoint. Second, the timing coincided with the point when agents begin heading back to the checkpoint for a shift change, which leaves the area unpatrolled. Stoddard knew that alien smugglers did extensive scouting and seemed to be most active when agents were en route back to the checkpoint. Another border patrol agent told Stoddard that the same sensor had gone off several weeks before and that he had apprehended a minivan using the same route and witnessed the occupants throwing bundles of marijuana out the door.

Stoddard drove eastbound on Rucker Canyon Road to investigate. As he did so, he received another radio report of sensor activity. It indicated that the vehicle that had triggered the first sensor was heading westbound on Rucker Canyon Road. He continued east, passing Kuykendall Cutoff Road. He saw the dust trail of an approaching vehicle about a half mile away. Stoddard had not seen any other vehicles and, based on the timing, believed that this was the one that had tripped the sensors. He pulled off to the side of the road at a slight slant so he could get a good look at the oncoming vehicle as it passed by.

It was a minivan, a type of automobile that Stoddard knew smugglers used. As it approached, it slowed dramatically, from about 50–55 to 25–30 miles per hour. He saw five occupants inside. An adult man was driving, an adult woman sat in the front passenger seat, and three children were in the back. The driver appeared stiff and his posture very rigid. He did not look at Stoddard and seemed to be trying to pretend that Stoddard was not there. Stoddard thought this suspicious because in his experience on patrol most persons look over and see what is going on, and in that area most drivers give border patrol agents a friendly wave. Stoddard noticed that the knees of the two children sitting in the very back seat were unusually high, as if their feet were propped up on some cargo on the floor.

At that point, Stoddard decided to get a closer look, so he began to follow the vehicle as it continued westbound on Rucker Canyon Road toward Kuykendall Cutoff Road. Shortly thereafter, all of the children, though still facing forward, put their hands up at the same time and began to wave at Stoddard in an abnormal pattern. It looked to Stoddard as if the children were being instructed. Their odd waving continued on and off for about four to five minutes.

Several hundred feet before the Kuykendall Cutoff Road intersection, the driver signaled that he would turn. At one point, the driver turned the signal off, but just as he approached the intersection he put it back on and abruptly turned north onto Kuykendall. The turn was significant to Stoddard because it was made at the last place that would have allowed the minivan to avoid the checkpoint. Also, Kuykendall, though passable by a sedan or van, is rougher than either Rucker Canyon or Leslie Canyon roads, and the normal traffic is four-wheel-drive vehicles. Stoddard did not recognize the minivan as part of the local traffic agents encounter on patrol, and he did not think it likely that the minivan was going to or coming from a picnic outing. He was not aware of any picnic grounds on Turkey Creek, which could be reached by following Kuykendall Cutoff all the way up. He knew of picnic grounds and a Boy Scout camp east of the intersection of Rucker Canyon and Leslie Canyon roads, but the minivan had turned west at that intersection. And he had never seen anyone picnicking or sightseeing near where the first sensor went off.

Stoddard radioed for a registration check and learned that the minivan was registered to an address in Douglas that was four blocks north of the border in an area notorious for alien and narcotics smuggling. After receiving the information, Stoddard decided to make a vehicle stop. He approached the driver and learned that his name was Ralph Arvizu. Stoddard asked if respondent would mind if he looked inside and searched the vehicle. Respondent agreed, and Stoddard discovered marijuana in a black duffel bag under the feet of the two children in the back seat. Another bag containing marijuana was behind the rear seat. In all, the van contained 128.85 pounds of marijuana, worth an estimated $ 99,080.

Respondent was charged with possession with intent to distribute marijuana * * *. He moved to suppress the marijuana, arguing among other things that Stoddard did not have reasonable suspicion to stop the vehicle as required by the Fourth Amendment. After holding a hearing where Stoddard and respondent testified, the District Court for the District of Arizona ruled otherwise. It pointed to a number of the facts described above and noted particularly that any recreational areas north of Rucker Canyon would have been accessible from Douglas via 191 and another paved road, making it unnecessary to take a 40-to-50-mile trip on dirt roads.

The Court of Appeals for the Ninth Circuit reversed. In its view, fact-specific weighing of circumstances or other multifactor tests introduced "a troubling degree of uncertainty and unpredictability" into the Fourth Amendment analysis. It therefore "attempted . . . to describe and clearly delimit the extent to which certain factors may be considered by law enforcement officers in making stops such as the stop involving" respondent. After characterizing the District Court's analysis as relying on a list of 10 factors, the Court of Appeals proceeded to examine each in turn. It held that 7 of the factors, including respondent's slowing down, his failure to acknowledge Stoddard, the raised position of the children's knees, and their odd waving carried little or no weight in the reasonable-suspicion calculus. The remaining factors—the road's use by smugglers, the temporal proximity between respondent's trip and the agents' shift change, and the use of minivans by smugglers—were not enough to render the stop permissible. We granted certiorari to review the decision of the Court of

Appeals because of its importance to the enforcement of federal drug and immigration laws. * * *

When discussing how reviewing courts should make reasonable-suspicion determinations, we have said repeatedly that they must look at the "totality of the circumstances" of each case to see whether the detaining officer has a "particularized and objective basis" for suspecting legal wrongdoing. This process allows officers to draw on their own experience and specialized training to make inferences from and deductions about the cumulative information available to them that "might well elude an untrained person." Although an officer's reliance on a mere " 'hunch' " is insufficient to justify a stop, the likelihood of criminal activity need not rise to the level required for probable cause, and it falls considerably short of satisfying a preponderance of the evidence standard. * * *

We think that the approach taken by the Court of Appeals here departs sharply from the teachings of these cases. The court's evaluation and rejection of seven of the listed factors in isolation from each other does not take into account the "totality of the circumstances," as our cases have understood that phrase. The court appeared to believe that each observation by Stoddard that was by itself readily susceptible to an innocent explanation was entitled to "no weight." *Terry*, however, precludes this sort of divide-and-conquer analysis. * * *

The Court of Appeals' view that it was necessary to "clearly delimit" an officer's consideration of certain factors to reduce "troubling . . . uncertainty," * * * underestimates the usefulness of the reasonable-suspicion standard in guiding officers in the field. * * *

* * * Take, for example, the court's positions that respondent's deceleration could not be considered because "slowing down after spotting a law enforcement vehicle is an entirely normal response that is in no way indicative of criminal activity" and that his failure to acknowledge Stoddard's presence provided no support because there were "no 'special circumstances' rendering 'innocent avoidance . . . improbable.' " We think it quite reasonable that a driver's slowing down, stiffening of posture, and failure to acknowledge a sighted law enforcement officer might well be unremarkable in one instance (such as a busy San Francisco highway) while quite unusual in another (such as a remote portion of rural southeastern Arizona). Stoddard was entitled to make an assessment of the situation in light of his specialized training and familiarity with the customs of the area's inhabitants. To the extent that a totality of the circumstances approach may render appellate review less circumscribed by precedent than otherwise, it is the nature of the totality rule.

In another instance, the Court of Appeals chose to dismiss entirely the children's waving on grounds that odd conduct by children was all too common to be probative in a particular case. Yet this case did not involve simply any odd act by children. At the suppression hearing, Stoddard testified about the children's waving several times, and the record suggests that he physically demonstrated it as well. The District Court Judge, who saw and heard Stoddard, then characterized the waving as "methodical," "mechanical," "abnormal," and "certainly . . . a fact that is odd and would lead a reasonable officer to wonder why they are doing this." Though the issue of this case does not turn on the children's idiosyncratic actions, the Court of Appeals should not have casually rejected this factor in light of the District Court's superior access to the evidence and the well-recognized inability of reviewing courts to reconstruct what happened in the courtroom.

Having considered the totality of the circumstances and given due weight to the factual inferences drawn by the law enforcement officer and District Court Judge, we hold that Stoddard had reasonable suspicion to believe that respondent was engaged in illegal activity. It was reasonable for Stoddard to infer from his observations, his registration check, and his experience as a border patrol agent that respondent had set out from Douglas along a little-traveled route used by smugglers to avoid the 191 checkpoint. Stoddard's knowledge further supported a commonsense inference that respondent intended to pass through the area at a time when officers would be leaving their backroads patrols to change shifts. The likelihood that respondent and his family were on a picnic outing was diminished by the fact that the minivan had turned away from the known recreational areas accessible to the east on Rucker Canyon Road. Corroborating this inference was the fact that recreational areas farther to the north would have been easier to reach by taking 191, as opposed to the 40-to-50-mile trip on unpaved and primitive roads. The children's elevated knees suggested the existence of concealed cargo in the passenger compartment. Finally, for the reasons we have given, Stoddard's assessment of respondent's reactions upon seeing him and the children's mechanical-like waving, which continued for a full four to five minutes, were entitled to some weight. * * *

The judgment of the Court of Appeals is therefore reversed, and the case is remanded for further proceedings consistent with this opinion.

It is so ordered.

JUSTICE SCALIA, concurring.

[Omitted.]

QUESTIONS, COMMENTS, CONCERNS?

1. **Reasonable suspicion at the border.** As warrantless border investigations have evolved, probable cause has played almost no role. Rather, as one district court has boldly declared, reasonable suspicion is the "highest

level of Fourth Amendment protection available" at the border. *United States v. Kolsuz*, 185 F. Supp. 3d 843, 859 (E.D. Va. 2016).

2.   Reasonable suspicion at the border and factors. Although the *Arvizu* Court criticized the Ninth Circuit's use of various factors to conclude that no reasonable suspicion existed to stop Arvizu's minivan, the Ninth Circuit's reliance on a factor test has roots in Supreme Court jurisprudence.

In *United States v. Brignoni-Ponce*, 422 U.S. 873 (1975), the Supreme Court held that officers on roving patrol may constitutionally stop a vehicle if they have "reasonable suspicion" to believe "that the vehicles contain aliens who may be illegally in the country." In making that calculation, *Brignoni-Ponce* provided a list of possible factors that, if present, would support a finding of reasonable suspicion: (1) the area of the stop and its relation to the border; (2) aspects of the vehicle itself (like those with large compartments); (3) whether the vehicle appears to be heavily loaded; and (4) "the characteristic appearance of persons who live in Mexico, relying on such factors as the mode of dress and haircut." As to that final factor, the Court wrote, "[t]he likelihood that any given person of Mexican ancestry is an alien is high enough to make Mexican appearance a relevant factor[.]"

Factors aside, note that *Brignoni-Ponce* talks about reasonable suspicion to believe that the driver or the vehicle's occupants are "illegally in the country," rather than engaged in criminal activity (as *Arvizu* focuses on).

3.   Reasonable suspicion—or not? Compare *Flores-Montano* to *Arvizu*. In the former, *Flores-Montano*, no suspicion was required to conduct a search of respondent's fuel tank because his vehicle was searched *at* the border. By contrast, *Arvizu* requires reasonable suspicion to believe that the driver or its occupants are "engaged in illegal activity" to support stopping the vehicle. Accordingly, the presence or absence of a reasonable suspicion protection depends on whether Border Patrol Agents search a suspect's vehicle *at* the border or while on "roving patrol."

4.   *Arvizu* and Ericksen. Technically, Ericksen was not at the border given that he never sought to cross. If that's right, did he miss the opportunity to argue that *Arvizu* applied to his stop because he was outside the border? That argument, if successful, would have obligated the prosecution to prove reasonable suspicion existed to believe Ericksen was engaged in illegal activity at the time he entered the secondary inspection area. Although Ericksen declined to raise the issue, the suppression court construed the area where Ericksen was stopped as "the functional equivalent of the border." [Casefile Document 4, at 5.] But a person is either at the border or not, right? Being there—or not—seems a binary proposition. Do you agree with the suppression court?

5.   The rest of the Ericksen story. Following the denial of Ericksen's motion to suppress, he appealed to the Circuit Court. [Casefile Document 5.] That court affirmed, holding that the warrantless search of Ericksen's vehicle was a lawful use of the border search exception. *Id.* at 6. In doing so, it rejected

Ericksen's claim that his "undisputed intent should act as a limitation on what is normally an unlimited border search." *Id.*

Following his criminal case, Ericksen, still represented by his father, filed a civil lawsuit in federal court on January 12, 2015, against members of the border patrol alleging that the search of his vehicle violated his Fourth Amendment rights. [Casefile Document 7, at 15.] While the lawsuit was pending, Ericksen pleaded guilty in state court to misdemeanor possession of drug paraphernalia and was sentenced to one-month of probation. [Casefile Document 10, at 3.] The district court dismissed the civil lawsuit months later on July 1, and Ericksen appealed to the Sixth Circuit. [Casefile Document 7, at 15–16.] He raised *nineteen* appellate issues. *Id.* at 11–13.

The Sixth Circuit, in affirming the district court, rejected all of Ericksen's appellate issues. On the border issue specifically, the court wrote as follows:

> That D.E. subjectively did not intend to cross the border is also irrelevant. There is no reliable way for the CBP officers to tell the difference between a motorist who has just crossed the border or who intends to cross the border and a "turnaround motorist" who is at the border area by mistake. It would be dangerous (and quite stupid) for CBP officers to assume that every traveler who claims to be there by mistake—or who possesses an easily fabricated laminated card—is telling the truth, especially considering that D.E.'s vehicle was in the same lane as motorists arriving from Canada. CBP officers are not infallible lie detectors capable of correctly determining the subjective intent of travelers at the border. Instead, because the "Government's interest in preventing the entry of unwanted persons and effects is at its zenith at the international border," *Flores-Montano*, 541 U.S. at 152, officers may conduct suspicionless searches of vehicles at the border (or at its functional equivalent, *Almeida-Sanchez v. United States*, 413 U.S. 266, 272 (1973)) without regard to the reasons why motorists are at the border.

[Casefile Document 10, at 4.] One concurring judge agreed with Ericksen that the border search exception was inapplicable because Ericksen "did not cross the border and was not in the process of crossing the border when his vehicle was searched." *Id.* at 8. Accordingly, the concurrence would require reasonable suspicion in order to lawfully search Ericksen's car. *Id.* at 9.

Despite having lost in criminal and civil court, Ericksen was not done. He sued—again—and lost—again. [Casefile Document 11.]

3. Checkpoints

ILLINOIS V. LIDSTER

540 U.S. 419
Supreme Court of the United States
November 5, 2003, Argued; January 13, 2004, Decided
No. 02-1060

JUSTICE BREYER delivered the opinion of the Court.

This Fourth Amendment case focuses upon a highway checkpoint where police stopped motorists to ask them for information about a recent hit-and-run accident. We hold that the police stops were reasonable, hence, constitutional.

I

The relevant background is as follows: On Saturday, August 23, 1997, just after midnight, an unknown motorist traveling eastbound on a highway in Lombard, Illinois, struck and killed a 70-year-old bicyclist. The motorist drove off without identifying himself. About one week later at about the same time of night and at about the same place, local police set up a highway checkpoint designed to obtain more information about the accident from the motoring public.

Police cars with flashing lights partially blocked the eastbound lanes of the highway. The blockage forced traffic to slow down, leading to lines of up to 15 cars in each lane. As each vehicle drew up to the checkpoint, an officer would stop it for 10 to 15 seconds, ask the occupants whether they had seen anything happen there the previous weekend, and hand each driver a flyer. The flyer said "ALERT . . . FATAL HIT & RUN ACCIDENT" and requested "assistance in identifying the vehicle and driver in this accident which killed a 70 year old bicyclist."

Robert Lidster, the respondent, drove a minivan toward the checkpoint. As he approached the checkpoint, his van swerved, nearly hitting one of the officers. The officer smelled alcohol on Lidster's breath. He directed Lidster to a side street where another officer administered a sobriety test and then arrested Lidster. Lidster was tried and convicted in Illinois state court of driving under the influence of alcohol.

Lidster challenged the lawfulness of his arrest and conviction on the ground that the government had obtained much of the relevant evidence through use of a checkpoint stop that violated the Fourth Amendment. The trial court rejected that challenge. But an Illinois appellate court reached the opposite conclusion. The Illinois Supreme Court agreed with the appellate court. It held * * * that our decision in *Indianapolis v. Edmond*, 531 U.S. 32 (2000), required it to find the stop unconstitutional.

Because lower courts have reached different conclusions about this matter, we granted certiorari. We now reverse the Illinois Supreme Court's determination.

II

The Illinois Supreme Court basically held that our decision in *Edmond* governs the outcome of this case. We do not agree. *Edmond* involved a checkpoint at which police stopped vehicles to look for evidence of drug crimes committed by occupants of those vehicles. After stopping a vehicle at the checkpoint, police would examine (from outside the vehicle) the vehicle's interior; they would walk a drug-sniffing dog around the exterior; and, if they found sufficient evidence of drug (or other) crimes, they would arrest the vehicle's occupants. We found that police had set up this checkpoint primarily for general "crime control" purposes, i.e., "to detect evidence of ordinary criminal wrongdoing." We noted that the stop was made without individualized suspicion. And we held that the Fourth Amendment forbids such a stop, in the absence of special circumstances.

The checkpoint stop here differs significantly from that in *Edmond*. The stop's primary law enforcement purpose was not to determine whether a vehicle's occupants were committing a crime, but to ask vehicle occupants, as members of the public, for their help in providing information about a crime in all likelihood committed by others. The police expected the information elicited to help them apprehend, not the vehicle's occupants, but other individuals.

Edmond's language, as well as its context, makes clear that the constitutionality of this latter, information-seeking kind of stop was not then before the Court. *Edmond* refers to the subject matter of its holding as "stops justified only by the generalized and ever-present possibility that interrogation and inspection may reveal that *any given motorist has committed some crime.*" *Ibid.* (emphasis added). We concede that *Edmond* describes the law enforcement objective there in question as a "general interest in crime control," but it specifies that the phrase "general interest in crime control" does not refer to every "law enforcement" objective. We must read this and related general language in *Edmond* as we often read general language in judicial opinions—as referring in context to circumstances similar to the circumstances then before the Court and not referring to quite different circumstances that the Court was not then considering.

Neither do we believe, *Edmond* aside, that the Fourth Amendment would have us apply an *Edmond*-type rule of automatic unconstitutionality to brief, information-seeking highway stops of the kind now before us. For one thing, the fact that such stops normally lack individualized suspicion cannot by itself determine the constitutional outcome. As in *Edmond*, the stop here at issue involves a motorist. The Fourth Amendment does not treat a motorist's car as his castle. And special law enforcement concerns will sometimes justify highway stops without individualized suspicion. *See Michigan Dep't of State Police v. Sitz*, 496 U.S. 444 (1990) (sobriety checkpoint); *Martinez-Fuerte, supra* (Border Patrol checkpoint). Moreover, unlike *Edmond*, the context here (seeking information from the public) is one in which, by definition, the concept of individualized suspicion has little role to play. Like certain other forms of police activity, say, crowd control or public safety, an information-seeking stop is not the kind of event that involves suspicion, or lack of suspicion, of the relevant individual.

For another thing, information-seeking highway stops are less likely to provoke anxiety or to prove intrusive. The stops are likely brief. The police are not likely to ask questions designed to elicit self-incriminating information. And citizens will often react positively when police simply ask for their help as "responsible citizen[s]" to "give whatever information they may have to aid in law enforcement." *Miranda v. Arizona*, 384 U.S. 436, 477–478 (1966).

Further, the law ordinarily permits police to seek the voluntary cooperation of members of the public in the investigation of a crime. * * * That, in part, is because voluntary requests play a vital role in police investigatory work.

The importance of soliciting the public's assistance is offset to some degree by the need to stop a motorist to obtain that help—a need less likely present where a pedestrian, not a motorist, is involved. The difference is significant in light of our determinations that such an involuntary stop amounts to a "seizure" in Fourth Amendment terms. *E.g., Edmond*, 531 U.S., at 40. That difference, however, is not important enough to justify an *Edmond*-type rule here. After all, as we have said, the motorist stop will likely be brief. Any accompanying traffic delay should prove no more onerous than many that typically accompany normal traffic congestion. And the resulting voluntary questioning of a motorist is as likely to prove important for police investigation as is the questioning of a pedestrian. Given these considerations, it would seem anomalous were the law (1) ordinarily to allow police freely to seek the voluntary cooperation of pedestrians but (2) ordinarily to forbid police to seek similar voluntary cooperation from motorists.

Finally, we do not believe that an *Edmond*-type rule is needed to prevent an unreasonable proliferation of police checkpoints. Practical considerations—namely, limited police resources and community hostility to related traffic tie-ups—seem likely to inhibit any such proliferation. And, of course, the Fourth Amendment's normal insistence that the stop be reasonable in context will still provide an important legal limitation on police use of this kind of information-seeking checkpoint.

These considerations, taken together, convince us that an *Edmond*-type presumptive rule of unconstitutionality does not apply here. That does not mean the stop is automatically, or even presumptively, constitutional. It simply means that we must judge its reasonableness, hence, its constitutionality, on the basis of the individual circumstances. * * *

III

* * * We hold that the stop was constitutional.

The relevant public concern was grave. Police were investigating a crime that had resulted in a human death. No one denies the police's need to obtain more information at that time. And the stop's objective was to help find the perpetrator of a specific and known crime, not of unknown crimes of a general sort.

The stop advanced this grave public concern to a significant degree. The police appropriately tailored their checkpoint stops to fit important criminal investigatory needs. The stops took place about one week after the hit-and-run accident, on the same highway near the location of the accident, and at about the same time of night. And police used the stops to obtain information from drivers, some of whom might well have been in the vicinity of the crime at the time it occurred.

Most importantly, the stops interfered only minimally with liberty of the sort the Fourth Amendment seeks to protect. Viewed objectively, each stop required only a brief wait in line—a very few minutes at most. Contact with the police lasted only a few seconds. Police contact consisted simply of a request for information and the distribution of a flyer. Viewed subjectively, the contact provided little reason for anxiety or alarm. The police stopped all vehicles systematically. And there is no allegation here that the police acted in a discriminatory or otherwise unlawful manner while questioning motorists during stops.

For these reasons we conclude that the checkpoint stop was constitutional.

The judgment of the Illinois Supreme Court is reversed.

JUSTICE STEVENS, with whom JUSTICE SOUTER and JUSTICE GINSBURG join, concurring in part and dissenting in part.

[Omitted.]

QUESTIONS, COMMENTS, CONCERNS?

1. **Spot checks instead of checkpoints?** In *Delaware v. Prouse*, 440 U.S. 648 (1979), a New Castle County, Delaware, patrolman pulled over respondent's vehicle "to check the driver's license and registration." The patrolman, however, had neither reasonable suspicion nor probable cause to believe that a traffic violation occurred or that criminal activity was afoot. The

patrolman smelled marijuana as he walked toward respondent's car and then saw marijuana in plain view on the vehicle's floor. The trial court suppressed the marijuana, "finding the stop and detention to have been wholly capricious," and the Delaware Supreme Court affirmed. The Supreme Court affirmed and held that, "except in those situations in which there is at least articulable and reasonable suspicion that a motorist is unlicensed or that an automobile is not registered, or that either the vehicle or an occupant is otherwise subject to seizure for violation of law, stopping an automobile and detaining the driver in order to check his driver's license and the registration of the automobile are unreasonable under the Fourth Amendment." The Court reasoned that "[t]he marginal contribution to roadway safety possibly resulting from a system of spot checks" did not outweigh concerns with the "unbridled discretion of law enforcement officials."

The Court did, however, leave the door open to the prospect of law enforcement using "spot checks" in the future. In particular, it cautioned:

> This holding does not preclude the State of Delaware or other States from developing methods for spot checks that involve less intrusion or that do not involve the unconstrained exercise of discretion. Questioning of all oncoming traffic at roadblock-type stops is one possible alternative. We hold only that persons in automobiles on public roadways may not for that reason alone have their travel and privacy interfered with at the unbridled discretion of police officers.

2. Other checkpoint cases. Unlike some other areas of the Fourth Amendment, the Supreme Court has not considered a voluminous number of checkpoint-related issues. In *Michigan Department of State Police v. Sitz*, 496 U.S. 444 (1990), the Court considered whether a state's use of highway sobriety checkpoints violated the Fourth Amendment. The Michigan checkpoint program at issue called for setting up sobriety checkpoints along selected state roads. All of the vehicles that passed through the particular checkpoint would be stopped, and drivers were examined for signs of intoxication. On the day before a checkpoint in Saginaw County became operational, respondents filed a complaint in state court "seeking declaratory and injunctive relief from potential subjection to the checkpoints." The Supreme Court held that Michigan's checkpoint program did not violate the Fourth Amendment. It reasoned, "the balance of the State's interest in preventing drunken driving, the extent to which this system can reasonably be said to advance that interest, and the degree of intrusion upon individual motorists who are briefly stopped, weighs in favor of the state program."

Notably, the Court's discretionary concerns in *Prouse* did not exist in *Sitz* because, unlike *Prouse*, the *Sitz* checkpoints were selected based on "guidelines, and uniformed police officers stop[ped] every approaching vehicle." Thus, unlike *Prouse*, respondents were not challenging "random highway stops."

3. Turning around at a checkpoint. After learning about *Sitz*, do you think drivers can turn around before approaching a DUI checkpoint? As a general rule, turning around by itself, and without more, does not provide reasonable suspicion to justify a traffic stop. *See, e.g., Hawaii v. Heapy*, 151 P.3d 764, 786 (Haw. 2007); *Bass v. Commonwealth*, 525 S.E.2d 921, 925 (Va. 2000); *Commonwealth v. Scavello*, 734 A.2d 386, 388 (Pa. 1999); *State v. McCleery*, 560 N.W.2d 789, 793 (Neb. 1997); *Howard v. Voshell*, 621 A.2d 804, 808 (Del. Super. Ct. 1992); *State v. Powell*, 591 A.2d 1306, 1308 (Me. 1991); *State v. Binion*, 900 S.W.2d 702, 706 (Tenn. Crim. App. 1994); *Jorgensen v. State*, 428 S.E.2d 440, 440 (Ga. Ct. App. 1993); *State v. Talbot*, 792 P.2d 489, 495 (Utah Ct. App. 1990); *Pooler v. Motor Vehicles Div.*, 746 P.2d 716, 718 (Or. Ct. App. 1987). Some courts, however, have held that a driver's avoidance of a highway checkpoint automatically gives an officer reasonable suspicion to detain the motorist. *See, e.g., State v. Thill*, 474 N.W.2d 86, 88 (S.D. 1991); *Smith v. State*, 515 So. 2d 149, 152 (Ala. Crim. App. 1987); *Coffman v. Arkansas*, 759 S.W.2d 573, 576 (Ark. Ct. App. 1988); *Boches v. Mississippi*, 506 So. 2d 254, 264 (Miss. 1987); *Steinbeck v. Commonwealth*, 862 S.W.2d 912, 914 (Ky. Ct. App. 1993).

But even in jurisdictions where avoiding a checkpoint does not provide reasonable suspicion for an officer to stop the avoiding vehicle, think back to *Whren v. United States* (Chapter 4). Remember that, pursuant to *Whren*, officers need, at most, probable cause to stop a vehicle for committing a traffic infraction. And following that lawful traffic stop, the officer can freely be on the lookout for signs of intoxication.

4. "Information seeking" vs. "crime control." At first blush, *Sitz* appears difficult to reconcile with *Lidster*. But the *Lidster* Court had little difficulty reconciling *Sitz*, noting as you read above that "special law enforcement concerns will sometimes justify highway stops without individualized suspicion."

Stepping back from this collection of cases—*Lidster, Sitz, Prouse*, and *Edmond*—there is at least one thread that runs through the cases that may help us synthesize why stop checkpoints violate the Fourth Amendment while others do not. The general rationale appears to turn on whether police checkpoints are premised on seeking information (*Lidster*) or roadway safety (*Sitz*) or, instead, seeking to engage in generic crime control (*Edmond*). The former is permissible whereas the latter is unconstitutional absent individualized suspicion.

5. The *Lidster* search was constitutional, but was it an unlawful seizure? Note a subtle secondary question in *Lidster* is whether Robert Lidster was seized at the information-seeking highway stop. The *Lidster* Court seemingly implied that he was not. Lidster, said the Court, was detained for only ten to fifteen seconds for what began as information-gathering purposes. But that's contrary to the Supreme Court's view of police checkpoints elsewhere. *United States v. Martinez-Fuerte*, 428 U.S. 543, 556 (1976) ("It is agreed that checkpoint stops are 'seizures' within the meaning of the Fourth Amendment."). And the Ninth Circuit, for example, has held that a seizure occurred at a national park entrance when the park ranger directed a vehicle to pull off the road following a routine interaction at the information station. *United States v. Faulkner*, 450 F.3d 466, 469–70 (9th Cir. 2006).

The *Faulkner* example reminds us that it is possible to analyze many of the cases in this chapter as seizure cases. That is important to remember because it offers defense litigants alternative arguments favoring application of the Fourth Amendment. *Accord Mills v. District of Columbia*, 571 F.3d 1304, 1308 (D.C. Cir. 2009) (noting that "a seizure occurs when a vehicle is stopped at a police checkpoint"). Remember, the Fourth Amendment applies when government conduct constitutes a "search" *or* "seizure." *E.g., Maxwell v. City of New York*, 102 F.3d 664, 668 n.2 (2d Cir. 1996) (considering whether a vehicle stop could constitute a search or seizure for Fourth Amendment purposes).

But even if a seizure occurred, that does not end the inquiry into whether the police conduct at issue is constitutional. Rather, the analysis shifts to determining whether the seizure was "reasonable." Evaluating the reasonableness of a seizure "involves a weighing of the gravity of the public concerns served by the seizure, the degree to which the seizure advances the public interest, and the severity of the interference with individual liberty." *Brown v. Texas*, 443 U.S. 47, 50–51 (1979).

6.   Was Ericksen "seized"? Let's apply the seizure theory discussed in the immediately preceding note. We know that police searched Ericksen's vehicle without a warrant and that the border search exception applied to justify that search. But what about the seizure analysis? Was Ericksen unlawfully seized while Border Patrol Agents searched his vehicle? Ericksen argued, in part, that no case "holds that it is reasonable for the Border Patrol to detain a motorist beyond the time needed to ascertain that he is turning back from a border crossing." [Casefile Document 2, at 9.] The issue seemingly gets conflated with the border search issue and receives very little attention from either the suppression court or the Circuit Court on appeal. [Casefile Document 4, at 11; Casefile Document 5, at 4.] In defense of those courts, however, arguing that Ericksen was unlawfully seized is an argument better left for checkpoints unrelated to the border. Indeed, the limited analysis from both the suppression court and Circuit Court is likely due to the understanding of the border search exception as permitting a limited seizure. That is, in the border context, a "routine border search" permits a corresponding Fourth Amendment seizure. *E.g., United States v. Montoya De Hernandez*, 473 U.S. 531, 539–40 (1985).

4. Schools

VERNONIA SCH. DIST. 47J v. ACTON

515 U.S. 646
Supreme Court of the United States
March 28, 1995, Argued; June 26, 1995, Decided
No. 94-590

JUSTICE SCALIA delivered the opinion of the Court.

The Student Athlete Drug Policy adopted by School District 47J in the town of Vernonia, Oregon, authorizes random urinalysis drug testing of students who participate in the District's school athletics programs. We granted certiorari to decide whether this violates the Fourth and Fourteenth Amendments to the United States Constitution.

I

A

Petitioner Vernonia School District 47J (District) operates one high school and three grade schools in the logging community of Vernonia, Oregon. As elsewhere in small-town America, school sports play a prominent role in the town's life, and student athletes are admired in their schools and in the community.

Drugs had not been a major problem in Vernonia schools. In the mid-to-late 1980's, however, teachers and administrators observed a sharp increase in drug use. Students began to speak out about their attraction to the drug culture, and to boast that there was nothing the school could do about it. Along with more drugs came more disciplinary problems. Between 1988 and 1989 the number of disciplinary referrals in Vernonia schools rose to more than twice the number reported in the early 1980's, and several students were suspended. Students became increasingly rude during class; outbursts of profane language became common.

Not only were student athletes included among the drug users but, as the District Court found, athletes were the leaders of the drug culture. This caused the District's administrators particular concern, since drug use increases the risk of sports-related injury. Expert testimony at the trial confirmed the deleterious effects of drugs on motivation, memory, judgment, reaction, coordination, and performance. The high school football and wrestling coach witnessed a severe sternum injury suffered by a wrestler, and various omissions of safety procedures and misexecutions by football players, all attributable in his belief to the effects of drug use.

Initially, the District responded to the drug problem by offering special classes, speakers, and presentations designed to deter drug use. It even brought in a specially trained dog to detect drugs, but the drug problem persisted. * * *

At that point, District officials began considering a drug-testing program. They held a parent "input night" to discuss the proposed Student Athlete Drug Policy (Policy), and the parents in attendance gave their unanimous approval. The school board approved the Policy for implementation in the fall of 1989. Its expressed purpose is to prevent student athletes from using drugs, to protect their health and safety, and to provide drug users with assistance programs.

B

The Policy applies to all students participating in interscholastic athletics. Students wishing to play sports must sign a form consenting to the testing and must obtain the written consent of their parents. Athletes are tested at the beginning of the season for their sport. In addition, once each week of the season the names of the athletes are placed in a "pool" from which a student, with the supervision of two adults, blindly draws the names of 10% of the athletes for random testing. Those selected are notified and tested that same day, if possible.

The student to be tested completes a specimen control form which bears an assigned number. Prescription medications that the student is taking must be identified by providing a copy of the prescription or a doctor's authorization. The student then enters an empty locker room accompanied by an adult monitor of the same sex. Each boy selected produces a sample at a urinal, remaining fully clothed with his back to the monitor, who stands approximately 12 to 15 feet behind the student. Monitors may (though do not always) watch the student while he produces the sample, and they listen for normal sounds of urination. Girls produce samples in an enclosed bathroom stall, so that they can be heard but not observed. After the sample is produced, it is given to the monitor, who checks it for temperature and tampering and then transfers it to a vial.

The samples are sent to an independent laboratory, which routinely tests them for amphetamines, cocaine, and marijuana. Other drugs, such as LSD, may be screened at the request of the District, but the identity of a particular student does not determine which drugs will be tested. The laboratory's procedures are 99.94% accurate. The District follows strict procedures regarding the chain of custody and access to test results. The laboratory does not know the identity of the students whose samples it tests. It is authorized to mail written test reports only to the superintendent and to provide test results to District personnel by telephone only after the requesting official recites a code confirming his authority. Only the superintendent, principals, vice-principals, and athletic directors have access to test results, and the results are not kept for more than one year.

If a sample tests positive, a second test is administered as soon as possible to confirm the result. If the second test is negative, no further action is taken. If the second test is positive, the athlete's parents are notified, and the school principal convenes a meeting with the student and his parents, at which the student is given the option of (1) participating for six weeks in an assistance program that includes weekly urinalysis, or (2) suffering suspension from athletics for the remainder of the current season and the next athletic season. The student is then retested prior to the start of the next athletic season for which he or she is eligible. The Policy states that a second offense results in automatic imposition of option (2); a third offense in suspension for the remainder of the current season and the next two athletic seasons.

C

In the fall of 1991, respondent James Acton, then a seventh grader, signed up to play football at one of the District's grade schools. He was denied participation, however, because he and his parents refused to sign the testing consent forms. The Actons filed suit, seeking declaratory and injunctive relief from enforcement of the Policy on the grounds that it violated the Fourth and Fourteenth Amendments to the United States Constitution and Article I, § 9, of the Oregon Constitution. After a bench trial, the District Court entered an order denying the claims on the merits and dismissing the action. The United States Court of Appeals for the Ninth Circuit reversed * * *. We granted certiorari.

II

The Fourth Amendment to the United States Constitution provides that the Federal Government shall not violate "the right of the people to be secure in their persons, houses, papers, and effects, against unreasonable searches and seizures . . . ." We have held that the Fourteenth Amendment extends this constitutional guarantee to searches and seizures by state officers, including public school officials, *New Jersey v. T. L. O.*, 469 U.S. 325, 336–337 (1985). * * *

As the text of the Fourth Amendment indicates, the ultimate measure of the constitutionality of a governmental search is "reasonableness." At least in a case such as this, where there was no clear practice, either approving or disapproving the type of search at issue, at the time the constitutional provision was enacted, whether a particular search meets the reasonableness standard " 'is judged by balancing its intrusion on the individual's Fourth Amendment interests against its promotion of legitimate governmental interests.' " Where a search is undertaken by law enforcement officials to discover evidence of criminal wrongdoing, this Court has said that reasonableness generally requires the obtaining of a judicial warrant. Warrants cannot be issued, of course, without the showing of probable cause required by the Warrant Clause. But a warrant is not required to establish the reasonableness of all government searches; and when a warrant is not required (and the Warrant Clause therefore not applicable), probable cause is not invariably required either. A search unsupported by probable cause can be constitutional, we have said, "when special needs, beyond the normal need for law enforcement, make the warrant and probable-cause requirement impracticable."

We have found such "special needs" to exist in the public school context. There, the warrant requirement "would unduly interfere with the maintenance of the swift and informal disciplinary procedures [that are] needed," and "strict adherence to the requirement that searches be based on probable cause" would undercut "the substantial need of teachers and administrators for freedom to maintain order in the schools." *T. L. O.*, 469 U.S. at 340, 341. The school search we approved in *T. L. O.*, while not based on probable cause, was based on individualized suspicion of wrongdoing. As we explicitly acknowledged, however, " 'the Fourth Amendment imposes no irreducible requirement of such suspicion.' " We have upheld suspicionless searches and seizures to conduct drug testing of railroad personnel involved in train accidents, to conduct random drug testing of federal customs officers who carry arms or are involved in drug interdiction, and to maintain automobile checkpoints looking for illegal immigrants and contraband.

III

The first factor to be considered is the nature of the privacy interest upon which the search here at issue intrudes. The Fourth Amendment does not protect all subjective expectations of privacy, but only those that society recognizes as "legitimate." *T. L. O.*, 469 U.S. at 338. What expectations are legitimate varies, of course, with context, depending, for example, upon whether the individual asserting the privacy interest is at home, at work, in a car, or in a public park. In addition, the legitimacy of certain privacy expectations vis-a-vis the State may depend upon the individual's legal relationship with the State. * * * Central, in our view, to the present case is the fact that the subjects of the Policy are (1) children, who (2) have been committed to the temporary custody of the State as schoolmaster.

Traditionally at common law, and still today, unemancipated minors lack some of the most fundamental rights of self-determination—including even the right of liberty in its narrow sense, i.e., the right to come and go at will. They are subject, even as to their physical freedom, to the control of their parents or guardians. When parents place minor children in private schools for their education, the teachers and administrators of those schools stand *in loco parentis* over the children entrusted to them. In fact, the tutor or schoolmaster is the very prototype of that status. * * *

In *T.L.O.* we rejected the notion that public schools, like private schools, exercise only parental power over their students, which of course is not subject to constitutional constraints. Such a view of things * * * is inconsistent with our prior decisions treating school officials as state actors for purposes of the Due Process and Free Speech Clauses. But while denying that the State's power over schoolchildren is formally no more than the delegated power of their parents, *T. L. O.* did not deny, but indeed emphasized, that the nature of that power is custodial and tutelary, permitting a degree of supervision and control that could not be exercised over free adults. * * *

Fourth Amendment rights, no less than First and Fourteenth Amendment rights, are different in public schools than elsewhere; the "reasonableness" inquiry cannot disregard the schools' custodial and tutelary responsibility for children. For their own good and that of their classmates, public school children are routinely required to submit to various physical examinations, and to be vaccinated against various diseases. * * * Particularly with regard to medical examinations and procedures, therefore, "students within the school environment have a lesser expectation of privacy than members of the population generally."

Legitimate privacy expectations are even less with regard to student athletes. School sports are not for the bashful. They require "suiting up" before each practice or event, and showering and changing afterwards. Public school locker rooms, the usual sites for these activities, are not notable for the privacy they afford. The locker rooms in Vernonia are typical: No individual dressing rooms are provided; shower heads are lined up along a wall, unseparated by any sort of partition or curtain; not even all the toilet stalls have doors. * * *

There is an additional respect in which school athletes have a reduced expectation of privacy. By choosing to "go out for the team," they voluntarily subject themselves to a degree of regulation even higher than that imposed on students generally. In Vernonia's public schools, they must submit to a preseason physical exam (James testified that his included the giving of a urine sample), they must acquire adequate insurance coverage or sign an insurance waiver, maintain a minimum grade point average, and comply with any "rules of conduct, dress, training hours and related matters as may be established for each sport by the head coach and athletic director with the principal's approval." Somewhat like adults who choose to participate in a "closely regulated industry," students who voluntarily participate in school athletics have reason to expect intrusions upon normal rights and privileges, including privacy.

IV

Having considered the scope of the legitimate expectation of privacy at issue here, we turn next to the character of the intrusion that is complained of. We [have] recognized * * * that collecting the samples for urinalysis intrudes upon "an excretory function traditionally shielded by great privacy." We noted, however, that the degree of intrusion depends upon the manner in which production of the urine sample is monitored. Under the

District's Policy, male students produce samples at a urinal along a wall. They remain fully clothed and are only observed from behind, if at all. Female students produce samples in an enclosed stall, with a female monitor standing outside listening only for sounds of tampering. These conditions are nearly identical to those typically encountered in public restrooms, which men, women, and especially school children use daily. Under such conditions, the privacy interests compromised by the process of obtaining the urine sample are in our view negligible.

The other privacy-invasive aspect of urinalysis is, of course, the information it discloses concerning the state of the subject's body, and the materials he has ingested. In this regard it is significant that the tests at issue here look only for drugs, and not for whether the student is, for example, epileptic, pregnant, or diabetic. Moreover, the drugs for which the samples are screened are standard, and do not vary according to the identity of the student. And finally, the results of the tests are disclosed only to a limited class of school personnel who have a need to know; and they are not turned over to law enforcement authorities or used for any internal disciplinary function. * * *

The General Authorization Form that respondents refused to sign, which refusal was the basis for James's exclusion from the sports program, said only (in relevant part): "I . . . authorize the Vernonia School District to conduct a test on a urine specimen which I provide to test for drugs and/or alcohol use. I also authorize the release of information concerning the results of such a test to the Vernonia School District and to the parents and/or guardians of the student." While the practice of the District seems to have been to have a school official take medication information from the student at the time of the test, that practice is not set forth in, or required by, the Policy, which says simply: "Student athletes who . . . are or have been taking prescription medication must provide verification (either by a copy of the prescription or by doctor's authorization) prior to being tested." It may well be that, if and when James was selected for random testing at a time that he was taking medication, the School District would have permitted him to provide the requested information in a confidential manner—for example, in a sealed envelope delivered to the testing lab. Nothing in the Policy contradicts that, and when respondents choose, in effect, to challenge the Policy on its face, we will not assume the worst. Accordingly, * * * the invasion of privacy was not significant.

V

Finally, we turn to consider the nature and immediacy of the governmental concern at issue here, and the efficacy of this means for meeting it. * * *

That the nature of the concern is important—indeed, perhaps compelling—can hardly be doubted. Deterring drug use by our Nation's schoolchildren is at least as important as enhancing efficient enforcement of the Nation's laws against the importation of drugs * * *. School years are the time when the physical, psychological, and addictive effects of drugs are most severe. * * * And of course the effects of a drug-infested school are visited not just upon the users, but upon the entire student body and faculty, as the educational process is disrupted. In the present case, moreover, the necessity for the State to act is magnified by the fact that this evil is being visited not just upon individuals at large, but upon children for whom it has undertaken a special responsibility of care and direction. Finally, it must not be lost sight of that this program is directed more narrowly to drug use by school athletes, where the risk of immediate physical harm to the drug user or those with whom he is playing his sport is particularly high. * * *

As for the immediacy of the District's concerns: We are not inclined to question—indeed, we could not possibly find clearly erroneous—the District Court's conclusion that "a large segment of the student body, particularly those involved in interscholastic athletics, was in a state of rebellion," that "disciplinary actions had reached 'epidemic proportions,'" and that "the rebellion was being fueled by alcohol and drug abuse as well as by the student's misperceptions about the drug culture." * * *

As to the efficacy of this means for addressing the problem: It seems to us self-evident that a drug problem largely fueled by the "role model" effect of athletes' drug use, and of particular danger to athletes, is effectively addressed by making sure that athletes do not use drugs. * * *

VI

Taking into account all the factors we have considered above—the decreased expectation of privacy, the relative unobtrusiveness of the search, and the severity of the need met by the search—we conclude Vernonia's Policy is reasonable and hence constitutional.

We caution against the assumption that suspicionless drug testing will readily pass constitutional muster in other contexts. The most significant element in this case is the first we discussed: that the Policy was undertaken in furtherance of the government's responsibilities, under a public school system, as guardian and tutor of children entrusted to its care. * * * Given the findings of need made by the District Court, we conclude that in the present case it is. * * *

* * *

* * * We therefore vacate the judgment, and remand the case to the Court of Appeals for further proceedings consistent with this opinion.

It is so ordered.

JUSTICE GINSBURG, concurring.

[Omitted.]

JUSTICE O'CONNOR, with whom JUSTICE STEVENS and JUSTICE SOUTER join, dissenting.

[Omitted.]

QUESTIONS, COMMENTS, CONCERNS?

1.   **The Fourth Amendment in private schools.** Notice the *Vernonia* Court's limitation: "the Policy was undertaken in furtherance of the government's responsibilities, *under a public school system*, as guardian and tutor of children entrusted to its care." That begs the obvious question: what about private schools? You may have caught that *Vernonia* also answers that question, noting that private schools "exercise only parental power over their students, which of course is not subject to constitutional constraints." Accordingly, although public school students retain some limited Fourth Amendment protections, those protections do not exist for students at private schools.

On a related note, you may be interested to know that most charter schools are considered public schools for constitutional analysis purposes. "Charter schools and 'traditional public schools' are similar in that they are directly subsidized by a combination of primarily state and local taxes based on their enrollments." Preston C. Green et al., *Having It Both Ways: How Charter Schools Try to Obtain Funding of Public Schools and the Autonomy of Private Schools*, 63 EMORY L.J. 303, 303 (2013).

2.   **Policing and schools.** In part because of the increase in school shootings, there has been an increase in police presence in schools. That, in turn, has blurred the line between traditional misbehavior and criminal behavior. "In some states, for example, a fistfight can mean a suspension while in North Carolina a simple affray, as it is called, can mean adult court for a 16-year-old." Gary Fields & John R. Emshwiller, *For More Teens, Arrests by Police Replace School Discipline*, WSJ.COM (Oct. 20, 2014), https://www.wsj.com/articles/for-more-teens-arrests-by-police-replace-school-discipline-1413858602. Apart from how a state might define school misbehavior, there are simply more police in schools today. According to a 2013 study from the Congressional Research Service, the number of school police officers rose 55% over a ten-year period from 1997 to 2007. *Id.*

Because of the increase of law enforcement personnel, it's critical to distinguish *who* conducts a school search. In practice, this distinction gives schools significant leeway to conduct searches, especially in this age of school shootings when students, teachers, and administrators are incredibly vigilant and on edge. As *T. L. O.* makes clear, searches of students by school administrators requires only reasonable suspicion. That is, according to *T. L. O.*, "reasonable grounds for suspecting that the search will turn up evidence that the student has violated or is violating either the law or the rules of the school." By contrast, the probable cause standard governs searches by law enforcement. *E.g., State v. Heirtzler*, 789 A.2d 634, 636 (N.H. 2001); *In re Thomas B.D.*, 486 S.E.2d 498, 500 (S.C. Ct. App. 1997); *State v. Tywayne H.*, 933 P.2d 251, 254 (N.M. Ct. App. 1997).

3.   What about competitive, *non*-athletic activities? In *Bd. of Educ. v. Earls*, 536 U.S. 822, 825 (2002), a school district required all students participating in competitive extracurricular activities to submit to drug testing. Activities subject to the policy included "the Academic Team, Future Farmers of America, Future Homemakers of America, band, choir, pom, cheerleading, and athletics." In a 5–4 opinion, a majority of the Court upheld the policy by finding it was "a reasonable means of furthering the School District's important interest in preventing and deterring drug use among its schoolchildren." The Court reasoned in part that urine collection, as the policy called for, was "minimally intrusive," and the test results were put to "limited uses."

As we consider the impact of *Earls*, recall that state law may provide a greater degree of protection than federal law. *See York v. Wahkiakum Sch. Dist. No. 200*, 178 P.3d 995 (Wash. 2008) (rejecting the special needs exception for a random drug test of student athletes and holding that, in the absence of individualized suspicion, the drug testing violated the students' right to privacy). *But see Hageman v. Goshen Cnty. Sch. Dist. No. 1*, 256 P.3d 487 (Wy. 2011) (treating a student's mere participation in an extracurricular activity as consent to search).

4.   Beyond the Fourth Amendment. Failing the drug policy in *Vernonia* called for participation in a remedial assistance program or suspension from athletic programming. But what if the policy automatically called for suspension or even dismissal of all students who fail their drug testing? Criminal law considerations aside, school-based punishment for drug possession/use presumably provides robust due process protections. But what precisely does that entail? Notice of the charges from the school district? A hearing? Notice of the standard of proof? Do you think an appellate process is also required? *See Goss v. Lopez*, 419 U.S. 565, 581–82 (1975) (holding that the imposition of ten-day high school student suspensions without a hearing violated the students' due process rights); N.Y. EDUC. LAW § 3214(3)(c)(1) (McKinney 2018) (mandating certain due process requirements before a school can suspend a student for more than five days). Admittedly, this is not a class on education law, but it is worth thinking about the considerable intersection in this block of material between criminal and civil law.

SAFFORD UNIFIED SCH. DIST. #1 V. REDDING

557 U.S. 364
Supreme Court of the United States
April 21, 2009, Argued; June 25, 2009, Decided
No. 08-479

JUSTICE SOUTER delivered the opinion of the Court.

The issue here is whether a 13-year-old student's Fourth Amendment right was violated when she was subjected to a search of her bra and underpants by school officials acting on reasonable suspicion that she had brought forbidden prescription and over-the-counter drugs to school. Because there were no reasons to suspect the drugs presented a danger or were concealed in her underwear, we hold that the search did violate the Constitution * * *.

I

The events immediately prior to the search in question began in 13-year-old Savana Redding's math class at Safford Middle School one October day in 2003. The assistant principal of the school, Kerry Wilson, came into the room and asked Savana to go to his office. There, he showed her a day planner, unzipped and open flat on his desk, in which there were several knives, lighters, a permanent marker, and a cigarette. Wilson asked Savana whether the planner was hers; she said it was, but that a few days before she had lent it to her friend, Marissa Glines. Savana stated that none of the items in the planner belonged to her.

Wilson then showed Savana four white prescription-strength ibuprofen 400-mg pills, and one over-the-counter blue naproxen 200-mg pill, all used for pain and inflammation but banned under school rules without advance permission. He asked Savana if she knew anything about the pills. Savana answered that she did not. Wilson then told Savana that he had received a report that she was giving these pills to fellow students; Savana denied it and agreed to let Wilson search her belongings. Helen Romero, an administrative assistant, came into the office, and together with Wilson they searched Savana's backpack, finding nothing.

At that point, Wilson instructed Romero to take Savana to the school nurse's office to search her clothes for pills. Romero and the nurse, Peggy Schwallier, asked Savana to remove her jacket, socks, and shoes, leaving her in stretch pants and a T-shirt (both without pockets), which she was then asked to remove. Finally, Savana was told to pull her bra out and to the side and shake it, and to pull out the elastic on her underpants, thus exposing her breasts and pelvic area to some degree. No pills were found.

Savana's mother filed suit against Safford Unified School District #1, Wilson, Romero, and Schwallier for conducting a strip search in violation of Savana's Fourth Amendment rights. The individuals (hereinafter petitioners) moved for summary judgment * * *. The District Court for the

District of Arizona granted the motion on the ground that there was no Fourth Amendment violation, and a panel of the Ninth Circuit affirmed.

A closely divided Circuit sitting en banc, however, reversed.

We granted certiorari * * *.

II

* * * In [*New Jersey v. T. L. O.*, 469 U.S. 325 (1985)], we recognized that the school setting "requires some modification of the level of suspicion of illicit activity needed to justify a search," and held that for searches by school officials "a careful balancing of governmental and private interests suggests that the public interest is best served by a Fourth Amendment standard of reasonableness that stops short of probable cause." We have thus applied a standard of reasonable suspicion to determine the legality of a school administrator's search of a student, and have held that a school search "will be permissible in its scope when the measures adopted are reasonably related to the objectives of the search and not excessively intrusive in light of the age and sex of the student and the nature of the infraction." * * *

III

A

In this case, the school's policies strictly prohibit the nonmedical use, possession, or sale of any drug on school grounds, including " '[a]ny prescription or over-the-counter drug, except those for which permission to use in school has been granted pursuant to Board policy.' "[1] A week before Savana was searched, another student, Jordan Romero (no relation of the school's administrative assistant), told the principal and Assistant Principal Wilson that "certain students were bringing drugs and weapons on campus," and that he had been sick after taking some pills that "he got from a classmate." On the morning of October 8, the same boy handed Wilson a white pill that he said Marissa Glines had given him. He told Wilson that students were planning to take the pills at lunch.

Wilson learned from Peggy Schwallier, the school nurse, that the pill was Ibuprofen 400 mg, available only by prescription. Wilson then called

---

[1] When the object of a school search is the enforcement of a school rule, a valid search assumes, of course, the rule's legitimacy. But the legitimacy of the rule usually goes without saying as it does here. The Court said plainly in *New Jersey v. T. L. O.*, 469 U.S. 325, 342, n.9 (1985), that standards of conduct for schools are for school administrators to determine without second-guessing by courts lacking the experience to appreciate what may be needed. Except in patently arbitrary instances, Fourth Amendment analysis takes the rule as a given, as it obviously should do in this case. There is no need here either to explain the imperative of keeping drugs out of schools, or to explain the reasons for the school's rule banning all drugs, no matter how benign, without advance permission. Teachers are not pharmacologists trained to identify pills and powders, and an effective drug ban has to be enforceable fast. The plenary ban makes sense, and there is no basis to claim that the search was unreasonable owing to some defect or shortcoming of the rule it was aimed at enforcing.

Marissa out of class. Outside the classroom, Marissa's teacher handed Wilson the day planner, found within Marissa's reach, containing various contraband items. Wilson escorted Marissa back to his office.

In the presence of Helen Romero, Wilson requested Marissa to turn out her pockets and open her wallet. Marissa produced a blue pill, several white ones, and a razor blade. Wilson asked where the blue pill came from, and Marissa answered, " 'I guess it slipped in when she gave me the IBU 400s.' " When Wilson asked whom she meant, Marissa replied, " 'Savana Redding.' " Wilson then enquired about the day planner and its contents; Marissa denied knowing anything about them. Wilson did not ask Marissa any followup questions to determine whether there was any likelihood that Savana presently had pills: neither asking when Marissa received the pills from Savana nor where Savana might be hiding them.

Schwallier did not immediately recognize the blue pill, but information provided through a poison control hotline indicated that the pill was a 200-mg dose of an anti-inflammatory drug, generically called naproxen, available over the counter. At Wilson's direction, Marissa was then subjected to a search of her bra and underpants by Romero and Schwallier, as Savana was later on. The search revealed no additional pills.

It was at this juncture that Wilson called Savana into his office and showed her the day planner. Their conversation established that Savana and Marissa were on friendly terms: while she denied knowledge of the contraband, Savana admitted that the day planner was hers and that she had lent it to Marissa. Wilson had other reports of their friendship from staff members, who had identified Savana and Marissa as part of an unusually rowdy group at the school's opening dance in August, during which alcohol and cigarettes were found in the girls' bathroom. Wilson had reason to connect the girls with this contraband, for Wilson knew that Jordan Romero had told the principal that before the dance, he had been at a party at Savana's house where alcohol was served. Marissa's statement that the pills came from Savana was thus sufficiently plausible to warrant suspicion that Savana was involved in pill distribution.

This suspicion of Wilson's was enough to justify a search of Savana's backpack and outer clothing.[3] If a student is reasonably suspected of giving out contraband pills, she is reasonably suspected of carrying them on her person and in the carryall that has become an item of student uniform in most places today. If Wilson's reasonable suspicion of pill distribution were not understood to support searches of outer clothes and backpack, it would not justify any search worth making. And the look into Savana's bag, in her

---

[3]   There is no question here that justification for the school officials' search was required in accordance with the *T. L. O.* standard of reasonable suspicion, for it is common ground that Savana had a reasonable expectation of privacy covering the personal things she chose to carry in her backpack, and that Wilson's decision to look through it was a "search" within the meaning of the Fourth Amendment.

presence and in the relative privacy of Wilson's office, was not excessively intrusive, any more than Romero's subsequent search of her outer clothing.

B

Here it is that the parties part company, with Savana's claim that extending the search at Wilson's behest to the point of making her pull out her underwear was constitutionally unreasonable. The exact label for this final step in the intrusion is not important, though strip search is a fair way to speak of it. Romero and Schwallier directed Savana to remove her clothes down to her underwear, and then "pull out" her bra and the elastic band on her underpants. Although Romero and Schwallier stated that they did not see anything when Savana followed their instructions, we would not define strip search and its Fourth Amendment consequences in a way that would guarantee litigation about who was looking and how much was seen. The very fact of Savana's pulling her underwear away from her body in the presence of the two officials who were able to see her necessarily exposed her breasts and pelvic area to some degree, and both subjective and reasonable societal expectations of personal privacy support the treatment of such a search as categorically distinct, requiring distinct elements of justification on the part of school authorities for going beyond a search of outer clothing and belongings.

Savana's subjective expectation of privacy against such a search is inherent in her account of it as embarrassing, frightening, and humiliating. The reasonableness of her expectation (required by the Fourth Amendment standard) is indicated by the consistent experiences of other young people similarly searched, whose adolescent vulnerability intensifies the patent intrusiveness of the exposure. The common reaction of these adolescents simply registers the obviously different meaning of a search exposing the body from the experience of nakedness or near undress in other school circumstances. Changing for gym is getting ready for play; exposing for a search is responding to an accusation reserved for suspected wrongdoers and fairly understood as so degrading that a number of communities have decided that strip searches in schools are never reasonable and have banned them no matter what the facts may be.

The indignity of the search does not, of course, outlaw it, but it does implicate the rule of reasonableness as stated in *T. L. O.*, that "the search as actually conducted [be] reasonably related in scope to the circumstances which justified the interference in the first place." The scope will be permissible, that is, when it is "not excessively intrusive in light of the age and sex of the student and the nature of the infraction."

Here, the content of the suspicion failed to match the degree of intrusion. Wilson knew beforehand that the pills were prescription-strength ibuprofen and over-the-counter naproxen, common pain relievers equivalent to two Advil, or one Aleve. He must have been aware of the nature and limited threat of the specific drugs he was searching for, and while just about anything can be taken in quantities that will do real harm, Wilson had no reason to suspect that large amounts of the drugs were being passed around, or that individual students were receiving great numbers of pills.

Nor could Wilson have suspected that Savana was hiding common painkillers in her underwear. Petitioners suggest, as a truth universally acknowledged, that "students . . . hid[e] contraband in or under their clothing," and cite a smattering of cases of students with contraband in their underwear. But when the categorically extreme intrusiveness of a search down to the body of an adolescent requires some justification in suspected facts, general background possibilities fall short; a reasonable search that extensive calls for suspicion that it will pay off. But nondangerous school contraband does not raise the specter of stashes in intimate places, and there is no evidence in the record of any general practice among Safford Middle School students of hiding that sort of thing in underwear; neither Jordan nor Marissa suggested to Wilson that Savana was doing that, and the preceding search of Marissa that Wilson ordered yielded nothing. Wilson never even determined when Marissa had received the pills from Savana; if it had been a few days before, that would weigh heavily against any reasonable conclusion that Savana presently had the pills on her person, much less in her underwear.

In sum, what was missing from the suspected facts that pointed to Savana was any indication of danger to the students from the power of the drugs or their quantity, and any reason to suppose that Savana was carrying pills in her underwear. We think that the combination of these deficiencies was fatal to finding the search reasonable. * * *

* * * [T]he *T. L. O.* concern to limit a school search to reasonable scope requires the support of reasonable suspicion of danger or of resort to underwear for hiding evidence of wrongdoing before a search can reasonably make the quantum leap from outer clothes and backpacks to exposure of intimate parts. The meaning of such a search, and the degradation its subject may reasonably feel, place a search that intrusive in a category of its own demanding its own specific suspicions. * * *

It is so ordered.

JUSTICE STEVENS, with whom JUSTICE GINSBURG joins, concurring in part and dissenting in part.

[Omitted.]

JUSTICE GINSBURG, concurring in part and dissenting in part.

[Omitted.]

JUSTICE THOMAS, concurring in the judgment in part and dissenting in part.

[Omitted.]

QUESTIONS, COMMENTS, CONCERNS?

1. **Concerns about public school strip searches.** As *Safford* makes clear, the same reasonable suspicion that may justify patting a student down does not necessarily extend to a strip search. But, in either a pat-down or strip search, reasonable suspicion remains the standard. Lower courts have therefore considered whether reasonable suspicion supported the particular strip search in a variety of cases.

In *Cornfield v. Consol. High Sch. Dist.*, 991 F.2d 1316 (7th Cir. 1993), for example, a teacher's aide caught sixteen-year-old plaintiff outside the school building in violation of school rules. The aide observed a bulge in his pants. The following day, believing that the plaintiff was "crotching" drugs, defendants strip-searched plaintiff without his parents' consent. As a preliminary matter, the court recognized that "[w]hat may constitute reasonable suspicion for a search of a locker or even a pocket or pocketbook may fall well short of reasonableness for a nude search." The Court nonetheless held that reasonable suspicion existed to support the strip search because, among other factors: plaintiff once previously stated he was dealing drugs; he was earlier found with a live bullet at school; plaintiff's bus driver reported smelling marijuana near plaintiff; a student reported plaintiff smoking marijuana on the bus; and there was an earlier report that plaintiff "crotched" drugs at a police raid on his mother's home.

By contrast, in *Beard v. Whitmore Lake Sch. Dist.*, 402 F.3d 598 (6th Cir. 2005), the Sixth Circuit held unconstitutional the strip search of over twenty male and female students that took place after a student reported that her prom money was stolen. As to the male students, the court commented, "The highly intrusive nature of the searches, the fact that the searches were undertaken to find missing money, the fact that the searches were performed on a substantial number of students, the fact that the searches were performed *in the absence of individualized suspicion*, and the lack of consent, taken together, demonstrate that the searches were not reasonable." The court likewise disapproved of searching the female students, holding, "The fact that the searches of the females were highly intrusive, the fact that the searches occurred in the presence of other students, the lack of consent, *the absence of individualized suspicion*, and the fact that the searches were undertaken to find money, taken together, demonstrate that the searches performed on the females in this case were not reasonable."

Courts have also wrestled, though less so, with whether reasonable suspicion exists to support less intrusive searches of the student's person. *Faber v. Monticello Cent. Sch. Dist.*, 10-CV-01812 (ER), 2013 U.S. Dist. LEXIS 79869, **13–14 (S.D.N.Y. June 6, 2013) (search of pockets); *Binder v. Cold Spring Harbor Cent. Sch. Dist.*, No. 09 Civ. 4181 (SJF) (ARL), 2010 U.S. Dist. LEXIS 83493, at *6 (E.D.N.Y. July 19, 2010) (search of backpack); *Bridgman v. New Trier High Sch. Dist. No. 203*, 128 F.3d 1146, 1150 (7th Cir. 1997) (medical assessment and search of outer clothing).

For any of these searches, do you see a conflict between the school's investigatory interest and its role to protect students? It seems odd that no constitutional duty exists requiring schools to protect students from harm while conducting these types of searches. That is, K–12 public schools owe no duty to protect students from harm even though they stand in a *in loco parentis* role. *See* Danielle Weatherby, *Opening the "Snake Pit": Arming Teachers in the War Against School Violence and the Government-Created Risk Doctrine*, 48 CONN. L. REV. 119, 131–34 (2015) (discussing the country's belief that "schools should protect schoolchildren from violence" though "no special relationship exists giving rise to a school's affirmative duty to protect").

2.   Strip searches and transgender students. The Supreme Court has yet to consider how the reasonable suspicion requirement applies to the strip search of a transgender student. But recall *T. L. O.*'s twofold requirement. First, a schoolhouse search must be "justified at its inception"—i.e., reasonable suspicion is required. *New Jersey v. T.L.O.*, 469 U.S. 325, 341 (1985). Second, the search must be "permissible in scope" in the sense that it must "not excessively [be] intrusive in light of the age *and* sex of the student and nature of the infraction." *Id.* (emphasis added).

Does the *T. L. O.* framework apply to the strip search of a transgender student? If it doesn't, how could the Supreme Court one day expand the framework to encompass the additional concerns raised by schoolhouse searches of transgender students?

CHAPTER 7

INTERROGATION METHODS & THE DUE PROCESS "VOLUNTARINESS" TEST

■ ■ ■

I. INTRODUCTION

A. INTERROGATION METHODS

Kill your woman and a good detective will come close to real tears as he touches your shoulder and tells you how he knows that you must have loved her, that it wouldn't be so hard for you to talk about if you didn't. Beat your child to death and a police detective will wrap his arm around you in the interrogation room, telling you about how he beats his own children all the time, how it wasn't your fault if the kid up and died on you. Shoot a friend over a poker hand and that same detective will lie about your dead buddy's condition, telling you that the victim is in stable condition at Hopkins and probably won't press charges, which wouldn't amount to more than assault with intent even if he does. Murder a man with an accomplice and the detective will walk your co-conspirator past the open door of your interrogation room, then say your bunky's going home tonight because he gave a statement making you the triggerman. And if that same detective thinks you can be bluffed, he might tell you that they've got your prints on the weapon, or that there are two eyewitnesses who have picked your photo from an array, or that the victim made a dying declaration in which he named you as his assailant.[1]

How do detectives know these tricks?[2] More than likely, investigators learned them from John E. Reid & Associates—teachers of "the leading interview and interrogation approach used today in both the law enforcement and business communities."[3] The prevalence of the Reid technique—as taught in seminars and described in the *Criminal*

---

[1] DAVID SIMON, HOMICIDE: A YEAR ON THE KILLING STREETS 203 (1991).

[2] Portions of the discussion that follows are taken with permission from Brian Gallini, *Police "Science" in the Interrogation Room: The Use of Pseudo-Psychological Interrogation Methods to Obtain Seventy Years of Inadmissible Confessions*, 61 HASTINGS L.J. 529 (2010). All footnotes are omitted.

[3] John E. Reid & Associates, Inc., *About*, REID.COM, https://reid.com/about (last visited Aug. 13, 2022).

Interrogation and Confessions text—cannot be overstated. Indeed, John E. Reid & Associates is the largest, best-known provider of interrogation training in the United States.

Officers from every state and Canadian province use the Reid method. One nationwide survey of police departments revealed that two-thirds of state police departments train some or all of their officers in the Reid method. The Reid technique also claims international reach. According to the most recent edition of Reid and Inbau's *Criminal Interrogation and Confessions*, "[t]he technique is now taught in seminars across the United States, Canada, Europe, and Asia."[4] Even the United States military law enforcement uses the Reid technique. In total, Reid & Associates boasts that over 500,000 law enforcement and security professionals have attended its interrogation seminars since they were first offered in 1974.[5]

Although there are of course competing training manuals, they too generally follow principles that are aligned with the Reid method. In a survey of police investigators from California, Texas, Maryland, Massachusetts, Florida, and Canada, investigators cited to the same room setup and interrogation techniques listed by the Reid method, regardless of whether the respondent knew the Reid name.

Training in the Reid technique is derived from the Reid textbook, *Criminal Interrogation and Confessions*. The fifth edition of the nearly five-hundred-page training manual begins by distinguishing an "interview" from an "interrogation." An interview, according to the text, is a non-accusatory information gathering exercise that may take place at the beginning of an investigation and in a variety of environments. The interview, more specifically described by the text as a "Behavior Analysis Interview," should be "free flowing and relatively unstructured" in order to allow the interviewer to collect unanticipated information and make a credibility determination by evaluating the suspect's behavioral responses. Along the way, the examiner should also "establish a level of rapport and trust with the suspect that cannot be accomplished during an accusatory interrogation."

By contrast, an interrogation takes place "only when the investigator is reasonably certain of the suspect's guilt," which certainty may arise from "the suspect's behavior during an interview." The interrogation itself must occur in a controlled environment, during which the interrogator displays an air of unwavering confidence in the suspect's guilt. The interrogator should employ the nine-step Reid technique, described below, during questioning.

---

[4] FRED E. INBAU ET AL., CRIMINAL INTERROGATION AND CONFESSIONS viii (5th ed. 2004).

[5] John E. Reid & Associates, Inc., *The Reid Technique of Interviewing and Interrogation*, REID.COM, https://reid.com/programs/program-descriptions/interview-and-interrogation-technique-1 (last visited Aug. 13, 2022).

The moment when a police officer elects to conclude an interview and commence an interrogation is critical. Given that interrogation is a "guilt-presumptive process," the investigators should make a determination during the Behavior Analysis Interview about the suspect's credibility before commencing a formal interrogation. To do so, the investigator should establish the suspect's normal behavioral patterns and then—in response to "behavior-provoking questions"—evaluate the suspect's attitudes, verbal behavior, paralinguistic behavior (i.e., the suspect's speech characteristics), and nonverbal behavior. In the words of Inbau et al., the examiner must give "analytical consideration" to the suspect's "behavioral responses."

Based on a suspect's responses to between ten to fifteen behavior-provoking questions, the investigator "will generally be able to classify the overall responses to those questions as either fitting the description of an innocent or guilty suspect." And, assuming the investigator is "unable to eliminate a suspect based on behavior assessments or investigative findings," that investigator should hastily follow up with a formal interrogation.

The Reid technique's nine-step method comes into play as soon as our hypothetical investigator elects to begin a formal interrogation. Before the investigator commences an interrogation, though, Inbau et al. advise the investigator to set up a private soundproof room within the police station that is free from distractions and furnished sparsely with straight-backed chairs. The room should also be equipped with a one-way observation mirror so that other detectives can evaluate the suspect's "behavior symptoms." Arranging the room in this manner isolates the suspect and removes the suspect from any familiar surroundings, thereby heightening the suspect's anxiety while incentivizing the suspect to extricate himself from the situation.

The interrogator should then "allow the suspect to sit in the interview room alone for about five minutes." Doing so will promote insecurity in the suspect and cause the suspect "additional doubts and concerns." The investigator should also preliminarily "prepare and have on hand an evidence case folder, or a simulation of one." Doing so will allow the investigator to make reference to the case file throughout the interrogation, even if the "file" contains nothing or simply contains blank paper. At the outset of the formal interrogation, the investigator should enter with an air of confidence and, if the suspect is not seated, instruct the suspect to sit.

Step one of the Reid technique directs the interrogator to "initiate the interrogation with a direct statement indicating absolute certainty in the suspect's guilt." Immediately thereafter, the interrogator should pause and say, "I want to sit down with you so that we can get this straightened out. Okay?" No matter what the suspect says in response, "the investigator will proceed to offer a reason as to why it is important for the suspect to tell the truth."

Step two of the Reid method directs the interrogator to begin developing a "theme." The theme should present the suspect with a moral—not legal—excuse for committing the offense. "The selected theme may be based on a simple, common sense analysis of a suspect's background and probable motive that triggered the criminal conduct." So, if a suspect admits during the Behavior Analysis Interview that he might be tempted to take money from someone at gunpoint if he were "desperate," the interrogator should consider a theme justifying the suspect's commission of robbery out of dire financial need or possible drug addiction. Or, if a suspect suggests during the Behavior Analysis Interview that certain circumstances may justify a homicide, the interrogator should thematically condemn the victim of the suspect's crime. Regardless, this "minimization" technique is designed to "offer a 'crutch' for the suspect as he moves toward a confession." Often, however, the suspect meets the interrogator's theme presentation with a denial.

The third step advises interrogators on how to handle a suspect's denial following the interrogator's direct positive confrontation (step one) or the interrogator's theme presentation (step two). Should a denial follow step one, Inbau et al. instructs interrogators to ignore a suspect's "weak denial." Should the suspect offer a more forceful denial, then the investigator should "reassert his confidence in the suspect's guilt" while directing the discussion back to the facts of the case. Little changes in the context of a post-theme denial: the interrogator is advised to evaluate the veracity of the denial while returning to the interrogation theme.

Step four addresses how interrogators should respond when a suspect's simple denial matures into an "objection." An objection, according to the text, "will ordinarily take the form of a reason as to why the accusation is wrong." Although it will not contain evidence of innocence, the objection is designed to shake the interrogator's confidence in the suspect's guilt. A suspect's willingness to resort to objections is a good thing, though, say Inbau et al., because "the suspect's move from a denial to an objection is a good indication of a concealment of the truth." Substantively, the interrogator should "act as though the statement was expected" (e.g., by saying, "I was hoping you'd say that" or "I'm glad you mentioned that"). Then, the interrogator should "reverse the significance of the suspect's objection and return to the interrogation theme without delay."

Step five of the approach turns to teaching the interrogator how to procure and retain the suspect's attention. This step is particularly important given the propensity of suspects "to psychologically withdraw from the interrogation and ignore the investigator's theme." To avoid that result, interrogators are advised to: (1) move their chairs physically closer to the suspect, (2) establish eye contact, (3) use visual aids, or (4) ask hypothetical questions.

Step six counsels interrogators on how to handle a suspect's passive mood. In short, this step first advises the interrogator to tailor the general theme established at step two specifically to this suspect. If, after hearing this theme restatement, the suspect "drifts into a passive mood," the interrogator should move closer to the suspect and begin urging the suspect to tell the truth. Working at the "peak of sincerity," the investigator should utilize "soft and warm" eye contact while speaking in a low tone and encouraging the suspect to "tell the truth for the sake of his own conscience, mental relief, or moral well-being, as well as 'for the sake of everybody concerned.'" The investigator should continue this process "until the suspect shows some physical sign of resignation, at which time step seven should immediately be employed."

At step seven, the officer should present to the suspect a so-called "alternative question," which provides the suspect "a choice between two explanations for possible commission of the crime." One explanation is designed to be more "acceptable" or "understandable" than the other. For example, in a theft case, the interrogator may ask "did you blow that money on booze . . . or did you need it to help out your family?" The interrogator should then follow with a statement supporting the more morally acceptable alternative. Inbau et al. suggest that "the alternative question has allowed [the suspect] the opportunity to tell the truth while saving face."

Step eight begins once the suspect accepts his involvement in the crime based on a morally understandable reason and instructs the interrogator on how to deduce details about the offense from the suspect. This step calls on the interrogator to "employ a great deal of patience" throughout several gradual stages, beginning with offering the suspect a "statement of reinforcement." The statement is a brief one like "good, that's what I thought it was all along," which should be followed by working to develop the suspect's gradual acknowledgement of guilt. The interrogator should then "return to the beginning of the crime and attempt to develop information that can be corroborated by further investigation." Finally, although only one interrogator should elicit the initial oral confession, another person should witness that oral confession once the first investigator "is satisfied that adequate details surrounding the commission of the crime have been obtained."

The ninth and final step counsels interrogators on how to convert the oral confession into a written one. Spanning more than twenty pages of text, this step: (1) emphasizes the importance of documentation, (2) teaches how to again provide the warnings required by *Miranda v. Arizona*,

(3) instructs how to prepare and form the confession, (4) outlines best practices for safeguarding the effectiveness of the confession, and (5) suggests engaging in a post-confession interview with the suspect.

B. SOCIAL SCIENCE RESPONDS

Unsurprisingly, perhaps, the Reid technique has been the subject of considerable scholarly commentary and criticism. That criticism has extended into the mainstream media, largely given the now widely-held belief that use of the Reid technique is linked to producing false confessions.[6] Most prominently, in March 2017, Wicklander-Zulawski & Associates, one of the largest consulting groups engaged in police training, announced that it will no longer teach the Reid technique.[7] Wicklander-Zulawski & Associates specifically cited the risk of false confessions as its reasoning for declining to continue teaching the Reid technique, which it had offered since 1984.

Leading confession expert Professor Richard A. Leo has argued that social science explains why the Reid technique is particularly apt to produce a false confession.[8] Professor Leo argues that the Reid technique, and other similar confrontation-based interrogation techniques, create a coercive interrogation environment—and therefore the potential for a false confession—through two separate steps. At step one, the investigator convinces the suspect that his situation is hopeless. Then, at step two, the investigator offers a series of "inducements" to confess; that is, reasons why confessing is in the suspect's best interests. Those inducements, Professor Leo explains, can take the form of low-end inducements, systemic inducements, and high-end inducements:

> Low-end inducements refer to interpersonal or moral appeals the interrogator uses to convince a suspect that he will feel better if he confesses. For example, an interrogator may tell a suspect that the truth will set him free if he confesses, that confessing will relieve his anxiety or guilt, that confessing is the moral or Christian thing to do, or that confessing will improve his standing in the eyes of the victim or the eyes of the community.
>
> Systemic inducements refer to appeals that the interrogator uses to focus the suspect's attention on the processes and outcomes of the criminal justice system in order to get the suspect to come to the conclusion that his case is likely to be processed more

---

[6]   Douglas Starr, *The Interview*, THE NEW YORKER (Dec. 9 2013), http://www.newyorker.com/magazine/2013/12/09/the-interview-7.

[7]   Eli Hager, *A Major Player In Law Enforcement Says It Will Stop Using a Method That's Been Linked to False Confessions*, BUSINESSINSIDER.COM (Mar. 9, 2017), http://www.business insider.com/reid-technique-false-confessions-law-enforcement-2017-3.

[8]   Richard A. Leo, *Police Interrogation, False Confessions, and Alleged Child Abuse Cases*, 50 U. MICH. J.L. REFORM 693 (2017).

favorably by all actors in the criminal justice system if he confesses. For example, an interrogator may tell a suspect that he is the suspect's ally and will try to help him out—both in his discussions with the prosecutor as well as in his role as a professional witness at trial—but can only do so if the suspect first admits his guilt. Or the interrogator may ask the suspect how he expects the prosecutor to look favorably on the suspect's case if the suspect does not cooperate with authorities. Or the interrogator may ask the suspect what a judge and jury are really going to think, and how they are likely to react, if he does not demonstrate remorse and admit his guilt to authorities. Interrogators often couple the use of systemic incentives with the assertion that this is the suspect's one and only chance—now or never—to tell his side of the story; if he passes up this opportunity, all the relevant actors in the system (police, prosecutor, judge, and jury) will no longer be open to the possibility of viewing his actions in their most favorable light. This tactic may incentivize a suspect to either falsely confess or confirm an incorrect story for the interrogator based on the belief that the suspect will not have the same opportunity to help himself again in the future. Interrogators rely on systemic inducements to persuade the suspect to reason to the conclusion that the justice system naturally confers rewards for those who admit guilt, demonstrate remorse, and cooperate with authorities, whereas it inevitably metes out punishment for those who do not.

Finally, high-end inducements refer to appeals that directly communicate the message that the suspect will receive less punishment, a lower prison sentence and/or some form of police, prosecutorial, judicial, or juror leniency and/or immunity if he complies with the interrogator's demand that he confess, but that the suspect will receive a higher sentence or greater punishment if he does not comply with the interrogator's demand that he confess. High-end inducements may either be implicit or explicit: the important question is whether the interrogation technique communicates the message, or is understood to communicate the message, that the suspect will receive a lower (or no) criminal charge and/or lesser (or no) punishment if he confesses as opposed to a higher criminal charge and/or greater amount of punishment if he does not. For example, if police interrogators lead a suspect to believe he will be able to go home and not be charged with a homicide if he confesses to witnessing the crime and fingering someone else as the triggerman, this would be a high-end inducement because it communicates immunity in exchange for making such a statement.

Explicit high-end incentives can include telling a suspect that there are several degrees of the alleged offense, each of which carry different amounts of punishment, and asking the suspect which version he would like to confess to. Or the interrogator may explicitly tell the suspect that he will receive a long prison sentence—or perhaps even the death penalty—if he does not confess to the interrogator's version of events. The interrogator may also point out what happens to men of the suspect's age, or men accused of crime, in prison if the suspect does not confess to the interrogator's minimized account. Sometimes interrogators who rely on high-end inducements will present the suspect with a simple two-choice situation (good vs. bad): if the suspect agrees to the good choice (a minimized version of the offense, such as involuntary manslaughter or self-defense, or the implication of another person), he will receive a lower amount of punishment or no punishment at all; but if he does not confess right then, criminal justice officials will impute to him the bad choice (a maximized version of the offense, such as pre-meditated first degree murder, or that the suspect was acting alone), and he will receive a higher level of punishment, or perhaps the harshest possible punishment. The purpose of high-end inducements is to communicate to a suspect that it is in his rational self-interest to confess to the minimized or less-incriminating version of events that the interrogator is suggesting because if the suspect does so, he will receive a lower charge, a lesser amount of punishment and/or no time in prison. If he fails to do so, he will receive a higher charge, a greater amount of punishment and more time in prison, perhaps even the death penalty.[9]

Professor Leo suggests that an interrogation's two primary steps—conveying hopelessness alongside the use of inducements—should be considered alongside the circumstances of the interrogation. That is, certain circumstances might present additional risk factors for a suspect making a false confession. He, for example, points specifically to the following:

- An officer beginning with or arriving at a premature presumption of guilt;

- Engaging in a lengthy interrogation that includes sleep deprivation;

- False evidence ploys (i.e., making up or lying about evidence); and/or

---

[9] *Id.* at 706–08.

- Minimization/maximizing the impact of the offense, depending on the situation, to encourage a confession.[10]

Now we turn to the question of why it's important to have some understanding of the Reid technique alongside the responsive critical social science literature. At the risk of over-simplifying, there are two primary means of challenging a confession: (1) the Fourteenth Amendment's voluntariness doctrine (discussed in this chapter), and (2) the Fifth Amendment's *Miranda v. Arizona* doctrine (discussed in the next two chapters). In the voluntariness context, understanding how the Reid technique was used in a particular interrogation may help determine whether the suspect's statement was voluntary. Similarly, spotting the use of the Reid technique and/or inducements may be relevant for analyzing whether the suspect was in custody for *Miranda* purposes. Fundamentally, it's not enough in modern suppression litigation to know the law; rather, you must also have a solid understanding of what's happening inside the interrogation room in order to craft persuasive legal arguments.

II. THE WEST MEMPHIS THREE[11]

On May 5, 1993, three eight-year-old boys set out for a bike ride around their hometown of West Memphis, Arkansas—never to be seen alive again. The following day, the mutilated bodies of Steve Branch, Michael Moore, and Christopher Byers were pulled from the wooded drainage ditch located just outside of the Rolling Hills community where the boys lived. Over the next month, rumors and allegations of satanic rituals and human sacrifice consumed both local and national media headlines, leading the West Memphis Police Department to believe the victims were sacrificed as part of a satanic murder ritual.

Mugshot of the West Memphis Three after their June 1993 arrest

The state would eventually charge Damien Echols, Jason Baldwin, and Jesse Misskelley Jr. with three counts of capital murder. At the time

---

[10] *Id.* at 710–14.

[11] Remember that you have access to the filings relevant to this chapter in your online repository.

of their arrests, Jessie Misskelley Jr. was seventeen years old, Jason Baldwin was sixteen, and Damien Echols was eighteen. Both Misskelley and Echols were high school dropouts. Baldwin, however, was a successful student who earned high grades in school. Baldwin and Echols were close friends who bonded over their love of Metallica and fantasy fiction. They were acquainted with Misskelley from their time at school, but were not close friends.

West Memphis

West Memphis sits in the Northeast corner of Arkansas on Interstate 40, just eight miles west of downtown Memphis. In 1993, West Memphis was an economically challenged community that saw property and violent crime rates well above the state average. According to the 1990 census, the West Memphis population was 28,259. West Memphis's median household income was only $22,052 with a per capita income of only $10,009, which put 22.9% of its residents below the national poverty level. Additionally, just 62.5% of individuals over the age of twenty-five had a high school degree. Manufacturing, transportation and retail trade made up nearly 43% of the town's work force.

The Crime

At around 8:00 p.m. on May 5, 1993, the West Memphis Police Department received a call from John Mark Byers reporting that his son, Christopher Byers, was missing. Within the next twenty minutes, both Dana Moore and Pamela Hobbs reported that their sons, Michael Moore and Steve Branch, were also missing. A preliminary investigation revealed that the boys were last seen riding off on their bikes together around 6:00 p.m.

007110 —

The victims' bikes are pulled from the water

The next morning, on May 6, Chief Inspector Gary Gitchell announced that a search for the missing boys was underway. In the early afternoon, Juvenile Officer Steve Jones reported a black children's tennis shoe floating in the water of Robin Hood Hills drainage stream, a four-acre wood near Interstate 40 where neighborhood children liked to play. Within the hour, the bodies of Chris Byers, Steven Branch, and Michael Moore were pulled out of the thick, muddy water of the drainage stream, along with their bikes.

The three boys had all been stripped naked and hogtied with their own shoelaces. Subsequent autopsies revealed that Byers died of "multiple injuries" and that Moore and Branch both died of "multiple injuries with drowning." Disturbingly, Mark Byers's penis, scrotal sac, and testicles were all missing, which led detectives to believe they were removed as a part of the satanic ritual rumored to have taken place. Although all three autopsy reports found that the boys had dilation of the anus, no visible injuries existed to suggest sexual contact. But a small concentration of semen was located on one of the boys' underwear that police recovered at the scene.

The Investigation

Based on the autopsy reports, West Memphis Detectives believed that the crime had "cult overtones." Officers also believed that the boys were sodomized prior to the murders due to the anal dilation and trace amounts of semen. Police immediately focused on a local teenager, Damien Echols, because of his interest in occultism. After police interrogated Echols, suspicions around Echols grew because, during the interrogation, Echols mentioned that one of the victims sustained genital wounds. That fact would lead to a false, but widely shared, rumor that Echols removed Byers's genitals and displayed them in a jar of formaldehyde inside his room.

The same day the victims' bodies were found, a woman named Vicki Hutcheson was coincidentally taking a polygraph exam in the neighboring town of Marion on a suspicion that she had stolen money from her West Memphis employer. Present at the polygraph exam was Hutcheson's young son who was a friend and playmate of the victims. During the exam, he told officers that the boys were killed at what he called "the playhouse." When the bodies of the boys were discovered, detectives questioned the boy, who told them that he had witnessed Spanish speaking Satanists murder the three victims, but could not identify Echols, Baldwin, or Misskelley. Although the boy's statements were wholly inconsistent, an officer leaked this information to the local press, perpetuating the rumor that the victims had been murdered as a part of a satanic ritual.

After a month passed without an arrest, Hutcheson agreed to place microphones in her home in order to record a staged interaction between Echols and Misskelley. When the recordings turned up inaudible, Hutcheson alleged that, about two weeks after the murders were committed, she, Echols, and Misskelley attended a Wiccan (i.e., pagan) meeting in a nearby town, where Echols openly bragged about killing the three boys. Hutcheson would later recant her story, stating that she implicated Echols and Misskelley in order to avoid the theft charges against her while obtaining a reward for helping to solve the murders.

The Interrogation

Based on Hutcheson's story, West Memphis Detectives interrogated Jessie Misskelley Jr. on June 3, 1993. At the time of his interrogation, Jessie Misskelley was only seventeen years old with a reported IQ of 72—categorizing him as "borderline" intellectual functioning. Although investigators interrogated Misskelley for nearly twelve hours, only two segments of the interrogation, totaling forty-six minutes, were recorded.

During the taped session of the interrogation, Misskelley admitted to being present while Echols and Baldwin tied up and murdered the three boys. After prompting and suggestion by detectives, Misskelley confessed that one victim, Michael Moore, had attempted to escape, but Misskelley chased him down and brought him back. In all, Misskelley would state that the victims were choked, hogtied, sodomized, and thrown into the drainage ditch—all as part of a satanic ritual. Misskelley would later recant his confession, citing police coercion, fatigue, and intimidation.

Misskelley's interrogation occurred in three stages: (1) a pre-polygraph test, where detectives asked about Misskelley's involvement with Satanism, drugs, and whether he was involved or suspected anyone in the murders; (2) a ten question polygraph examination; and (3) an intensive post polygraph interrogation lasting approximately eight hours. During the pre-polygraph and polygraph examinations, Misskelley denied having any involvement with Satanism or the victims' deaths. Although Misskelley's defense expert, Warren Holmes, a veteran homicide detective and FBI polygraph consultant, would later testify that Misskelley's tests indicated deception *only* with regard to whether he used illegal drugs, West Memphis detectives told Misskelley at the time that the polygraph results showed he was "lying his ass off." According to Misskelley, detectives told him that the polygraph machine could read people's minds. He commented, "I didn't know what was going on . . . . Because how could my brain be telling him that I was sitting there lying? It got me confused."

Once the polygraph concluded, detectives moved Misskelley to a separate interrogation room and began to question him about his alleged deception. During this portion of the interrogation, detectives drew a diagram for Misskelley of a circle surrounded by "X's" with three dots in the center. According to detectives' handwritten notes, not contained in their final report, investigators told Misskelley that the Xs were police and that he could either be inside the circle with Echols and Baldwin, or outside the circle with the police. Although Misskelley told detectives he wanted to be on the side of police, the interrogators persisted. When Misskelley would give a statement that failed to match facts known to police, the detectives would interrupt and accuse Misskelley of lying. If Misskelley remained silent without responding to questioning, detectives would present Misskelley with a picture of the murdered boys. The interrogation caused Misskelley to cry and state that he wanted to get out. Misskelley recounted his confession:

> Gitchell came and got me and took me to another room, and that's
> when he started talking to me. The whole time, the same
> questions that they'd already asked me, they kept asking over and

over again. . . . They kept saying they knew I had something to do with it, because other people done told 'em. After I told 'em what the boys were wearing, Gary Gitchell told me, was any of them tied up? That's when I went along with him. I repeated what he told me. I said, yes, they was tied up. He asked, "what was they tied up with." I told 'em rope. He got mad. He told me, "God damn it, Jessie, don't mess with me." He said, "No. They was tied up with shoestrings." I had to go all through the story again until I got it right. They hollered at me until I got it right.

Misskelley's Confession

Before trial, Misskelley's public defender, Dan Stidham, filed a motion to suppress Misskelley's June 3, 1993 confession by arguing that his statements were involuntary. The motion was denied. At trial, Stidham called Dr. Richard Ofshe, a social psychologist from Stanford University who specializes in interpersonal dynamics in police interrogations.[12] Dr. Ofshe testified that the inaccurate polygraph report began an escalating process that led "the statement by Jessie Misskelley [to be] the product of influence tactics" by interrogators. Specifically, Dr. Ofshe testified that the circle diagram, repeated refusals to believe Misskelley's statements, and presentation of the deceased victims' photographs, intensified Misskelley's "sense of helplessness" that could lead someone with a similar IQ to confess falsely. Dr. Ofshe concluded, "[T]hese statements are far more likely to be the product of influence than they are based on any memory that Mr. Misskelley has of the crime."

Misskelley was convicted of first degree murder for the death of Michael Moore and second-degree murder for the deaths of Christopher Byers and Stevie Branch. The jury sentenced Misskelley to life in prison without parole for the murder of Moore, and two twenty-year sentences, set to run consecutively, for the murders of Byers and Branch. In 1996, the Arkansas Supreme Court reviewed each tactic used by West Memphis Detectives, but nonetheless held that Misskelley's statements were voluntary.

---

[12] Richard Leo, discussed above, and Dr. Ofshe have collaborated together on numerous false confession pieces. *See, e.g.*, Richard A. Leo, *Inside the Interrogation Room*, 86 J. CRIM. L. & CRIMINOLOGY 300 (1996); Richard A. Leo & Richard J. Ofshe, *The Consequences of False Confessions: Deprivations of Liberty and Miscarriages of Justice in the Age of Psychological Interrogation*, 88 J. CRIM. L. & CRIMINOLOGY 429 (1998); Richard A. Leo & Richard J. Ofshe, *The Social Psychology of Police Interrogation: The Theory and Classification of True and False Confessions*, 16 STUD. L. POL. & SOC'Y 189 (1997); Richard J. Ofshe & Richard A. Leo, *The Decision to Confess Falsely: Rational Choice and Irrational Action*, 74 DEN. L. REV. 979 (1997).

III. VOLUNTARINESS & THE DUE PROCESS PROTECTION

The Supreme Court has long recognized—since 1884, to be exact—that "[a] confession, if freely and voluntarily made, is evidence of the most satisfactory character." *Hopt v. Utah*, 110 U.S. 574, 584 (1884). Involuntary confessions, by contrast, are inadmissible as evidence against the accused. At first, the requirement that a confession be made voluntarily was construed narrowly as merely a common-law evidentiary requirement having no relationship to the Constitution. Yet, in that context, an involuntary confession was one induced by a "threat or promise by or in the presence of such person, which, operating upon the fears or hopes of the accused, in reference to the charge, deprives him of that freedom of will or self-control essential to make his confession voluntary within the meaning of the law." The Court subsequently applied this early voluntariness rule to a number of cases in which the defendant was in custody, yet received no warnings about silence or counsel.

Thirteen years later, in *Bram v. United States*, 168 U.S. 532 (1897), the Court merged its common law voluntariness rule into the Fifth Amendment privilege against self-incrimination. The "generic" language of the Fifth Amendment, the Court reasoned, "was but a crystallization of the doctrine as to confessions." Although, after *Bram*, involuntary confessions were inadmissible in federal criminal trials as a matter of constitutional law, the Fifth Amendment was not yet considered a fundamental right applicable to the states. States were therefore free to ignore the *Bram* voluntariness requirement.

For roughly three decades thereafter, federal courts faithfully applied *Bram*, a proposition aided by the Supreme Court's extension of *Bram* in *Ziang Sung Wan v. United States*, 266 U.S. 1 (1924). In *Wan*, an ill defendant confessed after enduring almost two weeks of relentless, incommunicado police interrogation. Although the defendant's resulting confession was motivated by neither threat nor promise, the Court nonetheless held that "a confession obtained by compulsion must be excluded whatever may have been the character of the compulsion, and whether the compulsion was applied in a judicial proceeding or otherwise."

Notwithstanding the extension of *Bram* in *Wan*, there remained no constitutional basis for excluding a defendant's confession in state court until 1936. In *Brown v. Mississippi*, 297 U.S. 278 (1936), the Supreme Court—adhering to principles of federalism—held that due process mandated invalidating a confession obtained by "officers of the State [using] brutality and violence." Specifically, in *Brown*, officers (with the aid of an angry mob) hanged one and severely whipped three "ignorant negroes" until the trio confessed to committing a murder. After analogizing the state's conduct to "the rack and torture chamber," the Court had little trouble concluding that "[i]t would be difficult to conceive of methods more revolting to the sense of justice than those taken to procure the confessions of these petitioners, and the use of the confessions thus obtained as the basis for conviction and sentence was a clear denial of due process."

What remained missing after *Brown*, however, was any meaningful insight into how to distinguish a voluntary confession from an involuntary one. Indeed, given that the facts in *Brown* so clearly mandated discarding the defendants' confessions, the Court had no occasion to offer any guidance to courts in future, closer cases.

In many ways, decades later, the due process voluntariness doctrine remains an elusive one where seemingly everything is relevant, but nothing is dispositive. At its core, though, the voluntariness doctrine seeks to determine whether the suspect's confession was the product of an essentially free and unconstrained choice or, rather, whether the suspect's confession was coerced. When making this assessment, courts are advised to consider all of the surrounding circumstances of the interrogation, including the character of the accused and the character of the interrogation. As it relates to the accused, courts might consider the suspect's familiarity with the justice system, educational background, emotional stability, and age—among other factors. As for the character of the interrogation, courts might consider whether the interrogators used torture, false promises, tricks, or threats, and whether the interrogators deprived the suspect of food or sleep. The timing of the interrogation—day vs. night—the number of interrogators, and the duration of questioning might also be relevant.

As you will see, the fact that so many factors are relevant to the voluntariness analysis has produced dramatically different and inconsistent results.

A. ESTABLISHING THE DOCTRINE

Our first case in this chapter, *Spano v. New York*, illustrates law enforcement's movement away from "third degree" interrogation tactics. In the interrogation context, "third degree" is an umbrella term referring "to a variety of coercive interrogation strategies, ranging from psychological duress such as prolonged confinement to extreme physical violence and torture."[13] The third degree reigned as the prized interrogation method in the early 1900s. Then, in 1931, the National Commission on Law Observance in Law Enforcement issued a Report on Lawlessness in Law Enforcement to President Herbert Hoover documenting and decrying the

---

[13] Richard A. Leo, *The Third Degree and the Origins of Psychological Interrogation in the United States*, *in* 20 INTERROGATIONS, CONFESSIONS, AND ENTRAPMENT 37, 42 (G. Daniel Lassiter ed., 2004).

use of the third degree.[14] The Wickersham Report specifically documented, for example, use of hot lights, confinement in rancid rooms, and beating suspects with fists or phone books.[15] When it became clear through a series of Supreme Court cases, beginning in 1940,[16] that the Court would no longer tolerate the third degree, law enforcement turned to exerting psychological pressures on the suspect.

SPANO V. NEW YORK

360 U.S. 315
Supreme Court of the United States
April 27, 1959, Argued; June 22, 1959, Decided
No. 582

MR. CHIEF JUSTICE WARREN delivered the opinion of the Court.

This is another in the long line of cases presenting the question whether a confession was properly admitted into evidence under the Fourteenth Amendment. * * *

The State's evidence reveals the following: Petitioner Vincent Joseph Spano is a derivative citizen of this country, having been born in Messina, Italy. He was 25 years old at the time of the shooting in question and had graduated from junior high school. He had a record of regular employment. The shooting took place on January 22, 1957.

On that day, petitioner was drinking in a bar. The decedent, a former professional boxer weighing almost 200 pounds who had fought in Madison Square Garden, took some of petitioner's money from the bar.[17] Petitioner followed him out of the bar to recover it. A fight ensued, with the decedent knocking petitioner down and then kicking him in the head three or four times. Shock from the force of these blows caused petitioner to vomit. After the bartender applied some ice to his head, petitioner left the bar, walked to his apartment, secured a gun, and walked eight or nine blocks to a candy store where the decedent was frequently to be found. He entered the store in which decedent, three friends of decedent, at least two of whom were ex-convicts, and a boy who was supervising the store were present. He fired five shots, two of which entered the decedent's body, causing his death. The boy was the only eyewitness; the three friends of decedent did not see the person who fired the shot. Petitioner then disappeared for the next week or so.

---

[14] *See* Nat'l Comm. on Law Observance & Enforcement, Report on Lawlessness in Law Enforcement (1931).

[15] *Id.* at 31, 47, 126, 149.

[16] *Chambers v. Florida*, 309 U.S. 227, 238 n.11 (1940).

[17] *Ed. note*: Palermo began his professional campaign in 1945 and fought until 1951, earning an overall record of 29-13-2. Interestingly, he fought as a welterweight and, by the time of his death in 1957, Palermo had been out of the ring for six years. The welterweight weight class, a class in between lightweight and middleweight, is between 140–147 pounds.

On February 1, 1957, the Bronx County Grand Jury returned an indictment for first-degree murder against petitioner. * * *

On February 3, 1957, petitioner called one Gaspar Bruno, a close friend of 8 or 10 years' standing who had attended school with him. Bruno was a fledgling police officer, having at that time not yet finished attending police academy. According to Bruno's testimony, petitioner told him "that he took a terrific beating, that the deceased hurt him real bad and he dropped him a couple of times and he was dazed; he didn't know what he was doing and that he went and shot at him." Petitioner told Bruno that he intended to get a lawyer and give himself up. Bruno relayed this information to his superiors.

The following day, February 4, at 7:10 p. m., petitioner, accompanied by counsel, surrendered himself to the authorities in front of the Bronx County Building, where both the office of the Assistant District Attorney who ultimately prosecuted his case and the courtroom in which he was ultimately tried were located. His attorney had cautioned him to answer no questions, and left him in the custody of the officers. He was promptly taken to the office of the Assistant District Attorney and at 7:15 p. m. the questioning began, being conducted by Assistant District Attorney Goldsmith, Lt. Gannon, Detectives Farrell, Lehrer and Motta, and Sgt. Clarke. The record reveals that the questioning was both persistent and continuous. Petitioner, in accordance with his attorney's instructions, steadfastly refused to answer. Detective Motta testified: "He refused to talk to me." "He just looked up to the ceiling and refused to talk to me." Detective Farrell testified:

Q.   And you started to interrogate him?

A.   That is right.

. . . .

Q.   What did he say?

A.   He said 'you would have to see my attorney. I tell you nothing but my name.'

. . . .

Q.   Did you continue to examine him?

A.   Verbally, yes, sir.

He asked one officer, Detective Ciccone, if he could speak to his attorney, but that request was denied. Detective Ciccone testified that he could not find the attorney's name in the telephone book.[1] He was given two sandwiches, coffee and cake at 11 p. m.

At 12:15 a.m. on the morning of February 5, after five hours of questioning in which it became evident that petitioner was following his attorney's instructions, on the Assistant District Attorney's orders petitioner was transferred to the 46th Squad, Ryer Avenue Police Station. The Assistant District Attorney also went to the police station and to some extent continued to participate in the interrogation. Petitioner arrived at 12:30 and questioning was resumed at 12:40. The character of the questioning is revealed by the testimony of Detective Farrell:

Q.   Who did you leave him in the room with?

A.   With Detective Lehrer and Sergeant Clarke came in and Mr. Goldsmith came in or Inspector Halk came in. It was back and forth. People just came in, spoke a few words to the defendant or they listened a few minutes and they left.

But petitioner persisted in his refusal to answer, and again requested permission to see his attorney, this time from Detective Lehrer. His request was again denied.

It was then that those in charge of the investigation decided that petitioner's close friend, Bruno, could be of use. He had been called out on the case around 10 or 11 p. m., although he was not connected with the 46th Squad or Precinct in any way. Although, in fact, his job was in no way threatened, Bruno was told to tell petitioner that petitioner's telephone call had gotten him "in a lot of trouble," and that he should seek to extract sympathy from petitioner for Bruno's pregnant wife and three children. Bruno developed this theme with petitioner without success, and petitioner, also without success, again sought to see his attorney, a request which Bruno relayed unavailingly to his superiors. After this first session with petitioner, Bruno was again directed by Lt. Gannon to play on petitioner's sympathies, but again no confession was forthcoming. But the Lieutenant a third time ordered Bruno falsely to importune his friend to confess, but again petitioner clung to his attorney's advice. Inevitably, in the fourth such session directed by the Lieutenant, lasting a full hour, petitioner succumbed to his friend's prevarications and agreed to make a statement. Accordingly, at 3:25 a. m. the Assistant District Attorney, a stenographer, and several other law enforcement officials entered the room where petitioner was being questioned, and took his statement in question and answer form with the Assistant District Attorney asking the questions. The statement was completed at 4:05 a. m.

---

[1]   How this could be so when the attorney's name, Tobias Russo, was concededly in the telephone book does not appear. The trial judge sustained objections by the Assistant District Attorney to questions designed to delve into this mystery.

But this was not the end. At 4:30 a.m. three detectives took petitioner to Police Headquarters in Manhattan. On the way they attempted to find the bridge from which petitioner said he had thrown the murder weapon. They crossed the Triborough Bridge into Manhattan, arriving at Police Headquarters at 5 a. m., and left Manhattan for the Bronx at 5:40 a. m. via the Willis Avenue Bridge. When petitioner recognized neither bridge as the one from which he had thrown the weapon, they reentered Manhattan via the Third Avenue Bridge, which petitioner stated was the right one, and then returned to the Bronx well after 6 a. m. During that trip the officers also elicited a statement from petitioner that the deceased was always "on [his] back," "always pushing" him and that he was "not sorry" he had shot the deceased. All three detectives testified to that statement at the trial.

Court opened at 10 a. m. that morning, and petitioner was arraigned at 10:15.

At the trial, the confession was introduced in evidence over appropriate objections. The jury was instructed that it could rely on it only if it was found to be voluntary. The jury returned a guilty verdict and petitioner was sentenced to death. The New York Court of Appeals affirmed the conviction over three dissents, and we granted certiorari to resolve the serious problem presented under the Fourteenth Amendment. * * *

The abhorrence of society to the use of involuntary confessions does not turn alone on their inherent untrustworthiness. It also turns on the deep-rooted feeling that the police must obey the law while enforcing the law; that in the end life and liberty can be as much endangered from illegal methods used to convict those thought to be criminals as from the actual criminals themselves. Accordingly, the actions of police in obtaining confessions have come under scrutiny in a long series of cases. Those cases suggest that in recent years law enforcement officials have become increasingly aware of the burden which they share, along with our courts, in protecting fundamental rights of our citizenry, including that portion of our citizenry suspected of crime. The facts of no case recently in this Court have quite approached the brutal beatings in *Brown v. Mississippi*, 297 U.S. 278 (1936), or the 36 consecutive hours of questioning present in *Ashcraft v. Tennessee*, 322 U.S. 143 (1944). But as law enforcement officers become more responsible, and the methods used to extract confessions more sophisticated, our duty to enforce federal constitutional protections does not cease. It only becomes more difficult because of the more delicate judgments to be made. Our judgment here is that, on all the facts, this conviction cannot stand.

Petitioner was a foreign-born young man of 25 with no past history of law violation or of subjection to official interrogation, at least insofar as the record shows. He had progressed only one-half year into high school and the record indicates that he had a history of emotional instability.[3] He did not make a narrative statement, but was subject to the leading questions of a skillful prosecutor in a question and answer confession. He was subjected to questioning not by a few men, but by many. * * * All played some part, and the effect of such massive official interrogation must have been felt. Petitioner was questioned for virtually eight straight hours before he confessed, with his only respite being a transfer to an arena presumably considered more appropriate by the police for the task at hand. Nor was the questioning conducted during normal business hours, but began in early evening, continued into the night, and did not bear fruition until the not-too-early morning. The drama was not played out, with the final admissions obtained, until almost sunrise. In such circumstances slowly mounting fatigue does, and is calculated to, play its part. The questioners persisted in the face of his repeated refusals to answer on the advice of his attorney, and they ignored his reasonable requests to contact the local attorney whom he had already retained and who had personally delivered him into the custody of these officers in obedience to the bench warrant.

The use of Bruno, characterized in this Court by counsel for the State as a "childhood friend" of petitioner's, is another factor which deserves mention in the totality of the situation. Bruno's was the one face visible to petitioner in which he could put some trust. There was a bond of friendship between them going back a decade into adolescence. It was with this material that the officers felt that they could overcome petitioner's will. They instructed Bruno falsely to state that petitioner's telephone call had gotten him into trouble, that his job was in jeopardy, and that loss of his job would be disastrous to his three children, his wife and his unborn child. And Bruno played this part of a worried father, harried by his superiors, in not one, but four different acts, the final one lasting an hour. * * *

We conclude that petitioner's will was overborne by official pressure, fatigue and sympathy falsely aroused, after considering all the facts in their post-indictment setting. Here a grand jury had already found sufficient cause to require petitioner to face trial on a charge of first-degree murder, and the police had an eyewitness to the shooting. The police were not therefore merely trying to solve a crime, or even to absolve a suspect. They were rather concerned primarily with securing a statement from defendant on which they could convict him. The undeviating intent of the officers to extract a confession from petitioner is therefore patent. When such an intent is shown, this Court has held that the confession obtained

---

[3]   Medical reports from New York City's Fordham Hospital introduced by defendant showed that he had suffered a cerebral concussion in 1955. He was described by a private physician in 1951 as "an extremely nervous tense individual who is emotionally unstable and maladjusted," and was found unacceptable for military service in 1951, primarily because of "Psychiatric disorder." He failed the Army's AFQT-1 intelligence test. His mother had been in mental hospitals on three separate occasions.

must be examined with the most careful scrutiny, and has reversed a conviction on facts less compelling than these. Accordingly, we hold that petitioner's conviction cannot stand under the Fourteenth Amendment.

* * * The judgment must be

Reversed.

MR. JUSTICE DOUGLAS, with whom MR. JUSTICE BLACK and MR. JUSTICE BRENNAN join, concurring.

While I join the opinion of the Court, I add what for me is an even more important ground of decision.

* * * The question is whether after the indictment and before the trial the Government can interrogate the accused in secret when he asked for his lawyer and when his request was denied. This is a capital case; and under the rule of *Powell v. Alabama*, 287 U.S. 45, the defendant was entitled to be represented by counsel. This representation by counsel is not restricted to the trial. * * *

Depriving a person, formally charged with a crime, of counsel during the period prior to trial may be more damaging than denial of counsel during the trial itself.

We do not have here mere suspects who are being secretly interrogated by the police * * *, nor witnesses who are being questioned in secret administrative or judicial proceedings * * *. This is a case of an accused, who is scheduled to be tried by a judge and jury, being tried in a preliminary way by the police. This is a kangaroo court procedure whereby the police produce the vital evidence in the form of a confession which is useful or necessary to obtain a conviction. They in effect deny him effective representation by counsel. This seems to me to be a flagrant violation of the principle announced in *Powell v. Alabama*, *supra*, that the right of counsel extends to the preparation for trial, as well as to the trial itself. * * * When he is deprived of that right after indictment and before trial, he may indeed be denied effective representation by counsel at the only stage when legal aid and advice would help him. * * *

* * * [W]hat use is a defendant's right to effective counsel at every stage of a criminal case if, while he is held awaiting trial, he can be questioned in the absence of counsel until he confesses? In that event the secret trial in the police precincts effectively supplants the public trial guaranteed by the Bill of Rights.

MR. JUSTICE STEWART, whom MR. JUSTICE DOUGLAS and MR. JUSTICE BRENNAN join, concurring.

While I concur in the opinion of the Court, it is my view that the absence of counsel when this confession was elicited was alone enough to render it inadmissible under the Fourteenth Amendment.

Let it be emphasized at the outset that this is not a case where the police were questioning a suspect in the course of investigating an unsolved crime. When the petitioner surrendered to the New York authorities he was under indictment for first degree murder.

Under our system of justice an indictment is supposed to be followed by an arraignment and a trial. At every stage in those proceedings the accused has an absolute right to a lawyer's help if the case is one in which a death sentence may be imposed. *Powell v. Alabama*, 287 U.S. 45. Indeed the right to the assistance of counsel whom the accused has himself retained is absolute, whatever the offense for which he is on trial.

What followed the petitioner's surrender in this case was not arraignment in a court of law, but an all-night inquisition in a prosecutor's office, a police station, and an automobile. Throughout the night the petitioner repeatedly asked to be allowed to send for his lawyer, and his requests were repeatedly denied. He finally was induced to make a confession. That confession was used to secure a verdict sending him to the electric chair.

Our Constitution guarantees the assistance of counsel to a man on trial for his life in an orderly courtroom, presided over by a judge, open to the public, and protected by all the procedural safeguards of the law. Surely a Constitution which promises that much can vouchsafe no less to the same man under midnight inquisition in the squad room of a police station.

QUESTIONS, COMMENTS, CONCERNS?

1.   The Fifth Amendment and *Spano*. Notice that, at the time of *Spano*, the Fifth Amendment had not yet been incorporated. Remember, the Court issued *Malloy v. Hogan* (Chapter 1) in 1964. The *Spano* Court, then, must rely on the Fourteenth Amendment. It's also wrestling with how to address interrogation tactics that have replaced the third degree: i.e., those that are *psychologically* coercive, but do not rely on physical violence or torture.

2.   A (more) modern example of voluntariness. In *Arizona v. Fulminante*, 499 U.S. 279 (1991), Oreste Fulminante on September 14, 1982, called the police to report that his eleven-year-old stepdaughter, Jeneane Michelle Hunt, was missing. Hunt was found dead two days later; she had been shot twice in the head, and investigators found a ligature around her neck. Officers could not tell whether she had been sexually assaulted.

Although Fulminante was considered a suspect, he was not initially charged. He left Arizona for New Jersey, but was later convicted in New Jersey on federal charges of possession of a firearm by a felon. While incarcerated on that charge, he became friends with another inmate, Anthony Sarivola, who was a paid informant for the Federal Bureau of Investigation. Once Sarivola heard that Fulminante was suspected of killing a child in Arizona, Sarivola tried engaging Fulminante on the topic. Fulminante repeatedly denied his involvement in Hunt's death, but once told Sarivola that Hunt was killed by bikers looking for drugs. Yet during another conversation, Fulminante said he did not know what had happened. Sarivola passed this information on to an FBI agent who told Sarivola to find out more.

One evening in October 1983, Sarivola said that he knew Fulminante was "starting to get some tough treatment and whatnot" from other inmates because of the rumor about Fulminante killing Hunt. Sarivola later said that he responded by offering to protect Fulminante from the other inmates on one condition: " 'You have to tell me about it,' you know. I mean, in other words, 'For me to give you any help.' " Fulminante then confessed to Sarivola that he had drove Hunt to the desert on his motorcycle before choking her, sexually assaulting her, and shooting her twice in the head.

Fulminante was later indicted in Arizona for the first-degree murder of Hunt. He moved to suppress the confession he made to Sarivola, as well as a second confession he had given to Sarivola's fiancée. Fulminante argued that the confession to Sarivola was coerced and that his second confession was the "fruit" of the first. The trial court denied his motion, and the state introduced both confessions against Fulminante who was convicted of Hunt's murder and sentenced to death.

On certiorari, the Supreme Court held that Fulminante's confession to Sarivola was coerced in violation of the Fourteenth Amendment. Writing for a 5–4 majority, Justice White wrote:

> Although the question is a close one, we agree with the Arizona Supreme Court's conclusion that Fulminante's confession was coerced. The Arizona Supreme Court found a credible threat of physical violence unless Fulminante confessed. Our cases have made clear that a finding of coercion need not depend upon actual violence by a government agent; a credible threat is sufficient. As we have said, "coercion can be mental as well as physical, and . . . the blood of the accused is not the only hallmark of an unconstitutional inquisition." *Blackburn v. Alabama*, 361 U.S. 199, 206 (1960). *See also* * * * *Payne v. Arkansas*, 356 U.S. 560, 561 (1958). As in *Payne*, where the Court found that a confession was coerced because the interrogating police officer had promised that if the accused confessed, the officer would protect the accused from an angry mob outside the jailhouse door, so too here, the Arizona Supreme Court found that it was fear of physical violence, absent protection from his friend (and Government agent) Sarivola, which motivated Fulminante to confess. Accepting the Arizona court's finding, permissible on this record, that there was a credible threat of physical violence, we agree with its conclusion that Fulminante's will was overborne in such a way as to render his confession the product of coercion.

After the Supreme Court's opinion, Fulminante received a new trial and was again convicted. But his conviction was reversed *again* on appeal. *State v. Fulminante*, 975 P.2d 75 (Ariz. 1999).

The popular *Law & Order* show based an episode titled, "Confession" on the Supreme Court's *Fulminante* decision. *Confession (L&O)*, http://lawand order.wikia.com/wiki/Confession_(L%26O) (last visited Aug. 13, 2022). The episode was first aired on September 17, 1991 during season two.

3.   Evaluating Misskelley's confession. As you listen to Misskelley's confession [Casefile MP3 1], please follow along with the interrogation transcript, [Casefile Document 2]. Doing so creates a fuller picture by allowing you to assess both the officers' and Misskelley's demeanors. Let's consider some facets of that transcript.

a)   *Valid waiver?* At the outset of the interrogation, the detectives walk Misskelley through his *Miranda* rights. At one point, Detective Ridge says about Misskelley's *Miranda* waiver form, "we are informing you that we are Detective Sergeant Mark Fallon, and Detective Brian Ridge, and Detective Sergeant Mark Fallon is the one that read this form to you earlier, is that correct?" [Casefile Document 2, at 1.] What's the definition, do you think of "earlier"? Does it trouble you that officers secured a waiver of Misskelley's rights *before* starting the audio recording? How should that factor into the voluntariness analysis?

b)   *Feeding Misskelley details.* At numerous points, the officers feed details to Misskelley. Presumably, they learned those details in an earlier interrogation or, more problematically, from a different facet of the case. Consider a few examples. First, when discussing how to access the woods where the victims were killed, Misskelley never mentions a path. But Detective Ridge injects one: "Is there a path that you go down?" [Casefile Document 2, at 5.] Second, Detective Ridge suggests to Misskelley that Misskelley "saw somebody with a knife." *Id.* at 7. He also feeds Misskelley that the victims were cut: "Alright, another boy was cut I understand, where was he cut at?" *Id.* Third, Detective Mitchell seems to want one of the victims to be hit with a stick. He asks, without Misskelley previously discussing a stick, "[d]id you ever use, did anyone use a stick and hit the boys with?" *Id.* at 15. Fourth, and perhaps most problematically, Detective Mitchell feeds Misskelley a factual detail about a briefcase: "Did they have a briefcase with them?" *Id.* at 16. Other examples abound. *See, e.g., id.* at 16 ("Is that when you first saw the pictures of the little boys?"); *id.* at 18 ("Okay, the night you were in these woods, uh had you all been in the water?"); *id.* at 19 ("You've been back to this place since that murder?").

Are officers contaminating the record by feeding Misskelley these details or, rather, are they simply reminding him of their prior conversations to jog his memory? How does officer contamination factor into the *Spano* voluntariness test?

c) *Is Misskelley credible?* Misskelley stumbles at numerous points during his responses to the officers' questions. At one point, he is unable to correctly identify one of the victims. [Casefile Document 2, at 4.] At another point, officers ask him questions about anal sex, yet at another point, they appear so concerned about his knowledge of basic anatomy that they ask him, "Do you know what [a] penis is?" *Id.* at 7. Just a few lines later, Detective Ridge again asks, "Alright, do you know what a penis is?" *Id.* at 8.

Three other major factual issues persist. First, Misskelley states that the victims skipped school on the day they were killed. *Id.* at 9. That turned out to be false. [*See* Casefile Document 6, at 66–67.]

Second, Misskelley constantly changes when he left the murder scene. Early on in the interrogation, he says he left right after Echols and Baldwin tied the boys up. [Casefile Document 2, at 6.] As the interrogation progressed, though, Misskelley would say he left after he watched Echols and Baldwin cut the boys, *id.* at 8, though he returned to his answer that he left once the boys were tied up, *id.* at 13. Ultimately, Misskelley would say that, before running from the scene, he was there to witness Echols and Baldwin sexually assault and beat the victims. *Id.* at 21.

The final lingering factual issue surrounds Misskelley's ability perceive time. Throughout the interrogation—and then the clarification of statement beginning on page 27—Misskelley would provide differing answers about when the boys arrived at the scene. He first says he arrived at 9 a.m., *id.* at 11, but then says that Echols and Baldwin called him at 9 p.m., *id.* at 12. Officers are confused. *Id.* at 12 ("I've got some real confusion with the times you're telling me . . . ."). So much so that they stop the interrogation and return to try to clarify Misskelley's timeframe. *See id.* at 27 (Clarification Statement). That does not seem to help. Misskelley tells them the victims came to the woods between 5–6 p.m. *Id.* at 27. He then changes that to 7 p.m. *Id.* at 28.

Misskelley is unsure about other details, like when Echols and Baldwin called him later in the day after killing the victims. He also changes his recollection of what he and Baldwin were wearing on the day the victims were killed. If Misskelley cannot remember all of these basic details, how credible should his confession be? Is there a way to capture that concern in the voluntariness analysis?

d) *What exactly did Misskelley confess to?* Was Misskelley an active participant in the killings according to his own statements?

4. Recording interrogations. Notice a major—and obvious—problem with Misskelley's confession: law enforcement recorded only part of it, although presumably they had full capability to record *all* of it. They also only recorded the audio of Misskelley's confession—not the video. Consider a few questions related to that issue:

a) Why might officers decline to record all of their interrogation of a suspect?

b)   Is there a credible reason why officers might not record the totality of their interrogation?

c)   Who would define what constitutes "all" of an interrogation? After all, the savvy defense attorney would presumably want *any* conversation between Misskelley and the police recorded.

d)   Even if officers recorded "all" of the Misskelley interrogation, what might be problematic about having just an audio recording?

e)   Notice that, even in this recording, the officers appear to start and stop the tape a number of times. How does that impact the voluntariness of Misskelley's statements?

f)   How does Misskelley's attorney creatively frame law enforcement's failure to record the full interrogation as a constitutional problem? [*See* Casefile Document 7, at 25–30.]

As of 2014, nineteen states have mandated video recording interrogations at least for certain crimes. Jeff Kukucka, *Lights, Camera, Justice: The Value of Recording Police Interrogations*, HUFFINGTONPOST.COM (May 28, 2014), https://www.huffingtonpost.com/jeff-kukucka/lights-camera-justice-the_b_540 4579.html. Other departments have voluntarily adopted a recording policy. *Id.* And, since 2014, other mandatory recording laws have arisen. *E.g.*, Ayla Ferrone, *Police Now Must Record Interrogations in Serious Investigations*, NEWS10.COM (Apr. 11, 2018), http://www.news10.com/news/local-news/police-now-must-record-interrogations-in-serious-investigations/1104880505.

But despite the increasing number of jurisdictions adopting recording laws, troubling questions persist. How much should officers record? Should a recording take place in a particular room? Must the recording include the officers and the suspect or just the suspect? To many, that last question is particularly important given the norm of "camera bias." A 2015 study by Ohio University psychology professor G. Daniel Lassiter revealed that, when the camera focuses just on the suspect, "viewers are more likely to believe that any self-incriminating statement is voluntary." *A new perspective on police interrogations*, NSF.GOV (Sept. 3, 2015), https://www.nsf.gov/discoveries/disc_summ.jsp?cntn_id=136170&WT.mc_id=USNSF_1.

5.   More on *Spano*'s application to Misskelley. How does *Spano* apply to Misskelley's case? And more specifically, what statements does Misskelley make on June 3 that you think merit suppression? *Spano* teaches that the totality of the circumstances due process voluntariness test requires courts to consider the suspect's statement against both the circumstances of the interrogation alongside the character of the suspect.

What circumstances are relevant to the *Spano* analysis from the circumstances of the interrogation? Look at a handful of pages of the suppression hearing transcript. [*See* Casefile Document 6, at 17, 26 (discussion with Misskelley prior to providing *Miranda*); 29–30 (when Misskelley became a suspect); 35–36, 43–50, 58–62, 106–16 (role of the polygraph); 38–39, 117–18 (bringing up a reward for information to Misskelley); 66–67, 73–74 (inaccuracies in Misskelley's story); 68–70, 94 (using a controversial drawing to get Misskelley to talk); 82–85, 99 (events prior to the taped interrogation).]

And relatedly, what about the character of the accused? What do we learn about Misskelley that is relevant for purposes of *Spano*? [*See* Casefile Document 6, at 8, 12, 26–27 (intelligence); 9 (no guardian present); 10, 13 (age); 75 (having to explain "penis" to Misskelley).

   6.   Counsel for Misskelley. How did Misskelley's defense attorney do in specifying which statements should be suppressed? Can you tell when the *first* time Misskelley's attorney even mentioned the June 3 interrogation? [*See* Casefile Document 7, at 37.]

COLORADO V. CONNELLY
479 U.S. 157
Supreme Court of the United States
October 8, 1986, Argued; December 10, 1986, Decided
No. 85-660

CHIEF JUSTICE REHNQUIST delivered the opinion of the Court. * * *

I

On August 18, 1983, Officer Patrick Anderson of the Denver Police Department was in uniform, working in an off-duty capacity in downtown Denver. Respondent Francis Connelly approached Officer Anderson and, without any prompting, stated that he had murdered someone and wanted to talk about it. Anderson immediately advised respondent that he had the right to remain silent, that anything he said could be used against him in court, and that he had the right to an attorney prior to any police questioning. *See Miranda v. Arizona*, 384 U.S. 436 (1966). Respondent stated that he understood these rights but he still wanted to talk about the murder. Understandably bewildered by this confession, Officer Anderson asked respondent several questions. Connelly denied that he had been drinking, denied that he had been taking any drugs, and stated that, in the past, he had been a patient in several mental hospitals. Officer Anderson again told Connelly that he was under no obligation to say anything. Connelly replied that it was "all right," and that he would talk to Officer Anderson because his conscience had been bothering him. To Officer Anderson, respondent appeared to understand fully the nature of his acts.

Shortly thereafter, Homicide Detective Stephen Antuna arrived. Respondent was again advised of his rights, and Detective Antuna asked him "what he had on his mind." Respondent answered that he had come all the way from Boston to confess to the murder of Mary Ann Junta, a young girl whom he had killed in Denver sometime during November 1982. Respondent was taken to police headquarters, and a search of police records revealed that the body of an unidentified female had been found in April 1983. Respondent openly detailed his story to Detective Antuna and

Sergeant Thomas Haney, and readily agreed to take the officers to the scene of the killing. Under Connelly's sole direction, the two officers and respondent proceeded in a police vehicle to the location of the crime. Respondent pointed out the exact location of the murder. Throughout this episode, Detective Antuna perceived no indication whatsoever that respondent was suffering from any kind of mental illness.

Respondent was held overnight. During an interview with the public defender's office the following morning, he became visibly disoriented. He began giving confused answers to questions, and for the first time, stated that "voices" had told him to come to Denver and that he had followed the directions of these voices in confessing. Respondent was sent to a state hospital for evaluation. He was initially found incompetent to assist in his own defense. By March 1984, however, the doctors evaluating respondent determined that he was competent to proceed to trial.

At a preliminary hearing, respondent moved to suppress all of his statements. Dr. Jeffrey Metzner, a psychiatrist employed by the state hospital, testified that respondent was suffering from chronic schizophrenia and was in a psychotic state at least as of August 17, 1983, the day before he confessed. Metzner's interviews with respondent revealed that respondent was following the "voice of God." This voice instructed respondent to withdraw money from the bank, to buy an airplane ticket, and to fly from Boston to Denver. When respondent arrived from Boston, God's voice became stronger and told respondent either to confess to the killing or to commit suicide. Reluctantly following the command of the voices, respondent approached Officer Anderson and confessed.

Dr. Metzner testified that, in his expert opinion, respondent was experiencing "command hallucinations." This condition interfered with respondent's "volitional abilities; that is, his ability to make free and rational choices." Dr. Metzner further testified that Connelly's illness did not significantly impair his cognitive abilities. Thus, respondent understood the rights he had when Officer Anderson and Detective Antuna advised him that he need not speak. Dr. Metzner admitted that the "voices" could in reality be Connelly's interpretation of his own guilt, but explained that in his opinion, Connelly's psychosis motivated his confession.

On the basis of this evidence the Colorado trial court decided that respondent's statements must be suppressed because they were "involuntary." * * * Accordingly, respondent's initial statements and his custodial confession were suppressed.

The Colorado Supreme Court affirmed. * * *

II

The Due Process Clause of the Fourteenth Amendment provides that no State shall "deprive any person of life, liberty, or property, without due process of law." Just last Term * * * we held that by virtue of the Due Process Clause "certain interrogation techniques, either in isolation or as applied to the unique characteristics of a particular suspect, are so offensive to a civilized system of justice that they must be condemned."

Indeed, coercive government misconduct was the catalyst for this Court's seminal confession case, *Brown v. Mississippi*, 297 U.S. 278 (1936). In that case, police officers extracted confessions from the accused through brutal torture. The Court had little difficulty concluding that even though the Fifth Amendment did not at that time apply to the States, the actions of the police were "revolting to the sense of justice." The Court has retained this due process focus, even after holding, in *Malloy v. Hogan*, 378 U.S. 1 (1964), that the Fifth Amendment privilege against compulsory self-incrimination applies to the States.

Thus the cases considered by this Court over the 50 years since *Brown v. Mississippi* have focused upon the crucial element of police overreaching. While each confession case has turned on its own set of factors justifying the conclusion that police conduct was oppressive, all have contained a substantial element of coercive police conduct. Absent police conduct causally related to the confession, there is simply no basis for concluding that any state actor has deprived a criminal defendant of due process of law. Respondent correctly notes that as interrogators have turned to more subtle forms of psychological persuasion, courts have found the mental condition of the defendant a more significant factor in the "voluntariness" calculus. *See Spano v. New York*, 360 U.S. 315 (1959). But this fact does not justify a conclusion that a defendant's mental condition, by itself and apart from its relation to official coercion, should ever dispose of the inquiry into constitutional "voluntariness."

Respondent relies on *Blackburn v. Alabama*, 361 U.S. 199 (1960), and *Townsend v. Sain*, 372 U.S. 293 (1963), for the proposition that the "deficient mental condition of the defendants in those cases was sufficient to render their confessions involuntary." But respondent's reading of *Blackburn* and *Townsend* ignores the integral element of police overreaching present in both cases. In *Blackburn*, the Court found that the petitioner was probably insane at the time of his confession and the police learned during the interrogation that he had a history of mental problems. The police exploited this weakness with coercive tactics: "the eight- to nine-hour sustained interrogation in a tiny room which was upon occasion literally filled with police officers; the absence of Blackburn's friends, relatives, or legal counsel; [and] the composition of the confession by the Deputy Sheriff rather than by Blackburn." These tactics supported a finding that the confession was involuntary. Indeed, the Court specifically condemned police activity that "wrings a confession out of an accused against his will." *Townsend* presented a similar instance of police wrongdoing. In that case, a police physician had given Townsend a drug with truth-serum properties. The subsequent confession, obtained by officers who knew that Townsend had been given drugs, was held involuntary. These two cases demonstrate that while mental condition is surely relevant to an individual's susceptibility to police coercion, mere examination of the confessant's state of mind can never conclude the due process inquiry.

Our "involuntary confession" jurisprudence is entirely consistent with the settled law requiring some sort of "state action" to support a claim of violation of the Due Process Clause of the Fourteenth Amendment. The Colorado trial court, of course, found that the police committed no wrongful acts, and that finding has been neither challenged by respondent nor disturbed by the Supreme Court of Colorado. The latter court, however, concluded that sufficient state action was present by virtue of the admission of the confession into evidence in a court of the State.

The difficulty with the approach of the Supreme Court of Colorado is that it fails to recognize the essential link between coercive activity of the State, on the one hand, and a resulting confession by a defendant, on the other. The flaw in respondent's constitutional argument is that it would expand our previous line of "voluntariness" cases into a far-ranging requirement that courts must divine a defendant's motivation for speaking or acting as he did even though there be no claim that governmental conduct coerced his decision.

The most outrageous behavior by a private party seeking to secure evidence against a defendant does not make that evidence inadmissible under the Due Process Clause. * * *

* * * Respondent would now have us require sweeping inquiries into the state of mind of a criminal defendant who has confessed, inquiries quite divorced from any coercion brought to bear on the defendant by the State. We think the Constitution rightly leaves this sort of inquiry to be resolved by state laws governing the admission of evidence and erects no standard of its own in this area. A statement rendered by one in the condition of respondent might be proved to be quite unreliable, but this is a matter to be governed by the evidentiary laws of the forum, and not by the Due Process Clause of the Fourteenth Amendment. "The aim of the requirement of due process is not to exclude presumptively false evidence, but to prevent fundamental unfairness in the use of evidence, whether true or false."

We hold that coercive police activity is a necessary predicate to the finding that a confession is not "voluntary" within the meaning of the Due Process Clause of the Fourteenth Amendment. We also conclude that the taking of respondent's statements, and their admission into evidence, constitute no violation of that Clause. * * *

The judgment of the Supreme Court of Colorado is accordingly reversed, and the cause is remanded for further proceedings not inconsistent with this opinion.

It is so ordered.

JUSTICE BLACKMUN, concurring in part and concurring in the judgment.

[Omitted.]

JUSTICE STEVENS, concurring in the judgment in part and dissenting in part.

[Omitted.]

JUSTICE BRENNAN, with whom JUSTICE MARSHALL joins, dissenting.

Today the Court denies Mr. Connelly his fundamental right to make a vital choice with a sane mind, involving a determination that could allow the State to deprive him of liberty or even life. * * * Because I believe that the use of a mentally ill person's involuntary confession is antithetical to the notion of fundamental fairness embodied in the Due Process Clause, I dissent.

I

The respondent's seriously impaired mental condition is clear on the record of this case. At the time of his confession, Mr. Connelly suffered from a "longstanding severe mental disorder," diagnosed as chronic paranoid schizophrenia. He had been hospitalized for psychiatric reasons five times prior to his confession; his longest hospitalization lasted for seven months. Mr. Connelly heard imaginary voices and saw nonexistent objects. He believed that his father was God, and that he was a reincarnation of Jesus.

At the time of his confession, Mr. Connelly's mental problems included "grandiose and delusional thinking." He had a known history of "thought withdrawal and insertion." Although physicians had treated Mr. Connelly "with a wide variety of medications in the past including antipsychotic medications," he had not taken any antipsychotic medications for at least six months prior to his confession. Following his arrest, Mr. Connelly initially was found incompetent to stand trial because the court-appointed psychiatrist, Dr. Metzner, "wasn't very confident that he could consistently relate accurate information." Dr. Metzner testified that Mr. Connelly was unable "to make free and rational choices" due to auditory hallucinations: "[When] he was read his Miranda rights, he probably had the capacity to know that he was being read his Miranda rights [but] he wasn't able to use that information because of the command hallucinations that he had experienced." He achieved competency to stand trial only after six months of hospitalization and treatment with antipsychotic and sedative medications.

The state trial court found that the "overwhelming evidence presented by the Defense" indicated that the prosecution did not meet its burden of demonstrating by a preponderance of the evidence that the initial statement to Officer Anderson was voluntary. While the court found no police misconduct, it held:

> [There's] no question that the Defendant did not exercise free will in choosing to talk to the police. He exercised a choice both [sic] of which were mandated by auditory hallucination, had no basis in reality, and were the product of a psychotic break with reality. The Defendant at the time of the confession had absolutely in the Court's estimation no volition or choice to make.

* * *

The Supreme Court of Colorado affirmed after evaluating "the totality of circumstances" surrounding the unsolicited confession * * *.

II

The absence of police wrongdoing should not, by itself, determine the voluntariness of a confession by a mentally ill person. The requirement that a confession be voluntary reflects a recognition of the importance of free will and of reliability in determining the admissibility of a confession, and thus demands an inquiry into the totality of the circumstances surrounding the confession.

A

Today's decision restricts the application of the term "involuntary" to those confessions obtained by police coercion. Confessions by mentally ill individuals or by persons coerced by parties other than police officers are now considered "voluntary." The Court's failure to recognize all forms of involuntariness or coercion as antithetical to due process reflects a refusal to acknowledge free will as a value of constitutional consequence. But due process derives much of its meaning from a conception of fundamental fairness that emphasizes the right to make vital choices voluntarily: "The Fourteenth Amendment secures against state invasion . . . the right of a person to remain silent unless he chooses to speak in the unfettered exercise of his own will. . . ." *Malloy v. Hogan*, 378 U.S. 1, 8 (1964). This right requires vigilant protection if we are to safeguard the values of private conscience and human dignity.

* * *

A true commitment to fundamental fairness requires that the inquiry be "not whether the conduct of state officers in obtaining the confession is shocking, but whether the confession was 'free and voluntary'. . . ." *Malloy v. Hogan, supra,* at 7.

We have never confined our focus to police coercion, because the value of freedom of will has demanded a broader inquiry. The confession cases decided by this Court over the 50 years since *Brown v. Mississippi*, 297 U.S. 278 (1936), have focused upon both police overreaching and free will. While it is true that police overreaching has been an element of every confession case to date, it is also true that in every case the Court has made clear that ensuring that a confession is a product of free will is an independent concern. The fact that involuntary confessions have always been excluded in part because of police overreaching signifies only that this is a case of first impression. Until today, we have never upheld the admission of a confession that does not reflect the exercise of free will. * * *

This Court * * * favor[s] * * * the view that only confessions rendered involuntary by some state action are inadmissible, and that the only relevant form of state action is police conduct. But even if state action is required, police overreaching is not its only relevant form. * * *

* * * [W]e have traditionally examined the totality of the circumstances, including the motivation and competence of the defendant, in determining whether a confession is voluntary. Even today's Court admits that "as interrogators have turned to more subtle forms of psychological persuasion, courts have found the mental condition of the defendant a more significant factor in the 'voluntariness' calculus." The Court's holding that involuntary confessions are only those procured through police misconduct is thus inconsistent with the Court's historical insistence that only confessions reflecting an exercise of free will be admitted into evidence.

B

Since the Court redefines voluntary confessions to include confessions by mentally ill individuals, the reliability of these confessions becomes a central concern. A concern for reliability is inherent in our criminal justice system, which relies upon accusatorial rather than inquisitorial practices. While an inquisitorial system prefers obtaining confessions from criminal defendants, an accusatorial system must place its faith in determinations of "guilt by evidence independently and freely secured." * * *

Our distrust for reliance on confessions is due, in part, to their decisive impact upon the adversarial process. * * *

The instant case starkly highlights the danger of admitting a confession by a person with a severe mental illness. The trial court made no findings concerning the reliability of Mr. Connelly's involuntary confession, since it believed that the confession was excludable on the basis of involuntariness. However, the overwhelming evidence in the record points to the unreliability of Mr. Connelly's delusional mind. Mr. Connelly was found incompetent to stand trial because he was unable to relate accurate information, and the court-appointed psychiatrist indicated that

Mr. Connelly was actively hallucinating and exhibited delusional thinking at the time of his confession. The Court, in fact, concedes that "[a] statement rendered by one in the condition of respondent might be proved to be quite unreliable. . . ."

Moreover, the record is barren of any corroboration of the mentally ill defendant's confession. No physical evidence links the defendant to the alleged crime. Police did not identify the alleged victim's body as the woman named by the defendant. Mr. Connelly identified the alleged scene of the crime, but it has not been verified that the unidentified body was found there or that a crime actually occurred there. There is not a shred of competent evidence in this record linking the defendant to the charged homicide. There is only Mr. Connelly's confession.

Minimum standards of due process should require that the trial court find substantial indicia of reliability, on the basis of evidence extrinsic to the confession itself, before admitting the confession of a mentally ill person into evidence. I would require the trial court to make such a finding on remand. To hold otherwise allows the State to imprison and possibly to execute a mentally ill defendant based solely upon an inherently unreliable confession. * * *

I dissent.

QUESTIONS, COMMENTS, CONCERNS?

1.   **Voluntariness and "fruits".** In *Mincey v. Arizona*, 437 U.S. 385 (1978), undercover police officer Barry Headricks arranged to buy heroin from Rufus Mincey on the morning of October 28, 1974. Later that afternoon, Headricks and nine other plainclothes policemen returned to raid Mincey's apartment. As Headricks entered the apartment, he moved quickly to Mincey's bedroom in order to make an arrest. The other officers could only watch as a flurry of shots rang out from inside the bedroom and Officer Headricks collapsed on the floor. As the other officers rushed to help Headricks, they discovered Mincey wounded on the floor with an apparent gunshot wound. Officer Headricks died several hours later.

Mincey was brought to the hospital immediately after the shooting. As a result of Mincey's injuries, tubes were inserted into his throat to help him breathe. At about 8:00 p.m. that evening, Detective Hust of the Tucson Police Department went to the hospital, arrested Mincey, and informed him of his *Miranda* rights. Detective Hust began to question Mency, but because of the tubes in his mouth, Mincey responded to Hust's questions in writing. Although Mincey asked repeatedly for the interrogation to stop until he could speak with an attorney, Hust continued his questioning until almost midnight. At trial, Mincey's incriminating statements were used against him.

The Supreme Court held that the statements made by Mincey in the hospital were involuntary and could not be used against him. The Court wrote,

"It is hard to imagine a situation less conducive to the exercise of 'a rational intellect and free will' than Mincey's." The Court reasoned that Mincey, in his "debilitated and helpless condition," clearly expressed a desire not to be interrogated without the presence of an attorney. Accordingly, said the Court, Mincey's statements were not the product of his free and rational choice. Due process of law therefore required exclusion of Mincey's statements for *all* purposes—including impeachment—at his trial.

One year after *Mincey*, the Supreme Court in *New Jersey v. Portash*, 440 U.S. 450 (1979), reaffirmed that the prosecution may not rely on an involuntary confession or its fruit for any purpose in a criminal trial. It specifically held that "a defendant's compelled statements, as opposed to statements taken in violation of *Miranda*, may not be put to any testimonial use whatever against him in a criminal trial." Collectively, *Mincey* and *Portash* make clear that *Miranda*'s exclusionary rule is different from—and weaker than—*Spano*'s exclusionary rule.

    2. Misskelley and age. Misskelley is a juvenile. Should a different standard exist for measuring the voluntariness of a juvenile's confession?

    3. Psychological coercion. Officers relied on a polygraph to induce Misskelley into confessing on tape. According to Misskelley's attorney, officers told Misskelley that he was "lying his ass off." [Casefile Document 7, at 16.] In actuality, the results of the polygraph were less than clear. Does it matter to the voluntariness analysis if the officers lied to Misskelley about the results of his polygraph? Or rather, is the polygraph analogous to the voices respondent heard in *Connelly*?

    Those questions aside, you should be aware that the results of a polygraph are inadmissible as evidence in a criminal trial. *See, e.g., United States v. Gill*, 513 F.3d 836, 846 (8th Cir. 2008) ("Our cases make clear polygraph evidence is disfavored."); *United States v. Gardiner*, 463 F.3d 445, 469 n.8 (6th Cir. 2006) ("Admission of polygraph evidence is disfavored in this Circuit . . . ."); *United States v. Messina*, 131 F.3d 36, 42 (2d Cir. 1997) (refusing to admit polygraph results in sentencing proceedings). The logic for excluding polygraph results, in short, is that they are unreliable. Numerous studies cast doubt on the accuracy of polygraphs. *See, e.g.*, Council Report, *Polygraph*, 256 JAMA 1172, 1173 (1986) (concluding that there are "enough false-positives and false-negatives to make many applications [of the polygraph], perhaps even in criminal cases, of dubious value"); Douglas Carroll, *How Accurate Is Polygraph Lie Detection?, in* THE POLYGRAPH TEST: LIES, TRUTH AND SCIENCE 19, 22 (Anthony Gale ed., 1988) (reporting lab results that reflect a twenty-three percent chance for an innocent person to be classified as guilty); Kleinmuntz & Julian J. Szucko, *On the Fallibility of Lie Detection*, 17 LAW & SOC'Y REV. 85, 87 (1982) ("[T]here is no reason to believe that lying produces distinctive physiological changes that characterize it and only it.").

B.   THE DOCTRINE'S UNPREDICTABILITY

Our final case in this chapter illustrates a troubling reality—applying the voluntariness test produces, at best, unpredictable results. Perhaps that's unsurprising given that the voluntariness test relies on a totality of the circumstances approach where seemingly everything is relevant, but nothing is dispositive. Such an approach, in turn, leaves the police with little meaningful guidance. In many ways, that concern—to provide the police with more structure in the interrogation room—served as the basis for the Court's decision in *Miranda v. Arizona* (Chapter 8). But more on that later.

UNITED STATES V. LEBRUN

363 F.3d 715
United States Court of Appeals for the Eighth Circuit
April 16, 2003, Submitted; April 9, 2004, Filed
No. 01-4005

JUDGES: Before LOKEN, CHIEF JUDGE, MCMILLIAN, BOWMAN, WOLLMAN, HANSEN, MORRIS SHEPPARD ARNOLD, MURPHY, BYE, RILEY, MELLOY, and SMITH, CIRCUIT JUDGES. MORRIS SHEPPARD ARNOLD, CIRCUIT JUDGE, with whom MCMILLIAN, BYE, and SMITH, CIRCUIT JUDGES, join, dissenting.

HANSEN, CIRCUIT JUDGE.

After thirty-three minutes of questioning, Michael LeBrun confessed to naval investigators that in 1968, while he was enlisted in the United States Navy, he strangled to death his superior officer, Ensign Andrew Muns, on board the U.S.S. Cacapon after Ensign Muns caught LeBrun robbing the safe in the ship's disbursing office. The district court suppressed the confession on the ground that it was * * * coerced, and thus obtained in violation of LeBrun's due process rights. The government appealed, and a divided panel of this court affirmed the judgment of the district court. We granted the government's petition for rehearing en banc, vacated the panel opinion, and for the reasons stated below, now reverse the judgment of the district court.

I.

Muns and LeBrun served as shipmates during the Vietnam War aboard the U.S.S. Cacapon. Ensign Muns served as the disbursing officer, and LeBrun served as the disbursing clerk. On January 16 or 17, 1968, while the U.S.S. Cacapon was moored in the Subic Bay, Muns disappeared. After conducting an investigation into Muns' disappearance, the Navy concluded that Muns had stolen $ 8600 from the disbursing office and had deserted. Thirty years later, still unconvinced of her brother's wrong-doing, Muns' sister convinced Special Agent Peter Hughes of the Naval Criminal Investigative Service ("NCIS") Cold Case Homicide Unit to reopen the investigation.

In the fall of 1999, NCIS agents conducted four interviews with LeBrun. On each of these four occasions, LeBrun cooperated with the investigators and voluntarily answered questions regarding Muns' disappearance. On three of these occasions, he was given his *Miranda* warnings by the interviewers. During an interview conducted on November 20,1999, LeBrun told NCIS agents that he realized that he may have been involved in the death and disappearance of Ensign Muns. LeBrun also told the agents that he felt that he had repressed memories, and he asked Agent Hughes if he knew of a therapist who could help LeBrun recover those memories. After completing the first round of interviews, the NCIS agents did not have any further significant contact with LeBrun for approximately ten months as they continued to investigate other leads. By September of 2000, however, the NCIS had focused on LeBrun as the lead suspect in the case. At that time, NCIS agents decided to interview LeBrun again.

On September 21, 2000, NCIS Special Agent Early and Corporal Hunter of the Missouri Highway Patrol arrived unexpectedly at LeBrun's place of employment. Hunter told LeBrun that he and Early were conducting an investigation and requested that LeBrun accompany them to the Missouri Highway Patrol office to participate in an interview. Although the officers did not tell LeBrun the subject of their investigation, LeBrun agreed to accompany the officers because he thought that the officers might be investigating certain criminal allegations concerning LeBrun's employer. At the officers' suggestion, LeBrun rode in the front seat of an unmarked patrol car to the station house. The door was unlocked during the trip, and LeBrun was not restrained in any manner.

After they arrived at the patrol office, but before they went inside, Agent Early told LeBrun that he was not under arrest, that he was free to terminate the impending interview at any time, and that he was free to leave at any time. He was also told that he was subject to audio and visual recording anywhere inside the building. The officers then took LeBrun inside the office to a windowless interview room. The authorities had prepared the room prior to LeBrun's arrival, adorning the interview room walls with enlarged photographs of scenes from LeBrun's life. After LeBrun took a seat, NCIS Agents Early and Grebas identified themselves and initiated the interview. At no point immediately prior to or during the September 21, 2000, interview did the agents recite to LeBrun the *Miranda* warnings. The district court found that the decision not to warn was a conscious one made by the interviewers. Special Agent Early testified that no warning was thought necessary because it was not an under arrest custodial situation.

Despite the agents' failure to recite the *Miranda* warnings, LeBrun testified at the suppression hearing that at the time of the interview he understood what his *Miranda* rights were. LeBrun also testified that at the time the interview commenced he believed that he was not in custody and that he was free to leave at any time. The government concedes that the officers used psychological ploys during the course of the interview to facilitate a confession. For example, the agents told LeBrun that he was the prime suspect in Muns' death and that they had significant evidence establishing that LeBrun was the killer. The agents also told LeBrun that a protracted trial in a distant district would drain his financial resources and would ruin his family's reputation. At no point, however, did the agents shout at LeBrun or use physical force against him. After approximately thirty-three minutes of questioning, LeBrun confessed to the crime. LeBrun explained that while he was robbing the safe, Ensign Muns walked into the disbursing office. He confessed that he rushed Muns and killed him by strangling him and then smashing his head against the deck of the disbursing office. At the agents' urging, LeBrun then physically reenacted the robbery and attack. He also explained how he had dumped Muns' body and the missing money into a tank of caustic fuel oil to dispose of the evidence.

After LeBrun confessed to the killing, Agents Early and Grebas asked whether he wanted to apologize to Muns' sister, Mary Lou Taylor, who had flown in from Milwaukee to assist in the interrogation if it became necessary. He indicated that he did. Dr. Taylor, accompanied by Agent Billington, who was posing as Muns' brother and whom the agents had told LeBrun was stricken with cancer, then entered the interview room. LeBrun acknowledged to Taylor and Billington that he was responsible for Muns' death, and he apologized. After the agents had completed their questioning, LeBrun consented to having his house searched. LeBrun then withdrew a cellular telephone from his pocket and called his spouse. The agents drove LeBrun to his house and searched it. After conducting their search, the officers left LeBrun at home. They did not arrest him that day.

LeBrun was arrested at a later date and charged with felony murder * * *. He moved to suppress his confession, arguing that it was obtained in violation of * * * his due process rights. The district court agreed with LeBrun, concluding that * * * his confession was coerced. The district court granted the motion to suppress, the government appeals, and we reverse the judgment of the district court.

* * *

III.

"A statement is involuntary when it was extracted by threats, violence, or express or implied promises sufficient to overbear the defendant's will and critically impair his capacity for self-determination." Whether a confession is involuntary is judged by the totality of the circumstances. The court must look at the "conduct of the officers and the characteristics of the accused." The government bears the burden of persuasion and must prove by a preponderance of the evidence that the challenged statements were voluntary. We review the district court's findings of fact for clear error and its legal conclusion as to whether a confession was voluntary de novo.

The facts surrounding the confession are straightforward. LeBrun confessed to strangling Ensign Muns after only thirty-three minutes of questioning. Neither Agent Grebas nor Agent Early was armed during the interview. The agents never shouted at LeBrun or physically threatened him. The government concedes that it used psychological pressure to facilitate a confession. The district court correctly recognized that the type of psychological pressure Agents Grebas and Early exerted on LeBrun here did not alone render his confession involuntary. The district court concluded, however, that these tactics, when coupled with certain statements that Agents Early and Grebas made concerning nonprosecution, rendered LeBrun's confession involuntary. The critical exchange occurred as follows:

LEBRUN: So, am I hearing that I won't be prosecuted?

GREBAS: That's what you are hearing.

LEBRUN: Is that what I am hearing?

GREBAS: That's what you are hearing.

EARLY: If it's [the killing of Ensign Muns] spontaneous and that's the truth, you will not be prosecuted.

GREBAS: That's absolutely right.

LEBRUN: I am here to tell you there was no premeditation.

EARLY: All right.

LEBRUN: It was spontaneous.

EARLY: Okay.

GREBAS: So it was, let me get this clear. It was spontaneous?

LEBRUN: Correct.

GREBAS: If this is true, then you killed him and it was over, it was over the money; is that right?

LEBRUN: I don't know what it was over.

The district court noted that the agents qualified their representations by stating to LeBrun that it was only "possible" that LeBrun would not be prosecuted. The district court explicitly did not "make any findings as to what-if any-promise was actually made, or what the legal effect of any promise [was]." Instead, the district court found only that "LeBrun believed he would not be prosecuted if he confessed to a 'spontaneous' murder."

Applying the facts as found by the district court to the controlling legal standard, we conclude that LeBrun's confession was not compelled because a defendant's mistaken belief that he could not be prosecuted does not render a confession involuntary.

Even assuming that a reasonable person would view the Agents' statements as a promise, a promise made by law enforcement "does not render a confession involuntary per se." A promise is merely one factor in the totality of the circumstances. Whatever the facts of an individual case, our polestar always must be to determine whether or not the authorities overbore the defendant's will and critically impaired his capacity for self-determination. Thus, it is not enough to show that the authorities' representations were the but-for cause of a confession. Therefore, even assuming that the agents' statements could be construed as a promise and that the statements induced LeBrun's confession, our inquiry remains the same: whether the facts surrounding this interview demonstrate that the authorities overbore LeBrun's will and capacity for self-determination. This is a very demanding standard, and we are of the view that the facts of this case do not rise to that level.

We have previously concluded that a promise not to seek execution or a promise not to prosecute failed to render the confessions of similarly situated defendants involuntary. * * *

We place substantial weight on the fact that LeBrun confessed after a mere thirty-three minutes. Thus, this is not a situation where the officers wore down a defendant's will with persistent questioning over a considerable length of time. We also place significant weight on the fact that LeBrun testified that he had a subjective understanding of his *Miranda* rights at the time of the interview. We also place substantial weight on the fact that LeBrun was a sophisticated individual with legal training. LeBrun was fifty years old at the time of the interview. He has served in the military, attended five years of college and one year of law school, and worked as a manager in a real estate office. As we have noted, "one of the key concerns in judging whether confessions were involuntary, or the product of coercion, [is] the intelligence, mental state, or any other factors possessed by the defendant that might make him particularly suggestible, and susceptible to having his will overborne." Generally, we have concluded that where the defendant possessed at least average intelligence, then his inculpatory statements were not compelled.

In addition to possessing average intelligence, LeBrun did not display any unique sensitivity that would indicate that the agents might overbear his will. LeBrun had met with NCIS investigators on four prior occasions. The videotape of the interview demonstrates that LeBrun was composed and aware of his surroundings and the circumstances confronting him. In fact, as LeBrun and the Agents discussed the potential statute of limitations problems, LeBrun became more animated and much more interested in the interview. After watching the videotape, it is apparent that LeBrun is an intelligent, calculating person who erroneously perceived a potential loophole in the prosecution's case and tried to take advantage of it by confessing to "spontaneous" murder. Whatever his motivation, it is clear to us that LeBrun's capacity for self-determination was not impaired. Thus, the district court erred in concluding that LeBrun's confession was involuntary.

IV.

For the reasons stated above, we reverse the judgment of the district court and remand the case for further proceedings.

MORRIS SHEPPARD ARNOLD, CIRCUIT JUDGE, with whom MCMILLIAN, BYE, and SMITH, CIRCUIT JUDGES, join, dissenting.

* * * Because it appears to me that Mr. LeBrun's confession was the product of an overborne will, I would affirm the district court. Our panel opinion in this case, see United States v. LeBrun, 306 F.3d 545, 548–50, 552–56 (8th Cir. 2002), vacated and reh'g en banc granted (Dec. 31, 2002), very effectively rehearsed the tactics used to bring Mr. LeBrun to the point of confessing, which included threatening to ruin him financially, preying on fears related to his cancer, and vividly limning the effects that protracted civil and criminal litigation in a faraway place would have on his family, on its reputation, and in particular on his pregnant wife. I will therefore content myself with some observations on the court's opinion and on some matters that I think have not already received proper attention in previous opinions.

While, as the court notes, the agents never shouted at Mr. LeBrun or threatened him physically, the district court found on ample evidence that the atmosphere at the interrogation was police-dominated and that the agents frequently raised their voices and changed their tone when doing so. They also interrupted Mr. LeBrun in a bullying manner and demonstrated a threatening kind of impatience with him. * * *

The court * * * adverts to the fact that the district court made no findings as to what promises the interrogators actually made, but instead found only that Mr. LeBrun reasonably believed that he was promised that he would not be prosecuted if he would say that he had killed Mr. Muns "spontaneously." The court then looks for support in cases that hold that a mistaken belief as to what the law is will not render a confession involuntary. * * * But the clear purport of what the agents said in this case was that Mr. LeBrun would not be prosecuted if he said what the agents wanted him to say, and they even assured Mr. LeBrun that Mr. Muns's family approved of the deal. Indeed, they said that the family would not pursue civil remedies if he confessed and apologized. What the family wanted, the interrogators said, was simply to clear Mr. Muns's name.

In addition to the part of the interview that the court quotes in its opinion, the record reveals that, both before and after the exchange that the court isolates, the interviewers made reference to an alleged statute of limitations difficulty that would prevent prosecution for a "spontaneous" murder; and the officers intimated, moreover, that if Mr. LeBrun would simply admit to a spontaneous killing, they would call the United States Attorney in charge of the prosecution and tell him that there was no case against Mr. LeBrun. In addition, I respectfully suggest that the district court did not, as the court maintains, note that the agents qualified their representations by telling Mr. LeBrun that it was "only 'possible' " that he would not be prosecuted. In relevant part, the transcript of the interview reveals only that one of the agents said at one point that "it was possible, beyond possible" that no prosecution would take place if Mr. LeBrun would cooperate, which is significantly different from what the court asserts was said. Taken in their entirety, the agents' assurances, which operated both as representations of what the law was and as promises, were categorical.

The district court shrank from holding that an absolute promise not to prosecute was made, not because of this part of the exchange between Mr. LeBrun and his interrogators, but because the promise not to prosecute was fleetingly qualified at one point, by one agent, by the condition that Mr. LeBrun must be telling the truth that the killing was spontaneous before the government would refrain from prosecution. This transitory allusion to truth-telling does nothing to undermine the district court's factual finding that Mr. LeBrun believed that he would not be prosecuted. My own examination of the transcript and the video tape leaves little room for doubt that the agents were in fact making such a representation about the law and a promise that Mr. LeBrun would not be prosecuted, and indeed it appears that the entire interview was deliberately structured around this stratagem. But nothing in particular really turns on this point: The coercive effect, if any, of a reasonably perceived promise is exactly the same as that of an actual promise.

In addition to the coercive tactics that the court briefly rehearses, among the enlarged pictures displayed prominently on the wall of the small interrogation room was a picture of Mr. Muns's family at his gravesite. The agents, moreover, did not merely invent generic phantom witnesses to the killing; they contrived a bizarre tale of a suicide note implicating Mr. LeBrun, and even claimed that there were other witnesses to the killing who were so haunted that their lives had been ruined by what they had seen. These were all knowing falsehoods. None of this finds a place in the court's opinion. Finally, and perhaps most importantly, the court fails altogether to mention the district court's finding that, despite the agents' assurances, Mr. LeBrun did not feel free to leave as the interview progressed. This is a finding of fact that is supported by Mr. LeBrun's testimony and cannot be reasonably rejected as clearly erroneous. It is also a finding that weighs heavily in favor of the district court's conclusion that Mr. LeBrun's confession was involuntary.

This is probably the right juncture to observe that it is not immediately apparent why statements by interrogators that are untrue, and known to be false, are more "coercive" than statements that are true. Such techniques may be reprehensible, but that fact would not seem to contribute to their propensity to overwhelm the will. Perhaps it is enough simply to note that the Supreme Court has said that "the fact the police misrepresented the statements that [a witness] had made is . . . relevant," *Frazier v. Cupp*, 394 U.S. 731, 739 (1969), in circumstances like the present ones. But we need also to consider the possibility that what lies at the bottom of these kinds of cases is not merely an aversion to something called coercion, but a general uneasiness about the fairness of admitting confessions that were induced by knowing, lurid falsehoods and unfulfilled promises, whether "coercive" or not. In fact, the Supreme Court has specifically said that "the admissibility of a confession turns as much on whether the techniques for extracting the statements . . . are compatible with a system that presumes innocence and assures that a conviction will not be secured by inquisitorial means as on whether the defendant's will was in fact overborne." *Miller v. Fenton*, 474 U.S. 104, 116 (1985).

In sum, a consideration of the evidence in this case, including the kinds of pressure that were brought to bear on Mr. LeBrun, the assurances of leniency that went unfulfilled, and the deceit that the interrogators practiced, leads me to the conclusion that his confession was illegally obtained and should have been suppressed. At the very least, it seems to me relatively plain that the government has not carried its burden of showing that the relevant statements were voluntary.

I therefore respectfully dissent and would affirm the judgment of the district court. Affirming the judgment, not incidentally, has the effect of specifically performing the promise that an objective observer would conclude Mr. LeBrun's interrogators made to him, an altogether appropriate and equitable result.

QUESTIONS, COMMENTS, CONCERNS?

1. **Misskelley's confession on appeal.** The suppression court denied Misskelley's motion to suppress in a disappointing one-page order. [Casefile Document 8.] Misskelley was ultimately tried by a jury and found guilty of first-degree murder for the death of Michael Moore and second-degree murder for the deaths of Steven Branch and Christopher Byers. In all, Misskelley received a life sentence without the possibility of parole plus forty years. He would appeal to the Arkansas Supreme Court arguing, as he did before the suppression court, that his confession was involuntary. [Casefile Document 9.] That court candidly acknowledged, "The statements were the strongest evidence offered against the appellant at trial." *Misskelley v. State*, 915 S.W.2d

702, 707 (Ark. 1996). Nonetheless, the court affirmed Misskelley's convictions and held that his statements were voluntary.

Focus your attention on page 712 of the Arkansas Supreme Court's opinion. The sum and substance of the court's opinion on voluntariness is limited. What do you notice about the opinion? Does the court correctly state Misskelley's age at the time of the June 1993 interrogation? Does the court follow the *Spano* Court's instructions to break apart the circumstances of the interrogation from the characteristics of the accused? Does the court successfully navigate concerns around Misskelley's intelligence and educational background? Finally, what role does the investigators' reliance on the disputed polygraph results play in the court's analysis?

2.   The rest of the West Memphis Three story. It's hard to overstate how much media attention Misskelley's case got. His case, along with Echols and Baldwin, was the subject of three major HBO documentary films: *Paradise Lost: The Child Murders at Robin Hood Hills*; *Paradise Lost 2: Revelations*; and *Paradise Lost 3: Purgatory*. But those films hardly tell the full story of how much the media paid attention to the so-called "West Memphis Three." Other significant media efforts include *West of Memphis*, a movie that premiered at the 2012 Sundance Film Festival, and *Devil's Knot*, a dramatized film of the boys' case.

In 2010, after extensive appellate efforts, the Arkansas Supreme Court ordered an evidentiary hearing for Echols, at which the lower court was assigned to hear Echols's motion for a new trial and to consider DNA evidence exonerating him, Baldwin, and Misskelley to the crime. *Echols v. State*, 373 S.W.3d 892, 896, 902 (Ark. 2010). Ultimately, "the DNA material from the hair found in the ligature used to bind Moore was found to be consistent with Terry Hobbs, Branch's stepfather. The hair found on the tree stump was consistent with the DNA of David Jacoby, a friend of Terry Hobbs."

In the end—the very end—Misskelley, Baldwin, and Echols would enter what's called an *Alford* plea in 2011. Campbell Robertson, *Deal Frees 'West Memphis Three' in Arkansas*, N.Y. TIMES (Aug. 19, 2011), https://www.nytimes.com/2011/08/20/us/20arkansas.html. Although *North Carolina v. Alford*, 400 U.S. 25 (1970), is typically the subject of the Criminal Procedure II course, a brief definition is appropriate: an *Alford* plea is one where the defendant maintains innocence, but concedes that the prosecution has sufficient evidence to prove guilt beyond a reasonable doubt. On his release, Misskelley returned to Arkansas to be close to his father. Kim Severson, *West Memphis Three, a Year Out of Prison, Navigate New Paths*, N.Y. TIMES (Aug. 17, 2012), https://www.nytimes.com/2012/08/18/us/west-memphis-three-a-year-out-of-prison-navigate-new-paths.html.

CHAPTER 8

MIRANDA & ITS PRECURSOR (*ESCOBEDO*)

■ ■ ■

I. *MIRANDA*: THE HISTORY[1]

A. WHO WAS ERNESTO MIRANDA?[2]

Ernesto Arturo Miranda was born in Mesa, Arizona, on March 9, 1941. He had an eighth-grade education and a prison record based primarily on car thefts, burglaries, and armed robberies. That record also included an attempted rape and assault. Miranda joined the Army in 1958. He received an undesirable discharge in July 1959, after spending six of his fifteen months in the post stockade.

In January 1961, Miranda was released from a federal prison at Lompoc, California, where he had been confined following an interstate car theft conviction. He then met and moved in with Twila Hoffman who was separated from her husband and two children. Miranda and Hoffman also had a daughter of their own. They moved to Mesa in 1962. Hoffman began working in a local nursery school. Miranda held a series of motel and restaurant jobs, and then began working for United Produce in Phoenix in August 1962.

Eighteen-year-old Patricia Weir was kidnapped and raped shortly after midnight on March 3, 1963, while walking to her home from a bus stop in northeast Phoenix after working at a downtown movie theater. The Phoenix police suspected Miranda based on Weir's general description of her attacker and a partial license plate number the police traced to an old Packard registered to Hoffman that Miranda drove.

Acting on those suspicions, Phoenix Police Officers Carroll Cooley and Wilfred Young went to Miranda's Mesa home on March 13, 1963. They asked him to come to the police station to discuss a case they were investigating and stated they did not want to discuss it in front of Hoffman. Miranda agreed, not knowing whether he could decline to go with them.

---

[1]   Remember that you have access to the filings relevant to this chapter in your online repository. Also keep in mind that there are two casefiles associated with this chapter.

[2]   This subsection reprints with permission a version of Paul G. Ulrich, Miranda v. Arizona: *History, Memories, and Perspectives*, 7 PHOENIX L. REV. 203, 216–18 (2013). All footnotes are omitted.

Based on the limited information Cooley and Young then had, Cooley was doubtful Miranda was the man they were looking for.

At the police station, Miranda was immediately taken to Interrogation Room 2. At approximately 10:30 a.m., officers began questioning Miranda about the alleged kidnap-rape, an unrelated robbery, and an attempted robbery. Miranda initially denied committing all three crimes. He was then placed in a lineup before the kidnap-rape and robbery victims, but neither victim could positively identify him. Nevertheless, Cooley told Miranda that both victims had identified him.

Miranda therefore wrote and signed a confession to the kidnap-rape at 1:30 p.m. Although the written confession form Miranda signed stated that any statement he made could be used against him, he was not warned concerning his constitutional rights to counsel and to remain silent. Miranda also verbally confessed to the robbery and the attempted robbery. Cooley, however, did not ask for written confessions in those cases because he did not want to risk jeopardizing Miranda's prosecution in the kidnap-rape case.

Cooley then brought Weir and the robbery victim, separately, into the interrogation room to see if they could identify Miranda after hearing his voice. But before they could say anything, Miranda spontaneously identified each of them as the victims he was talking about. Based on those statements, both victims identified Miranda as their attacker. The victims later testified that they were "sure" Miranda was the man who had accosted them. Cooley and Young then formally arrested Miranda and booked him into jail. Until that time, he merely had been "in custody." The police also "cleared" their files in both the robbery and attempted robbery cases based on Miranda's confessions to those crimes. However, only the kidnap-rape and the robbery cases went to trial.

B. *MIRANDA* IN HISTORICAL CONTEXT[3]

The Supreme Court decided *Miranda v. Arizona* on June 13, 1966—as U.S. military involvement in Vietnam began to increase. As criticism of that involvement also increased, so too did the conflict itself; the conflict would peak with the Viet Cong Tet Offensive in early 1968, and Americans grew increasingly concerned about whether the war could be won following the Tet Offensive. Yet the public was also deeply concerned about poverty, civil rights, the threat of nuclear war, and environmental issues. The division in American popular thought was perhaps best illustrated by Richard Nixon winning the 1968 presidential election with only 43.5% of the popular vote.

---

[3] The next two subsections, with permission, are based on a portion of Brian Gallini, Schneckloth v. Bustamonte*: History's Unspoken Fourth Amendment Anomaly*, 79 TENN. L. REV. 233, 239–45 (2012). All footnotes are omitted.

Even as the Vietnam War began to deescalate at the close of the decade, societal chaos continued. On April 4, 1968, Dr. Martin Luther King Jr.'s assassination in Memphis sparked rioting in the city and required the aid of 4,000 National Guardsmen. Then, 1969 saw the beginnings of militant gay activism and a momentous push by the women's liberation movement prompting the adoption of the Equal Rights Amendment. Collectively, the social tensions arising from the Vietnam War and the civil rights movement gave rise to mass demonstrations and protests unlike any the country had ever seen.

The tenuous social environment surrounding *Miranda* was arguably heightened by the overall impact of the Warren Court. Although Earl Warren served as Chief Justice from 1953 until 1969, commentators often consider the "Warren Court" to span from 1961 (when Justice Arthur Goldberg replaced Justice Felix Frankfurter) to 1969 (when Chief Justice Warren retired). The Warren Court issued rulings on several controversial issues related to indigent criminal defense, marital privacy, and state voting rights. Those decisions, among others, sparked national public outcry. "Impeach Earl Warren" signs littered the countryside, and the Court endured criticism from prominent critics like the American Bar Association, the National Association of Attorneys General, and Judge Learned Hand of the U.S. Court of Appeals for the Second Circuit. Even Congress joined the fray by refusing to authorize a pay increase for the Justices and by seeking to limit the Court's jurisdiction.

Thus, although Ernesto Miranda's Supreme Court story began on June 13, 1966, the outcome in *Miranda* undoubtedly seems informed by the social impact of the Warren Court's decisions prior to 1966. Chief Justice Warren initially announced his retirement on June 13, 1968 and, to replace him, President Lyndon B. Johnson nominated sitting Associate Justice Abe Fortas. Yet, a Senate filibuster blocked his confirmation because of questionable off-bench conduct—most notably, his acceptance of a $20,000 fee from a friend under investigation for violating federal securities laws. Warren therefore remained as Chief for one additional year because Johnson's term as President was set to expire before he could consider another nominee. When Chief Justice Burger finally filled Warren's position on June 23, 1969, he was anxious to distance his tenure from Warren's legacy. Of particular note was Chief Justice Burger's criticism of the Warren Court's most famous decision—*Miranda*.

C. *MIRANDA* IN LEGAL CONTEXT

The seeds for *Miranda* were planted by the Warren Court's 1964 decision in *Escobedo v. Illinois*—a decision Justice Burger likewise disliked. Before *Escobedo*, law enforcement agencies nationwide were debating what limits existed—other than a prohibition against officers' use of the third degree—when interrogating a suspect. For years prior, the

Supreme Court dictated that a due process "voluntariness" standard governed the interrogation room. The voluntariness standard, however, allowed for considerable interpretive differences. The Supreme Court's desire to identify a more precise method of evaluating interrogation methods therefore persisted.

Enter Danny Escobedo, a twenty-two-year-old of Mexican descent working as a laborer in Chicago. When Escobedo's brother-in-law was killed on January 19, 1960, the police immediately suspected that Escobedo hired another individual, Benedict DiGerlando, to murder him because he frequently beat his wife—Escobedo's sister. The police arrested Escobedo at 2:30 a.m. the next morning at his sister's home, transported him to the police station, and questioned him for fourteen to fifteen hours. Remarkably, he made no statement, and the police released him.

Ten days later, on January 30, DiGerlando told police that Escobedo was the shooter. Police arrested Escobedo and his sister that same day at approximately 9:00 p.m. While on their way to the police station, officers told Escobedo that someone identified him as the shooter, but Escobedo did not take the bait. He instead requested to receive advice from his lawyer and to confront his accuser directly. Accordingly, officers arranged a stationhouse confrontation between Escobedo and DiGerlando at around 10:00 p.m., during which DiGerlando again accused Escobedo of the shooting. Escobedo responded, "I didn't shoot Manuel, you did it."

Outside the interrogation room, Escobedo's lawyer arrived at the police station at around 10:30 p.m. and sought permission from several officers to see Escobedo. His repeated requests were denied. At one point during the night, Escobedo and his lawyer saw one another through an open door and waved; police promptly shut the door. Escobedo's lawyer ultimately left the station at 1:00 a.m. without speaking to Escobedo. Afterward, Escobedo made additional incriminating statements.

Before trial, Escobedo unsuccessfully sought to suppress his confession. Although he conceded that no officer beat or threatened him, he contended that he incriminated himself for two reasons. First, he testified, "I seen that my sister was being put at the head of this crime and I knew she had not done it and I wanted to help my sister and that is the reason why I made the statement." Second, he contended that a Spanish-speaking officer claimed to be a friend of his brother and, outside the hearing of any other officer, promised that Escobedo would not be prosecuted if he agreed to testify against DiGerlando. A jury found Escobedo guilty, and he was sentenced to twenty years imprisonment.

On May 27, 1963, the Illinois Supreme Court affirmed the denial of Escobedo's motion to suppress, despite his contention that it should be inadmissible because of his previous requests for counsel. On July 1, 1963, Escobedo filed a petition for writ of certiorari to the Supreme Court. The

Court granted the petition on November 12, 1963, and set oral argument for April 29, 1964. The Court decided the case less than two months later.

D. THE PRECURSOR TO *MIRANDA*

ESCOBEDO V. ILLINOIS
378 U.S. 478
Supreme Court of the United States
April 29, 1964, Argued; June 22, 1964, Decided
No. 615

MR. JUSTICE GOLDBERG delivered the opinion of the Court.

The critical question in this case is whether, under the circumstances, the refusal by the police to honor petitioner's request to consult with his lawyer during the course of an interrogation constitutes a denial of "the Assistance of Counsel" in violation of the Sixth Amendment to the Constitution as "made obligatory upon the States by the Fourteenth Amendment," *Gideon v. Wainwright*, 372 U.S. 335, 342, and thereby renders inadmissible in a state criminal trial any incriminating statement elicited by the police during the interrogation. * * *

We conclude, for the reasons stated below, that it was not and, accordingly, we reverse the judgment of conviction.

In *Massiah v. United States*, 377 U.S. 201, this Court observed that "a Constitution which guarantees a defendant the aid of counsel at . . . trial could surely vouchsafe no less to an indicted defendant under interrogation by the police in a completely extrajudicial proceeding. Anything less . . . might deny a defendant 'effective representation by counsel at the only stage when legal aid and advice would help him.'"

The interrogation here was conducted before petitioner was formally indicted. But in the context of this case, that fact should make no difference. When petitioner requested, and was denied, an opportunity to consult with his lawyer, the investigation had ceased to be a general investigation of "an unsolved crime." *Spano v. New York*, 360 U.S. 315, 327 (STEWART, J., concurring). Petitioner had become the accused, and the purpose of the interrogation was to "get him" to confess his guilt despite his constitutional right not to do so. At the time of his arrest and throughout the course of the interrogation, the police told petitioner that they had convincing evidence that he had fired the fatal shots. Without informing him of his absolute right to remain silent in the face of this accusation, the police urged him to make a statement. As this Court observed many years ago:

It cannot be doubted that, placed in the position in which the accused was when the statement was made to him that the other suspected person had charged him with crime, the result was to produce upon his mind the fear that if he remained silent it would be considered an admission of guilt, and therefore render certain his being committed for trial as the guilty person, and it cannot be conceived that the converse impression would not also have naturally arisen, that by denying there was hope of removing the suspicion from himself. *Bram v. United States*, 168 U.S. 532, 562.

Petitioner, a layman, was undoubtedly unaware that under Illinois law an admission of "mere" complicity in the murder plot was legally as damaging as an admission of firing of the fatal shots. The "guiding hand of counsel" was essential to advise petitioner of his rights in this delicate situation. *Powell v. Alabama*, 287 U.S. 45, 69. This was the "stage when legal aid and advice" were most critical to petitioner. *Massiah v. United States, supra*, at 204. * * * It would exalt form over substance to make the right to counsel, under these circumstances, depend on whether at the time of the interrogation, the authorities had secured a formal indictment. Petitioner had, for all practical purposes, already been charged with murder. * * *

It is argued that if the right to counsel is afforded prior to indictment, the number of confessions obtained by the police will diminish significantly, because most confessions are obtained during the period between arrest and indictment, and "any lawyer worth his salt will tell the suspect in no uncertain terms to make no statement to police under any circumstances." This argument, of course, cuts two ways. The fact that many confessions are obtained during this period points up its critical nature as a "stage when legal aid and advice" are surely needed. The right to counsel would indeed be hollow if it began at a period when few confessions were obtained. There is necessarily a direct relationship between the importance of a stage to the police in their quest for a confession and the criticalness of that stage to the accused in his need for legal advice. Our Constitution, unlike some others, strikes the balance in favor of the right of the accused to be advised by his lawyer of his privilege against self-incrimination.

We have learned the lesson of history, ancient and modern, that a system of criminal law enforcement which comes to depend on the "confession" will, in the long run, be less reliable and more subject to abuses than a system which depends on extrinsic evidence independently secured through skillful investigation. As Dean Wigmore so wisely said:

> *Any system of administration which permits the prosecution to trust habitually to compulsory self-disclosure as a source of proof must itself suffer morally thereby.* The inclination develops to rely mainly upon such evidence, and to be satisfied with an incomplete investigation of the other sources. The exercise of the power to extract answers begets a forgetfulness of the just limitations of

that power. The simple and peaceful process of questioning breeds a readiness to resort to bullying and to physical force and torture. If there is a right to an answer, there soon seems to be a right to the expected answer,—that is, to a confession of guilt. Thus the legitimate use grows into the unjust abuse; ultimately, the innocent are jeopardized by the encroachments of a bad system. Such seems to have been the course of experience in those legal systems where the privilege was not recognized. 8 Wigmore, Evidence (3d ed. 1940), 309. (Emphasis in original.) * * *

We have also learned the companion lesson of history that no system of criminal justice can, or should, survive if it comes to depend for its continued effectiveness on the citizens' abdication through unawareness of their constitutional rights. No system worth preserving should have to fear that if an accused is permitted to consult with a lawyer, he will become aware of, and exercise, these rights. If the exercise of constitutional rights will thwart the effectiveness of a system of law enforcement, then there is something very wrong with that system.

We hold, therefore, that where, as here, the investigation is no longer a general inquiry into an unsolved crime but has begun to focus on a particular suspect, the suspect has been taken into police custody, the police carry out a process of interrogations that lends itself to eliciting incriminating statements, the suspect has requested and been denied an opportunity to consult with his lawyer, and the police have not effectively warned him of his absolute constitutional right to remain silent, the accused has been denied "the Assistance of Counsel" in violation of the Sixth Amendment to the Constitution as "made obligatory upon the States by the Fourteenth Amendment," *Gideon v. Wainwright*, 372 U.S., at 342, and that no statement elicited by the police during the interrogation may be used against him at a criminal trial. * * *

Nothing we have said today affects the powers of the police to investigate "an unsolved crime," *Spano v. New York*, 360 U.S. 315, 327 (STEWART, J., concurring), by gathering information from witnesses and by other "proper investigative efforts." We hold only that when the process shifts from investigatory to accusatory—when its focus is on the accused and its purpose is to elicit a confession—our adversary system begins to operate, and, under the circumstances here, the accused must be permitted to consult with his lawyer.

The judgment of the Illinois Supreme Court is reversed and the case remanded for proceedings not inconsistent with this opinion.

Reversed and remanded.

MR. JUSTICE HARLAN, dissenting.

[Omitted.]

MR. JUSTICE STEWART, dissenting. * * *

The confession which the Court today holds inadmissible was a voluntary one. It was given during the course of a perfectly legitimate police investigation of an unsolved murder. The Court says that what happened during this investigation "affected" the trial. I had always supposed that the whole purpose of a police investigation of a murder was to "affect" the trial of the murderer, and that it would be only an incompetent, unsuccessful, or corrupt investigation which would not do so. The Court further says that the Illinois police officers did not advise the petitioner of his "constitutional rights" before he confessed to the murder. This Court has never held that the Constitution requires the police to give any "advice" under circumstances such as these.

Supported by no stronger authority than its own rhetoric, the Court today converts a routine police investigation of an unsolved murder into a distorted analogue of a judicial trial. It imports into this investigation constitutional concepts historically applicable only after the onset of formal prosecutorial proceedings. By doing so, I think the Court perverts those precious constitutional guarantees, and frustrates the vital interests of society in preserving the legitimate and proper function of honest and purposeful police investigation.

Like my Brother CLARK, I cannot escape the logic of my Brother WHITE's conclusions as to the extraordinary implications which emanate from the Court's opinion in this case, and I share their views as to the untold and highly unfortunate impact today's decision may have upon the fair administration of criminal justice. I can only hope we have completely misunderstood what the Court has said.

MR. JUSTICE WHITE, with whom MR. JUSTICE CLARK and MR. JUSTICE STEWART join, dissenting.

In *Massiah v. United States*, 377 U.S. 201, the Court held that as of the date of the indictment the prosecution is disentitled to secure admissions from the accused. The Court now moves that date back to the time when the prosecution begins to "focus" on the accused. Although the opinion purports to be limited to the facts of this case, it would be naive to think that the new constitutional right announced will depend upon whether the accused has retained his own counsel, or has asked to consult with counsel in the course of interrogation. At the very least the Court holds that once the accused becomes a suspect and, presumably, is arrested, any admission made to the police thereafter is inadmissible in evidence unless the accused has waived his right to counsel. The decision is thus another major step in the direction of the goal which the Court seemingly has in mind—to bar from evidence all admissions obtained from an individual suspected of crime, whether involuntarily made or not. It does of course put us one step "ahead" of the English judges who have had the good sense to leave the matter a discretionary one with the trial court. I reject this step and the invitation to go farther which the Court has now issued.

By abandoning the voluntary-involuntary test for admissibility of confessions, the Court seems driven by the notion that it is uncivilized law enforcement to use an accused's own admissions against him at his trial. It attempts to find a home for this new and nebulous rule of due process by attaching it to the right to counsel guaranteed in the federal system by the Sixth Amendment and binding upon the States by virtue of the due process guarantee of the Fourteenth Amendment. The right to counsel now not only entitles the accused to counsel's advice and aid in preparing for trial but stands as an impenetrable barrier to any interrogation once the accused has become a suspect. From that very moment apparently his right to counsel attaches, a rule wholly unworkable and impossible to administer unless police cars are equipped with public defenders and undercover agents and police informants have defense counsel at their side. I would not abandon the Court's prior cases defining with some care and analysis the circumstances requiring the presence or aid of counsel and substitute the amorphous and wholly unworkable principle that counsel is constitutionally required whenever he would or could be helpful. * * * Under this new approach one might just as well argue that a potential defendant is constitutionally entitled to a lawyer before, not after, he commits a crime, since it is then that crucial incriminating evidence is put within the reach of the Government by the would-be accused. Until now there simply has been no right guaranteed by the Federal Constitution to be free from the use at trial of a voluntary admission made prior to indictment.

It is incongruous to assume that the provision for counsel in the Sixth Amendment was meant to amend or supersede the self-incrimination provision of the Fifth Amendment, which is now applicable to the States. That amendment addresses itself to the very issue of incriminating admissions of an accused and resolves it by proscribing only compelled statements. Neither the Framers, the constitutional language, a century of decisions of this Court nor Professor Wigmore provides an iota of support for the idea that an accused has an absolute constitutional right not to answer even in the absence of compulsion—the constitutional right not to incriminate himself by making voluntary disclosures.

Today's decision cannot be squared with other provisions of the Constitution which, in my view, define the system of criminal justice this Court is empowered to administer. The Fourth Amendment permits upon probable cause even compulsory searches of the suspect and his possessions and the use of the fruits of the search at trial, all in the absence of counsel. The Fifth Amendment and state constitutional provisions authorize, indeed require, inquisitorial grand jury proceedings at which a potential defendant, in the absence of counsel, is shielded against no more than compulsory incrimination. A grand jury witness, who may be a suspect, is interrogated and his answers, at least until today, are admissible in evidence at trial. And these provisions have been thought of as constitutional safeguards to persons suspected of an offense. Furthermore, until now, the Constitution has permitted the accused to be fingerprinted and to be identified in a line-up or in the courtroom itself.

The Court chooses to ignore these matters and to rely on the virtues and morality of a system of criminal law enforcement which does not depend on the "confession." No such judgment is to be found in the Constitution. It might be appropriate for a legislature to provide that a suspect should not be consulted during a criminal investigation; that an accused should never be called before a grand jury to answer, even if he wants to, what may well be incriminating questions; and that no person, whether he be a suspect, guilty criminal or innocent bystander, should be put to the ordeal of responding to orderly noncompulsory inquiry by the State. But this is not the system our Constitution requires. The only "inquisitions" the Constitution forbids are those which compel incrimination. Escobedo's statements were not compelled and the Court does not hold that they were.

This new American judges' rule, which is to be applied in both federal and state courts, is perhaps thought to be a necessary safeguard against the possibility of extorted confessions. To this extent it reflects a deep-seated distrust of law enforcement officers everywhere, unsupported by relevant data or current material based upon our own experience. Obviously law enforcement officers can make mistakes and exceed their authority, as today's decision shows that even judges can do, but I have somewhat more faith than the Court evidently has in the ability and desire of prosecutors and of the power of the appellate courts to discern and correct such violations of the law.

The Court may be concerned with a narrower matter: the unknowing defendant who responds to police questioning because he mistakenly believes that he must and that his admissions will not be used against him. But this worry hardly calls for the broadside the Court has now fired. The failure to inform an accused that he need not answer and that his answers may be used against him is very relevant indeed to whether the disclosures are compelled. Cases in this Court, to say the least, have never placed a premium on ignorance of constitutional rights. If an accused is told he must answer and does not know better, it would be very doubtful that the resulting admissions could be used against him. When the accused has not been informed of his rights at all the Court characteristically and properly looks very closely at the surrounding circumstances. I would continue to do so. But in this case Danny Escobedo knew full well that he did not have to answer and knew full well that his lawyer had advised him not to answer.

I do not suggest for a moment that law enforcement will be destroyed by the rule announced today. The need for peace and order is too insistent for that. But it will be crippled and its task made a great deal more difficult, all in my opinion, for unsound, unstated reasons, which can find no home in any of the provisions of the Constitution.

A Postscript to *Escobedo*[4]

The Court's decision in *Escobedo* served notice: procedure inside the interrogation room was going to change. The law enforcement community, however, was not anxious to embrace change. New York's police commissioner accused the *Escobedo* decision of joining a series of Supreme Court decisions that "unduly hampered" law enforcement, and the Philadelphia District Attorney opined that certain killings "were spawned by the Court's liberal interpretations of the Constitution."

The judiciary likewise did not receive *Escobedo* with uniform approval. Concededly, a handful of lower court decisions interpreted *Escobedo* broadly. California's Supreme Court interpreted *Escobedo* to require the provision of counsel—even in the absence of a defendant's request—by construing interrogation as a "critical stage" for Sixth Amendment purposes. The Supreme Court of Oregon held that *Escobedo* required law enforcement to warn a defendant of his right to remain silent. And finally, the Supreme Court of Tennessee applied *Escobedo*'s precise language to a case it believed was factually similar.

More representative of the cold reception that the judiciary gave *Escobedo* were the handful of lower courts that sought to limit its implications. For example, the Seventh Circuit and the state of Maryland both declined to extend *Escobedo* to factual scenarios where a defendant did not specifically request counsel during interrogation. The Supreme Court of Illinois concluded that a defendant's confession remained admissible despite law enforcement's failure to "affirmatively caution the accused of his right to have an attorney and his right to remain silent before his admissions of guilt." Finally, the Ohio Supreme Court declined to extend *Escobedo* to a defendant's request for counsel at the time of arrest.

But, perhaps the biggest *Escobedo*-related war waged inside the United States Court of Appeals for the District of Columbia. Inside that court, Republican-appointee Judge Warren Burger led a conservative bloc of judges against a separate liberal bloc led by Democratic-appointee Chief Judge David Bazelon. When given the opportunity, a Bazelon-led panel generally aligned itself with the *Escobedo* majority, whereas Burger-involved decisions applied rationale from the dissent. Of course, what made the ideological battle particularly interesting was that both judges' names

---

[4] This postscript is based with permission on a portion of Brian Gallini, Schneckloth v. Bustamonte: *History's Unspoken Fourth Amendment Anomaly*, 79 TENN. L. REV. 233, 246–49 (2012). All footnotes are omitted.

were, at varying times, floated in conversations about Supreme Court vacancies.

As the post-*Escobedo* judicial battle waged on, one influential academic saw *Escobedo* as a gateway to something more. In 1965, Professor Yale Kamisar had recently joined the law faculty at the University of Michigan after teaching for seven years at the University of Minnesota. Although he would go on to author many other influential articles and books in his still-ongoing illustrious career, Professor Kamisar penned what history would call his "masterpiece" that same year—*Equal Justice in the Gatehouses and Mansions of American Criminal Procedure: From* Powell *to* Gideon, *From* Escobedo *to* . . . In it, Professor Kamisar wrote that he "would not abolish all in-custody police interrogation," but rather, would impose on the police a duty to inform suspects subject to incommunicado interrogation of certain constitutional rights.

Amidst the post-*Escobedo* chaos, the Supreme Court followed Professor Kamisar's lead and dropped the *Miranda* bombshell on June 13, 1966.

II. AURORA & BOSTON

A. THE AURORA MOVIE THEATER SHOOTING[5]

Born in San Diego, California, on December 13, 1987, James "Jimmy" Eagan Holmes grew up in the middle-class neighborhood of Oak Hills near Castroville, California. Holmes is the son of well-educated parents. His father, Robert M. Holmes Sr., earned degrees from Stanford, UCLA, and Berkeley, and his mother, Arlene Rosemary Holmes, worked as a registered nurse. Growing up alongside his sister, Chris, Holmes attended Castroville Elementary School and enjoyed what was, by all accounts, a privileged childhood. But when Holmes turned twelve, he and his family relocated 400 miles south to the San Diego area, a move that Holmes expressed his disagreement with by trying to cut his wrist with cardboard.

Following the family's relocation, described later by his father as a "pivotal time" in Holmes's life, Holmes became more socially withdrawn despite his mother going door-to-door in their new neighborhood in an effort to find playmates. Holmes nonetheless remained engaged in his academic and extra-curricular life; he played trumpet in middle school, later ran for the cross-country team, and played both football and soccer. "He was happiest when he was playing soccer when he was a young kid," Holmes's father would later say. Described by those who knew him as "reserved," "a great team player," and "really sweet," Holmes completed his high school education at Westview High School where he excelled in the

---

[5] This subsection is based with permission on a portion of Brian Gallini, *The Languishing Public Safety Doctrine*, 68 RUTGERS L. REV. 957 (2016). All footnotes are omitted.

classroom. Described by classmates as "crazy smart," Holmes graduated from high school in 2006 and enrolled that fall in the University of California, Riverside as a scholarship student.

Holmes stood out for all the right reasons at UC-Riverside. "Academically, he was at the top of the top," said Chancellor Timothy P. White. Holmes declared a neuroscience major and fit in with his classmates. He took snowboarding trips to nearby mountains, went to dinner with friends, and generally "was no different from any other neuroscience student at UCR." Ironically, his program of study focused on "how we all behave." He graduated in 2010 with highest honors and a bachelor's degree in neuroscience.

Despite having assembled a deeply successful academic background, Holmes struggled personally and professionally after graduation. Holmes would ultimately take a factory job coating pharmaceutical pills. His mom and neighbors grew concerned that he was "troubled and lonely." Holmes's coworkers indicated that he often "looked spaced out" and "didn't socialize much with anyone."

Meanwhile, Holmes applied to a series of graduate schools, but received no offers of admission. After sending a second wave of applications, he was admitted to the University of Colorado-Denver's Ph.D. neuroscience program and enrolled in June 2011. As part of his admission, he received a $21,600 grant from the National Institute of Health and a $5,000 stipend from the University. But unlike his prior academic successes, Holmes struggled in the classroom. He came home over the semester break sick with mononucleosis, though by then he had found his first girlfriend—Gargi Datta. The pair would date until February 2012 when Datta terminated their relationship because, in her words, "I told him I saw no future for us . . . [;] He never had highs and lows of emotion."

Holmes was distraught after the breakup, though the two still maintained contact. During one Google Chat on March 25, 2012, Holmes wrote to her about "doing evil." He also told her about his "human capital" philosophy—a philosophy that, he believed, would cure his depression by adding to his human worth through the subtraction of human lives. Datta at first thought Holmes was joking, but she grew concerned as their exchange progressed; she advised Holmes to get help.

Unbeknownst to Datta, Holmes had begun seeing a psychiatrist— Lynne Fenton—four days earlier, March 21, 2012. Holmes had previously called student mental health services for what he said was social anxiety. After confessing homicidal thoughts to a social worker, Holmes was referred to Fenton, then the medical director. Fenton immediately began to worry when, during their first session, Holmes admitted that he thought about homicide three to four times per day. The two met seven more times, with one of Fenton's senior colleagues present at their last two sessions.

Although Fenton did not initially perceive Holmes as a threat, her opinion changed during their final session on June 11, when Holmes said he was dropping out of school, began making paranoid statements, and said he was "reading the writings of the Unabomber."

By the time of his June 11 session, Holmes had recently failed a June 7 oral exam, purchased a high-powered AR-15 semi-automatic assault rifle that same day, bought two tear gas grenades on May 10, and then began withdrawing from school on June 10. At the end of his final session with Fenton, which Holmes cut short, he walked out of her office without saying goodbye or shaking her hand. Fenton felt uncomfortable enough after that final session, during which Holmes exhibited an "an angry edge," that she broke confidentiality by contacting the campus threat assessment team.

Holmes's June 7 purchase of that AR-15 added to a growing arsenal that he began stockpiling on May 22 using his grant stipend to fund the purchases. Indeed, by the time Holmes purchased the AR-15, he had already bought a Remington 870 Express Tactical 12-gauge shotgun at a Bass Pro Shop and the first of two Glock pistols at Gander Mountain in Aurora.

Holmes would continue to stockpile weapons, tactical gear, and ammunition. He purchased a scope and non-firing dummy bullets on July 1. The next day, Holmes placed an online order with TacticalGear.com for an urban assault vest, a triple pistol magazine, an M16 magazine pouch, and a silver knife. His $306.99 bill included extra for two-day shipping. Then, on July 6, he returned to Bass Pro Shop to purchase a second Glock pistol. During this same period, Holmes also purchased nearly 6,300 rounds of ammunition through online retailers, beam laser lights, bomb-making materials, and handcuffs. Finally, he bought chemicals from a science store that he could combine to create sparks. Once complete, UPS had delivered roughly ninety packages to Holmes's apartment. All of his purchases were lawful.

With his arsenal complete, there was next the matter of his composition notebook. Characterized later by the *New York Times* as "a road map to murder," the notebook detailed Holmes's plans to carry out a "mass murder spree." After rejecting an airport bombing because, he wrote, airports have "too much of a terrorist history," Holmes settled on "mass murder at the movies." Other pages contain maps of the Century 16 movie theater in Aurora, Colorado, including theaters nine, ten, and twelve. In one troubling passage, Holmes implied which movie would accompany his attack:

> I was fear incarnate. Love gone, motivation directed to hate and obsessions, which didnt [sic] disapear [sic] for whatever reason with the drugs . . . . No consequences, no fear, alone, isolated, no

work for distractions, no reason to seek self-actualization. Embraced the hatred, a dark knight rises.

Addressed initially to his mother, father, and sister, Holmes would ultimately send its contents—twenty-nine pages in all—to his former psychiatrist, Lynne Fenton, on July 19.

Just hours later, Holmes purchased a ticket to the Century 16 movie theater's midnight screening of the film *The Dark Knight Rises* in theater nine. Holmes got up roughly twenty minutes into the movie and left the theater through an emergency exit door, which he propped open using a plastic tablecloth holder. After visiting his car, Holmes returned to the theater "dressed in black and wearing a ballistic helmet and vest, ballistic leggings, throat and groin protectors, and gas mask and black tactical gloves." He threw two canisters of tear gas and opened fire using his shotgun, AR-15, and Glock pistol. Although the AR-15 ultimately malfunctioned, he managed to fire sixty-five shots from it to go along with five from the handgun and six from the shotgun. His seventy-six total shots killed twelve people and injured seventy others.

The Century 16 theater in Aurora, CO

The first 911 call came over police radios at 12:39 a.m. and officers responded to the theater in less than one minute. Officers were never supposed to arrive so quickly. In an effort to delay officers' arrival on the scene, Holmes had previously set more than twenty homemade explosives in his apartment. Holmes set loud techno music to begin playing twenty-five minutes after he left for the theater that, he hoped, would prompt a neighbor to file a noise complaint. That complaint, Holmes hoped, would cause an officer to open his door into a fishing line tripwire, which would set off the explosives. Although a neighbor did knock on his door to complain, she did not open it and did not report the music to the police. The explosives, therefore, never detonated. Despite residents at the apartment complex remaining unharmed, officers found "complete chaos" and "[p]eople covered in blood" when they arrived at the theater. They apprehended Holmes at about 12:45 a.m.

Law enforcement then conducted three separate interrogations of Holmes that same day, July 20. Officers' first interrogation of Holmes was a brief one consisting of a few questions immediately following his apprehension and arrest. The scene preceding his arrest was chaotic to say the least. Officers Jason Oviatt and Jason Sweeney arrived at roughly 12:43 a.m. to find "a war zone" scene approximately ninety seconds after receiving the call from dispatch. After following a trail of blood on the backside of the complex, officers spotted Holmes standing next to a parked white car. Although officers initially assumed that Holmes, dressed in tactical gear, was a fellow officer, Sweeney noticed that the gas mask Holmes wore was not department-issued.

Officers approached Holmes from the passenger's side of the vehicle and pointed their guns at him. Officer Sweeney ordered Holmes to put his hands up; Holmes immediately complied. Officers ordered Holmes to put his face down on the ground; Holmes again complied. As Holmes was on the ground, another officer, Justin Grizzle, arrived to assist Oviatt with securing Holmes and placing him under arrest. After moving Holmes away from the car, Officer Oviatt removed Holmes's helmet and gas mask for the first time. Officer Sweeney asked Holmes "if there was anybody else with him." Holmes responded, "No, it's just me."

Following his arrest, officers moved Holmes to the back seat of a patrol car where Oviatt and a new officer, Officer Aaron Blue, remained with Holmes. While in the car, Blue opened Holmes's wallet and looked at his driver's license. Blue then asked Holmes if he had any weapons on him. Holmes replied that he had "four guns" and "didn't have any bombs [at the theater], but had improvised explosive devices at his house" that would not "go off unless [police officers] set them off." Blue asked Holmes if the address on his driver's license was the same address Holmes mentioned; Holmes answered "yes." Blue then asked Holmes if anybody else was with him, to which Holmes responded "no." Following a thorough search of Holmes's person, officers transported him to the station wearing only his underwear and t-shirt.

With the first interrogation complete, the second would not occur until 2:44 a.m. when Detectives Chuck Mehl and Craig Appel interviewed Holmes at the Aurora Police Department. At the outset of the interview, which lasted fewer than eight minutes, detectives greeted Holmes, asked if he needed anything to drink, and asked booking questions. Detective Mehl then asked, "Do you need us to get you some help or are you good to talk to us?" Holmes replied, "Help as in counsel?" Detective Mehl replied, "No, no. As in making sure you're ok physically. The paramedics check you out, are you okay there? You good to talk to us?" Holmes answered in the affirmative, which prompted Mehl to tell Holmes they first had "to get a couple things out of the way," namely, *Miranda* warnings.

Holmes at an early court appearance

As Detective Mehl prepared to read Holmes his *Miranda* rights, Holmes interrupted and asked, "There weren't any children hurt, were there?" Detective Mehl replied, "We'll get to that." Mehl commenced advising Holmes of his rights and then asked him if he understood his right to talk to a lawyer and to have the lawyer present during questioning. Holmes responded, "How do I get a lawyer?" Mehl replied that they would talk about that. At the end of the warnings, Holmes said he wanted to "invoke the Sixth Amendment." The detectives confirmed that he was invoking his right to counsel and acknowledged his affirmative response. But despite Holmes's invocation, the detectives asked Holmes three additional questions about accomplices. When asked if there was anyone with him at the theater, Holmes responded, "Except for the 100 people in the movie theater, no." The interview terminated at 2:51 a.m.

The third interrogation occurred when officers determined that they needed more information in order to safely defuse the explosives in Holmes's apartment. Holmes agreed to investigators' request that he answer questions related only to his apartment. The interrogation began around 3:35 p.m., roughly fifteen hours after the shooting, and lasted about forty minutes. Holmes described in detail two explosive systems in his apartment and told the officers that he set the bombs in his apartment to distract police officers while he carried out the theater shooting. Holmes would go on to answer all of the officers' questions in great detail.

B. THE BOSTON MARATHON BOMBING[6]

Patriots' Day is loaded with history. Generally observed on the third Monday of April, the day honors the centenary of the first American Revolution battles, otherwise known as the Battles of Lexington and Concord, which were fought in Middlesex County, Massachusetts, on April 19, 1775. In Boston, Patriots' Day also marks the running of the Boston Marathon and a Boston Red Sox home game at Fenway Park. The Marathon, however, stands as the giant of the two events. Although a sold-out Fenway Park holds 35,692 fans during day games, the Marathon draws approximately 30,000 runners and roughly 500,000 spectators annually.

On April 15, 2013, Patriots' Day called for the 117th running of the Boston Marathon. Shortly before 10:00 a.m., 23,181 runners gathered at the start line. Explaining the Boston Marathon experience to those who have not participated, either as a runner or spectator, is a challenge. The streets are lined with spectators in a manner unlike any other race, particularly so nearby the finish line. That April day, twenty-nine-year-old Krystle Campbell, eight-year-old Martin Richard, and twenty-three-year-old Lingzi Lu were among those gathered to watch the race. Tamerlan and Dzhokhar Tsarnaev also showed up near the finish line that day (referred to hereafter as "Tamerlan" for Tamerlan Tsarnaev and "Tsarnaev" for Dzhokhar Tsarnaev). But they were not there to watch the race.

Tamerlan moved with his family from Kyrgyzstan in 2003 seeking a new life in America. The transition to the United States began smoothly enough for the athletic Tamerlan who registered to fight with USA Boxing and worked as a pizza deliveryman. He attended Bunker Hill Community College part-time from fall 2006 to fall 2008. In 2010, he won a local

---

6   This subsection is based with permission on a portion of Brian Gallini, *The Unlikely Meeting Between Dzhokhar Tsarnaev and Benjamin Quarles*, 66 CASE W. RES. L. REV. 393 (2016). All footnotes are omitted.

heavyweight boxing title and married Katherine Russell. He and Katherine had a daughter that same year.

Meanwhile, though, Tamerlan's personality began to change. He had a falling out with friends and told his uncle that he was unconcerned with school or work because "God had a plan for him." Tamerlan traveled to Russia from New York for roughly seven months in 2012. Shortly after his return, he created a YouTube channel that included two videos under a category labeled "Terrorists." He then had separate confrontations with a religious leader at his local mosque when, at one point, he accused another leader of being a "non-believer."

Like his older brother, Tsarnaev immigrated to the United States from Kyrgyzstan but arrived one year earlier, in 2002. Unlike his brother, who some described as "angry" or "aggressive," Tsarnaev as a boy showed "virtually no signs of anger, let alone radical political ideology or any kind of deeply felt religious beliefs." Following success in high school both academically and athletically as a wrestler, Tsarnaev attended UMass-Dartmouth beginning in fall 2011. But his successes stopped there; after nearly four semesters, his transcript reflected that he was failing most of his classes. Tsarnaev then became angry.

The first blast seen from a second floor half a block away

The race began that morning without any signs foretelling an attack. A race within the race quickly emerged between the front-running Ethiopian and Kenyan runners. Following a three-way sprint down Boylston Street between Micah Kogo (Kenya), Lelisa Desisa (Ethiopia), and Gebre Gebremariam (Ethiopia), Desisa won the men's race with a finishing time of 2:10:22. The winner of the women's race, Rita Jeptoo, finished in 2:26:25. More than two hours later and with roughly 5,700 runners still on course, the first of two bombs went off at 2:49 p.m. Twelve to thirteen seconds later, and roughly a block away, a second explosion occurred. The detonations were so strong that they blew out windows in nearby buildings.

The marathon stopped, and chaos enveloped the streets of Boston. Rescue workers and medical personnel immediately began assisting the wounded. Many onlookers and other runners were confused, wondering if there was a shooting at the finish line or perhaps the stands had collapsed. According to Tyler Dodd's firsthand account, "There were people screaming, a lot of people with lower extremity injuries, and a lot of blood." Surviving victim Rebekah Gregory, who had to wheel past Tsarnaev's hospital room before each of her eleven operations, said, "All I could do was look around for [my son]. When I found him behind me, I reached out for him and saw all the bones sticking out of my left hand and blood dripping. It was at that moment that I really thought I was going to die." The smell of human flesh haunted the scene.

The blasts killed Campbell, Richard, and Lu. More than 260 others were also wounded including sixteen people who lost legs, the youngest of whom was a seven-year-old girl. After securing the scene, more than 1,000 members of state, federal, and local law enforcement officials immediately began investigating who was responsible. They promised to "go to the ends of the Earth" to identify the perpetrators.

After the bombings, Tsarnaev largely returned to his daily life. He took to social media less than three hours after the attack, tweeting, "Ain't no love in the heart of the city, stay safe people." In a more sinister tweet later that evening, he posted in part, "Lol those people are cooked." By now back on the campus of UMass-Dartmouth, Tsarnaev went to the gym the next day, attended his classes, and discussed the attacks with his friends. He commented to one friend on Tuesday evening, "It's crazy this is happening now. This is so easy to do. These tragedies happen all the time in Afghanistan and Iraq." He even went out to a college party Wednesday night, April 17.

But by then Tsarnaev's time was running out. That Wednesday, authorities had identified an image of a suspect carrying a black bag at the site of the second bombing. The FBI then released pictures of two male suspects to the public at approximately 5 p.m. on Thursday, April 18. Back at the dorm where Tsarnaev lived, students joked that Tsarnaev looked like the person pictured on the FBI photos. One specific friend, Dias Kadyrbayev, texted Tsarnaev to ask if Tsarnaev saw the news and whether "[yo]u saw [yo]urself there?" Tsarnaev responded in part, "y[o]u can go to my room and take what's there."

The picture the FBI released of Tsarnaev and his brother

At approximately 9 p.m. that evening, Kadyrbayev texted his roommate, Azamat Tazhayakov, and suggested that Tsarnaev was involved in the bombings. Kadyrbayev then texted another of their friends, Robel Phillipos, proposing that the three—Kadyrbayev, Tazhayakov, and Phillipos—meet in Tsarnaev's room. The trio agreed but, by the time they arrived, Tsarnaev's roommate reported that Tsarnaev had already left a few hours earlier.

Tsarnaev, meanwhile, had reunited with his brother, Tamerlan, and the pair hastily made plans for an escape to New York. At approximately 10:30 p.m., the pair approached twenty-seven-year-old MIT campus police officer Sean Collier's cruiser from behind and shot him to death using a borrowed gun. After unsuccessfully attempting to acquire Collier's weapon, Tsarnaev and his brother briefly split up; Tamerlan then carjacked the driver of a parked Mercedes-Benz SUV at around midnight. With the driver held hostage, Tamerlan forced him to drive in tandem with another vehicle, a green Honda Civic, driven by Tsarnaev to East Watertown where the brothers transferred "heavy objects" from the Civic to the Mercedes. With the Mercedes running low on gas, the three pulled into a gas station shortly after midnight. When the brothers became momentarily distracted, the hostage successfully fled to a nearby separate gas station where the cashier called 911.

With the carjacking victim's cell phone still inside the SUV, law enforcement began to track the stolen Mercedes as it stopped to pick up

Tsarnaev's green Honda Civic. An officer then spotted and began to follow the Mercedes, traveling in tandem with the Civic, shortly after 12:30 a.m. Just as additional officers arrived, Tsarnaev and Tamerlan abruptly stopped their vehicles and began shooting at the officers. The police and the Tsarnaev brothers exchanged more than 200 shots during the next five to ten minutes, a period that included one of the brothers throwing a pressure cooker bomb at law enforcement.

Suddenly, Tamerlan emerged and began shooting at officers "trying to get closer." An officer successfully tackled Tamerlan just after Tamerlan ran out of ammunition. But as officers began to handcuff Tamerlan, Tsarnaev sped the Mercedes toward them, ran over his brother (killing him), and escaped just after 1 a.m.

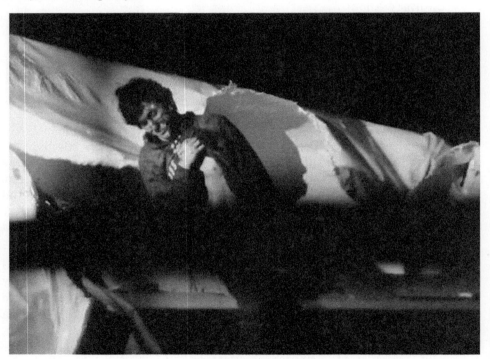

Tsarnaev emerges from the boat
Photo credit: Massachusetts State Police

With Tsarnaev presumably still close, Massachusetts Governor Deval Patrick shut the city down that morning, April 19, and ordered residents of Boston and Watertown to stay inside. The manhunt for Tsarnaev lasted all day, as officers went door to door in Watertown searching for Tsarnaev. That evening, shortly after Governor Patrick lifted the citywide lockdown, Dave Henneberry went outside his home to check on his boat. He saw "a good amount of blood" inside and promptly called 911. Thousands of officers converged on Henneberry's residence along with a police helicopter equipped with a thermal imaging camera, which determined that Tsarnaev was inside the boat. Following an exchange of gunfire and police use of flash-bang grenades, law enforcement employed a robotic arm to lift the tarp covering the boat. Tsarnaev then stood up and lifted his shirt to demonstrate that he was not wearing an explosive vest. Police finally took him into custody at approximately 8:45 p.m.

Following his capture, Tsarnaev arrived at the hospital "covered in blood" where he received treatment for substantial injuries, including a gunshot wound to the mouth and "multiple gunshot wounds to the extremities." Doctors worked to stabilize Tsarnaev who ultimately required intubation and emergency surgery. While Tsarnaev received treatment and was unable to speak, the government told the media of its intent to question him without first providing *Miranda* warnings.

Using a specialized FBI interrogation team, the government began interrogating Tsarnaev at approximately 7:22 p.m. on April 20 and continued with breaks until the morning of April 22. Before the interrogation began, lawyers from the Federal Public Defender's Office asked a federal district court to appoint them to represent Tsarnaev. Two lawyers from that office alongside a private lawyer went to the hospital in an effort to meet with Tsarnaev, but were turned away by law enforcement. Law enforcement also declined to accept a letter from defense lawyers addressed to Tsarnaev to inform him of counsels' availability.

When the unrecorded interrogation began, Tsarnaev was medicated and handcuffed to his bed with his jaw wired closed and one eye sutured shut. He was confused, writing his Cambridge address incorrectly and asking if the investigators could "hear some noise." During the lengthy questioning, Tsarnaev wrote answers to the investigators' questions in a notebook because he could not talk. He asserted that he was no longer a public safety threat and asked for time to rest. He wrote at one point, "I am tired. Leave me alone. I want a l[illegible]." His pen then trailed off the page. At other times, he wrote "I'm hurt," "I'm exhausted," "[c]an we do this later[,]" "[y]ou said you were gonna let me sleep[,]" and "I need to throw up."

Tsarnaev also "wrote the word 'lawyer' ten times, sometimes circling it." An FBI report confirmed that Tsarnaev "asked to speak to a lawyer on multiple occasions," but was told "he first needed to answer questions to ensure that the public safety was no longer in danger from other individuals, devices, or otherwise." Questioning persisted on a wide range of subjects, including how and where the bombs were assembled, his views about Islam, his career goals, his accomplishments in school, and U.S. foreign policy. Agents quickly obtained a confession. According to the government, "[f]rom the moment the agents began questioning Tsarnaev about the Marathon bombings, he readily admitted his own involvement[.]"

III. *MIRANDA*: THE BASICS

MIRANDA V. ARIZONA

384 U.S. 436
Supreme Court of the United States
February 28, 1966–March 1, 1966, Argued
June 13, 1966, Decided
No. 759

MR. CHIEF JUSTICE WARREN delivered the opinion of the Court.

* * * I

The constitutional issue we decide in each of these cases is the admissibility of statements obtained from a defendant questioned while in custody or otherwise deprived of his freedom of action in any significant way. In each, the defendant was questioned by police officers, detectives, or a prosecuting attorney in a room in which he was cut off from the outside world. In none of these cases was the defendant given a full and effective warning of his rights at the outset of the interrogation process. In all the cases, the questioning elicited oral admissions, and in three of them, signed statements as well which were admitted at their trials. They all thus share salient features—incommunicado interrogation of individuals in a police-dominated atmosphere, resulting in self-incriminating statements without full warnings of constitutional rights.

An understanding of the nature and setting of this in-custody interrogation is essential to our decisions today. * * * [T]he modern practice of in-custody interrogation is psychologically rather than physically oriented. * * * Interrogation still takes place in privacy. Privacy results in secrecy and this in turn results in a gap in our knowledge as to what in fact goes on in the interrogation rooms. A valuable source of information about present police practices, however, may be found in various police manuals and texts which document procedures employed with success in the past, and which recommend various other effective tactics.[8] These texts are used by law enforcement agencies themselves as guides.[9] It should be noted that

---

[8]   The manuals quoted in the text following are the most recent and representative of the texts currently available. Material of the same nature appears in Kidd, *Police Interrogation* (1940); Mulbar, *Interrogation* (1951); Dienstein, *Technics for the Crime Investigator* 97–115 (1952). Studies concerning the observed practices of the police appear in LaFave, *Arrest: The Decision To Take a Suspect Into Custody* 244–437, 490–521 (1965); LaFave, *Detention for Investigation by the Police: An Analysis of Current Practices*, 1962 Wash. U. L. Q. 331; Barrett, *Police Practices and the Law—From Arrest to Release or Charge*, 50 Calif. L. Rev. 11 (1962); Sterling, *supra*, n.7, at 47–65.

[9]   The methods described in *Inbau & Reid, Criminal Interrogation and Confessions* (1962), are a revision and enlargement of material presented in three prior editions of a predecessor text, *Lie Detection and Criminal Interrogation* (3d ed. 1953). The authors and their associates are officers of the Chicago Police Scientific Crime Detection Laboratory and have had extensive experience in writing, lecturing and speaking to law enforcement authorities over a 20-year period. They say that the techniques portrayed in their manuals reflect their experiences and are the most effective psychological stratagems to employ during interrogations. Similarly, the techniques described in O'Hara, *Fundamentals of Criminal Investigation* (1956), were gleaned from long

these texts professedly present the most enlightened and effective means presently used to obtain statements through custodial interrogation. By considering these texts and other data, it is possible to describe procedures observed and noted around the country.

The officers are told by the manuals that the "principal psychological factor contributing to a successful interrogation is privacy—being alone with the person under interrogation."[10] The efficacy of this tactic has been explained as follows:

> If at all practicable, the interrogation should take place in the investigator's office or at least in a room of his own choice. The subject should be deprived of every psychological advantage. In his own home he may be confident, indignant, or recalcitrant. He is more keenly aware of his rights and more reluctant to tell of his indiscretions or criminal behavior within the walls of his home. Moreover his family and other friends are nearby, their presence lending moral support. In his own office, the investigator possesses all the advantages. The atmosphere suggests the invincibility of the forces of the law.

To highlight the isolation and unfamiliar surroundings, the manuals instruct the police to display an air of confidence in the suspect's guilt and from outward appearance to maintain only an interest in confirming certain details. The guilt of the subject is to be posited as a fact. The interrogator should direct his comments toward the reasons why the subject committed the act, rather than court failure by asking the subject whether he did it. Like other men, perhaps the subject has had a bad family life, had an unhappy childhood, had too much to drink, had an unrequited desire for women. The officers are instructed to minimize the moral seriousness of the offense,[12] to cast blame on the victim or on society. These tactics are designed to put the subject in a psychological state where his story is but an elaboration of what the police purport to know already— that he is guilty. Explanations to the contrary are dismissed and discouraged.

The texts thus stress that the major qualities an interrogator should possess are patience and perseverance. * * * The manuals suggest that the suspect be offered legal excuses for his actions in order to obtain an initial

---

service as observer, lecturer in police science, and work as a federal criminal investigator. All these texts have had rather extensive use among law enforcement agencies and among students of police science, with total sales and circulation of over 44,000.

[10] Inbau & Reid, *Criminal Interrogation and Confessions* (1962), at 1.

[12] Inbau & Reid, *supra*, at 34–43, 87. For example, in *Leyra v. Denno*, 347 U.S. 556 (1954), the interrogator-psychiatrist told the accused, "We do sometimes things that are not right, but in a fit of temper or anger we sometimes do things we aren't really responsible for," *id.*, at 562, and again, "We know that morally you were just in anger. Morally, you are not to be condemned," *id.*, at 582.

admission of guilt. Where there is a suspected revenge-killing, for example, the interrogator may say:

> Joe, you probably didn't go out looking for this fellow with the purpose of shooting him. My guess is, however, that you expected something from him and that's why you carried a gun—for your own protection. You knew him for what he was, no good. Then when you met him he probably started using foul, abusive language and he gave some indication that he was about to pull a gun on you, and that's when you had to act to save your own life. That's about it, isn't it, Joe?

Having then obtained the admission of shooting, the interrogator is advised to refer to circumstantial evidence which negates the self-defense explanation. This should enable him to secure the entire story. One text notes that "Even if he fails to do so, the inconsistency between the subject's original denial of the shooting and his present admission of at least doing the shooting will serve to deprive him of a self-defense 'out' at the time of trial."

When the techniques described above prove unavailing, the texts recommend they be alternated with a show of some hostility. One ploy often used has been termed the "friendly-unfriendly" or the "Mutt and Jeff" act:

> . . . In this technique, two agents are employed. Mutt, the relentless investigator, who knows the subject is guilty and is not going to waste any time. He's sent a dozen men away for this crime and he's going to send the subject away for the full term. Jeff, on the other hand, is obviously a kindhearted man. He has a family himself. He has a brother who was involved in a little scrape like this. He disapproves of Mutt and his tactics and will arrange to get him off the case if the subject will cooperate. He can't hold Mutt off for very long. The subject would be wise to make a quick decision. The technique is applied by having both investigators present while Mutt acts out his role. Jeff may stand by quietly and demur at some of Mutt's tactics. When Jeff makes his plea for cooperation, Mutt is not present in the room.

The interrogators sometimes are instructed to induce a confession out of trickery. The technique here is quite effective in crimes which require identification or which run in series. In the identification situation, the interrogator may take a break in his questioning to place the subject among a group of men in a line-up. "The witness or complainant (previously coached, if necessary) studies the line-up and confidently points out the subject as the guilty party." Then the questioning resumes "as though there were now no doubt about the guilt of the subject." * * *

The manuals also contain instructions for police on how to handle the individual who refuses to discuss the matter entirely, or who asks for an attorney or relatives. The examiner is to concede him the right to remain silent. "This usually has a very undermining effect. First of all, he is disappointed in his expectation of an unfavorable reaction on the part of the interrogator. Secondly, a concession of this right to remain silent impresses the subject with the apparent fairness of his interrogator." After this psychological conditioning, however, the officer is told to point out the incriminating significance of the suspect's refusal to talk:

> Joe, you have a right to remain silent. That's your privilege and I'm the last person in the world who'll try to take it away from you. If that's the way you want to leave this, O. K. But let me ask you this. Suppose you were in my shoes and I were in yours and you called me in to ask me about this and I told you, 'I don't want to answer any of your questions.' You'd think I had something to hide, and you'd probably be right in thinking that. That's exactly what I'll have to think about you, and so will everybody else. So let's sit here and talk this whole thing over.

Few will persist in their initial refusal to talk, it is said, if this monologue is employed correctly. * * *

From these representative samples of interrogation techniques, the setting prescribed by the manuals and observed in practice becomes clear. In essence, it is this: To be alone with the subject is essential to prevent distraction and to deprive him of any outside support. The aura of confidence in his guilt undermines his will to resist. He merely confirms the preconceived story the police seek to have him describe. Patience and persistence, at times relentless questioning, are employed. To obtain a confession, the interrogator must "patiently maneuver himself or his quarry into a position from which the desired objective may be attained." When normal procedures fail to produce the needed result, the police may resort to deceptive stratagems such as giving false legal advice. It is important to keep the subject off balance, for example, by trading on his insecurity about himself or his surroundings. The police then persuade, trick, or cajole him out of exercising his constitutional rights.

Even without employing brutality, the "third degree" or the specific stratagems described above, the very fact of custodial interrogation exacts a heavy toll on individual liberty and trades on the weakness of individuals.[24] This fact may be illustrated simply by referring to three confession cases decided by this Court * * *. In *Townsend v. Sain*, 372 U.S.

---

[24] Interrogation procedures may even give rise to a false confession. The most recent conspicuous example occurred in New York, in 1964, when a Negro of limited intelligence confessed to two brutal murders and a rape which he had not committed. When this was discovered, the prosecutor was reported as saying: "Call it what you want—brain-washing, hypnosis, fright. They made him give an untrue confession. The only thing I don't believe is that Whitmore was beaten." N.Y. Times, Jan. 28, 1965, p. 1, col. 5. In two other instances, similar events had occurred. N.Y. Times, Oct. 20, 1964, p. 22, col. 1; N.Y. Times, Aug. 25, 1965, p. 1, col. 1. In general, see Borchard, *Convicting the Innocent* (1932); Frank & Frank, *Not Guilty* (1957).

293 (1963), the defendant was a 19-year-old heroin addict, described as a "near mental defective," *id.*, at 307–310. The defendant in *Lynumn v. Illinois*, 372 U.S. 528 (1963), was a woman who confessed to the arresting officer after being importuned to "cooperate" in order to prevent her children from being taken by relief authorities. This Court as in those cases reversed the conviction of a defendant in *Haynes v. Washington*, 373 U.S. 503 (1963), whose persistent request during his interrogation was to phone his wife or attorney. In other settings, these individuals might have exercised their constitutional rights. In the incommunicado police-dominated atmosphere, they succumbed.

In the cases before us today, given this background, we concern ourselves primarily with this interrogation atmosphere and the evils it can bring. In No. 759, *Miranda v. Arizona*, the police arrested the defendant and took him to a special interrogation room where they secured a confession. In No. 760, *Vignera v. New York*, the defendant made oral admissions to the police after interrogation in the afternoon, and then signed an inculpatory statement upon being questioned by an assistant district attorney later the same evening. In No. 761, *Westover v. United States*, the defendant was handed over to the Federal Bureau of Investigation by local authorities after they had detained and interrogated him for a lengthy period, both at night and the following morning. After some two hours of questioning, the federal officers had obtained signed statements from the defendant. Lastly, in No. 584, *California v. Stewart*, the local police held the defendant five days in the station and interrogated him on nine separate occasions before they secured his inculpatory statement.

In these cases, we might not find the defendants' statements to have been involuntary in traditional terms. Our concern for adequate safeguards to protect precious Fifth Amendment rights is, of course, not lessened in the slightest. In each of the cases, the defendant was thrust into an unfamiliar atmosphere and run through menacing police interrogation procedures. The potentiality for compulsion is forcefully apparent, for example, in *Miranda*, where the indigent Mexican defendant was a seriously disturbed individual with pronounced sexual fantasies, and in *Stewart*, in which the defendant was an indigent Los Angeles Negro who had dropped out of school in the sixth grade. To be sure, the records do not evince overt physical coercion or patent psychological ploys. The fact remains that in none of these cases did the officers undertake to afford appropriate safeguards at the outset of the interrogation to insure that the statements were truly the product of free choice.

It is obvious that such an interrogation environment is created for no purpose other than to subjugate the individual to the will of his examiner. This atmosphere carries its own badge of intimidation. To be sure, this is not physical intimidation, but it is equally destructive of human dignity.

The current practice of incommunicado interrogation is at odds with one of our Nation's most cherished principles—that the individual may not be compelled to incriminate himself. Unless adequate protective devices are employed to dispel the compulsion inherent in custodial surroundings, no statement obtained from the defendant can truly be the product of his free choice. * * *

III

Today, then, there can be no doubt that the Fifth Amendment privilege is available outside of criminal court proceedings and serves to protect persons in all settings in which their freedom of action is curtailed in any significant way from being compelled to incriminate themselves. We have concluded that without proper safeguards the process of in-custody interrogation of persons suspected or accused of crime contains inherently compelling pressures which work to undermine the individual's will to resist and to compel him to speak where he would not otherwise do so freely. In order to combat these pressures and to permit a full opportunity to exercise the privilege against self-incrimination, the accused must be adequately and effectively apprised of his rights and the exercise of those rights must be fully honored.

It is impossible for us to foresee the potential alternatives for protecting the privilege which might be devised by Congress or the States in the exercise of their creative rule-making capacities. Therefore we cannot say that the Constitution necessarily requires adherence to any particular solution for the inherent compulsions of the interrogation process as it is presently conducted. Our decision in no way creates a constitutional straitjacket which will handicap sound efforts at reform, nor is it intended to have this effect. We encourage Congress and the States to continue their laudable search for increasingly effective ways of protecting the rights of the individual while promoting efficient enforcement of our criminal laws. However, unless we are shown other procedures which are at least as effective in apprising accused persons of their right of silence and in assuring a continuous opportunity to exercise it, the following safeguards must be observed.

At the outset, if a person in custody is to be subjected to interrogation, he must first be informed in clear and unequivocal terms that he has the right to remain silent. For those unaware of the privilege, the warning is needed simply to make them aware of it—the threshold requirement for an intelligent decision as to its exercise. More important, such a warning is an absolute prerequisite in overcoming the inherent pressures of the interrogation atmosphere. It is not just the subnormal or woefully ignorant who succumb to an interrogator's imprecations, whether implied or expressly stated, that the interrogation will continue until a confession is obtained or that silence in the face of accusation is itself damning and will bode ill when presented to a jury. Further, the warning will show the individual that his interrogators are prepared to recognize his privilege should he choose to exercise it. * * *

The warning of the right to remain silent must be accompanied by the explanation that anything said can and will be used against the individual in court. This warning is needed in order to make him aware not only of the privilege, but also of the consequences of forgoing it. It is only through an awareness of these consequences that there can be any assurance of real understanding and intelligent exercise of the privilege. Moreover, this warning may serve to make the individual more acutely aware that he is faced with a phase of the adversary system—that he is not in the presence of persons acting solely in his interest.

The circumstances surrounding in-custody interrogation can operate very quickly to overbear the will of one merely made aware of his privilege by his interrogators. Therefore, the right to have counsel present at the interrogation is indispensable to the protection of the Fifth Amendment privilege under the system we delineate today. Our aim is to assure that the individual's right to choose between silence and speech remains unfettered throughout the interrogation process. A once-stated warning, delivered by those who will conduct the interrogation, cannot itself suffice to that end among those who most require knowledge of their rights. A mere warning given by the interrogators is not alone sufficient to accomplish that end. Prosecutors themselves claim that the admonishment of the right to remain silent without more "will benefit only the recidivist and the professional." Even preliminary advice given to the accused by his own attorney can be swiftly overcome by the secret interrogation process. *Cf. Escobedo v. Illinois,* 378 U.S. 478, 485, n. 5. Thus, the need for counsel to protect the Fifth Amendment privilege comprehends not merely a right to consult with counsel prior to questioning, but also to have counsel present during any questioning if the defendant so desires.

The presence of counsel at the interrogation may serve several significant subsidiary functions as well. If the accused decides to talk to his interrogators, the assistance of counsel can mitigate the dangers of untrustworthiness. With a lawyer present the likelihood that the police will practice coercion is reduced, and if coercion is nevertheless exercised the lawyer can testify to it in court. The presence of a lawyer can also help to guarantee that the accused gives a fully accurate statement to the police and that the statement is rightly reported by the prosecution at trial.

An individual need not make a pre-interrogation request for a lawyer. While such request affirmatively secures his right to have one, his failure to ask for a lawyer does not constitute a waiver. No effective waiver of the right to counsel during interrogation can be recognized unless specifically made after the warnings we here delineate have been given. The accused who does not know his rights and therefore does not make a request may be the person who most needs counsel. * * *

Accordingly we hold that an individual held for interrogation must be clearly informed that he has the right to consult with a lawyer and to have the lawyer with him during interrogation under the system for protecting the privilege we delineate today. As with the warnings of the right to remain silent and that anything stated can be used in evidence against him, this warning is an absolute prerequisite to interrogation. No amount of circumstantial evidence that the person may have been aware of this right will suffice to stand in its stead. Only through such a warning is there ascertainable assurance that the accused was aware of this right.

If an individual indicates that he wishes the assistance of counsel before any interrogation occurs, the authorities cannot rationally ignore or deny his request on the basis that the individual does not have or cannot afford a retained attorney. The financial ability of the individual has no relationship to the scope of the rights involved here. The privilege against self-incrimination secured by the Constitution applies to all individuals. The need for counsel in order to protect the privilege exists for the indigent as well as the affluent. In fact, were we to limit these constitutional rights to those who can retain an attorney, our decisions today would be of little significance. The cases before us as well as the vast majority of confession cases with which we have dealt in the past involve those unable to retain counsel.[40] * * *

In order fully to apprise a person interrogated of the extent of his rights under this system then, it is necessary to warn him not only that he has the right to consult with an attorney, but also that if he is indigent a lawyer will be appointed to represent him. Without this additional warning, the admonition of the right to consult with counsel would often be understood as meaning only that he can consult with a lawyer if he has one or has the funds to obtain one. * * *

Once warnings have been given, the subsequent procedure is clear. If the individual indicates in any manner, at any time prior to or during questioning, that he wishes to remain silent, the interrogation must cease. At this point he has shown that he intends to exercise his Fifth Amendment privilege; any statement taken after the person invokes his privilege cannot be other than the product of compulsion, subtle or otherwise. Without the right to cut off questioning, the setting of in-custody interrogation operates on the individual to overcome free choice in producing a statement after the privilege has been once invoked. If the individual states that he wants an attorney, the interrogation must cease

---

[40] Estimates of 50–90% indigency among felony defendants have been reported. Pollock, *Equal Justice in Practice*, 45 Minn. L. Rev. 737, 738–739 (1961); Birzon, Kasanof & Forma, *The Right to Counsel and the Indigent Accused in Courts of Criminal Jurisdiction in New York State*, 14 Buffalo L. Rev. 428, 433 (1965).

until an attorney is present. At that time, the individual must have an opportunity to confer with the attorney and to have him present during any subsequent questioning. If the individual cannot obtain an attorney and he indicates that he wants one before speaking to police, they must respect his decision to remain silent.

* * * If the interrogation continues without the presence of an attorney and a statement is taken, a heavy burden rests on the government to demonstrate that the defendant knowingly and intelligently waived his privilege against self-incrimination and his right to retained or appointed counsel. This Court has always set high standards of proof for the waiver of constitutional rights, *Johnson v. Zerbst*, 304 U.S. 458 (1938), and we re-assert these standards as applied to in-custody interrogation. Since the State is responsible for establishing the isolated circumstances under which the interrogation takes place and has the only means of making available corroborated evidence of warnings given during incommunicado interrogation, the burden is rightly on its shoulders.

An express statement that the individual is willing to make a statement and does not want an attorney followed closely by a statement could constitute a waiver. But a valid waiver will not be presumed simply from the silence of the accused after warnings are given or simply from the fact that a confession was in fact eventually obtained.

* * * Whatever the testimony of the authorities as to waiver of rights by an accused, the fact of lengthy interrogation or incommunicado incarceration before a statement is made is strong evidence that the accused did not validly waive his rights. In these circumstances the fact that the individual eventually made a statement is consistent with the conclusion that the compelling influence of the interrogation finally forced him to do so. It is inconsistent with any notion of a voluntary relinquishment of the privilege. Moreover, any evidence that the accused was threatened, tricked, or cajoled into a waiver will, of course, show that the defendant did not voluntarily waive his privilege. The requirement of warnings and waiver of rights is a fundamental with respect to the Fifth Amendment privilege and not simply a preliminary ritual to existing methods of interrogation.

The warnings required and the waiver necessary in accordance with our opinion today are, in the absence of a fully effective equivalent, prerequisites to the admissibility of any statement made by a defendant.

To summarize, we hold that when an individual is taken into custody or otherwise deprived of his freedom by the authorities in any significant way and is subjected to questioning, the privilege against self-incrimination is jeopardized. Procedural safeguards must be employed to protect the privilege, and unless other fully effective means are adopted to notify the person of his right of silence and to assure that the exercise of the right will be scrupulously honored, the following measures are required. He must be warned prior to any questioning that he has the right to remain silent, that anything he says can be used against him in a court of law, that he has the right to the presence of an attorney, and that if he cannot afford an attorney one will be appointed for him prior to any questioning if he so desires. Opportunity to exercise these rights must be afforded to him throughout the interrogation. After such warnings have been given, and such opportunity afforded him, the individual may knowingly and intelligently waive these rights and agree to answer questions or make a statement. But unless and until such warnings and waiver are demonstrated by the prosecution at trial, no evidence obtained as a result of interrogation can be used against him. * * *

Therefore, in accordance with the foregoing, the judgments of the Supreme Court of Arizona in No. 759, of the New York Court of Appeals in No. 760, and of the Court of Appeals for the Ninth Circuit in No. 761 are reversed. The judgment of the Supreme Court of California in No. 584 is affirmed.

It is so ordered.

MR. JUSTICE CLARK, dissenting in Nos. 759, 760, and 761, and concurring in the result in No. 584.

[Omitted.]

MR. JUSTICE WHITE, with whom MR. JUSTICE HARLAN and MR. JUSTICE STEWART join, dissenting.

I

The proposition that the privilege against self-incrimination forbids in-custody interrogation without the warnings specified in the majority opinion and without a clear waiver of counsel has no significant support in the history of the privilege or in the language of the Fifth Amendment. As for the English authorities and the common-law history, the privilege, firmly established in the second half of the seventeenth century, was never applied except to prohibit compelled judicial interrogations. The rule excluding coerced confessions matured about 100 years later, "but there is nothing in the reports to suggest that the theory has its roots in the privilege against self-incrimination. And so far as the cases reveal, the privilege, as such, seems to have been given effect only in judicial proceedings, including the preliminary examinations by authorized magistrates."

Our own constitutional provision provides that no person "shall be compelled in any criminal case to be a witness against himself." These words, when "considered in the light to be shed by grammar and the dictionary . . . appear to signify simply that nobody shall be compelled to give oral testimony against himself in a criminal proceeding under way in which he is defendant." And there is very little in the surrounding circumstances of the adoption of the Fifth Amendment or in the provisions of the then existing state constitutions or in state practice which would give the constitutional provision any broader meaning. * * *

Only a tiny minority of our judges who have dealt with the question, including today's majority, have considered in-custody interrogation, without more, to be a violation of the Fifth Amendment. And this Court, as every member knows, has left standing literally thousands of criminal convictions that rested at least in part on confessions taken in the course of interrogation by the police after arrest. * * *

Criticism of the Court's opinion, however, cannot stop with a demonstration that the factual and textual bases for the rule it propounds are, at best, less than compelling. Equally relevant is an assessment of the rule's consequences measured against community values. * * *

The obvious underpinning of the Court's decision is a deep-seated distrust of all confessions. As the Court declares that the accused may not be interrogated without counsel present, absent a waiver of the right to counsel, and as the Court all but admonishes the lawyer to advise the accused to remain silent, the result adds up to a judicial judgment that evidence from the accused should not be used against him in any way, whether compelled or not. This is the not so subtle overtone of the opinion—that it is inherently wrong for the police to gather evidence from the accused himself. And this is precisely the nub of this dissent. I see nothing wrong or immoral, and certainly nothing unconstitutional, in the police's asking a suspect whom they have reasonable cause to arrest whether or not he killed his wife or in confronting him with the evidence on which the arrest was based, at least where he has been plainly advised that he may remain completely silent, *see Escobedo v. Illinois*, 378 U.S. 478, 499 (dissenting opinion). Until today, "the admissions or confessions of the prisoner, when voluntarily and freely made, have always ranked high in the scale of incriminating evidence." Particularly when corroborated, as where the police have confirmed the accused's disclosure of the hiding place of implements or fruits of the crime, such confessions have the highest reliability and significantly contribute to the certitude with which we may believe the accused is guilty. Moreover, it is by no means certain that the process of confessing is injurious to the accused. To the contrary it may provide psychological relief and enhance the prospects for rehabilitation. * * *

The rule announced today will measurably weaken the ability of the criminal law to perform these tasks. It is a deliberate calculus to prevent interrogations, to reduce the incidence of confessions and pleas of guilty and to increase the number of trials.[5] Criminal trials, no matter how efficient the police are, are not sure bets for the prosecution, nor should they be if the evidence is not forthcoming. Under the present law, the prosecution fails to prove its case in about 30% of the criminal cases actually tried in the federal courts. But it is something else again to remove from the ordinary criminal case all those confessions which heretofore have been held to be free and voluntary acts of the accused and to thus establish a new constitutional barrier to the ascertainment of truth by the judicial process. There is, in my view, every reason to believe that a good many criminal defendants who otherwise would have been convicted on what this Court has previously thought to be the most satisfactory kind of evidence will now, under this new version of the Fifth Amendment, either not be tried at all or will be acquitted if the State's evidence, minus the confession, is put to the test of litigation.

I have no desire whatsoever to share the responsibility for any such impact on the present criminal process.

In some unknown number of cases the Court's rule will return a killer, a rapist or other criminal to the streets and to the environment which produced him, to repeat his crime whenever it pleases him. As a consequence, there will not be a gain, but a loss, in human dignity. The real concern is not the unfortunate consequences of this new decision on the criminal law as an abstract, disembodied series of authoritative proscriptions, but the impact on those who rely on the public authority for protection and who without it can only engage in violent self-help with guns, knives and the help of their neighbors similarly inclined. There is, of course, a saving factor: the next victims are uncertain, unnamed and unrepresented in this case.

Nor can this decision do other than have a corrosive effect on the criminal law as an effective device to prevent crime. A major component in its effectiveness in this regard is its swift and sure enforcement. The easier it is to get away with rape and murder, the less the deterrent effect on those who are inclined to attempt it. This is still good common sense. If it were

---

[5] Eighty-eight federal district courts (excluding the District Court for the District of Columbia) disposed of the cases of 33,381 criminal defendants in 1964. Only 12.5% of those cases were actually tried. Of the remaining cases, 89.9% were terminated by convictions upon pleas of guilty and 10.1% were dismissed. Stated differently, approximately 90% of all convictions resulted from guilty pleas. In the District Court for the District of Columbia a higher percentage, 27%, went to trial, and the defendant pleaded guilty in approximately 78% of the cases terminated prior to trial. No reliable statistics are available concerning the percentage of cases in which guilty pleas are induced because of the existence of a confession or of physical evidence unearthed as a result of a confession. Undoubtedly the number of such cases is substantial.

Perhaps of equal significance is the number of instances of known crimes which are not solved. In 1964, only 388,946, or 23.9% of 1,626,574 serious known offenses were cleared. The clearance rate ranged from 89.8% for homicides to 18.7% for larceny. Those who would replace interrogation as an investigatorial tool by modern scientific investigation techniques significantly overestimate the effectiveness of present procedures, even when interrogation is included.

not, we should posthaste liquidate the whole law enforcement establishment as a useless, misguided effort to control human conduct.

And what about the accused who has confessed or would confess in response to simple, noncoercive questioning and whose guilt could not otherwise be proved? Is it so clear that release is the best thing for him in every case? Has it so unquestionably been resolved that in each and every case it would be better for him not to confess and to return to his environment with no attempt whatsoever to help him? I think not. It may well be that in many cases it will be no less than a callous disregard for his own welfare as well as for the interests of his next victim.

There is another aspect to the effect of the Court's rule on the person whom the police have arrested on probable cause. The fact is that he may not be guilty at all and may be able to extricate himself quickly and simply if he were told the circumstances of his arrest and were asked to explain. This effort, and his release, must now await the hiring of a lawyer or his appointment by the court, consultation with counsel and then a session with the police or the prosecutor. Similarly, where probable cause exists to arrest several suspects, as where the body of the victim is discovered in a house having several residents, it will often be true that a suspect may be cleared only through the results of interrogation of other suspects. Here too the release of the innocent may be delayed by the Court's rule.

Much of the trouble with the Court's new rule is that it will operate indiscriminately in all criminal cases, regardless of the severity of the crime or the circumstances involved. It applies to every defendant, whether the professional criminal or one committing a crime of momentary passion who is not part and parcel of organized crime. It will slow down the investigation and the apprehension of confederates in those cases where time is of the essence, such as kidnapping, those involving the national security, and some of those involving organized crime. In the latter context the lawyer who arrives may also be the lawyer for the defendant's colleagues and can be relied upon to insure that no breach of the organization's security takes place even though the accused may feel that the best thing he can do is to cooperate.

At the same time, the Court's per se approach may not be justified on the ground that it provides a "bright line" permitting the authorities to judge in advance whether interrogation may safely be pursued without jeopardizing the admissibility of any information obtained as a consequence. Nor can it be claimed that judicial time and effort, assuming that is a relevant consideration, will be conserved because of the ease of application of the new rule. Today's decision leaves open such questions as whether the accused was in custody, whether his statements were spontaneous or the product of interrogation, whether the accused has effectively waived his rights, and whether nontestimonial evidence introduced at trial is the fruit of statements made during a prohibited interrogation, all of which are certain to prove productive of uncertainty during investigation and litigation during prosecution. For all these reasons, if further restrictions on police interrogation are desirable at this time, a more flexible approach makes much more sense than the Court's constitutional straitjacket which forecloses more discriminating treatment by legislative or rule-making pronouncements.

Applying the traditional standards to the cases before the Court, I would hold these confessions voluntary. I would therefore affirm in Nos. 759, 760, and 761, and reverse in No. 584.

QUESTIONS, COMMENTS, CONCERNS?

1. **The "fully effective equivalent" of *Miranda* warnings.** The *Miranda* Court advised that, pursuant to the Fifth Amendment, a suspect in a custodial interrogation setting "must be warned prior to any questioning that he has the right to remain silent, that anything he says can be used against him in a court of law, that he has the right to the presence of an attorney, and that if he cannot afford an attorney one will be appointed for him prior to any questioning if he so desires." But the Court also added that "a fully effective equivalent" would be sufficient to fulfill the *Miranda* Court's mandate.

The Court first considered what might constitute a "fully effective equivalent" in *California v. Prysock*, 453 U.S. 355 (1981). In *Prysock*, respondent, a juvenile, confessed to and was convicted of committing a brutal murder. Before he made incriminating statements, though, police warned respondent, "You have the right to talk to a lawyer before you are questioned, have him present with you while you are being questioned, and all during the questioning." Police also told him, "[Y]ou have the right to have a lawyer appointed to represent you at no cost to yourself." On appeal, respondent argued that these warnings did not properly advise him of his right to an appointed attorney before and during interrogation. The Supreme Court disagreed, holding that police "fully conveyed to respondent his rights as required by *Miranda*." In dicta, the Court suggested that *Miranda* warnings might be insufficient "if the reference to the right to appointed counsel was linked with some future point in time after the police interrogation."

The issue arose again in 1989. In *Duckworth v. Eagan*, 492 U.S. 195 (1989), respondent confessed to a stabbing after police read to him the following warnings:

Before we ask you any questions, you must understand your rights. You have the right to remain silent. Anything you say can be used against you in court. *You have a right to talk to a lawyer for advice before we ask you any questions, and to have him with you during questioning.* You have this right to the advice and presence of a lawyer even if you cannot afford to hire one. *We have no way of giving you a lawyer, but one will be appointed for you, if you wish, if and when you go to court.* If you wish to answer questions now without a lawyer present, you have the right to stop answering questions at any time. You also have the right to stop answering at any time until you've talked to a lawyer.

Before the Supreme Court, respondent contended that the warnings were unconstitutionally linked to providing him with a lawyer in the future—after the interrogation. The Supreme Court disagreed, reasoning:

> First, this instruction accurately described the procedure for the appointment of counsel in Indiana. Under Indiana law, counsel is appointed at the defendant's initial appearance in court, and formal charges must be filed at or before that hearing. We think it must be relatively commonplace for a suspect, after receiving *Miranda* warnings, to ask when he will obtain counsel. The "if and when you go to court" advice simply anticipates that question. Second, *Miranda* does not require that attorneys be producible on call, but only that the suspect be informed, as here, that he has the right to an attorney before and during questioning, and that an attorney would be appointed for him if he could not afford one.

In upholding the warnings, the Court concluded that they properly apprised respondent of his right to an attorney should he elect to answer questions.

2.   Unpacking the Holmes casefile. The organization of Holmes's casefile is confusing. Grouped into Casefile Document 1 are four motions to suppress. They are each listed below alongside the key evidence each seeks to suppress. Casefile Document 2 includes the prosecution's opposition filings, and Casefile Document 3 collects Holmes's replies. Casefile Document 4 is a large file comprising four separate orders from the district court.

- *D-124*: This is Holmes's first motion to suppress. It seeks to suppress Holmes's statements: (1) "It is just me," and (2) Holmes again acknowledging that he was alone and that he had four guns as well as explosives with him at his apartment. [Holmes Casefile Document 1, D-124 Motion, at 1–2.]

- *D-125*: This is Holmes's second motion to suppress. It seeks to suppress a comment from Officer Justin Grizzle who claims that, after he asked if anyone else was helping Holmes, Holmes replied with a "smirk." [Holmes Casefile Document 1, D-125 Motion, at 2.]

- *D-126*: This is Holmes's third motion to suppress. It seeks to suppress incriminating statements Holmes made (and an incriminating question he asked) at approximately 2:50 am on July 20 after he sought to "invoke the Sixth Amendment." [Holmes Casefile Document 1, D-126 Motion, at 2.] You can watch how detectives respond to that invocation in the interrogation video included in the Holmes casefile. [Holmes Casefile Video beginning at 5:45.]

- *D-127*: This is Holmes's fourth and final motion to suppress. After the brief July 20 video interrogation of Holmes, officers did not resume questioning him again until approximately 3:45 p.m. At that time, law enforcement acknowledged that Holmes had invoked his right to counsel, but told him they did not seek to ask him questions about the theater shooting. Rather, they sought to gain a better understanding of the booby traps that Holmes left in his apartment. This motion seeks to suppress the responses gave to those questions. [Holmes Casefile Document 1, D-127 Motion, at 2–3.]

3.   **Holmes and the form of his *Miranda* warnings.** Compare the holdings in *Prysock* and *Duckworth* to the *Miranda* warnings Holmes received during his second interrogation. [*See* Holmes Casefile Video beginning at 4:55.] Focus specifically on the *Miranda* right to counsel warning that Detective Mehl gives to Holmes. The pair have this exchange:

DETECTIVE MEHL: You have the right to talk to a lawyer and have him present with you while you're being questioned. Do you understand that?

HOLMES: How do I get a lawyer?

DETECTIVE MEHL: Well, we'll talk about that. . .

HOLMES: Well, yes, yes. . .

DETECTIVE MEHL: Ok. If you cannot afford to hire a lawyer, one will be appointed to represent you for any questioning if you wish.

HOLMES: Yes, yes.

What do you notice is different about the right to counsel warning Homes received as compared to the warnings in *Prysock* and *Duckworth*?

4.   **Holmes & "statements."** The *Miranda* Court makes clear that its new regime applies to "statements obtained from a defendant questioned while in custody or otherwise deprived of his freedom of action in any significant way." Consider Holmes's second motion to suppress, which seeks to suppress a "smirk" that Holmes made to an Officer Grizzle shortly after Holmes was detained. [Holmes Casefile Document 1, D-125 Motion, at 2.] Does a smirk qualify as a "statement" within the meaning of *Miranda*? How does the circuit court resolve that question? [*See* Holmes Casefile Document 4, Order on D-125, at 14.]

5.   **Tsarnaev & a procedural note.** Speaking generally, defendants charged in state court are arrested and *then* a criminal complaint is issued. In Tsarnaev's case, however, federal authorities proceeded in the opposite direction by filing a complaint before arresting Tsarnaev. Specifically, the government filed a criminal complaint and supporting affidavit against Tsarnaev on April 21, 2013, two days after his apprehension, charging him with (1) using a weapon of mass destruction, and (2) malicious destruction of property resulting in death. [See Tsarnaev Casefile Document 1.] Magistrate

Judge Marianna Bowler responsively issued an arrest warrant for Tsarnaev that same day. [See Tsarnaev Casefile Document 2.]

Federal Rule of Criminal Procedure 4 permits the issuance of an arrest warrant on the basis of a complaint. Rule 4 provides, in pertinent part, as follows: "If the complaint or one or more affidavits filed with the complaint establish probable cause to believe that an offense has been committed and that the defendant committed it, the judge must issue an arrest warrant to an officer authorized to execute it."

6.   Tsarnaev & the Fourth Amendment. Let's review. Consider how law enforcement discovered that Tsarnaev was one of the two bombers. As the affidavit in support of the criminal complaint filed against Tsarnaev reveals, law enforcement relied on the following: (1) "a security camera located on Boylston Street near the corner of Boylston and Gloucester Streets," (2) "security camera footage taken from a location farther east on Boylston Street, as well as contemporaneous photographs taken from across the street," and (3) "video footage taken from a security camera affixed above the doorway of the Forum Restaurant located at 755 Boylston Street." [See Affidavit in Tsarnaev Casefile Document 1, at 3–4.] Is use of any or all of that footage a Fourth Amendment "search" that implicates Tsarnaev's Fourth Amendment rights?

7.   Tsarnaev & voluntariness. Let's review. What is the significance—for purposes of the voluntariness analysis—of examining Tsarnaev's trauma surgeon, Dr. Stephen Odom? [*See* Tsarnaev Casefile Document 3.] Note *where* Dr. Odom was questioned. Speaking of voluntaries, was the Tsarnaev interrogation recorded? [*See* Tsarnaev Casefile Document 5, at 10.]

8.   Inside the boat. As you know, Dave Henneberry found Tsarnaev inside his boat on April 9, 2013. Later, law enforcement discovered that Tsarnaev wrote incriminating messages inside the boat, including: "The U.S. Government is killing our innocent civilians"; "I can't stand to see such evil go unpunished"; "We Muslims are one body, you hurt one you hurt us all"; "Now I don't like killing innocent people it is forbidden in Islam but due to said [unintelligible] it is allowed]"; and "Stop killing our innocent people and we will stop." [Tsarnaev Casefile Document 4, at 4.] Would *Miranda* or the Fourth Amendment prevent admission of those statements against Tsarnaev at trial?

9.   Quality of defense counsel. As you thumb through Tsarnaev's motion to suppress, what do you think of his attorneys' efforts? [*See* Tsarnaev Casefile Document 5.] Put yourself in his attorneys' shoes: Could you have served as a zealous advocate for Tsarnaev knowing the accusations he faced?

One of Tsarnaev's lawyers was Judy Clarke, a well-known death penalty lawyer whose client list includes Ted Kaczynski, Zacarias Moussaoui, and Jared Loughner. An excerpt from a September 2015 *New Yorker* piece gives some insight into her professional philosophy:

> Among death-penalty lawyers, Clarke is known, without irony, as St. Judy, on the basis of her humility, her generosity, and her devotion to her clients. She has not given an interview to the mainstream press

in twenty years. But, in a 2013 commencement speech at Gonzaga University School of Law, Clarke said that her clients have obliged her to "redefine what a win means." Victory usually means a life sentence. Even so, Clarke said, she owes a debt of gratitude to her clients, for "the lessons they've taught me—about human behavior and human frailty—and the constant reminder that there but for the grace of God go I."

Patrick Radden Keefe, *The Worst of the Worst*, NEWYORKER.COM (Sept. 14, 2015), https://www.newyorker.com/magazine/2015/09/14/the-worst-of-the-worst.

A Postscript to *Miranda*[7]

Given modern citizens' ability to recite those warnings, it is both easy and tempting to forget the profound impact the *Miranda* decision had on the public generally and on the interrogation room specifically. In short, the reaction was intense. A *New York Times* piece characterized the *Miranda* decision as providing "immunity from punishment for crime on a wholesale basis." Some police believed that the decision forced them to fight criminals "with two hands tied behind their back." The Chief of Police in Cleveland, Ohio, claimed that the Supreme Court made it impossible to obtain a suspect's voluntary statement, and the Los Angeles police chief predicted that "all confessions would soon be useless." Legislators proposed amending the constitution to overturn *Miranda*, and successfully passed legislation designed to overrule *Miranda*.

Amid the post-*Miranda* frustration, Judge Burger—then still a member of the U.S. Court of Appeals for the District of Columbia—gave an address on May 21, 1967, at Ripon College in Ripon, Wisconsin. His speech included these remarks:

> I assume that no one will take issue with me when I say that these North Europe countries are as enlightened as the United States in the value they place on the individual and on human dignity. When we look at the two stages of the administration of criminal justice in those countries, we find some interesting contrasts. They have not found it necessary to establish a system of procedure which makes a criminal trial so complex or so difficult or so long drawn out as in this country. They do not employ our system of 12 men and women as jurors. They do not consider it necessary to use a device like our 5th Amendment under which an accused person may not be required to testify. They go swiftly, efficiently and directly to the question of whether the accused is guilty. By our standards their system of finding the facts concerning guilt or innocence is almost ruthless. In those systems

---

[7]   This postscript is based with permission on a portion of Brian Gallini, Schneckloth v. Bustamonte: *History's Unspoken Fourth Amendment Anomaly*, 79 TENN. L. REV. 233, 250–53 (2012). All footnotes are omitted.

they do not have cases ... where the accused has countless hearings and trials and re-trials and reviews over 10 or 12 years. In these long drawn out cases everyone loses sight of the factor of guilt and even the most guilty convict comes to believe the press releases of his lawyer.

Judge Burger's remarks were later published in a 1967 U.S. News and World Report, and Republican nominee Richard M. Nixon was captivated when he read them; Nixon even began to integrate Burger's ideas into his own 1968 presidential campaign speeches. Burger himself viewed the speech as the primary reason that Nixon selected him to replace Warren as Chief Justice.

The 1968 election began to heat up alongside frustrations with *Miranda*. For example, in May of 1968, Senator John L. McClellan decried the *Miranda* and *Escobedo* decisions, arguing that they brought "confusion and disarray ... into law enforcement," and produced "deplorable and demoralizing" results. Moreover, he contended, the decisions "weakened intolerably the force and effect of our criminal laws" because they "set free many dangerous criminals" and "prevent[ed] the convictions of others [including] known, admitted, and confessed murderers, robbers, and rapists[.]" That same month, the New York County District Attorney professed that only 15% of defendants now gave incriminating statements post-Miranda—compared with 49% beforehand. Moreover, the Chief of Police in Fresno, California, indicated that convictions and guilty pleas had declined dramatically since Escobedo.

For Nixon himself, *Miranda* was likewise too much: "During the 1968 presidential election, Richard M. Nixon had run against Chief Justice Warren and his Court as much as he had run against his Democratic opponent, Hubert H. Humphrey." Indeed, Nixon believed that the courts "[had] gone too far in weakening the peace forces as against the criminal forces." He therefore made "law and order" a central issue in his campaign and gave speeches decrying the *Miranda* and *Escobedo* decisions. If elected, Nixon promised on the campaign trail, he would fill the Court with "strict constructionists."

As a dejected former President Lyndon Johnson would later concede, Nixon was ultimately elected in 1968 largely because of his law and order campaign. Thereafter, in early 1969, the search began for Chief Justice Warren's replacement; Nixon sought a judge who, among other characteristics, would "share[ ] his view that the Court should interpret the Constitution rather than amend it by judicial fiat." Coincidentally, in March of that year, the U.S. Court of Appeals for the District of Columbia reversed a defendant's conviction, citing an inability to determine whether the defendant waived his *Miranda* rights prior to his confession. Attacking the majority (and Miranda), Judge Burger issued a bitter dissent:

We are well on our way to forbidding any utterance of an accused to be used against him unless it is made in open court. Guilt or innocence becomes irrelevant in the criminal trial as we founder in a morass of artificial rules poorly conceived and often impossible of application.

Reports of Burger's dissent emerged in the local press, and Nixon noticed. He would ultimately nominate Burger to be Chief Justice on May 22, 1969; the Senate confirmed him eighteen days later.

IV. *MIRANDA* TRIGGERS

A. CUSTODY

BERKEMER V. MCCARTY
468 U.S. 420
Supreme Court of the United States
April 18, 1984, Argued; July 2, 1984, Decided
No. 83-710

JUSTICE MARSHALL delivered the opinion of the Court. * * *

I

A

* * * On the evening of March 31, 1980, Trooper Williams of the Ohio State Highway Patrol observed respondent's car weaving in and out of a lane on Interstate Highway 270. After following the car for two miles, Williams forced respondent to stop and asked him to get out of the vehicle. When respondent complied, Williams noticed that he was having difficulty standing. At that point, "Williams concluded that [respondent] would be charged with a traffic offense and, therefore, his freedom to leave the scene was terminated." However, respondent was not told that he would be taken into custody. Williams then asked respondent to perform a field sobriety test, commonly known as a "balancing test." Respondent could not do so without falling.

While still at the scene of the traffic stop, Williams asked respondent whether he had been using intoxicants. Respondent replied that "he had consumed two beers and had smoked several joints of marijuana a short time before." Respondent's speech was slurred, and Williams had difficulty understanding him. Williams thereupon formally placed respondent under arrest and transported him in the patrol car to the Franklin County Jail.

At the jail, respondent was given an intoxilyzer test to determine the concentration of alcohol in his blood. The test did not detect any alcohol whatsoever in respondent's system. Williams then resumed questioning respondent in order to obtain information for inclusion in the State

Highway Patrol Alcohol Influence Report. Respondent answered affirmatively a question whether he had been drinking. When then asked if he was under the influence of alcohol, he said, "I guess, barely." Williams next asked respondent to indicate on the form whether the marihuana he had smoked had been treated with any chemicals. In the section of the report headed "Remarks," respondent wrote, "No [angel] dust or PCP in the pot. Rick McCarty."

At no point in this sequence of events did Williams or anyone else tell respondent that he had a right to remain silent, to consult with an attorney, and to have an attorney appointed for him if he could not afford one.

B

Respondent was charged with operating a motor vehicle while under the influence of alcohol and/or drugs * * *. Under Ohio law, that offense is a first-degree misdemeanor and is punishable by fine or imprisonment for up to six months. Incarceration for a minimum of three days is mandatory.

Respondent moved to exclude the various incriminating statements he had made to Trooper Williams on the ground that introduction into evidence of those statements would violate the Fifth Amendment insofar as he had not been informed of his constitutional rights prior to his interrogation. When the trial court denied the motion, respondent pleaded "no contest" and was found guilty.[2] He was sentenced to 90 days in jail, 80 of which were suspended, and was fined $300, $100 of which were suspended.

On appeal to the Franklin County Court of Appeals, respondent renewed his constitutional claim. * * * [T]he Court of Appeals rejected respondent's argument and affirmed his conviction. The Ohio Supreme Court dismissed respondent's appeal on the ground that it failed to present a "substantial constitutional question."

Respondent then filed an action for a writ of habeas corpus in the District Court for the Southern District of Ohio. The District Court dismissed the petition, holding that "Miranda warnings do not have to be given prior to in custody interrogation of a suspect arrested for a traffic offense."

A divided panel of the Court of Appeals for the Sixth Circuit reversed, holding that "Miranda warnings must be given to all individuals prior to custodial interrogation, whether the offense investigated be a felony or a

---

[2] Ohio Rev. Code Ann. § 2937.07 (1982) provides, in pertinent part: "If the plea be 'no contest' or words of similar import in pleading to a misdemeanor, it shall constitute a stipulation that the judge or magistrate may make [a] finding of guilty or not guilty from the explanation of circumstances, and if guilt be found, impose or continue for sentence accordingly."

Ohio Rule of Criminal Procedure 12(H) provides: "The plea of no contest does not preclude a defendant from asserting upon appeal that the trial court prejudicially erred in ruling on a pretrial motion, including a pretrial motion to suppress evidence."

misdemeanor traffic offense." In applying this principle to the facts of the case, the Court of Appeals distinguished between the statements made by respondent before and after his formal arrest. The postarrest statements, the court ruled, were plainly inadmissible * * *. The court's treatment of respondent's prearrest statements was less clear. * * * [T]he Court of Appeals did not specify which statements, if any, could be used against respondent in a retrial.

We granted certiorari * * *.

II

* * * In the years since the decision in *Miranda*, we have frequently reaffirmed the central principle established by that case: if the police take a suspect into custody and then ask him questions without informing him of the rights enumerated above, his responses cannot be introduced into evidence to establish his guilt.

Petitioner asks us to carve an exception out of the foregoing principle. When the police arrest a person for allegedly committing a misdemeanor traffic offense and then ask him questions without telling him his constitutional rights, petitioner argues, his responses should be admissible against him. We cannot agree.

One of the principal advantages of the doctrine that suspects must be given warnings before being interrogated while in custody is the clarity of that rule. * * *

The exception to *Miranda* proposed by petitioner would substantially undermine this crucial advantage of the doctrine. The police often are unaware when they arrest a person whether he may have committed a misdemeanor or a felony. Consider, for example, the reasonably common situation in which the driver of a car involved in an accident is taken into custody. Under Ohio law, both driving while under the influence of intoxicants and negligent vehicular homicide are misdemeanors, while reckless vehicular homicide is a felony. When arresting a person for causing a collision, the police may not know which of these offenses he may have committed. Indeed, the nature of his offense may depend upon circumstances unknowable to the police, such as whether the suspect has previously committed a similar offense or has a criminal record of some other kind. It may even turn upon events yet to happen, such as whether a victim of the accident dies. It would be unreasonable to expect the police to make guesses as to the nature of the criminal conduct at issue before deciding how they may interrogate the suspect.

Equally importantly, the doctrinal complexities that would confront the courts if we accepted petitioner's proposal would be Byzantine. Difficult questions quickly spring to mind: For instance, investigations into seemingly minor offenses sometimes escalate gradually into investigations into more serious matters; at what point in the evolution of an affair of this sort would the police be obliged to give *Miranda* warnings to a suspect in custody? What evidence would be necessary to establish that an arrest for a misdemeanor offense was merely a pretext to enable the police to interrogate the suspect (in hopes of obtaining information about a felony) without providing him the safeguards prescribed by *Miranda*? The litigation necessary to resolve such matters would be time-consuming and disruptive of law enforcement. And the end result would be an elaborate set of rules, interlaced with exceptions and subtle distinctions, discriminating between different kinds of custodial interrogations. Neither the police nor criminal defendants would benefit from such a development.

Absent a compelling justification we surely would be unwilling so seriously to impair the simplicity and clarity of the holding of *Miranda*. * * * Petitioner * * * contends that *Miranda* warnings are unnecessary when a suspect is questioned about a misdemeanor traffic offense, because the police have no reason to subject such a suspect to the sort of interrogation that most troubled the Court in *Miranda*. We cannot agree that the dangers of police abuse are so slight in this context. For example, the offense of driving while intoxicated is increasingly regarded in many jurisdictions as a very serious matter. Especially when the intoxicant at issue is a narcotic drug rather than alcohol, the police sometimes have difficulty obtaining evidence of this crime. Under such circumstances, the incentive for the police to try to induce the defendant to incriminate himself may well be substantial. Similar incentives are likely to be present when a person is arrested for a minor offense but the police suspect that a more serious crime may have been committed.

We do not suggest that there is any reason to think improper efforts were made in this case to induce respondent to make damaging admissions. More generally, we have no doubt that, in conducting most custodial interrogations of persons arrested for misdemeanor traffic offenses, the police behave responsibly and do not deliberately exert pressures upon the suspect to confess against his will. But the same might be said of custodial interrogations of persons arrested for felonies. The purposes of the safeguards prescribed by *Miranda* are to ensure that the police do not coerce or trick captive suspects into confessing, to relieve the "inherently compelling pressures" generated by the custodial setting itself, "which work to undermine the individual's will to resist," and as much as possible to free courts from the task of scrutinizing individual cases to try to determine, after the fact, whether particular confessions were voluntary. Those purposes are implicated as much by in-custody questioning of persons suspected of misdemeanors as they are by questioning of persons suspected of felonies. * * *

We hold therefore that a person subjected to custodial interrogation is entitled to the benefit of the procedural safeguards enunciated in *Miranda*, regardless of the nature or severity of the offense of which he is suspected or for which he was arrested.

The implication of this holding is that the Court of Appeals was correct in ruling that the statements made by respondent at the County Jail were inadmissible. There can be no question that respondent was "in custody" at least as of the moment he was formally placed under arrest and instructed to get into the police car. Because he was not informed of his constitutional rights at that juncture, respondent's subsequent admissions should not have been used against him.

III

To assess the admissibility of the self-incriminating statements made by respondent prior to his formal arrest, we are obliged to address a second issue concerning the scope of our decision in *Miranda*: whether the roadside questioning of a motorist detained pursuant to a routine traffic stop should be considered "custodial interrogation." * * * Petitioner contends that a holding that every detained motorist must be advised of his rights before being questioned would constitute an unwarranted extension of the *Miranda* doctrine.

It must be acknowledged at the outset that a traffic stop significantly curtails the "freedom of action" of the driver and the passengers, if any, of the detained vehicle. Under the law of most States, it is a crime either to ignore a policeman's signal to stop one's car or, once having stopped, to drive away without permission. Certainly few motorists would feel free either to disobey a directive to pull over or to leave the scene of a traffic stop without being told they might do so.[25] Partly for these reasons, we have long acknowledged that "stopping an automobile and detaining its occupants constitute a 'seizure' within the meaning of [the Fourth] [Amendment], even though the purpose of the stop is limited and the resulting detention quite brief."

However, we decline to accord talismanic power to the phrase in the *Miranda* opinion emphasized by respondent. Fidelity to the doctrine announced in *Miranda* requires that it be enforced strictly, but only in those types of situations in which the concerns that powered the decision are implicated. Thus, we must decide whether a traffic stop exerts upon a detained person pressures that sufficiently impair his free exercise of his privilege against self-incrimination to require that he be warned of his constitutional rights.

Two features of an ordinary traffic stop mitigate the danger that a person questioned will be induced "to speak where he would not otherwise

---

[25] Indeed, petitioner frankly admits that "[no] reasonable person would feel that he was free to ignore the visible and audible signal of a traffic safety enforcement officer. . . . Moreover, it is nothing short of sophistic to state that a motorist ordered by a police officer to step out of his vehicle would reasonabl[y] or prudently believe that he was at liberty to ignore that command."

do so freely," *Miranda v. Arizona*, 384 U.S., at 467. First, detention of a motorist pursuant to a traffic stop is presumptively temporary and brief. The vast majority of roadside detentions last only a few minutes. A motorist's expectations, when he sees a policeman's light flashing behind him, are that he will be obliged to spend a short period of time answering questions and waiting while the officer checks his license and registration, that he may then be given a citation, but that in the end he most likely will be allowed to continue on his way. In this respect, questioning incident to an ordinary traffic stop is quite different from stationhouse interrogation, which frequently is prolonged, and in which the detainee often is aware that questioning will continue until he provides his interrogators the answers they seek.

Second, circumstances associated with the typical traffic stop are not such that the motorist feels completely at the mercy of the police. To be sure, the aura of authority surrounding an armed, uniformed officer and the knowledge that the officer has some discretion in deciding whether to issue a citation, in combination, exert some pressure on the detainee to respond to questions. But other aspects of the situation substantially offset these forces. Perhaps most importantly, the typical traffic stop is public, at least to some degree. Passersby, on foot or in other cars, witness the interaction of officer and motorist. This exposure to public view both reduces the ability of an unscrupulous policeman to use illegitimate means to elicit self-incriminating statements and diminishes the motorist's fear that, if he does not cooperate, he will be subjected to abuse. The fact that the detained motorist typically is confronted by only one or at most two policemen further mutes his sense of vulnerability. In short, the atmosphere surrounding an ordinary traffic stop is substantially less "police dominated" than that surrounding the kinds of interrogation at issue in *Miranda* itself, and in the subsequent cases in which we have applied *Miranda*.

In both of these respects, the usual traffic stop is more analogous to a so-called "*Terry* stop," *see Terry v. Ohio*, 392 U.S. 1 (1968), than to a formal arrest.[29] Under the Fourth Amendment, we have held, a policeman who lacks probable cause but whose "observations lead him reasonably to suspect" that a particular person has committed, is committing, or is about to commit a crime, may detain that person briefly in order to "investigate the circumstances that provoke suspicion." "[The] stop and inquiry must be 'reasonably related in scope to the justification for their initiation.' " Typically, this means that the officer may ask the detainee a moderate number of questions to determine his identity and to try to obtain

---

[29] No more is implied by this analogy than that most traffic stops resemble, in duration and atmosphere, the kind of brief detention authorized in *Terry*. We of course do not suggest that a traffic stop supported by probable cause may not exceed the bounds set by the Fourth Amendment on the scope of a *Terry* stop.

information confirming or dispelling the officer's suspicions. But the detainee is not obliged to respond. And, unless the detainee's answers provide the officer with probable cause to arrest him, he must then be released. The comparatively nonthreatening character of detentions of this sort explains the absence of any suggestion in our opinions that *Terry* stops are subject to the dictates of *Miranda*. The similarly noncoercive aspect of ordinary traffic stops prompts us to hold that persons temporarily detained pursuant to such stops are not "in custody" for the purposes of *Miranda*.

Respondent contends that to "exempt" traffic stops from the coverage of *Miranda* will open the way to widespread abuse. Policemen will simply delay formally arresting detained motorists, and will subject them to sustained and intimidating interrogation at the scene of their initial detention. The net result, respondent contends, will be a serious threat to the rights that the *Miranda* doctrine is designed to protect.

We are confident that the state of affairs projected by respondent will not come to pass. It is settled that the safeguards prescribed by *Miranda* become applicable as soon as a suspect's freedom of action is curtailed to a "degree associated with formal arrest." If a motorist who has been detained pursuant to a traffic stop thereafter is subjected to treatment that renders him "in custody" for practical purposes, he will be entitled to the full panoply of protections prescribed by *Miranda*. * * *

Turning to the case before us, we find nothing in the record that indicates that respondent should have been given *Miranda* warnings at any point prior to the time Trooper Williams placed him under arrest. For the reasons indicated above, we reject the contention that the initial stop of respondent's car, by itself, rendered him "in custody." And respondent has failed to demonstrate that, at any time between the initial stop and the arrest, he was subjected to restraints comparable to those associated with a formal arrest. Only a short period of time elapsed between the stop and the arrest. At no point during that interval was respondent informed that his detention would not be temporary. Although Trooper Williams apparently decided as soon as respondent stepped out of his car that respondent would be taken into custody and charged with a traffic offense, Williams never communicated his intention to respondent. A policeman's unarticulated plan has no bearing on the question whether a suspect was "in custody" at a particular time; the only relevant inquiry is how a reasonable man in the suspect's position would have understood his situation. Nor do other aspects of the interaction of Williams and respondent support the contention that respondent was exposed to "custodial interrogation" at the scene of the stop. From aught that appears in the stipulation of facts, a single police officer asked respondent a modest number of questions and requested him to perform a simple balancing test at a location visible to passing motorists. Treatment of this sort cannot fairly be characterized as the functional equivalent of formal arrest.

We conclude, in short, that respondent was not taken into custody for the purposes of *Miranda* until Williams arrested him. Consequently, the statements respondent made prior to that point were admissible against him. * * *

Accordingly, the judgment of the Court of Appeals is

Affirmed.

JUSTICE STEVENS, concurring in part and concurring in the judgment.

[Omitted.]

QUESTIONS, COMMENTS, CONCERNS?

1.   *Miranda* custody and telling the suspect he's not under arrest. After a residential burglary in Pendleton, Oregon, an Oregon State Police Officer in *Oregon v. Mathiason*, 429 U.S. 492 (1977), asked the victim if there was anyone who she suspected had committed the crime. The victim responded that she could think only of Carl Mathiason. Mathiason later agreed to meet with an officer with the state patrol office. Once there, the officer escorted Mathiason into an office and informed him that he was not under arrest. But without first advising Mathiason of his *Miranda* rights, the officer told Mathiason that he believed Mathiason was involved in the burglary. The officer also told Mathiason—falsely—that his fingerprints were found at the scene. After just a few minutes, Mathiason admitted to the robbery. He was then advised of his *Miranda* rights for the first time and gave a full confession. The confession was crucial to convicting Mathiason at a bench trial.

On appeal to the United States Supreme Court, the Court held that Mathiason's pre-*Miranda* statement was admissible because he was not in custody during the initial "interview." The Court reasoned, "[T]here is no indication that the questioning took place in a context where [Mathiason's] freedom to depart was restricted in any way." It further reasoned that Mathiason came to the police station voluntarily and was informed immediately before his confession that he was not under arrest. The Court added that the false statement about finding Mathiason's fingerprints at the scene was irrelevant to the question of whether Mathiason was in custody.

2.   An officer's subjective beliefs about custody. In *Stansbury v. California*, 511 U.S. 318 (1994), ten-year-old Robyn Jackson disappeared from a playground in Baldwin Park, California, on September 28, 1982. The following morning, Andrew Zimmerman observed a large man driving a turquoise sedan throw something into a flood control channel in Pasadena. Zimmerman relayed his observations to police, and officers later found Jackson's body in the channel. The evidence showed that Jackson was raped and that his cause of death was "asphyxia complicated by blunt force trauma to the head."

The ensuing investigation revealed that Jackson spoke with two ice cream truck drivers in the hours leading up to her disappearance, including Robert

Edward Stansbury. Initially, though, police viewed the other driver as the primary suspect and classified Stansbury as a witness. Stansbury agreed to accompany officers to the police station where two detectives interviewed him as a witness. But after Stansbury informed officers that his roommate drove a turquoise sedan and that he had prior convictions for rape and kidnapping, officers terminated the interview and read Stansbury his *Miranda* rights. Stansbury then refused to answer questioning and was arrested.

At trial, Stansbury moved to suppress his pre-*Miranda* statements. The trial court denied his motion, finding that Stansbury was not in custody. It reasoned that officers did not subjectively believe Stansbury was a suspect at the time of his statements. The Supreme Court reversed, holding that a police officer's subjective belief is not properly part of *Miranda*'s custody analysis. Rather, said the Court, the initial determination of custody "depends on the objective circumstances of the interrogation, not on the subjective views harbored by either the interrogating officers or the person being questioned." It reasoned that "one cannot expect the person under interrogation to probe the officer's innermost thoughts."

3. Tsarnaev and custody. Think about the scene inside the hospital where Tsarnaev was interrogated. His defense attorneys described it as follows:

> Before interrogation began, two lawyers from the Federal Public Defender Office and a private lawyer who had been appointed by the state public defender's office * * * attempted to meet with Mr. Tsarnaev at the hospital. They were turned away by FBI agents, who refused to accept a letter to Mr. Tsarnaev notifying him of counsel's availability.

[Tsarnaev Casefile Document 5, at 3.] Now consider that one FBI agent later claimed that Tsarnaev was not in custody. *Id.* Applying the Court's test in *Berkemer*, does that claim have any merit?

J. D. B. v. NORTH CAROLINA

564 U.S. 261
Supreme Court of the United States
March 23, 2011, Argued; June 16, 2011, Decided
No. 09-11121

JUSTICE SOTOMAYOR delivered the opinion of the Court.

This case presents the question whether the age of a child subjected to police questioning is relevant to the custody analysis of *Miranda v. Arizona*, 384 U.S. 436 (1966). It is beyond dispute that children will often feel bound to submit to police questioning when an adult in the same circumstances would feel free to leave. Seeing no reason for police officers or courts to blind themselves to that commonsense reality, we hold that a child's age properly informs the *Miranda* custody analysis.

I

* * * Petitioner J. D. B. was a 13-year-old, seventh-grade student attending class at Smith Middle School in Chapel Hill, North Carolina, when he was removed from his classroom by a uniformed police officer, escorted to a closed-door conference room, and questioned by police for at least half an hour.

This was the second time that police questioned J. D. B. in the span of a week. Five days earlier, two home break-ins occurred, and various items were stolen. Police stopped and questioned J. D. B. after he was seen behind a residence in the neighborhood where the crimes occurred. That same day, police also spoke to J. D. B.'s grandmother—his legal guardian— as well as his aunt.

Police later learned that a digital camera matching the description of one of the stolen items had been found at J. D. B.'s middle school and seen in J. D. B.'s possession. Investigator DiCostanzo, the juvenile investigator with the local police force who had been assigned to the case, went to the school to question J. D. B. Upon arrival, DiCostanzo informed the uniformed police officer on detail to the school (a so-called school resource officer), the assistant principal, and an administrative intern that he was there to question J. D. B. about the break-ins. Although DiCostanzo asked the school administrators to verify J. D. B.'s date of birth, address, and parent contact information from school records, neither the police officers nor the school administrators contacted J. D. B.'s grandmother.

The uniformed officer interrupted J. D. B.'s afternoon social studies class, removed J. D. B. from the classroom, and escorted him to a school conference room. There, J. D. B. was met by DiCostanzo, the assistant principal, and the administrative intern. The door to the conference room was closed. With the two police officers and the two administrators present, J. D. B. was questioned for the next 30 to 45 minutes. Prior to the commencement of questioning, J. D. B. was given neither *Miranda* warnings nor the opportunity to speak to his grandmother. Nor was he informed that he was free to leave the room.

Questioning began with small talk—discussion of sports and J. D. B.'s family life. DiCostanzo asked, and J. D. B. agreed, to discuss the events of the prior weekend. Denying any wrongdoing, J. D. B. explained that he had been in the neighborhood where the crimes occurred because he was seeking work mowing lawns. DiCostanzo pressed J. D. B. for additional detail about his efforts to obtain work; asked J. D. B. to explain a prior incident, when one of the victims returned home to find J. D. B. behind her house; and confronted J. D. B. with the stolen camera. The assistant principal urged J. D. B. to "do the right thing," warning J. D. B. that "the truth always comes out in the end."

Eventually, J. D. B. asked whether he would "still be in trouble" if he returned the "stuff." In response, DiCostanzo explained that return of the stolen items would be helpful, but "this thing is going to court" regardless. [Record cite] ("[W]hat's done is done[;] now you need to help yourself by making it right"). DiCostanzo then warned that he may need to seek a secure custody order if he believed that J. D. B. would continue to break into other homes. When J. D. B. asked what a secure custody order was, DiCostanzo explained that "it's where you get sent to juvenile detention before court."

After learning of the prospect of juvenile detention, J. D. B. confessed that he and a friend were responsible for the break-ins. DiCostanzo only then informed J. D. B. that he could refuse to answer the investigator's questions and that he was free to leave. Asked whether he understood, J. D. B. nodded and provided further detail, including information about the location of the stolen items. Eventually J. D. B. wrote a statement, at DiCostanzo's request. When the bell rang indicating the end of the school day, J. D. B. was allowed to leave to catch the bus home.

* * * After a suppression hearing at which DiCostanzo and J. D. B. testified, the trial court denied the motion, deciding that J. D. B. was not in custody at the time of the schoolhouse interrogation and that his statements were voluntary. As a result, J. D. B. entered a transcript of admission to all four counts, renewing his objection to the denial of his motion to suppress, and the court adjudicated J. D. B. delinquent. * * *

We granted certiorari to determine whether the *Miranda* custody analysis includes consideration of a juvenile suspect's age.

II

* * * Any police interview of an individual suspected of a crime has "coercive aspects to it." Only those interrogations that occur while a suspect is in police custody, however, "heighte[n] the risk" that statements obtained are not the product of the suspect's free choice. * * * [W]hether a suspect is "in custody" is an objective inquiry.

Two discrete inquiries are essential to the determination: first, what were the circumstances surrounding the interrogation; and second, given those circumstances, would a reasonable person have felt he or she was at liberty to terminate the interrogation and leave. Once the scene is set and the players' lines and actions are reconstructed, the court must apply an objective test to resolve the ultimate inquiry: was there a formal arrest or restraint on freedom of movement of the degree associated with formal arrest.

Rather than demarcate a limited set of relevant circumstances, we have required police officers and courts to "examine all of the circumstances surrounding the interrogation," including any circumstance that "would have affected how a reasonable person" in the suspect's position "would perceive his or her freedom to leave." On the other hand, the "subjective views harbored by either the interrogating officers or the person being questioned" are irrelevant. * * *

The State and its amici contend that a child's age has no place in the custody analysis, no matter how young the child subjected to police questioning. We cannot agree. In some circumstances, a child's age "would have affected how a reasonable person" in the suspect's position "would perceive his or her freedom to leave." That is, a reasonable child subjected to police questioning will sometimes feel pressured to submit when a reasonable adult would feel free to go. We think it clear that courts can account for that reality without doing any damage to the objective nature of the custody analysis.

A child's age is far "more than a chronological fact." It is a fact that "generates commonsense conclusions about behavior and perception." Such conclusions apply broadly to children as a class. And, they are self-evident to anyone who was a child once himself, including any police officer or judge. [The Court then engaged in a discussion about its treatment of children and the law.] * * *

As this discussion establishes, "[o]ur history is replete with laws and judicial recognition" that children cannot be viewed simply as miniature adults. We see no justification for taking a different course here. So long as the child's age was known to the officer at the time of the interview, or would have been objectively apparent to any reasonable officer, including age as part of the custody analysis requires officers neither to consider circumstances "unknowable" to them, nor to "anticipat[e] the frailties or idiosyncrasies" of the particular suspect whom they question. The same "wide basis of community experience" that makes it possible, as an objective matter, "to determine what is to be expected" of children in other contexts, likewise makes it possible to know what to expect of children subjected to police questioning.

In other words, a child's age differs from other personal characteristics that, even when known to police, have no objectively discernible relationship to a reasonable person's understanding of his freedom of action. * * * [I]n many cases involving juvenile suspects, the custody analysis would be nonsensical absent some consideration of the suspect's age. This case is a prime example. Were the court precluded from taking J. D. B.'s youth into account, it would be forced to evaluate the circumstances present here through the eyes of a reasonable person of average years. In other words, how would a reasonable adult understand his situation, after being removed from a seventh-grade social studies class by a uniformed school resource officer; being encouraged by his assistant principal to "do the right thing"; and being warned by a police investigator of the prospect of juvenile detention and separation from his guardian and primary caretaker? To describe such an inquiry is to demonstrate its absurdity. Neither officers nor courts can reasonably evaluate the effect of objective circumstances that, by their nature, are specific to children without accounting for the age of the child subjected to those circumstances.

* * * [Moreover,] the effect of the schoolhouse setting cannot be disentangled from the identity of the person questioned. A student—whose presence at school is compulsory and whose disobedience at school is cause for disciplinary action—is in a far different position than, say, a parent volunteer on school grounds to chaperone an event, or an adult from the community on school grounds to attend a basketball game. Without asking whether the person "questioned in school" is a "minor," the coercive effect of the schoolhouse setting is unknowable. * * *

Reviewing the question de novo today, we hold that so long as the child's age was known to the officer at the time of police questioning, or would have been objectively apparent to a reasonable officer, its inclusion in the custody analysis is consistent with the objective nature of that test. This is not to say that a child's age will be a determinative, or even a significant, factor in every case. It is, however, a reality that courts cannot simply ignore.

* * * The question remains whether J. D. B. was in custody when police interrogated him. We remand for the state courts to address that question, this time taking account of all of the relevant circumstances of the interrogation, including J. D. B.'s age at the time. The judgment of the North Carolina Supreme Court is reversed, and the case is remanded for proceedings not inconsistent with this opinion.

It is so ordered.

JUSTICE ALITO, with whom THE CHIEF JUSTICE, JUSTICE SCALIA, and JUSTICE THOMAS join, dissenting.

[Omitted.]

STATE V. BARTELT

906 N.W.2d 684
Supreme Court of Wisconsin
February 20, 2018, Filed
No. 2015AP2506-CR

PATIENCE DRAKE ROGGENSACK, C.J. This review concerns the point in time at which a person is "in custody" for purposes of *Miranda*. * * *

I. BACKGROUND

This case arises from two crimes committed in July 2013. On July 12, 2013, M.R. was assaulted by a male suspect with a knife while walking her dog in Richfield Historical Park in the Village of Richfield. M.R. was tackled to the ground and suffered several knife wounds before disarming the suspect, who fled the scene in a blue Dodge Caravan. Three days later, on July 15, 2013, Jessie Blodgett, a friend and former girlfriend of Bartelt, was found dead in her home in the City of Hartford. According to preliminary autopsy findings, the cause of death was ligature strangulation.

As of July 16, 2013, Clausing and Detective Richard Thickens of the Hartford Police Department had identified Bartelt as a person of interest in the attack on M.R. Earlier that month, a deputy had noticed a blue Dodge Caravan at the same park and had run the license plate, which revealed that the vehicle was registered to Bartelt's parents. Police learned that the Bartelts had a son, and were then able to match Bartelt's photograph from the Wisconsin Department of Transportation with the composite sketch drawn at M.R.'s direction. Clausing contacted Bartelt around 5:00 p.m. on July 16, and told him that the police were investigating an incident, and that they needed to speak with him. Bartelt was "very compliant," and agreed to meet with detectives at the Slinger Police Department.

The Slinger Police Department is located inside a municipal building that it shares with various other offices and departments. There is one main entrance to the building. Once inside, a separate entrance leads to the police department. Neither the main door to the building nor the door to the police department is secured during normal business hours, and there are no metal detectors or other security screening devices. Inside the police department, another door leads to the "internal portion" of the department. This door is locked from the outside, but one can freely exit. The interview room is located about twenty-five feet inside this secured area. The room is thirteen and one-half feet by ten and one-half feet, and contains a table, three chairs and a window. The room can be accessed by either of two doors, neither of which can be locked.

Bartelt was dropped off by two friends at the Slinger Police Department around 5:12 p.m. His friends waited outside. Clausing testified that Bartelt was escorted to the interview room but was not searched. Bartelt chose the seat on the far side of the table, while Clausing sat at the end, and Walsh sat opposite Bartelt. Clausing and Walsh were wearing civilian clothes; however, they both had their badges displayed on their belts, as well as their service weapons. Clausing testified that one of the doors to the room was left open. Unbeknownst to Bartelt, the interview was recorded by both audio and visual means.

Clausing began the interview by telling Bartelt that he was not in trouble, he was not under arrest, and he could leave at any time. Clausing did not read Bartelt his *Miranda* rights. Bartelt, who had just come from the Blodgett residence to pay his respects to the family, believed the police were meeting with him about Blodgett's murder. However, Clausing explained that law enforcement was investigating an attack that had occurred at Richfield Historic Park on the previous Friday. Bartelt was asked a number of preliminary questions and initially denied any involvement. Bartelt stated that he had been with his girlfriend on the day in question, although he could not "remember any specifics." Clausing then explained that cell phones "are kind of like GPS's," and told Bartelt, "I don't want any lies."

Clausing then observed some scrapes and a cut on Bartelt's hand and arm. Bartelt stated he did not remember how he scraped his arm, but that he had stabbed his hand "with a screw at work." The following exchange then occurred:

DET. CLAUSING: . . . So what do you think evidence is?

MR. BARTELT: Incriminating items, documents.

DET. CLAUSING: First—but I'm more of a nuts-and-bolts type of guy. Like, what would you consider to be evidence?

MR. BARTELT: Well—

DET. CLAUSING: Fingerprints?

MR. BARTELT: Yeah.

DET. CLAUSING: Okay. Fibers? Hairs?

MR. BARTELT: Yeah.

DET. CLAUSING: Any DNA? You know, footwear impressions?

MR. BARTELT: Yeah.

DET. CLAUSING: Witness statements, right? Video surveillance, stuff like that, right?

MR. BARTELT: Yeah.

DET. CLAUSING: Is there any evidence that we just talked about which would show that you would be in this park at the time of this incident that had occurred? Is there any evidence out there that would show that?

MR. BARTELT: I don't think so . . . What is this about?

After reminding Bartelt that police were investigating an incident at Richfield Historical Park, Clausing said, "What if I were to tell you that there might be something that links you there." Clausing then proceeded to explain "Locard's exchange principle," which holds that the perpetrator of a crime will bring something into the crime scene—such as fingerprints, sweat, DNA, or clothing fibers—and leave it behind. The detectives added that they had found evidence "from the person that was out there," which needed to be analyzed by the state crime laboratory.

Clausing next told Bartelt that they had an eyewitness, stating, "I would hate to put down your picture in front of the eyewitness and have them say, that's the guy that was out there." Further, Clausing stated, "I can prove that you were out there. It's not just a tip. I can prove it. And all I'm getting at is that if you were out there, just talk to us about what happened or what you saw or what you observed or whatever." Walsh told Bartelt they knew that his vehicle had been spotted at the park on several occasions when Bartelt was supposed to be at work. Bartelt admitted that he had been laid off for several months, and that the injury was actually the result of a cooking accident.

At this time Clausing moved his chair closer to Bartelt. When Clausing's face was about two feet from Bartelt's, Clausing told him, "No more lies. It just makes things worse. It is spiraling out of control right now . . . . Nobody in their right mind would lie about cutting themselves if it happened at home cooking . . . . What happened? Just be honest." Bartelt admitted that he had been to the park before and that he had seen the sketch on television, but that "it wasn't me."

Walsh then urged Bartelt to help bring closure to M.R. "Daniel, the truth is going to help us bring some resolution to this for everybody involved . . . . We have one scared person out there right now. . . and the easiest way to put some resolution to this is [for] the [ ] person that did this to take responsibility." Walsh added that he could understand why someone would do this, "especially if the person that did it explains to us what they were thinking, where they were in their life." For example, Bartelt had lost his job and hid that from his parents, and he had dropped out of college after only one semester. Walsh stated that "when things are not going well for people, they do things that are very out of character." He added, "I think you are a good person . . . [g]ood people can explain things away and we can understand why they do things. So tell us about the park."

Following a lengthy narrative from Clausing about the two types of people in this situation—those who take responsibility and those who say "prove it"—Bartelt admitted to being at the park and going "after that girl" because he "wanted to scare someone." Bartelt told the officers that he had been reading when he saw M.R., and in the "spur of the moment," he decided to "run at her and knock her down and scare her." Bartelt admitted there was no real explanation or motive for the attack; he was "just numb" and scared because "life scares me." Bartelt targeted M.R. because "[t]here was no one else there." Following this admission, Clausing asked Bartelt if he would be willing to provide a written statement of confession. Walsh explained that the written statement would be Bartelt's chance to apologize. When Bartelt asked what would happen after he gave his statement, Clausing responded, "I can't say what happens then. We'll probably have more questions for you, quite honestly." Clausing later testified that, once Bartelt had confessed, he "was going to be under arrest, and he probably wasn't free to get up and leave."

It was at this point that Bartelt asked, "Should I or can I speak to a lawyer or anything?" Clausing told him, "Sure, yes. That is your option." Bartelt responded, "I think I'd prefer that." At 5:45 p.m., roughly 33 minutes after Bartelt arrived at the station for questioning, Clausing and Walsh suspended the interview, took Bartelt's cell phone, and left the room. When the detectives returned seven or eight minutes later, Clausing told Bartelt he was under arrest, handcuffed him, and searched him. Bartelt was then transported to the Washington County Jail.

Clausing testified that, during the course of the interview, both he and Walsh spoke in a conversational tone, which did not change even after Bartelt's admission. Neither detective ever made reference to or unholstered their weapons. Bartelt never asked to use the restroom or take a break. At one point during the interview Clausing gave Bartelt permission to answer his cell phone, which Bartelt declined to do.

The following day, on July 17, 2013, Bartelt was brought to the interview room at the Washington County Sheriff's Department to be questioned by Thickens and Detective James Wolf regarding his relationship with Blodgett. Before commencing with questioning, Thickens read Bartelt his *Miranda* rights, which Bartelt knowingly and voluntarily waived.

Bartelt was questioned for approximately 90 minutes about his relationship with Blodgett and his whereabouts on the day of Blodgett's death. Bartelt denied being at the Blodgett residence on July 15, 2013, or having any knowledge of Blodgett's death. Bartelt stated that on the morning of July 15 he had left his house at 6:30 a.m. and drove "all over" before spending a few hours at Woodlawn Union Park. Bartelt then asked for an attorney, at which point the questioning stopped.

Thickens later drove to Woodlawn Union Park to investigate, and in doing so he collected garbage from the park's receptacles. In one container he found a Frosted Mini-Wheats cereal box containing paper toweling, numerous types of rope and tape, and antiseptic wipes with red stains. One of the ropes later revealed DNA that belonged to both Bartelt and Blodgett, and which matched the ligature marks on Blodgett's neck. Another rope matched the ligature marks on her wrists and ankles. Based on this evidence and the confession Bartelt made during his first interview, Bartelt was charged with attempted first-degree intentional homicide, first-degree reckless endangerment, and attempted false imprisonment for the attack on M.R., as well as first-degree intentional homicide for the murder of Blodgett.

Bartelt moved to suppress his statements, and any evidence derived from them, on the grounds that the officers had violated his *Miranda* rights when they questioned him. The circuit court denied Bartelt's motion, concluding that at the time of his July 16, 2013, interview, Bartelt had voluntarily agreed to speak with police. The circuit court concluded that Bartelt was not in custody until after he had requested an attorney, roughly ten minutes after his confession. Therefore, no *Miranda* warnings were necessary with respect to the July 16 interview, and police were free to initiate questioning on July 17 because "an assertion of *Miranda* . . . which a person makes while they are not in custody, does not prospectively prohibit law enforcement from attempting to interview an individual later." Further, with respect to the July 17 interview, the circuit court found that Bartelt was properly given his *Miranda* warning, which he voluntarily waived.

Following the denial of Bartelt's suppression motion, the circuit court ordered that the Blodgett homicide charge be separated from the charges related to M.R. After a seven-day jury trial, Bartelt was found guilty of Blodgett's murder. Consequently, he was sentenced to life imprisonment without the possibility of release to extended supervision. Shortly thereafter, the parties reached a plea agreement regarding the attempted murder, reckless endangerment, and false imprisonment charges. In exchange for Bartelt's guilty plea to first-degree reckless endangerment, the State agreed to dismiss and read-in the remaining counts, and Bartelt was sentenced to five years' imprisonment and five years' extended supervision consecutive to his life sentence.

Bartelt appealed his murder conviction on the grounds that the circuit court improperly denied his suppression motion. * * * The court of appeals rejected Bartelt's arguments and affirmed the circuit court's judgment. Bartelt sought review, which we granted. For the reasons explained below, we affirm the court of appeals.

II.   DISCUSSION

A.   Standard of Review

A determination of when custody begins presents a question of constitutional fact that we review under a two-part standard. The circuit court's findings of historical fact will be upheld unless they are clearly erroneous. Whether those findings support a determination of custody for purposes of *Miranda* is a question of law that we independently review.

B.   *Miranda* and Custody * * *

In *Miranda*, the Supreme Court defined custodial interrogation as "questioning initiated by law enforcement officers after a person has been taken into custody or otherwise deprived of his freedom of action in any significant way." The test to determine whether a person is in custody under *Miranda* is an objective test. The inquiry is "whether there is a formal arrest or restraint on freedom of movement of a degree associated with a formal arrest." Looking at the totality of the circumstances, courts will consider whether "a reasonable person would not feel free to terminate the interview and leave the scene."

We consider a variety of factors to determine whether under the totality of the circumstances a reasonable person would feel at liberty to terminate an interview and leave. Such factors include: the degree of restraint; the purpose, place, and length of the interrogation; and what has been communicated by police officers. "When considering the degree of restraint, we consider: whether the suspect is handcuffed, whether a weapon is drawn, whether a frisk is performed, the manner in which the suspect is restrained, whether the suspect is moved to another location, whether questioning took place in a police vehicle, and the number of officers involved."

If we determine that a suspect's freedom of movement is curtailed such that a reasonable person would not feel free to leave, we must then consider whether "the relevant environment presents the same inherently coercive pressures as the type of station house questioning at issue in *Miranda*." *Howes v. Fields*, 565 U.S. 499, 509 (2012). In other words, we must consider whether the specific circumstances presented a serious danger of coercion, because the "freedom-of-movement test identifies only a necessary and not a sufficient condition for *Miranda* custody." *Id.* Importantly, a noncustodial situation is not converted to one in which *Miranda* applies simply because the environment in which the questioning took place was coercive. "Any interview of one suspected of a crime by a police officer will have coercive aspects to it . . . [b]ut police officers are not required to administer *Miranda* warnings to everyone whom they question." Therefore, "*Miranda* warnings are not required 'simply because the questioning takes place in the station house, or because the questioned person is one whom the police suspect.'" And finally, "the initial determination of custody depends on the objective circumstances of the interrogation, not on the subjective views harbored by either the interrogating officers or the person being questioned."

C.   Bartelt and Custody

We now turn to whether, under the totality of the circumstances of this case, Bartelt was in custody at any time prior to Clausing taking his cell phone and telling him to remain in the interrogation room. Although the parties agree that the interview was not initially custodial, Bartelt argues that his confession to the attack on M.R. transformed his custody status into one in which a reasonable person would not have felt free to leave. As a result, all further questioning should have ceased once Bartelt invoked his right to counsel.[10] Accordingly, Bartelt alleges his constitutional rights were violated when detectives from the City of Hartford approached him

---

[10]   This argument assumes, although we do not decide, that Bartelt's request for counsel was unequivocal.

the following day about the murder of Blodgett without counsel present. Bartelt therefore argues that, under the exclusionary rule, all statements made during the July 17 interview and the evidence that was derived from those statements must be suppressed.

First, we consider the circumstances surrounding Clausing and Walsh's interrogation of Bartelt. Second, given those circumstances, we consider whether a reasonable person in Bartelt's position would have felt that he or she was at liberty to terminate the interview and leave. "Once the scene is set and the players' lines and actions are reconstructed, [we] must apply an objective test to resolve 'the ultimate inquiry': '[was] there a "formal arrest or restraint on freedom of movement" of the degree associated with a formal arrest[?]' "

As to Bartelt's custody status, the parties agree that Bartelt was not in custody at the beginning of the interview and up until the point that he confessed to attacking M.R. Bartelt came to the Slinger Police Department voluntarily. He was dropped off by two friends who waited for him in the parking lot, indicating that a reasonable person in Bartelt's position would have believed he or she would be free to leave at the end of the interview.

Once inside the building, Bartelt was taken through a secured door, locked from the outside only, to the internal portion of the police department. He was then led to an interview room that had two doors, neither of which could be locked, and one of which was left ajar during the interview itself. The detectives did not search Bartelt, and he was not restrained in any way. All of these circumstances imply he was not in custody.

At the outset of the interview, Clausing told Bartelt that he was "not in trouble" and that he was "not under arrest." Bartelt showed that he understood that when he nodded and responded, "that's good." Clausing further advised Bartelt that he could "get up and walk out of here any time [he] want[ed]." Additionally, Clausing testified that neither he nor Detective Walsh ever raised their voice or made a show of authority, such as referencing or removing their weapons.[11] When Bartelt's phone rang, he was given the opportunity to answer it. And finally, the interview lasted only thirty-five minutes. We agree that these factors support the conclusion that, prior to his confession, there was no restraint on Bartelt's freedom to the degree associated with an arrest.

Nonetheless, Bartelt argues that, as the interview progressed, he was increasingly treated as though he were the target of a serious felony investigation. At the outset of the interview, Clausing told Bartelt that he was investigating an "incident" that had occurred in Richfield Historical

---

[11] At one point, having caught Bartelt in a lie about his employment and the nature of the cut on his hand, Clausing moved his chair closer to Bartelt, from approximately four or five feet away to within two feet. The ambiance of the interview remained otherwise unchanged.

Park on the previous Friday. He did not specify the nature of the incident, nor did he accuse Bartelt of being involved. However, after Bartelt's initial denials and hesitations, the detectives began to insinuate that not only had Bartelt been at the park, but that they suspected—and indeed had evidence—that Bartelt was involved in an attack in the park. The detectives said they knew what happened and just wanted to understand why. Clausing testified that he and Walsh were attempting to minimize Bartelt's moral liability by offering justifications for his behavior. Bartelt argues that the inherently coercive nature of the interview, coupled with the fact that the detectives essentially told Bartelt they believed he was guilty, created an environment such that from the moment Bartelt confessed, no reasonable person would have felt free to leave.

The court of appeals acknowledged that the detectives "applied some psychological pressures on Bartelt to persuade him to confess . . . ." We agree that this factor tends to favor custody. However, when combined with all of the other circumstances present here, neither the use of certain interrogation techniques nor that the interview took place at a police station is enough to conclude that Bartelt could not have terminated the interview and left, even after his confession. * * *

Given the totality of the circumstances presented herein, we conclude that Bartelt was not in custody at the time of his confession.

We now turn to Bartelt's argument that from the moment of his confession no reasonable person in his position would have felt free to terminate the interview and leave. * * *

First, we note that both before and after Bartelt's confession, Clausing and Walsh spoke in a conversational tone. Although Clausing moved his chair closer to Bartelt after catching Bartelt in a series of lies, the discussion otherwise was not aggressive or confrontational. Rather, following Bartelt's admission, the detectives simply continued to ask for details about the attack, which Bartelt continued to supply.

Second, that Bartelt was arrested at the end of his interview does not necessarily mean that he was in custody at any point prior to his arrest. Stated otherwise, although Clausing and Walsh clearly suspected Bartelt and had enough evidence to arrest him when he confessed, that in itself did not restrain Bartelt's freedom of movement. * * *

We therefore conclude that although an admission of guilt to a serious crime is a factor to consider in a custody analysis, Bartelt's admission to attacking M.R. was not enough to transform his status to that of "in custody" given the totality of the circumstances. Because Bartelt was not in custody when he asked about counsel, his Fifth Amendment right to counsel did not attach. * * *

The decision of the court of appeals is affirmed.

ANN WALSH BRADLEY, J. (dissenting). "I committed a serious, violent felony." If suspects uttered these words, would law enforcement let them walk out of the station? Would a reasonable person feel free to simply get up and leave? Engaging in a work of fantasy, the majority says yes. Mired to the grips of reality, I say no.

Legal decisions regarding what the "reasonable person" would do in a given situation do not always reflect the real world. In reality, any reasonable person would not feel free to leave a police interrogation room after confessing to a serious, violent felony. Yet, the majority again finds "a perceived freedom to depart in circumstances when only the most thick-skinned of suspects would think such a choice was open to them."

To further the fantasy, the majority omits relevant facts from its analysis that would lead to the conclusion that Bartelt was in custody after confessing to the attack on M.R. As a result, it does not reach a critical issue in this case—whether the defendant clearly and unequivocally invoked his right to counsel. Unlike the majority, I would reach that issue.

I conclude that a reasonable person in Bartelt's position would not have felt free to leave the station house interrogation room, and that Bartelt clearly and unequivocally invoked his right to counsel. When considering the totality of the circumstances (namely all of the facts of record), I determine that Bartelt's Fifth Amendment rights were violated. Accordingly, I respectfully dissent.

I

The majority engages in fantasy by determining that a reasonable person would feel free to leave the police interrogation room under the circumstances presented here. Academic studies, the facts of this case, and common sense support a conclusion contrary to that of the majority.

A

A suspect is in custody for *Miranda* purposes if, under the totality of the circumstances, a reasonable person would not feel free to terminate the interview and leave the scene.

Studies demonstrate that the "free to leave" standard that courts apply does not generally reflect what reasonable people actually think and how they act when interacting with law enforcement.

Indeed, one study concluded that the average person does not feel free to leave even a simple interaction with law enforcement on a bus or sidewalk. This result held true even among people who knew they had the right to leave such an encounter.

Our jurisprudence should reflect reality. It should be based on true inclinations and thought processes rather than pushing the mythical "reasonable person" even further from the bounds of the real world. The majority in this case accomplishes the latter.

B

Although the majority correctly invokes analysis of the totality of the circumstances, it errs by ignoring relevant facts that, in the aggregate, support a determination that Bartelt was in custody immediately after confessing to the attack on M.R.

First, the majority correctly sets the scene by observing that "Bartelt chose the seat on the far side of the table, while Clausing sat at the end, and Walsh sat opposite Bartelt." The majority fails to mention, however, that in order to leave the room (unless he went under the table), Bartelt would have had to walk around either detective. Thus, from the outset of the interview, he would have had to squeeze by a detective in his path if he tried to leave the room.

Second, the majority observes that at one point during the interrogation, Detective Clausing "moved his chair closer to Bartelt, from approximately four or five feet away to within two feet." Yet, according to the majority, "[t]he ambiance of the interview remained otherwise unchanged." I disagree. Under the totality of the circumstances, cutting the distance by half and bringing the detective within arm's reach of the suspect changed the atmosphere of the room considerably.

Detective Clausing's movement in effect shrunk the size of the room and further blocked Bartelt's exit. Subsequently, in order to leave the room, Bartelt would have had not only to walk past either detective, but also if he chose to leave in Detective Clausing's direction, carefully maneuver around Detective Clausing, who now sat a mere two feet away from him.

Finally, the majority also fails to note an important shift in the tone of the conversation: Detective Clausing's language becomes coarser.[5] In fact, Detective Clausing does not utter a curse word over the course of the entire interview until after he pulls his chair closer to Bartelt. The change in language coupled with the close proximity of the detective to the suspect enhances coercive pressure. In other words, it puts more pressure on the suspect and weighs in favor of a custody determination, even if the officer's comments otherwise remain conversational.

To summarize: two detectives, one of them two feet away and now swearing at him, block Bartelt's exit path. Yet under the majority's

---

[5]   Detective Clausing lectured Bartelt:

There is [sic] two different types of people that are in your chair at this time. Okay? There is a person that says, no, f--- this. F--- you. Prove it. And, okay, we will. But there is a person, you know, I f---ed up, I made a mistake, I screwed up, but here is the reason why. Okay? Maybe I have a problem with A, maybe I have a problem with B. I was out of character. I'm making bad decisions, and I regret it, and I will do everything in my power to reverse what I did and make things right.

analysis, Bartelt should have felt free to stand up in the interrogation room, squeeze by a hovering detective, and walk out of the police station.

Add to this atmosphere the fact that the suspect confessed to a serious, violent felony—the assault of M.R. Essentially, the majority determines that a suspect in Bartelt's situation could state to the police, "I committed a serious, violent felony. I'm leaving, see you later," and then march past detectives on the way out of the interrogation room and the police station. This stretches the bounds of credulity.

Additionally, Detective Clausing testified that he subjectively believed that after Bartelt confessed, Bartelt would not have been free to leave.[7] Is Detective Clausing not a reasonable person?

I acknowledge that Detective Clausing's subjective view of when Bartelt was in custody is not dispositive. However, his view certainly provides a window into the perspective of one reasonable person with a front seat view of the situation. It further demonstrates law enforcement's expected response if Bartelt had simply walked out as the majority contends he could have done.

If even the interrogating detective testified that a suspect was not free to leave, would a reasonable suspect in such a position really think he could just get up and walk out? Only in a fantasy world would a suspect act in this manner. Common sense tells us that a real world suspect would do no such thing.

In sum, I determine that the totality of the circumstances clearly indicates that Bartelt was not free to leave. Rather, he was in custody for *Miranda* purposes immediately after confessing to the attack on M.R. * * *

Accordingly, I respectfully dissent.

I am authorized to state that JUSTICE SHIRLEY S. ABRAHAMSON joins this dissent.

---

[7] During an evidentiary hearing, Detective Clausing testified as follows:
COUNSEL FOR BARTELT: Okay. And when, from your perspective, did [Bartelt being able to walk out of the room] change during the course of this interview?
DET. CLAUSING: When he admitted to attacking [M.R.].
COUNSEL FOR BARTELT: So at that point in time, he was in trouble, he was going to be under arrest, and he probably wasn't free to get up and leave, true?
DET. CLAUSING: In my mind?
COUNSEL FOR BARTELT: Yes.
DET. CLAUSING: Yes.

B. INTERROGATION

RHODE ISLAND V. INNIS

446 U.S. 291
Supreme Court of the United States
October 30, 1979, Argued; May 12, 1980, Decided
No. 78-1076

MR. JUSTICE STEWART delivered the opinion of the Court.

In *Miranda v. Arizona*, 384 U.S. 436, 474, the Court held that, once a defendant in custody asks to speak with a lawyer, all interrogation must cease until a lawyer is present. The issue in this case is whether the respondent was "interrogated" in violation of the standards promulgated in the *Miranda* opinion.

I

On the night of January 12, 1975, John Mulvaney, a Providence, R.I., taxicab driver, disappeared after being dispatched to pick up a customer. His body was discovered four days later buried in a shallow grave in Coventry, R.I. He had died from a shotgun blast aimed at the back of his head.

On January 17, 1975, shortly after midnight, the Providence police received a telephone call from Gerald Aubin, also a taxicab driver, who reported that he had just been robbed by a man wielding a sawed-off shotgun. Aubin further reported that he had dropped off his assailant near Rhode Island College in a section of Providence known as Mount Pleasant. While at the Providence police station waiting to give a statement, Aubin noticed a picture of his assailant on a bulletin board. Aubin so informed one of the police officers present. The officer prepared a photo array, and again Aubin identified a picture of the same person. That person was the respondent. Shortly thereafter, the Providence police began a search of the Mount Pleasant area.

At approximately 4:30 a. m. on the same date, Patrolman Lovell, while cruising the streets of Mount Pleasant in a patrol car, spotted the respondent standing in the street facing him. When Patrolman Lovell stopped his car, the respondent walked towards it. Patrolman Lovell then arrested the respondent, who was unarmed, and advised him of his so-called *Miranda* rights. While the two men waited in the patrol car for other police officers to arrive, Patrolman Lovell did not converse with the respondent other than to respond to the latter's request for a cigarette.

Within minutes, Sergeant Sears arrived at the scene of the arrest, and he also gave the respondent the *Miranda* warnings. Immediately thereafter, Captain Leyden and other police officers arrived. Captain Leyden advised the respondent of his *Miranda* rights. The respondent stated that he understood those rights and wanted to speak with a lawyer. Captain Leyden then directed that the respondent be placed in a "caged wagon," a four-door police car with a wire screen mesh between the front and rear seats, and be driven to the central police station. Three officers, Patrolmen Gleckman, Williams, and McKenna, were assigned to accompany the respondent to the central station. They placed the respondent in the vehicle and shut the doors. Captain Leyden then instructed the officers not to question the respondent or intimidate or coerce him in any way. The three officers then entered the vehicle, and it departed.

While en route to the central station, Patrolman Gleckman initiated a conversation with Patrolman McKenna concerning the missing shotgun. As Patrolman Gleckman later testified:

> A.   At this point, I was talking back and forth with Patrolman McKenna stating that I frequent this area while on patrol and [that because a school for handicapped children is located nearby,] there's a lot of handicapped children running around in this area, and God forbid one of them might find a weapon with shells and they might hurt themselves.

Patrolman McKenna apparently shared his fellow officer's concern:

> A.   I more or less concurred with him [Gleckman] that it was a safety factor and that we should, you know, continue to search for the weapon and try to find it.

While Patrolman Williams said nothing, he overheard the conversation between the two officers:

> A.   He [Gleckman] said it would be too bad if the little—I believe he said a girl—would pick up the gun, maybe kill herself.

The respondent then interrupted the conversation, stating that the officers should turn the car around so he could show them where the gun was located. At this point, Patrolman McKenna radioed back to Captain Leyden that they were returning to the scene of the arrest, and that the respondent would inform them of the location of the gun. At the time the respondent indicated that the officers should turn back, they had traveled no more than a mile, a trip encompassing only a few minutes.

The police vehicle then returned to the scene of the arrest where a search for the shotgun was in progress. There, Captain Leyden again advised the respondent of his *Miranda* rights. The respondent replied that he understood those rights but that he "wanted to get the gun out of the way because of the kids in the area in the school." The respondent then led the police to a nearby field, where he pointed out the shotgun under some rocks by the side of the road.

On March 20, 1975, a grand jury returned an indictment charging the respondent with the kidnaping, robbery, and murder of John Mulvaney. Before trial, the respondent moved to suppress the shotgun and the statements he had made to the police regarding it. After an evidentiary hearing at which the respondent elected not to testify, the trial judge found that the respondent had been "repeatedly and completely advised of his *Miranda* rights." He further found that it was "entirely understandable that [the officers in the police vehicle] would voice their concern [for the safety of the handicapped children] to each other." The judge then concluded that the respondent's decision to inform the police of the location of the shotgun was "a waiver, clearly, and on the basis of the evidence that I have heard, and [sic] intelligent waiver, of his [*Miranda*] right to remain silent." Thus, without passing on whether the police officers had in fact "interrogated" the respondent, the trial court sustained the admissibility of the shotgun and testimony related to its discovery. That evidence was later introduced at the respondent's trial, and the jury returned a verdict of guilty on all counts.

On appeal, the Rhode Island Supreme Court, in a 3–2 decision, set aside the respondent's conviction. * * *

We granted certiorari to address for the first time the meaning of "interrogation" under *Miranda v. Arizona*.

II

In its *Miranda* opinion, the Court concluded that in the context of "custodial interrogation" certain procedural safeguards are necessary to protect a defendant's Fifth and Fourteenth Amendment privilege against compulsory self-incrimination. More specifically, the Court held that "the prosecution may not use statements, whether exculpatory or inculpatory, stemming from custodial interrogation of the defendant unless it demonstrates the use of procedural safeguards effective to secure the privilege against self-incrimination." Those safeguards included the now familiar *Miranda* warnings—namely, that the defendant be informed "that he has the right to remain silent, that anything he says can be used against him in a court of law, that he has the right to the presence of an attorney, and that if he cannot afford an attorney one will be appointed for him prior to any questioning if he so desires"—or their equivalent.

The Court in the *Miranda* opinion also outlined in some detail the consequences that would result if a defendant sought to invoke those procedural safeguards. With regard to the right to the presence of counsel, the Court noted:

Once warnings have been given, the subsequent procedure is clear. . . . If the individual states that he wants an attorney, the interrogation must cease until an attorney is present. At that time, the individual must have an opportunity to confer with the attorney and to have him present during any subsequent questioning. If the individual cannot obtain an attorney and he indicates that he wants one before speaking to police, they must respect his decision to remain silent.

In the present case, the parties are in agreement that the respondent was fully informed of his *Miranda* rights and that he invoked his *Miranda* right to counsel when he told Captain Leyden that he wished to consult with a lawyer. It is also uncontested that the respondent was "in custody" while being transported to the police station.

The issue, therefore, is whether the respondent was "interrogated" by the police officers in violation of the respondent's undisputed right under *Miranda* to remain silent until he had consulted with a lawyer. In resolving this issue, we first define the term "interrogation" under *Miranda* before turning to a consideration of the facts of this case.

A

The starting point for defining "interrogation" in this context is, of course, the Court's *Miranda* opinion. There the Court observed that "[by] custodial interrogation, we mean *questioning* initiated by law enforcement officers after a person has been taken into custody or otherwise deprived of his freedom of action in any significant way." (emphasis added). This passage and other references throughout the opinion to "questioning" might suggest that the *Miranda* rules were to apply only to those police interrogation practices that involve express questioning of a defendant while in custody.

We do not, however, construe the *Miranda* opinion so narrowly. The concern of the Court in *Miranda* was that the "interrogation environment" created by the interplay of interrogation and custody would "subjugate the individual to the will of his examiner" and thereby undermine the privilege against compulsory self-incrimination. The police practices that evoked this concern included several that did not involve express questioning. * * *

This is not to say, however, that all statements obtained by the police after a person has been taken into custody are to be considered the product of interrogation. * * *

It is clear therefore that the special procedural safeguards outlined in *Miranda* are required not where a suspect is simply taken into custody, but rather where a suspect in custody is subjected to interrogation. "Interrogation," as conceptualized in the *Miranda* opinion, must reflect a measure of compulsion above and beyond that inherent in custody itself.

We conclude that the *Miranda* safeguards come into play whenever a person in custody is subjected to either express questioning or its functional equivalent. That is to say, the term "interrogation" under *Miranda* refers not only to express questioning, but also to any words or actions on the part

of the police (other than those normally attendant to arrest and custody) that the police should know are reasonably likely to elicit an incriminating response from the suspect. The latter portion of this definition focuses primarily upon the perceptions of the suspect, rather than the intent of the police. This focus reflects the fact that the *Miranda* safeguards were designed to vest a suspect in custody with an added measure of protection against coercive police practices, without regard to objective proof of the underlying intent of the police. A practice that the police should know is reasonably likely to evoke an incriminating response from a suspect thus amounts to interrogation.[7] But, since the police surely cannot be held accountable for the unforeseeable results of their words or actions, the definition of interrogation can extend only to words or actions on the part of police officers that they should have known were reasonably likely to elicit an incriminating response.[8]

B

Turning to the facts of the present case, we conclude that the respondent was not "interrogated" within the meaning of *Miranda*. It is undisputed that the first prong of the definition of "interrogation" was not satisfied, for the conversation between Patrolmen Gleckman and McKenna included no express questioning of the respondent. Rather, that conversation was, at least in form, nothing more than a dialogue between the two officers to which no response from the respondent was invited.

Moreover, it cannot be fairly concluded that the respondent was subjected to the "functional equivalent" of questioning. It cannot be said, in short, that Patrolmen Gleckman and McKenna should have known that their conversation was reasonably likely to elicit an incriminating response from the respondent. There is nothing in the record to suggest that the officers were aware that the respondent was peculiarly susceptible to an appeal to his conscience concerning the safety of handicapped children. Nor is there anything in the record to suggest that the police knew that the respondent was unusually disoriented or upset at the time of his arrest.[9]

The case thus boils down to whether, in the context of a brief conversation, the officers should have known that the respondent would

---

[7] This is not to say that the intent of the police is irrelevant, for it may well have a bearing on whether the police should have known that their words or actions were reasonably likely to evoke an incriminating response. In particular, where a police practice is designed to elicit an incriminating response from the accused, it is unlikely that the practice will not also be one which the police should have known was reasonably likely to have that effect.

[8] Any knowledge the police may have had concerning the unusual susceptibility of a defendant to a particular form of persuasion might be an important factor in determining whether the police should have known that their words or actions were reasonably likely to elicit an incriminating response from the suspect.

[9] The record in no way suggests that the officers' remarks were designed to elicit a response. It is significant that the trial judge, after hearing the officers' testimony, concluded that it was "entirely understandable that [the officers] would voice their concern [for the safety of the handicapped children] to each other."

suddenly be moved to make a self-incriminating response. Given the fact that the entire conversation appears to have consisted of no more than a few offhand remarks, we cannot say that the officers should have known that it was reasonably likely that Innis would so respond. This is not a case where the police carried on a lengthy harangue in the presence of the suspect. Nor does the record support the respondent's contention that, under the circumstances, the officers' comments were particularly "evocative." It is our view, therefore, that the respondent was not subjected by the police to words or actions that the police should have known were reasonably likely to elicit an incriminating response from him.

The Rhode Island Supreme Court erred, in short, in equating "subtle compulsion" with interrogation. That the officers' comments struck a responsive chord is readily apparent. Thus, it may be said, as the Rhode Island Supreme Court did say, that the respondent was subjected to "subtle compulsion." But that is not the end of the inquiry. It must also be established that a suspect's incriminating response was the product of words or actions on the part of the police that they should have known were reasonably likely to elicit an incriminating response.[10] This was not established in the present case.

For the reasons stated, the judgment of the Supreme Court of Rhode Island is vacated, and the case is remanded to that court for further proceedings not inconsistent with this opinion.

It is so ordered.

MR. JUSTICE WHITE, concurring.

I would prefer to reverse the judgment for the reasons stated in my dissenting opinion in *Brewer v. Williams*, 430 U.S. 387 (1977); but given that judgment and the Court's opinion in *Brewer*, I join the opinion of the Court in the present case.

MR. CHIEF JUSTICE BURGER, concurring in the judgment.

[Omitted.]

MR. JUSTICE MARSHALL, with whom MR. JUSTICE BRENNAN joins, dissenting.

I am substantially in agreement with the Court's definition of "interrogation" within the meaning of *Miranda v. Arizona*, 384 U.S. 436 (1966). * * *

---

[10] By way of example, if the police had done no more than to drive past the site of the concealed weapon while taking the most direct route to the police station, and if the respondent, upon noticing for the first time the proximity of the school for handicapped children, had blurted out that he would show the officers where the gun was located, it could not seriously be argued that this "subtle compulsion" would have constituted "interrogation" within the meaning of the *Miranda* opinion.

I am utterly at a loss, however, to understand how this objective standard as applied to the facts before us can rationally lead to the conclusion that there was no interrogation. Innis was arrested at 4:30 a.m., handcuffed, searched, advised of his rights, and placed in the back seat of a patrol car. Within a short time he had been twice more advised of his rights and driven away in a four-door sedan with three police officers. Two officers sat in the front seat and one sat beside Innis in the back seat. Since the car traveled no more than a mile before Innis agreed to point out the location of the murder weapon, Officer Gleckman must have begun almost immediately to talk about the search for the shotgun.

The Court attempts to characterize Gleckman's statements as "no more than a few offhand remarks" which could not reasonably have been expected to elicit a response. If the statements had been addressed to respondent, it would be impossible to draw such a conclusion. The simple message of the "talking back and forth" between Gleckman and McKenna was that they had to find the shotgun to avert a child's death.

One can scarcely imagine a stronger appeal to the conscience of a suspect—any suspect—than the assertion that if the weapon is not found an innocent person will be hurt or killed. And not just any innocent person, but an innocent child—a little girl—a helpless, handicapped little girl on her way to school. The notion that such an appeal could not be expected to have any effect unless the suspect were known to have some special interest in handicapped children verges on the ludicrous. As a matter of fact, the appeal to a suspect to confess for the sake of others, to "display some evidence of decency and honor," is a classic interrogation technique. *See, e.g.*, F. Inbau & J. Reid, *Criminal Interrogation and Confessions* 60–62 (2d ed. 1967).

Gleckman's remarks would obviously have constituted interrogation if they had been explicitly directed to respondent, and the result should not be different because they were nominally addressed to McKenna. This is not a case where police officers speaking among themselves are accidentally overheard by a suspect. These officers were "talking back and forth" in close quarters with the handcuffed suspect, traveling past the very place where they believed the weapon was located. They knew respondent would hear and attend to their conversation, and they are chargeable with knowledge of and responsibility for the pressures to speak which they created.

I firmly believe that this case is simply and aberration, and that in future cases the Court will apply the standard adopted today in accordance with its plain meaning.

MR. JUSTICE STEVENS, dissenting.

* * * [I]n order to give full protection to a suspect's right to be free from any interrogation at all, the definition of "interrogation" must include any

police statement or conduct that has the same purpose or effect as a direct question. Statements that appear to call for a response from the suspect, as well as those that are designed to do so, should be considered interrogation. By prohibiting only those relatively few statements or actions that a police officer should know are likely to elicit an incriminating response, the Court today accords a suspect considerably less protection. Indeed, since I suppose most suspects are unlikely to incriminate themselves even when questioned directly, this new definition will almost certainly exclude every statement that is not punctuated with a question mark from the concept of "interrogation."

The difference between the approach required by a faithful adherence to *Miranda* and the stinted test applied by the Court today can be illustrated by comparing three different ways in which Officer Gleckman could have communicated his fears about the possible dangers posed by the shotgun to handicapped children. He could have:

(1)   directly asked Innis:

Will you please tell me where the shotgun is so we can protect handicapped schoolchildren from danger?

(2)   announced to the other officers in the wagon:

If the man sitting in the back seat with me should decide to tell us where the gun is, we can protect handicapped children from danger.

or (3)   stated to the other officers:

It would be too bad if a little handicapped girl would pick up the gun that this man left in the area and maybe kill herself.

In my opinion, all three of these statements should be considered interrogation because all three appear to be designed to elicit a response from anyone who in fact knew where the gun was located. Under the Court's test, on the other hand, the form of the statements would be critical. The third statement would not be interrogation because in the Court's view there was no reason for Officer Gleckman to believe that Innis was susceptible to this type of an implied appeal; therefore, the statement would not be reasonably likely to elicit an incriminating response. Assuming that this is true, then it seems to me that the first two statements, which would be just as unlikely to elicit such a response, should also not be considered interrogation. But, because the first statement is clearly an express question, it would be considered interrogation under the Court's test. The second statement, although just as clearly a deliberate appeal to Innis to reveal the location of the gun, would presumably not be interrogation because (a) it was not in form a direct question and (b) it does not fit within the "reasonably likely to elicit an incriminating response" category that applies to indirect interrogation.

As this example illustrates, the Court's test creates an incentive for police to ignore a suspect's invocation of his rights in order to make continued attempts to extract information from him. If a suspect does not appear to be susceptible to a particular type of psychological pressure, the police are apparently free to exert that pressure on him despite his request for counsel, so long as they are careful not to punctuate their statements with question marks. And if, contrary to all reasonable expectations, the suspect makes an incriminating statement, that statement can be used against him at trial. The Court thus turns *Miranda*'s unequivocal rule against any interrogation at all into a trap in which unwary suspects may be caught by police deception. * * *

Even if the Court's new definition of the term "interrogation" provided a proper standard for deciding this case, I find it remarkable that the Court should undertake the initial task of applying its new standard to the facts of the present case. * * * [G]iven the creation of a new standard of decision at this stage of the litigation, the proper procedure would be to remand to the trial court for findings on the basis of evidence directed at the new standard. * * *

QUESTIONS, COMMENTS, CONCERNS?

1. **Excluded from the definition of "interrogation."** Notice the *Innis* Court's definition of interrogation: "the term 'interrogation' under *Miranda* refers not only to express questioning, but also to any words or actions on the part of the police (other than those normally attendant to arrest and custody) that the police should know are reasonably likely to elicit an incriminating response from the suspect." That language in the parentheses— "other than those normally attendant to arrest and custody"—has become known as the "booking exception" to *Miranda*.

In *Pennsylvania v. Muniz*, 496 U.S. 582 (1990), police spotted Inocencio Muniz and a passenger parked on a highway shoulder. An officer stopped to speak with Muniz and smelled alcohol on his breath. Muniz performed poorly on a series of field sobriety tests, which Muniz explained happened because he had been drinking. The officer arrested Muniz and transported him to a central booking center. Pursuant to standard procedure, the booking process was recorded. Before Muniz received his *Miranda* warnings, officers asked him his address, height, weight, eye color, date of birth, and age. The officer then asked him, "Do you know what the date was of your sixth birthday?" Muniz offered an inaudible reply, prompting the officer to repeat, "When you turned six years old, do you remember what the date was?" Muniz replied, "No, I don't." Muniz was subsequently convicted for driving under the influence of alcohol.

On appeal, Muniz argued that his videotaped booking responses were admitted against him in violation of *Miranda*. The Supreme Court disagreed, holding that the "routine booking question" exception permitted admission of Muniz's responses against him. The Court reasoned in part that the questions were "reasonably related to the police's administrative concerns" and therefore fell outside the definition of "interrogation" for *Miranda* purposes.

2.   Holmes & the booking exception. Recall Holmes's third motion to suppress. [*See* Holmes Casefile Document 1, D-126 Motion.] It seeks to suppress statements that Holmes made during the video interrogation. *Id.* at 2–3. How does the state argue that the booking exception permits admission of at least some of Holmes's responses? [*See* Holmes Casefile Document 2, at 19–20.]

3.   Interrogation & Holmes. Holmes's third motion to suppress also seeks to suppress an incriminating question Holmes asked during the video interrogation. [Holmes Casefile Document 1, D-126 Motion, at 2–3.] During that interrogation, *before* Detective Mehl began to provide Holmes with his *Miranda* warnings, the pair had this exchange:

DETECTIVE MEHL: What I'd like to do here, uh, I'm sure you have some questions and we have some questions, ok? Before we have a chance to talk, ok, we gotta get a couple things out of the way. Then we'll have a chance to talk and I'll answer any questions you might have. Fair enough? Do you understand that?

HOLMES: Yes.

DETECTIVE MEHL: Ok. Umm . . . by the mere fact that you're here at the police department, I'm sure you've seen this on TV one-hundred times. I'm going to read this to you. If you have any questions, please, feel free to ask. Ok?

HOLMES: The sign said, uh, "victims services unit-children something". . .

DETECTIVE MEHL: Yeah, well, what about that?

HOLMES: There wasn't any children hurt, were there?

[Holmes Casefile Video, at 3:55–4:45.] At this point, Holmes is clearly in custody. Does this interaction between Detective Mehl and Holmes, however, meet the definition of "interrogation" under *Innis*? What does the state argue? [*See* Holmes Casefile Document 2, at 20.] Why does the circuit court ultimately permit admission of Holmes's question? [*See* Holmes Casefile Document 4, Order on D-126, at 26–28.]

ARIZONA V. MAURO

481 U.S. 520
Supreme Court of the United States
March 31, 1987, Argued; May 4, 1987, Decided
No. 85-2121

JUSTICE POWELL delivered the opinion of the Court. * * *

I

On November 23, 1982, the Flagstaff Police Department received a telephone call from a local K mart store. The caller stated that a man had entered the store claiming to have killed his son. When officers reached the store, respondent Mauro freely admitted that he had killed his son. He directed the officers to the child's body, and then was arrested and advised of his constitutional rights pursuant to *Miranda v. Arizona*, 384 U.S. 436 (1966). The officers then took Mauro to the police station, where he was advised of his *Miranda* rights again. At that point, Mauro told the officers that he did not wish to make any more statements without having a lawyer present. All questioning then ceased. As no secure detention area was available, Mauro was held in the office of the police captain.

At the same time, one of the officers, Detective Manson, was questioning Mauro's wife in another room. After she finished speaking with Manson, Mrs. Mauro asked if she could speak to her husband. Manson was reluctant to allow the meeting, but after Mrs. Mauro insisted, he discussed the request with his supervisor, Sergeant Allen. Allen testified that he "saw no harm in it and suggested to [Manson] that if she really sincerely wanted to talk to him to go ahead and allow it." Allen instructed Manson not to leave Mr. and Mrs. Mauro alone and suggested that Manson tape-record the conversation.

Manson then "told both Mr. and Mrs. Mauro that they could speak together only if an officer were present in the room to observe and hear what was going on." He brought Mrs. Mauro into the room and seated himself at a desk, placing a tape recorder in plain sight on the desk. He recorded their brief conversation, in which she expressed despair about their situation. During the conversation, Mauro told his wife not to answer questions until a lawyer was present.[1]

---

[1] The entire conversation proceeded as follows:

MRS. MAURO: Please—please, I don't know what to do. We should have put David [the victim] in the hospital. Please—I don't know what we're going to do. We should have went for help—we should have went for help.

[MR. MAURO]: You tried as best you could to stop it.

MRS. MAURO: I—

[MR. MAURO]: Shut up.

MRS. MAURO: —taken him to a mental hospital or something. What'll we do?

[MR. MAURO]: Shut up.

Mauro's defense at trial was that he had been insane at the time of the crime. In rebuttal, the prosecution played the tape of the meeting between Mauro and his wife, arguing that it demonstrated that Mauro was sane on the day of the murder. Mauro sought suppression of the recording on the ground that it was a product of police interrogation in violation of his *Miranda* rights. The trial court refused to suppress the recording. * * * Accordingly, the trial court admitted the evidence. Mauro was convicted of murder and child abuse, and sentenced to death.

The Arizona Supreme Court reversed. It found that by allowing Mauro to speak with his wife in the presence of a police officer, the detectives interrogated Mauro within the meaning of *Miranda*. * * * Therefore, it held that the tape recording was not properly admitted at Mauro's trial.

* * * Because the decision below appeared to misconstrue our decision in *Rhode Island v. Innis*, *supra*, we granted the petition. We now reverse. * * *

III

* * * The officers gave Mauro the warnings required by *Miranda*. Mauro indicated that he did not wish to be questioned further without a lawyer present. Mauro never waived his right to have a lawyer present. The sole issue, then, is whether the officers' subsequent actions rose to the level of interrogation—that is, in the language of *Innis*, whether they were the "functional equivalent" of police interrogation. We think it is clear under both *Miranda* and *Innis* that Mauro was not interrogated. The tape recording of the conversation between Mauro and his wife shows that Detective Manson asked Mauro no questions about the crime or his conduct.[4] Nor is it suggested—or supported by any evidence—that Sergeant Allen's decision to allow Mauro's wife to see him was the kind of

---

DET. MANSON: Do you know a reverend or a priest or someone you can talk to—take care of David?

MRS. MAURO: No.

[MR. MAURO]: Don't answer questions until you get rights of attorney before you find out whats [sic] going on. You tried to stop me as best you can. What are you going to do, kill me? You tried the best you can to stop me.

MRS. MAURO: I don't—we don't—I don't have money.

[MR. MAURO]: There's a public attorney.

MRS. MAURO: I don't know.

[MR. MAURO]: There's a public attorney. Why don't you just be quiet.

MRS. MAURO: I don't have any money to bury him. I don't have any money. All I got is enough money for the rent for the children and that's it.

DET. MANSON: Did you want to talk to your husband any more?

MRS. MAURO: No, I can't talk to him.

[MR. MAURO]: Then don't talk to me—get out.

MRS. MAURO: I don't know what to do. O.K.

[4] In the course of the conversation, that apparently lasted only a few minutes, Manson made two statements, both apparently directed at Mauro's wife.

psychological ploy that properly could be treated as the functional equivalent of interrogation.

There is no evidence that the officers sent Mrs. Mauro in to see her husband for the purpose of eliciting incriminating statements. As the trial court found, the officers tried to discourage her from talking to her husband, but finally "yielded to her insistent demands." Nor was Detective Manson's presence improper. His testimony, that the trial court found credible, indicated a number of legitimate reasons—not related to securing incriminating statements—for having a police officer present. Finally, the weakness of Mauro's claim that he was interrogated is underscored by examining the situation from his perspective. *Cf. Rhode Island v. Innis*, 446 U.S., at 301 (suggesting that the suspect's perspective may be relevant in some cases in determining whether police actions constitute interrogation). We doubt that a suspect, told by officers that his wife will be allowed to speak to him, would feel that he was being coerced to incriminate himself in any way.

The Arizona Supreme Court was correct to note that there was a "possibility" that Mauro would incriminate himself while talking to his wife. It also emphasized that the officers were aware of that possibility when they agreed to allow the Mauros to talk to each other. But the actions in this case were far less questionable than the "subtle compulsion" that we held not to be interrogation in *Innis*. Officers do not interrogate a suspect simply by hoping that he will incriminate himself. * * *

Mauro was not subjected to compelling influences, psychological ploys, or direct questioning. Thus, his volunteered statements cannot properly be considered the result of police interrogation.

In deciding whether particular police conduct is interrogation, we must remember the purpose behind * * * *Miranda* * * *: preventing government officials from using the coercive nature of confinement to extract confessions that would not be given in an unrestrained environment. The government actions in this case do not implicate this purpose in any way. Police departments need not adopt inflexible rules barring suspects from speaking with their spouses, nor must they ignore legitimate security concerns by allowing spouses to meet in private. In short, the officers in this case acted reasonably and lawfully by allowing Mrs. Mauro to speak with her husband. In this situation, the Federal Constitution does not forbid use of Mauro's subsequent statements at his criminal trial.

IV

The judgment of the Arizona Supreme Court is reversed. The case is remanded for further proceedings not inconsistent with this opinion.

It is so ordered.

JUSTICE STEVENS, with whom JUSTICE BRENNAN, JUSTICE MARSHALL, and JUSTICE BLACKMUN join, dissenting.

The Supreme Court of Arizona unanimously and unequivocally concluded that the police intended to interrogate respondent.[1] This Court reverses, finding that no interrogation occurred because Mauro "was not subjected to compelling influences, psychological ploys, or direct questioning." The record indicates, however, that the police employed a powerful psychological ploy; they failed to give respondent any advance warning that Mrs. Mauro was coming to talk to him, that a police officer would accompany her, or that their conversation would be recorded. As the transcript of the conversation reveals, respondent would not have freely chosen to speak with her. These facts compel the conclusion that the police took advantage of Mrs. Mauro's request to visit her husband, setting up a confrontation between them at a time when he manifestly desired to remain silent. Because they allowed respondent's conversation with his wife to commence at a time when they knew it was reasonably likely to produce an incriminating statement, the police interrogated him. The Court's opposite conclusion removes an important brick from the wall of protection against police overreaching that surrounds the Fifth Amendment rights of suspects in custody. * * *

. . . .

It is undisputed that a police decision to place two suspects in the same room and then to listen to or record their conversation may constitute a form of interrogation even if no questions are asked by any police officers. That is exactly what happened here.[5] The police placed respondent and his wife, who was also in police custody, in the same small area. Mr. and Mrs. Mauro were both suspects in the murder of their son. Each of them had been interrogated separately before the officers decided to allow them to

---

[1] Thus, the Arizona Supreme Court credited part, but not all, of the following testimony by Detective Manson:

Q. I'd like to ask you some questions concerning police interrogation techniques, if I might.

Do you have any experience in police interrogation techniques?

A. Yes, sir.

Q. Another technique, Byron, would be to, for example, if you are investigating a juvenile matter, to have the parents come down and speak to the juvenile in your presence?

A. That's correct.

Q. Along those same lines, it's not uncommon to ask a family member to come in and speak to someone in your presence?

A. That's correct.

Q. And, in fact, that technique was utilized in this case, isn't it true?

A. I don't believe so, no, sir. That was not our purpose. That was not an interrogation method.

[5] The regrettable irony in this case is that respondent endured the functional equivalent of interrogation while in the very process of advising his wife to exercise her own Fifth Amendment right to remain silent.

converse, an act that surely did not require a tape recorder or the presence of a police officer within hearing range. Under the circumstances, the police knew or should have known that Mrs. Mauro's encounter with respondent was reasonably likely to produce an incriminating response. Indeed, Officer Allen's supervisor testified that the police had a reasonable expectation that the spousal conversation would provide information on the murder investigation. When asked, "what was the purpose in having Detective Manson present during any interview or confrontation. . . between the defendant, Mr. Mauro, and his wife. . .?" Captain Latham replied:

> Well, one of the reasons would be to, for her protection, in case he attacked her or there was any violence that occurred. . . The other reason would be to see what the conversation was about. *She and he both were under investigation at that time, and any statements that she made or he made could shed light on our case.* (emphasis added).

In my opinion, it was not only likely, but highly probable, that one of the suspects would make a statement that the prosecutor might seek to introduce at trial. It follows that the police conduct in this case was the "functional equivalent" of deliberate, direct interrogation.

The State should not be permitted to set aside this conclusion with testimony that merely indicates that the evidence-gathering purpose of the police was mixed with other motives. For example, it is irrelevant to the inquiry whether the police had legitimate security reasons for having an officer present that were "not related to securing incriminating statements." Nor does it matter that the officers lacked a precise expectation of how the statements Mauro would make might be incriminating; much interrogation is exploratory rather than directed at the admission of a fact whose incriminatory import is already known to the officers.

The Court's final proffered reason for disregarding the findings of the Supreme Court of Arizona is that the suspect may not have felt coerced to incriminate himself. The police did not compel or even encourage Mauro to speak with his wife. When they brought her into the room without warning Mauro in advance, however, they expected that the resulting conversation "could shed light on our case." Under the circumstances, the mere fact that respondent's wife made the initial request leading to the conversation does not alter the correctness of the Supreme Court of Arizona's analysis. The officers exercised exclusive control over whether and when the suspects spoke with each other; the police knew that whatever Mauro might wish to convey to his wife at that moment, he would have to say under the conditions unilaterally imposed by the officers. In brief, the police exploited the custodial situation and the understandable desire of Mrs. Mauro to speak with respondent to conduct an interrogation.

I respectfully dissent.

ILLINOIS V. PERKINS

496 U.S. 292
Supreme Court of the United States
February 20, 1990, Argued; June 4, 1990, Decided
No. 88-1972

MR. JUSTICE KENNEDY delivered the opinion of the Court.

An undercover government agent was placed in the cell of respondent Perkins, who was incarcerated on charges unrelated to the subject of the agent's investigation. Respondent made statements that implicated him in the crime that the agent sought to solve. Respondent claims that the statements should be inadmissible because he had not been given *Miranda* warnings by the agent. We hold that the statements are admissible. *Miranda* warnings are not required when the suspect is unaware that he is speaking to a law enforcement officer and gives a voluntary statement.

I

In November 1984, Richard Stephenson was murdered in a suburb of East St. Louis, Illinois. The murder remained unsolved until March 1986, when one Donald Charlton told police that he had learned about a homicide from a fellow inmate at the Graham Correctional Facility, where Charlton had been serving a sentence for burglary. The fellow inmate was Lloyd Perkins, who is the respondent here. Charlton told police that, while at Graham, he had befriended respondent, who told him in detail about a murder that respondent had committed in East St. Louis. On hearing Charlton's account, the police recognized details of the Stephenson murder that were not well known, and so they treated Charlton's story as a credible one.

By the time the police heard Charlton's account, respondent had been released from Graham, but police traced him to a jail in Montgomery County, Illinois, where he was being held pending trial on a charge of aggravated battery, unrelated to the Stephenson murder. The police wanted to investigate further respondent's connection to the Stephenson murder, but feared that the use of an eavesdropping device would prove impracticable and unsafe. They decided instead to place an undercover agent in the cellblock with respondent and Charlton. The plan was for Charlton and undercover agent John Parisi to pose as escapees from a work release program who had been arrested in the course of a burglary. Parisi and Charlton were instructed to engage respondent in casual conversation and report anything he said about the Stephenson murder.

Parisi, using the alias "Vito Bianco," and Charlton, both clothed in jail garb, were placed in the cellblock with respondent at the Montgomery County jail. The cellblock consisted of 12 separate cells that opened onto a common room. Respondent greeted Charlton who, after a brief conversation with respondent, introduced Parisi by his alias. Parisi told respondent that he "wasn't going to do any more time," and suggested that the three of them escape. Respondent replied that the Montgomery County jail was "rinky-dink" and that they could "break out." The trio met in respondent's cell later that evening, after the other inmates were asleep, to refine their plan. Respondent said that his girlfriend could smuggle in a pistol. Charlton said "Hey, I'm not a murderer, I'm a burglar. That's your guys' profession." After telling Charlton that he would be responsible for any murder that occurred, Parisi asked respondent if he had ever "done" anybody. Respondent said that he had, and proceeded to describe at length the events of the Stephenson murder. Parisi and respondent then engaged in some casual conversation before respondent went to sleep. Parisi did not give respondent *Miranda* warnings before the conversations.

Respondent was charged with the Stephenson murder. Before trial, he moved to suppress the statements made to Parisi in the jail. The trial court granted the motion to suppress, and the State appealed. The Appellate Court of Illinois affirmed, holding that *Miranda v. Arizona*, 384 U.S. 436 (1966), prohibits all undercover contacts with incarcerated suspects which are reasonably likely to elicit an incriminating response.

We granted certiorari. * * *

II

In *Miranda v. Arizona, supra,* the Court held that the Fifth Amendment privilege against self-incrimination prohibits admitting statements given by a suspect during "custodial interrogation" without a prior warning. Custodial interrogation means "questioning initiated by law enforcement officers after a person was been taken into custody. . . . The warning mandated by *Miranda* was meant to preserve the privilege during "incommunicado interrogation of individuals in a police-dominated atmosphere." That atmosphere is said to generate "inherently compelling pressures which work to undermine the individual's will to resist and to compel him to speak where he would not otherwise do so freely." * * *

Conversations between suspects and undercover agents do not implicate the concerns underlying *Miranda*. The essential ingredients of a "police-dominated atmosphere" and compulsion are not present when an incarcerated person speaks freely to someone that he believes to be a fellow inmate. Coercion is determined from the perspective of the suspect. *Rhode Island v. Innis*, 446 U.S. 291, 301 (1980); *Berkemer v. McCarty*, 468 U.S. 420, 442 (1984). When a suspect considers himself in the company of cellmates and not officers, the coercive atmosphere is lacking. There is no empirical basis for the assumption that a suspect speaking to those whom he assumes are not officers will feel compelled to speak by the fear of reprisal for remaining silent or in the hope of more lenient treatment should be confess.

It is the premise of *Miranda* that the danger of coercion results from the interaction of custody and official interrogation. We reject the argument that *Miranda* warnings are required whenever a suspect is in custody in a technical sense and converses with someone who happens to be a government agent. Questioning by captors, who appear to control the suspect's fate, may create mutually reinforcing pressures that the Court has assumed will weaken the suspect's will, but where a suspect does not know that he is conversing with a government agent, these pressures do not exist. The State Court here mistakenly assumed that because the suspect was in custody, no undercover questioning could take place. When the suspect has no reason to think that the listeners have official power over him, it should not be assumed that his words are motivated by the reaction he expects from his listeners. * * *

Miranda forbids coercion, not mere strategic deception by taking advantage of a suspect's misplaced trust in one he supposes to be a fellow prisoner. As we recognized in *Miranda*, "confessions remain a proper element in law enforcement. Any statement given freely and voluntarily without any compelling influences is, of course, admissible in evidence." Ploys to mislead a suspect or lull him into a false sense of security that do not rise to the level of compulsion or coercion to speak are not within *Miranda*'s concerns.

Miranda was not meant to protect suspects from boasting about their criminal activities in front of persons whom they believe to be their cellmates. This case is illustrative. Respondent had no reason to feel that undercover agent Parisi had any legal authority to force him to answer questions or that Parisi could affect respondent's future treatment. Respondent viewed the cellmate-agent as an equal and showed no hint of being intimidated by the atmosphere of the jail. In recounting the details of the Stephenson murder, respondent was motivated solely by the desire to impress his fellow inmates. He spoke at his own peril.

The tactic employed here to elicit a voluntary confession from a suspect does not violate the Self-Incrimination Clause. * * *

Respondent can seek no help from his argument that a bright-line rule for the application of *Miranda* is desirable. Law enforcement officers will have little difficulty putting into practice our holding that undercover agents need not give *Miranda* warnings to incarcerated suspects. The use of undercover agents is a recognized law enforcement technique, often employed in the prison context to detect violence against correctional officials or inmates, as well as for the purposes served here. The interests protected by *Miranda* are not implicated in these cases, and the warnings are not required to safeguard the constitutional rights of inmates who make voluntary statements to undercover agents.

We hold that an undercover law enforcement officer posing as a fellow inmate need not give *Miranda* warnings to an incarcerated suspect before asking questions that may elicit an incriminating response. The statements at issue in this case were voluntary, and there is no federal obstacle to their admissibility at trial. We now reverse and remand for proceedings not inconsistent with our opinion.

It is so ordered.

JUSTICE BRENNAN, concurring in the judgment.

[Omitted.]

JUSTICE MARSHALL, dissenting.

* * * The Court does not dispute that the police officer here conducted a custodial interrogation of a criminal suspect. Perkins was incarcerated in county jail during the questioning at issue here; under these circumstances, he was in custody as that term is defined in *Miranda.* * * *

While Perkins was confined, an undercover police officer, with the help of a police informant, questioned him about a serious crime. Although the Court does not dispute that Perkins was interrogated, it downplays the nature of the 35-minute questioning by disingenuously referring to it as a "conversation." The officer's narration of the "conversation" at Perkins' trial, however, reveals that it clearly was an interrogation.

[Agent:] You ever do anyone?

[Perkins:] Yeah, once in East St. Louis, in a rich white neighborhood.

Informant: I didn't know they had any rich white neighborhoods in East St. Louis.

Perkins: It wasn't in East St. Louis, it was by a race track in Fairview Heights. . . .

[Agent]: You did a guy in Fairview Heights?

Perkins: Yeah in a rich white section where most of the houses look the same.

[Informant]: If all the houses look the same, how did you know you had the right house?

Perkins: Me and two guys cased the house for about a week. I knew exactly which house, the second house on the left from the corner.

[Agent]: How long ago did this happen?

Perkins: Approximately about two years ago. I got paid $5,000 for that job.

[Agent]: How did it go down?

Perkins: I walked up to . . . this guy['s] house with a sawed-off under my trench coat.

[Agent]: What type gun[?]

Perkins: A .12 gauge Remmington [sic] Automatic Model 1100 sawed-off.

The police officer continued the inquiry, asking a series of questions designed to elicit specific information about the victim, the crime scene, the weapon, Perkins' motive, and his actions during and after the shooting. This interaction was not a "conversation"; Perkins, the officer, and the informant were not equal participants in a free-ranging discussion, with each man offering his views on different topics. Rather, it was an interrogation: Perkins was subjected to express questioning likely to evoke an incriminating response. *Rhode Island v. Innis*, 446 U.S. 291, 300–301 (1980).

Because Perkins was interrogated by police while he was in custody, *Miranda* required that the officer inform him of his rights. In rejecting that conclusion, the Court finds that "conversations" between undercover agents and suspects are devoid of the coercion inherent in stationhouse interrogations conducted by law enforcement officials who openly represent the State. *Miranda* was not, however, concerned solely with police coercion. It dealt with any police tactics that may operate to compel a suspect in custody to make incriminating statements without full awareness of his constitutional rights. Thus, when a law enforcement agent structures a custodial interrogation so that a suspect feels compelled to reveal incriminating information, he must inform the suspect of his constitutional rights and give him an opportunity to decide whether or not to talk. * * *

The Court's holding today complicates a previously clear and straightforward doctrine. The Court opines that "law enforcement officers will have little difficulty putting into practice our holding that undercover agents need not give *Miranda* warnings to incarcerated suspects." Perhaps this prediction is true with respect to fact patterns virtually identical to the one before the Court today. But the outer boundaries of the exception created by the Court are by no means clear. Would *Miranda* be violated, for instance, if an undercover police officer beat a confession out of a suspect, but the suspect thought the officer was another prisoner who wanted the information for his own purposes?

Even if *Miranda*, as interpreted by the Court, would not permit such obviously compelled confessions, the ramifications of today's opinion are still disturbing. The exception carved out of the *Miranda* doctrine today may well result in a proliferation of departmental policies to encourage police officers to conduct interrogations of confined suspects through undercover agents, thereby circumventing the need to administer *Miranda* warnings. Indeed, if *Miranda* now requires a police officer to issue warnings only in those situations in which the suspect might feel compelled "to speak by the fear of reprisal for remaining silent or in the hope of more lenient treatment should he confess," presumably it allows custodial interrogation by an undercover officer posing as a member of the clergy or a suspect's defense attorney. Although such abhorrent tricks would play on a suspect's need to confide in a trusted adviser, neither would cause the suspect to "think that the listeners have official power over him." The Court's adoption of the "undercover agent" exception to the *Miranda* rule thus is necessarily also the adoption of a substantial loophole in our jurisprudence protecting suspects' Fifth Amendment rights.

I dissent.

C. EXCEPTIONS TO *MIRANDA*

NEW YORK V. QUARLES

467 U.S. 649
Supreme Court of the United States
January 18, 1984, Argued; June 12, 1984, Decided
No. 82-1213

JUSTICE REHNQUIST delivered the opinion of the Court.

Respondent Benjamin Quarles was charged in the New York trial court with criminal possession of a weapon. * * *

On September 11, 1980, at approximately 12:30 a. m., Officer Frank Kraft and Officer Sal Scarring were on road patrol in Queens, N.Y., when a young woman approached their car. She told them that she had just been raped by a black male, approximately six feet tall, who was wearing a black jacket with the name "Big Ben" printed in yellow letters on the back. She told the officers that the man had just entered an A & P supermarket located nearby and that the man was carrying a gun.

The officers drove the woman to the supermarket, and Officer Kraft entered the store while Officer Scarring radioed for assistance. Officer Kraft quickly spotted respondent, who matched the description given by the woman, approaching a checkout counter. Apparently upon seeing the officer, respondent turned and ran toward the rear of the store, and Officer Kraft pursued him with a drawn gun. When respondent turned the corner at the end of an aisle, Officer Kraft lost sight of him for several seconds, and upon regaining sight of respondent, ordered him to stop and put his hands over his head.

Although more than three other officers had arrived on the scene by that time, Officer Kraft was the first to reach respondent. He frisked him and discovered that he was wearing a shoulder holster which was then empty. After handcuffing him, Officer Kraft asked him where the gun was. Respondent nodded in the direction of some empty cartons and responded, "the gun is over there." Officer Kraft thereafter retrieved a loaded .38-caliber revolver from one of the cartons, formally placed respondent under arrest, and read him his *Miranda* rights from a printed card. Respondent indicated that he would be willing to answer questions without an attorney present. Officer Kraft then asked respondent if he owned the gun and where he had purchased it. Respondent answered that he did own it and that he had purchased it in Miami, Fla.

In the subsequent prosecution of respondent for criminal possession of a weapon, the judge excluded the statement, "the gun is over there," and the gun because the officer had not given respondent the warnings required by our decision in *Miranda v. Arizona*, 384 U.S. 436 (1966), before asking him where the gun was located. The judge excluded the other statements about respondent's ownership of the gun and the place of purchase, as evidence tainted by the prior *Miranda* violation. The Appellate Division of the Supreme Court of New York affirmed without opinion.

The Court of Appeals granted leave to appeal and affirmed by a 4–3 vote. * * * For the reasons which follow, we believe that this case presents a situation where concern for public safety must be paramount to adherence to the literal language of the prophylactic rules enunciated in *Miranda*.

* * * In *Miranda* this Court for the first time extended the Fifth Amendment privilege against compulsory self-incrimination to individuals subjected to custodial interrogation by the police. * * * The *Miranda* Court * * * presumed that interrogation in certain custodial circumstances is inherently coercive and held that statements made under those circumstances are inadmissible unless the suspect is specifically informed of his *Miranda* rights and freely decides to forgo those rights. The prophylactic *Miranda* warnings therefore are "not themselves rights protected by the Constitution but [are] instead measures to insure that the right against compulsory self-incrimination [is] protected." *Michigan v. Tucker*, 417 U.S. 433, 444 (1974). * * *

In this case * * * the only issue before us is whether Officer Kraft was justified in failing to make available to respondent the procedural safeguards associated with the privilege against compulsory self-incrimination since *Miranda*. * * *

We hold that on these facts there is a "public safety" exception to the requirement that *Miranda* warnings be given before a suspect's answers may be admitted into evidence, and that the availability of that exception does not depend upon the motivation of the individual officers involved. In a kaleidoscopic situation such as the one confronting these officers, where spontaneity rather than adherence to a police manual is necessarily the order of the day, the application of the exception which we recognize today should not be made to depend on post hoc findings at a suppression hearing concerning the subjective motivation of the arresting officer. Undoubtedly most police officers, if placed in Officer Kraft's position, would act out of a host of different, instinctive, and largely unverifiable motives—their own safety, the safety of others, and perhaps as well the desire to obtain incriminating evidence from the suspect.

Whatever the motivation of individual officers in such a situation, we do not believe that the doctrinal underpinnings of *Miranda* require that it be applied in all its rigor to a situation in which police officers ask questions reasonably prompted by a concern for the public safety. The *Miranda* decision was based in large part on this Court's view that the warnings which it required police to give to suspects in custody would reduce the likelihood that the suspects would fall victim to constitutionally impermissible practices of police interrogation in the presumptively coercive environment of the station house. The dissenters warned that the requirement of *Miranda* warnings would have the effect of decreasing the number of suspects who respond to police questioning. The *Miranda* majority, however, apparently felt that whatever the cost to society in terms of fewer convictions of guilty suspects, that cost would simply have to be borne in the interest of enlarged protection for the Fifth Amendment privilege.

The police in this case, in the very act of apprehending a suspect, were confronted with the immediate necessity of ascertaining the whereabouts of a gun which they had every reason to believe the suspect had just removed from his empty holster and discarded in the supermarket. So long as the gun was concealed somewhere in the supermarket, with its actual whereabouts unknown, it obviously posed more than one danger to the public safety: an accomplice might make use of it, a customer or employee might later come upon it.

In such a situation, if the police are required to recite the familiar *Miranda* warnings before asking the whereabouts of the gun, suspects in Quarles' position might well be deterred from responding. Procedural safeguards which deter a suspect from responding were deemed acceptable in *Miranda* in order to protect the Fifth Amendment privilege; when the primary social cost of those added protections is the possibility of fewer convictions, the *Miranda* majority was willing to bear that cost. Here, had *Miranda* warnings deterred Quarles from responding to Officer Kraft's question about the whereabouts of the gun, the cost would have been something more than merely the failure to obtain evidence useful in convicting Quarles. Officer Kraft needed an answer to his question not simply to make his case against Quarles but to insure that further danger to the public did not result from the concealment of the gun in a public area.

We conclude that the need for answers to questions in a situation posing a threat to the public safety outweighs the need for the prophylactic rule protecting the Fifth Amendment's privilege against self-incrimination. We decline to place officers such as Officer Kraft in the untenable position of having to consider, often in a matter of seconds, whether it best serves society for them to ask the necessary questions without the *Miranda* warnings and render whatever probative evidence they uncover inadmissible, or for them to give the warnings in order to preserve the admissibility of evidence they might uncover but possibly damage or destroy their ability to obtain that evidence and neutralize the volatile situation confronting them.[7]

In recognizing a narrow exception to the *Miranda* rule in this case, we acknowledge that to some degree we lessen the desirable clarity of that rule. At least in part in order to preserve its clarity, we have over the years refused to sanction attempts to expand our *Miranda* holding. As we have in other contexts, we recognize here the importance of a workable rule "to guide police officers, who have only limited time and expertise to reflect on and balance the social and individual interests involved in the specific circumstances they confront." But as we have pointed out, we believe that the exception which we recognize today lessens the necessity of that on-the-scene balancing process. The exception will not be difficult for police officers to apply because in each case it will be circumscribed by the exigency which justifies it. We think police officers can and will distinguish almost instinctively between questions necessary to secure their own safety or the safety of the public and questions designed solely to elicit testimonial evidence from a suspect.

The facts of this case clearly demonstrate that distinction and an officer's ability to recognize it. Officer Kraft asked only the question necessary to locate the missing gun before advising respondent of his rights. It was only after securing the loaded revolver and giving the warnings that he continued with investigatory questions about the ownership and place of purchase of the gun. The exception which we recognize today, far from complicating the thought processes and the on-the-scene judgments of police officers, will simply free them to follow their

---

[7]   The dissent argues that a public safety exception to *Miranda* is unnecessary because in every case an officer can simply ask the necessary questions to protect himself or the public, and then the prosecution can decline to introduce any incriminating responses at a subsequent trial. But absent actual coercion by the officer, there is no constitutional imperative requiring the exclusion of the evidence that results from police inquiry of this kind; and we do not believe that the doctrinal underpinnings of *Miranda* require us to exclude the evidence, thus penalizing officers for asking the very questions which are the most crucial to their efforts to protect themselves and the public.

legitimate instincts when confronting situations presenting a danger to the public safety.

We hold that the Court of Appeals in this case erred in excluding the statement, "the gun is over there," and the gun because of the officer's failure to read respondent his *Miranda* rights before attempting to locate the weapon. Accordingly we hold that it also erred in excluding the subsequent statements as illegal fruits of a *Miranda* violation. We therefore reverse and remand for further proceedings not inconsistent with this opinion.

It is so ordered.

JUSTICE O'CONNOR, concurring in the judgment in part and dissenting in part.

In *Miranda v. Arizona*, 384 U.S. 436 (1966), the Court held unconstitutional, because inherently compelled, the admission of statements derived from in-custody questioning not preceded by an explanation of the privilege against self-incrimination and the consequences of forgoing it. Today, the Court concludes that overriding considerations of public safety justify the admission of evidence—oral statements and a gun—secured without the benefit of such warnings. In so holding, the Court acknowledges that it is departing from prior precedent, and that it is "[lessening] the desirable clarity of [the *Miranda*] rule." Were the Court writing from a clean slate, I could agree with its holding. But *Miranda* is now the law and, in my view, the Court has not provided sufficient justification for departing from it or for blurring its now clear strictures. Accordingly, I would require suppression of the initial statement taken from respondent in this case. On the other hand, nothing in *Miranda* or the privilege itself requires exclusion of nontestimonial evidence derived from informal custodial interrogation, and I therefore agree with the Court that admission of the gun in evidence is proper.[1] * * *

The court below assumed, without discussion, that the privilege against self-incrimination required that the gun derived from respondent's statement also be suppressed, whether or not the State could independently link it to him. That conclusion was, in my view, incorrect. * * *

* * * What makes the question of [the gun's] admissibility difficult is the fact that, in asking respondent to produce the gun, the police also "compelled" him, in the *Miranda* sense, to create an incriminating testimonial response. In other words, the case is problematic because police compelled respondent not only to provide the gun but also to admit that he knew where it was and that it was his.

---

[1]   As to the statements elicited after the *Miranda* warnings were administered, admission should turn solely on whether the answers received were voluntary. * * *

It is settled that *Miranda* did not itself determine whether physical evidence obtained in this manner would be admissible. * * *

The harm caused by failure to administer *Miranda* warnings relates only to admission of testimonial self-incriminations, and the suppression of such incriminations should by itself produce the optimal enforcement of the *Miranda* rule. * * *

* * * I would * * * adhere to our precedents requiring that statements elicited in the absence of *Miranda* warnings be suppressed. But because nontestimonial evidence such as the gun should not be suppressed, I join in that part of the Court's judgment that reverses and remands for further proceedings with the gun admissible as evidence against the accused.

JUSTICE MARSHALL, with whom JUSTICE BRENNAN and JUSTICE STEVENS join, dissenting.

The police in this case arrested a man suspected of possessing a firearm in violation of New York law. Once the suspect was in custody and found to be unarmed, the arresting officer initiated an interrogation. Without being advised of his right not to respond, the suspect incriminated himself by locating the gun. The majority concludes that the State may rely on this incriminating statement to convict the suspect of possessing a weapon. I disagree. The arresting officers had no legitimate reason to interrogate the suspect without advising him of his rights to remain silent and to obtain assistance of counsel. By finding on these facts justification for unconsented interrogation, the majority abandons the clear guidelines enunciated in *Miranda v. Arizona*, 384 U.S. 436 (1966), and condemns the American judiciary to a new era of post hoc inquiry into the propriety of custodial interrogations. More significantly and in direct conflict with this Court's longstanding interpretation of the Fifth Amendment, the majority has endorsed the introduction of coerced self-incriminating statements in criminal prosecutions. * * *

The irony of the majority's decision is that the public's safety can be perfectly well protected without abridging the Fifth Amendment. If a bomb is about to explode or the public is otherwise imminently imperiled, the police are free to interrogate suspects without advising them of their constitutional rights. Such unconsented questioning may take place not only when police officers act on instinct but also when higher faculties lead them to believe that advising a suspect of his constitutional rights might decrease the likelihood that the suspect would reveal life-saving information. If trickery is necessary to protect the public, then the police may trick a suspect into confessing. While the Fourteenth Amendment sets limits on such behavior, nothing in the Fifth Amendment or our decision in *Miranda v. Arizona* proscribes this sort of emergency questioning. All the Fifth Amendment forbids is the introduction of coerced statements at trial.

To a limited degree, the majority is correct that there is a cost associated with the Fifth Amendment's ban on introducing coerced self-incriminating statements at trial. Without a "public-safety" exception, there would be occasions when a defendant incriminated himself by revealing a threat to the public, and the State was unable to prosecute because the defendant retracted his statement after consulting with counsel and the police cannot find independent proof of guilt. Such occasions would not, however, be common. The prosecution does not always lose the use of incriminating information revealed in these situations. After consulting with counsel, a suspect may well volunteer to repeat his statement in hopes of gaining a favorable plea bargain or more lenient sentence. The majority thus overstates its case when it suggests that a police officer must necessarily choose between public safety and admissibility.[9]

But however frequently or infrequently such cases arise, their regularity is irrelevant. The Fifth Amendment prohibits compelled self-incrimination.[10] As the Court has explained on numerous occasions, this prohibition is the mainstay of our adversarial system of criminal justice. Not only does it protect us against the inherent unreliability of compelled testimony, but it also ensures that criminal investigations will be conducted with integrity and that the judiciary will avoid the taint of official lawlessness. The policies underlying the Fifth Amendment's privilege against self-incrimination are not diminished simply because testimony is compelled to protect the public's safety. The majority should not be permitted to elude the Amendment's absolute prohibition simply by calculating special costs that arise when the public's safety is at issue. Indeed, were constitutional adjudication always conducted in such an ad hoc manner, the Bill of Rights would be a most unreliable protector of individual liberties. * * *

Having determined that the Fifth Amendment renders inadmissible Quarles' response to Officer Kraft's questioning, I have no doubt that our precedents require that the gun discovered as a direct result of Quarles' statement must be presumed inadmissible as well. The gun was the direct product of a coercive custodial interrogation. In *Silverthorne Lumber Co. v. United States*, 251 U.S. 385 (1920), and *Wong Sun v. United States*, 371

---

[9]   I also seriously question how often a statement linking a suspect to the threat to the public ends up being the crucial and otherwise unprovable element of a criminal prosecution. The facts of the current case illustrate this point. The police arrested respondent Quarles not because he was suspected of carrying a gun, but because he was alleged to have committed rape. Had the State elected to prosecute on the rape count alone, respondent's incriminating statement about the gun would have had no role in the prosecution. Only because the State dropped the rape count and chose to proceed to trial solely on the criminal-possession charge did respondent's answer to Officer Kraft's question become critical.

[10]   In this sense, the Fifth Amendment differs fundamentally from the Fourth Amendment, which only prohibits unreasonable searches and seizures. Accordingly, the various exceptions to the Fourth Amendment permitting warrantless searches under various circumstances should have no analogy in the Fifth Amendment context. * * *

U.S. 471 (1963), this Court held that the Government may not introduce incriminating evidence derived from an illegally obtained source. This Court recently explained the extent of the *Wong Sun* rule:

> Although Silverthorne and Wong Sun involved violations of the Fourth Amendment, the 'fruit of the poisonous tree' doctrine has not been limited to cases in which there has been a Fourth Amendment violation. The Court has applied the doctrine where the violations were of the Sixth Amendment as well as of the Fifth Amendment. *Nix v. Williams*

When they ruled on the issue, the New York courts were entirely correct in deciding that Quarles' gun was the tainted fruit of a nonconsensual interrogation and therefore was inadmissible under our precedents.

However, since the New York Court of Appeals issued its opinion, the scope of the *Wong Sun* doctrine has changed. In *Nix v. Williams*, *supra*, this Court construed *Wong Sun* to permit the introduction into evidence of constitutionally tainted "fruits" that inevitably would have been discovered by the government. In its briefs before this Court and before the New York courts, petitioner has argued that the "inevitable-discovery" rule, if applied to this case, would permit the admission of Quarles' gun. * * * I believe that the proper disposition of the matter is to vacate the order of the New York Court of Appeals to the extent that it suppressed Quarles' gun and remand the matter to the New York Court of Appeals for further consideration in light of *Nix v. Williams*.

Accordingly, I would affirm the order of the Court of Appeals to the extent that it found Quarles' incriminating statement inadmissible under the Fifth Amendment, would vacate the order to the extent that it suppressed Quarles' gun, and would remand the matter for reconsideration in light of *Nix v. Williams*.

QUESTIONS, COMMENTS, CONCERNS?

1. **A historic *Quarles* invocation.** Justice Rehnquist's majority opinion in *Quarles* seemingly contemplates a reactive scene where officers encounter a "kaleidoscopic situation." But shortly after capturing Tsarnaev on April 19, 2013, the government would *preemptively* "invoke" the public safety exception. As Tsarnaev was traveling to the hospital for treatment following his capture, a DOJ official made a short public statement explaining that there were no plans to read Tsarnaev his *Miranda* rights. The official commented, "[W]e plan to invoke the public-safety exception to *Miranda* in order to question the suspect extensively about other potential explosive devices or accomplices, and to gain critical intelligence." Amy Davidson Sorkin, *What Happened To The* Miranda *Warning In Boston?*, NEWYORKER.COM (Apr. 21,

2013),   https://www.newyorker.com/news/amy-davidson/what-happened-to-the-miranda-warning-in-boston.

Four days after the bombing, the government would interrogate Tsarnaev for at least sixteen hours without providing him *Miranda* warnings. In fact, only after judicial intervention was Tsarnaev read his rights. Little caselaw exists on the open question of whether law enforcement can *preemptively* invoke the public safety exception to intentionally avoid *Miranda*. *Cf. United States v. Peace*, 2014 U.S. Dist. LEXIS 169455, at **3–4 (N.D. Ga. Sept. 25, 2014); *United States v. Rogers*, No. 13-cr-130, 2013 U.S. Dist. LEXIS 173175 (D. Minn. Aug. 29, 2013).

2.   Holmes & Tsarnaev as test cases: *Quarles* & the *Miranda* right to counsel. During the Tsarnaev interrogation, and before he received his *Miranda* warnings, he wrote his answers to investigators' questions because he could not talk. In particular, he "wrote the word 'lawyer' ten times, sometimes circling it." [Tsarnaev Casefile Document 5, at 4.] Similarly, during the video recorded portion of Holmes's first stationhouse interrogation, Holmes clearly invoked his right to counsel. [Holmes Casefile Video beginning at 5:50.] In both cases, investigators continued their questioning and obtained incriminating statements. The admissibility of those statements raises an important question: If a suspect invokes the *Miranda* right to counsel during a *Quarles* interrogation, must investigators cease questioning? That too is an open question, and the lower courts have reached different answers. *Compare United States v. Mobley*, 40 F.3d 688, 692–93 (4th Cir. 1994), *with United States v. Guess*, 756 F. Supp. 2d 730, 745 (E.D. Va. 2010).

3.   The *Miranda* right to counsel vs. *Quarles* (redux). Tsarnaev's case provides no ruling on the question of whether *Quarles* trumps a suspect's invocation of counsel. The state court in Holmes's case, however, provides two rulings that seemingly point in opposite directions.

In the first ruling, the court was asked whether *Quarles* applied to admit the statements Holmes made to investigators after invoking his right to counsel during the recorded stationhouse interview. The court declined to apply *Quarles*. Why? [*See* Holmes Casefile Document 4, Order on D-126, at 2, 29–42.] Read carefully. Does the circuit court hold that Holmes's invocation trumped *Quarles* or, rather, more simply that *Quarles* does not apply given that the exigency created by the theater shooting had expired?

Compare that order to how the court answers the question of whether *Quarles* permits admission of the statements Holmes made during his third interrogation where investigators asked him about the explosives in his apartment. Although officers acknowledged that Holmes had invoked his right to counsel, they nonetheless began this interrogation roughly fifteen hours after the shooting. They questioned Holmes for forty minutes, and he answered all of their questions in detail. How does the circuit court justify admitting some of Holmes's responses despite his clear invocation of counsel? Focus on a particular portion of the court's order. [*See* Holmes Casefile Document 4, Order on D-127, at 68–76.]

4. Why did the government stipulate not to use the statements Tsarnaev made at the hospital? Notice that the government ultimately conceded not "to use [Tsarnaev's] statements in its case-in-chief." [Tsarnaev Casefile Document 6, at 2.] Why? It's speculation of course, but prosecutors may have abandoned introduction of the hospital statements in favor of showing the jury pictures of the incriminating statements Tsarnaev wrote into the side of the boat where he was captured. *See id.* at 24.

But even if that's the case, why did the government bother arguing that *Quarles* applied? *Id.* at 20–24. The question is important because it seems there is a disconnect between what the government is arguing—to use Tsarnaev's hospital statements as impeachment evidence—and what *Quarles* would admit. That is, if *Quarles* applies, would Tsarnaev's hospital statements be admissible in the government's case-in-chief? As you will learn in Chapter 9, the Supreme Court's decision in *Harris v. New York*, 401 U.S. 222 (1971), presumably offered the government with a more straightforward path to rely on Tsarnaev's hospital statements for its chosen purpose.

5. Events outside the record & application of *Quarles*. Consider the government's justification for preemptively invoking *Quarles* at the time they began interrogating Tsarnaev: "In light of the history of coordinated terrorist attacks (and planned attacks) such as the ones in Mumbai, India, Times Square, the New York subway system, and an on September 11, the FBI had a duty to investigate whether any additional attacks were imminent." [Tsarnaev Casefile Document 6, at 1.]

Like the government in Tsarnaev's case, events outside the record played a role in the application of *Quarles* to Holmes's case. This time, however, it was the circuit court that relied on outside events, in part, to hold that *Quarles* applied to admit statements Holmes made at the scene shortly after his apprehension. [Holmes Casefile Document 4, Order on D-124, at 24.] Of particular note, the court reasoned, "The officers were also aware—based on their training, experience, and knowledge of the Columbine High School shooting and similar incidents around the country—that mass shootings often involve multiple assailants." *Id.* at 24–25.

Is it proper for the government to point to factual events having nothing to do with Tsarnaev as a basis for invoking the public safety exception? What about when a *court*, as in Holmes's case, relies on outside events as a basis to deny a defendant's motion to suppress? Does Justice Rehnquist's majority opinion in *Quarles* provide any supporting rationale for doing so?

6. Revisiting the *Quarles* dissent. Recall Justice Marshall's dissent. He comments:

> If a bomb is about to explode or the public is otherwise imminently imperiled, the police are free to interrogate suspects without advising them of their constitutional rights. Such unconsented questioning may take place not only when police officers act on instinct but also when higher faculties lead them to believe that advising a suspect of

his constitutional rights might decrease the likelihood that the suspect would reveal life-saving information. If trickery is necessary to protect the public, then the police may trick a suspect into confessing. While the Fourteenth Amendment sets limits on such behavior, nothing in the Fifth Amendment or our decision in *Miranda v. Arizona* proscribes this sort of emergency questioning. All the Fifth Amendment forbids is the introduction of coerced statements at trial.

Notice that Justice Marshall impressively foresees the prospect of investigators intentionally avoiding *Miranda*. He makes the important point that a *Miranda* violation only prohibits introduction of the suspect's incriminating *statements* at trial. As a result, investigators are free to use statements taken in violation of *Miranda* to further investigate and to address the very public safety concerns voiced by the prosecution in both the Holmes and Tsarnaev cases. In light of Justice Marshall's comments, is the public safety exception necessary in your view?

7.   The rest of the Tsarnaev story. The district court ultimately filed a one sentence ruling on Tsarnaev's motion to suppress. On October 20, 2014, it ruled: "In light of the government's representations that it will not be using the defendant's statements at trial, the defendant's motion to suppress 295 is denied without prejudice."

Tsarnaev's trial began on March 4, 2015, and he was convicted on April 8, 2015. Following the sentencing phase, the jury recommended that Tsarnaev be sentenced to death by lethal injection. The district court formally pronounced the death sentence on June 24, 2015, which made Tsarnaev, at the age of twenty-one, the youngest member of death row. Tsarnaev is currently housed at the federal Administrative Maximum Facility—otherwise known as "ADX." Based in Florence, Colorado, ADX is the federal prison system's super-maximum-security penitentiary. Tsarnaev is housed there with the likes of Ted Kaczynski, Zacarias Moussaoui, and Eric Rudolf. A detailed piece in the *New York Times* described life at ADX, where inmates spend twenty-three hours of the day in solitary confinement, as follows:

The ADX can house up to 500 prisoners in its eight units. Inmates spend their days in 12-by-7-foot cells with thick concrete walls and double sets of sliding metal doors (with solid exteriors, so prisoners can't see one another). A single window, about three feet high but only four inches wide, offers a notched glimpse of sky and little else. Each cell has a sink-toilet combo and an automated shower, and prisoners sleep on concrete slabs topped with thin mattresses. Most cells also have televisions (with built-in radios), and inmates have access to books and periodicals, as well as certain arts-and-craft materials. Prisoners in the general population are allotted a maximum of 10 hours of exercise a week outside their cells, alternating between solo trips to an indoor "gym" (a windowless cell with a single chin-up bar) and group visits to the outdoor rec yard (where each prisoner nonetheless remains confined to an individual cage). All meals come through slots in the interior door, as does any face-to-face human interaction (with a guard or psychiatrist, chaplain or imam).

Mark Binelli, *Inside America's Toughest Federal Prison*, N.Y. TIMES (Mar. 26, 2015), https://www.nytimes.com/2015/03/29/magazine/inside-americas-toughest -federal-prison.html. If Tsarnaev's execution is carried out, he would be transferred to the Terre Haute, Indiana, facility where the last federal inmate was executed in 2004.

8.   The rest of the Holmes story. Holmes was tried on more than 165 charges before a jury in Colorado state court. Following more than twelve hours of deliberations, jurors found him guilty of twenty-four counts of first-degree murder, 140 counts of attempted murder, and one count of possession or control of an explosive or incendiary device. Holmes was sentenced to twelve consecutive life sentences plus more than 3,000 additional years imprisonment. In pronouncing the sentence, Judge Carlos Samour said the following to a crowded courtroom:

> I want to make it clear that it is the court's intention that the defendant never set foot in free society again. The intention of my sentences is that he spend every single day of the rest of his life in prison and that he be in prison without the possibility of parole. If there was ever a case that warranted the maximum sentences, this is the case. One of the victims said yesterday, "The defendant does not deserve any sympathy." I wholeheartedly agree. The defendant does not deserve any sympathy, and for that reason, the court imposes the maximum sentences the court can impose under the law.

Michael Roberts, *End of Aurora Theater Shooting Trial: "Get the Defendant Out of My Courtroom,"* WESTWORD.COM (Aug. 27, 2015), http://www.westword. com/news/end-of-aurora-theater-shooting-trial-get-the-defendant-out-of-my-courtroom-7075690. Judge Samour added, "Get the defendant out of my courtroom, please." The courtroom applauded.

Holmes began serving his sentence at the Colorado State Penitentiary in Canon City, but was transferred to San Carlos Correctional Facility in Pueblo. While housed at Pueblo, an inmate named Mark "Slim" Daniels attacked Holmes on October 8, 2015. Not only would Daniels then admit to the attack, he sent a letter to the media in which he wrote, "I would like to express my deepest condolences to all the victims and to the families." He added, "I'm so sorry I couldn't wipe him out and sent [sic] him packing to Satan's lake of fire. It was just impossible to do by myself with so many cops." Alan Prendergast, *James Holmes Attacker Sorry He Couldn't Send Killer to "Satan's Lake of Fire,"* WESTWORD.COM (Dec. 14, 2015), http://www.westword.com/news/james-holmes-attacker-sorry-he-couldnt-send-killer-to-satans-lake-of-fire-7419338. After the attack, Holmes was transferred to federal prison. He is currently serving his sentence at USP Allenwood, a high-security prison in Pennsylvania. Kieran Nicholson, *Aurora Theater Shooter Relocated to High-Security Federal Prison in Pennsylvania*, DENVERPOST.COM (Sept. 27, 2017), https://www.denverpost.com/2017/09/27/james-holmes-aurora-theater-shooting-transferred-to-federal-prison/.

A Postscript to *Quarles*

The Supreme Court has done nothing since *Quarles* to clarify the public safety exception. Acknowledged at the time as the "first time that the Court carved out an exception" to *Miranda*,[8] *Quarles* has since received no additional attention from the Supreme Court. But the Supreme Court has had its chances. Since 1984, for example, the Court has turned down requests to hear cases involving public safety interrogations that lasted two minutes,[9] thirty to forty-five minutes,[10] and three and one-half hours.[11] Moreover, the Court has declined opportunities to resolve the permissibility of public safety interrogations that began hours,[12] days,[13] and months after the commission of a defendant's crime.[14]

The Court has similarly passed on answering the question of what constitutes a proper public safety question,[15] and what impact, if any, a suspect's invocation of counsel or silence has on the *Quarles* analysis.[16] Less important, but still incompletely answered,[17] is whether *Quarles* permits admission of an involuntary statement.[18] Since *Quarles*, the Supreme Court has taken at least fourteen *Miranda*-related cases while turning down at least twenty-seven opportunities to clarify varying facets of the public safety exception.[19]

---

[8] *High Court Curbs Right of Suspect*, N.Y. TIMES (June 13, 1984), http://www.nytimes.com/1984/06/13/us/high-court-curbs-right-of-suspect.html (last visited Aug. 14, 2022).

[9] United States v. Duncan, 308 F. App'x 601, 608 (3d Cir.), *cert. denied*, 556 U.S. 1275 (2009).

[10] Derrington v. United States, 488 A.2d 1314, 1322 (D.C. Cir. 1985), *cert. denied sub nom.* Grayson v. United States, 486 U.S. 1009 (1988).

[11] People v. Coffman, 96 P.3d 30, 73–74 (Cal. 2004), *cert. denied*, 544 U.S. 1063 (2005).

[12] United States v. Ferguson, 702 F.3d 89, 96 (2d Cir. 2012) (interrogation began sixty to ninety minutes following commission of the crime), *cert. denied*, 571 U.S. 830 (2013).

[13] People v. Sims, 853 P.2d 992, 1019 (Cal. 1993) (interrogation began sixteen days after the crime), *cert. denied*, 112 U.S. 1253 (1994).

[14] United States v. Powell, 444 F. App'x 517, 520 (3d Cir. 2011) (interrogation began almost three and one-half months after commission of the crime), *cert. denied*, 566 U.S. 940 (2012).

[15] *See, e.g.*, United States v. Newsome, 475 F.3d 1221, 1225 (11th Cir.), *cert. denied*, 552 U.S. 899 (2007); United States v. Brady, 819 F.2d 884, 887 (9th Cir. 1987), *cert. denied*, 484 U.S. 1068 (1988); State v. Ramirez, 871 P.2d 237, 244 (Ariz.), *cert. denied*, 513 U.S. 968 (1994).

[16] *See, e.g.*, United States v. Mobley, 40 F.3d 688, 692–93 (4th Cir. 1994), *cert. denied*, 514 U.S. 1129 (1995); People v. Palmer, 693 N.Y.S.2d 539, 540 (App. Div.), *cert. denied*, 528 U.S. 1051 (1999); State v. Stanley, 809 P.2d 944, 949 (Ariz.), *cert. denied*, 502 U.S. 1014 (1991).

[17] *Cf.* New York v. Quarles, 467 U.S. 649, 685 (1984) (Marshall, J., dissenting) ("The 'public-safety' exception is efficacious precisely because it permits police officers to coerce criminal defendants into making involuntary statements.").

[18] *See, e.g.*, United States v. Carroll, 207 F.3d 465, 472 (8th Cir.), *cert. denied*, 531 U.S. 849 (2000); People v. Panah, 107 P.3d 790, 841 (Cal. 2005), *cert. denied*, 546 U.S. 1216 (2006); People v. Coffman, 96 P.3d 30, 76–79 (Cal. 2004), *cert. denied*, 544 U.S. 1063 (2005).

[19] There are technically over 100 cases involving *Quarles* where the Court denied certiorari. Brian Gallini, *The Languishing Public Safety Doctrine*, 68 RUTGERS L. REV. 957, 1011 n.460 (2016).

CHAPTER 9

MIRANDA IN PRACTICE

■ ■ ■

I. BRENDAN DASSEY MEETS TERESA HALBACH—OR DOES HE?[1]

Dassey during his April 2007 trial

Brendan Ray Dassey was born in Manitowoc County, Wisconsin, on October 19, 1989, to parents Barbara and Peter Dassey. Dassey lived with his family in a trailer located on Avery Salvage with his brothers—Bryan, Bobby, and Blaine—and his half-brother—Brad. As you will recall from Chapter 5, Avery Salvage was located on a forty-acre property that housed numerous buildings and roughly 4,000 junked automobiles.

In fall 2005, Dassey was a sixteen-year-old sophomore at Mishicot High School. Apart from his intense desire to attend his classes, Dassey struggled in school. At the time photographer Teresa Halbach was reported missing, October 31, 2005, Dassey was enrolled in special education classes and was failing three of his courses.

Dassey's limited academic capabilities have a history. He began receiving special education services almost a decade earlier—in 1996— after intelligence testing revealed a full-scale IQ of 74 with a verbal IQ of

---

[1] Remember that you have access to the filings relevant to this chapter in your online repository.

65 and performance IQ of 87. Follow-up testing three years later indicated similar scores: a full-scale IQ of 73, a verbal IQ of 69, and a performance IQ of 82. In 2002, Mishicot School District School Psychologist Kris Schoenenberger-Gross evaluated Dassey using the Woodcock-Johnson test for cognitive abilities. That evaluation placed Dassey in the borderline to below average range. Additionally, Schoenenberger-Gross reported that Dassey suffered from a speech and language impairment and had difficulty expressing himself as well as understanding some facets of language.

Dassey was first questioned by law enforcement on November 6, 2005. By then, the Manitowoc County Sheriff's Department's (MCSD) investigation into Halbach's disappearance was already focused on Avery Salvage and, in particular, Dassey's uncle, Steven Avery. For many reasons, MCSD's focus on Avery was not surprising. After all, Halbach visited Avery Salvage on the day of her disappearance, and law enforcement thought Avery was the last one to see her alive. That visit, alongside Avery's three calls to Halbach on the day she disappeared, caused law enforcement to obtain a search warrant for Avery's trailer and Avery Salvage on November 5, which officers began executing that same day.

The following morning, as law enforcement began a second day of searching the large property, Marinette County Detectives Anthony J. O'Neill and Todd Baldwin spotted two young men driving Avery's car—the subject of a separate search warrant—and stopped them. After identifying the car's occupants as Avery's nephews, Bryan Dassey and Brendan Dassey, the detectives seized the vehicle and asked Brendan if he would sit and talk with them in an unmarked squad car. Detective O'Neill informed Dassey that he was not under arrest and that he was free to leave at any time. Neither Detective O'Neill nor Detective Baldwin advised Dassey of his *Miranda* rights.

The conversation that followed cemented law enforcement's belief that Dassey was involved in Halbach's murder. At the outset, Dassey told the detectives that, on the day Halbach disappeared, he got off the bus at 3:45 p.m. He was aware at the time that Avery was trying to sell a van for his mother and knew that Halbach planned to take pictures of the van. After initially denying seeing Halbach on the day of her disappearance, Dassey later conceded that, indeed, he saw her:

> DET. O'NEILL: You remember that girl taking that picture. You're gettin' off the bus, it's a beautiful day, it's daylight and everybody sees her, you do too. Do you remember seeing that girl there taking a picture?
>
> BRENDAN: Maybe, I don't know. . .don't remember.
>
> DET. BALDWIN: Brendan, come on.

DET. O'NEILL: . . .You do know, don't you? Brendan, you're not going to disappoint any of us. Think about that girl, was that girl standing there taking a picture that day?

BRENDAN: Maybe.

DET. O'NEILL: Ah, it's either a yes or no, I mean I'm not puttin' nothin' in your mind. You tell me if you remember that girl standing there taking pictures.

BRENDAN: [silence]

DET. O'NEILL: Was she? Huh? Why won't you tell me?

BRENDAN: I was just trying to think of if I seen her.

DET. O'NEILL: Well did you see her standing there taking a picture?

BRENDAN: Yeah.

DET. O'NEILL: Why didn't you tell me that? You scared?

BRENDAN: . . .Yeah.[ ]

Additionally, Dassey indicated that he saw Halbach's car and that he knew a bonfire in Avery's yard was planned for the week of October 31. Dassey also admitted to speaking with Avery on October 31 and to seeing Avery in his garage that evening. The interview concluded after nearly fifty-four minutes.

In his written report following the interview, Detective O'Neill acknowledged several inconsistencies in Dassey's statements:

During the interview, Brendan told us that he lives with his mother on Avery Road next to his uncle Steven Avery. He told us that he had never seen Teresa Halbach nor her Toyota SUV at their property on Avery Rd. When I asked Brendan specifically about seeing either Halbach or her vehicle on Monday (October 31st 2005) he again told us that he had not seen either. * * *

When I confronted Brendan about seeing Teresa Halbach when he had gotten off the bus with his brother on that Monday, Brendan now said that he had seen Teresa Halbach and her vehicle and that he did not tell us because he did not want to go to jail. When I asked Brendan as to what he had seen of Teresa, Brendan said that while he was walking down the driveway with his brother they had moved off to the side of the driveway to allow the Toyota SUV to go by. Brendan told us that the vehicle had been traveling out of the driveway toward the road and that it had only been on the property for five minutes.

> When asked again as to if he had seen Teresa out of the vehicle by the van by his and his uncles home Brendan now told us that while he was in his home after walking down the driveway to his home, from the kitchen by the kitchen sink window Brendan had seen his uncle Steven Avery and the girl taking pictures by the van parked in front of his home.

Ultimately, Dassey's November 6 roadside encounter with law enforcement marked the beginning of a long interrogation journey—a journey that ended with his conviction and life sentence for participating in Halbach's murder. But we are getting ahead of ourselves.

Law enforcement interviewed Dassey again just four days later. The transcript from this interview is discussed in Dassey's appellate brief:

> During a second interview on November 10, 2005, Brendan told police that he attended a bonfire in Steven's yard around November 1. He stated that he and Steven had burned branches, wood, a few old tires, and a junked car seat-but he had seen no sign of Halbach while he was there. Brendan had been at the fire for only an hour or two and had left when it was still burning steadily.

After these interviews, investigators left Dassey alone for several months.

Meanwhile, in January 2006, Kayla Avery, Dassey's fifteen-year-old-cousin, walked into Susan Brandt's office at Mishicot High School. At the time, Brandt was interning at both the high school and Mishicot Middle School as part of completing her Master's Degree in Counselor Education. According to Brandt, Kayla entered her office and said she "was scared" because Avery had asked Brendan for help moving a body. The following month, Calumet County Investigators Mark Wiegert and Wendy Baldwin interviewed Kayla. During that interview, Kayla told investigators that Dassey was "acting up lately" and, in particular, that Dassey "would just stare into space and start crying, basically uncontrollably." She also opined that Dassey had recently lost roughly forty pounds.

Based on Kayla's interview, Detective Wiegert decided to question Dassey a third time. On February 27, Detective Wiegert and FBI Special Agent Fassbender pulled Dassey out of class at Mishicot High School and questioned him on campus for nearly two hours. At the outset of the interview, Detective Wiegert and Agent Fassbender told Dassey that he was not under arrest, that he was free to leave, and that he did not have to answer their questions. Neither a lawyer nor a guardian was present.

During his third interview, Dassey told a story much different from the one he told during his November 2005 interviews. He stated that Steven Avery tied up and stabbed Halbach in her truck and then put the knife under the truck's seat. According to Dassey, Avery burned Halbach's body in a burn pit located on the Avery Salvage property before hiding the truck. Dassey also reported that he saw blood on Halbach's clothing.

But to get that story from Dassey, Detective Wiegert and Agent Fassbender relied on a handful of techniques from the Reid method. The investigators took turns developing a theme with Dassey, sought to blame Avery for what happened, and often appeared to contaminate Dassey's answers by asking detail-laden questions. At one point, Detective Wiegert asked, "[W]as there blood on those clothes?" Later, Agent Fassbender told Dassey that he "saw some body parts," to which Dassey responded, "Toes." Perhaps most troublingly, though, the officers came close to promising Dassey leniency: "Did you help him put that body in the fire? If you did it's OK." At the end of the interview, Detective Wiegert and Agent Fassbender permitted Dassey to return to class.

When Dassey's school day finished a few hours later, the investigators decided to drive Dassey just down the road (7.7 miles, to be exact) to the Two Rivers Police Station to conduct a videotaped interview. Dassey's mother, Barb Janda, agreed to the stationhouse interview, unaware that Dassey was a suspect at that time. Janda met Dassey and the investigators at the school and accompanied them to the station, but declined to be present in the interrogation room during Dassey's questioning.

During his fourth interview, which lasted from 3:21 p.m. to 4:03 p.m. Dassey sat at the far end of a formal interrogation room—if he wanted to leave, he would need to pass by both officers—and the investigators advised him of his *Miranda* rights. Additionally, Detective Wiegert asked Dassey to sign a waiver, and Dassey complied. Dassey then generally repeated what he said hours earlier at the school, though he changed his story with respect to where Avery placed Halbach's clothing, where Avery hid Halbach's vehicle, and how Avery moved Halbach's body.

Concerned about the safety of Dassey and Janda along with the prospect of them tampering with evidence, law enforcement arranged for Dassey and Janda to spend the night at a hotel near the police station. There, investigators again visited Janda and Dassey. That conversation, however, was not recorded. Janda and Dassey left the hotel the next morning, February 28.

Dassey returned to school on Wednesday, March 1. But with Janda's permission, the investigators retrieved Dassey from school for a videotaped interview—this time 11.6 miles away at the Manitowoc County Sheriff's Department. Dassey's fifth interview, which became famous after the release of Netflix documentary, *Making a Murderer*, lasted from 10:45 a.m. to 3:40 p.m. During that time, Dassey made several key statements that the state later used against him at trial, including that he raped Halbach and slit her throat on his uncle's instruction. Once again, Dassey had neither a guardian nor an attorney present. Dassey's fifth interview concluded with his arrest.

II. INVOKING & WAIVING *MIRANDA* RIGHTS

We move now into the caselaw governing how, practically, a suspect invokes and waives their *Miranda* rights. Our first case, *Michigan v. Mosley*, specifically considers what happens when a suspect invokes the *Miranda* right to silence. *Edwards v. Arizona*, our second case, addresses the consequences of a suspect's invocation of the *Miranda* right to counsel. *Edwards* also considers what standard should govern the waiver of a suspect's *Miranda* rights. Given that between eighty to ninety percent of suspects waive their *Miranda* rights, you should pay close attention to the waiver standard. Jan Hoffman, *Police Tactics Chipping Away at Suspects' Rights*, N.Y. TIMES, Mar. 29, 1998, at A1.

Both *Davis v. United States* and *Berghuis v. Thompkins* each address what standard governs *how* a suspect invokes each of the rights. Then, the notes following each case encourage you to dive deeply into the varied Dassey interrogations. This chapter's casefile provides access to audio, video, and transcripts associated with each interrogation so that you can follow along with the questions raised in each note.

MICHIGAN V. MOSLEY

423 U.S. 96
Supreme Court of the United States
Argued October 6, 1975; December 9, 1975
No. 74-653

MR. JUSTICE STEWART delivered the opinion of the Court.

The respondent, Richard Bert Mosley, was arrested in Detroit, Mich., in the early afternoon of April 8, 1971, in connection with robberies that had recently occurred at the Blue Goose Bar and the White Tower Restaurant on that city's lower east side. The arresting officer, Detective James Cowie of the Armed Robbery Section of the Detroit Police Department, was acting on a tip implicating Mosley and three other men in the robberies. After effecting the arrest, Detective Cowie brought Mosley to the Robbery, Breaking and Entering Bureau of the Police Department, located on the fourth floor of the departmental headquarters building. The officer advised Mosley of his rights under this Court's decision in *Miranda v. Arizona*, 384 U.S. 436, and had him read and sign the department's constitutional rights notification certificate. After filling out the necessary arrest papers, Cowie began questioning Mosley about the robbery of the White Tower Restaurant. When Mosley said he did not want to answer any questions about the robberies, Cowie promptly ceased the interrogation. The completion of the arrest papers and the questioning of Mosley together took approximately 20 minutes. At no time during the questioning did Mosley indicate a desire to consult with a lawyer, and there is no claim that the procedures followed to this point did not fully comply with the strictures of the *Miranda* opinion. Mosley was then taken to a ninth-floor cell block.

Shortly after 6 p.m., Detective Hill of the Detroit Police Department Homicide Bureau brought Mosley from the cell block to the fifth-floor office of the Homicide Bureau for questioning about the fatal shooting of a man named Leroy Williams. Williams had been killed on January 9, 1971, during a holdup attempt outside the 101 Ranch Bar in Detroit. Mosley had not been arrested on this charge or interrogated about it by Detective Cowie. Before questioning Mosley about this homicide, Detective Hill carefully advised him of his "*Miranda* rights." Mosley read the notification form both silently and aloud, and Detective Hill then read and explained the warnings to him and had him sign the form. Mosley at first denied any involvement in the Williams murder, but after the officer told him that Anthony Smith had confessed to participating in the slaying and had named him as the "shooter," Mosley made a statement implicating himself in the homicide. The interrogation by Detective Hill lasted approximately 15 minutes, and at no time during its course did Mosley ask to consult with a lawyer or indicate that he did not want to discuss the homicide. In short, there is no claim that the procedures followed during Detective Hill's interrogation of Mosley, standing alone, did not fully comply with the strictures of the *Miranda* opinion.

Mosley was subsequently charged in a one-count information with first-degree murder. Before the trial he moved to suppress his incriminating statement on a number of grounds, among them the claim that under the doctrine of the *Miranda* case it was constitutionally impermissible for Detective Hill to question him about the Williams murder after he had told Detective Cowie that he did not want to answer any questions about the robberies. * * * We granted the writ because of the important constitutional question presented. * * *

The issue in this case * * * is whether the conduct of the Detroit police that led to Mosley's incriminating statement did in fact violate the *Miranda* "guidelines," so as to render the statement inadmissible in evidence against Mosley at his trial. Resolution of the question turns almost entirely on the interpretation of a single passage in the *Miranda* opinion, upon which the Michigan appellate court relied in finding a per se violation of *Miranda*[.] * * *

[That] passage states that "the interrogation must cease" when the person in custody indicates that "he wishes to remain silent." It does not state under what circumstances, if any, a resumption of questioning is permissible. The passage could be literally read to mean that a person who has invoked his "right to silence" can never again be subjected to custodial interrogation by any police officer at any time or place on any subject. Another possible construction of the passage would characterize "any statement taken after the person invokes his privilege" as "the product of compulsion" and would therefore mandate its exclusion from evidence, even if it were volunteered by the person in custody without any further interrogation whatever. Or the passage could be interpreted to require only the immediate cessation of questioning, and to permit a resumption of interrogation after a momentary respite.

It is evident that any of these possible literal interpretations would lead to absurd and unintended results. To permit the continuation of custodial interrogation after a momentary cessation would clearly frustrate the purposes of *Miranda* by allowing repeated rounds of questioning to undermine the will of the person being questioned. At the other extreme, a blanket prohibition against the taking of voluntary statements or a permanent immunity from further interrogation, regardless of the circumstances, would transform the *Miranda* safeguards into wholly irrational obstacles to legitimate police investigative activity, and deprive suspects of an opportunity to make informed and intelligent assessments of their interests. Clearly, therefore, neither this passage nor any other passage in the *Miranda* opinion can sensibly be read to create a per se proscription of indefinite duration upon any further questioning by any police officer on any subject, once the person in custody has indicated a desire to remain silent.

A reasonable and faithful interpretation of the *Miranda* opinion must rest on the intention of the Court in that case to adopt "fully effective means. . .to notify the person of his right of silence and to assure that the exercise of the right will be scrupulously honored. . ." The critical safeguard identified in the passage at issue is a person's "right to cut off questioning." Through the exercise of his option to terminate questioning he can control the time at which questioning occurs, the subjects discussed, and the duration of the interrogation. The requirement that law enforcement authorities must respect a person's exercise of that option counteracts the coercive pressures of the custodial setting. We therefore conclude that the admissibility of statements obtained after the person in custody has decided to remain silent depends under *Miranda* on whether his "right to cut off questioning" was "scrupulously honored."

A review of the circumstances leading to Mosley's confession reveals that his "right to cut off questioning" was fully respected in this case. Before his initial interrogation, Mosley was carefully advised that he was under no obligation to answer any questions and could remain silent if he wished. He orally acknowledged that he understood the *Miranda* warnings and then signed a printed notification-of-rights form. When Mosley stated that he did not want to discuss the robberies, Detective Cowie immediately ceased the interrogation and did not try either to resume the questioning or in any way to persuade Mosley to reconsider his position. After an interval of more than two hours, Mosley was questioned by another police officer at another location about an unrelated holdup murder. He was given full and complete *Miranda* warnings at the outset of the second interrogation. He was thus reminded again that he could remain silent and could consult with a lawyer, and was carefully given a full and fair opportunity to exercise these options. The subsequent questioning did not undercut Mosley's previous decision not to answer Detective Cowie's inquiries. Detective Hill did not resume the interrogation about the White Tower Restaurant robbery or inquire about the Blue Goose Bar robbery, but instead focused exclusively on the Leroy Williams homicide, a crime different in nature and in time and place of occurrence from the robberies for which Mosley had been arrested and interrogated by Detective Cowie. Although it is not clear from the record how much Detective Hill knew about the earlier interrogation, his questioning of Mosley about an unrelated homicide was quite consistent with a reasonable interpretation of Mosley's earlier refusal to answer any questions about the robberies.

This is not a case, therefore, where the police failed to honor a decision of a person in custody to cut off questioning, either by refusing to discontinue the interrogation upon request or by persisting in repeated efforts to wear down his resistance and make him change his mind. In contrast to such practices, the police here immediately ceased the interrogation, resumed questioning only after the passage of a significant period of time and the provision of a fresh set of warnings, and restricted the second interrogation to a crime that had not been a subject of the earlier interrogation. * * *

For these reasons, we conclude that the admission in evidence of Mosley's incriminating statement did not violate the principles of *Miranda v. Arizona*. Accordingly, the judgment of the Michigan Court of Appeals is vacated, and the case is remanded to that court for further proceedings not inconsistent with this opinion.

It is so ordered.

MR. JUSTICE WHITE, concurring in the result.

[Omitted.]

MR. JUSTICE BRENNAN, with whom MR. JUSTICE MARSHALL joins, dissenting.

[Omitted.]

QUESTIONS, COMMENTS, CONCERNS?

1.   **The *Miranda* right to silence.** Apart from providing a standard governing how officers must respect a suspect's invocation of the *Miranda* right

to silence, *Mosley* stands for a different and more important proposition: the *Miranda* right to silence is crime specific. That is, in Mosely's case, the fact that he invoked his right to silence when questioned about the robberies did not prevent officers from asking Mosely about his involvement in the death of Leroy Williams.

2.   **The Dassey Casefile organization.** The Dassey casefile is a bit larger than some others, and the series of questions throughout this chapter will really only scratch the surface of the issues raised by Dassey's interrogations. But know that the casefile has two major structural parts: first are the interrogation videos and transcripts. When you watch an interrogation video, be sure to have the relevant transcript in front of you. You may wish to make notes on what the transcript includes that perhaps the corresponding video does *not* include. The second piece of the casefile includes the relevant filings from Dassey's case, a case that continues to this day. The file is over-inclusive for those who wish to explore Dassey's case in more detail. For purposes of this chapter, though, our focus will be on the major *Miranda*-based issues raised by Dassey's interrogations.

3.   **Reviewing *Miranda* custody: Dassey's first "interview."** Spend just a minute reviewing the custody standard from *Berkemer* and think through how *J. D. B.* impacts that standard. After all, *J. D. B.* suddenly takes center stage in Dassey's case. As you review this first interaction between Dassey and the police, consider the location of the interaction, the number of officers, the tone the officers take, whether they ask informational or accusatory questions, Dassey's age, and his intelligence level.

Next, pull up Dassey's first statement, which he made during his first interview. [*See* Casefile Interrogation Transcripts Document 1.] Be sure to also follow along by opening the first file in the interrogation recordings casefile folder. [*See* Casefile Interrogation Recordings Recording 1.] You will hear an obnoxious clicking sound throughout the recording, which is the sound of the officer's squad car flashers.

By November 6, law enforcement has entered its fourth day into investigating the disappearance of Teresa Halbach. Investigators are also into day two of executing the November 5 warrant we studied in Chapter 5. At the time police stopped Dassey on November 6, Dassey and his brother Blaine were leaving the Avery property to pick up sodas in Crivitz, Wisconsin. Police towed the car away and detectives separated Dassey from his brother. Dassey and his brother are then separately interviewed by a pair of detectives in the squad car (Detectives O'Neill and Baldwin who are referenced in the transcript).

Notice the rough flow of Dassey's story during that first interaction with Detectives O'Neill and Baldwin. At first, you'll hear Dassey say that he never saw Halbach. But then, he says he saw her leaving the Avery property because she drove by him while he was walking home. Dassey changes his story again later in the interview by saying that he saw Halbach leave from outside his window once he got home from school.

Let's look at some particular facets of the interview. Each of the clips below includes an approximate timestamp along with a general description of what you should expect to hear. Please consider, at each bullet point, whether Dassey is in police custody subject to interrogation.

- [~1:56–2:30; pg. 2 ("So you're not certain if it was Monday?")] Dassey denies seeing Halbach but admits to learning about her on the news. He says he has not seen her vehicle.

- [~9:08–10:05; pg. 8 ("All right you didn't ah. . .")] Dassey says he got home from school at 3:45 p.m. and played PlayStation with his brother.

- [19:00–19:34; pg. 15 ("You take the bus to school?")] Dassey says the bus dropped him off by the mailboxes and he did not see a green Toyota at that time.

- [20:35–24:45; pg. 17 ("You don't know. . .")] There's a long pause. O'Neill challenges Dassey's story about not seeing Halbach taking pictures of the van.

- [25:37–26:47; pg. 21 ("Brendan, listen this girl has. . .")] Detectives accuse Dassey of lying to them and they imply that they'll find Brendan's fingerprints when they sweep the RAV4.

- [28:31–31:14; pg. 23 ("We're gonna talk to Blaine, too. . .")] Dassey says Halbach drove by him and Blaine on her way off the property. The detectives accuse him of changing his story.

- [38:43–40:37; pg. 29 ("Tell me what you do know.")] Officers tell Dassey that "no one needs to know" what they talk about. At the very end (on page 48 of the transcript), they tell him they will keep Dassey's story "between us."

- [49:30–50:43; pg. 36 ("Then you said you saw her leave.")] Dassey now he says he saw Halbach leave while he was standing in his kitchen looking out the window. The detectives challenge him and tell Dassey he is not going to go to jail.

Do you think Dassey felt free to leave throughout his first interview?

4. Reviewing *Miranda* interrogation: Dassey's first "interview." Did the tenor in the clips you just listened to change at any point? In other words, was there a point where the interaction between Detectives Baldwin and O'Neill moved from an "interview" to an "interrogation"? Could you identify any areas where Detectives Baldwin and O'Neill relied on the Reid method to question Dassey? If so, how do your observations about the officers' use of the Reid method intersect with the governing law? That is, does it make it more or less likely that what took place in the squad car was, in fact, police interrogation?

Looking ahead for just a moment, there is reason to believe that the chief interrogators in Dassey's case, Detective Mark Wiegert and Special Agent Tom

Fassbender, thought that this first interaction may have been problematic. Look for a minute at the transcript of Dassey's second interview, which occurred at his school on February 27, 2006. [*See* Casefile Interrogation Transcripts Document 2.] On the very first page, Agent Fassbender opens with this comment: "We're not here ta, ta jump in your face or get into ya or anything like that. I know that may have happened before and stuff like that, we're, we're not here to do that." *Id.* at 440 (note that references to this and other transcripts will follow the pagination of the transcript in the upper right-hand corner).

5. **Miranda, Mosley, and Dassey's first "interview."** What do the preceding notes have to do with *Mosley*? Well, if Dassey is not in custody and what's happening in the squad car does not qualify as interrogation, then nothing. But if what took place in the squad car was custodial interrogation, then minimally Dassey was entitled to receive *Miranda* warnings—including his right to silence before question began. And interestingly, there are portions of the November 6 transcript that suggest Dassey may well have been interested in remaining silent. At more than one point, he admits to detectives that he is "scared," yet detectives consistently challenge his accounts and ask him "[w]hat happened to that girl?"

Let's assume that *Miranda* applies to Dassey's first interview. Did Dassey say anything incriminating? After all, *Miranda*'s remedy contemplates exclusion of "statements," so it's important to keep in mind what Dassey's counsel should seek to suppress, if anything.

6. **Reviewing *Miranda* custody: Dassey's third "interview."** Let's look in more depth at Dassey's third interview (recall: November 10, 2005, was Dassey's second interview). Pull up Dassey's third statement, which is an audio-only file, and the accompanying transcript. [*See* Casefile Interrogation Recordings Recording 2; Casefile Interrogation Transcripts Document 2.] Each of the clips below include an approximate timestamp alongside a general description of what you should expect to hear. Some of the noted clips also include questions for your consideration. Those specific questions aside, you should be thinking generally about whether Dassey is in police custody subject to interrogation during this third interview. Please also consider whether the officers' more prominent use of the Reid interrogation technique in this interview impacts your analysis.

- [0:00–2:04; pg. 440 ("Mark's obviously. . .")]: Agent Fassbender tells Dassey he's free to leave. What role should the "free to leave" statement play in the *Miranda* custody analysis? Would you like to know where they officers are sitting relative to where Dassey is sitting? Would you also like to know how the room is setup and where the exits are located? Finally, what else happens during Agent Fassbender's opening statement? Can you tell which Reid step Agent Fassbender is already using?

- [4:13–5:03; pg. 442 ("Did you see any body parts?")]: Agent Fassbender asks Dassey about a bonfire on October 31, 2005.

Who is the first to mention "body parts"? Was it Dassey or Agent Fassbender? If the latter, is that problematic?

- [5:10–7:02; pg. 442 ("As I said, we're not gonna say. . .")]: Agent Fassbender and Detective Wiegert raise the prospect that Dassey could be arrested and charged with the crime if he does not provide investigators with an acceptable factual account. Agent Fassbender specifically references the prosecutor's office looking at Dassey's involvement in Halbach's death. Thinking back to the introductory readings in Chapter 7, could this qualify as a systemic inducement?

- [7:51–12:53; pg. 443 ("Yeah I know how hard this is. . .")] During this segment, you'll hear Agent Fassbender blame Steven Avery for Halbach's death and mutilation while minimizing the moral seriousness of Dassey's involvement and blameworthiness. Investigators also during this segment suggest that Halbach's hand, foot, or something else of hers was in the fire. Dassey does not offer that. Can you spot any problematic inducements during that exchange? If so, are they communicating to Dassey that he would receive more favorable treatment from the detectives or the criminal justice system if he provided the account they desired?

- [17:29–19:04; pg. 446 ("Did he tell you what to say?")]: In this segment, the officer questioning Dassey changes. Now Detective Wiegert is the one to emphasize the importance of Dassey being honest. Can you spot which step of the Reid technique Detective Wiegert is using?

- [22:45–26:33; pg. 448 ("I'm really. . .by the garage)]: Investigators during this exchange get Dassey to admit that he saw some clothes "like a blue shirt, some pants." He then says, after investigators suggest it to him, that there was blood on the clothes. It is perhaps worth noting that Halbach was actually wearing blue jeans, a white button-down shirt, and a summer jacket.

- [29:56–33:40; pg. 451 ("Yeah, it's not your fault. . .")]: Dassey will admit here that he saw toes. Does this exchange remind you of step six of the Reid technique?

After reviewing these clips, what in your opinion has Dassey admitted to that is self-incriminating? Should his statement(s) be suppressed because he was in custody subject to interrogation and therefore should have received *Miranda* warnings? As you answer that question, consider that Dassey was reminded that he was "not under arrest" about an hour into the interview. [Casefile Interrogation Transcripts Document 2, at 467.] You may also wish to look back to see whether officers promised Dassey anything. *E.g., id.* at 453. Finally, look at the end of the "interview" and consider whether Dassey understands the gravity of what took place during his conversation with the investigators. *Id.* at 479.

7. Previewing *Miranda* exclusion. If you concluded that Dassey should have received *Miranda* warnings during his first interview (roadside) or third interview (schoolhouse), the remedy seems straightforward: Suppress Dassey's incriminating statements from both interviews, right? Well, maybe. As we will learn, *Miranda's* exclusionary rule does not reach as far as does the Fourth Amendment's exclusionary. The complexities of *Miranda* exclusion aside, trial counsel never argued the reach of *Miranda* exclusion on Dassey's behalf because, quite unbelievably, Dassey's trial counsel conceded that Dassey was not in custody during any of the interrogations. [See Casefile Litigation Files Document 3, at 6–7.] Yes, you read that correctly. The exchange you will read in the cited casefile pages is quite unlike any that you have likely ever read before. This seems like a great point to remind you of why we began our journey in Chapter 1 by discussing the quality of lawyering.

EDWARDS V. ARIZONA
451 U.S. 477
Supreme Court of the United States
November 5, 1980, Argued; May 18, 1981, Decided
No. 79-5269

JUSTICE WHITE delivered the opinion of the Court. * * *

I.

On January 19, 1976, a sworn complaint was filed against Edwards in Arizona state court charging him with robbery, burglary, and first-degree murder. An arrest warrant was issued pursuant to the complaint, and Edwards was arrested at his home later that same day. At the police station, he was informed of his rights as required by *Miranda v. Arizona*, 384 U.S. 436 (1966). Petitioner stated that he understood his rights, and was willing to submit to questioning. After being told that another suspect already in custody had implicated him in the crime, Edwards denied involvement and gave a taped statement presenting an alibi defense. He then sought to "make a deal." The interrogating officer told him that he wanted a statement, but that he did not have the authority to negotiate a deal. The officer provided Edwards with the telephone number of a county attorney. Petitioner made the call, but hung up after a few moments. Edwards then said: "I want an attorney before making a deal." At that point, questioning ceased and Edwards was taken to county jail.

At 9:15 the next morning, two detectives, colleagues of the officer who had interrogated Edwards the previous night, came to the jail and asked to see Edwards. When the detention officer informed Edwards that the detectives wished to speak with him, he replied that he did not want to talk to anyone. The guard told him that "he had" to talk and then took him to meet with the detectives. The officers identified themselves, stated they wanted to talk to him, and informed him of his *Miranda* rights. Edwards was willing to talk, but he first wanted to hear the taped statement of the alleged accomplice who had implicated him. After listening to the tape for several minutes, petitioner said that he would make a statement so long as it was not tape-recorded. The detectives informed him that the recording was irrelevant since they could testify in court concerning whatever he said. Edwards replied: "I'll tell you anything you want to know, but I don't want it on tape." He thereupon implicated himself in the crime.

Prior to trial, Edwards moved to suppress his confession on the ground that his *Miranda* rights had been violated when the officers returned to question him after he had invoked his right to counsel. The trial court initially granted the motion to suppress, but reversed its ruling when presented with a supposedly controlling decision of a higher Arizona court. The court stated without explanation that it found Edwards' statement to be voluntary. Edwards was tried twice and convicted. Evidence concerning his confession was admitted at both trials.

On appeal, the Arizona Supreme Court held that Edwards had invoked both his right to remain silent and his right to counsel during the interrogation conducted on the night of January 19. The court then went on to determine, however, that Edwards had waived both rights during the January 20 meeting when he voluntarily gave his statement to the detectives after again being informed that he need not answer questions and that he need not answer without the advice of counsel: "The trial court's finding that the waiver and confession were voluntarily and knowingly made is upheld."

II.

In *Miranda v. Arizona*, the Court determined that the Fifth and Fourteenth Amendments' prohibition against compelled self-incrimination required that custodial interrogation be preceded by advice to the putative defendant that he has the right to remain silent and also the right to the presence of an attorney. The Court also indicated the procedures to be followed subsequent to the warnings. If the accused indicates that he wishes to remain silent, "the interrogation must cease." If he requests counsel, "the interrogation must cease until an attorney is present."

Miranda thus declared that an accused has a Fifth and Fourteenth Amendment right to have counsel present during custodial interrogation. Here, the critical facts as found by the Arizona Supreme Court are that Edwards asserted his right to counsel and his right to remain silent on January 19, but that the police, without furnishing him counsel, returned the next morning to confront him and, as a result of the meeting, secured incriminating oral admissions. Contrary to the holdings of the state courts, Edwards insists that having exercised his right on the 19th to have counsel present during interrogation, he did not validly waive that right on the 20th. For the following reasons, we agree.

First, the Arizona Supreme Court applied an erroneous standard for determining waiver where the accused has specifically invoked his right to counsel. It is reasonably clear under our cases that waivers of counsel must not only be voluntary, but must also constitute a knowing and intelligent relinquishment or abandonment of a known right or privilege, a matter which depends in each case "upon the particular facts and circumstances surrounding that case, including the background, experience, and conduct of the accused." * * *

Here, however sound the conclusion of the state courts as to the voluntariness of Edwards' admission may be, neither the trial court nor the Arizona Supreme Court undertook to focus on whether Edwards understood his right to counsel and intelligently and knowingly relinquished it. It is thus apparent that the decision below misunderstood the requirement for finding a valid waiver of the right to counsel, once invoked.

Second, although we have held that after initially being advised of his *Miranda* rights, the accused may himself validly waive his rights and respond to interrogation, *see North Carolina v. Butler*, the Court has strongly indicated that additional safeguards are necessary when the accused asks for counsel; and we now hold that when an accused has invoked his right to have counsel present during custodial interrogation, a valid waiver of that right cannot be established by showing only that he responded to further police-initiated custodial interrogation even if he has been advised of his rights. We further hold that an accused, such as Edwards, having expressed his desire to deal with the police only through counsel, is not subject to further interrogation by the authorities until counsel has been made available to him, unless the accused himself initiates further communication, exchanges, or conversations with the police.

Miranda itself indicated that the assertion of the right to counsel was a significant event and that once exercised by the accused, "the interrogation must cease until an attorney is present." Our later cases have not abandoned that view. In *Michigan v. Mosley*, 423 U.S. 96 (1975), the Court noted that *Miranda* had distinguished between the procedural safeguards triggered by a request to remain silent and a request for an attorney and had required that interrogation cease until an attorney was present only if the individual stated that he wanted counsel. We reconfirm * * * that it is inconsistent with *Miranda* and its progeny for the authorities, at their instance, to reinterrogate an accused in custody if he has clearly asserted his right to counsel.

In concluding that the fruits of the interrogation initiated by the police on January 20 could not be used against Edwards, we do not hold or imply that Edwards was powerless to countermand his election or that the authorities could in no event use any incriminating statements made by Edwards prior to his having access to counsel. Had Edwards initiated the meeting on January 20, nothing in the Fifth and Fourteenth Amendments would prohibit the police from merely listening to his voluntary, volunteered statements and using them against him at the trial. The Fifth Amendment right identified in *Miranda* is the right to have counsel present at any custodial interrogation. Absent such interrogation, there would have been no infringement of the right that Edwards invoked and there would be no occasion to determine whether there had been a valid waiver. *Rhode Island v. Innis* makes this sufficiently clear.

But this is not what the facts of this case show. Here, the officers conducting the interrogation on the evening of January 19 ceased interrogation when Edwards requested counsel as he had been advised he had the right to do. The Arizona Supreme Court was of the opinion that this was a sufficient invocation of his *Miranda* rights, and we are in accord. It is also clear that without making counsel available to Edwards, the police returned to him the next day. This was not at his suggestion or request. Indeed, Edwards informed the detention officer that he did not want to talk to anyone. At the meeting, the detectives told Edwards that they wanted to talk to him and again advised him of his *Miranda* rights. Edwards stated that he would talk, but what prompted this action does not appear. He listened at his own request to part of the taped statement made by one of his alleged accomplices and then made an incriminating statement, which was used against him at his trial. We think it is clear that Edwards was subjected to custodial interrogation on January 20 within the meaning of *Rhode Island v. Innis, supra,* and that this occurred at the instance of the authorities. His statement, made without having had access to counsel, did not amount to a valid waiver and hence was inadmissible.

Accordingly, the holding of the Arizona Supreme Court that Edwards had waived his right to counsel was infirm, and the judgment of that court is reversed.

So ordered.

CHIEF JUSTICE BURGER, concurring in the judgment.

[Omitted.]

JUSTICE POWELL, with whom JUSTICE REHNQUIST joins, concurring in the result.

[Omitted.]

QUESTIONS, COMMENTS, CONCERNS?

1.   **The reach of *Edwards*.** Unlike the *Miranda* right to silence, the *Miranda* right to counsel is not crime specific. Once a suspect invokes the *Miranda* right to counsel, questioning on *all* crimes must cease. In *Arizona v. Roberson*, 486 U.S. 675 (1988), respondent was arrested for burglary and invoked counsel. Three days later, a different officer interrogated respondent about a different burglary—without knowledge that respondent had invoked his right to counsel. Respondent made an incriminating statement about this second burglary. The trial court suppressed respondent's statement, and following the prosecution's appeal, the Supreme Court affirmed. The Court held that "the presumption raised by a suspect's request for counsel—that he considers himself unable to deal with the pressures of custodial interrogation without legal assistance—does not disappear simply because the police have approached the suspect, still in custody, still without counsel, about a separate investigation."

With *Roberson* in mind, return briefly to the James Holmes casefile. Recall that Holmes sought a "court-appointed attorney" toward the end of his videotaped interrogation on July 20, 2012. [Chapter 8 Holmes Casefile Video, beginning at 7:10.] Detectives recognized his invocation and terminated the interview at 2:51 a.m. *Id.* But hours later, at 3:45 p.m., investigators approached Holmes to ask him about the explosives at his apartment. [Chapter 8 Holmes Casefile Document 1, D-127 Motion, at 2.] They acknowledged Holmes's invocation of counsel and indicated that they would not question him about the theater shooting. Rather, they wanted to discuss only the booby traps in his apartment. They proceeded to interrogate him for thirty-eight minutes, during which Holmes made incriminating statements. Was that subsequent interrogation permissible under *Edwards-Roberson*?

2.   ***Edwards* and waiver of the *Miranda* right to counsel.** Notice that the *Edwards* Court also holds that a suspect does not waive *Miranda* rights by merely responding to police questioning. Thus, for post-*Miranda* statements to be admissible at trial, the prosecution must prove that the suspect knowingly and intentionally waived the *Miranda* right to counsel. This rule applies even where the suspect invokes neither the *Miranda* right to counsel nor the *Miranda* right to silence. Or, stated differently, waiver and invocation are separate issues.

3.   **Dassey and the form of *Miranda* warnings.** Recall our discussion in Chapter 8 of *California v. Prysock*, 453 U.S. 355 (1981) and *Duckworth v. Eagan*, 492 U.S. 195 (1989). Now consider the *Miranda* warnings Dassey received during his stationhouse interrogation on February 27, 2006. [*See* Casefile Interrogation Transcripts Document 3, at 484.] In relevant part, those warnings included the following statement:

> You have this right to the advice and presence of a lawyer even though you cannot afford to hire one. We have no way of getting you a lawyer but one will be appointed for you if you wish and if and when you go to court.

Id. Is that warning problematic under *Prysock* or *Duckworth*?

Now compare that warning to the warning Dassey received during his March 1, 2006 interrogation:

> You have the right to consult a lawyer and have him present with you while you're being questioned. If you cannot afford to hire an attorney, one will be appointed to represent you before any questioning.

[Casefile Interrogation Transcripts Document 4, at 526.] How is the March 1 warning critically different from the February 27 warning? Does one version suggest more specifically that counsel could be provided to Dassey *before* questioning begins?

4.   Waiver and Dassey (part 1). Dassey's second February 27, 2006 interrogation provides us with the first real-life window into how interrogators might secure a *Miranda* waiver. Remember that, under *Edwards*, a suspect's waiver is valid if it is voluntary, and knowingly and intelligently made based on the totality of the circumstances. After Detective Wiegert finished reading Dassey's *Miranda* rights to him, the pair had this exchange:

> WIEGERT: * * * I have read the above statement of my rights I understand what my rights are, I am willing to answer questions and to make statements. I do not want a lawyer. I understand and know what I am doing. No promises or threats have been made to me and no pressure of any kind has been used against me. Do you agree with that?
>
> BRENDAN: Yeah.
>
> WIEGERT: You have to speak up a little bit.
>
> BRENDAN: Yeah.
>
> WIEGERT: Yes?
>
> BRENDAN: Yes.
>
> WIEGERT: Then if you agree with making a statement, I need you to sign right there and if you wanna read it, you can read it there. (pause) Why don't you put your initials here and put your initials here. These are the two things I read to you. (pause) Ok, and I'm just going to put the place up here, Two Rivers Police Department, and the date is 2/27/06, and the time is approximately 3:21 p.m. OK. Let's put that over there for now. * * *

[Casefile Interrogation Transcripts Document 3, at 484.] Do you think Detective Wiegert secured a voluntary, knowing, and intelligent waiver from Dassey based on that exchange? What else could Detective Wiegert have done to ensure that Dassey did, in fact, understand *each* of his *Miranda* rights?

5.   Waiver and Dassey (part 2). Let's look at Dassey's *Miranda* waiver on March 1, 2006. Bring up the first March 1 interrogation file and follow along with the paper transcript. [*See* Casefile Interrogation Transcripts Document 4;

Casefile Interrogation Recordings Recording 4a.] The first thing you should notice in watching the video is that it does not match the first several pages of the transcript. That's because officers administered Dassey's *Miranda* warnings before turning on the video recorder. After providing Dassey with the warnings, Detective Wiegert asks, "I just got two questions to ask you from there: Do you know and understand each of these rights, your rights, which I have explained?" Dassey replies simply, "Yeah," before signing a waiver form at approximately 10:05 a.m. Is that sufficient for *Edwards* purposes?

The video turns on at 10:56 a.m. At that point, Detective Wiegert and Dassey have the following exchange:

> WIEGERT: Um, I just wanted to just, just go over this real quick again. Do you remember these rights, your *Miranda* Rights that I read to you? (Brendan nods "yes")
>
> BRENDAN: Yeah. (nods "yes")
>
> WIEGERT: Um, you still want to talk to us.
>
> BRENDAN: Yeah. (nods "yes")
>
> WIEGERT: OK. Just wanted to make sure of that. (Brendan nods "yes")

[Casefile Interrogation Transcripts Document 4, at 539.] Has Dassey, as a juvenile, validly waived his *Miranda* warnings under *Edwards*?

DAVIS V. UNITED STATES

512 U.S. 452
Supreme Court of the United States
March 29, 1994, Argued; June 24, 1994, Decided
No. 92-1949

JUSTICE O'CONNOR delivered the opinion of the Court.

In *Edwards v. Arizona*, 451 U.S. 477 (1981), we held that law enforcement officers must immediately cease questioning a suspect who has clearly asserted his right to have counsel present during custodial interrogation. In this case we decide how law enforcement officers should respond when a suspect makes a reference to counsel that is insufficiently clear to invoke the *Edwards* prohibition on further questioning.

I.

Pool brought trouble—not to River City, but to the Charleston Naval Base. Petitioner, a member of the United States Navy, spent the evening of October 2, 1988, shooting pool at a club on the base. Another sailor, Keith Shackleton, lost a game and a $30 wager to petitioner, but Shackleton refused to pay. After the club closed, Shackleton was beaten to death with a pool cue on a loading dock behind the commissary. The body was found early the next morning.

The investigation by the Naval Investigative Service (NIS) gradually focused on petitioner. Investigative agents determined that petitioner was at the club that evening, and that he was absent without authorization from his duty station the next morning. The agents also learned that only privately-owned pool cues could be removed from the club premises, and that petitioner owned two cues—one of which had a bloodstain on it. The agents were told by various people that petitioner either had admitted committing the crime or had recounted details that clearly indicated his involvement in the killing.

On November 4, 1988, petitioner was interviewed at the NIS office. As required by military law, the agents advised petitioner that he was a suspect in the killing, that he was not required to make a statement, that any statement could be used against him at a trial by court-martial, and that he was entitled to speak with an attorney and have an attorney present during questioning. Petitioner waived his rights to remain silent and to counsel, both orally and in writing.

About an hour and a half into the interview, petitioner said, "Maybe I should talk to a lawyer." According to the uncontradicted testimony of one of the interviewing agents, the interview then proceeded as follows:

> [We m]ade it very clear that we're not here to violate his rights, that if he wants a lawyer, then we will stop any kind of questioning with him, that we weren't going to pursue the matter unless we have it clarified is he asking for a lawyer or is he just making a comment about a lawyer, and he said, ["]No, I'm not asking for a lawyer," and then he continued on, and said, "No, I don't want a lawyer."

After a short break, the agents reminded petitioner of his rights to remain silent and to counsel. The interview then continued for another hour, until petitioner said, "I think I want a lawyer before I say anything else." At that point, questioning ceased.

At his general court-martial, petitioner moved to suppress statements made during the November 4 interview. The Military Judge denied the motion * * *. Petitioner was convicted on one specification of unpremeditated murder * * *. He was sentenced to confinement for life, a dishonorable discharge, forfeiture of all pay and allowances, and a reduction to the lowest pay grade. The convening authority approved the findings and sentence. The Navy-Marine Corps Court of Military Review affirmed.

The United States Court of Military Appeals granted discretionary review and affirmed. * * *

We granted certiorari * * *.

II.

* * * [W]e held in *Miranda v. Arizona*, that a suspect subject to custodial interrogation has the right to consult with an attorney and to have counsel present during questioning, and that the police must explain this right to him before questioning begins. * * *

The right to counsel recognized in *Miranda* is sufficiently important to suspects in criminal investigations, we have held, that it "requir[es] the special protection of the knowing and intelligent waiver standard." *Edwards v. Arizona*, 451 U.S. at 483. If the suspect effectively waives his right to counsel after receiving the *Miranda* warnings, law enforcement officers are free to question him. But if a suspect requests counsel at any time during the interview, he is not subject to further questioning until a lawyer has been made available or the suspect himself reinitiates conversation. *Edwards v. Arizona*, 451 U.S. at 484–485. This "second layer of prophylaxis for the *Miranda* right to counsel," is "designed to prevent police from badgering a defendant into waiving his previously asserted *Miranda* rights." To that end, we have held that a suspect who has invoked the right to counsel cannot be questioned regarding any offense unless an attorney is actually present. * * *

The applicability of the " 'rigid' prophylactic rule" of *Edwards* requires courts to "determine whether the accused *actually invoked* his right to counsel." (emphasis added). To avoid difficulties of proof and to provide guidance to officers conducting interrogations, this is an objective inquiry. Invocation of the *Miranda* right to counsel "requires, at a minimum, some statement that can reasonably be construed to be an expression of a desire for the assistance of an attorney." But if a suspect makes a reference to an attorney that is ambiguous or equivocal in that a reasonable officer in light of the circumstances would have understood only that the suspect might be invoking the right to counsel, our precedents do not require the cessation of questioning.

Rather, the suspect must unambiguously request counsel. As we have observed, "a statement either is such an assertion of the right to counsel or it is not." Although a suspect need not "speak with the discrimination of an Oxford don," he must articulate his desire to have counsel present sufficiently clearly that a reasonable police officer in the circumstances would understand the statement to be a request for an attorney. If the statement fails to meet the requisite level of clarity, *Edwards* does not require that the officers stop questioning the suspect.

We decline petitioner's invitation to extend *Edwards* and require law enforcement officers to cease questioning immediately upon the making of an ambiguous or equivocal reference to an attorney. The rationale underlying *Edwards* is that the police must respect a suspect's wishes regarding his right to have an attorney present during custodial interrogation. But when the officers conducting the questioning reasonably do not know whether or not the suspect wants a lawyer, a rule requiring the immediate cessation of questioning "would transform the *Miranda* safeguards into wholly irrational obstacles to legitimate police investigative activity," because it would needlessly prevent the police from questioning a suspect in the absence of counsel even if the suspect did not wish to have a lawyer present. Nothing in *Edwards* requires the provision of counsel to a suspect who consents to answer questions without the assistance of a lawyer. In *Miranda* itself, we expressly rejected the suggestion "that each police station must have a 'station house lawyer' present at all times to advise prisoners," and held instead that a suspect must be told of his right to have an attorney present and that he may not be questioned after invoking his right to counsel. We also noted that if a suspect is "indecisive in his request for counsel," the officers need not always cease questioning.

We recognize that requiring a clear assertion of the right to counsel might disadvantage some suspects who—because of fear, intimidation, lack of linguistic skills, or a variety of other reasons—will not clearly articulate their right to counsel although they actually want to have a lawyer present. But the primary protection afforded suspects subject to custodial interrogation is the *Miranda* warnings themselves. * * * A suspect who knowingly and voluntarily waives his right to counsel after having that right explained to him has indicated his willingness to deal with the police unassisted. Although *Edwards* provides an additional protection—if a suspect subsequently requests an attorney, questioning must cease—it is one that must be affirmatively invoked by the suspect.

* * * The *Edwards* rule—questioning must cease if the suspect asks for a lawyer—provides a bright line that can be applied by officers in the real world of investigation and interrogation without unduly hampering the gathering of information. But if we were to require questioning to cease if a suspect makes a statement that might be a request for an attorney, this clarity and ease of application would be lost. Police officers would be forced to make difficult judgment calls about whether the suspect in fact wants a lawyer even though he has not said so, with the threat of suppression if they guess wrong. We therefore hold that, after a knowing and voluntary waiver of the *Miranda* rights, law enforcement officers may continue questioning until and unless the suspect clearly requests an attorney.

Of course, when a suspect makes an ambiguous or equivocal statement it will often be good police practice for the interviewing officers to clarify whether or not he actually wants an attorney. That was the procedure followed by the NIS agents in this case. Clarifying questions help protect the rights of the suspect by ensuring that he gets an attorney if he wants one and will minimize the chance of a confession being suppressed due to subsequent judicial second-guessing as to the meaning of the suspect's statement regarding counsel. But we decline to adopt a rule requiring officers to ask clarifying questions. If the suspect's statement is not an unambiguous or unequivocal request for counsel, the officers have no obligation to stop questioning him. * * *

The courts below found that petitioner's remark to the NIS agents—"Maybe I should talk to a lawyer"—was not a request for counsel, and we see no reason to disturb that conclusion. The NIS agents therefore were not required to stop questioning petitioner, though it was entirely proper for them to clarify whether petitioner in fact wanted a lawyer. Because there is no ground for suppression of petitioner's statements, the judgment of the Court of Military Appeals is

Affirmed.

JUSTICE SCALIA, concurring.

[Omitted.]

JUSTICE SOUTER, with whom JUSTICE BLACKMUN, JUSTICE STEVENS, and JUSTICE GINSBURG join, concurring in the judgment.

[Omitted.]

QUESTIONS, COMMENTS, CONCERNS?

1.   **Interrogation room setup and the likelihood of invocation.** Let's consider the manner in which investigators setup the interrogation room on February 27, 2006. Open the February 27 stationhouse interrogation recording. [*See* Casefile Interrogation Recordings Recording 3.] Consider the room setup—Dassey is at the far end of the room. If he wanted to leave, he would need to pass by both officers to access the exit.

The setup of Dassey's interrogation room was likely no accident. The *Criminal Interrogation and Confessions* text, on which the Reid technique is based, dedicates an entire chapter to discussing how to setup an interrogation room. FRED E. INBAU ET AL., CRIMINAL INTERROGATION AND CONFESSIONS 43–53 (5th ed. 2013). In that chapter, investigators are advised to setup a private, soundproof room within the police station that is free from distractions and furnished sparsely with straight-backed chairs. The room should also be equipped with a one-way observation mirror so that other detectives can evaluate the suspect's "behavior symptoms." Doing so isolates the suspect and removes the suspect from any familiar surroundings.

Compare that description to the setup of Dassey's interrogation room. Look familiar? Do you think a suspect is more or less likely to invoke one of the *Miranda* rights in a room designed to raise the suspect's anxiety while incentivizing the suspect to extricate themself from the situation? Does that matter? But more specifically, how likely is a suspect like Dassey—a juvenile with limited intelligence—to invoke *Miranda* rights?

By the way, if you have any doubt about how important room setup is to interrogators, go back to the Holmes interrogation video and watch the first couple minutes as investigators reorganize where Holmes is sitting before they begin questioning him. [*See* Chapter 8 Holmes Casefile Video, beginning at 0:49–1:40.]

2. What counts as invocation? Think back for a moment to the Tsarnaev and Holmes casefiles in Chapter 8. The former wrote the word "lawyer" ten times in a notebook (because he was unable to speak due to his injuries) during his first hospital-based interrogation. Sometimes, Tsarnaev even circled the word. [Chapter 8 Tsarnaev Casefile Document 5, at 4.] Surely that counts as an invocation under *Davis*, right?

But what about Holmes? Recall that, as Detective Mehl read Holmes's *Miranda* warnings, Holmes asked, "How do I get a lawyer?" [Chapter 8 Holmes Casefile Video beginning at 5:18–5:23.] Mehl responded, "Well, we'll talk about that." *Id.* Holmes would later argue that, by asking how to get a lawyer, he "unambiguously asserted his right to counsel." [Chapter 8 Holmes Casefile Document 1, D-126 Motion, at 2.] Do you agree?

The judge resolving Holmes's motion to suppress didn't reach the issue because the prosecution never challenged the validity of Holmes's invocation. [Chapter 8 Holmes Casefile Document 4, Order on D-126, at 42 n.22.]

BERGHUIS V. THOMPKINS
560 U.S. 370
Supreme Court of the United States
March 1, 2010, Argued; June 1, 2010, Decided
No. 08-1470

JUSTICE KENNEDY delivered the opinion of the Court.

* * * The warden of a Michigan correctional facility is the petitioner here, and Van Chester Thompkins, who was convicted, is the respondent.

I.

A.

On January 10, 2000, a shooting occurred outside a mall in Southfield, Michigan. Among the victims was Samuel Morris, who died from multiple gunshot wounds. The other victim, Frederick France, recovered from his injuries and later testified. Thompkins, who was a suspect, fled. About one year later he was found in Ohio and arrested there.

Two Southfield police officers traveled to Ohio to interrogate Thompkins, then awaiting transfer to Michigan. The interrogation began around 1:30 p.m. and lasted about three hours. The interrogation was conducted in a room that was 8 by 10 feet, and Thompkins sat in a chair that resembled a school desk (it had an arm on it that swings around to provide a surface to write on). At the beginning of the interrogation, one of the officers, Detective Helgert, presented Thompkins with a form derived from the *Miranda* rule. It stated:

1.   You have the right to remain silent.

2.   Anything you say can and will be used against you in a court of law.

3.   You have a right to talk to a lawyer before answering any questions and you have the right to have a lawyer present with you while you are answering any questions.

4.   If you cannot afford to hire a lawyer, one will be appointed to represent you before any questioning, if you wish one.

5.   You have the right to decide at any time before or during questioning to use your right to remain silent and your right to talk with a lawyer while you are being questioned.

Helgert asked Thompkins to read the fifth warning out loud. Thompkins complied. Helgert later said this was to ensure that Thompkins could read, and Helgert concluded that Thompkins understood English. Helgert then read the other four *Miranda* warnings out loud and asked Thompkins to sign the form to demonstrate that he understood his rights. Thompkins declined to sign the form. The record contains conflicting evidence about whether Thompkins then verbally confirmed that he understood the rights listed on the form.

Officers began an interrogation. At no point during the interrogation did Thompkins say that he wanted to remain silent, that he did not want to talk with the police, or that he wanted an attorney. Thompkins was "[l]argely" silent during the interrogation, which lasted about three hours. He did give a few limited verbal responses, however, such as "yeah," "no," or "I don't know." And on occasion he communicated by nodding his head. Thompkins also said that he "didn't want a peppermint" that was offered to him by the police and that the chair he was "sitting in was hard."

About 2 hours and 45 minutes into the interrogation, Helgert asked Thompkins, "Do you believe in God?" Thompkins made eye contact with Helgert and said "Yes," as his eyes "well[ed] up with tears." Helgert asked, "Do you pray to God?" Thompkins said "Yes." Helgert asked, "Do you pray to God to forgive you for shooting that boy down?" Thompkins answered "Yes" and looked away. Thompkins refused to make a written confession, and the interrogation ended about 15 minutes later.

Thompkins was charged with first-degree murder, assault with intent to commit murder, and certain firearms-related offenses. He moved to suppress the statements made during the interrogation. He argued that he had invoked his Fifth Amendment right to remain silent, requiring police to end the interrogation at once, *see Michigan v. Mosley*, 423 U.S. 96, 103

(1975), that he had not waived his right to remain silent, and that his inculpatory statements were involuntary. The trial court denied the motion. * * * The jury found Thompkins guilty on all counts. He was sentenced to life in prison without parole.

B.

* * * Thompkins appealed * * * the trial court's refusal to suppress his pretrial statements under *Miranda*. The Michigan Court of Appeals rejected the *Miranda* claim, ruling that Thompkins had not invoked his right to remain silent and had waived it. * * * The Michigan Supreme Court denied discretionary review.

Thompkins filed a petition for a writ of habeas corpus in the United States District Court for the Eastern District of Michigan. The District Court rejected Thompkins's *Miranda* * * * claim[ ]. It noted that, under the Antiterrorism and Effective Death Penalty Act of 1996 (AEDPA), a federal court cannot grant a petition for a writ of habeas corpus unless the state court's adjudication of the merits was "contrary to, or involved an unreasonable application of, clearly established Federal law." The District Court reasoned that Thompkins did not invoke his right to remain silent and was not coerced into making statements during the interrogation. It held further that the Michigan Court of Appeals was not unreasonable in determining that Thompkins had waived his right to remain silent.

The United States Court of Appeals for the Sixth Circuit reversed * * *. The Court of Appeals ruled that the state court, in rejecting Thompkins's *Miranda* claim, unreasonably applied clearly established federal law and based its decision on an unreasonable determination of the facts. The Court of Appeals acknowledged that a waiver of the right to remain silent need not be express, as it can be " 'inferred from the actions and words of the person interrogated.' " The panel held, nevertheless, that the state court was unreasonable in finding an implied waiver in the circumstances here. The Court of Appeals found that the state court unreasonably determined the facts because "the evidence demonstrates that Thompkins was silent for two hours and forty-five minutes." According to the Court of Appeals, Thompkins's "persistent silence for nearly three hours in response to questioning and repeated invitations to tell his side of the story offered a clear and unequivocal message to the officers: Thompkins did not wish to waive his rights." * * *

We granted certiorari. * * *

II.

Under AEDPA, a federal court may not grant a habeas corpus application "with respect to any claim that was adjudicated on the merits in State court proceedings," unless the state court's decision "was contrary to, or involved an unreasonable application of, clearly established Federal law, as determined by the Supreme Court of the United States," or "was based on an unreasonable determination of the facts in light of the evidence presented in the State court proceeding." * * * The relevant state-court decision here is the Michigan Court of Appeals's decision affirming Thompkins's conviction and rejecting his *Miranda* and ineffective-assistance-of-counsel claims on the merits.

III. * * *

A.

Thompkins makes various arguments that his answers to questions from the detectives were inadmissible. He first contends that he "invoke[d] his privilege" to remain silent by not saying anything for a sufficient period of time, so the interrogation should have "cease[d]" before he made his inculpatory statements.

This argument is unpersuasive. In the context of invoking the *Miranda* right to counsel, the Court in *Davis v. United States*, 512 U.S. 452, 459 (1994), held that a suspect must do so "unambiguously." If an accused makes a statement concerning the right to counsel "that is ambiguous or equivocal" or makes no statement, the police are not required to end the interrogation, or ask questions to clarify whether the accused wants to invoke his or her *Miranda* rights.

The Court has not yet stated whether an invocation of the right to remain silent can be ambiguous or equivocal, but there is no principled reason to adopt different standards for determining when an accused has invoked the *Miranda* right to remain silent and the *Miranda* right to counsel at issue in *Davis*. Both protect the privilege against compulsory self-incrimination by requiring an interrogation to cease when either right is invoked.

There is good reason to require an accused who wants to invoke his or her right to remain silent to do so unambiguously. A requirement of an unambiguous invocation of *Miranda* rights results in an objective inquiry that "avoid[s] difficulties of proof and . . . provide[s] guidance to officers" on how to proceed in the face of ambiguity. *Davis*, 512 U.S., at 458–459. If an ambiguous act, omission, or statement could require police to end the interrogation, police would be required to make difficult decisions about an accused's unclear intent and face the consequence of suppression "if they guess wrong." Suppression of a voluntary confession in these circumstances would place a significant burden on society's interest in prosecuting criminal activity. Treating an ambiguous or equivocal act, omission, or statement as an invocation of *Miranda* rights "might add marginally to *Miranda*'s goal of dispelling the compulsion inherent in custodial interrogation." But "as *Miranda* holds, full comprehension of the rights to remain silent and request an attorney are sufficient to dispel whatever coercion is inherent in the interrogation process."

Thompkins did not say that he wanted to remain silent or that he did not want to talk with the police. Had he made either of these simple, unambiguous statements, he would have invoked his "right to cut off questioning." *Mosley*. Here he did neither, so he did not invoke his right to remain silent.

B.

We next consider whether Thompkins waived his right to remain silent. Even absent the accused's invocation of the right to remain silent, the accused's statement during a custodial interrogation is inadmissible at trial unless the prosecution can establish that the accused "in fact knowingly and voluntarily waived [*Miranda*] rights" when making the statement. The waiver inquiry "has two distinct dimensions": waiver must be "voluntary in the sense that it was the product of a free and deliberate choice rather than intimidation, coercion, or deception," and "made with a full awareness of both the nature of the right being abandoned and the consequences of the decision to abandon it."

Some language in *Miranda* could be read to indicate that waivers are difficult to establish absent an explicit written waiver or a formal, express oral statement. *Miranda* said, "a valid waiver will not be presumed simply from the silence of the accused after warnings are given or simply from the fact that a confession was in fact eventually obtained." In addition, the *Miranda* Court stated that "a heavy burden rests on the government to demonstrate that the defendant knowingly and intelligently waived his privilege against self-incrimination and his right to retained or appointed counsel."

The course of decisions since *Miranda*, informed by the application of *Miranda* warnings in the whole course of law enforcement, demonstrates that waivers can be established even absent formal or express statements of waiver that would be expected in, say, a judicial hearing to determine if a guilty plea has been properly entered. The main purpose of *Miranda* is to ensure that an accused is advised of and understands the right to remain silent and the right to counsel. * * *

One of the first cases to decide the meaning and import of *Miranda* with respect to the question of waiver was *North Carolina v. Butler*. The *Butler* Court, after discussing some of the problems created by the language in *Miranda*, established certain important propositions. *Butler* interpreted the *Miranda* language concerning the "heavy burden" to show waiver in accord with usual principles of determining waiver, which can include waiver implied from all the circumstances. And in a later case, the Court stated that this "heavy burden" is not more than the burden to establish waiver by a preponderance of the evidence.

The prosecution therefore does not need to show that a waiver of *Miranda* rights was express. An "implicit waiver" of the "right to remain silent" is sufficient to admit a suspect's statement into evidence. *Butler* made clear that a waiver of *Miranda* rights may be implied through "the defendant's silence, coupled with an understanding of his rights and a course of conduct indicating waiver." The Court in *Butler* therefore "retreated" from the "language and tenor of the *Miranda* opinion," which "suggested that the Court would require that a waiver . . . be 'specifically made.'"

If the State establishes that a *Miranda* warning was given and the accused made an uncoerced statement, this showing, standing alone, is insufficient to demonstrate "a valid waiver" of *Miranda* rights. The prosecution must make the additional showing that the accused understood these rights. Where the prosecution shows that a *Miranda* warning was given and that it was understood by the accused, an accused's uncoerced statement establishes an implied waiver of the right to remain silent. * * *

The record in this case shows that Thompkins waived his right to remain silent. There is no basis in this case to conclude that he did not understand his rights; and on these facts it follows that he chose not to invoke or rely on those rights when he did speak. First, there is no contention that Thompkins did not understand his rights; and from this it follows that he knew what he gave up when he spoke. There was more than enough evidence in the record to conclude that Thompkins understood his *Miranda* rights. Thompkins received a written copy of the *Miranda* warnings; Detective Helgert determined that Thompkins could read and understand English; and Thompkins was given time to read the warnings. Thompkins, furthermore, read aloud the fifth warning, which stated that "you have the right to decide at any time before or during questioning to use your right to remain silent and your right to talk with a lawyer while you are being questioned." He was thus aware that his right to remain silent would not dissipate after a certain amount of time and that police would have to honor his right to be silent and his right to counsel during the whole course of interrogation. Those rights, the warning made clear, could be asserted at any time. Helgert, moreover, read the warnings aloud.

Second, Thompkins's answer to Detective Helgert's question about whether Thompkins prayed to God for forgiveness for shooting the victim is a "course of conduct indicating waiver" of the right to remain silent. If Thompkins wanted to remain silent, he could have said nothing in response to Helgert's questions, or he could have unambiguously invoked his *Miranda* rights and ended the interrogation. The fact that Thompkins made a statement about three hours after receiving a *Miranda* warning does not overcome the fact that he engaged in a course of conduct indicating waiver. Police are not required to rewarn suspects from time to time. Thompkins's answer to Helgert's question about praying to God for forgiveness for shooting the victim was sufficient to show a course of conduct indicating waiver. This is confirmed by the fact that before then Thompkins had given sporadic answers to questions throughout the interrogation.

Third, there is no evidence that Thompkins's statement was coerced. Thompkins does not claim that police threatened or injured him during the interrogation or that he was in any way fearful. The interrogation was conducted in a standard-sized room in the middle of the afternoon. It is true that, apparently, he was in a straight-backed chair for three hours, but there is no authority for the proposition that an interrogation of this length is inherently coercive. Indeed, even where interrogations of greater duration were held to be improper, they were accompanied, as this one was not, by other facts indicating coercion, such as an incapacitated and sedated suspect, sleep and food deprivation, and threats. The fact that Helgert's question referred to Thompkins's religious beliefs also did not render Thompkins's statement involuntary. * * * In these circumstances, Thompkins knowingly and voluntarily made a statement to police, so he waived his right to remain silent.

C.

Thompkins next argues that, even if his answer to Detective Helgert could constitute a waiver of his right to remain silent, the police were not allowed to question him until they obtained a waiver first. *Butler* forecloses this argument. The *Butler* Court held that courts can infer a waiver of *Miranda* rights "from the actions and words of the person interrogated." This principle would be inconsistent with a rule that requires a waiver at the outset. The *Butler* Court thus rejected the rule proposed by the *Butler* dissent, which would have "requir[ed] the police to obtain an express waiver of [*Miranda* rights] before proceeding with interrogation." This holding also makes sense given that "the primary protection afforded suspects subject[ed] to custodial interrogation is the *Miranda* warnings themselves." The *Miranda* rule and its requirements are met if a suspect receives adequate *Miranda* warnings, understands them, and has an opportunity to invoke the rights before giving any answers or admissions. Any waiver, express or implied, may be contradicted by an invocation at any time. If the right to counsel or the right to remain silent is invoked at any point during questioning, further interrogation must cease. * * *

In order for an accused's statement to be admissible at trial, police must have given the accused a *Miranda* warning. If that condition is established, the court can proceed to consider whether there has been an express or implied waiver of *Miranda* rights. In making its ruling on the admissibility of a statement made during custodial questioning, the trial court, of course, considers whether there is evidence to support the conclusion that, from the whole course of questioning, an express or implied waiver has been established. Thus, after giving a *Miranda* warning, police may interrogate a suspect who has neither invoked nor waived his or her *Miranda* rights. On these premises, it follows the police were not required to obtain a waiver of Thompkins's *Miranda* rights before commencing the interrogation.

D.

In sum, a suspect who has received and understood the *Miranda* warnings, and has not invoked his *Miranda* rights, waives the right to remain silent by making an uncoerced statement to the police. Thompkins did not invoke his right to remain silent and stop the questioning. Understanding his rights in full, he waived his right to remain silent by making a voluntary statement to the police. The police, moreover, were not required to obtain a waiver of Thompkins's right to remain silent before interrogating him. The state court's decision rejecting Thompkins's *Miranda* claim was thus correct under de novo review and therefore necessarily reasonable under the more deferential AEDPA standard of review. * * *

The judgment of the Court of Appeals is reversed, and the case is remanded with instructions to deny the petition.

It is so ordered.

JUSTICE SOTOMAYOR, with whom JUSTICE STEVENS, JUSTICE GINSBURG, and JUSTICE BREYER join, dissenting. * * *

The Court concludes today that a criminal suspect waives his right to remain silent if, after sitting tacit and uncommunicative through nearly three hours of police interrogation, he utters a few one-word responses. The Court also concludes that a suspect who wishes to guard his right to remain silent against such a finding of "waiver" must, counterintuitively, speak—and must do so with sufficient precision to satisfy a clear-statement rule that construes ambiguity in favor of the police. Both propositions mark a substantial retreat from the protection against compelled self-incrimination that *Miranda v. Arizona*, 384 U.S. 436 (1966), has long provided during custodial interrogation. * * *

I.   * * *

The strength of Thompkins's *Miranda* claims depends in large part on the circumstances of the 3-hour interrogation, at the end of which he made inculpatory statements later introduced at trial. The Court's opinion downplays record evidence that Thompkins remained almost completely silent and unresponsive throughout that session. One of the interrogating officers, Detective Helgert, testified that although Thompkins was administered *Miranda* warnings, the last of which he read aloud, Thompkins expressly declined to sign a written acknowledgment that he had been advised of and understood his rights. There is conflicting evidence in the record about whether Thompkins ever verbally confirmed understanding his rights. The record contains no indication that the officers sought or obtained an express waiver.

As to the interrogation itself, Helgert candidly characterized it as "very, very one-sided" and "nearly a monologue." Thompkins was "[p]eculiar," "[s]ullen," and "[g]enerally quiet." Helgert and his partner "did most of the talking," as Thompkins was "not verbally communicative" and "[l]argely" remained silent. To the extent Thompkins gave any response, his answers consisted of "a word or two. A 'yeah,' or a 'no,' or 'I don't know'. . .And sometimes. . .he simply sat down. . .with [his] head in [his] hands looking down. Sometimes. . .he would look up and make eye-contact would be the only response." After proceeding in this fashion for approximately 2 hours and 45 minutes, Helgert asked Thompkins three questions relating to his faith in God. The prosecution relied at trial on Thompkins's one-word answers of "yes."

Thompkins's nonresponsiveness is particularly striking in the context of the officers' interview strategy, later explained as conveying to Thompkins that "this was his opportunity to explain his side [of the story]" because "[e]verybody else, including [his] co-[d]efendants, had given their version," and asking him "[w]ho is going to speak up for you if you don't speak up for yourself?" Yet, Helgert confirmed that the *only* thing [Thompkins said] relative to his involvement [in the shooting]" occurred near the end of the interview—i.e., in response to the questions about God. (emphasis added). The only other responses Helgert could remember Thompkins giving were that "[h]e didn't want a peppermint" and "the chair that he was sitting in was hard." * * *

* * * It is undisputed here that Thompkins never expressly waived his right to remain silent. His refusal to sign even an acknowledgment that he understood his *Miranda* rights evinces, if anything, an intent not to waive those rights. That Thompkins did not make the inculpatory statements at issue until after approximately 2 hours and 45 minutes of interrogation serves as "strong evidence" against waiver. *Miranda* and *Butler* expressly preclude the possibility that the inculpatory statements themselves are sufficient to establish waiver.

In these circumstances, Thompkins's "actions and words" preceding the inculpatory statements simply do not evidence a "course of conduct indicating waiver" sufficient to carry the prosecution's burden. * * * I believe it is objectively unreasonable under our clearly established precedents to conclude the prosecution met its "heavy burden" of proof on a record consisting of three one-word answers, following 2 hours and 45 minutes of silence punctuated by a few largely nonverbal responses to unidentified questions.

II. * * *

B.

Perhaps because our prior *Miranda* precedents so clearly favor Thompkins, the Court today goes beyond AEDPA's deferential standard of review and announces a new general principle of law. Any new rule, it must be emphasized, is unnecessary to the disposition of this case. * * *

Today's dilution of the prosecution's burden of proof to the bare fact that a suspect made inculpatory statements after *Miranda* warnings were given and understood takes an unprecedented step away from the "high standards of proof for the waiver of constitutional rights" this Court has long demanded. When waiver is to be inferred during a custodial interrogation, there are sound reasons to require evidence beyond inculpatory statements themselves. *Miranda* and our subsequent cases are premised on the idea that custodial interrogation is inherently coercive. Requiring proof of a course of conduct beyond the inculpatory statements themselves is critical to ensuring that those statements are voluntary admissions and not the dubious product of an overborne will.

Today's decision thus ignores the important interests *Miranda* safeguards. * * *

III.

Thompkins separately argues that his conduct during the interrogation invoked his right to remain silent, requiring police to terminate questioning. * * * I cannot agree with the Court's much broader ruling that a suspect must clearly invoke his right to silence by speaking. Taken together with the Court's reformulation of the prosecution's burden of proof as to waiver, today's novel clear-statement rule for invocation invites police to question a suspect at length—notwithstanding his persistent refusal to answer questions—in the hope of eventually obtaining a single inculpatory response which will suffice to prove waiver of rights. Such a result bears little semblance to the "fully effective" prophylaxis that *Miranda* requires. * * *

B.

The Court * * * extend[s] *Davis* to hold that police may continue questioning a suspect until he unambiguously invokes his right to remain silent. Because Thompkins neither said "he wanted to remain silent" nor said "he did not want to talk with the police," the Court concludes, he did not clearly invoke his right to silence.

I disagree with this novel application of *Davis*. Neither the rationale nor holding of that case compels today's result. *Davis* involved the right to counsel, not the right to silence. The Court in *Davis* reasoned that extending *Edwards'* "rigid" prophylactic rule to ambiguous requests for a lawyer would transform *Miranda* into a "wholly irrational obstacl[e] to legitimate police investigative activity" by "needlessly prevent[ing] the police from questioning a suspect in the absence of counsel even if [he] did not wish to have a lawyer present." *Davis, supra*, at 460. But *Miranda* itself "distinguished between the procedural safeguards triggered by a request to remain silent and a request for an attorney." *Mosley*, 423 U.S., at 104, n.10. *Mosley* upheld the admission of statements when police immediately stopped interrogating a suspect who invoked his right to silence, but reapproached him after a 2-hour delay and obtained inculpatory responses relating to a different crime after administering fresh *Miranda* warnings. The different effects of invoking the rights are consistent with distinct standards for invocation. To the extent *Mosley* contemplates a more flexible form of prophylaxis than *Edwards*—and, in particular, does not categorically bar police from reapproaching a suspect who has invoked his right to remain silent—*Davis's* concern about "wholly irrational obstacles" to police investigation applies with less force.

In addition, the suspect's equivocal reference to a lawyer in *Davis* occurred only after he had given express oral and written waivers of his rights. *Davis's* holding is explicitly predicated on that fact. The Court ignores this aspect of *Davis*, as well as the decisions of numerous federal and state courts declining to apply a clear-statement rule when a suspect has not previously given an express waiver of rights.

In my mind, a more appropriate standard for addressing a suspect's ambiguous invocation of the right to remain silent is the constraint *Mosley* places on questioning a suspect who has invoked that right: The suspect's "right to cut off questioning" must be "scrupulously honored." Such a standard is necessarily precautionary and fact specific. The rule would acknowledge that some statements or conduct are so equivocal that police may scrupulously honor a suspect's rights without terminating questioning—for instance, if a suspect's actions are reasonably understood to indicate a willingness to listen before deciding whether to respond. But other statements or actions—in particular, when a suspect sits silent throughout prolonged interrogation, long past the point when he could be deciding whether to respond—cannot reasonably be understood other than as an invocation of the right to remain silent. Under such circumstances, "scrupulous" respect for the suspect's rights will require police to terminate questioning under *Mosley*.

To be sure, such a standard does not provide police with a bright-line rule. But, as we have previously recognized, *Mosley* itself does not offer clear guidance to police about when and how interrogation may continue after a suspect invokes his rights. Given that police have for nearly 35 years applied *Mosley's* fact-specific standard in questioning suspects who have invoked their right to remain silent; that our cases did not during that time resolve what statements or actions suffice to invoke that right; and that neither Michigan nor the Solicitor General has provided evidence in this case that the status quo has proved unworkable, I see little reason to believe today's clear-statement rule is necessary to ensure effective law enforcement.

Davis's clear-statement rule is also a poor fit for the right to silence. Advising a suspect that he has a "right to remain silent" is unlikely to convey that he must speak (and must do so in some particular fashion) to ensure the right will be protected. By contrast, telling a suspect "he has the right to the presence of an attorney, and that if he cannot afford an attorney one will be appointed for him prior to any questioning if he so desires," *Miranda*, 384 U.S. at 479, implies the need for speech to exercise that right. *Davis's* requirement that a suspect must "clearly reques[t] an attorney" to terminate questioning thus aligns with a suspect's likely understanding of the *Miranda* warnings in a way today's rule does not. The Court suggests Thompkins could have employed the "simple, unambiguous" means of saying "he wanted to remain silent" or "did not want to talk with the police." But the *Miranda* warnings give no hint that a suspect should use those magic words, and there is little reason to believe police—who have ample incentives to avoid invocation—will provide such guidance.

Conversely, the Court's concern that police will face "difficult decisions about an accused's unclear intent" and suffer the consequences of "guess[ing] wrong," is misplaced. If a suspect makes an ambiguous statement or engages in conduct that creates uncertainty about his intent to invoke his right, police can simply ask for clarification. It is hardly an unreasonable burden for police to ask a suspect, for instance, "Do you want to talk to us?" The majority in *Davis* itself approved of this approach as protecting suspects' rights while "minimiz[ing] the chance of a confession [later] being suppressed." Given this straightforward mechanism by which police can "scrupulously hono[r]" a suspect's right to silence, today's clear-statement rule can only be seen as accepting "as tolerable the certainty that some poorly expressed requests [to remain silent] will be disregarded," without any countervailing benefit. Police may well prefer not to seek clarification of an ambiguous statement out of fear that a suspect will invoke his rights. But "our system of justice is not founded on a fear that a suspect will exercise his rights. 'If the exercise of constitutional rights will thwart the effectiveness of a system of law enforcement, then there is something very wrong with that system.' " * * *

For these reasons, I believe a precautionary requirement that police "scrupulously hono[r]" a suspect's right to cut off questioning is a more faithful application of our precedents than the Court's awkward and needless extension of *Davis*. * * *

I respectfully dissent.

QUESTIONS, COMMENTS, CONCERNS?

1.   **Holmes and post-arrest silence.** Return to the Holmes casefile once more. Following Holmes's arrest outside the movie theater, officers asked him several times whether anyone else was there helping him. He did not reply with a verbal response to one of the officers. In one of his motions to suppress, Holmes contends that his responses constituted "post-arrest silence." [Chapter 8 Holmes Casefile Document 1, D-125 Motion, at 2.] Would that non-response be sufficient under *Berghuis* to invoke Holmes's *Miranda* right to silence?

2.   ***Miranda* 2.0.** After reading the *Miranda* waiver and invocation cases, do you think that the classic *Miranda* warnings capture the modern Court's concerns? That is, do you think officers should have to update the warnings to tell a suspect that affirmative invocation is required to utilize a *Miranda* right? And on the subject of waiver, is it sufficient for law enforcement to obtain a general waiver of *Miranda*—as the officers did twice in Dassey's case. Or instead, should officers obtain independent waivers for each individual *Miranda* right?

3.   **The Fifth Amendment as a separate interrogation room protection?** In *Salinas v. Texas*, 570 U.S. 178 (2013), the Supreme Court considered whether the Fifth Amendment's privilege against self-incrimination—*Miranda* aside—could offer additional constitutional protection to a suspect in the interrogation room.

On the morning of December 18, 1992, two brothers were shot and killed in their Houston home. During the ensuing investigation, police recovered six shotgun shells at the scene and began to suspect petitioner. Investigators visited petitioner at his home. He agreed to submit his shotgun to investigators for ballistics testing and to accompany police to the station for questioning. Police questioned petitioner in a noncustodial setting for one hour without giving him *Miranda* warnings. For the most part, petitioner answered the officer's questions. When police asked if his weapon "would match the shells recovered at the scene of the murder," petitioner did not answer. Rather, he "[l]ooked down at the floor, shuffled his feet, bit his bottom lip, cl[e]nched his hands in his lap, [and] began to tighten up." The officer later asked additional questions, which petitioner answered.

Petitioner was charged with the double-murder, and prosecutors used his silence in response to the officer's question during the noncustodial interview as evidence of guilt. The jury found petitioner guilty. Before the Supreme Court, petitioner argued that use of his silence as evidence of guilt violated the Fifth Amendment (not *Miranda*). A plurality of the Supreme Court held that petitioner's silence was properly admitted against him, reasoning that a witness cannot invoke the Fifth Amendment's privilege against self-incrimination "by simply standing mute."

Justices Thomas wrote a concurring opinion, which Justice Scalia joined, making clear that, in his view, petitioner's "claim would fail even if he had invoked the privilege because the prosecutor's comments regarding his precustodial silence did not compel him to give self-incriminating testimony."

On some level, *Salinas* is intriguing because it leaves open the prospect that the Fifth Amendment's privilege against self-incrimination *might*, in certain circumstances, offer a suspect a constitutional protection before *Miranda* attaches. But as Justice Breyer asked in dissent, "[D]oes it really mean that the suspect must use the exact words 'Fifth Amendment'? How can an individual who is not a lawyer know that these particular words are legally magic?"

III. (RE)INITIATION

In this next pair of cases, we consider so-called "re-initiation" fact patterns. The facts are typically straightforward: the suspect invokes the *Miranda* right to silence or the *Miranda* right to counsel; the suspect or police later re-initiate questioning; and, during the re-initiated encounter, the suspect makes an incriminating statement. Analytically, these fact patterns raise two questions.

First, did the suspect or police reinitiate the encounter? That matters because, as you will recall, the right to silence is crime specific, but the right to counsel is not. Accordingly, there are some right to silence re-initiation fact patterns where police-based re-initiation is constitutionally permissible, but there are *no* permissible police-based re-initiation fact patterns in the right to counsel context. For right to counsel re-initiation fact patterns, only the suspect can reinitiate the interrogation. Second, assuming re-initiation was proper, did the suspect voluntarily, knowingly, and intelligently waive *Miranda* (think, *Edwards*) before making an incriminating statement?

This short block of cases pertains to the first question. Our first case, *Oregon v. Bradshaw*, defines what constitutes re-initiation. Our second case, *Maryland v. Shatzer*, evaluates whether police are *forever* barred from re-approaching a suspect who invokes the *Miranda* right to counsel or, instead, whether there is some leeway. Disclaimer: *Shatzer*, along with its answer, is an oddity.

OREGON V. BRADSHAW
462 U.S. 1039
Supreme Court of the United States
March 28, 1983, Argued; June 23, 1983, Decided
No. 81-1857

JUSTICE REHNQUIST announced the judgment of the Court and delivered an opinion, in which THE CHIEF JUSTICE, JUSTICE WHITE, and JUSTICE O'CONNOR joined.

After a bench trial in an Oregon trial court, respondent James Edward Bradshaw was convicted of the offenses of first-degree manslaughter, driving while under the influence of intoxicants, and driving while his license was revoked. The Oregon Court of Appeals reversed his conviction, holding that an inquiry he made of a police officer at the time he was in custody did not "initiate" a conversation with the officer, and that therefore statements by the respondent growing out of that conversation should have been excluded from evidence under *Edwards v. Arizona*, 451 U.S. 477 (1981). We granted certiorari to review this determination.

In September 1980, Oregon police were investigating the death of one Lowell Reynolds in Tillamook County. Reynolds' body had been found in his wrecked pickup truck, in which he appeared to have been a passenger at the time the vehicle left the roadway, struck a tree and an embankment, and finally came to rest on its side in a shallow creek. Reynolds had died from traumatic injury, coupled with asphyxia by drowning. During the investigation of Reynolds's death, respondent was asked to accompany a police officer to the Rockaway Police Station for questioning.

Once at the station, respondent was advised of his rights as required by *Miranda v. Arizona*, 384 U.S. 436 (1966). Respondent then repeated to the police his earlier account of the events of the evening of Reynolds's death, admitting that he had provided Reynolds and others with liquor for a party at Reynolds's house, but denying involvement in the traffic accident that apparently killed Reynolds. Respondent suggested that Reynolds might have met with foul play at the hands of the assailant whom respondent alleged had struck him at the party.

At this point, respondent was placed under arrest for furnishing liquor to Reynolds, a minor, and again advised of his *Miranda* rights. A police officer then told respondent the officer's theory of how the traffic accident that killed Reynolds occurred; a theory which placed respondent behind the wheel of the vehicle. Respondent again denied his involvement and said, "I do want an attorney before it goes very much further." The officer immediately terminated the conversation.

Sometime later respondent was transferred from the Rockaway Police Station to the Tillamook County Jail, a distance of some 10 or 15 miles. Either just before, or during, his trip from Rockaway to Tillamook, respondent inquired of a police officer, "Well, what is going to happen to me now?" The officer answered by saying, "You do not have to talk to me. You have requested an attorney and I don't want you talking to me unless you so desire because anything you say—because—since you have requested an attorney, you know, it has to be at your own free will." Respondent said he understood. There followed a discussion between respondent and the officer concerning where respondent was being taken and the offense with which he would be charged. The officer suggested that respondent might help himself by taking a polygraph examination. Respondent agreed to take such an examination, saying that he was willing to do whatever he could to clear up the matter.

The next day, following another reading to respondent of his *Miranda* rights, and respondent's signing a written waiver of those rights, the polygraph was administered. At its conclusion, the examiner told respondent that he did not believe respondent was telling the truth. Respondent then recanted his earlier story, admitting that he had been at the wheel of the vehicle in which Reynolds was killed, that he had consumed a considerable amount of alcohol, and that he had passed out at the wheel before the vehicle left the roadway and came to rest in the creek.

Respondent was charged with first-degree manslaughter, driving while under the influence of intoxicants, and driving while his license was revoked. His motion to suppress the statements described above was denied, and he was found guilty after a bench trial. The Oregon Court of Appeals, relying on our decision in *Edwards v. Arizona, supra,* reversed, concluding that the statements had been obtained in violation of respondent's Fifth Amendment rights. We now conclude that the Oregon Court of Appeals misapplied our decision in *Edwards.* * * *

Respondent's question in the present case, "Well, what is going to happen to me now?", admittedly was asked prior to respondent's being "[subjected] to further interrogation by the authorities." The Oregon Court of Appeals stated that it did not "construe defendant's question about what was going to happen to him to have been a waiver of his right to counsel, invoked only minutes before. . ." The Court of Appeals, after quoting relevant language from *Edwards,* concluded that "under the reasoning enunciated in *Edwards,* defendant did not make a valid waiver of his Fifth Amendment rights, and his statements were inadmissible."

We think the Oregon Court of Appeals misapprehended the test laid down in *Edwards.* We did not there hold that the "initiation" of a conversation by a defendant such as respondent would amount to a waiver of a previously invoked right to counsel; we held that after the right to counsel had been asserted by an accused, further interrogation of the accused should not take place "unless the accused himself initiates further communication, exchanges, or conversations with the police." This was in effect a prophylactic rule, designed to protect an accused in police custody from being badgered by police officers in the manner in which the defendant in *Edwards* was. We recently restated the requirement in *Wyrick v. Fields,* 459 U.S. 42, 46 (1982) (per curiam), to be that before a suspect in custody can be subjected to further interrogation after he requests an attorney there must be a showing that the "suspect himself initiates dialogue with the authorities."

But even if a conversation taking place after the accused has "expressed his desire to deal with the police only through counsel," is initiated by the accused, where reinterrogation follows, the burden remains upon the prosecution to show that subsequent events indicated a waiver of the Fifth Amendment right to have counsel present during the interrogation. * * *

Thus, the Oregon Court of Appeals was wrong in thinking that an "initiation" of a conversation or discussion by an accused not only satisfied the *Edwards* rule, but *ex proprio vigore* sufficed to show a waiver of the previously asserted right to counsel. The inquiries are separate, and clarity of application is not gained by melding them together.

There can be no doubt in this case that in asking, "Well, what is going to happen to me now?", respondent "initiated" further conversation in the ordinary dictionary sense of that word. While we doubt that it would be desirable to build a superstructure of legal refinements around the word "initiate" in this context, there are undoubtedly situations where a bare inquiry by either a defendant or by a police officer should not be held to "initiate" any conversation or dialogue. There are some inquiries, such as a request for a drink of water or a request to use a telephone, that are so routine that they cannot be fairly said to represent a desire on the part of an accused to open up a more generalized discussion relating directly or indirectly to the investigation. Such inquiries or statements, by either an accused or a police officer, relating to routine incidents of the custodial relationship, will not generally "initiate" a conversation in the sense in which that word was used in *Edwards*.

Although ambiguous, the respondent's question in this case as to what was going to happen to him evinced a willingness and a desire for a generalized discussion about the investigation; it was not merely a necessary inquiry arising out of the incidents of the custodial relationship. It could reasonably have been interpreted by the officer as relating generally to the investigation. That the police officer so understood it is apparent from the fact that he immediately reminded the accused that "[you] do not have to talk to me," and only after the accused told him that he "understood" did they have a generalized conversation. On these facts we believe that there was not a violation of the *Edwards* rule.

Since there was no violation of the *Edwards* rule in this case, the next inquiry was "whether a valid waiver of the right to counsel and the right to silence had occurred, that is, whether the purported waiver was knowing and intelligent and found to be so under the totality of the circumstances, including the necessary fact that the accused, not the police, reopened the dialogue with the authorities." *Edwards v. Arizona*, 451 U.S., at 486, n.9. As we have said many times before, this determination depends upon "the particular facts and circumstances surrounding [the] case, including the background, experience, and conduct of the accused."

The state trial court made this inquiry and, in the words of the Oregon Court of Appeals, "found that the police made no threats, promises or inducements to talk, that defendant was properly advised of his rights and understood them and that within a short time after requesting an attorney he changed his mind without any impropriety on the part of the police. The court held that the statements made to the polygraph examiner were voluntary and the result of a knowing waiver of his right to remain silent."

We have no reason to dispute these conclusions, based as they are upon the trial court's firsthand observation of the witnesses to the events involved. The judgment of the Oregon Court of Appeals is therefore reversed, and the cause is remanded for further proceedings.

It is so ordered.

JUSTICE POWELL, concurring in the judgment.

[Omitted.]

JUSTICE MARSHALL, with whom JUSTICE BRENNAN, JUSTICE BLACKMUN, and JUSTICE STEVENS join, dissenting.

Because in my view the plurality has misapplied *Edwards v. Arizona*, 451 U.S. 477 (1981), I respectfully dissent.

I.

* * * In this case, respondent invoked his right to have counsel during custodial interrogation. Shortly thereafter, he asked a police officer, "Well, what is going to happen to me now?" The Oregon Court of Appeals concluded that respondent's question was not "a waiver of his right to counsel, invoked only minutes before, or anything other than a normal reaction to being taken from the police station and placed in a police car, obviously for transport to some destination." Relying on *Edwards*, the Oregon court held that respondent had not initiated the subsequent interrogation.

The Oregon Court of Appeals properly applied *Edwards*. When this Court in *Edwards* spoke of "[initiating] further communication" with the police and "[reopening] the dialogue with the authorities," it obviously had in mind communication or dialogue about the subject matter of the criminal investigation. The rule announced in *Edwards* was designed to ensure that any interrogation subsequent to an invocation of the right to counsel be at the instance of the accused, not the authorities. Thus, a question or statement which does not invite further interrogation before an attorney is present cannot qualify as "initiation" under *Edwards*. To hold otherwise would drastically undermine the safeguards that *Miranda* and

Edwards carefully erected around the right to counsel in the custodial setting.

The safeguards identified in *Edwards* hardly pose an insurmountable obstacle to an accused who truly wishes to waive his rights after invoking his right to counsel. A waiver can be established, however, only when the accused himself reopens the dialogue about the subject matter of the criminal investigation. Since our decision in *Edwards*, the lower courts have had no difficulty in identifying such situations.

II.

I agree with the plurality that, in order to constitute "initiation" under *Edwards*, an accused's inquiry must demonstrate a desire to discuss the subject matter of the criminal investigation. I am baffled, however, at the plurality's application of that standard to the facts of this case. The plurality asserts that respondent's question, "[What] is going to happen to me now?", evinced both "a willingness and a desire for a generalized discussion about the investigation." If respondent's question had been posed by Jean-Paul Sartre before a class of philosophy students, it might well have evinced a desire for a "generalized" discussion. But under the circumstances of this case, it is plain that respondent's only "desire" was to find out where the police were going to take him. * * *

To hold that respondent's question in this case opened a dialogue with the authorities flies in the face of the basic purpose of the *Miranda* safeguards. When someone in custody asks, "What is going to happen to me now?", he is surely responding to his custodial surroundings. The very essence of custody is the loss of control over one's freedom of movement. The authorities exercise virtually unfettered control over the accused. To allow the authorities to recommence an interrogation based on such a question is to permit them to capitalize on the custodial setting. Yet *Miranda*'s procedural protections were adopted precisely in order "to dispel the compulsion inherent in custodial surroundings."

Accordingly, I dissent.

MARYLAND V. SHATZER

559 U.S. 98
Supreme Court of the United States
October 5, 2009, Argued; February 24, 2010, Decided
No. 08-680

JUSTICE SCALIA delivered the opinion of the Court.

We consider whether a break in custody ends the presumption of involuntariness established in *Edwards v. Arizona*, 451 U.S. 477, 101 S. Ct. 1880, 68 L. Ed. 2d 378 (1981).

I.

In August 2003, a social worker assigned to the Child Advocacy Center in the Criminal Investigation Division of the Hagerstown Police Department referred to the department allegations that respondent Michael Shatzer, Sr., had sexually abused his 3-year-old son. At that time, Shatzer was incarcerated at the Maryland Correctional Institution-Hagerstown, serving a sentence for an unrelated child-sexual-abuse offense. Detective Shane Blankenship was assigned to the investigation and interviewed Shatzer at the correctional institution on August 7, 2003. Before asking any questions, Blankenship reviewed Shatzer's *Miranda* rights with him and obtained a written waiver of those rights. When Blankenship explained that he was there to question Shatzer about sexually abusing his son, Shatzer expressed confusion—he had thought Blankenship was an attorney there to discuss the prior crime for which he was incarcerated. Blankenship clarified the purpose of his visit, and Shatzer declined to speak without an attorney. Accordingly, Blankenship ended the interview, and Shatzer was released back into the general prison population. Shortly thereafter, Blankenship closed the investigation.

Two years and six months later, the same social worker referred more specific allegations to the department about the same incident involving Shatzer. Detective Paul Hoover, from the same division, was assigned to the investigation. He and the social worker interviewed the victim, then eight years old, who described the incident in more detail. With this new information in hand, on March 2, 2006, they went to the Roxbury Correctional Institute, to which Shatzer had since been transferred, and interviewed Shatzer in a maintenance room outfitted with a desk and three chairs. Hoover explained that he wanted to ask Shatzer about the alleged incident involving Shatzer's son. Shatzer was surprised because he thought that the investigation had been closed, but Hoover explained they had opened a new file. Hoover then read Shatzer his *Miranda* rights and obtained a written waiver on a standard department form.

Hoover interrogated Shatzer about the incident for approximately 30 minutes. Shatzer denied ordering his son to perform fellatio on him but admitted to masturbating in front of his son from a distance of less than three feet. Before the interview ended, Shatzer agreed to Hoover's request that he submit to a polygraph examination. At no point during the interrogation did Shatzer request to speak with an attorney or refer to his prior refusal to answer questions without one.

Five days later, on March 7, 2006, Hoover and another detective met with Shatzer at the correctional facility to administer the polygraph examination. After reading Shatzer his *Miranda* rights and obtaining a written waiver, the other detective administered the test and concluded that Shatzer had failed. When the detectives then questioned Shatzer, he became upset, started to cry, and incriminated himself by saying, "I didn't force him. I didn't force him." After making this inculpatory statement, Shatzer requested an attorney, and Hoover promptly ended the interrogation.

The State's Attorney for Washington County charged Shatzer with second-degree sexual offense, sexual child abuse, second-degree assault, and contributing to conditions rendering a child in need of assistance. Shatzer moved to suppress his March 2006 statements pursuant to *Edwards*. The trial court held a suppression hearing and later denied Shatzer's motion. The *Edwards* protections did not apply, it reasoned, because Shatzer had experienced a break in custody for *Miranda* purposes between the 2003 and 2006 interrogations. Shatzer pleaded not guilty, waived his right to a jury trial, and proceeded to a bench trial based on an agreed statement of facts. In accordance with the agreement, the State described the interview with the victim and Shatzer's 2006 statements to the detectives. Based on the proffered testimony of the victim and the "admission of the defendant as to the act of masturbation," the trial court found Shatzer guilty of sexual child abuse of his son.

Over the dissent of two judges, the Court of Appeals of Maryland reversed and remanded. The court held that "the passage of time alone is insufficient to [end] the protections afforded by *Edwards*," and that, assuming, *arguendo*, a break-in-custody exception to *Edwards* existed, Shatzer's release back into the general prison population between interrogations did not constitute a break in custody. We granted certiorari.

II. * * *

It is easy to believe that a suspect may be coerced or badgered into abandoning his earlier refusal to be questioned without counsel in the paradigm *Edwards* case. That is a case in which the suspect has been arrested for a particular crime and is held in uninterrupted pretrial custody while that crime is being actively investigated. After the initial interrogation, and up to and including the second one, he remains cut off from his normal life and companions, "thrust into" and isolated in an "unfamiliar," "police-dominated atmosphere," *Miranda*, where his captors "appear to control [his] fate," *Illinois v. Perkins*, 496 U.S. 292, 297 (1990). That was the situation confronted by * * * *Edwards* * * *. Edwards was arrested pursuant to a warrant and taken to a police station, where he was interrogated until he requested counsel. The officer ended the interrogation and took him to the county jail,[2] but at 9:15 the next morning, two of the officer's colleagues reinterrogated Edwards at the jail. * * * [Edwards

---

[2] Jail is a "local government's detention center where persons awaiting trial or those convicted of misdemeanors are confined." BLACK'S LAW DICTIONARY 910 (9th ed. 2009). Prison, by contrast, is a "state or federal facility of confinement for convicted criminals, esp. felons." *Id.* at 1314.

never] regained a sense of control or normalcy after [he was] initially taken into custody for the crime under investigation.

When, unlike what happened in [that case], a suspect has been released from his pretrial custody and has returned to his normal life for some time before the later attempted interrogation, there is little reason to think that his change of heart regarding interrogation without counsel has been coerced. He has no longer been isolated. He has likely been able to seek advice from an attorney, family members, and friends. And he knows from his earlier experience that he need only demand counsel to bring the interrogation to a halt; and that investigative custody does not last indefinitely. In these circumstances, it is farfetched to think that a police officer's asking the suspect whether he would like to waive his *Miranda* rights will any more "wear down the accused," than did the first such request at the original attempted interrogation—which is of course not deemed coercive. His change of heart is less likely attributable to "badgering" than it is to the fact that further deliberation in familiar surroundings has caused him to believe (rightly or wrongly) that cooperating with the investigation is in his interest. Uncritical extension of *Edwards* to this situation would not significantly increase the number of genuinely coerced confessions excluded. The "justification for a conclusive presumption disappears when application of the presumption will not reach the correct result most of the time."

At the same time that extending the *Edwards* rule yields diminished benefits, extending the rule also increases its costs: the in-fact voluntary confessions it excludes from trial, and the voluntary confessions it deters law enforcement officers from even trying to obtain. * * *

The only logical endpoint of *Edwards* disability is termination of *Miranda* custody and any of its lingering effects. Without that limitation— and barring some purely arbitrary time—every *Edwards* prohibition of custodial interrogation of a particular suspect would be eternal. The prohibition applies, of course, when the subsequent interrogation pertains to a different crime, when it is conducted by a different law enforcement authority, and even when the suspect has met with an attorney after the first interrogation. And it not only prevents questioning *ex ante*; it would render invalid, *ex post*, confessions invited and obtained from suspects who (unbeknownst to the interrogators) have acquired *Edwards* immunity previously in connection with any offense in any jurisdiction. In a country that harbors a large number of repeat offenders, this consequence is disastrous.

We conclude that such an extension of *Edwards* is not justified * * *. The protections offered by *Miranda*, which we have deemed sufficient to ensure that the police respect the suspect's desire to have an attorney present the first time police interrogate him, adequately ensure that result when a suspect who initially requested counsel is reinterrogated after a break in custody that is of sufficient duration to dissipate its coercive effects.

If Shatzer's return to the general prison population qualified as a break in custody (a question we address in Part III, *infra*), there is no doubt that it lasted long enough (two years) to meet that durational requirement. But what about a break that has lasted only one year? Or only one week? It is impractical to leave the answer to that question for clarification in future case-by-case adjudication; law enforcement officers need to know, with certainty and beforehand, when renewed interrogation is lawful. And while it is certainly unusual for this Court to set forth precise time limits governing police action, it is not unheard of. * * *

* * * We think it appropriate to specify a period of time to avoid the consequence that continuation of the *Edwards* presumption "will not reach the correct result most of the time." It seems to us that period is 14 days. That provides plenty of time for the suspect to get reacclimated to his normal life, to consult with friends and counsel, and to shake off any residual coercive effects of his prior custody.

The 14-day limitation meets Shatzer's concern that a break-in-custody rule lends itself to police abuse. He envisions that once a suspect invokes his *Miranda* right to counsel, the police will release the suspect briefly (to end the *Edwards* presumption) and then promptly bring him back into custody for reinterrogation. But once the suspect has been out of custody long enough (14 days) to eliminate its coercive effect, there will be nothing to gain by such gamesmanship—nothing, that is, except the entirely appropriate gain of being able to interrogate a suspect who has made a valid waiver of his *Miranda* rights. * * *

Because Shatzer experienced a break in *Miranda* custody lasting more than two weeks between the first and second attempts at interrogation, *Edwards* does not mandate suppression of his March 2006 statements. Accordingly, we reverse the judgment of the Court of Appeals of Maryland and remand the case for further proceedings not inconsistent with this opinion.

It is so ordered.

JUSTICE THOMAS, concurring in part and concurring in the judgment.

[Omitted.]

JUSTICE STEVENS, concurring in the judgment.

While I agree that the presumption from *Edwards v. Arizona*, 451 U.S. 477 (1981), is not "eternal," and does not mandate suppression of Shatzer's statement made after a 2-year break in custody, I do not agree with the

Court's newly announced rule: that *Edwards* always ceases to apply when there is a 14-day break in custody. * * *

I.

The most troubling aspect of the Court's time-based rule is that it disregards the compulsion caused by a second (or third, or fourth) interrogation of an indigent suspect who was told that if he requests a lawyer, one will be provided for him. When police tell an indigent suspect that he has the right to an attorney, that he is not required to speak without an attorney present, and that an attorney will be provided to him at no cost before questioning, the police have made a significant promise. If they cease questioning and then reinterrogate the suspect 14 days later without providing him with a lawyer, the suspect is likely to feel that the police lied to him and that he really does not have any right to a lawyer.

When officers informed Shatzer of his rights during the first interrogation, they presumably informed him that if he requested an attorney, one would be appointed for him before he was asked any further questions. But if an indigent suspect requests a lawyer, "any further interrogation" (even 14 days later) "without counsel having been provided will surely exacerbate whatever compulsion to speak the suspect may be feeling." When police have not honored an earlier commitment to provide a detainee with a lawyer, the detainee likely will "understan[d] his (expressed) wishes to have been ignored" and "may well see further objection as futile and confession (true or not) as the only way to end his interrogation." Simply giving a "fresh se[t] of *Miranda* warnings" will not " 'reassure' a suspect who has been denied the counsel he has clearly requested that his rights have remained untrammeled."

II.

The Court never explains why its rule cannot depend on, in addition to a break in custody and passage of time, a concrete event or state of affairs, such as the police's having honored their commitment to provide counsel. Instead, the Court simply decides to create a time-based rule, and in so doing, disregards much of the analysis upon which Edwards and subsequent decisions were based. * * *

* * * [T]he Court engages in its own speculation that a 14-day break in custody eliminates the compulsion that animated *Edwards*. But its opinion gives no strong basis for believing that this is the case. A 14-day break in custody does not eliminate the rationale for the initial *Edwards* rule: The detainee has been told that he may remain silent and speak only through a lawyer and that if he cannot afford an attorney, one will be provided for him. He has asked for a lawyer. He does not have one. He is in custody. And police are still questioning him. A 14-day break in custody does not change the fact that custodial interrogation is inherently compelling. It is unlikely to change the fact that a detainee "considers himself unable to deal

with the pressures of custodial interrogation without legal assistance." And in some instances, a 14-day break in custody may make matters worse "[w]hen a suspect understands his (expressed) wishes to have been ignored" and thus "may well see further objection as futile and confession (true or not) as the only way to end his interrogation."[10]

The Court ignores these understandings from the *Edwards* line of cases and instead speculates that if a suspect is reinterrogated and eventually talks, it must be that "further deliberation in familiar surroundings has caused him to believe (rightly or wrongly) that cooperating with the investigation is in his interest." But it is not apparent why that is the case. The answer, we are told, is that once a suspect has been out of *Miranda* custody for 14 days, "[h]e has likely been able to seek advice from an attorney, family members, and friends." This speculation, however, is overconfident and only questionably relevant. As a factual matter, we do not know whether the defendant has been able to seek advice: First of all, suspects are told that if they cannot afford a lawyer, one will be provided for them. Yet under the majority's rule, an indigent suspect who took the police at their word when he asked for a lawyer will nonetheless be assumed to have "been able to seek advice from an attorney." Second, even suspects who are not indigent cannot necessarily access legal advice (or social advice as the Court presumes) within 14 days. Third, suspects may not realize that they need to seek advice from an attorney. Unless police warn suspects that the interrogation will resume in 14 days, why contact a lawyer? When a suspect is let go, he may assume that the police were satisfied. * * *

III.

Because, at the very least, we do not know whether Shatzer could obtain a lawyer, and thus would have felt that police had lied about providing one, I cannot join the Court's opinion. I concur in today's judgment, however, on another ground: Even if Shatzer could not consult a lawyer and the police never provided him one, the 2-year break in custody is a basis for treating the second interrogation as no more coercive than the first. Neither a break in custody nor the passage of time has an inherent, curative power. But certain things change over time. An indigent suspect who took police at their word that they would provide an attorney probably will feel that he has "been denied the counsel he has clearly requested," when police begin to question him, without a lawyer, only 14 days later. But, when a suspect has been left alone for a significant period of time, he

---

[10] Not only is this a likely effect of reinterrogation, but police may use this effect to their advantage. Indeed, the Court's rule creates a strange incentive to delay formal proceedings, in order to gain additional information by way of interrogation after the time limit lapses. * * * [T]he reality is that police may operate within the confines of the Fifth Amendment in order to extract as many confessions as possible. With a time limit as short as 14 days, police who hope that they can eventually extract a confession may feel comfortable releasing a suspect for a short period of time. The resulting delay will only increase the compelling pressures on the suspect.

is not as likely to draw such conclusions when the police interrogate him
again. It is concededly "impossible to determine with precision" where to
draw such a line. In the case before us, however, the suspect was returned
to the general prison population for two years. I am convinced that this
period of time is sufficient. I therefore concur in the judgment.

IV. THE LIMITS OF *MIRANDA* EXCLUSION: *MIRANDA* FRUITS & SEQUENTIAL CONFESSIONS

In this block of material, we explore the strength of *Miranda*'s
exclusionary rule. Remember, the *Miranda* Court originally said that,
"unless and until such warnings and waiver are demonstrated by the
prosecution at trial, no evidence obtained as a result of interrogation can
be used against him." We know from that language that *Miranda* excludes
the suspect's primary statement; that is, the statement obtained in
violation of *Miranda*. But a much harder question, and the one we focus on
below, is whether *Miranda*'s exclusionary rule also suppresses the "fruits"
of the suspect's statement.

Miranda fruit typically takes one of three forms: (1) witnesses—e.g.,
the suspect's primary statement reveals the name of a person who later
testifies against the suspect; (2) repeated statements—e.g., after making a
primary statement, the suspect receives *Miranda* warnings and then
repeats the primary statement; or (3) physical evidence—e.g., the suspect's
primary statement mentions the location of tangible, incriminating
evidence.

The cases below follow that organizational framework. A word of
warning: this material is challenging. For that reason, this chapter
provides a more detailed inquiry into the accompanying Casefile. The hope
is that it will provide you with ample opportunity to practice applying the
complexities of *Miranda*'s vast framework.

A. WITNESSES AS A *MIRANDA* "FRUIT"

MICHIGAN V. TUCKER

417 U.S. 433
Supreme Court of the United States
March 20, 1974, Argued; June 10, 1974, Decided
No. 73-482

MR. JUSTICE REHNQUIST delivered the opinion of the Court.

This case presents the question whether the testimony of a witness in
respondent's state court trial for rape must be excluded simply because
police had learned the identity of the witness by questioning respondent at
a time when he was in custody as a suspect but had not been advised that

counsel would be appointed for him if he was indigent. The questioning took place before this Court's decision in *Miranda v. Arizona*, 384 U.S. 436 (1966), but respondent's trial, at which he was convicted, took place afterwards. * * * *Miranda* is applicable to this case. The United States District Court for the Eastern District of Michigan reviewed respondent's claim on a petition for habeas corpus and held that the testimony must be excluded. The Court of Appeals affirmed.

I.

On the morning of April 19, 1966, a 43-year-old woman in Pontiac, Michigan, was found in her home by a friend and coworker, Luther White, in serious condition. At the time she was found the woman was tied, gagged, and partially disrobed, and had been both raped and severely beaten. She was unable to tell White anything about her assault at that time and still remains unable to recollect what happened.

While White was attempting to get medical help for the victim and to call for the police, he observed a dog inside the house. This apparently attracted White's attention for he knew that the woman did not own a dog herself. Later, when talking with police officers, White observed the dog a second time, and police followed the dog to respondent's house. Neighbors further connected the dog with respondent.

The police then arrested respondent and brought him to the police station for questioning. Prior to the actual interrogation the police asked respondent whether he knew for what crime he had been arrested, whether he wanted an attorney, and whether he understood his constitutional rights. Respondent replied that he did understand the crime for which he was arrested, that he did not want an attorney, and that he understood his rights. The police further advised him that any statements he might make could be used against him at a later date in court. The police, however, did not advise respondent that he would be furnished counsel free of charge if he could not pay for such services himself.

The police then questioned respondent about his activities on the night of the rape and assault. Respondent replied that during the general time period at issue he had first been with one Robert Henderson and then later at home, alone, asleep. The police sought to confirm this story by contacting Henderson, but Henderson's story served to discredit rather than to bolster respondent's account. Henderson acknowledged that respondent had been with him on the night of the crime but said that he had left at a relatively early time. Furthermore, Henderson told police that he saw respondent the following day and asked him at that time about scratches on his face—"asked him if he got hold of a wild one or something." Respondent answered, "Something like that." Then, Henderson said, he asked respondent "who it was," and respondent said, "Some woman lived the next block over," adding, "She is a widow woman" or words to that effect.

These events all occurred prior to the date on which this Court handed down its decision in *Miranda v. Arizona, supra*, but respondent's trial occurred afterwards. Prior to trial respondent's appointed counsel made a motion to exclude Henderson's expected testimony because respondent had revealed Henderson's identity without having received full *Miranda* warnings. Although respondent's own statements taken during interrogation were excluded, the trial judge denied the motion to exclude Henderson's testimony. Henderson therefore testified at trial, and respondent was convicted of rape and sentenced to 20 to 40 years' imprisonment. His conviction was affirmed by both the Michigan Court of Appeals and the Michigan Supreme Court.

Respondent then sought habeas corpus relief in Federal District Court. That court, noting that respondent had not received the full *Miranda* warnings and that the police had stipulated Henderson's identity was learned only through respondent's answers, "reluctantly" concluded that Henderson's testimony could not be admitted. Application of such an exclusionary rule was necessary, the court reasoned, to protect respondent's Fifth Amendment right against compulsory self-incrimination. The court therefore granted respondent's petition for a writ of habeas corpus unless petitioner retried respondent within 90 days. The Court of Appeals for the Sixth Circuit affirmed. We granted certiorari and now reverse.

II.

Although respondent's sole complaint is that the police failed to advise him that he would be given free counsel if unable to afford counsel himself, he did not, and does not now, base his arguments for relief on a right to counsel under the Sixth and Fourteenth Amendments. * * *

Respondent's argument, and the opinions of the District Court and Court of Appeals, instead rely upon the Fifth Amendment right against compulsory self-incrimination and the safeguards designed in *Miranda* to secure that right. In brief, the position urged upon this Court is that proper regard for the privilege against compulsory self-incrimination requires, with limited exceptions not applicable here, that all evidence derived solely from statements made without full *Miranda* warnings be excluded at a subsequent criminal trial. * * *

III. * * *

A comparison of the facts in this case with the historical circumstances underlying the privilege against compulsory self-incrimination strongly indicates that the police conduct here did not deprive respondent of his privilege against compulsory self-incrimination as such, but rather failed to make available to him the full measure of procedural safeguards associated with that right since *Miranda*. * * *

Our determination that the interrogation in this case involved no compulsion sufficient to breach the right against compulsory self-incrimination does not mean there was not a disregard, albeit an inadvertent disregard, of the procedural rules later established in *Miranda*. The question for decision is how sweeping the judicially imposed consequences of this disregard shall be. This Court said in *Miranda* that statements taken in violation of the *Miranda* principles must not be used to prove the prosecution's case at trial. That requirement was fully complied with by the state court here: respondent's statements, claiming that he was with Henderson and then asleep during the time period of the crime were not admitted against him at trial. This Court has also said, in *Wong Sun v. United States*, 371 U.S. 471 (1963), that the "fruits" of police conduct which actually infringed a defendant's Fourth Amendment rights must be suppressed. But * * * the police conduct at issue here did not abridge respondent's constitutional privilege against compulsory self-incrimination, but departed only from the prophylactic standards later laid down by this Court in *Miranda* to safeguard that privilege. Thus, in deciding whether Henderson's testimony must be excluded, there is no controlling precedent of this Court to guide us. We must therefore examine the matter as a question of principle.

IV.

Just as the law does not require that a defendant receive a perfect trial, only a fair one, it cannot realistically require that policemen investigating serious crimes make no errors whatsoever. The pressures of law enforcement and the vagaries of human nature would make such an expectation unrealistic. Before we penalize police error, therefore, we must consider whether the sanction serves a valid and useful purpose.

We have recently said, in a search-and-seizure context, that the exclusionary rule's "prime purpose is to deter future unlawful police conduct and thereby effectuate the guarantee of the Fourth Amendment against unreasonable searches and seizures." *United States v. Calandra*, 414 U.S. 338, 347 (1974). * * *

In a proper case this rationale would seem applicable to the Fifth Amendment context as well.

The deterrent purpose of the exclusionary rule necessarily assumes that the police have engaged in willful, or at the very least negligent, conduct which has deprived the defendant of some right. By refusing to admit evidence gained as a result of such conduct, the courts hope to instill in those particular investigating officers, or in their future counterparts, a greater degree of care toward the rights of an accused. Where the official action was pursued in complete good faith, however, the deterrence rationale loses much of its force.

We consider it significant to our decision in this case that the officers' failure to advise respondent of his right to appointed counsel occurred prior to the decision in *Miranda*. Although we have been urged to resolve the broad question of whether evidence derived from statements taken in violation of the *Miranda* rules must be excluded regardless of when the interrogation took place, we instead place our holding on a narrower ground. For at the time respondent was questioned these police officers were guided, quite rightly, by the principles established in *Escobedo v. Illinois*, 378 U.S. 478 (1964), particularly focusing on the suspect's opportunity to have retained counsel with him during the interrogation if he chose to do so. Thus, the police asked respondent if he wanted counsel, and he answered that he did not. The statements actually made by respondent to the police, as we have observed, were excluded at trial * * *. Whatever deterrent effect on future police conduct the exclusion of those statements may have had, we do not believe it would be significantly augmented by excluding the testimony of the witness Henderson as well.

When involuntary statements or the right against compulsory self-incrimination are involved, a second justification for the exclusionary rule also has been asserted: protection of the courts from reliance on untrustworthy evidence. Cases which involve the Self-Incrimination Clause must, by definition, involve an element of coercion, since the Clause provides only that a person shall not be compelled to give evidence against himself. And cases involving statements often depict severe pressures which may override a particular suspect's insistence on innocence. Fact situations ranging from classical third-degree torture, *Brown v. Mississippi*, 297 U.S. 278 (1936), to prolonged isolation from family or friends in a hostile setting, *Gallegos v. Colorado*, 370 U.S. 49 (1962), or to a simple desire on the part of a physically or mentally exhausted suspect to have a seemingly endless interrogation end, *Watts v. Indiana*, 338 U.S. 49 (1949), all might be sufficient to cause a defendant to accuse himself falsely.

But those situations are a far cry from that presented here. The pressures on respondent to accuse himself were hardly comparable even with the least prejudicial of those pressures which have been dealt with in our cases. More important, the respondent did not accuse himself. The evidence which the prosecution successfully sought to introduce was not a confession of guilt by respondent, or indeed even an exculpatory statement by respondent, but rather the testimony of a third party who was subjected to no custodial pressures. There is plainly no reason to believe that Henderson's testimony is untrustworthy simply because respondent was not advised of his right to appointed counsel. Henderson was both available at trial and subject to cross-examination by respondent's counsel, and counsel fully used this opportunity, suggesting in the course of his cross-examination that Henderson's character was less than exemplary and that he had been offered incentives by the police to testify against respondent. Thus, the reliability of his testimony was subject to the normal testing process of an adversary trial. * * *

Reversed.

MR. JUSTICE STEWART, concurring.

[Omitted.]

MR. JUSTICE BRENNAN, with whom MR. JUSTICE MARSHALL joins, concurring in the judgment.

[Omitted.]

MR. JUSTICE WHITE, concurring in the judgment.

[Omitted.]

MR. JUSTICE DOUGLAS, dissenting. * * *

I.

I cannot agree when the Court says that the interrogation here "did not abridge respondent's constitutional privilege against compulsory self-incrimination but departed only from the prophylactic standards later laid down by this Court in *Miranda* to safeguard that privilege." The Court is not free to prescribe preferred modes of interrogation absent a constitutional basis. We held the "requirement of warnings and waiver of rights [to be] fundamental with respect to the Fifth Amendment privilege," and without so holding we would have been powerless to reverse *Miranda's* conviction. While *Miranda* recognized that police need not mouth the precise words contained in the Court's opinion, such warnings were held necessary "unless other fully effective means are adopted to notify the person" of his rights. There is no contention here that other means were adopted. * * *

II.

With the premise that respondent was subjected to an unconstitutional interrogation, there remains the question whether not only the testimony elicited in the interrogation but also the fruits thereof must be suppressed. * * *

The testimony of the witness in this case was no less a fruit of unconstitutional police action than the photographs in *Silverthorne* or the narcotics in *Wong Sun*. The petitioner has stipulated that the identity and the whereabouts of the witness and his connection with the case were learned about only through the unconstitutional interrogation of the respondent. His testimony must be excluded to comply with *Miranda's* mandate that "*no* evidence obtained as a result of interrogation [not preceded by adequate warnings] can be used against" an accused. (emphasis added). * * *

I would affirm the judgment below.

QUESTIONS, COMMENTS, CONCERNS?

1. **The "fruits" of a *Miranda* violation.** *Tucker* clarifies that the *Miranda* exclusionary rule and corresponding fruits doctrine operate differently from the Fourth Amendment. Put candidly, *Tucker* makes the *Miranda* fruits doctrine considerably weaker than its Fourth Amendment counterpart—a trend that will continue in the subsequent cases we will read. But please remember that *Miranda* fruits is a fundamentally different doctrine than the fruits doctrine associated with due process voluntariness. That is, *Tucker* and its corresponding logic apply to an initial, voluntary statement made in violation of *Miranda*; *Tucker* is inapplicable to involuntary statements.

B. REPEATED STATEMENTS AS A *MIRANDA* "FRUIT"

OREGON V. ELSTAD

470 U.S. 298
Supreme Court of the United States
October 3, 1984, Argued; March 4, 1985, Decided
No. 83-773

JUSTICE O'CONNOR delivered the opinion of the Court.

This case requires us to decide whether an initial failure of law enforcement officers to administer the warnings required by *Miranda v. Arizona*, 384 U.S. 436 (1966), without more, "taints" subsequent admissions made after a suspect has been fully advised of and has waived his *Miranda* rights. * * *

I.

In December 1981, the home of Mr. and Mrs. Gilbert Gross, in the town of Salem, Polk County, Ore., was burglarized. Missing were art objects and furnishings valued at $150,000. A witness to the burglary contacted the Polk County Sheriff's Office, implicating respondent Michael Elstad, an 18-year-old neighbor and friend of the Grosses' teenage son. Thereupon, Officers Burke and McAllister went to the home of respondent Elstad, with a warrant for his arrest. Elstad's mother answered the door. She led the officers to her son's room where he lay on his bed, clad in shorts and listening to his stereo. The officers asked him to get dressed and to accompany them into the living room. Officer McAllister asked respondent's mother to step into the kitchen, where he explained that they had a warrant for her son's arrest for the burglary of a neighbor's residence. Officer Burke remained with Elstad in the living room. He later testified:

> I sat down with Mr. Elstad and I asked him if he was aware of why Detective McAllister and myself were there to talk with him.

He stated no, he had no idea why we were there. I then asked him if he knew a person by the name of Gross, and he said yes, he did, and also added that he heard that there was a robbery at the Gross house. And at that point I told Mr. Elstad that I felt he was involved in that, and he looked at me and stated, "Yes, I was there."

The officers then escorted Elstad to the back of the patrol car. As they were about to leave for the Polk County Sheriff's office, Elstad's father arrived home and came to the rear of the patrol car. The officers advised him that his son was a suspect in the burglary. Officer Burke testified that Mr. Elstad became quite agitated, opened the rear door of the car and admonished his son: "I told you that you were going to get into trouble. You wouldn't listen to me. You never learn."

Elstad was transported to the Sheriff's headquarters and approximately one hour later, Officers Burke and McAllister joined him in McAllister's office. McAllister then advised respondent for the first time of his *Miranda* rights, reading from a standard card. Respondent indicated he understood his rights, and, having these rights in mind, wished to speak with the officers. Elstad gave a full statement, explaining that he had known that the Gross family was out of town and had been paid to lead several acquaintances to the Gross residence and show them how to gain entry through a defective sliding glass door. The statement was typed, reviewed by respondent, read back to him for correction, initialed and signed by Elstad and both officers. As an afterthought, Elstad added and initialed the sentence, "After leaving the house Robby & I went back to [the] van & Robby handed me a small bag of grass." Respondent concedes that the officers made no threats or promises either at his residence or at the Sheriff's office.

Respondent was charged with first-degree burglary. He was represented at trial by retained counsel. Elstad waived his right to a jury, and his case was tried by a Circuit Court Judge. Respondent moved at once to suppress his oral statement and signed confession. He contended that the statement he made in response to questioning at his house "let the cat out of the bag," * * * and tainted the subsequent confession as "fruit of the poisonous tree," citing *Wong Sun v. United States*, 371 U.S. 471 (1963). The judge ruled that the statement, "I was there," had to be excluded because the defendant had not been advised of his *Miranda* rights. The written confession taken after Elstad's arrival at the Sheriff's office, however, was admitted in evidence. * * *

Elstad was found guilty of burglary in the first degree. He received a 5-year sentence and was ordered to pay $18,000 in restitution.

Following his conviction, respondent appealed to the Oregon Court of Appeals, relying on *Wong Sun* * * *. * * * The Court of Appeals reversed respondent's conviction, identifying the crucial constitutional inquiry as "whether there was a sufficient break in the stream of events between [the] inadmissible statement and the written confession to insulate the latter statement from the effect of what went before." * * *

Because of the brief period separating the two incidents, the "cat was sufficiently out of the bag to exert a coercive impact on [respondent's] later admissions."

The State of Oregon petitioned the Oregon Supreme Court for review, and review was declined. * * *

II.

The arguments advanced in favor of suppression of respondent's written confession rely heavily on metaphor. One metaphor, familiar from the Fourth Amendment context, would require that respondent's confession, regardless of its integrity, voluntariness, and probative value, be suppressed as the "tainted fruit of the poisonous tree" of the *Miranda* violation. A second metaphor questions whether a confession can be truly voluntary once the "cat is out of the bag." Taken out of context, each of these metaphors can be misleading. They should not be used to obscure fundamental differences between the role of the Fourth Amendment exclusionary rule and the function of Miranda in guarding against the prosecutorial use of compelled statements as prohibited by the Fifth Amendment. The Oregon court assumed, and respondent here contends, that a failure to administer *Miranda* warnings necessarily breeds the same consequences as police infringement of a constitutional right, so that evidence uncovered following an unwarned statement must be suppressed as "fruit of the poisonous tree." We believe this view misconstrues the nature of the protections afforded by *Miranda* warnings and therefore misreads the consequences of police failure to supply them. * * *

Respondent's contention that his confession was tainted by the earlier failure of the police to provide *Miranda* warnings and must be excluded as "fruit of the poisonous tree" assumes the existence of a constitutional violation. This figure of speech is drawn from *Wong Sun v. United States*, 371 U.S. 471 (1963), in which the Court held that evidence and witnesses discovered as a result of a search in violation of the Fourth Amendment must be excluded from evidence. The *Wong Sun* doctrine applies as well when the fruit of the Fourth Amendment violation is a confession. It is settled law that "a confession obtained through custodial interrogation after an illegal arrest should be excluded unless intervening events break the causal connection between the illegal arrest and the confession so that the confession is 'sufficiently an act of free will to purge the primary taint.'"

But as we explained in *Quarles* and *Tucker*, a procedural *Miranda* violation differs in significant respects from violations of the Fourth Amendment, which have traditionally mandated a broad application of the "fruits" doctrine. The purpose of the Fourth Amendment exclusionary rule is to deter unreasonable searches, no matter how probative their fruits. * * * Where a Fourth Amendment violation "taints" the confession, a finding of voluntariness for the purposes of the Fifth Amendment is merely a threshold requirement in determining whether the confession may be admitted in evidence. Beyond this, the prosecution must show a sufficient break in events to undermine the inference that the confession was caused by the Fourth Amendment violation.

The *Miranda* exclusionary rule, however, serves the Fifth Amendment and sweeps more broadly than the Fifth Amendment itself. It may be triggered even in the absence of a Fifth Amendment violation. The Fifth Amendment prohibits use by the prosecution in its case in chief only of compelled testimony. Failure to administer *Miranda* warnings creates a presumption of compulsion. Consequently, unwarned statements that are otherwise voluntary within the meaning of the Fifth Amendment must nevertheless be excluded from evidence under *Miranda*. Thus, in the individual case, *Miranda*'s preventive medicine provides a remedy even to the defendant who has suffered no identifiable constitutional harm.

But the *Miranda* presumption, though irrebuttable for purposes of the prosecution's case in chief, does not require that the statements and their fruits be discarded as inherently tainted. Despite the fact that patently voluntary statements taken in violation of *Miranda* must be excluded from the prosecution's case, the presumption of coercion does not bar their use for impeachment purposes on cross-examination. *Harris v. New York*, 401 U.S. 222 (1971). The Court in *Harris* rejected as an "extravagant extension of the Constitution," the theory that a defendant who had confessed under circumstances that made the confession inadmissible, could thereby enjoy the freedom to "deny every fact disclosed or discovered as a 'fruit' of his confession, free from confrontation with his prior statements" and that the voluntariness of his confession would be totally irrelevant. Where an unwarned statement is preserved for use in situations that fall outside the sweep of the *Miranda* presumption, "the primary criterion of admissibility [remains] the 'old' due process voluntariness test."

* * * We believe that this reasoning applies with equal force when the alleged "fruit" of a noncoercive *Miranda* violation is neither a witness nor an article of evidence but the accused's own voluntary testimony. As in *Tucker*, the absence of any coercion or improper tactics undercuts the twin rationales—trustworthiness and deterrence—for a broader rule. Once warned, the suspect is free to exercise his own volition in deciding whether or not to make a statement to the authorities. * * *

* * * If errors are made by law enforcement officers in administering the prophylactic *Miranda* procedures, they should not breed the same irremediable consequences as police infringement of the Fifth Amendment

itself. It is an unwarranted extension of *Miranda* to hold that a simple failure to administer the warnings, unaccompanied by any actual coercion or other circumstances calculated to undermine the suspect's ability to exercise his free will, so taints the investigatory process that a subsequent voluntary and informed waiver is ineffective for some indeterminate period. Though *Miranda* requires that the unwarned admission must be suppressed, the admissibility of any subsequent statement should turn in these circumstances solely on whether it is knowingly and voluntarily made. * * *

III.

* * * Respondent * * * has argued that he was unable to give a fully informed waiver of his rights because he was unaware that his prior statement could not be used against him. Respondent suggests that Officer McAllister, to cure this deficiency, should have added an additional warning to those given him at the Sheriff's office. Such a requirement is neither practicable nor constitutionally necessary. In many cases, a breach of *Miranda* procedures may not be identified as such until long after full *Miranda* warnings are administered and a valid confession obtained. The standard *Miranda* warnings explicitly inform the suspect of his right to consult a lawyer before speaking. Police officers are ill-equipped to pinch-hit for counsel, construing the murky and difficult questions of when "custody" begins or whether a given unwarned statement will ultimately be held admissible. * * *

IV.

When police ask questions of a suspect in custody without administering the required warnings, *Miranda* dictates that the answers received be presumed compelled and that they be excluded from evidence at trial in the State's case in chief. The Court has carefully adhered to this principle, permitting a narrow exception only where pressing public safety concerns demanded. *See New York v. Quarles.* The Court today in no way retreats from the bright-line rule of *Miranda.* We do not imply that good faith excuses a failure to administer *Miranda* warnings; nor do we condone inherently coercive police tactics or methods offensive to due process that render the initial admission involuntary and undermine the suspect's will to invoke his rights once they are read to him. * * * The relevant inquiry is whether, in fact, the second statement was also voluntarily made. As in any such inquiry, the finder of fact must examine the surrounding circumstances and the entire course of police conduct with respect to the suspect in evaluating the voluntariness of his statements. The fact that a suspect chooses to speak after being informed of his rights is, of course, highly probative. We find that the dictates of *Miranda* and the goals of the Fifth Amendment proscription against use of compelled testimony are fully satisfied in the circumstances of this case by barring use of the unwarned statement in the case in chief. No further purpose is served by imputing "taint" to subsequent statements obtained pursuant to a voluntary and knowing waiver. We hold today that a suspect who has once responded to unwarned yet uncoercive questioning is not thereby disabled from waiving his rights and confessing after he has been given the requisite *Miranda* warnings.

The judgment of the Court of Appeals of Oregon is reversed, and the case is remanded for further proceedings not inconsistent with this opinion.

It is so ordered.

JUSTICE BRENNAN, with whom JUSTICE MARSHALL joins, dissenting. * * *

Today's decision * * * threatens disastrous consequences far beyond the outcome in this case. * * *

I. * * *

This Court has had long experience with the problem of confessions obtained after an earlier confession has been illegally secured. Subsequent confessions in these circumstances are not per se inadmissible, but the prosecution must demonstrate facts "sufficient to insulate the [subsequent] statement from the effect of all that went before." If the accused's subsequent confession was merely the culmination of "one continuous process," or if the first confession was merely "filled in and perfected by additional statements given in rapid succession," the subsequent confession is inadmissible even though it was not obtained through the same illegal means as the first. The question in each case is whether the accused's will was "overborne at the time he confessed," and the prosecution must demonstrate that the second confession "was an act independent of the [earlier] confession." * * *

Our precedents did not develop in a vacuum. They reflect an understanding of the realities of police interrogation and the everyday experience of lower courts. Expert interrogators, far from dismissing a first admission or confession as creating merely a "speculative and attenuated" disadvantage for a suspect understand that such revelations frequently lead directly to a full confession. Standard interrogation manuals advise that "[the] securing of the first admission is the biggest stumbling block. . ." If this first admission can be obtained, "there is every reason to expect that the first admission will lead to others, and eventually to the full confession." * * *

Interrogators describe the point of the first admission as the "breakthrough" and the "beachhead," which once obtained will give them enormous "tactical advantages," F. Inbau & J. Reid, *Criminal Interrogation and Confessions* 82 (2d ed. 1967). Thus "[the] securing of incriminating admissions might well be considered as the beginning of the final stages in crumbling the defenses of the suspect," and the process of obtaining such admissions is described as "the spadework required to motivate the subject into making the full confession." * * *

The practical experience of state and federal courts confirms the experts' understanding. From this experience, lower courts have concluded that a first confession obtained without proper *Miranda* warnings, far from creating merely some "speculative and attenuated" disadvantage for the accused frequently enables the authorities to obtain subsequent confessions on a "silver platter."

* * * The variations of this practice are numerous, but the underlying problem is always the same: after hearing the witness testimony and considering the practical realities, courts have confirmed the time-honored wisdom of presuming that a first illegal confession "taints" subsequent confessions, and permitting such subsequent confessions to be admitted at trial only if the prosecution convincingly rebuts the presumption. * * * For all practical purposes, the prewarning and postwarning questioning are often but stages of one overall interrogation. Whether or not the authorities explicitly confront the suspect with his earlier illegal admissions makes no significant difference, of course, because the suspect knows that the authorities know of his earlier statements and most frequently will believe that those statements already have sealed his fate. * * *

I would have thought that the Court, instead of dismissing the "cat out of the bag" presumption out of hand, would have accounted for these practical realities. * * *

The correct approach, administered for almost 20 years by most courts with no untoward results, is to presume that an admission or confession obtained in violation of *Miranda* taints a subsequent confession unless the prosecution can show that the taint is so attenuated as to justify admission of the subsequent confession. * * *

* * * [T]oday's opinion marks an evisceration of the established fruit of the poisonous tree doctrine, but its reasoning is sufficiently obscure and qualified as to leave state and federal courts with continued authority to combat obvious flouting by the authorities of the privilege against self-incrimination. I am confident that lower courts will exercise this authority responsibly, as they have for the most part prior to this Court's intervention.

II.

Not content merely to ignore the practical realities of police interrogation and the likely effects of its abolition of the derivative-evidence presumption, the Court goes on to assert that nothing in the Fifth Amendment or the general judicial policy of deterring illegal police conduct "ordinarily" requires the suppression of evidence derived proximately from a confession obtained in violation of *Miranda*. The Court does not limit its analysis to successive confessions, but recurrently refers generally to the "fruits" of the illegal confession. Thus, the potential impact of the Court's reasoning might extend far beyond the "cat out of the bag" context to include the discovery of physical evidence and other derivative fruits of *Miranda* violations as well.

* * *

As the Executive Director of the National District Attorneys Association Foundation emphasized shortly after *Miranda*, merely to exclude the statement itself while putting no curbs on the admission of derivative evidence "would destroy the whole basis for the rule in the first instance." Yet that is precisely the result that today's disastrous opinion threatens to encourage. How can the Court possibly expect the authorities to obey *Miranda* when they have every incentive now to interrogate suspects without warnings or an effective waiver, knowing that the fruits of such interrogations "ordinarily" will be admitted, that an admissible subsequent confession "ordinarily" can be obtained simply by reciting the *Miranda* warnings shortly after the first has been procured and asking the accused to repeat himself, and that unless the accused can demonstrate otherwise his confession will be viewed as an "act of free will" in response to "legitimate law enforcement activity"? By condoning such a result, the Court today encourages practices that threaten to reduce *Miranda* to a mere "form of words," *Silverthorne Lumber Co. v. United States*, 251 U.S., at 392, and it is shocking that the Court nevertheless disingenuously purports that it "in no way retreats" from the *Miranda* safeguards. * * *

I dissent.

JUSTICE STEVENS, dissenting. * * *

As I read the Court's opinion, it expressly accepts the proposition that routine *Miranda* warnings will not be sufficient to overcome the presumption of coercion and thereby make a second confession admissible when an earlier confession is tainted by coercion "by physical violence or other deliberate means calculated to break the suspect's will." Even in such a case, however, it is not necessary to assume that the earlier confession will always "effectively immunize" a later voluntary confession. But surely the fact that an earlier confession was obtained by unlawful methods should add force to the presumption of coercion that attaches to subsequent custodial interrogation and should require the prosecutor to shoulder a heavier burden of rebuttal than in a routine case. Simple logic, as well as the interest in not providing an affirmative incentive to police misconduct, requires that result. I see no reason why the violation of a rule that is as well recognized and easily administered as the duty to give *Miranda* warnings should not also impose an additional burden on the prosecutor. If we are faithful to the holding in *Miranda* itself, when we are considering the admissibility of evidence in the prosecutor's case in chief, we should not try to fashion a distinction between police misconduct that warrants a finding of actual coercion and police misconduct that establishes an irrebuttable presumption of coercion. * * *

I respectfully dissent.

QUESTIONS, COMMENTS, CONCERNS?

1. **Is *Miranda* a "constitutional" decision?** Language from the Court's opinions in *Tucker, Harris, Quarles,* and *Elstad* abounds to suggest that *Miranda* is not a constitutional decision. Rather, as you read, Justice O'Connor's majority opinion in *Elstad* described a *Miranda* violation as a "procedural" one only that "differs in significant respects from violations of the Fourth Amendment, which have traditionally mandated a broad application of the 'fruits' doctrine." *Elstad* likewise continued the use of *Tucker*'s language to describe *Miranda* as proscribing only "prophylactic" warnings that are "not themselves rights protected by the Constitution."

But then came *Dickerson v. United States*, 530 U.S. 428, 431 (2000), which held that *Miranda* is "a constitutional decision." Despite that holding, however, *Dickerson* upheld *Quarles, Elstad, Tucker,* and *Harris* as good law. *Dickerson* candidly acknowledged that "there is language in some of our opinions that supports the view" that *Miranda* is not a constitutional decision. Yet the *Dickerson* Court reasoned that its prior opinions merely "illustrate the principle" that no constitutional rule (including *Miranda*) "is immutable."

MISSOURI V. SEIBERT

542 U.S. 600
Supreme Court of the United States
December 9, 2003, Argued; June 28, 2004, Decided
No. 02-1371

JUSTICE SOUTER announced the judgment of the Court and delivered an opinion, in which JUSTICE STEVENS, JUSTICE GINSBURG, and JUSTICE BREYER join.

This case tests a police protocol for custodial interrogation that calls for giving no warnings of the rights to silence and counsel until interrogation has produced a confession. Although such a statement is generally inadmissible, since taken in violation of *Miranda v. Arizona*, 384 U.S. 436 (1966), the interrogating officer follows it with *Miranda* warnings and then leads the suspect to cover the same ground a second time. The question here is the admissibility of the repeated statement. Because this midstream recitation of warnings after interrogation and unwarned confession could not effectively comply with *Miranda*'s constitutional requirement, we hold that a statement repeated after a warning in such circumstances is inadmissible.

I.

Respondent Patrice Seibert's 12-year-old son Jonathan had cerebral palsy, and when he died in his sleep she feared charges of neglect because of bedsores on his body. In her presence, two of her teenage sons and two of their friends devised a plan to conceal the facts surrounding Jonathan's death by incinerating his body in the course of burning the family's mobile home, in which they planned to leave Donald Rector, a mentally ill teenager living with the family, to avoid any appearance that Jonathan had been unattended. Seibert's son Darian and a friend set the fire, and Donald died.

Five days later, the police awakened Seibert at 3 a.m. at a hospital where Darian was being treated for burns. In arresting her, Officer Kevin Clinton followed instructions from Rolla, Missouri, Officer Richard Hanrahan that he refrain from giving *Miranda* warnings. After Seibert had been taken to the police station and left alone in an interview room for 15 to 20 minutes, Hanrahan questioned her without *Miranda* warnings for 30 to 40 minutes, squeezing her arm and repeating "Donald was also to die in his sleep." After Seibert finally admitted she knew Donald was meant to die in the fire, she was given a 20-minute coffee and cigarette break. Officer Hanrahan then turned on a tape recorder, gave Seibert the *Miranda* warnings, and obtained a signed waiver of rights from her. He resumed the questioning with "Ok, 'trice, we've been talking for a little while about what happened on Wednesday the twelfth, haven't we?" and confronted her with her prewarning statements:

HANRAHAN: Now, in discussion you told us, you told us that there was a[n] understanding about Donald.

SEIBERT: Yes.

HANRAHAN: Did that take place earlier that morning?

SEIBERT: Yes.

HANRAHAN: And what was the understanding about Donald?

SEIBERT: If they could get him out of the trailer, to take him out of the trailer.

HANRAHAN: And if they couldn't?

SEIBERT: I, I never even thought about it. I just figured they would.

HANRAHAN: 'Trice, didn't you tell me that he was supposed to die in his sleep?

SEIBERT: If that would happen, 'cause he was on that new medicine, you know. . .

HANRAHAN: The Prozac? And it makes him sleepy. So he was supposed to die in his sleep?

SEIBERT: Yes.

After being charged with first-degree murder for her role in Donald's death, Seibert sought to exclude both her prewarning and postwarning statements. At the suppression hearing, Officer Hanrahan testified that he made a "conscious decision" to withhold *Miranda* warnings, thus resorting to an interrogation technique he had been taught: question first, then give the warnings, and then repeat the question "until I get the answer that she's already provided once." He acknowledged that Seibert's ultimate statement was "largely a repeat of information. . . obtained" prior to the warning.

* * * [T]he Missouri Court of Appeals affirmed, treating this case as indistinguishable from *Oregon v. Elstad*, 470 U.S. 298 (1985). The Supreme Court of Missouri reversed[.] * * * We granted certiorari to resolve a split in the Courts of Appeals. We now affirm.

II.

* * * In *Miranda*, we explained that the "voluntariness doctrine in the state cases. . .encompasses all interrogation practices which are likely to exert such pressure upon an individual as to disable him from making a free and rational choice." We appreciated the difficulty of judicial enquiry post hoc into the circumstances of a police interrogation, and recognized that "the coercion inherent in custodial interrogation blurs the line between voluntary and involuntary statements, and thus heightens the risk" that the privilege against self-incrimination will not be observed. Hence our concern that the "traditional totality-of-the-circumstances" test posed an "unacceptably great" risk that involuntary custodial confessions would escape detection.

Accordingly, "to reduce the risk of a coerced confession and to implement the Self-Incrimination Clause," this Court in *Miranda* concluded that "the accused must be adequately and effectively apprised of his rights and the exercise of those rights must be fully honored." *Miranda* conditioned the admissibility at trial of any custodial confession on warning a suspect of his rights: failure to give the prescribed warnings and obtain a waiver of rights before custodial questioning generally requires exclusion of any statements obtained. Conversely, giving the warnings and getting a waiver has generally produced a virtual ticket of admissibility; maintaining that a statement is involuntary even though given after warnings and voluntary waiver of rights requires unusual stamina, and litigation over voluntariness tends to end with the finding of a valid waiver. To point out the obvious, this common consequence would not be common at all were it not that *Miranda* warnings are customarily given under circumstances allowing for a real choice between talking and remaining silent.

III.

* * * The technique of interrogating in successive, unwarned and warned phases raises a new challenge to *Miranda*. Although we have no statistics on the frequency of this practice, it is not confined to Rolla, Missouri. An officer of that police department testified that the strategy of withholding *Miranda* warnings until after interrogating and drawing out a confession was promoted not only by his own department, but by a national police training organization and other departments in which he had worked. Consistently with the officer's testimony, the Police Law Institute, for example, instructs that "officers may conduct a two-stage interrogation... At any point during the pre-*Miranda* interrogation, usually after arrestees have confessed, officers may then read the *Miranda* warnings and ask for a waiver. If the arrestees waive their *Miranda* rights, officers will be able to repeat any subsequent incriminating statements later in court." The upshot of all this advice is a question-first practice of some popularity, as one can see from the reported cases describing its use, sometimes in obedience to departmental policy.

IV.

* * * The object of question-first is to render *Miranda* warnings ineffective by waiting for a particularly opportune time to give them, after the suspect has already confessed.

Just as "no talismanic incantation [is] required to satisfy [*Miranda's*] strictures," it would be absurd to think that mere recitation of the litany suffices to satisfy *Miranda* in every conceivable circumstance. "The inquiry is simply whether the warnings reasonably 'conve[y] to [a suspect] his rights as required by *Miranda*.'" The threshold issue when interrogators question first and warn later is thus whether it would be reasonable to find that in these circumstances the warnings could function "effectively" as *Miranda* requires. Could the warnings effectively advise the suspect that he had a real choice about giving an admissible statement at that juncture? Could they reasonably convey that he could choose to stop talking even if he had talked earlier? For unless the warnings could place a suspect who has just been interrogated in a position to make such an informed choice, there is no practical justification for accepting the formal warnings as compliance with *Miranda*, or for treating the second stage of interrogation as distinct from the first, unwarned and inadmissible segment.

There is no doubt about the answer that proponents of question-first give to this question about the effectiveness of warnings given only after successful interrogation, and we think their answer is correct. By any objective measure, applied to circumstances exemplified here, it is likely that if the interrogators employ the technique of withholding warnings until after interrogation succeeds in eliciting a confession, the warnings will be ineffective in preparing the suspect for successive interrogation, close in time and similar in content. After all, the reason that question-first is catching on is as obvious as its manifest purpose, which is to get a confession the suspect would not make if he understood his rights at the outset; the sensible underlying assumption is that with one confession in hand before the warnings, the interrogator can count on getting its duplicate, with trifling additional trouble. Upon hearing warnings only in the aftermath of interrogation and just after making a confession, a suspect would hardly think he had a genuine right to remain silent, let alone persist in so believing once the police began to lead him over the same ground again. A more likely reaction on a suspect's part would be perplexity about the reason for discussing rights at that point, bewilderment being an unpromising frame of mind for knowledgeable decision. What is worse, telling a suspect that "anything you say can and will be used against you," without expressly excepting the statement just given, could lead to an entirely reasonable inference that what he has just said will be used, with subsequent silence being of no avail. Thus, when *Miranda* warnings are inserted in the midst of coordinated and continuing interrogation, they are likely to mislead and "depriv[e] a defendant of knowledge essential to his ability to understand the nature of his rights and the consequences of abandoning them." * * *

V.

Missouri argues that a confession repeated at the end of an interrogation sequence envisioned in a question-first strategy is admissible on the authority of *Oregon v. Elstad*, 470 U.S. 298 (1985), but the argument disfigures that case. In *Elstad*, the police went to the young suspect's house to take him into custody on a charge of burglary. Before the arrest, one officer spoke with the suspect's mother, while the other one joined the suspect in a "brief stop in the living room," where the officer said he "felt" the young man was involved in a burglary. The suspect acknowledged he had been at the scene. This Court noted that the pause in the living room "was not to interrogate the suspect but to notify his mother of the reason for his arrest," and described the incident as having "none of the earmarks of coercion." The Court, indeed, took care to mention that the officer's initial failure to warn was an "oversight" that "may have been the result of confusion as to whether the brief exchange qualified as 'custodial interrogation' or. . .may simply have reflected. . .reluctance to initiate an alarming police procedure before [an officer] had spoken with respondent's mother." At the outset of a later and systematic station house interrogation going well beyond the scope of the laconic prior admission, the suspect was given *Miranda* warnings and made a full confession. In holding the second statement admissible and voluntary, *Elstad* rejected the "cat out of the bag" theory that any short, earlier admission, obtained in arguably innocent neglect of *Miranda*, determined the character of the later, warned confession, on the facts of that case, the Court thought any causal connection between the first and second responses to the police was "speculative and attenuated." Although the *Elstad* Court expressed no explicit conclusion about either officer's state of mind, it is fair to read *Elstad* as treating the living room conversation as a good-faith *Miranda* mistake, not only open to correction by careful warnings before systematic questioning in that particular case, but posing no threat to warn-first practice generally.

The contrast between *Elstad* and this case reveals a series of relevant facts that bear on whether *Miranda* warnings delivered midstream could be effective enough to accomplish their object: the completeness and detail of the questions and answers in the first round of interrogation, the overlapping content of the two statements, the timing and setting of the first and the second, the continuity of police personnel, and the degree to which the interrogator's questions treated the second round as continuous with the first. In *Elstad*, it was not unreasonable to see the occasion for questioning at the station house as presenting a markedly different experience from the short conversation at home; since a reasonable person in the suspect's shoes could have seen the station house questioning as a new and distinct experience, the *Miranda* warnings could have made sense as presenting a genuine choice whether to follow up on the earlier admission.

At the opposite extreme are the facts here, which by any objective measure reveal a police strategy adapted to undermine the *Miranda* warnings.[6] The unwarned interrogation was conducted in the station house, and the questioning was systematic, exhaustive, and managed with psychological skill. When the police were finished there was little, if anything, of incriminating potential left unsaid. The warned phase of questioning proceeded after a pause of only 15 to 20 minutes, in the same place as the unwarned segment. When the same officer who had conducted the first phase recited the *Miranda* warnings, he said nothing to counter the probable misimpression that the advice that anything Seibert said could be used against her also applied to the details of the inculpatory statement previously elicited. In particular, the police did not advise that her prior statement could not be used. Nothing was said or done to dispel the oddity of warning about legal rights to silence and counsel right after the police had led her through a systematic interrogation, and any uncertainty on her part about a right to stop talking about matters previously discussed would only have been aggravated by the way Officer Hanrahan set the scene by saying "we've been talking for a little while

---

[6]   Because the intent of the officer will rarely be as candidly admitted as it was here (even as it is likely to determine the conduct of the interrogation), the focus is on facts apart from intent that show the question-first tactic at work.

about what happened on Wednesday the twelfth, haven't we?" The impression that the further questioning was a mere continuation of the earlier questions and responses was fostered by references back to the confession already given. It would have been reasonable to regard the two sessions as parts of a continuum, in which it would have been unnatural to refuse to repeat at the second stage what had been said before. These circumstances must be seen as challenging the comprehensibility and efficacy of the *Miranda* warnings to the point that a reasonable person in the suspect's shoes would not have understood them to convey a message that she retained a choice about continuing to talk.[8]

VI.

* * * Because the question-first tactic effectively threatens to thwart *Miranda*'s purpose of reducing the risk that a coerced confession would be admitted, and because the facts here do not reasonably support a conclusion that the warnings given could have served their purpose, Seibert's postwarning statements are inadmissible. The judgment of the Supreme Court of Missouri is affirmed.

It is so ordered.

JUSTICE BREYER, concurring.

[Omitted.]

JUSTICE KENNEDY, concurring in the judgment.

The interrogation technique used in this case is designed to circumvent *Miranda v. Arizona*, 384 U.S. 436 (1966). It undermines the *Miranda* warning and obscures its meaning. The plurality opinion is correct to conclude that statements obtained through the use of this technique are inadmissible. Although I agree with much in the careful and convincing opinion for the plurality, my approach does differ in some respects, requiring this separate statement.

In my view, *Elstad* was correct in its reasoning and its result. *Elstad* reflects a balanced and pragmatic approach to enforcement of the *Miranda* warning. An officer may not realize that a suspect is in custody and warnings are required. The officer may not plan to question the suspect or may be waiting for a more appropriate time. Skilled investigators often interview suspects multiple times, and good police work may involve referring to prior statements to test their veracity or to refresh recollection. In light of these realities it would be extravagant to treat the presence of one statement that cannot be admitted under *Miranda* as sufficient reason to prohibit subsequent statements preceded by a proper warning. That approach would serve "neither the general goal of deterring improper police

---

[8] Because we find that the warnings were inadequate, there is no need to assess the actual voluntariness of the statement.

conduct nor the Fifth Amendment goal of assuring trustworthy evidence would be served by suppression of the. . .testimony."

This case presents different considerations. The police used a two-step questioning technique based on a deliberate violation of *Miranda*. The *Miranda* warning was withheld to obscure both the practical and legal significance of the admonition when finally given. * * * When an interrogator uses this deliberate, two-step strategy, predicated upon violating *Miranda* during an extended interview, postwarning statements that are related to the substance of prewarning statements must be excluded absent specific, curative steps.

The plurality concludes that whenever a two-stage interview occurs, admissibility of the postwarning statement should depend on "whether [the] *Miranda* warnings delivered midstream could have been effective enough to accomplish their object" given the specific facts of the case. This test envisions an objective inquiry from the perspective of the suspect and applies in the case of both intentional and unintentional two-stage interrogations. In my view, this test cuts too broadly. *Miranda*'s clarity is one of its strengths, and a multifactor test that applies to every two-stage interrogation may serve to undermine that clarity. I would apply a narrower test applicable only in the infrequent case, such as we have here, in which the two-step interrogation technique was used in a calculated way to undermine the *Miranda* warning.

The admissibility of postwarning statements should continue to be governed by the principles of *Elstad* unless the deliberate two-step strategy was employed. If the deliberate two-step strategy has been used, postwarning statements that are related to the substance of prewarning statements must be excluded unless curative measures are taken before the postwarning statement is made. Curative measures should be designed to ensure that a reasonable person in the suspect's situation would understand the import and effect of the *Miranda* warning and of the *Miranda* waiver. For example, a substantial break in time and circumstances between the prewarning statement and the *Miranda* warning may suffice in most circumstances, as it allows the accused to distinguish the two contexts and appreciate that the interrogation has taken a new turn. Alternatively, an additional warning that explains the likely inadmissibility of the prewarning custodial statement may be sufficient. No curative steps were taken in this case, however, so the postwarning statements are inadmissible and the conviction cannot stand.

For these reasons, I concur in the judgment of the Court.

JUSTICE O'CONNOR, with whom THE CHIEF JUSTICE, JUSTICE SCALIA, and JUSTICE THOMAS join, dissenting.

The plurality devours *Oregon v. Elstad*, 470 U.S. 298 (1985), even as it accuses petitioner's argument of "disfigur[ing]" that decision. I believe that we are bound by *Elstad* to reach a different result, and I would vacate the judgment of the Supreme Court of Missouri. * * *

QUESTIONS, COMMENTS, CONCERNS?

1.   **Understanding *Seibert*.** Understanding the relationship between *Seibert* and *Elstad* presents one of the most formidable challenges of the Casebook. To begin, recall that *Elstad* contemplates exclusion of a second statement under some circumstances: "[A]bsent deliberately coercive or improper tactics in obtaining the initial statement, the mere fact that a suspect has made an unwarned admission does not warrant a presumption of compulsion." *Seibert*, then, seemingly illustrates what might constitute "improper tactics" and when such tactics would justify suppressing a repeated primary statement.

2.   **Dassey and fruits.** The question of how *Elstad-Seibert* might apply to Dassey's case is compelling. Put simply, the *Elstad-Seibert* analysis boils down to whether the police acted in good faith or bad faith. Ask yourself: did Detective Wiegert and Agent Fassbender act in good or bad faith when interrogating Dassey? The next few notes consider that question in more depth.

3.   **Dassey and *Seibert* (part 1).** Consider how Dassey's February 27, 2006 interrogations match up with the facts in *Seibert*. Remember that Seibert was interrogated without *Miranda* warnings for thirty to forty minutes, given a twenty-minute break, and then interrogated following *Miranda* warnings during which she repeated her incriminating primary statements. Sounds familiar, right?

At Mishicot High School, Dassey was interrogated without *Miranda* warnings from roughly 12:30 p.m. to 2:14 p.m., during which time he made incriminating statements. A few hours later, Officers again interrogated Dassey at the police station from 3:21 p.m. to 4:03 p.m. This time, Dassey received and waived *Miranda*. He then generally repeated the incriminating statements he made at the schoolhouse.

Assume that the state sought to introduce statements from that second interview. Assume further that you represent Dassey and have filed a motion to suppress. How would you apply *Seibert* to seek exclusion of Dassey's stationhouse statements? How would you distinguish *Elstad*?

4.   **Dassey and *Seibert* (part 2).** Is there *any* way to argue that statements taken from Dassey on March 1—the statements introduced against him at trial—are inadmissible under *Seibert*? Probably not. But remember that *Seibert* is concerned fundamentally with bad faith "police practices." Are those present in Dassey's case?

To remind you, Dassey was interrogated at his high school from 12:30–2:14 p.m. He is interrogated again later that day at the Two Rivers Police Department from 3:21–4:03 p.m. After the stationhouse interview, you'll recall that the state paid for Dassey and his mother to stay overnight at a nearby hotel where Detective Wiegert and Agent Fassbender would visit them that evening for an unknown duration. But, they must have talked for longer than a quick hello. At the end of the March 1 interrogation, Agent Fassbender would make reference to that visit, commenting "you ate that whole pizza the other night." [Casefile Interrogation Recordings Recording 4c at ~19:50.] In any event, Dassey returned home on February 28, but Agent Fassbender and Detective Wiegert removed Dassey from school at 9:50 a.m. on March 1.

Were those police contacts all one interrogation for *Seibert* purposes or separate interactions? Could the presumably unconstitutional February 27 high school interrogation keep out the statements Dassey made on March 1?

5. **A juvenile *Seibert*?** Notice a critical omission from our conversation thus far. At no point have we discussed Dassey's juvenile status or the role of his IQ of 72. The Supreme Court has not addressed whether the *Elstad-Seibert* analysis changes in the context of a juvenile with limited educational capability. That's presumably important given that the Supreme Court has acknowledged in other contexts that the law treats juveniles differently. *See, e.g., Miller v. Alabama*, 567 U.S. 460 (2012) (holding that mandatory life without parole sentences for juveniles are unconstitutional); *Roper v. Simmons*, 543 U.S. 551 (2005) (holding that imposition of the death penalty on juvenile offenders is unconstitutional). The role of educational capacity has likewise mattered in the Eighth Amendment context. *E.g., Atkins v. Virginia*, 536 U.S. 304 (2002) (prohibiting the execution of a mentally retarded person).

Equally problematic is that there is no separate Reid technique for juveniles. The Reid method concedes that interrogating juvenile suspects is, in part, different from interrogating adult suspects—but not much. FRED E. INBAU ET AL., CRIMINAL INTERROGATION AND CONFESSIONS 418–20 (5th ed. 2013). At one point, the technique acknowledges that, "[d]ue to immaturity and the corresponding lack of values and sense of responsibility, the behavior symptoms displayed by a youthful suspect may be unreliable." *Id.* at 250. It also advises that investigators should take special note of distinctions in *Miranda* waiver and voluntariness for the child suspect (defined as between ages 1–9) and the adolescent suspect (defined as aged 10–15). *Id.* at 254. Yet the technique simultaneously contends that "the principles and many of the case examples ... discussed with respect to adult suspects are just as applicable to the young ones." *Id.* at 250.

For the most part, the Reid method advocates not for a change in technique, but rather a change in the *approach* to the technique—specifically in the context of theme development. *Id.* at 250–55. Appropriate juvenile themes, the Reid method suggests, include having the investigator help the juvenile suspect blame commission of the crime on, for example, "family life and ensuing difficulties" or "[t]he neighborhood in which the suspect lived as a child may be blamed for not providing suitable alternatives to mischievous conduct." *Id.* at 251.

Perhaps the Reid technique's suggested juvenile themes surrounding "family life and ensuing difficulties" sound familiar. Consider some of the representative themes that Agent Fassbender and Detective Wiegert sought to develop when they questioned Dassey at his high school on February 27, 2006. Early on, Agent Fassbender provided Dassey with a lengthy Reid Step 2 theme statement, which included the following comments:

> And I've got . . . kids somewhat your age, I'm lookin' at you and I see you in him and I see him in you, I really do, and I know how that would hurt me too. I know how much he would hurt because of what he did know and how, how he felt for the person and what he saw and what he knows. I'm not here, like I said I'm not here to. . .I'm not, I'm here to give you the opportunity to get this off your chest. Mark and I, yeah we're cops, we're investigators and stuff like that, but I'm not right now. I'm a father that has a kid your age too. I wanna be here for you. There's nothing I'd like more than to come over and give you a hug cuz I know you're hurtin'.

[Casefile Interrogation Transcripts Document 2, at 443.] Later, in that same interview, Detective Wiegert would take his turn:

> Obviously, it's bothering you, this whole thing is bothering you and the rest of your family, but you'll never ever get over it unless you're honest about it, cuz this will bug you 'til the day that you die, unless you're honest about it. But we wanna go back and tell people that, you know, Brendan told us what he knew. We wanna be able to tell people that Brendan was honest, he's not like Steve, he's honest, he's a good guy.

Id. at 446. Wiegert would add shortly thereafter, "Steve doesn't care about you right now, he cares about himself." *Id.* at 447.

In many ways, the law on *Miranda*—not Reid—is to blame for permitting the use on juvenile suspects of psychologically coercive interrogation methods designed for use on adults. Unlike in the Eighth Amendment context, the Supreme Court has not yet seen fit to treat juveniles differently for *Miranda* purposes. In *Fare v. Michael C.*, 442 U.S. 707, 725 (1979), a *Miranda* waiver case, the Court expressly stated, "We discern no persuasive reasons why any other approach is required where the question is whether a juvenile has waived his rights, as opposed to whether an adult has done so."

Seibert makes no change to the *Miranda* fruits analysis based on the suspect's age. Admittedly, the offender's age was not an express issue in *Seibert*, but the point remains: Dassey's status as a juvenile remarkably contributes nothing to the *Seibert* analysis. Sure, *J. D. B.* teaches us that a juvenile's age is relevant to *Miranda* custody, but similar considerations do not pervade in the context of a *Miranda* fruits issue, where *Seibert* teaches litigants to look for a problematic interrogation practice or pattern generally— without regard to the suspect's age.

6.   Revisiting Daniel Ericksen. Remember Daniel Ericksen from Chapter 6? You will recall that Border Patrol Agents found drugs and drug paraphernalia in his vehicle after searching his car pursuant to the border search exception. While agents searched his car, Ericksen was questioned without *Miranda* rights by Agent Vittorini. Ericksen falsely stated that he "wasn't sure" if he had contraband in his vehicle. [Ericksen Casefile Document 4, at 1.] After Ericksen was transferred to the custody of the Port Huron state police, officer Thomas Rumley provided Ericksen with his *Miranda* rights, and Ericksen again made an incriminating statement. [Ericksen Casefile Document 2, at 3.] Ericksen argued in his motion to suppress that his unwarned statement was inadmissible because he was in custody subject to interrogation. But he *also* argued that *Elstad-Seibert* precluded admission of his second statement. [Ericksen Casefile Document 3, at 3–7.]

Both the suppression court and Circuit Court held that Ericksen was not in custody at the time of his initial statement at the border, rendering his *Seibert* argument inapplicable. Let's assume, though, that Ericksen was in custody at the time of his "wasn't sure" statement. Would *Seibert* keep out the incriminating statement he later made to Thomas Rumley—a different officer who worked for a different branch of law enforcement?

C. PHYSICAL EVIDENCE AS A *MIRANDA* "FRUIT"

UNITED STATES V. PATANE

542 U.S. 630
Supreme Court of the United States
December 9, 2003, Argued; June 28, 2004, Decided
No. 02-1183

JUSTICE THOMAS announced the judgment of the Court and delivered an opinion, in which the CHIEF JUSTICE and JUSTICE SCALIA join.

In this case we must decide whether a failure to give a suspect the warnings prescribed by *Miranda v. Arizona*, requires suppression of the physical fruits of the suspect's unwarned but voluntary statements. * * * Because the *Miranda* rule protects against violations of the Self-Incrimination Clause, which, in turn, is not implicated by the introduction at trial of physical evidence resulting from voluntary statements, we answer the question presented in the negative.

I.

In June 2001, respondent, Samuel Francis Patane, was arrested for harassing his ex-girlfriend, Linda O'Donnell. He was released on bond, subject to a temporary restraining order that prohibited him from contacting O'Donnell. Respondent apparently violated the restraining order by attempting to telephone O'Donnell. On June 6, 2001, Officer Tracy Fox of the Colorado Springs Police Department began to investigate the matter. On the same day, a county probation officer informed an agent of the Bureau of Alcohol, Tobacco and Firearms (ATF) that respondent, a convicted felon, illegally possessed a .40 Glock pistol. The ATF relayed this information to Detective Josh Benner, who worked closely with the ATF.

Together, Detective Benner and Officer Fox proceeded to respondent's residence.

After reaching the residence and inquiring into respondent's attempts to contact O'Donnell, Officer Fox arrested respondent for violating the restraining order. Detective Benner attempted to advise respondent of his *Miranda* rights but got no further than the right to remain silent. At that point, respondent interrupted, asserting that he knew his rights, and neither officer attempted to complete the warning.[1]

Detective Benner then asked respondent about the Glock. Respondent was initially reluctant to discuss the matter, stating: "I am not sure I should tell you anything about the Glock because I don't want you to take it away from me." Detective Benner persisted, and respondent told him that the pistol was in his bedroom. Respondent then gave Detective Benner permission to retrieve the pistol. Detective Benner found the pistol and seized it.

A grand jury indicted respondent for possession of a firearm by a convicted felon. The District Court granted respondent's motion to suppress the firearm, reasoning that the officers lacked probable cause to arrest respondent for violating the restraining order. It therefore declined to rule on respondent's alternative argument that the gun should be suppressed as the fruit of an unwarned statement.

The Court of Appeals reversed the District Court's ruling with respect to probable cause but affirmed the suppression order on respondent's alternative theory. The court rejected the Government's argument that this Court's decisions in *[Oregon v.] Elstad* and *[Michigan v.] Tucker* foreclosed application of the fruit of the poisonous tree doctrine of *Wong Sun v. United States* to the present context. * * * [W]e reverse the judgment of the Court of Appeals and remand the case for further proceedings.

II.

The Self-Incrimination Clause provides: "No person. . .shall be compelled in any criminal case to be a witness against himself." U.S. Const., Amdt. 5. * * * [T]he core protection afforded by the Self-Incrimination Clause is a prohibition on compelling a criminal defendant to testify against himself at trial. * * * To be sure, the Court has recognized and applied several prophylactic rules designed to protect the core privilege against self-incrimination.

[For example], in *Miranda*, the Court concluded that the possibility of coercion inherent in custodial interrogations unacceptably raises the risk that a suspect's privilege against self-incrimination might be violated. To

---

[1] The Government concedes that respondent's answers to subsequent on-the-scene questioning are inadmissible at trial under *Miranda v. Arizona*, 384 U.S. 436 (1966), despite the partial warning and respondent's assertions that he knew his rights.

protect against this danger, the *Miranda* rule creates a presumption of coercion, in the absence of specific warnings, that is generally irrebuttable for purposes of the prosecution's case in chief.

But because these prophylactic rules (including the *Miranda* rule) necessarily sweep beyond the actual protections of the Self-Incrimination Clause, any further extension of these rules must be justified by its necessity for the protection of the actual right against compelled self-incrimination. Indeed, at times the Court has declined to extend *Miranda* even where it has perceived a need to protect the privilege against self-incrimination.

It is for these reasons that statements taken without *Miranda* warnings (though not actually compelled) can be used to impeach a defendant's testimony at trial, *see Elstad, supra,* at 307–308; *Harris v. New York,* 401 U.S. 222 (1971), though the fruits of actually compelled testimony cannot, *see New Jersey v. Portash,* 440 U.S. 450, 458–459 (1979). More generally, the *Miranda* rule "does not require that the statements [taken without complying with the rule] and their fruits be discarded as inherently tainted," *Elstad,* 470 U.S., at 307. Such a blanket suppression rule could not be justified by reference to the "Fifth Amendment goal of assuring trustworthy evidence" or by any deterrence rationale, *id.,* at 308; *see Tucker, supra,* at 446–449; *Harris, supra,* at 225–226, and n.2, and would therefore fail our close-fit requirement. * * *

III.

Our cases also make clear the related point that a mere failure to give *Miranda* warnings does not, by itself, violate a suspect's constitutional rights or even the *Miranda* rule. * * * It follows that police do not violate a suspect's constitutional rights (or the *Miranda* rule) by negligent or even deliberate failures to provide the suspect with the full panoply of warnings prescribed by *Miranda*. Potential violations occur, if at all, only upon the admission of unwarned statements into evidence at trial. And, at that point, "[t]he exclusion of unwarned statements. . .is a complete and sufficient remedy" for any perceived *Miranda* violation.[3]

Thus, unlike unreasonable searches under the Fourth Amendment or actual violations of the Due Process Clause or the Self-Incrimination Clause, there is, with respect to mere failures to warn, nothing to deter. There is therefore no reason to apply the "fruit of the poisonous tree" doctrine of *Wong Sun,* 371 U.S., at 488. * * *

---

[3]   We acknowledge that there is language in some of the Court's post-*Miranda* decisions that might suggest that the *Miranda* rule operates as a direct constraint on police. But *Miranda* itself made clear that its focus was the admissibility of statements, a view the Court reaffirmed in *Dickerson v. United States,* 530 U.S. 428, 443–444 (2000) (equating the *Miranda* rule with the proposition that "unwarned statements may not be used as *evidence* in the prosecution's case in chief" (emphasis added)).

IV.

In the present case, the Court of Appeals, relying on *Dickerson*, wholly adopted the position that the taking of unwarned statements violates a suspect's constitutional rights. And, of course, if this were so, a strong deterrence-based argument could be made for suppression of the fruits.

But *Dickerson's* characterization of *Miranda* as a constitutional rule does not lessen the need to maintain the closest possible fit between the Self-Incrimination Clause and any judge-made rule designed to protect it. And there is no such fit here. Introduction of the nontestimonial fruit of a voluntary statement, such as respondent's Glock, does not implicate the Self-Incrimination Clause. The admission of such fruit presents no risk that a defendant's coerced statements (however defined) will be used against him at a criminal trial. In any case, "[t]he exclusion of unwarned statements. . .is a complete and sufficient remedy" for any perceived *Miranda* violation. There is simply no need to extend (and therefore no justification for extending) the prophylactic rule of *Miranda* to this context.

Similarly, because police cannot violate the Self-Incrimination Clause by taking unwarned though voluntary statements, an exclusionary rule cannot be justified by reference to a deterrence effect on law enforcement, as the Court of Appeals believed. Our decision not to apply *Wong Sun* to mere failures to give *Miranda* warnings was sound at the time *Tucker* and *Elstad* were decided, and we decline to apply *Wong Sun* to such failures now. * * *

Accordingly, we reverse the judgment of the Court of Appeals and remand the case for further proceedings.

It is so ordered.

JUSTICE KENNEDY, with whom JUSTICE O'CONNOR joins, concurring in the judgment.

In *Oregon v. Elstad*, 470 U.S. 298 (1985), *New York v. Quarles*, 467 U.S. 649 (1984), and *Harris v. New York*, 401 U.S. 222 (1971), evidence obtained following an unwarned interrogation was held admissible. This result was based in large part on our recognition that the concerns underlying the *Miranda v. Arizona*, 384 U.S. 436 (1966), rule must be accommodated to other objectives of the criminal justice system. I agree with the plurality that *Dickerson v. United States*, 530 U.S. 428 (2000), did not undermine these precedents and, in fact, cited them in support. Here, it is sufficient to note that the Government presents an even stronger case for admitting the evidence obtained as the result of Patane's unwarned statement. Admission of nontestimonial physical fruits (the Glock in this case), even more so than the postwarning statements to the police in *Elstad* and *Michigan v. Tucker*, 417 U.S. 433 (1974), does not run the risk of admitting into trial an accused's coerced incriminating statements against himself. In light of the important probative value of reliable physical evidence, it is doubtful that exclusion can be justified by a deterrence rationale sensitive to both law enforcement interests and a suspect's rights during an in-custody interrogation. Unlike the plurality, however, I find it unnecessary to decide whether the detective's failure to give Patane the full *Miranda* warnings should be characterized as a violation of the *Miranda* rule itself, or whether there is "anything to deter" so long as the unwarned statements are not later introduced at trial.

With these observations, I concur in the judgment of the Court.

JUSTICE SOUTER, with whom JUSTICE STEVENS and JUSTICE GINSBURG join, dissenting.

[Omitted.]

QUESTIONS, COMMENTS, CONCERNS?

1.   Placement of the camera during recorded interrogations. Did you notice the different placement of the camera in the varied Dassey interrogations? During the February 27, 2006, stationhouse interrogation, the camera captures Dassey, Agent Fassbender, and Detective Wiegert. By comparison, though, the March 1 camera recording focuses solely on Dassey, and for most of the interrogation, the viewer can see neither Detective Wiegert nor Agent Fassbender. A 2014 piece in the *New York Times* summarizes the concern with focusing the camera solely on Dassey:

> In a series of experiments led by the psychologist G. Daniel Lassiter of Ohio University, mock juries were shown exactly the same interrogation, but some saw only the defendant, while others had a wider-angle view that included the interrogator. When the interrogator isn't shown on camera, jurors are significantly less likely to find an interrogation coercive, and more likely to believe in the truth and accuracy of the confession that they hear—even when the interrogator explicitly threatens the defendant.

Jennifer L. Mnookin, *Can a Jury Believe What It Sees?*, N.Y. TIMES (July 13, 2014), https://www.nytimes.com/2014/07/14/opinion/videotaped-confessions-can -be-misleading.html.

2.   The rest of the Dassey story. After Dassey's trial counsel, Len Kachinsky, conceded that Dassey was not in custody during any of the interrogations, Dassey was left with just one meaningful argument: that his March 1 confession was involuntary. As if conceding the custody issue was not bad enough, Kachinsky also set up a follow-up interrogation for Agent Fassbender and Detective Wiegert to question Dassey on May 13, 2006. If you can believe it, Kachinsky even agreed not to be there. Dassey's statements on May 13 were so inconsistent with his March 1 statements that the prosecution elected not to use anything from the May 13 interrogation. Before trial,

Kachinsky was removed from the case as a result of his decision not to attend the May 13 interrogation.

In any event, Kachinsky's motion to suppress sought to suppress statements Dassey made on February 27 and March 1 on the basis that they were involuntary. [Casefile Litigation Files Document 1.] The motion cited one case. *Id.* at 6. After the state filed a response, the circuit court held a hearing on Dassey's motion. [See Casefile Litigation Files Document 3.] At the hearing, the court heard from Detective Wiegert who testified to that, in his opinion, Dassey understood his *Miranda* warnings before waiving them. *Id.* at 27. The circuit court ultimately denied Dassey's motion and held that his statements were voluntary. [Casefile Litigation Files Document 4.] In doing so, the circuit court noted that Dassey waived his *Miranda* warnings and that he, along with the prosecution, stipulated that his interrogations were non-custodial. *Id.* at 7, 11.

Dassey was tried over the course of nine days beginning on April 16, 2007. Before his trial, on November 15, 2006, Dassey was evaluated by Dr. Robert Gordon, a licensed psychologist, who relayed that Dassey scored on the "low average" range of intelligence. [Casefile Litigation Files Document 5, at 3.] Based on his evaluation, Dr. Gordon reached the following conclusion:

> Brendan is somewhat intellectually limited, passive, anxious, avoidant and reserved. If he is presented with leading questions during an interview and/or presented with interrogative pressure, his personality, as shown by interview data, behavior during the police interview and interview by the present psychologist, research regarding adolescents and suggestibility, and current test data, is very susceptible to suggestibility.

Id. at 5. False confessions expert Dr. Lawrence T. White also examined the Dassey interrogations prior to trial. [Casefile Litigation Files Document 6.] In his extensive twenty-page report, he concluded that there were "many reasons to question the trustworthiness and voluntariness of Brendan Dassey's so-called "confession." *Id.* Nevertheless, Dassey was convicted of first-degree intentional homicide, rape, and mutilation of a corpse on April 25, 2007. [Casefile Litigation Files Document 7.] Seventeen-years-old Dassey was sentenced to life in prison with the possibility of parole in 2048. *Id.* at 2.

His case has since followed a winding road. Briefly stated, his direct appeals through the state courts were unsuccessful. *E.g., State v. Dassey*, 827 N.W.2d 928 (Wisc. Ct. App. 2013) (per curiam). With new counsel, Dassey transitioned into the federal courts. On October 20, 2014, he filed a petition for a writ of habeas corpus arguing that his March 1 statements were involuntary and that he received ineffective assistance of counsel. [Casefile Litigation Files Document 8.]

In an opinion spanning nearly one-hundred pages, the United States District Court for the Eastern District of Wisconsin granted Dassey's writ on August 12, 2016. [Casefile Litigation Files Document 9.] Although it rejected

Dassey's ineffective assistance of counsel claim (remember you were warned in Chapter 1 that *Strickland* is worthless!), the court held that Dassey's confession was involuntary. *Id.* at 74–89. The court ordered his release from custody within ninety days pending the state's decision to retry him. *Id.* at 90.

The state appealed. In an extensive 104-page opinion, the Seventh Circuit affirmed the district court's decision. [Casefile Litigation Files Document 10.] The panel majority agreed that Dassey's confession was involuntarily and concluded that "the investigators promised Dassey freedom and alliance if he told the truth[,] and all signs suggest that Dassey took that promise literally." *Id.* at 101. Sitting *en banc*, however, the Seventh Circuit reversed the panel opinion, holding that the state court's finding of voluntariness, though debatable, was "reasonable" for purposes of the deferential habeas standard. *Id.* at 3.

On February 20, 2018, Dassey petitioned for review before the United States Supreme Court. [Casefile Litigation Files Document 12.] The Court denied his petition.

Dassey remains in prison.

V. BRINGING *MIRANDA* TOGETHER:
A REVIEW CHART

Miranda Review Chart

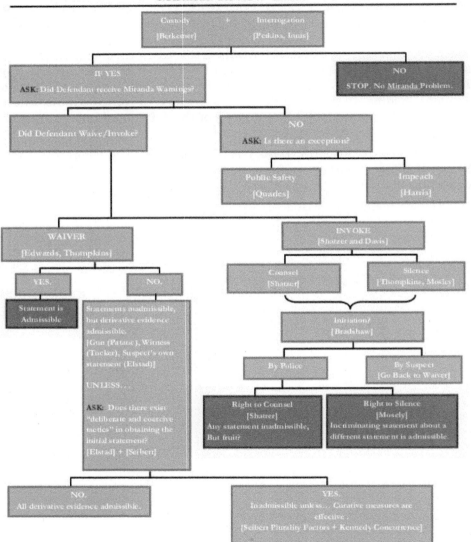

CHAPTER 10

CONFESSIONS & THE SIXTH AMENDMENT

■ ■ ■

I. INTRODUCTION[1]

A. CHAPTER ORGANIZATION

This introduction and casefile are a bit different. Rather than peer behind the curtain of litigants' filings or the manner in which a lower court evaluated a particular issue, this casefile—premised on the famous Supreme Court case of *Brewer v. Williams*—offers a rare look behind the scenes into how the Court operates. The look is particularly compelling given that, as discussed below, most thought *Brewer* would be the case to overrule *Miranda*. How wrong they were.

How the Supreme Court Operates (A General Overview)

We begin with some general insights into how the Supreme Court operates. Under Article III, Section 2, of the Constitution, the Supreme Court has both original and appellate jurisdiction. The Court's original jurisdiction, however, encompasses only a few types of cases, including disputes between two or more States.[2] In such cases, parties can file suit directly with the Supreme Court.

By contrast, the Court's appellate jurisdiction extends to cases first heard by lower courts. A party who is dissatisfied with a lower court ruling must petition (i.e., ask) the Court to hear their case; the primary means to petition the Court for review is to ask it to grant a *writ of certiorari*.[3] Four of the nine Justices must vote in favor of granting the petition in order for the Court to hear the case.

As petitions come into the Court, they are typically divided among the Justices and then further divided among the Justices' three to four judicial law clerks. A law clerk will read the petition and draft a bench memorandum recommending whether the case should be accepted.

---

[1] Remember that you have access to the filings relevant to this chapter in your online repository.

[2] 28 U.S.C. § 1251.

[3] *Supreme Court Procedures*, U.S. COURTS, http://www.uscourts.gov/about-federal-courts/educational-resources/about-educational-outreach/activity-resources/supreme-1 (last visited Aug. 27, 2022).

Assuming the case is accepted, the parties will brief the issues in advance of oral argument. By law, the Court's term begins on the first Monday in October and runs through the Sunday before the first Monday in October of the following year. That said, the Court typically sits in recess from late June/early July until that first Monday in October. Oral arguments occur from October through April.

After argument, the Justices hold a conference on the case. The current Supreme Court holds two conferences per week when in session. Only the Justices are permitted in the Conference. To begin, as a sign of collegiality, it is tradition for the Justices to shake hands. During the conference, the Justices speak without interruption in descending order of seniority. Votes are then cast, beginning with the Chief Justice and descending in order of seniority.

After voting is complete, the Chief or the most senior Justice in the majority assigns the opinion. The most senior Justice in dissent may assign the dissenting opinion. Opinions are published no later than the last day of the Court's term—that is, typically the day before Court goes into summer recess. No opinion is considered final until the Court delivers it in open Court or makes the opinion publicly available.

As you review the *Brewer* Casefile, you should be able to track this organization throughout each of the Justices' papers. Some of the Justices' files will be more organized and contain more information than others. Particulars aside, the *Brewer* Casefile provides considerable insight into the Supreme Court's internal and very private operations.

More on the Brewer *Casefile*

The *Brewer* Casefile is large—very large—and constitutes a compilation of private internal papers kept by six of the Justices who were on the Court at the time of *Brewer*. For the sake of organization, what constitutes several folders or, in some cases, boxes of material have been consolidated into a single PDF bearing the name of the individual Justice. That PDF was then assigned a page number at the bottom of the page in the center. That page number is solely attributable to this Casebook and not associated with the original materials.

Within each file, you will notice a couple of things. First, you will see that the Justices shared, retained, and kept their many draft opinions. As such, there is considerable duplication in the files. But the Justices' exchange of drafts opinions, and the letters that accompany them, provide a window into what it looks like for the Court to decide an incredibly important issue and then reduce its collective thought into a published opinion.

Second, you will notice that some of the Justices kept correspondences in their files. Some of those correspondences, we will discover, consist of direct letters from upset citizens, constituents, and even Pamela's brother. Oftentimes, a Justice's election to retain certain correspondence (and, in some cases, respond to it) shows just how passionately that Justice felt about the case alongside the position he took on the case.

Third, we will have the opportunity review bench memoranda filed by the Justices' judicial law clerks. This provides some insight into the relationship each Justice had with his particular clerk. Ideally, as you review the work submitted by the clerks, you will have a renewed appreciation for the important work done by judicial law clerks.

Finally, you will note that the *Brewer* Casefile includes private papers for Justices Blackmun, Brennan, Marshall, Stewart, Powell, and White. But what about the other three? Tracking down the Justices' papers is an endeavor—and an inconsistent one. Many of the Justices' papers are kept at the Library of Congress, but others are spread out at various locations across the country. One reason for the inconsistency is that the Justices' working papers have never been legislatively regulated.[4] The "longstanding historical default," instead, "embraces private ownership of judicial papers and gives individual judges and their heirs complete control over the fate of their papers."[5]

In the case of *Brewer*, we are missing papers from Chief Justice Burger, Justice Stevens, and Justice Rehnquist. The Chief's papers are housed at the College of William & Mary and are unavailable to researchers until at least 2032.[6] Justice Rehnquist's papers are closed during the lifetime of any member of the Supreme Court who served with him.[7] Justice Stevens's papers are unavailable because he is, of course, still alive.

A final reminder about our objectives. Our goals in this Casefile are relatively modest. Rather than make a critical assessment of litigants' arguments or writing, as we have done in previous Chapters, our goal here is to gain a better understanding of the inner workings of the Supreme Court. Think like a tourist and take it in.

B. AN INTRODUCTION TO *BREWER*

The idea that the *Sixth* Amendment—a trial right, after all—would have a role in the interrogation room was largely a foreign concept until 1964 when the Supreme Court issued *Massiah v. United States*. Well, foreign to everyone except Justice Potter Stewart. Recall that Justice

---

[4] Kathryn A. Watts, *Judges and Their Papers*, 88 N.Y.U. L. REV. 1666, 1669 (2013).

[5] *Id.*

[6] W&M Libraries Exhibits, *Introduction*, WARREN E. BURGER, https://exhibits.libraries.wm.edu/exhibits/show/warren-burger/intro (last visited Dec. 16, 2022).

[7] *Rehnquist Papers: Finding Aid for Materials from 1947 to 1974 Available to Researchers on November 17, 2008*, HOOVER INST., https://www.hoover.org/press-releases/rehnquist-papers-finding-aid-materials-1947-1974-available-researchers-november-17.

Stewart wrote a concurrence in *Spano v. New York*—a 1959 voluntariness case—wherein he wrote, in part, "[I]t is my view that the absence of counsel when [Spano's] confession was elicited was alone enough to render it inadmissible."[8] That view—that the Constitution limits police conduct after the filing of formal charges—crystalized more precisely in *Massiah*. As *Massiah*'s majority author, Justice Stewart wrote, "[The defendant] was denied the basic protections of [the Sixth Amendment] when there was used against him at his trial evidence of his own incriminating words, which federal agents had deliberately elicited from him after he had been indicted and in the absence of his counsel."[9]

But in the absence of formal charges, Justice Stewart was adamant that neither the Sixth Amendment nor the Fifth Amendment should have a role in the interrogation room. That to some extent explains his dissents in both *Miranda* and *Escobedo*, and it largely clarifies that, prior to a formal charge, Justice Stewart was comfortable measuring the admissibility of a defendant's incriminating statements using the voluntariness test. For the most part, though, he alone held that view—at least until *Brewer*. After all, the *Massiah* doctrine sat untouched for fourteen years until the Court decided *Brewer* in 1977. *Brewer* made clear that, in certain contexts, the Sixth Amendment would serve as a barrier to police behavior in the interrogation room.

As you move through these materials, make notes on how the Sixth Amendment right, as established through *Massiah* and its progeny, differs from the *Miranda* rights. Try to also note where the Fifth and Sixth Amendment rights overlap.

The Death and Discovery of Pamela Powers[10]

Christmas Eve 1968. By then, law enforcement was already familiar with Robert Williams. At the time, Williams was twenty-four-years-old and had a police record dating back six years. His record included auto theft, passing bad checks, molestation, attempted rape, and statutory rape. In total, Williams, from Kansas City, Missouri, had accrued fourteen different arrests while operating under numerous aliases.

By the time of Christmas Eve, Williams found himself in Des Moines, Iowa, having recently escaped in July 1968 from the Fulton State Hospital in Fulton, Missouri, where he was committed after being declared guilty but insane in the rape of two girls, aged eight and six. Since his arrival, Williams had become a licensed minister and joined the Maple Street Baptist Church where he played the organ, read devotions, preached a few times, and performed odd jobs for the church. Williams moved into the Des

---

8   360 U.S. 315, 326 (1959) (Stewart, J., concurring).

9   *Massiah v. United States*, 377 U.S. 201, 206 (1964).

10   Unless otherwise noted, the following story relies exclusively on THOMAS N. McINNIS, THE CHRISTIAN BURIAL CASE: AN INTRODUCTION TO CRIMINAL AND JUDICIAL PROCEDURE 2–11 (2001).

Moines YMCA on October 26, 1968, where he paid $16.83 in weekly rent. He began work on December 16 at Blue Cross as a unit clerk involved in billing.

Meanwhile, that same Christmas Eve, the Powers family, consisting of Mr. and Mrs. Merlin Powers, their daughter Vickie (15), son Mark (14), and daughter Pamela (10), were in Des Moines to attend a wrestling tournament at the local YMCA where Mark was competing. While at the tournament, Pamela left to wash her hands before eating a candy bar, but never returned. Her family searched for her for roughly twenty minutes before calling the police.

As the search for Pamela began, a security officer who worked at the YMCA, John Knapp, observed a YMCA resident carrying a blanket-wrapped bundle. Knapp, unaware that Pamela was missing, asked the man what he was carrying, to which the man responded a mannequin. The man proceeded to load the blanket and its contents into a nearby car. As the man loaded the blanket into the vehicle, fourteen-year-old witness Kevin Sanders would later say that the man's doing so exposed "skinny white legs." The man drove off in a 1959 green Buick with Iowa license plate number 63-2904. Knapp called the police.

Having now received two calls from the YMCA, the police realized the calls were likely related. As police collected preliminary information, Pamela was described as "4-feet-9 inches tall, weighing 63 pounds, with blond hair and blue eyes. She had been wearing an orange, striped blouse and orange slacks."[11] Knapp identified "Robert Anthony" as the man who carried the bundled blanket into the car. He described Robert Anthony, one of the aliases Williams used, for police, noting that he was roughly 5'7", had short hair, weighed 175 pounds, and was a light-skinned black man. Knapp further described the car Williams left in and told police that Williams was a resident at the YMCA. Police launched a search for Pamela and, for obvious reasons, police also focused their suspicions around Williams.

---

[11] *Id.* at 3.

Pamela Powers   Robert Williams

Nineteen-year veteran and chief of detectives, Captain Cleatus Leaming, was assigned to the case. Leaming instructed investigators to search the YMCA generally and Williams's room specifically, though the search failed to locate Pamela. But based on witness accounts, an arrest warrant was issued for Robert Williams on a charge of "child stealing."

Police thereafter enlarged the search area. The search for Pamela, which included twenty patrolmen from the Des Moines Police Department, extended overnight and into Christmas morning when the FBI joined the investigation. Investigators found Williams's car mid-morning on Christmas day in Davenport, Iowa, roughly 160 miles east of Des Moines. From there, the investigation became increasingly productive—a maintenance man would find "a pair of orange slacks, a white bobby sock, a man's shirt, a pair of men's trousers with the name 'Anthony' sewed on the inside, a handkerchief, and a Y.M.C.A. blanket in a garbage can at a rest stop on Interstate 80 near Grinnell, about 40 miles east of Des Moines."[12] Later that day, Pamela's father would identify certain items of clothing as the ones Pamela was wearing when she disappeared.

Meanwhile, Williams, in Davenport on Christmas Eve, went to the home of Sadie Wakefield Cade, who he had known for several years and who was unaware of the manhunt. The two made the short trip to Rock Island, Illinois, and went to the Clover Club where Williams, who ordinarily did not drink, consumed several alcoholic drinks. The pair stayed until 3 a.m. Cade and Williams celebrated Christmas together the

---

[12] *Id.* at 4.

next day and made plans to return to the Clover Club that night, this time with another couple. But when they arrived at the club at roughly 10 p.m., Williams refused to enter—choosing instead to remain in the car. When Cade exited the club at 11:30 p.m. to check on Williams, Williams was gone.

Williams called Henry McKnight the next morning, December 26, at around 8 a.m. McKnight was a Des Moines attorney and knew Williams from church. Williams, who was still in Rock Island, listened as McKnight told him that the community was upset about Pamela's disappearance. Williams replied by asking for help, to which McKnight replied that he would help Williams only if Williams turned himself in. McKnight also added, "You must give me the facts about the girl when you get here." When their call finished, McKnight then called the Davenport Police Department to let them know that Williams intended to surrender.

For his part, Williams took a cab from Rock Island back to Davenport. He arrived following the short ride at the Davenport police department at 9 a.m. With just $2.64 on him to pay for the $3.60 fare, the police would pay the cab driver the extra dollar after Williams walked into the precinct and identified himself.

As Williams completed his surrender, McKnight began arranging for Williams's transportation back to Des Moines. McKnight traveled to the Des Moines police station where he received a phone call from Williams. In the presence of the Chief of Police, Wendell Nichols, and Detective Leaming, McKnight told Williams that Des Moines officers would pick Williams up from Davenport and return him to Des Moines.

McKnight told Williams he "would not be mistreated or grilled and that he should make no statement until he reached Des Moines and they had a chance to consult."[13] McKnight would contend later that an agreement existed between him and Leaming that Williams would not be questioned until McKnight had a chance to speak with Williams. Leaming would disagree, asserting that no such deal existed.

In any event, Williams for the first time received his *Miranda* warnings following his phone call with McKnight. At 11 a.m. that morning, Williams appeared in state court before a judge who again provided to Williams his *Miranda* warnings. During that proceeding, Williams approached Thomas Kelly, a Davenport attorney, "because Kelly was the only other black person in the courtroom."[14] Kelly advised McKnight to make no statement until he could speak with McKnight back in Des Moines.

---

[13] *Id.* at 7.

[14] Philip E. Johnson, *The Return of the Christian Burial Speech Case*, 32 EMORY L.J. 349, 370 n.73 (1983).

As the proceeding unfolded, Detective Leaming and Detective Arthur Nelson, a fifteen-year law enforcement veteran who was working homicides, drove to Davenport. At 1 p.m., Leaming and Nelson arrived to retrieve Williams and had a conversation with both Williams and Thomas Kelly. Leaming again gave Williams his *Miranda* rights and indicated that they would be "visiting" on the return drive to Des Moines. Kelly would claim later that he received assurances that Leaming would not question Williams and, moreover, that he, Kelly, was denied the opportunity to ride back to Des Moines with Williams and the detectives in order to safeguard Williams's rights.

Williams was handcuffed and placed in the back seat of the car with his hands behind his back. Williams told Detective Leaming that he would speak with the officers after he had an opportunity to speak with McKnight. Despite Williams's comment, Leaming, who knew of Williams's mentally unstable and religious background, engaged Williams in a wide range of topics, including religion. Williams shared that he too "had religious training as a child."[15] Leaming believed that Pamela's body was somewhere in Mitchellville, a suburb of Des Moines—an area they would pass on the return trip to Des Moines.[16] Given that the trip ultimately took between five to six hours because of the bad weather, Leaming had plenty of time to work. According to Leaming's testimony, "in an effort to obtain statements from Williams concerning the missing girl, Leaming addressed Williams as 'Reverend' and went into what has become known as the Christian burial speech."[17]

The record of Williams's case does not reflect with clarity when the Christian burial speech occurred. But according to Professor Yale Kamisar, the "best reading of the record" suggests that "it occurred only a short time after they left the Davenport area and entered the freeway."[18] The United States Supreme Court and four other courts would analyze this speech, but as Professor Kamisar has observed, none discussed that Leaming offered two versions of the speech:

> [Leaming's] first version was given on April 2, 1969, at a pretrial hearing to suppress evidence; his second version, which was the only one quoted and discussed by the Supreme Court and lower federal courts, was given at the trial held four weeks later. Evidently, nobody noticed at the trial that the version Leaming then gave differed in several respects from his earlier version. He was not asked to explain any inconsistencies and did not do so.[19]

---

[15] McINNIS, *supra* note 10, at 8.

[16] Yale Kamisar, *Foreword: Brewer v. Williams—A Hard Look at a Discomfiting Record*, 66 GEO. L.J. 209, 212 (1977).

[17] McINNIS, *supra* note 10, at 8.

[18] Kamisar, *supra* note 16, at 215.

[19] *Id.* at 216.

Compare the two versions. In the first version, Leaming testified that he said the following to Williams:

> I said to Mr. Williams, I said, "Reverend, I'm going to tell you something. I don't want you to answer me, but I want you to think about it when we're driving down the road." I said, "I want you to observe the weather. It's raining and it's sleeting and it's freezing. Visibility is very poor. They are predicting snow for tonight. I think that we're going to be going right past where that body is, and if we should stop and find out where it is on the way in, her parents are going to be able to have a good Christian burial for their little daughter. If we don't and it does snow and if you're the only person knows where this is and if you have only been there once, it's very possible that with show on the ground you might not be able to find it. Now I just want you to think about that when we're driving down the road." That's all I said.[20]

At Williams's trial, Leaming recounted the speech as follows:

> Eventually, as we were traveling along there, I said to Mr. Williams that "I want to give you something to think about while we're traveling down the road." I said, "Number one, I want you to observe the weather conditions, it's raining, it's sleeting, it's freezing, driving is very treacherous, visibility is poor, it's going to be dark early this evening. They are predicting several inches of snow for tonight, and I feel that you yourself are the only person that knows where this little girl's body is, that you yourself have only been there once, and if you get a snow on top of it you yourself may be unable to find it. And, since we will be going right past the area on the way into Des Moines, I feel that we could stop and locate the body, that the parents of this little girl should be entitled to a Christian burial for the little girl who was snatched away from them on Christmas [E]ve and murdered. And I feel we should stop and locate it on the way in rather than waiting until morning and trying to come back out after a snow storm and possibly not being able to find it at all."[21]

Professor Kamisar has argued that the different versions of the speech are important. He, for example, has observed the following: "The first thing that strikes one about the earlier version of the Christian burial speech is the very first word—'Reverend.' *Why* did Leaming call Williams that? *How many times* did he do so on the drive back to Des Moines? These questions

---

[20] *Id.* at 216–17.

[21] *Id.*

were never asked. *No* questions about Williams being addressed as Reverend were ever asked."[22]

Inconsistencies in the speech aside, police had expanded their search efforts considerably as Williams was making his return trip to Des Moines. Specifically, by that time, roughly 250 people were looking for Pamela, including law enforcement, other state agents, the Boy Scouts, and volunteers. And as Williams's drive made its way toward Grinnell, Iowa, Williams asked the investigators whether they had found Pamela's shoes and offered to show them the shoes at a gas station where he claimed to have hidden them. But when the shoes could not be found following a stop, Williams offered to lead Leaming and Nelson to a blanket at a rest stop. Upon stopping at the rest stop, however, they learned the blanket had already been found. Finally, as they continued down the interstate, Williams offered to show Leaming and Nelson where Pamela's body was.

Based on Williams's offer to assist with the search, it was called off at approximately 3 p.m. on December 26. By 5:45 p.m., with Williams's cooperation, Pamela's body was discovered on a gravel road in Polk County. She was bare from the waist down and partially covered in snow, but dressed in an orange and white striped blouse.

Believing no interrogation would occur, McKnight was upset when, at 7:30 p.m., Detective Leaming arrived at the Des Moines Police Department with Williams. In his words, McKnight claimed that the police "really double-crossed me. They violated all the gentlemen's agreements we had."[23] Williams made his second appearance before a judge, this time on a murder charge. The charge of child stealing—the charge that supported the original arrest warrant—was dropped. McKnight was appointed as Williams's lawyer and Williams was held without bail. A subsequent autopsy reflected that Pamela was likely sexually assaulted and that she died from suffocation—probably before she was taken from the YMCA.

A Look at Williams's Procedural History[24]

Williams was charged and convicted of murder following a jury trial. He received a life sentence. But before trial, counsel for Williams filed a motion to suppress the statements Williams made during the drive from Davenport to Des Moines. The motion also sought to suppress evidence

---

[22] *Id.* at 221. Interestingly, Professor Kamisar noticed that Justice Stewart's majority opinion in *Brewer*, as you'll read, "describes the Christian burial speech as follows: 'Addressing Williams as 'Reverend,' the Detective said. . .' Justice Stewart then gives the second version of the speech and related testimony in its entirety. But Leaming did not address Williams as Reverend in the second version, only in the first." *Id.* at 223. Professor Kamisar cannot explain the inconsistency but openly wonders, "Why is the earlier version * * * ignored except for the very first word? Why does the second version become the official version?" *Id.*

[23] MCINNIS, *supra* note 10, at 9.

[24] Unless noted otherwise, this portion of the story relies on Tom N. McInnis, *Nix v. Williams and the Inevitable Discovery Exception: Creation of a Legal Safety Net*, 28 ST. LOUIS U. PUB. L. REV. 397, 406–12 (2009).

derived from those statements. For support, the motion relied jointly on the Fifth Amendment right against self-incrimination and the Sixth Amendment right to counsel. The trial court denied the motion, reasoning that Williams understood and voluntarily waived his rights before he gave information to the police.

Following the trial, McKnight filed an appeal to the Supreme Court of Iowa, arguing that Williams's conviction should be reversed because his statements were taken in violation of *Miranda*.[25] In a 5–4 decision, the Iowa Supreme Court held that Williams waived his Fifth and Sixth Amendment rights. It therefore upheld Williams's conviction.

In response, Williams filed a writ of habeas corpus in the United States District Court for the Southern District of Iowa. The question remained whether the statements Williams gave on his trip from Davenport to Des Moines violated the Fifth and Sixth Amendments. Answering that question in the affirmative, the federal district court granted Williams's petition. The court reasoned that officers knew Williams was represented by counsel and that there was no "affirmative indication" that Williams waived his rights.[26] The court therefore ordered that Williams be released from custody within sixty days pending an appeal or the pursuit of a new trial by the State of Iowa.

The State chose to file an appeal. In a 2–1 panel decision, the Eighth Circuit affirmed. The majority opinion, which focused largely on the Fifth Amendment, held that no *Miranda* waiver existed because Williams indicated during the trip that he would tell detectives the full story only after he consulted with counsel. The majority reasoned that, despite Williams's clear statement, Detective Leaming inappropriately "persisted in his 'conversation' with appellee with the admitted intent of obtaining information before their arrival in Des Moines and appellee's consultation with his attorney there. By means of a subtle form of interrogation, Leaming did obtain the incriminating statements from appellee."[27]

The Supreme Court granted the State's petition for certiorari in December 1975. The State's brief, "along with twenty-one other states acting as *amici curiae*, urged the Court to re-examine and overrule *Miranda v. Arizona*."[28] That seemed an appropriate manner to posture the case. *Miranda*, after all, was a 5–4 decision, and by the time of *Brewer* in 1977, there were just two members of the *Miranda* majority who were still on the Court. Moreover, And, moreover, the replacement Justices—four of whom were Nixon appointees—showed an affinity toward voting

---

[25] *Iowa v. Williams*, 182 N.W.2d 396 (Iowa 1971).

[26] *Williams v. Brewer*, 375 F. Supp. 170, 182 (S.D. Iowa 1974).

[27] *Williams v. Brewer*, 509 F.2d 227, 233–34 (8th Cir. 1974).

[28] McInnis, *supra* note 24, at 411.

together.[29] President Nixon himself had long ago expressed a desire to overrule *Miranda*. Even on the campaign trail, he gave speeches that attacked both *Miranda* and *Escobedo*. He promised that, if elected, he would fill the Court with "strict constructionists."[30]

Brewer therefore appeared to be the perfect storm as the case to fulfill President Nixon's campaign promises. The state even argued that *Brewer* was a *Miranda* case.[31] In the "Questions Presented" portion of its brief, the state framed the first issue as follows: "Should the oft-challenged doctrine of *Miranda v. Arizona*, 384 U.S. 436 (1966) now be disapproved?"

II. *MASSIAH*: THE BASICS

We now turn to a pair of foundational cases. The first, *Massiah v. United States*, established the Sixth Amendment firmly in the realm of pretrial investigations, and particularly so in the context of interrogations. Another Warren Court decision, *Massiah* was decided just two years before *Miranda* and, like *Miranda*, was not well-received. *E.g.*, Daniel Gutman, *The Criminal Gets the Breaks*, N.Y. TIMES, Nov. 29, 1964, at SM36 120–21. Whether because of its cold reception or something else, the *Massiah* doctrine sat untouched for more than a decade until our second case— *Brewer v. Williams*. In 1977, *Brewer* resurrected the *Massiah* doctrine and further expanded the right to counsel.

At its core, *Massiah* holds that investigators violate the Sixth Amendment by "deliberately eliciting" statements from a previously indicted or otherwise charged suspect in the absence of counsel. From that core holding, *Massiah* and *Brewer* collectively raise four primary questions:

1. When does *Massiah* attach?

2. What does "deliberate elicitation" mean?

3. How does as a suspect waive and invoke *Massiah*?

4. What does the *Massiah* exclusionary rule suppress?

---

[29] Johnson, *supra* note 12, at 352 n.13.

[30] Evan Thomas, *Inside the High Court*, TIME MAGAZINE, Nov. 5, 1979.

[31] Although this introductory text uses the term "state" to refer to petitioner, the petitioner in *Brewer* was actually Lou V. Brewer, the Warden of the Iowa State Penitentiary at Fort Madison, Iowa. By the time *Brewer* reached the Supreme Court, it had procedurally matured into a habeas case. At the risk of over-simplifying, the issue in a habeas case fundamentally asks whether something that took place in a *state* criminal proceeding violates the *federal* constitution. A writ of habeas corpus, then, proceeds as a civil action against the state agent holding the defendant— usually the warden—in order to determine whether the defendant is lawfully imprisoned.

While we are on the subject of habeas proceedings, you may notice in the *Brewer* Casefile that the Justices periodically debate the applicability of a case called *Stone v. Powell*, 428 U.S. 465 (1976). In *Stone v. Powell*, the Court held that "a federal court need not apply the exclusionary rule on habeas corpus review of a Fourth Amendment claim absent a showing that the state prisoner was denied an opportunity for a full and fair litigation of that claim at trial and on direct review." *Brewer v. Williams*, 430 U.S. 387, 413 (1977) (Marshall, J., concurring). Given that we are focused on the reach of *Massiah*, you may properly ignore those references for purposes of this chapter.

We begin with *Massiah*.

MASSIAH V. UNITED STATES

377 U.S. 201
Supreme Court of the United States
March 3, 1964, Argued; May 18, 1964, Decided
No. 199

MR. JUSTICE STEWART delivered the opinion of the Court.

The petitioner was indicted for violating the federal narcotics laws. He retained a lawyer, pleaded not guilty, and was released on bail. While he was free on bail a federal agent succeeded by surreptitious means in listening to incriminating statements made by him. Evidence of these statements was introduced against the petitioner at his trial over his objection. He was convicted, and the Court of Appeals affirmed. We granted certiorari to consider whether, under the circumstances here presented, the prosecution's use at the trial of evidence of the petitioner's own incriminating statements deprived him of any right secured to him under the Federal Constitution.

The petitioner, a merchant seaman, was in 1958 a member of the crew of the S. S. Santa Maria. In April of that year federal customs officials in New York received information that he was going to transport a quantity of narcotics aboard that ship from South America to the United States. As a result of this and other information, the agents searched the Santa Maria upon its arrival in New York and found in the afterpeak of the vessel five packages containing about three and a half pounds of cocaine. They also learned of circumstances, not here relevant, tending to connect the petitioner with the cocaine. He was arrested, promptly arraigned, and subsequently indicted for possession of narcotics aboard a United States vessel. In July a superseding indictment was returned, charging the petitioner and a man named Colson with the same substantive offense, and in separate counts charging the petitioner, Colson, and others with having conspired to possess narcotics aboard a United States vessel, and to import, conceal, and facilitate the sale of narcotics. The petitioner, who had retained a lawyer, pleaded not guilty and was released on bail, along with Colson.

A few days later, and quite without the petitioner's knowledge, Colson decided to cooperate with the government agents in their continuing investigation of the narcotics activities in which the petitioner, Colson, and others had allegedly been engaged. Colson permitted an agent named Murphy to install a Schmidt radio transmitter under the front seat of Colson's automobile, by means of which Murphy, equipped with an appropriate receiving device, could overhear from some distance away conversations carried on in Colson's car.

On the evening of November 19, 1959, Colson and the petitioner held a lengthy conversation while sitting in Colson's automobile, parked on a New York street. By prearrangement with Colson, and totally unbeknown to the petitioner, the agent Murphy sat in a car parked out of sight down the street and listened over the radio to the entire conversation. The petitioner made several incriminating statements during the course of this conversation. At the petitioner's trial these incriminating statements were brought before the jury through Murphy's testimony, despite the insistent objection of defense counsel. The jury convicted the petitioner of several related narcotics offenses, and the convictions were affirmed by the Court of Appeals.

The petitioner argues that it was an error of constitutional dimensions to permit the agent Murphy at the trial to testify to the petitioner's incriminating statements which Murphy had overheard under the circumstances disclosed by this record. * * * [I]t is said that the petitioner's Fifth and Sixth Amendment rights were violated by the use in evidence against him of incriminating statements which government agents had deliberately elicited from him after he had been indicted and in the absence of his retained counsel. * * *

In *Spano v. New York*, 360 U.S. 315, this Court reversed a state criminal conviction because a confession had been wrongly admitted into evidence against the defendant at his trial. In that case the defendant had already been indicted for first-degree murder at the time he confessed. The Court held that the defendant's conviction could not stand under the Fourteenth Amendment. While the Court's opinion relied upon the totality of the circumstances under which the confession had been obtained, four concurring Justices pointed out that the Constitution required reversal of the conviction upon the sole and specific ground that the confession had been deliberately elicited by the police after the defendant had been indicted, and therefore at a time when he was clearly entitled to a lawyer's help. * * *

Ever since this Court's decision in the *Spano* case, the New York courts have unequivocally followed this constitutional rule. * * *

Here we deal not with a state court conviction, but with a federal case, where the specific guarantee of the Sixth Amendment directly applies. We hold that the petitioner was denied the basic protections of that guarantee when there was used against him at his trial evidence of his own incriminating words, which federal agents had deliberately elicited from him after he had been indicted and in the absence of his counsel. It is true that in the *Spano* case the defendant was interrogated in a police station, while here the damaging testimony was elicited from the defendant without his knowledge while he was free on bail. But, as Judge Hays pointed out in his dissent in the Court of Appeals, "if such a rule is to have any efficacy it must apply to indirect and surreptitious interrogations as well as those conducted in the jailhouse. In this case, Massiah was more seriously imposed upon. . .because he did not even know that he was under interrogation by a government agent."

* * * We do not question that in this case, as in many cases, it was entirely proper to continue an investigation of the suspected criminal activities of the defendant and his alleged confederates, even though the defendant had already been indicted. All that we hold is that the defendant's own incriminating statements, obtained by federal agents under the circumstances here disclosed, could not constitutionally be used by the prosecution as evidence against him at his trial.

Reversed.

MR. JUSTICE WHITE, with whom MR. JUSTICE CLARK and MR. JUSTICE HARLAN join, dissenting. * * *

It is * * * a rather portentous occasion when a constitutional rule is established barring the use of evidence which is relevant, reliable and highly probative of the issue which the trial court has before it—whether the accused committed the act with which he is charged. Without the evidence, the quest for truth may be seriously impeded and in many cases the trial court, although aware of proof showing defendant's guilt, must nevertheless release him because the crucial evidence is deemed inadmissible. This result is entirely justified in some circumstances because exclusion serves other policies of overriding importance, as where evidence seized in an illegal search is excluded, not because of the quality of the proof, but to secure meaningful enforcement of the Fourth Amendment. *Weeks v. United States*, 232 U.S. 383; *Mapp v. Ohio*, 367 U.S. 643. But this only emphasizes that the soundest of reasons is necessary to warrant the exclusion of evidence otherwise admissible and the creation of another area of privileged testimony. With all due deference, I am not at all convinced that the additional barriers to the pursuit of truth which the Court today erects rest on anything like the solid foundations which decisions of this gravity should require. * * *

Whatever the content or scope of the rule may prove to be, I am unable to see how this case presents an unconstitutional interference with Massiah's right to counsel. Massiah was not prevented from consulting with counsel as often as he wished. No meetings with counsel were disturbed or spied upon. Preparation for trial was in no way obstructed. It is only a sterile syllogism—an unsound one, besides—to say that because Massiah had a right to counsel's aid before and during the trial, his out-of-court conversations and admissions must be excluded if obtained without counsel's consent or presence. The right to counsel has never meant as much before and its extension in this case requires some further explanation, so far unarticulated by the Court.

Since the new rule would exclude all admissions made to the police, no matter how voluntary and reliable, the requirement of counsel's presence or approval would seem to rest upon the probability that counsel would foreclose any admissions at all. This is nothing more than a thinly disguised constitutional policy of minimizing or entirely prohibiting the use in evidence of voluntary out-of-court admissions and confessions made by the accused. Carried as far as blind logic may compel some to go, the notion that statements from the mouth of the defendant should not be used in evidence would have a severe and unfortunate impact upon the great bulk of criminal cases.

Viewed in this light, the Court's newly fashioned exclusionary principle goes far beyond the constitutional privilege against self-incrimination, which neither requires nor suggests the barring of voluntary pretrial admissions. * * *

The Court presents no facts, no objective evidence, no reasons to warrant scrapping the voluntary-involuntary test for admissibility in this area. Without such evidence I would retain it in its present form. * * *

Meanwhile, of course, the public will again be the loser and law enforcement will be presented with another serious dilemma. The general issue lurking in the background of the Court's opinion is the legitimacy of penetrating or obtaining confederates in criminal organizations. For the law enforcement agency, the answer for the time being can only be in the form of a prediction about the future application of today's new constitutional doctrine. More narrowly, and posed by the precise situation involved here, the question is this: when the police have arrested and released on bail one member of a criminal ring and another member, a confederate, is cooperating with the police, can the confederate be allowed to continue his association with the ring or must he somehow be withdrawn to avoid challenge to trial evidence on the ground that it was acquired after rather than before the arrest, after rather than before the indictment?

* * * Massiah and those like him receive ample protection from the long line of precedents in this Court holding that confessions may not be introduced unless they are voluntary. In making these determinations the courts must consider the absence of counsel as one of several factors by which voluntariness is to be judged. This is a wiser rule than the automatic rule announced by the Court, which requires courts and juries to disregard voluntary admissions which they might well find to be the best possible evidence in discharging their responsibility for ascertaining truth.

QUESTIONS, COMMENTS, CONCERNS?

1. ***Miranda's* applicability to *Massiah*.** Does the *Fifth Amendment* right to counsel apply to the statements made by petitioner?

2. *Massiah* fruits. What if police learned about a witness or a weapon from petitioner's statements? Could police introduce that "fruit" against petitioner?

3. "Deliberate elicitation." Is the Sixth Amendment *Massiah* right to counsel violated if the police or prosecutors have *any* contact with a person formally accused of a crime without a lawyer present?

BREWER V. WILLIAMS

430 U.S. 387
Supreme Court of the United States
Argued October 4, 1976; March 23, 1977
No. 74-1263

MR. JUSTICE STEWART delivered the opinion of the Court. * * *

I.

On the afternoon of December 24, 1968, a 10-year-old girl named Pamela Powers went with her family to the YMCA in Des Moines, Iowa, to watch a wrestling tournament in which her brother was participating. When she failed to return from a trip to the washroom, a search for her began. The search was unsuccessful.

Robert Williams, who had recently escaped from a mental hospital, was a resident of the YMCA. Soon after the girl's disappearance Williams was seen in the YMCA lobby carrying some clothing and a large bundle wrapped in a blanket. He obtained help from a 14-year-old boy in opening the street door of the YMCA and the door to his automobile parked outside. When Williams placed the bundle in the front seat of his car the boy "saw two legs in it and they were skinny and white." Before anyone could see what was in the bundle Williams drove away. His abandoned car was found the following day in Davenport, Iowa, roughly 160 miles east of Des Moines. A warrant was then issued in Des Moines for his arrest on a charge of abduction.

On the morning of December 26, a Des Moines lawyer named Henry McKnight went to the Des Moines police station and informed the officers present that he had just received a long-distance call from Williams, and that he had advised Williams to turn himself in to the Davenport police. Williams did surrender that morning to the police in Davenport, and they booked him on the charge specified in the arrest warrant and gave him the warnings required by *Miranda v. Arizona*, 384 U.S. 436. The Davenport police then telephoned their counterparts in Des Moines to inform them that Williams had surrendered. McKnight, the lawyer, was still at the Des Moines police headquarters, and Williams conversed with McKnight on the telephone. In the presence of the Des Moines chief of police and a police detective named Leaming, McKnight advised Williams that Des Moines police officers would be driving to Davenport to pick him up, that the officers would not interrogate him or mistreat him, and that Williams was not to talk to the officers about Pamela Powers until after consulting with McKnight upon his return to Des Moines. As a result of these conversations, it was agreed between McKnight and the Des Moines police officials that Detective Leaming and a fellow officer would drive to Davenport to pick up Williams, that they would bring him directly back to Des Moines, and that they would not question him during the trip.

In the meantime, Williams was arraigned before a judge in Davenport on the outstanding arrest warrant. The judge advised him of his *Miranda* rights and committed him to jail. Before leaving the courtroom, Williams conferred with a lawyer named Kelly, who advised him not to make any statements until consulting with McKnight back in Des Moines.

Detective Leaming and his fellow officer arrived in Davenport about noon to pick up Williams and return him to Des Moines. Soon after their arrival they met with Williams and Kelly, who, they understood, was acting as Williams's lawyer. Detective Leaming repeated the *Miranda* warnings, and told Williams:

> [W]e both know that you're being represented here by Mr. Kelly and you're being represented by Mr. McKnight in Des Moines, and. . .I want you to remember this because we'll be visiting between here and Des Moines.

Williams then conferred again with Kelly alone, and after this conference Kelly reiterated to Detective Leaming that Williams was not to be questioned about the disappearance of Pamela Powers until after he had consulted with McKnight back in Des Moines. When Leaming expressed some reservations, Kelly firmly stated that the agreement with McKnight was to be carried out—that there was to be no interrogation of Williams during the automobile journey to Des Moines. Kelly was denied permission to ride in the police car back to Des Moines with Williams and the two officers.

The two detectives, with Williams in their charge, then set out on the 160-mile drive. At no time during the trip did Williams express a willingness to be interrogated in the absence of an attorney. Instead, he stated several times that "[w]hen I get to Des Moines and see Mr. McKnight, I am going to tell you the whole story." Detective Leaming knew that Williams was a former mental patient and knew also that he was deeply religious.

The detective and his prisoner soon embarked on a wide-ranging conversation covering a variety of topics, including the subject of religion. Then, not long after leaving Davenport and reaching the interstate highway, Detective Leaming delivered what has been referred to in the briefs and oral arguments as the "Christian burial speech." Addressing Williams as "Reverend," the detective said:

I want to give you something to think about while we're traveling down the road. . . Number one, I want you to observe the weather conditions, it's raining, it's sleeting, it's freezing, driving is very treacherous, visibility is poor, it's going to be dark early this evening. They are predicting several inches of snow for tonight, and I feel that you yourself are the only person that knows where this little girl's body is, that you yourself have only been there once, and if you get a snow on top of it you yourself may be unable to find it. And, since we will be going right past the area on the way into Des Moines, I feel that we could stop and locate the body, that the parents of this little girl should be entitled to a Christian burial for the little girl who was snatched away from them on Christmas [E]ve and murdered. And I feel we should stop and locate it on the way in rather than waiting until morning and trying to come back out after a snow storm and possibly not being able to find it at all.

Williams asked Detective Leaming why he thought their route to Des Moines would be taking them past the girl's body, and Leaming responded that he knew the body was in the area of Mitchellville—a town they would be passing on the way to Des Moines.[1] Leaming then stated: "I do not want you to answer me. I don't want to discuss it any further. Just think about it as we're riding down the road."

As the car approached Grinnell, a town approximately 100 miles west of Davenport, Williams asked whether the police had found the victim's shoes. When Detective Leaming replied that he was unsure, Williams directed the officers to a service station where he said he had left the shoes; a search for them proved unsuccessful. As they continued towards Des Moines, Williams asked whether the police had found the blanket, and directed the officers to a rest area where he said he had disposed of the blanket. Nothing was found. The car continued towards Des Moines, and as it approached Mitchellville, Williams said that he would show the officers where the body was. He then directed the police to the body of Pamela Powers.

Williams was indicted for first-degree murder. Before trial, his counsel moved to suppress all evidence relating to or resulting from any statements Williams had made during the automobile ride from Davenport to Des Moines. After an evidentiary hearing the trial judge denied the motion. He found that "an agreement was made between defense counsel and the police officials to the effect that the Defendant was not to be questioned on the return trip to Des Moines," and that the evidence in question had been elicited from Williams during "a critical stage in the proceedings requiring the presence of counsel on his request." The judge ruled, however, that

---

[1]   The fact of the matter, of course, was that Detective Leaming possessed no such knowledge.

Williams had "waived his right to have an attorney present during the giving of such information."

The evidence in question was introduced over counsel's continuing objection at the subsequent trial. The jury found Williams guilty of murder, and the judgment of conviction was affirmed by the Iowa Supreme Court, a bare majority of whose members agreed with the trial court that Williams had "waived his right to the presence of his counsel" on the automobile ride from Davenport to Des Moines. * * *

Williams then petitioned for a writ of habeas corpus in the United States District Court for the Southern District of Iowa. Counsel for the State and for Williams stipulated that "the case would be submitted on the record of facts and proceedings in the trial court, without taking of further testimony." The District Court made findings of fact as summarized above, and concluded as a matter of law that the evidence in question had been wrongly admitted at Williams's trial. This conclusion was based on three alternative and independent grounds: (1) that Williams had been denied his constitutional right to the assistance of counsel; (2) that he had been denied the constitutional protections defined by this Court's decisions in *Escobedo v. Illinois*, 378 U.S. 478, and *Miranda v. Arizona*, 384 U.S. 436; and (3) that in any event, his self-incriminatory statements on the automobile trip from Davenport to Des Moines had been involuntarily made. Further, the District Court ruled that there had been no waiver by Williams of the constitutional protections in question.

The Court of Appeals for the Eighth Circuit, with one judge dissenting, affirmed this judgment and denied a petition for rehearing en banc. We granted certiorari to consider the constitutional issues presented.

II.   * * *

* * * [T]here is no need to review in this case the doctrine of *Miranda v. Arizona*, a doctrine designed to secure the constitutional privilege against compulsory self-incrimination. * * * For it is clear that the judgment before us must in any event be affirmed upon the ground that Williams was deprived of a different constitutional right—the right to the assistance of counsel.

This right, guaranteed by the Sixth and Fourteenth Amendments, is indispensable to the fair administration of our adversary system of criminal justice. * * *

There has occasionally been a difference of opinion within the Court as to the peripheral scope of this constitutional right. * * * Whatever else it may mean, the right to counsel granted by the Sixth and Fourteenth Amendments means at least that a person is entitled to the help of a lawyer at or after the time that judicial proceedings have been initiated against him—"whether by way of formal charge, preliminary hearing, indictment, information, or arraignment."

There can be no doubt in the present case that judicial proceedings had been initiated against Williams before the start of the automobile ride from Davenport to Des Moines. A warrant had been issued for his arrest, he had been arraigned on that warrant before a judge in a Davenport courtroom, and he had been committed by the court to confinement in jail. The State does not contend otherwise.

There can be no serious doubt, either, that Detective Leaming deliberately and designedly set out to elicit information from Williams just as surely as—and perhaps more effectively than—if he had formally interrogated him. Detective Leaming was fully aware before departing for Des Moines that Williams was being represented in Davenport by Kelly and in Des Moines by McKnight. Yet he purposely sought during Williams's isolation from his lawyers to obtain as much incriminating information as possible. Indeed, Detective Leaming conceded as much when he testified at Williams's trial:

> Q. In fact, Captain, whether he was a mental patient or not, you were trying to get all the information you could before he got to his lawyer, weren't you?
>
> A. I was sure hoping to find out where that little girl was, yes, sir.
>
> . . . . .
>
> Q. Well, I'll put it this way: You was [sic] hoping to get all the information you could before Williams got back to McKnight, weren't you?
>
> A. Yes, sir.[6]

The state courts clearly proceeded upon the hypothesis that Detective Leaming's "Christian burial speech" had been tantamount to interrogation. Both courts recognized that Williams had been entitled to the assistance of counsel at the time he made the incriminating statements. Yet no such constitutional protection would have come into play if there had been no interrogation.

---

[6] Counsel for petitioner, in the course of oral argument in this Court, acknowledged that the "Christian burial speech" was tantamount to interrogation:

Q: But isn't the point, really, Mr. Attorney General, what you indicated earlier, and that is that the officer wanted to elicit information from Williams. . .

A: Yes, sir.

Q: . . .by whatever techniques he used, I would suppose a lawyer would consider that he were pursuing interrogation.

A: It is, but it was very brief.

The circumstances of this case are thus constitutionally indistinguishable from those presented in *Massiah v. United States, supra.* * * *

That the incriminating statements were elicited surreptitiously in the *Massiah* case, and otherwise here, is constitutionally irrelevant. Rather, the clear rule of *Massiah* is that once adversary proceedings have commenced against an individual, he has a right to legal representation when the government interrogates him.[8] It thus requires no wooden or technical application of the *Massiah* doctrine to conclude that Williams was entitled to the assistance of counsel guaranteed to him by the Sixth and Fourteenth Amendments.

III.

The Iowa courts recognized that Williams had been denied the constitutional right to the assistance of counsel. They held, however, that he had waived that right during the course of the automobile trip from Davenport to Des Moines. * * *

In its lengthy opinion affirming this determination, the Iowa Supreme Court applied "the totality-of-circumstances test for a showing of waiver of constitutionally-protected rights in the absence of an express waiver," and concluded that "evidence of the time element involved on the trip, the general circumstances of it, and the absence of any request or expressed desire for the aid of counsel before or at the time of giving information, were sufficient to sustain a conclusion that defendant did waive his constitutional rights as alleged."

In the federal habeas corpus proceeding the District Court, believing that the issue of waiver was not one of fact but of federal law, held that the Iowa courts had "applied the wrong constitutional standards" in ruling that Williams had waived the protections that were his under the Constitution. The court held "that it is the *government* which bears a heavy burden. . .but that is the burden which explicitly was placed on [Williams] by the state courts." (emphasis in original). After carefully reviewing the evidence, the District Court concluded:

> [U]nder the proper standards for determining waiver, there simply is no evidence to support a waiver. . .[T]here is no affirmative indication. . .that [Williams] did waive his rights. . .

---

[8] The only other significant factual difference between the present case and *Massiah* is that here the police had agreed that they would not interrogate Williams in the absence of his counsel. This circumstance plainly provides petitioner with no argument for distinguishing away the protection afforded by *Massiah.*

It is argued that this agreement may not have been an enforceable one. But we do not deal here with notions of offer, acceptance, consideration, or other concepts of the law of contracts. We deal with constitutional law. And every court that has looked at this case has found an "agreement" in the sense of a commitment made by the Des Moines police officers that Williams would not be questioned about Pamela Powers in the absence of his counsel.

[T]he state courts' emphasis on the absence of a demand for counsel was not only legally inappropriate, but factually unsupportable as well, since Detective Leaming himself testified that [Williams], on several occasions during the trip, indicated that he would talk after he saw Mr. McKnight. * * *

The Court of Appeals approved the reasoning of the District Court[.] * * *

The District Court and the Court of Appeals were correct in the view that the question of waiver was not a question of historical fact, but one which, in the words of Mr. Justice Frankfurter, requires "application of constitutional principles to the facts as found. . ."

The District Court and the Court of Appeals were also correct in their understanding of the proper standard to be applied in determining the question of waiver as a matter of federal constitutional law—that it was incumbent upon the State to prove "an intentional relinquishment or abandonment of a known right or privilege." That standard has been reiterated in many cases. * * *

We conclude, finally, that the Court of Appeals was correct in holding that, judged by these standards, the record in this case falls far short of sustaining petitioner's burden. It is true that Williams had been informed of and appeared to understand his right to counsel. But waiver requires not merely comprehension but relinquishment, and Williams's consistent reliance upon the advice of counsel in dealing with the authorities refutes any suggestion that he waived that right. He consulted McKnight by long-distance telephone before turning himself in. He spoke with McKnight by telephone again shortly after being booked. After he was arraigned, Williams sought out and obtained legal advice from Kelly. Williams again consulted with Kelly after Detective Leaming and his fellow officer arrived in Davenport. Throughout, Williams was advised not to make any statements before seeing McKnight in Des Moines and was assured that the police had agreed not to question him. His statements while in the car that he would tell the whole story after seeing McKnight in Des Moines were the clearest expressions by Williams himself that he desired the presence of an attorney before any interrogation took place. But even before making these statements, Williams had effectively asserted his right to counsel by having secured attorneys at both ends of the automobile trip, both of whom, acting as his agents, had made clear to the police that no interrogation was to occur during the journey. Williams knew of that agreement and, particularly in view of his consistent reliance on counsel, there is no basis for concluding that he disavowed it.

Despite Williams's express and implicit assertions of his right to counsel, Detective Leaming proceeded to elicit incriminating statements from Williams. Leaming did not preface this effort by telling Williams that he had a right to the presence of a lawyer and made no effort at all to ascertain whether Williams wished to relinquish that right. The circumstances of record in this case thus provide no reasonable basis for finding that Williams waived his right to the assistance of counsel.

The Court of Appeals did not hold, nor do we, that under the circumstances of this case Williams could not, without notice to counsel, have waived his rights under the Sixth and Fourteenth Amendments. It only held, as do we, that he did not. * * *

The judgment of the Court of Appeals is affirmed.[12]

It is so ordered.

MR. JUSTICE MARSHALL, concurring.

[Omitted.]

MR. JUSTICE POWELL, concurring. * * *

I join the opinion of the Court which * * * finds that the efforts of Detective Leaming "to elicit information from Williams," as conceded by counsel for petitioner at oral argument, were a skillful and effective form of interrogation. Moreover, the entire setting was conducive to the psychological coercion that was successfully exploited. Williams was known by the police to be a young man with quixotic religious convictions and a history of mental disorders. The date was the day after Christmas, the weather was ominous, and the setting appropriate for Detective Leaming's talk of snow concealing the body and preventing a "Christian burial." Williams was alone in the automobile with two police officers for several hours. It is clear from the record, as both of the federal courts below found, that there was no evidence of a knowing and voluntary waiver of the right to have counsel present beyond the fact that Williams ultimately confessed. It is settled law that an inferred waiver of a constitutional right is disfavored. I find no basis in the record of this case—or in the dissenting opinions for disagreeing with the conclusion of the District Court that "the State has produced no affirmative evidence whatsoever to support its claim of waiver."

The dissenting opinion of THE CHIEF JUSTICE states that the Court's holding today "conclusively presumes a suspect is legally incompetent to

---

[12]   The District Court stated that its decision "does not touch upon the issue of what evidence, if any, beyond the incriminating statements themselves must be excluded as 'fruit of the poisonous tree.' " We, too, have no occasion to address this issue, and in the present posture of the case there is no basis for the view of our dissenting Brethren that any attempt to retry the respondent would probably be futile. While neither Williams's incriminating statements themselves nor any testimony describing his having led the police to the victim's body can constitutionally be admitted into evidence, evidence of where the body was found and of its condition might well be admissible on the theory that the body would have been discovered in any event, even had incriminating statements not been elicited from Williams. In the event that a retrial is instituted, it will be for the state courts in the first instance to determine whether particular items of evidence may be admitted.

change his mind and tell the truth until an attorney is present." I find no justification for this view. On the contrary, the opinion of the Court is explicitly clear that the right to assistance of counsel may be waived, after it has attached, without notice to or consultation with counsel. We would have such a case here if petitioner had proved that the police officers refrained from coercion and interrogation, as they had agreed, and that Williams freely on his own initiative had confessed the crime. * * *

MR. JUSTICE STEVENS, concurring.

* * * [T]he strong language in the dissenting opinions prompts me to add this brief comment about the Court's function in a case such as this.

Nothing that we write, no matter how well reasoned or forcefully expressed, can bring back the victim of this tragedy or undo the consequences of the official neglect which led to the respondent's escape from a state mental institution. The emotional aspects of the case make it difficult to decide dispassionately, but do not qualify our obligation to apply the law with an eye to the future as well as with concern for the result in the particular case before us.

Underlying the surface issues in this case is the question whether a fugitive from justice can rely on his lawyer's advice given in connection with a decision to surrender voluntarily. The defendant placed his trust in an experienced Iowa trial lawyer who in turn trusted the Iowa law enforcement authorities to honor a commitment made during negotiations which led to the apprehension of a potentially dangerous person. Under any analysis, this was a critical stage of the proceeding in which the participation of an independent professional was of vital importance to the accused and to society. At this stage—as in countless others in which the law profoundly affects the life of the individual—the lawyer is the essential medium through which the demands and commitments of the sovereign are communicated to the citizen. If, in the long run, we are seriously concerned about the individual's effective representation by counsel, the State cannot be permitted to dishonor its promise to this lawyer.*

MR. CHIEF JUSTICE BURGER, dissenting.

The result in this case ought to be intolerable in any society which purports to call itself an organized society. It continues the Court—by the narrowest margin—on the much-criticized course of punishing the public for the mistakes and misdeeds of law enforcement officers, instead of punishing the officer directly, if in fact he is guilty of wrongdoing. It mechanically and blindly keeps reliable evidence from juries whether the claimed constitutional violation involves gross police misconduct or honest human error.

---

*   The importance of this point is emphasized by the State's refusal to permit counsel to accompany his client on the trip from Davenport to Des Moines.

Williams is guilty of the savage murder of a small child; no member of the Court contends he is not. While in custody, and after no fewer than five warnings of his rights to silence and to counsel, he led police to the concealed body of his victim. The Court concedes Williams was not threatened or coerced and that he spoke and acted voluntarily and with full awareness of his constitutional rights. In the face of all this, the Court now holds that because Williams was prompted by the detective's statement—not interrogation but a statement—the jury must not be told how the police found the body.

* * *   With JUSTICES WHITE, BLACKMUN, and REHNQUIST, I categorically reject the remarkable notion that the police in this case were guilty of unconstitutional misconduct, or any conduct justifying the bizarre result reached by the Court. * * *

Under well-settled precedents which the Court freely acknowledges, it is very clear that Williams had made a valid waiver of his Fifth Amendment right to silence and his Sixth Amendment right to counsel when he led police to the child's body. Indeed, even under the Court's analysis I do not understand now a contrary conclusion is possible.

The Court purports to apply as the appropriate constitutional waiver standard the familiar "intentional relinquishment or abandonment of a known right or privilege" test of *Johnson v. Zerbst*, 304 U.S. 458, 464 (1938). The Court assumes, without deciding, that Williams's conduct and statements were voluntary. It concedes, as it must, that Williams had been informed of and fully understood his constitutional rights and the consequences of their waiver. Then, having either assumed or found every element necessary to make out a valid waiver under its own test, the Court reaches the astonishing conclusion that no valid waiver has been demonstrated. * * *

The evidence is uncontradicted that Williams had abundant knowledge of his right to have counsel present and of his right to silence. Since the Court does not question his mental competence, it boggles the mind to suggest that Williams could not understand that leading police to the child's body would have other than the most serious consequences. All of the elements necessary to make out a valid waiver are shown by the record and acknowledged by the Court; we thus are left to guess how the Court reached its holding.

One plausible but unarticulated basis for the result reached is that once a suspect has asserted his right not to talk without the presence of an attorney, it becomes legally impossible for him to waive that right until he has seen an attorney. But constitutional rights are personal, and an otherwise valid waiver should not be brushed aside by judges simply because an attorney was not present. The Court's holding * * * conclusively presumes a suspect is legally incompetent to change his mind and tell the truth until an attorney is present. It denigrates an individual to a nonperson whose free will has become hostage to a lawyer so that until the lawyer consents, the suspect is deprived of any legal right or power to decide for himself that he wishes to make a disclosure. It denies that the rights to counsel and silence are personal, nondelegable, and subject to a waiver only by that individual. The opinions in support of the Court's judgment do not enlighten us as to why police conduct—whether good or bad—should operate to suspend Williams's right to change his mind and "tell all" at once rather than waiting until he reached Des Moines. * * *

MR. JUSTICE WHITE, with whom MR. JUSTICE BLACKMUN and MR. JUSTICE REHNQUIST join, dissenting.

The respondent in this case killed a 10-year-old child. The majority sets aside his conviction, holding that certain statements of unquestioned reliability were unconstitutionally obtained from him, and under the circumstances probably makes it impossible to retry him. Because there is nothing in the Constitution or in our previous cases which requires the Court's action, I dissent. * * *

II.

The strictest test of waiver which might be applied to this case is that set forth in *Johnson v. Zerbst*, 304 U.S. 458, 464 (1938), and quoted by the majority. In order to show that a right has been waived under this test, the State must prove "an intentional relinquishment or abandonment of a known right or privilege." The majority creates no new rule preventing an accused who has retained a lawyer from waiving his right to the lawyer's presence during questioning. The majority simply finds that no waiver was proved in this case. I disagree. That respondent knew of his right not to say anything to the officers without advice and presence of counsel is established on this record to a moral certainty. He was advised of the right by three officials of the State—telling at least one that he understood the right—and by two lawyers. Finally, he further demonstrated his knowledge of the right by informing the police that he would tell them the story in the presence of McKnight when they arrived in Des Moines. The issue in this case, then, is whether respondent relinquished that right intentionally.

Respondent relinquished his right not to talk to the police about his crime when the car approached the place where he had hidden the victim's clothes. Men usually intend to do what they do, and there is nothing in the record to support the proposition that respondent's decision to talk was anything but an exercise of his own free will. Apparently, without any prodding from the officers, respondent—who had earlier said that he would tell the whole story when he arrived in Des Moines—spontaneously changed his mind about the timing of his disclosures when the car approached the places where he had hidden the evidence. However, even if his statements were influenced by Detective Leaming's above-quoted statement, respondent's decision to talk in the absence of counsel can hardly be viewed as the product of an overborne will. The statement by Leaming was not coercive; it was accompanied by a request that respondent not respond to it; and it was delivered hours before respondent decided to make any statement. Respondent's waiver was thus knowing and intentional.

The majority's contrary conclusion seems to rest on the fact that respondent "asserted" his right to counsel by retaining and consulting with one lawyer and by consulting with another. How this supports the conclusion that respondent's later relinquishment of his right not to talk in the absence of counsel was unintentional is a mystery. The fact that respondent consulted with counsel on the question whether he should talk to the police in counsel's absence makes his later decision to talk in counsel's absence better informed and, if anything, more intelligent.

The majority recognizes that even after this "assertion" of his right to counsel, it would have found that respondent waived his right not to talk in counsel's absence if his waiver had been express—i.e., if the officers had asked him in the car whether he would be willing to answer questions in counsel's absence and if he had answered "yes." But waiver is not a formalistic concept. Waiver is shown whenever the facts establish that an accused knew of a right and intended to relinquish it. Such waiver, even if not express, was plainly shown here. The only other conceivable basis for the majority's holding is the implicit suggestion that the right involved in *Massiah v. United States*, 377 U.S. 201 (1964), as distinguished from the right involved in *Miranda v. Arizona*, 384 U.S. 436 (1966), is a right not to be asked any questions in counsel's absence rather than a right not to answer any questions in counsel's absence, and that the right not to be asked questions must be waived before the questions are asked. Such wafer-thin distinctions cannot determine whether a guilty murderer should go free. The only conceivable purpose for the presence of counsel during questioning is to protect an accused from making incriminating answers. Questions, unanswered, have no significance at all. Absent coercion—no matter how the right involved is defined—an accused is amply protected by a rule requiring waiver before or simultaneously with the giving by him of an answer or the making by him of a statement.

III.

The consequence of the majority's decision is, as the majority recognizes, extremely serious. A mentally disturbed killer whose guilt is not in question may be released. Why? Apparently, the answer is that the majority believes that the law enforcement officers acted in a way which involves some risk of injury to society and that such conduct should be deterred. However, the officers' conduct did not, and was not likely to, jeopardize the fairness of respondent's trial or in any way risk the conviction of an innocent man—the risk against which the Sixth Amendment guarantee of assistance of counsel is designed to protect. The police did nothing "wrong," let alone anything "unconstitutional." To anyone not lost in the intricacies of the prophylactic rules of *Miranda v. Arizona*, the result in this case seems utterly senseless; and for the reasons stated in Part II, *supra*, even applying those rules as well as the rule of *Massiah v. United States*, *supra*, the statements made by respondent were properly admitted. In light of these considerations, the majority's protest that the result in this case is justified by a "clear violation" of the Sixth and Fourteenth Amendments has a distressing hollow ring. I respectfully dissent.

MR. JUSTICE BLACKMUN, with whom MR. JUSTICE WHITE and MR. JUSTICE REHNQUIST join, dissenting.

[Omitted.]

QUESTIONS, COMMENTS, CONCERNS?

1.   ***Massiah*'s applicability to Williams.** Can you identify why the *Massiah* doctrine applied to Williams to begin with?

2.   **The evolution of a legal issue before the Supreme Court.** The briefs before the Supreme Court in *Brewer* were not the only ones that assumed that *Brewer* was actually a *Miranda* case. In his bench memorandum to Justice Powell, then-judicial law clerk, Gene Comey, plainly stated that the first issue was whether "this Court's landmark decision in *Miranda v. Arizona* [should] be modified or overruled." [Casefile Powell Papers, at 14.] Other parts of the Justices' materials suggest that, within the *Miranda* context, the real issue in *Brewer* was whether Williams had waived his *Miranda* rights. [Casefile Blackmun Papers, at 130]. And still another view of the issue was whether the Court's *Miranda* right-to-silence case, *Michigan v. Mosley*, disposed of the matter. *Id.* at 34. An alternative view suggests that the issue was whether Williams voluntarily gave incriminating statements. [Casefile Powell Papers, at 49.] Some of the materials also suggest that the Justices should consider whether the Christian Burial speech constituted interrogation within the meaning of *Miranda. Id.* at 55.

If we look closely, Justice Stewart is the one who injects *Massiah* into the *Brewer* discussion. At the Justices' December 12, 1975 conference on whether to grant certiorari in *Brewer*, a handwritten note on Justice Powell's vote sheet says, "Stewart says this is not a 4th Amend case nor is it a 5th Amend case. It was decided on 6th Amend. Not controlled by *Mosley*. Does not involve *the* Exclusionary Rule." [Casefile Powell Papers, at 13.]

Appointed Counsel for Williams, Robert Bartels, seemingly picked up on the Court's leanings. At oral argument, Bartels argued at one point as follows:

That kind of purposeful attempt to obtain information, given all his background about the agreement, the other indications that there should be no questioning, the fact that defendant had counsel with regard to a crime with which he had been charged.

That purposeful interrogation in light of all those facts clearly is a violation of the defendant's right to counsel under the Sixth and Fourteenth Amendments.

And that is quite apart for any considerations of *Miranda* versus Arizona here.

Even if the case did not exist, we would still have the same result. Now, at the same time it is true that *Miranda* provides an alternative basis.

Justice Powell would seek to clarify Bartels's position later in the argument:

STEWART: Up to now you have not been talking. I am asking this question, up to now your argument has not relied on the *Miranda* case and . . .

BARTELS: No, Your Honor, I think it . . .

STEWART: It is rely rather on the *Massiah* and *Escobedo* and basically on the Sixth and Fourteenth Amendments.

BARTELS: That is correct Your Honor. Everything I have said, I think about the facts also relates to the *Miranda* claim, but clearly there is the violation here quite apart from *Miranda* or *Escobedo*.

Even when challenged by other members of the Court about his view of the case, Bartels stood his ground.

At the conference following oral argument on October 6, 1976, the Justices were hardly uniform in their view about the primary issue in the case. Justice Powell's handwritten conference notes indicate that Chief Justice Burger would decide the case on *Stone v. Powell* grounds, while Justice Stewart would affirm because "*Massiah* controls." [Casefile Powell Papers, at 62.] For his part, Justice Powell wrote that he had "no thought of reversing *Miranda*." *Id.* at 63. Based on those handwritten notes, the Court probably had a better idea of the majority opinion's direction when it was finally assigned to Justice Stewart. *Id.* at 64.

    3.   The evolution of an opinion. Justice Stewart's papers provide us with a rare and detailed look inside the mind of a Justice working through an exceptionally controversial and important case. Indeed, the first 102 pages of his materials see him painstakingly make his way through several drafts, along the way handwriting large portions of the opinion in doing so. [Casefile Stewart Papers, at 1–102.] You can even see the use of whiteout in some of these early drafts. *Id.* at 72. Given the prevalence of computers in modern opinion drafting, it seems unlikely that a Justice's editing process today would be similarly preserved.

As you skim Justice Stewart's early drafts, you may wish to pay special attention to a few of his edits:

- Justice Stewart's early work specifically struggled—a struggle that persisted in the published *Brewer* opinion—with how to characterize the detectives' interactions with Williams during the drive to Des Moines. Notice that he alternates between calling what took place "questioning" and "interrogation." *Id.* at 6.

- Concerns about using the word "interrogation" persisted in Justice Stewart's drafting efforts. He would ultimately remove a particularly bold sentence from the majority opinion: "It was the act of interrogation that violated Williams's rights, and any statements that derived therefrom could not constitutionally be admitted at trial against him." *Id.* at 26.

- In the *Brewer* majority, Justice Stewart takes a position on whether an "agreement" existed that detectives would not question Williams during the 160-mile drive. You can see the early seeds of him thinking through the role of the controversial "agreement" in his opinion drafts. *Id.* at 9.

- After his first draft, Justice Stewart catches a critical omission—that first draft did not explain why *Miranda* is inapplicable. He drafts—by hand—his explanation in his first revision. *Id.* at 50. His initial handwritten explanation of why *Miranda* was inapplicable would largely remain intact in the final published version.

Justice Stewart was assigned the case on October 7, 1976. [Casefile Powell Papers, at 64.] He circulated the first draft on November 24, 1976. [Casefile Stewart Papers, at 108.]

4. Catching the Justices disagreeing. We have in the Justices papers a rare moment to see some confrontation, albeit limited. In an early draft of Justice Blackmun's dissent, he included a footnote, later removed, quoting from Charles Dickens's second novel, *Oliver Twist:* "If the law supposes that, . . .that law is a ass—a idiot. If that's the eye of the law, the law's a bachelor; and the worse I wish the law is, that his eye may be opened by experience—by experience." [See Casefile Brennan Papers, at 22.] Chief Justice Burger appreciated that quote and, in his first draft dissent, he commented that the majority's decision "fully justifies judges occasionally recalling Mr. Bumble's blunt conclusion quoted by Mr. Justice Blackmun." [See Casefile Marshall Papers, at 56.]

But on February 22, 1977, Justice Blackmun realized that, in a different pending case, Justice Stevens also relied on a Charles Dickens reference. He therefore wrote to the Conference indicating that he intended to remove the footnote because he saw "no purpose in its double use in substantially contemporaneous cases." [See Casefile Brennan Papers, at 55.] Justice Stevens replied directly to Justice Blackmun that same day offering to delete his "Bumble reference" in the other opinion. [See Casefile Blackmun Papers, at 20.] In a letter also dated February 22, Justice Blackmun replied to Justice Stevens, abruptly commenting, "[t]hat is just the point. If you now delete, I shall reinstate." *Id.* at 22. It is unclear whether Justice Blackmun sent the letter. It is neither signed nor written on U.S. Supreme Court stationery.

5. **Trying to distinguish *Miranda* from *Massiah*.** You may find challenging the task of distinguishing a suspect's *Miranda* rights from his *Massiah* rights. Even Justice Powell had that difficulty. Look back at his private papers and, in a particular note to himself, he struggles with the applicability of interrogating a suspect following the attachment of *Massiah*— but where a suspect has not asserted his right to counsel. Rather than resolve it in his notes, he writes plainly, "I think we should dodge it in this case." [Casefile Powell Papers, at 65.]

6. ***Brewer* is announced.** Justice Stewart announced the *Brewer* decision publicly on March 23, 1977. It took Justice Stewart just three minutes to announce the opinion. In a candid display of just how displeased Chief Justice Burger was with the *Brewer* majority, he then took roughly the next eleven minutes to publicly chastise the opinion. Chief Justice Burger would specifically call attention to Justice Powell's concurrence:

> In his opinion—in his separate opinion in which he concurs in the judgment of the Court and the opinion of the Court, and the exclusion of this evidence of the body, Mr. Justice Powell intimates that he agrees that there is little sense in applying the exclusionary rule where the evidence suppressed is typically reliable and often the most probative information bearing on the guilt or the innocence of the defendant.

> And since he seems to concede that the evidence in question here is highly reliable and probative, his joining the Court's opinion can be explained as I see it only by an insistence that the question has not been presented in the briefs and arguments submitted to us.

Speaking for the four-member dissent, he added, "It is often been said the law goes by trial and error and perhaps that's the way it must be. But in the view of four us, today's case is one of those errors." According to one of Justice Powell's biographers, Chief Justice Burger was "glaring down the bench at Powell as he read excerpts from his dissent." JOHN CALVIN JEFFRIES, JUSTICE LEWIS F. POWELL, JR. 401 (2001).

Later that day, Justice Powell's clerks wrote a short memorandum to the Justice commending him for not responding to Chief Justice Burger. They wrote, "We vote unanimously that you showed considerable restraint given the Chief's 'performance.' We have sent out for a bushel of rotten tomatoes." [Casefile Powell Papers, at 129.]

Why *exactly* is Chief Justice Burger upset? What evidence is he so passionately angry about being excluded? Would *Miranda* exclude that same evidence?

III. WHEN THE RIGHT ATTACHES

In *Massiah*, Justice Stewart's holding was in part premised on the fact that, at the time agents overheard Winston Massiah's conversations, he had already been indicted. Justice Stewart expanded the prospect of when *Massiah* could attach when he wrote, in *Brewer*, that "the right to counsel granted by the Sixth and Fourteenth Amendments means at least that a person is entitled to the help of a lawyer at or after the time that judicial proceedings have been initiated against him—'whether by way of formal charge, preliminary hearing, indictment, information, or arraignment.'" *Brewer v. Williams*, 430 U.S. 387, 398 (1977).

But a question persisted: what is included—or excluded—by *Brewer*'s use of phrases like "judicial proceedings" or "formal charge"? Stated succinctly, when and how *exactly* does *Massiah* attach? We consider that question in our next pair of cases.

TEXAS V. COBB

532 U.S. 162
Supreme Court of the United States
January 16, 2001, Argued; April 2, 2001, Decided
No. 99-1702

CHIEF JUSTICE REHNQUIST delivered the opinion of the Court. * * *

In December 1993, Lindsey Owings reported to the Walker County, Texas, Sheriff's Office that the home he shared with his wife, Margaret, and their 16-month-old daughter, Kori Rae, had been burglarized. He also informed police that his wife and daughter were missing. Respondent Raymond Levi Cobb lived across the street from the Owings. Acting on an anonymous tip that respondent was involved in the burglary, Walker County investigators questioned him about the events. He denied involvement. In July 1994, while under arrest for an unrelated offense, respondent was again questioned about the incident. Respondent then gave a written statement confessing to the burglary, but he denied knowledge relating to the disappearances. Respondent was subsequently indicted for the burglary, and Hal Ridley was appointed in August 1994 to represent respondent on that charge.

Shortly after Ridley's appointment, investigators asked and received his permission to question respondent about the disappearances. Respondent continued to deny involvement. Investigators repeated this process in September 1995, again with Ridley's permission and again with the same result.

In November 1995, respondent, free on bond in the burglary case, was living with his father in Odessa, Texas. At that time, respondent's father contacted the Walker County Sheriff's Office to report that respondent had confessed to him that he killed Margaret Owings in the course of the burglary. Walker County investigators directed respondent's father to the Odessa police station, where he gave a statement. Odessa police then faxed the statement to Walker County, where investigators secured a warrant for respondent's arrest and faxed it back to Odessa. Shortly thereafter, Odessa police took respondent into custody and administered warnings pursuant to *Miranda v. Arizona*, 384 U.S. 436 (1966). Respondent waived these rights.

After a short time, respondent confessed to murdering both Margaret and Kori Rae. Respondent explained that when Margaret confronted him as he was attempting to remove the Owings' stereo, he stabbed her in the stomach with a knife he was carrying. Respondent told police that he dragged her body to a wooded area a few hundred yards from the house. Respondent then stated:

> I went back to her house and I saw the baby laying on its bed. I took the baby out there and it was sleeping the whole time. I laid the baby down on the ground four or five feet away from its mother. I went back to my house and got a flat edge shovel. That's all I could find. Then I went back over to where they were and I started digging a hole between them. After I got the hole dug, the baby was awake. It started going toward its mom and it fell in the hole. I put the lady in the hole and I covered them up. I remember stabbing a different knife I had in the ground where they were. I was crying right then.

Respondent later led police to the location where he had buried the victims' bodies.

Respondent was convicted of capital murder for murdering more than one person in the course of a single criminal transaction. He was sentenced to death. On appeal to the Court of Criminal Appeals of Texas, respondent argued, inter alia, that his confession should have been suppressed because it was obtained in violation of his Sixth Amendment right to counsel. * * * [R]espondent contended that his right to counsel had attached when Ridley was appointed in the burglary case and that Odessa police were therefore required to secure Ridley's permission before proceeding with the interrogation.

The Court of Criminal Appeals reversed respondent's conviction by a divided vote and remanded for a new trial. The court held that "once the right to counsel attaches to the offense charged, it also attaches to any other offense that is very closely related factually to the offense charged." Finding the capital murder charge to be "factually interwoven with the burglary," the court concluded that respondent's Sixth Amendment right to counsel had attached on the capital murder charge even though respondent had not yet been charged with that offense. The court further found that respondent had asserted that right by accepting Ridley's appointment in the burglary case. Accordingly, it deemed the confession inadmissible and found that its introduction had not been harmless error. * * *

The State sought review in this Court, and we granted certiorari to consider first whether the Sixth Amendment right to counsel extends to crimes that are "factually related" to those that have actually been charged * * *. * * *

The Sixth Amendment provides that "in all criminal prosecutions, the accused shall enjoy the right. . .to have the Assistance of Counsel for his defence." In *McNeil v. Wisconsin*, 501 U.S. 171 (1991), we explained when this right arises:

> The Sixth Amendment right [to counsel]. . .is offense specific. It cannot be invoked once for all future prosecutions, for it does not attach until a prosecution is commenced, that is, at or after the initiation of adversary judicial criminal proceedings—whether by way of formal charge, preliminary hearing, indictment, information, or arraignment.

Accordingly, we held that a defendant's statements regarding offenses for which he had not been charged were admissible notwithstanding the attachment of his Sixth Amendment right to counsel on other charged offenses.

Some state courts and Federal Courts of Appeals, however, have read into McNeil's offense-specific definition an exception for crimes that are "factually related" to a charged offense. * * *

Respondent suggests that *Brewer* implicitly held that the right to counsel attached to the factually related murder when the suspect was arraigned on the abduction charge. The Court's opinion, however, simply did not address the significance of the fact that the suspect had been arraigned only on the abduction charge, nor did the parties in any way argue this question. Constitutional rights are not defined by inferences from opinions which did not address the question at issue. * * *

Respondent predicts that the offense-specific rule will prove "disastrous" to suspects' constitutional rights and will "permit law enforcement officers almost complete and total license to conduct unwanted and uncounseled interrogations." Besides offering no evidence that such a parade of horribles has occurred in those jurisdictions that have not enlarged upon *McNeil*, he fails to appreciate the significance of two critical considerations. First, there can be no doubt that a suspect must be apprised of his rights against compulsory self-incrimination and to consult with an attorney before authorities may conduct custodial interrogation. *See Miranda v. Arizona*, 384 U.S. at 479. In the present case, police scrupulously followed *Miranda's* dictates when questioning respondent. Second, it is critical to recognize that the Constitution does not negate society's interest in the ability of police to talk to witnesses and suspects, even those who have been charged with other offenses. * * *

It remains only to apply these principles to the facts at hand. At the time he confessed to Odessa police, respondent had been indicted for burglary of the Owings residence, but he had not been charged in the murders of Margaret and Kori Rae. As defined by Texas law, burglary and capital murder are not the same offense * * *. Accordingly, the Sixth Amendment right to counsel did not bar police from interrogating respondent regarding the murders, and respondent's confession was therefore admissible.

The judgment of the Court of Criminal Appeals of Texas is reversed.

It is so ordered.

JUSTICE KENNEDY, with whom JUSTICE SCALIA and JUSTICE THOMAS join, concurring.

[Omitted.]

JUSTICE BREYER, with whom JUSTICE STEVENS, JUSTICE SOUTER, and JUSTICE GINSBURG join, dissenting. * * *

The majority's rule permits law enforcement officials to question those charged with a crime without first approaching counsel, through the simple device of asking questions about any other related crime not actually charged in the indictment. Thus, the police could ask the individual charged with robbery about, say, the assault of the cashier not yet charged, or about any other uncharged offense * * *, all without notifying counsel. Indeed, the majority's rule would permit law enforcement officials to question anyone charged with any crime in any one of the examples just given about his or her conduct on the single relevant occasion without notifying counsel unless the prosecutor has charged every possible crime arising out of that same brief course of conduct. What Sixth Amendment sense—what common sense—does such a rule make? What is left of the "communicate through counsel" rule? The majority's approach is inconsistent with any common understanding of the scope of counsel's representation. It will undermine the lawyer's role as "medium" between the defendant and the government. And it will, on a random basis, remove a significant portion of the protection that this Court has found inherent in the Sixth Amendment. * * *

In *Brewer v. Williams*, the effect of the majority's rule would have been * * * dramatic. Because * * * at the time of the impermissible interrogation

Williams had been charged only with abduction of a child, Williams' murder conviction should have remained undisturbed. This is not to suggest that this Court has previously addressed and decided the question presented by this case. Rather, it is to point out that the Court's conception of the Sixth Amendment right at the time that * * * *Brewer* [was] decided naturally presumed that it extended to factually related but uncharged offenses.

* * * We can, and should, define "offense" in terms of the conduct that constitutes the crime that the offender committed on a particular occasion, including criminal acts that are "closely related to" or "inextricably intertwined with" the particular crime set forth in the charging instrument. * * *

One cannot say in favor of this commonly followed approach that it is perfectly clear—only that, because it comports with common sense, it is far easier to apply than that of the majority. One might add that, unlike the majority's test, it is consistent with this Court's assumptions in previous cases. And, most importantly, the "closely related" test furthers, rather than undermines, the Sixth Amendment's "right to counsel," a right so necessary to the realization in practice of that most "noble ideal," a fair trial.

The Texas Court of Criminal Appeals, following this commonly accepted approach, found that the charged burglary and the uncharged murders were "closely related." All occurred during a short period of time on the same day in the same basic location. The victims of the murders were also victims of the burglary. Cobb committed one of the murders in furtherance of the robbery, the other to cover up the crimes. The police, when questioning Cobb, knew that he already had a lawyer representing him on the burglary charges and had demonstrated their belief that this lawyer also represented Cobb in respect to the murders by asking his permission to question Cobb about the murders on previous occasions. The relatedness of the crimes is well illustrated by the impossibility of questioning Cobb about the murders without eliciting admissions about the burglary. Nor, in my view, did Cobb waive his right to counsel. These considerations are sufficient. The police officers ought to have spoken to Cobb's counsel before questioning Cobb. I would affirm the decision of the Texas court.

Consequently, I dissent.

QUESTIONS, COMMENTS, CONCERNS?

1. **Comparing *Edwards* and *Cobb*.** Does *Cobb* make the Sixth Amendment right to counsel weaker in some ways than its *Miranda* right to counsel counterpart as explained in *Edwards*?

2. The scope of "offense-specific." Assume Cobb committed a separate burglary *before* breaking into the Owings home and killing Margaret and Kori Rae Owings. Assuming Cobb has been formally charged in connection with his role in killing Margaret and Kori Rae and burglarizing their home, can police deliberately elicit incriminating statements from Cobb about the uncharged prior burglary?

3. The impact of *Cobb* on *Brewer*. Remember that Williams was formally charged and arraigned on a charge of "child stealing," but that he ultimately gave incriminating statements about the death of Pamela Williams—that is, a different uncharged offense. Does *Brewer* come out the same way after *Cobb*?

4. A note on Raymond Cobb. Cobb was just seventeen-years-old when he killed Margaret Owings and her sixteen-month-old child. Cobb was initially sentenced to death, but his death sentence was commuted to life in prison in 2005 following the Supreme Court's decision in *Roper v. Simmons*, 543 U.S. 551 (2005). In *Roper*, the Supreme Court held that the Eighth and Fourteenth Amendments prohibit executing individuals under the age of eighteen.

The *Roper* decision and the corresponding commuting of Cobb's sentence caused considerable debate in Texas. David Weeks, the district attorney who secured a death sentence against Cobb said about Cobb's crime that it "was the most horrendous thing I have ever seen." Scott Gold, *Death Penalty Ruling Hits Texas Hard*, LATIMES.COM (Mar. 2, 2005), http://articles.latimes.com/2005/mar/02/nation/na-death2. Even after *Roper*, Weeks said, "If ever there was a crime that the death penalty was designed to punish, that was it." *Id.* Born in 1976, Cobb is now 41 and remains in prison.

ROTHGERY v. GILLESPIE COUNTY

554 U.S. 191
Supreme Court of the United States
March 17, 2008, Argued; June 23, 2008, Decided
No. 07-440

JUSTICE SOUTER delivered the opinion of the Court.

This Court has held that the right to counsel guaranteed by the Sixth Amendment applies at the first appearance before a judicial officer at which a defendant is told of the formal accusation against him and restrictions are imposed on his liberty. *See Brewer v. Williams*, 430 U.S. 387, 398–99 (1977). The question here is whether attachment of the right also requires that a public prosecutor (as distinct from a police officer) be aware of that initial proceeding or involved in its conduct. We hold that it does not.

I.

A.

Although petitioner Walter Rothgery has never been convicted of a felony, a criminal background check disclosed an erroneous record that he had been, and on July 15, 2002, Texas police officers relied on this record to arrest him as a felon in possession of a firearm. The officers lacked a warrant, and so promptly brought Rothgery before a magistrate, as required by [Texas law]. Texas law has no formal label for this initial appearance before a magistrate, which is sometimes called the "article 15.17 hearing"; it combines the Fourth Amendment's required probable-cause determination with the setting of bail, and is the point at which the arrestee is formally apprised of the accusation against him.

Rothgery's article 15.17 hearing followed routine. The arresting officer submitted a sworn "Affidavit Of Probable Cause" that described the facts supporting the arrest and "charge[d] that . . . Rothgery . . . commit[ted] the offense of unlawful possession of a firearm by a felon—3rd degree felony [Tex. Penal Code Ann. § 46.04]." After reviewing the affidavit, the magistrate "determined that probable cause existed for the arrest." The magistrate informed Rothgery of the accusation, set his bail at $5,000, and committed him to jail, from which he was released after posting a surety bond. The bond, which the Gillespie County deputy sheriff signed, stated that "Rothgery stands charged by complaint duly filed. . .with the offense of a. . .felony, to wit: Unlawful Possession of a Firearm by a Felon." The release was conditioned on the defendant's personal appearance in trial court "for any and all subsequent proceedings that may be had relative to the said charge in the course of the criminal action based on said charge."

Rothgery had no money for a lawyer and made several oral and written requests for appointed counsel, which went unheeded. The following January, he was indicted by a Texas grand jury for unlawful possession of a firearm by a felon, resulting in rearrest the next day, and an order increasing bail to $15,000. When he could not post it, he was put in jail and remained there for three weeks.

On January 23, 2003, six months after the article 15.17 hearing, Rothgery was finally assigned a lawyer, who promptly obtained a bail reduction (so Rothgery could get out of jail), and assembled the paperwork confirming that Rothgery had never been convicted of a felony. Counsel relayed this information to the district attorney, who in turn filed a motion to dismiss the indictment, which was granted.

B.

Rothgery then brought this 42 U.S.C. § 1983 action against respondent Gillespie (County), claiming that if the County had provided a lawyer within a reasonable time after the article 15.17 hearing, he would not have been indicted, rearrested, or jailed for three weeks. The County's failure is said to be owing to its unwritten policy of denying appointed counsel to indigent defendants out on bond until at least the entry of an information or indictment. Rothgery sees this policy as violating his Sixth Amendment right to counsel.

The District Court granted summary judgment to the County and the Court of Appeals affirmed. * * *

We granted certiorari and now vacate and remand.

II.

The Sixth Amendment right of the "accused" to assistance of counsel in "all criminal prosecutions" is limited by its terms: "it does not attach until a prosecution is commenced." *McNeil v. Wisconsin*, 501 U.S. 171, 175 (1991). We have, for purposes of the right to counsel, pegged commencement to "the initiation of adversary judicial criminal proceedings—whether by way of formal charge, preliminary hearing, indictment, information, or arraignment." The rule is not "mere formalism," but a recognition of the point at which "the government has committed itself to prosecute," "the adverse positions of government and defendant have solidified," and the accused "finds himself faced with the prosecutorial forces of organized society, and immersed in the intricacies of substantive and procedural criminal law." The issue is whether Texas's article 15.17 hearing marks that point, with the consequent state obligation to appoint counsel within a reasonable time once a request for assistance is made.

A.

When the Court of Appeals said no, because no prosecutor was aware of Rothgery's article 15.17 hearing or involved in it, the court effectively focused not on the start of adversarial judicial proceedings, but on the activities and knowledge of a particular state official who was presumably otherwise occupied. This was error.

* * * [T]he right to counsel attaches at the initial appearance before a judicial officer. This first time before a court, also known as the "preliminary arraignment" or "arraignment on the complaint," is generally the hearing at which "the magistrate informs the defendant of the charge in the complaint, and of various rights in further proceedings," and "determine[s] the conditions for pretrial release." Texas's article 15.17 hearing is an initial appearance: Rothgery was taken before a magistrate, informed of the formal accusation against him, and sent to jail until he posted bail. * * *

B.

Our latest look at the significance of the initial appearance was *McNeil*, 501 U.S. 171, which is no help to the County. In *McNeil* the State had conceded that the right to counsel attached at the first appearance before a county court commissioner, who set bail and scheduled a preliminary examination. But we did more than just accept the concession; we went on to reaffirm that "[t]he Sixth Amendment right to counsel attaches at the first formal proceeding against an accused," and observed that "in most States, at least with respect to serious offenses, free counsel is made available at that time. . ."

That was 17 years ago, the same is true today, and the overwhelming consensus practice conforms to the rule that the first formal proceeding is the point of attachment. * * *

III.

Our holding is narrow. We do not decide whether the 6-month delay in appointment of counsel resulted in prejudice to Rothgery's Sixth Amendment rights and have no occasion to consider what standards should apply in deciding this. We merely reaffirm what we have held before and what an overwhelming majority of American jurisdictions understand in practice: a criminal defendant's initial appearance before a judicial officer, where he learns the charge against him and his liberty is subject to restriction, marks the start of adversary judicial proceedings that trigger attachment of the Sixth Amendment right to counsel. Because the Fifth Circuit came to a different conclusion on this threshold issue, its judgment is vacated, and the case is remanded for further proceedings consistent with this opinion.

It is so ordered.

CHIEF JUSTICE ROBERTS, with whom JUSTICE SCALIA joins, concurring.

[Omitted.]

JUSTICE ALITO, with whom THE CHIEF JUSTICE and JUSTICE SCALIA join, concurring.

I join the Court's opinion because I do not understand it to hold that a defendant is entitled to the assistance of appointed counsel as soon as his Sixth Amendment right attaches. As I interpret our precedents, the term "attachment" signifies nothing more than the beginning of the defendant's prosecution. It does not mark the beginning of a substantive entitlement to the assistance of counsel. I write separately to elaborate on my understanding of the term "attachment" and its relationship to the Amendment's substantive guarantee of "the Assistance of Counsel for [the] defence." * * *

Because pretrial criminal procedures vary substantially from jurisdiction to jurisdiction, there is room for disagreement about when a "prosecution" begins for Sixth Amendment purposes. As the Court, notes, however, we have previously held that "arraignments" that were functionally indistinguishable from the Texas magistration marked the point at which the Sixth Amendment right to counsel "attached."

It does not follow, however, and I do not understand the Court to hold, that the county had an obligation to appoint an attorney to represent petitioner within some specified period after his magistration. To so hold, the Court would need to do more than conclude that petitioner's criminal prosecution had begun. It would also need to conclude that the assistance of counsel in the wake of a Texas magistration is part of the substantive guarantee of the Sixth Amendment. That question lies beyond our reach, petitioner having never sought our review of it. * * *

JUSTICE THOMAS, dissenting.

[Omitted.]

IV. DELIBERATE ELICITATION

Remember that *Massiah* applies, in the words of Justice Stewart, only when police "deliberately elicit" incriminating statements from a suspect. That means investigators can, in some circumstances, interact with a suspect after the suspect has been "formally charged." But as *Kuhlman v. Wilson* and *Fellers v. United States*, our next two cases, demonstrate, the line between a permissible officer-suspect interaction and unconstitutional "deliberate elicitation" is often thin. Pay attention also as you move through this material to how "deliberate elicitation" for *Massiah* purposes differs from *Miranda* "interrogation."

KUHLMANN V. WILSON
477 U.S. 436
Supreme Court of the United States
January 14, 1986, Argued; June 26, 1986, Decided
No. 84-1479

JUSTICE POWELL announced the judgment of the Court and delivered the opinion of the Court with respect to Parts I, IV, and V, and an opinion with respect to Parts II and III in which THE CHIEF JUSTICE, JUSTICE REHNQUIST, and JUSTICE O'CONNOR join. * * *

I.

In the early morning of July 4, 1970, respondent and two confederates robbed the Star Taxicab Garage in the Bronx, New York, and fatally shot the night dispatcher. Shortly before, employees of the garage had observed respondent, a former employee there, on the premises conversing with two other men. They also witnessed respondent fleeing after the robbery, carrying loose money in his arms. After eluding the police for four days, respondent turned himself in. Respondent admitted that he had been present when the crimes took place, claimed that he had witnessed the robbery, gave the police a description of the robbers, but denied knowing them. Respondent also denied any involvement in the robbery or murder, claiming that he had fled because he was afraid of being blamed for the crimes.

After his arraignment, respondent was confined in the Bronx House of Detention, where he was placed in a cell with a prisoner named Benny Lee. Unknown to respondent, Lee had agreed to act as a police informant. Respondent made incriminating statements that Lee reported to the police. Prior to trial, respondent moved to suppress the statements on the ground that they were obtained in violation of his right to counsel. The trial court held an evidentiary hearing on the suppression motion, which revealed that the statements were made under the following circumstances.

Before respondent arrived in the jail, Lee had entered into an arrangement with Detective Cullen, according to which Lee agreed to listen to respondent's conversations and report his remarks to Cullen. Since the police had positive evidence of respondent's participation, the purpose of placing Lee in the cell was to determine the identities of respondent's confederates. Cullen instructed Lee not to ask respondent any questions, but simply to "keep his ears open" for the names of the other perpetrators. Respondent first spoke to Lee about the crimes after he looked out the cellblock window at the Star Taxicab Garage, where the crimes had occurred. Respondent said, "someone's messing with me," and began talking to Lee about the robbery, narrating the same story that he had given the police at the time of his arrest. Lee advised respondent that this explanation "didn't sound too good,"[1] but respondent did not alter his story. Over the next few days, however, respondent changed details of his original account. Respondent then received a visit from his brother, who mentioned that members of his family were upset because they believed that respondent had murdered the dispatcher. After the visit, respondent again described the crimes to Lee. Respondent now admitted that he and two other men, whom he never identified, had planned and carried out the robbery, and had murdered the dispatcher. Lee informed Cullen of respondent's statements and furnished Cullen with notes that he had written surreptitiously while sharing the cell with respondent.

---

[1]   At the suppression hearing, Lee testified that, after hearing respondent's initial version of his participation in the crimes, "I think I remember telling him that the story wasn't—it didn't sound too good. Things didn't look too good for him." At trial, Lee testified to a somewhat different version of his remark: "Well, I said, look, you better come up with a better story than that because that one doesn't sound too cool to me, that's what I said."

After hearing the testimony of Cullen and Lee, the trial court found that Cullen had instructed Lee "to ask no questions of [respondent] about the crime but merely to listen as to what [respondent] might say in his presence." The court determined that Lee obeyed these instructions, that he "at no time asked any questions with respect to the crime," and that he "only listened to [respondent] and made notes regarding what [respondent] had to say." The trial court also found that respondent's statements to Lee were "spontaneous" and "unsolicited." Under state precedent, a defendant's volunteered statements to a police agent were admissible in evidence because the police were not required to prevent talkative defendants from making incriminating statements. The trial court accordingly denied the suppression motion.

The jury convicted respondent of common-law murder and felonious possession of a weapon. On May 18, 1972, the trial court sentenced him to a term of 20 years to life on the murder count and to a concurrent term of up to 7 years on the weapons count. The Appellate Division affirmed without opinion and the New York Court of Appeals denied respondent leave to appeal.

On December 7, 1973, respondent filed a petition for federal habeas corpus relief. Respondent argued, among other things, that his statements to Lee were obtained pursuant to police investigative methods that violated his constitutional rights. After considering *Massiah v. United States*, 377 U.S. 201 (1964), the District Court for the Southern District of New York denied the writ on January 7, 1977. * * *

A divided panel of the Court of Appeals for the Second Circuit affirmed. The court noted that a defendant is denied his Sixth Amendment rights when the trial court admits in evidence incriminating statements that state agents "had deliberately elicited from him after he had been indicted and in the absence of counsel." Relying in part on *Brewer v. Williams*, 430 U.S. 387 (1977), the court reasoned that the "deliberately elicited" test of *Massiah* requires something more than incriminating statements uttered in the absence of counsel. On the facts found by the state trial court, * * * the court held that respondent had not established a violation of his Sixth Amendment rights. We denied a petition for a writ of certiorari.

Following this Court's decision in *United States v. Henry*, 447 U.S. 264 (1980), which applied the *Massiah* test to suppress statements made to a paid jailhouse informant, respondent decided to relitigate his Sixth Amendment claim. On September 11, 1981, he filed in state trial court a motion to vacate his conviction. The judge denied the motion, on the grounds that *Henry* was factually distinguishable from this case, and that under state precedent *Henry* was not to be given retroactive effect. The Appellate Division denied respondent leave to appeal.

On July 6, 1982, respondent returned to the District Court for the Southern District of New York on a habeas petition, again arguing that admission in evidence of his incriminating statements to Lee violated his Sixth Amendment rights. Respondent contended that the decision in *Henry* constituted a new rule of law that should be applied retroactively to this case. The District Court found it unnecessary to consider retroactivity because it decided that *Henry* did not undermine the Court of Appeals' prior disposition of respondent's Sixth Amendment claim. Noting that *Henry* reserved the question whether the Constitution forbade admission in evidence of an accused's statements to an informant who made "no effort to stimulate conversations about the crime charged," *see United States v. Henry, supra,* at 271, n.9, the District Court believed that this case presented that open question and that the question must be answered negatively. * * *

A different, and again divided, panel of the Court of Appeals reversed. * * * The court * * * reasoned that the circumstances under which respondent made his incriminating statements to Lee were indistinguishable from the facts of *Henry.* Finally, the court decided that *Henry* was fully applicable here because it did not announce a new constitutional rule, but merely applied settled principles to new facts. Therefore, the court concluded that all of the judges who had considered and rejected respondent's claim had erred and remanded the case to the District Court with instructions to order respondent's release from prison unless the State elected to retry him.

We granted certiorari * * *. We now reverse. * * *

II.

* * * [W]e conclude that [the Court of Appeals] erred in holding that respondent was entitled to relief under *United States v. Henry,* 447 U.S. 264 (1980). * * *

A.   * * *

The Court in *Massiah* * * * held that, once a defendant's Sixth Amendment right to counsel has attached, he is denied that right when federal agents "deliberately elicit" incriminating statements from him in the absence of his lawyer. The Court adopted this test, rather than one that turned simply on whether the statements were obtained in an "interrogation," to protect accused persons from "indirect and surreptitious interrogations as well as those conducted in the jailhouse. * * *"

In *United States v. Henry,* the Court applied the *Massiah* test to incriminating statements made to a jailhouse informant. The Court of Appeals in that case found a violation of *Massiah* because the informant had engaged the defendant in conversations and "had developed a relationship of trust and confidence with [the defendant] such that [the defendant] revealed incriminating information." This Court affirmed, holding that the Court of Appeals reasonably concluded that the Government informant "deliberately used his position to secure incriminating information from [the defendant] when counsel was not present." Although the informant had not questioned the defendant, the informant had "stimulated" conversations with the defendant in order to "elicit" incriminating information. The Court emphasized that those facts, like the facts of *Massiah*, amounted to "indirect and surreptitious [interrogation]" of the defendant.

Earlier this Term, we applied the *Massiah* standard in a case involving incriminating statements made under circumstances substantially similar to the facts of *Massiah* itself. In *Maine v. Moulton*, 474 U.S. 159 (1985), the defendant made incriminating statements in a meeting with his accomplice, who had agreed to cooperate with the police. During that meeting, the accomplice, who wore a wire transmitter to record the conversation, discussed with the defendant the charges pending against him, repeatedly asked the defendant to remind him of the details of the crime, and encouraged the defendant to describe his plan for killing witnesses. The Court concluded that these investigatory techniques denied the defendant his right to counsel on the pending charges.[21] Significantly, the Court emphasized that, because of the relationship between the defendant and the informant, the informant's engaging the defendant "in active conversation about their upcoming trial was certain to elicit" incriminating statements from the defendant. Thus, the informant's participation "in this conversation was 'the functional equivalent of interrogation.' "

As our recent examination of this Sixth Amendment issue in *Moulton* makes clear, the primary concern of the *Massiah* line of decisions is secret interrogation by investigatory techniques that are the equivalent of direct police interrogation. Since "the Sixth Amendment is not violated whenever—by luck or happenstance—the State obtains incriminating statements from the accused after the right to counsel has attached," a defendant does not make out a violation of that right simply by showing that an informant, either through prior arrangement or voluntarily, reported his incriminating statements to the police. Rather, the defendant must demonstrate that the police and their informant took some action, beyond merely listening, that was designed deliberately to elicit incriminating remarks.

---

[21] The Court observed, however, that where the defendant makes "[incriminating] statements pertaining to other crimes, as to which the Sixth Amendment right has not yet attached," those statements "are, of course, admissible at a trial of those offenses."

B.

It is thus apparent that the Court of Appeals erred in concluding that respondent's right to counsel was violated under the circumstances of this case. * * *

The state court found that Officer Cullen had instructed Lee only to listen to respondent for the purpose of determining the identities of the other participants in the robbery and murder. The police already had solid evidence of respondent's participation. The court further found that Lee followed those instructions, that he "at no time asked any questions" of respondent concerning the pending charges, and that he "only listened" to respondent's "spontaneous" and "unsolicited" statements. The only remark made by Lee that has any support in this record was his comment that respondent's initial version of his participation in the crimes "didn't sound too good." * * * [T]he Court of Appeals focused on that one remark and gave a description of Lee's interaction with respondent that is completely at odds with the facts found by the trial court. In the Court of Appeals's view, "[subtly] and slowly, but surely, Lee's ongoing verbal intercourse with [respondent] served to exacerbate [respondent's] already troubled state of mind." After thus revising some of the trial court's findings, and ignoring other more relevant findings, the Court of Appeals concluded that the police "deliberately elicited" respondent's incriminating statements. This conclusion conflicts with the decision of every other state and federal judge who reviewed this record * * *.

III.

The judgment of the Court of Appeals is reversed, and the case is remanded for further proceedings consistent with this opinion.

It is so ordered.

CHIEF JUSTICE BURGER, concurring.

[Omitted.]

JUSTICE BRENNAN, with whom JUSTICE MARSHALL joins, dissenting. * * *

The Sixth Amendment guarantees an accused, at least after the initiation of formal charges, the right to rely on counsel as the "medium" between himself and the State. *Maine v. Moulton*, 474 U.S. 159, 176 (1985). Accordingly, the Sixth Amendment "imposes on the State an affirmative obligation to respect and preserve the accused's choice to seek [the assistance of counsel]," and therefore "[the] determination whether particular action by state agents violates the accused's right to. . .counsel must be made in light of this obligation." To be sure, the Sixth Amendment is not violated whenever, "by luck or happenstance," the State obtains incriminating statements from the accused after the right to counsel has attached. It is violated, however, when "the State obtains incriminating statements by knowingly circumventing the accused's right to have counsel present in a confrontation between the accused and a state agent." As we explained in *Henry*, where the accused has not waived his right to counsel, the government knowingly circumvents the defendant's right to counsel where it "deliberately [elicits]" inculpatory admissions, that is, "intentionally [creates] a situation likely to induce [the accused] to make incriminating statements without the assistance of counsel."

In *Henry*, we found that the Federal Government had "deliberately elicited" incriminating statements from Henry based on the following circumstances. The jailhouse informant, Nichols, had apparently followed instructions to obtain information without directly questioning Henry and without initiating conversations concerning the charges pending against Henry. We rejected the Government's argument that because Henry initiated the discussion of his crime, no Sixth Amendment violation had occurred. We pointed out that under *Massiah v. United States*, 377 U.S. 201 (1964), it is irrelevant whether the informant asks pointed questions about the crime or "merely engage[s] in general conversation about it." Nichols, we noted, "was not a passive listener. . .he had 'some conversations with Mr. Henry' while he was in jail and Henry's incriminatory statements were 'the product of this conversation.' "

In deciding that Nichols's role in these conversations amounted to deliberate elicitation, we also found three other factors important. First, Nichols was to be paid for any information he produced and thus had an incentive to extract inculpatory admissions from Henry. Second, Henry was not aware that Nichols was acting as an informant. "Conversation stimulated in such circumstances," we observed, "may elicit information that an accused would not intentionally reveal to persons known to be Government agents." Third, Henry was in custody at the time he spoke with Nichols. This last fact is significant, we stated, because "custody imposes pressures on the accused [and] confinement may bring into play subtle influences that will make him particularly susceptible to the ploys of undercover Government agents." We concluded that by "intentionally creating a situation likely to induce Henry to make incriminating statements without the assistance of counsel, the Government violated Henry's Sixth Amendment right to counsel."

In the instant case, as in *Henry*, the accused was incarcerated and therefore was "susceptible to the ploys of undercover Government agents." Like Nichols, Lee was a secret informant, usually received consideration for the services he rendered the police, and therefore had an incentive to produce the information which he knew the police hoped to obtain. Just as Nichols had done, Lee obeyed instructions not to question respondent and to report to the police any statements made by the respondent in Lee's presence about the crime in question. And, like Nichols, Lee encouraged respondent to talk about his crime by conversing with him on the subject over the course of several days and by telling respondent that his exculpatory story would not convince anyone without more work. However, unlike the situation in *Henry*, a disturbing visit from respondent's brother, rather than a conversation with the informant, seems to have been the immediate catalyst for respondent's confession to Lee. While it might appear from this sequence of events that Lee's comment regarding respondent's story and his general willingness to converse with respondent about the crime were not the immediate causes of respondent's admission, I think that the deliberate-elicitation standard requires consideration of the entire course of government behavior.

The State intentionally created a situation in which it was foreseeable that respondent would make incriminating statements without the assistance of counsel, *Henry*, 447 U.S., at 274—it assigned respondent to a cell overlooking the scene of the crime and designated a secret informant to be respondent's cellmate. The informant, while avoiding direct questions, nonetheless developed a relationship of cellmate camaraderie with respondent and encouraged him to talk about his crime. While the coup de grace was delivered by respondent's brother, the groundwork for respondent's confession was laid by the State. Clearly the State's actions had a sufficient nexus with respondent's admission of guilt to constitute deliberate elicitation within the meaning of Henry. I would affirm the judgment of the Court of Appeals.

JUSTICE STEVENS, dissenting.

[Omitted.]

QUESTIONS, COMMENTS, CONCERNS?

1. **The secret agent fact patterns.** Cases like *Massiah* and *Wilson* raise a question: how can the defendant assert or invoke his Sixth Amendment right to counsel if the defendant is unaware that he is talking to a law enforcement agent? Investigators essentially face choices in these undercover investigations. Essentially, police must make sure that any post-charging investigations do not involve "deliberate elicitation." That is, if what takes place is *not* deliberate elicitation, then *Massiah* is not triggered. But the government avoids *Massiah* by doing as it did in *Wilson*: instructing the jailhouse informant "not to ask respondent any questions, but simply to 'keep his ears open' for the names of the other perpetrators."

That approach is to be contrasted against the informant's approach in *Henry*. The *Henry* informant "developed a relationship of trust and confidence" with the defendant and " 'stimulated' conversations with the defendant in order to 'elicit' incriminating information." The *Massiah* exclusionary rule applies to the *Henry* informant, thereby rendering the defendant's statements to the informant inadmissible. By contrast, statements to the informant in *Wilson* do not violate *Massiah*.

FELLERS V. UNITED STATES

540 U.S. 519
Supreme Court of the United States
December 10, 2003, Argued; January 26, 2004, Decided
No. 02-6320

JUSTICE O'CONNOR delivered the opinion of the Court.

After a grand jury indicted petitioner John J. Fellers, police officers arrested him at his home. During the course of the arrest, petitioner made several inculpatory statements. He argued that the officers deliberately elicited these statements from him outside the presence of counsel, and that the admission at trial of the fruits of those statements therefore violated his Sixth Amendment right to counsel. Petitioner contends that in rejecting this argument, the Court of Appeals for the Eighth Circuit improperly held that the Sixth Amendment right to counsel was "not applicable" because "the officers did not interrogate [petitioner] at his home." We granted the petition for a writ of certiorari and now reverse.

I.

On February 24, 2000, after a grand jury indicted petitioner for conspiracy to distribute methamphetamine, Lincoln Police Sergeant Michael Garnett and Lancaster County Deputy Sheriff Jeff Bliemeister went to petitioner's home in Lincoln, Nebraska, to arrest him. The officers knocked on petitioner's door and, when petitioner answered, identified themselves and asked if they could come in. Petitioner invited the officers into his living room.

The officers advised petitioner they had come to discuss his involvement in methamphetamine distribution. They informed petitioner that they had a federal warrant for his arrest and that a grand jury had indicted him for conspiracy to distribute methamphetamine. The officers told petitioner that the indictment referred to his involvement with certain individuals, four of whom they named. Petitioner then told the officers that he knew the four people and had used methamphetamine during his association with them.

After spending about 15 minutes in petitioner's home, the officers transported petitioner to the Lancaster County jail. There, the officers advised petitioner for the first time of his rights under *Miranda v. Arizona* * * *. Petitioner and the two officers signed a *Miranda* waiver form, and petitioner then reiterated the inculpatory statements he had made earlier, admitted to having associated with other individuals implicated in the charged conspiracy, and admitted to having loaned money to one of them even though he suspected that she was involved in drug transactions.

Before trial, petitioner moved to suppress the inculpatory statements he made at his home and at the county jail. A Magistrate Judge conducted a hearing and recommended that the statements petitioner made at his home be suppressed because the officers had not informed petitioner of his *Miranda* rights. The Magistrate Judge found that petitioner made the statements in response to the officers' "implici[t] questions," noting that the officers had told petitioner that the purpose of their visit was to discuss his use and distribution of methamphetamine. The Magistrate Judge further recommended that portions of petitioner's jailhouse statement be suppressed as fruits of the prior failure to provide *Miranda* warnings.

The District Court suppressed the "unwarned" statements petitioner made at his house but admitted petitioner's jailhouse statements pursuant to *Oregon v. Elstad*, 470 U.S. 298 (1985), concluding petitioner had knowingly and voluntarily waived his *Miranda* rights before making the statements.

Following a jury trial at which petitioner's jailhouse statements were admitted into evidence, petitioner was convicted of conspiring to possess with intent to distribute methamphetamine. Petitioner appealed, arguing that his jailhouse statements should have been suppressed as fruits of the statements obtained at his home in violation of the Sixth Amendment. The Court of Appeals affirmed. * * *

II.

The Sixth Amendment right to counsel is triggered "at or after the time that judicial proceedings have been initiated. . .'whether by way of formal charge, preliminary hearing, indictment, information, or arraignment.' " *Brewer v. Williams*, 430 U.S. 387, 398 (1977). We have held that an accused is denied "the basic protections" of the Sixth Amendment "when there [is] used against him at his trial evidence of his own incriminating words, which federal agents. . .deliberately elicited from him after he had been indicted and in the absence of his counsel." *Massiah v. United States*, 377 U.S. 201, 206 (1964).

We have consistently applied the deliberate-elicitation standard in subsequent Sixth Amendment cases, *see United States v. Henry*, 447 U.S. 264, 270 (1980) ("The question here is whether under the facts of this case a Government agent 'deliberately elicited' incriminating statements. . .within the meaning of Massiah"); *Brewer, supra*, at 399 (finding a Sixth Amendment violation where a detective "deliberately and designedly set out to elicit information from [the suspect]"), and we have expressly distinguished this standard from the Fifth Amendment custodial-interrogation standard, *see Michigan v. Jackson*, 475 U.S. 625, 632, n.5 (1986) ("[T]he Sixth Amendment provides a right to counsel. . .even when there is no interrogation and no Fifth Amendment applicability"); *Rhode Island v. Innis*, 446 U.S. 291, 300, n.4 (1980) ("The definitions of 'interrogation' under the Fifth and Sixth Amendments, if indeed the term 'interrogation' is even apt in the Sixth Amendment context, are not necessarily interchangeable").

The Court of Appeals erred in holding that the absence of an "interrogation" foreclosed petitioner's claim that the jailhouse statements should have been suppressed as fruits of the statements taken from petitioner at his home. First, there is no question that the officers in this case "deliberately elicited" information from petitioner. Indeed, the officers, upon arriving at petitioner's house, informed him that their purpose in coming was to discuss his involvement in the distribution of methamphetamine and his association with certain charged co-conspirators. Because the ensuing discussion took place after petitioner had been indicted, outside the presence of counsel, and in the absence of any waiver of petitioner's Sixth Amendment rights, the Court of Appeals erred in holding that the officers' actions did not violate the Sixth Amendment standards established in *Massiah*, and its progeny.

Second, because of its erroneous determination that petitioner was not questioned in violation of Sixth Amendment standards, the Court of Appeals improperly conducted its "fruits" analysis under the Fifth Amendment. Specifically, it applied *Elstad*, to hold that the admissibility of the jailhouse statements turns solely on whether the statements were "knowingly and voluntarily made." The Court of Appeals did not reach the question whether the Sixth Amendment requires suppression of petitioner's jailhouse statements on the ground that they were the fruits of previous questioning conducted in violation of the Sixth Amendment deliberate-elicitation standard. We have not had occasion to decide whether the rationale of *Elstad* applies when a suspect makes incriminating statements after a knowing and voluntary waiver of his right to counsel notwithstanding earlier police questioning in violation of Sixth Amendment standards. We therefore remand to the Court of Appeals to address this issue in the first instance.

Accordingly, the judgment of the Court of Appeals is reversed, and the case is remanded for further proceedings consistent with this opinion.

It is so ordered.

QUESTIONS, COMMENTS, CONCERNS?

1. **Interrogation vs. deliberate elicitation.** Recall Justice Stewart's struggles with the use of "interrogation" in the context of his majority opinion in *Brewer*. His periodic use of the term "interrogation" in *Brewer* raised a question: is "deliberate elicitation" for *Massiah* purposes the same as *Miranda* interrogation? As you now know from *Rhode Island v. Innis* (Chapter 8), the answer is no. The *Innis* Court, as Justice O'Connor highlights in *Fellers*, stated, "The definitions of 'interrogation' under the Fifth and Sixth Amendments, if indeed the term 'interrogation' is even apt in the Sixth Amendment context, are not necessarily interchangeable, since the policies underlying the two constitutional protections are quite distinct."

Knowing that "deliberate elicitation" is something different from "interrogation" raises a new question: *how* are they different? Well, *Innis* defines interrogation as "either express questioning or its functional equivalent. By contrast, *Massiah*'s deliberate elicitation focuses more broadly on the *environment* surrounding a defendant's incriminating statement. Express questioning, as *Fellers* contemplates, is also deliberate elicitation. But as *Williams* and *Henry* make clear, deliberate elicitation also includes circumstances where investigators obtain incriminating statements through informants, false friends, or jailhouse plants. As *Williams* indicates, those circumstances must show some *deliberate* effort on the part of law enforcement to obtain incriminating statements from the defendant.

2.   Elicitation aside, what is "deliberate"? The precise definition of "deliberate" is a bit of a moving target, but the Court's decision in *Maine v. Moulton*, 474 U.S. 159 (1985), as summarized above in *Wilson*, offers some guidance. In *Moulton*, Justice Brennan offered the following insight:

> [T]he Sixth Amendment is not violated whenever—by luck or happenstance—the State obtains incriminating statements from the accused after the right to counsel has attached. However, knowing exploitation by the State of an opportunity to confront the accused without counsel being present is as much a breach of the State's obligation not to circumvent the right to the assistance of counsel as is the intentional creation of such an opportunity. Accordingly, the Sixth Amendment is violated when the State obtains incriminating statements by knowingly circumventing the accused's right to have counsel present in a confrontation between the accused and a state agent.

Id. at 176.

3.   *Elstad*'s applicability to *Massiah*(?). To jog your memory, and at the risk of over-simplifying, *Oregon v. Elstad* (Chapter 9) held that, in a sequential confession fact pattern, a "good faith" *Miranda* mistake does not preclude admission of a subsequent warned statement. *Fellers* looks like a repeat of *Elstad*. The difference, of course, is that a grand jury indicted Fellers before he talked to the police.

You may remember that Justice O'Connor wrote the majority *Elstad* opinion. It is therefore likely no accident that Justice O'Connor injects the prospect of *Elstad*'s applicability to *Massiah*. She teases, "We have not had occasion to decide whether the rationale of *Elstad* applies when a suspect makes incriminating statements after a knowing and voluntary waiver of his right to counsel notwithstanding earlier police questioning in violation of Sixth Amendment standards." But is Justice O'Connor correct? *Brewer*, after all, made clear that *Massiah* exclusion suppressed both Williams's statements (the primary illegality) *and* Pamela's body (the fruit). By contrast, *Elstad* assumed that *Miranda* warnings are merely "prophylactic." Applying that rationale, the *Miranda* exclusionary rule, according to *Elstad*, justifies only suppression of a suspect's initial unwarned statement (the primary illegality), but *not* a second warned statement (the fruit). The inference, then, seems clear: the Sixth Amendment's exclusionary rule is stronger than its Fifth Amendment counterpart.

Is there any room to argue, as Justice O'Connor implies, that *Elstad* could somehow support admission of secondary "fruits" evidence?

V. WAIVING & INVOKING *MASSIAH*

In *Patterson v. Illinois* and *Montejo v. Louisiana*, our next two cases, we take up the question of how a suspect waives and invokes *Massiah*. Those questions necessarily raise a separate question: must police inform the suspect about *Massiah*? In other words, do we need separate *Miranda* rights for *Massiah*? Or instead, does *Miranda* also convey *Massiah*? Answering those questions matters, of course, because, if the suspect does not know about *Massiah*, it's hard to imagine the suspect invoking its protections. Knowledge of *Massiah* rights also matters, it would seem, for waiver purposes. After all, can a suspect *knowingly* waive *Massiah* if the suspect was never told about *Massiah* to begin with?

Collectively, notice that the answers to these questions will either align *Massiah* with *Miranda* on waiver/invocation questions or cause the doctrines to diverge. We begin with *Patterson v. Illinois*.

PATTERSON V. ILLINOIS
487 U.S. 285
Supreme Court of the United States
March 22, 1988, Argued; June 24, 1988, Decided
No. 86-7059

JUSTICE WHITE delivered the opinion of the Court. * * *

I.

Before dawn on August 21, 1983, petitioner and other members of the "Vice Lords" street gang became involved in a fight with members of a rival gang, the "Black Mobsters." Some time after the fight, a former member of the Black Mobsters, James Jackson, went to the home where the Vice Lords had fled. A second fight broke out there, with petitioner and three other Vice Lords beating Jackson severely. The Vice Lords then put Jackson into a car, drove to the end of a nearby street, and left him face down in a puddle of water. Later that morning, police discovered Jackson, dead, where he had been left.

That afternoon, local police officers obtained warrants for the arrest of the Vice Lords, on charges of battery and mob action, in connection with the first fight. One of the gang members who was arrested gave the police a statement concerning the first fight; the statement also implicated several of the Vice Lords (including petitioner) in Jackson's murder. A few hours later, petitioner was apprehended. Petitioner was informed of his rights under *Miranda v. Arizona*, 384 U.S. 436 (1966), and volunteered to answer questions put to him by the police. Petitioner gave a statement concerning the initial fight between the rival gangs but denied knowing anything about Jackson's death. Petitioner was held in custody the following day, August 22, as law enforcement authorities completed their investigation of the Jackson murder.

On August 23, a Cook County grand jury indicted petitioner and two other gang members for the murder of James Jackson. Police Officer Michael Gresham, who had questioned petitioner earlier, removed him from the lockup where he was being held, and told petitioner that because he had been indicted he was being transferred to the Cook County jail. Petitioner asked Gresham which of the gang members had been charged with Jackson's murder, and upon learning that one particular Vice Lord had been omitted from the indictments, asked: "[W]hy wasn't he indicted, he did everything." Petitioner also began to explain that there was a witness who would support his account of the crime.

At this point, Gresham interrupted petitioner, and handed him a *Miranda* waiver form. The form contained five specific warnings, as suggested by this Court's *Miranda* decision, to make petitioner aware of his right to counsel and of the consequences of any statement he might make to police. Gresham read the warnings aloud, as petitioner read along with him. Petitioner initialed each of the five warnings and signed the waiver form. Petitioner then gave a lengthy statement to police officers concerning the Jackson murder; petitioner's statement described in detail the role of each of the Vice Lords—including himself—in the murder of James Jackson.

Later that day, petitioner confessed involvement in the murder for a second time. This confession came in an interview with Assistant State's Attorney (ASA) George Smith. At the outset of the interview, Smith reviewed with petitioner the Miranda waiver he had previously signed, and petitioner confirmed that he had signed the waiver and understood his rights. Smith went through the waiver procedure once again: reading petitioner his rights, having petitioner initial each one, and sign a waiver form. In addition, Smith informed petitioner that he was a lawyer working with the police investigating the Jackson case. Petitioner then gave another inculpatory statement concerning the crime.

Before trial, petitioner moved to suppress his statements, arguing that they were obtained in a manner at odds with various constitutional guarantees. The trial court denied these motions, and the statements were used against petitioner at his trial. The jury found petitioner guilty of murder, and petitioner was sentenced to a 24-year prison term.

On appeal, petitioner argued that he had not "knowingly and intelligently" waived his Sixth Amendment right to counsel before he gave his uncounseled post-indictment confessions. Petitioner contended that the warnings he received, while adequate for the purposes of protecting his Fifth Amendment rights as guaranteed by *Miranda*, did not adequately inform him of his Sixth Amendment right to counsel. The Illinois Supreme Court, however, rejected this theory * * *.

In reaching this conclusion, the Illinois Supreme Court noted that this Court had reserved decision on this question on several previous occasions and that the lower courts are divided on the issue. We granted this petition for certiorari to resolve this split of authority and to address the issues we had previously left open.

II.

There can be no doubt that petitioner had the right to have the assistance of counsel at his post-indictment interviews with law enforcement authorities. Our cases make it plain that the Sixth Amendment guarantees this right to criminal defendants. Petitioner asserts that the questioning that produced his incriminating statements violated his Sixth Amendment right to counsel in two ways.

A.

Petitioner's first claim is that because his Sixth Amendment right to counsel arose with his indictment, the police were thereafter barred from initiating a meeting with him. He equates himself with a preindictment suspect who, while being interrogated, asserts his Fifth Amendment right to counsel; under *Edwards v. Arizona*, 451 U.S. 477 (1981), such a suspect may not be questioned again unless he initiates the meeting.

Petitioner, however, at no time sought to exercise his right to have counsel present. The fact that petitioner's Sixth Amendment right came into existence with his indictment, i.e., that he had such a right at the time of his questioning, does not distinguish him from the preindictment interrogatee whose right to counsel is in existence and available for his exercise while he is questioned. Had petitioner indicated he wanted the assistance of counsel, the authorities' interview with him would have stopped, and further questioning would have been forbidden (unless petitioner called for such a meeting). * * *

At bottom, petitioner's theory cannot be squared with our rationale in *Edwards*, the case he relies on for support. *Edwards* rested on the view that once "an accused. . .ha[s] expressed his desire to deal with the police only through counsel" he should "not [be] subject to further interrogation by the authorities until counsel has been made available to him, unless the accused himself initiates further communication." *Edwards, supra,* at 484–485. Preserving the integrity of an accused's choice to communicate with police only through counsel is the essence of *Edwards* and its progeny—not barring an accused from making an initial election as to whether he will face the State's officers during questioning with the aid of counsel, or go it alone. If an accused "knowingly and intelligently" pursues the latter course, we see no reason why the uncounseled statements he then makes must be excluded at his trial.

B.

Petitioner's principal and more substantial claim is that questioning him without counsel present violated the Sixth Amendment because he did not validly waive his right to have counsel present during the interviews. Since it is clear that after the *Miranda* warnings were given to petitioner, he not only voluntarily answered questions without claiming his right to silence or his right to have a lawyer present to advise him but also executed a written waiver of his right to counsel during questioning, the specific issue posed here is whether this waiver was a "knowing and intelligent" waiver of his Sixth Amendment right.

* * * [T]he key inquiry in a case such as this one must be: Was the accused, who waived his Sixth Amendment rights during post-indictment questioning, made sufficiently aware of his right to have counsel present during the questioning, and of the possible consequences of a decision to forgo the aid of counsel? In this case, we are convinced that by admonishing petitioner with the *Miranda* warnings, respondent has met this burden and that petitioner's waiver of his right to counsel at the questioning was valid.[5]

First, the *Miranda* warnings given petitioner made him aware of his right to have counsel present during the questioning. By telling petitioner that he had a right to consult with an attorney, to have a lawyer present while he was questioned, and even to have a lawyer appointed for him if he could not afford to retain one on his own, Officer Gresham and ASA Smith conveyed to petitioner the sum and substance of the rights that the Sixth Amendment provided him. "Indeed, it seems self-evident that one who is told he" has such rights to counsel "is in a curious posture to later complain" that his waiver of these rights was unknowing. There is little more petitioner could have possibly been told in an effort to satisfy this portion of the waiver inquiry.

Second, the *Miranda* warnings also served to make petitioner aware of the consequences of a decision by him to waive his Sixth Amendment rights during post-indictment questioning. Petitioner knew that any statement that he made could be used against him in subsequent criminal proceedings. This is the ultimate adverse consequence petitioner could

---

[5] We emphasize the significance of the fact that petitioner's waiver of counsel was only for this limited aspect of the criminal proceedings against him—only for post-indictment questioning. Our decision on the validity of petitioner's waiver extends only so far.

have suffered by virtue of his choice to make uncounseled admissions to the authorities. This warning also sufficed—contrary to petitioner's claim here—to let petitioner know what a lawyer could "do for him" during the post-indictment questioning: namely, advise petitioner to refrain from making any such statements.[6] By knowing what could be done with any statements he might make, and therefore, what benefit could be obtained by having the aid of counsel while making such statements, petitioner was essentially informed of the possible consequences of going without counsel during questioning. If petitioner nonetheless lacked "a full and complete appreciation of all of the consequences flowing" from his waiver, it does not defeat the State's showing that the information it provided to him satisfied the constitutional minimum. * * *

As a general matter, then, an accused who is admonished with the warnings prescribed by this Court in *Miranda* has been sufficiently apprised of the nature of his Sixth Amendment rights, and of the consequences of abandoning those rights, so that his waiver on this basis will be considered a knowing and intelligent one.[9] We feel that our conclusion in a recent Fifth Amendment case is equally apposite here: "Once it is determined that a suspect's decision not to rely on his rights was uncoerced, that he at all times knew he could stand mute and request a lawyer, and that he was aware of the State's intention to use his statements to secure a conviction, the analysis is complete and the waiver is valid as a matter of law."

C.

We consequently reject petitioner's argument, which has some acceptance from courts and commentators, that since "the sixth amendment right [to counsel] is far superior to that of the fifth amendment right" and since "[t]he greater the right the greater the loss from a waiver of that right," waiver of an accused's Sixth Amendment right to counsel should be "more difficult" to effectuate than waiver of a suspect's Fifth

---

[6] An important basis for our analysis is our understanding that an attorney's role at post-indictment questioning is rather limited, and substantially different from the attorney's role in later phases of criminal proceedings. At trial, an accused needs an attorney to perform several varied functions—some of which are entirely beyond even the most intelligent layman. Yet during post-indictment questioning, a lawyer's role is rather unidimensional: largely limited to advising his client as to what questions to answer and which ones to decline to answer. * * *

[9] This does not mean, of course, that all Sixth Amendment challenges to the conduct of post-indictment questioning will fail whenever the challenged practice would pass constitutional muster under *Miranda*. For example, we have permitted a *Miranda* waiver to stand where a suspect was not told that his lawyer was trying to reach him during questioning; in the Sixth Amendment context, this waiver would not be valid. *See Moran v. Burbine*, 475 U.S., at 424, 428. Likewise, a surreptitious conversation between an undercover police officer and an unindicted suspect would not give rise to any *Miranda* violation as long as the "interrogation" was not in a custodial setting; however, once the accused is indicted, such questioning would be prohibited. *See United States v. Henry*, 447 U.S. 264, 273, 274–75 (1980).

Thus, because the Sixth Amendment's protection of the attorney-client relationship—"the right to rely on counsel as a 'medium' between [the accused] and the State"—extends beyond *Miranda*'s protection of the Fifth Amendment right to counsel, there will be cases where a waiver which would be valid under *Miranda* will not suffice for Sixth Amendment purposes.

Amendment rights. While our cases have recognized a "difference" between the Fifth Amendment and Sixth Amendment rights to counsel, and the "policies" behind these constitutional guarantees, we have never suggested that one right is "superior" or "greater" than the other, nor is there any support in our cases for the notion that because a Sixth Amendment right may be involved, it is more difficult to waive than the Fifth Amendment counterpart.

Instead, we have taken a more pragmatic approach to the waiver question—asking what purposes a lawyer can serve at the particular stage of the proceedings in question, and what assistance he could provide to an accused at that stage—to determine the scope of the Sixth Amendment right to counsel, and the type of warnings and procedures that should be required before a waiver of that right will be recognized. * * *

Applying this approach, it is our view that whatever warnings suffice for *Miranda's* purposes will also be sufficient in the context of post-indictment questioning. The State's decision to take an additional step and commence formal adversarial proceedings against the accused does not substantially increase the value of counsel to the accused at questioning, or expand the limited purpose that an attorney serves when the accused is questioned by authorities. With respect to this inquiry, we do not discern a substantial difference between the usefulness of a lawyer to a suspect during custodial interrogation, and his value to an accused at post-indictment questioning.

* * * Because the role of counsel at questioning is relatively simple and limited, we see no problem in having a waiver procedure at that stage which is likewise simple and limited. So long as the accused is made aware of the "dangers and disadvantages of self-representation" during post-indictment questioning, by use of the *Miranda* warnings, his waiver of his Sixth Amendment right to counsel at such questioning is "knowing and intelligent."

III.

Before confessing to the murder of James Jackson, petitioner was meticulously informed by authorities of his right to counsel, and of the consequences of any choice not to exercise that right. On two separate occasions, petitioner elected to forgo the assistance of counsel, and speak directly to officials concerning his role in the murder. Because we believe that petitioner's waiver of his Sixth Amendment rights was "knowing and intelligent," we find no error in the decision of the trial court to permit petitioner's confessions to be used against him. Consequently, the judgment of the Illinois Supreme Court is

Affirmed.

JUSTICE BLACKMUN, dissenting.

[Omitted.]

JUSTICE STEVENS, with whom JUSTICE BRENNAN and JUSTICE MARSHALL join, dissenting. * * *

The majority premises its conclusion that *Miranda* warnings lay a sufficient basis for accepting a waiver of the right to counsel on the assumption that those warnings make clear to an accused "what a lawyer could 'do for him' during the post-indictment questioning: namely, advise [him] to refrain from making any [incriminating] statements." Yet, this is surely a gross understatement of the disadvantage of proceeding without a lawyer and an understatement of what a defendant must understand to make a knowing waiver. The *Miranda* warnings do not, for example, inform the accused that a lawyer might examine the indictment for legal sufficiency before submitting his or her client to interrogation or that a lawyer is likely to be considerably more skillful at negotiating a plea bargain and that such negotiations may be most fruitful if initiated prior to any interrogation. Rather, the warnings do not even go so far as to explain to the accused the nature of the charges pending against him—advice that a court would insist upon before allowing a defendant to enter a guilty plea with or without the presence of an attorney. Without defining precisely the nature of the inquiry required to establish a valid waiver of the Sixth Amendment right to counsel, it must be conceded that at least minimal advice is necessary—the accused must be told of the "dangers and disadvantages of self-representation."

Yet, once it is conceded that certain advice is required and that after indictment the adversary relationship between the state and the accused has solidified, it inescapably follows that a prosecutor may not conduct private interviews with a charged defendant. As at least one Court of Appeals has recognized, there are ethical constraints that prevent a prosecutor from giving legal advice to an uncounseled adversary. Thus, neither the prosecutor nor his or her agents can ethically provide the unrepresented defendant with the kind of advice that should precede an evidence-gathering interview after formal proceedings have been commenced. Indeed, in my opinion even the *Miranda* warnings themselves are a species of legal advice that is improper when given by the prosecutor after indictment.

Moreover, there are good reasons why such advice is deemed unethical, reasons that extend to the custodial, post-indictment setting with unequaled strength. First, the offering of legal advice may lead an accused to underestimate the prosecuting authorities' true adversary posture. For an incarcerated defendant—in this case, a 17-year-old who had been in custody for 44 hours at the time he was told of the indictment—the assistance of someone to explain why he is being held, the nature of the charges against him, and the extent of his legal rights, may be of such importance as to overcome what is perhaps obvious to most, that the prosecutor is a foe and not a friend. Second, the adversary posture of the parties, which is not fully solidified until formal charges are brought, will inevitably tend to color the advice offered. As hard as a prosecutor might try, I doubt that it is possible for one to wear the hat of an effective adviser to a criminal defendant while at the same time wearing the hat of a law enforcement authority. Finally, regardless of whether or not the accused actually understands the legal and factual issues involved and the state's role as an adversary party, advice offered by a lawyer (or his or her agents) with such an evident conflict of interest cannot help but create a public perception of unfairness and unethical conduct. * * *

In sum, without a careful discussion of the pitfalls of proceeding without counsel, the Sixth Amendment right cannot properly be waived. An adversary party, moreover, cannot adequately provide such advice. As a result, once the right to counsel attaches and the adversary relationship between the state and the accused solidifies, a prosecutor cannot conduct a private interview with an accused party without "dilut[ing] the protection afforded by the right to counsel," *Maine v. Moulton*, 474 U.S. 159, 171 (1985). Although this ground alone is reason enough to never permit such private interviews, the rule also presents the added virtue of drawing a clear and easily identifiable line at the point between the investigatory and adversary stages of a criminal proceeding. * * * I think it clear that such private communications are intolerable not simply during trial, but at any point after adversary proceedings have commenced.

I therefore respectfully dissent.

QUESTIONS, COMMENTS, CONCERNS?

1. **Returning to *Brewer*.** Look back at *Brewer* for a moment. On the subject of waiver, key language from Justice Stewart's majority opinion clarifies that the majority agreed with the lower courts' conception of Sixth Amendment waiver: "an intentional relinquishment or abandonment of a known right or privilege." In applying that language to Robert Williams, do you think the *Brewer* Court thought *Miranda* and *Massiah* waiver were equivalent? As you consider your answer, remember that Williams received his *Miranda* warnings multiple times before telling authorities where to find Pamela's body.

Justice White may have viewed the waivers as equivalent. Note that he dissented in *Massiah* and *Brewer*, but wrote the majority opinion in *Patterson*.

2. **The role of counsel prior to charging.** You no doubt recall after reading *Spano*, *Massiah*, and *Brewer* that Justice Stewart felt passionately about the strength of the right to counsel post-indictment. But what about the role of (not right to) counsel pre- and post-charging—most importantly, in the interrogation room. The *Patterson* majority hardly seems persuaded. Look in particular at footnote six, where the majority comments, "An important basis

for our analysis is our understanding that an attorney's role at post-indictment questioning is rather limited, and substantially different from the attorney's role in later phases of criminal proceedings." Given law enforcement's frequent reliance on confessions as evidence of guilt, does that statement seem accurate? Had Justice Stewart still been on the Court at the time of *Patterson*, how do you think he would have voted? Note that Justice Stewart stepped down from his role on the Court in 1981 at the age of sixty-six. He passed away in 1985 after suffering a stroke. Justice O'Connor replaced Justice Stewart—and she voted to join what became the slim five-member *Patterson* majority.

3. *Miranda* and *Massiah* rights after *Patterson*. Is it fair to say that *Miranda* warnings, after *Patterson*, by themselves also convey the Sixth Amendment *Massiah* right to counsel?

4. *Miranda* and *Massiah* waiver after *Patterson*. Does a suspect's waiver of the *Miranda* right to counsel post-*Patterson* also count as a waiver of the *Massiah* right to counsel?

MONTEJO V. LOUISIANA

556 U.S. 778
Supreme Court of the United States
January 13, 2009, Argued; May 26, 2009, Decided
No. 07-1529

JUSTICE SCALIA delivered the opinion of the Court.

We consider in this case the scope and continued viability of the rule announced by this Court in *Michigan v. Jackson*, 475 U.S. 625 (1986), forbidding police to initiate interrogation of a criminal defendant once he has requested counsel at an arraignment or similar proceeding.

I.

Petitioner Jesse Montejo was arrested on September 6, 2002, in connection with the robbery and murder of Lewis Ferrari, who had been found dead in his own home one day earlier. Suspicion quickly focused on Jerry Moore, a disgruntled former employee of Ferrari's dry cleaning business. Police sought to question Montejo, who was a known associate of Moore.

Montejo waived his rights under *Miranda v. Arizona*, 384 U.S. 436 (1966), and was interrogated at the sheriff's office by police detectives through the late afternoon and evening of September 6 and the early morning of September 7. During the interrogation, Montejo repeatedly changed his account of the crime, at first claiming that he had only driven Moore to the victim's home, and ultimately admitting that he had shot and killed Ferrari in the course of a botched burglary. These police interrogations were videotaped.

On September 10, Montejo was brought before a judge for what is known in Louisiana as a "72-hour hearing"—a preliminary hearing required under state law. Although the proceedings were not transcribed, the minute record indicates what transpired: "The defendant being charged with First Degree Murder, Court ordered N[o] Bond set in this matter. Further, Court ordered the Office of Indigent Defender be appointed to represent the defendant."

Later that same day, two police detectives visited Montejo back at the prison and requested that he accompany them on an excursion to locate the murder weapon (which Montejo had earlier indicated he had thrown into a lake). After some back-and-forth, the substance of which remains in dispute, Montejo was again read his *Miranda* rights and agreed to go along; during the excursion, he wrote an inculpatory letter of apology to the victim's widow. Only upon their return did Montejo finally meet his court-appointed attorney, who was quite upset that the detectives had interrogated his client in his absence.

At trial, the letter of apology was admitted over defense objection. The jury convicted Montejo of first-degree murder, and he was sentenced to death.

The Louisiana Supreme Court affirmed the conviction and sentence. As relevant here, the court rejected Montejo's argument that under the rule of *Jackson, supra* the letter should have been suppressed. *Jackson* held that "if police initiate interrogation after a defendant's assertion, at an arraignment or similar proceeding, of his right to counsel, any waiver of the defendant's right to counsel for that police-initiated interrogation is invalid."

* * * [T]he Louisiana Supreme Court reasoned that the prophylactic protection of *Jackson* is not triggered unless and until the defendant has actually requested a lawyer or has otherwise asserted his Sixth Amendment right to counsel. Because Montejo simply stood mute at his 72-hour hearing while the judge ordered the appointment of counsel, he had made no such request or assertion. So the proper inquiry, the court ruled, was only whether he had knowingly, intelligently, and voluntarily waived his right to have counsel present during the interaction with the police. And because Montejo had been read his *Miranda* rights and agreed to waive them, the Court answered that question in the affirmative and upheld the conviction.

We granted certiorari. * * *

II. * * *

The only question raised by this case, and the only one addressed by the *Jackson* rule, is whether courts must presume that such a waiver is invalid under certain circumstances. We created such a presumption in *Jackson* by analogy to a similar prophylactic rule established to protect the Fifth Amendment-based *Miranda* right to have counsel present at any custodial interrogation. *Edwards v. Arizona*, 451 U.S. 477 (1981), decided that once "an accused has invoked his right to have counsel present during custodial interrogation. . .[he] is not subject to further interrogation by the authorities until counsel has been made available," unless he initiates the contact.

The *Edwards* rule is "designed to prevent police from badgering a defendant into waiving his previously asserted *Miranda* rights." It does this by presuming his post-assertion statements to be involuntary, "even where the suspect executes a waiver and his statements would be considered voluntary under traditional standards." *McNeil v. Wisconsin*, 501 U.S. 171, 177 (1991). * * *

Jackson represented a "wholesale importation of the *Edwards* rule into the Sixth Amendment." The *Jackson* Court decided that a request for counsel at an arraignment should be treated as an invocation of the Sixth Amendment right to counsel "at every critical stage of the prosecution," despite doubt that defendants "actually inten[d] their request for counsel to encompass representation during any further questioning," because doubts must be "resolved in favor of protecting the constitutional claim." Citing *Edwards*, the Court held that any subsequent waiver would thus be "insufficient to justify police-initiated interrogation." In other words, we presume such waivers involuntary "based on the supposition that suspects who assert their right to counsel are unlikely to waive that right voluntarily" in subsequent interactions with police. * * *

With this understanding of what *Jackson* stands for and whence it came, it should be clear that Montejo's interpretation of that decision—that no represented defendant can ever be approached by the State and asked to consent to interrogation—is off the mark. When a court appoints counsel for an indigent defendant in the absence of any request on his part, there is no basis for a presumption that any subsequent waiver of the right to counsel will be involuntary. There is no "initial election" to exercise the right that must be preserved through a prophylactic rule against later waivers. No reason exists to assume that a defendant like Montejo, who has done nothing at all to express his intentions with respect to his Sixth Amendment rights, would not be perfectly amenable to speaking with the police without having counsel present. And no reason exists to prohibit the police from inquiring. *Edwards* and *Jackson* are meant to prevent police from badgering defendants into changing their minds about their rights, but a defendant who never asked for counsel has not yet made up his mind in the first instance. * * *

In practice, Montejo's rule would prevent police-initiated interrogation entirely once the Sixth Amendment right attaches, at least in those States that appoint counsel promptly without request from the defendant. As the dissent in *Jackson* pointed out, with no expressed disagreement from the majority, the opinion "most assuredly [did] not hold that the *Edwards* per se rule prohibiting all police-initiated interrogations applies from the moment the defendant's Sixth Amendment right to counsel attaches, with or without a request for counsel by the defendant." * * *

III. * * *

It is true, as Montejo points out in his supplemental brief, that the doctrine established by *Miranda* and *Edwards* is designed to protect Fifth Amendment, not Sixth Amendment, rights. But that is irrelevant. What matters is that these cases, like *Jackson*, protect the right to have counsel during custodial interrogation—which right happens to be guaranteed (once the adversary judicial process has begun) by two sources of law. Since the right under both sources is waived using the same procedure, doctrines ensuring voluntariness of the Fifth Amendment waiver simultaneously ensure the voluntariness of the Sixth Amendment waiver.

Montejo also correctly observes that the *Miranda-Edwards* regime is narrower than *Jackson* in one respect: The former applies only in the context of custodial interrogation. If the defendant is not in custody then those decisions do not apply; nor do they govern other, non-interrogative types of interactions between the defendant and the State (like pretrial lineups). However, those uncovered situations are the least likely to pose a risk of coerced waivers. When a defendant is not in custody, he is in control, and need only shut his door or walk away to avoid police badgering. And non-interrogative interactions with the State do not involve the "inherently compelling pressures," *Miranda, supra,* that one might reasonably fear could lead to involuntary waivers. * * *

On the other side of the equation are the costs of adding the bright-line *Jackson* rule on top of *Edwards* and other extant protections. The principal cost of applying any exclusionary rule "is, of course, letting guilty and possibly dangerous criminals go free. . ." *Jackson* not only "operates to invalidate a confession given by the free choice of suspects who have received proper advice of their *Miranda* rights but waived them nonetheless," but also deters law enforcement officers from even trying to obtain voluntary confessions. The "ready ability to obtain uncoerced confessions is not an evil but an unmitigated good." Without these confessions, crimes go unsolved and criminals unpunished. These are not negligible costs, and in our view the *Jackson* Court gave them too short shrift.

Notwithstanding this calculus, Montejo and his amici urge the retention of *Jackson*. Their principal objection to its elimination is that the *Edwards* regime which remains will not provide an administrable rule. But this Court has praised *Edwards* precisely because it provides " 'clear and unequivocal' guidelines to the law enforcement profession." Our cases make clear which sorts of statements trigger its protections, *see Davis v.*

United States, 512 U.S. 452, 459 (1994), and once triggered, the rule operates as a bright line. Montejo expresses concern that courts will have to determine whether statements made at preliminary hearings constitute *Edwards* invocations * * *. That concern is misguided. "We have in fact never held that a person can invoke his *Miranda* rights anticipatorily, in a context other than 'custodial interrogation'. . ." What matters for *Miranda* and *Edwards* is what happens when the defendant is approached for interrogation, and (if he consents) what happens during the interrogation—not what happened at any preliminary hearing.

In sum, when the marginal benefits of the *Jackson* rule are weighed against its substantial costs to the truth-seeking process and the criminal justice system, we readily conclude that the rule does not "pay its way," *United States v. Leon*, 468 U.S. 897, 907–908, n.6 (1984). *Michigan v. Jackson* should be and now is overruled.

IV.

Although our holding means that the Louisiana Supreme Court correctly rejected Montejo's claim under Jackson, we think that Montejo should be given an opportunity to contend that his letter of apology should still have been suppressed under the rule of *Edwards*. If Montejo made a clear assertion of the right to counsel when the officers approached him about accompanying them on the excursion for the murder weapon, then no interrogation should have taken place unless Montejo initiated it. Even if Montejo subsequently agreed to waive his rights, that waiver would have been invalid had it followed an "unequivocal election of the right." * * *

The judgment of the Louisiana Supreme Court is vacated, and the case is remanded for further proceedings not inconsistent with this opinion.

It is so ordered.

JUSTICE ALITO, with whom JUSTICE KENNEDY joins, concurring.

[Omitted.]

JUSTICE STEVENS, with whom JUSTICE SOUTER and JUSTICE GINSBURG join, and with whom JUSTICE BREYER joins except for footnote 5, dissenting. * * *

The majority's decision to overrule *Jackson* rests on its assumption that *Jackson's* protective rule was intended to "prevent police from badgering defendants into changing their minds about their rights," just as the rule adopted in *Edwards v. Arizona*, 451 U.S. 477 (1981), was designed to prevent police from coercing unindicted suspects into revoking their requests for counsel at interrogation. Operating on that limited understanding of the purpose behind *Jackson's* protective rule, the Court concludes that *Jackson* provides no safeguard not already secured by this

Court's Fifth Amendment jurisprudence. *See Miranda v. Arizona*, 384 U.S. 436.

The majority's analysis flagrantly misrepresents *Jackson's* underlying rationale and the constitutional interests the decision sought to protect. While it is true that the rule adopted in *Jackson* was patterned after the rule in *Edwards*, the *Jackson* opinion does not even mention the anti-badgering considerations that provide the basis for the Court's decision today. Instead, *Jackson* relied primarily on cases discussing the broad protections guaranteed by the Sixth Amendment right to counsel—not its Fifth Amendment counterpart. *Jackson* emphasized that the purpose of the Sixth Amendment is to "protec[t] the unaided layman at critical confrontations with his adversary," by giving him "the right to rely on counsel as a 'medium' between him[self] and the State." Underscoring that the commencement of criminal proceedings is a decisive event that transforms a suspect into an accused within the meaning of the Sixth Amendment, we concluded that arraigned defendants are entitled to "at least as much protection" during interrogation as the Fifth Amendment affords unindicted suspects. Thus, although the rules adopted in *Edwards* and *Jackson* are similar, *Jackson* did not rely on the reasoning of *Edwards* but remained firmly rooted in the unique protections afforded to the attorney-client relationship by the Sixth Amendment.

Once *Jackson* is placed in its proper Sixth Amendment context, the majority's justifications for overruling the decision crumble. * * *

Despite the fact that the rule established in *Jackson* remains relevant, well grounded in constitutional precedent, and easily administrable, the Court today rejects it *sua sponte*. Such a decision can only diminish the public's confidence in the reliability and fairness of our system of justice. * * *

Even if *Jackson* had never been decided, it would be clear that Montejo's Sixth Amendment rights were violated. Today's decision eliminates the rule that "any waiver of Sixth Amendment rights given in a discussion initiated by police is presumed invalid" once a defendant has invoked his right to counsel. Nevertheless, under the undisputed facts of this case, there is no sound basis for concluding that Montejo made a knowing and valid waiver of his Sixth Amendment right to counsel before acquiescing in police interrogation following his 72-hour hearing. Because police questioned Montejo without notice to, and outside the presence of, his lawyer, the interrogation violated Montejo's right to counsel even under pre-*Jackson* precedent. * * *

The Court avoids confronting the serious Sixth Amendment concerns raised by the police interrogation in this case by assuming that Montejo validly waived his Sixth Amendment rights before submitting to interrogation. It does so by summarily concluding that "doctrines ensuring voluntariness of the Fifth Amendment waiver simultaneously ensure the voluntariness of the Sixth Amendment waiver"; thus, because Montejo was given *Miranda* warnings prior to interrogation, his waiver was presumptively valid. Ironically, while the Court faults *Jackson* for blurring the line between this Court's Fifth and Sixth Amendment jurisprudence, it commits the same error by assuming that the *Miranda* warnings given in this case, designed purely to safeguard the Fifth Amendment right against self-incrimination, were somehow adequate to protect Montejo's more robust Sixth Amendment right to counsel.

The majority's cursory treatment of the waiver question rests entirely on the dubious decision in *Patterson*, in which we addressed whether, by providing *Miranda* warnings, police had adequately advised an indicted but unrepresented defendant of his Sixth Amendment right to counsel. The majority held that "[a]s a general matter. . .an accused who is admonished with the warnings prescribed. . .in *Miranda*. . .has been sufficiently apprised of the nature of his Sixth Amendment rights, and of the consequences of abandoning those rights." The Court recognized, however, that "because the Sixth Amendment's protection of the attorney-client relationship. . .extends beyond *Miranda's* protection of the Fifth Amendment right to counsel, . . .there will be cases where a waiver which would be valid under *Miranda* will not suffice for Sixth Amendment purposes." This is such a case.

As I observed in *Patterson*, the conclusion that *Miranda* warnings ordinarily provide a sufficient basis for a knowing waiver of the right to counsel rests on the questionable assumption that those warnings make clear to defendants the assistance a lawyer can render during post-indictment interrogation. Because *Miranda* warnings do not hint at the ways in which a lawyer might assist her client during conversations with the police, I remain convinced that the warnings prescribed in *Miranda*, while sufficient to apprise a defendant of his Fifth Amendment right to remain silent, are inadequate to inform an unrepresented, indicted defendant of his Sixth Amendment right to have a lawyer present at all critical stages of a criminal prosecution. The inadequacy of those warnings is even more obvious in the case of a represented defendant. While it can be argued that informing an indicted but unrepresented defendant of his right to counsel at least alerts him to the fact that he is entitled to obtain something he does not already possess, providing that same warning to a defendant who has already secured counsel is more likely to confound than enlighten.[8] By glibly assuming that the *Miranda* warnings given in this

---

[8] With respect to vulnerable defendants, such as juveniles and those with mental impairments of various kinds, amici National Association of Criminal Defense Lawyers et al. assert that "[o]verruling *Jackson* would be particularly detrimental. . .because of the confusing instructions regarding counsel that they would receive. At the initial hearing, they would likely learn that an attorney was being appointed for them. In a later custodial interrogation, however, they would be informed in the traditional manner of 'their right to counsel' and right to have

case were sufficient to ensure Montejo's waiver was both knowing and voluntary, the Court conveniently avoids any comment on the actual advice Montejo received, which did not adequately inform him of his relevant Sixth Amendment rights or alert him to the possible consequences of waiving those rights.

A defendant's decision to forgo counsel's assistance and speak openly with police is a momentous one. Given the high stakes of making such a choice and the potential value of counsel's advice and mediation at that critical stage of the criminal proceedings, it is imperative that a defendant possess "a full awareness of both the nature of the right being abandoned and the consequences of the decision to abandon it," before his waiver is deemed valid. Because the administration of *Miranda* warnings was insufficient to ensure Montejo understood the Sixth Amendment right he was being asked to surrender, the record in this case provides no basis for concluding that Montejo validly waived his right to counsel, even in the absence of *Jackson's* enhanced protections. * * *

I respectfully dissent.

JUSTICE BREYER, dissenting.

[Omitted.]

QUESTIONS, COMMENTS, CONCERNS?

1.   **The impact of *Massiah* attachment.** How does *Montejo* impact the assertion of a suspect's Sixth Amendment right to counsel post-charging?

2.   ***Brewer's* legacy.** If Justice Stewart might struggle with the result in *Patterson*, one can only imagine what reaction he might have to *Montejo*. Do you think, at the time of *Brewer*, that the *Brewer* majority viewed the scope of the *Massiah* right to counsel as equivalent to the *Miranda* right to counsel?

3.   **Is *Edwards* at risk post-*Montejo*?** If the modern Supreme Court is willing to overrule *Michigan v. Jackson*, do you think, if given the chance, that it would reconsider *Edwards v. Arizona*? As you consider your answer, you might like to know that *Jackson* relied heavily on *Edwards*. Writing for the majority in *Jackson*, Justice Stevens said:

> *Edwards* is grounded in the understanding that "the assertion of the right to counsel [is] a significant event," and that "additional safeguards are necessary when the accused asks for counsel." We conclude that the assertion is no less significant, and the need for additional safeguards no less clear, when the request for counsel is made at an arraignment and when the basis for the claim is the Sixth Amendment. We thus hold that, if police initiate interrogation after

---

counsel 'appointed' if they are indigent, notwithstanding that counsel had already been appointed in open court. These conflicting statements would be confusing to anyone but would be especially baffling to defendants with mental disabilities or other impairments."

a defendant's assertion, at an arraignment or similar proceeding, of his right to counsel, any waiver of the defendant's right to counsel for that police-initiated interrogation is invalid.

Although the *Edwards* decision itself rested on the Fifth Amendment and concerned a request for counsel made during custodial interrogation, the Michigan Supreme Court correctly perceived that the reasoning of that case applies with even greater force to these cases.

Michigan v. Jackson, 475 U.S. 625, 636 (1986).

VI. *MASSIAH* EXCLUSION

We close this chapter with a single case—*Kansas v. Ventris*—that helps to clarify the strength of the Sixth Amendment exclusionary rule. There is some good news here as we unpack *Ventris*. Unlike *Miranda* exclusion, the *Massiah* exclusion is generally more straightforward. Given that a violation of *Massiah* is also a violation of the Sixth Amendment, as opposed a violation of the "prophylactic" *Miranda* warnings (*Dickerson* notwithstanding), the fruit of the poisonous tree doctrine applies. *E.g.*, *United States v. Terzado-Madruga*, 897 F.2d 1099, 1112–14 (11th Cir. 1990). But so too do the exceptions to the fruit of the poisonous tree doctrine we learned in Chapter 2—namely, attenuation, inevitable discovery, and independent source.

Viewed within that framework, then, you should view *Ventris* as an exception to those general rules.

KANSAS V. VENTRIS
556 U.S. 586
Supreme Court of the United States
January 21, 2009, Argued; April 29, 2009, Decided
No. 07-1356

JUSTICE SCALIA delivered the opinion of the Court.

We address in this case the question whether a defendant's incriminating statement to a jailhouse informant, concededly elicited in violation of Sixth Amendment strictures, is admissible at trial to impeach the defendant's conflicting statement.

I.

In the early hours of January 7, 2004, after two days of no sleep and some drug use, Rhonda Theel and respondent Donnie Ray Ventris reached an ill-conceived agreement to confront Ernest Hicks in his home. The couple testified that the aim of the visit was simply to investigate rumors that Hicks abused children, but the couple may have been inspired by the potential for financial gain: Theel had recently learned that Hicks carried large amounts of cash.

The encounter did not end well. One or both of the pair shot and killed Hicks with shots from a .38-caliber revolver, and the companions drove off in Hicks's truck with approximately $300 of his money and his cell phone. On receiving a tip from two friends of the couple who had helped transport them to Hicks's home, officers arrested Ventris and Theel and charged them with various crimes, chief among them murder and aggravated robbery. The State dropped the murder charge against Theel in exchange for her guilty plea to the robbery charge and her testimony identifying Ventris as the shooter.

Prior to trial, officers planted an informant in Ventris's holding cell, instructing him to "keep [his] ear open and listen" for incriminating statements. According to the informant, in response to his statement that Ventris appeared to have "something more serious weighing in on his mind," Ventris divulged that "[h]e'd shot this man in his head and in his chest" and taken "his keys, his wallet, about $350.00, and. . .a vehicle."

At trial, Ventris took the stand and blamed the robbery and shooting entirely on Theel. The government sought to call the informant, to testify to Ventris's prior contradictory statement; Ventris objected. The State conceded that there was "probably a violation" of Ventris's Sixth Amendment right to counsel but nonetheless argued that the statement was admissible for impeachment purposes because the violation "doesn't give the Defendant. . .a license to just get on the stand and lie." The trial court agreed and allowed the informant's testimony, but instructed the jury to "consider with caution" all testimony given in exchange for benefits from the State. The jury ultimately acquitted Ventris of felony murder and misdemeanor theft but returned a guilty verdict on the aggravated burglary and aggravated robbery counts.

The Kansas Supreme Court reversed the conviction, holding that "[o]nce a criminal prosecution has commenced, the defendant's statements made to an undercover informant surreptitiously acting as an agent for the State are not admissible at trial for any reason, including the impeachment of the defendant's testimony." We granted the State's petition for certiorari.

II.

* * * The State has conceded throughout these proceedings that Ventris's confession was taken in violation of *Massiah's* dictates and was therefore not admissible in the prosecution's case in chief. Without affirming that this concession was necessary, *see Kuhlmann v. Wilson*, 477 U.S. 436, 459–460 (1986), we accept it as the law of the case. The only question we answer today is whether the State must bear the additional consequence of inability to counter Ventris's contradictory testimony by placing the informant on the stand.

A.

Whether otherwise excluded evidence can be admitted for purposes of impeachment depends upon the nature of the constitutional guarantee that is violated. Sometimes that explicitly mandates exclusion from trial, and sometimes it does not. The Fifth Amendment guarantees that no person shall be compelled to give evidence against himself, and so is violated whenever a truly coerced confession is introduced at trial, whether by way of impeachment or otherwise. The Fourth Amendment, on the other hand, guarantees that no person shall be subjected to unreasonable searches or seizures, and says nothing about excluding their fruits from evidence; exclusion comes by way of deterrent sanction rather than to avoid violation of the substantive guarantee. Inadmissibility has not been automatic, therefore, but we have instead applied an exclusionary-rule balancing test. The same is true for violations of the Fifth and Sixth Amendment prophylactic rules forbidding certain pretrial police conduct. * * *

Our opinion in *Massiah*, to be sure, was equivocal on what precisely constituted the violation. It quoted various authorities indicating that the violation occurred at the moment of the post-indictment interrogation because such questioning "contravenes the basic dictates of fairness in the conduct of criminal causes." But the opinion later suggested that the violation occurred only when the improperly obtained evidence was "used against [the defendant] at his trial." That question was irrelevant to the decision in *Massiah* in any event. Now that we are confronted with the question, we conclude that the *Massiah* right is a right to be free of uncounseled interrogation and is infringed at the time of the interrogation. That, we think, is when the "Assistance of Counsel" is denied.

It is illogical to say that the right is not violated until trial counsel's task of opposing conviction has been undermined by the statement's admission into evidence. A defendant is not denied counsel merely because the prosecution has been permitted to introduce evidence of guilt—even evidence so overwhelming that the attorney's job of gaining an acquittal is rendered impossible. In such circumstances the accused continues to enjoy the assistance of counsel; the assistance is simply not worth much. The assistance of counsel has been denied, however, at the prior critical stage which produced the inculpatory evidence. Our cases acknowledge that reality in holding that the stringency of the warnings necessary for a waiver of the assistance of counsel varies according to "the usefulness of counsel to the accused at the particular [pretrial] proceeding." *Patterson v. Illinois*, 487 U.S. 285, 298 (1988). It is that deprivation which demands a remedy.

The United States insists that "post-charge deliberate elicitation of statements without the defendant's counsel or a valid waiver of counsel is not intrinsically unlawful." That is true when the questioning is unrelated to charged crimes—the Sixth Amendment right is "offense specific," *McNeil v. Wisconsin*, 501 U.S. 171, 175 (1991). We have never said, however, that officers may badger counseled defendants about charged crimes so long as they do not use information they gain. The constitutional violation occurs when the uncounseled interrogation is conducted.

B.

This case does not involve, therefore, the prevention of a constitutional violation, but rather the scope of the remedy for a violation that has already occurred. Our precedents make clear that the game of excluding tainted evidence for impeachment purposes is not worth the candle. The interests safeguarded by such exclusion are "outweighed by the need to prevent perjury and to assure the integrity of the trial process." "It is one thing to say that the Government cannot make an affirmative use of evidence unlawfully obtained. It is quite another to say that the defendant can. . .provide himself with a shield against contradiction of his untruths." Once the defendant testifies in a way that contradicts prior statements, denying the prosecution use of "the traditional truth-testing devices of the adversary process" is a high price to pay for vindication of the right to counsel at the prior stage.

On the other side of the scale, preventing impeachment use of statements taken in violation of *Massiah* would add little appreciable deterrence. Officers have significant incentive to ensure that they and their informants comply with the Constitution's demands, since statements lawfully obtained can be used for all purposes rather than simply for impeachment. And the *ex ante* probability that evidence gained in violation of *Massiah* would be of use for impeachment is exceedingly small. An investigator would have to anticipate both that the defendant would choose to testify at trial (an unusual occurrence to begin with) and that he would testify inconsistently despite the admissibility of his prior statement for impeachment. Not likely to happen—or at least not likely enough to risk squandering the opportunity of using a properly obtained statement for the prosecution's case in chief.

In any event, even if "the officer may be said to have little to lose and perhaps something to gain by way of possibly uncovering impeachment material," we have multiple times rejected the argument that this "speculative possibility" can trump the costs of allowing perjurious statements to go unchallenged. We have held in every other context that tainted evidence—evidence whose very introduction does not constitute the constitutional violation, but whose obtaining was constitutionally invalid—is admissible for impeachment. We see no distinction that would alter the balance here.

* * *

We hold that the informant's testimony, concededly elicited in violation of the Sixth Amendment, was admissible to challenge Ventris's inconsistent testimony at trial. The judgment of the Kansas Supreme Court is reversed, and the case is remanded for further proceedings not inconsistent with this opinion.

It is so ordered.

JUSTICE STEVENS, with whom JUSTICE GINSBURG joins, dissenting.

* * * [M]y view * * * is * * * that "the Sixth Amendment is violated when the fruits of the State's impermissible encounter with the represented defendant are used for impeachment just as it is when the fruits are used in the prosecutor's case in chief."

In this case, the State has conceded that it violated the Sixth Amendment as interpreted in *Massiah v. United States*, 377 U.S. 201, 206 (1964), when it used a jailhouse informant to elicit a statement from the defendant. No *Miranda* warnings were given to the defendant, nor was he otherwise alerted to the fact that he was speaking to a state agent. Even though the jury apparently did not credit the informant's testimony, the Kansas Supreme Court correctly concluded that the prosecution should not be allowed to exploit its pretrial constitutional violation during the trial itself. The Kansas court's judgment should be affirmed.

This Court's contrary holding relies on the view that a defendant's pretrial right to counsel is merely "prophylactic" in nature. The majority argues that any violation of this prophylactic right occurs solely at the time the State subjects a counseled defendant to an uncounseled interrogation, not when the fruits of the encounter are used against the defendant at trial. This reasoning is deeply flawed. * * *

Treating the State's actions in this case as a violation of a prophylactic right, the Court concludes that introducing the illegally obtained evidence at trial does not itself violate the Constitution. I strongly disagree. While the constitutional breach began at the time of interrogation, the State's use of that evidence at trial compounded the violation. The logic that compels the exclusion of the evidence during the State's case in chief extends to any attempt by the State to rely on the evidence, even for impeachment. The use of ill-gotten evidence during any phase of criminal prosecution does damage to the adversarial process—the fairness of which the Sixth Amendment was designed to protect.

When counsel is excluded from a critical pretrial interaction between the defendant and the State, she may be unable to effectively counter the potentially devastating, and potentially false, evidence subsequently introduced at trial. Inexplicably, today's Court refuses to recognize that this is a constitutional harm. Yet in *Massiah*, the Court forcefully explained that a defendant is "denied the basic protections of [the Sixth

Amendment] guarantee when there [is] used against him at his trial evidence of his own incriminating words" that were "deliberately elicited from him after he had been indicted and in the absence of his counsel." Sadly, the majority has retreated from this robust understanding of the right to counsel.

Today's decision is lamentable not only because of its flawed underpinnings, but also because it is another occasion in which the Court has privileged the prosecution at the expense of the Constitution. Permitting the State to cut corners in criminal proceedings taxes the legitimacy of the entire criminal process. "The State's interest in truthseeking is congruent with the defendant's interest in representation by counsel, for it is an elementary premise of our system of criminal justice. . .that partisan advocacy on both sides of a case will best promote the ultimate objective that the guilty be convicted and the innocent go free." Although the Court may not be concerned with the use of ill-gotten evidence in derogation of the right to counsel, I remain convinced that such shabby tactics are intolerable in all cases. I respectfully dissent.

QUESTIONS, COMMENTS, CONCERNS?

1.   **Note the *Ventris* dissenter.** Note that the lone dissent in *Ventris* comes from Justice Stevens. By 2009, when *Ventris* was published, Justice Stevens was the last Justice remaining from the *Brewer* majority. Although Justice Stevens was not yet on the Court at the time of *Massiah*, you see his respect for the opinion shine through in his dissent. You can likewise see his understanding of the strength of the *Massiah* right to counsel and his argument that *Ventris* inappropriately undermines the strength of *Massiah*'s exclusionary rule.

2.   **Vote trading and foreshadowing other holes in the exclusionary rule.** As you may recall from Chapter 2, *Brewer* preceded Williams's second appearance before the Supreme Court in *Nix v. Williams*, 467 U.S. 431 (1984). *Nix*, as you may remember, established the inevitable discovery exception to the exclusionary rule. *Nix* ultimately held that the condition of Pamela's body—the fruit of Williams's incriminating statements—was properly admitted at Williams's retrial because volunteer searchers would have discovered Pamela's body without the statements. *Nix* therefore had the ultimate effect of affirming Williams's life sentence.

But the more interesting story resides in the Justices' *Brewer* papers—particularly told through an exchange between Chief Justice Burger and Justice Powell. That exchange seems clearly to have planted the seeds for *Nix* and the inevitable discovery doctrine. After Justice Stewart circulated his draft majority opinion on November 24, 1976, Chief Justice Burger wrote an angry memorandum to the full Court on December 29, 1976. In part, he wrote:

I will probably write separately focusing on the utter irrationality of fulfilling Cardozo's half-century old prophecy—which he really made in jest—that some day some court would carry the Suppression Rule to the absurd extent of suppressing evidence of a murder victim's body.

That is what is being done here—at least as of now. My thrust will be that even accepting the view of the present majority—which I do not—it is indeed irrational for the Court to extend the Suppression Rule to exclude evidence of the body.

[Casefile Marshall Papers, at 123.] After that memorandum, Justice Powell authored and circulated his concurring opinion on January 6, 1977. [Casefile Powell Papers, at 96.] Upon reviewing the opinion, Chief Justice Burger saw an opportunity to sway Powell's vote. In a personal letter to Justice Powell, dated February 10, 1977, Chief Justice Burger wrote in part:

[The victim's body] is at once the most reliable and most probative we could conceivably have bearing on Respondent's guilt or innocence. It is far more probative than a confession due to the objective facts disclosed. * * *

As you know, Byron, Harry and Bill Rehnquist are on record as favoring a remand for reconsideration in light of the voluntariness issue, which the Court of Appeals did not reach. Your concurrence prompts me to say that if five would agree, we ought to dispose of the case with a per curiam order vacating the judgment below and remanding the case for reconsideration both of the voluntariness issue and the Stone v. Powell exclusionary question. For me that would be infinitely preferable to the present proposed disposition of the case, which is inconclusive.

Id. at 102–03. Justice Powell responded to the Chief's letter the next day. By way of his own personal letter, Justice Powell wrote in pertinent part the following:

But *Brewer v. Williams*, at least as I view it, is a poor vehicle for modifying the exclusionary rule. I would have difficulty defending the police conduct, although I appreciate that you and others have a different view.

I would let *Brewer v. Williams* come down as written, with the various concurring and dissenting opinions. As my concurrence makes clear, the case is highly fact specific. There is little difference among us as to the applicable principle. *It will not foreclose our considering a modification of the exclusionary rule in a more appropriate case. When such a case arises, I think you will find me a congenial spirit.*

Id. at 105 (second emphasis added). As it would turn out, *Nix* was the case to modify the exclusionary rule. Chief Justice Burger wrote the majority opinion in *Nix*, which Justice Powell joined. Justice Powell's doing so is perhaps evidence that he does not hold a grudge (you will recall reading about Chief Justice Burger calling attention to Justice Powell's concurrence on the day *Brewer* was announced).

3. **Do the Justices read law review articles?** Justices Powell and Blackmun did. Look at the end of Justice Powell's file and you will see the cover to the 1977 *Georgetown Law Journal* article authored by Professor Yale Kamisar. [Casefile Powell Papers, at 133.] Cited in the introductory materials to this chapter, the article is titled, "Brewer v. Williams—*A Hard Look at a Discomfiting Record.*" On the cover is a handwritten note from Professor Kamisar that reads, "For Justice Powell, with warm regard and best wishes, Yale. What really happened on the long drive back to Des Moines?"

For his part, Justice Blackmun retained a memorandum, apparently from his law clerk, reviewing and assessing Professor Kamisar's law review article. [Casefile Blackmun Papers, at 5–6.]

4. **What about media reports—do the Justices read those?** Well, Justice Powell did. So too did Justices Brennan and Blackmun. *Brewer* was published on March 23, 1977. On March 28, 1977, Justice Powell authored a short memorandum to his law clerk, Gene Comey, indicating that "Columnist George Will (Sunday's Post) did not seem terribly enthusiastic about the majority opinion in the above case. He even suggested, as I read him, that I did not know the difference between the day before and the day after Christmas." [Casefile Powell Papers, at 130.]

You can read a copy of Will's article. Remarkably, Justice Brennan kept a copy. [Casefile Brennan Papers, at 197.] Justice Brennan also retained a handful of other news clippings that were published after *Brewer*, including an editorial published in *The Washington Post* by Professor Yale Kamisar. *Id.* at 196–99. Justice Blackmun also retained a news article that was brutally critical of the *Brewer* majority. [Casefile Blackmun Papers, at 141 ("If Williams does walk and kills again, the blood of his victims will be on the heads of Marshall, Brennan, Stevens, Stewart, and Powell.").]

5. **Public access to the Justices.** It is hard to imagine in today's world, but several of the Justices retained personal correspondence from a member of the public in their working papers. Justice Brennan, for example, saved a letter from a father who apparently met Justice Brennan only briefly. [Casefile Brennan Papers, at 195.] The father wrote to complain that his son disparaged Justice Brennan after *Brewer* was published. *Id.* Not only did Justice Brennan save the letter, he even authored a reply. *Id.* at 194.

Justice Blackmun also saved personal letters from the public. In one example, Justice Blackmun retained a note from a private practitioner who appreciated his dissent in *Brewer*. [Casefile Blackmun Papers, at 140.] Justice Blackmun would also receive a letter from a surgeon who was concerned about "why the high Courts continue to protect the criminal as opposed to the injured. *Id.* at 161. Justice Blackmun replied to the doctor's letter with a note of his own, which acknowledged, "The division in the Court was deep[.]" *Id.* at 160.

There are other periodic examples of the Court's engagement with the public, including a letter to Justice Powell from a concerned citizen who expressed that he was "extremely disappointed" in the Justice's decision to concur. *Id.* at 164. But perhaps the most fascinating letter included in the Justices' files came from Mark Alan Powers, Pamela's brother, who was competing in the wrestling tournament when Pamela was taken. *Id.* at 167–68. He wrote with disappointment in the *Brewer* opinion, noting, "[I]t appears to me as though guilt or innocence has lost its significance." *Id.* at 168.

VII. COMPARING *MASSIAH* & *MIRANDA*: A REVIEW CHART

Massiah Review Chart

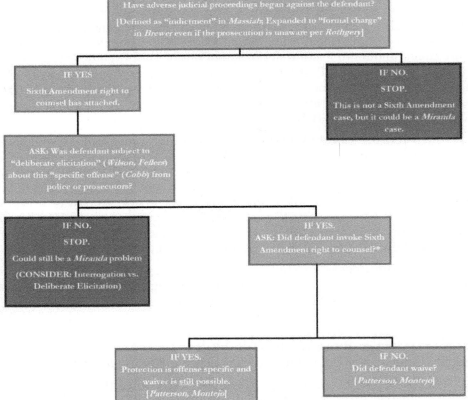

CHAPTER 11

IDENTIFICATIONS & MISIDENTIFICATIONS

■ ■ ■

I. INTRODUCTION: UNDERSTANDING THE (MIS)IDENTIFICATION PROBLEM[1]

A. THE AVAILABLE PROCEDURES[2]

Eyewitnesses can be crucial evidence of guilt in robbery, assault, rape, and other commonly prosecuted offenses. Each year as many as 80,000 eyewitnesses make identifications of suspects in criminal investigations.

How do police determine whether an eyewitness can identify a culprit? Police know full well that eyewitness memory is fallible, just as judges, lawyers, and social scientists have long known this fact. Police try to test the eyewitness's memory and use a range of techniques to get a suspect identified via an eyewitness.

If a suspect is found shortly after the crime, police may present that suspect to the eyewitness directly. Such a one-on-one procedure, called a showup, is inherently suggestive. Police may use such a procedure only in the hours immediately following an incident, in order to quickly identify the perpetrator or rule out the suspect and continue their investigation. Showups are particularly risky for the police. Because there are no fillers, or other known-innocent people included in addition to the suspect, a mistake is more likely to result in the witness identifying an innocent person as the guilty party. And if the eyewitness is unsure, there is a greater risk that a guilty person might not be identified.

If police do not immediately locate a suspect, they may try to show an eyewitness books or computerized collections of mug shots. If that also fails, police may ask the witness to work with a police sketch artist or with a computer program to generate a composite image that can be used in "wanted" postings.

When police eventually locate a suspect, they conduct an identification procedure to test the eyewitness's memory. In a live lineup, a suspect stands in a row of "filler" individuals and the witness looks at the group

---

[1]   Remember that you have access to the filings relevant to this chapter in your online repository.

[2]   This subsection is adapted with permission from a portion of Brandon L. Garrett, *Eyewitnesses and Exclusion*, 65 VAND. L. REV. 451, 457–60 (2012). All footnotes are omitted.

from behind one-way glass. In the past few decades, police have mostly stopped using live lineups because it is so difficult and time-consuming to find people who look similar to a suspect. Instead, they use photo arrays, typically a standard set of six photos (called a "six-pack").

Procedures for creating photo arrays and conducting lineups were traditionally passed on by senior officers through word of mouth. Although police departments have detailed procedures, manuals, and training on a host of subjects—ranging from traffic stops to use of force—many, if not most, police departments still do not have any written procedures or formal training on how to conduct lineups or photo arrays. Perhaps, however, this is starting to change in reaction to high-profile eyewitness misidentifications. Unfortunately, archival studies also suggest that unnecessary showups are quite common together with other flawed identification procedures.

If there is a trial, identifications may occur in court. The courtroom identification is obviously highly suggestive. The defendant is sitting at the counsel's table, perhaps in prison clothing. There are no fillers and there is no lineup. And the identification may follow emotionally charged testimony by the victim describing a crime—a victim who, in the conclusion of the testimony, points out the culprit to the jury.

The courtroom identification may simply serve to confirm what came before. The procedures that came before may have been suggestive or shoddy. The eyewitness may have previously been uncertain. But in court, the eyewitness may appear supremely confident and will have no trouble picking out the defendant and pointing him out to the jury. As the Tenth Circuit has explained:

> Because the jurors are not present to observe the pretrial identification, they are not able to observe the witness making that initial identification. The certainty or hesitation of the witness when making the identification, the witness's facial expressions, voice inflection, body language, and the other normal observations one makes in everyday life when judging the reliability of a person's statements, are not available to the jury during this pretrial proceeding. There is a danger that the identification in court may only be a confirmation of the earlier identification, with much greater certainty expressed in court than initially.

B. THE PROBLEM

According to the Innocence Project,[3] "[m]istaken eyewitness identifications contributed to approximately 70% of the more than 350

---

[3] Founded in 1992, the Innocence Project works to exonerate wrongfully convicted inmates through the use of DNA testing. It likewise advocates for criminal justice reform. To date, the

wrongful convictions in the United States overturned by post-conviction DNA evidence."[4] A state court has helpfully summarized the leading available research that helps us to understand *why* eyewitness identifications are so problematic:

> Since the first cases addressing the reliability of eyewitness testimony were decided in the 1970s, a robust body of research in the area of eyewitness identification has emerged. Many studies now confirm that false identifications are more common than was previously believed. For example, Professor Brandon L. Garrett concluded in a [2011] study involving 250 exonerated defendants that "[e]yewitnesses misidentified 76% of the exonerees (190 of 250 cases)." Professor Garrett's original study of 200 such cases in 2008 concluded that eyewitness identification testimony was the leading contributing factor to wrongful convictions and was four times more likely to contribute to a wrongful conviction than a false confession. Other studies have reached similar results.

> Researchers have found that several variables tend to affect the reliability of an eyewitness's identification. These include the passage of time, witness stress, duration of exposure, distance, "weapon focus" (visual attention eyewitnesses give to a perpetrator's weapon during crime), and cross-race (eyewitnesses are more accurate at identifying persons of their own race). Juries, however, may not be aware of the extent to which these factors affect an individual's ability to make an accurate identification, and thus tend to "over believe" witness identification testimony. In a 1983 study, for example, researchers presented individuals with crime scenarios derived from previous empirical studies. Researchers found that the study's respondents estimated an average accuracy rate of 71 percent for a highly unreliable scenario in which only 12.5 percent of eyewitnesses had in fact made a correct identification.

> Empirical research has also undermined the common sense notion that the confidence of the witness is a valid indicator of the accuracy of the identification. However, courts and juries continue to place great weight on the confidence expressed by the witness in assessing reliability.[5]

Innocence Project has freed 356 wrongfully convicted individuals while helping to identify 153 real perpetrators. *Exonerate the Innocent*, INNOCENCEPROJECT.ORG, https://www.innocenceproject. org/exonerate/ (last visited Aug. 28, 2018).

[4] *Mistaken Identifications are the Leading Factor in Wrongful Convictions*, INNOCENCE PROJECT.ORG, https://www.innocenceproject.org/eyewitness-identification-reform (last visited Aug. 28, 2022).

[5] State v. Cabagbag, 277 P.3d 1027, 1035–36 (Haw. 2012) (internal citations and footnotes omitted).

C. IMPROVING EYEWITNESS IDENTIFICATIONS[6]

The Innocence Project endorses a range of procedural reforms to improve the accuracy of eyewitness identification. These reforms have been recognized by police, prosecutors, the judiciary, as well as national justice organizations, including the National Institute of Justice and the American Bar Association. The benefits of these reforms are corroborated by over 30 years of peer-reviewed comprehensive research.

1. **The "Double-blind" Procedure/Use of a Blind Administrator:** A "double-blind" lineup is one in which neither the administrator nor the eyewitness knows who the suspect is. This prevents the administrator of the lineup from providing inadvertent or intentional verbal or nonverbal cues to influence the eyewitness to pick the suspect.

2. **Instructions:** "Instructions" are a series of statements issued by the lineup administrator to the eyewitness that deter the eyewitness from feeling compelled to make a selection. They also prevent the eyewitness from looking to the lineup administrator for feedback during the identification procedure. One of the recommended instructions includes the directive that the suspect may or may not be present in the lineup.

3. **Composing the Lineup:** Suspect photographs should be selected that do not bring unreasonable attention to them. That is, the suspect should not unduly stand out from the fillers. Non-suspect photographs and/or live lineup members (fillers) should also be selected based on their resemblance to the description provided by the eyewitness—as opposed to their resemblance to the police suspect. (More detailed recommendations can be provided upon request by the Innocence Project.)

4. **Confidence Statements:** Immediately following the lineup procedure, the eyewitness should provide a statement that, in their own words, articulates the level of confidence they have in the identification made.

5. **The Lineup Procedure Should Be Documented:** Ideally, the lineup procedure should be video recorded. If this is impractical, an audio or written record should be made.

---

[6] This subsection is adapted with permission from *Eyewitness Identification Reform: Mistaken Identifications are the Leading Factor in Wrongful Convictions*, INNOCENCEPROJECT. ORG, https://www.innocenceproject.org/eyewitness-identification-reform/ (last visited Aug. 28, 2022).

Numerous states including Georgia, Texas, Oregon, Maryland, New Jersey, North Carolina, and Connecticut, as well as jurisdictions ranging in size from Dallas, Minneapolis, Boston, Philadelphia, San Diego, San Francisco, Tucson, and Denver to Northampton, MA, have implemented evidence-based practices as standard procedure.

West Virginia, Virginia, Rhode Island, and other jurisdictions have recommended/promulgated voluntary guidelines that comport with scientifically-supported best practices and incorporated them into law enforcement training.

D. THE LAW'S RESPONSE

The law has not been quick to respond to the problem of misidentifications. That said, there exist essentially two sources of law relevant to challenging witness identification procedures: (1) the Sixth Amendment, and (2) the Due Process Clause. Both sources are severely limited. The first, the Sixth Amendment, provides a limited pretrial right to counsel at a lineup proceeding. The second, due process, is a more widely available tool that enables a defendant to challenge any identification procedure. The materials below discuss each source in turn. The chapter closes by looking very briefly at the state's responsibility, if any, should it wrongfully convict the defendant.

II. MEET RONNIE LONG[7]

In April 1976, Ronnie Long was a young, twenty-one-year-old African American working as a cement mason in Concord, North Carolina. He was born in Charlotte but grew up in Concord along with seven brothers and sisters. His dad was a concrete contractor and the vice president of the Southern Conference Educational Fund. He played sports at Concord City High School and followed in his father's footsteps by enrolling in masonry courses that taught him how to set stone. Beyond being concerned about the racial dynamics in his town, he would say later, "I was just your average teenager." But that April, Long had recently been arrested for misdemeanor trespassing in a public park and was scheduled to appear in district court on May 10. His life would forever change on that date.

---

[7] Ronnie Long's story, as told in the text, comes from numerous sources in addition to the Casefile documents. *E.g.*, Erica Hellerstein, *Ronnie Long Has Spent Four Decades Behind Bars for a Rape He Says He Didn't Commit*, INDY WEEK (Feb. 21, 2018), https://indyweek.com/news/north carolina/ronnie-long-spent-four-decades-behind-bars-rape-says-commit.-reason-think-got-raw-deal./; Michael Gordon, *Halfway through 80-year rape sentence, Concord man gets new shot at freedom*, THE CHARLOTTE OBSERVER (Oct. 25, 2017), http://www.charlotteobserver.com/news/local/article180850171.html.

Long's mugshot after he was arrested for trespassing

At nearly 10:00 p.m. on April 25, 1976, in Concord, Sarah Bost, the fifty-four-year-old widow of a Cannon Mills executive, was raped by someone who broke into her home. The now defunct Cannon Mills, which went bankrupt in 2003, was an American textile company headquartered in the neighboring town of Kannapolis, though it maintained plants all over the country. Locally, it served as the area's biggest employer.

Bost was hurt. Badly. She was admitted to Cabarrus Memorial Hospital where she was treated for various injuries. Her "fingernails were all sore" and some "had been bent backward," which she reported having sustained while fighting and scratching the rapist. She further relayed that the rapist slammed her head on the ground and that he likely would have persisted had the phone not rang, which startled the attacker. She stumbled naked to a neighbor's house where the neighbor's husband called the police.

The hospital staff obtained biological evidence from Bost, including a rape kit. She initially indicated that her assailant wore a leather jacket and knit cap. Two hours later, just past midnight, Bost spoke with Sgt. David J. Taylor and offered a more detailed description:

A black male, height, five foot five to five foot nine, slender build, slim hips. Subject was plain spoken, used correct English and at times spoke very softly. No speech defect, accent, or noticeable brogue evident. Subject was wearing a dark waist length leather jacket, blue jeans with a dark toboggan pulled over his head. Could possibly have been wearing gloves.

She would later add at trial that her attacker was "yellow-looking" in complexion and "just not totally black. Not like, you know, a blue-black, black man." Sgt. Taylor gave Bost a photo lineup of thirteen possible suspects—all black men aged twenty to thirty. Taylor did not include Long in the lineup, and Bost did not identify her attacker in the array.

Several days passed until, on May 5, Sgt. Taylor and Lt. George Vogler asked Bost to accompany them to district court on May 10. The officers knew Long would be in court that morning to answer for the trespassing charge, and they suggested to Bost that her rapist may be present. When the morning of May 10 arrived, the officers took Bost and her neighbor to the courthouse. Before entering, though, investigators disguised Bost in a red wig and glasses.

According to Bost, the officers instructed her to "sit [in the gallery] and to look around and see if [she] saw anybody that [she] knew, or the man that raped [her]." Meanwhile, Taylor and Vogler watched from the jury box. There were between thirty-five and fifty people in the courtroom that day, roughly a dozen of whom were black. Long sat in middle of the gallery for roughly an hour to an hour and a half while Bost was "constantly just looking." When the judge called Long to come forward for his trespassing case, which was dismissed, Bost identified him as her attacker. "That's the one," she whispered to her neighbor. Taylor and Vogler asked her about her level of confidence, to which she replied, "There is no doubt in my mind."

Roughly twenty minutes later, the officers brought Bost to the police station where they showed her between six and eight photos. Long was the only one in the photo lineup wearing a black leather jacket. When the officers asked Bost whether there was "anything distinctive about the dress of any of those individuals . . . that drew [her] attention to them," she said, "[It] was the jacket . . . if it wasn't the jacket, it was the identical, one identical to it. It was a leather jacket."

That same evening, May 10, Sgt. Taylor and Sgt. Marshall Lee went to Long's home. They instructed him to come to the station to "straighten out" the trespassing warrant. They arrested Long for the rape and burglary once he arrived.

By October 1, 1976, despite a strong alibi defense, Long was tried before an all-white jury and convicted. Long's case attracted considerable attention—even before the verdict. At a pro-Long rally of roughly three hundred people two months before his sentencing, a speaker declared,

"We're gonna let them rich folks that run this town know they're gonna free Ronnie Long." Another said, "We're gonna let this Klansman judge get an idea . . . . We're gonna start dealing with all these racists."

Long was sentenced to two concurrent life sentences.

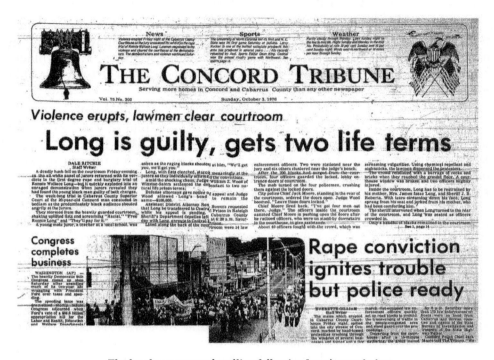

The local newspaper headline following Long's conviction

III. THE RIGHT TO COUNSEL AT LINEUPS

We begin this chapter's limited caselaw by considering what role the Sixth Amendment plays in the context of in-person (i.e., corporeal) lineups. Consider two themes as you move through these materials. First, be mindful of what role counsel should play at a lineup. There is, you will remember from Chapter 1, a difference between having a lawyer and having a *good* lawyer. If having a good lawyer is important to you, then pay careful attention to the logic of *Kirby v. Illinois*.

Second, notice the impact of changing personnel on how the Court views the importance of counsel at lineups. Justice Brennan wrote the *United States v. Wade* majority in 1967—a close 5–4 decision rendered at the peak of the Warren Court. By the time of 1972 when *Kirby v. Illinois* was decided, three of the Justices in the *Wade* majority (Warren, Clark, and Fortas) had been replaced. Although *Kirby* was also close, another 5–4 opinion, the remaining *Wade* majority Justices (Douglas and Brennan) found themselves together in the *Kirby* dissent. Moreover, the Justices who replaced outgoing Warren Court Justices voted as a block in the *Kirby* majority. That group, comprised of Burger, Blackmun, Powell, and Rehnquist, were all Nixon appointees and, as a block, they often voted together. In their first term together, the 1972–1973 term when *Kirby* was decided, they agreed in more than 100 of all the 177 cases the Court heard.[8] They were even more closely aligned in the context of criminal procedure cases.[9]

A. BEFORE CHARGING

UNITED STATES V. WADE

388 U.S. 218
Supreme Court of the United States
February 16, 1967, Argued; June 12, 1967, Decided
No. 334

MR. JUSTICE BRENNAN delivered the opinion of the Court.

The question here is whether courtroom identifications of an accused at trial are to be excluded from evidence because the accused was exhibited to the witnesses before trial at a post-indictment lineup conducted for identification purposes without notice to and in the absence of the accused's appointed counsel.

The federally insured bank in Eustace, Texas, was robbed on September 21, 1964. A man with a small strip of tape on each side of his face entered the bank, pointed a pistol at the female cashier and the vice president, the only persons in the bank at the time, and forced them to fill a pillowcase with the bank's money. The man then drove away with an accomplice who had been waiting in a stolen car outside the bank. On March 23, 1965, an indictment was returned against respondent, Wade, and two others for conspiring to rob the bank, and against Wade and the accomplice for the robbery itself. Wade was arrested on April 2, and counsel was appointed to represent him on April 26. Fifteen days later an FBI agent, without notice to Wade's lawyer, arranged to have the two bank employees observe a lineup made up of Wade and five or six other prisoners and conducted in a courtroom of the local county courthouse. Each person in the line wore strips of tape such as allegedly worn by the robber and upon direction each said something like "put the money in the bag," the words allegedly uttered by the robber. Both bank employees identified Wade in the lineup as the bank robber.

---

[8] Paul C. Bartholomew, *The Supreme Court of the United States, 1972–1973*, 27 W. POL. Q. 164, 164 (1974); *see also* Fred P. Graham, *The "Nixon Court": A Premature Label?*, N.Y. TIMES, Jan. 7, 1972, at 8.

[9] *See* STEPHEN L. WASBY, CONTINUITY AND CHANGE: FROM THE WARREN COURT TO THE BURGER COURT 68 (1976).

At trial, the two employees, when asked on direct examination if the robber was in the courtroom, pointed to Wade. The prior lineup identification was then elicited from both employees on cross-examination. At the close of testimony, Wade's counsel moved for a judgment of acquittal or, alternatively, to strike the bank officials' courtroom identifications on the ground that conduct of the lineup, without notice to and in the absence of his appointed counsel, violated * * * his Sixth Amendment right to the assistance of counsel. The motion was denied, and Wade was convicted. The Court of Appeals for the Fifth Circuit reversed the conviction and ordered a new trial at which the in-court identification evidence was to be excluded, holding that * * * "the lineup, held as it was, in the absence of counsel, already chosen to represent appellant, was a violation of his Sixth Amendment rights . . . ." We granted certiorari * * *. * * *

IV.

* * * [T]he confrontation compelled by the State between the accused and the victim or witnesses to a crime to elicit identification evidence is peculiarly riddled with innumerable dangers and variable factors which might seriously, even crucially, derogate from a fair trial. The vagaries of eyewitness identification are well-known; the annals of criminal law are rife with instances of mistaken identification. * * * A major factor contributing to the high incidence of miscarriage of justice from mistaken identification has been the degree of suggestion inherent in the manner in which the prosecution presents the suspect to witnesses for pretrial identification. * * * Suggestion can be created intentionally or unintentionally in many subtle ways. And the dangers for the suspect are particularly grave when the witness' opportunity for observation was insubstantial, and thus his susceptibility to suggestion the greatest.

Moreover, "it is a matter of common experience that, once a witness has picked out the accused at the line-up, he is not likely to go back on his word later on, so that in practice the issue of identity may (in the absence of other relevant evidence) for all practical purposes be determined there and then, before the trial."

The pretrial confrontation for purpose of identification may take the form of a lineup, also known as an "identification parade" or "showup," as in the present case, or presentation of the suspect alone to the witness * * *. It is obvious that risks of suggestion attend either form of confrontation and increase the dangers inhering in eyewitness identification. But as is the case with secret interrogations, there is serious difficulty in depicting what transpires at lineups and other forms of identification confrontations. "Privacy results in secrecy and this in turn results in a gap in our knowledge as to what in fact goes on . . . ." For the same reasons, the defense can seldom reconstruct the manner and mode of lineup identification for judge or jury at trial. Those participating in a lineup with the accused may often be police officers; in any event, the participants' names are rarely recorded or divulged at trial. The impediments to an objective observation are increased when the victim is the witness. Lineups are prevalent in rape and robbery prosecutions and present a particular hazard that a victim's understandable outrage may excite vengeful or spiteful motives. In any event, neither witnesses nor lineup participants are apt to be alert for conditions prejudicial to the suspect. And if they were, it would likely be of scant benefit to the suspect since neither witnesses nor lineup participants are likely to be schooled in the detection of suggestive influences. Improper influences may go undetected by a suspect, guilty or not, who experiences the emotional tension which we might expect in one being confronted with potential accusers. Even when he does observe abuse, if he has a criminal record he may be reluctant to take the stand and open up the admission of prior convictions. Moreover, any protestations by the suspect of the fairness of the lineup made at trial are likely to be in vain; the jury's choice is between the accused's unsupported version and that of the police officers present. In short, the accused's inability effectively to reconstruct at trial any unfairness that occurred at the lineup may deprive him of his only opportunity meaningfully to attack the credibility of the witness' courtroom identification.

What facts have been disclosed in specific cases about the conduct of pretrial confrontations for identification illustrate both the potential for substantial prejudice to the accused at that stage and the need for its revelation at trial. * * *

* * * [S]tate reports, in the course of describing prior identifications admitted as evidence of guilt, reveal numerous instances of suggestive procedures, for example, that all in the lineup but the suspect were known to the identifying witness, that the other participants in a lineup were grossly dissimilar in appearance to the suspect, that only the suspect was required to wear distinctive clothing which the culprit allegedly wore, that the witness is told by the police that they have caught the culprit after which the defendant is brought before the witness alone or is viewed in jail, that the suspect is pointed out before or during a lineup, and that the participants in the lineup are asked to try on an article of clothing which fits only the suspect.

The potential for improper influence is illustrated by the circumstances, insofar as they appear, surrounding the prior identifications in the three cases we decide today. In the present case, the testimony of the identifying witnesses elicited on cross-examination revealed that those witnesses were taken to the courthouse and seated in the courtroom to await assembly of the lineup. The courtroom faced on a hallway observable to the witnesses through an open door. The cashier testified that she saw Wade "standing in the hall" within sight of an FBI agent. Five or six other prisoners later appeared in the hall. The vice president testified that he saw a person in the hall in the custody of the agent who "resembled the person that we identified as the one that had entered the bank." * * *

The few cases that have surfaced therefore reveal the existence of a process attended with hazards of serious unfairness to the criminal accused and strongly suggest the plight of the more numerous defendants who are unable to ferret out suggestive influences in the secrecy of the confrontation. We do not assume that these risks are the result of police procedures intentionally designed to prejudice an accused. Rather we assume they derive from the dangers inherent in eyewitness identification and the suggestibility inherent in the context of the pretrial identification. * * *

Insofar as the accused's conviction may rest on a courtroom identification in fact the fruit of a suspect pretrial identification which the accused is helpless to subject to effective scrutiny at trial, the accused is deprived of that right of cross-examination which is an essential safeguard to his right to confront the witnesses against him. And even though cross-examination is a precious safeguard to a fair trial, it cannot be viewed as an absolute assurance of accuracy and reliability. Thus in the present context, where so many variables and pitfalls exist, the first line of defense must be the prevention of unfairness and the lessening of the hazards of eyewitness identification at the lineup itself. The trial which might determine the accused's fate may well not be that in the courtroom but that at the pretrial confrontation, with the State aligned against the accused, the witness the sole jury, and the accused unprotected against the overreaching, intentional or unintentional, and with little or no effective appeal from the judgment there rendered by the witness—"that's the man."

Since it appears that there is grave potential for prejudice, intentional or not, in the pretrial lineup, which may not be capable of reconstruction at trial, and since presence of counsel itself can often avert prejudice and assure a meaningful confrontation at trial, there can be little doubt that for Wade the post-indictment lineup was a critical stage of the prosecution at which he was "as much entitled to such aid [of counsel] . . . as at the trial itself." Thus both Wade and his counsel should have been notified of the impending lineup, and counsel's presence should have been a requisite to conduct of the lineup, absent an "intelligent waiver." No substantial countervailing policy considerations have been advanced against the requirement of the presence of counsel. Concern is expressed that the requirement will forestall prompt identifications and result in obstruction of the confrontations. As for the first, we note that in the two cases in which the right to counsel is today held to apply, counsel had already been appointed and no argument is made in either case that notice to counsel would have prejudicially delayed the confrontations. Moreover, we leave open the question whether the presence of substitute counsel might not suffice where notification and presence of the suspect's own counsel would result in prejudicial delay. And to refuse to recognize the right to counsel for fear that counsel will obstruct the course of justice is contrary to the basic assumptions upon which this Court has operated in Sixth Amendment cases. * * *

In our view counsel can hardly impede legitimate law enforcement; on the contrary, for the reasons expressed, law enforcement may be assisted by preventing the infiltration of taint in the prosecution's identification evidence. That result cannot help the guilty avoid conviction but can only help assure that the right man has been brought to justice.

Legislative or other regulations, such as those of local police departments, which eliminate the risks of abuse and unintentional suggestion at lineup proceedings and the impediments to meaningful confrontation at trial may also remove the basis for regarding the stage as "critical." But neither Congress nor the federal authorities have seen fit to provide a solution. * * *

V.

We come now to the question whether the denial of Wade's motion to strike the courtroom identification by the bank witnesses at trial because of the absence of his counsel at the lineup required, as the Court of Appeals held, the grant of a new trial at which such evidence is to be excluded. We do not think this disposition can be justified without first giving the Government the opportunity to establish by clear and convincing evidence that the in-court identifications were based upon observations of the suspect other than the lineup identification. Where, as here, the admissibility of evidence of the lineup identification itself is not involved, a per se rule of exclusion of courtroom identification would be unjustified. A rule limited solely to the exclusion of testimony concerning identification at the lineup itself, without regard to admissibility of the courtroom identification, would render the right to counsel an empty one. The lineup is most often used, as in the present case, to crystallize the witnesses' identification of the defendant for future reference. We have already noted that the lineup identification will have that effect. The State may then rest upon the witnesses' unequivocal courtroom identification, and not mention the pretrial identification as part of the State's case at trial. Counsel is then in the predicament in which Wade's counsel found himself—realizing that possible unfairness at the lineup may be the sole means of attack upon the unequivocal courtroom identification, and having to probe in the dark in an attempt to discover and reveal unfairness, while bolstering the government witness' courtroom identification by bringing out and dwelling upon his prior identification. Since counsel's presence at the lineup would equip him to attack not only the lineup identification but the courtroom identification as well, limiting the impact of violation of the right to counsel to exclusion of evidence only of identification at the lineup itself disregards a critical element of that right.

We think it follows that the proper test to be applied in these situations is that quoted in *Wong Sun v. United States*, 371 U.S. 471, 488, " 'Whether, granting establishment of the primary illegality, the evidence to which instant objection is made has been come at by exploitation of that illegality or instead by means sufficiently distinguishable to be purged of the primary taint.' " Application of this test in the present context requires consideration of various factors; for example, the prior opportunity to observe the alleged criminal act, the existence of any discrepancy between any pre-lineup description and the defendant's actual description, any identification prior to lineup of another person, the identification by picture of the defendant prior to the lineup, failure to identify the defendant on a prior occasion, and the lapse of time between the alleged act and the lineup identification. It is also relevant to consider those facts which, despite the absence of counsel, are disclosed concerning the conduct of the lineup.

We doubt that the Court of Appeals applied the proper test for exclusion of the in-court identification of the two witnesses. The court stated that "it cannot be said with any certainty that they would have recognized appellant at the time of trial if this intervening lineup had not occurred," and that the testimony of the two witnesses "may well have been colored by the illegal procedure [and] was prejudicial." Moreover, the court was persuaded, in part, by the "compulsory verbal responses made by Wade at the instance of the Special Agent." This implies the erroneous holding that Wade's privilege against self-incrimination was violated so that the denial of counsel required exclusion.

On the record now before us we cannot make the determination whether the in-court identifications had an independent origin. This was not an issue at trial, although there is some evidence relevant to a determination. That inquiry is most properly made in the District Court. We therefore think the appropriate procedure to be followed is to vacate the conviction pending a hearing to determine whether the in-court identifications had an independent source, or whether, in any event, the introduction of the evidence was harmless error, and for the District Court to reinstate the conviction or order a new trial, as may be proper.

The judgment of the Court of Appeals is vacated and the case is remanded to that court with direction to enter a new judgment vacating the conviction and remanding the case to the District Court for further proceedings consistent with this opinion.

It is so ordered.

THE CHIEF JUSTICE joins the opinion of the Court except for Part I, from which he dissents for the reasons expressed in the opinion of MR. JUSTICE FORTAS.

MR. JUSTICE DOUGLAS joins the opinion of the Court except for Part I. * * *

MR. JUSTICE CLARK, concurring.

[Omitted.]

MR. JUSTICE BLACK, dissenting in part and concurring in part.

[Omitted.]

MR. JUSTICE WHITE, whom MR. JUSTICE HARLAN and MR. JUSTICE STEWART join, dissenting in part and concurring in part.

[Omitted.]

MR. JUSTICE FORTAS, with whom THE CHIEF JUSTICE and MR. JUSTICE DOUGLAS join, concurring in part and dissenting in part.

[Omitted.]

QUESTIONS, COMMENTS, CONCERNS?

1.   The strength of *Wade*. The *Wade* opinion provides a suspect with a strong Sixth Amendment right to counsel protection—in the proper context, that is. Notice that the *Wade* right to counsel rule applies to so-called "corporeal" (or in-person) lineups where the suspect has already been indicted or otherwise formally charged. Assuming those conditions are met, notice the case that the *Wade* Court relies on—*Wong Sun*. We can therefore say that the Sixth Amendment exclusionary rule is more analogous to Fourth Amendment exclusion than to Fifth Amendment *Miranda* exclusion. Thus, when *Wade* applies, the prosecution may not use an in-court lineup that is derived from the pretrial corporeal post-charging lineup unless the prosecution can prove by clear and convicting evidence that the in-court identification has an "independent origin."

2.   Why did Concord police focus on Long to begin with? The Casefile documents do not make clear why Concord police came to focus on Long. Neither does the complete record. Long likely became the chief suspect because, several months before the assault on Bost, the Metropolitan Police Department (MPD) in Washington, D.C. contacted the Concord Police Department. The MPD was investigating Long as a possible assailant in a Washington, D.C. rape.

Long was living in D.C. at the time of the alleged rape and was identified as a suspect because his social security card was found in the victim's apartment, though Long had reportedly lost his wallet several weeks before the rape. The assault in D.C. occurred in an apartment complex, and witnesses chased the perpetrator after hearing the victim's screams. The Concord Police Department provided a photo of Long to the D.C. police, but the victim and witnesses could not identify him. Long was never arrested in the incident, and it is believed (though unconfirmed) that someone else was ultimately arrested for the crime.

When Long was arrested for the trespassing charge that brought him to court when Bost made her identification, the Concord Police Department recalled being contacted by the D.C. police. Although Concord authorities had no idea what happened in the D.C. case, they assumed Long must have committed a similar crime in their town and made him a suspect.

3.   **Ronnie Long and types of lineups.** There were essentially three lineups in Long's case. First, Sgt. Taylor and Lt. Vogler went to see Bost in the hospital shortly after the incident. They showed her a handful of pictures. [Casefile Document 2.] Second, Sgt. Taylor and Lt. Vogler asked Bost to identify Long in court. Finally, Bost picked Long out of an additional handful of photographs. [Casefile Document 13.] What type of lineup was each? Were any, in the *Wade* Court's words, a "showup," an "identification parade," or something else? Would the *Wade* right to counsel apply to any of them?

B. AFTER CHARGING

KIRBY V. ILLINOIS
406 U.S. 682
Supreme Court of the United States
November 11, 1971, Argued; June 7, 1972, Decided
No. 70-5061

MR. JUSTICE STEWART announced the judgment of the Court and an opinion in which THE CHIEF JUSTICE, MR. JUSTICE BLACKMUN, and MR. JUSTICE REHNQUIST join.

In *United States v. Wade*, 388 U.S. 218, and *Gilbert v. California*, 388 U.S. 263, this Court held "that a post-indictment pretrial lineup at which the accused is exhibited to identifying witnesses is a critical stage of the criminal prosecution; that police conduct of such a lineup without notice to and in the absence of his counsel denies the accused his Sixth [and Fourteenth] Amendment right to counsel and calls in question the admissibility at trial of the in-court identifications of the accused by witnesses who attended the lineup." Those cases further held that no "in-court identifications" are admissible in evidence if their "source" is a lineup conducted in violation of this constitutional standard. "Only a per se exclusionary rule as to such testimony can be an effective sanction," the Court said, "to assure that law enforcement authorities will respect the accused's constitutional right to the presence of his counsel at the critical lineup." In the present case we are asked to extend the *Wade-Gilbert* per se exclusionary rule to identification testimony based upon a police station showup that took place before the defendant had been indicted or otherwise formally charged with any criminal offense.

On February 21, 1968, a man named Willie Shard reported to the Chicago police that the previous day two men had robbed him on a Chicago street of a wallet containing, among other things, traveler's checks and a

Social Security card. On February 22, two police officers stopped the petitioner and a companion, Ralph Bean, on West Madison Street in Chicago. When asked for identification, the petitioner produced a wallet that contained three traveler's checks and a Social Security card, all bearing the name of Willie Shard. Papers with Shard's name on them were also found in Bean's possession. When asked to explain his possession of Shard's property, the petitioner first said that the traveler's checks were "play money," and then told the officers that he had won them in a crap game. The officers then arrested the petitioner and Bean and took them to a police station.

Only after arriving at the police station, and checking the records there, did the arresting officers learn of the Shard robbery. A police car was then dispatched to Shard's place of employment, where it picked up Shard and brought him to the police station. Immediately upon entering the room in the police station where the petitioner and Bean were seated at a table, Shard positively identified them as the men who had robbed him two days earlier. No lawyer was present in the room, and neither the petitioner nor Bean had asked for legal assistance, or been advised of any right to the presence of counsel.

More than six weeks later, the petitioner and Bean were indicted for the robbery of Willie Shard. Upon arraignment, counsel was appointed to represent them, and they pleaded not guilty. A pretrial motion to suppress Shard's identification testimony was denied, and at the trial Shard testified as a witness for the prosecution. In his testimony he described his identification of the two men at the police station on February 22, and identified them again in the courtroom as the men who had robbed him on February 20. He was cross-examined at length regarding the circumstances of his identification of the two defendants. The jury found both defendants guilty, and the petitioner's conviction was affirmed on appeal. The Illinois appellate court held that the admission of Shard's testimony was not error, relying upon an earlier decision of the Illinois Supreme Court holding that the *Wade-Gilbert* per se exclusionary rule is not applicable to pre-indictment confrontations.

We granted certiorari, limited to this question.

I   * * *

The initiation of judicial criminal proceedings is far from a mere formalism. It is the starting point of our whole system of adversary criminal justice. For it is only then that the government has committed itself to prosecute, and only then that the adverse positions of government and defendant have solidified. It is then that a defendant finds himself faced with the prosecutorial forces of organized society, and immersed in the intricacies of substantive and procedural criminal law. It is this point, therefore, that marks the commencement of the "criminal prosecutions" to which alone the explicit guarantees of the Sixth Amendment are applicable.

In this case we are asked to import into a routine police investigation an absolute constitutional guarantee historically and rationally applicable only after the onset of formal prosecutorial proceedings. We decline to do so. Less than a year after *Wade* and *Gilbert* were decided, the Court explained the rule of those decisions as follows: "The rationale of those cases was that an accused is entitled to counsel at any 'critical stage of the *prosecution*,' and that a post-indictment lineup is such a 'critical stage.' " (Emphasis supplied.) We decline to depart from that rationale today by imposing a per se exclusionary rule upon testimony concerning an identification that took place long before the commencement of any prosecution whatever.

II

What has been said is not to suggest that there may not be occasions during the course of a criminal investigation when the police do abuse identification procedures. Such abuses are not beyond the reach of the Constitution. As the Court pointed out in *Wade* itself, it is always necessary to "scrutinize any pretrial confrontation . . . ." The Due Process Clause of the Fifth and Fourteenth Amendments forbids a lineup that is unnecessarily suggestive and conducive to irreparable mistaken identification. When a person has not been formally charged with a criminal offense, *Stovall* strikes the appropriate constitutional balance between the right of a suspect to be protected from prejudicial procedures and the interest of society in the prompt and purposeful investigation of an unsolved crime.

The judgment is affirmed.

MR. CHIEF JUSTICE BURGER, concurring.

[Omitted.]

MR. JUSTICE POWELL, concurring in the result.

[Omitted.]

MR. JUSTICE BRENNAN, with whom MR. JUSTICE DOUGLAS and MR. JUSTICE MARSHALL join, dissenting.

After petitioner and Ralph Bean were arrested, police officers brought Willie Shard, the robbery victim, to a room in a police station where petitioner and Bean were seated at a table with two other police officers. Shard testified at trial that the officers who brought him to the room asked him if petitioner and Bean were the robbers and that he indicated they were. The prosecutor asked him, "And you positively identified them at the police station, is that correct?" Shard answered, "Yes." Consequently, the question in this case is whether, under *Gilbert v. California*, 388 U.S. 263

(1967), it was constitutional error to admit Shard's testimony that he identified petitioner at the pretrial station-house showup when that showup was conducted by the police without advising petitioner that he might have counsel present. *Gilbert* held, in the context of a post-indictment lineup, that "only a per se exclusionary rule as to such testimony can be an effective sanction to assure that law enforcement authorities will respect the accused's constitutional right to the presence of his counsel at the critical lineup." I would apply *Gilbert* and the principles of its companion case, *United States v. Wade*, 388 U.S. 218 (1967), and reverse. * * *

In view of *Wade*, it is plain, and the plurality today does not attempt to dispute it, that there inhere in a confrontation for identification conducted after arrest the identical hazards to a fair trial that inhere in such a confrontation conducted "after the onset of formal prosecutorial proceedings." The plurality apparently considers an arrest, which for present purposes we must assume to be based upon probable cause, to be nothing more than part of "a routine police investigation," and thus not "the starting point of our whole system of adversary criminal justice." An arrest, according to the plurality, does not face the accused "with the prosecutorial forces of organized society," nor immerse him "in the intricacies of substantive and procedural criminal law." Those consequences ensue, says the plurality, only with "the initiation of judicial criminal proceedings," "for it is only then that the government has committed itself to prosecute, and only then that the adverse positions of government and defendant have solidified." If these propositions do not amount to "mere formalism," it is difficult to know how to characterize them. An arrest evidences the belief of the police that the perpetrator of a crime has been caught. A post-arrest confrontation for identification is not "a mere preparatory step in the gathering of the prosecution's evidence." *Wade, supra.* A primary, and frequently sole, purpose of the confrontation for identification at that stage is to accumulate proof to buttress the conclusion of the police that they have the offender in hand. The plurality offers no reason, and I can think of none, for concluding that a post-arrest confrontation for identification, unlike a post-charge confrontation, is not among those "critical confrontations of the accused by the prosecution at pretrial proceedings where the results might well settle the accused's fate and reduce the trial itself to a mere formality."

The highly suggestive form of confrontation employed in this case underscores the point. This showup was particularly fraught with the peril of mistaken identification. In the setting of a police station squad room where all present except petitioner and Bean were police officers, the danger was quite real that Shard's understandable resentment might lead him too readily to agree with the police that the pair under arrest, and the only persons exhibited to him, were indeed the robbers. "It is hard to imagine a situation more clearly conveying the suggestion to the witness that the one presented is believed guilty by the police." The State had no case without Shard's identification testimony, and safeguards against that consequence were therefore of critical importance. Shard's testimony itself demonstrates the necessity for such safeguards. On direct examination, Shard identified petitioner and Bean not as the alleged robbers on trial in the courtroom, but as the pair he saw at the police station. His testimony thus lends strong support to the observation, quoted by the Court in *Wade*, that "it is a matter of common experience that, once a witness has picked out the accused at the line-up, he is not likely to go back on his word later on, so that in practice the issue of identity may (in the absence of other relevant evidence) for all practical purposes be determined there and then, before the trial." * * *

Wade and *Gilbert*, of course, happened to involve post-indictment confrontations. Yet even a cursory perusal of the opinions in those cases reveals that nothing at all turned upon that particular circumstance. In short, it is fair to conclude that rather than "declin[ing] to depart from [the] rationale" of *Wade* and *Gilbert*, the plurality today, albeit purporting to be engaged in "principled constitutional adjudication," refuses even to recognize that "rationale." For my part, I do not agree that we "extend" *Wade* and *Gilbert* by holding that the principles of those cases apply to confrontations for identification conducted after arrest. Because Shard testified at trial about his identification of petitioner at the police station showup, the exclusionary rule of *Gilbert* requires reversal.

MR. JUSTICE WHITE, dissenting.

[Omitted.]

QUESTIONS, COMMENTS, CONCERNS?

1. **Does the rationale of *Kirby* make sense?** It's hard to read *Kirby* as anything other than a retreat from *Wade*—at least in the right to counsel context. After *Kirby*, a suspect is not entitled to counsel for corporeal identifications conducted before the suspect is indicted or otherwise formally charged. But does that make sense? As Justice Brennan notes in dissent, "[T]here inhere in a confrontation for identification conducted after arrest the identical hazards to a fair trial that inhere in such a confrontation conducted 'after the onset of formal prosecutorial proceedings.'"

Long's case seemingly emphasizes Justice Brennan's point. Remember that, in Long's case, there were three separate identifications, the second of which took place in court where Long appeared on a misdemeanor trespassing charge. Although we will explore that identification in more depth in the notes below, it would be an understatement to say the circumstances surrounding that identification are concerning. What does the fact that Long had not yet been arrested have to do with the troubling context of Bost's in-court identification?

UNITED STATES V. ASH

413 U.S. 300
Supreme Court of the United States
January 10, 1973, Argued; June 21, 1973, Decided
No. 71-1255

MR. JUSTICE BLACKMUN delivered the opinion of the Court.

In this case the Court is called upon to decide whether the Sixth Amendment grants an accused the right to have counsel present whenever the Government conducts a post-indictment photographic display, containing a picture of the accused, for the purpose of allowing a witness to attempt an identification of the offender. The United States Court of Appeals for the District of Columbia Circuit, sitting en banc, held, by a 5-to-4 vote, that the accused possesses this right to counsel. The Court's holding is inconsistent with decisions of the courts of appeals of nine other circuits. We granted certiorari to resolve the conflict and to decide this important constitutional question. We reverse and remand.

I

On the morning of August 26, 1965, a man with a stocking mask entered a bank in Washington, D.C., and began waving a pistol. He ordered an employee to hang up the telephone and instructed all others present not to move. Seconds later a second man, also wearing a stocking mask, entered the bank, scooped up money from tellers' drawers into a bag, and left. The gunman followed, and both men escaped through an alley. The robbery lasted three or four minutes.

A Government informer, Clarence McFarland, told authorities that he had discussed the robbery with Charles J. Ash, Jr., the respondent here. Acting on this information, an FBI agent, in February 1966, showed five black-and-white mug shots of Negro males of generally the same age, height, and weight, one of which was of Ash, to four witnesses. All four made uncertain identifications of Ash's picture. At this time Ash was not in custody and had not been charged. On April 1, 1966, an indictment was returned charging Ash and a codefendant, John L. Bailey, in five counts related to this bank robbery * * *.

Trial was finally set for May 1968, almost three years after the crime. In preparing for trial, the prosecutor decided to use a photographic display to determine whether the witnesses he planned to call would be able to make in-court identifications. Shortly before the trial, an FBI agent and the prosecutor showed five color photographs to the four witnesses who previously had tentatively identified the black-and-white photograph of Ash. Three of the witnesses selected the picture of Ash, but one was unable to make any selection. None of the witnesses selected the picture of Bailey which was in the group. This post-indictment identification provides the basis for respondent Ash's claim that he was denied the right to counsel at a "critical stage" of the prosecution.

No motion for severance was made, and Ash and Bailey were tried jointly. The trial judge held a hearing on the suggestive nature of the pretrial photographic displays. The judge did not make a clear ruling on suggestive nature, but held that the Government had demonstrated by "clear and convincing" evidence that in-court identifications would be "based on observation of the suspect other than the intervening observation."

At trial, the three witnesses who had been inside the bank identified Ash as the gunman, but they were unwilling to state that they were certain of their identifications. None of these made an in-court identification of Bailey. The fourth witness, who had been in a car outside the bank and who had seen the fleeing robbers after they had removed their masks, made positive in-court identifications of both Ash and Bailey. Bailey's counsel then sought to impeach this in-court identification by calling the FBI agent who had shown the color photographs to the witnesses immediately before trial. Bailey's counsel demonstrated that the witness who had identified Bailey in court had failed to identify a color photograph of Bailey. During the course of the examination, Bailey's counsel also, before the jury, brought out the fact that this witness had selected another man as one of the robbers. At this point the prosecutor became concerned that the jury might believe that the witness had selected a third person when, in fact, the witness had selected a photograph of Ash. After a conference at the bench, the trial judge ruled that all five color photographs would be admitted into evidence. The Court of Appeals held that this constituted the introduction of a post-indictment identification at the prosecutor's request and over the objection of defense counsel.

McFarland testified as a Government witness. He said he had discussed plans for the robbery with Ash before the event and, later, had discussed the results of the robbery with Ash in the presence of Bailey. McFarland was shown to possess an extensive criminal record and a history as an informer.

The jury convicted Ash on all counts. It was unable to reach a verdict on the charges against Bailey, and his motion for acquittal was granted. Ash received concurrent sentences on the several counts, the two longest being 80 months to 12 years.

The five-member majority of the Court of Appeals held that Ash's right to counsel, guaranteed by the Sixth Amendment, was violated when his attorney was not given the opportunity to be present at the photographic displays conducted in May 1968 before the trial. * * *

The majority did not reach the issue of suggestiveness; their opinion implies, however, that they would order a remand for additional findings by the District Court. * * *

II

The Court of Appeals relied exclusively on that portion of the Sixth Amendment providing, "In all criminal prosecutions, the accused shall enjoy the right . . . to have the Assistance of Counsel for his defence." The right to counsel in Anglo-American law has a rich historical heritage, and this Court has regularly drawn on that history in construing the counsel guarantee of the Sixth Amendment. We re-examine that history in an effort to determine the relationship between the purposes of the Sixth Amendment guarantee and the risks of a photographic identification. * * *

The Court frequently has interpreted the Sixth Amendment to assure that the "guiding hand of counsel" is available to those in need of its assistance. * * *

This historical background suggests that the core purpose of the counsel guarantee was to assure "Assistance" at trial, when the accused was confronted with both the intricacies of the law and the advocacy of the public prosecutor. Later developments have led this Court to recognize that "Assistance" would be less than meaningful if it were limited to the formal trial itself.

This extension of the right to counsel to events before trial has resulted from changing patterns of criminal procedure and investigation that have tended to generate pretrial events that might appropriately be considered to be parts of the trial itself. At these newly emerging and significant events, the accused was confronted, just as at trial, by the procedural system, or by his expert adversary, or by both. * * *

Throughout this expansion of the counsel guarantee to trial-like confrontations, the function of the lawyer has remained essentially the same as his function at trial. In all cases considered by the Court, counsel has continued to act as a spokesman for, or advisor to, the accused. The accused's right to the "Assistance of Counsel" has meant just that, namely, the right of the accused to have counsel acting as his assistant. * * *

The function of counsel in rendering "Assistance" continued at the lineup under consideration in *Wade* and its companion cases. Although the accused was not confronted there with legal questions, the lineup offered opportunities for prosecuting authorities to take advantage of the accused. Counsel was seen by the Court as being more sensitive to, and aware of, suggestive influences than the accused himself, and as better able to reconstruct the events at trial. Counsel present at lineup would be able to remove disabilities of the accused in precisely the same fashion that counsel compensated for the disabilities of the layman at trial. Thus, the

Court mentioned that the accused's memory might be dimmed by "emotional tension," that the accused's credibility at trial would be diminished by his status as defendant, and that the accused might be unable to present his version effectively without giving up his privilege against compulsory self-incrimination. *United States v. Wade*, 388 U.S., at 230–231. It was in order to compensate for these deficiencies that the Court found the need for the assistance of counsel.

This review of the history and expansion of the Sixth Amendment counsel guarantee demonstrates that the test utilized by the Court has called for examination of the event in order to determine whether the accused required aid in coping with legal problems or assistance in meeting his adversary. * * *

IV

A substantial departure from the historical test would be necessary if the Sixth Amendment were interpreted to give Ash a right to counsel at the photographic identification in this case. Since the accused himself is not present at the time of the photographic display, and asserts no right to be present, no possibility arises that the accused might be misled by his lack of familiarity with the law or overpowered by his professional adversary. Similarly, the counsel guarantee would not be used to produce equality in a trial-like adversary confrontation. Rather, the guarantee was used by the Court of Appeals to produce confrontation at an event that previously was not analogous to an adversary trial.

Even if we were willing to view the counsel guarantee in broad terms as a generalized protection of the adversary process, we would be unwilling to go so far as to extend the right to a portion of the prosecutor's trial-preparation interviews with witnesses. Although photography is relatively new, the interviewing of witnesses before trial is a procedure that predates the Sixth Amendment. * * * The traditional counterbalance in the American adversary system for these interviews arises from the equal ability of defense counsel to seek and interview witnesses himself.

That adversary mechanism remains as effective for a photographic display as for other parts of pretrial interviews. No greater limitations are placed on defense counsel in constructing displays, seeking witnesses, and conducting photographic identifications than those applicable to the prosecution. Selection of the picture of a person other than the accused, or the inability of a witness to make any selection, will be useful to the defense in precisely the same manner that the selection of a picture of the defendant would be useful to the prosecution. In this very case, for example, the initial tender of the photographic display was by Bailey's counsel, who sought to demonstrate that the witness had failed to make a photographic identification. Although we do not suggest that equality of access to photographs removes all potential for abuse, it does remove any inequality in the adversary process itself and thereby fully satisfies the historical spirit of the Sixth Amendment's counsel guarantee.

The argument has been advanced that requiring counsel might compel the police to observe more scientific procedures or might encourage them to utilize corporeal rather than photographic displays. This Court has recognized that improved procedures can minimize the dangers of suggestion. Commentators have also proposed more accurate techniques.

Pretrial photographic identifications, however, are hardly unique in offering possibilities for the actions of the prosecutor unfairly to prejudice the accused. Evidence favorable to the accused may be withheld; testimony of witnesses may be manipulated; the results of laboratory tests may be contrived. In many ways the prosecutor, by accident or by design, may improperly subvert the trial. The primary safeguard against abuses of this kind is the ethical responsibility of the prosecutor, who, as so often has been said, may "strike hard blows" but not "foul ones." If that safeguard fails, review remains available under due process standards. These same safeguards apply to misuse of photographs.

We are not persuaded that the risks inherent in the use of photographic displays are so pernicious that an extraordinary system of safeguards is required.

We hold, then, that the Sixth Amendment does not grant the right to counsel at photographic displays conducted by the Government for the purpose of allowing a witness to attempt an identification of the offender. This holding requires reversal of the judgment of the Court of Appeals. * * *

Reversed and remanded.

MR. JUSTICE STEWART, concurring in the judgment.

The issue in the present case is whether, under the Sixth Amendment, a person who has been indicted is entitled to have a lawyer present when prosecution witnesses are shown the person's photograph and asked if they can identify him. * * *

A photographic identification is quite different from a lineup, for there are substantially fewer possibilities of impermissible suggestion when photographs are used, and those unfair influences can be readily reconstructed at trial. It is true that the defendant's photograph may be markedly different from the others displayed, but this unfairness can be demonstrated at trial from an actual comparison of the photographs used or from the witness' description of the display. Similarly, it is possible that the photographs could be arranged in a suggestive manner, or that by comment or gesture the prosecuting authorities might single out the defendant's picture. But these are the kinds of overt influence that a witness can easily recount and that would serve to impeach the identification testimony. In short, there are few possibilities for unfair suggestiveness—and those rather blatant and easily reconstructed. Accordingly, an accused would not be foreclosed from an effective cross-examination of an identification witness simply because his counsel was not present at the photographic display. For this reason, a photographic display cannot fairly be considered a "critical stage" of the prosecution. * * *

Preparing witnesses for trial by checking their identification testimony against a photographic display is little different, in my view, from the prosecutor's other interviews with the victim or other witnesses before trial. While these procedures can be improperly conducted, the possibility of irretrievable prejudice is remote, since any unfairness that does occur can usually be flushed out at trial through cross-examination of the prosecution witnesses. The presence of defense counsel at such pretrial preparatory sessions is neither appropriate nor necessary under our adversary system of justice "to preserve the defendant's basic right to a fair trial as affected by his right meaningfully to cross-examine the witnesses against him and to have effective assistance of counsel at the trial itself."

MR. JUSTICE BRENNAN, with whom MR. JUSTICE DOUGLAS and MR. JUSTICE MARSHALL join, dissenting.

The Court holds today that a pretrial display of photographs to the witnesses of a crime for the purpose of identifying the accused, unlike a lineup, does not constitute a "critical stage" of the prosecution at which the accused is constitutionally entitled to the presence of counsel. In my view, today's decision is wholly unsupportable in terms of such considerations as logic, consistency, and, indeed, fairness. As a result, I must reluctantly conclude that today's decision marks simply another step towards the complete evisceration of the fundamental constitutional principles established by this Court, only six years ago, in *United States v. Wade*, 388 U.S. 218 (1967); *Gilbert v. California*, 388 U.S. 263 (1967); and *Stovall v. Denno*, 388 U.S. 293 (1967). I dissent. * * *

II

In June 1967, this Court decided a trilogy of "lineup" cases which brought into sharp focus the problems of pretrial identification. *See United States v. Wade, supra; Gilbert v. California, supra; Stovall v. Denno, supra*. In essence, those decisions held (1) that a pretrial lineup is a "critical stage" in the criminal process at which the accused is constitutionally entitled to the presence of counsel; (2) that evidence of an identification of the accused at such an uncounseled lineup is *per se* inadmissible; and (3) that evidence of a subsequent in-court identification of the accused is likewise inadmissible unless the Government can demonstrate by clear and convincing evidence that the in-court identification was based upon observations of the accused independent of the prior uncounseled lineup identification. * * *

III

As the Court of Appeals recognized, "the dangers of mistaken identification . . . set forth in *Wade* are applicable in large measure to photographic as well as corporeal identifications." To the extent that misidentification may be attributable to a witness' faulty memory or perception, or inadequate opportunity for detailed observation during the crime, the risks are obviously as great at a photographic display as at a lineup. But "because of the inherent limitations of photography, which presents its subject in two dimensions rather than the three dimensions of reality, . . . a photographic identification, even when properly obtained, is clearly inferior to a properly obtained corporeal identification." Indeed, noting "the hazards of initial identification by photograph," we have expressly recognized that "a corporeal identification . . . is normally more accurate" than a photographic identification. Thus, in this sense at least, the dangers of misidentification are even greater at a photographic display than at a lineup.

Moreover, as in the lineup situation, the possibilities for impermissible suggestion in the context of a photographic display are manifold. Such suggestion, intentional or unintentional, may derive from three possible sources. First, the photographs themselves might tend to suggest which of the pictures is that of the suspect. For example, differences in age, pose, or other physical characteristics of the persons represented, and variations in the mounting, background, lighting, or markings of the photographs all might have the effect of singling out the accused.

Second, impermissible suggestion may inhere in the manner in which the photographs are displayed to the witness. The danger of misidentification is, of course, "increased if the police display to the witness . . . the pictures of several persons among which the photograph of a single such individual recurs or is in some way emphasized." And, if the photographs are arranged in an asymmetrical pattern, or if they are displayed in a time sequence that tends to emphasize a particular photograph, "any identification of the photograph which stands out from the rest is no more reliable than an identification of a single photograph, exhibited alone."

Third, gestures or comments of the prosecutor at the time of the display may lead an otherwise uncertain witness to select the "correct" photograph. For example, the prosecutor might "indicate to the witness that [he has] other evidence that one of the persons pictured committed the crime," and might even point to a particular photograph and ask whether the person pictured "looks familiar." More subtly, the prosecutor's inflection, facial expressions, physical motions, and myriad other almost imperceptible means of communication might tend, intentionally or unintentionally, to compromise the witness' objectivity. Thus, as is the case with lineups, "improper photographic identification procedures, . . . by exerting a suggestive influence upon the witnesses, can often lead to an erroneous identification . . . ." And "regardless of how the initial misidentification comes about, the witness thereafter is apt to retain in his memory the image of the photograph rather than of the person actually seen . . . ." As a result, " 'the issue of identity may (in the absence of other relevant evidence) for all practical purposes be determined there and then, before the trial.' "

Moreover, as with lineups, the defense can "seldom reconstruct" at trial the mode and manner of photographic identification. It is true, of course, that the photographs used at the pretrial display might be preserved for examination at trial. But "it may also be said that a photograph can preserve the record of a lineup; yet this does not justify a lineup without counsel." Indeed, in reality, preservation of the photographs affords little protection to the unrepresented accused. For, although retention of the photographs may mitigate the dangers of misidentification due to the suggestiveness of the photographs themselves, it cannot in any sense reveal to defense counsel the more subtle, and therefore more dangerous, suggestiveness that might derive from the manner in which the photographs were displayed or any accompanying comments or gestures. Moreover, the accused cannot rely upon the witnesses themselves to expose these latter sources of suggestion, for the witnesses are not "apt to be alert for conditions prejudicial to the suspect. And if they were, it would likely be of scant benefit to the suspect" since the witnesses are hardly "likely to be schooled in the detection of suggestive influences."

Finally, and unlike the lineup situation, the accused himself is not even present at the photographic identification, thereby reducing the likelihood that irregularities in the procedures will ever come to light. * * *

Thus, the difficulties of reconstructing at trial an uncounseled photographic display are at least equal to, and possibly greater than, those involved in reconstructing an uncounseled lineup. * * * As a result, both photographic and corporeal identifications create grave dangers that an innocent defendant might be convicted simply because of his inability to expose a tainted identification. This being so, considerations of logic, consistency, and, indeed, fairness compel the conclusion that a pretrial photographic identification, like a pretrial corporeal identification, is a "critical stage of the prosecution at which [the accused is] 'as much entitled to such aid [of counsel] . . . as at the trial itself.' "

IV

Ironically, the Court does not seriously challenge the proposition that presence of counsel at a pretrial photographic display is essential to preserve the accused's right to a fair trial on the issue of identification. Rather, in what I can only characterize a triumph of form over substance, the Court seeks to justify its result by engrafting a wholly unprecedented—and wholly unsupportable—limitation on the Sixth Amendment right of "the accused . . . to have the Assistance of Counsel for his defence." Although apparently conceding that the right to counsel attaches, not only at the trial itself, but at all "critical stages" of the prosecution, the Court holds today that, in order to be deemed "critical," the particular "stage of the prosecution" under consideration must, at the very least, involve the physical "presence of the accused," at a "trial-like confrontation" with the Government, at which the accused requires the "guiding hand of counsel." According to the Court a pretrial photographic identification does not, of course, meet these criteria. * * *

There is something ironic about the Court's conclusion today that a pretrial lineup identification is a "critical stage" of the prosecution because counsel's presence can help to compensate for the accused's deficiencies as an observer, but that a pretrial photographic identification is not a "critical stage" of the prosecution because the accused is not able to observe at all. In my view, there simply is no meaningful difference, in terms of the need for attendance of counsel, between corporeal and photographic identifications. And applying established and well-reasoned Sixth Amendment principles, I can only conclude that a pretrial photographic display, like a pretrial lineup, is a "critical stage" of the prosecution at which the accused is constitutionally entitled to the presence of counsel.

QUESTIONS, COMMENTS, CONCERNS?

1. *Ash* and Long. Notice that *Ash* essentially dooms any chance of Long arguing that he was entitled to counsel at the time police showed Bost an array of seven pictures at the police station on May 10, 1976. Can you see why? And from Long's standpoint, why might he view that photo array as problematic and therefore desire counsel to be present as Bost reviews the photos? [*See* Casefile Document 13.] Why does Justice Brennan think counsel would be helpful during a non-corporeal photo lineup?

2. **Pop quiz—remember *Edwards v. Arizona*?** Speaking of lawyers, officers would arrest Long for first-degree rape and first-degree burglary on May 10, 1976—the same day that Bost identified him in court and via photo lineup. [Casefile Document 10.] Following Long's arrest, officers sought to obtain a statement from Long. Long agreed and signed a Concord Police Department *Miranda* waiver. [Casefile Document 11.] Do you remember the standard for evaluating a waiver of *Miranda* rights? With that standard in mind, what is your opinion of the Concord Police Department's form? An officer report on Long's first statement elaborates on the circumstances surrounding Long's *Miranda* waiver. [Casefile Document 12.] Does that solidify the constitutionality of Long's waiver?

3. **Long's first statement.** Look again at Long's first statement denying any involvement in Bost's rape. [Casefile Document 12.] Notice that

officers searched Long's vehicle and retrieved a toboggan, a pair of gloves, and a black leather coat. *Id.* at 2. Forensic testing of the seized items failed to reveal the presence of any hair, carpet fibers, or paint fragments from Bost's home. [Casefile Document 19, at 4–5.] In 2008, new counsel for Long would contend that the state failed to disclose the results of that testing to Long's trial counsel. *Id.* at 1. The Superior Court of North Carolina nevertheless declined to vacate Long's convictions and give him a new trial. *Id.* at 14.

4.   Long's second statement. Long would make a second statement the day after he was indicted for first-degree rape and first-degree burglary. [Casefile Document 15.] This time accompanied by his father and represented by counsel, Long again denied involvement, volunteered to submit to a polygraph test, and named Carl Young as the perpetrator. *Id.* Based on Long's second statement, should officers have constructed an additional lineup for Bost that included Carl Young's photo?

IV. CHALLENGING THE IDENTIFICATION

We finish our journey together by looking at a pair of cases that provide the standard for how to challenge witness identification procedures. Notice the change in our source of law. Unlike the right to counsel materials, which are grounded in the Sixth Amendment, *Manson v. Brathwaite* and *Perry v. New Hampshire* are Fourteenth Amendment due process cases. Accordingly, both cases focus on challenges to witness procedures more broadly, as opposed to the Sixth Amendment cases that focus on the narrower category of corporeal identifications.

MANSON V. BRATHWAITE
432 U.S. 98
Supreme Court of the United States
Argued November 29, 1976; June 16, 1977; as amended
No. 75-871

MR. JUSTICE BLACKMUN delivered the opinion of the Court.

This case presents the issue as to whether the Due Process Clause of the Fourteenth Amendment compels the exclusion, in a state criminal trial, apart from any consideration of reliability, of pretrial identification evidence obtained by a police procedure that was both suggestive and unnecessary. This Court's decision in *Stovall v. Denno*, 388 U.S. 293 (1967), and *Neil v. Biggers*, 409 U.S. 188 (1972), are particularly implicated.

I

Jimmy D. Glover, a full-time trooper of the Connecticut State Police, in 1970 was assigned to the Narcotics Division in an undercover capacity. On May 5 of that year, about 7:45 p.m., e.d.t., and while there was still daylight, Glover and Henry Alton Brown, an informant, went to an apartment building at 201 Westland, in Hartford, for the purpose of purchasing narcotics from "Dickie Boy" Cicero, a known narcotics dealer. Cicero, it was thought, lived on the third floor of that apartment building. Glover and Brown entered the building, observed by backup Officers D'Onofrio and Gaffey, and proceeded by stairs to the third floor. Glover knocked at the door of one of the two apartments served by the stairway. The area was illuminated by natural light from a window in the third floor hallway. The door was opened 12 to 18 inches in response to the knock. Glover observed a man standing at the door and, behind him, a woman. Brown identified himself. Glover then asked for "two things" of narcotics. The man at the door held out his hand, and Glover gave him two $10 bills. The door closed. Soon the man returned and handed Glover two glassine bags. While the door was open, Glover stood within two feet of the person from whom he made the purchase and observed his face. Five to seven minutes elapsed from the time the door first opened until it closed the second time.

Glover and Brown then left the building. This was about eight minutes after their arrival. Glover drove to headquarters where he described the seller to D'Onofrio and Gaffey. Glover at that time did not know the identity of the seller. He described him as being "a colored man, approximately five feet eleven inches tall, dark complexion, black hair, short Afro style, and having high cheekbones, and of heavy build. He was wearing at the time blue pants and a plaid shirt." D'Onofrio, suspecting from this description that respondent might be the seller, obtained a photograph of respondent from the Records Division of the Hartford Police Department. He left it at Glover's office. D'Onofrio was not acquainted with respondent personally, but did know him by sight and had seen him "[s]everal times" prior to May 5. Glover, when alone, viewed the photograph for the first time upon his return to headquarters on May 7; he identified the person shown as the one from whom he had purchased the narcotics.

The toxicological report on the contents of the glassine bags revealed the presence of heroin. The report was dated July 16, 1970.

Respondent was arrested on July 27 while visiting at the apartment of a Mrs. Ramsey on the third floor of 201 Westland. This was the apartment at which the narcotics sale had taken place on May 5.

Respondent was charged, in a two-count information, with possession and sale of heroin * * *. At his trial in January 1971, the photograph from which Glover had identified respondent was received in evidence without objection on the part of the defense. Glover also testified that, although he had not seen respondent in the eight months that had elapsed since the sale, "there [was] no doubt whatsoever" in his mind that the person shown on the photograph was respondent. Glover also made a positive in-court identification without objection.

No explanation was offered by the prosecution for the failure to utilize a photographic array or to conduct a lineup.

Respondent, who took the stand in his own defense, testified that on May 5, the day in question, he had been ill at his Albany Avenue apartment ("a lot of back pains, muscle spasms . . . a bad heart . . . high blood pressure . . . neuralgia in my face, and sinus"), and that at no time on that particular day had he been at 201 Westland. His wife testified that she recalled, after her husband had refreshed her memory, that he was home all day on May 5. Doctor Wesley M. Vietzke, an internist and assistant professor of medicine at the University of Connecticut, testified that respondent had consulted him on April 15, 1970, and that he took a medical history from him, heard his complaints about his back and facial pain, and discovered that he had high blood pressure. The physician found respondent, subjectively, "in great discomfort." Respondent in fact underwent surgery for a herniated disc at L5 and S1 on August 17.

The jury found respondent guilty on both counts of the information. He received a sentence of not less than six nor more than nine years. His conviction was affirmed per curiam by the Supreme Court of Connecticut. * * *

Fourteen months later, respondent filed a petition for habeas corpus in the United States District Court for the District of Connecticut. He alleged that the admission of the identification testimony at his state trial deprived him of due process of law to which he was entitled under the Fourteenth Amendment. The District Court, by an unreported written opinion based on the court's review of the state trial transcript, dismissed respondent's petition. On appeal, the United States Court of Appeals for the Second Circuit reversed, with instructions to issue the writ unless the State gave notice of a desire to retry respondent and the new trial occurred within a reasonable time to be fixed by the District Judge.

In brief summary, the court felt that evidence as to the photograph should have been excluded, regardless of reliability, because the examination of the single photograph was unnecessary and suggestive. And, in the court's view, the evidence was unreliable in any event. We granted certiorari.

II

Stovall v. Denno, supra, decided in 1967, concerned a petitioner who had been convicted in a New York court of murder. He was arrested the day following the crime and was taken by the police to a hospital where the victim's wife, also wounded in the assault, was a patient. After observing Stovall and hearing him speak, she identified him as the murderer. She later made an in-court identification. On federal habeas, Stovall claimed the identification testimony violated his Fifth, Sixth, and Fourteenth Amendment rights. The District Court dismissed the petition, and the

Court of Appeals, en banc, affirmed. This Court also affirmed. On the identification issue, the Court reviewed the practice of showing a suspect singly for purposes of identification, and the claim that this was so unnecessarily suggestive and conducive to irreparable mistaken identification that it constituted a denial of due process of law. The Court noted that the practice "has been widely condemned," but it concluded that "a claimed violation of due process of law in the conduct of a confrontation depends on the totality of the circumstances surrounding it." In that case, showing Stovall to the victim's spouse "was imperative." The Court then quoted the observations of the Court of Appeals to the effect that the spouse was the only person who could possibly exonerate the accused; that the hospital was not far from the courthouse and jail; that no one knew how long she might live; that she was not able to visit the jail; and that taking Stovall to the hospital room was the only feasible procedure, and, under the circumstances, "the usual police station line-up. . . was out of the question."

Neil v. Biggers, supra, decided in 1972, concerned a respondent who had been convicted in a Tennessee court of rape, on evidence consisting in part of the victim's visual and voice identification of Biggers at a station-house showup seven months after the crime. The victim had been in her assailant's presence for some time and had directly observed him indoors and under a full moon outdoors. She testified that she had "no doubt" that Biggers was her assailant. She previously had given the police a description of the assailant. She had made no identification of others presented at previous showups, lineups, or through photographs. On federal habeas, the District Court held that the confrontation was so suggestive as to violate due process. The Court of Appeals affirmed. This Court reversed on that issue, and held that the evidence properly had been allowed to go to the jury. * * * The Court concluded that * * * "admission of evidence of a showup without more does not violate due process." The Court expressed concern about the lapse of seven months between the crime and the confrontation and observed that this "would be a seriously negative factor in most cases." The "central question," however, was "whether under the 'totality of the circumstances' the identification was reliable even though the confrontation procedure was suggestive." Applying that test, the Court found "no substantial likelihood of misidentification. The evidence was properly allowed to go to the jury."

Biggers well might be seen to provide an unambiguous answer to the question before us: The admission of testimony concerning a suggestive and unnecessary identification procedure does not violate due process so long as the identification possesses sufficient aspects of reliability. In one passage, however, the Court observed that the challenged procedure occurred pre-*Stovall* and that a strict rule would make little sense with regard to a confrontation that preceded the Court's first indication that a suggestive procedure might lead to the exclusion of evidence. One perhaps might argue that, by implication, the Court suggested that a different rule could apply post-*Stovall*. The question before us, then, is simply whether the *Biggers* analysis applies to post-*Stovall* confrontations as well to those pre-*Stovall*. * * *

IV

Petitioner at the outset acknowledges that "the procedure in the instant case was suggestive [because only one photograph was used] and unnecessary" [because there was no emergency or exigent circumstance]. The respondent * * * proposes a *per se* rule of exclusion that he claims is dictated by the demands of the Fourteenth Amendment's guarantee of due process. He rightly observes that this is the first case in which this Court has had occasion to rule upon strictly post-*Stovall* out-of-court identification evidence of the challenged kind. * * *

There are, of course, several interests to be considered and taken into account. The driving force behind *United States v. Wade*, 388 U.S. 218 (1967), *Gilbert v. California*, 388 U.S. 263 (1967) (right to counsel at a post-indictment lineup), and *Stovall*, all decided on the same day, was the Court's concern with the problems of eyewitness identification. Usually the witness must testify about an encounter with a total stranger under circumstances of emergency or emotional stress. The witness' recollection of the stranger can be distorted easily by the circumstances or by later actions of the police. Thus, *Wade* and its companion cases reflect the concern that the jury not hear eyewitness testimony unless that evidence has aspects of reliability. It must be observed that both approaches before us are responsive to this concern. The *per se* rule, however, goes too far since its application automatically and peremptorily, and without consideration of alleviating factors, keeps evidence from the jury that is reliable and relevant.

The second factor is deterrence. Although the *per se* approach has the more significant deterrent effect, the totality approach also has an influence on police behavior. The police will guard against unnecessarily suggestive procedures under the totality rule, as well as the per se one, for fear that their actions will lead to the exclusion of identifications as unreliable.

The third factor is the effect on the administration of justice. Here the per se approach suffers serious drawbacks. Since it denies the trier reliable evidence, it may result, on occasion, in the guilty going free. Also, because of its rigidity, the *per se* approach may make error by the trial judge more likely than the totality approach. And in those cases in which the admission of identification evidence is error under the per se approach but not under the totality approach—cases in which the identification is reliable despite an unnecessarily suggestive identification procedure—reversal is a

Draconian sanction. Certainly, inflexible rules of exclusion that may frustrate rather than promote justice have not been viewed recently by this Court with unlimited enthusiasm. * * *

The standard, after all, is that of fairness as required by the Due Process Clause of the Fourteenth Amendment. *Stovall*, with its reference to "the totality of the circumstances," and *Biggers*, with its continuing stress on the same totality, did not, singly or together, establish a strict exclusionary rule or new standard of due process. * * *

We therefore conclude that reliability is the linchpin in determining the admissibility of identification testimony for both pre- and post-*Stovall* confrontations. The factors to be considered * * * include the opportunity of the witness to view the criminal at the time of the crime, the witness' degree of attention, the accuracy of his prior description of the criminal, the level of certainty demonstrated at the confrontation, and the time between the crime and the confrontation. Against these factors is to be weighed the corrupting effect of the suggestive identification itself.

V

We turn, then, to the facts of this case and apply the analysis:

1.   The opportunity to view. Glover testified that for two to three minutes he stood at the apartment door, within two feet of the respondent. The door opened twice, and each time the man stood at the door. The moments passed, the conversation took place, and payment was made. Glover looked directly at his vendor. It was near sunset, to be sure, but the sun had not yet set, so it was not dark or even dusk or twilight. Natural light from outside entered the hallway through a window. There was natural light, as well, from inside the apartment.

2.   The degree of attention. Glover was not a casual or passing observer, as is so often the case with eyewitness identification. Trooper Glover was a trained police officer on duty—and specialized and dangerous duty—when he called at the third floor of 201 Westland in Hartford on May 5, 1970. Glover himself was a Negro and unlikely to perceive only general features of "hundreds of Hartford black males," as the Court of Appeals stated. It is true that Glover's duty was that of ferreting out narcotics offenders and that he would be expected in his work to produce results. But it is also true that, as a specially trained, assigned, and experienced officer, he could be expected to pay scrupulous attention to detail, for he knew that subsequently he would have to find and arrest his vendor. In addition, he knew that his claimed observations would be subject later to close scrutiny and examination at any trial.

3.   The accuracy of the description. Glover's description was given to D'Onofrio within minutes after the transaction. It included the vendor's race, his height, his build, the color and style of his hair, and the high

cheekbone facial feature. It also included clothing the vendor wore. No claim has been made that respondent did not possess the physical characteristics so described. D'Onofrio reacted positively at once. Two days later, when Glover was alone, he viewed the photograph D'Onofrio produced and identified its subject as the narcotics seller.

4. The witness' level of certainty. There is no dispute that the photograph in question was that of respondent. Glover, in response to a question whether the photograph was that of the person from whom he made the purchase, testified: "There is no question whatsoever." This positive assurance was repeated.

5. The time between the crime and the confrontation. Glover's description of his vendor was given to D'Onofrio within minutes of the crime. The photographic identification took place only two days later. We do not have here the passage of weeks or months between the crime and the viewing of the photograph.

These indicators of Glover's ability to make an accurate identification are hardly outweighed by the corrupting effect of the challenged identification itself. Although identifications arising from single-photograph displays may be viewed in general with suspicion, we find in the instant case little pressure on the witness to acquiesce in the suggestion that such a display entails. D'Onofrio had left the photograph at Glover's office and was not present when Glover first viewed it two days after the event. There thus was little urgency and Glover could view the photograph at his leisure. And since Glover examined the photograph alone, there was no coercive pressure to make an identification arising from the presence of another. The identification was made in circumstances allowing care and reflection.

Although it plays no part in our analysis, all this assurance as to the reliability of the identification is hardly undermined by the facts that respondent was arrested in the very apartment where the sale had taken place, and that he acknowledged his frequent visits to that apartment.

Surely, we cannot say that under all the circumstances of this case there is "a very substantial likelihood of irreparable misidentification." Short of that point, such evidence is for the jury to weigh. We are content to rely upon the good sense and judgment of American juries, for evidence with some element of untrustworthiness is customary grist for the jury mill. Juries are not so susceptible that they cannot measure intelligently the weight of identification testimony that has some questionable feature.

Of course, it would have been better had D'Onofrio presented Glover with a photographic array including "so far as practicable . . . a reasonable number of persons similar to any person then suspected whose likeness is included in the array." The use of that procedure would have enhanced the force of the identification at trial and would have avoided the risk that the evidence would be excluded as unreliable. But we are not disposed to view D'Onofrio's failure as one of constitutional dimension to be enforced by a rigorous and unbending exclusionary rule. The defect, if there be one, goes to weight and not to substance.

We conclude that the criteria laid down in *Biggers* are to be applied in determining the admissibility of evidence offered by the prosecution concerning a post-*Stovall* identification, and that those criteria are satisfactorily met and complied with here.

The judgment of the Court of Appeals is reversed.

It is so ordered.

MR. JUSTICE STEVENS, concurring.

[Omitted.]

MR. JUSTICE MARSHALL, with whom MR. JUSTICE BRENNAN joins, dissenting. * * *

* * * In assessing the reliability of the identification, the Court mandates weighing "the corrupting effect of the suggestive identification itself" against the "indicators of [a witness'] ability to make an accurate identification." The Court holds * * * that a due process identification inquiry must take account of the suggestiveness of a confrontation and the likelihood that it led to misidentification, as recognized in *Stovall* and *Wade*. Thus, even if a witness did have an otherwise adequate opportunity to view a criminal, the later use of a highly suggestive identification procedure can render his testimony inadmissible. Indeed, it is my view that, assuming applicability of the totality test enunciated by the Court, the facts of the present case require that result.

I consider first the opportunity that Officer Glover had to view the suspect. Careful review of the record shows that he could see the heroin seller only for the time it took to speak three sentences of four or five short words, to hand over some money, and later after the door reopened, to receive the drugs in return. The entire face-to-face transaction could have taken as little as 15 or 20 seconds. But during this time, Glover's attention was not focused exclusively on the seller's face. He observed that the door was opened 12 to 18 inches, that there was a window in the room behind the door, and, most importantly, that there was a woman standing behind the man. Glover was, of course, also concentrating on the details of the transaction—he must have looked away from the seller's face to hand him the money and receive the drugs. The observation during the conversation thus may have been as brief as 5 or 10 seconds.

As the Court notes, Glover was a police officer trained in and attentive to the need for making accurate identifications. Nevertheless, both common sense and scholarly study indicate that while a trained observer such as a police officer "is somewhat less likely to make an erroneous identification than the average untrained observer, the mere fact that he has been so trained is no guarantee that he is correct in a specific case. His identification testimony should be scrutinized just as carefully as that of the normal witness." Moreover, "identifications made by policemen in highly competitive activities, such as undercover narcotic agents . . . , should be scrutinized with special care." Yet it is just such a searching inquiry that the Court fails to make here.

Another factor on which the Court relies—the witness' degree of certainty in making the identification—is worthless as an indicator that he is correct. Even if Glover had been unsure initially about his identification of respondent's picture, by the time he was called at trial to present a key piece of evidence for the State that paid his salary, it is impossible to imagine his responding negatively to such questions as "is there any doubt in your mind whatsoever" that the identification was correct. * * *

Next, the Court finds that because the identification procedure took place two days after the crime, its reliability is enhanced. While such temporal proximity makes the identification more reliable than one occurring months later, the fact is that the greatest memory loss occurs within hours after an event. After that, the dropoff continues much more slowly. Thus, the reliability of an identification is increased only if it was made within several hours of the crime. If the time gap is any greater, reliability necessarily decreases.

Finally, the Court makes much of the fact that Glover gave a description of the seller to D'Onofrio shortly after the incident. Despite the Court's assertion that because "Glover himself was a Negro and unlikely to perceive only general features of 'hundreds of Hartford black males,' as the Court of Appeals stated," the description given by Glover was actually no more than a general summary of the seller's appearance. We may discount entirely the seller's clothing, for that was of no significance later in the proceeding. Indeed, to the extent that Glover noticed clothes, his attention was diverted from the seller's face. Otherwise, Glover merely described vaguely the seller's height, skin color, hairstyle, and build. He did say that the seller had "high cheekbones," but there is no other mention of facial features, nor even an estimate of age. Conspicuously absent is any indication that the seller was a native of the West Indies, certainly something which a member of the black community could immediately recognize from both appearance and accept.

From all of this, I must conclude that the evidence of Glover's ability to make an accurate identification is far weaker than the Court finds it. In contrast, the procedure used to identify respondent was both extraordinarily suggestive and strongly conducive to error. In dismissing "the corrupting effect of the suggestive identification" procedure here, the

Court virtually grants the police license to convict the innocent. By displaying a single photograph of respondent to the witness Glover under the circumstances in this record almost everything that could have been done wrong was done wrong.

In the first place, there was no need to use a photograph at all. Because photos are static, two-dimensional, and often outdated, they are "clearly inferior in reliability" to corporeal procedures. While the use of photographs is justifiable and often essential where the police have no knowledge of an offender's identity, the poor reliability of photos makes their use inexcusable where any other means of identification is available. Here, since Detective D'Onofrio believed that he knew the seller's identity, further investigation without resort to a photographic showup was easily possible. With little inconvenience, a corporeal lineup including Brathwaite might have been arranged. Properly conducted, such a procedure would have gone far to remove any doubt about the fairness and accuracy of the identification.

Worse still than the failure to use an easily available corporeal identification was the display to Glover of only a single picture, rather than a photo array. With good reason, such single-suspect procedures have "been widely condemned." They give no assurance that the witness can identify the criminal from among a number of persons of similar appearance, surely the strongest evidence that there was no misidentification. * * *

The use of a single picture (or the display of a single live suspect, for that matter) is a grave error, of course, because it dramatically suggests to the witness that the person shown must be the culprit. Why else would the police choose the person? And it is deeply ingrained in human nature to agree with the expressed opinions of others—particularly others who should be more knowledgeable—when making a difficult decision. In this case, moreover, the pressure was not limited to that inherent in the display of a single photograph. Glover, the identifying witness, was a state police officer on special assignment. He knew that D'Onofrio, an experienced Hartford narcotics detective, presumably familiar with local drug operations, believed respondent to be the seller. There was at work, then, both loyalty to another police officer and deference to a better-informed colleague. Finally, of course, there was Glover's knowledge that without an identification and arrest, government funds used to buy heroin had been wasted.

The Court discounts this overwhelming evidence of suggestiveness, however. It reasons that because D'Onofrio was not present when Glover viewed the photograph, there was "little pressure on the witness to acquiesce in the suggestion." That conclusion blinks psychological reality. There is no doubt in my mind that even in D'Onofrio's absence, a clear and powerful message was telegraphed to Glover as he looked at respondent's photograph. He was emphatically told that "this is the man," and he responded by identifying respondent then and at trial "whether or not he was in fact 'the man.' "

I must conclude that this record presents compelling evidence that there was "a very substantial likelihood of misidentification" of respondent Brathwaite. * * *

QUESTIONS, COMMENTS, CONCERNS?

1. **Applying the *Manson* framework to Long's case.** In many ways, *Manson* is a difficult decision to accept. *Manson* makes clear that even a suggestive out-of-court identification procedure is insufficient to prove a due process violation. Rather, the lineup procedure must be both suggestive and unreliable. Proving reliability, says the Court, revolves around a host of factors, including "the opportunity of the witness to view the criminal at the time of the crime, the witness' degree of attention, the accuracy of his prior description of the criminal, the level of certainty demonstrated at the confrontation, and the time between the crime and the confrontation."

Consider Bost's third identification against the *Manson* framework—the one at the police station on May 10, 1976. [Casefile Document 13.] How long did Bost have to view her attacker at the time of the crime? Check her testimony during the hearing on Long's motion to suppress the identification. [*See* Casefile Document 16, at 17–18.] What was Bost's "degree of attention"? That is, did Bost have ample opportunity—in good lighting—during the incident to look at her assailant? *See id.* Does it matter that Bost wore glasses? *See id.* at 24. Can you tell if she had them on at the time she was attacked?

How about the accuracy of Bost's prior description of her assailant relative to Long's physical characteristics? Compare Bost's initial statement [Casefile Document 1] to Long's booking photo [Casefile Document 13, at Picture #4]. Notice that some booking photos in the police station photo lineup have measurements behind the suspect, but others do not. Why might that be relevant?

And what level of certainty does Bost have about identifying Long? [*See* Casefile Document 8, at 1–2.] How much time had passed between the crime and the day Bost had an opportunity to identify Long at the police station? [*See* Casefile Document 7 (handwritten note).]

As you assess the *Manson* reliability factors, consider also how Bost's in-court lineup impacts her later police station identification. If Bost identified Long in court, what was the point of identifying him at the police station just a few hours after she saw him in person? In other words, should we be concerned that Bost was identifying the person who she saw in court rather than the person who attacked her?

Other concerns abound. Bost said with certainty that Long was the rapist. [Casefile Document 16, at 20.] But there's reason for concern about the accuracy of her identification. Consider, for example, the role of the jacket Bost said her attacker wore. Beginning with her initial statement, Bost relayed that the "[s]ubject was wearing [a] dark, waist length leather jacket." [Casefile Document 1.] She said the same thing to one of the responding officers, noting that the assailant wore "a leather coat." [Casefile Document 5.] The officers would write in their progress report a few days later that the suspect was wearing "a black leather jacket (waist length)." [Casefile Document 6.]

Long was wearing "a medium brown leather coat" when he appeared in court on May 10, 1976. [Casefile Document 9.] When she viewed the officers' photo lineup at the police station a few hours later, Long was the only one pictured wearing a leather coat. [Casefile Document 13, at Picture #4 (providing the photos); Casefile Document 8, at 1 (providing the timing between the courthouse and stationhouse identifications).] At the hearing on Long's motion to suppress the identification, Long's attorney had this exchange with Bost:

Q   Mrs. Bost, when Ronnie Long got up, do you recall what he had on?

A   He was dressed in a short, light colored, maybe a shade of brown, and light colored pants. They could have been beige, or on the yellow side.

Q   What kind of jacket was it that he had on? Was it a leather jacket?

A   I don't know. I didn't touch it or feel it or . . .

Q   Now, you said he passed about two feet in front of you, did you not?

A   I was looking at his face.

Q   Didn't notice his jacket?

A   Oh, no. It wasn't what he had on when he attacked me. It made no difference.

[Casefile Document 16, at 47.] What do you make of Bost's suppression hearing testimony? Does her failure to notice (or admit noticing) Long's jacket undermine her claims of certainty about identifying him? Remember, the officers saw the jacket and noted it in their report. [Casefile Document 9.]

Bottom line: did Bost provide a reliable identification pursuant to *Manson*?

PERRY V. NEW HAMPSHIRE

565 U.S. 228
Supreme Court of the United States
November 2, 2011, Argued; January 11, 2012, Decided
No. 10-8974

JUSTICE GINSBURG delivered the opinion of the Court. * * *

I

A

Around 3 a.m. on August 15, 2008, Joffre Ullon called the Nashua, New Hampshire, Police Department and reported that an African-American male was trying to break into cars parked in the lot of Ullon's apartment building. Officer Nicole Clay responded to the call. Upon arriving at the parking lot, Clay heard what "sounded like a metal bat hitting the ground." She then saw petitioner Barion Perry standing between two cars. Perry walked toward Clay, holding two car-stereo amplifiers in his hands. A metal bat lay on the ground behind him. Clay asked Perry where the amplifiers came from. "[I] found them on the ground," Perry responded.

Meanwhile, Ullon's wife, Nubia Blandon, woke her neighbor, Alex Clavijo, and told him she had just seen someone break into his car. Clavijo immediately went downstairs to the parking lot to inspect the car. He first observed that one of the rear windows had been shattered. On further inspection, he discovered that the speakers and amplifiers from his car stereo were missing, as were his bat and wrench. Clavijo then approached Clay and told her about Blandon's alert and his own subsequent observations.

By this time, another officer had arrived at the scene. Clay asked Perry to stay in the parking lot with that officer, while she and Clavijo went to talk to Blandon. Clay and Clavijo then entered the apartment building and took the stairs to the fourth floor, where Blandon's and Clavijo's apartments were located. They met Blandon in the hallway just outside the open door to her apartment.

Asked to describe what she had seen, Blandon stated that, around 2:30 a.m., she saw from her kitchen window a tall, African-American man roaming the parking lot and looking into cars. Eventually, the man circled Clavijo's car, opened the trunk, and removed a large box.

Clay asked Blandon for a more specific description of the man. Blandon pointed to her kitchen window and said the person she saw breaking into Clavijo's car was standing in the parking lot, next to the police officer. Perry's arrest followed this identification.

About a month later, the police showed Blandon a photographic array that included a picture of Perry and asked her to point out the man who had broken into Clavijo's car. Blandon was unable to identify Perry.

B

Perry was charged in New Hampshire state court with one count of theft by unauthorized taking and one count of criminal mischief. Before trial, he moved to suppress Blandon's identification on the ground that admitting it at trial would violate due process. Blandon witnessed what amounted to a one-person showup in the parking lot, Perry asserted, which all but guaranteed that she would identify him as the culprit.

The New Hampshire Superior Court denied the motion. * * * On appeal, Perry repeated his challenge to the admissibility of Blandon's out-of-court identification. The trial court erred, Perry contended, in requiring an initial showing that the police arranged the suggestive identification procedure. Suggestive circumstances alone, Perry argued, suffice to trigger the court's duty to evaluate the reliability of the resulting identification before allowing presentation of the evidence to the jury.

The New Hampshire Supreme Court rejected Perry's argument and affirmed his conviction. * * * We granted certiorari to resolve a division of opinion on the question whether the Due Process Clause requires a trial judge to conduct a preliminary assessment of the reliability of an eyewitness identification made under suggestive circumstances not arranged by the police.

II

A

The Constitution, our decisions indicate, protects a defendant against a conviction based on evidence of questionable reliability, not by prohibiting introduction of the evidence, but by affording the defendant means to persuade the jury that the evidence should be discounted as unworthy of credit. Constitutional safeguards available to defendants to counter the State's evidence include the Sixth Amendment rights to counsel, compulsory process, and confrontation plus cross-examination of witnesses. Apart from these guarantees, we have recognized, state and federal statutes and rules ordinarily govern the admissibility of evidence, and juries are assigned the task of determining the reliability of the evidence presented at trial. Only when evidence "is so extremely unfair that its admission violates fundamental conceptions of justice," have we imposed a constraint tied to the Due Process Clause.

Contending that the Due Process Clause is implicated here, Perry relies on a series of decisions involving police-arranged identification procedures. In *Stovall v. Denno*, 388 U.S. 293 (1967), first of those decisions, a witness identified the defendant as her assailant after police officers brought the defendant to the witness' hospital room. At the time the witness made the identification, the defendant—the only African-American in the room—was handcuffed and surrounded by police officers. Although the police-arranged showup was undeniably suggestive, the Court held that no due process violation occurred. Crucial to the Court's decision was the procedure's necessity: The witness was the only person who could identify or exonerate the defendant; the witness could not leave her hospital room; and it was uncertain whether she would live to identify the defendant in more neutral circumstances. Ibid.

A year later, in *Simmons v. United States*, 390 U.S. 377 (1968), the Court addressed a due process challenge to police use of a photographic array. When a witness identifies the defendant in a police-organized photo lineup, the Court ruled, the identification should be suppressed only where "the photographic identification procedure was so [unnecessarily] suggestive as to give rise to a very substantial likelihood of irreparable misidentification." Satisfied that the photo array used by Federal Bureau of Investigation agents in Simmons was both necessary and unlikely to have led to a mistaken identification, the Court rejected the defendant's due process challenge to admission of the identification. In contrast, the Court held in *Foster v. California*, 394 U.S. 440 (1969), that due process required the exclusion of an eyewitness identification obtained through police-arranged procedures that "made it all but inevitable that [the witness] would identify [the defendant]."

Synthesizing previous decisions, we set forth in *Neil v. Biggers*, 409 U.S. 188 (1972), and reiterated in *Manson v. Brathwaite*, 432 U.S. 98 (1977), the approach appropriately used to determine whether the Due Process Clause requires suppression of an eyewitness identification tainted by police arrangement. The Court emphasized, first, that due process concerns arise only when law enforcement officers use an identification procedure that is both suggestive and unnecessary. Even when the police use such a procedure, the Court next said, suppression of the resulting identification is not the inevitable consequence.

A rule requiring automatic exclusion, the Court reasoned, would "g[o] too far," for it would "kee[p] evidence from the jury that is reliable and relevant," and "may result, on occasion, in the guilty going free."

Instead of mandating a per se exclusionary rule, the Court held that the Due Process Clause requires courts to assess, on a case-by-case basis, whether improper police conduct created a "substantial likelihood of misidentification." "[R]eliability [of the eyewitness identification] is the linchpin" of that evaluation, the Court stated in *Brathwaite*. Where the "indicators of [a witness'] ability to make an accurate identification" are "outweighed by the corrupting effect" of law enforcement suggestion, the identification should be suppressed. Otherwise, the evidence (if admissible in all other respects) should be submitted to the jury.[5]

Applying this "totality of the circumstances" approach, the Court held in *Biggers* that law enforcement's use of an unnecessarily suggestive showup did not require suppression of the victim's identification of her assailant. Notwithstanding the improper procedure, the victim's identification was reliable: She saw her assailant for a considerable period of time under adequate light, provided police with a detailed description of her attacker long before the showup, and had "no doubt" that the defendant was the person she had seen. Similarly, the Court concluded in *Brathwaite* that police use of an unnecessarily suggestive photo array did not require exclusion of the resulting identification. The witness, an undercover police officer, viewed the defendant in good light for several minutes, provided a thorough description of the suspect, and was certain of his identification. Hence, the "indicators of [the witness'] ability to make an accurate identification [were] hardly outweighed by the corrupting effect of the challenged identification."

B

Perry concedes that, in contrast to every case in the *Stovall* line, law enforcement officials did not arrange the suggestive circumstances surrounding Blandon's identification. He contends, however, that it was mere happenstance that each of the *Stovall* cases involved improper police action. The rationale underlying our decisions, Perry asserts, supports a rule requiring trial judges to prescreen eyewitness evidence for reliability any time an identification is made under suggestive circumstances. We disagree.

Perry's argument depends, in large part, on the Court's statement in *Brathwaite* that "reliability is the linchpin in determining the admissibility of identification testimony." If reliability is the linchpin of admissibility under the Due Process Clause, Perry maintains, it should make no difference whether law enforcement was responsible for creating the suggestive circumstances that marred the identification.

Perry has removed our statement in Brathwaite from its mooring, and thereby attributes to the statement a meaning a fair reading of our opinion does not bear. As just explained, the *Brathwaite* Court's reference to reliability appears in a portion of the opinion concerning the appropriate remedy when the police use an unnecessarily suggestive identification procedure. The Court adopted a judicial screen for reliability as a course preferable to a per se rule requiring exclusion of identification evidence

---

[5]   Among "factors to be considered" in evaluating a witness' " ability to make an accurate identification," the Court listed: "the opportunity of the witness to view the criminal at the time of the crime, the witness' degree of attention, the accuracy of his prior description of the criminal, the level of certainty demonstrated at the confrontation, and the time between the crime and the confrontation."

whenever law enforcement officers employ an improper procedure. The due process check for reliability, *Brathwaite* made plain, comes into play only after the defendant establishes improper police conduct. The very purpose of the check, the Court noted, was to avoid depriving the jury of identification evidence that is reliable, notwithstanding improper police conduct.

Perry's contention that improper police action was not essential to the reliability check *Brathwaite* required is echoed by the dissent. Both ignore a key premise of the *Brathwaite* decision: A primary aim of excluding identification evidence obtained under unnecessarily suggestive circumstances, the Court said, is to deter law enforcement use of improper lineups, showups, and photo arrays in the first place. Alerted to the prospect that identification evidence improperly obtained may be excluded, the Court reasoned, police officers will "guard against unnecessarily suggestive procedures." This deterrence rationale is inapposite in cases, like Perry's, in which the police engaged in no improper conduct. * * *

Perry's argument * * * would open the door to judicial preview, under the banner of due process, of most, if not all, eyewitness identifications. External suggestion is hardly the only factor that casts doubt on the trustworthiness of an eyewitness' testimony. As one of Perry's amici points out, many other factors bear on "the likelihood of misidentification"—for example, the passage of time between exposure to and identification of the defendant, whether the witness was under stress when he first encountered the suspect, how much time the witness had to observe the suspect, how far the witness was from the suspect, whether the suspect carried a weapon, and the race of the suspect and the witness. There is no reason why an identification made by an eyewitness with poor vision, for example, or one who harbors a grudge against the defendant, should be regarded as inherently more reliable, less of a "threat to the fairness of trial," than the identification Blandon made in this case. To embrace Perry's view would thus entail a vast enlargement of the reach of due process as a constraint on the admission of evidence.

Perry maintains that the Court can limit the due process check he proposes to identifications made under "suggestive circumstances." Even if we could rationally distinguish suggestiveness from other factors bearing on the reliability of eyewitness evidence, Perry's limitation would still involve trial courts, routinely, in preliminary examinations. Most eyewitness identifications involve some element of suggestion. Indeed, all in-court identifications do. Out-of-court identifications volunteered by witnesses are also likely to involve suggestive circumstances. For example, suppose a witness identifies the defendant to police officers after seeing a photograph of the defendant in the press captioned "theft suspect," or hearing a radio report implicating the defendant in the crime. Or suppose the witness knew that the defendant ran with the wrong crowd and saw him on the day and in the vicinity of the crime. Any of these circumstances might have "suggested" to the witness that the defendant was the person the witness observed committing the crime.

C

In urging a broadly applicable due process check on eyewitness identifications, Perry maintains that eyewitness identifications are a uniquely unreliable form of evidence. We do not doubt either the importance or the fallibility of eyewitness identifications. Indeed, in recognizing that defendants have a constitutional right to counsel at postindictment police lineups, we observed that "the annals of criminal law are rife with instances of mistaken identification."

We have concluded in other contexts, however, that the potential unreliability of a type of evidence does not alone render its introduction at the defendant's trial fundamentally unfair. We reach a similar conclusion here: The fallibility of eyewitness evidence does not, without the taint of improper state conduct, warrant a due process rule requiring a trial court to screen such evidence for reliability before allowing the jury to assess its creditworthiness.

Our unwillingness to enlarge the domain of due process as Perry and the dissent urge rests, in large part, on our recognition that the jury, not the judge, traditionally determines the reliability of evidence. We also take account of other safeguards built into our adversary system that caution juries against placing undue weight on eyewitness testimony of questionable reliability. These protections include the defendant's Sixth Amendment right to confront the eyewitness. Another is the defendant's right to the effective assistance of an attorney, who can expose the flaws in the eyewitness' testimony during cross-examination and focus the jury's attention on the fallibility of such testimony during opening and closing arguments. Eyewitness-specific jury instructions, which many federal and state courts have adopted, likewise warn the jury to take care in appraising identification evidence. The constitutional requirement that the government prove the defendant's guilt beyond a reasonable doubt also impedes convictions based on dubious identification evidence.

State and federal rules of evidence, moreover, permit trial judges to exclude relevant evidence if its probative value is substantially outweighed by its prejudicial impact or potential for misleading the jury. In appropriate cases, some States also permit defendants to present expert testimony on the hazards of eyewitness identification evidence.

Many of the safeguards just noted were at work at Perry's trial. During her opening statement, Perry's court-appointed attorney cautioned the jury about the vulnerability of Blandon's identification. While cross-examining Blandon and Officer Clay, Perry's attorney constantly brought up the weaknesses of Blandon's identification. She highlighted: (1) the significant distance between Blandon's window and the parking lot; (2) the lateness of the hour; (3) the van that partly obstructed Blandon's view; (4) Blandon's concession that she was "so scared [she] really didn't pay attention" to what Perry was wearing; (5) Blandon's inability to describe Perry's facial features or other identifying marks; (6) Blandon's failure to pick Perry out of a photo array; and (7) Perry's position next to a uniformed, gun-bearing police officer at the moment Blandon made her identification. Perry's counsel reminded the jury of these frailties during her summation.

After closing arguments, the trial court read the jury a lengthy instruction on identification testimony and the factors the jury should consider when evaluating it. The court also instructed the jury that the defendant's guilt must be proved beyond a reasonable doubt, and specifically cautioned that "one of the things the State must prove [beyond a reasonable doubt] is the identification of the defendant as the person who committed the offense."

Given the safeguards generally applicable in criminal trials, protections availed of by the defense in Perry's case, we hold that the introduction of Blandon's eyewitness testimony, without a preliminary judicial assessment of its reliability, did not render Perry's trial fundamentally unfair.

For the foregoing reasons, * * * we hold that the Due Process Clause does not require a preliminary judicial inquiry into the reliability of an eyewitness identification when the identification was not procured under unnecessarily suggestive circumstances arranged by law enforcement. Accordingly, the judgment of the New Hampshire Supreme Court is

Affirmed.

JUSTICE THOMAS, concurring.

[Omitted.]

JUSTICE SOTOMAYOR, dissenting.

[Omitted.]

QUESTIONS, COMMENTS, CONCERNS?

1. **"Suggestiveness" and Long.** What do you make of Bost's courtroom identification of Long? In many ways, *Perry* brings the Court's due process identification caselaw together by summarizing that a lineup procedure must be *both* suggestive and unreliable to violate due process. But notice what *Perry* says about the suggestiveness portion of the inquiry: "An identification infected by improper police influence * * * is not automatically excluded." Rather, there must exist "a very substantial likelihood of irreparable misidentification."

Reliability concerns aside, did the circumstances surrounding Bost's in-court identification of Long produce "a very substantial likelihood of irreparable misidentification"? Before you answer that question, look at the

May 5, 1976 interview by law enforcement of Bost. [Casefile Document 7.] Is that document truly an "interview" or, rather, were officers trying to cover their tracks? Consider also Bost's own conception of the in-court identification. [Casefile Document 16, at 21–30.] Although she indicated that the officers told her "we don't know what, whether he'll be there[,]" she also testified at the pretrial suppression hearing, in part, that she thought it was "strange" for the officers to ask her to come to court. *Id.* at 23.

Remember also the circumstances surrounding the in-court identification. According to Bost, there were "[t]hirty-five, maybe forty-five, or fifty" people in court on that date. [Casefile Document 7, at 27.] She added that "there were blacks in there, like maybe, a dozen." *Id.* at 28. The officer's report, however, suggests there were between sixty and sixty-five people in attendance, including "12 adult black males in the general age group of the suspect." [Casefile Document 9.] Recall, also, note 1 following *Manson*, which more specifically lays out the potentially problematic role Long's jacket played in Bost's identification.

In any event, are these circumstances collectively "suggestive" to trigger the reliability portion of the *Perry* analysis? What did the suppression court think? [*See* Casefile Document 16, at 58.] Did Long have any better luck in his direct appeal in front of the Supreme Court of North Carolina? [*See* Casefile Document 18, at 731.]

2.   The sources of wrongful convictions. People are wrongfully convicted for a range of reasons, including false confessions, perjury, withholding exculpatory evidence, other prosecutorial misconduct, ineffective representation, and eyewitness misidentifications. Of that list, "[e]yewitness misidentifications contributed to the initial convictions in over 80 percent of documented DNA exonerations." Steven A. Krieger, *Why Our Justice System Convicts Innocent People, and the Challenges Faced by Innocence Projects Trying to Exonerate Them*, 14 NEW CRIM. L. REV. 333, 341 (2011) (quoting Daniel S. Medwed, *Anatomy of a Wrongful Conviction: Theoretical Implications and Practical Solutions*, 51 VILL. L. REV. 337, 339 (2006)).

3.   The rest of the Long story. After his 1976 conviction, Long remained in prison until December 2020. In 2005, the UNC Innocence Project filed a motion to preserve evidence in Cabarrus County Superior Court. That court ordered that certain evidence be preserved and disclosed to the defense. Of particular note, Long learned that none of the items taken from the crime scene were connected to him, including hair samples, a leather jacket, gloves, and a beanie cap. The fact that Long was not a match with the seized items was never disclosed to his defense team prior to the 1976 trial. The defense, moreover, was never told about the Cabarrus Memorial Hospital rape kit. By 2005, though, it was gone. Those discoveries were not enough to free Long; the North Carolina court system held that the evidence was not sufficiently "material" and would not have changed the outcome of the trial.

There's more. In 2015, the North Carolina Innocence Inquiry Commission, a state agency that investigates inmates' innocence claims, learned that investigators back in 1976 collected almost seventy fingerprints from the crime scene, but none matched Long's. In 2016, Long filed what was by then a third petition for a writ of habeas corpus arguing that the fingerprints were new evidence of innocence. The petition further argued that Bost's initial identification of Long was inherently flawed. The district court denied Long's petition and a three-judge panel of the U.S. Court of Appeals voted 2–1 to reject Long's appeal on January 8, 2020.

Long then petitioned the Fourth Circuit for *en banc* review and, by a 9–6 margin, the judges voted on August 24, 2020 to reverse the dismissal of Long's writ. Judge Stephanie Thacker wrote for a majority of the court, in part, that "A man has been incarcerated for 44 years because, quite simply, the judicial system has failed him." Following the reversal, on August 27, 2020, the district court granted Long's petition for a writ of habeas corpus. He was released from prison that same day.

Long was then granted a pardon of innocence on December 17, 2020, which enabled him to receive compensation for his wrongful conviction. Finally, in March 2021, Long received $750,00 from the state of North Carolina, the maximum amount allowed under North Carolina law. Jordan Mendoza & Dustin Barnes, *North Carolina Just Paid a Man for 15 Years of Wrongful Imprisonment. He was in Prison for 44 Years*, USATODAY.COM (Apr. 8, 2021), https://www.usatoday.com/story/news/nation/2021/04/08/north-carolina-pays-ronnie-long-750-k-44-years-prison/7122295002/.

4. Compensating the wrongfully convicted. Once an inmate is exonerated—typically by DNA—the question shifts to what the state should (or must) do about the wrongful conviction. Thirty-two states have so-called "recompensation" statutes, but eighteen offer no form of relief to wrongfully convicted defendants. As the Innocence Project has noted, the following states have no statute available to the wrongfully convicted: Alaska, Arizona, Arkansas, Delaware, Georgia, Idaho, Indiana, Kansas, Kentucky, Nevada, New Mexico, North Dakota, Oregon, Pennsylvania, Rhode Island, South Carolina, South Dakota, and Wyoming. But in the states that do provide some relief, the coverage is by no means uniform. According to the Innocence Project, "Texas compensates the wrongfully convicted $80,000 per year of incarceration and an annuity set at the same amount, whereas Wisconsin gives $5,000 per year of incarceration, with a maximum of $25,000 total, no matter how many years were spent in prison." Rebecca Brown & Carlita Salazar, *Wrongful Conviction Day 2017: Taking a Closer Look at Compensation Laws in the U.S.*, INNOCENCEPROJECT.ORG (Oct. 2, 2017), https://www.innocenceproject.org/wrongful-conviction-day-2017-taking-closer-look-compensation-laws-u-s/.

INDEX

References are to Pages